CME PROJECT

Algebra 2
COMMON CORE

The Center for Mathematics Education Project was developed at Education Development Center, Inc. (EDC) within the Center for Mathematics Education (CME), with partial support from the National Science Foundation.

 Learning transforms lives. Education Development Center, Inc.
Center for Mathematics Education
Newton, Massachusetts

 This material is based upon work supported by the National Science Foundation under Grant No. ESI-0242476, Grant No. MDR-9252952, and Grant No. ESI-9617369. Any opinions, findings, and conclusions or recommendations expressed in this material are those of the author(s) and do not necessarily reflect the views of the National Science Foundation.

Cover Art: 9 Surf Studios; Alamy/RubberBall

Taken from:

CME Project: Algebra 2
By the CME Project Development Team
Copyright ©2009 by Educational Development Center, Inc.
Published by Pearson Education, Inc.
Upper Saddle River, New Jersey 07458

CME Common Core Additional Lessons: Algebra 2
By the CME Project Development Team
Copyright ©2012 by Educational Development Center, Inc.
Published by Pearson Education, Inc.
Upper Saddle River, New Jersey 07458

CME Project Development Team
Lead Developer: **Al Cuoco**

Core Development Team: Anna Baccaglini-Frank, Jean Benson, Nancy Antonellis D'Amato, Daniel Erman, Brian Harvey, Wayne Harvey, Bowen Kerins, Doreen Kilday, Ryota Matsuura, Stephen Maurer, Sarah Sword, Audrey Ting, and Kevin Waterman

Others who contributed include Steve Benson, Paul D'Amato, Robert Devaney, Andrew Golay, Paul Goldenberg, Jane Gorman, C. Jud Hill, Eric Karnowski, Helen Lebowitz, Joseph Leverich, Melanie Palma, Mark Saul, Nina Shteingold, and Brett Thomas.

Pearson Learning Solutions, 501 Boylston Street, Suite 900, Boston, MA 02116
A Pearson Education Company
www.pearsoned.com

Printed in the United States of America

2 3 4 5 6 7 8 9 10 V011 17 16 15

000200010271661100

MD

 **PEARSON**
ISBN 10: 1-256-74147-7
ISBN 13: 978-1-256-74147-3

Contents in Brief

Introduction to the CME Project

CME PROJECT

The CME Project, developed by EDC's Center for Mathematics Education, is a new NSF-funded high school program, organized around the familiar courses of algebra 1, geometry, algebra 2, and precalculus. The CME Project provides teachers and schools with a third alternative to the choice between traditional texts driven by basic skill development and more progressive texts that have unfamiliar organizations. This program gives teachers the option of a problem-based, student-centered program, organized around the mathematical themes with which teachers and parents are familiar. Furthermore, the tremendous success of NSF-funded middle school programs has left a need for a high school program with similar rigor and pedagogy. The CME Project fills this need.

The goal of the CME Project is to help students acquire a deep understanding of mathematics. Therefore, the mathematics here is rigorous. We took great care to create lesson plans that, while challenging, will capture and engage students of all abilities and improve their mathematical achievement.

The Program's Approach

The organization of the CME Project provides students the time and focus they need to develop fundamental mathematical ways of thinking. Its primary goal is to develop in students robust mathematical proficiency.

- The program employs innovative instructional methods, developed over decades of classroom experience and informed by research, that help students master mathematical topics.

- One of the core tenets of the CME Project is to focus on developing students' Habits of Mind, or ways in which students approach and solve mathematical challenges.

- The program builds on lessons learned from high-performing countries: develop an idea thoroughly and then revisit it only to deepen it; organize ideas in a way that is faithful to how they are organized in mathematics; and reduce clutter and extraneous topics.

- It also employs the best American models that call for grappling with ideas and problems as preparation for instruction, moving from concrete problems to abstractions and general theories, and situating mathematics in engaging contexts.

- The CME Project is a comprehensive curriculum that meets the dual goals of mathematical rigor and accessibility for a broad range of students.

About CME

EDC's Center for Mathematics Education, led by mathematician and teacher **Al Cuoco**, brings together an eclectic staff of mathematicians, teachers, cognitive scientists, education researchers, curriculum developers, specialists in educational technology, and teacher educators, internationally known for leadership across the entire range of K–16 mathematics education. We aim to help students and teachers in this country experience the thrill of solving problems and building theories, understand the history of ideas behind the evolution of mathematical disciplines, and appreciate the standards of rigor that are central to mathematical culture.

Contributors to the CME Project

National Advisory Board The National Advisory Board met early in the project, providing critical feedback on the instructional design and the overall organization. Members include

Richard Askey, University of Wisconsin
Edward Barbeau, University of Toronto
Hyman Bass, University of Michigan
Carol Findell, Boston University
Arthur Heinricher, Worcester Polytechnic Institute
Roger Howe, Yale University
Barbara Janson, Janson Associates
Kenneth Levasseur, University of Massachusetts, Lowell
James Madden, Louisiana State University, Baton Rouge
Jacqueline Miller, Education Development Center
James Newton, University of Maryland
Robert Segall, Greater Hartford Academy of Mathematics and Science
Glenn Stevens, Boston University
Herbert Wilf, University of Pennsylvania
Hung-Hsi Wu, University of California, Berkeley

Core Mathematical Consultants **Dick Askey,** **Ed Barbeau,** and **Roger Howe** have been involved in an even more substantial way, reviewing chapters and providing detailed and critical advice on every aspect of the program. Dick and Roger spent many hours reading and criticizing drafts, brainstorming with the writing team, and offering advice on everything from the logical organization to the actual numbers used in problems. We can't thank them enough.

Teacher Advisory Board The Teacher Advisory Board for the CME Project was essential in helping us create an effective format for our lessons that embodies the philosophy and goals of the program. Their debates about pedagogical issues and how to develop mathematical topics helped to shape the distinguishing features of the curriculum so that our lessons work effectively in the classroom. The advisory board includes

**Jayne Abbas, Richard Coffey,
Charles Garabedian, Dennis Geller,
Eileen Herlihy, Doreen Kilday,
Gayle Masse, Hugh McLaughlin,
Nancy McLaughlin, Allen Olsen,
Kimberly Osborne, Brian Shoemaker,
and Benjamin Sinwell**

Field-Test Teachers Our field-test teachers gave us the benefit of their classroom experience by teaching from our draft lessons and giving us extensive, critical feedback that shaped the drafts into realistic, teachable lessons. They shared their concerns, questions, challenges, and successes and kept us focused on the real world. Some of them even welcomed us into their classrooms as co-teachers to give us the direct experience with students that we needed to hone our lessons. Working with these expert professionals has been one of the most gratifying parts of the development—they are "highly qualified" in the most profound sense.

California Barney Martinez, Jefferson High School, Daly City; **Calvin Baylon** and **Jaime Lao,** Bell Junior High School, San Diego; **Colorado Rocky Cundiff,** Ignacio High School, Ignacio; **Illinois Jeremy Kahan, Tammy Nguyen,** and **Stephanie Pederson,** Ida Crown Jewish Academy, Chicago; **Massachusetts Carol Martignette, Chris Martino,** and **Kent Werst,** Arlington High School, Arlington; **Larry Davidson,** Boston University Academy, Boston; **Joe Bishop** and **Carol Rosen,** Lawrence High School, Lawrence; **Maureen Mulryan,** Lowell High School, Lowell; **Felisa Honeyman,** Newton South High School, Newton Centre; **Jim Barnes** and **Carol Haney,** Revere High School, Revere; **New Hampshire Jayne Abbas** and **Terin Voisine,** Cawley Middle School, Hooksett; **New Mexico Mary Andrews,** Las Cruces High School, Las Cruces; **Ohio James Stallworth,** Hughes Center, Cincinnati; **Texas Arnell Crayton,** Bellaire High School, Bellaire; **Utah Troy Jones,** Waterford School, Sandy; **Washington Dale Erz, Kathy Greer, Karena Hanscom,** and **John Henry,** Port Angeles High School, Port Angeles; **Wisconsin Annette Roskam,** Rice Lake High School, Rice Lake.

Special thanks go to our colleagues at Pearson, most notably Elizabeth Lehnertz, Joe Will, and Stewart Wood. The program benefits from their expertise in every way, from the actual mathematics to the design of the printed page.

1

Fitting Functions to Tables

2 Functions and Polynomials

3 Complex Numbers

4 Linear Algebra

5

Exponential and Logarithmic Functions

6

Graphs and Transformations

Contents

7 Sequences and Series

8 Introduction to Trigonometry

CME Project
Student Handbook

What Makes CME Different

Welcome to the CME Project! The goal of this program is to help you develop a deep understanding of mathematics. Throughout this book, you will engage in many different activities to help you develop that deep understanding. Some of these instructional activities may be different from ones you are used to. Below is an overview of some of these elements and why they are an important part of the CME Project.

The Habits of Mind Experience

Mathematical Habits of Mind are the foundation for serious questioning, solid thinking, good problem solving, and critical analysis. These Habits of Mind are what will help you become a mathematical thinker. Throughout the CME Project, you will focus on developing and refining these Habits of Mind.

Developing Habits of Mind

Develop thinking skills. This feature provides you with various methods and approaches to solving problems.

You will develop, use, and revisit specific Habits of Mind throughout the course. These include

- **Process** (how you work through problems)
- **Visualization** (how you "picture" problems)
- **Representation** (what you write down)
- **Patterns** (what you find)
- **Relationships** (what you find or use)

Developing good habits will help you as problems become more complicated.

Habits of Mind

Think. These special margin notes highlight key thinking skills and prompt you to apply your developing Habits of Mind.

You can find Developing Habits of Mind on pages 8, 9, 17, 23, 47, 48, 62, 77, 78, 104, 105, 110, 118, 120, 131, 153, 162, 164, 169, 178, 184, 213, 219, 230, 232, 241, 250, 255, 274, 287, 311, 324, 325, 341, 343, 359, 363, 364, 377, 428, 445, 457, 464, 478, 491, 497, 541, 550, 562, 563, 577, 625, 683, 695, 711, 721, 725, 736, 745, 748, 768, 774, 786.

Minds in Action

Discussion of mathematical ideas is an effective method of learning. The Minds in Action feature exposes you to ways of communicating about mathematics.

Join Sasha, Tony, Derman, and others as they think, calculate, predict, and discuss their way towards understanding.

Minds in Action	prologue

Sasha, Tony, and Derman have just skimmed through their CME Project Algebra 2 book.

Sasha   Did you notice the student dialogs throughout the book?

Derman   Sure did!

Tony   They talk and think just the way we do.

Sasha   I know! And they even make mistakes sometimes, the way we do.

Tony   But I like how they help each other to learn from those mistakes. I bet they use the Habits of Mind I saw all over the book, too.

Sasha   That's great! They should help a lot.

You can find Minds in Action **on pages** 16, 32, 60, 115, 125, 143, 151, 169, 185, 191, 219, 247, 258, 272, 287, 303, 333, 353, 360, 406, 432, 444, 463, 465, 504, 531, 539, 548, 565, 572, 574, 576, 588, 598, 619, 635, 637, 658, 676, 735, 780.

Exploring Mathematics

Throughout the CME Project, you will engage in activities that extend your learning and allow you to explore the concepts you learn in greater depth. Two of these activities are In-Class Experiments and Chapter Projects.

In-Class Experiment

In-Class Experiments allow you to explore new concepts and apply the Habits of Mind.

You will explore math as mathematicians do. You start with a question and develop answers through experimentation.

You can find In-Class Experiments on pages 55, 115, 249, 455, 462, 470, 510, 597, 623, 624, 665, 675, 750.

Chapter Projects

Chapter Projects allow you to apply your Habits of Mind to the content of the chapter. These projects cover many different topics and allow you to explore and engage in greater depth.

Chapter Projects
Using Mathematical Habits

Here is a list of the Chapter Projects and page numbers.

Using Your CME Book

To help you make the most of your CME experience, we are providing the following overview of the organization of your book.

Focusing Your Learning

In *Algebra 2*, there are 8 chapters, with each chapter devoted to a mathematical concept. With only 8 chapters, your class will be able to focus on these core concepts and develop a deep understanding of them.

Within each chapter, you will explore a series of Investigations. Each Investigation focuses on an important aspect of the mathematical concept for that chapter.

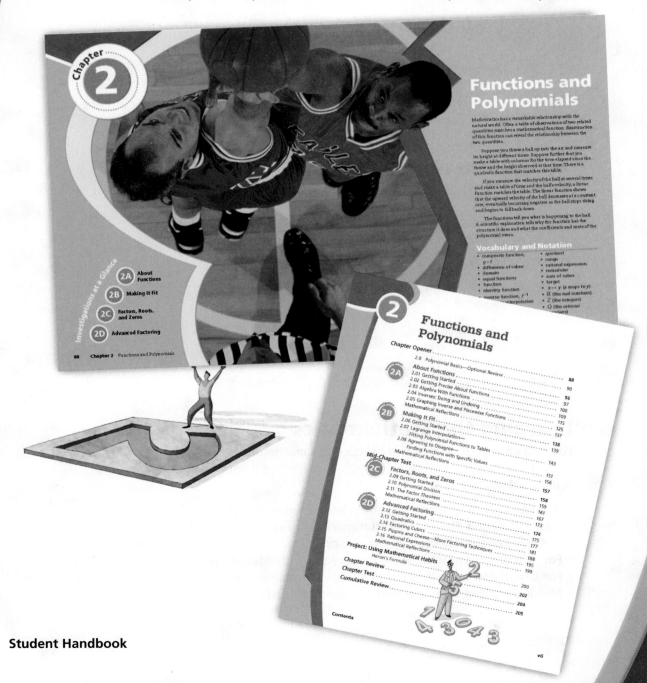

The CME Investigation

The goal of each mathematical Investigation is for you to formalize your understanding of the mathematics being taught. There are some common instructional features in each Investigation.

Getting Started

You will launch into each Investigation with a Getting Started lesson that activates prior knowledge and explores new ideas. This lesson provides you the opportunity to grapple with ideas and problems. The goal of these lessons is for you to explore—not all your questions will be answered in these lessons.

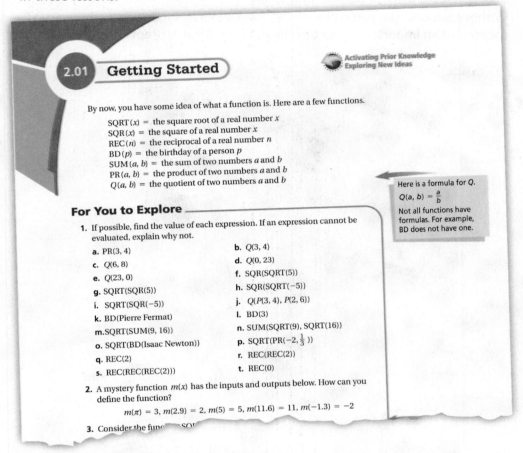

2.01 Getting Started

Activating Prior Knowledge
Exploring New Ideas

By now, you have some idea of what a function is. Here are a few functions.

SQRT(x) = the square root of a real number x
SQR(x) = the square of a real number x
REC(n) = the reciprocal of a real number n
BD(p) = the birthday of a person p
SUM(a, b) = the sum of two numbers a and b
PR(a, b) = the product of two numbers a and b
Q(a, b) = the quotient of two numbers a and b

Here is a formula for Q.

$$Q(a, b) = \frac{a}{b}$$

Not all functions have formulas. For example, BD does not have one.

For You to Explore

1. If possible, find the value of each expression. If an expression cannot be evaluated, explain why not.

a. PR(3, 4)
b. Q(3, 4)
c. Q(6, 8)
d. Q(0, 23)
e. Q(23, 0)
f. SQR(SQRT(5))
g. SQRT(SQR(5))
h. SQR(SQRT(−5))
i. SQRT(SQR(−5))
j. Q(P(3, 4), P(2, 6))
k. BD(Pierre Fermat)
l. BD(3)
m. SQRT(SUM(9, 16))
n. SUM(SQRT(9), SQRT(16))
o. SQRT(BD(Isaac Newton))
p. SQRT(PR(−2, $\frac{1}{3}$))
q. REC(2)
r. REC(REC(2))
s. REC(REC(REC(2)))
t. REC(0)

2. A mystery function $m(x)$ has the inputs and outputs below. How can you define the function?

$$m(\pi) = 3, m(2.9) = 2, m(5) = 5, m(11.6) = 11, m(−1.3) = −2$$

3. Consider the func... SQ...

Learning the Mathematics

You will engage in, learn, and practice the mathematics in a variety of ways. The types of learning elements you will find throughout this course include

- **Worked-Out Examples** that model how to solve problems
- **Definitions and Theorems** to summarize key concepts
- **In-Class Experiments** to explore the concepts
- **For You to Do** assignments to check your understanding
- **For Discussion** questions to encourage communication
- **Minds in Action** to model mathematical discussion

Communicating the Mathematics

Student dialogs

By featuring dialogs between characters, the CME Project exposes you to a way of communicating about mathematics. These dialogs will then become a real part of your classroom!

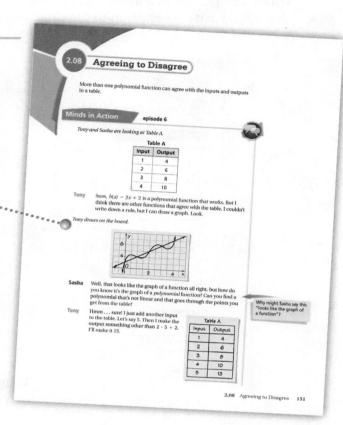

Reflecting on the Mathematics

At the end of each Investigation, Mathematical Reflections give you an opportunity to put ideas together. This feature allows you to demonstrate your understanding of the Investigation and reflect on what you learn.

Practice

The CME Project views extensive practice as a critical component of a mathematics curriculum. You will have daily opportunities to practice what you learn.

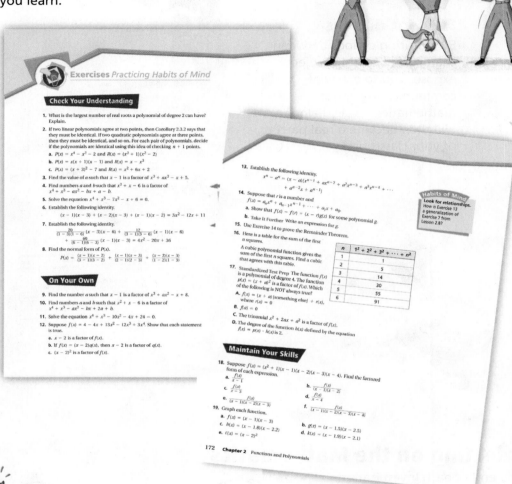

Check Your Understanding

Assess your readiness for independent practice by working through these problems in class.

On Your Own

Practice and continue developing the mathematical understanding you learn in each lesson.

Maintain Your Skills

Review and reinforce skills from previous lessons.

Also Available

An additional Practice Workbook is available separately.

Go Online

With PearsonSuccessNet your teachers have selected the best tools and features to help you succeed in your classes.

Log-in to www.pearsonsuccessnet.com to find:

- **an online Pearson eText version of your textbook**
- **extra practice and assessments**
- **worksheets and activities**
- **multimedia**

Check out PearsonSuccessNet

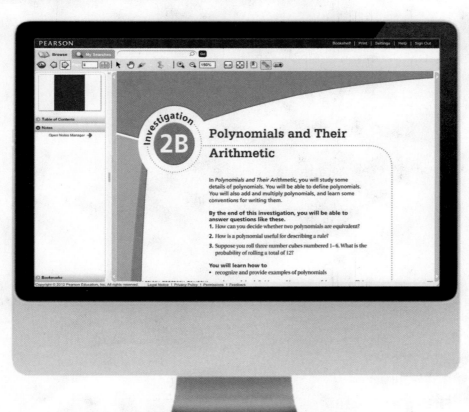

Fitting Functions to Tables

You might buy all of your cars with cash, but most people take out a loan when they buy a car. Shopping for the right car loan is a complicated process, full of choices. The techniques you will learn in this chapter will help you to compare your options.

To buy a car, you need to know how much you can afford as a down payment, what you can afford to pay per month on the loan, the interest rate, and the length of the loan. These variables can depend on the model of car you want to buy, the lender, and your credit rating. You can borrow the money through the car dealer, through a bank, or get a personal loan from a family member.

Sometimes car dealers have special promotional interest rates for certain models. Some dealers offer a rebate that you can use as all or part of your down payment. You are likely to have several different financing offers to consider. The financing might even influence your choice of car.

Vocabulary

- balance point
- closed-form definition
- cubic function
- difference table
- factorial function, n!
- hockey stick property
- line of best fit
- mean absolute error
- mean squared error
- outlier
- quadratic function
- recursive definition
- slope
- standard error
- up-and-over property

Tables

In *Tables*, you will use algebra to describe patterns that you see in tables of numbers. You can describe mathematics as the "science of patterns." That is a big oversimplification, but it is true that the ability to find patterns in data is an important skill for mathematicians and people who use mathematical thinking in their work and in their lives.

By the end of this investigation, you will be able to answer questions like these.

1. How can you tell whether there is a linear function that fits a table?

2. How can you use differences to decide what type of function fits a table?

3. What polynomial function agrees with this table?

Input	Output
0	1
1	5
2	11
3	19
4	29
5	41

You will learn how to

- identify and describe specific patterns in input-output tables

- determine whether a linear function matches a table

- use differences to decide what type of function can fit a table

- compare recursive and closed-form rules for functions

You will develop these habits and skills:

- Look for patterns and describe them with algebra.

- "Work like a mathematician"—search for hidden regularities, describe the patterns explicitly, and explain inconsistencies.

- Generalize methods so that they work in a greater number of situations.

- Find laws and principles based on patterns in tables.

- Make conjectures using the guess and check method.

You can record a jumping frog's height in a table. Then you can fit a polynomial function to the table.

Getting Started

You can write a rule for a function based on the input and output values in a table.

For You to Explore

The object of the game is to find a simple function that agrees with each table.

> Some examples of simple functions are linear, quadratic, reciprocal, and square-root functions. You can also describe a simple function with words, such as "each output is 2 more than the previous output."

Table A

Input, n	Output, $A(n)$
0	0
1	2
2	4
3	6
4	8

Table B

Input, n	Output, $B(n)$
0	0
1	2
2	6
3	12
4	20

Table C

Input, n	Output, $C(n)$
0	2
1	1
2	0
3	−1
4	−2

Table D

Input, n	Output, $D(n)$
0	0
1	3
2	8
3	15
4	24

1. For each table above, find a rule that produces these outputs. Do not worry about the notation or vocabulary you use to describe the rule. You can use an equation such as

    output = 3 × input

    or a sentence such as "each output is the output above it plus 4."

2. Richard notices there is more than one rule for Table A. He says, "Sure, I can find a rule that works: Double the input. But there are other functions that make that same table from 0 to 4 and produce different outputs for inputs greater than 4."

    a. Draw a graph with the 5 points of Table A. Then draw the graph of the function $n \mapsto 2n$.

    b. **Write About It** Do you agree or disagree with Richard? Explain your answer using additional graphs or tables as needed.

    c. **Take It Further** Find a function that supports Richard's claim. If no such function exists, explain why.

> Richard claims that there are many functions that agree with Table A.

Exercises *Practicing Habits of Mind*

On Your Own

For Exercises 3–20, find a function that agrees with each table. Keep track of the functions you find, because the solution for one exercise may be useful in a later exercise.

Habits of Mind

Think about it another way. There are many ways to think about these exercises. For example, you can suppose there is a mystery function generating each table. You want to find it.

3.
Table E

Input	Output
0	3
1	5
2	7
3	9
4	11

4.
Table F

Input	Output
0	-2
1	$-1\frac{1}{2}$
2	-1
3	$-\frac{1}{2}$
4	0

5.
Table G

Input	Output
0	-7
1	-4
2	-1
3	2
4	5

6.
Table H

Input	Output
0	3
1	8
2	13
3	18
4	23

7.
Table I

Input	Output
0	0
1	1
2	4
3	9
4	16

8.
Table J

Input	Output
0	0
1	2
2	8
3	18
4	32

9.
Table K

Input	Output
0	1
1	2
2	5
3	10
4	17

10.
Table L

Input	Output
0	-25
1	-24
2	-21
3	-16
4	-9

11.
Table M

Input	Output
0	9
1	15
2	21
3	27
4	33

Go Online
Video Tutor
Pearsonsuccessnet.com

12.

Table N

Input	Output
0	9
1	16
2	25
3	36
4	49

13.

Table O

Input	Output
0	0
1	5
2	20
3	45
4	80

14.

Table P

Input	Output
0	1
1	5
2	9
3	13
4	17

15.

Table Q

Input	Output
0	1
1	10
2	29
3	58
4	97

16.

Table R

Input	Output
0	0
1	1
2	8
3	27
4	64

17.

Table S

Input	Output
0	3
1	4
2	11
3	30
4	67
5	128

18.

Table T

Input	Output
0	1
1	3
2	9
3	27
4	81
5	243

19.

Table U

Input	Output
0	1
1	2
2	4
3	8
4	16
5	32

20.

Table V

Input	Output
0	0
1	1
2	3
3	7
4	15
5	31

Maintain Your Skills

21. Make a table for the inputs 0 through 5 for each of the following functions.

a. $a(x) = x^2$ **b.** $b(x) = x^2 - 1$ **c.** $c(x) = x^2 - 4$ **d.** $d(x) = x^2 - 9$

22. Find a number c that makes $f(x) = x^2 - c$ equal to zero when $x = 5$.

23. Show that the following identity is true.

$$(x + 1)^2 - x^2 = 2x + 1$$

Two Types of Definitions

The table below is from Exercise 6 of Lesson 1.01.

Table H

Input	Output
0	3
1	8
2	13
3	18
4	23

You can describe a function that agrees with this table in more than one way. For example,

- If the input n is zero, the output is 3. To get the next output, add 5 to the previous output.

- $g(n) = 5n + 3$

Developing Habits of Mind

Look for patterns. In Chapter 2, you will learn that Table H itself is a function. The set of possible inputs is $\{0, 1, 2, 3, 4\}$ and nothing else. When you think of the table as a function, you can write $H(2) = 13$, but $H(6)$ is not defined.

In this lesson, you are looking for something different—a way to express some regularity in the table. Finding and describing a pattern can allow you to extend the domain from $\{0, 1, 2, 3, 4\}$ to a larger set of numbers. Both bulleted descriptions above do this. When you match a table with a polynomial or another simple rule, you are uncovering a hidden relationship in the numbers. This is something that mathematicians really prize.

> You learned that the domain of a function is *the set of allowable inputs.* You will learn a more precise definition in Chapter 2.

For You to Do

1. When the input is 9, what is the output of each of the two functions described above?

2. Can you use each function to find the output when the input is −2? Explain.

Facts and Notation

A function definition such as "$g(n) = 5n + 3$" is a **closed-form definition**. A closed-form definition lets you find any output $g(n)$ for any input n by direct calculation.

A function definition such as "$f(0) = 3$ and any output is 5 more than the previous output" is a **recursive definition**. Recursive definitions are useful for expressing patterns in the outputs of a function. The notation below is a useful way to write a recursive definition.

$$f(n) = \begin{cases} 3 & \text{if } n = 0 \\ f(n-1) + 5 & \text{if } n > 0 \end{cases}$$

Notice that f is a recursive function and g is a closed-form function. Do the two definitions give the same function?

Developing Habits of Mind

Use a model. The closed-form definition below matches Table H from Exercise 6 of the Getting Started lesson.

$$g(n) = 5n + 3$$

You can build a computer or calculator model for function g in your function-modeling language. Then you can experiment with the model. You can do the following:

- Evaluate the function.
- Graph the function.
- Make a table of the function in a spreadsheet window.

It is a good habit to build models like these for the functions you use, especially when you want to get a feel for how the functions behave.

How you build a model depends on your computer or calculator. See the TI-Nspire™ Handbook, p. 804.

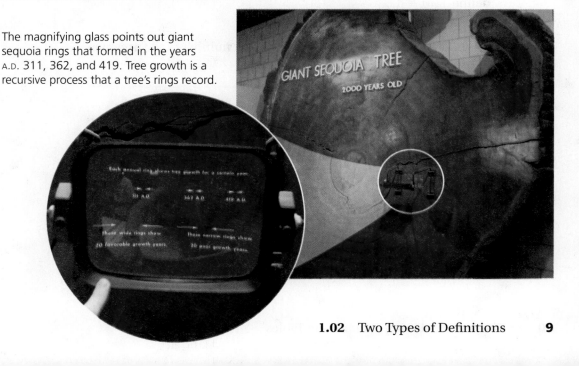

The magnifying glass points out giant sequoia rings that formed in the years A.D. 311, 362, and 419. Tree growth is a recursive process that a tree's rings record.

GIANT SEQUOIA TREE
2000 YEARS OLD

For You to Do

3. Build a model for *g* in your function-modeling language.

4. Make a table of your model for inputs between 0 and 10.

5. Graph your model in your graphing environment.

A recursive definition lets you calculate any output in terms of previous outputs. The simplest kind of recursive definition for a function *f* tells you how to compute $f(n)$ for an integer *n* in terms of $f(n-1)$. You need a place to start. The definition below tells you to start at 3 (when $n = 0$) and to add 5 to get from one output to the next.

$$f(n) = \begin{cases} 3 & \text{if } n = 0 \\ f(n-1) + 5 & \text{if } n > 0 \end{cases}$$

- $f(0) = 3$, because $n = 0$
- $f(1) = f(1-1) + 5 = f(0) + 5 = 3 + 5 = 8$
- $f(2) = f(2-1) + 5 = f(1) + 5 = 8 + 5 = 13$

> Read the second line as "the current output is the previous output plus five." This recursively defined function fits all the entries in Table H.

For You to Do

You can use function-modeling language to model a recursive definition. Your technology may even provide a template like the one below. For help, see the TI-Nspire™ Handbook, p. 804.

$$\text{define } f(n) = \begin{cases} \blacksquare, \blacksquare \\ \blacksquare, \blacksquare \end{cases}$$

You just fill in the boxes.

$$\text{define } f(n) = \begin{cases} 3, & \text{if } n = 0 \\ f(n-1) + 5, & \text{if } n > 0 \end{cases}$$

> Recursive definitions tell you how the outputs are related. Closed-form definitions tell you how inputs are related to outputs. Each tells you something interesting. In some cases, you can convert one to the other. Later in this investigation you will see how.

6. Build a model for *f* and experiment with it. What numbers will *f* accept as inputs? Explain. How does *g* compare to *f*?

Difference Tables

A **difference table** can help you see patterns that lead to recursive definitions. Use Table H from Exercise 6 of Lesson 1.01.

Table H

Input	Output
0	3
1	8
2	13
3	18
4	23

To make a difference table, add a third column marked with the Δ symbol. Write the difference between one output and the next in the third column.

The Δ symbol is the capital Greek letter delta. It represents change or difference.

Input	Output	Δ
0	3	$8 - 3 = 5$
1	8	$13 - 8 = 5$
2	13	$18 - 13 = 5$
3	18	$23 - 18 = 5$
4	23	

The differences are exactly what you need to write a recursively defined function that matches Table H. In this case, all the differences are the same number, 5. The following recursive definition fits Table H.

$$f(n) = \begin{cases} 3 & \text{if } n = 0 \\ f(n - 1) + 5 & \text{if } n > 0 \end{cases}$$

In some tables the differences are not constant, as in the table below.

Table D

Input, n	Output, $d(n)$	Δ
0	0	3
1	3	5
2	8	7
3	15	9
4	24	11
5	35	13
6	48	

In Lesson 1.05, you will see that you can still use the Δ column to find a recursive function that matches the table. Here is a recursive definition for d.

What function matches the Δ column?

$$d(n) = \begin{cases} 0 & \text{if } n = 0 \\ d(n - 1) + 2n + 1 & \text{if } n > 0 \end{cases}$$

For You to Do

7. Show that the function d fits Table D.

Exercises *Practicing Habits of Mind*

Check Your Understanding

For Exercises 1–3, use Table B from Lesson 1.01.

Table B

Input, n	Output, $B(n)$
0	0
1	2
2	6
3	12
4	20

1. Make a difference table for Table B.

2. Decide whether each recursive definition fits Table B.

a. $b(n) = \begin{cases} 0 & \text{if } n = 0 \\ b(n-1) + 2 & \text{if } n > 0 \end{cases}$

b. $b(n) = \begin{cases} 0 & \text{if } n = 0 \\ b(n-1) + 2(n-1) & \text{if } n > 0 \end{cases}$

c. $b(n) = \begin{cases} 0 & \text{if } n = 0 \\ b(n-1) + 2n & \text{if } n > 0 \end{cases}$

d. $b(n) = \begin{cases} 2 & \text{if } n = 0 \\ b(n-1) + 2n & \text{if } n > 0 \end{cases}$

3. Decide whether each closed-form definition fits Table B.

a. $b(n) = 2n$

b. $b(n) = n^2 + n$

c. To find each output, take the input and multiply by one more than the input.

d. $b(n) = 2^{n+1} - 2$

For Exercises 4–6, copy and complete each difference table.

4.

Input	Output	Δ
0	5	6
1	11	■
2	19	10
3	■	15
4	■	

5.

Input	Output	Δ
0	■	3
1	■	3
2	■	3
3	■	3
4	18	

6.

Input	Output	Δ
0	5	-3
1	■	■
2	17	■
3	■	-5
4	-1	

7. Use the recursive definition below.

$$f(n) = \begin{cases} 1 & \text{if } n = 0 \\ n \cdot f(n-1) & \text{if } n > 0 \end{cases}$$

a. Find the values of $f(1)$ through $f(6)$ for this function.

b. What preprogrammed function on your calculator agrees with f?

8. The table at the right is an incomplete input-output table for a function.

You can use each rule to complete the table. Make a completed table for each rule.

Input	Output
0	2
1	6
2	■
3	■
4	■

a. To get each output, take the previous output and add four.

b. To get each output, take the previous output and multiply by three.

c. $n \mapsto 2(3^n)$

d. To get each output, take the input, multiply by four, and then add two.

9. Write About It Consider the tables in Lesson 1.01. Find three tables that are related. Describe how they are related. You may find it helpful to make difference tables.

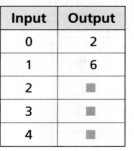
Remember...
$a^0 = 1$ for any nonzero number a, so $3^0 = 1$.

The *triangular numbers* are numbers determined by the pattern shown below. The number of dots in a triangular pattern with *n* dots on a side is the *n*th triangular number.

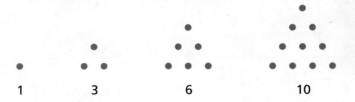

1   3   6   10

This pattern results when you arrange the counting numbers in a spiral and color the triangular numbers.

Here is a table for the triangular numbers.

10. Make a difference table for the triangular numbers.

11. a. Write a recursive function definition that fits the table of triangular numbers.

b. Take It Further Find a closed-form definition for a function that generates the triangular numbers.

Side Length	Number of Dots
0	0
1	1
2	3
3	6
4	10
5	15

12. a. Copy and complete the difference table below.

Input, *x*	Output, *ax* + *b*	Δ
0	*b*	▪
1	*a* + *b*	▪
2	2*a* + *b*	▪
3	3*a* + *b*	▪
4	4*a* + *b*	▪
5	5*a* + *b*	

b. Find a formula for $f(x + 1) - f(x)$ when $f(x) = ax + b$.

You can define $f(x) = ax + b$ in your computer algebra system (CAS) and ask for $f(x + 1) - f(x)$. Make sure you have not assigned any values to *a*, *b*, or *x*.

13. a. Copy and complete the difference table below.

Input, x	Output, $ax^2 + bx + c$	Δ
0	c	▪
1	$a + b + c$	▪
2	$4a + 2b + c$	▪
3	$9a + 3b + c$	▪
4	$16a + 4b + c$	▪
5	$25a + 5b + c$	

Habits of Mind

Look for relationships. What is the connection between the two parts of this exercise?

b. Find a formula for $f(x + 1) - f(x)$ when $f(x) = ax^2 + bx + c$.

14. Standardized Test Prep Find the output of the function $g(n)$ below for the input $n = 4$.

$$g(n) = \begin{cases} 1 & \text{if } n = 1 \\ g(n - 1) + 2n - 1 & \text{if } n > 1 \end{cases}$$

Go Online
Pearsonsuccessnet.com

A. 1　　　　　　　　　　　　**B.** 4

C. 10　　　　　　　　　　　**D.** 16

Maintain Your Skills

15. In each table below, the input-output pairs represent points on the graph of a linear function. Find the slope of each graph.

a.

Input	Output
0	-7
1	-4
2	-1
3	2
4	5
5	8

b.

Input	Output
0	-7
1	-11
2	-15
3	-19
4	-23
5	-27

c.

Input	Output
0	2
1	$1\frac{1}{2}$
2	1
3	$\frac{1}{2}$
4	0
5	$-\frac{1}{2}$

Remember...

Slope is the ratio of the change in the y-coordinates to the change in the x-coordinates.

d. Describe how you can find the slope of a linear function when you have a table for the function in which the inputs are consecutive integers.

In this lesson, you will explore a specific type of difference table. The inputs are consecutive integers and all the differences between the outputs are constant. Here is Table H from Lesson 1.01.

Below is a difference table for Table H.

Table H

Input	Output
0	3
1	8
2	13
3	18
4	23

Input	Output	Δ
0	3	5
1	8	5
2	13	5
3	18	5
4	23	

In Lesson 1.02, you saw that the recursively defined function below fits the table.

$$f(n) = \begin{cases} 3 & \text{if } n = 0 \\ f(n - 1) + 5 & \text{if } n > 0 \end{cases}$$

You can use a recursive definition that has constant differences to find a closed form that also fits the table.

Leslie explains how she finds a closed-form definition that fits the table.

Leslie Say I'm looking for $f(4)$ and all I know is the recursive definition.

$$f(4) = f(3) + 5$$

So if I want to know $f(4)$, I just need to know what $f(3)$ was. But $f(3)$ depends on $f(2)$. Oh, I have to use the recursive definition *again*.

$$f(3) = f(2) + 5$$

And I can combine those two: $f(4) = f(2) + 5 + 5$. Two steps, two fives. Every step I take is another five. So if I go all the way back, that's four steps.

$$f(4) = f(0) + 4 \cdot 5$$

The definition tells me $f(0) = 3$, so $f(4)$ is 3 plus 4 fives. What's great about this is there isn't anything special about finding $f(4)$. If I want to find $f(17)$, I add 3 plus 17 fives. If I want to find $f(n)$, I add 3 plus n fives.

$$f(n) = 3 + n \cdot 5$$

I think I'd rather write that as $f(n) = 5n + 3$.

Input	Output	Δ
0	3	5
1	8	5
2	13	5
3	18	5
4	23	

Leslie used the numbers highlighted in this difference table to find $f(4) = f(0) + 4 \cdot 5$.

Developing Habits of Mind

Visualize. The two properties below apply to any difference table, whether or not it has constant differences.

- **Up-and-over property.** An output is the sum of two numbers above it: the output directly above and the difference above and to the right.

- **Hockey stick property.** An output is the sum of all the differences above it to the right and the single output at the top of the table.

The properties are easier to see than to describe. Here is an example of the up-and-over property for Table Q from Lesson 1.01.

Input	Output	Δ
0	1	9
1	10	19
2	29	29
3	58	39
4	97	

$10 + 19 = 29$

When you highlight all the numbers you add up, it looks like a hockey stick. Otherwise, this property has nothing to do with hockey!

The output for an input of 2 is the sum of the output for 1 and the difference next to the output for 1.

Here is an example of the hockey stick property for Table Q.

Input	Output	Δ
0	1	9
1	10	19
2	29	29
3	58	39
4	97	

$1 + (9 + 19 + 29) = 58$

The output for an input of 3 is the sum of all the differences in the column leading up to $Q(3)$ and the output for 0.

The hockey stick property leads to Theorem 1.1.

Theorem 1.1

You can match an input-output table with constant differences with a linear function. The slope of the graph of the function is the constant difference in the table.

In this chapter, assume that the inputs in the table are {0, 1, 2, 3, . . . } unless stated otherwise.

For Discussion

1. Show that the up-and-over property is a result of the way you construct difference tables.

2. Show that the hockey stick property is a result of the way you construct difference tables.

3. Use the hockey stick property to prove Theorem 1.1.

Theorem 1.2 is the converse of Theorem 1.1.

Theorem 1.2

If $f(x) = ax + b$ is a linear function, its differences are constant.

Habits of Mind

Detect the key characteristics. What is the value of the constant difference?

For You to Do

4. Prove Theorem 1.2.

You can use the hockey stick property to quickly find a closed-form definition for a function that fits a table with constant differences. Here is Table H again with a hockey stick illustrated.

Input	Output	Δ
0	3	5
1	8	5
2	13	5
3	18	5
4	23	

The output is the number at the tip of the hockey stick plus the sum of the numbers on the handle.

For You to Do

5. Describe how you can find the number 23 using the hockey stick property.

6. How can you use the hockey stick property to find a closed form that agrees with the table?

Exercises Practicing Habits of Mind

For Exercises 1–4, use Table G from this investigation's Getting Started lesson.

Table G

Input	Output
0	−7
1	−4
2	−1
3	2
4	5

1. Make a difference table for Table G.

2. Write a recursive definition for a function that fits Table G.

3. Write a closed-form definition for a function that fits Table G.

4. Use the functions from Exercises 2 and 3. What does each function give as output for each input below?

    a. 10

    b. 10.1

> **Habits of Mind**
>
> **Look for relationships.**
> Model your recursive and closed-form rules in your function modeling language. Do they agree for all inputs?

5. **What's Wrong Here?** Leslie built a difference table for the input-output table at the right.

    Leslie says, "All the differences are 6. So, this table has constant differences. Then the rule for the table is $f(n) = 6n + 11$. Hmm, that doesn't seem right. That rule says $f(4)$ is 35, but it's not."

    Find the flaw in Leslie's logic.

n	f(n)
0	11
1	5
2	11
3	5
4	11

6. The table at the right has constant differences. Copy and complete the table.

7. Suppose the table from Exercise 6 continues with constant differences. Find the values of $p(10)$, $p(100)$, and $p(263)$.

n	p(n)	Δ
0	3	■
1	■	■
2	■	■
3	■	■
4	−4	

8. **Standardized Test Prep** Suppose you have a table with constant differences. The input 2 gives the output 11. The input 3 gives the output 14. What is the output for the input 7?

    A. 10   **B.** 17

    C. 21   **D.** 26

9. Use the function table for $F(n)$.

  a. Build a difference table for $F(n)$.

  b. How are the differences related to the outputs?

  c. Predict the value of $F(10)$ by extending the pattern in the table.

n	F(n)
0	1
1	1
2	2
3	3
4	5
5	8
6	13

Can you model this function in your function-modeling language?

On Your Own

For Exercises 10–12, use Table M from Lesson 1.01.

10. Make a difference table for Table M.

11. Write a recursive definition for a function that fits Table M.

12. Write a closed-form definition for a function that fits Table M.

13. Model your recursive and closed-form definitions from Exercises 10 and 11 in your function-modeling language. Do they agree for all inputs?

14. Use the function table for $D(n)$.

  a. Build a difference table for $D(n)$.

  b. How are the differences related to the outputs?

  c. Predict the value of $D(10)$ by extending the pattern.

Table M

Input	Output
0	9
1	15
2	21
3	27
4	33

n	D(n)
0	1
1	2
2	4
3	8
4	16
5	32
6	64

Habits of Mind

Experiment. In Exercise 13, what does each model give as an output when you input 7? What does each model give as an output when you input -7?

You can use a keyboard or voice-recognition software. If the words you input are the same, then the outputs will be the same.

Go Online
Pearsonsuccessnet.com

15. **Write About It** Describe how to find a closed-form definition for a function that fits a table with constant differences. Include an example.

16. Which of the Tables A–V in Lesson 1.01 have constant differences?

17. A table with integer inputs has constant differences. When the input is 3, the output is 9. When the input is 11, the output is −3. Calculate the constant difference.

18. **Take It Further** Suppose you reverse the inputs and outputs of Table M. You get the input-output table at the right.

    a. Find a function that fits the table.

    b. Using your function, copy and complete the difference table below that has integer inputs from 0 to 4.

Inverse of Table M

Input	Output
9	0
15	1
21	2
27	3
33	4

Input	Output	Δ
0	▪	▪
1	▪	▪
2	▪	▪
3	▪	▪
4	▪	

c. How is the constant difference in the table from part (b) related to the constant difference in the original Table M?

Maintain Your Skills

19. The table at the right has constant differences. Copy and complete the table.

20. Find the slope between each pair of points.

    a. $A(2, -5)$ and $B(5, 22)$

    b. $C(7, -5)$ and $D(10, 22)$

    c. $E(-5, 2)$ and $F(22, 5)$

Input	Output	Δ
0	▪	▪
1	▪	▪
2	−5	▪
3	▪	▪
4	▪	▪
5	22	▪
6	▪	

1.04 Tables and Slope

In the last lesson, you saw that you can fit a linear function to a table with constant differences. In this lesson, you will learn the relationship between difference tables and slope.

Example

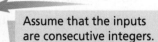

Problem An input-output table has constant differences. When the input is 2, the output is 9. When the input is 7, the output is −6. Find the constant difference.

Solution Suppose the constant difference is k. You can make this difference table.

Input	Output	Δ
0	?	k
1	?	k
2	9	k
3	?	k
4	?	k
5	?	k
6	?	k
7	−6	

Assume that the inputs are consecutive integers.

Since the table has a constant difference, you can label every entry in the Δ column k.

Now that you have labeled the difference column, you can write other outputs as expressions in terms of k. For example, you can use the up-and-over property of difference tables to find the output when the input is 3.

Input	Output	Δ
0	?	k
1	?	k
2	**9**	k
3	**9 + k**	k
4	?	k
5	?	k
6	?	k
7	−6	

You can calculate the other outputs in the same way. When the input is 4, the output is $9 + 2k$. The completed table at the right shows the outputs written in terms of k.

Now you know two expressions for the output when the input is 7. The up-and-over property gives $9 + 5k$, but the output is supposed to be -6. These must be equal.

$$9 + 5k = -6$$

Solve for k to find the constant difference.

$$9 + 5k = -6$$
$$5k = -15$$
$$k = -3$$

Input	Output	Δ
0	$9 - 2k$	k
1	$9 - k$	k
2	9	k
3	$9 + k$	k
4	$9 + 2k$	k
5	$9 + 3k$	k
6	$9 + 4k$	k
7	$9 + 5k$	

For Discussion

1. Can you use the hockey stick property, instead, to find the constant difference? Explain.

2. Find a linear function that fits the table.

Developing Habits of Mind

Consider more than one strategy. There is another way to find the constant difference.

Theorem 1.1 says that you can match a table with constant differences with a *linear* function. The graph of the function is a line with slope equal to the constant difference in the table.

You can calculate the slope of that line by finding the slope between any two points on the line. Any input-output pair from the table gives the coordinates of a point on that line.

Therefore, you can calculate the constant difference as $\dfrac{\text{change in output}}{\text{change in input}}$.

For You to Do

3. A table has constant differences. When the input is 6, the output is 10. When the input is 15, the output is also 15. Find the constant difference.

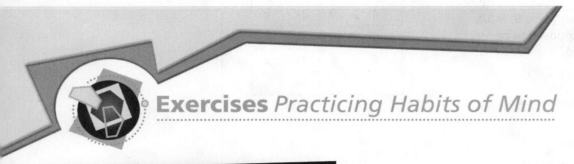

Exercises *Practicing Habits of Mind*

Check Your Understanding

1. An input-output table has constant differences. When the input is 3, the output is 10. When the input is 7, the output is 24.

  a. Find the constant difference.

  b. Find the output when the input is 0.

  c. Find the linear function that fits the table.

2. A line passes through the points (3, 10) and (7, 24).

  a. Find the slope of the line.

  b. Find an equation for the line.

3. **Write About It** Is there a line that contains the points (0, −12), (3, 5), and (4, 10)? Explain.

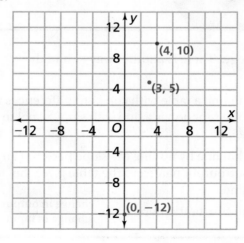

4. Some entries are missing from the table below. Can a linear function generate the table? Explain.

Input	Output
0	−12
1	?
2	?
3	5
4	10

5. A linear function generated the table below left. Find the values of a and b.

Input	Output
0	?
1	4
2	a
3	?
4	?
5	?
6	−21
7	b

Input	Output
0	−4
1	$-3\frac{1}{2}$
2	−3
3	$-2\frac{1}{2}$
4	−2

6. Find a linear function that agrees with the table above right.

7. An input-output table has constant difference 5. When the input is 6, the output is −3.

   a. Find the output when the input is 7.

   b. Find the output when the input is 3.

   c. Find a linear function that fits the input-output table.

8. Use differences to prove that you cannot find a linear function that matches Table K from Lesson 1.01.

Table K

Input	Output
0	1
1	2
2	5
3	10
4	17

9. Copy and complete the difference table from Table K. Complete the last column by finding the differences of the numbers in the Δ column.

x	K(x)	Δ	Δ²
0	1	1	2
1	2	3	■
2	5	■	■
3	10	7	
4	17		

The symbol Δ² means "Δ of the Δ." Find the differences of the difference column.

On Your Own

10. A line contains the points (1, 4) and (6, −21).

   a. Find the slope of the line.

   b. Find the value of a such that the point (2, a) lies on the line.

   c. Find the value of b such that the point (7, b) lies on the line.

11. **Write About It** Does the table below have constant differences? Explain.

Input, x	Output, y
0	11
1	11
2	11
3	11
4	11

Habits of Mind

Look for patterns. What is the value of c such that (6, c) lies on the line?

12. A line connects the points (3, 7) and (−2, 7).

   a. Draw the line on a coordinate plane.

   b. Find the slope of the line.

   c. Write an equation for the line.

13. A line connects the points (7, 3) and (7, −2).

   a. Draw the line on a coordinate plane.

   b. Explain why the slope of this line is undefined.

   c. Write an equation for the line.

14. Make a difference table for Table O from Lesson 1.01. Explain why Table O *cannot* come from a linear function.

Table O

Input	Output
0	0
1	5
2	20
3	45
4	80

Go Online
Pearsonsuccessnet.com

15. Use differences to find a linear rule that agrees with Table P from Lesson 1.01.

Table P

Input	Output
0	1
1	5
2	9
3	13
4	17

16. Take It Further Here is a difference table for Table Q from Lesson 1.01.

a. Describe the relationship between Tables O, P, and Q.

b. Describe the relationship between the difference tables that come from Tables O, P, and Q.

n	Q(n)	Δ
0	1	9
1	10	19
2	29	29
3	58	39
4	97	

17. The table below comes from the function $R(w) = w^3$. You can find the entries in the Δ, Δ^2, and Δ^3 difference columns by finding the differences of the numbers in the respective previous columns.

Copy and complete the table.

w	R(w)	Δ	Δ²	Δ³
0	0	1	6	■
1	1	■	■	■
2	8	19	■	■
3	27	■	24	6
4	64	61	30	■
5	125	91	■	
6	216	■		
7	343			

Each difference column will have one entry fewer than the one before it.

The Sudbury Neutrino Observatory is enclosed in this sphere with a 9-m radius. You can use the cubic function $V = \frac{4}{3}\pi r^3$ to find the volume of the sphere.

18. Derman is making a table for the function below.

$$d(x) = x^4 - 6x^3 + 11x^2 - 4x + 3$$

x	d(x)	Δ
0	■	■
1	■	■
2	■	■
3	■	

   a. Copy and complete Derman's table for him.

   b. Derman says, "What? Do I have a linear function?" How can you help Derman figure this out?

19. **Standardized Test Prep** Ramon accidentally shredded his physics homework. He knows the relationship he was graphing is linear. He is able to reconstruct two table values. For the input of 2, the output is 17. For the input of 11, the output is 38. What is the slope of the relationship Ramon was graphing?

   A. $\frac{39}{17}$ **B.** $\frac{3}{7}$ **C.** $\frac{7}{3}$ **D.** $\frac{9}{5}$

Maintain Your Skills

20. Make a difference table for each function. Include inputs 0 through 4.

   a. $a(x) = x^2$

   b. $b(x) = 2x^2$

   c. $c(x) = 5x^2$

   d. $d(x) = -10x^2$

   e. Find an integer k such that the function $e(x) = kx^2$ has the number 50 in its difference column.

   f. **Take It Further** Find all integers k such that the function $e(x) = kx^2$ has the number 50 in its difference column.

21. Make a difference table for each function. Use inputs 0, 1, 2, 3, and 4.

   a. $f(x) = 3x + 2$

   b. $g(x) = f(x + 1) - f(x)$

   c. $h(x) = x^2 + 3x$

   d. $k(x) = h(x + 1) - h(x)$

   e. $r(x) = x^3$

   f. $s(x) = r(x + 1) - r(x)$

Habits of Mind

Organize what you know. How can you use your CAS for this exercise?

Here is a difference table for the function $D(n) = n^2 + 2n$.

You can look at the first and third columns at the right as a new table. You can match this new table with $n \mapsto 2n + 3$. Then you can make another difference column showing the differences of the new outputs. These "differences of the differences" are second differences.

Input, n	Output, $D(n)$	Δ
0	0	3
1	3	5
2	8	7
3	15	9
4	24	11
5	35	13
6	48	

So far in this chapter, you have found functions that match a table. In this lesson, you will also start with a function and use it to generate a table.

Here is the table with a second differences column.

You can continue this process to find third differences and even more differences. For the table that comes from $D(n)$, all the third differences are equal to zero. So are any fourth differences, fifth differences, and so on.

Input, n	Output, $D(n)$	Δ	Δ^2
0	0	3	2
1	3	5	2
2	8	7	2
3	15	9	2
4	24	11	2
5	35	13	
6	48		

Habits of Mind

Understand the notation. The second differences are in the column labeled Δ^2. This notation means you perform the Δ operation twice. It does not mean to square the differences.

Example

Problem Use difference tables to find a recursive definition for a function that matches the following table.

Input	Output
0	−2
1	0
2	16
3	46
4	90

Solution A recursive definition for a function that fits this table might look something like the one below.

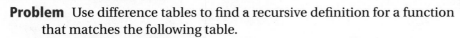

$$f(x) = \begin{cases} -2 & \text{if } x = 0 \\ f(x-1) + (\text{■}) & \text{if } x > 0 \end{cases}$$

Here is the difference table. The Δ column tells you what to add to move from one output to the next. So finding a rule for the Δ column gives the missing information for the recursive definition.

Input	Output	Δ
0	-2	2
1	0	16
2	16	30
3	46	44
4	90	

Now you need to find a function that fits the Δ column. Try finding the second differences.

Input	Output	Δ	Δ^2
0	-2	2	14
1	0	16	14
2	16	30	14
3	46	44	
4	90		

The second differences are constant. Therefore, you can find a linear function that gives the first differences in the Δ column as outputs. In this case, a linear function that matches the input column with the Δ column is $x \mapsto 14x + 2$.

New "Output"

Input	Δ	Δ^2
0	2	14
1	16	14
2	30	14
3	44	
4		

> Ignore the output column. Think of the Δ column as a new output column.

Before you write down the recursive definition, you may find it helpful to write out a few specific examples with numbers. This can give you the rhythm of how to produce the outputs.

$$f(1) = f(0) + 14 \cdot 0 + 2$$
$$f(2) = f(1) + 14 \cdot 1 + 2$$
$$f(3) = f(2) + 14 \cdot 2 + 2$$
$$f(4) = f(3) + 14 \cdot 3 + 2$$
$$f(5) = f(4) + 14 \cdot 4 + 2$$
$$\vdots \qquad\qquad \vdots$$
$$f(175) = f(174) + 14 \cdot 174 + 2$$

The rhythm of the outputs suggests this general definition.

$$f(x) = \begin{cases} -2 & \text{if } x = 0 \\ f(x - 1) + 14(x - 1) + 2 & \text{if } x > 0 \end{cases}$$

or

$$f(x) = \begin{cases} -2 & \text{if } x = 0 \\ f(x - 1) + 14x - 12 & \text{if } x > 0 \end{cases}$$

> Where did the expression $14x - 12$ come from?

For You to Do

Derman looks at all this and says, "I have a closed-form definition for a function that matches the table." Here is Derman's definition:

$$f(x) = 7x^2 - 5x - 2$$

1. Does Derman's function match the table?

2. How do you think he found his definition?

"He guessed" is not the best answer to Problem 2.

A **quadratic function** is a function defined by a polynomial of degree 2. For example, $f(x) = 3x^2 + 5x - 7$ is quadratic. But $g(x) = 3x^2 + 5x - 7x^3$ is not quadratic—it has degree 3.

So far, you have seen two quadratic functions in this lesson. The first, $D(n) = n^2 + 2n$, has constant second differences equal to 2. The second, $f(x) = 7x^2 - 5x - 2$, has constant second differences equal to 14. Notice that 14 is twice 7, and 7 is the coefficient of x^2.

Look at another example. Here is a difference table for $s(t) = -16t^2 + 150t$.

Input, t	Output, $s(t)$	Δ	Δ^2
0	0	134	-32
1	134	102	-32
2	236	70	-32
3	306	38	
4	344		

The function $s(t)$ gives the height of an object thrown up in the air at 150 feet per second. Here, t is the number of seconds since the throw, and $s(t)$ is the height of the object.

The leading coefficient is the coefficient of the highest-degree term. For $s(t) = -16t^2 + 150t$, the leading coefficient is -16. The second differences in the table are constant and twice the leading coefficient.

You can use the general quadratic $p(x) = ax^2 + bx + c$ to show that this happens in general. In the table below, note that the second differences are constant and twice the leading coefficient.

Input, x	Output, $ax^2 + bx + c$	Δ	Δ^2
0	c	$a + b$	$2a$
1	$a + b + c$	$3a + b$	$2a$
2	$4a + 2b + c$	$5a + b$	$2a$
3	$9a + 3b + c$	$7a + b$	$2a$
4	$16a + 4b + c$	$9a + b$	
5	$25a + 5b + c$		

This table suggests that the second differences for any quadratic function are constant.

Theorem 1.3

For any quadratic function $p(x) = ax^2 + bx + c$, the second differences are constant. The constant second difference is $2a$, twice the coefficient of the squared term.

Proof Basically, you want to show that the pattern in the above table continues. First, compute the entry in the Δ column for any input n.

Input	Output	Δ
$\vdots$	$\vdots$	$\vdots$
n	$p(n) = an^2 + bn + c$	?
$n + 1$	$p(n + 1) = a(n + 1)^2 + b(n + 1) + c$	$\vdots$
$\vdots$	$\vdots$	$\vdots$

Use the up-and-over property.

$$p(n + 1) - p(n) = (a(n + 1)^2 + b(n + 1) + c) - (an^2 + bn + c)$$
$$= a((n + 1)^2 - n^2) + b((n + 1) - n) + (c - c)$$
$$= a(2n + 1) + b = 2an + a + b$$

This gives you a formula for the Δ column. It agrees with the table above for the general quadratic. Also, as predicted, the formula for the Δ column defines a linear function.

$$n \mapsto 2an + (a + b)$$

Here, a and b are constants. By Theorem 1.2, the first differences of this linear function—that is, the second differences of the original function p—are constant. Below, you will finish the proof by finding the value of the constant difference.

> Use the identity from Exercise 23 in Lesson 1.01. You can also define $p(x) = ax^2 + bx + c$ in your CAS and ask for $p(n + 1) - p(n)$. Make sure you have not assigned any values to a, b, c, or d.

For You to Do

3. Finish the proof by showing that the value of the constant second difference is twice the coefficient of x^2.

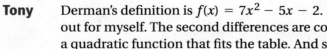

Minds in Action episode 2

Tony is trying to figure out how Derman got that function in the For You to Do section on the previous page.

Tony Derman's definition is $f(x) = 7x^2 - 5x - 2$. I think I can figure it out for myself. The second differences are constant, so I bet there's a quadratic function that fits the table. And since the second difference is 14, the coefficient of x^2 would be 7.

So now I'm going to make a table with the inputs and outputs for $f(x)$, and an extra column with just the values of $7x^2$.

Input, x	Output, $f(x)$	Output, $7x^2$
0	−2	0
1	0	7
2	16	28
3	46	63
4	90	112

The real rule is $f(x)$ equals $7x^2$ plus something. I can figure out that something by subtracting $7x^2$ from all the outputs of $f(x)$. I'll make a new column for that.

Input, x	Output, $f(x)$	Output, $7x^2$	$f(x) - 7x^2$
0	−2	0	−2
1	0	7	−7
2	16	28	−12
3	46	63	−17
4	90	112	−22

> Try using your function-modeling language to do this experiment.

Check it out: −2, −7, −12, −17, and −22. Those numbers can be matched with a linear function, and I know how to find one. The linear function is $x \mapsto -5x - 2$. So the whole thing must be

$$f(x) = 7x^2 + (-5x - 2)$$

And this works! It's like breaking down the problem into a simpler one. Once you subtract $7x^2$, the rest of it has to be linear.

For Discussion

4. Use Tony's ideas to find a closed-form definition for a function that fits Table R from Lesson 1.01.

Table R

Input	Output
0	0
1	1
2	8
3	27
4	64

Tony suspects that if the second differences are constant, a quadratic function will fit the table.

Theorem 1.4

If a table has constant second differences, there is some quadratic function that agrees with the table.

This is the converse of Theorem 1.3. It is true, and you can use Tony's method to prove it.

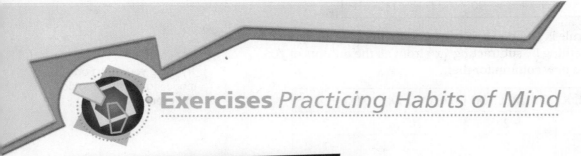

Exercises *Practicing Habits of Mind*

Check Your Understanding

1. Is there a quadratic function that fits the table below? If so, find one. If not, explain why.

n	y(n)
0	−2
1	6
2	24
3	52
4	90

2. Find a quadratic function that fits the table below.

n	y(n)
0	10
1	22
2	28
3	28
4	22

Copy and complete the difference table for each function.

3. $R(w) = w^3$

w	R(w)	Δ	Δ²	Δ³
0	0	1	6	■
1	1	■	■	■
2	8	19	■	■
3	27	■	24	6
4	64	61	30	■
5	125	91	■	
6	216	■		
7	343			

4. $m(x) = 5x^3 + 2x^2 - 10x + 4$

x	m(x)	Δ	Δ²	Δ³
0	4	■	■	■
1	1	■	■	■
2	32	■	■	■
3	127	■	■	■
4	316	■	■	■
5	629	■	■	
6	1096	■		
7	1747			

Can you use your spreadsheet tool to create the difference table for you?

5. Write About It Make a difference table for a cubic function of your choice. Answer the following questions based on your tables from Exercises 3 and 4.

A **cubic function** is a polynomial in which the highest-degree term is cubed.
$f(x) = 3x^3 + 5x - 7$ is cubic, while
$g(x) = 3x^2 + 5x - 7$ is quadratic.

a. When does a cubic function yield constant differences?

b. What is the relationship between the constant difference and the leading coefficient?

6. Take It Further Sasha thinks she has an efficient way to do Exercise 4. She says, "I make a record of the formulas for the Δs of the basic powers like x^3, x^2, and so on.

- The Δ for $x \mapsto x^3$ is $x \mapsto 3x^2 + 3x + 1$.
- The Δ for $x \mapsto x^2$ is $x \mapsto 2x + 1$.
- The Δ for $x \mapsto x$ is $x \mapsto 1$.
- The Δ for $x \mapsto 1$ is $x \mapsto 0$.

So, the Δ for $x \mapsto 5x^3 + 2x^2 - 10x + 4$ is

$x \mapsto 5(3x^2 + 3x + 1) + 2(2x + 1) - 10(1) + 4(0)$."

Does Sasha's method work for all cubic functions? Justify your answer with a proof or a counterexample.

7. Take It Further Make a difference table for the general cubic function $f(x) = ax^3 + bx^2 + cx + d$. Include enough inputs and difference columns to show the constant difference.

8. a. Find three values of x that make the following equation true.

$$(x - 3)(x - 5)(x - 6) = 0$$

b. Expand the expression $(x - 3)(x - 5)(x - 6)$ so that it has no parentheses.

9. Copy and complete the difference table for the following function.

$$v(x) = (x - 3)(x - 5)(x - 6)$$

x	v(x)	Δ	Δ²	Δ³
0	−90	■	■	■
1	−40	■	■	■
2	−12	■	■	■
3	0	■	■	■
4	2	■	■	■
5	0	■	■	
6	0	■		
7	8			

Habits of Mind

Look for patterns.
What is the degree of $(x - 3)(x - 5)(x - 6)$? What is the constant term? Can you answer these questions without expanding or using a CAS?

You can define $v(x)$ in your CAS and ask for $v(x + 1) - v(x)$. Make sure you have not assigned any value to x.

10. Find a quadratic function that fits the table below.

Input	Output
0	7
1	−6
2	1
3	28
4	75

11. Use this table for $F(n)$ from Lesson 1.03. Use difference tables to answer the following questions.

a. Could the table have come from a cubic function?

b. Describe any patterns you find in the repeated difference that comes from the function.

n	F(n)
0	1
1	1
2	2
3	3
4	5
5	8
6	13

12. Take It Further Find a function that fits the
table at the right.

Input	Output
0	−3
1	−5
2	−5
3	9
4	49
5	127

On Your Own

13. Could the table at the right have come from a quadratic
function? Explain.

n	y(n)
0	−7
1	−5
2	3
3	23
4	61

For Exercises 14 and 15, find a function that agrees with each table.

14.

Input, a	Output, b
0	25
1	11
2	−3
3	−17
4	−31

15.

n	c(n)
0	−8
1	0
2	4
3	4
4	0

Go Online
Pearsonsuccessnet.com

16. Use the table at the right for $D(n)$ from Lesson 1.03.

Use difference tables to answer these questions.

  a. Could the table have come from a cubic function?

  b. Describe any patterns you find in the difference table.

n	D(n)
0	1
1	2
2	4
3	8
4	16
5	32
6	64

For Exercises 17–19, use the input-output table below.

Input, x	Output, y
0	1
1	1
2	4
3	7
4	12

17. Show that the table could not have come from a linear, quadratic, or cubic function.

18. None of the rules below exactly matches the input-output table, but which rule is the closest fit? Explain.

Rule 1: $y = 2x - 5$ **Rule 2:** $y = 2.8x - 0.6$

Rule 3: $y = x^2 - x + 1$ **Rule 4:** $y = x^3 - 3x^2 - 2x + 1$

19. Take It Further Find a polynomial function that fits the table exactly.

20. Standardized Test Prep What is the value of the constant third differences of the cubic function $f(x) = x^3 + 2x^2 + 7$?

A. 0   **B.** 3

C. 6   **D.** 7

Maintain Your Skills

21. Make an input-output table for each function. Use the inputs 0 through 5.

  a. $f(x) = (x - 7)(x - 2)$ **b.** $g(x) = (x - 6)(x - 13)$

  c. $h(x) = x(x - 9)$ **d.** $j(x) = 3(x - 1)(x - 3)$

  e. a function $k(x)$ for which $k(5)$ and $k(6)$ both equal zero

  f. Take It Further a function $m(x)$ for which
    $m(0) = 0, m(1) = 0, m(2) = 0,$ and $m(3) = 24$

22. Make an input-output table for each function. Use the inputs 0 through 4.

  a. $f(x) = 3x$ **b.** $g(x) = 3x + x$

  c. $h(x) = 3x + x(x - 1)$ **d.** $j(x) = 3x + x(x - 1)(x - 2)$

  e. a function $k(x)$ that is different from $f(x)$, but has the same outputs for the inputs 0 through 4 (For example, the two functions might have different outputs for an input of 5.)

In this investigation, you learned how to find closed-form and recursive function definitions that fit tables and how to use difference tables to decide whether a linear or quadratic function fits a given table. These questions will help you summarize what you have learned.

Use Table B for Exercises 1 and 2.

1. Find a recursively defined function g that agrees with Table B.

2. Find a closed-form definition for a function f that agrees with Table B.

Table B

Input, n	Output, $B(n)$
0	1
1	3
2	7
3	13
4	21

3. Find an equation for the line that contains $(2, 5)$ and $(-4, 8)$.

4. How can you tell whether there is a linear function that fits a table?

5. How can you use differences to decide what type of function fits a table?

6. What polynomial function agrees with this table?

Input	Output
0	1
1	5
2	11
3	19
4	29
5	41

You can use the polynomial function that describes the frog's motion to predict the time the frog will land.

Vocabulary

In this investigation, you learned these terms.
Make sure you understand what each one means and how to use it.

- closed-form definition
- cubic function
- difference table
- hockey stick property

- quadratic function
- recursive definition
- slope
- up-and-over property

Fitting and Data

In *Fitting and Data,* you will learn to analyze data. This includes real data that you quite likely cannot fit with a simple rule. For some types of real data, you will learn how to find a line that best fits the data. You will use the line of best fit to analyze the data and make predictions.

By the end of this investigation, you will be able to answer questions like these:

1. How do you find a line that fits a set of data?

2. What is the definition of the line of best fit?

3. What is the line of best fit for the data in the table at the right?

You will learn how to:

- decide whether a linear function reasonably represents a data set

- calculate the balance point of a data set

- estimate the slope of a fitting line

- calculate error, given a data set and a fitting function

- calculate the mean absolute error, mean squared error, and standard error

- use algebra to find the line of best fit for a set of data

Men's 1500-meter Olympic Gold Medal Times (seconds)

Year	Time	Year	Time	Year	Time
1896	273.2	1932	231.2	1972	216.3
1900	246.2	1936	227.8	1976	219.2
1904	245.4	1948	229.8	1980	218.4
1908	243.4	1952	225.1	1984	212.5
1912	236.8	1956	221.2	1988	215.96
1920	241.8	1960	215.6	1992	220.12
1924	233.6	1964	218.1	1996	215.78
1928	233.2	1968	214.9	2000	212.07

SOURCE: *2007 ESPN Sports Almanac*

You will develop these habits and skills:

- Compare measures of error in data.

- Approximate scatter plots with graphs of simple functions.

- Graph linear equations.

- Evaluate the quality of a function's agreement with data.

- Use absolute value and square roots in calculations of error.

The problems in this lesson are about an experiment with a number cube. You will build a table that shows the number of rolls of the number cube and the cumulative total for all the rolls. For example, your table might look like the one below after 5 rolls.

Rolls	Total
0	0
1	5
2	10
3	14
4	16
5	22
⋮	⋮

> Why is the total zero after zero rolls, and not some other number?

For You to Explore

With a partner, roll a number cube 20 times.

1. Record the cumulative totals in a table like the one above. Then make a difference table for your results. It might look like the table below.

Rolls	Total	Δ
0	0	5
1	5	5
2	10	4
3	14	2
4	16	6
5	22	

> How do the numbers in the Δ column relate to the results of the rolls?

2. **Write About It** Look at the difference table you made in Problem 1. Is there a linear function that matches the table? Justify your answer.

3. Bethany rolls a number cube 100 times and records the total. Which of these totals is the most likely after 100 rolls? Explain.

A. 98

B. 256

C. 354

D. 412

4. Draw a scatter plot with the number of rolls *r* on the horizontal axis and the total *T* on the vertical axis. Here is a plot for the number cube example on the previous page.

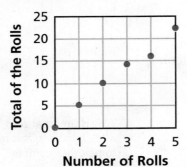

Your graph should go from 0 to 20 on the horizontal axis.

Describe your graph. How does your graph compare with the graphs of other groups?

5. On the same coordinate axes as your data, plot *T* against *r* for each of the functions below. Which function best fits the trends in your data? Which fits the worst?

a. $T = r + 30$

b. $T + 3r = 60$

c. $T = 2.5r$

d. $T = 3.5r$

e. $T = 4.5r$

6. Think about a ruler with weights hanging from it.

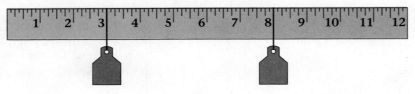

For the purpose of this exercise, assume the ruler is weightless and all the weights are equal.

a. Suppose the ruler has two weights on it, at 3 inches and 8 inches. Where can you place the ruler on your finger to balance the weights?

b. Suppose the two weights are at *x* inches and *y* inches. Write a rule that tells you where the ruler's balance point is.

c. Suppose the ruler has three weights on it, at 1 inch, 3 inches, and 8 inches. Where is the ruler's balance point?

Exercises *Practicing Habits of Mind*

On Your Own

7. Write About It There were no Olympic Games held in 1916, 1940, or 1944, due to the two world wars. How can you make a guess about what the winning time would have been for the 1500-meter run in 1944? How can you make the same sort of predictions for Olympic Games in the future?

8. a. Lisa takes three tests. She gets scores of 85, 82, and 91. What is her average?

b. A meter stick has three weights on it, at 85 cm, 82 cm, and 91 cm. Where is the ruler's balance point?

> Assume the ruler is weightless and all the weights are equal.

9. Every 10 years, the U.S. Census is taken. One of the reported calculations is the location in the United States that is the center of population. The report says,

> The concept of the center of population as used by the U.S. Census Bureau is that of a balance point. That is, the center of population is the point at which [a map of the country] would balance if weights of identical size were placed on it so that each weight represented the location of one person.

Habits of Mind

Look for relationships. In geometry, you called balance points *centroids*. Is there a connection here?

a. According to the Census Bureau, the population center of the U.S. has moved west in every census since its inception in 1790. Give some possible reasons why this has happened.

b. A Census Bureau report explains how to calculate the center.

> [T]he latitude of the center of population was determined by multiplying the population of each unit of area by the latitude of its population center, then adding all these products and dividing this total by the total population of the United States. The result is the latitude of the population center.

What mathematical calculation is the Census Bureau describing?

10. The table below shows the coordinates of some points (x, y).

a. How do you know that these points lie on a line?

b. Find the equation of the line.

c. Find the balance point for these five points by calculating the mean of the x-coordinates and the mean of the y-coordinates.

d. Show that the balance point is on the line.

x	y
0	4
1	7
2	10
5	19
8	28

> Do not forget about the zero in the input list when calculating the mean of the five inputs.

11. The table below shows the coordinates of some points (x, y).

x	y
3	2
6	3
8	5
11	5
12	6

Habits of Mind

Communicate by context. Points are collinear if they lie on the same line. What do you think *linear trend* might mean?

a. Plot the five points. How do you know that the points are not collinear?

b. These points follow a linear trend. Estimate the slope of a line that closely approximates the data.

c. Find the balance point for these five points.

d. Plot the balance point on the same graph as the five points. Explain why the balance point might be a good anchor for a line of best fit.

12. Find the value of p that minimizes each function.

a. $p \mapsto 158.86 - 47.2p + 4p^2$ **b.** $p \mapsto 52.26 - 27.2p + 4p^2$

c. $p \mapsto 5.66 - 7.2p + 4p^2$ **d.** $p \mapsto 19.06 + 12.8p + 4p^2$

Maintain Your Skills

The **balance point** $(\bar{x}, \bar{y})$ is the point with x-coordinate that is the average of the x-coordinates in the table and with y-coordinate that is the average of the y-coordinates in the table.

For Exercises 13–16, do the following steps.

Step 1: Compute the balance point $(\bar{x}, \bar{y})$.

Step 2: Build a new table by subtracting $\bar{x}$ from each x-value and subtracting $\bar{y}$ from each y-value.

Step 3: Compute the balance point for the new (x, y) values.

Step 4: Make and justify some conjectures about this process.

13.

x	y
0	4
1	7
2	10
5	19
8	28

$x - \bar{x}$	$y - \bar{y}$
▦	▦
▦	▦
▦	▦
▦	▦
▦	▦

14.

x	y
3	2
6	3
8	5
11	5
12	6

→

$x - \bar{x}$	$y - \bar{y}$
■	■
■	■
■	■
■	■
■	■

15.

x	y
1900	246.2
1904	245.4
1908	243.4
1912	236.8
1920	241.8
1924	233.6
1928	233.2

→

$x - \bar{x}$	$y - \bar{y}$
■	■
■	■
■	■
■	■
■	■
■	■
■	■

16.

x	y
73	6
22	66
16	54
60	18
6	9
73	13
10	82
6	85
8	73
33	57

→

$x - \bar{x}$	$y - \bar{y}$
■	■
■	■
■	■
■	■
■	■
■	■
■	■
■	■
■	■
■	■

17. Show that the following identity is true.

$$(a - b)^2 = 2(a^2 + b^2) - (a + b)^2$$

To slide along a grind rail, a skateboarder finds a balance point. How is a physical balance point related to the balance point of a data set?

1.07 Fitting Lines to Data

The table below shows the winning times for the men's 1500-meter run at each Olympics from 1896 until 2000.

Men's 1500-meter Olympic Gold Medal Times (seconds)

Year	Time	Year	Time	Year	Time
1896	273.2	1932	231.2	1972	216.3
1900	246.2	1936	227.8	1976	219.2
1904	245.4	1948	229.8	1980	218.4
1908	243.4	1952	225.1	1984	212.5
1912	236.8	1956	221.2	1988	215.96
1920	241.8	1960	215.6	1992	220.12
1924	233.6	1964	218.1	1996	215.78
1928	233.2	1968	214.9	2000	212.07

SOURCE: *2007 ESPN Sports Almanac*

Go Online
Pearsonsuccessnet.com

Here is a scatter plot for the data.

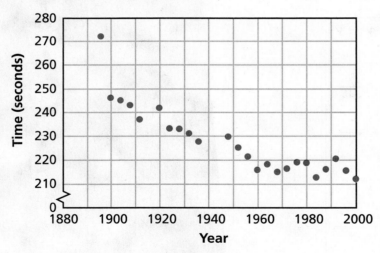

The data point for the 1896 Olympics is far away from the rest. Such a point is an **outlier**. Except for the 1896 data point, there is a general downward trend that seems to follow a straight path. It makes sense to approximate the data with a line.

On the other hand, the trend after 1960 seems to level out. You will investigate this idea in Exercise 6.

In your first-year algebra course, you learned that a line with slope m through the point (h, k) has the following equation.

$$y - k = m(x - h)$$

In order to use this method for finding the equation of a fitting line, you need a point on the line and a slope.

When the data seem to follow a linear trend, a good anchor point for your fitting line is the balance point of the data. For the gold medal data, the balance point is (1949.8, 227.82). Throwing out the 1896 data point gives a slightly different balance point of (1952.2, 225.85).

Right now, you do not have a good definition of the best possible fitting line, so all you can do is approximate the slope of a fitting line that looks good to you. Later in this investigation, you will develop the definition of the line of best fit, and explore the reasons why that definition makes sense.

Remember...

The balance point (or centroid) has x-coordinate equal to the average of the x-coordinates of the data. Its y-coordinate is equal to the average of the y-coordinates of the data.

For You to Do

Copy the scatter plot of the gold medal data.

1. Use the balance point that excludes (1896, 273.2) and a slope that you estimate to draw a fitting line for the 1500-meter data. Find the equation of your line.

2. The Olympic Games were not held in 1944 because of World War II. Use your equation to estimate what a winning time in the 1944 Olympics might have been.

Habits of Mind

Look for relationships. Later in this course, you will do arithmetic and algebra with points. Then the balance point will just be the average of the data points. What would be a good way to add (3, 2) and (5, −1)?

Developing Habits of Mind

Establish a process. Start thinking about how to decide whether one fitting line is better than another. Then you can develop the definition of the best-fit line.

Look at the table of gold medal times. When you plot the data, the vertical axis tells you the outcome of each race. The horizontal axis tells you when each outcome happened. If you want to use a line to predict future outcomes, you want the line's y-height at each year to be close to the y-height for the data point for that year. For example, you want the height of the line at 1920 to be close to 241.8.

You want a line that comes as close as possible to all the outcomes. So, you want to somehow minimize the overall differences between the data and the line's y-values.

The table below shows the calculation of the errors for one possible fitting line for the 1500-meter data. In the equation, x is the year and y is the time in seconds.

Data vs. Line Fit
$$y = -0.34x + 892.1$$

Year	Actual Time	Predicted Time	Error: Actual – Predicted
1900	246.2	246.1	0.1
1904	245.4	244.7	0.7
1908	243.4	243.4	0.0
1912	236.8	242.0	−5.2
1920	241.8	239.3	2.5
1924	233.6	237.9	−4.3
⋮	⋮	⋮	⋮
1992	220.12	214.8	5.32
1996	215.78	213.5	2.28
2000	212.07	212.1	−0.03

You often cannot make all the numbers in the error column small with one linear function. A line that makes one error small may make another error large. So you need some idea of overall error. Calculating the overall error is not as simple as just adding all the numbers in the error column, since negative and positive errors can cancel each other.

In fact, for any line that contains the balance point, the total sum of all the errors equals 0. See Exercise 9.

For Discussion

3. Think of a function you can apply to the numbers in the error column so you can add them together to get one measure of total error.

Developing Habits of Mind

Consider more than one strategy. You can always draw a line to approximate the data in a scatter plot. Sometimes, however, curves do a better job of minimizing error.

Even when lines do a good job of approximating the data, they often do it only locally. For example, you cannot use the line for $y = -0.34x + 892.1$ to predict 1500-meter times too far into the future. It would predict negative times. For what year does this first happen?

Exercises *Practicing Habits of Mind*

Check Your Understanding

1. a. Find the equations of three different lines that contain the point (3, 6).

  b. Find the equation of the one line that contains (3, 6) and (8, −1).

For Exercises 2 and 3, do parts (a)–(c).

  a. Draw a scatter plot for the points in the table.

  b. Calculate and plot the balance point.

  c. Explain whether it is reasonable to fit a line to the data.

2.

Time (seconds)	Distance (meters)
0	0
1	4.9
2	19.6
3	44.1
4	78.4

3.

Time (seconds)	$\sqrt{}$Distance ($\sqrt{}$meters)
0	0
1	2.21
2	4.43
3	6.64
4	8.85

The numbers in the second column in Exercise 3 are the approximate square roots of the distances in Exercise 2.

4. Use the table of data at the right.

Plot the data points and the four lines given below on the same axes. Which line do you think fits the data best? Explain your choice.

  A. $y = x + 1$ **B.** $y = 0.5x + 2.5$

  C. $y = 0.9x + 0.9$ **D.** $y = x + 0.5$

Input	Output
1	1.8
2	1.7
3	3.6
5	5.4
6	7.3
7	7.2

5. On a coordinate plane, City A is at (300, 20), City B is at (700, 100), and City C is at (1000, −400).

   a. If the three cities have about the same population, what is a good spot to call the "population center" for the cities?

   b. If City A has 100,000 people, City B has 200,000 people, and City C has 50,000 people, what is a good spot to call the population center for the cities?

6. Roger is looking at the gold medal data from the beginning of the lesson. He says, "I disagree with the claim that a single line fits the data. It seems to me, both from the table and the scatter plot, that there is a good fit to a line from 1900 to 1960, decreasing at about $\frac{1}{2}$ second per year. Then times were nearly static from 1960 to 2000."

   Divide the data set into two parts. For each part, calculate the balance point and plot a good fitting line. Compare this piecewise fit to the linear fit with equation $y = -0.34x + 892.1$.

   Part A: 1900–1960   **Part B:** 1960–2000

   a. What does the piecewise fit suggest might have happened in the years when there were no Olympics?

   b. What does it predict for the year 2624?

On Your Own

7. The table below shows an analysis of the first fitting line from Exercise 4.

   ### Data vs. Line Fit: $y = x + 1$

Input	Actual	Predicted: $y = x + 1$	Error: Actual − Predicted
1	1.8	2	−0.2
2	1.7	3	−1.3
3	3.6	4	−0.4
5	5.4	6	−0.6
6	7.3	7	0.3
7	7.2	8	−0.8

   a. Does the line $y = x + 1$ contain any of the six data points?

   b. The error column is negative for some entries. Are those points above or below the line $y = x + 1$?

   c. **Write About It** Use the table and the graph from Exercise 4. Decide whether $y = x + 1$ is a good fitting line for the six data points.

Go Online
Pearsonsuccessnet.com

8. In Exercise 4, there are four fitting lines suggested for a table of data. In Exercise 7, there is a table of errors for the first line, $y = x + 1$.

   a. Build a table of errors for each of the other three lines listed in Exercise 4.

   b. Which line has the fewest errors?   **c.** Which line has the smallest errors?

9. Use the data in Exercise 4.

   a. Find the equation of a line that contains the balance point.

   b. Show that the sum of the differences between the data and the corresponding points on your line is 0.

   c. **Take It Further** Show that the sum of the differences between the data and the corresponding points on any line that contains the balance point is 0.

   > For part (a), you get to pick the slope.

10. **a.** Where is the balance point of a ruler?

    b. Where is the balance point of a coin?

    c. **Write About It** Is it possible for an object to have a balance point that is not part of the object? Describe an example, or explain why it is impossible.

    > A line that contains the balance point has an equation of the form $y - \bar{y} = m(x - \bar{x})$.

11. Harvey rolls a number cube 85 times and writes down the outcomes. He counts 10 ones, 15 twos, 19 threes, 16 fours, and 11 fives.

    a. How many sixes does Harvey roll?

    b. Find the mean, median, and mode for Harvey's 85 rolls.

12. The table of data below comes from an experiment by Tor Carlson in 1913 on *Saccharomyces cerevisiae* (a type of yeast). The data show the number of hours elapsed and the number of yeast cells per square unit of area in a Petri dish.

Hours	Yeast Density
0	9.6
1	18.3
2	29.0
3	47.2
4	71.1
5	119.1
6	174.6
7	257.3

Where is the balance point of the forks and the blue toothpick?

   a. Draw a scatter plot for the eight data points.

   b. Calculate and plot the balance point.

   c. Is using a fitting line reasonable for these data? Explain your reasoning.

13. a. For the table in Exercise 12, a graphing calculator gives the best-fit line $y = 33.4476x - 26.2917$. Copy and complete the table of errors.

Calculate the error as the actual value minus the predicted value.

Data vs. Line Fit: $y = 33.4476x - 26.2917$

Hours, x	Actual Yeast Density	Predicted Yeast Density, y	Error
0	9.6	▦	▦
1	18.3	▦	▦
2	29.0	▦	▦
3	47.2	▦	▦
4	71.1	▦	▦
5	119.1	▦	▦
6	174.6	▦	▦
7	257.3	▦	▦

b. Calculate the following numbers and arrange the list of numbers from least to greatest.

   I. the average of the absolute values of the errors

   II. the average of the errors

   III. the average of the squares of the errors

14. Standardized Test Prep Which line contains the point $(-1, 2)$ and has a slope of 4?

  A. $y = 4x$ **B.** $y = 2x + 4$

  C. $y = 2(2x - 1)$ **D.** $y = 4x + 6$

Maintain Your Skills

For Exercises 15–18, do parts (a)–(d).

a. Make a table of the function for integer inputs from 0 to 4.

b. Make a graph of the five input-output pairs in your table.

c. Find and plot the balance point of the five points in your table.

d. Decide whether the balance point is on the graph of the function.

Habits of Mind

Look for relationships. As usual, your job in these exercises is to practice calculations and to look for hidden theorems.

15. $f(x) = 3x + 1$ **16.** $x \mapsto 3x + 4$

17. $x \mapsto x^2$ **18.** $g(x) = x^2 + 3$

1.08 The Line of Best Fit, Part 1

Some calculators can find a *line of best fit* for any data set with two variables. How exactly do they do it? In this lesson and the next, you will learn what the line of best fit is and how to find it.

The data table below shows the weight losses of ten people on the same diet and the number of months it took them to lose the weight.

Months	Pounds
5	18
2	2
15	54
10	39
18	65
8	25
5	12
13	41
23	72
11	46

The scatter plot below left suggests that a line might approximate the data well. To figure out the best line, you need to measure how good a line is. For example, the scatter plot below right shows the graph of $y = 3x - 1$ and the data.

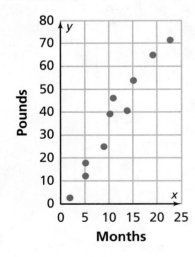

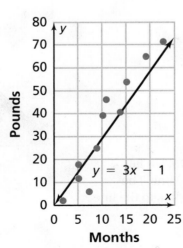

As you did in the previous lesson,
you can calculate the errors from the
approximating line.

Data vs. Line Fit: $y = 3x - 1$

Months	Pounds	Predicted	Error
5	18	14	4
2	2	5	−3
15	54	44	10
10	39	29	10
18	65	53	12
8	25	23	2
5	12	14	−2
13	41	38	3
23	72	68	4
11	46	32	14

You can show the error column of the table on
the graph. Each error is the vertical distance
between the actual data and the
approximating line.

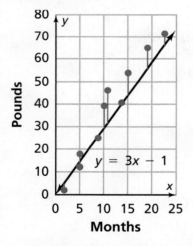

For example, the data point (15, 54) lies
above the point (15, 45) on the line. The
height of the "stick" from the data to the line
is the error, which is 9.

Facts and Notation

One measure of overall error is the average length of the sticks. The lengths are the absolute values of the errors. Their average is the **mean absolute error**.

A calculator does something different to find the line of best fit. It sums the squares of the lengths of the sticks—the squares of the errors. The average of the squares of the errors is the **mean squared error**. The line of best fit minimizes the mean squared error.

Another useful measure of error is **standard error** or *root mean squared error*. It is just the square root of the mean squared error.

Why do you take the square root? One reason is that it preserves units. For example, in the weight-loss data, the standard error is a measure of pounds, not pounds^2.

For You to Do

1. Calculate the mean squared error for the graph of $y = 3x - 1$ and the weight loss data. Can you find a line that has a smaller mean squared error?

In-Class Experiment

Here is a useful way to think about finding the line of best fit.

Suppose you have a moveable line on a scatter plot. You also have vertical sticks between the line and the data points. As you move the line, some sticks grow in length, while others shrink. If you keep track of the sums of the squares of the stick lengths, you can fine-tune the line position. You can adjust the line to make the overall error small.

2. You can turn this thought experiment into a real experiment. Use your dynamic geometry software and the data in the table at the beginning of this lesson.

For more details, see the TI-Nspire Handbook, p. 804.

Step 1 Make a scatter plot of the data.

Step 2 Construct a moveable line on the plot. Translating the line keeps the slope the same. Rotating the line changes the slope.

Step 3 Construct a vertical segment from each of the ten data points to the moveable line.

Step 4 Ask the system to calculate the sum of the squares of the vertical segment lengths.

Step 5 Adjust the line. Try to make it so that the sum in Step 4 is as small as possible.

Theorem 1.5 *Invariance Under Translation*

Suppose *a* and *b* are fixed numbers and you have a set of data labeled (x, y). If you perform the transformation $(x, y) \mapsto (x + a, y + b)$ on the data set, the lines of best fit for the two data sets will have the same slope.

Remember...

The notation $(x, y) \mapsto (x + a, y + b)$ means that you add *a* to all the *x*-values and add *b* to all the *y*-values.

For You to Do

3. Write a convincing argument to support Theorem 1.5.

For Discussion

4. The mean squared error is the average of the squares of the errors. Why does making the sum of the squares of the errors as small as possible also minimize the mean squared error?

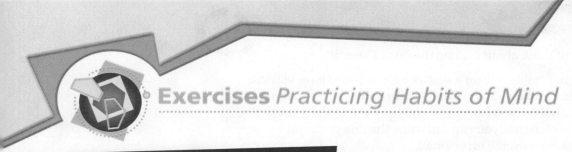

Exercises *Practicing Habits of Mind*

Check Your Understanding

1. Use the graph of data points at the right. Which line best fits the data in the graph?

A. $y = 2x + 3$

B. $y = \frac{1}{2}x + 3$

C. $y = 2x - 3$

D. $y = -2x + 3$

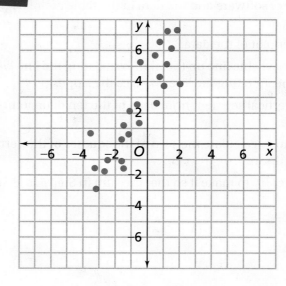

2. Use the table of data at the right.

   a. Which equation has a graph that best fits the data?

   A. $y = 3x - 1$ **B.** $y = -x + 8.4$

   b. For each equation in part (a), compare the following.

   - the sum of the errors
   - the mean absolute error
   - the mean squared error

Input	Output
1	3
2	4.5
3	8.1
4	8

3. Tony looks at the data in Exercise 2 and wonders, "If I keep the slope at 3, which line will give me the smallest mean squared error?" Sasha says, "Every line with slope 3 has an equation $y = 3x + b$ for some number b. So, let's keep b variable and calculate the sum of the squares of the errors as a function of b."

   a. Copy and complete the following table for Tony and Sasha.

   Data vs. Line Fit: $y = 3x + b$

Input	Output	Predicted	Error
1	3	$3 \cdot 1 + b = 3 + b$	$3 - (3 + b) = -b$
2	4.5	▨	▨
3	8.1	$3 \cdot 3 + b = 9 + b$	▨
4	8	▨	$-4 - b$

   b. What is the sum of the squares of the errors in terms of b?

   c. What value of b minimizes the sum in part (b)?

   d. What is the equation of the line that Tony wants?

   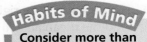

   Your CAS can be a great help here.

4. Use the data from Exercise 2 and the method from Exercise 3. Find the equation of the line with the given slope that minimizes the sum of the squares of the errors.

   a. slope $= 1$ **b.** slope $= 2$ **c.** slope $= 0$

Habits of Mind

Consider more than one strategy.
What is the balance point of the data?

5. Make a table like the one shown here using your solutions to Exercises 3 and 4.

   How does the constant term in the equation of the best-fitting line depend on the slope?

Slope	Equation of Best Line
0	▨
1	▨
2	▨
3	▨

6. Plot each data set below. Then use the plot to decide whether a line would be a good fit to the data.

Table 1

Input	Output
1	2
2	4
3	7
4	9
5	12

Table 2

Input	Output
2	1
5	3
7	4
10	6
13	8

Table 3

Input	Output
2	0
3	6
4	8
5	6
6	0
7	−10

Table 4

Input	Output
1	−5
2	−1
2	2
3	4
4	9

Go Online
Pearsonsuccessnet.com

7. For each table in Exercise 6, calculate the balance point $(\bar{x}, \bar{y})$. Plot it along with the data.

> **Remember...**
> $\bar{x}$ is the mean (average) of the *x*-values.

8. Show that all the lines you found in Exercises 3 and 4 are concurrent. Is their common point significant with respect to the data?

> Lines are concurrent if they all intersect in the same point.

9. The data set at the right follows a linear trend. Find the mean absolute error for the graph of each equation.

   a. $y = x + 3$ b. $y = x + 2$

   c. $y = x + 4$ d. $y = 2x - 2$

Input	Output
0	4
2	4
4	5
5	7
5	9
6	11
8	12
10	12

10. Find the standard error for the first three lines in Exercise 9. According to standard error, which one is the best fit?

11. **Standardized Test Prep**   What is the balance point of the data set below?

    (5, 1), (6, 22), (14, 17), (23, 29), (34, 27), (38, 42)

    A. (6, 6)   **B.** (20, 23)   **C.** (120, 138)   **D.** (114, 132)

12. Write About It There is an old saying: The mean squared error downplays small errors and magnifies large ones.

   a. Explain what the statement means and why it is true. (*Hint:* What do you know about the squares of positive numbers less than 1 and greater than 1?)

   b. What are the advantages of a measure of error that downplays small errors and magnifies large ones?

13. Take It Further Use Tor Carlson's data from Lesson 1.07, shown below.

   a. Use a graphing calculator to find the best-fit quadratic function of the form $y = Ax^2 + Bx + C$.

   b. Find the best-fit exponential function of the form $y = A \cdot B^x$.

   c. Which function has the smaller standard error?

Hours	Yeast Density
0	9.6
1	18.3
2	29.0
3	47.2
4	71.1
5	119.1
6	174.6
7	257.3

For help, see the TI-Nspire Handbook, p. 804.

yeast cells magnified 3000 times

Maintain Your Skills

14. a. Find five numbers that have a mean of 23.

   b. Find five numbers that have a mean of 23 and a median of 25.

   c. Take It Further Find five numbers that have a mean of 23, a median of 25, and a mode of 27.

   d. Take It Further Find a different set of five numbers that also has a mean of 23, a median of 25, and a mode of 27.

15. Consider the five numbers you found in Exercise 13a.

   a. If you increase each number by 7, what is the new mean?

   b. If you double each number, what is the new mean?

   c. Use the five numbers to build a new set that has a mean of 1.

   d. Use the five numbers to build a new set that has a mean of 0.

16. Find the mean, median, and mode for each data set.

   a. 6, 6, 7, 7, 10, 10, 10   **b.** 4, 5, 6, 7, 10, 10, 14   **c.** −2, 3, 5, 7, 10, 10, 23

Remember...

The *median* is the middle number in a sorted list of the data. The *mode* is the most common data value.

Go Online
Video Tutor
Pearsonsuccessnet.com

1.09 The Line of Best Fit, Part 2

You can use the fact that the line of best fit contains the balance point to develop a definition for the line of best fit.

Minds in Action   episode 3

Tony and Sasha used a calculator to plot the data from Lesson 1.08, shown below. The trend looked linear, so Tony asked the calculator for the line of best fit. They saw the graphs pictured here.

Months	Pounds
5	18
2	2
15	54
10	39
18	65
8	25
5	12
13	41
23	72
11	46

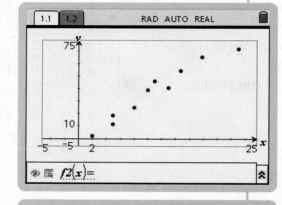

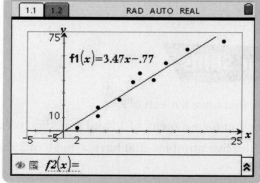

Tony So, the best-fit line has equation $y = 3.47x - 0.77$. How'd it get that?

Sasha The work we've done already makes me think that the line of best fit goes through the centroid. Let's see, the centroid is . . .

They calculate.

Tony The balance point is $(11, 37.4)$. And, yes, $(11, 37.4)$ is on the graph of $y = 3.47x - 0.77$. But $(11, 37.4)$ is on many lines.

Sasha But all the lines have equations with the same form. The equations of all the lines that go through the balance point look similar.

$$y - 37.4 = m(x - 11)$$

$$\text{or } y = m(x - 11) + 37.4$$

How does Tony know that $(11, 37.4)$ is on the graph of $y = 3.47x - 0.77$?

Hey, this is like Exercise 3 in Lesson 1.08. The only unknown is m. Let's go back to our error table and fill in the errors in terms of m. Then we'll calculate the mean squared error as a function of m and see if we can find an m that minimizes the mean squared error.

Tony   Sounds tricky, but let's try it and see what we get.

For You to Do

1. Help Tony and Sasha carry out their plan by copying and completing the error table below.

> Some entries are filled in for you.

Data vs. Line Fit: $y = m(x - 11) + 37.4$

Months	Pounds	Predicted	Error
5	18	$m(5 - 11) + 37.4$ $= -6m + 37.4$	$18 - (-6m + 37.4)$ $= 6m - 19.4$
2	2	▨	▨
15	54	▨	▨
10	39	$m(10 - 11) + 37.4$ $= -m + 37.4$	$39 - (-m + 37.4)$ $= m + 1.6$
18	65	▨	▨
8	25	$m(8 - 11) + 37.4$ $= -3m + 37.4$	$25 - (-3m + 37.4)$ $= 3m - 12.4$
5	12	▨	▨
13	41	▨	▨
23	72	$m(23 - 11) + 37.4$ $= 12m + 37.4$	$72 - (12m + 37.4)$ $= -12m + 34.6$
11	46	▨	▨

Sasha and Tony look at the completed table.

Tony   See, it *is* tricky. So the sum of the squares of the errors is

$(6m - 19.4)^2 + (9m - 35.4)^2 + (-4m + 16.6)^2 + (m + 1.6)^2$

$+ (-7m + 27.6)^2 + (3m - 12.4)^2 + (6m - 25.4)^2$

$+ (-2m + 3.6)^2 + (-12m + 34.6)^2 + (8.6)^2$

What a mess! What does that tell us?

Sasha   It's a mess all right, but look. It is a quadratic expression in m, and we know how to minimize a quadratic. If we have a CAS, we can use it to expand all this and see what we get.

Tony   And if we don't have a CAS, we can ask some friends to help—it's only a bunch of squares of binomials to expand.

Sasha uses her CAS to expand the sum of squares expression.

> **Habits of Mind**
>
> **Look for relationships.** How can you tell from the expression that its normal form is a quadratic in m?

Tony   Wow, much better. We get $4752.4 - 2610m + 376m^2$.

I know how to minimize that—it's just the vertex result we learned in our first-year algebra course. The vertex of the graph of $x \mapsto ax^2 + bx + c$ has x-coordinate $\frac{-b}{2a}$.

Sasha   Right. And $\dfrac{-(-2610)}{2 \cdot 376}$ is . . .

Sasha types it into the calculator.

Check the answer.

Tony   The suspense is too much.

Sasha   . . . approximately 3.47074. Great! That's where the 3.47 comes from.

Tony   And the best-fit line has equation $y = 3.47(x - 11) + 37.4$.

Sure enough, this gives us $y = 3.47x - 0.77$. Very smooth. This method will work for any data set. But even with a CAS, I wouldn't want to try it on sets with huge amounts of data.

Sasha   Maybe we can do it in general, once and for all, and get a formula for the best-fit line.

Tony   Let's save that for another day. It's lunch time.

Developing Habits of Mind

Check your assumptions. Tony and Sasha have discovered a method for finding a line that minimizes the sum of the squares of the errors for any data set. Their method rests on one assumption that you have not proved: All best-fit lines contain the balance point (centroid). It is not hard to prove this. In fact, if you try the project in Chapter 7 of this course, you will work through a proof. The proof is a bit technical, so consider it a reasonable but unproved conjecture for now.

Conjecture 1.1

For any set of data, the line of best fit contains the balance point.

Finally, you have a definition of *line of best fit*.

Definition

Given a set of data, the **line of best fit** is the line that minimizes the sum of the squares of the errors. It minimizes the mean squared error.

For most reasonable sets of data, there is exactly one line that satisfies this definition.

Exercises Practicing Habits of Mind

Check Your Understanding

1. Find the equation of the line of best fit for each table.

Habits of Mind

Look for relationships. Look for connections among your answers. Make conjectures.

Table 1

Input	Output
1	−10
2	8
3	12
4	2

Table 2

Input	Output
4	−10
5	8
6	12
7	2

Table 3

Input	Output
1	−22
2	58
3	40
4	24

Table 4

Input	Output
3	−22
4	58
5	40
6	24

2. Find the equation for the line of best fit for the table from Exercise 2 of Lesson 1.08 shown at the right.

Input	Output
1	3
2	4.5
3	8.1
4	8

3. Use the data set at the right.

   a. Find the best-fit line.

   b. **Take It Further** Find the best-fit quadratic and best-fit exponential. Determine which has the lesser mean squared error.

Input	Output
1	20
2	30
3	50
4	100
5	150
6	200
7	300
8	400

result

On Your Own

4. Find the equation of the line of best fit for each table.

Table 1

Input	Output
1	0
2	90
3	50
4	60

Table 2

Input	Output
−1	0
0	90
1	50
2	60

Table 3

Input	Output
−1	−1
0	89
1	49
2	59

Table 4

Input	Output
−1.5	−50
−0.5	40
0.5	0
1.5	10

5. Plot the data set in each table below. Then use the plot to decide whether a line would be a good approximation of the data.

Table 1

Input	Output
1	2
2	4
3	7
4	9
5	12

Table 2

Input	Output
2	1
5	3
7	4
10	6
13	8

Table 3

Input	Output
2	0
3	6
4	8
5	6
6	0
7	−10

Table 4

Input	Output
1	−5
2	−1
2	2
3	4
4	9

The relationship between the height and the age of a giant sequoia tree is linear. A plot of height against age will suggest a line.

result

6. For each table in Exercise 5, calculate the balance point $(\bar{x}, \bar{y})$ and plot it along with the data.

7. For each table in Exercise 5 with a linear trend, estimate the slope of the trend. Then use the balance point you found in Exercise 6 to write the equation of the line that best fits the data. Check your answer against the actual slope of the best-fit line.

8. The data set at the right follows a linear trend.

   Find the mean absolute error for each line.

   a. $y = x + 3$ **b.** $y = x + 2$

   c. $y = x + 4$ **d.** $y = 2x - 2$

Input	Output
0	4
2	4
4	5
5	7
5	9
6	11
8	12
10	12

9. Find the standard error for the first three lines in Exercise 8. Which one is the best fit according to standard error?

Remember...

The standard error is the square root of the mean squared error.

10. **Standardized Test Prep** Which statement about a line of best fit is true?

    A. The line of best fit must contain all the points in the data set.

    B. The line of best fit cannot contain any points in the data set.

    C. The line of best fit contains the balance point of the data set.

    D. The line of best fit contains the origin.

11. Pick one table from Exercise 4. Build a different table that has the same line of best fit.

12. **Take It Further** Find a set of data that has more than one line of best fit.

Find more than one line that satisfies the definition.

Maintain Your Skills

Exercises 13 and 14 lead to an algebraic identity that is useful in many statistical calculations.

13. Establish each algebraic identity.

    a. $(x_1 - x_2)^2 = 2((x_1)^2 + (x_2)^2) - (x_1 + x_2)^2$

    b. $(x_1 - x_2)^2 + (x_1 - x_3)^2 + (x_2 - x_3)^2$
       $= 3((x_1)^2 + (x_2)^2 + (x_3)^2) - (x_1 + x_2 + x_3)^2$

    c. $(x_1 - x_2)^2 + (x_1 - x_3)^2 + (x_1 - x_4)^2 + (x_2 - x_3)^2 + (x_2 - x_4)^2$
       $+ (x_3 - x_4)^2 = 4((x_1)^2 + (x_2)^2 + (x_3)^2 + (x_4)^2) - (x_1 + x_2 + x_3 + x_4)^2$

14. What might the next identity be? What is the general identity?

The name of the general identity is the Lagrange Identity.

In this investigation, you learned how linear functions can represent some data sets. You calculated the balance point for a data set and found the line of best fit. These questions will help you summarize what you have learned.

1. Find the line of best fit for the data in Table N.

Table N

Input	Output
−1	−2
2	88
5	48
6	58

2. How do you find a line that fits a set of data?

3. What is the definition of the line of best fit?

4. What is the line of best fit for data in the table below?

Men's 1500-meter Olympic Gold Medal Times (seconds)

Year	Time	Year	Time	Year	Time
1896	273.2	1932	231.2	1972	216.3
1900	246.2	1936	227.8	1976	219.2
1904	245.4	1948	229.8	1980	218.4
1908	243.4	1952	225.1	1984	212.5
1912	236.8	1956	221.2	1988	215.96
1920	241.8	1960	215.6	1992	220.12
1924	233.6	1964	218.1	1996	215.78
1928	233.2	1968	214.9	2000	212.07

SOURCE: *2007 ESPN Sports Almanac*

Vocabulary

In this investigation you learned these terms. Make sure you understand what each one means and how to use it.

- **balance point**
- **line of best fit**
- **mean absolute error**
- **mean squared error**
- **outlier**
- **standard error**

Multiple Choice

1. A linear function generates the input-output table below. What is the missing output?

Input	Output
1	5
−2	6
7	■

A. 7 **B.** 3 **C.** 4 **D.** 2

2. Which of the following lines best fits the data in the graph below?

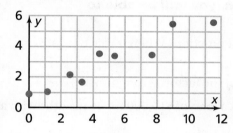

A. $y = \frac{1}{2}x - 1$ **B.** $y = 2x + 1$

C. $y = \frac{1}{2}x + \frac{1}{2}$ **D.** $y = -x + 0.6$

3. Which of the following points is the balance point for the data set below?

x	y
−1	4
2	6
3	−2
8	8

A. (3.5, 5) **B.** (3, 4) **C.** (12, 16) **D.** (2.5, 2)

Open Response

4. Find a closed-form function and a recursive function that match the following table.

n	d(n)
0	−7
1	−4.5
2	−2
3	0.5
4	3

5. Make a difference table for the input-output table below. Include enough columns to show a constant difference. Use your difference table to find a closed-form function that matches the table. Explain how you used the information in the table to find the function.

x	e(x)
0	5
1	10
2	17
3	26
4	37
5	50

6. Find the equation for the line with a slope of 2 that has the least standard error for the data set below.

x	y
0	−4
1	2
2	3
3	5

Does the line you found contain the balance point of the data set?

More About Recursive Models

In *More About Recursive Models,* you will analyze the following question.

How does a bank figure out the monthly payment on a loan?

You will answer this question with a recursively defined function that calculates the balance you owe in any month of a car loan.

You will also see a function that has no simple closed form—its recursive model is its primary definition. This is the factorial function. Its value at *n* is the product of all integers between 1 and *n*.

$$f(n) = 1 \cdot 2 \cdot 3 \cdot \cdots \cdot n$$

By the end of this investigation, you will be able to answer questions like these.

1. What is a recursive definition of a function? When is this type of definition useful?

2. What is the recursive definition of the factorial function?

3. What is the monthly payment on a loan of $10,000 for 36 months with an interest rate of 5%?

You will learn how to

- find the monthly payment on a loan given the interest rate, term, and amount you borrow

- understand how the monthly payment on a loan changes with the amount you borrow

- build a recursively defined function that agrees with a table

- use the recursive model for the factorial function

You will develop these habits and skills:

- Build and modify recursive definitions for functions.

- Search for hidden regularity in tables of numbers.

- Reason about algebraic forms.

- Build models for recursively defined functions in your function-modeling language.

You have to set the table. There are 3 · 2 · 1, or 6, possible arrangements of three utensils.

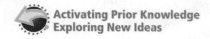

You can use a table to help you rewrite a recursive definition for a function as a closed-form definition.

For You to Explore

For Exercises 1–5, make a table of the function values for inputs between 0 and 10. Then find a closed-form definition that agrees with the table. Use your closed-form definition to find the outputs at 103, 104, and 245.

1. $g(n) = \begin{cases} 5 & \text{if } n = 0 \\ g(n-1) + 7 & \text{if } n > 0 \end{cases}$

You can build models of the functions in your function-modeling language.

2. $t(n) = \begin{cases} 1 & \text{if } n = 0 \\ 2 \cdot t(n-1) & \text{if } n > 0 \end{cases}$

3. $j(n) = \begin{cases} 0 & \text{if } n = 0 \\ j(n-1) + 2n - 1 & \text{if } n > 0 \end{cases}$

4. $k(n) = \begin{cases} 0 & \text{if } n = 0 \\ k(n-1) + 2n & \text{if } n > 0 \end{cases}$

5. $\ell(n) = \begin{cases} 0 & \text{if } n = 0 \\ \ell(n-1) + n & \text{if } n > 0 \end{cases}$

For Exercises 6–8, find a recursively defined function that agrees with each table. Make a table of the function values for inputs from 0 to 10.

6.

Input	Output
0	6
1	9
2	12
3	15
4	18
5	21

7.

Input	Output
0	7
1	11
2	15
3	19
4	23
5	27

8.

Input	Output
0	7
1	18
2	33
3	52
4	75
5	102

Exercises *Practicing Habits of Mind*

On Your Own

For Exercises 9–12, make a table of the function values for inputs between 0 and 10. Then find a closed-form definition that agrees with the table. Use your closed-form definition to find the outputs at 103, 104, and 245.

9. $g(n) = \begin{cases} 0 & \text{if } n = 0 \\ g(n-1) + 1 & \text{if } n > 0 \end{cases}$

> You can build models of the functions in your function language.

10. $t(n) = \begin{cases} 1 & \text{if } n = 0 \\ 3 \cdot t(n-1) & \text{if } n > 0 \end{cases}$

11. $j(n) = \begin{cases} 1 & \text{if } n = 0 \\ j(n-1) + 2n + 1 & \text{if } n > 0 \end{cases}$

12. $k(n) = \begin{cases} 0 & \text{if } n = 0 \\ k(n-1) + \dfrac{n(n-1)}{2} & \text{if } n > 0 \end{cases}$

13. Find a recursively defined function that agrees with the table below. Make a table of the function values for inputs from 0 to 10.

Input	Output
0	1
1	1
2	2
3	6
4	24
5	120

> **Go Online**
> **Video Tutor**
> Pearsonsuccessnet.com

14. Make a table of the function f defined below for inputs from 0 to 10.

$$f(n) = \begin{cases} 1 & \text{if } n = 0 \\ 1 & \text{if } n = 1 \\ f(n-1) + f(n-2) & \text{if } n > 1 \end{cases}$$

> For advice on modeling recursive functions, see the TI-Nspire Handbook, p. 804.

15. a. Use your function-modeling language to model the function b defined below. For what value of n is $b(n)$ closest to 0?

$$b(n) = \begin{cases} 10,000 & \text{if } n = 0 \\ \frac{12.05}{12} \cdot b(n-1) - 438.71 & \text{if } n > 0 \end{cases}$$

b. Find the value of x that makes $b(36)$ closest to 0 for the definition of b below.

$$b(n) = \begin{cases} 10,000 & \text{if } n = 0 \\ \frac{12.02}{12} \cdot b(n-1) - x & \text{if } n > 0 \end{cases}$$

Maintain Your Skills

16. How many ways are there to arrange the letters in each word?

a. TO

b. MOP

c. FORM

d. SHOWN

e. CLOSED

17. How many ways are there to arrange the letters in "ABCDEFHIJ"?

18. Show that the following identity is true.

$$\frac{n(n+1)}{2} - \frac{(n-1)n}{2} = n$$

Recursion Using Mirrors

1.11 Monthly Payments

Suppose you want to buy a car. You can put $1000 down and pay $250 per month. The interest rate is 5%, and the dealer wants the loan paid off in three years. How much can you afford to spend on the car?

A recursive approach lets you experiment using your function modeling language. Can you afford a $10,000 car? Well, after you pay $1000 down, you can borrow $9000. At the end of 36 months, you want the balance to be 0.

Begin with a simpler model, one that would hold in an ideal world where you did not have to pay any interest.

- At the end of Month 0, you owe $9000 (that is how much you borrowed, and Month 0 is when the loan starts).

- For any month after Month 0, you owe $250 less than the month before (because you paid $250).

If $b(n)$ is the balance in dollars at the end of the nth month, then

$$b(n) = \begin{cases} 9000 & \text{if } n = 0 \\ b(n-1) - 250 & \text{if } n > 0 \end{cases}$$

> Every now and then, car dealers offer a 0% interest rate.

For You to Do

For Problems 1–4, find how much you owe after each time span.

1. 1 month
2. 2 months
3. 6 months
4. 1 year
5. Can you pay off your car in 36 months? If not, how much do you still owe?

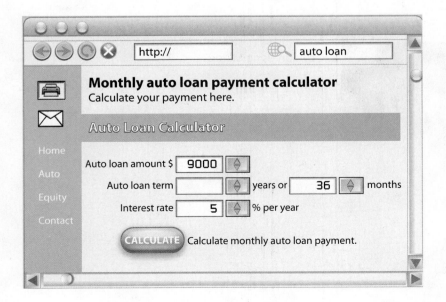

> Go Online
> Pearsonsuccessnet.com

For Discussion

6. Find a closed form for the function b on the previous page.

What happens when you take the 5% interest into account?

- Month 0 is when the loan starts. At the end of Month 0, you owe $9000. That amount is how much you borrowed.

- For any month after Month 0, you owe the balance from the previous month, plus the interest on that balance, minus $250.

The interest for one month is one twelfth the interest for a whole year. The interest for a year is 5%, so the interest for a month is $\frac{0.05}{12}$ times the balance for that month.

You can now refine the definition of b.

$$b(n) = \begin{cases} \$9000 & \text{if } n = 0 \\ b(n-1) + \frac{0.05}{12} \cdot b(n-1) - \$250 & \text{if } n > 0 \end{cases}$$

At the end of the first month you owe

- $9000 (what you owed at the beginning of the month)
- plus $\frac{0.05}{12} \cdot \$9000$ (which is $45.83)
- minus $250 (your monthly payment)

$$\$9000 + \left(\frac{0.05}{12} \cdot \$9000 \right) - \$250 = \$8787.50$$

> Banks use the following rule: What you owe at the end of the month is what you owed at the start of the month, plus $\frac{1}{12}$ of the yearly interest on that amount, minus the monthly payment.

For You to Do

7. What do you owe at the end of Month 2?

8. What do you owe at the end of Month 3?

The Memory Error

When you model the new recursive definition for b, your system can quickly run out of memory. Why?

> Your calculator may return a message such as "Recursion too deep."

How does a computer find $b(4)$ using this definition? You tell it that $n = 4$, and, as it scans the definition, it notes what it needs to do. It sees two places where it will need to compute $b(3)$.

$$b(4) = b(3) + \frac{0.05}{12} \cdot b(3) - 250$$

$$b(2) + \frac{0.05}{12} \cdot b(2) - 250 \qquad b(2) + \frac{0.05}{12} \cdot b(2) - 250$$

$$? \qquad ? \qquad ? \qquad ?$$

In each of these 2 computations of $b(3)$, the computer needs to compute $b(2)$ twice, for a total of 4 times. Continuing, it computes $b(1)$ 8 times, and the base case $b(0)$ 16 times. Then it feeds this information back through three layers of computation to do 1 last calculation to get $b(4)$.

Adding the number of evaluations of b, you have

$$1 + 2 + 4 + 8 + 16 = 31 = 2^{(4+1)} - 1$$

That is how many computations the computer needs to compute $b(4)$. In general, calculating $b(n)$ requires tracking $2^{(n+1)} - 1$ evaluations of b. No wonder your calculator or computer runs into trouble quickly.

But where your calculator sees two calculations to be done separately, a person would notice that they are the same—both $b(n - 1)$. You can figure it out once and then plug it in both places.

$$b(4) = b(3) + \frac{0.05}{12} \cdot b(3) - 250$$

$$b(2) + \frac{0.05}{12} \cdot b(2) - 250$$

You can force the computer to do the calculation the smart way as well. If you take the expression $b(n - 1) + \frac{0.05}{12} \cdot b(n - 1)$ and factor out $b(n - 1)$, you get the following expression.

$$b(n - 1) + \frac{0.05}{12} \cdot b(n - 1) = 1 \cdot b(n - 1) + \frac{0.05}{12} \cdot b(n - 1)$$

$$= b(n - 1)\left(1 + \frac{0.05}{12}\right)$$

Now the computer only needs to track $n + 1$ evaluations of b in order to find $b(n)$. This change makes the computation manageable.

Estimate. Estimating shows that $2^{10} > 1000$ and $2^{20} > 1,000,000$.

Smart calculation does not guarantee you will never get the memory error, just that you will not get it as soon!

For You to Do

9. Build a model in your function-modeling language for the function b below.

$$b(n) = \begin{cases} 9000 & \text{if } n = 0 \\ \left(1 + \frac{0.05}{12}\right) \cdot b(n - 1) - 250 & \text{if } n > 0 \end{cases}$$

You can add extra inputs that will let you change the monthly payment, the amount of the loan, or the interest rate on the loan. See the TI-Nspire Handbook, p. 804.

10. How much do you owe after 6 months? How long does it take you to pay the loan down to $8000?

Exercises *Practicing Habits of Mind*

Check Your Understanding

For Exercises 1–3, suppose you take a $9000 loan at 5% interest with a $250 monthly payment.

1. How much do you owe at the end of one year?

2. Can you pay off the loan in 36 months?

3. What monthly payment will let you pay off the loan in each amount of time?

    a. 36 months   **b.** 39 months   **c.** 48 months

4. If you can only afford to pay $250 per month, and you must pay your loan off in 36 months at 5% interest, how much money can you borrow?

5. What does the interest rate have to be so that you can afford a $12,000 car with $1000 down and payments of $310 per month for 36 months?

On Your Own

6. Suppose you want to pay off a car loan in 36 months. Pick an interest rate and keep it constant. Investigate how the monthly payment changes with the cost of the car.

> Make sure you state what interest rate you are using. You can find a rate in a newspaper car ad.

    a. Make a table like the one below and complete it.

Cost of Car (thousands of dollars)	Monthly Payment
10	▪
11	▪
12	▪
13	▪
14	▪
15	▪
16	▪
⋮	⋮

Go Online
Pearsonsuccessnet.com

    b. Find either a closed-form or a recursive definition for a function that agrees with your table. Build a model of your function.

    c. Use your model to find the monthly payment on a $26,000 car.

> If this function works for all inputs, you can use it to calculate the monthly payment in terms of the cost of the car.

7. A local car dealer has an ad each week that offers two deals on its cars.

- You can get a $2000 rebate on the list price of the car. You then pay off the rest in 36 months at 5% interest.

- Instead of the rebate, you can get a low 0.9% interest rate and then pay off the full list price of the car in 36 months.

Cars on the lot sell at prices between $20,000 and $40,000. For which cars is it better to take the rebate? For which cars is it better to take the low interest rate? For what price are the deals the same?

8. Standardized Test Prep Suppose you take a $10,000 loan at 5% interest. How much do you owe after three monthly payments of $500?

A. $1500.00   **B.** $8500.00   **C.** $8619.27   **D.** $8925.00

Habits of Mind

Organize what you know. Make a table for prices between $20,000 and $40,000 in increments of $1000. Figure out the monthly payment for each price. You can use your function-modeling language and a spreadsheet.

Maintain Your Skills

9. Evaluate each sum.

a. $1 + 2$

b. $1 + 2 + 2^2$

c. $1 + 2 + 2^2 + 2^3$

d. $1 + 2 + 2^2 + 2^3 + 2^4$

e. $1 + 2 + 2^2 + 2^3 + 2^4 + 2^5$

f. $1 + 2 + 2^2 + 2^3 + 2^4 + 2^5 + \cdots + 2^9$

10. Use the description of s below.

$$s(n) = 1 + 2 + 2^2 + 2^3 + \cdots + 2^n$$

a. Find a recursive definition for s.

b. Find a closed form for s.

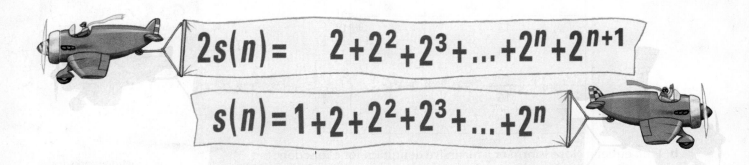

$$2s(n) = 2 + 2^2 + 2^3 + \ldots + 2^n + 2^{n+1}$$

$$s(n) = 1 + 2 + 2^2 + 2^3 + \ldots + 2^n$$

1.12 The Factorial Function

Not all useful functions have both closed forms and recursive models. In this lesson, you will study a very useful function that has no simple closed form.

Suppose you have three books, labeled A, B, and C. In how many ways can you arrange them on a shelf? Well, you could make a systematic list.

A	B	C
A	C	D
B	A	C
B	C	A
C	A	B
C	B	A

So there are six arrangements. But what if you have 5 books? Or 8 books? Making a list of all possible arrangements would take a long time.

Developing Habits of Mind

Establish a process. One way to think about the arrangement problem is to model it with a function. Let

$f(n) =$ the number of ways to arrange n books on a shelf

You can think about f and try to get a closed-form or recursive definition for it. For example, since there is one way to arrange a single book, two ways to arrange 2 books, and six ways to arrange 3 books, you have the start of a table for f.

n	$f(n)$
1	1
2	2
3	6

> This is an example of a counting problem. In many counting problems, recursive definitions are easier to find than closed forms.

There are many functions that agree with f for inputs 1, 2, and 3. You want one that counts arrangements of any number of books.

Look for a recursive relation. Can you use the fact that there are six ways to arrange 3 books to find how many ways there are to arrange 4 books? Consider the following steps.

> Just for fun, make a table for
> $$g(x) = \frac{5x^2 - 15x + 12}{2}$$
> with inputs 1, 2, and 3. What is $g(4)$?

Step 1 Suppose your books are labeled A, B, C, and D. First place D. There are four places to do that. Pick one.

Step 2 Now you have three books left and three spots in which you can place them. But you have already solved that problem. There are $f(3)$, or 6, ways to arrange 3 books.

Step 3 So, for each of your four choices for Book D, there are $f(3)$, or 6, ways to arrange the rest of the books. There must be $4 \cdot f(3) = 24$ ways to arrange the four books.

For You to Do

1. Write out the 24 arrangements of four books in a list. Start by placing D, and then fill out the shelf with all six arrangements of A, B, and C.

For Discussion

2. Come up with an argument to show that $f(n) = n \cdot f(n - 1)$ for $n > 1$.

This leads to the definition of a function that appears throughout mathematics.

Definition

The recursive rule below defines the **factorial function.**

$$f(n) = \begin{cases} 1 & \text{if } n = 0 \\ n \cdot f(n - 1) & \text{if } n > 0 \end{cases}$$

In how many ways can you arrange 0 books on a shelf?

For Discussion

3. Build a model for f in your function-modeling language. Make a table of f for inputs between 1 and 6.

Is there a closed form for f? Look at $f(5)$.

$$f(5) = 5 \cdot f(4) \qquad \text{But } f(4) = 4 \cdot f(3).$$
$$= 5 \cdot 4 \cdot f(3) \qquad \text{But } f(3) = 3 \cdot f(2).$$
$$= 5 \cdot 4 \cdot 3 \cdot f(2) \qquad \text{But } f(2) = 2 \cdot f(1).$$
$$= 5 \cdot 4 \cdot 3 \cdot 2 \cdot f(1) \quad \text{You know } f(1) = 1.$$
$$= 5 \cdot 4 \cdot 3 \cdot 2 \cdot 1 \qquad \text{Now you can compute.}$$
$$= 120$$

You can work out $f(n)$ for other positive integers n. You will see that $f(n)$ is the product of all the integers from 1 to n.

Developing Habits of Mind

Detect the key characteristics. So, is $f(n) = 1 \cdot 2 \cdot 3 \cdots \cdot n$ a closed-form definition for the factorial function?

It does not seem to use $f(n - 1)$. But the dots conceal the true nature of f. You cannot use this equation to build a model for f in your function-modeling language. A machine cannot guess what the missing numbers are.

Can you write a closed-form definition for the factorial function? The answer is no. In a closed-form definition, you can calculate the output of the function at n by a fixed number of operations regardless of the value of n. But computing the factorial function requires more operations for larger values of the input. The factorial function has no simple closed form.

Computer scientists use this distinction between closed-form and recursive definitions.

The factorial function is so useful that it has a formal notation. You represent the factorial of n as $n!$. So, $n!$ is the product of all the integers from 1 to n.

For You to Do

Just to get used to the notation, find the numerical value of each expression.

4. $5!$ **5.** $7!$ **6.** $\dfrac{7!}{5!}$ **7.** $\dfrac{100!}{98!}$

Your calculator has a model of the factorial function built in. Or you can use your own recursive model.

Exercises Practicing Habits of Mind

Check Your Understanding

1. Use the definition of g below.

   $$g(n) = \frac{n!}{(n-1)!}$$

   Make a table for g with inputs from 2 to 10. Find a closed form for g.

2. Use the definition of h below.

   $$h(n) = \frac{n!}{(n-2)!}$$

   Make a table for h with inputs from 3 to 10. Find a closed form for h.

3. Express $k(n) = n(n-1)(n-2)(n-3)$ in terms of factorials.

4. Express $q(n)$ below in terms of $n!$.

   $$q(n) = \begin{cases} 1 & \text{if } n = 0 \\ n^2 \cdot q(n-1) & \text{if } n > 0 \end{cases}$$

5. Without computing the numbers exactly, find how many zeros are at the end of each number.

   a. $5!$ **b.** $10!$ **c.** $20!$

On Your Own

6. Solve each equation for n.

a. $\frac{n!}{(n-2)!} = 56$ **b.** $\frac{(n-1)!}{(n-3)!} = 56$ **c.** $\frac{(n+1)!}{(n-1)!} = 56$ **d.** $\frac{(n+1)!}{n!} = 56$

7. Find a recursively defined function that agrees with the table at the right.

8. Standardized Test Prep The formula for the number of possible ways to choose r objects from a set of n objects is $\frac{n!}{r!(n-r)!}$. How many different ways can you choose a group of 3 students from a group of 8 students?

A. 24   **B.** 56

C. 120   **D.** 336

Input	Output
1	2
2	4
3	12
4	48
5	240
6	1440

Is there a closed form?

9. How many zeros are at the end of 150!?

Go Online
Pearsonsuccessnet.com

For each function in Exercises 10–13, do parts (a)–(c).

  a. Make an input-output table for whole-number inputs from 1 to 5.

  b. Find a recursive model for the function.

  c. Decide whether there is a closed form. Explain.

10. $r(n) = 1 + 2 + \ldots + n$

11. $s(n) = 1 + 3 + 5 + \ldots + (2n + 1)$

12. $t(n) = 1 \cdot 3 \cdot 5 \cdot \ldots \cdot (2n + 1)$

13. $r(n) = 1 + 3 + 3^2 + \ldots + 3^n$

14. Take It Further Are there any values of n such that $n! > 100^n$?

Hint: If S is the sum of the powers of 3 from 1 to 3^n, then what is $3S$?

Maintain Your Skills

For the expanded form of each expression, find the coefficient of the second-highest power of x and the constant term.

15. $(x - 1)(x - 2)$

16. $(x - 1)(x - 2)(x - 3)$

17. $(x - 1)(x - 2)(x - 3)(x - 4)$

18. $(x - 1)(x - 2)(x - 3)(x - 4)(x - 5)(x - 6)(x - 7)(x - 8)$

In this investigation, you learned to evaluate recursive functions, including the factorial function. You calculated the balance on a loan and solved for an unknown variable in a monthly payment situation. These questions will help you summarize what you have learned.

1. Find a closed form for the following function.

$$k(n) = \begin{cases} 0 & \text{if } n = 0 \\ k(n-1) + 4n & \text{if } n > 0 \end{cases}$$

For Exercises 2 and 3, find a recursively defined function that agrees with each table. Make a table of the function for inputs from 1 to 10.

2.

Input	Output
0	3
1	8
2	13
3	18
4	23
5	28

3.

Input	Output
0	3
1	11
2	24
3	42
4	65
5	93

4. Make a table for the function b below with inputs from 1 to 10.

$$b(n) = \begin{cases} 12{,}000 & \text{if } n = 0 \\ \dfrac{12.06}{12} \cdot b(n-1) - 400 & \text{if } n > 0 \end{cases}$$

There are 4!, or 24, possible arrangements of four utensils.

a. Suppose $b(n)$ is a model for the balance on a loan at the end of month n. What is the amount of the loan? What is the interest rate?

b. For what value of n is $b(n)$ closest to 0?

5. What is a recursive definition of a function? When is this type of definition useful?

6. What is the recursive definition of the factorial function?

7. What is the monthly payment on a loan of $10,000 for 36 months with an interest rate of 5%?

Vocabulary and Notation

In this investigation, you learned this term and symbol. Make sure you understand what each one means and how to use it.

• **factorial function, $n!$**

Project: Using Mathematical Habits

More On Monthly Payments

You need to consider several variables when you use a loan to buy a car:

- the cost of the car
- the interest rate
- the monthly payment
- the number of months that you will take to pay off the loan

The general function b below relates these variables. It gives the balance at the end of n months on a loan amount of c dollars at an interest rate of i% (represented by a decimal) with a monthly payment of m dollars.

$$b(n, c, i, m) = \begin{cases} c & \text{if } n = 0 \\ (1 + i)b(n - 1, c, i, m) - m & \text{if } n > 0 \end{cases}$$

In this project, you will look at the effects of two of the variables on the rest.

- If i and n are constant, how does c depend on m?
- If c and n are constant, how does m depend on i?
- If i and c are constant, how does m depend on n?

If you finance $9000 at 5% interest for 36 months to buy this car, you will pay $9710.57 in all.

Cost and Monthly Payment

1. Pick an interest rate and keep it constant. Suppose you want to pay off a car loan in 36 months. Investigate how much you can spend on a car for a given monthly payment.

a. Make a table like the one below.

Monthly Payment	Cost of Car
200	▪
210	▪
220	▪
230	▪
240	▪
250	▪
260	▪
270	▪
280	▪
⋮	⋮

b. Find either a closed-form or a recursive definition that lets you calculate the cost of the car in terms of the monthly payment. Build a model for your function.

c. Use your model from part (b) to find the cost of a car you can afford with a $360 monthly payment. Check your result with the original model for b.

Interest Rate and Monthly Payment

2. Investigate the effect of interest on the monthly payment. Pick a car price and keep it constant. Suppose you want to pay off a car in 36 months. The interest rate might range from 0% to 15%.

a. Make a table like the one below.

Interest Rate (%)	Monthly Payment
0	■
1	■
2	■
3	■
4	■
5	■
6	■
7	■
8	■
⋮	⋮

b. Find the monthly payment on the car when the interest rate is 13%.

c. **Take It Further** Find either a closed-form or a recursive definition that lets you calculate the monthly payment in terms of the interest rate. Express the interest rate as a decimal or a percent. Build a model for your function.

d. **Take It Further** Use the model you wrote in part (c) to find the monthly payment on your car when the interest rate is 13%. Check your result with the original model for *b*.

Length of Loan and Monthly Payment

3. Investigate the effect of the length of the loan on the monthly payment. Pick a car price and keep it constant. Find the monthly payment on the car as the number of months varies.

a. Make a table like the one below.

Term (months)	Monthly Payment
24	■
28	■
32	■
36	■
40	■
44	■
48	■
52	■
56	■
⋮	⋮

b. Find the monthly payment on the car when the term of the loan is five years.

c. **Take It Further** Find either a closed-form or a recursive definition that lets you calculate the monthly payment in terms of the length of the loan. Build a model for your function.

d. **Take It Further** Use the model you wrote in part (c) to find the monthly payment on the car when the length of the loan is five years. Check your result with the original model for *b*.

In **Investigation 1A,** you learned how to

- find closed-form and recursive functions to fit input-output tables
- use difference tables to determine whether a linear or a quadratic function will fit a given table
- use the up-and-over and hockey stick properties of difference tables

The following questions will help you check your understanding.

1. Write a closed-form and a recursive rule to match the table below. Use either rule to find $a(15)$.

n	a(n)
0	1
1	5
2	25
3	125
4	625
5	3125

2. Copy and complete the difference table below.

x	b(x)	Δ	Δ²
0	1	2	3
1	▦	▦	▦
2	▦	8	▦
3	▦	▦	3
4	▦	▦	
5	41		

What kind of function agrees with the inputs and outputs in the table?

3. Make a difference table for the input-output table below. Include enough columns to show a constant difference. Use your difference table to find a closed-form function that matches the table. Explain how you used the information in the table to find the function.

x	c(x)
0	−3
1	4
2	15
3	30
4	49

In **Investigation 1B,** you learned how to

- decide whether a linear function can reasonably represent a data set
- calculate error measures for a given data set and fitting line
- find the balance point and line of best fit for a data set

The following questions will help you check your understanding.

4. Graph the data in the following data set.

Find the balance point for the data set. Include it in your graph. Would a linear function be a good fit for the data?

x	y
0	11
0.5	8
1	6
2	4
4	2
5	1.5
6	1
7	0.5
10	0
12	0

5. Find the mean absolute error, mean squared error, and standard error for the data in the following table and the fitting line $y = 3x - 2$.

x	y
1	0.2
4	8.8
6	17
7	21.1

6. Calculate the line of best fit for the following data set.

x	y
1	−6
2	2
3	8
4	12

In **Investigation 1C,** you learned how to

- define, identify, and evaluate recursive functions including the factorial function

- calculate the balance on a loan given a loan amount, interest rate, length, and monthly payment

- solve for an unknown variable in a monthly payment situation

The following questions will help you check your understanding.

7. Make a table of the function

$$g(n) = \frac{n!}{(n-2)!2!}$$ with inputs from 3 to 10.

8. Find recursive and closed-form functions that agree with your table from Exercise 7.

9. Suppose that you can afford to pay $1000 down and $300 per month. You can get a 36-month loan at 3%. What is the maximum price of a car that you can buy in this situation?

10. The car Maya wants to buy costs $12,000. The dealer offers her a choice of loans. She can get a $1000 rebate that she can use as her down payment. She can then take out a loan at 5% interest for 36 months to pay off the loan. Or, she can choose a zero down payment option with a 0.9% interest rate for 36 months. Which loan has the lower monthly payment?

Multiple Choice

1. Which of the following recursive functions best fits the table below?

Input, n	Output, $a(n)$
0	2
1	−1
2	−7
3	−19
4	−43

A. $a(n) = \begin{cases} 2 & \text{if } n = 0 \\ a(n - 1) - 3 & \text{if } n > 0 \end{cases}$

B. $a(n) = \begin{cases} 2 & \text{if } n = 0 \\ 2 \cdot a(n - 1) - 5 & \text{if } n > 0 \end{cases}$

C. $a(n) = \begin{cases} 2 & \text{if } n = 0 \\ a(n - 1) + 2n - 5 & \text{if } n > 0 \end{cases}$

D. $a(n) = \begin{cases} 2 & \text{if } n = 0 \\ a(n - 1) - 2n - 2 & \text{if } n > 0 \end{cases}$

2. Which of the following lines best fits the data in the graph below?

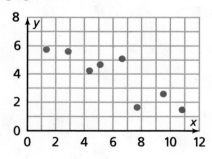

A. $y = -\frac{1}{2}x - 2$ **B.** $y = -2x + 6$

C. $y = -0.6x + 7$ **D.** $y = x - 3$

3. The table below is part of a difference table for a function $b(n)$. The table has constant first differences. Find $b(20)$.

Input, n	Output, $b(n)$
0	■
1	−3
2	■
3	■
4	24

A. 168

B. 177

C. 180

D. You cannot determine the value of $b(20)$ from the information given.

4. Which of the following statements about the line of best fit for a table of data is false?

A. The line of best fit contains the centroid of the data.

B. The line of best fit is the line with the least possible standard error.

C. The line of best fit must contain at least two data points.

D. The line of best fit may not have the least mean absolute error of any fitting line.

5. Solve the equation below for n.

$$\frac{(n + 1)!}{(n - 1)!} = 72$$

A. $n = 7$ **B.** $n = 8$

C. $n = 9$ **D.** $n = 10$

6. Dana bought a car for $12,000. She put $1000 down and got a 36-month loan at 4% interest. How much is her car payment each month?

A. $305.56   **B.** $324.76

C. $329.68   **D.** $359.62

Open Response

7. Make a table of the following recursive function with inputs from 0 to 10.

$$m(n) = \begin{cases} 4 & \text{if } n = 0 \\ 2 \cdot m(n-1) + 3n - 10 & \text{if } n > 0 \end{cases}$$

Find a closed-form function that agrees with your table. Use it to find $m(80)$.

8. Find a recursive function definition and a closed-form function definition that agree with the table below.

n	p(n)
0	−8
1	−5
2	−2
3	1
4	4

9. Copy and complete the difference table below.

x	g(x)	Δ	Δ²
0	4	▦	▦
1	7	▦	▦
2	8	▦	▦
3	7	▦	
4	4		

Find a closed-form function definition that agrees with the table. Explain how you can find the coefficients of the function from the difference table.

Use Table R for Exercises 10 and 11.

Table R

Input	Output
−2.1	−8.2
1.3	−0.6
4	4.8
5.2	7.4

10. Calculate the mean absolute error, the mean squared error, and the standard error for the data in Table R and the fitting line $y = 2x - 3$.

11. Find the balance point for the data in Table R. Does the line with equation $y = 2x - 3$ pass through the balance point? Is the line with equation $y = 2x - 3$ the line of slope 2 that minimizes the standard error for Table R?

12. Find an equation for the line of best fit for the following set of data.

x	y
5	18
2	12
8	23
5	12

13. Use your knowledge of the factorial function to show that the following equation is true.

$$\frac{n!}{(n-1)! \cdot 1!} + \frac{n!}{(n-2)! \cdot 2!} = \frac{(n+1)!}{(n-1)! \cdot 2!}$$

14. Shawn can put $1200 down and pay $300 a month on a loan. He can get a 36-month loan at 5% interest. How much can Shawn afford to pay for a car?

15. Shawn found a car for the exact price you calculated in Exercise 14. How much will Shawn pay over the life of the loan? If Shawn pays $350 each month instead of $300 with the same loan, how many months will it take him to pay off the loan? How much will he save over the life of the loan?

Functions and Polynomials

Mathematics has a remarkable relationship with the natural world. Often a table of observations of two related quantities matches a mathematical function. Examination of this function can reveal the relationship between the two quantities.

Suppose you throw a ball up into the air and measure its height at different times. Suppose further that you make a table with columns for the time elapsed since the throw and the height observed at that time. There is a quadratic function that matches this table.

If you measure the velocity of the ball at several times and make a table of time and the ball's velocity, a linear function matches the table. The linear function shows that the upward velocity of the ball decreases at a constant rate, eventually becoming negative as the ball stops rising and begins to fall back down.

The functions tell you what is happening to the ball. A scientific explanation tells why the function has the structure it does and what the coefficients and roots of the polynomial mean.

Vocabulary and Notation

- composite function, $g \circ f$
- difference of cubes
- domain
- equal functions
- function
- identity function
- inverse function, f^{-1}
- Lagrange interpolation
- one-to-one
- piecewise-defined function
- quadratic formula
- quotient
- range
- rational expression
- remainder
- sum of cubes
- target
- $x \mapsto y$ (x maps to y)
- $\mathbb{R}$ (the real numbers)
- $\mathbb{Z}$ (the integers)
- $\mathbb{Q}$ (the rational numbers)

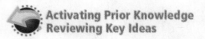
In your first-year algebra course, you studied the basic facts about polynomials—what they are, how to talk about them, and how to calculate with them. This lesson reviews that material.

Start by reviewing some vocabulary.

First, pick a set of variables. The variables are just placeholders, and their meaning does not matter at the moment. The variables can be letters or expressions, such as x, y, $\sqrt{x}$, $\frac{1}{z}$, or more complicated expressions.

A **monomial** is an expression that you can write as a product of a nonzero number (this is the **coefficient**), and one or more variables, each raised to a nonnegative integer exponent.

> The **degree of a monomial** is the sum of the exponents of each variable in the monomial.

When you want to specify the variables, you say that a monomial is a "monomial in something." For example, $4x^2y^3$ is a monomial in x and y.

A **polynomial** is a sum of monomials. The monomials are the **terms** of the polynomial.

The **degree of a polynomial** is the degree of all of its terms.

Here are a few examples:

- $3x^2$ is a monomial in x of degree 2. Its coefficient is 3.
- The monomial $7x^2y^3$ has coefficient 7, variables x and y, and degree 5.
- $7x^6 + 5x^3 - 3$ is a polynomial in x of degree 6.
- $7x^6 + 5x^3 - 3$ is also polynomial in x^3 of degree 2, because you can rewrite it as $7(x^3)^2 + 5(x^3) - 3$.
- The monomial b^3 has coefficient 1, variable b, and degree 3.
- The monomial $-\frac{1}{2}$ has coefficient $-\frac{1}{2}$ and degree 0. One way to think about this is that $x^0 = 1$, so $-\frac{1}{2}$ is equivalent to $-\frac{1}{2}x^0$.

>
> $b^3 = 1b^3$

- You can say that $3a + a^2b + 2ab^3 + 9b + 3$ is a polynomial in a and b. You can also say it is a quadratic polynomial in a with coefficients that are polynomials in b.

$$(9b + 3) + (3 + 2b^3)a + ba^2$$

You can also say that $3a + a^2b + 2ab^3 + 9b + 3$ is a cubic polynomial in b with coefficients that are polynomials in a.

$$(3a + 3) + (a^2 + 9)b + 2ab^3$$

For You to Do

Consider the polynomial $\frac{1}{x^2} + \frac{3}{x^6}$.

1. Explain why it is not a polynomial in x.

2. It is a polynomial in $\frac{1}{x}$. What is its degree?

3. It is also a polynomial in $\frac{1}{x^2}$. What is its degree?

Facts and Notation

There are several points to remember.

- Two polynomials are equivalent if you can transform one into another with the basic rules of algebra. These rules include the commutative properties for addition and multiplication, the associative properties for addition and multiplication, and the Distributive Property.

- An *identity* is a statement that two polynomials are equivalent. For example, $x(x - 1) = x^2 - x$ is an identity. You can transform one side of the equation into the other using the basic rules of algebra.

- The form implies function principle says that if two polynomials are equivalent, then they define equal functions. They produce the same output for the same input. For example, $f(x) = x(x - 1)$ and $g(x) = x^2 - x$ produce the same output for any given input.

- The **normal form** of a polynomial in one variable is what you get when you apply the basic rules of algebra, collect like terms, and write the terms from highest to lowest degree. For example, the normal form of $f(x) = (x - 2)(x - 1)$ is $f(x) = x^2 - 3x + 2$.

> You may have learned the commutative and associative properties as the any-order-any-grouping principle. What are the other basic rules?

> You can define normal form for polynomials in more than one variable, too. Each CAS has its own way of doing this.

For Discussion

4. Determine whether each expression is a polynomial in x. For expressions that are not polynomials in x, explain how they fail to meet the definition. For those that are polynomials in x, give the degree.

a. $5x$

b. $\frac{5}{x}$

c. $\frac{x}{5}$

d. $x + \sqrt{5}$

e. $5 + \sqrt{x}$

f. $xyz - z^{1999} - 0.093$

g. $(x^2 + x + 1)(y - 1)$

h. $x^{2.5} - 1.414$

i. $x^3 + 3^x$

For You to Do

5. Explain why two polynomials are equivalent if they have the same normal form.

Calculations with Polynomials

There are two ways to think about polynomials.

- You can think about them as formal expressions, in which the variables have no particular meaning.

- You can think about them as functions, in which the variables are placeholders for inputs.

Algebra involves thinking about polynomials in both ways. When you calculate with polynomials, you often think about them as expressions. The variables help you to keep the terms straight in your mind. When you substitute a number for the variable, you are thinking of the polynomial as a function.

> *Calculate* here means to apply the basic rules of algebra.

Example 1

Problem Find the normal form of $(1 - x)(1 + x + x^2)$.

Solution
$$(1 - x)(1 + x + x^2) = 1 \cdot (1 + x + x^2) - x(1 + x + x^2)$$
$$= 1 + x + x^2 + (-x - x^2 - x^3)$$
$$= 1 - x^3$$

For You to Do

6. Find the normal form of $(x - 1)(1 + x + x^2 + x^3)$.

One kind of polynomial identity results from factoring a polynomial. You can use this kind of identity in conjunction with the following property of real numbers to solve equations.

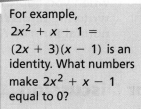

For example,
$2x^2 + x - 1 =$
$(2x + 3)(x - 1)$ is an identity. What numbers make $2x^2 + x - 1$ equal to 0?

Theorem 2.0 The Zero Product Property

If a and b are real numbers with a product of 0, then either a or b (or both) must be 0.

Put another way, the Zero Product Property (ZPP) says that if $ab = 0$, then at least one of the numbers a and b has to be 0.

Proof Suppose $ab = 0$.

If $a = 0$, you are done.

Suppose $a \neq 0$. Then by the basic rules of arithmetic, a has a reciprocal, $\frac{1}{a}$.

Multiply both sides of the equation $ab = 0$ by $\frac{1}{a}$. You find that $b = 0$.

So, if a is not 0, then b must be 0.

Example 2

Problem Find the solutions of each equation.

    a. $x^2 - 5x + 6 = 0$

    b. $x^2 - 10x + 10 = -14$

Solution

    a. To solve the equation $x^2 - 5x + 6 = 0$, factor the polynomial.
$$x^2 - 5x + 6 = (x - 2)(x - 3)$$

So you can rewrite the equation as $(x - 2)(x - 3) = 0$. By the ZPP, either
$$x - 2 = 0 \text{ or } x - 3 = 0$$
So $x = 2$ or $x = 3$.

b. To solve the equation $x^2 - 10x + 10 = -14$ with the ZPP, you cannot just factor. If $ab = -14$, you cannot conclude that $a = -14$ or $b = -14$. You need to use basic moves of algebra to rewrite the equation.
$$x^2 - 10x + 24 = 0$$
Then you factor.
$$x^2 - 10x + 24 = (x - 6)(x - 4)$$
So $x = 6$ or $x = 4$.

> If you substitute 2 or 3 into the original equation, you get $0 = 0$.

For You to Do

Solve each equation.

7. $(5x - 3)(x^2 - 5x + 6) = 0$

8. $x^2 - 15x + 30 = -26$

Exercises *Practicing Habits of Mind*

Check Your Understanding

1. Determine which of these equations are identities.

    a. $x^3 - 27 = (x - 3)(x^2 + 3x + 9x)$

    b. $x^2 - 16 = (x - 4)(x - 4)$

    c. $x^2 - 16 = (4 - x)(-4 - x)$

    d. $4x^2 - 16 = (2x - 4)(2x + 4)$

    e. $(2x - 5)(4x + 3) = 10x^2 - 14x - 15$

2. Without expanding, find the coefficient of x^{11} in the normal form of each polynomial.

    a. $(x + x^2 + x^3 + x^4 + x^5 + x^6)^2$

    b. $(x + x^2 + x^3 + x^4 + x^5 + x^6)^3$

3. Consider the function below.

$$g(n) = \left(\frac{n(n+1)}{2} + \frac{n(n-1)}{2} \right)\left(\frac{n(n+1)}{2} - \frac{n(n-1)}{2} \right)$$

Find a much simpler expression that defines g.

4. Expand each product and combine like powers of x.

   a. $(1 + x)(1 + x^2)$

   b. $(1 + x)(1 + x^2)(1 + x^4)$

   c. $(1 + x)(1 + x^2)(1 + x^4)(1 + x^8)$

   d. $(1 + x)(1 + x^2)(1 + x^4)(1 + x^8)(1 + x^{16})$

5. Solve each equation.

   a. $x^2 - 7x + 12 = 0$ **b.** $x^2 + 16x - 30 = 50$

   c. $x^2 - 9 = 10x - 33$

On Your Own

6. Consider the polynomial $f(x) = x^2 + 4x - 5$.

   a. Find $f(1)$.

   b. Show that $(x - 1)$ is a factor of $f(x)$.

7. Consider the polynomial $g(x) = x^2 - 14x - 51$.

   a. Find $g(17)$.

   b. Show that $(x - 17)$ is a factor of $g(x)$.

8. Consider the polynomial $f(x) = x^2 + 4x - 5$.

   a. Find $f(3)$.   **b.** Find $f(x) - f(3)$.

   c. Show that $(x - 3)$ is a factor of the polynomial $h(x) = f(x) - f(3)$.

9. Consider the polynomial $g(x) = x^2 - 14x - 51$.

   a. Find $g(5)$.   **b.** Find $g(x) - g(5)$.

   c. Show that $(x - 5)$ is a factor of the polynomial $m(x) = g(x) - g(5)$.

10. a. Without expanding, find the coefficient of x^8 in the normal form of $(1 + x + x^2 + x^3 + x^4 + x^5)^2$.

     b. Without expanding, find the coefficient of x^8 in the normal form of $(1 + x + x^2 + x^3 + x^4 + x^5)^3$.

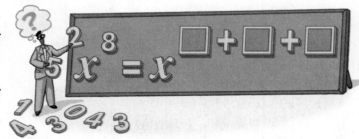

11. Let $\deg p$ be the degree of a polynomial p. Suppose f and g are arbitrary polynomials in x. For each part, find a relationship among the given values.

   a. $\deg fg$, $\deg f$, and $\deg g$

   b. $\deg 2g$ and $\deg g$

   c. $\deg(f + g)$, $\deg f$, and $\deg g$

Habits of Mind

Experiment. Try some concrete examples. What are the polynomials of degree 0?

12. If possible, find two polynomials, each of degree 6, such that the degree of their sum is 4.

13. If possible, find two polynomials, each of degree 6, such that the degree of their sum is 8.

14. Find the normal form for $(r + s)^3 - 3rs(r + s)$.

This is a polynomial in two variables. Think of it as a polynomial in one of the variables.

Maintain Your Skills

15. Find the degree of each polynomial.

   a. $(x - 2)$

   b. $(x - 2)(x + 3)$

   c. $(x - 2)(x + 3)(x - 4)$

   d. $(x - 2)(x + 3)(x - 4)(x - 5)$

   e. $(x - 2)(x + 3)(x - 4)(x - 5)(x - 6)(x - 12)(x - 15)$

   f. $(x - 2)(x + 3)^2$

   g. $(x - 2)(x + 3)^2(x - 4)^3(x - 5)$

   h. $(x - 2)^{20}$

16. Expand each product.

   a. $(a - b)(a + b)$

   b. $(a - b)(a^2 + ab + b^2)$

   c. $(a - b)(a^3 + a^2b + ab^2 + b^3)$

   d. $(a - b)(a^4 + a^3b + a^2b^2 + ab^3 + b^4)$

   e. What is the pattern?

17. Expand each product.

   a. $(1 + x)(1 - x)$ b. $(1 + x)(1 - x + x^2)$

   c. $(1 + x)(1 - x + x^2 - x^3)$ d. What is the pattern?

About Functions

In *About Functions*, you will build on your understanding of functions as machines that accept inputs and produce outputs. You will also see that the definition of a function is not complete unless you specify the set of allowable inputs.

By the end of this investigation, you will be able to answer questions like these.

1. What is a function?

2. How do you compose two functions to make a new function?

3. What function undoes $x \mapsto 3x + 7$?

You will learn how to

- decide whether a table, graph, or closed-form rule is a function

- use function notation

- decide whether two rules define the same function

- determine the domain, target, and range of a function

- compose functions

- decide whether a given function has an inverse

- find the inverse of a one-to-one function

- graph piecewise-defined functions

You will develop these habits and skills:

- Write, compose, and invert functions.

- Model functions in a function-modeling language.

- Develop an algebraic perspective on functions.

- "Work like a mathematician"— search for hidden regularities, describe the patterns explicitly, and explain inconsistencies.

- Establish properties of functions.

A function machine can double the size of the input.

**Activating Prior Knowledge
Exploring New Ideas**

2.01 Getting Started

By now, you have some idea of what a function is. Here are a few functions.

SQRT(x) = the square root of a real number x
SQR(x) = the square of a real number x
REC(n) = the reciprocal of a real number n
BD(p) = the birthday of a person p
SUM(a, b) = the sum of two numbers a and b
PR(a, b) = the product of two numbers a and b
QUO(a, b) = the quotient of two numbers a and b

Here is a formula for QUO.

$$QUO(a, b) = \frac{a}{b}$$

Not all functions have formulas. For example, BD does not have one.

For You to Explore

1. If possible, find the value of each expression. If an expression cannot be evaluated, explain why not.

   a. PR(3, 4)

   b. QUO(3, 4)

   c. QUO(6, 8)

   d. QUO(0, 23)

   e. QUO(23, 0)

   f. SQR(SQRT(5))

   g. SQRT(SQR(5))

   h. SQR(SQRT(−5))

   i. SQRT(SQR(−5))

   j. QUO(PR(3, 4), PR(2, 6))

   k. BD(Pierre de Fermat)

   l. BD(3)

   m. SQRT(SUM(9, 16))

   n. SUM(SQRT(9), SQRT(16))

   o. SQRT(BD(Isaac Newton))

   p. SQRT(PR$\left(-2, \frac{1}{3}\right)$)

   q. REC(2)

   r. REC(REC(2))

   s. REC(REC(REC(2)))

   t. REC(0)

2. A mystery function $m(x)$ has the inputs and outputs below. How can you define the function?

   $m(\pi) = 3 \quad m(2.9) = 2 \quad m(5) = 5 \quad m(11.6) = 11 \quad m(-1.3) = -2$

3. Consider the function SQRT.

   a. Is the following equation true?

   $$SQRT(a + b) = SUM(SQRT(a), SQRT(b))$$

   b. **Take It Further** If the equation above is true for all numbers, prove it. If it is not, find the conditions on a and b that make it true.

   SQRT(Joseph-Louis Lagrange) does not make sense. The largest set of inputs for which a function produces an output is the function's natural domain.

4. Find the natural domain of each function. Describe the domain in detail.

   a. BD

   b. SQRT

   c. QUO

   d. REC

   e. $f(x) = \dfrac{\sqrt{x}}{x - 2}$

You can restrict the domain even further. For example, the function $A(r) = \pi r^2$ gives the area of a circle with radius r. You want to restrict the domain to positive numbers.

The key property of a function is that it turns each input into a well-defined output. The inputs are members of the domain. The set of all outputs is the *range* of the function.

5. For each function in Problem 4, you defined a domain. Using that domain, describe each function's range.

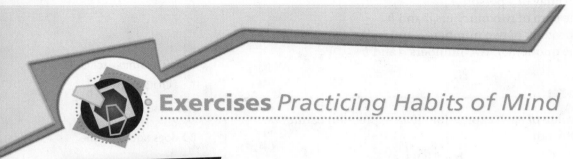

Exercises Practicing Habits of Mind

On Your Own

6. Suppose each function gives an output of 9. Do you have enough information to determine the input? Explain.

    a. PR   **b.** SQRT   **c.** SQR

7. If possible, find two different inputs for each function that give the same output.

    a. SQR   **b.** BD   **c.** QUO

    d. SQRT   **e.** REC

8. Use the definition of function D below.

$$D(x, y) = \sqrt{x^2 + y^2}$$

Find each value.

> What is the natural domain of D?

    a. $D(0, 0)$ **b.** $D(3, 4)$ **c.** $D(-3, 4)$ **d.** $D(4, 3)$

    e. Find another input that makes $D(x, y) = 5$.

    f. **Take It Further** Draw a graph of all the coordinate pairs (x, y) that make $D(x, y) = 5$.

> Can you find a pair of irrational numbers (x, y) that makes $D(x, y) = 5$?

9. Suppose you define the function $B(x, y, z)$ in terms of $D(x, y)$ from Exercise 8 as follows.

$$B(x, y, z) = D(x, y) + z$$

For example, $B(3, 4, 10) = 15$, since $D(3, 4) = 5$.

Find each value.

    a. $B(0, 0, 0)$ **b.** $B(3, 4, 5)$ **c.** $B(4, 3, 5)$ **d.** $B(-3, 4, -5)$

    e. Find the value of z such that $B(5, 12, z) = 7$.

    f. Find all triples (x, y, z) such that $B(x, y, z) = 0$.

10. a. Is it possible for the output of $D(x, y)$ to be negative? Explain.

  b. Is it possible for the output of $B(x, y, z)$ to be negative? Explain.

Maintain Your Skills

11. Use the definitions of functions f and g below.

$$f(x) = 3x - 7$$

$$g(x) = \frac{x + 7}{3}$$

Find each value.

a. $f(10)$ **b.** $g(23)$

c. $f(f(0))$ **d.** $g(g(-28))$

e. $f(g(172))$ **f.** $g(f(0.27))$

g. $f(g(f(g(1000))))$

12. Use the definitions of functions h and j below.

$$h(x) = (x - 1)^2$$

$$j(x) = \sqrt{x} + 1$$

Find each value.

a. $h(4)$ **b.** $j(9)$

c. $h(h(3))$ **d.** $j(j(16))$

e. $j(h(5))$ **f.** $j(h(-5))$

g. $h(j(-3))$

> What are the natural domains of h and j?

13. Suppose $f(x) = x + 4$. Find each value.

a. $f(3)$ **b.** $f(f(3))$

c. $f(f(f(3)))$ **d.** $f(f(f(f(3))))$

e. $\dfrac{f(f(\ldots(f(3)))))))))))))}{12\ f\text{'s}}$

14. Suppose $g(x) = \frac{x + 1}{x}$. Find each value.

a. $g(1)$ **b.** $g(g(1))$

c. $g(g(g(1)))$ **d.** $g(g(g(g(1))))$

e. $g(g(g(g(g(1)))))$ **f.** $\dfrac{g(g(\ldots(g(1)))))))))))}{10\ g\text{'s}}$

2.02 Getting Precise About Functions

The algebra 1 point of view

You may think of functions as machines that take inputs and produce outputs.

The function is the machine. An input is anything you pass into a function, and the corresponding output is whatever the machine produces. You can define many functions with rules or algorithms, sets of instructions about what to do to an input to produce an output.

You put in x.

Out comes $x + 2$.

Input

The function is the machine.

The rule is what the machine does to the input to get the output.

Output

Remember...

An algorithm or rule is a recipe. Two kinds of rules are especially useful in algebra: polynomial rules and recursive rules.

You can use arrow notation to write a function.

$$x \mapsto \frac{1}{x}$$

You say "x maps to 1 over x."

For this function, the input is a nonzero number x and the output at x is the reciprocal of x.

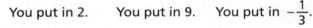

You put in 2.   You put in 9.   You put in $-\frac{1}{3}$.

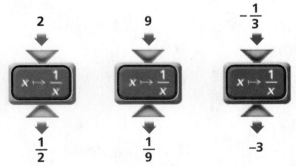

Out comes $\frac{1}{2}$.   Out comes $\frac{1}{9}$.   Out comes -3.

Habits of Mind

Detect the key characteristics. Why does the input have to be a nonzero number?

Another way to describe functions is to name the machine, usually with a letter, such as *f*, or a shorthand, such as ABS. Then you can use the name of the function to describe the output. If you call a function *f* and you give it an input of 3, the output is *f*(3).

If the input is *x* and the function is *f*, then the output is *f*(x).

In mathematics, it is customary to name a function with a single letter. In computer science, it is customary to name a function with a short abbreviation for what it does. So, ABS might stand for absolute value. How does your calculator name functions?

Not every rule gives a function. The rule "to find *f*(x), flip a coin; if it comes up heads, output $x + 2$; otherwise output $x + 3$" does not define a function.

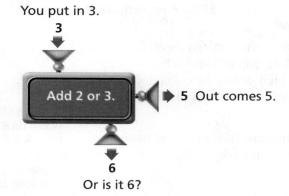

You put in 3.

3

Add 2 or 3. **5** Out comes 5.

6

Or is it 6?

A good example of a function on your calculator is the square root function. You give it an input, and it gives you exactly one output.

For You to Do

1. Experiment with the square root function on your calculator. Find the outputs for the inputs 4, 8, and −4. What numbers are their own square roots?

2. Pick a positive number. Take its square root. Take the square root of the result. Keep going. What happens?

You can also define your own function in a function-modeling language. You give the function a name and a rule for finding outputs.

$$\text{define } g(x) = \frac{1}{x} + 1$$

You can then use this model just like a built-in function—give it inputs, tabulate it, graph it, and experiment with it.

Try evaluating
$5 + 2*g(6)$.

For You to Do

3. Pick a positive number. Take *g* of it. Take *g* of the result. Keep going. What happens?

In your first-year algebra course, you may have learned that the set of all possible inputs that cause a function to produce an output is the domain of the function.

The calculator model of $g(x) = \frac{1}{x} + 1$ can take any input except 0. Asking for $g(0)$ generates an error. This means that 0 is not in the domain of g.

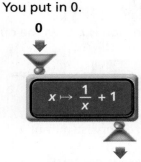

You put in 0.

0

ERROR: no reciprocal.

Building on the algebra 1 point of view

In this course, it is essential to make some finer distinctions about functions and to state things in a more precise way. Here, you will revisit the working definitions of *function* and *domain*. You will talk about the collection of outputs for a function. This discussion focuses on two of the finer distinctions about functions.

The domain of a function is part of its definition. Take a piece of paper, say 5 inches × 8 inches. Cut a little square out of each corner. Fold up the sides to make a box.

In the next lesson, you will do a kind of algebra with functions. You will need a better and more precise language for talking about functions.

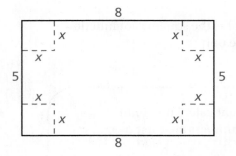

If the side length of the cutout is x, the volume V of the box is a function of x.

For You to Do

4. Let $V(x)$ be the volume of the box when a square of side length x is cut from each corner. Show that $V(x) = x(5 - 2x)(8 - 2x)$.

There is a problem here. The natural domain for V is all real numbers, $\mathbb{R}$. But, in terms of the box, an input of -2 makes no sense. You cannot cut -2 inches from the corners of the rectangle. In fact, the only numbers that make sense for the size of a cutout are $0 \leq x \leq \frac{5}{2}$. So, a complete definition of V is

Besides, $V(-2) = -216$.

> V is the function defined on the domain $0 \leq x \leq \frac{5}{2}$ such that $V(x) = x(5 - 2x)(8 - 2x)$.

Functions on different domains are different functions, even if they share the same formula. The function defined on all of $\mathbb{R}$ by

$$f(x) = x(5 - 2x)(8 - 2x)$$

is different from V. In fact, since the domain for f contains the domain for V, you call V a restriction of f and you call f an extension of V.

Functions are determined by their behavior. Look at these machine models for two functions.

Habits of Mind

Consider the context. Sometimes you use the same expression to define a function on different domains. The appropriate domain depends on the context.

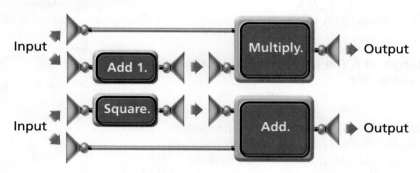

The domain for both functions is all of $\mathbb{R}$. These networks look as if they do very different things to their inputs. But if you build models for the functions in a function-modeling language and display tables of them side by side, you cannot tell them apart.

For You to Do

5. Try it. Build a model for each network above. Call the models f and g. Make a table for f and g. Then graph them. Do you see any difference? Can you prove that the two functions act the same for all inputs?

For advice on modeling, graphing, and making tables of functions, see the TI-Nspire™ Handbook, p. 804.

For all practical purposes, these two functions are the same. This point of view—two functions are the same if they give the same outputs for all inputs is—is the one that people use in most parts of mathematics and science today. As long as two functions refer to the same input-output pairings, it does not matter how the rule works on the inside.

For You to Do

6. Suppose f has domain $\mathbb{R}^+$ and the rule $f(x) = 3x + 7$. Show that the two functions below agree with f on its domain.

- $x \mapsto 3|x| + 7$
- $x \mapsto |3x + 7|$

Does either of them agree with f on all of $\mathbb{R}$?

In this course, $\mathbb{R}^+$ stands for the nonnegative real numbers.

To define a function, you must first specify two sets: a *domain A* and a *target B*. Then a function from *A* to *B* is a recipe that produces, for each member of *A*, a unique member of *B*.

Definitions

Suppose *A* and *B* are two sets of objects. A **function** from *A* to *B* is a pairing between *A* and *B* such that each element in *A* pairs with exactly one element of *B*.

This notation denotes a function *f* from set *A* to set *B*:

$$f : A \rightarrow B$$

A is the **domain** of *f*. *B* is the **target** of *f*. The set of objects in *B* that are paired with objects in *A* is the **range** of *f*.

Remember...

A and *B* can be sets of numbers, points, people, triangles, and so on. Any pairing between *A* and *B* is a *relation*, while a *function* is a pairing that involves each element of *A* exactly once.

If the domain of a function is not stated explicitly, assume that its domain is as large as possible. This is the natural domain of a function. For example, the natural domain of $f(x) = \frac{1}{x} + 1$ is all real numbers other than 0.

Developing Habits of Mind

Visualize. The key idea here is that a function assigns each object in *A* to exactly one object in *B*. Here is a picture of a function from *A* to *B*.

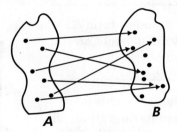

Each element of *A* is paired with exactly one element of *B*.
Note the following:

This is a "potato-and-arrow" diagram.

- Not every element of *B* is an output. The range (things that are outputs) does not have to match the entire target (things that might be outputs).

- Two elements of *A* can be paired with the same element of B. The definition of a function only prohibits one element of A from being paired with more than one element of *B*.

Think about the birthday function from Lesson 2.01. One possible domain (Set *A*) might be the students in your class. The target (Set *B*) is the days of the year. The range is not all days in the year, however. It is only those days that actually get paired. The range for that domain is the days of the year that are birthdays for at least one person in your class.

Note that it is still a function if two students in the same class have the same birthday. It would not be a function if one student had two birthdays!

Example

Problem Find the domain, target, and range for the function $f : \mathbb{R} \to \mathbb{R}$, where $f(x) = x^2$.

Solution The domain and target are given by the function statement. The domain is $\mathbb{R}$, and so is the target.

The rule $f(x) = x^2$ determines the range. This function produces squares. No squares are negative. So the range is the set of all nonnegative real numbers, $\mathbb{R}^+$.

> **Remember...**
>
> The domain is the first set, and the target is the second.

So, when are two functions the same? You now have the language to talk about this.

Definition

Two functions f and g are **equal functions** if both these conditions are satisfied.

- f and g have the same domain.
- $f(a) = g(a)$ for every a in the common domain.

> If f and g are equal functions, you write $f = g$. This means the functions satisfy the conditions in this definition.

Developing Habits of Mind

Look for relationships. Two functions may be different (not equal) on their natural domains and yet be equal if you restrict their domains to some smaller set. For example, the two functions below are not equal.

$$f : \mathbb{R} \to \mathbb{R}, \text{ where } f = 2x + 1$$

$$g : \mathbb{R} \to \mathbb{R}, \text{ where } g(x) = 2x + 1 + (x - 1)(x - 2)(x - 3)$$

For example, $f(5) = 11$ and $g(5) = 35$. But f and g are equal if you restrict the domain to the numbers 1, 2, and 3. So you can say $f = g$ on the domain $\{1, 2, 3\}$.

For You to Do

7. Suppose you have the following function.

$$f(x) = \begin{cases} 3 & \text{if } x = 0 \\ f(x - 1) + 5 & \text{if } x > 0 \end{cases}$$

What is the natural domain of f? Find a function $g : \mathbb{R} \to \mathbb{R}$ that is equal to f on the natural domain of f.

Exercises Practicing Habits of Mind

Check Your Understanding

1. Let $f : \mathbb{R} \to \mathbb{R}$ and $f(x) = 72x - x^2$.

   a. What is the range of f?

   b. Graph f over its domain.

2. There are many rectangles with perimeter 144. Let x be the length of such a rectangle and let $A(x)$ be the area of the rectangle in terms of x.

   a. Express $A(x)$ as a function of x.

   b. What is the domain of A?

   c. What is the range of A?

   d. Graph A over its domain.

3. **Write About It** Are the functions in Exercises 1 and 2 equal? Explain.

> Use the definition of equal functions from this lesson.

4. Here are two functions.

   $$H(n) = 3 + 5n$$

   $$K(n) = \begin{cases} 3 & \text{if } n = 0 \\ K(n - 1) + 5 & \text{if } n > 0 \end{cases}$$

   a. Make a table of values for H and K that includes inputs from 0 to 5.

   b. What is the natural domain of H? What is the natural domain of K?

   c. Are H and K equal functions? Explain.

5. Consider the function $h(x) = \sqrt{x^3}$.

   a. What is the natural domain of h?

   b. Find the range of h using the natural domain.

6. Let $f : \mathbb{R}^2 \to \mathbb{R}$ and $f(a, b) = 2a + 3b$.

   a. Find the domain and target of f.

   b. Find some pairs (x, y) that make $f(x, y) = 12$.

   c. Graph the set of all points (x, y) for which $f(x, y) = 12$.

> $\mathbb{R}^2$ means that the function takes two real numbers as inputs. The SUM, PR, and QUO functions from the Getting Started lesson have $\mathbb{R}^2$ as their domains.

7. Let $f : \mathbb{R} \to \mathbb{R}$ and $f(x) = 3x^2$.

   a. Calculate $f(3)$ and $f(-3)$.

   b. Find all values of x for which $f(x) = 12$.

   c. Calculate $f(11) - f(10)$.

   d. Show that you can write $f(x + 1)$ as $f(x + 1) = 3x^2 + 6x + 3$.

   e. Write a simplified expression for $f(x + 1) - f(x)$.

   f. If $g(x) = f(x + 1) - f(x)$, what is $g(10)$?

8. Suppose $g(x) = f(x + 1) - f(x)$, where f is another function. For each $f(x)$, find a polynomial formula in normal form for $g(x)$.

a. $f(x) = 5x$

b. $f(x) = 5x + 7$

c. $f(x) = 10x - 12$

d. $f(x) = Ax + B$

e. $f(x) = x^2$

f. $f(x) = 3x^2$

g. $f(x) = 10x^2$

h. $f(x) = x^2 + 10x - 12$

i. $f(x) = 3x^2 + 10x - 12$

> **Remember...**
>
> A polynomial is in normal form if it contains no parentheses, like terms have been combined, and the degrees of the terms go from highest to lowest.

9. Suppose you define function f in two pieces.

$$f(x) = \begin{cases} x & \text{if } x < 0 \\ 2x & \text{if } 0 \le x \le 6 \end{cases}$$

a. What is the natural domain of f? 　b. Sketch the graph of f.

On Your Own

10. Consider the function $j(x) = (\sqrt{x})^3$.

a. What is the natural domain of j?

b. Find the range of j using the natural domain.

11. A recipe takes a date as input, such as May 12. The output is the day of the week (Sunday, Monday, and so on) on which that date next occurs.

a. Find the output for your birthday.

b. Find the output for the day after your birthday.

c. Does this recipe define a function? Explain.

12. Suppose $N : \mathbb{R}^2 \to \mathbb{R}$ and $N(a, b) = a^2 + b^2$.

a. Find the domain and target of N.

b. Find some pairs (x, y) that make $N(x, y) = 25$.

c. Find all pairs (x, y) that make $N(x, y) = 0$.

d. Graph the set of all points (x, y) that make $N(x, y) = 25$.

e. **Take It Further** What is the range of N? Explain.

13. **What's Wrong Here?** While using a calculator, Derman noticed that $(\sqrt{3})^2 = 3$ and $(\sqrt{9})^2 = 9$ and $(\sqrt{10})^2 = 10$. He says that the function $t(x) = (\sqrt{x})^2$ is the same function as $f(x) = x$. Why is this incorrect?

14. For each function, find the natural domain, target, and range.

a. $f(x) = 6x^2 - x - 2$ 　b. $f(x) = \sqrt{x - 3}$ 　c. $f(x) = \dfrac{1}{\sqrt{x - 3}}$

d. $f(x) = \frac{1}{x} + 1$ 　e. $f(x, y) = x + 3y$ 　f. $f(x) = (x, x^3)$

g. $f(x, y) = (y, x)$

15. Suppose $f(x) = x^2 - 4x$ and $g(x) = x - 6$. Find each value.

   a. $f(g(2))$ **b.** $g(f(2))$ **c.** $f(g(z))$

   d. $g(f(z))$ **e.** $f(f(z))$ **f.** $g(g(z))$

   g. Find all numbers a such that $f(a) = g(a)$.

   h. Find all numbers b such that $f(g(b)) = g(f(b))$.

16. Suppose $f : \mathbb{R} \to \mathbb{R}$ and $f(x) = 3x + 2$. Find the value of a in each case.

   a. $2f(a) + 3 = 5$ **b.** $f(2a + 3) = 5$ **c.** $f(2a + 3) = a + 3$

17. For each function, find all values of x such that $f(x) = 12{,}290$.

   a. $f(x) = 3x + 2$ **b.** $f(x) = 3x^2 + 2$

   c. $f(x) = 3x^3 + 2$ **d.** $f(x) = 3x^6 + 2$

18. Derman says that for any function $f : \mathbb{R} \to \mathbb{R}$, if $f(r) = f(s)$, then $r = s$. Check Derman's conjecture for each function.

   a. $f(x) = 3x + 2$ **b.** $f(x) = 3x^2 + 2$

   c. $f(x) = 3x^3 + 2$ **d.** $f(x) = 3x^6 + 2$

19. **Standardized Test Prep** What is the natural domain of the function
$f(x) = \dfrac{1}{x^2 - 5x + 4}$?

   A. $x \geq -3$ **B.** $x > 5$

   C. $x > 4$ **D.** $x \neq 1$ and $x \neq 4$

20. Spiro the Spectacular has a number trick: A player picks a number, adds 3, divides by 2, subtracts 3, and multiplies by 4. Find the inverse of Spiro's trick.

> The inverse of Spiro's trick lets you figure out what number the player picked.

21. Suppose $f : \mathbb{R} \to \mathbb{R}$ and $f(3a + 1) = a - 2$. Find each value.

   a. $f(7)$ **b.** $f(14)$ **c.** $f(16)$ **d.** $f(z)$ (in terms of z)

22. Find two different functions f and g such that $f(g(x)) = g(f(x))$ for every number x.

Maintain Your Skills

23. Each of these functions has a domain of $\mathbb{R}$. Which functions have a range of $\mathbb{R}$?

   a. $f(x) = x^2$ **b.** $g(x) = x^3$ **c.** $h(x) = x^4$ **d.** $j(x) = x^5$

   e. **Take It Further** $k(x) = x^3 - 4x$

24. **Take It Further** Suppose $g : \mathbb{R}^2 \to \mathbb{R}$ and $g(x, y) = \dfrac{f(x) - f(y)}{x - y}$.

   For each function f, find $g(x, y)$.

   a. $f(x) = 3x + 5$ **b.** $f(x) = 5x + 5$ **c.** $f(x) = 12x + 5$

   d. $f(x) = x^2$ **e.** $f(x) = x^2 + x$ **f.** $f(x) = 3x^2 + 2x - 1$

Algebra With Functions

The basic rules of algebra tell you how the operations of addition and multiplication behave. Addition and multiplication are operations that combine numbers. In this lesson, you will learn about an operation that combines functions. Here are two functions.

- $B(p)$ is the birthday of person p. The domain is all people, and the target is the days of the year.

- $W(d)$ is the day of the week on which a date d will occur next year. The domain is the days of the year, and the target is the seven days of the week.

You can compose these two functions to form a third function.

- $C(p)$ is the day of the week of person p's birthday next year. The domain is all people, and the target is the seven days of the week.

C is a composition of functions W and B. To find $C(p)$, you start with the person, find that person's birthday, and then find the day of the week of that date next year. In other words, C is the result of running an input through B, taking the output, and running that output through W.

> So B(Carl Gauss) = April 30.

For You to Do

Find each value.

1. B(you) **2.** W(you) **3.** C(you)

You can express the relationship between these functions with the equation

$$C(p) = W(B(p))$$

This tells you how to compute the output of C for any input. If you just want to say that C is the composition of W and B, you write it as $C = W \circ B$.

Composing functions together by using the output of one as the input of the next is very common. You can do this with any two functions for which the domain of one function contains the target of another. If $f : A \to B$ and $g : B \to C$, you can define a new function that maps inputs in A to outputs in C with the following rule.

$$x \mapsto g(f(x))$$

This new function has domain A and target C. Instead of using a new letter to name it, you can just call the composition $g \circ f$. You read $g \circ f$ as "g circle f" or "g composed with f."

> **Remember...**
> When you evaluate $g(f(x))$, first you do f and then you do g.

Look for relationships. You can think of functions as objects on which you can perform operations, just as you do with numbers.

- $g \circ f$ is a function.
- $g(f(x))$ is the output of that function for input x.

Composition takes two functions and produces a third function. The concept of an operation with two inputs and one output is very common in algebra. Composition of functions is another example.

The addition and the multiplication of two numbers are two more examples of a binary operation. Some of the concepts that apply to addition and multiplication may carry over to composition. Here are some questions to consider.

- Addition and multiplication have identity elements. You can add 0 to a number and it does not change. You can multiply a number by 1 and it does not change. Is there an identity function for composition?

- Addition and multiplication have inverses (with one exception). All numbers have opposites that sum to 0, the identity. All numbers other than 0 have reciprocals. Do compositions of functions have inverses?

- Addition and multiplication are commutative. You can add or multiply in either order: $3 + 5 = 5 + 3$ and $3 \cdot 5 = 5 \cdot 3$. Is composition commutative?

When you work on these questions, you are thinking about functions as objects rather than machines. Composition is an operation on these objects, just as addition and multiplication are operations on numbers.

> Operations that take two inputs and produce one output are binary operations. They are functions, too, as long as they always produce the same output given the same two inputs.

> Artist's rendition of $f \circ g$

Here is the formal definition of composition.

Definition

For two functions $f : A \rightarrow B$ and $g : B \rightarrow C$, the **composite function** $g \circ f$ meets the following conditions.

- $g \circ f : A \rightarrow C$
- $g \circ f(x) = g(f(x))$

For You to Do

Suppose $f, g, h: \mathbb{R} \to \mathbb{R}$ and

$$f(x) = 2x^2 - 1$$

$$g(x) = x + 1$$

$$h(x) = 4x^3 - 3x$$

4. Build models for the three functions in your function-modeling language.

5. Show that $f \circ g(5) = 71$.

6. Find $g \circ f(5)$, $f \circ h(5)$, and $h \circ f(5)$.

7. Find formulas for $f \circ g$ and $g \circ f$. Are these functions the same?

> The notation
> $f, g, h: \mathbb{R} \to \mathbb{R}$ means
> that f, g, and h all have
> domain $\mathbb{R}$ and target $\mathbb{R}$.

Historical Perspective

Algebra began as a collection of methods for finding unknown numbers—for solving equations. The object was to find general formulas, like the quadratic formula, that provided recipes for solving a class of equations. Mathematicians stated the recipes in terms of the operations of arithmetic. (Take the *negative* of the coefficient of *x*, *add* it to the *square root* of the *square* of that coefficient *minus* . . .) The goal was to make the recipe independent of the actual numbers in the equations. Over time, mathematicians began to look for similar formulas in systems other than numbers that had different operations. Gradually, the focus shifted from the formulas to the operations themselves. This systems approach to algebra led people to investigate properties of operations and to make lists of the properties that are useful in calculating—properties that are very similar to the basic rules of arithmetic.

Algebra today deals with all kinds of systems—numbers, polynomials, matrices, functions, and more exotic objects. Each system has one or more operations that allow for calculations. One such system is the set of functions, all with the same domain and target, in which the operation is composition.

The output is dependent on the input, but the recipe itself is independent of both.

Exercises Practicing Habits of Mind

Check Your Understanding

1. Consider the functions $f(x) = 2x + 3$ and $g(x) = 5x + 1$. Find each value.

   a. $f(3)$ b. $g(3)$ c. $f(g(3))$

   d. $f \circ g(3)$ e. $g \circ f(3)$ f. $f(3) \cdot g(3)$

   > Unless otherwise stated, all functions in these exercises have domain $\mathbb{R}$ and target $\mathbb{R}$.

2. Let $f(x) = 2x + 3$ and $g(x) = 5x + 1$.

   a. Find a formula for $g \circ f(x)$.

   b. Find a formula for $f \circ g(x)$.

3. Suppose you drop a stone into a pond. It makes concentric circular ripples. The radius of a ripple as a function of time is $r = 4t$, where r is the radius in inches and t is the time in seconds.

   a. Express the area of a ripple as a function of its radius.

   b. Express the area of a ripple as a function of time.

4. Suppose $f : \mathbb{R} \to \mathbb{R}$ and $f(x) = x$. For each definition of g, find formulas for $f \circ g(x)$ and $g \circ f(x)$.

   a. $g(x) = x^2 + 3$

   b. $g(x) = 2x - 7$

   c. $g(x) = (x - 4)^3$

   d. **Write About It** Explain what it might mean to say that the function f is the identity function on $\mathbb{R}$.

5. Suppose $f(x) = 3x - 1$. If possible, find a function g such that $f \circ g(x) = x$.

6. Suppose $f(x) = 2x + 3$. If possible, find a function g such that $g \circ f(x) = x$.

7. Suppose $f(x) = 2x + 5$. If possible, find a function g that makes each equation true.

   a. $f \circ g(x) = 4x^2 + 1$

   b. $g \circ f(x) = 4x^2 + 1$

8. **Take It Further** Let $f(x) = ax + b$ and $g(x) = cx + d$.

   a. Find formulas for $f \circ g(x)$ and $g \circ f(x)$.

   b. Find conditions on $a, b, c,$ and d that make $f \circ g = g \circ f$.

9. **Take It Further** Find a linear function $f(x) = ax + b$ such that $f \circ f(x) = 4x + 9$.

> **Go Online**
> Pearsonsuccessnet.com

10. Consider the functions $f(x) = x^2 - 1$ and $g(x) = 3x + 1$. Find each value.

a. $f(4)$

b. $g(4)$

c. $f(4) \cdot g(4)$

d. $f(g(4))$

e. $f \circ g(4)$

f. $g \circ f(4)$

Go Online
Pearsonsuccessnet.com

11. Suppose $h : \mathbb{R} \to \mathbb{R}$ and $h(x) = \sqrt{x^2}$. Show that $h = a$, where $a(x) = |x|$.

12. Suppose $f(x) = x^2 - 5x + 6$ and $g(x) = x - 2$. Find each value.

a. $f \circ g(3)$

b. $g \circ f(3)$

c. $f \circ g(a)$

d. $g \circ f(a)$

e. $(f \circ g) \circ f(a)$

f. $f \circ (g \circ f)(a)$

g. Find all numbers a such that $f \circ g(a) = 0$.

h. Find all numbers a such that $g \circ f(a) = 0$.

13. Use the functions below.

$$f(x) = x^2 - 6x + 8$$
$$g(x) = x + 3$$
$$h(x) = x + 1$$

Find a formula for each composition.

a. $h \circ (f \circ g)(x)$

b. $(h \circ f) \circ g(x)$

14. Suppose $f(x) = x^2 - 10x + 21$. If possible, find linear functions g and h that make each equation true.

a. $f \circ g(x) = x^2 - 4$

b. $h \circ (f \circ g)(x) = x^2$

15. If $f(x) = x^2$, find a function g, that is not equal to f, such that $f \circ g = g \circ f$.

16. **Standardized Test Prep** Suppose $f(x) = x - 5$. Find a function g such that $g \circ f(x) = 3x^2 - 11x - 20$.

A. $g(x) = 3x^2 + 19x$

B. $g(x) = 3x^2 + 4$

C. $g(x) = (3x - 4)$

D. $g(x) = (3x + 4)$

Remember...

A linear function is a function in the form $x \mapsto ax + b$ for some numbers a and b. Why do you call it linear?

17. Consider these three functions.

$$a(x) = 3x + 1$$
$$b(x) = x^2 - 7$$
$$c(x) = x - 5$$

Find a formula for each composition.

a. $a \circ b$

b. $b \circ c$

c. $(a \circ b) \circ c$

d. $a \circ (b \circ c)$

18. Suppose $a, b, c : \mathbb{R} \to \mathbb{R}$. Show that $(a \circ b) \circ c = a \circ (b \circ c)$.

19. **Take It Further** Suppose $f(x) = 2x + 3$ and $g(x) = x^2$. Find a way to construct the graph of $f \circ g$ from the graphs of f and g.

> In arithmetic, addition is associative. For any numbers a, b, and c,
> $(a + b) + c = a + (b + c)$.

Maintain Your Skills

20. For each function f, find a function g such that $f \circ g(x) = x$.

a. $f(x) = x + 3$

b. $f(x) = x - 3$

c. $f(x) = 3x + 5$

d. $f(x) = 3x - 5$

e. $f(x) = 2x + 5$

f. $f(x) = Ax + B$, where $A \neq 0$

21. For each function f, find a function g such that $g \circ f(x) = x$.

a. $f(x) = x + 3$

b. $f(x) = x - 3$

c. $f(x) = 3x + 5$

d. $f(x) = 3x - 5$

e. $f(x) = 2x + 5$

f. $f(x) = Ax + B$, where $A \neq 0$

Go **Online**
Video Tutor
Pearsonsuccessnet.com

2.04 Inverses: Doing and Undoing

Suppose you have an output and you want to find the input that generated it. Can you always find it?

In-Class Experiment

Have everyone think of an integer from 1 to 20. Then, follow these steps:

- Subtract 10 from your number.
- Square the result.
- Add 7 to the squared result to get an ending number.

List everyone's starting and ending numbers.

1. Did any students get the same ending number? More important, did any two students who got the same ending number start with different numbers?

2. If a student gives you an ending number, can you always find the starting number? Explain.

Try the experiment again. This time, cube the number in the second step.

3. Did any students get the same ending number this time? Did any two students who got the same ending number start with different numbers?

4. If a student gives you an ending number, can you always find the starting number? Explain.

Minds in Action   episode 4

Sasha and Derman are looking at the results from the In-Class Experiment.

Derman Tony and Michelle got the same number at the end, and they started with different numbers: Tony had 13 and Michelle had 7.

Sasha Maybe we should look at what they did with their numbers.

	Tony	Michelle
Starting number	13	7
After subtracting 10	3	−3
After squaring	9	9
After adding 7	16	16

Derman Either way, they end up with 16. I wonder if we can retrace the steps from the output 16.

	Tony	Michelle
Ending number	16	16
After undoing addition by 7	9	9
After undoing squaring	???	???

Derman Hmm. We can't undo the squaring. If $x^2 = 9$, then x could be 3 or -3.

Sasha It looks like there's no way to decide. If you only told me Tony and Michelle ended up with 16, I couldn't figure out what their original numbers were.

Derman It's weird. That didn't happen the second time we ran the experiment. If two people started with different numbers, they always got different results. That time, Tony started with 5 and Michelle started with 12.

	Tony	Michelle
Starting number	5	12
After subtracting 10	−5	2
After cubing	−125	8
After adding 7	−118	15

Sasha What happens if we try to undo the operations?

	Tony	Michelle
Ending number	−118	15
After undoing addition by 7	−125	8
After undoing cubing	−5	2
After undoing subtraction by 10	5	12

Derman No problems this time. We found their starting numbers. I think you could do this with any ending number.

Sasha To go from the ending number back to the starting number, we should start with the last operation. So we have these steps:

- Subtract seven from the ending number.
- Take the cube root of that.
- Add ten to *that*.

We *will* be able to get back the starting number!

> Why can Sasha and Derman undo cubing but not squaring?

Derman As long as all the steps can be undone. I wonder how we can decide whether or not a step can be undone.

For Discussion

5. In the second experiment, why can Sasha and Derman always derive the starting number from the ending number?

6. Change the first experiment in some way to make its process reversible.

The second In-Class Experiment amounted to evaluating the function $f(x) = (x - 10)^3 + 7$ for different starting values of x. When your class evaluated this function in the In-Class Experiment, you found that, if two students got the same output, they must have started with the same input. When a function has this behavior, it is *one-to-one*.

Definition

A function is **one-to-one** if its ouputs are unique. That is, a function f is one-to-one if $f(r) = f(s)$ only when $r = s$.

Habits of Mind

Establish a process.
To check if a function f is one-to-one, assume that $f(r) = f(s)$ and try to show that $r = s$.

The function from the first In-Class Experiment is not one-to-one, since the different inputs 13 and 7 both give the same output, 16. That is, $f(13) = f(7)$. But $13 \neq 7$.

For You to Do

7. Which of these functions are one-to-one?

$$P(x) = x^2 \qquad Q(x) = x^3 \qquad R(x) = |x - 10| \qquad S(x) = \sqrt{x + 15}$$

Is P one-to-one? That is, if $P(r) = P(s)$, does r have to equal s?
If $r^2 = s^2$, does $r = s$?
No, not necessarily!

You can sometimes tell that a function from $\mathbb{R}$ to $\mathbb{R}$ is not one-to-one from its graph. Here is the graph of a function $g : \mathbb{R} \to \mathbb{R}$.

From the graph, you can see that there are different inputs that give the same output. If two points on the graph have the same y-height, they correspond to different inputs that produce the same output. This graph shows two different inputs a and b with $g(a) = g(b)$.

If a horizontal line crosses the graph of a function in more than one place, the function cannot be one-to-one.

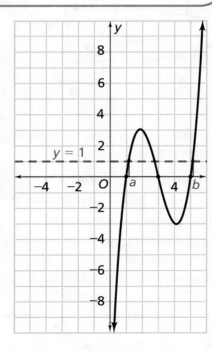

Habits of Mind

Be careful. The graph of an $\mathbb{R}$-to-$\mathbb{R}$ function cannot tell you with certainty that a function *is* one-to-one, because you can never see the complete graph. For example, suppose $f(x) = x^3 - x$ and $g(x) = f(x - 20)$. Graph g over the interval $-10 \leq x \leq 10$. No horizontal line cuts the graph twice. But is g one-to-one? Check out the graph over the interval $-10 \leq x \leq 30$.

For You to Do

Use graphs to determine which functions are not one-to-one. Which functions are one-to-one? Explain.

8. $A(x) = x$

9. $B(x) = x^2$

10. $C(x) = x^3$

11. $D(x) = \frac{1}{x}$

12. $E(x) = |x|$

13. $F(x) = \sqrt{x}$

14. $G(x) = x^3 - x$

15. $H(x) = x^3 + x$

Developing Habits of Mind

Visualize. Here is a potato-and-arrow diagram for a one-to-one function.

One important fact about one-to-one functions is that they are reversible, as Derman and Sasha noticed. In the diagram, if you pick any output in Set B, it is always possible to determine where it came from.

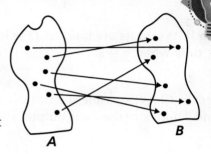

Any two arrows from A end at different objects in B. Only a one-to-one function has this property.

This means there is another function, an *inverse function*, from Set B to Set A. In a potato-and-arrow diagram, the inverse function looks similar, but all the arrows reverse direction.

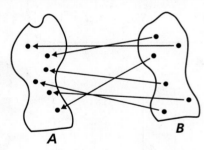

The domain and range switch. If you follow an arrow in the original function and then the corresponding arrow of the inverse function, you are back where you started.

You will see the formal definition of an inverse function in a moment. Derman and Sasha used inverse functions in their dialog.

- The function "add 7" has an inverse: "subtract 7."

- The function "cube the number" has an inverse: "take the cube root."

- The function "subtract 10" has an inverse: "add 10."

It might appear that the squaring and square root functions are inverses, but they are not. When the domain is $\mathbb{R}$, the squaring function is not one-to-one, so the squaring step cannot be inverted. What do you find if the domain is different?

See Exercise 4.

You can write the inverse of f as f^{-1}. Here is the formal definition.

Definition

**Suppose f is a one-to-one function with domain A and range B.
The inverse function f^{-1} is a function with these properties:**

- **f^{-1} has domain B and range A.**
- **For all x in B, $f(f^{-1}(x)) = x$.**

There is another way to state this definition that puts the emphasis on the function rather than on its output. The **identity function** on a set is the function id that simply returns its input.

$$\text{id}(x) = x$$

There is an identity function for each domain, but they all behave the same way: They do nothing to an input. What is the graph of id : $\mathbb{R} \to \mathbb{R}$?

Definition

(Alternate Version) Suppose f is a one-to-one function with domain A and range B. The inverse function f^{-1} is a function with these properties:

- **f^{-1} has domain B and range A.**
- **For all x in B, $f \circ f^{-1} = \text{id}$.**

Derman's description of the function $f(x) = (x - 10)^3 + 7$ refers to f as a composition of three simpler functions, in this order.

- Subtract 10.
- Cube.
- Add 7.

Sasha and Derman then describe how to recover the original input from the output.

- Subtract 7.
- Take the cube root.
- Add 10.

This process describes the inverse function of $f(x) = (x - 10)^3 + 7$. You can build the inverse function by starting with x and applying the three reversing rules in the order above.

$$f^{-1}(x) = \sqrt[3]{x - 7} + 10$$

When an inverse function exists, you can often find it by describing the steps to reverse the process.

The original function f is the composition $f = c \circ b \circ a$ of the steps listed. Then the inverse f^{-1} is $f^{-1} = a^{-1} \circ b^{-1} \circ c^{-1}$. You invert each function and reverse their order.

Example

Problem Find the inverse function of $f(x) = \frac{x}{2} + 5$.

Solution

Method 1 One way to do this is to describe $f(x)$ as steps: Divide by 2 and then add 5. The inverse function f^{-1} takes an input, subtracts 5, and then multiplies by 2.

$$f^{-1}(x) = 2(x - 5)$$

Method 2 The other way to find an inverse function is to use the definition.

$$f(f^{-1}(x)) = x$$

If $f(x) = \frac{x}{2} + 5$, then

$$f(f^{-1}(x)) = \frac{f^{-1}(x)}{2} + 5$$

Since $x = f(f^{-1}(x))$, you have

$$x = \frac{f^{-1}(x)}{2} + 5$$

Solve for $f^{-1}(x)$ as you would for any variable. You can subtract 5 from each side and then multiply by 2.

$$x = \frac{f^{-1}(x)}{2} + 5$$

$$x - 5 = \frac{f^{-1}(x)}{2}$$

$$2(x - 5) = f^{-1}(x)$$

Habits of Mind

Represent a function.
You can think of this equation as
$f(\text{anything}) = \frac{\text{anything}}{2} + 5$.

For You to Do

16. Find the inverse of $g(x) = 2(x - 5)$.

For Discussion

17. What happens when you try to find the inverse of $h(x) = (x - 10)^2 + 7$?

Developing Habits of Mind

Look for relationships. In arithmetic, numbers have additive inverses. When you add a number to its additive inverse, you get 0, the identity for addition. The additive inverse of a number is its opposite.

Nonzero numbers have multiplicative inverses. When you multiply a number by its multiplicative inverse, you get 1, the identity for multiplication. The multiplicative inverse of a number is its reciprocal.

One-to-one functions have inverses with respect to composition. When you compose a function with its inverse, you get id, the identity for composition. There is one hitch: composition, unlike addition and multiplication, is not commutative. $f \circ g \neq g \circ f$ unless f and g are special functions. For a function and its inverse, though, the story is much simpler, thanks to the following theorem.

Remember...

The functions $f \circ g$ and $g \circ f$ do not necessarily have the same domain.

Theorem 2.1

Suppose $f : A \rightarrow B$ is one-to-one. Then

- $f^{-1} : B \rightarrow A$ is one-to-one
- $(f^{-1})^{-1} = f$

Proof

- Suppose $f^{-1}(r) = f^{-1}(s)$. Take f of each side to conclude that $r = s$.
- For f to be the inverse of f^{-1} (that is, $f = (f^{-1})^{-1}$), f must have a domain A and range B (which it does).

  Also, $f^{-1}(f(a))$ must equal a for all a in A.

  You know $f \circ f^{-1}$ is the identity, so

  $$f(f^{-1}(f(a))) = f \circ f^{-1}(f(a)) = \text{id}(f(a) = f(a).$$

  The fact that f is one-to-one and $f(f^{-1}(f(a))) = f(a)$ means that

  $$f^{-1}(f(a)) = a.$$

  Thus f fits the definition of the inverse of f^{-1}. So, $f = (f^{-1})^{-1}$.

Habits of Mind

Detect the key characteristics. Study the two characteristics of f proved in the second part. They meet the requirements for f to be the inverse of f^{-1}. That is why you can conclude $f = (f^{-1})^{-1}$.

Exercises *Practicing Habits of Mind*

Check Your Understanding

1. The basic functions below are all from $\mathbb{R}$ to $\mathbb{R}$. For each function, determine whether the function has an inverse. If it does, find the inverse function. If it does not, explain why not.

   a. $f(x) = x$
   b. $g(x) = \frac{1}{x}$
   c. $h(x) = x^2$
   d. $k(x) = x^3$
   e. $\ell(x) = x^3 - x$
   f. $m(x) = \sqrt{x}$
   g. $n(x) = |x|$

2. Use the graph of a function and its inverse at the right.

  a. The point (1, 5) is on the graph of the function. What point must be on the graph of the inverse function?

  b. If $f : \mathbb{R} \to \mathbb{R}$, describe how you get the graph of f^{-1} from the graph of f.

  c. How does this graph connect to the statement of Theorem 2.1?

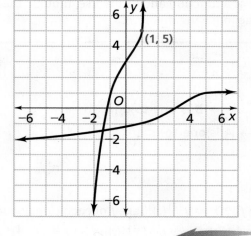

3. Use the definition of f below.

$$f(x) = \begin{cases} x & \text{if } x < 0 \\ 2x & \text{if } 0 \le x \le 6 \end{cases}$$

This is the function from Exercise 9 in Lesson 2.02.

  a. What is the natural domain of f?

  b. Sketch the graph of f.

  c. Extend the definition of f so that its domain is all of $\mathbb{R}$ and f is one-to-one.

  d. Extend the definition of f so that its domain is all of $\mathbb{R}$ and f is not one-to-one.

4. The function $x \mapsto x^2$ is not one-to-one on its natural domain.

  a. Restrict its domain to a set on which the function is one-to-one.

  b. On this restricted domain, what is the inverse of $x \mapsto x^2$?

5. The table at the right defines the function t.

  a. What is the domain of t?

  b. Draw a potato-and-arrow diagram that illustrates $t(x)$.

  c. Why is t a function?

  d. Does t have an inverse? If so, give the table for t^{-1}. If not, change the table to make a new function that is one-to-one.

x	t(x)
1	3
5	7
9	11
13	11

Remember...

In exercises like this, the table is the entire function. If an input is not in the table, then it is not in the domain of t.

6. Find the inverse of $f(x) = \dfrac{x}{x-1}$, where $x \ne 1$.

7. Functions h and j are defined on $\mathbb{R}^+$.

$$h(x) = x^2$$
$$j(x) = \sqrt{x}$$

Graph $h(x)$ and $j(x)$. Is h equal to j^{-1}?

8. Suppose $f, g : \mathbb{R} \to \mathbb{R}$, with $f(x) = 5x^2 - 17x + 6$ and $g(x) = 5x$.

   a. Find a formula for $g \circ f(x)$.

   b. Find a formula for $h(x) = g \circ f \circ g^{-1}(x)$.

   c. Draw the graphs of f and h on the same axes.

   d. Find the zeros of h and the zeros of f.

9. **Take It Further** Prove or disprove the following statement.

   If $f(x) = f^{-1}(x)$ for an input x, then $f(x) = x$.

On Your Own

10. Here are the graphs of four functions. Which functions are definitely not one-to-one?

   a.

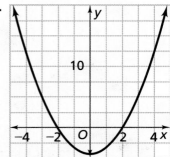

   b.

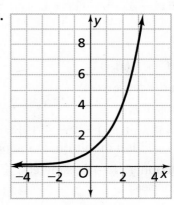

   c.

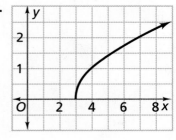

   d.

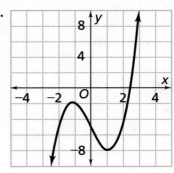

11. **Standardized Test Prep** Function $f(x)$ is one-to-one, with $f(3) = 7$ and $f(7) = 5$. Which equation must be true?

   A. $f^{-1}(3) = \frac{1}{7}$ **B.** $f^{-1}(3) = 7$

   C. $f^{-1}(7) = 5$ **D.** $f^{-1}(7) = 3$

12. Prove that, if functions $f, g : \mathbb{R} \to \mathbb{R}$ are one-to-one, then $f \circ g$ is one-to-one.

Go Online
Pearsonsuccessnet.com

13. Functions f and g are one-to-one. Which function is the inverse function of $f \circ g$?

A. $f^{-1} \circ g^{-1}$ **B.** $g^{-1} \circ f^{-1}$

C. $f^{-1} \circ g$ **D.** $g^{-1} \circ f$

14. Find the inverse of each function.

   a. $m(x) = 5x + 3$ **b.** $n(x) = 2x - 11$

   c. $p(x) = -3x + 4$ **d.** $q(x) = \frac{x}{5} - 0.6$

> The domain of each function is $\mathbb{R}$.

15. The graph of the function $f(x) = ax + b$ is a line with slope a.

   a. If $a \neq 0$, show that f is one-to-one.

   b. Find a formula for $f^{-1}(x)$.

   c. Find the slope of the graph of the inverse function f^{-1}.

   d. Find three linear functions g, h, and j such that each is its own inverse.

16. Suppose $f, g, k : \mathbb{R} \to \mathbb{R}$, $f(x) = 5x^3 - 12x^2 - 11x + 6$, $g(x) = 25x$, and $k(x) = 5x$.

   a. Find a formula for $g \circ f(x)$.

   b. Find a formula for $h(x) = g \circ f \circ k^{-1}(x)$.

   c. Draw the graphs of f and h on the same axes.

   d. Find the zeros of f and the zeros of h.

17. Take It Further Suppose $f : \mathbb{R} \to \mathbb{R}$ and $f(x) = 7x^2 - 15x + 2$. Find a linear function g such that $g \circ f \circ g^{-1}$ is a monic quadratic polynomial.

18. Write About It The graph of function $f : \mathbb{R} \to \mathbb{R}$ is increasing, which means that as x increases, $f(x)$ also increases.

> A quadratic is monic if the coefficient of x^2 is 1.

   a. Draw a possible graph of function f.

   b. Roy says that any increasing function, no matter what its graph looks like, must be one-to-one. Do you agree? Explain.

Maintain Your Skills

19. Let $f(x) = 4x + 3$. Find each value.

   a. $f(10)$ **b.** $f^{-1}(43)$ **c.** $f(f(0))$

   d. $f^{-1}(f^{-1}(15))$ **e.** $f(f^{-1}(289))$ **f.** $f^{-1}(f(-162.3))$

   g. $f(f^{-1}(f(10)))$

20. Let $f(x) = 4x + 3$. Find each value in terms of r.

   a. $f(r)$ **b.** $f(f(r))$ **c.** $f(f(f(r)))$

   d. $f(f(f(f(r))))$ **e.** $f(f(f(f(f(r)))))$ **f.** $f^{12}(r)$

> The notation $f^{12}(r)$ means "compose 12 copies of f and apply the composition to r."

Graphing Inverse and Piecewise Functions

There is a relationship between the graphs of a function and its inverse.

Minds in Action

Tony and Sasha are discussing Exercise 2 from Lesson 2.04.

Sasha   Tony, how did you answer part (b)?

Tony   Well, when you look at the two graphs, they're mirror images of each other.

Tony copies the graphs onto his graph paper.

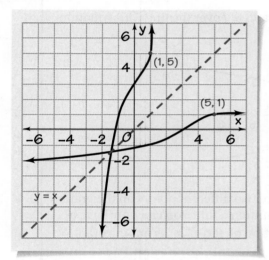

Tony   See, if you fold the paper on the diagonal, the graphs line up.

Sasha   What you're really doing is folding it so that the *x*-axis and the *y*-axis line up, right?

Tony   Um, yeah, that's right. Hey, that's what part (a) is getting at . . . if (1, 5) is on the graph of *f*, then (5, 1) is on the graph of f^{-1}.

Sasha   Right, because *f* maps 1 to 5, so f^{-1} maps 5 back to 1.

Tony   Good. Okay, so now when you fold it along that diagonal . . .

Sasha   Which is the graph of $y = x$, by the way . . .

Tony   Right, when you fold it along $y = x$, (1, 5) and (5, 1) will line up since the *x* from the first point is equal to the *y* of the second, and vice versa.

Sasha   Cool. So we're reflecting over the line $y = x$. We can reflect anything over that line, can't we?

Tony   I don't see why not. How does that help us figure out if a function has an inverse?

For Discussion

1. Reflect the graph on page 117 over the line with equation $y = x$. Is the reflection the graph of a function? Why or why not?

Example 1

Problem

a. Draw the graph of $f(x) = x^2$. Sketch the reflection of the graph of f over the line $y = x$. Is the reflection the graph of a function? Why or why not?

b. Draw the graph of $g(x) = x^3$. Sketch the reflection of the graph of g over the line $y = x$. Is the reflection the graph of a function? Why or why not?

Solution

a. Here is a sketch of the reflection of the graph of f over the line with equation $y = x$.

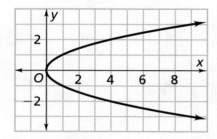

From the graph, you can see that there are two different points on the graph for every positive value of x. Since by definition a function can only have a single output for a given input, the reflection of $f(x) = x^2$ is not the graph of a function.

If you draw just the top part of the reflection (the part where $y \geq 0$), you get the graph of the equation $y = \sqrt{x}$.

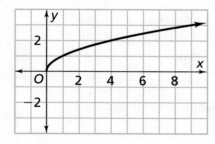

The square root function is a function from $\mathbb{R}^+ \to \mathbb{R}^+$.

> What do you get if you reflect the graph of the square root function over the line with equation $y = x$?

b. Here is a sketch of the reflection of the graph of g over the line with equation $y = x$.

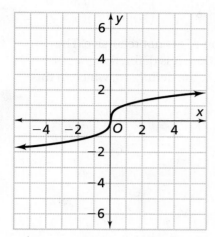

The reflection does appear to be the graph of a function. And, in fact, since $g(x) = x^3$ is one-to-one, its inverse is a function. The graph above is the graph of the function $h(x) = \sqrt[3]{x}$.

> You showed this fact in Lesson 2.04 Exercise 1.

For You to Do

2. Find the inverse of $r(x) = 2x^3 - 5$. Draw a graph of both r and r^{-1}.

In Chapter 1, you looked at a number of functions that were defined recursively. Consider $f(n)$ below, for whole number values of n.

$$f(n) = \begin{cases} 3, & \text{if } n = 0 \\ f(n-1) + 5, & \text{if } n > 0 \end{cases}$$

A graph of the function $f(n)$ is shown below.

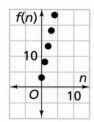

The graph of any function with a recursive definition will simply be a set of discrete points. In this case, since the natural domain of the function is $\mathbb{Z}^+$, the x-coordinate of each point will be a whole number.

Compare the definitions of the functions below.

$$f(n) = \begin{cases} 3, & \text{if } n = 0 \\ f(n-1) + 5, & \text{if } n > 0 \end{cases} \qquad g(x) = \begin{cases} 3, & \text{if } x < 0 \\ 5x + 3, & \text{if } x \geq 0 \end{cases}$$

They are similar in structure, but the definition of g is not recursive. The function g is called a **piecewise-defined function**. It is defined in pieces. The domain of g is the union of each domain in the definition, which in this case is all real numbers. Here is a graph of g.

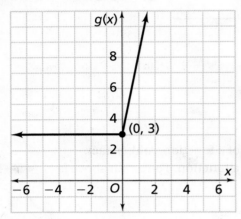

You have to make sure the domains for each piece do not overlap; otherwise you might not be defining a function. Why?

You may be familiar with this function:

$$a(x) = \begin{cases} -x, & \text{if } x < 0 \\ x, & \text{if } x \geq 0 \end{cases}$$

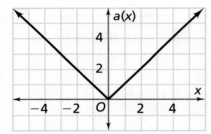

Function f from Lesson 2.04 Exercise 3 is also a piecewise function. You know the function a by its more familiar notation, $a(x) = |x|$.

Example 2

Problem Sketch the graph of the function k shown below.

$$k(x) = \begin{cases} 2 - x, & \text{if } x \leq 1 \\ \frac{1}{2}x - 1, & \text{if } 1 < x \leq 4 \\ -3x + 11, & \text{if } x > 4 \end{cases}$$

Solution This graph has three pieces, and each piece is linear. The key part of graphing piecewise-defined functions is to be attentive to the end points of each domain interval. For instance, the first part of the definition is for $x \leq 1$. The graph will include the point $(1, 1)$, which is the rightmost point on the section of the graph that includes the line with the equation $y = 2 - x$. Indicate this by drawing a solid circle at $(1, 1)$, the endpoint of that piece of the graph.

The second domain interval is $1 < x \le 4$, so the second piece will not include the leftmost endpoint, but will include the rightmost. Draw an open circle at the point $\left(1, -\frac{1}{2}\right)$ and a solid circle at $(4, 1)$.

The last domain interval is $x > 4$. For the third piece, use an open circle at the point $(4, -1)$.

Now, when you look at the graph, it satisfies the conditions for being a function. No vertical line passes through more than one point on the graph.

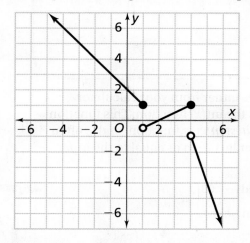

For Discussion

3. What are the domain and range of k? Does k have an inverse function? Explain your reasoning. If not, how can you change the definition of k so that it does have an inverse function?

Each piece of a piecewise-defined function can be any kind of function, not just lines. For instance, the graph below represents a piecewise-defined function.

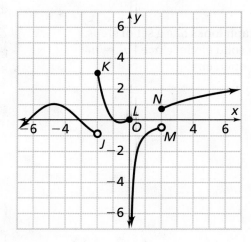

For You to Do

4. Sketch a graph of each of the following functions. Indicate whether the function is one-to-one.

a. $f(x) = \begin{cases} 3, & \text{if } x \le -1 \\ -2, & \text{if } x > -1 \end{cases}$

b. $g(x) = \begin{cases} 2x - 4, & \text{if } x < 0 \\ 2x + 4, & \text{if } x \ge 0 \end{cases}$

c. $k(x) = \begin{cases} x^2, & \text{if } x \le -1 \\ |x|, & \text{if } -1 < x \le 1 \\ x^2, & \text{if } x > 1 \end{cases}$

Another function you may be familiar with, either from your calculator or from a computer programming class, is the int(x) function. This function is also called the *floor* function, or the *greatest integer* function, and is often written as $\lfloor x \rfloor$. It returns the greatest integer less than or equal to the input. For instance:

$$\lfloor 2.5 \rfloor = 2, \lfloor \pi \rfloor = 3, \text{ and } \lfloor -4.08 \rfloor = -5$$

The graph of the equation $y = \lfloor x \rfloor$ is shown below.

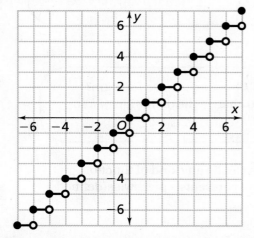

You might see the greatest integer function represented as [x] or as [[x]].

This is called a step function because its graph looks like a set of steps. Notice that for each step, the left side has a solid circle (since $\lfloor n \rfloor = n$ if n is an integer), and the right side has an open circle.

Be careful! Some people think of the floor function as "stripping off the fractional part," but that isn't true when the input is negative.

Look for relationships. One way to think of the floor function is that it is a piecewise-defined function with infinitely many pieces.

$$\lfloor x \rfloor = \begin{cases} \vdots \\ -1, & \text{if } -1 \le x < 0 \\ 0, & \text{if } 0 \le x < 1 \\ 1, & \text{if } 1 \le x < 2 \\ 2, & \text{if } 2 \le x < 3 \\ \vdots \end{cases}$$

For You to Do

5. Evaluate each of the following.

 a. $\lfloor 2.17 \rfloor$ b. $\lfloor -6.85 \rfloor$ c. $\lfloor 2\pi \rfloor$ d. $\lfloor -\frac{\pi}{2} \rfloor$

 e. $\lfloor \frac{112}{2} \rfloor$ f. $\lfloor 14\frac{1}{2} \rfloor$ g. $\lfloor -8\frac{2}{3} \rfloor$

For Discussion

6. Suppose $\lfloor x \rfloor = 17$. What are possible values for x?

Exercises *Practicing Habits of Mind*

Check Your Understanding

1. Use the floor function to write the following functions.

 a. a function that rounds a number to the nearest integer

 b. a function that rounds to the nearest $\frac{1}{100}$

 c. a function that rounds to the nearest multiple of 5

There are several different conventions for rounding halfway numbers like 4.5 or −7.5. Use the rounding rule that halfway numbers always round up, so 4.5 rounds to 5 and −7.5 rounds to −7.

2. What are the domain and range of $f(x) = \lfloor x \rfloor$? Does the floor function have an inverse?

3. Here is the graph of a piecewise-defined function.

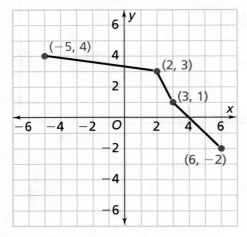

 a. Write a function for this graph.

 b. Explain why the function has an inverse function.

 c. Write the piecewise definition for the inverse of this function.

 d. Carefully sketch the graph of the inverse of this function.

 e. Write About It Compare the rule for the function with the rule for the inverse. How are they similar?

4. Sketch a graph for each function and its inverse.

 a. $f(x) = \sqrt{x + 3}$

 b. $f(x) = \sqrt{x} + 3$

 c. $f(x) = \sqrt{2x}$

 d. $f(x) = 2\sqrt{x}$

 e. $f(x) = \sqrt[3]{x - 5}$

 f. $f(x) = \sqrt[3]{8x}$

 g. $f(x) = 2\sqrt[3]{x}$

 h. $f(x) = \sqrt{x^2}$

 i. $f(x) = \sqrt[3]{x^3}$

5. Consider the following story.

 Colleen is going on a field trip at school today. She rode her bike to school at 10 mi/h for 15 minutes. She waited 7 minutes for the bus. She then rode in the bus for 35 minutes at a speed of 35 mi/h.

 Write a piecewise-defined function s that represents Colleen's speed t minutes after she left her house. Sketch a graph of s.

6. Compare the following two functions. Are they equivalent? Explain your reasoning.

$$f(x) = \lfloor x + 4 \rfloor \text{ and } g(x) = \lfloor x \rfloor + 4$$

7. What's Wrong Here? Derman wrote the following piecewise definition:

$$f(x) = \begin{cases} -2x & \text{if } x < 1 \\ 2x & \text{if } x \geq -1 \end{cases}$$

Is *f* a function? Explain your reasoning.

8. Determine whether each function is one-to-one. Explain your reasoning.

a. $f(x) = x - \lfloor x \rfloor$

b. $f(x) = x - 2\lfloor x \rfloor$

c. $f(x) = x - \lfloor 2x \rfloor$

d. $f(x) = x + \lfloor x \rfloor$

e. $f(x) = x + 2\lfloor x \rfloor$

f. $f(x) = 2x - \lfloor x \rfloor$

Sketching a graph of the function may help you decide.

On Your Own

9. The "ceiling" function, written $\lceil x \rceil$, is similar to the floor function. Given an input of a real number, it returns the smallest integer greater than or equal to the given number. So, $\lceil 2 \rceil = 2$, $\lceil 3.53 \rceil = 4$, $\lceil 1.00001 \rceil = 2$, and $\lceil -5.39 \rceil = -5$.

a. Sketch a graph of the equation $y = \lceil x \rceil$.

b. Write the ceiling function in terms of the floor function.

10. Here is the graph of a piecewise-defined function.

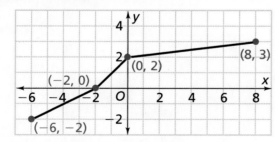

a. Write a function *f* that represents this graph.

b. Translate the graph of *f* to the right 5 units. Write a function to represent this new graph.

c. Translate the graph of *f* up 3 units. Write a function to represent this new graph.

11. Joe was looking at the data plan for his smartphone.

> **Joe** I pay \$60 a month, and with that I get 5 gigabytes of data that I can download. If I go past that, I pay \$5 per gigabyte. But that means that if I go over even by a little bit, I pay the extra charge. So if I download 6.02 gigabytes, I have to pay for 7 gigabytes.

Hint: One of the pieces is a step function. You can use any of the step functions from this lesson.

Write a piecewise-defined function c that returns Joe's bill for d gigabytes of data downloaded in one month. Sketch a graph of c.

12. Compare the two functions below. Are they equivalent? Explain your reasoning.

$$f(x) = \lfloor 2x \rfloor \text{ and } g(x) = 2\lfloor x \rfloor$$

13. Compare the functions below. Are they equivalent? If not, for what values (if any) are they equal? Explain your reasoning.

$$f(x) = \lfloor x^2 \rfloor \text{ and } g(x) = \lfloor x \rfloor^2$$

Try sketching the graph of each function. Some graphing calculators have a *floor* function.

Another way to describe a piecewise-defined function is to use the

Heaviside step function $h_a(x) = \begin{cases} 0, & \text{if } x < a \\ 1, & \text{if } x \geq a \end{cases}$. You can use a Heaviside step

function to write piecewise-defined functions on a single line. For example,

$f(x) = \begin{cases} 2, & \text{if } x < 1 \\ 5x + 2, & \text{if } x \geq 1 \end{cases}$ can be written as $f(x) = 2 + h_1(x) \cdot 5x$. When

$x < 1$, $h_1(x) = 0$, so $f(x) = 2$. When $x \geq 1$, $h_1(x) = 1$, so $f(x) = 2 + 5x$, as desired.

14. Write the following piecewise-defined functions on a single line using one or more Heaviside step functions.

a. $f(x) = \begin{cases} 4, & \text{if } x < -2 \\ 4 - 3x, & \text{if } x \geq -2 \end{cases}$

b. $f(x) = \begin{cases} -6, & \text{if } x < 3 \\ 7x + 1, & \text{if } x \geq 3 \end{cases}$

c. $f(x) = \begin{cases} 2x + 4, & \text{if } x < -1 \\ 3, & \text{if } x \geq -1 \end{cases}$

d. $f(x) = \begin{cases} 2, & \text{if } x < -3 \\ x + 1, & \text{if } -3 \leq x < 4 \\ 6, & \text{if } x \geq 4 \end{cases}$

e. $f(x) = \begin{cases} 1 - x^2, & \text{if } x \leq 1 \\ 1, & \text{if } 1 < x < 5 \\ 1 + x^2, & \text{if } x \geq 5 \end{cases}$

15. Write the function $a(x) = |x|$ using one or more Heaviside step functions.

16. Write the floor function on the domain $-3 \le x < 3$ using a Heaviside step function.

> There are at least two ways of writing this function. One way has only one term.

Maintain Your Skills

17. Evaluate the expression $(x - 4)(x - 1)(x + 3)(x + 5)(x + 9)$ for each x-value.

a. 1

b. -5

c. 4

d. -9

e. -3

f. What is similar about these five cases? Is there a sixth similar case? Explain.

18. Evaluate the expressions

$$2x^2 - 3x + 4$$
$$2x^2 - 3x + 4 + (x - 4)(x - 1)(x + 3)(x + 5)(x + 9)$$

for each x-value below.

a. 1

b. -5

c. 0

d. 4

e. What are the x-values that produce the same result in both expressions?

In this investigation, you learned how to determine whether a table, graph, or closed-form rule is a function; compose functions; find the inverse of a function if it exists; and graph piecewise-defined functions. These exercises will help you summarize what you have learned.

1. Suppose $f : \mathbb{R} \to \mathbb{R}$ and $f(x) = 3x^2 - 6x + 1$.

   a. Calculate $f(3)$ and $f(-3)$.

   b. Find all values of x for which $f(x) = 12$.

   c. Calculate $f(11) - f(10)$.

   d. Show that you can write $f(x + 1)$ as $f(x + 1) = 3x^2 - 2$.

   e. Write a simplified expression for $f(x + 1) - f(x)$.

   f. If $g(x) = f(x + 1) - f(x)$, what is $g(10)$?

2. Consider the functions $f(x) = 3x + 2$ and $g(x) = x + 5$. Calculate each value.

   a. $f(3)$ b. $g(3)$ c. $f(g(3))$ d. $f \circ g(3)$ e. $g \circ f(3)$ f. $f(3) \cdot g(3)$

3. Consider the function $f(x) = 3x + 2$. Find a function g that makes each equation true.

   a. $f \circ g(x) = x$ b. $g \circ f(x) = x$ c. $f \circ g(x) = x^2$

   d. $g \circ f(x) = x^2$ e. $g \circ f(x) = f(x)$ f. $f \circ g(x) = f(x)$

4. Suppose $f, g, k : \mathbb{R} \to \mathbb{R}$, $f(x) = -3 + x + 8x^2 + 4x^3$, $g(x) = 16x$, and $k(x) = 4x$.

   a. Find a formula for $g \circ f(x)$.

   b. Find a formula for $h(x) = g \circ f \circ k^{-1}(x)$.

   c. Draw the graphs of f and h on the same axes.

   d. Find the zeros of h and the zeros of f.

5. What is a function?

6. How do you compose two functions to make a new function?

7. What function undoes $x \mapsto 3x + 7$?

8. What is a piecewise-defined function?

Vocabulary and Notation

In this investigation you learned these terms and symbols. Make sure you understand what each one means and how to use it.

- composite function, $g \circ f$
- domain
- equal functions
- function
- identity function
- inverse function, f^{-1}

- piecewise-defined function
- one-to-one
- range
- target
- $x \mapsto y$ (x maps to y)
- $\mathbb{R}$ (the real numbers)

Making It Fit

In Chapter 1, you learned how to find a simple function that fits a table if the inputs increase in a regular way. In *Making It Fit,* you will learn a general-purpose technique called Lagrange interpolation. You can use this technique to fit a polynomial function to any table.

By the end of this investigation, you will be able to answer questions like these.

1. How can you find a polynomial that agrees with a table?

2. How can you find two different functions that agree with the same table?

3. What number comes next in the sequence 1, 4, 9, . . . ?

You will learn how to

- fit polynomials to tables
- work with linear combinations

You will develop these habits and skills:

- Use linear combinations of polynomials to determine new polynomials.
- Use zeros of polynomials to determine factors of polynomials.
- Find several functions that agree with a given table.
- Predict the results of calculations without having to carry them out.

Viewed from above, the bridge and its shadow suggest polynomial-function graphs that agree at two points.

In Chapter 1, you learned some techniques for finding polynomial functions that agree with tables. Usually the tables started with 0 and had inputs that increased by 1. How do you handle inputs that are not arranged that way? What do you do if the inputs do not follow a simple pattern? Suppose you have to work with a graph like this.

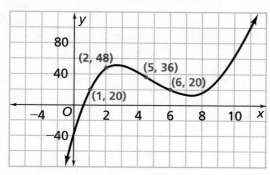

In this investigation, you will learn *Lagrange interpolation*. This technique will handle any data set that can come from a polynomial function.

For You to Explore

In Problems 1–3, find a polynomial function that agrees with each table.

1.

n	f(n)
2	5
5	11
7	15

2.

n	g(n)
2	6
5	30
7	56

3.

x	h(x)
2	10
5	55
7	105

> How can you check that the functions you find actually agree with the tables?

4. a. Find a quadratic function that agrees with the following table.

x	k(x)
1	0
3	0

b. Is the function you found the only quadratic function that agrees with the table? If it is, explain why. If not, find another one.

5. Find a quadratic function that agrees with each table.

a.
x	j(x)
1	20
3	0
6	0

b.
x	n(x)
1	0
3	12
6	0

c.
x	m(x)
1	0
3	0
6	60

d. Copy and complete the following table.

x	j(x) + n(x) + m(x)
1	▪
3	▪
6	▪

6. Find a quadratic function *f* that agrees with this table.

x	f(x)
1	20
3	12
6	60

7. Find a polynomial function *k* that agrees with this table.

x	k(x)
1	10
3	12
6	45

8. Find a polynomial function *t* that agrees with this table.

x	t(x)
1	84
5	48
8	42

9. Find a quadratic function *f* such that the graph of *f* contains the points in the graph.

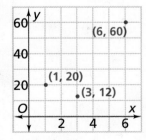

Exercises Practicing Habits of Mind

10. Suppose $f(x) = A(x - 1)(x - 4) + B(x - 1)(x - 6) + C(x - 4)(x - 6)$ for some numbers A, B, and C.

> Sketch the graph of f.

   a. Find the numbers A, B, and C such that the graph of f contains the points $(1, 45)$, $(4, 12)$, and $(6, 60)$.

   b. Find the normal form of the polynomial that defines f.

11. Find a function that agrees with this table.

x	r(x)
1	45
4	12
6	60

12. Consider these two functions.

$$f(x) = 3x + 1$$
$$g(x) = 3x + 1 + 7(x - 1)(x - 2)(x - 4)(x + 1)$$

   a. Copy and complete the following table.

x	f(x)	g(x)
−2	■	■
−1	■	■
0	■	■
1	■	■
2	■	■
3	■	■
4	■	■
5	■	■

   b. On which inputs do f and g agree?

   c. Are the inputs you found in part (a) the only inputs on which f and g agree? Explain.

   d. Find the normal form of the polynomial that defines g.

   e. Sketch the graphs of f and g.

13. Let $f(x) = 4x - 3$.

    a. Find a polynomial function that agrees with f for the input 2 but differs from it for every other input.

    b. Find a polynomial function that agrees with f for the inputs 2, 5, and 7 but differs from f for every other input.

Maintain Your Skills

Suppose $f(x) = A(x - 1)(x - 4) + B(x - 1)(x - 6) + C(x - 4)(x - 6)$ for some numbers A, B, and C. For Exercises 14–18, use the information given about f to do parts (a)–(d).

a. Find A, B, and C.

b. Find the normal form of the polynomial that defines f.

c. Sketch the graph of f.

d. Take It Further Find the minimum or maximum output of f.

14.

x	f(x)
1	60
4	−18
6	20

15.

x	f(x)
1	60
4	−18
6	10

16. The graph of f contains $(1, 0)$, $(4, 6)$, and $(6, 30)$.

17. The graph of f contains $(1, 0)$, $(4, 6)$, and $(6, -30)$.

18.

x	f(x)
1	30
4	−6
6	−30

The cars are approaching the roller coaster's maximum.

2.07 Lagrange Interpolation

In Chapter 1, you found rules to match the entries in tables. You developed some methods for fitting functions to tables. The methods were not general for two reasons.

You learned that a constant first difference means there is an exact linear fit. A constant nonzero second difference means there is an exact quadratic fit.

- Most of the tables in Chapter 1 had inputs that started with 0 and increased by 1 in each row.

- The methods relied on your ability to spot patterns.

In this lesson you will develop a way of matching the values in a table for any n distinct points using a polynomial of degree less than n. If you just rely on cleverness, it can be hard to find a function that agrees with a table (very hard for some tables), so it is very useful to have a method that will work for all tables.

The polynomial you get using this method may not be the simplest function that matches the n values in your table. It may look so messy that you want to use a computer or calculator to simplify it. But the method always works. Given a table, you will be able to find a function every time. And if the simplest function that matches the table is a polynomial, the method gives you the unique simplest rule for the table.

You will prove that the rule you get is unique in a later lesson.

Minds in Action   episode 5

Derman and Sasha are working on Problem 6 from the Getting Started lesson.

Table A

Input, x	Output, f(x)
1	20
3	12
6	60

Derman I wish a couple of these outputs were 0. Then this would be easy.

Sasha   Derman, that gives me an idea. We could split up Table A this way.

Sasha writes the following three tables on the board.

x	g(x)
1	20
3	0
6	0

\+

x	h(x)
1	0
3	12
6	0

\+

x	j(x)
1	0
3	0
6	60

Sasha   I can find polynomials that fit these tables. Look what happens if we add $g(x) + h(x) + j(x)$.

x	g(x) + h(x) + j(x)
1	20 + 0 + 0 = 20
3	0 + 12 + 0 = 12
6	0 + 0 + 60 = 60

We're back to Table A. So if we can figure out polynomials that fit the three simpler tables, we can get a polynomial that fits Table A. Let's look at the first table.

x	g(x)
1	20
3	0
6	0

Let's start with $x \mapsto (x - 3)(x - 6)$. At least that agrees with our table for $x = 3$ and $x = 6$.

Derman   Well, in that function, $1 \mapsto 10$, so that doesn't agree with the table.

Sasha   OK, what about a multiple of that function? Try $g(x) = A(x - 3)(x - 6)$ for some A. Let's figure out what A has to be in order for $g(1)$ to be 20.

$$20 = g(1) = A(1 - 3)(1 - 6)$$
$$20 = A(-2)(-5)$$
$$20 = 10A$$
$$A = 2$$

So $g(x) = 2(x - 3)(x - 6) = 2x^2 - 18x + 36$.

Derman   OK, that works. And $h(x)$ could be $B(x - 1)(x - 6)$ for some number B. Then I can figure out what B is.

$$12 = h(3) = B(3 - 1)(3 - 6)$$
$$12 = B(2)(-3)$$
$$12 = -6B$$
$$B = -2$$

So $h(x) = -2(x - 1)(x - 6) = -2x^2 + 14x - 12$.

Habits of Mind

Determine the process. How might Sasha have known that $x \mapsto (x - 3)(x - 6)$ agrees with their table for $x = 3$ and $x = 6$? How does Derman know that $1 \mapsto 10$?

Do you agree with Derman that $g(x) = 2(x - 3)(x - 6)$ works?

Sasha   While you were doing that, I figured out a function for the last table.

$$j(x) = 4(x - 1)(x - 3) = 4x^2 - 16x + 12$$

Derman   Adding $g(x) + h(x) + j(x)$, we get $f(x) = 4x^2 - 20x + 36$.

And here is its graph.

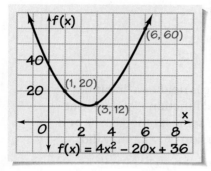

Habits of Mind

Establish a process. How can you check that the function $f(x)$ fits the original table?

Sasha   Hey, if we write $f(x)$ without expanding all the pieces, we can see more.

Sasha writes an equation on the board.

$$f(x) = 2(x - 3)(x - 6) - 2(x - 1)(x - 6) + 4(x - 1)(x - 3)$$

Derman   That looks much more complicated.

Sasha   Yes, but it lets you see the way it all works. Look what happens if you replace x with 1.

Derman   Oh yeah—everything disappears except the first bit.

Sasha   So, if we had another table with inputs 1, 3, and 6, and if the output for 1 were 30, I could change the $2(x - 3)(x - 6)$ to $3(x - 3)(x - 6)$.

Derman   And you could adjust the other numbers to make this expression work for any table with inputs 1, 3, and 6. So I guess the complicated form is pretty useful.

Why would Sasha change the 2 to a 3?

For You to Do

1. Find a polynomial function with a graph that contains (1, 80), (3, 36), and (6, 30).

Remember to check that the polynomial you find actually agrees with the input-output pairs.

Problem Suppose you have the following table.

Input, x	Output, $f(x)$
1	20
2	48
5	36
6	20

If you graph the data, you can determine that there is neither a linear nor a quadratic fit. So, you are looking for a polynomial function—of degree at least 3—that agrees with the table. You can use the same method Sasha and Derman used. Here is a somewhat streamlined version of what they did.

Solution Suppose the following strange rule gives a function $f(x)$. You will determine the numbers A, B, C, and D later.

$$f(x) = A(x - 1)(x - 2)(x - 5) + B(x - 1)(x - 2)(x - 6)$$
$$+ C(x - 1)(x - 5)(x - 6) + D(x - 2)(x - 5)(x - 6)$$

> Notice that, no matter what the values for A, B, C, and D are, this function cannot have degree greater than 3.

Why would anyone write a function this way? This is just a sum of functions, like the sum of functions Sasha and Derman found. Now you can find expressions for $f(1)$, $f(2)$, $f(5)$, and $f(6)$.

$$f(1) = A(1 - 1)(1 - 2)(1 - 5) + B(1 - 1)(1 - 2)(1 - 6)$$
$$+ C(1 - 1)(1 - 5)(1 - 6) + D(1 - 2)(1 - 5)(1 - 6)$$
$$= 0 + 0 + 0 + D(1 - 2)(1 - 5)(1 - 6)$$
$$= D(-1)(-4)(-5)$$
$$= -20D$$

In the same way, you can find $f(2)$, $f(5)$, and $f(6)$.

$$f(2) = C(2 - 1)(2 - 5)(2 - 6) = 12C$$
$$f(5) = B(5 - 1)(5 - 2)(5 - 6) = -12B$$
$$f(6) = A(6 - 1)(6 - 2)(6 - 5) = 20A$$

But you know $f(1)$, $f(2)$, $f(5)$, and $f(6)$. They are in the table.

$$f(1) = 20 = -20D, \text{ so } D = -1$$
$$f(2) = 48 = 12C, \text{ so } C = 4$$
$$f(5) = 36 = -12B, \text{ so } B = -3$$
$$f(6) = 20 = 20A, \text{ so } A = 1$$

By substituting in these values, you find a formula for $f(x)$.

$$f(x) = (x - 1)(x - 2)(x - 5) - 3(x - 1)(x - 2)(x - 6)$$
$$+ 4(x - 1)(x - 5)(x - 6) - 1(x - 2)(x - 5)(x - 6)$$

Too messy, you say. But a CAS can simplify this with no trouble. You could too, if you needed to. The formula simplifies to

$$f(x) = x^3 - 16x^2 + 69x - 34$$

This is a well-behaved cubic that agrees with the table. How is this similar to the method Sasha and Derman used?

$y = x^3 - 16x^2 + 69x - 34$

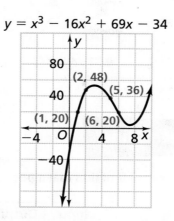

Here is the graph.

This method of finding a polynomial to agree with a table is **Lagrange interpolation.**

For You to Do

2. Use Lagrange interpolation to find a polynomial function with a graph that contains $(1, 20)$, $(2, 48)$, and $(5, 36)$.

Historical Perspective

Joseph-Louis Lagrange was born in Turin, Italy, in 1736, and died in Paris, France, in 1813. His interest in advanced mathematics began when he read a calculus book by Edmond Halley (of Halley's comet fame).

Lagrange was a professor of geometry at the Royal Artillery School in Turin from 1755 (at age 19) to 1766 and helped to found the Royal Academy of Sciences there in 1757. In 1766, when Leonhard Euler left his post as director of the Berlin Academy of Sciences, Lagrange succeeded him. In 1787, Lagrange left Berlin to become a member of the French Academy of Sciences, where he remained for the rest of his career.

Lagrange contributed many results and techniques to the field of algebra. Lagrange interpolation is one of these contributions. Another contribution was a new proof that every integer is the sum of the squares of at most four integers. His interest in physics and mechanics led him to devise a new way of writing down Newton's laws of motion.

Joseph-Louis Lagrange

Exercises *Practicing Habits of Mind*

Check Your Understanding

In Exercises 1–4, find a polynomial function that agrees with each table.

1.

Input	Output
1	12
2	8
4	36

2.

Input	Output
1	2
2	11
3	20

3.

Input	Output
1	2
2	11
3	28

4.

Input	Output
1	1
2	22
3	61
4	124

5. Sasha has a method for solving Exercise 4. She writes
$f(x) = A + B(x - 1) + C(x - 1)(x - 2) + D(x - 1)(x - 2)(x - 3)$.
Then she uses $f(1) = 1$ to find A, $f(2) = 22$ to find B, and so on.

  a. Find A, B, C, and D using Sasha's method.

  b. Do you get the same rule for f as you got in Exercise 4?

6. Write About It Sometimes, when you might expect a cubic, Lagrange interpolation produces a polynomial of lesser degree. How might this happen? (*Hint:* You can use Exercise 2 as an example.)

A curved underground hose joining 4 sprinkler heads could suggest a unique polynomial function of degree 3 or less.

On Your Own

7. A radio show offers a prize to the first caller who can predict the next term in this sequence.

  {1, 2, 4, 8, 16}

  a. What do you get if you use common sense?

  b. What do you get if you use Lagrange interpolation? (You will need a CAS for this one.)

8. Find a polynomial function that agrees with this table.

Input	Output
1	−6
3	166
6	7159
8	31,291
9	56,938
12	243,787

Go Online
Pearsonsuccessnet.com

9. **Write About It** Explain Lagrange interpolation in your own words.

10. Suppose you have a table that has five entries. What is the greatest possible degree of polynomial that you would need to match the table using Lagrange interpolation? What is the least possible degree of polynomial that you would need?

11. Find a nonconstant polynomial function h such that

$$h(1) = h(2) = h(3) = h(4) = 0$$

12. Find a nonconstant polynomial function j such that

$$j(1) = j(2) = j(3) = 3$$

For Exercises 11 and 12, sketch the graphs!

13. **Standardized Test Prep** Tony has the graph of a cubic function through the four points $(−2, 0)$, $(0, −6)$, $(1, −12)$, and $(3, 30)$. He has written the following formula to approximate the function.

$$f(x) = Ax(x − 1)(x − 3) + B(x + 2)(x − 1)(x − 3)$$
$$+ Cx(x + 2)(x − 3) + Dx(x + 2)(x − 1)$$

If the value of C is 2 and the value of D is 1, what are the values of A and B?

A. $A = −1, B = 0$ **B.** $A = 0, B = −1$

C. $A = 1, B = −1$ **D.** $A = 1, B = 1$

14. You may know a formula for the sum of the numbers from 1 to n. If you do not know it, you can figure it out. You can model the sum of the first n numbers with a recursively defined function s.

$$s(n) = \begin{cases} 1 & \text{if } n = 1 \\ s(n − 1) + n & \text{if } n > 1 \end{cases}$$

a. Explain why the recursion above yields the following sum.

$$s(n) = 1 + 2 + 3 + \cdots + (n − 1) + n$$

This is the sum of the integers between 1 and n.

b. Make a table of $s(n)$. Find a simple polynomial function S that agrees with s for all values in your table.

15. Take It Further Use the method in Exercise 14 to find a formula for the sum of the squares between 1 and n. The recursive function below gives the sum of the squares of the numbers from 1 to n.

$$q(n) = \begin{cases} 1 & \text{if } n = 1 \\ q(n-1) + n^2 & \text{if } n > 1 \end{cases}$$

Find a closed-form polynomial function Q that agrees with q.

Maintain Your Skills

16. For each function f, find $f(5)$ and $f(7)$. Then write f in normal form.

a. $f(x) = \dfrac{6}{7-5}(x-5) + \dfrac{3}{5-7}(x-7)$

b. $f(x) = \dfrac{12}{7-5}(x-5) + \dfrac{-20}{5-7}(x-7)$

c. $f(x) = \dfrac{b_2}{7-5}(x-5) + \dfrac{b_1}{5-7}(x-7)$

d. Take It Further Suppose $f(x) = \dfrac{b_2}{a_2-a_1}(x-a_1) + \dfrac{b_1}{a_1-a_2}(x-a_2)$.
Find $f(a_1)$ and $f(a_2)$. Write f in normal form.

17. For each function f, find $f(3)$, $f(5)$, and $f(7)$. Then write f in normal form.

a. $f(x) = \dfrac{6}{(7-3)(7-5)}(x-3)(x-5) + \dfrac{4}{(5-3)(5-7)}(x-3)(x-7)$
$\qquad + \dfrac{9}{(3-5)(3-7)}(x-5)(x-7)$

b. $f(x) = \dfrac{16}{(7-3)(7-5)}(x-3)(x-5) + \dfrac{-9}{(5-3)(5-7)}(x-3)(x-7)$
$\qquad + \dfrac{29}{(3-5)(3-7)}(x-5)(x-7)$

c. $f(x) = \dfrac{b_3}{(7-3)(7-5)}(x-3)(x-5) + \dfrac{b_2}{(5-3)(5-7)}(x-3)(x-7)$
$\qquad + \dfrac{b_1}{(3-5)(3-7)}(x-5)(x-7)$

d. Take It Further Suppose $f(x) = \dfrac{b_3}{(a_3-a_1)(a_3-a_2)}(x-a_1)(x-a_2)$

$\qquad + \dfrac{b_2}{(a_2-a_1)(a_2-a_3)}(x-a_1)(x-a_3)$

$\qquad + \dfrac{b_1}{(a_1-a_2)(a_1-a_3)}(x-a_2)(x-a_3)$. Find $f(a_1)$, $f(a_2)$, and $f(a_3)$.

Write f in normal form.

Agreeing to Disagree

More than one polynomial function can agree with the inputs and outputs in a table.

Minds in Action episode 6

Tony and Sasha are looking at Table A.

Table A

Input	Output
1	4
2	6
3	8
4	10

Tony Sure, $h(x) = 2x + 2$ is a polynomial function that works. But I think there are other functions that agree with the table. I couldn't write down a rule, but I can draw a graph. Look.

Tony draws on the board.

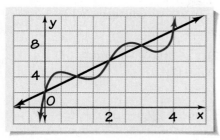

Sasha Well, that looks like the graph of a function, all right, but how do you know it's the graph of a *polynomial* function? Can you find a polynomial that's not linear and that goes through the points you get from the table?

Tony Hmm . . . sure! I just add another input to the table. Let's say 5. Then I make the output something other than $2 \cdot 5 + 2$. I'll make it 13.

Why might Sasha say this "looks like the graph of a function"?

Table A

Input	Output
1	4
2	6
3	8
4	10
5	13

Tony and Sasha . . . and then use Lagrange interpolation!

Sasha So, all those problems on the standardized tests that ask you to find the next term in a sequence are misleading—*any* number could be the next term in a sequence.

Tony The test writers must not know about Lagrange interpolation.

For You to Do

1. Find a polynomial function that agrees with Tony's extension of Table A.

A CAS might be helpful here.

Tony and Sasha are still thinking about the original Table A.

Sasha I think I have another way to trick the table, a way that might be easier than Lagrange interpolation. We know that $x \mapsto 2x + 2$ fits what we have. If I add to that another polynomial that outputs zero for the inputs 1, 2, 3, and 4, the result will still produce the outputs of Table A.

Tony How are you going to find a function like that?

Sasha I remember we did that a few days ago.

Sasha thumbs through her notebook.

Sasha Here it is: Exercise 11 from Lesson 2.07. This will do the trick.

$$x \mapsto (x - 1)(x - 2)(x - 3)(x - 4)$$

Tony So $r(x) = 2x + 2 + (x - 1)(x - 2)(x - 3)(x - 4)$ will agree with Table A. And it is not linear—it has degree 4.

Sasha So will $t(x) = 2x + 2 + 3(x - 1)(x - 2)(x - 3)(x - 4)$ and $q(x) = 2x + 2 + 275(x - 1)(x - 2)(x - 3)(x - 4)$.

For that matter,
$x \mapsto 2x + 2 + \text{(any polynomial)} \cdot (x - 1)(x - 2)(x - 3)(x - 4)$
will work.

Why does Tony's polynomial have degree 4?

Tony I think we're onto something. I wonder if every polynomial function that agrees with the table can be built by this method.

Sasha We need to think about that.

For Discussion

2. Can you write the polynomial Tony got using Lagrange interpolation in Sasha's form below? Explain.

$$x \mapsto 2x + 2 + \text{(any polynomial)} \cdot (x - 1)(x - 2)(x - 3)(x - 4)$$

Establish a process. You can use Tony and Sasha's new method to find a polynomial that agrees with a given function on any finite set of inputs but that takes on a different specific value at some other input. For example, suppose you want a function f that agrees with $x \mapsto 3x$ for x-values of 1, 3, and 4, but you want $f(2)$ to be 12. Start with the following equation.

$$f(x) = 3x + A(x - 1)(x - 3)(x - 4)$$

This function agrees with $x \mapsto 3x$ for x-values of 1, 3, and 4. Then you can figure out A from the equation below.

$$12 = f(2) = 3 \cdot 2 + A(2 - 1)(2 - 3)(2 - 5)$$

For You to Do

3. Find the value of A.

4. Find a function that agrees with $x \mapsto 3x$ at 1, 3, and 5 but that takes on the value 21 at $x = 2$.

Exercises *Practicing Habits of Mind*

Check Your Understanding

1. Graph the functions f and h with equations
$f(x) = 2x + 2 + 3(x - 1)(x - 2)(x - 3)$ and $h(x) = 2x + 2$. List the points where the graphs intersect.

2. Find and graph two different functions j and k that agree with $h(x) = 2x + 2$ for x-values of 1, 2, and 3. How can you produce more functions like these?

3. Consider the function with outputs 1, 3, and 5 for $x = 1, 2, 3$.

a. If someone asked you to come up with the next term, what would you say? What simple rule could define this function?

b. Give another possible next term and the rule that produces it.

c. Find a rule that gives 19 as the next term.

d. Find a rule that gives 1 as the next term.

4. Suppose you see the following problem on a multiple-choice test.

What is the next number in the sequence?

   2, 4, 6, . . .

A. 0   **B.** 8   **C.** 10   **D.** 80

Show that any of these answers could be correct. To do this, you may want to set up tables like the one at the right.

Input	Output
1	2
2	4
3	6
4	▪

5. Use the following rules to play the Polynomial Game. This game requires at least three players.

- Choose one player to be the Polynomial Keeper. The other players are the Finders.

- The Polynomial Keeper writes down a (secret) polynomial function and gives one input-output pair to the Finders.

- The Finders guess a polynomial function. If they are successful, the Keeper gets one point. If they are not successful, the Keeper gives them another input-output pair.

- The Keeper continues to give out pairs until the Finders figure out the polynomial. The Keeper scores one point for every pair the Finders need to figure out the polynomial. Then the Keeper becomes a Finder and a new Keeper is chosen.

- The player with the most points at the end of the game wins.

a. How many points is a Keeper likely to get for a quadratic function?

b. How many points is a Keeper likely to get for a quintic function? A quintic function is a polynomial of degree 5.

c. How many points is a Keeper likely to get for a polynomial of degree n?

On Your Own

For Exercises 6–9, find a function that agrees with the given function for the given inputs but is not equal to the given function. Graph your function and the given function on the same set of axes. Identify the points where the graphs intersect.

Go Online
Pearsonsuccessnet.com

6. $x \mapsto 3x - 1$; $x = 0, 1, 2, 3$ **7.** $x \mapsto 3x - 1$; $x = 0, 1, 2, 3, 4$

8. $x \mapsto 4 - x^2$; $x = 0, 1, 2, 3$ **9.** $x \mapsto 4 - x^2$; $x = 0, 1, 2, 3, 4$

10. Is there another linear function that agrees with $x \mapsto 3x - 1$ at the inputs 1 and 2? Explain.

11. **a.** Is there another quadratic function that agrees with $x \mapsto 4 - x^2$ at the inputs 1 and 2? Explain.

    b. Is there another quadratic function that agrees with $x \mapsto 4 - x^2$ at the inputs 1, 2, and 3? Explain.

12. **Write About It** Describe two methods for finding a function that agrees with $x \mapsto x^2$ at $x = 1, 2,$ and 3 and that takes on the value 7 at $x = 4$.

13. **Standardized Test Prep** You are given three points on a line. You wish to find a function that has the same values as the linear function at those three points but is different everywhere else. What is the least possible degree of a polynomial function through those points?

    A. 2   **B.** 3

    C. 4   **D.** 5

14. **Write About It** Is there a nonconstant polynomial that takes on the value 0 at every integer? Explain.

Maintain Your Skills

15. Expand each product. Describe and explain at least two patterns among the coefficients in the collection of answers.

    a. $(x - 1)(x - 2)$

    b. $(x - 1)(x - 2)(x - 3)$

    c. $(x - 1)(x - 2)(x - 3)(x - 4)$

    d. $(x - 1)(x - 2)(x - 3)(x - 4)(x - 5)$

    e. $(x - 1)(x - 2)(x - 3)(x - 4)(x - 5)(x - 6)$

    f. $(x - 1)(x - 2)(x - 3)(x - 4)(x - 5)(x - 6)(x - 7)$

    g. $(x - 1)(x - 2)(x - 3)(x - 4)(x - 5)(x - 6)(x - 7)(x - 8)$

Use each answer to help you get the next one.

Go Online
Video Tutor
Pearsonsuccessnet.com

In this investigation, you learned how to use linear combinations of polynomials to determine new polynomials and find polynomials that agree with a given table. These exercises will help you summarize what you have learned.

In Exercises 1 and 2, find a polynomial function that agrees with each table.

1.

Input	Output
1	3
2	7
4	21

2.

Input	Output
1	4
3	40
5	156

3. Find a nonconstant polynomial h such that $h(1) = h(2) = h(4) = 7$.

4. Find a polynomial function that agrees with $x \rightarrow x^3 - x$ at $x = 1, 2$, and 3 but has the value 0 at $x = 4$.

5. **Take It Further** Suppose you define the function q for nonnegative integers using the following rule.

$$q(x) = \begin{cases} 1 & \text{if } x = 0 \\ q(x-1) + 3x^2 - x + 1 & \text{if } x > 0 \end{cases}$$

Find a polynomial function that agrees with q on its domain.

6. How can you find a polynomial that agrees with a table?

7. How can you find two different functions that agree with the same table?

8. What number comes next in the sequence $1, 4, 9, \ldots$?

Vocabulary

In this investigation, you learned this term. Make sure you understand what it means and how to use it.

• **Lagrange interpolation**

Multiple Choice

1. Suppose f and g are functions with $f(x) = 3x$ and $g(x) = f(x + 1) - f(x)$. Which expression is equal to $g(x)$?

   A. 1

   B. 3

   C. x

   D. $2x + 1$

2. Suppose $N : \mathbb{R}^2 \to \mathbb{R}$ and $N(a, b) = a^2 + b^2$. Which of the following ordered pairs does NOT give an output of 169?

   A. $(-5, 12)$

   B. $(12, 5)$

   C. $(1, 12)$

   D. $(-5, -12)$

3. Let $f(x) = 3x - 4$ and $g(x) = 2x + 5$. Which value is equal to $f \circ g(2)$?

   A. 9

   B. 11

   C. 18

   D. 23

4. Let $m(x) = 2x - 7$. Which expression is equal to $m^{-1}(x)$?

   A. $2x + 7$

   B. $-2x + 7$

   C. $\frac{x + 7}{2}$

   D. $\frac{1}{2}x + 7$

5. Let $f(x) = 3x - 5 + 4(x - 1)(x - 6)$ and $g(x) = 3x - 5$. Find the x-coordinates of the points at which the graphs of f and g intersect.

   A. 1, 4, or 6

   B. $\frac{5}{3}$

   C. 0, 1, or 6

   D. 1 or 6

Open Response

6. Suppose $f : \mathbb{R} \to \mathbb{R}$ and $f(x) = 3x^2 + 1$.

   a. Calculate $f(2)$ and $f(-2)$.

   b. Find all values of x that make $f(x) = 49$.

   c. Calculate $f(5) - f(4)$.

   d. Show that you can write $f(x + 1)$ as $f(x + 1) = 3x^2 + 6x + 4$.

   e. Write a simplified expression for $f(x + 1) - f(x)$.

   f. If $g(x) = f(x + 1) - f(x)$, what is $g(4)$?

7. Suppose $f(x) = 3x + 4$. If possible, find a function g such that $g \circ f(x) = x$.

8. Use the definition of function f below.
   $$f(x) = \begin{cases} 2x & \text{if } x < 0 \\ x^2 & \text{if } 0 \le x \le 2 \end{cases}$$

   a. What is the natural domain of f?

   b. Sketch a graph of f.

   c. Extend the definition of f so that its domain is all of $\mathbb{R}$ and f is one-to-one.

   d. Extend the definition of f so that its domain is all of $\mathbb{R}$ and f is not one-to-one.

9. Suppose $f(x) = \frac{1}{x + 2}$, where $x \ne -2$. Find the inverse of f.

10. Find a polynomial function f that agrees with this table.

Input	Output
1	6
2	15
3	36

11. What is a function?

Factors, Roots, and Zeros

In *Factors, Roots, and Zeros*, you will discover some important facts about polynomials and polynomial functions. You will study the connection between the zeros of a polynomial function and the factors of the polynomial. In your first-year algebra course, you may have learned the "form-implies-function" principle:

> If you can transform one polynomial into another with the basic rules of algebra, the polynomials define the same function.

In this investigation, you will see a partial converse:

> If two polynomial functions agree for enough inputs (depending on their degree), then they are equivalent under the basic rules of algebra.

By the end of this investigation, you will be able to answer questions like these.

1. How are the zeros of a polynomial related to its factors?

2. How can you tell if two polynomials are equivalent without using the form-implies-function principle?

3. What is the greatest-degree polynomial you need to fit a table with four inputs?

You will learn how to

- understand the relationship between roots and factors of a polynomial
- divide polynomials by monic linear polynomials
- state and use the Remainder Theorem and the Factor Theorem
- check that two polynomials of degree n are equivalent by checking $n + 1$ function values
- write the general form of a function that fits a table

You will develop these habits and skills:

- Make conjectures and create proofs.
- Formalize previous experiences.
- Connect the algebra in this investigation to Lagrange interpolation.

Activating Prior Knowledge
Exploring New Ideas

These exercises look like ordinary calculations, but they give a preview of some important themes in this investigation.

For You to Explore

1. Suppose $f(x) = (x - 5)(x - 3)(x^2 - 1) + 219$.

   a. Find $f(5)$.

   b. List four values of x for which $f(x) = 219$.

2. **a.** Find a nonconstant polynomial that agrees with the table at the right. You do not need to find the normal form.

   b. What is the degree of the polynomial you found in part (a)?

   c. Find a nonconstant polynomial that agrees with the table at the right. You do not need to find the normal form.

   d. What is the degree of the polynomial you found in part (c)?

x	q(x)
1	0
3	0

x	r(x)
1	0
3	0
5	0
7	0
9	0

3. **a.** Find two different polynomials $j(x)$ and $g(x)$ such that the degree of each polynomial is greater than 1 and $j(5) = g(5) = 0$.

   b. Suppose $h(x) = j(x) - g(x)$. What is $h(5)$?

4. Use the three functions below. Find the degree of each polynomial.

   $$t(x) = x^5 - 1 \qquad u(x) = x^5 + x^2 + 3 \qquad v(x) = x^4 + 7$$

   a. $t(x) + u(x)$

   b. $t(x) - u(x)$

   c. $t(x) + v(x)$

   d. $t(x) - v(x)$

   e. $t(x) \cdot u(x)$

5. Find k if $m(x) = (x - 8)\left(7x^3 + 12x^2 - 13x + \frac{22}{5}\right) + 7(k + 1)$ and $m(8) = 21$.

6. Find a polynomial $g(x)$ such that $x^3 - 1 = (x - 1)g(x)$.

7. Show that if n is a positive integer,
   $$x^n - 1 = (x - 1)(x^{n-1} + x^{n-2} + \cdots + x^2 + x + 1).$$

This is an important identity that you will use throughout this course.

Exercises *Practicing Habits of Mind*

On Your Own

8. Suppose $h(x) = (x - 1)(x + 3)(x^5 + x^4 + x^3 + x^2 + x + 1) + 5x - 2$.

   a. For what inputs a can you easily find $h(a)$ without using a calculator?

   b. Find the output of h for each of your answers to part (a).

9. If a is some fixed number, find the normal form of $(x - a)(x^2 + ax + a^2)$.

10. If a is some fixed number, find the normal form of
    $(x - a)(x^3 + ax^2 + a^2x + a^3)$.

11. Find a polynomial $g(x)$ such that $\frac{x^5 - 1}{x - 1} = g(x)$.

> **Habits of Mind**
>
> **Look for patterns.**
> What is a general result suggested by Exercises 9 and 10?

Maintain Your Skills

In Exercises 12–14, expand each expression and write the result in normal form.

12. $(x^2 - 1)(x^4 + x^2 + 1)$

13. $(x^3 - 1)(x^6 + x^3 + 1)$

14. $(x^4 - 1)(x^8 + x^4 + 1)$

> **Go Online**
> **Video Tutor**
> Pearsonsuccessnet.com

2.10 Polynomial Division

After you learned to multiply numbers, you learned to "undo" multiplication with division. The same thing can be done with polynomials. If you know that $x^3 + 10x^2 + 18x - 35 = (x + 5)(x^2 + 5x + 7)$, then you also know that $\dfrac{x^3 + 10x^2 + 18x - 35}{x + 5} = x^2 + 5x - 7$.

When you divide one polynomial by another, you get a quotient and a remainder. In the example above, the quotient is $x^2 + 5x - 7$ and the remainder is 0.

Example

Problem Find the quotient and the remainder when you divide $x^3 + 2x^2 + 4x + 6$ by $x - 2$.

Solution You can do a calculation that looks just like long division.

$$
\begin{array}{r}
x^2 + 4x + 12 \\
x - 2 \overline{) \ x^3 + 2x^2 + 4x + \ 6} \\
\underline{x^3 - 2x^2 } \\
4x^2 + 4x + \ 6 \\
\underline{4x^2 - 8x } \\
12x + \ 6 \\
\underline{12x - 24} \\
30
\end{array}
$$

So, the quotient is $x^2 + 4x + 12$ and the remainder is 30.

For information on dividing polynomials, see the TI-Nspire Handbook, p. 804.

Habits of Mind

Establish a process. In the long division process, how do you know when to stop?

For You to Do

1. Find the quotient and the remainder when you divide $x^3 + 2x^2 + 4x + 10$ by $x - 2$.

2. If $g(x) = x^3 + 2x^2 + 4x + 10$, what is $g(2)$?

3. Find a polynomial $q(x)$ and a number r such that $x^3 + 2x^2 + 4x + 10 = (x - 2)q(x) + r$.

When you divide 37 by 7, the quotient is 5 and the remainder is 2.

You can summarize the division by writing $37 = 7 \cdot 5 + 2$.

$$
\begin{array}{r}
5 \\
7 \overline{) \ 37} \\
\underline{35} \\
2
\end{array}
$$

You could also say $37 = 7 \cdot 4 + 9$.

$$
\begin{array}{r}
4 \\
7 \overline{) \ 37} \\
\underline{28} \\
9
\end{array}
$$

While $37 = 7 \cdot 4 + 9$ is correct, this is not standard division. When you divide, the remainder must be less than the divisor (less than 7, in this example). In general, an important property of integers is the Euclidean Property.

Property *Euclidean Property*

Given positive integers a and b, there are unique nonnegative integers q (the **quotient**) and r (the **remainder**) such that

- $b = a \cdot q + r$
- $0 \le r < a$

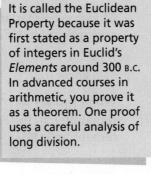

It is called the Euclidean Property because it was first stated as a property of integers in Euclid's *Elements* around 300 B.C. In advanced courses in arithmetic, you prove it as a theorem. One proof uses a careful analysis of long division.

In the example above, $b = 37$, $a = 7$, $q = 5$, and $r = 2$.

There is a Euclidean Property for polynomials, too. It comes from the fact that you can divide and get a remainder with degree less than the degree of the divisor. In the example, the result is an identity.

$$x^3 + 2x^2 + 4x + 6 = (x - 2)(x^2 + 4x + 12) + 30$$

For You to Do

4. Use the basic rules of algebra to show that $(x - 2)(x^2 + 4x + 12) + 30$ is, in fact, equal to $x^3 + 2x^2 + 4x + 6$.

5. If $h(x) = x^3 + 2x^2 + 4x + 6$, find $h(2)$.

Property *Euclidean Property for Polynomials*

Given polynomials $f(x)$ and $g(x)$, there are unique polynomials $q(x)$ (the quotient) and $r(x)$ (the remainder) such that

- $f(x) = g(x) \cdot q(x) + r(x)$
- deg $(r(x))$ < deg $(g(x))$

Developing Habits of Mind

Use an equation to represent a process. The identity $f(x) = g(x) \cdot q(x) + r(x)$ is just another way to state the division.

$$g(x) \overline{)\begin{array}{l} q(x) \\ f(x) \\ \underline{g(x) \cdot q(x)} \\ r(x) \end{array}}$$

The polynomial $g(x)$ is the divisor. It is what gets divided into $f(x)$. The condition deg $(r(x))$ < deg $(g(x))$ guarantees that the degree of the remainder is less than the degree of the divisor.

For You to Do

6. Using the above notation, find $q(x)$ and $r(x)$ if $f(x) = 2x^3 - 7x^2 - 8x - 34$ and $g(x) = x - 5$.

The most important case for this investigation is when the divisor is of the form $x - a$ for some number a. Suppose $f(x)$ is a polynomial and you divide it by $x - a$. Then the remainder has degree less than 1, so it must be a constant. The constant turns out to be very useful. It is equal to $f(a)$. Here are the details.

Working with greater-degree divisors is important, especially in calculus. In general, though, it is more important to be able to reason about the division process than to be skilled at carrying it out.

Theorem 2.2 The Remainder Theorem

If you divide a polynomial $f(x)$ by $x - a$, where a is a number, the remainder is the number $f(a)$.

Proof First look at a concrete example. Use the polynomial from the example at the beginning of the lesson. Suppose $f(x) = x^3 + 2x^2 + 4x + 6$ and you divide it by $x - 2$.

$$
\begin{array}{r}
x^2 + 4x + 12 \\
x - 2 \overline{)\, x^3 + 2x^2 + 4x + 6} \\
\underline{x^3 - 2x^2} \\
4x^2 + 4x + 6 \\
\underline{4x^2 - 8x} \\
12x + 6 \\
\underline{12x - 24} \\
30
\end{array}
$$

So you can summarize the division by writing

$$f(x) = x^3 + 2x^2 + 4x + 6 = (x - 2)(x^2 + 4x + 12) + 30$$

Use the far right side as the form that defines f.

$$f(2) = (2 - 2)(2^2 + 2x + 12) + 30$$

$$= 0 \cdot \text{(some number)} + 30$$

$$= 30$$

The proof amounts to carrying out this argument generally, without using specific polynomials. It goes this way.

Suppose you divide $f(x)$ by $x - a$. The remainder is a number, because you are dividing by $x - a$. You cannot stop until you get a polynomial of degree less than 1 (that is, a constant). Call the remainder r. The main point of the theorem is that the remainder r is the same as $f(a)$. So the division looks like this.

$$
\begin{array}{r}
q(x) \\
x - a \overline{)\, f(x)} \\
\underline{(x - a)q(x)} \\
r
\end{array}
$$

You can summarize the division by writing $f(x) = (x - a)q(x) + r$.

Now replace x with a.

$$f(a) = (a - a) \cdot q(a) + r$$
$$= 0 \cdot (\text{some number}) + r$$
$$= r$$

So, $f(a) = r$.

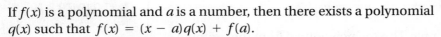 The remainder r is a number, so it does not change when you replace x with a.

Developing Habits of Mind

Think about it another way. You can restate the Remainder Theorem this way.

If $f(x)$ is a polynomial and a is a number, then there exists a polynomial $q(x)$ such that $f(x) = (x - a)q(x) + f(a)$.

For You to Do

7. Find the quotient and the remainder when you divide
   $f(x) = x^3 + x^2 + x$ by $x - 2$.

8. Find $f(2)$.

9. What are the zeros of f?

Remember...

The zeros of f are the numbers a that make $f(a) = 0$.

 **Exercises** *Practicing Habits of Mind*

Check Your Understanding

1. **a.** Find the quotient and the remainder when you divide
   $h(x) = x^3 + 2x^2 - 3x - 6$ by $x + 2$.

   b. Use your result to find $h(-2)$.

2. Find the remainder of $x^{105} + x + 1$ divided by $x - 1$.

3. Find the remainder of $x^{105} + x + 1$ divided by $x + 1$.

Long division takes too long in these cases. Some CAS systems will have trouble, too.

4. Suppose $(x - 10)$ divides evenly into some polynomial $P(x)$. What is $P(10)$?

5. At Sasha's party, Tony presents the following puzzle: "I'm thinking of a number. If I divide it by 3, the remainder is 2. If I divide it by 5, the remainder is 3. If I divide it by 7, the remainder is 1. What's my number?"

   a. What number might Tony be thinking of?

   b. Is there more than one integer that fits Tony's puzzle? If so, name two of them. If not, explain why.

6. Later that night, Derman takes the floor and presents the following puzzle: "I'm thinking of a polynomial. If I divide it by $x - 3$, the remainder is 16. If I divide it by $x - 5$, the remainder is 42. If I divide it by $x - 7$, the remainder is 84. What's my polynomial?"

   a. What polynomial might Derman be thinking of?

   b. Is there more than one polynomial that fits Derman's puzzle? If so, name two of them. If not, explain why.

On Your Own

7. a. Find the quotient and the remainder when you divide
   $f(x) = x^3 + x^2 + x$ by $x + 2$.

   b. Find $f(-2)$.

8. Find the remainders when you divide each polynomial by $x - 3$.

   a. $x^3 - 1$ **b.** $x - 1$ **c.** $x^2 + x + 1$

   d. $x^4 + x^2 + 1$ **e.** $(x^4 + x^2 + 1)(x - 1)$ **f.** $x^4 + x^3 + x^2$

Habits of Mind

Consider more than one strategy. Is long division really necessary?

9. Suppose that f and g are polynomials and that $f(2) = 5$ and $g(2) = -4$. Find the remainder when you divide each polynomial by $x - 2$.

   a. $3f + g$

   b. fg^2

   c. $(x^2 + x + 1)f(x) + g(x)$

10. Suppose $f(x) = 5(x - 2)^3 + 3(x - 2)^2 - 6(x - 2) + 8$.

   a. What is $f(2)$?

   b. What is the remainder when you divide $f(x)$ by $x - 2$?

   c. Suppose $g(x)$ is the quotient when you divide $f(x)$ by $x - 2$. What is $g(2)$?

   d. What is the remainder when you divide $g(x)$ by $x - 2$?

   e. Suppose $h(x)$ is the quotient when you divide $g(x)$ by $x - 2$. What is $h(2)$?

   f. What is the remainder when you divide $h(x)$ by $x - 2$?

   g. Suppose $m(x)$ is the quotient when you divide $h(x)$ by $x - 2$. What is $m(2)$?

   h. What is the remainder when you divide $m(x)$ by $x - 2$?

11. Standardized Test Prep Let $g(x) = x^3 - 12x^2 + 21x + 98$ and $g(-2) = 0$. Find the zeros of $g(x)$.

   A. -2 and -7

   B. -2 and 7

   C. 2 and -7

   D. 2 and 7

12. Take It Further Suppose $f(x)$ is a polynomial such that $f(2) = 5$ and $f(3) = 7$. What is the remainder when you divide $f(x)$ by $(x - 2)(x - 3)$?

13. Find numbers B, C, and D such that
$x^3 + x^2 - 8x + 13 = (x - 1)^3 + B(x - 1)^2 + C(x - 1) + D$.

14. Suppose $P(x) = x^3 - 3x^2 + 2x + 5$. Use the Remainder Theorem to show that $P(x) - P(7)$ is divisible by $x - 7$.

15. Take It Further Suppose $P(x)$ is any polynomial and a is a number. Use the Remainder Theorem to show that $P(x) - P(a)$ is divisible by $x - a$.

Maintain Your Skills

16. Find each quotient.

   a. $\dfrac{x^2 - 1}{x - 1}$ **b.** $\dfrac{x^3 - 1}{x - 1}$ **c.** $\dfrac{x^4 - 1}{x - 1}$ **d.** $\dfrac{x^5 - 1}{x - 1}$ **e.** $\dfrac{x^{12} - 1}{x - 1}$

17. Suppose $f(x) = 2x^2 + 5x - 1$. Simplify each expression.

   a. $\dfrac{f(x) - f(1)}{x - 1}$ **b.** $\dfrac{f(x) - f(2)}{x - 2}$ **c.** $\dfrac{f(x) - f(3)}{x - 3}$

   d. $\dfrac{f(x) - f(4)}{x - 4}$ **e.** $\dfrac{f(x) - f(5)}{x - 5}$ **f.** $\dfrac{f(x) - f(6)}{x - 6}$

What is the pattern?

Suppose you want to find all roots of the equation below.

$$x^3 + 4x^2 - 9x - 36 = 0$$

You can start by factoring the left side of the equation.

$$x^3 + 4x^2 - 9x - 36 = (x^2 - 9)(x + 4) = (x - 3)(x + 3)(x + 4)$$

Suppose a is a root of the equation. Then $a^3 + 4a^2 - 9a - 36 = 0$.

By the form-implies-function principle, $(a - 3)(a + 3)(a + 4) = 0$.

By the Zero Product Property, one of the factors must be 0.

$$a - 3 = 0 \text{ or } a + 3 = 0 \text{ or } a + 4 = 0$$

If $a - 3 = 0$, then $a = 3$. If $a + 3 = 0$, then $a = -3$. If $a + 4 = 0$, then $a = -4$. So, the roots of the equation are 3, -3, and -4. Notice that each root a of the equation corresponds to a factor $(x - a)$ of the polynomial on the left side. This happens for any root.

Theorem 2.3 The Factor Theorem

Suppose $f(x)$ is a polynomial. Then the number a is a root of the equation $f(x) = 0$ if and only if $x - a$ is a factor of $f(x)$.

Remember...

The form-implies-function principle says that if two expressions are the same under the basic rules of algebra, then they define functions that produce the same output for the same input.

The Zero Product Property states that if $ab = 0$, then at least one of the numbers a and b has to be zero.

For Discussion

1. Use the Remainder Theorem to prove the Factor Theorem.

For You to Do

2. Suppose $p(x)$ is a polynomial of degree 3 with three zeros at $x = 1, 2,$ and 3. Find $p(x)$ if $p(5) = 48$.

There are many corollaries to the Factor Theorem that have a wide range of applications in algebra. Here are a few.

Corollary 2.3.1

A polynomial of degree n can have at most n distinct real-number zeros.

Proof Suppose $f(x)$ is a polynomial of degree n and a is a zero. Then, by the Factor Theorem, there is a polynomial $q(x)$ such that

$$f(x) = (x - a)q(x)$$

Because the degree of a product is the sum of the degrees (see Problem 4 from Lesson 2.09), the degree of $q(x)$ has to be $n - 1$.

Suppose b is another zero of $f(x)$, different from a. Then, using the above equation,

$$0 = f(b) = (b - a)q(b)$$

Since $b - a \neq 0$, $q(b) = 0$ by the Zero Product Property. Apply the Factor Theorem and the result of Problem 4 from Lesson 2.09. There is a polynomial $p(x)$ of degree $n - 2$ such that

$$q(x) = (x - b)p(x)$$

Substituting $f(x) = (x - a)q(x)$, you have

$$f(x) = (x - a)(x - b)p(x)$$

Keep doing this until you run out of real zeros.

$$f(x) = (x - a)(x - b)(x - c)\ldots \ell(x)$$

The polynomial $\ell(x)$ has no real zeros. Since the degree of $f(x)$ is n, the sum of the degrees on the right side must be n. Since each zero of $f(x)$ contributes 1 to this sum, there can be at most n of them.

For You to Do

3. Carefully write out the steps for applying this proof to
$f(x) = x^3 - 2x^2 - x + 2$.

Corollary 2.3.2

If two polynomials of degree n agree at $n + 1$ inputs, they are identical.

For Discussion

4. Prove Corollary 2.3.2. Why might you call Corollary 2.3.2 the "function-implies-form" principle?

Developing Habits of Mind

Use a different process to get the same answer. Corollary 2.3.2 will save you time and effort. It provides an alternative to the form-implies-function principle.

For example, suppose you have two polynomials of degree 5. You want to show that they will always give the same output for a given input. One way to do that is to show that they are equivalent under the basic rules of algebra. Another way is to show that they agree at six inputs. Corollary 2.3.2 says that, if two fifth-degree polynomials agree for six inputs, they are automatically identical. That is, they are equivalent under the basic rules.

So, to check that two polynomial functions are equal for all real inputs, all you have to do is to show that they agree on enough inputs. *Enough* means 1 more than their degree. This is quite a remarkable fact. It is not often that only a few checks of a result guarantee the result for infinitely many other cases.

Corollary 2.3.3

A polynomial of degree *n* is completely determined by its output values for *n* + 1 inputs.

Minds in Action   episode 7

Tony and Sasha are picking up where they left off in Lesson 2.08.

Tony   So, we have a way to build as many polynomials as we want that agree with this table for $f(x) = 2x + 2$.

x	f(x)
1	4
2	6
3	8
4	10

Sasha   Right. We just take another function of the form

$$r(x) = 2x + 2 + (\text{something}) \cdot (x - 1)(x - 2)(x - 3)(x - 4).$$

And I think this is the only way to get such a function.

Tony   Me too, but I don't see why.

Sasha Suppose we have a function $g(x)$ that agrees with f on the table. Then if I subtract $g(x)$ from $f(x)$, I get a polynomial that outputs zero for all the input values in the table.

x	f(x)	g(x)	f(x) − g(x)
1	4	4	0
2	6	6	0
3	8	8	0
4	10	10	0

What do we know about a polynomial that has 1, 2, 3, and 4 as zeros?

Tony We know it looks like

$$(\text{something}) \cdot (x - 1)(x - 2)(x - 3)(x - 4)$$

Why do they know this?

Sasha Right. So,

$$f(x) - g(x) = (\text{something}) \cdot (x - 1)(x - 2)(x - 3)(x - 4)$$

So . . .

Tony Oh.

$$f(x) = g(x) + (\text{something}) \cdot (x - 1)(x - 2)(x - 3)(x - 4)$$

and $g(x)$ comes from our method. Very smooth.

Derman enters the discussion.

Derman But I have another function that agrees with f at 1, 2, 3, and 4. Look.

$$d(x) = 338 - 698x + 490x^2 - 140x^3 + 14x^4$$

For You to Do

5. Write Derman's function in a way that shows how it comes from Tony and Sasha's method.

Exercises *Practicing Habits of Mind*

Check Your Understanding

1. What is the greatest number of real roots a polynomial of degree 2 can have? Explain.

2. If two linear polynomials agree at two points, then Corollary 2.3.2 says that they must be identical. If two quadratic polynomials agree at three points, then they must be identical, and so on. For each pair of polynomials, decide if the polynomials are identical using this idea of checking $n + 1$ points.

   a. $P(x) = x^4 - x^2 - 2$ and $R(x) = (x^2 + 1)(x^2 - 2)$

   b. $P(x) = x(x + 1)(x - 1)$ and $R(x) = x - x^3$

   c. $P(x) = (x + 3)^2 - 7$ and $R(x) = x^2 + 6x + 2$

3. Find the value of a such that $x - 1$ is a factor of $x^3 + ax^2 - x + 5$.

4. Find numbers a and b such that $x^2 + x - 6$ is a factor of $x^4 + x^3 - ax^2 - bx + a - b$.

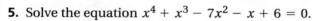

$x^2 + x - 6 =$
$(x - 2)(x + 3)$

5. Solve the equation $x^4 + x^3 - 7x^2 - x + 6 = 0$.

6. Establish the following identity.

$$(x - 1)(x - 3) + (x - 2)(x - 3) + (x - 1)(x - 2) = 3x^2 - 12x + 11$$

7. Establish the following identity.

$$\frac{20}{(1 - 3)(1 - 6)} (x - 3)(x - 6) + \frac{12}{(3 - 1)(3 - 6)} (x - 1)(x - 6)$$
$$+ \frac{60}{(6 - 1)(6 - 3)} (x - 1)(x - 3) = 4x^2 - 20x + 36$$

Can you do Exercises 6 and 7 without expanding the left sides?

8. Find the normal form of $P(x)$.

$$P(x) = \frac{(x - 1)(x - 2)}{(3 - 1)(3 - 2)} + \frac{(x - 1)(x - 3)}{(2 - 1)(2 - 3)} + \frac{(x - 2)(x - 3)}{(1 - 2)(1 - 3)}$$

On Your Own

9. Find the number a such that $x - 1$ is a factor of $x^3 + ax^2 - x + 8$.

10. Find numbers a and b such that $x^2 + x - 6$ is a factor of $x^4 + x^3 - ax^2 - bx + 2a + b$.

11. Solve the equation $x^4 + x^3 - 10x^2 - 4x + 24 = 0$.

12. Suppose $f(x) = 4 - 4x + 13x^2 - 12x^3 + 3x^4$. Show that each statement is true.

    a. $x - 2$ is a factor of $f(x)$.   **b.** $(x - 2)^2$ is a factor of $f(x)$.

    c. If $f(x) = (x - 2)q(x)$, then $x - 2$ is a factor of $q(x)$.

Go Online
Pearsonsuccessnet.com

13. Establish the following identity.

$$x^n - a^n = (x - a)(x^{n-1} + ax^{n-2} + a^2x^{n-3} + a^3x^{n-4} + \cdots$$
$$+ a^{n-2}x + a^{n-1})$$

Habits of Mind

Look for relationships.
How is Exercise 13
a generalization
of Exercise 7 from
Lesson 2.09?

14. Suppose that r is a number and
$$f(x) = a_nx^n + a_{n-1}x^{n-1} + \cdots + a_1x + a_0.$$

a. Show that $f(x) - f(r) = (x - r)g(x)$ for some polynomial g.

b. Take It Further Write an expression for g.

15. Use Exercise 14 to prove the Remainder Theorem.

16. Here is a table for the sum of the first n squares.

A cubic polynomial function gives the sum of the first n squares. Find a cubic that agrees with this table.

n	$1^2 + 2^2 + \cdots + n^2$
1	1
2	5
3	14
4	30
5	55
6	91

17. Standardized Test Prep The function $f(x)$ is a polynomial of degree 4. The function $p(x) = (x + a)^2$ is a factor of $f(x)$. Which of the following is NOT always true?

A. $f(x) = (x + a) \cdot$ (something else) $+ r(x)$, where $r(x) = 0$

B. $f(a) = 0$

C. The trinomial $x^2 + 2ax + a^2$ is a factor of $f(x)$.

D. The degree of the function $h(x)$ defined by the equation $f(x) = p(x) \cdot h(x)$ is 2.

Maintain Your Skills

18. Suppose $f(x) = (x^2 + 1)(x - 1)(x - 2)(x - 3)(x - 4)$. Find the factored form of each expression.

a. $\dfrac{f(x)}{x - 1}$

b. $\dfrac{f(x)}{(x - 1)(x - 2)}$

c. $\dfrac{f(x)}{x - 3}$

d. $\dfrac{f(x)}{x - 4}$

e. $\dfrac{f(x)}{(x - 1)(x - 2)(x - 3)}$

f. $\dfrac{f(x)}{(x - 1)(x - 2)(x - 3)(x - 4)}$

19. Graph each function.

a. $f(x) = (x - 1)(x - 3)$

b. $g(x) = (x - 1.5)(x - 2.5)$

c. $h(x) = (x - 1.8)(x - 2.2)$

d. $k(x) = (x - 1.9)(x - 2.1)$

e. $\ell(x) = (x - 2)^2$

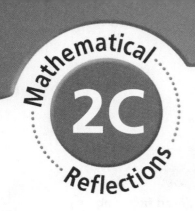

In this investigation, you learned how to divide polynomials by linear polynomials and how to use the Remainder Theorem and the Factor Theorem. You also learned about the relationship between roots and factors of polynomials. These exercises will help you summarize what you have learned.

1. Find the polynomial $g(x)$ such that $x^8 - 1 = (x - 1)g(x)$.

2. Find the polynomial $g(x)$ such that $x^8 - 1 = (x - 1)(x + 1)g(x)$.

3. Find the remainder of $x^{105} - 3x + 1$ divided by $x + 1$.

4. Find numbers B and C such that $x^2 + 2x = (x - 1)^2 + B(x - 1) + C$.

5. **Take It Further** Find numbers r and s if $(x - 2)^2$ is a factor of $2x^3 + rx^2 + sx + 4$.

6. How are the zeros of a polynomial related to its factors?

7. How can you tell if two polynomials are equal without using the form-implies-function principle?

8. What is the greatest-degree polynomial you need to fit a table with four inputs?

Vocabulary

In this investigation, you learned these terms. Make sure you understand what each one means and how to use it.

- **quotient**
- **remainder**

The posts determine a unique fence line. A set of points can determine a unique function.

Investigation 2D

Advanced Factoring

In *Advanced Factoring*, you will develop some advanced factoring methods. Many of them depend on the connection between roots and factors. Factoring a polynomial is important because it simplifies the problem of finding the zeros of the polynomial.

By the end of this investigation, you will be able to answer questions like these.

1. How do you factor nonmonic quadratics?

2. How do you factor differences and sums of cubes?

3. Does $x^4 + 4$ factor over $\mathbb{Z}$?

You will learn how to

- factor polynomials by scaling

- factor polynomials using the differences and sums of squares

- factor polynomials using the differences and sums of cubes

- factor polynomials using grouping

- factor polynomials by identifying quadratic-like or cubic-like polynomials

- factor polynomials by finding roots

You will develop these habits and skills:

- Rearrange polynomials into more useful forms. Sometimes a factored form of a polynomial is more useful than an expanded form.

- Use several techniques for factoring polynomials.

Breaking a house into parts makes it easier to move. Breaking a polynomial into factors makes it easier to identify roots.

The following problems and exercises ask you to review some ideas from your first-year algebra course and to preview some ideas from this investigation.

You can decide if a problem or exercise is a review, a preview, or both.

For You to Explore

1. Factor each quadratic polynomial over $\mathbb{Z}$. If a polynomial does not factor, explain why not.

   The symbol $\mathbb{Z}$ means the integers.

   a. $x^2 + 10x + 25$

   b. $x^2 + 10x + 24$

   c. $z^2 + 10z + 23$

   d. $u^2 + 10u + 21$

   e. $y^2 + 10y + 26$

2. Factor each polynomial over $\mathbb{Z}$. If a polynomial does not factor, explain why not.

   a. $x^2 + 18x + 45$

   b. $4x^2 + 36x + 45$

   c. $(x - 3)^2 + 18(x - 3) + 45$

   d. $z^2 - 121$

   e. $9u^2 - 121$

   f. $(y + 5)^2 - 121$

   g. $y^2(y + 5) - 4(y + 5)$

   h. $y^2(y + 5) - 3(y + 5)$

3. Suppose α and β are roots of this equation.

   $$x^2 - 6x + 5 = 0$$

   Find each value.

   a. $\alpha + \beta$

   b. $\alpha\beta$

4. Suppose α and β are two numbers with a sum of 6 and a product of -3. Show that α and β are roots of the equation $x^2 - 6x - 3 = 0$.

Exercises *Practicing Habits of Mind*

On Your Own

Habits of Mind

Look for patterns.
Generalize the identities you find.

5. Factor these quadratic polynomials over $\mathbb{Z}$. If a polynomial does not factor, explain why not.

a. $x^2 + 6x + 5$ **b.** $x^2 - 6x + 9$ **c.** $x^2 + 12x + 20$

d. $x^2 + 10x - 20$ **e.** $x^2 - 5x - 24$ **f.** $x^2 + 10x + 30$

6. Find the normal form for each polynomial.

a. $(x - 1)(x^2 + x + 1)$ **b.** $(x + 1)(x^2 - x + 1)$

7. Factor each polynomial over $\mathbb{Z}$.

a. $x^3 - 1$ **b.** $x^3 + 1$ **c.** $x^3 - 8$

d. $x^3 + 8$ **e.** $8x^3 - 1$ **f.** $8x^3 + 1$

g. $x^3 - a^3$ **h.** $x^3 + a^3$ **i.** $(x + 1)^3 - 1$

j. $(x - 1)^3 + 1$

In parts (g) and (h), *a* stands for an integer.

8. Show that if the equation $x^2 - 10x + 7 = 0$ has roots p and q, then the following statement must be true.

$$p + q = 10 \quad \text{and} \quad pq = 7$$

Is the converse true?

9. Find a quadratic equation with solutions $3 + \sqrt{7}$ and $3 - \sqrt{7}$.

10. Find A, B, C, and D such that

$$-37 + 40x - 18x^2 + 3x^3 = A(x - 2)^3 + B(x - 2)^2 + C(x - 2) + D$$

Maintain Your Skills

11. Find the normal form for each polynomial.

a. $x^2 - 9$ **b.** $(2x)^2 - 9$

c. $9 - x^2$ **d.** $(x + 1)^2 - 9$

e. $(x + 1)^2 - x^2$ **f.** $(x^2 + 1)^2 - x^2$

g. $(x^2 + 1)^3 - x^3$ **h.** $(x^2 + 1)^3 - x^6$

12. Factor each polynomial over $\mathbb{Z}$.

a. $x^2 - 9$ **b.** $(2x)^2 - 9$

c. $9 - x^2$ **d.** $(x + 1)^2 - 9$

e. $(x + 1)^2 - x^2$ **f.** $(x^2 + 1)^2 - x^2$

g. $(x^2 + 1)^3 - x^3$ **h.** $(x^2 + 1)^3 - x^6$

2.13 Quadratics

In your first-year algebra course, you learned to factor quadratic polynomials in order to solve quadratic equations. Most of the quadratics you factored were monic—the coefficient of x^2 was 1. In this lesson, you will build on the methods you used to factor monics to find the factors of any quadratic polynomial. The new methods will extend to polynomials of higher degrees.

Factoring to solve was the original motivation for factoring, but, like most topics in mathematics, factoring has become an interesting problem in its own right.

First, you will quickly review the basic factoring techniques for monic quadratics. If you want to factor $x^2 - 7x + 12$, you look for two numbers with sum of 7 and a product of 12. To understand why you do this, suppose the equation is in factored form.

$$x^2 - 7x + 12 = (x - r)(x - s)$$

If you multiply out the right side, you get

$$x^2 - 7x + 12 = x^2 - (r + s)x + rs$$

So, in this case, $r + s = 7$ and $rs = 12$.

Make sure you know how to multiply out the right side.

For You to Do

1. Factor $x^2 - 7x + 12$.

Now, what can you do if the quadratic is not monic? A good mathematical habit is to make use of something you already know how to do. The scaling method is a good example of this habit.

You can scale up to make a process—such as removing bunny ears—easier to do. After you have fixed the problem, you can scale back down.

Example

Problem Factor $6x^2 + 11x - 10$.

Solution You can use the scaling method to transform nonmonic polynomials into monic ones. Here are the steps.

Step 1 Multiply the polynomial by 6 to make the leading coefficient a perfect square.

$$6(6x^2 + 11x - 10) = 36x^2 + 11 \cdot 6x - 60 = (6x)^2 + 11(6x) - 60$$

Step 2 Think of $6x$ as the variable. Let $z = 6x$.

$$z^2 + 11z - 60$$

Step 3 This expression factors.

$$z^2 + 11z - 60 = (z + 15)(z - 4)$$

Step 4 Replace z with $6x$.

$$(6x + 15)(6x - 4)$$

So

$$6(6x^2 + 11x - 10) = (6x + 15)(6x - 4)$$
$$= 3(2x + 5) \cdot 2(3x - 2)$$
$$= 6(2x + 5)(3x - 2)$$

Step 5 Divide both sides by 6 to obtain the factored form.

$$6x^2 + 11x - 10 = (2x + 5)(3x - 2)$$

> **Habits of Mind**
>
> **Look for relationships.** Dividing by 6 undoes the multiplication by 6 that you did in Step 1.

Developing Habits of Mind

Change variables. This idea of lumping part of an expression into one unit is very useful in mathematics. You can say that $(2x)^2 + 18(2x) + 45$ is a monic quadratic in $2x$. This means that if you think of $2x$ as the variable instead of x, the quadratic looks monic.

For You to Do

2. Factor $6x^2 - 31x + 35$.

For Discussion

3. State the scaling method as an algorithm, a sequence of steps that describes exactly what to do.

Exercises *Practicing Habits of Mind*

Check Your Understanding

1. Factor each polynomial.

   a. $9x^2 + 18x - 7$

   c. $15x^2 + 16x - 7$

   e. $-18x^2 - 65x - 7$

   g. $9x^4 + 62x^2 - 7$

   i. $18x^3 - 61x^2 - 7x$

   b. $6x^2 - 31x + 35$

   d. $9x^2 + 62x - 7$

   f. $-18x^2 + 61x + 7$

   h. $25 - 4x^2$

   > For more on factoring polynomials, see the TI-Nspire Handbook, p. 804.

2. Factor each polynomial.

   a. $9x^2 + 18xy - 7y^2$

   c. $15x^2 + 16xa - 7a^2$

   e. $-18x^2 - 65xa - 7a^2$

   g. $25y^2 - 4x^2$

   b. $6x^2 - 31xy + 35y^2$

   d. $9x^2 + 62xb - 7b^2$

   f. $-18x^2 + 61xy + 7y^2$

   h. $18x^3 - 61x^2y - 7xy^2$

On Your Own

3. Factor each polynomial.

   a. $4x^2 - 13x + 3$

   b. $4x^2 - 8x + 3$

   c. $4x^2 + 4x - 3$

   d. $4(x + 1)^2 + 4(x + 1) - 3$

   e. $4x^4 - 13x^2 + 3$

   f. $4(x - 1)^4 - 13(x - 1)^2 + 3$

   g. $4(x - 1)^{12} - 13(x - 1)^6 + 3$

   h. $(x^2 + 1)^2 - x^2$

4. Solve $2x - \frac{3}{x} = 5$ for x.

5. In the equation $x^2 - 6x + 7 = 0$, let $z = x - 3$.

   a. Express the equation in terms of z.

   b. Solve the equation for z.

   c. Use the result from part (b) to solve the original equation.

   > If $z = x - 3$, then $x = z + 3$.

6. **Standardized Test Prep** Sasha has a number of rules for factoring quadratic polynomial of the form $ax^2 + bx + c$. Which of the following is NOT always true?

 A. If $a > 0$ and $c < 0$, then one real root is positive and one real root is negative.

 B. If $a = 1$ and $b < 0$ and d and e are the roots, with $|d| > |e|$, then $(x - d)$ is a factor of the polynomial.

 C. If a is an integer greater than 1, then multiplying c by a^2 converts the polynomial into a monic polynomial.

 D. If a, b, and c are integers and all are greater than zero, then any real roots, if they exist, are less than zero.

7. Derman wants to use the scaling method to factor $18x^2 + 7x - 1$. He multiplies the polynomial by 2 to make 18 a perfect square. Will this work?

Maintain Your Skills

8. Solve each pair of equations and compare the solutions.

 a. $x^2 - 8x + 7 = 0$ and $x^2 - 24x + 63 = 0$

 b. $2x^2 + 11x - 21 = 0$ and $2x^2 + 22x - 84 = 0$

 c. $2x^2 + 11x - 21 = 0$ and $2x^2 + 33x - 189 = 0$

 d. $2x^2 + 11x - 21 = 0$ and $2x^2 + 55x - 525 = 0$

 e. $2x^2 + 11x - 21 = 0$ and $x^2 + 11x - 42 = 0$

 f. $3x^2 + 16x - 35 = 0$ and $x^2 + 16x - 105 = 0$

 g. $3x^2 + 16x - 32 = 0$ and $x^2 + 16x - 96 = 0$

How are the equations in each pair related?

9. Find an equation with solutions scaled in each of the following ways.

 a. 7 times the solutions of $x^2 - 8x + 7 = 0$

 b. 7 times the solutions of $2x^2 + 11x - 21 = 0$

 c. 2 times the solutions of $2x^2 + 11x - 21 = 0$

 d. 3 times the solutions of $3x^2 + 11x - 21 = 0$

 e. 5 times the solutions of $5x^2 + 11x - 21 = 0$

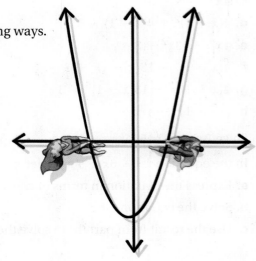

2.14 Factoring Cubics

In your first-year algebra course, you learned some basic identities that allow you to factor most quadratics that factor over $\mathbb{Z}$. Some of these identities included

- the difference-of-squares identity

$$x^2 - y^2 = (x - y)(x + y)$$

- the perfect-square identities

$$x^2 + 2xy + y^2 = (x + y)^2$$
$$x^2 - 2xy + y^2 = (x - y)^2$$

> Only one of these perfect-square identities is really necessary.

- the sum-and-product identity

$$x^2 - (a + b)x + ab = (x - a)(x - b)$$

Equipped with these identities, the **quadratic formula,** the Factor Theorem, and the scaling method, you can tackle any quadratic, often in more than one way.

> If all else fails, you can use the quadratic formula to get the roots.
> $$x = \frac{-b \pm \sqrt{b^2 - 4ac}}{2a}$$
> If the roots are rational numbers, you can factor the quadratic over $\mathbb{Z}$.

But how can you handle cubics?

In this lesson, you will learn some methods for factoring certain cubics. There is a formula, similar to the quadratic formula, that you can use to find the roots, and therefore the factors, of any cubic. But this cubic formula often leads to solutions that are in such an unrecognizable form that they are useless, so factoring special cubics is still worthwhile. Besides, it is fun.

Sums and Differences of Cubes

By now, you have seen the following theorem several times in exercises.

Theorem 2.4

The following identities show the factoring for the **difference of cubes** and the **sum of cubes.**

- $x^3 - y^3 = (x - y)(x^2 + xy + y^2)$
- $x^3 + y^3 = (x + y)(x^2 - xy + y^2)$

> **Habits of Mind**
>
> **Look for relationships.**
> You need only one of these identities.

For Discussion

1. Prove Theorem 2.4.

For You to Do

2. Factor $x^3 - 27$ and $8x^3 + 27$ over $\mathbb{Z}$.

Example 1

Problem Factor $(x + 1)^3 - 1$ over $\mathbb{Z}$.

Solution You can look at this two different ways.

Method 1 Difference of Cubes

If you lump things together and think of $x + 1$ as z, you get

$$z^3 - 1 = z^3 - 1^3$$

By Theorem 2.4, you can factor this as a difference of cubes.

$$z^3 - 1^3 = (z - 1)(z^2 + z + 1)$$

Now replace z with $(x + 1)$ and simplify.

$$(z - 1)(z^2 + z + 1) = ((x + 1) - 1)((x + 1)^2 + (x + 1) + 1)$$
$$= x((x^2 + 2x + 1) + (x + 1) + 1)$$
$$= x(x^2 + 3x + 3)$$

Since $x^2 + 3x + 3$ does not factor over $\mathbb{Z}$, this is the factored form.

Method 2 Expand and Simplify

For this method, you just expand $(x + 1)^3$, subtract 1, simplify, and factor the result.

$$(x + 1)^3 = (x + 1)(x + 1)^2$$
$$= (x + 1)(x^2 + 2x + 1)$$
$$= x^3 + 2x^2 + x + x^2 + 2x + 1$$
$$= x^3 + 3x^2 + 3x + 1$$

So

$$(x + 1)^3 - 1 = (x^3 + 3x^2 + 3x + 1) - 1 = x^3 + 3x^2 + 3x$$

Now factor out the common factor of x.

$$x^3 + 3x^2 + 3x = x(x^2 + 3x + 3)$$

Habits of Mind

Check your work. It is a good thing that both methods give the same answer, because there is only one factorization of a polynomial over $\mathbb{Z}$.

3. Factor $(3x + 2)^3 + 8$ over $\mathbb{Z}$.

Grouping

Grouping is a technique in which you lump a few terms of a polynomial together so that you can factor that piece. Sometimes the factors of that piece are also factors of the whole polynomial.

> You can apply grouping to any polynomial. Cubics with four terms are convenient because sometimes you can group them in pairs.

Example 2

Problem Factor the following two polynomials over $\mathbb{Z}$.

a. $x^3 - 8x^2 + 4x - 32$

b. $x^3 - 2x^2 + x - 2$

Solution

a. Factor $x^3 - 8x^2 + 4x - 32$.

Group the first two terms and the last two terms together.

$$x^3 - 8x^2 + 4x - 32 = (x^3 - 8x^2) + (4x - 32)$$

Factor out the common factor in each group.

$$(x^3 - 8x^2) + (4x - 32) = x^2(x - 8) + 4(x - 8)$$

Each group has a factor of $x - 8$, so you can pull it out.

$$x^2(x - 8) + 4(x - 8) = (x - 8)(x^2 + 4)$$

The polynomial $x^2 + 4$ does not factor over $\mathbb{Z}$, so you are done.

> If $f(x) = x^3 - 8x^2 + 4x - 32$, what is $f(8)$?

b. Factor $x^3 - 2x^2 + x - 2$.

Just for variety, group the first and third terms together, and then the second and fourth terms.

$$x^3 - 2x^2 + x - 2 = (x^3 + x) + (-2x^2 - 2)$$

Factor out the common factor in each group.

$$(x^3 + x) + (-2x^2 - 2) = x(x^2 + 1) - 2(x^2 + 1)$$

Each group has a factor of $x^2 + 1$, so you can pull it out.

$$x(x^2 + 1) - 2(x^2 + 1) = (x - 2)(x^2 + 1)$$

The polynomial $x^2 + 1$ does not factor over $\mathbb{Z}$, so you are done.

> If $f(x) = x^3 - 2x^2 + x - 2$, what is $f(2)$?

For You to Do

4. Factor $x^3 - 2x^2 + x - 2$ another way: Group the first two terms together and the last two terms together.

For Discussion

5. Factor the expression $(r + s)^3 - 3rs(r + s)$ by grouping.

6. Use your factoring to establish the identity below.

$$(r + s)^3 - 3rs(r + s) - (r^3 + s^3) = 0$$

Developing Habits of Mind

Consider more than one strategy. Some warnings:

- Not all cubics can be factored by grouping, but they may still factor. For example, you can try every grouping combination for $2x^3 - 13x^2 + x + 21$ and nothing will work, but it still factors.

$$2x^3 - 13x^2 + x + 21 = (2x - 3)(x^2 - 5x - 7)$$

- Sometimes a combination of methods can be useful. For example, look at the following polynomial.

$$27x^3 + 27x^2 + 9x + 1$$

Grouping the first and second terms looks promising, but it does not lead anywhere. You can group the first and last terms, factor that pair as a sum of cubes, and then factor out the common factor from the middle two terms.

$$
\begin{aligned}
27x^3 + 27x^2 + 9x + 1 &= \left(27x^3 + 1\right) + 27x^2 + 9x \\
&= (3x + 1)\left((3x)^2 - (3x) + 1\right) + 9x(3x + 1) \\
&= (3x + 1)\left(9x^2 - 3x + 1\right) + 9x(3x + 1) \\
&= (3x + 1)\left(9x^2 - 3x + 1 + 9x\right) \\
&= (3x + 1)\left(9x^2 + 6x + 1\right) \\
&= (3x + 1)(3x + 1)^2 \\
&= (3x + 1)^3
\end{aligned}
$$

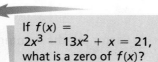 If $f(x) = 2x^3 - 13x^2 + x = 21$, what is a zero of $f(x)$?

So $27x^3 + 27x^2 + 9x + 1$ is a perfect cube.

Find a Root, Find a Factor

The Factor Theorem sets up a correspondence between roots and factors. For cubics, if you can find a root a of the equation $f(x) = 0$, you have found a factor of $f(x)$, namely $x - a$. So, you know $f(x) = (x - a)g(x)$, where $g(x)$ is a quadratic. And you know how to handle quadratics.

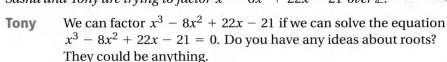

Minds in Action   episode 8

Sasha and Tony are trying to factor $x^3 - 8x^2 + 22x - 21$ over $\mathbb{Z}$.

Tony   We can factor $x^3 - 8x^2 + 22x - 21$ if we can solve the equation $x^3 - 8x^2 + 22x - 21 = 0$. Do you have any ideas about roots? They could be anything.

Sasha   Let's use the trick of working backward. Suppose we have a root a. Then $x - a$ is a factor, so we'd get something like

$$x^3 - 8x^2 + 8x + 21 = (x - a)(rx^2 + sx + t)$$

for integers r, s, and t.

Tony   I know that r would have to be 1, because if you multiplied it back out, the leading term would be rx^3. May be we could figure out the other coefficients in the same way.

Sasha   I'm looking at the constant term. It would have to be $-at$. So, $-at = 21$, and $at = -21$.

> Why does the constant term have to be $-at$?

Derman joins the discussion.

Derman   Well, there are millions of pairs of numbers with a product of -21. Like -100 and $\frac{21}{100}$, for example. Or $\frac{21}{\sqrt{2}}$ and $\sqrt{2}$.

Sasha   Yes, Derman, but a and t have to be integers. That narrows the field.

Tony   Right. We're basically looking at factors of 21. So a can only be 1, 3, or 7.

Sasha   Or their opposites. So, we only have six numbers to try. Let's do it.

They split up the numbers—three for Sasha, two for Tony, and one for Derman.

Tony   I've got it: 3 is a root. So, $x - 3$ is a factor. Now we can either figure out s from $x^3 - 8x^2 + 8x + 21 = (x - 3)(x^2 + sx - 7)$, or we can use long division.

> Why is the second factor $x^2 + sx - 7$?

They try it both ways and get the same answer.

Tony   So here's how it factors.

$$x^3 - 8x^2 + 8x + 21 = (x - 3)(x^2 - 5x - 7)$$

Derman   Does the quadratic factor some more?

For You to Do

7. What are the roots of $x^2 - 5x - 7$?

8. Answer Derman's question from the dialog.

For Discussion

9. Can you use the scaling method to turn nonmonic cubics into monic cubics? Try it with $2x^3 - 13x^2 + x + 21$.

For You to Do

10. Find all real roots of $2x^3 - 13x^2 + x + 21$.

Exercises *Practicing Habits of Mind*

Check Your Understanding

1. Prove the following theorem that shows how to cube a binomial.

Theorem 2.5

The following are identities.

- $(x + y)^3 = x^3 + 3x^2y + 3xy^2 + y^3$
- $(x - y)^3 = x^3 - 3x^2y + 3xy^2 - y^3$

2. Factor each polynomial over $\mathbb{Z}$.

a. $x^3 - 64$ **b.** $x^3 + 64$ **c.** $27x^3 - 64$

d. $27x^3 + 64$ **e.** $(x + 1)^3 - 64$

f. $(2x - 3)^3 + 64$ **g.** $x^3 + 3x^2 - 9x - 27$

h. $x^3 + ax^2 - a^2x - a^3$ **i.** $x^2 - (3x + 1)^2$

j. $x^2 - y^2 + 2yz - z^2$ **k.** $x^3 - 4x^2 - 31x + 70$

l. $x^3 - 4x^2y - 31xy^2 + 70y^3$ **m.** $(x + 1)^3 - 3x(x + 1)$

3. Use the scaling method to transform $5x^2 + 3x^2 + 3x - 2$ into a monic cubic. Then use the transformed cubic to factor $5x^3 + 3x^2 + 3x - 2$.

On Your Own

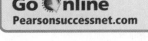

4. Factor each polynomial over $\mathbb{Z}$.

  a. $x^3 - 27$ **b.** $x^3 + 27$

  c. $64x^3 - 27$ **d.** $64x^3 + 27$

  e. $(x - 1)^3 - 125$ **f.** $(2x - 3)^3 + 125$

  g. $x^3 + 5x^2 - 25x - 125$ **h.** $5x^3 - 7x^2 + 7x - 2$

  i. $x^4 - (3x + 1)^4$ **j.** $x^2 - y^2 - 2yz - z^2$

  k. $(x + 1)^3 + x^3$ **l.** $x^3 - 3x^2 + 3x - 2$

  m. $x^3 - 3x^2z + 3xz^2 - 2z^3$ **n.** $x^3 - 12x^2 + 48x - 64$

5. Factor $x^3 - 15x - 4$ over $\mathbb{Z}$.

6. Factor $(x - 1)^3 - 15(x - 1) - 4$ over $\mathbb{Z}$.

7. **Take It Further** Factor $x^4 - x^3 - 2x^2 + x + 1$ over $\mathbb{Z}$.

8. **Standardized Test Prep** What is the difference $(x + 4)^3 - (x^3 + 4^3)$?

  A. $x^2 - 4x + 4$ **B.** $x^2 - 4x + 16$

  C. $3x^2 + 48$ **D.** $12x^2 + 48x$

Maintain Your Skills

9. Find the normal form of each polynomial.

  a. $x + 1$

  b. $(x + 1)^2$

  c. $(x + 1)^3$

  d. $(x + 1)^4$

  e. $(x + 1)^5$

What patterns do you see?

2.15 Pippins and Cheese

There are many more methods of factoring, some of them quite involved. You will learn about a few more very beautiful ones later. For now, you will look at three more topics to round out the discussion.

Quadratic-like and Cubic-like Polynomials

In Exercise 3a from Lesson 2.13, you factored this quadratic.

$$4x^2 - 13x + 3 = (4x - 1)(x - 3)$$

Then in Exercise 3e, you factored this fourth-degree polynomial.

$$4x^4 - 13x^2 + 3$$

One way to factor is to notice that this is a quadratic in x^2.

$$4x^4 - 13x^2 + 3 = 4(x^2)^2 - 13(x^2) + 3$$

So, if you let $z = x^2$, you have the same form as in Exercise 3a.

$$4z^2 - 13z + 3 = (4z - 1)(z - 3)$$

Now $z = x^2$, so you can convert to a polynomial in x.

$$4x^4 - 13x^2 + 3 = (4x^2 - 1)(x^2 - 3)$$

Then $4x^2 - 1$ factors some more over $\mathbb{Z}$, but $x^2 - 3$ does not.

Remember...

A fourth-degree polynomial is a quartic. Some people call a quartic that is a quadratic in x^2 a biquadratic.

For You to Do

1. Factor $9x^4 - 37x^2 + 4$ over $\mathbb{Z}$.

There are other kinds of quadratic-like polynomials—polynomials that are quadratic in some power of x.

Example 1

Problem Factor $x^6 - 7x^3 - 8$ over $\mathbb{Z}$.

Solution Is it a sixth degree polynomial? Well, yes, but it is a quadratic in x^3.

$$x^6 - 7x^3 - 8 = (x^3)^2 - 7(x^3) - 8$$

This is like $z^2 - 7z - 8$, where $z = x^3$. Write $z^2 - 7z - 8 = (z - 8)(z + 1)$.

For You to Do

2. Finish the example. Replace z with x^3 and finish the factorization.

So, some polynomials are quadratic-like. And some are cubic-like.

Example 2

Problem Factor $x^9 - 8x^6 + 4x^3 - 32$ over $\mathbb{Z}$.

Solution This is a cubic in x^3.

$$x^9 - 8x^6 + 4x^3 - 32 = (x^3)^3 - 8(x^3)^2 + 4(x^3) - 32$$

Let $z = x^3$. Then you get $x^9 - 8x^6 + 4x^3 - 32 = z^3 - 8z^2 + 4z - 32$.

In Example 2 from Lesson 2.14, you factored this cubic by grouping.

$$z^3 - 8z^2 + 4z - 32 = (z - 8)(z^2 + 4)$$

Now replace z with x^3.

$$(z - 8)(z^2 + 4) = (x^3 - 8)((x^3)^2 + 4) = (x^3 - 8)(x^6 + 4)$$

The polynomial $x^3 - 8$ factors as a difference of cubes.

$$(x^3 - 8) = (x - 2)(x^2 + 2x + 4)$$

So you have $x^9 - 8x^6 + 4x^3 - 32 = (x - 2)(x^2 + 2x + 4)(x^6 + 4)$.

> Well, in Lesson 2.14 it was a different variable.

For Discussion

3. Are you done? Does either $x^2 + 2x + 4$ or $x^6 + 4$ factor over $\mathbb{Z}$?

Difference of Squares in Disguise

There is a class of biquadratics that you can factor as the difference of two squares if you add and subtract a perfect square. Here is how it works.

Example 3

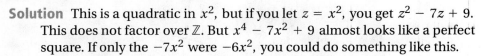

Problem Factor $x^4 - 7x^2 + 9$ over $\mathbb{Z}$.

Solution This is a quadratic in x^2, but if you let $z = x^2$, you get $z^2 - 7z + 9$. This does not factor over $\mathbb{Z}$. But $x^4 - 7x^2 + 9$ almost looks like a perfect square. If only the $-7x^2$ were $-6x^2$, you could do something like this.

$$x^4 - 6x^2 + 9 = (x^2 - 3)^2$$

Well, you can make the middle term $-6x^2$ by adding and subtracting x^2.

$$x^4 - 7x^2 + 9 = x^4 - 6x^2 + 9 - x^2 = (x^2 - 3)^2 - x^2$$

> Can you factor either of these factors any more?

That did it. This is a difference of squares, so now you can factor it.

$$x^4 - 7x^2 + 9 = (x^2 - 3)^2 - x^2 = (x^2 - 3 - x)(x^2 - 3 + x)$$

You can write each factor in normal form.

$$x^4 - 7x^2 + 9 = (x^2 - x - 3)(x^2 + x - 3)$$

For You to Do

4. Factor $x^4 + 4$ over $\mathbb{Z}$.

For Discussion

5. Suppose you want to factor $x^6 - 1$ over $\mathbb{Z}$. You have at least two ways to do it:

- as a difference of squares

$$x^6 - 1 = (x^3)^2 - 1$$
$$= (x^3 - 1)(x^3 + 1)$$
$$= (x - 1)(x^2 + x + 1)(x + 1)(x^2 - x + 1)$$

- as a difference of cubes

$$x^6 - 1 = (x^2)^3 - 1$$
$$= (x^2 - 1)((x^2)^2 + (x^2) + 1)$$
$$= (x - 1)(x + 1)(x^4 + x^2 + 1)$$

These look like two different factorizations. Are they?

Factoring Over Extensions

Throughout this investigation, the verb *factor* has meant "to factor over $\mathbb{Z}$." If you allow for polynomials with real-number coefficients, some polynomials that do not factor over $\mathbb{Z}$ will factor over $\mathbb{R}$. For example, $x^2 - 3$ is irreducible over $\mathbb{Z}$, but if you "move up" to $\mathbb{R}$, you can factor it.

$$x^2 - 3 = (x - \sqrt{3})(x + \sqrt{3})$$

Factoring over $\mathbb{R}$ is often the right setting for applying the Factor Theorem.

Another way to say that a polynomial does not factor over $\mathbb{Z}$ is to say that a polynomial is *irreducible* over $\mathbb{Z}$.

Sometimes you have to search a larger set of objects to find what you are looking for.

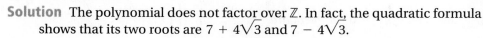

Example 4

Problem Factor $x^2 - 14x + 1$ over $\mathbb{R}$.

Solution The polynomial does not factor over $\mathbb{Z}$. In fact, the quadratic formula shows that its two roots are $7 + 4\sqrt{3}$ and $7 - 4\sqrt{3}$.

Check that the quadratic formula gives these roots.

The Factor Theorem says that if $7 + 4\sqrt{3}$ is a root, $(x - (7 + 4\sqrt{3}))$, or $(x - 7 - 4\sqrt{3})$, must be a factor.

Similarly, another factor must be

$$(x - (7 - 4\sqrt{3})) = (x - 7 + 4\sqrt{3})$$

Since the original is a monic quadratic, the factorization must be

$$x^2 - 14x + 1 = (x - 7 - 4\sqrt{3})(x - 7 + 4\sqrt{3})$$

For You to Do

6. Expand the product $(x - 7 - 4\sqrt{3})(x - 7 + 4\sqrt{3})$. (*Hint:* Why is this equal to $(x - 7)^2 - 48$?)

For Discussion

7. Find real numbers a and b such that $(a + b\sqrt{3})^2 = 7 + 4\sqrt{3}$.
8. Find four real roots for the equation $x^4 - 14x^2 + 1 = 0$.

Factoring over the real numbers can sometimes lead to puzzling situations.

Minds in Action   episode 9

Tony and Sasha are discussing Exercise 5 from Lesson 2.14.

Tony   We want to factor $x^3 - 15x - 4$. Well, I know that 4 is a root of $x^3 - 15x - 4 = 0$, so $(x - 4)$ is a factor.

Sasha   And I can use polynomial division to find that the other factor is $x^2 + 4x + 1$.

Tony   If we apply the quadratic formula to $x^2 + 4x + 1 = 0$, we get the roots $2 + \sqrt{3}$ and $2 - \sqrt{3}$. So, the factorization over $\mathbb{R}$ is

$$(x - 4)(x - 2 - \sqrt{3})(x - 2 + \sqrt{3})$$

How did Tony get this factorization?

Sasha I've been thinking. I wonder if we could find the roots of the cubic $x^3 - 15x - 4$ another way. Let's use my favorite identity from the For Discussion Problem 6 in Lesson 2.14.

Sasha writes $(r + s)^3 - 3rs(r + s) - (r^3 + s^3) = 0$ on the board.

Tony Huh?

Sasha My idea is to think of the root as $r + s$—call this z. So the identity is

$$z^3 - 3rs \cdot z - (r^3 + s^3) = 0$$

Now match this up with the equation

$$x^3 - 15x - 4 = 0$$

I want to find numbers r and s such that

$$3rs = 15 \text{ and } r^3 + s^3 = 4$$

or

$$rs = 5 \text{ and } r^3 + s^3 = 4$$

Tony I get it. This almost looks like a sum-and-product problem. So, let's cube the first equation.

$$r^3 s^3 = 125 \text{ and } r^3 + s^3 = 4$$

Now we can find r^3 and s^3, since we know their sum and product. When we're done, we just need to take the cube roots of the answers and we'll have r and s. And then we should be able to recover our three roots: 4 and $2 \pm \sqrt{3}$.

Sasha Well, by the sum-and-product identity, r^3 and s^3 are roots of $x^2 - 4x + 125 = 0$.

So we can apply the quadratic formula and get

$$r^3 = \frac{4 + \sqrt{16 - 500}}{2} \text{ and } r^3 = \frac{4 - \sqrt{16 - 500}}{2}$$

When we simplify r and s, we get something very odd.

$$r^3 = \frac{4 + \sqrt{-484}}{2} \text{ and } r^3 = \frac{4 - \sqrt{-484}}{2}$$

How can this be? We know the roots, and they are all real.

Tony I have no idea. The next chapter in this book is "Complex Numbers." Well, $\frac{4 + \sqrt{-484}}{2}$ is certainly as complex as they come. Let's wait until Chapter 3 and then come back to this.

Sasha agrees, very reluctantly.

For You to Do

9. Suppose that $\frac{4 + \sqrt{-484}}{2}$ and $\frac{4 - \sqrt{-484}}{2}$ actually exist and that they obey the basic rules of algebra. What are their sum and their product?

Exercises *Practicing Habits of Mind*

Check Your Understanding

1. Factor each polynomial over $\mathbb{Z}$.

    a. $x^4 - x^2 - 6$

    b. $x^6 - 9x^3 + 8$

    c. $x^4 - 16$

    d. $x^6 - 8$

    e. $x^4 - 16y^4$

    f. $x^6 + 8$

    g. $x^4 - 9x^2 + 16$

    h. $x^4 + x^2 + 1$

2. Factor each polynomial over $\mathbb{R}$.

    a. $x^2 - 2x - 4$

    b. $x^2 - x - 1$

3. Find a polynomial with integer coefficients that has a zero for each given value.

    a. $2 + \sqrt{3}$

    b. $2 - \sqrt{3}$

    c. **Take It Further** $\sqrt{2} + \sqrt{3}$

4. Can a polynomial be irreducible over $\mathbb{Z}$ but factor over $\mathbb{Q}$? Explain.

> Think of quadratics, for example. The symbol $\mathbb{Q}$ means the rational numbers.

On Your Own

5. Factor each polynomial over $\mathbb{Z}$.

    a. $x^4 - 11x^2 + 28$

    b. $x^6 - 6x^3 + 9$

    c. $x^6 - 27$

    d. $x^6 + 3x^4 + 3x^2 + 1$

    e. $x^4 + 9x^2 + 25$

    f. $x^4 - 3a^2x^2 + a^4$

    g. $x^6 - 1$

    h. $x^8 - 1$

6. Solve each equation.

    a. $\sqrt{x} = 7$

    b. $\sqrt{x - 3} = 7$

    c. $\sqrt{x - 3} = \sqrt{78}$

    d. $\sqrt{x - 3} = \sqrt{x^2 - 15}$

    e. **Take It Further** $\sqrt{2x - 5} - \sqrt{x - 2} = 2$

7. Derman is thinking about For Discussion Problem 5. He says, "I have a third way to factor $x^6 - 1$. I remember it from a homework problem a long time ago.

$$x^6 - 1 = (x - 1)(x^5 + x^4 + x^3 + x^2 + x + 1)$$

This is different from both answers."

Is Derman's factorization really different?

Go Online
Pearsonsuccessnet.com

8. **Standardized Test Prep** What is the greatest number of binomial factors over $\mathbb{Z}$ that you can use in a product to get $x^4 - 1$?

   A. 2

   B. 3

   C. 4

   D. 5

9. **Take It Further** Find real numbers a and b such that

$$x^4 + x^3 + x^2 + x + 1 = (x^2 + ax + 1)(x^2 + bx + 1)$$

Maintain Your Skills

10. Factor each polynomial over $\mathbb{Z}$.

    a. $1 + x + x^2 + x^3$

    b. $1 + x + x^2 + x^3 + x^4 + x^5$

    c. $1 + x + x^2 + x^3 + x^4 + x^5 + x^6 + x^7$

    d. $1 + x + x^2 + x^3 + x^4 + x^5 + x^6 + x^7 + x^8 + x^9$

Is there a general method here?

2.16 Rational Expressions

Polynomials have an arithmetic that is similar to the arithmetic of ordinary integers. In both systems, you can add, subtract, multiply, and divide, and these operations obey the same basic rules. You also have long division in both systems. You can use these facts to show that you can factor anything (into primes for an integer and into irreducibles for a polynomial) in exactly one way.

> There may be more than one way to carry out the factorization, but there will only be one final result.

Factoring polynomials is useful when you want to solve polynomial equations. Factoring integers is useful when you want to do arithmetic with fractions. That is, when you want to simplify a fraction and when you want to add two fractions.

For You to Do

1. Just for old-time's sake, simplify $\frac{25,725}{86,625}$.

2. Find the sum $\frac{18}{49} + \frac{5}{21}$.

Because polynomials have an arithmetic (the basic rules of algebra) that is so much like the arithmetic of $\mathbb{Z}$, you can do arithmetic with fractions of polynomials.

Example 1

Problem Simplify $\dfrac{x^2 - 5x + 6}{x^2 - 9}$.

Solution

$$\frac{x^2 - 5x + 6}{x^2 - 9} = \frac{(x - 3)(x - 2)}{(x - 3)(x + 3)}$$

$$= \frac{\cancel{(x - 3)}(x - 2)}{\cancel{(x - 3)}(x + 3)}$$

$$= \frac{(x - 2)}{(x + 3)}$$

Notice that this expression is equivalent to the original everywhere except at $x = 3$. At $x = 3$, the original rational expression was undefined, but this new expression is equal to $\frac{1}{6}$ at $x = 3$.

For You to Do

3. Simplify $\dfrac{x^3 - 1}{x^2 - 1}$.

Example 2

Problem Write this sum as a single rational expression.

$$\frac{5x + 1}{x^2 - 1} + \frac{3}{x - 1} + \frac{2}{x + 1}$$

Solution Just as with integers, you need to find a common denominator. Since $x^2 - 1 = (x - 1)(x + 1)$, all three denominators are factors of $x^2 - 1$. You can use that expression as the denominator. Multiply each fraction by a form of 1 that makes its denominator $x^2 - 1$.

$$\frac{5x + 1}{x^2 - 1} + \frac{3}{x - 1} + \frac{2}{x + 1} = \frac{5x + 1}{x^2 - 1} + \frac{3}{x - 1} \cdot \frac{(x + 1)}{(x + 1)} + \frac{2}{x + 1} \cdot \frac{(x - 1)}{(x - 1)}$$

$$= \frac{5x + 1}{x^2 - 1} + \frac{3(x + 1)}{x^2 - 1} + \frac{2(x - 1)}{x^2 - 1}$$

$$= \frac{(5x + 1) + 3(x + 1) + 2(x - 1)}{x^2 - 1}$$

$$= \frac{10x + 2}{x^2 - 1}$$

$$= \frac{2(5x + 1)}{x^2 - 1}$$

Habits of Mind

Think about it more than one way. If you are thinking of the polynomials as expressions, you call fractions like these **rational expressions.** If you are thinking of the polynomials as functions, you call them rational functions.

For You to Do

4. Write this difference as a single rational expression.

$$\frac{10}{x + 2} - \frac{6}{x - 2}$$

Exercises Practicing Habits of Mind

Check Your Understanding

1. Simplify each rational expression.

   a. $\dfrac{15x}{5x^2}$

   b. $\dfrac{x^2 - y^2}{(x + y)}$

   c. $\dfrac{x^2 - y^2}{(x + y)^2}$

   d. $\dfrac{x^2 - 1}{x^4 - 1}$

   e. $\dfrac{2x^2 + x - 6}{3x^2 + 4x - 4}$

   f. $\dfrac{3 - x - 3x^4 + x^5}{3 - x - 3x^3 + x^4}$

2. Let $f(x) = \dfrac{2x^2 + x - 6}{3x^2 + 4x - 4}$.

   Suppose you define $g(x)$ by the same fraction, except the fraction is in simplest form. How do the graphs of $f(x)$ and $g(x)$ compare?

3. Write each sum as a single rational expression.

   a. $\dfrac{b}{b - a} + \dfrac{a}{a - b}$

   b. $\dfrac{1}{(x - a)(a - b)} + \dfrac{1}{(x - b)(b - a)}$

4. Write each sum as a single rational expression.

   a. $\dfrac{1 + 2x}{3x - 3} + \dfrac{5 - x}{x^2 - 5x + 4}$

   b. $\dfrac{2}{x - 3} - \dfrac{2}{x + 3} - \dfrac{1}{x}$

   c. $\dfrac{1}{(a - b)(b - c)} + \dfrac{1}{(b - c)(c - a)} + \dfrac{1}{(c - a)(a - b)}$

5. **Take It Further** Find numbers A and B such that

   $$\dfrac{1}{(x - 1)(x - 3)} = \dfrac{A}{(x - 1)} + \dfrac{B}{(x - 3)}$$

On Your Own

6. Simplify each rational expression.

   a. $\dfrac{x^2 - 1}{x - 1}$

   b. $\dfrac{x^4 - 1}{x^2 - 1}$

   c. $\dfrac{x^6 - 1}{x^3 - 1}$

   d. $\dfrac{x^8 - 1}{x^4 - 1}$

   e. $\dfrac{x^{10} - 1}{x^5 - 1}$

7. Write each expression as the quotient of two polynomials.

a. $1 + \dfrac{1}{x-1} - \dfrac{1}{1+x}$

b. $1 - \dfrac{2}{1+x^2}$

c. $\dfrac{1}{x-2} - \dfrac{1}{x-1}$

d. $\dfrac{1}{2(x-3)} - \dfrac{1}{x-2} + \dfrac{1}{2(x-1)}$

e. $\dfrac{2}{(x-1)^2} + \dfrac{1}{x-1} - \dfrac{1}{x-2}$

Go Online
Pearsonsuccessnet.com

8. **Take It Further** Find numbers A and B such that

$$\dfrac{1}{(x-1)(x-2)} = \dfrac{A}{x-1} + \dfrac{B}{x-2}$$

9. **Standardized Test Prep** What is $\dfrac{x^2 - 9x + 20}{-x^2 + 6x - 8}$ written in lowest terms?

A. $\dfrac{x-5}{2-x}$

B. $\dfrac{x-5}{x-2}$

C. $\dfrac{x-4}{x-2}$

D. $\dfrac{x-5}{x-4}$

Maintain Your Skills

10. Simplify each rational expression.

a. $\dfrac{x^3 - 1}{x - 1}$

b. $\dfrac{x^4 - 1}{(x-1)(x+1)}$

c. $\dfrac{x^5 - 1}{x - 1}$

d. $\dfrac{x^6 - 1}{(x-1)(x+1)(x^2+x+1)}$

e. $\dfrac{x^8 - 1}{(x-1)(x+1)(x^2+1)}$

f. $\dfrac{x^9 - 1}{(x-1)(x^2+x+1)}$

g. $\dfrac{x^{10} - 1}{(x-1)(x+1)(x^4+x^3+x^2+x+1)}$

h. $\dfrac{x^{12} - 1}{(x-1)(x+1)(x^2+x+1)(x^2+1)(x^2-x+1)}$

Go Online
Video Tutor
Pearsonsuccessnet.com

11. **Take It Further** Suppose that $f(x) = \dfrac{1}{(x-1)(x-2)}$. Find each value.

a. $f(3) + f(4) + f(5)$

b. $f(3) + f(4) + f(5) + f(6)$

c. $f(3) + f(4) + f(5) + f(6) + f(7)$

d. $f(3) + f(4) + f(5) + f(6) + f(7) + \cdots + f(23)$

e. $f(3) + f(4) + f(5) + f(6) + f(7) + \cdots + f(n)$ (in terms of n)

Mathematical 2D Reflections

In this investigation, you learned to factor polynomials by scaling, by finding roots, by using the sums and differences of squares and cubes, by grouping, and by identifying quadratic-like or cubic-like polynomials. These questions will help you summarize what you have learned.

1. Factor each polynomial.

   a. $6x^2 - x - 15$ b. $6x^2 + x - 15$ c. $35x^2 + 79x + 42$

2. Factor each polynomial over $\mathbb{Z}$.

   a. $x^3 - 125$

   b. $x^3 + 125$

   c. $27x^3 - 64$

   d. $27x^3 + 64$

   e. $(x - 1)^3 - 27$

   f. $(2x - 3)^3 + 27$

   g. $x^3 + 3x^2 - 9x - 27$

   h. $x^3 - 4x^2 + 4x - 3$

   i. $x^4 - (2x + 1)^4$

   j. $x^2 - y^2 + 2yz - z^2$

3. Factor each polynomial over $\mathbb{Z}$.

   a. $35x^4 + 79x^2 + 42$

   b. $6x^6 + x^3 - 15$

   c. $x^4 - 81$

   d. $x^6 - 27$

   e. $4x^4 - 5x^2 + 1$

   f. $x^4 + 5x^2 + 9$

4. For each number, find an equation with integer coefficients that has that number as a solution.

   a. $\sqrt{5}$

   b. $\sqrt{5} + \sqrt{7}$

   c. **Take It Further** $3 + \sqrt{5} + \sqrt{7}$

5. Write each expression as a single rational expression.

   a. $1 - \dfrac{x + 2}{x^2 + x + 1}$

   b. $1 - \dfrac{2}{3(1 + x)} + \dfrac{2(x - 2)}{3(1 - x + x^2)}$

6. How do you factor nonmonic quadratics?

7. How do you factor differences and sums of cubes?

8. Does $x^4 + 4$ factor over $\mathbb{Z}$?

Vocabulary and Notation

In this investigation, you learned these terms and symbols. Make sure you understand what each one means and how to use it.

- difference of cubes
- quadratic formula
- rational expression
- sum of cubes
- $\mathbb{Z}$ (the integers)
- $\mathbb{Q}$ (the rational numbers)

Project Using Mathematical Habits

Heron's Formula

One of the most beautiful theorems in geometry is named after Heron of Alexandria, who lived about A.D. 62. It gives a formula for finding the area of a triangle in terms of the lengths of its three sides. The purpose of this project is to derive Heron's formula by using the ideas of this chapter.

Heron's Formula

If the sides of a triangle have lengths a, b, and c, the area of the triangle is

$$\sqrt{s(s-a)(s-b)(s-c)}$$

where $s = \frac{1}{2}(a+b+c)$.

Before you look at the proof, you can look at some reasons that the formula makes sense.

1. Show that you can also write Heron's formula as

$$\frac{1}{4}\sqrt{(a+b+c)(a+b-c)(a+c-b)(b+c-a)}$$

2. Use Heron's formula to find the area of an equilateral triangle with side length 8. Check this against the result of the formula $A = \frac{1}{2}bh$.

3. What is the area of a "triangle" with sides of length 4, 5, and 9? What happens when you apply Heron's formula to these numbers?

4. Under what conditions on a, b, and c will the output of Heron's formula be 0? What kinds of triangles give these inputs?

5. You can think of Heron's formula as a function of three inputs.

$$H(a, b, c) =$$
$$\frac{1}{4}\sqrt{(a+b+c)(a+b-c)(a+c-b)(b+c-a)}$$

Show that $H(a, b, c) = H(a, c, b) = H(b, a, c) = H(b, c, a) = H(c, a, b) = H(c, b, a)$. Why does this make sense geometrically?

6. From the formula

$$H(a, b, c) =$$
$$\frac{1}{4}\sqrt{(a+b+c)(a+b-c)(a+c-b)(b+c-a)}$$

you can conclude that

$$16(H(a, b, c))^2 =$$
$$(a+b+c)(a+b-c)(a+c-b)(b+c-a)$$

a. Expand the right side, removing the parentheses.

b. Show that $H(a, b, c)^2 = H(\pm a, \pm b, \pm c)$.

c. If $c^2 = a^2 + b^2$, the triangle is a right triangle. How does the expression for $16(H(a, b, c))^2$ simplify if $c^2 = a^2 + b^2$?

Now try the proof. Suppose you label the triangle this way, where h is the altitude from side c.

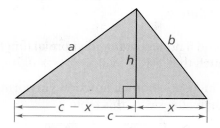

The area of the triangle is $\frac{1}{2}ch$. So, you need to find an expression for h in terms of a, b, and c. Apply the Pythagorean Theorem to the two right triangles in the figure.

$$h^2 + x^2 = b^2$$
$$h^2 + (c - x)^2 = a^2$$

Expand the second equation.

$$h^2 + c^2 - 2cx + x^2 = a^2$$

7. Show that this implies that $x = \frac{c^2 + b^2 - a^2}{2c}$.

Since $h^2 + x^2 = b^2$,

$$h^2 = b^2 - x^2$$
$$= b^2 - \left(\frac{c^2 + b^2 - a^2}{2c}\right)^2$$

8. Show that this implies that
$$h^2 = \frac{1}{4c^2}(4b^2c^2 - (c^2 + b^2 - a^2)^2)$$

The expression inside the parentheses is a difference of squares.

$$h^2 = \frac{1}{4c^2}\left(2bc - \left(c^2 + b^2 - a^2\right)\right) \cdot$$
$$\left(2bc + \left(c^2 + b^2 - a^2\right)\right)$$
$$= \frac{1}{4c^2}(a^2 - (c^2 - 2bc + b^2)) \cdot$$
$$((c^2 + 2bc + b^2) - a^2)$$

9. Finish the factorization to show that $h^2 = \frac{1}{4c^2} \cdot$
$$(a - c + b)(a + c - b)(c + b - a)(c + b + a)$$

10. Finally, use the previous exercises to derive Heron's formula. Write up your solutions and derivations as a report.

You can use Heron's formula to find the areas of the roof sections of this theater.

In **Investigation 2A,** you learned how to

- determine whether a table, graph, or closed-form rule is a function
- compose functions
- find the inverse of a function, if it exists
- find a piecewise-defined function

The following questions will help you check your understanding.

1. Consider the functions *f* and *g*.

   $$f(x) = 3x + 7$$

   $$g(x) = \frac{x + 1}{3}$$

   Calculate each value.

   a. $f(2)$ **b.** $g(2)$

   c. $f(g(2))$ **d.** $g(f(2))$

   e. $f \circ g(2)$ **f.** $f(2) \cdot g(2)$

2. Use the definitions of functions *f* and *g* below.

   $$f(x) = x - 2$$

   $$g(x) = x^2 + 4x + 1$$

   a. Find a formula for $f \circ g(x)$.

   b. Find a formula for $g \circ f(x)$.

3. Use the definitions of functions *f, g,* and *h* below.

   $$f(x) = \frac{x}{2} + 3$$

   $$g(x) = x^2$$

   $$h(x) = -3x$$

   a. Sketch the graph of each function.

   b. Determine whether each function is one-to-one.

   c. For each function that is one-to-one, find the inverse function.

In **Investigation 2B,** you learned how to

- use linear combinations of polynomials to determine new polynomials
- use zeros of polynomials to determine factors of polynomials
- find polynomials that agree with a given table

The following questions will help you check your understanding.

4. Find a nonconstant polynomial function *h* such that $h(1) = h(3) = h(4) = 0$.

5. Find a polynomial function *f* in normal form that agrees with this table.

Input	Output
1	−24
3	16
4	9
5	−8

6. **a.** Find a quadratic function *g* that agrees with $f: x \mapsto 3x - 5$ only at inputs $x = -1$ and $x = 2$.

   b. Sketch the graphs of *f* and *g* on the same set of axes.

In **Investigation 2C,** you learned how to

- understand the relationship between roots and factors of polynomials
- divide polynomials by monic linear polynomials
- state and use the Remainder Theorem and the Factor Theorem
- write the general form of a function that fits a table

The following questions will help you check your understanding.

7. a. Find the quotient and remainder when you divide $p(x) = x^3 - 8x^2 + 3x - 5$ by $x + 3$.

   b. Use your answer to find $p(-3)$.

8. Find the number a such that $x - 2$ is a factor of $p(x) = x^3 + 3x^2 + 4x + a$.

9. Find the numbers B and C such that $x^2 - 8x = (x - 1)^2 + B(x - 1) + C$.

In **Investigation 2D,** you learned how to

- factor polynomials by scaling and by finding roots
- factor polynomials using the sums and differences of squares and cubes
- factor polynomials by grouping and by identifying quadratic-like or cubic-like polynomials

The following questions will help you check your understanding.

10. Factor each polynomial over $\mathbb{Z}$.

   a. $4x^2 + 4x - 3$

   b. $6x^2 + 23x + 21$

   c. $36x^2 - 49y^2$

   d. $3(x - 2)^2 + 5(x - 2) + 2$

   e. $x^3 + 8$

   f. $x^3 - 2x^2 + 3x - 6$

11. Factor each polynomial over $\mathbb{R}$.

   a. $x^4 - 2x^2 + 1$

   b. $x^2 - x - 4$

12. Write each expression as a single rational expression.

   a. $\dfrac{2}{x - 4} + \dfrac{x}{x + 4}$

   b. $2 - \dfrac{x + 3}{x - 2}$

Multiple Choice

1. Use functions f and g below.

   $$f(x) = 2x - 3$$
   $$g(x) = 4x + 1$$

   Which value is equal to $f \circ g(3)$?

   A. 3

   B. 13

   C. 23

   D. 39

2. Suppose $f(x) = \sqrt[3]{x} + 1$. Which expression is equal to $f^{-1}(x)$?

   A. $x^3 - 1$

   B. $(x - 1)^3$

   C. $-\sqrt[3]{x} - 1$

   D. $(x + 1)^3$

3. Suppose the graph of $f: x \mapsto A(x - 2)(x - 3)$ contains the points $(2, 0)$, $(3, 0)$, and $(4, -6)$. What is the value of A?

   A. -6

   B. -3

   C. $-\frac{1}{3}$

   D. 3

4. When you divide $p(x) = 2x^3 - 3x^2 + 5x - 1$ by $x - 2$, what is the remainder?

   A. -1

   B. 0

   C. 13

   D. 36

5. Which expression is the factored form of $x^3 - 8$?

   A. $(x + 2)(x^2 + 2x + 4)$

   B. $(x - 2)^3$

   C. $(x - 2)(x^2 + 2x + 4)$

   D. $(x - 2)(x^2 + 4x + 4)$

Open Response

6. The functions f and g are defined as

   $$f(x) = \frac{2x + 1}{3}$$
   $$g(x) = x^2 - 1$$

   a. Find $f \circ g(x)$.

   b. Find $g \circ f(x)$.

   c. Find the inverse of f. Show that $f \circ f^{-1}(x) = x$.

7. Find a polynomial function in normal form that agrees with the table.

Input, x	Output, $f(x)$
1	4
2	-2
3	20

8. **a.** Find the quotient and remainder when you divide $f(x) = 2x^3 + 4x^2 - 5x + 6$ by $x - 3$.

   b. Use your answer to find $f(3)$.

9. Factor each polynomial over $\mathbb{Z}$.

   a. $8x^2 + 22x + 15$

   b. $x^4 - 13x^2 + 36$

   c. $x^3 + 1$

10. Find the difference.

    $$\frac{x}{x + 3} - \frac{3}{x - 2}$$

11. Write the piecewise-defined function for this graph.

    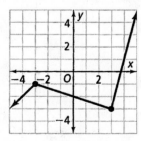

Cumulative Review

1. Which of the following recursive functions best fits the data in the table?

Input, n	Output, $a(n)$
0	3
1	5
2	7
3	9
4	11

A. $a(n) = \begin{cases} 0 & \text{if } n = 0 \\ a(n-1) & \text{if } n > 0 \end{cases}$

B. $a(n) = \begin{cases} 3 & \text{if } n = 0 \\ a(n-1) + 2 & \text{if } n > 0 \end{cases}$

C. $a(n) = \begin{cases} 3 & \text{if } n = 0 \\ a(n-1) + 1 & \text{if } n > 0 \end{cases}$

D. $a(n) = \begin{cases} 0 & \text{if } n = 0 \\ a(n-1) + 2 & \text{if } n > 0 \end{cases}$

2. The input-output table below models a function with a constant first difference. Find $a(50)$ and $a(100)$.

Input, n	Output, $a(n)$
0	58
1	■
2	■
3	■
4	■
5	−22

3. Which line best fits the data in the graph?

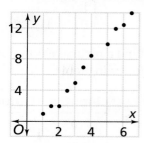

A. $y = \frac{3}{2}x - 1$

B. $y = 2x + 1$

C. $y = 2.5x - 2$

D. $y = x - 3$

4. Evaluate $\frac{2n!}{(n-1)!}$ for each value.

a. $n = 100$

b. $n = 500$

5. Molly took out a loan for college and is making more than the minimum monthly payment each month. Molly's loan was for $20,000. Her interest rate is 3.5% and she pays $400 per month. How long will it take Molly to pay off the loan?

A. 50 months

B. 52 months

C. 55 months

D. 60 months

6. Copy and complete the difference table.

Input, n	Output, $a(n)$	Δ	Δ^2
0	■	8	3
1	12	■	3
2	■	■	3
3	■	■	
4	■		

7. Make a difference table for the following function from $n = 0$ to $n = 4$. Include enough columns to show a constant difference. Use your table to find a closed-form function that agrees with the inputs and outputs in the table.

$$f(n) = \begin{cases} 1 & \text{if } n = 0 \\ f(n-1) + 2n + 1 & \text{if } n > 0 \end{cases}$$

8. Find a recursive function that agrees with the following table.

Input, n	Output, $a(n)$
0	2
1	4
2	12
3	48
4	240

9. Find the mean absolute error, mean squared error, and standard error for this data set, using the line with equation $y = x - 1$.

x	y
0	-3
1	-1
2	2
3	4
4	5

10. Find the line of slope 2 that has the least standard error for the data set below.

x	y
2	3
5	7
8	12
11	15
14	19

11. Find the line of best fit for the data set below.

x	y
3	48
7	27
9	15
14	9
20	1

12. Make a table for this function for $n = 1$ to $n = 10$. Then find closed-form and recursive functions that agree with your table.

$$r(n) = \frac{(n+1)!}{2(n-1)!}$$

13. Joan took out a loan for $12,000 from her parents to buy a used car. She agreed to pay back the loan over 4 years.

   a. At first, Joan's parents do not want to charge interest. What would be her monthly payment on a 0% interest loan?

   b. Joan feels she should pay some interest. After discussing it, her parents decide that 5% interest is reasonable. What are Joan's monthly payments under this agreement?

   c. How much interest in all will Joan pay?

14. Thomas can put $2500 down and pay $450 per month for a new car. He has qualified for a four-year, 3% loan. What is the most expensive car he can afford?

15. Use functions f and g below to find each value.

$$f(x) = x^2 + 1$$
$$g(x) = 2x - 3$$

   a. $f(-1)$

   b. $f \circ g(4)$

   c. $g \circ f(x)$

   d. $g^{-1}(x)$

16. The graph of $f : x \mapsto A(x + 2)(x - 3)$ passes through points $(0, -18)$, $(-2, 0)$ and $(3, 0)$. Find the value of A.

17. What is the remainder when you divide $p(x) = 2x^3 - 3x^2 + x - 2$ by $x + 2$?

18. Factor each expression.

   a. $27x^3 - 64$

   b. $125x^3 + 8y^3$

19. Given the function $f(x) = -3x + 1$, find its inverse and show that $f \circ f^{-1}(x) = x$.

20. Find a polynomial function in normal form that agrees with the following table.

Input, x	Output, $p(x)$
0	3
1	7
2	15

21. Use the polynomial $p(x) = -x^3 + 2x^2 + 3x - 1$.

   a. Find the quotient and remainder when $p(x)$ is divided by $x + 3$.

   b. Use your answer to find $p(-3)$.

22. Factor each polynomial over $\mathbb{Z}$.

   a. $12x^2 - 3x - 9$

   b. $10x^2 + 11x + 3$

   c. $x^8 - 5x^4 + 4$

23. Does $x^6 + 64$ factor over $\mathbb{Z}$? Explain.

24. Find each sum or difference.

   a. $2 + \frac{x-1}{x+1}$

   b. $\frac{3x}{2x+3} - 1$

Chapter 3

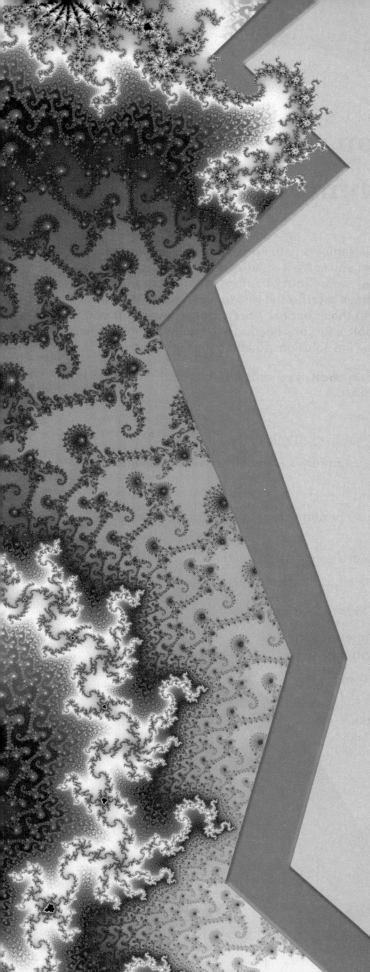

Complex Numbers

Fractals are self-similar geometric objects. This means that if you zoom in on a picture of a fractal, you will see small-scale details similar to the large-scale characteristics of the whole shape. Fractals have incredibly complex boundaries that reveal even more complexity under magnification.

One particularly beautiful and famous fractal is the Mandelbrot set. This set develops from a series of repeated calculations with complex numbers. Images of the Mandelbrot set often have color. The shading assigned to each point is based on the number of repeated calculations at that point required to achieve a particular goal.

Vocabulary

- argument, arg z
- complex numbers, $\mathbb{C}$
- complex plane
- conjugate, $\bar{z}$
- direction
- Fundamental Theorem of Algebra

- irrational numbers
- magnitude, $|z|$
- natural numbers, $\mathbb{N}$
- roots of unity
- $i\left(\sqrt{-1}\right)$
- $a + bi$ (complex number)

Introduction to Complex Numbers

In *Introduction to Complex Numbers*, you will begin your exploration of complex numbers. When you solve a quadratic equation, you sometimes end up with the square root of a negative number in your solution. In the past, you have interpreted this to mean that there are no real-number solutions to the equation. That is true. However, if you expand your set of allowable solutions beyond the real numbers to the complex numbers, you can find solutions to all quadratic equations.

By the end of this investigation, you will be able to answer questions like these.

1. What are complex numbers?

2. What two numbers have a sum of 20 and a product of 109?

3. How can you use complex numbers to solve any quadratic equation?

You will learn how to

- understand the set of complex numbers as an extension of the real numbers

- use complex numbers as tools for solving equations

- be fluent in complex number arithmetic

You will develop these habits and skills:

- Think like an algebraist by examining extensions of number systems.

- Work with properties of complex numbers.

- Prove facts about operations on complex numbers and their conjugates.

In the Flammarion woodcut, a man peers beyond the familiar world. In this chapter, you will explore beyond $\mathbb{R}$.

Activating Prior Knowledge
Exploring New Ideas

You can construct a quadratic equation by using the sum and product of its roots.

For You to Explore

1. **a.** Is there a real number with a square -16? Explain.

   b. Is there a real number with a square -1? Explain.

2. The quadratic equation $x^2 - 12x + 27 = 0$ has two roots.

   a. What is the sum of the roots?   **b.** What is the product of the roots?

   c. What is the sum of the squares of the roots?

3. The quadratic equation $x^2 - 12x + 34 = 0$ has two roots.

   a. What is the sum of the roots?   **b.** What is the product of the roots?

   c. What is the sum of the squares of the roots?

4. **a.** Show that the identity $x^2 + y^2 = (x + y)^2 - 2xy$ is true.

   b. **Take It Further** Write $x^3 + y^3$ in terms of the expressions $(x + y)$ and xy.

5. For each quadratic equation, find the sum of the roots, the product of the roots, and the sum of the squares of the roots.

   a. $x^2 - 12x + 35 = 0$ **b.** $x^2 - 12x + 32 = 0$

   c. $x^2 - 12x + 33 = 0$ **d.** $x^2 + 12x + 32 = 0$

   e. $x^2 - 25 = 0$ **f.** $x^2 - 10 = 0$

   g. $x^2 + 8x - 33 = 0$

6. For the general monic quadratic $x^2 + bx + c$, find each quantity in terms of the coefficients b and c.

   a. the sum of the roots   **b.** the product of the roots

   c. the sum of the squares of the roots

7. **Take It Further** For each quadratic equation, find the sum of the cubes of the roots.

   a. $x^2 - 12x + 35 = 0$ **b.** $x^2 - 12x + 32 = 0$

   c. $x^2 - 12x + 33 = 0$

8. Consider the quadratic $x^2 - 14x + 50$.

   a. If two real numbers sum to 14, what is their largest possible product?

   b. What happens if you use the quadratic formula to solve $x^2 - 14x + 50 = 0$?

Habits of Mind

Establish a process.
Can you find the sum of the cubes of the roots without finding the roots?

Exercises *Practicing Habits of Mind*

On Your Own

9. Suppose $a + b = 14$ and $ab = 47$. Find the value of $a^2 + b^2$ in two ways.

    a. Use the identity from Problem 4.   **b.** Find a and b first.

10. Write About It Decide whether each statement is true or false. Explain.

    a. If $r + s$ is an integer, and rs is an integer, then $r^2 + s^2$ is an integer.

    b. If $r + s$ and rs are integers, then r and s are integers.

11. Explain why the graph of $y = x^2 - 10x + 29$ cannot cross the x-axis.

12. Suppose $a + b = 10$ and $ab = 29$.

    a. Find the value of $a^2 + b^2$. Use the identity from Problem 4.

    b. What happens if you try to find $a^2 + b^2$ by finding a and b first?

> What happens if you use the quadratic formula to find the roots of $x^2 - 10x + 29 = 0$?

13. Take It Further The quadratic $x^2 - 10x + 22$ has two roots. Find a quadratic with roots that are the *squares* of the roots of $x^2 - 10x + 22$.

14. Find two numbers with sum p and product q.

    a. $p = 7, q = 10$ **b.** $p = 2, q = -15$ **c.** $p = 2, q = \frac{3}{4}$ **d.** $p = 2, q = -1$

    e. Take It Further Express the two numbers in terms of p and q.

> These problems are all sum-and-product problems. However, you need different types of numbers for each one. Can you determine which type of numbers you need in each case?

Maintain Your Skills

15. Expand each expression.

    a. $(\sqrt{7} + \sqrt{3})(\sqrt{7} - \sqrt{3})$ **b.** $(\sqrt{5} + \sqrt{2})(\sqrt{5} - \sqrt{2})$

    c. $(3 + \sqrt{7})(3 - \sqrt{7})$ **d.** $(2\sqrt{3} + \sqrt{5})(2\sqrt{3} - \sqrt{5})$

    e. $(\sqrt{m} + \sqrt{n})(\sqrt{m} - \sqrt{n})$ **f.** $(a + \sqrt{b})(a - \sqrt{b})$

> Give exact answers, not decimal approximations.

16. Rewrite each fraction so that it has an integer denominator.

    a. $\dfrac{1}{\sqrt{7} + \sqrt{3}}$ **b.** $\dfrac{1}{\sqrt{5} + \sqrt{2}}$

17. Simplify each expression without using a calculator.

    a. $(\sqrt{2})^2 + (-\sqrt{2})^2$ **b.** $(1 + \sqrt{2})^2 + (1 - \sqrt{2})^2$

    c. $\sqrt{2} \cdot \sqrt{5}$ **d.** $\sqrt{3} \cdot \sqrt{5}$ **e.** $\sqrt{7} \cdot \sqrt{7}$

    f. $(b\sqrt{2}) \cdot (b\sqrt{2})$ **g.** $\sqrt{a} \cdot \sqrt{b}$ **h.** $\sqrt{k} \cdot \sqrt{k}$

3.02 Extending Number Systems

The set of complex numbers is a number system that is an extension of the real numbers. In this lesson, you will examine why and how such extensions come about.

The earliest records of mathematics point to the system of counting numbers (1, 2, 3, . . .) and the operations of addition and multiplication. This system of counting numbers is referred to as the **natural numbers,** $\mathbb{N}$.

This system is closed under addition and multiplication. If you add or multiply two counting numbers, the result is a counting number. The counting numbers are not closed under other operations, but the results may still have meaning. This leads to extensions of $\mathbb{N}$.

- Consider $3 - 5 + 8$. The result is 6, but $3 - 5$ is not a counting number. So, you must "dip into" negative numbers in the middle of this calculation. However, the original expression and its result are both in $\mathbb{N}$. This type of calculation leads to the system of integers, $\mathbb{Z}$.

- Consider $28 \div 5 \times 10$. The result is 56, but $28 \div 5$, or $\frac{28}{5}$, is not an integer. This leads to the system of rational numbers, $\mathbb{Q}$. The rational numbers are closed under addition, subtraction, multiplication, and division (except division by 0).

> $\mathbb{Q}$ stands for "quotient." $\mathbb{Q}$ consists of all numbers $\frac{p}{q}$ where p and q are integers and $q \neq 0$.

Developing Habits of Mind

Experiment. You can define new numbers and incorporate them into an existing number system by extending the rules of calculation.

For example, start with $\mathbb{N}$ and extend to include 0, the identity for addition. Now you can define other numbers by how they operate under addition and multiplication.

- -5 is a new number defined by the fact that when you add it to 5, you get 0.

- $\frac{1}{5}$ is a new number defined by the fact that when you multiply it by 5, you get 1.

A number is something you can point to on the number line. The number line is a representation of all real numbers. Real numbers contain the rational numbers $\mathbb{Q}$ and **irrational numbers** that you cannot express as a quotient of integers. Irrational numbers include numbers such as $\sqrt{2}$ and π.

> **Remember...**
> Use $\mathbb{R}$ to represent the real numbers. So, you have $\mathbb{N}$, $\mathbb{Z}$, $\mathbb{Q}$, and $\mathbb{R}$.

You have already seen problems where even real numbers are not enough. Take a closer look at Exercise 12 in Lesson 3.01.

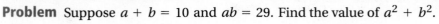

Example

Problem Suppose $a + b = 10$ and $ab = 29$. Find the value of $a^2 + b^2$.

Solution 1 Use the identity $x^2 + y^2 = (x + y)^2 - 2xy$.

If $a + b = 10$ and $ab = 29$, then

$$
\begin{aligned}
a^2 + b^2 &= (a + b)^2 - 2ab \\
&= 10^2 - 2 \cdot 29 \\
&= 100 - 58 \\
&= 42
\end{aligned}
$$

The value of $a^2 + b^2$ is 42.

Solution 2 Another idea is to find a and b first. Think of it as a sum-and-product problem. If $a + b = 10$ and $ab = 29$, then a and b are the two roots of the equation $x^2 - 10x + 29 = 0$.

To find a and b, use the quadratic formula. This results in two strange-looking roots.

$$
\frac{10 \pm \sqrt{100 - 4 \cdot 29}}{2} = \frac{10 \pm \sqrt{100 - 116}}{2} = \frac{10 \pm \sqrt{-16}}{2}
$$

The expression $\sqrt{-16}$ seems to make no sense because there is no real number with square -16. But suppose that the roots are numbers. So, there are two numbers a and b.

$$
a = \frac{10 + \sqrt{-16}}{2} \quad \text{and} \quad b = \frac{10 - \sqrt{-16}}{2}
$$

There are still several steps to do to show that $a^2 + b^2 = 42$. Consider this method a work in progress.

> **Remember...**
>
> An *identity* is an equation that is true for any substitution for its variables.

> In algebra, you sometimes make believe certain numbers exist to help you solve problems.

For Discussion

1. What steps might you try next to show that $a^2 + b^2 = 42$? Do you have to make any assumptions about how $\sqrt{-16}$ behaves?

Often a problem and its solution are in the same number system, but the process of solving the problem requires you to leave the system. Sometimes you must invent new objects that cancel out at the end of the process.

Gradually, mathematicians regarded numbers such as $\sqrt{-16}$ as more than just convenient devices that might cancel out in a calculation. Mathematicians found more and more uses for such numbers. These types of numbers fill in many of the algebraic holes in $\mathbb{R}$, in a way similar to how the numbers in $\mathbb{R}$ fill in the geometric holes in $\mathbb{Q}$.

In this chapter you will work with square roots of negative numbers until you begin to feel comfortable working with them. Then you can use them to solve problems in algebra and geometry.

> **Habits of Mind**
>
> **Look for relationships.** Sometimes, you get answers that are familiar, but the computations go through unfamiliar territory. Other times, you get answers that come from unfamiliar territory.

Exercises *Practicing Habits of Mind*

Check Your Understanding

1. For each equation, find the solutions, if any, that are in $\mathbb{N}$ (the natural numbers).

   a. $x^2 + 24 = 10x$ **b.** $x^2 = 10x$

   c. $x^2 + 10x + 24 = 0$ **d.** $24x^2 + 1 = 10x$

   e. $x^2 = 10$ **f.** $x^2 + 10 = 0$

   g. $x^2 + x + 1 = 0$ **h.** $x^3 = 1$

2. For each equation in Exercise 1, find the solutions, if any, that are in $\mathbb{Z}$ (the integers) but not in $\mathbb{N}$.

3. For each equation in Exercise 1, find the solutions, if any, that are in $\mathbb{Q}$ (the rational numbers) but not in $\mathbb{Z}$.

4. For each equation in Exercise 1, find the solutions, if any, that are in $\mathbb{R}$ (the real numbers) but not in $\mathbb{Q}$.

5. For each equation in Exercise 1, find the solutions, if any, that are not in $\mathbb{R}$.

6. For each equation, determine the number of real solutions.

   a. $x^2 + 4x + 3 = 0$ **b.** $x^2 + 4x + 4 = 0$

   c. $x^2 + 4x + 5 = 0$ **d.** $3x^2 - 10x + 8 = 0$

7. Graph each equation. Find the coordinates of all intercepts.

   a. $y = x^2 + 4x + 3$ **b.** $y = x^2 + 4x + 4$

   c. $y = x^2 + 4x + 5$ **d.** $y = 3x^2 - 10x + 8$

> **Remember...**
> An intercept is a point where a graph crosses either the *x*- or *y*-axis.

8. Suppose there is a number i with square -1.

   a. Simplify $(1 + i)^2 - 2(1 + i) + 2$.

   b. Explain why the number $1 + i$ is a solution of the equation $x^2 - 2x + 2 = 0$.

> Every time you see an i^2, replace it with -1.

9. Use the function $a(n)$. The domain is the whole numbers $\{0, 1, 2, 3, \ldots\}$.

$$a(n) = (\sqrt{3})^n + (-\sqrt{3})^n$$

   a. Find $a(n)$ for $n = 0$ through $n = 6$.

   b. Find $a(10)$ and $a(101)$.

   c. Is there a polynomial that agrees with this function a on all of $\mathbb{N}$? Explain.

10. Use the function $f(n)$. The domain is the whole numbers $\{0, 1, 2, 3, \ldots\}$.

$$f(n) = (1 + \sqrt{2})^n + (1 - \sqrt{2})^n$$

Determine whether each number is rational or irrational.

a. $(1 + \sqrt{2})^0$ **b.** $(1 + \sqrt{2})^1$ **c.** $(1 + \sqrt{2})^2$

d. Find $f(n)$ for $n = 0$ through $n = 6$.

e. Find an equation with integer coefficients that has $1 + \sqrt{2}$ as a solution.

f. **Take It Further** Show that $f(n) = 2f(n - 1) + f(n - 2)$ for any positive integer $n > 2$.

11. Suppose there is a number $\sqrt{-1}$, with square -1, that obeys the basic rules of arithmetic. The domain of the function $g(n)$ below is the whole numbers.

$$g(n) = (2 + \sqrt{-1})^n + (2 - \sqrt{-1})^n$$

For convenience, you might use some letter instead of $\sqrt{-1}$. Many people use i.

a. Find $g(n)$ for $n = 0$ through $n = 6$.

b. Show that $(2 + \sqrt{-1})^2 = 3 + 4\sqrt{-1}$.

c. Find an equation with integer coefficients that has $2 + \sqrt{-1}$ as a root.

d. **Take It Further** Show that $g(n) = 4g(n - 1) - 5g(n - 2)$ for any positive integer $n > 2$.

On Your Own

12. For each case, give two examples of a calculation with two numbers.

a. The inputs are not positive integers, but the result is a positive integer.

b. The inputs are not integers, but the result is an integer.

c. The inputs are not rational numbers, but the result is a rational number.

d. The inputs are not real numbers, but the result is a real number.

e. The inputs are positive integers, but the result is not a positive integer.

f. The inputs are integers, but the result is not an integer.

g. The inputs are rational numbers, but the result is not a rational number.

h. The inputs are real numbers, but the result is not a real number.

13. For each equation, find the solutions, if any, that are in $\mathbb{N}$.

a. $x^2 + 5 = 6x$ **b.** $x^2 + 6x + 5 = 0$ **c.** $x^2 + 4x = -2$

d. $5x^2 + x = 6$ **e.** $x^2 = 5$ **f.** $x^2 + 11 = 6x$

14. For each equation in Exercise 13, find the solutions, if any, that meet the given condition.

a. in $\mathbb{Z}$ but not in $\mathbb{N}$ **b.** in $\mathbb{Q}$ but not in $\mathbb{Z}$

c. in $\mathbb{R}$ but not in $\mathbb{Q}$ **d.** not in $\mathbb{R}$

Go Online
Pearsonsuccessnet.com

15. Calculate the sum and product of each pair of numbers.

    a. 13 and -23

    b. $1 + 3$ and $1 - 3$

    c. $1 + \sqrt{3}$ and $1 - \sqrt{3}$

    d. $1 + \sqrt{n}$ and $1 - \sqrt{n}$

    e. $1 + \sqrt{-3}$ and $1 - \sqrt{-3}$

> You should give the answers for Exercise 15d in terms of n.

16. **Standardized Test Prep** What is the product of $3 + \sqrt{-2}$ and $3 - \sqrt{-2}$?

    A. 1   **B.** 7   **C.** 9   **D.** 11

Maintain Your Skills

17. Decide whether each calculation results in a real number. Explain.

    a. $(2 + \sqrt{-1}) + (2 - \sqrt{-1})$

    b. $(2 + \sqrt{-1}) - (2 - \sqrt{-1})$

    c. $(2 + \sqrt{-1})(2 + \sqrt{-1})$

    d. $(2 + \sqrt{-1})(2 - \sqrt{-1})$

    e. $\dfrac{2 + \sqrt{-1}}{2 + \sqrt{-1}}$

> Again, assume you have a number $\sqrt{-1}$ that obeys the basic rules of arithmetic.

18. Suppose $x^2 = -1$. Write each expression in the form $A + Bx$, for real numbers A and B.

    a. $(2 + 3x) + (5 + 6x)$ **b.** $(2 + 3x) + (2 - 3x)$ **c.** $(2 + 3x) - (2 - 3x)$

    d. $(2 + 3x)(5 + 6x)$ **e.** $(2 + 3x)^2$ **f.** $(2 + 3x)(2 - 3x)$

Go Online
Pearsonsuccessnet.com

Historical Perspective

Square roots of negative numbers were first studied in the early 1500s. Mathematicians wanted to find a formula, similar to the quadratic formula, to solve cubic equations. Girolamo Cardano (1501–1576), Nicolo Tartaglia (1500–1557), and others developed and refined such a formula.

When they applied the formula to cubic functions with real roots, such as $x^3 - 15x - 4$, they ended up with expressions involving square roots of negative numbers.

The mathematicians did not let this strange result stop them. They imagined that they could calculate with these expressions, using the basic rules and the theorems of algebra.

Girolamo Cardano   Nicolo Tartaglia

Making the Extension: $\sqrt{-1}$

To find two numbers with a sum of 4 and a product of 16, you can solve the quadratic equation $x^2 - 4x + 16 = 0$. Use the quadratic formula to find the two solutions.

$$x = \frac{4 \pm \sqrt{4^2 - 4 \cdot 16}}{2} = \frac{4 \pm \sqrt{-48}}{2}$$

Because you cannot take the square root of a negative number in the real number system, no real solutions exist for the equation. So you cannot find two real numbers with a sum of 4 and a product of 16. However, if you allow for square roots of negatives, the two roots you found with the quadratic formula may solve the problem.

For You to Do

Evaluate each expression.

1. $\dfrac{4 + \sqrt{-48}}{2} + \dfrac{4 - \sqrt{-48}}{2}$

2. $\dfrac{4 + \sqrt{-48}}{2} \cdot \dfrac{4 - \sqrt{-48}}{2}$

> Assume that the basic rules for calculating with numbers still work, and that $(\sqrt{-48})^2 = -48$.

Example

Problem Rewrite $\dfrac{4 + \sqrt{-48}}{2}$ as an expression without a denominator.

Solution Note that $-48 = 16 \cdot -3$.

$$\sqrt{-48} = \sqrt{16 \cdot -3} = \sqrt{16} \cdot \sqrt{-3} = 4\sqrt{-3}$$

Rewrite $\sqrt{-48}$ to simplify the expression.

$$\frac{4 + \sqrt{-48}}{2} = \frac{4 + 4\sqrt{-3}}{2}$$
$$= \frac{2(2 + 2\sqrt{-3})}{2}$$
$$= 2 + 2\sqrt{-3}$$

Developing Habits of Mind

Check your work. Look more carefully at the calculation below.

$$\sqrt{-48} \overset{(1)}{=} \sqrt{16 \cdot -3} \overset{(2)}{=} \sqrt{16} \cdot \sqrt{-3} \overset{(3)}{=} 4\sqrt{-3}$$

Step (1) and Step (3) seem fine. But is Step (2) legitimate? Is the square root of a product always equal to the product of the square roots? It is true when the numbers are positive, but that is because of a convention. There are two numbers with a square 9, but we defined the symbol $\sqrt{9}$ to mean the positive number with a square 9.

You can use the "duck principle" to see if the ends of the calculation agree. Do you get -48 when you square $4\sqrt{-3}$?

$$(4\sqrt{-3})^2 = 4\sqrt{-3} \cdot 4\sqrt{-3} = 16 \cdot \sqrt{-3} \cdot \sqrt{-3} = 16 \cdot (-3) = -48$$

Since $\sqrt{-3} \cdot \sqrt{-3} = -3$, it seems reasonable for you to say that $\sqrt{-48} = 4\sqrt{-3}$. But what happens when both square roots are of negative numbers?

> The duck principle: If it walks like a duck and quacks like a duck, then it probably is a duck.

For Discussion

3. Find the value of $\sqrt{-12} \cdot \sqrt{-3}$.

4. Find the value of $\sqrt{-12} \cdot \sqrt{-12}$.

Minds in Action   episode 10

Tony and Sasha debate their answers to the For Discussion problems.

Tony   I solved the first one. It's 6.

Sasha   I solved it too. It's -6.

Tony   Well, then you're wrong. It can't be both 6 *and* -6.

Sasha   No, you're wrong. I replaced $\sqrt{-12}$ with $2\sqrt{-3}$ and calculated.

$$\sqrt{-12}\sqrt{-3} = \sqrt{4 \cdot -3}\sqrt{-3} = \sqrt{4}\sqrt{-3}\sqrt{-3} = 2\sqrt{-3} \cdot \sqrt{-3}$$

The square roots $\sqrt{-3}$ and $\sqrt{-3}$ multiply to make -3. Then 2 times -3 is -6, and that's the answer.

Tony   Hmm. That looks pretty solid, actually.

Sasha   As I said, I'm right and you're wrong. What did you do?

Tony   I used the fact that $\sqrt{a}$ times $\sqrt{b}$ is $\sqrt{ab}$. So, $\sqrt{-12} \cdot \sqrt{-3}$ is the same as $\sqrt{-12 \cdot -3}$. I multiplied and got $\sqrt{36}$. Then $\sqrt{36}$ is 6, and that's my answer.

Sasha Hmm. That looks pretty solid too. That's trouble. Did you get -12 for the second one?

Tony Sure. That one was easier, $\sqrt{x} \cdot \sqrt{x}$ is just x, no matter what x is.

Sasha Why didn't you use the rule you used for the first one?

Tony I don't know, I guess I could have. Then $\sqrt{-12} \cdot \sqrt{-12}$ is the same as $\sqrt{-12 \cdot -12}$. That's . . . uh oh, that's $\sqrt{144}$ which is 12, not -12.

Sasha Maybe you can't trust that $\sqrt{ab}$ rule after all . . .

Sasha and Tony's discussion leads to an important consequence. Known rules for calculation may no longer work in an extended system. The rule $\sqrt{a} \cdot \sqrt{b} = \sqrt{ab}$ works for nonnegative real numbers, but leads to a contradiction when both a and b are negative. Sasha and Tony discovered this contradiction when they compared their answers to Problem 3. Both 6 and -6 seem to make sense as values of $\sqrt{-12} \cdot \sqrt{-3}$. You need a more precise rule for handling square roots of negative numbers.

Think about the square roots of positive numbers. What does $\sqrt{49}$ mean? Your answer may be "a number with a square of 49," but there are two of these, 7 and -7. By convention, people decided that $\sqrt{49}$ represents the positive square root. Once you accept this convention, you can use it to prove theorems such as $\sqrt{a} \cdot \sqrt{b} = \sqrt{ab}$ (when a and b are nonnegative).

> What does this use of *convention* mean?

You need a similar convention for negative numbers in order to avoid Tony and Sasha's contradiction. The following definition does the trick.

- Start with the real numbers, $\mathbb{R}$. $\mathbb{R}$ already contains the square roots of positive numbers.
- Introduce one new number, $\sqrt{-1}$. This is just a symbol. The only property of $\sqrt{-1}$ is that its square is -1.
- If n is positive, define $\sqrt{-n}$ as $\sqrt{-n} = \sqrt{n} \cdot \sqrt{-1}$.

> **Remember...**
>
> You can use the letter i to represent $\sqrt{-1}$.

The following are some examples of numbers using this definition of $\sqrt{-n}$.

$$\sqrt{-4} = \sqrt{4} \cdot \sqrt{-1} = 2\sqrt{-1}$$
$$\sqrt{-6} = \sqrt{6} \cdot \sqrt{-1}$$
$$\sqrt{-100} = 10 \cdot \sqrt{-1}$$

This convention takes care of Tony and Sasha's contradiction. There is only one value for $\sqrt{-12} \cdot \sqrt{-3}$.

$$\sqrt{-12} \cdot \sqrt{-3} = \left(\sqrt{12} \cdot \sqrt{-1}\right) \cdot \left(\sqrt{3} \cdot \sqrt{-1}\right)$$
$$= \left(\sqrt{12} \cdot \sqrt{3}\right) \cdot \left(\sqrt{-1} \cdot \sqrt{-1}\right)$$
$$= \left(\sqrt{12 \cdot 3}\right) \cdot (-1)$$
$$= 6 \cdot -1$$
$$= -6$$

For You to Do

Simplify. Each product is an integer.

5. $\sqrt{-2} \cdot \sqrt{-8}$

6. $\sqrt{-9} \cdot \sqrt{-1}$

7. $\sqrt{-18} \cdot \sqrt{-8}$

The convention eliminates the ambiguity in multiplying square roots of negative numbers. Clearly the theorem $\sqrt{ab} = \sqrt{a} \cdot \sqrt{b}$ stops working in this new system. Moving forward, you will work with *complex numbers.* Complex numbers are expressions of the form

$$a + b\sqrt{-1}$$

where *a* and *b* are real numbers.

In some of the exercises that follow, you will test whether other basic results extend to complex numbers. In others, you will investigate the nature of this new arithmetic.

> You will explore a more formal definition of the complex numbers in the next lesson.

Exercises Practicing Habits of Mind

Check Your Understanding

1. Expand each expression.

   a. $(a + b)(a - b)$

   b. $(a + b\sqrt{2})(a - b\sqrt{2})$

   c. $(a + b\sqrt{3})(a - b\sqrt{3})$

   d. $(a + b\sqrt{c})(a - b\sqrt{c})$

   e. $(a + b\sqrt{-1})(a - b\sqrt{-1})$

2. Sketch the graphs of $y = x^2$ and $y = 6x - 11$. How many times do the graphs intersect?

3. When you include square roots of negative numbers, the equation $x^2 = 6x - 11$ has two solutions.

   a. Find the solutions. Express the solutions without denominators.

   b. Find the sum and the product of the solutions.

4. Does every quadratic equation with real coefficients have a solution if you include square roots of negative numbers? Explain.

5. What two numbers have squares of 34? Provide approximations rounded to the nearest hundredth for these two numbers.

6. Decide whether the following statement is true. Explain.

For every nonnegative real number a, there are two numbers with squares equal to a.

7. Show that the equation $x^3 - 5x^2 + 8x - 6 = 0$ has the following solutions.
$$x = 3, x = 1 + \sqrt{-1}, x = 1 - \sqrt{-1}$$

8. Simplify each expression.

a. $3 + (1 + \sqrt{-1}) + (1 - \sqrt{-1})$

b. $3(1 + \sqrt{-1}) + 3(1 - \sqrt{-1}) + (1 + \sqrt{-1})(1 - \sqrt{-1})$

c. $3(1 + \sqrt{-1})(1 - \sqrt{-1})$

On Your Own

9. Simplify each product.

a. $\sqrt{-4} \cdot \sqrt{-9}$ **b.** $\sqrt{-9} \cdot \sqrt{-4}$

c. $\sqrt{-3} \cdot \sqrt{-27}$ **d.** $\sqrt{-27} \cdot \sqrt{-3}$

e. $(2 + \sqrt{-3}) \cdot \sqrt{-3}$ **f.** $\sqrt{-3} \cdot (2 + \sqrt{-3})$

10. **Write About It** Does the Commutative Property of Multiplication apply to this new arithmetic? Explain. Use examples or proof.

11. Write each expression in the form $a + b\sqrt{-1}$, where a and b are real numbers.

a. $(3 + 4\sqrt{-1}) + (4 + 5\sqrt{-1})$ **b.** $(3 + \sqrt{-16}) + (4 + \sqrt{-25})$

c. $(5 + \sqrt{-1})(5 + 2\sqrt{-1})$ **d.** $(3 + \sqrt{-2}) + (3 - \sqrt{-2})$

e. $(3 + \sqrt{-2})(3 - \sqrt{-2})$

12. **Standardized Test Prep** What are the solutions to $x^2 - 10x + 26 = 0$?

A. $x = 5$ and $x = -5$

B. $x = 5 + \sqrt{2}$ and $x = 5 - \sqrt{2}$

C. $x = 5 + \sqrt{-1}$ and $x = 5 - \sqrt{-1}$

D. $x = 5 + \sqrt{-2}$ and $x = 5 - \sqrt{-2}$

Go Online
Pearsonsuccessnet.com

13. The equation $x^3 - 8 = 0$ has one solution in $\mathbb{R}$, $x = 2$.

When you include square roots of negative numbers, the equation has three solutions.

   a. Factor $x^3 - 8$.

   b. Use the factored form to find all three solutions to the equation $x^3 - 8 = 0$.

   c. Find the three solutions to $x^3 - 1 = 0$.

14. a. Use factoring to find the solutions to the equation $x^3 - 64 = 0$.

   b. Compare the solutions with the solutions to $x^3 - 8 = 0$ and $x^3 - 1 = 0$.

15. Take It Further Find all six solutions to the equation $x^6 - 64 = 0$.

You can start by factoring the left side as a difference of squares.

Maintain Your Skills

16. Simplify each expression.

   a. $(3 + 4\sqrt{-1})(3 - 4\sqrt{-1})$ **b.** $(12 + 5\sqrt{-1})(12 - 5\sqrt{-1})$

   c. $(7 + \sqrt{-1})(7 - \sqrt{-1})$ **d.** $(x + y\sqrt{-1})(x - y\sqrt{-1})$

Go Online
Video Tutor
Pearsonsuccessnet.com

17. Simplify each expression.

   a. $\sqrt{-1} \cdot \sqrt{-1}$ **b.** $\sqrt{-1} \cdot \sqrt{-1} \cdot \sqrt{-1} \cdot \sqrt{-1}$

   c. $(\sqrt{-1})^6$ **d.** $(\sqrt{-1})^8$

   e. $(\sqrt{-1})^9$

Extension to Complex Numbers

Lesson 3.03 introduced the number $\sqrt{-1}$ to allow you to work with square roots of negative numbers. This number is just a symbol defined by its behavior.

$$(\sqrt{-1})^2 = -1$$

Rather than writing $\sqrt{-1}$, you can use the letter i. Again, this is just a symbol defined by its behavior.

If a and b are real numbers, a number written in the form $a + bi$ is a *complex number*. Here is the formal definition.

Definition

The system of **complex numbers** $\mathbb{C}$ consists of all expressions in the form $a + bi$ with the following properties.

- a and b are real numbers.
- $i^2 = -1$
- You can use addition and multiplication as if $a + bi$ were a polynomial.

> A real number is also a complex number. For example, $3 = 3 + 0i$.

For Discussion

1. Explain how you know that i is not a real number.

2. Is $(2 + 3i)(5 - 4i)$ a complex number? Explain.

The following examples show that calculating with complex numbers is very similar to calculating with polynomials.

Example 1

Problem Write each expression as a complex number in the form $a + bi$.

  a. $(3 + 2i) + (2 - 5i)$ **b.** $(3 + 2i) - (2 - 5i)$ **c.** $(3 + 2i)(2 - 5i)$

Solution

  a. Use the associative and commutative properties of addition. Then combine like terms.

$$(3 + 2i) + (2 - 5i) = 3 + 2 + 2i - 5i$$
$$= 5 + (2 - 5)i$$
$$= 5 - 3i$$

b. Distribute the negative. Then combine like terms.

$$(3 + 2i) - (2 - 5i) = 3 + 2i - 2 + 5i$$
$$= 1 + 2i + 5i$$
$$= 1 + 7i$$

c. Multiply. Then combine like terms.

$$(3 + 2i)(2 - 5i) = 6 - 15i + 4i - 10i^2$$
$$= 6 - 11i - 10i^2$$
$$= 6 - 11i - 10(-1)$$
$$= 6 - 11i + 10$$
$$= 16 - 11i$$

Habits of Mind

Establish a process.
Treat the expressions
as polynomials. Use the
basic rules.

Remember...

Replace i^2 with -1.

For You to Do

Write each expression as a complex number in the form $a + bi$.

3. $(10 - 11i) + (3 - 2i)$ **4.** $(5 + 7i) - (5 - 3i)$ **5.** $(3 - 2i)(2 + 5i)$

You can represent a generic complex number with a single letter. So,
if $z = 3 + 2i$ and $w = -1 + i$, you can think about the expressions
$z + w$, which equals $(2 + 3i)$, and zw, which equals $(-5 + i)$.

But, how do you know that there is only one way you can write a complex
number in the form $a + bi$ with a and b real? Maybe you can find other real
numbers x and y such that $x + yi$ is equal to $3 + 2i$. The following theorem
and proof show that you cannot find such numbers.

Theorem 3.1

If a, b, c, and d are real numbers, then $a + bi = c + di$ only when $a = c$
and $b = d$.

Proof Suppose $a + bi = c + di$. Prove that $a = c$ and $b = d$. You can prove this
with indirect reasoning. Suppose $b \neq d$. Then solve the equation for i.

$$a + bi = c + di$$
$$bi - di = c - a$$
$$i = \frac{c - a}{b - d}$$

The expression $\frac{c - a}{b - d}$ represents a real number. This is a contradiction
because i is not a real number. Therefore, b must equal d.

Since $b = d$, then $bi = di$. You can subtract terms bi and di from each side
of the original equation. This leaves $a = c$. So, if $a + bi = c + di$, then
$a = c$ and $b = d$.

Because of Theorem 3.1, there is only one way you can write a complex number as $a + bi$, where a and b are real. So, every complex number is determined by two numbers—its real part and its imaginary part. Using this language, you can state Theorem 3.1 as follows.

Two complex numbers are equal if and only if their real parts are equal and their imaginary parts are equal.

> When you write a complex number in the form $a + bi$, you are expressing the number in standard form.

Example 2

Problem Find the complex number z that satisfies the equation below.

$$z \cdot (2 - i) = 21 + i$$

Solution Write $z = a + bi$ and multiply.

$$
\begin{aligned}
(a + bi)(2 - i) &= 2a - ai + 2bi - bi^2 \\
&= 2a - ai + 2bi + b \\
&= (2a + b) + (-a + 2b)i
\end{aligned}
$$

So, $2a + b = 21$, and $-a + 2b = 1$. Now you have a system of two equations and two unknowns.

$$
\begin{aligned}
2a + b &= 21 \\
-a + 2b &= 1
\end{aligned}
$$

You can solve this system of equations in several ways. One way is to multiply each side of the second equation by 2 and then add.

$$
\begin{array}{r}
2a + b = 21 \\
+ \quad -2a + 4b = 2 \\
\hline
5b = 23 \\
b = \frac{23}{5}
\end{array}
$$

> Complex numbers have two parts, the real part and the imaginary part. So, equations with complex numbers may result in two equations and two unknowns.

You can substitute to find the value $a = \frac{41}{5}$. The complex number z is $\frac{41}{5} + \frac{23}{5}i$.

For You to Do

6. Find the complex number w that satisfies the equation $w + (3 - i) = 4i$.

You have extended $\mathbb{R}$ to include the square roots of all real numbers, keeping the basic rules intact. But you discovered that not all familiar properties hold true in this new number system. For example, you gave up $a^2 \geq 0$. This is similar to giving up the idea that multiplication makes things bigger in passing from $\mathbb{N}$ to $\mathbb{Z}$.

By extending $\mathbb{R}$ to $\mathbb{C}$, you now have a system in which all quadratic equations with real coefficients have roots. Over the centuries, mathematicians discovered that even more is true. $\mathbb{C}$ not only contains all roots of any quadratic equation, it also contains all roots of any polynomial equation with real coefficients. This was a big discovery, and it took mathematicians generations to fully understand its meaning. It is now called the **Fundamental Theorem of Algebra**. It was first proved by Carl Friedrich Gauss in the 1800s.

Go Online
Pearsonsuccessnet.com

Exercises *Practicing Habits of Mind*

Check Your Understanding

1. Simplify each expression. Write your answer in the form $a + bi$, where a and b are real numbers.

   a. $(3 + 2i) + (9 - i)$ **b.** $(3 + 2i)(9 + i)$

   c. $(5 + 2i) + (5 - 2i)$ **d.** $(5 + 2i)(5 - 2i)$

   e. $(4 + 2i) + (2 + 4i)$ **f.** $(4 + 2i)(2 + 4i)$

2. The complex number $3 - 5i$ is the *conjugate* of $3 + 5i$. Simplify each expression involving conjugates.

   a. $(3 + 5i) + (3 - 5i)$ **b.** $(3 + 5i)(3 - 5i)$

   c. $(-7 + 2i) + (-7 - 2i)$ **d.** $(-7 + 2i)(-7 - 2i)$

   e. $(12 + 5i) + (12 - 5i)$ **f.** $(12 + 5i)(12 - 5i)$

3. **a.** What is the conjugate of $(a + bi)$?

   b. Show that when you add a complex number and its conjugate, the result is a real number.

   c. Show that when you multiply a complex number by its conjugate, the result is a real number.

   d. When is the sum of a number and its conjugate 0?

   e. When is the product of a number and its conjugate 0?

4. **What's Wrong Here?** Derman does not think that if two complex numbers are equal, their parts must be equal.

   Derman says, "I've got a really simple counterexample. If $a = i$ and $b = i$, it's the same as having $c = -1$ and $d = 1$. Try it, and you'll see. If $a + bi = c + di$, it doesn't mean $a = c$ and $b = d$."

   What happened? Is Derman correct? Explain.

5. Find the complex number $a + bi$ that satisfies the following equation.

$$(a + bi)(1 + i) = 11 - 3i$$

6. Every real number x has an opposite, a number that when added to x results in a sum of 0.

   a. Does $2 + 3i$ have an opposite? Explain.

   b. What complex numbers have opposites?

7. The conjugate of z is represented by $\overline{z}$. Show that if z and $\overline{z}$ are conjugates, then $z^2 + (\overline{z})^2$ is a real number.

8. **Take It Further** For each part, find an equation with real coefficients that has the listed numbers among its roots. Remember that when you add or multiply a complex number and its conjugate, the result is real.

   a. $3 + 2i$ **b.** $3 - 2i$

   c. $1 + 5i$ and $3 + 2i$ **d.** $1 + 5i$ and $-1 + 5i$

   e. $1 + i\sqrt{3}$ **f.** $\sqrt{2} + \sqrt{3}$

   g. $\sqrt{2} + i\sqrt{3}$

On Your Own

9. **Standardized Test Prep** If a and b are real numbers, what is the product $(a + bi)(b - ai)$?

   A. $(b^2 - a^2)i$ **B.** 0

   C. $2ab$ **D.** $2ab + (b^2 - a^2)i$

10. You can use the rule $i^2 = -1$ to simplify other powers of i.

   a. Express i^3 in simplest form without using an exponent.

   b. Express i^4 in simplest form without using an exponent.

   c. Simplify i^5, i^6, i^7, and i^8.

   d. What is i^{210}?

   e. **Take It Further** Express $\frac{1}{i}$ without a denominator.

11. Solve each equation. The solutions are complex numbers.

   a. $z + (3 - i) = 6 + 2i$ **b.** $w - 3 = 6 + i$

   c. $x^2 = -9$ **d.** $z^2 = 6z - 34$

Go Online
Pearsonsuccessnet.com

12. Find a complex number z such that the product $z \cdot (3 + 2i)$ is a real number.

13. Find a number that meets each set of given conditions. If no such number exists, explain why.

   a. a complex number that is not real

   b. a rational number that is also real

   c. a real number that is not rational

   d. a rational number that is not complex

   e. a real number that is also complex

14. a. Show that $x^2 + 1 = (x + i)(x - i)$.

   b. **Write About It** You may have learned in a previous course that $x^2 + 1$ does not factor. Does this statement contradict part (a)? Explain.

15. a. Use the quadratic formula to find the two solutions to the equation $x^2 - 10x + 34 = 0$.

   b. Find the sum and product of the solutions.

   c. Find the sum of the squares of the solutions.

16. Take It Further Find all complex numbers $a + bi$ that satisfy this equation.
$$(a + bi)^2 = -11 + 60i$$

Maintain Your Skills

17. Find each sum or difference.

   a. $(2 + i) + (3 + i)$ **b.** $(3 + i) + (2 + i)$

   c. $(5 + i) - (4 + 3i)$ **d.** $(4 + 3i) - (5 + i)$

   e. $(5 + 3i) + (8 - 3i)$ **f.** $\left(3 + i\sqrt{2}\right) + \left(3 - i\sqrt{2}\right)$

18. Find each product.

   a. $(2 + i)(3 + i)$ **b.** $(3 + i)(2 + i)$

   c. $(5 + i)(5 - i)$ **d.** $(2 + i)^2$

   e. $(3 + 2i)^2$ **f.** $(4 + i)^2$

19. Find the complex number z that satisfies each equation.

   a. $z \cdot (2 - i) = 3 + i$ **b.** $z \cdot (2 - i) = 6 + 2i$

   c. $z \cdot (2 - i) = 9 + 3i$ **d.** $z \cdot (2 - i) = 5$

   e. $z \cdot (2 - i) = 10$ **f.** $z \cdot (2 - i) = 15$

3.05 Reciprocals and Division

Addition and multiplication of complex numbers share the following important properties with addition and multiplication of polynomials. Let z, w, and u be complex numbers.

Distributive Property: $z(w + u) = zw + zu$

Properties of Addition and Multiplication

Addition	Property	Multiplication
$z + w = w + z$	Commutative	$zw = wz$
$z + (w + u) = (z + w) + u$	Associative	$z(wu) = (zw)u$
$z + 0 = z$	Identity	$z \cdot 1 = z$
z has an opposite in $\mathbb{C}$.	Inverse	You will explore this now.

Developing Habits of Mind

Look for relationships. The fact that these properties hold for complex numbers is not anything magical. Remember the following from the definition of complex numbers in Lesson 3.04.

You can use addition and multiplication as if $a + bi$ were a polynomial.

This more or less forces complex numbers to obey the rules for calculating that hold for polynomials.

Complex numbers have the structure of polynomials and the extra rule $i^2 = -1$. This is enough extra structure to guarantee that every nonzero complex number has a reciprocal. The following definition explains why.

Every complex number $a + bi$ has a **conjugate** $a - bi$. The product of a complex number and its conjugate is a real number. "Taking the conjugate" is the key operation that will allow you to divide complex numbers and to find their reciprocals.

When you extend the playing field, you have to adjust the rules to cover new situations.

Example 1

Problem Find the complex number z that satisfies $z \cdot (2 - i) = 21 + i$.

Solution In Lesson 3.04, you solved the same problem using a system of equations. It is simpler to solve using conjugates. Multiply the left and right sides of the equation by the conjugate of $(2 - i)$, which is $(2 + i)$.

$$z \cdot (2 - i) = 21 + i$$

$$z \cdot (2 - i)(2 + i) = (21 + i)(2 + i)$$

$$z \cdot 5 = 41 + 23i$$

The reason you want to multiply by $2 + i$ is that the product $(2 - i)(2 + i)$ is the real number 5. To solve the new equation $5z = 41 + 23i$, you just divide each side by 5.

$$z = \frac{41 + 23i}{5}$$

> You can also express this number as $\frac{41}{5} + \frac{23}{5}i$.

Multiplying a complex number by its conjugate always results in a real number. This property is the key to simplifying fractions involving complex numbers.

Example 2

Problem Express $\frac{18 + i}{3 - 4i}$ in the form $a + bi$.

Solution The denominator is a complex number. If you multiply the denominator by its conjugate, $3 + 4i$, the result is a real number. Since you do not want to affect the value of the original fraction, multiply both the numerator and the denominator by $3 + 4i$.

$$\frac{18 + i}{3 - 4i} \cdot \frac{3 + 4i}{3 + 4i} = \frac{50 + 75i}{25} = 2 + 3i$$

The fraction simplifies to $2 + 3i$. You can multiply to check the result.

$$(2 + 3i)(3 - 4i) = 6 - 8i + 9i - 12i^2 = 18 + i$$

Since $(2 + 3i)(3 - 4i) = 18 + i$, it is also true that $\frac{18 + i}{3 - 4i} = 2 + 3i$.

Remember...

When you multiply the numerator and denominator of a fraction by the same number, you are multiplying the fraction by 1.

For You to Do

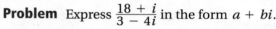

1. Find the reciprocal of $2 + 3i$.

Represent conjugates. The symbol $\overline{z}$ represents the conjugate of z. This notation helps you to describe more simply the relationships between complex numbers and their conjugates. For example, you can state the multiplication property from this lesson in an abbreviated manner.

$$z\overline{z} \text{ is a real number.}$$

> $z\overline{z}$ is the product of a complex number and its conjugate.

Conjugation is a function in which the input is a complex number and the output is a complex number. Here is a statement you will prove in the exercises.

$$\overline{z + w} = \overline{z} + \overline{w}$$

This statement illustrates the order of operations. The left side is the result of adding two complex numbers and then taking the conjugate. The right side is the result of taking both conjugates and adding them together.

Some of the exercises ask you to find or prove other statements about conjugation.

For Discussion

2. Suppose z is some nonzero complex number. Show that z has a reciprocal in $\mathbb{C}$. Does 0 have a reciprocal? Explain.

You can now complete the Properties of Addition and Multiplication table from the beginning of the lesson. For the Inverse Property under multiplication, you can include the following statement.

$$\text{If } z \neq 0, \text{ then } z \text{ has a reciprocal in } \mathbb{C}.$$

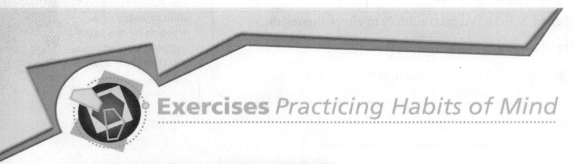

Exercises *Practicing Habits of Mind*

Check Your Understanding

1. Rewrite the following statement using z and $\overline{z}$.

The sum of a complex number and its conjugate is a real number.

2. a. What is the conjugate of $2i$? **b.** What is the conjugate of 7?

   c. Show that the statement $\overline{z + w} = \overline{z} + \overline{w}$ is true when $z = 2i$ and $w = 7$.

3. Suppose $z = a + bi$ and $w = c + di$.

   a. Write expressions for $\overline{z}$ and $\overline{w}$.

   b. Prove that $\overline{z + w} = \overline{z} + \overline{w}$ is true for any complex numbers z and w.

Remember...

A real number is also a complex number.

4. Suppose $z = 3 + 2i$ and $w = 4 - 5i$. Write each of the following as $r + si$, where r and s are real numbers.

   a. $\overline{z}$
   b. $\overline{(\overline{z})}$
   c. $\overline{z + w}$
   d. $\overline{z} + \overline{w}$

   e. $\overline{zw}$
   f. $(\overline{z})(\overline{w})$
   g. $z + \overline{z}$
   h. $w\overline{w}$

5. Express each fraction in the form $a + bi$.

   a. $\dfrac{11 - 3i}{1 + i}$
         b. $\dfrac{4 + i}{2 - i}$

   c. $\dfrac{8 + 4i}{2 + i}$
         d. $\dfrac{3 + i}{3 - i}$

   e. $\dfrac{3 - i}{3 + i}$
         f. Take It Further $\dfrac{c + di}{a + bi}$

6. Find each product.

   a. $(3 + 4i)(5 + 6i)$
         b. $(3 - 4i)(5 - 6i)$

   c. $(2 + 7i)(8 - 3i)$
         d. $(2 - 7i)(8 + 3i)$

   e. $(-10 + 3i)(2 - 7i)$
         f. $(-10 - 3i)(2 + 7i)$

7. The results in Exercise 6 suggest the following relationship for conjugates.

$$\overline{zw} = (\overline{z})(\overline{w})$$

Prove that this statement is true for any complex numbers z and w.

8. Let $z = a + bi$. Show that each statement is true.

   a. $z + \overline{z} = 2a$
         b. $z\overline{z} = a^2 + b^2$

9. a. Find two real numbers a and b such that $2a = 14$ and $a^2 + b^2 = 74$.

   b. Find two complex numbers with a sum of 14 and a product of 74.

These results prove that the sum and the product of conjugates are always real numbers.

On Your Own

10. Express each quotient in the form $a + bi$.

   a. $\dfrac{1}{1 + i}$
     b. $\dfrac{1}{1 - i}$
     c. $\dfrac{1}{2 + 3i}$
     d. $\dfrac{1}{5 + 6i}$

11. Suppose $z = a + bi$, where a and b are real numbers, and $z \neq 0$. Write $\frac{1}{z}$ in the form $c + di$ for real numbers c and d.

12. Consider the function $f(x) = x^2$, where the domain is $\mathbb{C}$. Write each output in the form $a + bi$.

    a. $f(i)$ **b.** $f(-i)$ **c.** $f(2 + i)$

    d. $f(2 - i)$ **e.** $f(3 + i)$ **f.** $f(3 - i)$

    g. $f(-5 + 4i)$ **h.** $f(-5 - 4i)$

13. The results in Exercise 12 suggest the relationship $\overline{z^2} = (\overline{z})^2$.

    a. Prove that this statement is true for any complex number z.

    b. **Take It Further** Explain how this relationship is a consequence of the result in Exercise 7.

14. Write each complex number in the form $r + si$.

    a. $\dfrac{4 + i}{4 - i}$ **b.** $\dfrac{2 + 3i}{2 - 3i}$ **c.** $\dfrac{a + bi}{a - bi}$

15. **Standardized Test Prep** Complex number w is the reciprocal of complex number z. If $z = x + yi$ and $w = u + vi$, what are the values of u and v in terms of x and y?

    A. $u = x$ and $v = y$ **B.** $u = \dfrac{x}{x^2 + y^2}$ and $v = \dfrac{-y}{x^2 + y^2}$

    C. $u = \dfrac{x}{x^2 - y^2}$ and $v = \dfrac{-y}{x^2 - y^2}$ **D.** $u = \dfrac{x}{x^2 + y^2}$ and $v = \dfrac{y}{x^2 + y^2}$

16. a. Show that $(a + bi)^2 = (a^2 - b^2) + (2ab)i$.

    b. Show that $(a^2 + b^2)^2 = (a^2 - b^2)^2 + (2ab)^2$.

    c. Let $a = 3$ and $b = 2$ in the equation from part (b). What are the values of $a^2 + b^2$, $a^2 - b^2$, and $2ab$?

17. List three quadratic equations with real coefficients and roots that are nonreal complex numbers. Then find the roots for each equation.

18. Prove that if z is a root of a quadratic polynomial with real coefficients, then $\overline{z}$ is also a root.

Maintain Your Skills

19. Express each quotient in the form $a + bi$.

    a. $\dfrac{8 + i}{2 + i}$ **b.** $\dfrac{8 - i}{2 - i}$ **c.** $\dfrac{3 + 5i}{2 - 3i}$

    d. $\dfrac{3 - 5i}{2 + 3i}$ **e.** $\dfrac{17 - 4i}{6 - 5i}$ **f.** $\dfrac{17 + 4i}{6 + 5i}$

20. Simplify each expression.

    a. $\dfrac{1}{1 + i} + \dfrac{1}{1 - i}$ **b.** $\dfrac{1}{2 + 3i} + \dfrac{1}{2 - 3i}$ **c.** $\dfrac{1}{5 + i} + \dfrac{1}{5 - i}$

    d. **Take It Further** Prove that if z is a nonzero complex number, then $\dfrac{1}{\overline{z}} + \dfrac{1}{z}$ is a real number.

Mathematical 3A Reflections

In this investigation, you explored the set of complex numbers. You learned to calculate with complex numbers and you used complex numbers as tools to solve equations. These exercises will help you summarize what you have learned.

1. Find the solutions, if they exist, to $x^4 - 121 = 0$ that meet each of the following conditions.

   a. The solution is in $\mathbb{N}$.

   b. The solution is in $\mathbb{Z}$ but not in $\mathbb{N}$.

   c. The solution is in $\mathbb{Q}$ but not in $\mathbb{Z}$.

   d. The solution is in $\mathbb{R}$ but not in $\mathbb{Q}$.

   e. The solution is not in $\mathbb{R}$.

2. Use the quadratic polynomial $x^2 - 4x + 13$.

   a. Find its roots.

   b. Find the sum of its roots.

   c. Find the product of its roots.

   d. Find the sum of the squares of its roots.

3. Find all roots of the polynomial $x^3 - 64$.

4. Find a complex number $z = a + bi$, with a and b real numbers, that satisfies each equation.

   a. $z + (4 - 3i) = 6 + 8i$

   b. $z \cdot (4 - 3i) = 6 + 8i$

5. Given two complex numbers, $z = 2 - 5i$ and $w = -3 + 7i$, show that $\overline{zw} = (\overline{z})(\overline{w})$.

6. What are complex numbers?

7. What two numbers have a sum of 20 and a product of 109?

8. How can you use complex numbers to solve any quadratic equation?

Vocabulary and Notation

In this investigation, you learned these terms and symbols. Make sure you understand what each one means and how to use it.

- **complex numbers, $\mathbb{C}$**
- **conjugate, $\overline{z}$**
- **Fundamental Theorem of Algebra**
- **irrational numbers**
- **natural numbers, $\mathbb{N}$**
- **i ($\sqrt{-1}$)**
- **$a + bi$ (complex number)**

The Complex Plane

In *The Complex Plane*, you will visualize complex numbers as points or vectors on a coordinate plane. This visual representation of complex numbers will help you develop new insights into addition, multiplication, and conjugation of complex numbers. By translating algebraic calculations into geometric operations, you can form a new understanding of the algebraic calculations.

By the end of this investigation, you will be able to answer questions like these.

1. How do you represent a complex number graphically?

2. What is the graphical effect of adding two complex numbers?

3. What is the graphical effect of multiplying a complex number by i?

You will learn how to

- graph complex numbers on the complex plane

- visualize operations on complex numbers as transformations on the complex plane

- develop greater fluency with complex number calculations, which include finding magnitude and direction

You will develop these habits and skills:

- Extend the concept of absolute value in the real numbers to magnitude in the complex numbers.

- Visualize complex numbers and operations on them in the context of the complex plane.

- Represent complex numbers as points or as vectors, depending upon the context.

a Julia set fractal on the complex plane

3.06 Getting Started

You can use properties of geometry and trigonometry to find angle measures and segment lengths on the coordinate plane.

For You to Explore

1. A triangle on the coordinate plane has vertices $O(0, 0)$, $A(4, 0)$, and $B(4, 3)$.

   a. Explain why this is a right triangle.

   b. Find the length of the hypotenuse.

   c. Angle B has a measure of approximately 53.13°. Find the approximate measure of angle O.

   d. Use a calculator in degree mode to find the value of $\tan^{-1}\left(\frac{3}{4}\right)$ to two decimal places.

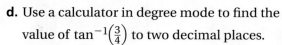

Remember...

The hypotenuse of a right triangle is the side opposite the right angle.

2. A triangle has vertices $O(0, 0)$, $P(\sqrt{3}, 1)$, and $Q(\sqrt{3}, -1)$.

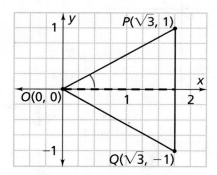

   a. Show that all three sides have the same length.

   b. Find the measure of the marked angle between $\overline{OP}$ and the x-axis.

3. A line segment on the coordinate plane has endpoints at $(0, 0)$ and $(7, 24)$.

   a. Find the slope of the line segment.

   b. Find the length of the line segment.

   c. Estimate the measure of the marked angle.

   d. Use a calculator in degree mode to find the value of $\tan^{-1}\left(\frac{24}{7}\right)$ to two decimal places.

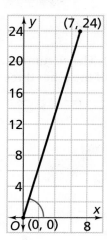

Habits of Mind

Look for relationships. What does part (d) have to do with the other parts of this problem?

4. A triangle has vertices $A(2, 0)$, $P(-1, \sqrt{3})$, and $Q(-1, -\sqrt{3})$. Its circumcenter is $O(0, 0)$.

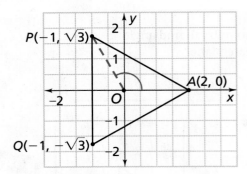

Remember...

The circumcenter of a polygon is the center of the circle that contains the vertices of the polygon.

a. Show that all three sides have the same length.

b. Find the measure of the marked angle between $\overline{OP}$ and the x-axis.

5. For each triangle, find the coordinates of points A and B.

a.

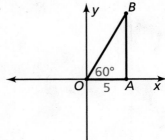

b.

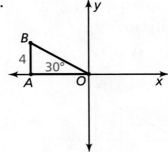

c.

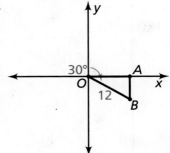

6. A square has a vertex at $(1, 0)$. The circumcenter of the square is at the origin. Find the coordinates of the other three vertices of the square.

Exercises *Practicing Habits of Mind*

On Your Own

Remember...

Exact means no approximations. For example, $\sqrt{13}$ is exact, but 3.60555 is an approximation to $\sqrt{13}$.

7. Graph each line segment. Then find the exact length of each segment.

   a. endpoints at $(0, 0)$ and $(4, 1)$

   b. endpoints at $(0, 0)$ and $(2, 1)$

   c. endpoints at $(0, 0)$ and $(7, 6)$

   d. endpoints at $(0, 0)$ and $(3, 4)$

   e. endpoints at $(0, 0)$ and $(6, 8)$

   f. endpoints at $(0, 0)$ and $(1, \sqrt{3})$

8. Find each product.

   a. $(4 + i)(4 - i)$ **b.** $(2 + i)(2 - i)$

   c. $(4 + i)(2 + i)$ **d.** $(7 + 6i)(7 - 6i)$

   e. $(3 + 4i)(3 - 4i)$ **f.** $(1 + i\sqrt{3})(1 - i\sqrt{3})$

9. Use the inverse tangent function on a calculator. Find the measure of each marked angle to two decimal places.

   a.

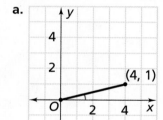

   b.

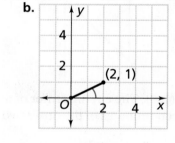

   c.

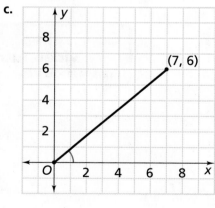

   d.

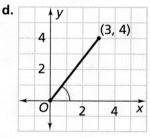

10. An isosceles right triangle has a right angle and two 45° angles.

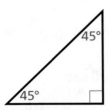

a. If one leg has length 4, find the length of the hypotenuse.

b. If one leg has length 10, find the length of the hypotenuse.

c. If one leg has length a, find the length of the hypotenuse.

d. If the hypotenuse has length 4, find the length of each leg.

e. If the hypotenuse has length 10, find the length of each leg.

f. If the hypotenuse has length b, find the length of each leg.

Remember...

The legs in a right triangle are the sides adjacent to the right angle.

11. For each triangle, find the coordinates of points A and B.

a.

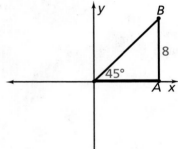

b.

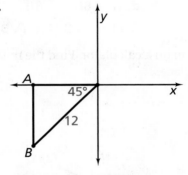

12. An equilateral triangle has a vertex at $(1, 0)$. The circumcenter of the triangle is at the origin. Find the exact coordinates of the other two vertices.

Maintain Your Skills

13. Evaluate each expression.

a. $(-1 + i\sqrt{3})^3$ **b.** $(-1 - i\sqrt{3})^3$ **c.** 2^3

d. $2(-1 + i\sqrt{3})(-1 - i\sqrt{3})$ **e.** $2 + (-1 + i\sqrt{3}) + (-1 - i\sqrt{3})$

14. For each point A, find the coordinates of point A', which you locate by rotating A 90° counterclockwise about the origin.

a. $A(1, 0)$ **b.** $A(0, -1)$ **c.** $A(3, 5)$ **d.** $A(6, -1)$

15. Write each complex number in the form $a + bi$, where a and b are real numbers.

a. $(3 + 4i)^2$ **b.** $(3 + 4i)^3$ **c.** $(3 + 4i)^4$ **d.** $(3 + 4i)^5$

Go Online
Video Tutor
Pearsonsuccessnet.com

Graphing Complex Numbers

Throughout the 1600s and 1700s, mathematicians used "imaginary" numbers as tools to solve problems involving real numbers. However, they did not feel that these numbers had any existence on their own.

Around 1800, mathematicians invented a geometric representation for numbers like $2 + i$. This graphic representation of complex numbers led to an explosion of activity in mathematics—many new fields were born.

> The geometric representation, along with the use of i, was made popular by Gauss in the early 1800s.

On the number line, you represent real numbers as points. For example, here is how you represent 5 on the number line.

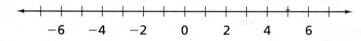

And here is -3.

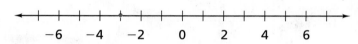

Developing Habits of Mind

Look for relationships. How do you represent a complex number geometrically? To know a complex number, you need to know two numbers—the real part and the imaginary part.

Two complex numbers are equal if and only if both their real and imaginary parts are equal by Theorem 3.1. So there is a one-to-one correspondence between complex numbers and pairs of real numbers. And how do you represent ordered pairs of real numbers? You represent ordered pairs as points on the coordinate plane.

So, take the number line and make a second axis, perpendicular to the first, to record multiples of i. This is the **complex plane**. Each complex number $a + bi$ is represented on the complex plane by a point at the coordinates (a, b).

> The complex plane is sometimes called the *Argand plane* in honor of Jean Argand, the author of one of the first papers about it.

Example

Problem Graph each complex number.

- $3i$
- $2 + i$
- $4 - 3i$
- -3

Solution The complex plane below shows the four points that correspond to the given numbers.

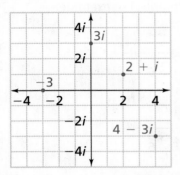

Note that you still represent a real number as a point on the real number line.

For You to Do

1. Identify the complex number represented by each point.

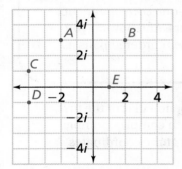

2. Which two points on the complex plane above are conjugates of each other?

3. If z is a complex number, compare the locations of z and $-z$ on the complex plane.

Exercises *Practicing Habits of Mind*

1. Graph and label each complex number on the same complex plane.

   a. $4 + 3i$ **b.** $4 - 3i$

   c. $-4 + 3i$ **d.** $-4 - 3i$

2. You can write a complex number as $z = a + bi$. What can you say about a and b if z is located in the given quadrant?

   a. Quadrant I   **b.** Quadrant II

   c. Quadrant III   **d.** Quadrant IV

3. **a.** Graph both solutions to the equation $x^2 + 13 = 4x$ on the complex plane.

   b. Compute the sum and product of the two solutions.

4. **a.** Graph all three solutions to the equation $x^3 - 8 = 0$ on the complex plane.

   b. The roots lie on the vertices of a triangle. Is this triangle equilateral, isosceles, or scalene? Justify your answer.

   c. Compute the sum and product of the three solutions.

5. Find four complex numbers that lie on the vertices of a square on the complex plane.

6. Graph and label each complex number on the same complex plane.

   a. i^0 **b.** i^1 **c.** i^2

   d. i^3 **e.** i^4 **f.** i^5

> **Habits of Mind**
>
> **Look for relationships.**
> How are the graphs of
> the solutions related?

On Your Own

For Exercises 7 and 8, graph and label the four complex numbers on a single complex plane.

7. **a.** $3 + 2i$ **b.** $3 - 2i$

   c. $-3 - 2i$ **d.** $-3 + 2i$

8. **a.** $2 + i$ **b.** $(2 + i)^2$

   c. $(2 + i)^3$ **d.** $(2 + i)^4$

> **Go Online**
> Pearsonsuccessnet.com

9. Suppose a and b are positive real numbers.

   a. Graph what $a + bi$ and $a - bi$ might look like on the same complex plane.

   b. Graph the sum of $z = a + bi$ and $\bar{z} = a - bi$.

   c. Describe how the sum $z + \bar{z}$ is geometrically related to z and $\bar{z}$.

   d. Describe how the difference $z - \bar{z}$ is geometrically related to z and $\bar{z}$.

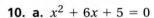

In Exercises 10 and 11, solve each equation. Then graph the solutions on the complex plane.

10. a. $x^2 + 6x + 5 = 0$

    b. $x^2 + 6x + 8 = 0$

    c. $x^2 + 6x + 10 = 0$

    d. $x^2 + 6x + 13 = 0$

    e. $x^2 + 6x + 18 = 0$

11. a. $x^4 - 1 = 0$

    b. $x^4 - 16 = 0$

    c. $x^4 - 81 = 0$

    d. $x^4 - 256 = 0$

12. Graph each complex number on the same complex plane.

    a. i^{10} b. i^{11} c. i^{243}

    d. i^{-1} e. i^{-11} f. i^{-243}

13. Suppose $z = 3 + i$ and $w = 2 - i$. Graph each group of numbers on the complex plane.

    a. $w, 2w, 3w$

    b. $z + w, z + 2w, z + 3w$

    c. $\bar{w}, \overline{2w}, \overline{3w}$

    d. $\overline{z + w}, \overline{z + 2w}, \overline{z + 3w}$

14. **Standardized Test Prep** Suppose $z = 5 + i$ and $w = 4 - i$. Which of the following numbers is NOT in Quadrant IV on the complex plane?

   A. zw **B.** w^2

   C. $\bar{z}$ **D.** $3z + 2w$

15. **Take It Further** Suppose $z = \dfrac{\sqrt{2}}{2} + \dfrac{\sqrt{2}}{2}i$. Simplify each expression. Then graph all the numbers on the same complex plane.

   a. z^0 **b.** z^1 **c.** z^2 **d.** z^3

   e. z^4 **f.** z^8 **g.** z^{27} **h.** z^{275}

Maintain Your Skills

16. Graph and label each complex number on the same complex plane.

   a. $-3 + i$

   b. $2(-3 + i)$

   c. $3(-3 + i)$

   d. $4(-3 + i)$

   e. $-1(-3 + i)$

17. Write each expression as a complex number $a + bi$. Then graph and label each complex number on the same complex plane.

   a. $3 + 5i$

   b. $(3 + 5i) \cdot i$

   c. $(3 + 5i) \cdot i^2$

   d. $(3 + 5i) \cdot i^3$

   e. $(3 + 5i) \cdot i^4$

3.08 Arithmetic in the Complex Plane

Once mathematicians realized that there is a one-to-one correspondence between points on a plane and complex numbers, they started asking questions about visualizing operations on complex numbers.

Suppose z and w are complex numbers, represented as points on the complex plane. How can you locate the following numbers?

- $z + w$

- $3z$

- zw

- $\bar{z}$

- $-z$

You have already explored some of these questions. In this lesson, you will focus on addition, and you will begin to explore multiplication.

Addition

The graph below shows $z = 2 + 3i$, $w = 6 + i$, and the sum $z + w = 8 + 4i$ on the complex plane.

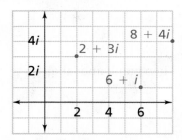

These may look like three random points, but if you draw vectors from the origin to z and w, you see more structure.

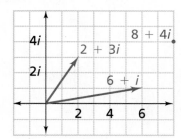

Remember...

A vector is an arrow from the origin to a point. You can use vectors to bring clarity to figures like this one.

Tony draws the vector for the sum $8 + 4i$.

Tony   Hey, look, Sasha. If I draw in the vector for the sum, I get this.

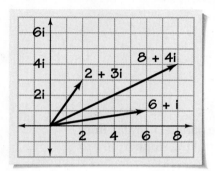

Sasha draws on Tony's graph.

Sasha   And if I connect the dots, it looks like a parallelogram.

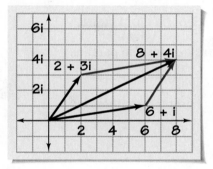

For You to Do

1. Prove Sasha correct. Show that if $z = 2 + 3i$ and $w = 6 + i$, then 0, z, w, and $z + w$ are the vertices of a parallelogram.

The following theorem shows that Sasha's parallelogram law always works. The proof is just a general version of what you did above with $2 + 3i$ and $6 + i$.

Theorem 3.2

Suppose $z = a + bi$ and $w = c + di$ are complex numbers. Then, on the complex plane, the numbers 0, z, w, and $z + w$ form the vertices of a parallelogram.

Proof $z + w = (a + c) + (b + d)i$, so the coordinates of the point corresponding to $z + w$ are $(a + c, b + d)$.

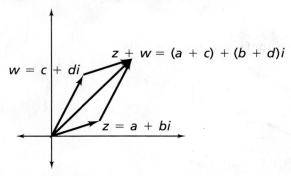

A figure is a parallelogram if its opposite sides are parallel. Parallel lines have the same slope. The slope from 0 to w is $\frac{d}{c}$, and the slope from z to $z + w$ is

$$\frac{(b + d) - b}{(a + c) - a} = \frac{d}{c}$$

So these two sides are parallel.

For You to Do

2. Complete the proof by showing that the other two sides are also parallel.

> Or you can show that the sides you proved parallel are also congruent.

You can also use the parallelogram law to subtract complex numbers by adding the opposite.

Multiplication: First Steps

How do you visualize multiplication? This is more difficult. Given z and w on the complex plane, can you locate zw? In this lesson, you will look at two special cases: when w is a real number, and when $w = i$.

You can visualize multiplication of a complex number z by a positive real number k as stretching or shrinking the vector by a factor of k. For example, for $z = -3 + i$, the graph below shows vectors for z and $4z$.

> Stretches and shrinks by a factor of k are dilations.

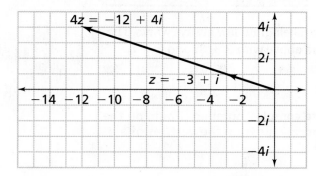

For Discussion

3. In the graph, $4z$, z, and 0 appear to be collinear. Prove that this is, in fact, true.

How do you prove that three points are collinear?

You can multiply z by a negative real number $-k$ by graphing $-z$ and then scaling that vector by k. For example, the graph below shows $-3 + i$ and $-2 \cdot (-3 + i)$ drawn as vectors.

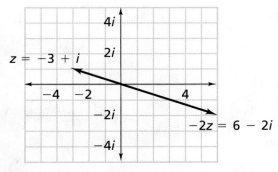

This works since $z \cdot (-k) = (-z) \cdot k$.

In-Class Experiment

For each z, graph z and iz as vectors on the same complex plane.

4. $z = 3 + 5i$

5. $z = -2 + i$

6. $z = -3 - 4i$

7. Describe how the graph of iz compares to the graph of z in the complex plane.

Habits of Mind

Experiment. Try more examples if you need to. Choose other complex numbers for z.

The In-Class Experiment above suggests the following relationship.

Theorem 3.3 Multiplication by i

If z is a complex number, iz is obtained from z by rotating it 90° counterclockwise about the origin.

The fact that the rotation is counterclockwise instead of clockwise is surprisingly technical. Ask your teacher if you are curious about the details.

Proof Show that the vectors representing iz and z are perpendicular and are the same distance from the origin. Then you obtain iz from z by a $90°$ rotation.

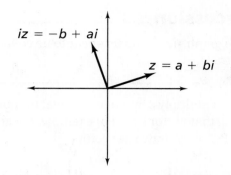

$iz = -b + ai$

$z = a + bi$

Start by writing $z = a + bi$. Then $iz = -b + ai$.

You can use slope to prove that the two vectors are perpendicular. The slope of the vector representing z is $\frac{b}{a}$. The slope of the vector representing iz is $\frac{a}{-b}$. These slopes are negative reciprocals.

$$\frac{b}{a} \cdot \frac{a}{-b} = -1$$

Therefore, the vectors are perpendicular, and the angle between z and iz is $90°$.

In the exercises, you will prove that $z = a + bi$ and $iz = -b + ai$ are the same distance from the origin.

You can use vectors to describe the magnitude and direction of the wind, currents, and movement of the ship.

Developing Habits of Mind

Represent complex numbers graphically. You can think about a complex number graphically in two ways: as a point and as a vector. By thinking about complex numbers as points, you can apply all the machinery of geometry. This representation helps you perform algebraic tasks, such as solving equations.

By thinking about complex numbers as vectors, you can visualize operations, such as adding or multiplying by i. Vectors also help you compare the relative sizes of complex numbers.

It is important that you become comfortable with both representations and that you develop a sense of when it is appropriate to "think point" or to "think vector."

You use vectors extensively in navigation and physics. Complex numbers are also key in analyzing signals, such as radio waves or electric current.

For You to Do

8. Which of these four complex numbers has the longest vector?

$$-5 - 6i \qquad 6 + i \qquad 4 + 5i \qquad 8$$

Exercises *Practicing Habits of Mind*

Check Your Understanding

1. Illustrate each addition equation on the complex plane.

   a. $(4 + i) + (2i) = 4 + 3i$

   b. $(2i) + (4 + i) = 4 + 3i$

   c. $(4 + i) + (4 - i) = 8$

   d. $(4 + i) + (-3 + i) = 1 + 2i$

   e. $-8 + 3 = -5$

2. The graph below shows two complex numbers z and w.

   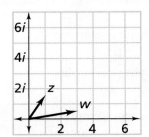

   Graph each expression.

   a. $z + w$

   b. $2z$

   c. $-w$

   d. $2z + 2w$

   e. $2z - w$

   f. Take It Further $z + wi$

3. If $z = a + bi$ is a complex number, show that z and iz are the same distance from the origin.

4. For each complex number, find the distance to the origin on the complex plane.

   a. $4 + i$

   b. $2 + i$

   c. $3 - 2i$

   d. $6 + 5i$

5. Find each product.

   a. $(4 + i)(4 - i)$

   b. $(2 + i)(2 - i)$

   c. $(3 - 2i)(3 + 2i)$

   d. $(6 + 5i)(6 - 5i)$

Go Online
Pearsonsuccessnet.com

6. Consider the triangle with the following vertices.

$$-18 + 49i \qquad 15 - 7i \qquad 30 - 15i$$

  a. Find the lengths of the sides of the triangle.

  b. If you multiply each vertex by −1, what is the position of the resulting triangle compared to the original triangle in the complex plane? Draw a picture to support your answer.

  c. If you multiply each vertex by i, what is the position of the resulting triangle compared to the original triangle in the complex plane? Draw a picture to support your answer.

7. For each complex number z, graph z and iz as vectors on the same complex plane.

  a. $z = 3 + 2i$ **b.** $z = -1 + 4i$

  c. $z = -1 - 3i$ **d.** $z = 2 - 3i$

8. a. Describe the effect, in the complex plane, of multiplying a complex number by i^2.

  b. Describe the effect, in the complex plane, of multiplying a complex number by $-i$.

9. Write About It For each statement, decide whether you would represent the complex numbers as points or as vectors. Give reasons for your choice. Then draw a diagram.

  a. The numbers 1, i, -1, and $-i$ lie on the vertices of a square on the complex plane.

  b. You can use the parallelogram law to visualize the sum $(3 + 2i) + (7 - 6i)$.

  c. If you multiply the vertices of a triangle by i, the new triangle is congruent to the original.

  d. The distance from $5 + 12i$ to the origin is greater than the distance from $3 + 4i$ to the origin.

On Your Own

10. Illustrate the following equation graphically.

$$(3 - i) + (3 - i) + (3 - i) = 9 - 3i$$

11. For each complex number, find its distance from the origin on the complex plane.

  a. $3 + i$ **b.** $4 - i$ **c.** $(3 + i)(4 - i)$

  d. $(2 + i)^2$ **e.** $(2 + i)^3$

Go Online
Pearsonsuccessnet.com

12. Does Theorem 3.2 work for two real numbers? Explain.

13. Order the following complex numbers from least to greatest, based on how far each number is from the origin.

$$5 + 3i \qquad 2 - 7i \qquad 8 \qquad -6 - 4i$$

14. **Standardized Test Prep** Here is a graph of $2iz$, for a complex number z, on the complex plane. Which of the following numbers is z?

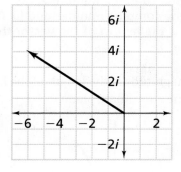

A. $-3 + 2i$

B. $2 + 3i$

C. $3 - 2i$

D. $4 + 6i$

15. Suppose $z = \frac{\sqrt{2}}{2} + \frac{\sqrt{2}}{2} i$. Graph each pair of complex numbers.

a. $1 + i$ and $(1 + i) \cdot z$ **b.** $3 + 5i$ and $(3 + 5i) \cdot z$

c. $-2 + i$ and $(-2 + i) \cdot z$ **d.** $-3 - 4i$ and $(-3 - 4i) \cdot z$

16. a. **Write About It** Describe the effect, in the complex plane, of multiplying by $z = \frac{\sqrt{2}}{2} + \frac{\sqrt{2}}{2} i$ in Exercise 15.

b. **Take It Further** Describe the effect, in the complex plane, of multiplying by $z^2 = \left(\frac{\sqrt{2}}{2} + \frac{\sqrt{2}}{2} i \right)^2$.

Maintain Your Skills

17. Solve each equation.

a. $x^3 - 1 = 0$ **b.** $x^3 - 8 = 0$ **c.** $x^3 = 27$ **d.** $x^3 = 64$

e. Find an equation with integer coefficients having solutions that include 8 and $-4 + 4i\sqrt{3}$.

> For Exercise 17 help, see the TI-Nspire™ Handbook, p. 804.

18. Suppose $z = 1 + i$. For each value of w, draw a diagram that shows z, w, and zw.

a. $w = 3 + 4i$ **b.** $w = -3 + 4i$

c. $w = -5 + 12i$ **d.** $w = 7$

e. $w = 3i$

> **Habits of Mind**
>
> **Make strategic choices.** You can represent complex numbers as vectors or as points. Decide which form is most helpful to you in each case.

3.09 Magnitude and Direction

In the last lesson, you represented complex numbers as vectors. Now you will focus on two properties of vectors, *magnitude* and *direction*.

Definition

The **magnitude** of the complex number *z*, denoted by $|z|$, is the distance between the complex number and (0, 0) in the complex plane. In other words, $|z|$ is the length of the vector that represents *z*.

If $z = a + bi$, the magnitude is the length of the line segment connecting (0, 0) and (a, b) in the coordinate plane.

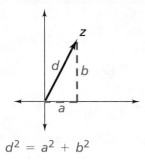

$$d^2 = a^2 + b^2$$

For You to Do

1. Find $|-3 + 5i|$.

2. Find a complex number in the fourth quadrant with magnitude 5.

3. Show that the magnitude of $z = a + bi$ is $|z| = \sqrt{a^2 + b^2}$.

To calculate magnitude, see the TI-Nspire Handbook, p. 804.

Theorem 3.4 *Magnitude and Conjugates*

The magnitude $|z|$ of a complex number is given by

$$|z| = \sqrt{z\overline{z}}$$

Proof Let $z = a + bi$. The conjugate is $\overline{z} = a - bi$. Find $\sqrt{z\overline{z}}$.

$$\sqrt{z\overline{z}} = \sqrt{(a + bi)(a - bi)} = \sqrt{a^2 + b^2}$$

This is the same as the expression for magnitude that you verified in Problem 3. So, $|z| = \sqrt{z\overline{z}}$.

Look for relationships. The symbol for magnitude is the same as the symbol for absolute value. There are at least two reasons that this makes sense.

- Find the magnitude of a real number $a + 0i$.

$$|a + 0i| = \sqrt{a^2 + 0^2} = \sqrt{a^2}$$

This satisfies one definition of absolute value: $|a| = \sqrt{a^2}$. For real numbers, magnitude and absolute value are equal.

- The absolute value of a real number is its distance from (0, 0) on a number line. Magnitude is also distance from (0, 0), but on the complex plane.

By defining $|z|$ as the distance between z and (0, 0), you extend the definition of absolute value from $\mathbb{R}$ to $\mathbb{C}$.

Remember...

Real numbers are still complex numbers. They have imaginary parts equal to 0.

For You to Do

4. Find as many complex numbers as you can with magnitude 5. Are any of them also real numbers?

Example 1

Problem Graph each complex number as a vector and find its magnitude.

  a. $(2 + i)^0$

  b. $(2 + i)^1$

  c. $(2 + i)^2$

  d. $(2 + i)^3$

  e. $(2 + i)^4$

For help with the calculations, see the TI-Nspire Handbook, p. 804.

Solution Evaluate each expression to find the real and imaginary parts of each number.

  a. A number raised to the zero power is 1, so $(2 + i)^0 = 1$.

  b. A number raised to the first power is itself, so $(2 + i)^1 = 2 + i$.

  c. $(2 + i)^2 = 3 + 4i$

  d. $(2 + i)^3 = (3 + 4i)(2 + i) = 2 + 11i$

  e. $(2 + i)^4 = (2 + 11i)(2 + i) = -7 + 24i$

This plot shows all five complex numbers drawn as vectors.

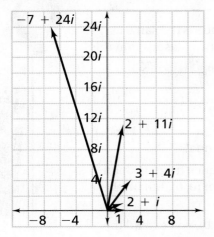

To find the magnitude of each number, use the expression $\sqrt{a^2 + b^2}$ or the Pythagorean Theorem.

a. $|1| = 1$

b. $|2 + i| = \sqrt{2^2 + 1^2} = \sqrt{5}$

c. $|3 + 4i| = \sqrt{3^2 + 4^2} = \sqrt{25} = 5$

d. $|2 + 11i| = \sqrt{2^2 + 11^2} = \sqrt{125} = 5\sqrt{5}$

e. $|-7 + 24i| = \sqrt{(-7)^2 + 24^2} = \sqrt{625} = 25$

For You to Do

5. Find the magnitude of $2 + 3i$ and $(2 + 3i)^2$.

For real numbers, the absolute value $|x - y|$ is defined as the distance between x and y on the number line. If magnitude is an extension of absolute value from $\mathbb{R}$ to $\mathbb{C}$, this should still apply in $\mathbb{C}$. The distance between two complex numbers z and w is $|z - w|$, the magnitude of the difference between the two numbers.

Example 2

Problem Find the distance between $3 + 2i$ and $4 - i$ on the complex plane.

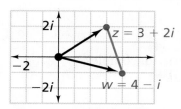

Solution Draw a right triangle with z and w as two vertices.

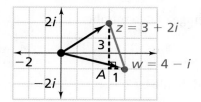

Using the Pythagorean theorem, the length of the segment joining z and w is $\sqrt{1^2 + 3^2} = \sqrt{10}$.

Alternately, you can calculate $|z - w|$ to find the distance between $3 + 2i$ and $4 - i$.

$$|(3 + 2i) - (4 - i)| = |-1 + 3i| = \sqrt{(-1)^2 + 3^2} = \sqrt{10}$$

Both methods give the same answer.

> A similar diagram can be used to find the distance between any two points in the plane: the distance between $A = (x_1, y_1)$ and $B = (x_2, y_2)$ is $\sqrt{(x_2 - x_1)^2 + (y_2 - y_1)^2}$

For You to Do

6. Find the distance between $-2 + 5i$ and $1 + i$.

> **Remember...**
>
> The magnitude of $a + bi$ is $\sqrt{a^2 + b^2}$.

Tony and Derman are working on some complex arithmetic problems.

Derman So this magnitude rule is like the distance formula. What's that other formula? It's got *x* over 2 and *y* over 2.

Tony The midpoint formula?

Derman Yeah! I wonder if the midpoint formula works for complex numbers. Here, I'll draw $6 + 5i$ and $10 + 3i$.

Derman draws a sketch of his two complex numbers.

Derman What complex number is halfway between those?

Tony On the number line, you can take the average of two numbers by adding them up and dividing by 2.

Derman Can you take averages of complex numbers?

Tony I don't see why not. Let's add them up and divide by 2. I get

$$\frac{(6 + 5i) + (10 + 3i)}{2} = \frac{16 + 8i}{2} = 8 + 4i.$$

Derman Here, let me graph it.

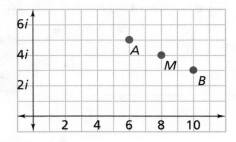

Tony That looks like it works to me.

Derman Me too, but how can we be sure?

For Discussion

7. Prove that $8 + 4i$ is the midpoint between $6 + 5i$ and $10 + 3i$.

Use what you know about the coordinate plane to help.

A complex number has magnitude. But, if you think of a complex number as a vector, it also has a specific direction. How should you define direction? You can define direction by using the counterclockwise angle measured from the positive real axis.

Definition

The **direction** of the complex number *z* is the angle measured from the positive real axis in a counterclockwise direction.

Generally, you express direction with a measure at least 0° and less than 360°. What does a direction of 450° mean?

Example 3

Problem Find the magnitude and direction of each complex number.

a. $-2i$

b. $-1 + i$

c. $1 + 3i$

d. $(1 + 3i)^2 = -8 + 6i$

Habits of Mind

Visualize. Graphing a complex number as a vector helps to illustrate its magnitude and direction.

Solution

a. The magnitude of $-2i$ is 2. Since $-2i$ lies directly along the negative imaginary axis, its direction angle is three-fourths of a full circle. The direction is 270°.

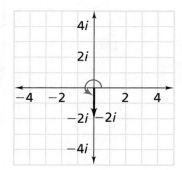

b. $|-1 + i| = \sqrt{2}$ because

$$|-1 + i| = \sqrt{(-1 + i)(-1 - i)} = \sqrt{(-1)^2 + 1^2} = \sqrt{2}.$$

By dropping an altitude from the point $(-1, 1)$, you make an isosceles right triangle. The measures of the angles in this triangle are 45°, 45°, and 90°.

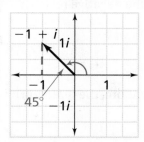

Where is $|-1 + i|$ in this picture?

The direction angle is supplementary to the 45° angle in the isosceles right triangle. Therefore, the direction is 135°.

c. The magnitude of $1 + 3i$ is $\sqrt{10}$ because $\sqrt{1^2 + 3^2} = \sqrt{10}$. By dropping an altitude from the point $(1, 3)$, you make a right triangle.

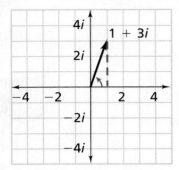

This triangle is not a special right triangle. So use trigonometry to approximate the measure of the marked angle. Since you know the lengths of all the sides, you can use any of the trigonometric ratios. For example, find the angle measure by using tangent.

$$\tan x = \frac{3}{1}$$
$$x = \tan^{-1}\left(\frac{3}{1}\right)$$
$$x \approx 71.565°$$

So, $71.565°$ is the approximate direction.

d. The magnitude of $-8 + 6i$ is 10 because $\sqrt{(-8)^2 + 6^2} = 10$. Drop an altitude from the point $(-8, 6)$ to make a right triangle.

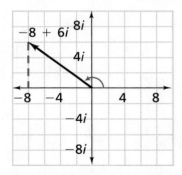

This triangle is not a special right triangle. So use trigonometry to approximate the angle formed by the hypotenuse and the negative real axis.

$$\tan x = \frac{6}{8}$$
$$x = \tan^{-1}\left(\frac{6}{8}\right)$$
$$x \approx 36.870°$$

The direction angle is supplementary to this angle. Therefore, the direction angle is approximately $180° - 36.870° = 143.130°$.

Why should you use tangent? The numbers involved in the tangent calculation come directly from the original complex number. Still, you could use sine, cosine, or tangent.

Facts and Notation

You will typically use the word *direction* when referring to vectors. However, when the vectors stand for complex numbers, it is more conventional to use the older term **argument** and the notation "arg." Below are some examples.

- $\arg(-2i) = 270°$
- $\arg(-1 + i) = 135°$
- $\arg(1 + 3i) \approx 71.565°$

For help calculating the argument of a complex number, see the TI-Nspire Handbook, p. 804.

For You to Do

Find $|z|$ and $\arg z$ for each complex number z.

8. $z = 2 + 2i$

9. $z = (1 + 3i)^3$

10. $z = 3$

11. $z = 1 - i\sqrt{3}$

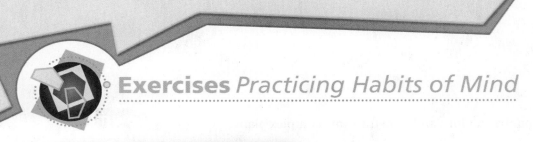

Exercises *Practicing Habits of Mind*

Check Your Understanding

1. Find the magnitude and direction of each complex number.

   a. $4 + 3i$

   b. $4 - 3i$

   c. $-4 + 3i$

   d. $-4 - 3i$

2. Find $|w|$ and $\arg w$ for each complex number w.

   a. $w = 2 + 2i$

   b. $w = 2 - 2i$

   c. $w = -2 + 2i$

   d. $w = -2 - 2i$

3. Without using a calculator, estimate the direction of each complex number to within 10°.

   a. $5 + 4i$

   b. $-5 + 4i$

   c. $5 - 4i$

   d. $-5 - 4i$

Throughout these exercises, calculate the direction to the nearest thousandth degree if you cannot find the exact angle.

4. Describe what happens to the magnitude and direction of a complex number when you double the complex number.

5. For real numbers x and y, absolute value is multiplicative.

$$|xy| = |x| \cdot |y|$$

With a partner, test two examples to see if $|zw| = |z| \cdot |w|$ is true when z and w are complex numbers.

6. Let $z = 1 + i$ and $w = -2 - 7i$. Calculate each value.

   a. $|z|$

   b. $|w|$

   c. $|z + w|$

   d. the distance from z to w

   e. the midpoint of the segment with endpoints at z and w

   f. the midpoint of the segment with endpoints at the origin and at $z + w$

7. For each complex number z, find the magnitude and direction of z and of z^2.

   a. $z = 2i$

   b. $z = -1 + i$

   c. $z = 4 + i$

   d. $z = -4 + i$

8. For each complex number z, plot z and $\frac{1}{z}$ on the same complex plane.

   a. $z = 1 + i$

   b. $z = 2 + i$

   c. $z = 1 + i\sqrt{3}$

   d. $z = -1 - i$

> **Remember...**
>
> The expression $\frac{1}{z}$ is the reciprocal of a complex number z. You worked with reciprocals in Lesson 3.05.

9. For each complex number z in Exercise 8, find the magnitude and direction of z and of $\frac{1}{z}$.

10. Write each complex number as a product of a positive real number and a complex number of magnitude 1.

   a. $4 + 3i$ **b.** $5 + 12i$ **c.** $1 + i$

   d. $1 - i$ **e.** $2 + 3i$ **f.** $-1 + i\sqrt{3}$

11. Show that you can write any nonzero complex number as the product of a positive real number and a complex number of magnitude 1.

12. Find the magnitude and direction of each complex number.

   a. $3 + 2i$ **b.** $3 - 2i$

   c. $-3 - 2i$ **d.** $-3 + 2i$

13. Find $|z|$ and arg z for each complex number z.

   a. $z = 1 + i\sqrt{3}$ **b.** $z = 1 - i\sqrt{3}$

   c. $-z = 1 + i\sqrt{3}$ **d.** $z = \left(1 + i\sqrt{3}\right)\left(1 - i\sqrt{3}\right)$

14. Let $z = 1 + 2i$ and $w = -3 + 6i$. Calculate each value.

   a. $|z|$ **b.** $|w|$

   c. $|z + w|$ **d.** the distance from z to w

   e. the midpoint of the segment with endpoints at z and w

   f. the midpoint of the segment with endpoints at the origin and at $z + w$

   g. What kind of quadrilateral is formed by the origin, z, w, and $z + w$?

15. In Geometry, you learned that if the diagonals of a quadrilateral bisect each other, then the quadrilateral is a parallelogram. Prove Theorem 3.4 using this property of quadrilaterals.

16. **Standardized Test Prep** To the nearest degree, arg $(-2 + 5i)$ is 112°. Which is the direction of $-2 - 5i$?

   A. 202°   **B.** 224°   **C.** 248°   **D.** 292°

17. A complex number z has magnitude 5 and direction 50°.

   a. Graph z as a vector on the complex plane.

   b. Graph the conjugate $\bar{z}$ on the same complex plane.

   c. Find the magnitude and direction of $\bar{z}$.

18. Describe what happens to the magnitude and direction of a complex number when you multiply the number by i.

19. Find the direction of each of these complex numbers from Example 1.

   a. $(2 + i)^0$ **b.** $(2 + i)^1$

   c. $(2 + i)^2$ **d.** $(2 + i)^3$

   e. $(2 + i)^4$

Go Online
Pearsonsuccessnet.com

Use approximations if necessary.

20. Consider the complex numbers $a = 3 + i$, $b = 9 + i$, and $c = 5 + 7i$.

   a. Plot these three numbers as points in the complex plane.

   b. Determine d, the complex number halfway between a and b, and e, the complex number halfway between a and c. Plot d and e in the same complex plane.

   c. Calculate the distance between b and c.

   d. Calculate the distance between d and e.

   e. What do you notice about the distances you found in parts (c) and (d)?

21. Consider the complex numbers $a = 3 + i$ and $b = 2 - 6i$.

   a. Draw a diagram showing a, b, and $a - b$ in the complex plane.

   b. Show that, for these values of a and b, $|a|^2 + |b|^2 = |a - b|^2$.

   c. **Take It Further** Show that for any complex number a and real number k, if $b = (ki)a$, then $|a|^2 + |b|^2 = |a - b|^2$.

22. For each pair of complex numbers, calculate $|z|$, $|w|$, and $|zw|$.

   a. $z = 2 + i$ and $w = 3 + i$

   b. $z = 2 + i$ and $w = 3 + 2i$

   c. $z = 5i$ and $w = 3i$

   d. $z = 2 + i$ and $w = \dfrac{2 - i}{5}$

23. a. Based on your results from Exercise 22, make a conjecture about the relationship among $|z|$, $|w|$, and $|zw|$.

   b. **Take It Further** Prove your conjecture.

Maintain Your Skills

24. Find the magnitude of each complex number.

a. $(1 + i)^2$

b. $(2 + i)^2$

c. $(3 + i)^2$

d. $(7 + i)^2$

e. $(2 + 3i)^2$

f. Find a complex number $a + bi$, with nonzero a and b, that has magnitude 29.

25. For each equation, find the magnitude and direction of all the solutions.

a. $x^2 - 1 = 0$

b. $x^3 - 1 = 0$

c. $x^4 - 1 = 0$

The equation $x^4 - 1 = 0$ has four solutions in $\mathbb{C}$.

Mathematical 3B Reflections

In this investigation, you graphed complex numbers as points and as vectors on the complex plane. You also calculated magnitude and direction of complex numbers. These exercises will help you summarize what you have learned.

1. Graph and label each pair of numbers on the same complex plane.

   a. $u = 2 - 3i$ and $\bar{u}$ **b.** $v = -2$ and $\bar{v}$

   c. $w = 4i$ and $\bar{w}$ **d.** $z = -3 + i$ and $\bar{z}$

2. For $z = -1 + i$ and $w = 4 + 2i$, graph and label z, w, $z + w$, $-w$, iw, zw, and z^2 on the same complex plane.

3. Prove that, for any nonzero real number r and nonzero complex number z, the product rz is collinear with 0 and z on the complex plane.

4. Find the magnitude and direction of each complex number.

   a. $1 + 2i$ **b.** $(1 + 2i)^2$ **c.** $(1 + 2i)^3$

5. A complex number has magnitude 4 and direction 120°. Write this complex number in the form $a + bi$, where a and b are exact real numbers.

6. How do you represent a complex number graphically?

7. What is the graphical effect of adding two complex numbers?

8. What is the graphical effect of multiplying a complex number by i?

Vocabulary and Notation

In this investigation, you learned these terms and symbols. Make sure you understand what each one means and how to use it.

- **argument, arg z**
- **complex plane**

- **direction**
- **magnitude, $|z|$**

another Julia set fractal

Multiple Choice

1. What is the value of $\sqrt{-5} \cdot \sqrt{-20}$?

   A. -5 **B.** -10

   C. $10\sqrt{-1}$ **D.** 10

2. What is the value of $2(1 + \sqrt{-1})$ $+ 2(-\sqrt{-1}) + (1 + \sqrt{-1})(1 - \sqrt{-1})$?

   A. 4   **B.** $6\sqrt{-1}$

   C. 6   **D.** $4\sqrt{-1}$

3. Which of the following is a complex number, but NOT a real number?

   A. 2   **B.** $3i^2$

   C. $4 - 2i$ **D.** 0

4. What is the magnitude of $2 + 3i$?

   A. $\sqrt{5}$ **B.** $\sqrt{13}$

   C. 4   **D.** $2 - 3i$

5. Which is the approximate argument of $2 + 3i$?

   A. $33.7°$ **B.** $56.3°$

   C. $26.2°$ **D.** $0.011°$

Open Response

6. Use the equation $x^2 + 2x + 5 = 0$.

   a. Find the solutions of the equation.

   b. Find the sum of the solutions of the equation.

   c. Find the product of the solutions of the equation.

   d. Find the sum of the squares of the solutions of the equation.

7. **a.** What are the three solutions to $x^3 + 27 = 0$?

   b. Graph the solutions on the complex plane.

8. Simplify each expression. Write your answer in the form $a + bi$.

   a. $(3 + 4i) + (3 - 4i)$

   b. $(3 + 4i) - (3 - 4i)$

   c. $(3 + 4i)(3 - 4i)$

   d. $\dfrac{3 + 4i}{3 - 4i}$

   e. $\dfrac{3 - 4i}{3 + 4i}$

9. Solve each equation. The solutions are complex numbers.

   a. $z + (3 - 2i) = 5 - 8i$

   b. $x^2 = -25$

   c. $2x^2 + 3x = -5$

   d. $z \cdot (3 + i) = 4 - i$

10. Use the complex number $z = 1 + i\sqrt{3}$.

    a. Find $\bar{z}$.

    b. Find $2z$.

    c. Find z^2.

    d. Graph z, $\bar{z}$, $2z$, and z^2 on the complex plane.

    e. Copy and complete this table.

Vector	Magnitude	Direction
z	▪	▪
$\bar{z}$	▪	▪
$2z$	▪	▪
z^2	▪	▪

11. Describe the set of complex numbers.

Complex Numbers, Geometry, and Algebra

In *Complex Numbers, Geometry, and Algebra,* you will connect many of the results you have proved about complex numbers and develop them further. You will also prove some conjectures you made in previous investigations.

By the end of this investigation, you will be able to answer questions like these.

1. How are the magnitude and argument of the product of two complex numbers related to the magnitude and argument of the original numbers?

2. If $-2 + i$ is a root of the polynomial $x^3 + 7x^2 + 17x + 15$, what is another root?

3. How can you graph the solutions to the equation $x^{10} - 1 = 0$ on the complex plane without doing many calculations?

You will learn how to

- describe relationships between magnitudes and arguments of factors and products

- prove the relationship between the function values of complex conjugates

- find and graph the roots of equations of the form $x^n - 1 = 0$ on the complex plane

You will develop these habits and skills:

- Visualize algebraic calculations as geometric transformations.

- Tinker with complex number calculations to find patterns and develop conjectures.

- Reason deductively to prove conjectures about the complex numbers.

Activating Prior Knowledge
Exploring New Ideas

You can find relationships between the magnitudes and directions of two complex numbers and the magnitude and direction of their product.

For You to Explore

1. For each complex number, find the exact magnitude and the direction to the nearest tenth of a degree.

   a. $3 + i$ **b.** $2 + i$ **c.** $(3 + i)(2 + i)$

   d. $4 + 3i$ **e.** $1 + 2i$ **f.** $(4 + 3i)(1 + 2i)$

2. Complex number z has magnitude 5 and direction 60°.
   Complex number w has magnitude 2 and direction 150°.

   a. Graph z and w on the complex plane.

   b. Estimate the magnitude and direction of the product zw.

   c. **Take It Further** Determine zw and write it in the form $a + bi$.

3. Graph each complex number on the complex plane. Then find its direction.

   a. $1 + i\sqrt{3}$ **b.** $-1 + i\sqrt{3}$ **c.** $-1 - i\sqrt{3}$ **d.** $1 - i\sqrt{3}$

   > What is the magnitude of each number?

4. Establish the following identity.
   $$(ac - bd)^2 + (bc + ad)^2 = \left(a^2 + b^2\right)\left(c^2 + d^2\right)$$

5. You can write a cubic with three roots in either expanded or factored form, where r, s, and t are the roots.
   $$x^3 + ax^2 + bx + c = (x - r)(x - s)(x - t)$$

   > **Remember...**
   >
   > What does the Factor Theorem say?

   a. Expand the right side of the equation.

   b. Write a in terms of r, s, and t.

   c. Write b in terms of r, s, and t.

   d. Write c in terms of r, s, and t.

6. For $f(x) = x^3 - 4x^2 - 2x + 20$, how are the following outputs related?

   a. $f(2 + i)$ and $f(2 - i)$ **b.** $f(4 + i)$ and $f(4 - i)$

   c. $f(-1 + 3i)$ and $f(-1 - 3i)$

   d. Evaluate $f(3 + i)$ and use it to calculate $f(3 - i)$.

7. **Take It Further** Find two complex numbers with the indicated sum and product. Graph them on the coordinate plane.

   a. sum $\dfrac{-1 + \sqrt{5}}{2}$, product 1 **b.** sum $\dfrac{-1 - \sqrt{5}}{2}$, product 1

   c. Expand the following product.
   $$\left(x - 1\right)\left(x^2 + \frac{1 + \sqrt{5}}{2}x + 1\right)\left(x^2 + \frac{1 - \sqrt{5}}{2}x + 1\right)$$

   > For expansion help, see the TI-Nspire Handbook, p. 804.

Exercises Practicing Habits of Mind

On Your Own

8. Graph each complex number. Then calculate its direction to the nearest degree.

    a. $4 + i$ **b.** $4 - i$

    c. $-4 + i$ **d.** $-4 - i$

9. Find the direction of each complex number.

    a. $\sqrt{3} + i$

    b. $\sqrt{2} + i\sqrt{2}$

    c. $\left(\sqrt{3} + i\right)\left(\sqrt{2} + i\sqrt{2}\right)$

    d. Take It Further $\left(\sqrt{3} + i\right)^2\left(\sqrt{2} + i\sqrt{2}\right)^2$

10. Use the complex numbers $z = 2 + 3i$ and $w = 1 + i$. Find each of the following.

    a. $\bar{z}$ **b.** $\bar{z} \cdot \bar{w}$ **c.** $\overline{zw}$

    d. z^2 **e.** $\overline{z^2}$ **f.** $\left(\bar{z}\right)^2$

11. If w and z are any two complex numbers, then $\bar{z} \cdot \bar{w} = \overline{zw}$.

    a. Express the statement in words.

    b. Prove that the statement is true.

> **Remember...**
>
> $\bar{z}$ is the conjugate of the complex number z. The conjugate of $a + bi$ is $a - bi$.

Maintain Your Skills

12. Use the complex number $w = \dfrac{1 + i\sqrt{3}}{2}$. Graph each of the following on the same complex plane.

    a. w **b.** w^2 **c.** w^3 **d.** w^4

    e. w^5 **f.** w^6 **g.** w^7 **h.** w^{12}

3.11 Multiplying Complex Numbers

In the last investigation, you learned that representing a complex number as a vector helps to show three operations.

- Add two numbers by completing the parallelogram.

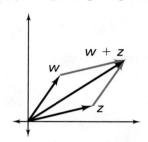

Remember...

The other way to represent a complex number is as a point.

- Multiply a complex number by a real number k by dilating the vector for the complex number by a factor of k.

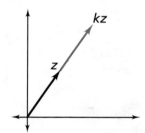

If $k > 0$, the head of the vector is k times as far from the origin in the same direction. If $k < 0$, the head of the vector is k times as far from the origin in the opposite direction.

- Multiply a complex number by i by rotating the complex number $90°$ counterclockwise.

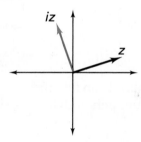

Some of the questions in Lesson 3.10 asked you to look at the relationship between the magnitude and direction of complex numbers and their products. Here is an example, using the product of $1 + 2i$ and $1 + 3i$.

$$(1 + 2i)(1 + 3i) = -5 + 5i$$

Number z	Magnitude $|z|$	Direction: arg z (within 0.001°)
$1 + 2i$	$\sqrt{5}$	63.435°
$1 + 3i$	$\sqrt{10}$	71.565°
$-5 + 5i$	$\sqrt{50}$	135.000°

Habits of Mind

Establish a process. To find the direction, first build a right triangle. Then use trigonometry, geometry, or the complex number functions on your calculator.

The magnitude of the product is the product of the magnitudes.

$$\sqrt{5} \cdot \sqrt{10} = \sqrt{50}$$

The direction of the product is the sum of the directions.

$$63.435° + 71.565° = 135°$$

This suggests the following theorem about the magnitude and direction of products.

Habits of Mind

Experiment. If you are not convinced it works, try another example.

Theorem 3.5

Given complex numbers *z* and *w*, the following statements are true.

- $|zw| = |z| \cdot |w|$

- arg *zw* = arg *z* + arg *w*.

In other words, magnitudes multiply and directions add when you consider the product of two complex numbers.

Remember...

The terms *argument* and *direction* have the same meaning when you refer to a complex number vector.

For Discussion

1. The argument of the product is the sum of the arguments. If arg *z* = 150° and arg *w* = 310°, arg *zw* = 460°. What does it mean to have an argument of 460°? In what quadrant is *zw*?

You can prove Theorem 3.5 using the properties of addition and multiplication you learned in the last lesson.

Minds in Action   episode 12

Sasha helps Tony prove Theorem 3.5.

Tony   Let's say I want to multiply $(4 + 3i)$ and $(1 + 2i)$. I can find the product $-2 + 11i$. Then I can graph the two numbers and their product. Now what do I do?

Sasha   We know how to add, so let's break it up.

$$(4 + 3i)(1 + 2i) = 4(1 + 2i) + 3i(1 + 2i)$$

That's four $(1 + 2i)$'s and $3i$ more $(1 + 2i)$'s. Well, I can make $4(1 + 2i)$ by extending $1 + 2i$ to four times its original size.

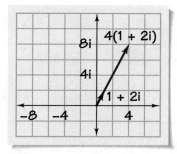

Now I need $3i(1 + 2i)$'s. I multiply by i by rotating 90° counterclockwise. So multiplying by $3i$ is rotating 90° and scaling by 3.

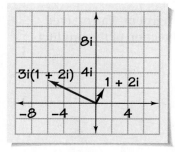

Then I can use the parallelogram law to add. I've got it.

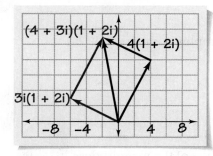

The parallelogram law is Theorem 3.2 from Lesson 3.08.

This dark triangle looks a lot like the triangle I drew in Lesson 3.10 to measure $4 + 3i$. Here, I'll show you what I mean.

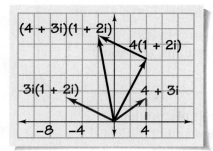

The big triangle for $(4 + 3i)(1 + 2i)$ looks just like the smaller triangle for $4 + 3i$. It's just larger and rotated a little. I'll bet I can prove those triangles are similar. Then I'll have enough evidence to prove Theorem 3.5.

For You to Do

2. Explain why the two drawn triangles both have a 90° angle.

3. Explain why each leg in the larger triangle is $\sqrt{5}$ times as long as each leg in the smaller triangle.

4. Explain why the two right triangles are similar.

The triangle similarity in the dialog above has two important consequences.

- The sides in similar triangles are proportional. Each side in the larger triangle is $\sqrt{5}$ times as long as the corresponding side in the smaller triangle. The magnitude of the product is $5\sqrt{5}$. This is also the product of the magnitudes of the original numbers $4 + 3i$ and $1 + 2i$.

- Corresponding angles in similar triangles are congruent. The marked angles on the graph below are congruent. The direction of the product is the sum of the two original angles.

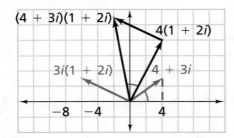

A formal proof of Theorem 3.5 uses the generic complex numbers $(a + bi)$ and $(c + di)$, but the ideas are the same.

Developing Habits of Mind

Visualize. The magnitude of a product is the product of the magnitudes. The argument of a product is the sum of the arguments.

If z and w are complex numbers, you obtain zw from z by a rotation and a scaling. The angle of rotation is arg w and the scale factor is $|w|$.

For example, if you multiply by $(1 + i)$, you are rotating by 45° (the argument of $1 + i$) and scaling by $\sqrt{2}$. If you multiply by i, you are rotating by 90° and scaling by 1.

You can also use algebra to prove that the magnitude of a product is the product of the magnitudes. The product of $a + bi$ and $c + di$ is $(ac - bd) + (bc + ad)i$. Find the magnitude of the product.

$$\sqrt{(ac - bd)^2 + (bc + ad)^2}$$

Then find the product of the magnitudes.

$$\sqrt{a^2 + b^2} \cdot \sqrt{c^2 + d^2}$$

The numbers under the square roots are not negative. Rewrite the expression above as $\sqrt{(a^2 + b^2)(c^2 + d^2)}$.

The result follows from an identity you established in Lesson 3.10.

Another algebraic method is to use the fact that the magnitude equals $\sqrt{z\bar{z}}$, where $\bar{z}$ is the conjugate.

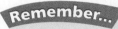
$$|zw| = \sqrt{zw\,\overline{zw}}$$
$$= \sqrt{zw\,\bar{z}\,\bar{w}}$$
$$= \sqrt{z\bar{z}\,w\bar{w}}$$
$$= \sqrt{z\bar{z}}\sqrt{w\bar{w}} = |z||w|$$

For Discussion

5. Give reasons for every step in the calculation above. At one point, a square root becomes the product of two square roots. Is that a legal step? Explain.

For You to Do

6. Describe multiplication by each number, in terms of rotation and scaling.

$$2 + i \qquad -i \qquad -1$$

Exercises *Practicing Habits of Mind*

Check Your Understanding

1. Complex number z has magnitude 3 and direction $120°$.

   a. Find the magnitude and direction of z^2.

   b. Find the magnitude and direction of z^3.

   c. Find an equation with integer coefficients such that z is a solution of the equation.

2. **Write About It** Suppose you know the magnitude and direction of complex number z. Describe how to find the magnitude and direction of z^2, z^3, and the general number z^n.

3. A complex number z^3 has magnitude 27 and direction 180°. Which of the following statements could be true about z?

A. z has magnitude 9 and direction 60°.

B. z has magnitude 3 and direction 60°.

C. z has magnitude 3 and direction 180°.

D. z has magnitude 3 and direction 300°.

For Exercises 4 and 5, use the following complex numbers.

- w, with magnitude 5 and direction 40°
- $x = 1 - i$
- $y = -w$
- $z = -x$

4. Sketch w, $\overline{w}$, y, and $\overline{y}$ on the same complex plane. Label each vector with its magnitude and direction.

5. a. Find the exact magnitude and direction of wx.

    b. Find the exact magnitude and direction of yz.

    c. Use algebra to show that $wx = yz$.

6. The graph below shows two complex numbers z and w. Estimate the magnitude and direction of zw.

Electrical engineers use complex numbers to describe the voltage and current in a circuit.

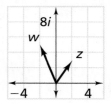

7. Write About It Suppose you have two complex numbers with directions that add to more than 360°. Describe how to find the magnitude and direction of their product.

8. For each z, graph the first few powers of z (z^0, z^1, z^2, ...). Describe what happens if you graph higher powers of z. Explain why.

    a. $z = i$

    b. $z = -i$

    c. $z = 1 + i$

    d. $z = 1 - i$

    e. $z = 2 + i$

    f. $z = 2 - i$

On Your Own

9. Suppose z and w are complex numbers with magnitude 1. Determine whether each number must also have magnitude 1.

    a. zw b. $z + w$ c. $\overline{w}$

    d. $\frac{1}{z}$ e. z^2 f. $2z$

Go Online
Pearsonsuccessnet.com

10. **a.** Graph the triangle with vertices $2 + 3i$, $4 + 6i$, and $7 - i$.

    b. Graph the triangle that results if you multiply each vertex by i.

    c. Graph the triangle that results if you multiply each vertex by $1 + i$.

    d. Graph the triangle that results if you add $1 + i$ to each vertex.

11. Two complex numbers have product $10i$. Neither number is a real number.

    a. Find one possible pair of numbers that fits this description.

    b. **Take It Further** Given any nonzero complex number z, explain how to find w such that $zw = 10i$.

12. The graph below shows two complex numbers z and w. Estimate the magnitude and direction of zw.

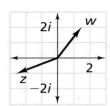

13. **a.** On the complex plane, graph, as points, four different numbers with direction 210°.

    b. Graph the set of all points with direction 210°.

    c. What complex number has magnitude 10 and direction 210°?

14. **Standardized Test Prep** Which of the following describes multiplication by $4 + 4i$?

    A. Rotate by 90° and scale by $4\sqrt{2}$.

    B. Rotate by 45° and scale by $2\sqrt{2}$.

    C. Rotate by 45° and scale by $4\sqrt{2}$.

    D. Rotate by 90° and scale by 4.

15. Use the complex numbers $z = 3 - 2i$ and $w = 1 + 3i$.

    a. Graph z and w as vectors. Determine the magnitude and direction of each.

    b. Find the magnitude and direction of zw.

    c. Find the magnitude and direction of $\overline{zw}$ and $\frac{1}{zw}$.

16. You learned how to find the magnitude and direction of the product of two complex numbers, but how do you find the quotient? Use the complex numbers $z = 4 + 2i$ and $w = 3 + i$.

   a. Write $\frac{z}{w}$ in the form $a + bi$, where a and b are in $\mathbb{R}$.

   b. Find the magnitude and direction of $\frac{z}{w}$.

   c. Describe the relationship between the magnitude and direction of z, w, and $\frac{z}{w}$.

17. **a.** Find five complex numbers with magnitude 13.

   b. **Take It Further** Graph the set of all complex numbers z such that $|z| = 13$.

18. **Take It Further** For each equation or inequality, graph the set of all complex numbers that satisfy the equation or inequality.

   a. $|z| = 3$ **b.** $|z| = 1$ **c.** $|z| < 1$ **d.** $|z| > 1$

   e. $|z| = \left|\frac{1}{z}\right|$ **f.** $z^2 = z$ **g.** $\bar{z} = z$ **h.** $|z^2| = |z|$

Maintain Your Skills

19. For each polynomial $p(x)$, calculate $p(2 + i)$ and $p(2 - i)$.

   a. $p(x) = x^2$ **b.** $p(x) = x^2 + 5x + 7$

   c. $p(x) = x^3$ **d.** $p(x) = x^3 + x^2$

   e. $p(x) = x^3 + x^2 - 15x + 25$ **f.** $p(x) = x^3 - 3x^2 + x + 5$

Is $x^2 - 4x + 5$ a factor of any these polynomials?

20. Write each sum in the form $a + bi$, where a and b are in $\mathbb{R}$.

   a. $1 + i + i^2$

   b. $1 + i + i^2 + i^3$

   c. $1 + i + i^2 + i^3 + i^4$

   d. $1 + i + i^2 + i^3 + i^4 + i^5$

   e. $1 + i + i^2 + i^3 + i^4 + i^5 + i^6$

   f. $1 + i + i^2 + i^3 + i^4 + i^5 + i^6 + i^7 + \cdots + i^{67}$

21. **Take It Further** Suppose that $w = -\frac{1}{2} + \frac{\sqrt{3}}{2}i$. Write each sum in the form $a + bi$, where a and b are in $\mathbb{R}$.

   a. $1 + w + w^2$

   b. $1 + w + w^2 + w^3$

   c. $1 + w + w^2 + w^3 + w^4$

   d. $1 + w + w^2 + w^3 + w^4 + w^5$

   e. $1 + w + w^2 + w^3 + w^4 + w^5 + w^6$

   f. $1 + w + w^2 + w^3 + w^4 + w^5 + w^6 + w^7 + \cdots + w^{67}$

3.12 Conjugates and Roots

One focus of this chapter is the properties of the conjugate of a complex number. This lesson explores an important property of conjugates that you can apply to find the roots of polynomials. In Exercise 18 of Lesson 3.05, you showed that if z is a root of a quadratic polynomial with real coefficients, so is $\bar{z}$. This result holds for higher-degree polynomials as well.

Theorem 3.6 lists the main algebraic properties of conjugation.

> One root of
> $x^2 - 4x + 5$ is $2 + i$.
> The other root is
> $2 - i = \overline{2 + i}$.

Theorem 3.6

Suppose that z and w are complex numbers. Then the following statements are true.

- $\bar{z} + \bar{w} = \overline{z + w}$

  When you add conjugates, the result is the conjugate of the sum of the original numbers.

- $\bar{z} \cdot \bar{w} = \overline{zw}$

  When you multiply conjugates, the result is the conjugate of the product of the original numbers.

- $(\bar{z})^2 = \overline{z^2}$

  When you square a conjugate, the result is the conjugate of the square of the original number.

- **If z is a real number, then $\bar{z} = z$.**

> **Remember...**
>
> The sum of the conjugates is the conjugate of the sum. And the product of the conjugates is the conjugate of the product.

For Discussion

1. Why does $(\bar{z})^2 = \overline{z^2}$ follow from $\bar{z} \cdot \bar{w} = \overline{zw}$?

2. Explain why $(\bar{z})^3 = \overline{z^3}$.

In the exercises, you will explain why $(\bar{z})^k = \overline{z^k}$ for any positive integer k. This fact leads to the following theorem about conjugates.

Theorem 3.7 Polynomials and Conjugates

For any polynomial f with real coefficients and any complex number z,
$\overline{f(z)} = f(\overline{z})$.

Proof Consider the case in which f is a cubic polynomial.

$$f(x) = ax^3 + bx^2 + cx + d$$
$$\overline{f(z)} = \overline{az^3 + bz^2 + cz + d}$$
$$= \overline{az^3} + \overline{bz^2} + \overline{cz} + \overline{d}$$
$$= \overline{a} \cdot \overline{z^3} + \overline{b} \cdot \overline{z^2} + \overline{c} \cdot \overline{z} + \overline{d}$$
$$= a\overline{z^3} + b\overline{z^2} + c\overline{z} + d$$
$$= a(\overline{z})^3 + b(\overline{z})^2 + c\overline{z} + d$$
$$= f(\overline{z})$$

So $\overline{f(z)} = f(\overline{z})$. The proof of the general case involves the same ideas.

For Discussion

3. Theorem 3.7 states that the polynomial has real coefficients. Which step of the proof uses this requirement?

Corollary 3.7.1 Conjugate Pairs

If f is a polynomial with real coefficients, and $f(z) = 0$, then $f(\overline{z}) = 0$.

For Discussion

4. Prove Corollary 3.7.1 using Theorem 3.7.

Corollary 3.7.1 says that complex roots come in conjugate pairs. If $2 + i$ is a root of a polynomial with real coefficients, then $2 - i$ must be another root.

Example 1

Problem Use the polynomial $f(x) = x^3 - 2x^2 - 14x + 40$.

  a. Show that $z = 3 + i$ is a root of f.   **b.** Find the other two roots.

Solution

  a. Let $x = 3 + i$ in $f(x)$.

$$f(3 + i) = (3 + i)^3 - 2(3 + i)^2 - 14(3 + i) + 40$$
$$= (18 + 26i) - 2(8 + 6i) - 14(3 + i) + 40$$
$$= (18 + 26i) + (-16 - 12i) + (-42 - 14i) + 40$$
$$= (18 - 16 - 42 + 40) + (26 - 12 - 14)i$$
$$= 0$$

Since $f(3 + i) = 0$, then $3 + i$ is a root of f.

  b. Since f has real coefficients, the conjugate is also a root. So, $3 - i$ is a root.

> You can confirm this by showing that $f(3 - i) = 0$.

There are a few ways to find the third root. One is to use the sum property. The sum of the three roots is 2. If the third root is r, then $(3 + i) + (3 - i) + r = 2$.

Combine like terms and solve to get $r = -4$. So, -4 is the third root.

For You to Do

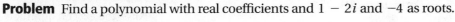

5. How do you solve the equation $x^3 - 5x^2 + 11x - 15 = 0$ if you do not know any of the roots of the polynomial $x^3 - 5x^2 + 11x - 15$?

> For this polynomial, the sum of the three roots is 5 and the product is 15.

Example 2

Problem Find a polynomial with real coefficients and $1 - 2i$ and -4 as roots.

Solution Since $1 - 2i$ is a root, $1 + 2i$ must also be a root.

$$f(x) = (x - (1 - 2i))(x - (1 + 2i))(x + 4)$$

Multiply the first two terms. The sum of $1 - 2i$ and $1 + 2i$ is 2, and the product is 5.

$$(x - (1 - 2i))(x - (1 + 2i)) = x^2 - 2x + 5$$

To find $f(x)$, expand the entire expression.

$$f(x) = (x^2 - 2x + 5)(x + 4)$$
$$= x^3 + 2x^2 - 3x + 20$$

Note that this is not the only possible polynomial with these roots, but it is the polynomial with the least possible degree.

Exercises Practicing Habits of Mind

Check Your Understanding

1. At the right is the graph of $f(x) = x^3 + 6x + 20$.

   a. Use the graph to find a root of $f(x)$.

   b. Find the other two roots.

2. Find a polynomial equation with real coefficients that has $4 - i$ as one of its solutions.

3. Find a polynomial equation with real coefficients that has $4 - i$ and 7 as solutions.

4. a. Show that $-1 + 2i$ is a root of $g(x) = x^3 - 4x^2 - 7x - 30$.

   b. Find the other two roots.

5. a. Show that $3 + i$ is a solution to the equation $x^2 - (8 + 6i) = 0$.

   b. **What's Wrong Here?** Gina says that because $3 + i$ is a solution, then $3 - i$ must also be a solution. Is Gina correct? Explain.

6. **Take It Further** Given p is a polynomial with real coefficients, prove the following statement.

   The product of all the roots of p is positive if and only if the product of all the real roots of p is positive.

On Your Own

7. Use the complex numbers $z = 5 + i$ and $w = 2 + 3i$.

   a. Find the magnitude and direction of z and w.

   b. Find the magnitude and direction of zw without finding zw.

   c. Find the magnitude and direction of z^2 and w^2.

   > Give the exact magnitude and approximate the direction to the nearest degree.

8. a. Show that $4 - i$ is a root of $x^3 - 5x^2 - 7x + 51 = 0$.

   b. Find the other two roots.

   c. Graph the three roots as points on the complex plane.

   > To find complex roots, see the TI-Nspire Handbook, p. 804.

9. Use the function $p(x) = (x - 3)^3 - 5(x - 3)^2 - 7(x - 3) + 51$.

   a. Show that $7 - i$ is a root of $p(x)$.

   b. Find the other two roots.

   c. Plot the three roots as points on the complex plane.

10. Suppose $f(x)$ is a polynomial with real coefficients and z is a complex number. Find $f(\bar{z})$ for each value of $f(z)$.

a. $f(z) = 0$ **b.** $f(z) = 7$

c. $f(z) = 1 + 3i$ **d.** $f(z) = -5i$

11. Find a polynomial function with real coefficients that has $4 - i$ and -5 as roots.

Historical Perspective

Complex numbers first emerged in mathematics as algebraic objects, useful in solving cubic equations. Once mathematicians got used to them as numbers, they realized that they could solve every quadratic equation with real coefficients in the complex numbers.

Not only does every quadratic equation with real coefficients have all its roots in $\mathbb{C}$, every polynomial of any degree n with real coefficients has exactly n roots in $\mathbb{C}$. This fact is the Fundamental Theorem of Algebra. The first rigorous proof of the theorem was given by Gauss in his doctoral thesis in 1799.

This important development in mathematics history is still relevant today. Of course, if you need complex numbers to solve polynomial equations with real coefficients, you probably think you need some other kind of number to solve polynomial equations with complex coefficients. Amazingly, this is not the case. Even if you allow the coefficients of a polynomial to be complex numbers, you still have exactly n roots for a polynomial of degree n, and you can find all those roots in the complex number system.

This number system, in which any polynomial with coefficients from the system has all its roots in the system, is considered algebraically closed. So, the Fundamental Theorem of Algebra states that $\mathbb{C}$ is algebraically closed.

The Fundamental Theorem of Algebra is an existence theorem. It states that an nth-degree polynomial has all its roots in $\mathbb{C}$, but it does not tell you how to find them. In fact, for polynomials of degree five or more, there is no analog to the quadratic formula that allows you to solve all polynomials of a given degree.

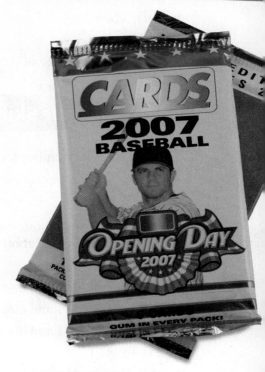

The packaging is like the Fundamental Theorem of Algebra. It tells you how many cards you get, but not what they are.

12. **Standardized Test Prep** If $3 + 4i$ is a root of $f(x) = x^3 - 2x^2 + x + 100$, which are the other two roots?

    A. $3 - 4i$ and 4   **B.** $3 - 5i$ and -4

    C. $-3 - 5i$ and 8   **D.** $3 - 4i$ and -4

13. **a.** Find a cubic function with real coefficients for which one root is $2 + 7i$ and the sum of the roots is 0.

    b. Find a cubic function with real coefficients for which one root is $2 + 7i$ and the product of the roots is 106.

14. Use the function $g(x) = x^6 - 1$. Calculate each value.

    a. $g(-1)$

    b. $g(w)$, where $w = \dfrac{1 + i\sqrt{3}}{2}$

    c. $g(w^2)$

    d. **Take It Further** Plot all six complex numbers that make $g(x) = 0$.

Maintain Your Skills

15. For each complex number z, calculate the magnitude and direction of z^4.

    a. $z = 1 + i$ **b.** $z = 1 - i$

    c. $z = -1 + i$ **d.** $z = -1 - i$

16. Suppose z^5 has magnitude 1 and direction 0°. Determine whether each statement could be true about z.

This is a more complicated way to say $z^5 = 1$.

    a. $z = 1$

    b. z has magnitude 1 and direction 72°.

    c. z has magnitude 1 and direction 120°.

    d. z has magnitude 1 and direction 144°.

    e. $z = -1$

    f. z has magnitude 1 and direction 216°.

Roots of Unity

In Chapter 2, you learned how to factor polynomials of the form $x^n - 1$. This lesson focuses on the roots of those polynomials.

Example

Problem Find and graph all solutions to each equation as points on the complex plane.

    a. $x^2 = 1$

    b. $x^3 = 1$

    c. $x^4 = 1$

    d. $x^6 = 1$

Solution Set each equation equal to zero and then factor it. Use the Zero-Product Property to find the solutions.

    a. Solve $x^2 - 1 = (x - 1)(x + 1)$ using difference of squares. The two roots are $x = 1$ and $x = -1$.

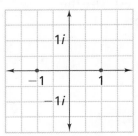

The Ferris wheel cars suggest the roots of $x^{12} - 1$.

    b. Solve $x^3 - 1 = (x - 1)(x^2 + x + 1)$ using difference of cubes. The first factor gives the root $x = 1$. Use the quadratic formula with the second factor to find the other roots.

$$x = \frac{-1 \pm \sqrt{1 - 4}}{2} = \frac{-1 \pm i\sqrt{3}}{2}$$

The other two roots are complex conjugates with magnitude 1 and directions 120° and 240°.

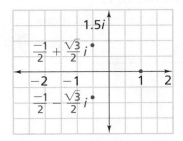

c. Solve $x^4 - 1 = \left(x^2 - 1\right)\left(x^2 + 1\right)$ using difference of squares. Use difference of squares again to factor $x^2 - 1$.

$$x^4 - 1 = (x - 1)(x + 1)(x^2 + 1)$$

The first two factors give the roots $x = 1$ and $x = -1$. Use the quadratic formula with the third factor to find the other roots.

$$x = \frac{0 \pm \sqrt{-4}}{2} = \frac{0 \pm 2i}{2} = \pm i$$

The four roots are 1, i, -1, and $-i$.

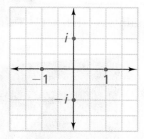

d. Solve $x^6 - 1 = \left(x^3 - 1\right)\left(x^3 + 1\right)$ using difference of squares. Use sum and difference of cubes to factor $x^3 - 1$ and $x^3 + 1$.

$$x^6 - 1 = (x - 1)\left(x^2 + x + 1\right)(x + 1)\left(x^2 - x + 1\right)$$

The first and third factors give the roots $x = 1$ and $x = -1$. Use the quadratic formula for the quadratic factors. The six roots are 1, -1, $\frac{-1 \pm i\sqrt{3}}{2}$, and $\frac{1 \pm i\sqrt{3}}{2}$.

For You to Do

1. Find the magnitude and direction for each of the six solutions to $x^6 = 1$.

2. Show that all the complex numbers in the above example are also solutions of $x^{12} - 1 = 0$.

Developing Habits of Mind

Look for relationships. The solutions to $x^n = 1$ are **roots of unity.**
Solving the equation involves taking a root of 1.

$$x^n = 1 \text{ or } x = \sqrt[n]{1}$$

In the real numbers, the only possible solutions to such an equation are
$x = 1$ and $x = -1$. But there are many other complex numbers with
magnitude 1, and there are many other ways for x^n to equal 1.

Think about how you represent 1 on the complex plane. It has magnitude
1 and direction $0°$. But you can also think of 1 as having magnitude 1
and direction $360°$, by going all the way around. Or you can think of the
direction as $720°$, or $1080°$, and so on.

In an exercise in Lesson 3.11, you found that the direction of z^3 is three
times the direction of z. If $z^3 = 1$, then three times the direction of z must
be a multiple of $360°$.

> $x = 1$ is always a
> solution. When is
> $x = -1$ a solution?

Minds in Action   episode 13

Tony is trying to find the solutions to $x^5 = 1$.

Tony   The example skips right over $x^5 = 1$, but I can find those
solutions by magnitude and direction. If $x^5 = 1$, then x has to
have magnitude 1. So now I just need to know the directions. The
direction of x^5 is five times the direction of x. That means I know
one possible direction for x.

$$\frac{360°}{5} = 72°$$

Five times at $72°$ is one trip all the way around and back to 1. The
next one is two trips all the way around, which is $720°$. So I divide
by 5 to find the direction.

$$\frac{720°}{5} = 144°$$

They just come equally spaced
like that. The directions are all the
multiples of $72°$ and the magnitudes
are always 1. Here's what it looks like
in the complex plane.

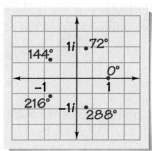

If I connect the points, I make a
regular pentagon. The others from
the example all work that way, too.
The point at 1 is always going to be a
vertex, since $1^n = 1$ for any power. I like this because I don't have
to factor. This even works for stuff that doesn't factor.

For You to Do

3. Find the magnitude and direction of all solutions to $x^9 = 1$.

Tony's method works in general. For example, below are the seventh roots of unity, which all satisfy $x^7 = 1$.

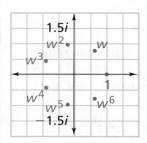

You can call the equation $x^n - 1 = 0$ the *cyclotomic* equation. This means that the roots of the equation divide a circle of radius 1 in the complex plane into n congruent arcs.

These seven numbers are all solutions to $x^7 - 1 = 0$. Since this equation can have at most seven solutions, this is the entire list of the solutions to the equation. And these seven roots of unity form a regular 7-gon in the complex plane.

Exercises *Practicing Habits of Mind*

Check Your Understanding

1. Suppose $w^n = 1$.

    a. Use the properties of exponents to show that $(w^2)^n = 1$.

    b. Show that for any positive integer k, $(w^k)^n = 1$.

2. Graph the ten solutions to $x^{10} = 1$ as points on the complex plane.

3. a. Graph the twelve solutions to $x^{12} = 1$ on the complex plane.

    b. Is $x = \frac{-1}{2} - \frac{\sqrt{3}}{2}i$ a solution to $x^{12} = 1$? Explain.

This proves that if w is a root of unity, then w^k is also a root of unity.

4. a. Find the three solutions to $x^3 = 8$. Then graph them on the complex plane.

   b. Describe how the solutions to $x^3 = 8$ are related to the solutions to $x^3 = 1$.

5. Use magnitude and direction to find two complex numbers z such that $z^2 = i$.

These numbers are the square roots of i.

6. a. Find a complex number z such that $z^3 = i$.

   b. Find all three complex numbers that are solutions to $x^3 = i$. Then plot them as points on the complex plane.

   c. Describe how the solutions to $x^3 = i$ are related to the solutions to $x^3 = 1$.

7. Find the sum of the sixth roots of unity.

8. Sasha says that if w is a fifth root of unity, so is $\overline{w}$. Is she correct? Explain.

9. Take It Further Some roots of unity repeat. For example, the cube roots of unity (solutions to $x^3 = 1$) are also sixth roots of unity (solutions to $x^6 = 1$). Also, $x = 1$ always repeats. But some roots of unity are new for a particular power. For example, i and $-i$ are solutions to $x^4 = 1$, but not of any lower-degree equations.

   a. Copy and complete the table below with the number of new roots of unity for each equation.

Equation	Number of New Roots
$x = 1$	1
$x^2 = 1$	1
$x^3 = 1$	2
$x^4 = 1$	2
$x^5 = 1$	▧
$x^6 = 1$	▧
$x^7 = 1$	▧
$x^8 = 1$	▧
$x^9 = 1$	▧
$x^{10} = 1$	▧

   b. Describe any relationships you notice in the table. Describe a rule for the number of new roots of unity for $x^n = 1$.

10. **Standardized Test Prep** Which angle is the difference in direction between consecutive solutions to $x^9 = 1$?

    A. $20°$ **B.** $30°$ **C.** $40°$ **D.** $45°$

11. A complex number z has magnitude 1 and direction $20°$. The powers of z are the vertices of a regular polygon on the complex plane. How many sides does this polygon have?

12. Consider the complex number $z = \frac{1 + i\sqrt{3}}{2}$.

    a. Find the magnitude and direction of z.

    b. Find a power n such that $z^n = 1$.

    c. Graph the powers of z as points on the complex plane.

13. The graph below shows the eight solutions to $x^8 = 1$.

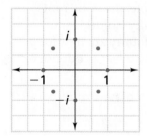

    a. Find the magnitude and direction of each solution.

    b. Write each complex number in the form $a + bi$. Use radicals where needed.

14. **Take It Further** Show that all eight numbers in Exercise 13 are powers of the same number.

Maintain Your Skills

15. For each complex number z, calculate z^2. Then find the magnitude of z^2.

    a. $z = 2 + i$ **b.** $z = 3 + 2i$ **c.** $z = 4 + i$

    d. $z = 4 + 3i$ **e.** $z = m + ni$

16. **a.** Find $1 + i + i^2 + i^3 + i^4$. Justify your answer.

    b. If $w^3 = 1$, find $1 + w + w^2$. Justify your answer.

    c. If $z^5 = 1$, find $1 + z + z^2 + z^3 + z^4$. Justify your answer.

    d. If $w^6 = 1$, find $1 + w + w^2 + w^3 + w^4 + w^5$. Justify your answer.

In this investigation, you found relationships between magnitudes and arguments of factors and products. You also graphed the solutions to equations in the form $x^n - 1 = 0$. These exercises will help you summarize what you have learned.

1. Use $z = 1 - \sqrt{3}i$. Find the magnitude and direction for each power of z.

    a. z **b.** z^2 **c.** z^3 **d.** z^4

    e. Which, if any, of the powers of z that you found is a real number? Explain.

2. A complex number z has magnitude 6 and direction 135°. A complex number w has magnitude 2 and direction 240°.

    a. Find the magnitude and direction of the product zw.

    b. Find the magnitude and direction of v such that zv has magnitude 3 and direction 30°.

3. Find a polynomial with real coefficients that has $2 - i$ and 3 among its roots. Is your polynomial the only possible polynomial? If so, explain why. If not, find another polynomial.

4. Show that $6i$ is a root of the polynomial $x^3 + 2x^2 + 36x + 72$. Then find the other roots.

5. Find the magnitude and direction of all solutions to the equation $x^5 - 1 = 0$. If there are any solutions in Quadrant II, express them in the form $a + bi$, where a and b are real numbers. Approximate to the nearest hundredth if you cannot find an exact answer.

6. How are the magnitude and argument of the product of two complex numbers related to the magnitude and argument of the original numbers?

7. If $-2 + i$ is a root of the polynomial $x^3 + 7x^2 + 17x + 15$, what is another root?

8. How can you graph the solution to the equation $x^{10} - 1 = 0$ on the complex plane without doing many calculations?

Vocabulary

In this investigation, you learned this term. Make sure you understand what it means and how to use it.

• **roots of unity**

Project: Using Mathematical Habits

Factoring a Sequence of Polynomials

Consider the following polynomials.

$$\{x^2 - 1, x^3 - 1, x^4 - 1, x^5 - 1, \ldots, x^n - 1, \ldots\}$$

For this project, you are to investigate how these polynomials factor over $\mathbb{Z}$.

Factor over $\mathbb{Z}$ means that the factors have integer coefficients. Integers are probably what your CAS gives by default when you tell it to factor things.

Note that not all the factors will be linear polynomials. You could have a factor like $(x^2 + x + 1)$, which does not factor further in $\mathbb{Z}$.

1. Make a table like the one below and complete it.

n	Number of Factors of $x^n - 1$
1	▪
2	▪
3	▪
4	▪
5	▪
6	▪
⋮	▪
20	▪

2. Describe at least two patterns you see in your table.

3. For what values of n does it seem that $x^n - 1$ factors into exactly two factors?

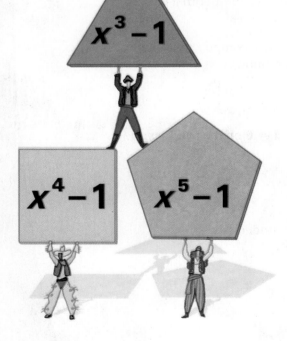

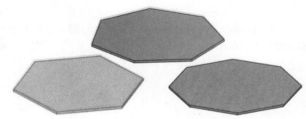

Review

Go Online
Pearsonsuccessnet.com

In **Investigation 3A,** you learned how to

- understand complex numbers as an extension of the real numbers
- use complex numbers as tools for solving equations
- be fluent in complex-number arithmetic

The following questions will help you check your understanding.

1. Use the equation $x^5 - 36x = 0$. Find the solutions, if they exist, that meet each of the following conditions.

   a. The solution is in $\mathbb{N}$.

   b. The solution is in $\mathbb{Z}$ but not in $\mathbb{N}$.

   c. The solution is in $\mathbb{Q}$ but not in $\mathbb{Z}$.

   d. The solution is in $\mathbb{R}$ but not in $\mathbb{Q}$.

   e. The solution is not in $\mathbb{R}$.

2. a. Solve $2x^2 - x + 5 = 0$ over $\mathbb{C}$.

   b. Find a complex number $z = a + bi$, where a and b are real numbers, that satisfies $z + (3 - 7i) = -2 - 11i$.

   c. Find a complex number $z = a + bi$, where a and b are real numbers, that satisfies $(1 - i) \cdot z = 3$.

3. Given two complex numbers $z = -1 + 3i$ and $w = 4 + 2i$, find each of the following.

   a. $z + w$

   b. $\overline{w}$

   c. $z \cdot w$

   d. $2z \cdot \overline{w}$

   e. z^2

   f. $\frac{1}{z}$

In **Investigation 3B,** you learned how to

- graph complex numbers on the complex plane
- visualize operations on complex numbers as transformations on the complex plane
- develop greater fluency with complex number calculations, which include finding magnitude and direction

The following questions will help you check your understanding.

4. For $z = 4 - 3i$ and $w = 2 + 2i$, graph and label each on the complex plane.

   a. z and $-z$

   b. z and $\overline{z}$

   c. z, w, and $z + w$

   d. w and $2w$

   e. w, $i \cdot w$

   f. z, w, and $z \cdot w$

5. Graph $2i$, $(2i)^2$, and $(2i)^3$ on the same complex plane.

6. Let $z = -1 + i$. Copy and complete the following table.

	$a + bi$	Magnitude	Direction
z	$-1 + i$	▦	▦
$-z$	▦	▦	▦
$\overline{z}$	▦	▦	▦
$i \cdot z$	▦	▦	▦
$3z$	▦	▦	▦
z^2	▦	▦	▦

In **Investigation 3C,** you learned how to

- describe relationships between magnitudes and arguments of factors and products
- prove the relationship between the function values of complex conjugates
- find and graph the solutions to equations of the form $x^n - 1 = 0$ on the complex plane

The following questions will help you check your understanding.

7. Complex number z has magnitude 3 and direction 30°. Complex number w has magnitude 2 and direction 120°.

   Find the magnitude and direction of each number.

   a. zw **b.** z^2

   c. z^3 **d.** $-w$

   e. $4w$ **f.** $\bar{z}$

8. Find a quadratic equation with real coefficients that has $2 + 3i$ as one of its solutions.

9. Without actually solving the equation, find the magnitude and direction of all solutions to the equation $x^6 - 1 = 0$.

Multiple Choice

1. What is the value of $\sqrt{-4} \cdot \sqrt{-9}$?

   A. 6

   B. -6

   C. $6i$

   D. $-6i$

2. If $z = 4 + 6i$, what is $z - \bar{z}$?

   A. 0

   B. 8

   C. $12i$

   D. $8 + 12i$

3. If $z = a + bi$ is in Quadrant III, then $i \cdot z$ is in which quadrant?

   A. I

   B. II

   C. III

   D. IV

4. What is the value of $|5 - 12i|$?

   A. $\sqrt{119}$

   B. 7

   C. 13

   D. 17

5. One solution of $ax^2 + bx + c = 0$, where a, b, and c are real numbers, is $4 - 6i$. Which of the following is another solution?

   A. $-4 + 6i$

   B. $\sqrt{52}$

   C. $-4 - 6i$

   D. $4 + 6i$

Open Response

6. Find the solutions of $x^2 - 2x + 10 = 0$ that are in each number system.

   a. $\mathbb{R}$ b. $\mathbb{C}$

7. Solve each equation over $\mathbb{C}$. Express your answer in the form $a + bi$, where a and b are real numbers.

   a. $z + 4i = 2(3 - i)$

   b. $z \cdot (5 + i) = 11 - 3i$

8. Use $z = -2 + 2i$ and $w = 1 + i$.

   a. Find $z \cdot w$.

   b. On the complex plane, graph z, w, and $z \cdot w$.

   c. Copy and complete the table below.

	$a + bi$	Magnitude	Direction
z	$-2 + 2i$	■	■
w	$1 + i$	■	■
$z \cdot w$	■	■	■

9. A complex number z has magnitude 4 and direction 30°. Find the magnitude and direction of each power of z.

   a. z^2 b. z^3 c. z^4

10. Find a cubic equation with real coefficients that has $3 - i$ and 1 as two of its solutions.

Chapter **4**

4

Linear Algebra

The World Wide Web consists of hundreds of millions of pages of content. New pages are added at any time without notice. How does anyone ever find anything he or she wants? One popular search engine determined that text matching alone would not be enough to help people find relevant information quickly. Its developers decided to rank pages by importance as well as using text matching techniques.

You can determine the importance of a Web page with an equation that counts contributions from every other page on the Web. To find the importance of a particular page, look at every page that links to it. Each linking page contributes the amount of its own importance divided by the number of pages it links to. This means that links from more important pages carry greater weight. To keep track of all these equations, one for every page, each with millions of terms, you can use a gigantic matrix. Then, every time a search engine crawls the Web to rebuild its index, it can use sophisticated linear algebra techniques to recalculate the matrix.

Vocabulary and Notation

- absorbing state
- determinant
- dimension
- dot product
- elimination
- Gaussian Elimination
- identity matrix, I
- inverse, A^{-1}
- linear combination
- matrix
- matrix multiplication

- matrix transformation
- n-tuple
- probability transition matrix
- row-reduced echelon form (rref)
- scalar multiplication
- steady state
- substitution
- transition matrix
- zero matrix, 0

Gaussian Elimination

In *Gaussian Elimination*, you will review several methods for solving systems of equations. You will also learn about matrices and how to use them to solve systems of equations.

By the end of this investigation, you will be able to answer questions like these.

1. Why is it possible to solve systems of linear equations in matrix form?

2. What is the process of Gaussian Elimination?

3. Find x, y, and z such that

$$4x - y + 4z = 1$$
$$2x - y + 8z = 11$$
$$2x - 2y + 4z = 0$$

You will learn how to

• solve a system of three equations in three unknowns

• write a system of linear equations in matrix form or translate a matrix into a system of equations

• describe and apply the process of Gaussian Elimination and apply it both by hand and with technology to solve a system

You will develop these habits and skills:

• Connect the results from substitution and elimination methods and show that the methods are equivalent.

• Strategize to solve a system of equations systematically.

• Reason about how to describe an algorithm generally as a series of steps that you can apply to any situation.

The scoreboard shows the score of the baseball game in matrix form.

Getting Started

In your first-year algebra course, you learned several ways to solve a system of equations.

For You to Explore

1. Solve the following system in at least two ways.

$$x + y = 4$$
$$2x - y = -1$$

2. Solve the following system.

$$2x + y = 1$$
$$3x + 2y = 1$$

3. Find the point where the lines given by the following equations intersect.

$$y = 3x + 2$$
$$y = -2x + 1$$

4. Find an x-value for which these two functions have the same output.

$$f(x) = 3x + 2$$
$$g(x) = -2x + 1$$

5. In Chapter 2, you learned how to use Lagrange Interpolation to find a polynomial that fits a set of data points. Find a polynomial $p(x)$ with a graph that passes through the points $(0, 1)$, $(1, -1)$, and $(3, 1)$.

6. Another way to find a polynomial with a graph that passes through the points $(0, 1)$, $(1, -1)$, and $(3, 1)$ is to first realize that the highest-degree polynomial you need to fit these three points is a quadratic. Then you can begin with a general form of a quadratic function, $q(x) = ax^2 + bx + c$. Use the data points to write a system of equations for finding the coefficients a, b, and c.

Habits of Mind

Detect the key characterisitics. Why do three points determine a quadratic?

a. Explain why $q(3) = 1$ implies that $9a + 3b + c = 1$.

b. Find two more equations involving a, b, and c using the other data points.

c. Find an equation for the polynomial.

Exercises Practicing Habits of Mind

On Your Own

7. Solve the following system.

$$2x + 3y = 1$$
$$\tfrac{1}{2}x + \tfrac{1}{3}y = 1$$

8. Find the point of intersection of the line with equation $\frac{y-1}{x-1} = 2$ and the line with slope -1 and x-intercept 3.

Remember...

If a line has x-intercept a, that means that the graph of the line intersects the x-axis at the point $(a, 0)$.

9. The simplest graph that goes through two points is a line. You know many ways to find an equation for this line. Here is a technique that uses a system of equations. Suppose the two points are $(1, 4)$ and $(3, 2)$. The polynomial must be of the form $p(x) = ax + b$. Use the two points to find two equations in a and b. Then solve them to find the polynomial.

10. Solve the following system.

$$x + y + z = 2$$
$$2x - y + z = 5$$
$$x + 2y + 3z = 5$$

Habits of Mind

Use a consistent process. Exercise 9 is like Problem 6. To understand a method, one good habit is to apply it in simpler situations.

11. Take It Further The system below has more unknowns than equations. However, you can still use the methods for solving two equations in two unknowns to find all the solutions.

$$x + 2y + 3z = 4$$
$$2x + y - z = -2$$

a. Solve the first equation for x and substitute into the second equation, eliminating x.

b. Eliminate x from the second equation another way: by subtracting a multiple of the first equation.

c. After using either method, solve the new second equation for y in terms of z.

d. Substitute your result from part (c) into the original first equation to eliminate y. Then express x in terms of z.

e. Explain why there is one solution (x, y, z) of the original system of equations for each value of z.

The solutions to part (e) form a *one-parameter family*. You can express all the solutions in terms of the single variable z. This gives you a way to manage an infinite set of solutions.

Habits of Mind

Consider more than one strategy. Along with the algebraic solution methods you have been reviewing, you might want to solve these systems graphically, too.

12. Solve each system. What new situations arise? How would you describe each solution?

a. $x + 2y = 3$
$2x + 4y = 6$

b. $x + 2y = 3$
$2x + 4y = 7$

Maintain Your Skills

Solve each system.

13. $x + 2y + 3z = 1$
$3y - z = 4$
$2z = -2$

14. $2x - 3y + 5z - 2t = 9$
$5y - z + 3t = 1$
$7z - t = 3$
$2t = 8$

15. 4×4 systems (four equations in four unknowns) are usually quite difficult to solve by hand, but the one in Exercise 14 is not. Explain.

Solve each system.

16. $\quad 2x = 4$
$x - y = 3$
$-x + 2y + z = 2$

17. $\quad x + 2z = 4$
$3z = -3$
$x + 2y - z = 1$

18. Consider the following system.

$$x + 2y + 3z = 4$$
$$-3y - 7z = -10$$

You can rewrite it with z's on the right side.

$$x + 2y = 4 - 3z$$
$$-3y = -10 + 7z$$

a. What does this new system now have in common with other Maintain Your Skills exercises?

b. Use this similarity to solve for x and y in terms of z.

19. Solve the following system.

$$x - 2y + z = 7$$
$$2x - y + 4z = 17$$
$$3x - 2y + 2z = 14$$

Go Online
Video Tutor
Pearsonsuccessnet.com

Solving Systems Systematically

Exercise 10 in Lesson 4.01 asked you to solve the system

$$x + y + z = 2 \qquad (1)$$
$$2x - y + z = 5 \qquad (2)$$
$$x + 2y + 3z = 5 \qquad (3)$$

This is a 3 × 3 system—three linear equations in three unknowns. It is natural to try the methods you used on two equations in two unknowns. The two main methods were *substitution* and *elimination*. In **substitution,** you solve one equation for one variable and substitute that solution into the other equation. Then you have an equation in the other variable alone, which you can solve. In **elimination,** you add or subtract the two equations so that one variable cancels out, again resulting in an equation in the other variable alone.

In a 3 × 3 system, both methods allow many more choices. Say you solve Equation (1) for x and substitute the result into (2). That still gives an equation in two unknowns, y and z, so what do you do next? You can do another substitution, but if you are not careful you may go in circles. The way to succeed is to substitute the same expression for x into the third equation. That gives you two equations in the same two unknowns, which you know how to solve.

Specifically, solving (1) for x gives

$$x = 2 - y - z \qquad (4)$$

Substituting into (2) gives

$$2(2 - y - z) - y + z = 5$$
$$4 - 2y - 2z - y + z = 5$$
$$-3y - z = 1$$

Substituting (4) into (3) gives

$$(2 - y - z) + 2y + 3z = 5$$
$$2 + y + 2z = 5$$
$$y + 2z = 3$$

Substitution has given you a 2 × 2 system.

$$-3y - z = 1$$
$$y + 2z = 3$$

> The numbers in parentheses are equation labels. They are helpful when you want to discuss several equations at once, or describe operations involving two equations. Remember to distinguish the number 2 from the equation (2).

Habits of Mind

Make strategic choices. Going from three equations in three unknowns to two equations in two unknowns is an instance of *reducing a problem to a simpler case*.

For You to Do

1. Solve the 2 × 2 system above.

Once you solve the 2 × 2 system, substitute the values of y and z into (4) to find x. In this problem, the final result is $x = 1$, $y = -1$, and $z = 2$.

> You can also write $(x, y, z) = (1, -1, 2)$.

Minds in Action episode 14

Sasha and Derman are trying to solve the same system (1)–(3) using the elimination method.

Sasha I think this will be easiest if we follow the method just shown as closely as possible.

Derman How can it be close? In elimination, you add and subtract equations, you don't substitute.

Sasha Right, but I mean let's use the same equations in the same order. I think that's our best chance to get down to two equations in y and z.

Derman I don't think it would have to be y and z, but yeah, let's do that. In the substitution method, we solved Equation (1) for x and substituted the result into Equations (2) and (3).

Sasha So let's try adding or subtracting (1) from (2) and (1) from (3) to eliminate x twice.

Derman But we've got to eliminate $2x$ from (2).

Sasha So let's multiply (1) by 2 and then subtract the result from (2).

$$
\begin{array}{r}
2x - y + z = 5 \\
(-)\,2x + 2y + 2z = 4 \\
\hline
-3y - z = 1
\end{array}
$$

Derman It's easier to eliminate x from (3)—just subtract (1) as it is.

$$
\begin{array}{r}
x + 2y + 3z = 5 \\
(-)\,x + y + z = 2 \\
\hline
y + 2z = 3
\end{array}
$$

Derman So the reduced system we get is

$$
-3y - z = 1
$$
$$
y + 2z = 3
$$

It's the same as before. Hmm.

Sasha That's good. We'll get the same solution as before, and we should.

Derman But lots of 2 × 2 systems have the same solution $y = -1$, $z = 2$. Do the two methods always give the same reduced system?

For Discussion

2. Think about Derman's question. Can you explain why the substitution and elimination methods ended up with the same 2×2 reduced system? Look carefully at the work shown in the text for solving the system (1)–(3).

This lesson has been about extending the methods you know for solving two equations in two unknowns to larger systems. It is time to put the pieces together and do one example from start to finish.

Example

Problem Solve the following system.

$$x - y + z = 0 \qquad (5)$$
$$x + y + 2z = 1 \qquad (6)$$
$$-x + 2y - 3z = 3 \qquad (7)$$

Solution This solution uses the elimination method. Subtract (5) from (6) and add (5) to (7). You get

$$2y + z = 1 \qquad (8)$$
$$y - 2z = 3 \qquad (9)$$

Now subtract (9) multiplied by 2 from (8).

$$5z = -5$$

So $z = -1$. Substitute this value into (9).

$$y + 2 = 3 \qquad \text{so} \qquad y = 1$$

> Substituting into (8) would also work.

Now substitute the y- and z-values into any one of the original equations, for example (5).

$$x - 1 - 1 = 0 \qquad \text{so} \qquad x = 2$$

Conclusion: $(x, y, z) = (2, 1, -1)$

> You can describe this process by saying that you solved the system by eliminating x first and then y.

Exercises Practicing Habits of Mind

Check Your Understanding

Consider the system (5)–(7) from the Example.

1. Solve the system again, this time eliminating y first by adding or subtracting (5) from (6) and (5) from (7).

2. Solve the system again, this time eliminating z first.

3. Solve the system again, this time by the substitution method. Solve for x from (5) and substitute into the other equations. Do you get the same 2×2 reduced system as in the solution by elimination in the Example?

4. Solve the system again, this time by the substitution method. Solve for y from (5) and substitute into the other equations. Do you get the same 2×2 reduced system as in Exercise 1? Can you explain why?

5. A quadratic function $f(x) = ax^2 + bx + c$ passes through the points (1, 1), (2, 3), and (3, 6). Find a, b, and c.

On Your Own

6. **Standardized Test Prep** Which is the solution to the system of equations at the right?

   $$x - 3y + 6z = 2$$
   $$-2x + 2y + z = 9$$
   $$-x + 3y - 7z = -3$$

   A. $(-7, 1, 2)$ **B.** $(-7.75, -3.25, 0)$

   C. $(-4, 0, 1)$ **D.** $(5, 7.8, 3.4)$

7. Consider the 4×4 system at the right.

   $$x + y + z - w = -1$$
   $$x + y - z + w = 0$$
   $$x - y + z + w = 1$$
   $$-x + y + z + w = 2$$

   a. Reduce this system to a 3×3 system by elimination, eliminating x.

   b. Reduce this system to a 3×3 system by substitution, again eliminating x.

   c. Solve the 3×3 system you got in part (a).

   d. Solve the original 4×4 system.

   > You may have gotten different systems for parts (a) and (b). Do the two systems have the same solution?

8. Solve the 4×4 system at the right.

   $$u + 2x - y + z = 1$$
   $$x + y + z = 2$$
   $$2x - y + z = 5$$
   $$x + 2y + 3z = 5$$

9. Try using both substitution and elimination to solve the following system. What happens?

$$x + 2y = 3$$
$$2x + 4y = 4$$

Go Online
Pearsonsuccessnet.com

10. Take It Further Consider this system.

$$x + 2y + z = 2$$
$$2x + 4y + 3z = 5$$

The last time you had two equations in three unknowns (see Lesson 4.01, Exercise 18), there was one solution for every value of z. What happens for this system?

11. Take It Further You write the equation for the graph of a circle in the form $(x - a)^2 + (y - b)^2 = r^2$, where (a, b) is the center and r is the radius.

a. By solving a system of equations, find the center and radius of the circle that goes through the points $(-4, 0)$, $(0, 2)$, and $(4, 0)$.

b. Find the center and radius using geometric methods.

These equations are not linear equations, but the method of adding and subtracting equations still works.

Maintain Your Skills

12. Solve this system.

$$x = y + z$$
$$y = x + z$$
$$z = x + y$$

13. Solve each system. Compare the solutions to the ones from the dialog.

a. $x + y + z = 2$
$2x - y + z = 5$
$3x + y + 4z = 10$

b. $x + y + z = 2$
$2x - y + z = 5$
$2x + 3y + 4z = 7$

14. In Exercise 13 from Lesson 4.01, you solved the following system.

$$x + 2y + 3z = 1$$
$$3y - z = 4$$
$$2z = -2$$

The natural way to solve such a triangular system is to solve for z and then substitute. However, you have learned that adding and subtracting equations can accomplish the same thing as substitution. Solve this system again without any substitutions.

15. Solve this system using addition and subtraction.

$$2x - 3y + 5z - 2t = 9$$
$$5y - z + 3t = 1$$
$$7z - t = 3$$
$$2t = 8$$

It is more work to add and subtract equations, but there is a reason for doing it. Stay tuned for the next lesson.

Solving Again, in Matrix Form

Substitution and elimination are effectively the same—if you apply them to the equations in the same order, you get the same key equations along the way. So, is there any reason to recommend one method over the other?

For large systems, it is much easier to implement elimination. You can describe elimination as a consistent series of steps that you always apply in the same order.

In the elimination method, you can consistently put each variable in the same place. For instance, you can always make the x's be first and the y's second. Also, the variables play almost no role! Only the coefficients and the constants on the right side of the equations change. The only role the variables play is as labels for the coefficients. For instance, if you subtract $2x + 4y = 6$ from $2x + 5y = 2$, the y's tell you that the 4 and the 5 both belong to the same variable and you can subtract them from each other.

But if the variables are always in the same place, then the position alone determines which coefficient goes with which variable. You do not need to write the variables at all! For instance, consider again Sasha and Derman's old friend.

> You can more easily implement elimination methods with technology.

$$x + y + z = 2 \tag{1}$$

$$2x - y + z = 5 \tag{2}$$

$$x + 2y + 3z = 5 \tag{3}$$

You can instead write

$$A = \begin{pmatrix} 1 & 1 & 1 & \Big| & 2 \\ 2 & -1 & 1 & \Big| & 5 \\ 1 & 2 & 3 & \Big| & 5 \end{pmatrix}$$

Now, instead of subtracting 2 times (1) from (2), multiply row 1 of A by 2 and subtract the result from row 2, entry by entry. Instead of writing a new system of equations with a new second equation, write a new matrix A' with a new second row.

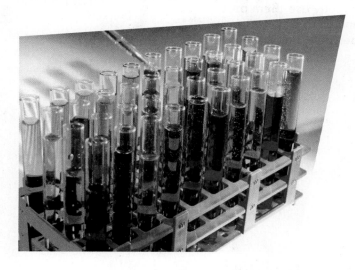

Sometimes it makes sense to record data from experiments in matrix form.

Look at the process up close.

$$\begin{pmatrix} 1 & 1 & 1 & \bigm| & 2 \\ 2 & -1 & 1 & \bigm| & 5 \\ 2 & 2 & 2 & \bigm| & 4 \\ 1 & 2 & 3 & \bigm| & 5 \end{pmatrix} \longrightarrow A' = \begin{pmatrix} 1 & 1 & 1 & \bigm| & 2 \\ 0 & -3 & -1 & \bigm| & 1 \\ 1 & 2 & 3 & \bigm| & 5 \end{pmatrix}$$

In the diagram, you see matrix A in black. Then, two times row 1 is shown in blue below row 2. Subtract term by term and replace row 2 with the result. The new resulting row is shown in blue in the second matrix.

To continue, instead of subtracting (1) from (3), subtract row 1 from row 3 to make a new row that replaces row 3.

$$A' = \begin{pmatrix} 1 & 1 & 1 & \bigm| & 2 \\ 0 & -3 & -1 & \bigm| & 1 \\ 1 & 2 & 3 & \bigm| & 5 \\ 1 & 1 & 1 & \bigm| & 2 \end{pmatrix} \longrightarrow A'' = \begin{pmatrix} 1 & 1 & 1 & \bigm| & 2 \\ 0 & -3 & -1 & \bigm| & 1 \\ 0 & 1 & 2 & \bigm| & 3 \end{pmatrix}$$

The bottom two rows now correspond to

$$-3y - z = 1$$
$$y + 2z = 3$$

These are the same equations as before.

Facts and Notation

A rectangular array like A is a **matrix**. This matrix has 3 rows (the horizontals) and 4 columns (the verticals). The vertical bar is an augmentation line. The whole matrix A is an augmented matrix. The thing that is augmented in A is the coefficient matrix of the linear system (1)–(3). The matrix below shows what that coefficient matrix looks like by itself.

$$B = \begin{pmatrix} 1 & 1 & 1 \\ 2 & -1 & 1 \\ 1 & 2 & 3 \end{pmatrix}$$

Matrix B does not have an augmentation line. In fact, even in an augmented matrix, the augmentation line is just a convenient reminder. Some books do not use them. (You cannot usually use them on a calculator.) The augmented matrix A has **dimension** 3×4 (3 rows, 4 columns). The coefficient matrix B has dimension 3×3.

The plural of *matrix* is *matrices*.

This book shows matrices enclosed by parentheses. In some books they are enclosed in square brackets, [ ].

For You to Do

1. Write down (but do not solve) the coefficient matrix and the augmented matrix for the linear system below.

$$x - 2y + z = 7$$
$$2x - y + 4z = 17$$
$$3x - 2y + 2z = 14$$

2. Write down (but do not solve) the system of equations corresponding to matrix M below. Let the variables be x, y, z in that order.

$$M = \left(\begin{array}{ccc|c} 1 & 2 & -3 & 2 \\ 2 & 0 & -1 & 4 \\ -3 & 1 & 2 & -5 \end{array} \right)$$

3. Start with matrix M from Problem 2. Make a new matrix M' by subtracting 2 times row 1 from row 2. (The row you subtract from is always the one you change.) Then, from M', make M'' by adding 3 times row 1 to row 3.

Now you have reduced Sasha and Derman's problem to a 2×2 system. You can continue to solve it in matrix form starting from

$$C = \left(\begin{array}{cc|c} -3 & -1 & 1 \\ 1 & 2 & 3 \end{array} \right)$$

Remember, the variables here are y and z. Eliminate y by adding 3 times the second row of C to the first row. You get

$$D = \left(\begin{array}{cc|c} 0 & 5 & 10 \\ 1 & 2 & 3 \end{array} \right)$$

The first row of D says that $5z = 10$, so $z = 2$. You can now substitute in the equation for the second row to find y. Then you can substitute in the original equation (1) to find x.

> You could also say that you subtracted -3 times the second row from the first row. Why be so complicated? Because in some contexts it is cleaner to always solve systems with the same operation.

There is just one problem with this method. You deal partly with matrices and partly with equations. You jump around picking information from different matrices and different equations. Also, you use matrices of different sizes. None of this is good for calculators or computers. For them, it is much easier and more efficient if all matrices for a given situation are the same size, operations are always done in the same order, and all the information ever needed is kept in the current matrix (so they can discard any earlier matrices).

You can solve Sasha and Derman's problem entirely in the matrix world. The expressions over the arrows summarize what steps you take. You will learn their meaning shortly. The first half goes like this.

$$A = \begin{pmatrix} 1 & 1 & 1 & | & 2 \\ 2 & -1 & 1 & | & 5 \\ 1 & 2 & 3 & | & 5 \end{pmatrix} \xrightarrow{(2)-2(1)} \begin{pmatrix} 1 & 1 & 1 & | & 2 \\ 0 & -3 & -1 & | & 1 \\ 1 & 2 & 3 & | & 5 \end{pmatrix}$$

$$\xrightarrow{(3)-(1)} \begin{pmatrix} 1 & 1 & 1 & | & 2 \\ 0 & -3 & -1 & | & 1 \\ 0 & 1 & 2 & | & 3 \end{pmatrix} \xrightarrow{\text{Switch }(2),(3)} \begin{pmatrix} 1 & 1 & 1 & | & 2 \\ 0 & 1 & 2 & | & 3 \\ 0 & -3 & -1 & | & 1 \end{pmatrix}$$

$$\xrightarrow{(3)+3(2)} \begin{pmatrix} 1 & 1 & 1 & | & 2 \\ 0 & 1 & 2 & | & 3 \\ 0 & 0 & 5 & | & 10 \end{pmatrix} \xrightarrow{(3) \div 5} \begin{pmatrix} 1 & 1 & 1 & | & 2 \\ 0 & 1 & 2 & | & 3 \\ 0 & 0 & 1 & | & 2 \end{pmatrix}$$

Now the third row says that $z = 2$. You can begin the process of substitution. Both the matrix and the corresponding equations are in triangular form, so you could easily solve for z, y, and x in that order by returning to equations and using substitution.

But you have already learned that you can accomplish substitution by elimination—adding and subtracting equations. So you can also carry out the substitution in matrix form. Machines do that easily. So continue.

$$\begin{pmatrix} 1 & 1 & 1 & | & 2 \\ 0 & 1 & 2 & | & 3 \\ 0 & 0 & 1 & | & 2 \end{pmatrix} \xrightarrow{(2)-2(3)} \begin{pmatrix} 1 & 1 & 1 & | & 2 \\ 0 & 1 & 0 & | & -1 \\ 0 & 0 & 1 & | & 2 \end{pmatrix} \xrightarrow[\substack{(1)-(3)}]{(1)-(2)} \begin{pmatrix} 1 & 0 & 0 & | & 1 \\ 0 & 1 & 0 & | & -1 \\ 0 & 0 & 1 & | & 2 \end{pmatrix}$$

This final matrix corresponds to the three equations $x = 1$, $y = -1$, and $z = 2$, so you have solved the original problem by using only matrices.

Can you figure out the expressions over and under the arrows? For instance, between matrix A and the next one, you see the expression $(2) - 2(1)$. This means replace row 2 of A with row 2 minus two times row 1.

For Discussion

4. Figure out the meanings of all the other expressions over and under the arrows.

This solution method is called **Gaussian Elimination**. Gaussian Elimination is an algorithm that transforms the matrix of any given system of linear equations through a sequence of other matrices. It ends in a final matrix from which the solution to the corresponding system is obvious. You call it Gaussian Elimination because the first stage (the reduction to triangular form) corresponds on the equation level to eliminating the variables one at a time.

Experiment. Is this pure matrix approach an improvement? Some people like the time saving from not having to write variables and equations. However, they do not like the extra work of keeping all the rows and columns. But remember, this is not a method intended for humans, except for small examples. So why take you through it? Because, like most good algorithms, it can tell you a lot. For instance, thinking about the patterns that could appear in the final matrix can lead to insights about the theory of solutions to equations. But you cannot think about what the final form might look like without understanding the algorithm. So, the point of the following exercises is to help you develop a feel for the algorithm.

In Gaussian Elimination, the transformations from one system of equations (or one matrix) to another use only three kinds of steps:

- *Scaling.* Replace one equation (row) with a multiple of itself.

- *Switching.* Switch the order of two equations (rows).

- *Subtracting.* Subtract or add a multiple of one equation (row) from another and replace the other equation with the result.

Not only do these steps allow you to go forward, they allow you to go backward: You can reverse every step. For instance, if you subtract three times (1) from (2), you can reverse this by adding three times (1) to the new (2). This means that you can always get from the last system back to the first.

Facts and Notation

Since you can get from the first system of equations to the last, any solution to the first system is a solution to the last. Since you can get from the last system to the first, any solution to the last system is a solution to the first. This means that the first and last systems are equivalent. They have the same solutions. Usually the last system has exactly one solution—for instance, in Sasha and Derman's example $(x, y, z) = (1, -1, 2)$. In that case, Gaussian Elimination has revealed for us the one and only solution to the original system.

> Each step you take preserves the solution set.

This situation is like the situation with basic moves for equations in one variable: You can reverse a basic move, and a basic move preserves the solution set. Therefore, you might call scaling, switching, and subtracting the basic moves for linear systems. The formal name is *elementary row operations.*

The final matrix you get to in Gaussian Elimination is in **row-reduced echelon form**, abbreviated *rref*. For instance, the last matrix in Sasha and Derman's example is

> You can call row-reduced echelon form just "row-reduced form." You can describe a matrix as "row reduced."

$$\begin{pmatrix} 1 & 0 & 0 & | & 1 \\ 0 & 1 & 0 & | & -1 \\ 0 & 0 & 1 & | & 2 \end{pmatrix}$$

Most graphing calculators are also matrix calculators. They can store matrices and do many matrix computations, such as finding row-reduced echelon form. Look for an **rref** command in the matrix menus. Find out how to input matrices and how to get your calculator to display their row-reduced forms. You cannot input the augmentation line, but you know where it goes.

In the example, the part of the row-reduced echelon form before the augmentation line is an **identity matrix**: a square matrix with all entries 0 except for 1's along the main diagonal from top left to lower right. This always happens when there is a unique solution. However, not every linear system has a unique solution, so the row-reduced form is not always so simple.

For instructions for using the rref command, see the TI-Nspire™ Handbook, p. 804.

Some of the exercises will illustrate what happens when there is not a unique solution and begin to hint at the general pattern.

Exercises *Practicing Habits of Mind*

Check Your Understanding

1. Consider this augmented matrix.

$$\left(\begin{array}{ccc|c} 1 & -1 & 2 & 5 \\ 2 & -3 & 1 & 3 \\ 1 & 0 & 7 & 16 \end{array}\right)$$

   a. What system of equations does it correspond to?

   b. Solve this system in matrix form.

2. Solve the following system using Gaussian Elimination on matrices.

$$x + y + z = 1$$
$$2y + z = 2$$
$$3z = 3$$

3. Go back to the complete matrix solution of system (1)–(3) to the point where the system was

$$\begin{pmatrix} 1 & 1 & 1 & \bigm| & 2 \\ 0 & -3 & -1 & \bigm| & 1 \\ 0 & 1 & 2 & \bigm| & 3 \end{pmatrix}$$

Instead of then switching the last two rows, add or subtract a multiple of the second row from the third to eliminate y. Then continue with the type of steps shown in the lesson until you reach a matrix in the form below.

$$\begin{pmatrix} 1 & 0 & 0 & \bigm| & \blacksquare \\ 0 & 1 & 0 & \bigm| & \blacksquare \\ 0 & 0 & 1 & \bigm| & \blacksquare \end{pmatrix}$$

Do you get the same solution you got before?

4. Illustrate the claim that you can reverse every step in a matrix solution. Reverse every step in the complete matrix solution of Sasha and Derman's problem. That is, show that using just scaling, switching, and subtracting, you can get from the matrix form of the final system back to the matrix form of the original system.

$$\begin{array}{ccc} x = 1 & & x + y + z = 2 \\ y = -1 & \longrightarrow & 2x - y + z = 5 \\ z = 2 & & x + 2y + 3z = 5 \end{array}$$

5. **Write About It** Subtracting a multiple of one equation from another is a basic move for systems. Yet sometimes it would be best to add a multiple of one equation to another. Explain why you do not have to list adding as a fourth basic move.

6. Solve this system by Gaussian Elimination in matrix form.

$$x + 2y = -3$$
$$2x - y = 4$$

7. The function $f(n) = a2^n + b3^n$, where a and b are constants, satisfies the conditions $f(1) = 1$ and $f(2) = 10$. Find a and b.

8. If you think of equations representing lines in the plane, you have a geometric interpretation for 2×2 systems. This interpretation helps explain why the solution to most, but not all, 2×2 systems is a single pair (x, y).

   a. How can you interpret the solution of a 2×2 system geometrically?

   b. Use that interpretation to help you to conjecture what can happen with $m \times 2$ systems. Remember, an $m \times 2$ system has m equations and two unknowns.

   c. **Take It Further** Make a conjecture about a geometric interpretation for $m \times 3$ systems.

Habits of Mind

Check your method. When mathematicians come up with a new approach, one of the things they do to test it out is to try it on a simpler system that they already know how to solve by other methods.

You might want to make a table for f and apply the methods of Chapter 1. Can you find any patterns? Your main task here, however, is to determine the function by the methods of the current chapter.

9. **Standardized Test Prep** In Gaussian Elimination, which of the following transformations can you NOT use?

   A. scaling
   B. subtracting
   C. switching columns
   D. switching rows

10. Solve the following system.

$$x + y + z = 3$$
$$2x - y + z = 2$$
$$x + 2y + 3z = 6$$

> Notice that this system is the same as Sasha and Derman's problem (1)–(3) except that the constants on the right are different.

11. Solve each system.

   a.
   $$x + y + z = 1$$
   $$2x - y + z = -2$$
   $$x + 2y + 3z = 4$$

   b.
   $$x + y + z = 1$$
   $$2x - y + z = 3$$
   $$x + 2y + 3z = -1$$

12. Find the unique linear function that goes through the points $(2, 2)$ and $(5, 8)$. You know several ways to solve this type of problem. Use Gaussian Elimination in matrix form.

> **Go Online**
> Pearsonsuccessnet.com

13. Solve the following system by matrix methods.

$$x + y = 2$$
$$y + z = 4$$
$$z + x = 6$$

14. Derman is thinking of three numbers. He says, "The average of the first two numbers is 1. The average of the last two numbers is 2. The average of the first number and last number is 3." What are Derman's numbers?

15. Rewrite the following system in a form to which you can apply Gaussian Elimination. You do not need to solve the system.

$$x + y + 2(y + z) = 3$$
$$x = \frac{1}{2}(y + z + 2)$$
$$x + \frac{y + \frac{1}{2}z}{3} = 1$$

16. Solve the following system.

$$x + y + 2z = 2$$
$$x - y + z = 5$$
$$2x + 2y + 3z = 5$$

> Notice that this problem has the same constants on the right as Sasha and Derman's problem (1)–(3), but the rest is different.

17. Take It Further Solve the system represented by the following augmented matrix without using a calculator. Even though it is 4×4, you can solve it by hand with Gaussian Elimination.

$$\left(\begin{array}{cccc|c} 1 & -1 & -1 & 0 & 1 \\ 0 & 1 & -1 & -1 & 1 \\ -1 & 0 & 1 & -1 & 1 \\ -1 & -1 & 0 & 1 & 1 \end{array}\right)$$

18. Do Exercise 5 from Lesson 4.02 in matrix form.

19. A rectangular box has six sides that come in three congruent pairs. Suppose the perimeters of the three different rectangular sides are 20 in., 24 in., and 28 in., respectively. What are the dimensions (length, width, and height) of the box?

20. Take It Further Consider another rectangular box. Suppose that the perimeters of all six sides of the box are the same. Does the box have to be a cube? Explain.

21. Find the unique polynomial of degree 3 or less that goes through the points (1, 1), (2, 3), (3, 6), and (4, 10).

> Solve this exercise using the rref command. See the TI-Nspire Handbook, p. 804.

22. Solve each system. If you use Gaussian Elimination, what situations arise?

a. $x + 2y = 3$

$2x + 4y = 6$

b. $x + 2y = 3$

$2x + 4y = 7$

Maintain Your Skills

23. What is the system of equations associated with the following augmented matrix? Assume the variables are x and y.

$$\left(\begin{array}{cc|c} 1 & 3 & 5 \\ 2 & 4 & 6 \end{array}\right)$$

24. Use Gaussian Elimination to solve the system from Exercise 23.

25. Do Exercise 12 from Lesson 4.02 again, this time in matrix form.

26. Use your calculator to compute the rref of each matrix below. Divide up the work with your friends so that no one has many to do. Describe any patterns you discover about the form of rrefs. Randomly create some more matrices and find their rrefs with your calculator. Do the rrefs of these matrices confirm the patterns you have found?

a. $\begin{pmatrix} 1 & -2 & | & -8 \\ -3 & 5 & | & 21 \end{pmatrix}$

b. $\begin{pmatrix} 1 & -2 & | & -8 \\ -3 & 6 & | & 21 \end{pmatrix}$

c. $\begin{pmatrix} 1 & -2 & | & -2 \\ -3 & 6 & | & 6 \end{pmatrix}$

d. $\begin{pmatrix} 1 & 2 & 3 & | & 5 \\ 2 & 3 & 4 & | & 8 \\ 3 & 2 & 1 & | & 7 \end{pmatrix}$

e. $\begin{pmatrix} 3 & 1 & -1 & | & 5 \\ 1 & -4 & -9 & | & -7 \\ 4 & 0 & -4 & | & 4 \end{pmatrix}$

f. $\begin{pmatrix} 1 & 2 & 3 & | & 8 \\ 2 & 3 & 4 & | & 12 \\ 3 & 2 & 1 & | & 6 \end{pmatrix}$

g. $\begin{pmatrix} 3 & 1 & -1 & | & 4 \\ 1 & -4 & -9 & | & 2 \\ 4 & 0 & -4 & | & 3 \end{pmatrix}$

h. $\begin{pmatrix} 1 & -2 & 2 & | & 4 \\ 2 & -4 & 3 & | & 5 \\ 3 & -6 & 2 & | & 0 \end{pmatrix}$

i. $\begin{pmatrix} 3 & -6 & 1 & | & -3 \\ 1 & -2 & -4 & | & -14 \\ 4 & -8 & 0 & | & -8 \end{pmatrix}$

j. $\begin{pmatrix} 1 & 3 & 2 & | & 4 \\ 2 & 6 & 3 & | & 5 \\ 3 & 9 & 2 & | & 0 \end{pmatrix}$

k. $\begin{pmatrix} 3 & 9 & 1 & | & -3 \\ 1 & 3 & -4 & | & -14 \\ 4 & 12 & 0 & | & -8 \end{pmatrix}$

l. $\begin{pmatrix} 1 & 2 & -2 & | & 8 \\ 2 & 3 & -3 & | & 13 \\ 3 & 2 & -2 & | & 12 \end{pmatrix}$

m. $\begin{pmatrix} 3 & 1 & -1 & | & 9 \\ 1 & -4 & 4 & | & -10 \\ 4 & 0 & 0 & | & 8 \end{pmatrix}$

n. $\begin{pmatrix} 1 & 2 & 3 & | & 9 \\ 2 & 3 & 4 & | & 13 \\ 3 & 2 & -1 & | & 1 \end{pmatrix}$

o. $\begin{pmatrix} 3 & 1 & -1 & | & 2 \\ 1 & -4 & 9 & | & 33 \\ 4 & 0 & -1 & | & 5 \end{pmatrix}$

p. $\begin{pmatrix} 1 & 2 & 9 & 3 & | & 14 \\ 2 & 3 & 15 & 4 & | & 20 \\ 3 & 2 & 15 & -1 & | & 4 \\ 3 & 1 & 12 & 2 & | & 11 \end{pmatrix}$

q. $\begin{pmatrix} 1 & 2 & 3 & -5 & | & -6 \\ 2 & 3 & 4 & -5 & | & -8 \\ 3 & 2 & -1 & 9 & | & 0 \\ 3 & 1 & 2 & 4 & | & -1 \end{pmatrix}$

r. $\begin{pmatrix} 1 & -2 & 3 & 0 & 1 & | & 4 \\ 0 & 0 & 0 & 1 & 3 & | & 5 \end{pmatrix}$

27. For parts (d), (f), (h), and (j) of Exercise 26, write down the equations that the original matrix represents and the equations that the rref represents. In what sense do the equations represented by the rref solve the problem?

In this investigation, you learned how to solve a system of three equations in three unknowns. You also learned how to use matrices and Gaussian Elimination to solve systems. These questions will help you summarize what you have learned.

1. Show how to solve this system using each technique.

$$2x - y = 3$$
$$x + 3y = 5$$

   a. substitution **b.** elimination

2. Solve this system.

$$3x - y + 2z = 4$$
$$4y - 3z = 3$$
$$6z = -6$$

3. Write the following system of equations as an augmented matrix.

$$x - 3z = 5$$
$$6y = 7 - z$$
$$2y + 6 = x$$

4. Find the row-reduced echelon form for this matrix. $\begin{pmatrix} 1 & 1 & 1 & | & 1 \\ 0 & 1 & 2 & | & 4 \\ 3 & 0 & 2 & | & 6 \end{pmatrix}$

You can use a matrix to organize a large amount of information, such as a bus schedule.

5. Sasha used Gaussian Elimination to solve a system of equations. She ended up with the following matrix. How should she interpret these results? $\begin{pmatrix} 1 & 0 & 0 & | & -2 \\ 0 & 1 & 0 & | & 4 \\ 0 & 0 & 0 & | & 3 \end{pmatrix}$

6. Why is it possible to solve systems of linear equations in matrix form?

7. What is the process of Gaussian Elimination?

8. Find x, y, and z such that

$$4x - y + 4z = 1$$
$$2x - y + 8z = 11$$
$$2x - 2y + 4z = 0$$

Vocabulary

In this investigation, you learned these terms. Make sure you understand what each one means and how to use it.

- **dimension**
- **elimination**
- **Gaussian Elimination**

- **matrix**
- **row-reduced echelon form (rref)**
- **substitution**

Matrix Algebra

In *Matrix Algebra*, you will learn how to perform basic operations with matrices. You will explore and prove properties of matrix algebra. You will compare matrix properties to the properties of real numbers.

By the end of this investigation, you will be able to answer questions like these.

1. What is a dot product? How can you represent matrix multiplication using dot products?

2. What are some special cases in which $AB = BA$ is true for matrices A and B?

3. How can you solve this system of equations using matrix inverses? What is the solution?

$$x + 4y - z = -3$$
$$2x - 2y + z = 0$$
$$3x + y - 3z = -9$$

You will learn how to

- communicate and prove results about matrices, including the ideas of rows and columns and indices

- compute sums, differences, dot products, products, and inverses of matrices

- interpret and solve problems using matrix calculations

You will develop these habits and skills:

- Visualize an operation on a matrix as a product.

- Explore the algebraic structure of matrices and n-tuples.

- Reason deductively to prove properties about matrices or find counterexamples.

What is the sum of the different colors at each point on the cover?

You can use tables to organize data.

For You to Explore

1. On the side of a box of cereal, there is a table that shows what percent of recommended daily food values are provided by 1 ounce of the cereal.

Daily Value

Carbohydrates	7%
Vitamin A	10%
Vitamin B$_{12}$	25%

Suppose for breakfast you eat 3 ounces of the cereal. Make your own personal table of the percent of your daily value you have met.

2. Cereal boxes usually give two columns in their daily percents table: one column for a standard serving of the cereal alone, and the other for the cereal and a standard amount of milk. Suppose the standard serving is 1 ounce of cereal, with or without one half cup of milk, and the table looks like this

	Cereal	Cereal With Milk
Carbohydrates	7%	9%
Vitamin A	10%	15%
Vitamin B$_{12}$	25%	35%

Make a bigger table with a column showing the percents for the one half cup of milk alone.

3. The weather bureau collects climate data for many U.S. cities. One set of data concerns cloudiness. Each day is classified as clear, partly cloudy, or cloudy. In an average year, Boston has 98 clear days and 164 cloudy days. On the other hand, Philadelphia has 93 clear days and 160 cloudy days, while San Francisco has 160 clear days and only 105 cloudy days.

Determine the average annual number of partly cloudy days in each of these cities. (Assume there are 365 days in a year.)

4. Return to the data in Problem 3. Suppose you want to determine the average number of clear, partly cloudy, and cloudy days for each of the three cities for

- two years

- the first half of the year (January to June)

Can you use the results of Problem 3 to calculate these numbers? If so, explain how. If not, explain why not.

> Put the given information and the information you compute into a labeled table.

5. The swim team buys swimsuits and goggles for its members. The team is going to buy 30 women's suits, 25 men's suits, and 55 pairs of goggles. The prices per item are $20 for a woman's suit, $15 for a man's, and $8 for a pair of goggles. You can display this information in a table.

	W	M	G
Number	30	25	55
Price ($)	20	15	8

What is the total amount the swim team will spend buying these things? Does the format of the table make it easy to describe the calculation?

6. The school cafeteria buys food wholesale. The following table shows a typical order.

	Beef	Pork	Chicken	Fish
Weight (lb)	200	50	250	100
Price ($/lb)	3.50	2.00	1.50	3.00

How much will the order cost?

Exercises *Practicing Habits of Mind*

On Your Own

7. The following table shows passenger car sales for various auto companies during a certain year.

Passenger Car Sales (millions of cars)

	Company A	Company B	Company C	Company D	Company E
Europe	0.4	0.2	0.2	0.2	1
United States	2	1.5	0.6	1	0.3
Asia	0.2	0.1	0.8	3.5	0.1

The table below shows the year's sales for other personal motor vehicles, including SUVs, vans, and light trucks.

Other Vehicle Sales (millions of vehicles)

	Company A	Company B	Company C	Company D	Company E
Europe	0.2	0.05	0.1	0.1	0.3
United States	2.6	1.8	0.8	1.2	0.1
Asia	0.1	0.05	0.5	1	0

Make a table of all personal motor vehicle sales for the year.

8. Here are tables of revenue (total money taken in) and expenditures (total money paid out) for the same auto companies during the same year.

Revenue (billions of dollars)

	Company A	Company B	Company C	Company D	Company E
Europe	18	7.5	9	10	38
United States	129	92.5	37	70	12
Asia	8	4.5	40	131	3

Expenditures (billions of dollars)

	Company A	Company B	Company C	Company D	Company E
Europe	17	7	9	9	32
United States	127	93	35	67	12
Asia	9	5	32	120	4

a. Make a table for profit (revenues minus expenditures).

b. For each company, calculate the total profit for all regions combined.

c. For each region of the world, calculate the total profit of all the companies combined.

Habits of Mind

Make strategic choices. For parts (b) and (c), what is a good way to display the results? In terms of the table, what are you doing?

9. Use the first set of data from Exercise 7.

    a. Suppose experts predict that sales of passenger cars will increase across the board by 5% in the following year. Make a table of predicted passenger car sales for the following year. How did you get it?

    b. Suppose it turns out that only Company D's sales increased by 5%. Company B's sales increased 3%, Company E's sales 2%, and the others had no change. Make a table for the actual sales. How did you get it?

    c. Suppose it turned out that growth is regional: All companies had 6% growth in Asia, but only 1% growth in the U.S., and a 1% decline in Europe. Make a table for the actual sales. How did you get it?

10. A local bakery has four trucks of different sizes. Their gas tanks hold different amounts of gas, and they get different miles per gallon, as shown in the table below.

	Trucks			
Tank Size (gal)	15	18	20	25
mi/gal	20	18	12	15

    If the bakery fills up all the tanks, how many miles of driving can it get from its fleet of trucks?

11. Return to the swim team from Problem 5. That table was just for the varsity squad. The team also buys suits and goggles for the JV squad at the same prices. These tables present the data a somewhat different way.

	W	M	G		
Varsity Numbers	30	25	55	20
JV Numbers	25	22	47	15
				8

    a. What is the total amount the swim team will spend buying these things? Does the format of the tables make it easy to describe the calculation?

    b. There are at least two methods to calculate the answer to part (a). You can compute the cost for varsity and JV separately, or you can add the numbers in each category (women's suits, men's suits, goggles) first. Repeat part (a) using each method. Which method feels like less work? Explain.

For the matrices in Exercises 12 and 13, do parts (a)–(d).

a. Suppose you had to describe the matrix to a friend over the phone. How would you do it?

b. Write down or describe a 4×4 matrix that follows the same pattern as the given matrix.

c. Repeat part (b), but describe a 10×12 matrix.

d. You may have used many words to describe the general pattern in parts (a), (b), and (c). Can you think of a way to use symbols to be just as precise without as much explanation?

12. $M = \begin{pmatrix} 1 & 2 & 3 \\ 2 & 3 & 4 \\ 3 & 4 & 5 \end{pmatrix}$

13. $N = \begin{pmatrix} 1 & 1 & 1 \\ 2 & 4 & 8 \\ 3 & 9 & 27 \end{pmatrix}$

14. Consider the matrix below.

$$I = \begin{pmatrix} 1 & 0 & 0 \\ 0 & 1 & 0 \\ 0 & 0 & 1 \end{pmatrix}$$

This is the 3×3 identity matrix.

a. Suppose you had to describe this matrix to a friend over the phone. How would you do it?

b. Write down or describe a 6×6 matrix that follows the same pattern as the one you described for I.

c. If n is an unknown positive integer, how would you describe an $n \times n$ matrix with the same pattern?

15. Consider this 1×20 matrix.

$$A = (10 \quad 7 \quad 4 \quad 1 \quad -2 \quad -5 \quad \dots)$$

a. What might be the last entry in the matrix? Explain.

b. How would you describe this matrix to a friend without showing it? Can you do this with symbols?

c. **Take It Further** Now consider this 1×20 matrix.

$$B = (2 \quad 4 \quad 6 \quad 8 \quad \dots)$$

Suppose you wanted to combine these two matrices in the same way you combined the two rows in Problem 5. How would you describe to a friend what you need to do without showing the calculations? Can you do this with symbols?

Basic Matrix Operations

You call the data displays in Lesson 4.04 tables, or sometimes two-way tables, but to mathematicians they are just matrices with labels! Indeed, you can show such tables with all sorts of formatting.

Passenger Car Sales (millions of cars)

	Company A	Company B	Company C	Company D	Company E
Europe	0.4	0.2	0.2	0.2	1
United States	2	1.5	0.6	1	0.3
Asia	0.2	0.1	0.8	3.5	0.1

But the tables are still just matrices. So you can write them as such.

$$\begin{pmatrix} 0.4 & 0.2 & 0.2 & 0.2 & 1 \\ 2 & 1.5 & 0.6 & 1 & 0.3 \\ 0.2 & 0.1 & 0.8 & 3.5 & 0.1 \end{pmatrix}$$

Or, if it is helpful, you can keep the labels.

$$\begin{array}{c} \\ \text{Europe} \\ \text{U.S.} \\ \text{Asia} \end{array} \begin{array}{ccccc} A & B & C & D & E \\ \begin{pmatrix} 0.4 & 0.2 & 0.2 & 0.2 & 1 \\ 2 & 1.5 & 0.6 & 1 & 0.3 \\ 0.2 & 0.1 & 0.8 & 3.5 & 0.1 \end{pmatrix} \end{array}$$

Developing Habits of Mind

Look for relationships. The tables help organize calculations people want to do. This means useful mathematical definitions are lurking! Try to identify the kinds of calculations that seem to be useful. See if you can define them for matrices independent of their particular use. Then you probably have concepts that will be useful in many places you have not yet imagined.

Consider Exercise 7 in Lesson 4.04, where you combined tables of passenger car sales with other vehicle sales to get total sales of all personal motor vehicles. Abstractly, what did you do? You started with two matrices.

$$\begin{pmatrix} 0.4 & 0.2 & 0.2 & 0.2 & 1 \\ 2 & 1.5 & 0.6 & 1 & 0.3 \\ 0.2 & 0.1 & 0.8 & 3.5 & 0.1 \end{pmatrix} \text{ and } \begin{pmatrix} 0.2 & 0.05 & 0.1 & 0.1 & 0.3 \\ 2.6 & 1.8 & 0.8 & 1.2 & 0.1 \\ 0.1 & 0.05 & 0.5 & 1 & 0 \end{pmatrix}$$

You got the matrix below.

$$\begin{pmatrix} 0.6 & 0.25 & 0.3 & 0.3 & 1.3 \\ 4.6 & 3.3 & 1.4 & 2.2 & 0.4 \\ 0.3 & 0.15 & 1.3 & 4.5 & 0.1 \end{pmatrix}$$

So, mathematically, you took two matrices of the same size and added the corresponding entries. The result was another matrix of the same size.

To make an algebra out of this, you need to use symbols. The sum $A + B$ of matrices A and B is the matrix you get by adding the corresponding entries.

The entries of a matrix are the numbers inside it.

For Discussion

1. Consider Exercise 8 from Lesson 4.04. Define another matrix operation based on this exercise.

Exercise 9a in Lesson 4.04 suggests another operation that takes one matrix and returns another matrix of the same size. You increase each entry by 5%. You can represent a percent increase as multiplication, in this case by 1.05. Since each entry of the matrix is multiplied by 1.05, the matrix is scaled. If you call the original matrix A, you can call the result $1.05A$. The process is **scalar multiplication.**

Scalar is another word for a number that you use when working with matrices. The product kA, where k is a number and A is a matrix, is another matrix you can get from A by multiplying each of its entries by k.

For You to Do

2. Use the matrices below.

$$A = \begin{pmatrix} 1 & 2 & 3 \\ 4 & 5 & 6 \end{pmatrix} \qquad B = \begin{pmatrix} 1 & 0 & 1 \\ 0 & -1 & 0 \end{pmatrix} \qquad C = \begin{pmatrix} 1 & 3 \\ 2 & 4 \end{pmatrix}$$

Compute $A + B$, $A - B$, $A + C$, $2A$, and $(-1)A$. Some of these expressions may be undefined.

Developing Habits of Mind

Detect the key characteristics. The definition of $A + B$ talks about "corresponding entries." In some cases, this may be clear. In other cases, such as in the definition of matrix multiplication, "corresponding entries" may not be clear. While it may be evident that you cannot add A and C in For You to Do Problem 2, shouldn't a good definition say something about that instead of leaving it for you to figure out? To address such clarity issues, you need more notation.

First, the size of matrix A is the number of its rows and its columns. Matrices A and B are the same size if they both have the same number of rows, m, and the same number of columns, n. More briefly, A and B are the same size if they are both $m \times n$. Two matrices must be the same size in order for you to add or subtract them.

Second, you need a way to talk about specific entries. Entries in a matrix need two coordinates—their row number and their column number. These numbers are listed as subscripts, called indices. So a 3×4 matrix A might be

The singular of *indices* is *index*.

$$A = \begin{pmatrix} a_{11} & a_{12} & a_{13} & a_{14} \\ a_{21} & a_{22} & a_{23} & a_{24} \\ a_{31} & a_{32} & a_{33} & a_{34} \end{pmatrix}$$

The first number in the subscript is the row number and the second is the column number. So, more generally, an $m \times n$ matrix could be

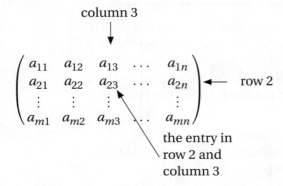

column 3

$$\begin{pmatrix} a_{11} & a_{12} & a_{13} & \cdots & a_{1n} \\ a_{21} & a_{22} & a_{23} & \cdots & a_{2n} \\ \vdots & \vdots & \vdots & & \vdots \\ a_{m1} & a_{m2} & a_{m3} & \cdots & a_{mn} \end{pmatrix} \leftarrow \text{row 2}$$

the entry in row 2 and column 3

For Discussion

3. Indices are like coordinates, in a way. How are they similar to coordinates? How are they different?

With this index notation comes a nice shorthand. You can write

Let $A = (a_{ij})$.

This notation tells us two things:

- The entries of A will all be a-something.
- For this matrix, i will be the index of the rows and j will be the index of the columns. That is, you will use i when referring to a typical row of A and j when referring to a typical column.

With this notation, you can indicate the size of A at the same time. You can write

Let A be the 3×5 matrix (a_{pq}).

or

Let $A = (a_{pq})$, $p = 1, 2, 3$, and $q = 1, 2, 3, 4, 5$.

You do not always have to use *i* and *j* as your indices. Sometimes there is a good reason not to.

For You to Do

4. Define $B = (b_{ij})$ to be the 3×2 matrix in which $b_{ij} = i^j$. Explain why this means that B is the matrix below.

$$B = \begin{pmatrix} 1 & 1 \\ 2 & 4 \\ 3 & 9 \end{pmatrix}$$

So what good is all this? The subscript notation is good for at least two reasons. First, it allows you to define matrices, even very big ones, without listing all the entries. Second, it allows you to give precise definitions of matrix operations such as sum and scalar product.

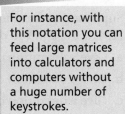

For instance, with this notation you can feed large matrices into calculators and computers without a huge number of keystrokes.

Definition

If $A = (a_{ij})$ and $B = (b_{ij})$ are both $m \times n$ matrices, then their sum $A + B$ is defined to be the $m \times n$ matrix with ij entry $a_{ij} + b_{ij}$. In other words, if $C = A + B$, then $c_{ij} = a_{ij} + b_{ij}$.

In such definitions, it is understood that any statement about entry ij is true for every such entry, but you can also be explicit and say $c_{ij} = a_{ij} + b_{ij}$ for all i from 1 to m and all j from 1 to n.

$$c_{ij} = a_{ij} + b_{ij}, \ i = 1, 2, \ldots, m \text{ and } j = 1, 2, \ldots, n$$

For You to Do

5. Give similarly precise definitions for $A - B$ and kA.

Exercises Practicing Habits of Mind

Check Your Understanding

1. Identify each value for the matrix A.

$$A = (a_{ij}) = \begin{pmatrix} 1 & 2 & 3 \\ 4 & 5 & 6 \end{pmatrix}$$

a. the size of A **b.** a_{12} **c.** a_{21}

d. a_{23} **e.** a_{32}

2. Let $E = (e_{pq})$ with $e_{pq} = p^2 + 2^q$.

    a. Write out E if it is 4×1.   **b.** Write out E if it is 1×4.

3. Come up with formulas for the entries of each matrix.

    a. $A = \begin{pmatrix} 2 & 3 & 4 \\ 3 & 4 & 5 \end{pmatrix}$ **b.** $B = \begin{pmatrix} 1 & 2 & 3 \\ 3 & 4 & 5 \end{pmatrix}$ **c.** $C = \begin{pmatrix} 1 & 2 & 3 & 4 \\ 4 & 9 & 16 & 25 \end{pmatrix}$

4. Suppose you want to add single-row matrices such as $(1, 2, 3, 4, 5)$ and $(1, 4, 9, 16, 25)$. You do not need two indices to define addition.

    a. Give a definition of $A + B$ for single-row matrices.

    b. Give a definition of $A - B$ for single-row matrices.

    c. Give a definition of scalar multiplication for single-row matrices.

> Of course, the same approach works for single-column matrices.

5. On the side of a box of cereal, there is a table that shows what percent of recommended daily food values are provided by 1 ounce of the cereal.

        Carbohydrates 7%   Vitamin A 10%   Vitamin B_{12} 25%

If you eat 3 ounces, what percents do you get? What matrix and what matrix operation are involved in your calculation?

6. A mathematics teacher keeps a record of each student's points on homework and points on tests. For three students, here are the homework points and test points for the first and second marking periods.

> Of course, you can do this calculation without thinking about matrices. The point here is to illustrate that matrices are everywhere and, in some sense, you have been using them all your life.

First Marking Period Points

	Tony	Sasha	Derman
Homework	127	143	107
Tests	181	170	165

Second Marking Period Points

	Tony	Sasha	Derman
Homework	144	139	126
Tests	184	192	175

The teacher now wants to compute the homework points and test points for both marking periods combined. Help the teacher and do the computations. What matrix operation do you use?

7. Another mathematics teacher keeps records as percents. For three students, here are the homework percents and test percents for the first and second marking periods.

Tony, Sasha, and Derman take more than one mathematics course.

First Marking Period Percents

	Sasha	Tony	Derman
Homework	94	98	85
Tests	95	91	83

Second Marking Period Percents

	Sasha	Tony	Derman
Homework	95	96	89
Tests	94	92	85

The teacher now wants to compute the homework percents and test percents for both marking periods combined. Can you compute this information from these tables? Explain.

On Your Own

8. Suppose $D = (d_{ij})$ is 3×3 and $d_{ij} = 2j$. Write out D.

9. Define the 2×4 matrix $C = (c_{jk})$ as $c_{jk} = k^j$. Write out C.

10. Define a matrix $M = (m_{ij})$ as $m_{ij} = \begin{cases} 1 & \text{if } i = j \\ 0 & \text{otherwise} \end{cases}$
For each size, write out the matrix M.

a. 4×4 **b.** 2×2 **c.** 4×3

This is your first example of a case statement defining a matrix. This type of definition is quite common.

11. Standardized Test Prep Define $D = (d_{jk})$ to be the 3×3 matrix in which $d_{jk} = (-j)^{(j+k)}$. Define $F = (f_{jk})$ to be the 3×3 matrix in which $f_{jk} = (2)^{(j-k)}$. If $G = D + F$, which is the entry in the second column of the third row of G?

A. -241 **B.** -31.5 **C.** 85 **D.** 730

12. In Exercise 7 of Lesson 4.04, you got one table about auto sales from two others. Viewing the tables as matrices, what matrix operation did you use?

13. In Exercise 8 of Lesson 4.04, you got one table about auto industry finances from two others. Viewing the tables as matrices, what matrix operation did you use?

14. In Problem 4 of Lesson 4.04, you got one table about weather from another. Viewing the tables as matrices, what matrix operation did you use?

Go Online
Pearsonsuccessnet.com

15. For three baseball players, Andre, Bobby, and Carlos, here are the RBIs and BAs for the first half and the second half of last season.

> RBI is the total number of runs batted in. BA, or batting average, is the ratio $\dfrac{\text{total hits}}{\text{total at bats}}$.

First Half of Season

	A	B	C
RBI	31	37	42
BA	.263	.294	.283

Second Half of Season

	A	B	C
RBI	26	36	53
BA	.243	.291	.314

Suppose you want to know their RBIs and BAs for the entire season. Can you get them from these tables? Explain.

Maintain Your Skills

16. Suppose $z = 2y_1 + 5y_2$ and

$$y_1 = 3x$$
$$y_2 = -x$$

Express z in terms of x.

17. Suppose

$$z = 2y_1 + 5y_2 - 3y_3 \quad \text{and} \quad \begin{aligned} y_1 &= 3x \\ y_2 &= -x \\ y_3 &= 4x \end{aligned}$$

Express z in terms of x. Is there a common pattern in this exercise and in Exercise 16? Explain.

18. Suppose again that $z = 2y_1 + 5y_2 - 3y_3$, but now $y_1 = 3$, $y_2 = -1$, and $y_3 = 4$. Evaluate z.

19. On a shopping spree in Europe, Bob spends 100 pounds in England, 150 euros in France, and 200 francs in Switzerland. At the time, a pound is worth \$1.80, a euro is worth \$1.25 and a Swiss franc is worth \$.75.

   a. In dollars, how much does Bob spend?

   b. How does this exercise connect to Exercises 16–18?

20. Suppose

$$z = a_1y_1 + a_2y_2 + a_3y_3 \quad \text{and} \quad \begin{aligned} y_1 &= b_1x \\ y_2 &= b_2x \\ y_3 &= b_3x \end{aligned}$$

Express z in terms of x.

21. Suppose

$$\begin{aligned} z &= a_1y_1 + a_2y_2 + a_3y_3 \\ w &= b_1y_1 + b_2y_2 + b_3y_3 \end{aligned} \quad \text{and} \quad \begin{aligned} y_1 &= c_1x \\ y_2 &= c_2x \\ y_3 &= c_3x \end{aligned}$$

Express the matrix $\begin{pmatrix} z \\ w \end{pmatrix}$ in terms of x.

> **Habits of Mind**
>
> **Look for relationships.** Exercise 20 is meant to give you a general statement of something you have done several times already in this investigation. What is it?

4.06 Dot Products

The exercises in the Maintain Your Skills section in Lesson 4.05 led to this general result in Exercise 20.

If

$$z = a_1y_1 + a_2y_2 + b_3y_3 \quad \text{and} \quad \begin{aligned} y_1 &= b_1x \\ y_2 &= b_2x \\ y_3 &= b_3x \end{aligned}$$

then

$$z = (a_1b_1 + a_2b_2 + a_3b_3)x$$

When there are just two intermediate variables y_1 and y_2, the result is $z = (a_1b_1 + a_2b_2)x$. (This is the result in Exercise 16. What are the values of a_1, a_2, b_1, and b_2 there?)

If there are n intermediate variables y_1 through y_n, then the result is

$$z = (a_1b_1 + a_2b_2 + \cdots + a_{n-1}b_{n-1} + a_nb_n)x$$

So what should you make of all this? You can write some definitions!

First, a string of n numbers, say $(a_1, a_2, \ldots, a_n)$, is an **n-tuple**. Second, given two n-tuples $A = (a_1, a_2, \ldots, a_n)$ and $B = (b_1, b_2, \ldots, b_n)$, define their **dot product** $A \cdot B$ to be the number

$$a_1b_1 + a_2b_2 + \cdots + a_nb_n$$

This is exactly the expression you got for the coefficient of x in Exercise 20, with $n = 3$. Dot products have plenty of uses, as you will soon see. In fact, you have already seen dot products in some word problems, such as Exercise 19 in Lesson 4.05.

Remember...

The most common name mathematicians use for an *n*-tuple is *vector*. The algebra of *n*-tuples is *vector algebra*. However, you are used to thinking of vectors as geometric objects—ordered pairs of points in a coordinate system.

Note that when $n = 2$, you have another geometric interpretation of *n*-tuples as points on the plane or as complex numbers represented as points on the complex plane. Also, when $n = 2$, you usually say "ordered pair" instead of "2-tuple."

For You to Do

Find each dot product, or explain why the calculation does not make sense.

1. $(1, 2) \cdot (-3, 4)$

2. $(2, 3) \cdot (-3, 2)$

3. $(1, 0, -1, 2) \cdot (3, 2, 1, x)$

4. $(1, 2) \cdot (2, -3, 4)$

You can view n-tuples as special thin matrices, either single rows or single columns, whichever seems more appropriate. For instance, the format of Exercise 20 suggests that you write the following.

$$\begin{pmatrix} y_1 \\ y_2 \\ y_3 \end{pmatrix} = \begin{pmatrix} b_1 \\ b_2 \\ b_3 \end{pmatrix} x$$

Do you see how viewing (y_1, y_2, y_3) as a matrix allows you to regard the x as a scalar and put it on the outside? In Exercise 20, if you regard $A = (a_1, a_2, a_3)$ as a row, then the expression $a_1b_1 + a_2b_2 + a_3b_3$ is the dot product of a row and a column. For dot products, it does not matter whether you think of the n-tuples as rows or as columns, so long as they both have the same number of elements.

When you multiply two n-tuples together, you do not get another n-tuple, you get a number. Usually, when you combine two things, you get the same sort of thing. For example, when you add two matrices, you get a matrix. When you multiply two complex numbers, you get a complex number. However, this is not the case for dot products.

> Not only do dot products show up in several places in this chapter, but they will show up in later math courses.

For You to Do

Do each set of computations. For each set, what is the relationship? How can you express the pattern?

5. $(1, 2, 3) \cdot (4, 5, 6)$ and $(4, 5, 6) \cdot (1, 2, 3)$

6. $(1, 0, 2) \cdot (x(1, -2, 2)), (x(1, 0, 2)) \cdot (1, -1, 2),$ and $x((1, 0, 2) \cdot (1, -1, 2))$

7. $(2, 3, 4) \cdot (c_1, c_2, c_3) + (3, 4, 5) \cdot (c_1, c_2, c_3)$ and $((2, 3, 4) + (3, 4, 5)) \cdot (c_1, c_2, c_3)$

Go back to the equations from Exercise 20 of Lesson 4.05. You can think of this in terms of the following matrices.

$$A = (a_1, a_2, a_3)$$
$$B = (b_1, b_2, b_3)$$
$$Y = (y_1, y_2, y_3)$$

The exercise says

$$z = A \cdot Y, \ Y = Bx, \text{ and } z = A \cdot (Bx)$$

The solution to Exercise 20 is $z = (a_1 b_1 + a_2 b_2 + a_3 b_3)x$, which you can write as

$$z = (A \cdot B)x$$

So in this case, $A \cdot (Bx) = (A \cdot B)x$. A similar equality showed up in Problem 6 above.

> You can also write $x(A \cdot B)$. Since both x and $(A \cdot B)$ are numbers, they commute.

Is the following statement a rule about dot products?

$$(kA) \cdot B = A \cdot (kB) = (A \cdot B)k$$

Yes, this is a rule, or theorem, about dot products. And it is easy to remember because it looks similar to one of the basic rules of algebra. Although, if it is so familiar, what is left to prove? In the following dialog, Tony and Sasha grapple with some of these basic rules. In the exercises, you will discover and explain several other basic rules about n-tuples and dot products.

Tony and Sasha have been asked to justify, or find counterexamples to, two proposed rules for n-tuples.

$$(kA) \cdot B = k(A \cdot B) \text{ and } A + B = B + A$$

Tony   Hey, Sasha, what's there to show? This is just basic algebra. Everybody knows that $(ka)b = k(ab)$ and $a + b = b + a$. These are just the basic rules of associativity and commutativity.

Sasha   Yes, we already know them for real-number addition and multiplication, but here we have n-tuples and dot products.

Tony   Ugh! If all the rules are the same and we know them, I don't see why we should have to show them again.

Sasha   Well, they aren't really the same, because n-tuples aren't numbers, so their sum isn't quite a number sum. Maybe the rules aren't even true. Though I hope they are, because their form is so familiar— something we would want to use. So how should we start?

Tony   I still don't get it. What do you mean that the sum isn't a number sum?

Sasha   Well, when we say $a + b = b + a$ for numbers, we are saying $3 + 7 = 7 + 3$ and old stuff like that. But when we say $A + B = B + A$ for n-tuples, we are saying $(1, 2, 3) + (2, 4, 1) = (2, 4, 1) + (1, 2, 3)$ and new stuff like that. This is a new use of the plus sign, so we've got to think about whether it's right. So the first issue is, what does the plus sign mean for n-tuples? Our teacher never really told us.

Tony   If they're just thin matrices, then it should be the same meaning as for matrices: Add corresponding entries.

Sasha   So A and B would have to be the same size, say $1 \times n$, and we could write

$$A = (a_1, a_2, \ldots, a_n)$$
$$B = (b_1, b_2, \ldots, b_n)$$

Those old indices again, but only one at a time, thank goodness.

Tony $A + B$ is $(a_1 + b_1, a_2 + b_2, \ldots)$. Each entry is $a_i + b_i$.

Sasha   Hey, each entry of $B + A$ is $b_i + a_i$. I think we're done, because $a_i + b_i = b_i + a_i$.

Tony   No way! You're going in circles. You're saying that A and B commute because a_i and b_i commute.

Sasha   No, I'm not going in circles, because A and B are n-tuples and a_i and b_i are numbers. We already know that numbers commute. We've reduced it to the previous case!

Tony   Okay, I see what you mean. I guess they are different. It still feels like we're just doing the same thing, but let's go on to the other rule.

Sasha   Well, I see an important difference here. Both sides of $(kA) \cdot B = k(A \cdot B)$ are numbers. Both sides of $A + B = B + A$ are thin matrices.

Tony   Good news. To show that two matrices are equal, we had to show that they were equal entry by entry. Now we just have two numbers that have to be equal.

Sasha   Yeah, but each number is constructed in a complicated way. On the left, $(kA) \cdot B$, we start with A. Suppose $A = (a_1, a_2, a_3)$. Then we multiply by some number k. Then we dot with some other 3-tuple B. Let's say $B = (b_1, b_2, b_3)$.

Tony   Who says these vectors are 3-tuples?

Sasha   No one, but if we see what is going on for 3-tuples, maybe the general pattern won't be much different. Try it. You compute $(kA) \cdot B$.

Tony   All right. $kA = (ka_1, ka_2, ka_3)$, so then $(kA) \cdot B$ would be

$$(ka_1)b_1 + (ka_2)b_2 + (ka_3)b_3$$

Sasha   Thanks. Now the right side of the rule, $k(A \cdot B)$, is

$$k(a_1b_1 + a_2b_2 + a_3b_3)$$

So are the two sides the same or not?

For Discussion

8. Are the two expressions that Tony and Sasha found actually the same?

Exercises *Practicing Habits of Mind*

Check Your Understanding

1. There were several dot-product exercises in Lesson 4.04—you just did not know they were dot products. Which exercises involved dot products? Explain.

2. Find each dot product.

   a. $(1, 2, 3) \cdot (4, 5, 6)$

   b. $(4, 5, 6) \cdot (1, 2, 3)$

   c. $(1, 2, 3) \cdot \begin{pmatrix} 4 \\ 5 \\ 6 \end{pmatrix}$

   d. $\begin{pmatrix} 3 \\ 2 \\ 1 \end{pmatrix} \cdot \begin{pmatrix} 6 \\ 5 \\ 4 \end{pmatrix}$

   e. $\begin{pmatrix} 1 \\ 2 \\ 3 \end{pmatrix} \cdot (4, 5, 6)$

   f. $(1, 2) \cdot (3, 4, 5)$

3. Find each dot product.

   a. $(3, 4) \cdot (3, 4)$

   b. $(a, b) \cdot (a, b)$

   c. $(2, 3, 4) \cdot (2, 3, 4)$

4. Find an n-tuple Z that satisfies each equation.

   a. $(1, 2) + Z = (1, 2)$

   b. $(x, y) + Z = (x, y)$

   c. $(1, 2, -3, \pi) + Z = (1, 2, -3, \pi)$

5. Generalize from Exercise 4. Show that for each n-tuple X, there is another n-tuple Z such that $X + Z = X$.

   > Not surprisingly, you call such a Z a zero.

6. **a.** Compute $(1, 0, 1) \cdot (x, y, z) + (0, 2, 1) \cdot (x, y, z) - (1, 2, 2) \cdot (x, y, z)$.

   b. Without actually computing any dot product, explain why the answer to part (a) has to be 0.

7. The Distributive Property of dot products says

   $$A \cdot (B \pm C) = A \cdot B \pm A \cdot C$$

   and

   $$(A \pm B) \cdot C = A \cdot C \pm B \cdot C$$

   That is, the dot product distributes over n-tuple addition and subtraction. You worked out a specific example of this property in Problem 5 in the For You to Do section.

   Assuming this property, show that

   $$(A + B) \cdot (A + B) = A \cdot A + 2A \cdot B + B \cdot B$$

   > The sign $\pm$ means "plus or minus." When it appears more than once in an equation, you must make the same choice in every case. For instance, in the equation to the left, either use plus both times or use minus both times.

8. Again assuming the Distributive Property, show that

$$(A + B) \cdot (A - B) = A \cdot A - B \cdot B$$

9. Show that, for all n-tuples X (actually, for all matrices X), $(-1)X = -X$. While this should be true if matrix algebra is to behave properly, note that it is not automatically true, because the two sides mean entirely different things. The left side means the result of multiplying X by the scalar -1. The right side means whatever n-tuple W satisfies $X + W = (0, 0, \dots)$.

10. Use Exercise 9 to show that $A \cdot (-B) = -(A \cdot B) = (-A) \cdot B$ is a special case of the general rule $A \cdot (kB) = k(A \cdot B) = (kA) \cdot B$.

On Your Own

11. **Standardized Test Prep** Find the following dot product.

$$(3, -5, 4) \cdot (2, 6, 7)$$

    A. $(5, 1, 11)$ **B.** $(6, -30, 28)$ **C.** 4 **D.** 17

12. Find each dot product.

    a. $(1, 0, 0) \cdot (x, y, z)$ **b.** $(0, 1, 0) \cdot (x, y, z)$ **c.** $(x, y, z) \cdot (0, 0, 1)$

13. Is there an associative property for dot products? That is, is the statement below true? Explain.

$$A \cdot (B \cdot C) = (A \cdot B) \cdot C$$

14. In parts (a)–(d), find each dot product.

    a. $(3, 4) \cdot (4, -3)$ **b.** $(3, 4) \cdot (-4, 3)$

    c. $(3, 4) \cdot (8, -6)$ **d.** $(a, b) \cdot (b, -a)$

    e. In your first-year algebra class, you learned the Zero Product Property. If $ab = 0$, then what can you conclude? What does this exercise have to do with the Zero Product Property?

15. **Take It Further** For parts (a)–(d) of Exercise 14, represent each ordered pair as a point on the plane and draw the vectors from the origin to those points. Do you notice anything? Pick some other pairs of ordered pairs, compute their dot products, and draw the associated vectors. Report on your findings.

16. **a.** Find A such that $A \cdot (1, 2) = 5$.

    b. Check that this same A satisfies $A \cdot (3, 6) = 15$.

    c. Find B such that $B \cdot (2, 4) = 10$.

    d. **Take It Further** Classify all A such that $A \cdot (1, 2) = 5$.

Go Online
Pearsonsuccessnet.com

17. The dot product satisfies the commutative property:
$$A \cdot B = B \cdot A$$
Explain why. Perhaps you can begin with $A = (a_1, a_2)$ and $B = (b_1, b_2)$ and work up to $A = (a_1, a_2, \ldots, a_n)$ and $B = (b_1, b_2, \ldots, b_n)$.

18. Find an n-tuple W that satisfies each equation.

a. $(1, 2) + W = (0, 0)$

b. $(x, y) + W = 0$

c. $(1, 2, -3, \pi) + W = 0$

19. Every number x has an additive inverse $-x$, which satisfies the property $x + (-x) = 0$. Generalize from Exercise 18 to define an additive inverse $-X$ for every n-tuple X. Show that $-X$ exists for every X. That is, for $X = (x_1, x_2, \ldots, x_n)$, find the coordinates of $-X$.

Habits of Mind

Try a specific case.
You might set $n = 3$.
If you can answer the question in a way that does not use any particular property of 3, your argument is correct for any n.

20. Show that the dot product distributes over n-tuple addition and subtraction.
$$A \cdot (B \pm C) = A \cdot B \pm A \cdot C$$

21. For real-number multiplication, there is an inverse, so you can solve $ax = b$ for x by multiplying both sides by a^{-1} to get $x = a^{-1}b$, assuming that $a \neq 0$, of course. Do n-tuples have dot-product inverses? That is, can you solve the equation $A \cdot X = b$ by taking the dot product with some n-tuple A^{-1}? Explain.

22. Write About It To what extent are dot-product rules the same as number rules? Is there a pattern to which rules are the same and which are not?

Maintain Your Skills

23. Consider the linear system below. Show how to represent z_1 and z_2 as a dot product using the vector $Y = (y_1, y_2, y_3)$.
$$z_1 = 2y_1 + 3y_2 + 4y_3$$
$$z_2 = 3y_1 - 2y_2 + 5y_3$$

24. Use the equations below.
$$z_1 = 2y_1 + 5y_2 - 3y_3 \qquad \qquad y_1 = 3x$$
$$z_2 = 3y_1 - y_2 + y_3 \qquad \text{and} \qquad y_2 = -x$$
$$y_3 = 4x$$

Express z_1 and z_2 in terms of x. What is the common pattern in this exercise and in Exercises 16 and 17 of Lesson 4.05? Can you use dot products to do this exercise? Explain.

25. Suppose $a = 3p + 7q$ and $\begin{aligned} p &= 2x - 3y \\ q &= 5x + 4y \end{aligned}$

Express a in terms of x and y. Can you express your calculation using dot products? Explain.

26. Suppose $\begin{aligned} a &= 3p + 7q \\ b &= p - 2q \end{aligned}$ and $\begin{aligned} p &= 2x - 3y \\ q &= 5x + 4y \end{aligned}$

Express a and b in terms of x and y. Look for dot products again.

27. Exercise 24 gave you two sets of equations and asked you to find a third set by substitution. Suppose you represent each given set of equations with its matrix of coefficients. Putting the two matrices side by side, they are

$$\begin{pmatrix} 2 & 5 & -3 \\ 3 & -1 & 1 \end{pmatrix} \begin{pmatrix} 3 \\ -1 \\ 4 \end{pmatrix}$$

The solution to Exercise 24 is the set of equations

$$\begin{aligned} z_1 &= -11x \\ z_2 &= 14x \end{aligned}$$

You can represent this solution with the matrix

$$\begin{pmatrix} -11 \\ 14 \end{pmatrix}$$

Can you explain a method for getting the final matrix directly from the two given matrices?

28. Exercise 25 gave you two sets of equations and asked you to find another equation by substitution. Suppose you represent each given set of equations with its matrix of coefficients. Putting the two matrices side by side, they are

$$\begin{pmatrix} 3 & 7 \end{pmatrix} \begin{pmatrix} 2 & -3 \\ 5 & 4 \end{pmatrix}$$

The resulting equation was $a = 41x + 19y$, so the resulting matrix is the row matrix $(41 \ 19)$. Can you explain a method for getting this row matrix directly from the two given matrices?

29. Exercise 26 gave you two sets of equations and asked you to find a third set by substitution. Suppose you represent each given set of equations with its matrix of coefficients. Putting the two matrices side by side, they are

$$\begin{pmatrix} 3 & 7 \\ 1 & -2 \end{pmatrix} \begin{pmatrix} 2 & -3 \\ 5 & 4 \end{pmatrix}$$

a. Write the matrix of coefficients of the resulting set of equations.

b. Can you explain a method for getting the final matrix directly from the two given matrices? Try to be as general as you can.

Matrix addition is defined by adding corresponding entries. It might make sense to define *matrix multiplication* the same way, entry-wise. It would be easy, but it is not done that way. Why not? A different, much less obvious definition turns out to be much more valuable. You will begin to see how valuable it is in this lesson, and you will see even more uses later as the chapter continues. Of course, historically it took time for mathematicians to realize which definition would be the most useful.

The "correct" definition grew out of the problem of linear substitutions. All the Maintain Your Skills exercises in the last two lessons were about linear substitutions. Consider Exercise 25 from Lesson 4.06. The variables a and b are linear in p and q. That is, a and b are both sums of multiples of p and q. There are no squares, square roots, exponentials, or constant terms. Moreover, the variables p and q are linear in x and y. What are a and b when expressed directly in terms of x and y? In Exercise 25, you substituted the expressions for p and q into the equations for a and b and got the answer. In particular, a and b turned out to be linear in x and y as well. And the computation involved dot products. For instance, in Exercise 25, a turned out to equal $41x + 19y$, where

$$41 = (3, 7) \cdot (2, 5) \quad \text{and} \quad 19 = (3, 7) \cdot (-3, 4)$$

> Another way to say this is to say a and b are **linear combinations** of p and q.

If linear substitutions occurred rarely, then each time you could do the work from scratch, as in Exercise 25. But, in fact, linear substitutions occur quite frequently in applications (see Example 2), so it is worth finding a time saver. Exercise 28 from Lesson 4.06 suggests how. Just as you can speed up solving linear systems by writing matrices instead of equations, you can speed up substitutions by getting the final matrix directly from the two original matrices, as in Exercise 28. The method is to dot rows of the first matrix with columns of the second. This result is defined to be the matrix product.

For instance, continuing with Exercise 25, the matrices associated with the two sets of equations (a and b in terms of p and q and then p and q in terms of x and y) are

$$A = \begin{pmatrix} 3 & 7 \\ 1 & -2 \end{pmatrix} \quad \text{and} \quad B = \begin{pmatrix} 2 & -3 \\ 5 & 4 \end{pmatrix}$$

The matrix associated with the resulting set of equations (a and b in terms of x and y) is

$$C = \begin{pmatrix} 41 & 19 \\ -8 & -11 \end{pmatrix}$$

Note that the dot product of the first row of A with the first column of B is $(3, 7) \cdot (2, 5) = 41$, which is the coefficient of x in $a = 41x + 19y$ and the top left entry of C. Then note that $19 = (3, 7) \cdot (-3, 4)$, which is the dot product of the first row of A and the second column of B, and 19 is the top right entry of C. In all four cases, the dot product of the ith row of A and the jth column of B results in the ij entry of C. (Check this!) So taking the dot product of rows of the left matrix with columns of the right matrix does seem to be the thing to do.

Here is the definition of **matrix multiplication.**

Definition

Let A have as many columns as B has rows. Suppose A is $m \times n$ and B is $n \times p$. Let the rows of A be called $R_1, R_2, \ldots, R_m$. Let the columns of B be called $C_1, C_2, \ldots, C_p$. The product AB is defined to be the $m \times p$ matrix with an ij entry that is the number $R_i \cdot C_j$.

$$AB = \begin{pmatrix} R_1 \cdot C_1 & R_1 \cdot C_2 & \cdots & R_1 \cdot C_p \\ R_2 \cdot C_1 & R_2 \cdot C_2 & \cdots & R_2 \cdot C_p \\ \vdots & \vdots & \ddots & \vdots \\ R_m \cdot C_1 & R_m \cdot C_2 & \cdots & R_m \cdot C_p \end{pmatrix}$$

Example 1

Problem Let $A = \begin{pmatrix} 1 & 2 & 3 \\ 2 & 3 & 4 \end{pmatrix}$ and $B = \begin{pmatrix} 1 \\ -1 \\ 2 \end{pmatrix}$. Compute AB.

Solution A is 2×3 with rows $R_1 = (1, 2, 3)$ and $R_2 = (2, 3, 4)$.

B is 3×1 with the one column

$$C_1 = \begin{pmatrix} 1 \\ -1 \\ 2 \end{pmatrix}$$

So,

$$AB = \begin{pmatrix} R_1 \cdot C_1 \\ R_2 \cdot C_1 \end{pmatrix} = \begin{pmatrix} 5 \\ 7 \end{pmatrix}$$

In terms of the letters in the definition, $m = 2$, $n = 3$, and $p = 1$.

Go Online
Pearsonsuccessnet.com

For You to Do

Compute each product, or explain why it cannot be computed.

1. $\begin{pmatrix} 1 & 2 \\ 2 & 3 \\ 3 & 4 \end{pmatrix} \begin{pmatrix} 1 & -2 \\ -3 & 4 \end{pmatrix}$

2. $(1 \quad 2) \begin{pmatrix} 1 & -2 & 1 & 2 \\ 2 & 1 & -1 & 3 \end{pmatrix}$

3. $\begin{pmatrix} 1 & -2 & 1 & 2 \\ 2 & 1 & -1 & 3 \end{pmatrix} \begin{pmatrix} 1 & -2 \\ -3 & 4 \end{pmatrix}$

Visualize. Some people think about the matrix product *AB* as shown in the figure below. *A* is on the left and *B* is on top. The matrix that just fits on the bottom right between them is *AB*. The size is correct. To compute any entry in the product (represented by the large dot), you multiply the row in *A* directly to its left (represented by a segment) by the column in *B* directly above it. As usual, multiplying a row by a column means finding the dot product.

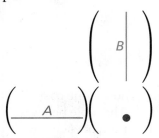

For Discussion

4. Why is *A* required to have as many columns as *B* has rows?

Mathematicians wrote the definition of a matrix product to mimic exactly what happens when you summarize the results of linear substitutions with matrices. So the following theorem should not be a surprise. In fact, the definition is constructed to make this theorem true!

Habits of Mind

Make strategic choices. In mathematics, you can pick your definition in order to make a theorem. As Georg Cantor said, "The essence of mathematics lies in its freedom."

Theorem 4.1

Suppose matrix *A* represents a system where the *z*'s are linear combinations of *y*'s. Suppose matrix *B* represents a system where these *y*'s are linear combinations of *x*'s.

Then, by substitution, the *z*'s are linear combinations of the *x*'s, and the matrix that represents this system is the product *AB*.

Make sure you understand what it means to *represent* a linear system with a matrix. Write the system in the usual way in rows.

$$y_1 = 2x_1 + 3x_2 - 4x_3$$
$$y_2 = -5x_1 + x_2 + 8x_3$$

Then the matrix is $\begin{pmatrix} 2 & 3 & -4 \\ -5 & 1 & 8 \end{pmatrix}$.

You take the coefficients from the equations and arrange them in the matrix in the same order they appear, one row for each equation.

Problem A steel company makes stainless steel and tempered steel. For either type, the raw ingredients are iron and coal, but in different amounts. The table below shows how many tons of iron and how many tons of coal the company needs to produce each ton of steel.

Tons of Raw Material per Ton of Steel

	Stainless Steel	Tempered Steel
Iron	1.1	1.3
Coal	0.5	0.3

In turn, there are costs associated with these raw goods. There is the cost of buying them, and there is also the cost of storing them. The table below shows the costs and the amount of space needed to store 1 ton of each raw good. The price is given in dollars and the space is given in cubic yards.

	Iron	Coal
Cost ($)	120	95
Space (yd^3)	20	52

a. Turn the first table into a system of linear equations. Let s and t be the amounts in tons of stainless and tempered steel, respectively. The other two variables are i and c. What do they stand for?

b. Similarly, turn the second table into a linear system.

c. What the steel company would really like to know is the direct relationship among how much steel they produce, how much money they need to spend, and how much space they need. Figure this out. Express it as a table.

Solution

a. Let i be the number of tons of iron and c be the number of tons of coal. Then

$$i = 1.1s + 1.3t$$
$$c = 0.5s + 0.3t \tag{10}$$

Notice you can read these equations from the rows of the table.

b. Let p be the cost in dollars and q be the number of cubic yards of space needed. You get

$$p = 120i + 95c$$
$$q = 20i + 52c \tag{11}$$

c. To find the direct relationship between steel amounts and cost, you need to eliminate the intermediate variables i and c. As shown in parts (a) and (b), the dollar cost p and amount of space q are linear combinations of the amounts of iron i and coal c. Also, i and c are linear combinations of amounts of steel s and t. You could do the elimination by substitution, but Theorem 4.1 says you can do it by matrix multiplication instead.

A real steel company would make many more types of steel and would use many more raw ingredients. But the form of the example is real. The main difference in actual practice is that the matrices are much bigger. Linear substitutions arise in real life whenever one set of things (here steel outputs) determines a second set (raw goods required) and that second set determines a third (costs).

The theorem says to compute AB, where A is the matrix of p and q in terms of i and c, and B is the matrix for i and c in terms of s and t. From system (11),

$$A = \begin{pmatrix} 120 & 95 \\ 20 & 52 \end{pmatrix}$$

From system (10),

$$B = \begin{pmatrix} 1.1 & 1.3 \\ 0.5 & 0.3 \end{pmatrix}$$

According to the definition of matrix multiplication,

$$AB = \begin{pmatrix} 120 \cdot 1.1 + 95 \cdot 0.5 & 120 \cdot 1.3 + 95 \cdot 0.3 \\ 20 \cdot 1.1 + 52 \cdot 0.5 & 20 \cdot 1.3 + 52 \cdot 0.3 \end{pmatrix} = \begin{pmatrix} 179.5 & 184.5 \\ 48 & 41.6 \end{pmatrix}$$

So

$$p = 179.5s + 184.5t$$
$$q = 48s + 41.6t$$

The table below shows the information the company wants to use.

	Stainless Steel	Tempered Steel
Cost ($)	179.5	184.5
Space (yd³)	48	41.6

For Discussion

5. Why is there such a fuss about which set of equations became matrix A on the left in the product? Is it true for matrices that $AB = BA$?

Developing Habits of Mind

Detect the key characteristics. To get the correct matrices when using Theorem 4.1, you must write the equations in rows. But not every table translates to row equations. For instance, the steel company could have represented the original data about raw goods with this table.

Raw Materials per Ton of Steel

	Iron	Coal
Stainless Steel	1.1	0.5
Tempered Steel	1.3	0.3

If you then used the matrix $\begin{pmatrix} 1.1 & 0.5 \\ 1.3 & 0.3 \end{pmatrix}$, you would be in trouble! Always make sure you know which way the equations go before converting to matrices. If the equations correspond to the columns, as in the table above, you have to first flip them into rows.

Matrix Equations

So far in this investigation, you have used matrices to represent the coefficients of equations but not the equations themselves. But with matrix multiplication, you can also easily represent systems of equations.

$$4x - 5y = 3$$
$$3x + y = -1$$

becomes

$$\begin{pmatrix} 4 & -5 \\ 3 & 1 \end{pmatrix}\begin{pmatrix} x \\ y \end{pmatrix} = \begin{pmatrix} 3 \\ -1 \end{pmatrix}$$

$$z_1 = 2y_1 + 5y_2 - 3y_3$$
$$z_2 = 3y_1 - y_2 + y_3$$

becomes

$$\begin{pmatrix} z_1 \\ z_2 \end{pmatrix} = \begin{pmatrix} 2 & 5 & 3 \\ 3 & -1 & 1 \end{pmatrix}\begin{pmatrix} y_1 \\ y_2 \\ y_3 \end{pmatrix}$$

When equations have numbers on one side, you usually write the numbers on the right. When equations have single variables on one side, you usually write the variables on the left.

For Discussion

Go the other way: Translate each equation into a linear system. Were you more comfortable with one translation than the other? Explain.

6. $\begin{pmatrix} x \\ y \\ z \end{pmatrix} = \begin{pmatrix} 1 & 2 \\ 3 & 4 \\ 5 & 6 \end{pmatrix}\begin{pmatrix} u \\ v \end{pmatrix}$

7. $(x \ y \ z)\begin{pmatrix} 1 & 2 & 3 \\ 2 & 3 & 4 \\ -3 & -4 & -5 \end{pmatrix} = (3 \ 5 \ 7)$

In short, if you allow yourself to put variables as well as constants into matrices and make use of single columns (or, less conveniently, single rows), you can express any linear system, no matter how big, as a single matrix equation. For instance, $Y = AX$.

It is cute, but does it really help? Time will tell.

And by the way, what happened to Gaussian Elimination? Matrices started out as a shorthand for solving linear systems, but solving systems has not played a role since Investigation 4A.

Matrix Operations on Calculators

Your calculator can do all the matrix and n-tuple operations discussed so far and more. See the TI-Nspire™ Handbook on p. 804 to find out how. Mathematicians and scientists routinely use calculators (or, more likely, computers) to do any matrix calculations bigger than about three rows or columns. For now, do all calculations by hand except where a calculator is requested. It takes a while to get a feel for all the things matrix multiplication can do, and the best way to get that feel is through hands-on practice.

Exercises *Practicing Habits of Mind*

The text has explained where matrix multiplication comes from. In this exercise set, you will begin to get a feel for all the things matrix multiplication can do. As always, look for patterns.

Check Your Understanding

1. Compute each product.

a. $\begin{pmatrix} a & b \\ c & d \end{pmatrix}\begin{pmatrix} 1 & 0 \\ 0 & 1 \end{pmatrix}$

b. $\begin{pmatrix} 1 & 0 \\ 0 & 1 \end{pmatrix}\begin{pmatrix} a & b \\ c & d \end{pmatrix}$

c. $\begin{pmatrix} a & b \\ c & d \end{pmatrix}\begin{pmatrix} 2 & 0 \\ 0 & -3 \end{pmatrix}$

d. $\begin{pmatrix} 2 & 0 \\ 0 & -3 \end{pmatrix}\begin{pmatrix} a & b \\ c & d \end{pmatrix}$

2. You can think of ordered pairs as representing points on the plane. Here you will begin to investigate what matrix multiplication does to points. You will return to this idea in Investigation 4C.

Throughout this exercise, let

$$U = \begin{pmatrix} 1 \\ 0 \end{pmatrix}, \ V = \begin{pmatrix} 1 \\ 3 \end{pmatrix}, \ W = \begin{pmatrix} 2 \\ 6 \end{pmatrix}, \ X = \begin{pmatrix} -1 \\ -3 \end{pmatrix}, \ Y = \begin{pmatrix} 3 \\ 4 \end{pmatrix}, \text{ and } Z = \begin{pmatrix} -1 \\ 1 \end{pmatrix}.$$

a. Plot $U, \ldots, Z$ as points on the plane.

b. Let $A = \begin{pmatrix} 1 & 0 \\ 0 & -1 \end{pmatrix}$. Compute $AU, \ldots, AZ$.

c. Plot the points in part (b) on the plane. Match the pairs U and AU, then V and AV, and so on. How is each point related to its match?

d. Now let $B = \begin{pmatrix} 0 & -1 \\ 1 & 0 \end{pmatrix}$. Compute $BU, \ldots, BZ$. Plot the results on the plane.

Match the pairs U and BU, then V and BV, and so on. How is each point related to its match?

3. Compute each product.

a. $\begin{pmatrix} 1 & 2 & 3 \\ 4 & 5 & 6 \\ 5 & 3 & 1 \end{pmatrix}\begin{pmatrix} 0 \\ 1 \\ 0 \end{pmatrix}$

b. $\begin{pmatrix} 1 & 2 & 3 \\ 4 & 5 & 6 \\ 5 & 3 & 1 \end{pmatrix}\begin{pmatrix} 1 \\ 1 \\ 1 \end{pmatrix}$

c. $(0 \ \ 0 \ \ 1)\begin{pmatrix} 1 & 2 & 3 \\ 4 & 5 & 6 \\ 5 & 3 & 1 \end{pmatrix}$

d. $(1 \ \ 0 \ \ -1)\begin{pmatrix} 1 & 2 & 3 \\ 4 & 5 & 6 \\ 5 & 3 & 1 \end{pmatrix}$

e. $\begin{pmatrix} 1 & 2 \\ 4 & 5 \\ 5 & 3 \end{pmatrix}\begin{pmatrix} 0 & 0 \\ 0 & 0 \end{pmatrix}$

f. $\begin{pmatrix} 0 & 0 \\ 0 & 0 \\ 0 & 0 \end{pmatrix}\begin{pmatrix} 3 & 5 \\ -2 & 6 \end{pmatrix}$

> Any matrix with all entries 0 is a **zero matrix**. You usually call it 0.

4. Translate each equation into a system of linear equations.

a. $\begin{pmatrix} p \\ q \end{pmatrix} = \begin{pmatrix} 1 & -1 \\ 3 & -2 \end{pmatrix} \begin{pmatrix} x \\ y \end{pmatrix}$

b. $\begin{pmatrix} 2 & 1 \\ 4 & 3 \\ 0 & 6 \end{pmatrix} \begin{pmatrix} a \\ b \end{pmatrix} = \begin{pmatrix} 3 \\ 5 \\ 7 \end{pmatrix}$

5. Translate each system into matrix form with the variables in a column.

a. $x = 2u - 3v + 4w$
$y = -u + 2v + \pi w$
$z = 7u - 4v - 2w$

b. $p = 2x + 3y - 4z$
$q = x - 3y$

c. $y_1 = 3x$
$y_2 = -x$
$y_3 = 4x$

6. Which of the following matrix operations are possible? Since only shape matters for this question, actual entries are not shown.

a. $\begin{pmatrix} \blacksquare & \blacksquare \\ \blacksquare & \blacksquare \end{pmatrix} + \begin{pmatrix} \blacksquare & \blacksquare \\ \blacksquare & \blacksquare \end{pmatrix}$

b. $\begin{pmatrix} \blacksquare \\ \blacksquare \end{pmatrix} + \begin{pmatrix} \blacksquare & \blacksquare \\ \blacksquare & \blacksquare \end{pmatrix}$

c. $k \begin{pmatrix} \blacksquare & \blacksquare & \blacksquare \\ \blacksquare & \blacksquare & \blacksquare \end{pmatrix}$

d. $\begin{pmatrix} \blacksquare \\ \blacksquare \end{pmatrix} \begin{pmatrix} \blacksquare & \blacksquare \\ \blacksquare & \blacksquare \end{pmatrix}$

e. $\begin{pmatrix} \blacksquare & \blacksquare \\ \blacksquare & \blacksquare \end{pmatrix} \begin{pmatrix} \blacksquare \\ \blacksquare \end{pmatrix}$

f. $\begin{pmatrix} \blacksquare & \blacksquare \\ \blacksquare & \blacksquare \end{pmatrix} (\blacksquare \quad \blacksquare)$

g. $(\blacksquare \quad \blacksquare) \begin{pmatrix} \blacksquare & \blacksquare \\ \blacksquare & \blacksquare \end{pmatrix}$

h. $(\blacksquare \quad \blacksquare \quad \blacksquare) \begin{pmatrix} \blacksquare & \blacksquare \\ \blacksquare & \blacksquare \end{pmatrix}$

7. Your calculator knows how to multiply matrices. See the TI-Nspire Handbook on p. 804 for advice on doing matrix multiplication.

- Use your calculator to check your work on Exercise 3.

- Create a matrix multiplication problem that would be difficult to do by hand but that a calculator can handle. Do the multiplication with your calculator.

Anyone can make a mistake when entering a problem into a calculator. What are some ways you can check the calculator's result without doing the entire calculation by hand?

Sometimes dimensions are important.

8. Matrices A and B are *conformable* for multiplication in the order AB if the product AB is defined. Suppose $A = \begin{pmatrix} 1 & 3 & 5 \\ 2 & 4 & 6 \end{pmatrix}$.

   a. What size matrices B are conformable for multiplication with A in the order AB?

   b. What size matrices B are conformable for multiplication with A in the order BA?

   c. What size matrices B are conformable for multiplication with A in either order?

9. For what size matrix A is it true that whenever B is the same size as A, then AB exists?

10. For what size matrix A is it true that whenever B is the same size as A, then BA exists?

11. Consider the equations below.

$$z_1 = y_1 + 2y_2 \qquad y_1 = 2x_1 - x_2$$
$$z_2 = 3y_1 - 4y_2 \qquad y_2 = 3x_1 + x_2$$

Use matrix multiplication (not direct substitution) to find formulas for z_1 and z_2 in terms of x_1 and x_2.

12. Return to Exercise 8 in Lesson 4.04 and regard the profit table from part (a) as a matrix. How could you add down columns as in part (b) by matrix multiplication? How could you add across rows as in part (c) by matrix multiplication?

13. For fundraisers, Local High School has a car wash and a play. All students are encouraged to sell tickets at $5 for a car wash and $10 for the play. The bordered matrix below shows how many tickets each class has sold.

$$\begin{array}{c} \\ \text{Car} \\ \text{Play} \end{array} \begin{array}{ccc} \text{Sr} & \text{Jr} & \text{Soph} \\ \begin{pmatrix} 200 & 150 & 50 \\ 100 & 100 & 85 \end{pmatrix} \end{array}$$

   a. Copy and complete the following matrix. Use a matrix product to compute the entries.

$$\begin{array}{c} \\ \text{Revenue} \\ \text{Total tickets} \end{array} \begin{array}{ccc} \text{Sr} & \text{Jr} & \text{Soph} \\ \begin{pmatrix} \blacksquare & \blacksquare & \blacksquare \\ \blacksquare & \blacksquare & \blacksquare \end{pmatrix} \end{array}$$

   b. Use another matrix product to determine the total revenue and total ticket sales for all three classes together.

You may be able to easily compute the entries in this matrix in your head, but the point is to recognize how you can use matrix multiplication in this situation.

14. Cereals A and B are multigrain cereals. The table below left shows how many ounces of certain grains are in one ounce of each cereal. The table on the right shows how many grams of vitamins X, Y and Z are in one ounce of those same grains.

	A	B
Wheat	0.3	0.5
Rice	0.3	0.2
Oats	0.3	0.3

	Wheat	Rice	Oats
Vitamin X	2	1	3
Vitamin Y	3	4	2
Vitamin Z	2	2	1

Use matrix multiplication to devise a table that shows how many grams of each vitamin is in one ounce of each cereal. That is, copy and complete the following table using matrix algebra.

	A	B
Vitamin X	■	■
Vitamin Y	■	■
Vitamin Z	■	■

On Your Own

Go Online
Pearsonsuccessnet.com

For Exercises 15 and 16, compute each pair of matrix products.

15.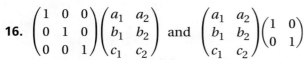
$$\begin{pmatrix} a & b & c \\ d & e & f \\ g & h & i \end{pmatrix} \begin{pmatrix} 1 & 0 & 0 \\ 0 & 1 & 0 \\ 0 & 0 & 1 \end{pmatrix} \text{ and } \begin{pmatrix} 1 & 0 & 0 \\ 0 & 1 & 0 \\ 0 & 0 & 1 \end{pmatrix} \begin{pmatrix} a & b & c \\ d & e & f \\ g & h & i \end{pmatrix}$$

16. $$\begin{pmatrix} 1 & 0 & 0 \\ 0 & 1 & 0 \\ 0 & 0 & 1 \end{pmatrix} \begin{pmatrix} a_1 & a_2 \\ b_1 & b_2 \\ c_1 & c_2 \end{pmatrix} \text{ and } \begin{pmatrix} a_1 & a_2 \\ b_1 & b_2 \\ c_1 & c_2 \end{pmatrix} \begin{pmatrix} 1 & 0 \\ 0 & 1 \end{pmatrix}$$

17. Standardized Test Prep Suppose A is a 3×2 matrix, B is a 2×4 matrix, and C is a 4×3 matrix. What are the dimensions of $B(CA)$?

A. 2×2 **B.** 3×3

C. 4×4 **D.** $B(CA)$ is not possible.

18. Use the matrices below. Compute AB and BA.

$$A = \begin{pmatrix} 3 & 4 \\ 1 & -2 \end{pmatrix} \qquad B = \begin{pmatrix} 2 & -3 \\ 3 & 4 \end{pmatrix}$$

19. Use the matrices below.

$$A = \begin{pmatrix} 1 & 2 \\ 3 & 4 \end{pmatrix} \quad B = \begin{pmatrix} 2 \\ -1 \end{pmatrix} \quad C = \begin{pmatrix} 3 \\ 4 \end{pmatrix}$$

a. Compute $AB + AC$. Compute it exactly as it is written. Find AB first, then AC, and then add.

b. Compute $A(B + C)$. Again, do the computation exactly as written.

20. Use the matrices below.

$$A = \begin{pmatrix} 1 & 3 \\ 2 & 4 \end{pmatrix} \quad B = (2 \ -1) \quad C = (3 \ 4)$$

a. Compute $BA + CA$. Compute it exactly as it is written. Find BA first, then find CA, and then add.

b. Compute $(B + C)A$. Again, do the computation exactly as written.

21. Use the matrices below to compute each product.

$$A = \begin{pmatrix} 1 & 2 \\ 3 & 4 \end{pmatrix} \quad B = \begin{pmatrix} 2 & 3 \\ 4 & 5 \end{pmatrix} \quad C = \begin{pmatrix} 1 & 0 \\ -1 & -2 \end{pmatrix}$$

a. $A(BC)$ **b.** $(AB)C$

22. Do part (c) of the steel company example in this lesson again, but this time do it by substitution, not matrix multiplication. Which method do you prefer?

23. The following table shows the enrollments last year by gender at Local High School.

	Sophomores	Juniors	Seniors
Male	154	148	136
Female	162	155	150

a. Compute the total number of students per class. Show how you can express this computation as matrix multiplication.

b. Compute the total number of males and the total number of females in the high school. Show how you can express this computation as matrix multiplication.

c. Use parts (a) and (b) to compute the total enrollment two ways. Show how you can express each way as matrix multiplication.

Matrix multiplication is not necessarily the best way to do this calculation, but it is valuable to realize that you can use matrix multiplication to do it. You can use matrix multiplication for an amazing number of calculations.

24. Return to Exercise 9 in Lesson 4.04 and regard the passenger car sales table as a matrix. Explain how to get each matrix for the following year by using matrix operations on the matrix for the original year.

25. Assume that the following table shows the number of grams of nutrients in one ounce of food indicated.

	Meat	Potato	Cabbage
Protein	5.5	0.5	3
Fat	5.5	0.03	0.02
Carbohydrates	0.1	6	1.5

a. If you eat a meal consisting of 9 ounces of meat, 20 ounces of potatoes, and 5 ounces of cabbage, how many grams of each nutrient do you get?

b. Why is this exercise in an investigation on matrices?

26. Continuing with the data from Exercise 25, suppose the military wants to use these same foods to feed new recruits a dinner providing 45 grams of protein, 35 grams of fat, and 100 grams of carbohydrates.

a. Write a system of equations, in traditional form, with a solution that would determine how much of each food the military should prepare for each recruit.

b. Rewrite your system of equations as a single matrix equation.

> Do not solve the system right now. The calculations are messy. Later you will learn some methods for solving systems like this. See Exercise 9 in Lesson 4.08.

27. Consider again Exercise 24 in Lesson 4.06. Translate both sets of given equations into matrix equations. Translate the solution set of equations into a matrix equation.

28. Consider again Exercise 26 in Lesson 4.06. Translate both sets of given equations into matrix equations. Translate the solution set of equations into a matrix equation.

29. Take It Further Suppose you have z's that equal linear expressions in y and y's that equal linear expressions in x. You know you can write the first linear system as $Z = AY$ and the second as $Y = BX$. Furthermore, you know from Theorem 4.1 that the matrix for the z's in terms of the x's is AB. That is,

$$Z = (AB)X$$

But wait a minute. Now that you have matrix equations, you can just substitute $Y = BX$ into $Z = AY$. The result is

$$Z = A(BX)$$

Compare the two equations for Z in terms of A, B, and X. What do you conclude? Is this a proof of something?

30. Use the matrices below.

$$A = \begin{pmatrix} 1 & 2 & 1 \\ 2 & 5 & 1 \\ -1 & 1 & 2 \end{pmatrix} \qquad B = \begin{pmatrix} 1 & 0 & 0 \\ -2 & 1 & 0 \\ 1 & 0 & 1 \end{pmatrix} \qquad C = \begin{pmatrix} 1 & 0 & 0 \\ 0 & 1 & 0 \\ 0 & -3 & 1 \end{pmatrix}$$

a. Compute $D = BA$.

b. Compute $E = C(BA)$.

c. Compute $(CB)A$.

d. Do you recognize D and E? Explain.

Maintain Your Skills

31. Use matrix A below. Compute AB for each matrix B.

$$A = \begin{pmatrix} 1 & 2 & 3 \\ 4 & 5 & 6 \\ 7 & 8 & 9 \end{pmatrix}$$

a. $B = \begin{pmatrix} 0 \\ 1 \\ 0 \end{pmatrix}$

b. $B = \begin{pmatrix} 0 \\ 0 \\ -1 \end{pmatrix}$

c. $B = \begin{pmatrix} 0 & 0 & 0 \\ 0 & 0 & 1 \\ 0 & 0 & 0 \end{pmatrix}$

d. $B = \begin{pmatrix} 0 & 0 & 1 \\ 0 & 1 & 0 \\ 1 & 0 & 0 \end{pmatrix}$

32. Use the matrices below. Compute AB, AC, and AD.

$$A = \begin{pmatrix} 1 & 2 \\ 3 & 4 \\ 5 & 6 \end{pmatrix} \qquad B = \begin{pmatrix} 2 \\ -3 \end{pmatrix} \qquad C = \begin{pmatrix} 0 \\ 1 \end{pmatrix} \qquad D = \begin{pmatrix} 2 & 0 \\ -3 & 1 \end{pmatrix}$$

33. Use matrix A below. Compute CA for each matrix C.

$$A = \begin{pmatrix} 1 & 2 & 3 \\ 4 & 5 & 6 \\ 7 & 8 & 9 \end{pmatrix}$$

a. $C = (0 \ \ 1 \ \ 0)$

b. $C = (0 \ \ 0 \ \ -1)$

c. $C = \begin{pmatrix} 0 & 0 & 0 \\ 0 & 0 & 0 \\ 0 & 1 & 0 \end{pmatrix}$

d. $C = \begin{pmatrix} 0 & 0 & 1 \\ 0 & 1 & 0 \\ 1 & 0 & 0 \end{pmatrix}$

34. Use the matrices below. Compute EA, FA, and GA.

$$A = \begin{pmatrix} 1 & 2 \\ 3 & 4 \\ 5 & 6 \end{pmatrix} \qquad E = (1 \ \ 0 \ \ -1) \qquad F = (-1 \ \ 2 \ \ -1) \qquad G = \begin{pmatrix} 1 & 0 & -1 \\ -1 & 2 & -1 \end{pmatrix}$$

35. Compute each product.

a. $\begin{pmatrix} a & b \\ c & d \end{pmatrix}\begin{pmatrix} d & -b \\ -c & a \end{pmatrix}$

b. $\begin{pmatrix} d & -b \\ -c & a \end{pmatrix}\begin{pmatrix} a & b \\ c & d \end{pmatrix}$

36. Use the matrices below.

$$A = (a_1 \quad a_2 \quad a_3) \qquad B = \begin{pmatrix} b_1 \\ b_2 \\ b_3 \end{pmatrix}$$

a. Compute AB or explain why it does not exist.

b. Compute BA or explain why it does not exist.

37. Compute $\begin{pmatrix} 1 & 3 \\ 2 & 6 \end{pmatrix}\begin{pmatrix} 3 & -6 \\ -1 & 2 \end{pmatrix}$. Do you notice anything surprising about the result? Explain.

38. Check the following equation.

$$\begin{pmatrix} 1 & 3 \\ 2 & 6 \end{pmatrix}\begin{pmatrix} 2 \\ 3 \end{pmatrix} = \begin{pmatrix} 1 & 3 \\ 2 & 6 \end{pmatrix}\begin{pmatrix} 5 \\ 2 \end{pmatrix}$$

Do you notice anything surprising about this equation? Explain.

39. Use the matrices below.

$$A = \begin{pmatrix} 1 & 2 \\ 3 & 4 \end{pmatrix} \qquad B = \begin{pmatrix} -1 \\ 1 \end{pmatrix}$$

Compute $A(AB)$ and $(AA)B$. Are the answers the same? Was the amount of work the same?

Just as in real-number algebra, you can write AA as A^2.

40. Square each matrix.

a. $I = \begin{pmatrix} 1 & 0 \\ 0 & 1 \end{pmatrix}$

b. $B = \begin{pmatrix} 1 & 0 \\ 0 & -1 \end{pmatrix}$

c. $C = \begin{pmatrix} 0 & 1 \\ 1 & 0 \end{pmatrix}$

d. $D = \begin{pmatrix} \frac{\sqrt{2}}{2} & \frac{\sqrt{2}}{2} \\ \frac{\sqrt{2}}{2} & -\frac{\sqrt{2}}{2} \end{pmatrix}$

e. $E = \begin{pmatrix} \frac{1}{2} & \frac{\sqrt{3}}{2} \\ \frac{\sqrt{3}}{2} & -\frac{1}{2} \end{pmatrix}$

Matrix notation gives you another way to solve systems of equations.

Sasha is doing her matrix homework in the cafeteria when Xavier wanders up and looks over her shoulder. Xavier is taking first-year algebra.

Xavier   Hey Sasha, that looks pretty hard.

Sasha   That's what I thought. We're solving several equations at the same time, with several variables. But at least now we've learned a shorthand for writing it. We can write a system of equations of any size as simple as this: $AX = B$.

Xavier   I don't know anything about that several-equations stuff, but come on, $AX = B$ is easy.

Sasha   What do you mean?

Xavier   Just divide by A. We learned that in first-year algebra. So $X = \frac{B}{A}$.

Sasha   Nice try, Xavier, but you don't understand. We're not talking about $ax = b$ where a, b, and x are numbers. Why do you think I wrote capital letters? A and B are matrices.

Xavier   So what? Just do a basic move and divide by A.

Sasha   You can't divide by matrices. It hasn't been defined.

Xavier   Well, can you multiply by matrices, whatever they are?

Sasha   Yes.

Xavier   You can undo multiplication by using the inverse. Multiplying by 5 is undone by multiplying by $\frac{1}{5}$. So find the inverse A^{-1}.

Sasha   Who says there's an inverse matrix?

Xavier   Well, every number a has an inverse a^{-1}, where $a^{-1}a = 1$. So if you multiply both sides of $ax = b$ by a^{-1}, you get $1x = x = a^{-1}b$. Just do the same with your matrices, whatever they are—you still haven't told me.

> Well, 0 does not have a multiplicative inverse.

Sasha   Look, they're these two-way tables on my paper. They're not numbers and you can't multiply them to get numbers, so there's no way there's going to be some A^{-1} that you can multiply by A to get 1. You've got to do a lot more, like row reduce or add and subtract equations.

Xavier   Sorry! But it looked so simple, written $AX = B$.

Using good notation has several advantages. Yes, it makes complicated things easier to write, but it also suggests a way to think about an idea. The matrix equation notation made Xavier think about solving equations as in first-year algebra. As it turns out, he is right!

This was his argument: You solve $ax = b$ by multiplying both sides by a^{-1} to get $x = a^{-1}b$. Sasha objected because she thinks there is no matrix C such that $CA = 1$, so there cannot be a matrix that deserves to be called A^{-1}.

There is a matrix I such that $IX = X$. Such a matrix is an **identity matrix**, because multiplying by it gives you back what you start with identically.

What does I look like? Perhaps you know from earlier exercises. Consider the following equations.

$$\begin{pmatrix} 1 & 0 \\ 0 & 1 \end{pmatrix}\begin{pmatrix} x \\ y \end{pmatrix} = \begin{pmatrix} x \\ y \end{pmatrix} \qquad \begin{pmatrix} 1 & 0 & 0 \\ 0 & 1 & 0 \\ 0 & 0 & 1 \end{pmatrix}\begin{pmatrix} x \\ y \\ z \end{pmatrix} = \begin{pmatrix} x \\ y \\ z \end{pmatrix}$$

If X is $m \times 1$, then I is the $m \times m$ matrix with 0's everywhere except for 1's along the main diagonal. You denote all these matrices as I and call each one an identity matrix. If it is important to indicate the size, you can write I_2, I_3, etc.

So, Sasha was mistaken. You do not need the number 1. You need something that serves the same function as 1 in the matrix context. It exists: I.

If there is a matrix M such that $MA = I$, then M will serve the same role as a^{-1}, and Xavier's method for solving matrix equations will work. Starting with $AX = B$, multiply on the left by M, you get

$$X = IX = MAX = MB$$

Example

Problem See if Xavier's method works for the following system.

$$s + 2t = 5$$
$$3s + 4t = 6$$

Solution First, rewrite the system in matrix form.

$$\begin{pmatrix} 1 & 2 \\ 3 & 4 \end{pmatrix}\begin{pmatrix} s \\ t \end{pmatrix} = \begin{pmatrix} 5 \\ 6 \end{pmatrix} \tag{12}$$

Now you need a 2×2 matrix M such that

$$M\begin{pmatrix} 1 & 2 \\ 3 & 4 \end{pmatrix} = \begin{pmatrix} 1 & 0 \\ 0 & 1 \end{pmatrix}$$

In Exercise 12, you will show that there is such a matrix.

$$M = \begin{pmatrix} -2 & 1 \\ \frac{3}{2} & -\frac{1}{2} \end{pmatrix}$$

$\begin{pmatrix} 1 & 0 \\ 0 & 1 \end{pmatrix}$ is the 2×2 identity matrix.

Therefore, multiply both sides of (12) by M, just as you would to solve a real-number equation.

$$\begin{pmatrix} 1 & 2 \\ 3 & 4 \end{pmatrix} \begin{pmatrix} s \\ t \end{pmatrix} = \begin{pmatrix} 5 \\ 6 \end{pmatrix}$$

$$\begin{pmatrix} -2 & 1 \\ \frac{3}{2} & -\frac{1}{2} \end{pmatrix} \begin{pmatrix} 1 & 2 \\ 3 & 4 \end{pmatrix} \begin{pmatrix} s \\ t \end{pmatrix} = \begin{pmatrix} -2 & 1 \\ \frac{3}{2} & -\frac{1}{2} \end{pmatrix} \begin{pmatrix} 5 \\ 6 \end{pmatrix}$$

$$\begin{pmatrix} 1 & 0 \\ 0 & 1 \end{pmatrix} \begin{pmatrix} s \\ t \end{pmatrix} = \begin{pmatrix} -2 & 1 \\ \frac{3}{2} & -\frac{1}{2} \end{pmatrix} \begin{pmatrix} 5 \\ 6 \end{pmatrix} = \begin{pmatrix} -4 \\ \frac{9}{2} \end{pmatrix}$$

$$\begin{pmatrix} s \\ t \end{pmatrix} = \begin{pmatrix} -4 \\ \frac{9}{2} \end{pmatrix}$$

The solution is $s = -4$ and $t = 4\frac{1}{2}$.

For You to Do

1. It is often easier to check a possible solution than to find it. In the example above, check that M really is the inverse of $A = \begin{pmatrix} 1 & 2 \\ 3 & 4 \end{pmatrix}$ by computing MA.

   Then check that $\begin{pmatrix} s \\ t \end{pmatrix} = \begin{pmatrix} -4 \\ 4\frac{1}{2} \end{pmatrix}$ really does solve the original equations.

When a matrix A has a companion matrix M such that $MA = I$, this companion matrix is the **inverse**. You write it as A^{-1}.

Good news and bad news The good news is that your calculator knows how to find matrix inverses. Therefore, your calculator provides a quick way to solve the matrix system $AX = B$.

Step 1 Input A.

Step 2 Press one or more keys to get A^{-1}.

Step 3 Compute the product $A^{-1}B$.

The answer appears on your screen.

The bad news is that the inverse method does not always work, because A^{-1} does not always exist. The inverse never exists if A is not square, and it often does not exist even if A is square. This is quite different from the situation with real numbers, where only 0 has no multiplicative inverse. In contrast, Gaussian Elimination always works when solving the system $AX = B$ for any matrix A. It turns out A^{-1} exists precisely when the system $AX = B$ has a unique solution. Gaussian Elimination handles those systems, as well as systems with no solution or many solutions. On the other hand, in this course, you will mostly consider systems with unique solutions, so the inverse matrix method will generally work for you.

Habits of Mind

Check your definition. This is a working definition. As you will see in Exercise 5, you have to say a little more.

You can always press the exponent key ($\wedge$) followed by -1. On some calculators, there is an x^{-1} button that allows you to find inverses with a single keystroke. See the TI-Nspire Handbook, p. 804.

The 2 × 2 case In general, there is no simple formula for A^{-1} in terms of A, although there is a straightforward algorithm to determine whether A has an inverse and to find A^{-1} when it does—a variant of Gaussian Elimination! However, in the 2 × 2 case, there is a nice formula, which is worth knowing. Recall the result you discovered in Exercise 34 of Lesson 4.07.

If $A = \begin{pmatrix} a & b \\ c & d \end{pmatrix}$ and $B = \begin{pmatrix} d & -b \\ -c & a \end{pmatrix}$, then $BA = AB = (ad - bc)I$.

Therefore, as long as $ad - bc \neq 0$,

$$A^{-1} = \frac{1}{ad - bc} \begin{pmatrix} d & -b \\ -c & a \end{pmatrix}$$

What can you do if $ad - bc = 0$? It turns out there is never an inverse when $ad - bc = 0$, so the 2 × 2 case is completely resolved: A^{-1} exists if and only if $ad - bc \neq 0$, in which case you use the formula above for A^{-1}. See Exercise 14.

Exercises *Practicing Habits of Mind*

Check Your Understanding

1. Return again to Sasha and Derman's favorite problem.

$$x + y + z = 2$$
$$2x - y + z = 5$$
$$x + 2y + 3z = 5$$

Solve this system using inverses.

2. Solve Exercise 21 from Lesson 4.03 again, this time using the inverse.

3. Consider the system below.

$$\begin{pmatrix} 1 & 2 \\ 2 & 4 \end{pmatrix}\begin{pmatrix} x \\ y \end{pmatrix} = \begin{pmatrix} 1 \\ 1 \end{pmatrix}$$

   a. Attempt to solve it geometrically, that is, by graphing the line corresponding to each equation. What happens?
   b. Attempt to solve it by Gaussian Elimination. What happens?
   c. Attempt to solve it by the inverse method. What happens?

There is one matrix equation here, but there are two linear equations.

4. **Write About It** In proposing how to solve $AX = B$, Xavier initially wrote $\frac{1}{A}$ and put the A directly under the B, as in $\frac{B}{A}$. Why does the book only show the notation A^{-1}, and why always on the left, as in $A^{-1}B$, instead of BA^{-1} or $\frac{B}{A}$?

5. Let $A = \begin{pmatrix} 1 & 0 \\ 3 & 4 \\ 0 & 1 \end{pmatrix}$ and $M = \begin{pmatrix} 1 & 0 & 0 \\ 0 & 0 & 1 \end{pmatrix}$.

Check that $MA = I$ and $AM \neq I$. So M is only a one-sided inverse of A, something that does not happen with number multiplication.

6. In the example, you showed that $M = \begin{pmatrix} -2 & 1 \\ \frac{3}{2} & -\frac{1}{2} \end{pmatrix}$ is the inverse of $A = \begin{pmatrix} 1 & 2 \\ 3 & 4 \end{pmatrix}$ in the sense that $MA = I$. Check whether $AM = I$.

7. Xavier said that every real number a has an inverse $\frac{1}{a}$. Is his statement true or false? Explain.

8. Consider the following equation: $\begin{pmatrix} 3 & -1 \\ -2 & 2 \end{pmatrix}\begin{pmatrix} 1 \\ 2 \end{pmatrix} = \begin{pmatrix} 1 \\ 2 \end{pmatrix}$

Does this mean that $\begin{pmatrix} 3 & -1 \\ -2 & 2 \end{pmatrix}$ is also an identity matrix? Explain.

On Your Own

9. Use inverses to solve the system of equations you set up for Exercise 26 of Lesson 4.07.

10. Suppose in Exercise 26 of Lesson 4.07 the military wants each meal to have 120 grams of carbohydrates instead of 150, but otherwise everything else stays the same. How many ounces of each food should the military now prepare for each recruit?

11. Show that the only matrix $\begin{pmatrix} a & b \\ c & d \end{pmatrix}$ that satisfies $\begin{pmatrix} a & b \\ c & d \end{pmatrix}\begin{pmatrix} x \\ y \end{pmatrix} = \begin{pmatrix} x \\ y \end{pmatrix}$ for all x and y is the 2×2 identity matrix $\begin{pmatrix} 1 & 0 \\ 0 & 1 \end{pmatrix}$.

Historical Perspective
Linear Equations and CAT Scans

When you get a CAT scan, the machine shoots X-rays through a slice of you from various angles. The strength of each beam when it comes out the other side reports the sum of the densities of matter along the ray. But your doctor is not interested in sums of densities. Your doctor wants to know the density at each point in the slice. The density indicates what sort of tissue, bone, or tumor is there. So, the software that creates the picture from the CAT scan essentially has to solve a system of summation equations similar to the one in Exercise 15, only much bigger.

12. Is there a matrix $\begin{pmatrix} x & y \\ z & w \end{pmatrix}$ that solves the following equation?

$$\begin{pmatrix} x & y \\ z & w \end{pmatrix}\begin{pmatrix} 1 & 2 \\ 3 & 4 \end{pmatrix} = \begin{pmatrix} 1 & 0 \\ 0 & 1 \end{pmatrix}$$

Write this single matrix equation as four ordinary equations. This gives you four linear equations in four unknowns. However, if you look at it carefully, you will see that this particular system is not hard to solve even by hand. Do it.

13. Is there a matrix $\begin{pmatrix} x & y \\ z & w \end{pmatrix}$ that solves the following equation?

$$\begin{pmatrix} 1 & 2 \\ 3 & 4 \end{pmatrix}\begin{pmatrix} x & y \\ z & w \end{pmatrix} = \begin{pmatrix} 1 & 0 \\ 0 & 1 \end{pmatrix}$$

Find out by converting this single matrix equation into four ordinary equations.

14. You already know that if $ad - bc \neq 0$, then $M = \begin{pmatrix} a & b \\ c & d \end{pmatrix}$ has the inverse $\frac{1}{ad - bc}\begin{pmatrix} d & -b \\ -c & a \end{pmatrix}$. Now show that you have not missed any matrices. Prove that M has an inverse only if $ad - bc \neq 0$.

15. Standardized Test Prep Suppose a_1 is the sum of x_1 and x_2, a_2 is the sum of x_2 and x_3, and a_3 is the sum of x_3 and x_1. If $(a_1, a_2, a_3) = (1, 2, 3)$, what are x_1, x_2, and x_3?

A. $(1, 2, 2)$ **B.** $(1, 2, 3)$ **C.** $(1, 0, 2)$ **D.** $(0, 1, 2)$

16. Take It Further Continuing with Exercise 15, forget all the work to find the individual x values. Is it possible to find the sum $x_1 + x_2 + x_3$ by adding the given equations? Explain.

17. Suppose b_1 is the sum of x_1 and x_2, b_2 is the sum of x_2 and x_3, b_3 is the sum of x_3 and x_4, and b_4 is the sum of x_4 and x_1. If $(b_1, b_2, b_3, b_4) = (1, 2, 3, 4)$, what are x_1, x_2, x_3, and x_4?

Go Online
Pearsonsuccessnet.com

Remember...

The system
$$ax + by = e$$
$$cx + dy = f$$
where a, b, c, d, e and f are known constants, has the unique solution $(x, y) =$
$$\left(\frac{de - bf}{ad - bc}, \frac{af - ce}{ad - bc} \right)$$

Maintain Your Skills

18. Compute the inverse of each matrix.

a. $\begin{pmatrix} 1 & 0 & 0 \\ 0 & 2 & 0 \\ 0 & 0 & \frac{1}{3} \end{pmatrix}$ **b.** $\begin{pmatrix} 1 & 1 \\ 0 & 1 \end{pmatrix}$ **c.** $\begin{pmatrix} 1 & 2 & 3 \\ 0 & 4 & 5 \\ 0 & 0 & 6 \end{pmatrix}$ **d.** $\begin{pmatrix} 1 & 0 & 0 \\ 2 & 1 & 0 \\ 2 & 1 & 2 \end{pmatrix}$

e. $\begin{pmatrix} 1 & 2 & 0 & 0 \\ 3 & 4 & 0 & 0 \\ 0 & 0 & 1 & 2 \\ 0 & 0 & 3 & 4 \end{pmatrix}$ **f.** $\begin{pmatrix} 1 & \frac{1}{2} \\ \frac{1}{2} & \frac{1}{3} \end{pmatrix}$ **g.** $\begin{pmatrix} 1 & \frac{1}{2} & \frac{1}{3} \\ \frac{1}{2} & \frac{1}{3} & \frac{1}{4} \\ \frac{1}{3} & \frac{1}{4} & \frac{1}{5} \end{pmatrix}$

4.09 Matrix Properties

With addition and multiplication of matrices defined, there is a whole algebra of matrices. You can write expressions such as $(X + Y)^2$, equations such as $X^2 + 3X = B$, and even systems of matrix equations such as

$$AX + BY = C$$

$$DX + EY = F$$

Do the rules of ordinary algebra apply? For instance, are the following equations true?

$$(3X + 4Y) - 2(X - Y) = X + 6Y$$

$$(X + Y)^2 = X^2 + 2XY + Y^2$$

Also, does $AB = 0$ imply $A = 0$ or $B = 0$?

If the usual rules do apply, that would make it much easier to do matrix algebra.

Developing Habits of Mind

Make strategic choices. There are many moves you can make in ordinary algebra. Do you have to verify each of them from scratch to apply them to matrices? No, not necessarily. Instead, you can find a few basic rules and deduce the other valid rules from them. This deductive approach is one of the great achievements of mathematics. You have probably already used it in your first-year algebra course to prove properties of real numbers. First, you can identify some key properties as basic rules, for instance, the commutative properties of addition and multiplication and the Distributive Property.

$a + b = b + a$ and $ab = ba$ for all real numbers a and b

$a(b + c) = ab + ac$ for all real numbers a, b, and c

Then you can show that many other properties followed from the full set of basic rules. For instance, you can prove the expansion principle: To multiply two sums, multiply each term in the first sum by each term in the second sum and add the results.

$$(x + y + z)(a + b) = xa + xb + ya + yb + za + zb$$

Similarly, if all the same basic rules held for matrix algebra, then so would the expansion principle.

It turns out that most, but not all, of the basic rules for real numbers hold for matrices as well. You will see the consequences shortly.

Tony and Sasha have been asked to justify, or find counterexamples to, the matrix versions of the two commutative properties.

Tony   We're half done, because we have already seen in Exercise 17 from Lesson 4.07 tha $AB \neq BA$. So let's conside $A + B = B + A$. That's always been true in all the examples I've seen.

Sasha   But that's not a proof.

Tony   True, but I've caught on to how this is done. We already worked this out for n-tuples. Matrices $A + B$ and $B + A$ will be equal if the real numbers inside them are equal entry by entry. So consider a typical entry.

Sasha   I see. For the typical entry of $A + B$, you add the A-entry and the B-entry. For $B + A$, you add the B-entry and the A-entry. Since these entries are numbers, and we already know that number addition commutes, we're done.

Tony   It helps me to build an example. Let $A = \begin{pmatrix} 1 & 2 \\ 3 & 4 \end{pmatrix}$ and $B = \begin{pmatrix} 5 & 6 \\ 7 & 8 \end{pmatrix}$. The row-1, column-2 entry of $A + B$ is $2 + 6$. The row-1, column-2 entry of $B + A$ is $6 + 2$. But good old number addition commutes.

Sasha   I like that. And since there was nothing special about the row-1, column-2 entry, we've shown that corresponding entries agree in all cases, so $A + B$ and $B + A$ are equal.

Tony   Great! Now we're done, because we already know that matrix multiplication doesn't commute.

Sasha   Yes, we have a specific example where $AB \neq BA$, but I'm not happy with that.

Tony   Why not? A claim is false if there is even just one counterexample.

Sasha   Yes, but I don't think I understand yet why order matters for matrix multiplication. I don't know whether failure to commute is rare or common.

Tony   Let's look at the definition of matrix multiplication and see if it gives us any clues.

Sasha   I like to think about the definition with the dot product of rows and columns. So I think of the ij entry of AB this way.

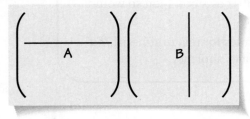

The horizontal and vertical lines I drew show how to compute a typical element of *A* times *B*: a dot product of the *i*th row of *A* and the *j*th column of *B*.

Tony   Looks good.

Sasha   Let's find the same entry of *B* times *A*.

Tony   OK, now the picture looks like this.

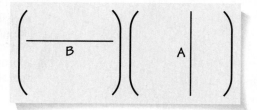

It looks about the same.

Sasha   It only looks the same if you ignore that the matrices have been switched! See, the numbers that you multiply are all different. Here, let me draw in the row and column of numbers that we took the dot product of when the product was *AB*.

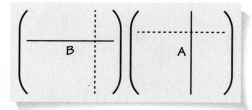

Look, they're almost completely different from the solid line entries that we used to compute *BA*. No wonder it is different!

Tony   Hmm. Now I'm surprised that *AB* ever equals *BA* in any entry!

Sasha   But we know it sometimes does, as in $AI = IA$ for an identity matrix. I guess those must be rare exceptions.

Tony   I wonder if we can explain with your pictures why *I* commutes with other matrices.

You will give an explanation in Exercise 8.

For Discussion

1. While thinking about why $AB \neq BA$, Sasha drew a picture with square matrices. If you look at nonsquare matrices, you can argue just from the sizes and the products that you cannot have equality. Explain.

Facts and Notation

You can now summarize the properties of matrix algebra, as compared to the properties of real numbers.

Commutative Properties:

- $A + B = B + A$ **True**
- $AB = BA$ **False** (It is not true for all A and B.)

Associative Properties:

- $(A + B) + C = A + (B + C)$ **True**
- $(AB)C = A(BC)$ **True**

Distributive Property:

- $A(B + C) = AB + AC$ and $(B + C)A = BA + CA$ **True**

Because matrix algebra has both matrix multiplication and scalar multiplication, some of the basic rules of real numbers split into several matrix rules. Consider the Distributive Property. Along with the version above, there are also two scalar versions:

- $a(B + C) = aB + aC$ **True**
- $(a + b)C = aC + bC$ **True**

Again, because there are two types of multiplication, some rules may look like associative properties, but they are not.

- $a(BC) = (aB)C = B(aC)$ **True**
- $a(bC) = (ab)C = b(aC)$ **True**

Additive Identity:

- For each matrix A, there exists a matrix 0 of the same size such that $A + 0 = A$. The matrix 0 has the number 0 in every entry. **True**

Additive Inverse:

- For every matrix A there exists another matrix $-A$ of the same size such that $A + (-A) = 0$. In fact, if $A = (a_{ij})$, then $-A = (-a_{ij})$. **True**

Multiplicative Identity:

- For each square matrix A, there exists a matrix I such that $AI = IA = A$. If A is $m \times n$, and I_k is the $k \times k$ identity matrix, with 1's on the main diagonal and 0's elsewhere, then $I_m A = A I_n = A$. **True**

Multiplicative Inverses:

- For each matrix A, where $A \neq 0$, there exists a matrix A^{-1} such that $AA^{-1} = A^{-1}A = I$. **False**

> When you consider a property with a sum like $A + B$ or a product like AB, you may assume that A and B are of the appropriate sizes for the operation.

Habits of Mind

Experiment. Where have you already seen examples for which the last rule is false?

Look for relationships. As Tony and Sasha noted, for those rules that are true, there are proofs. For those that are false, there are counterexamples and maybe some sort of intuitive way to see that there should be counterexamples.

But what do the proofs look like? The proof Tony and Sasha found for $A + B = B + A$ uses one standard matrix technique: Look at a typical entry (the ij entry). See whether the matrix identity reduces to a known numeric identity. In a similar way, proofs of facts about scalar multiplication often work out to be proofs about sums. See, for instance, Exercise 9.

Claims involving matrix multiplication are much more complicated to prove or disprove. This is because the formula for the typical entry of a product matrix is complicated.

Perhaps the most difficult basic rule to justify is the associative property of multiplication. Some earlier exercises illustrated instances of this property. They explained that the definition of matrix multiplication was tailored to make $A(BX) = (AB)X$ true, at least when X is a single column. You can accept the associative property of matrix multiplication as a working conjecture.

In particular, Exercise 26 in Lesson 4.06

You will explore some of the multiplication rules in the exercises.

Beyond the Basics

Any matrix claim that just involves addition, subtraction, and scalar multiplication is correct if the basic algebra version of it is correct. But claims that involve matrix multiplication may be wrong.

For instance, the matrix equation

$$a(X + Y) - b(X + 2Y) = (a - b)X + (a - 2b)Y \qquad (13)$$

corresponds to the number equation

$$a(x + y) - b(x + 2y) = (a - b)x + (a - 2b)y \qquad (14)$$

Equation (13) uses just matrix addition and subtraction and scalar multiplication. Equation (14) is correct, therefore (13) is correct. Why is it? The basic rules for matrix addition, subtraction, and scalar multiplication are the same as the basic rules for number addition, subtraction, and multiplication. So however you justify (14) from the basic algebra rules, exactly the same justification works for (13) using the basic matrix rules.

However, the following matrix-product statement is false even though the corresponding statement for real numbers is true.

If $AB = 0$, then $A = 0$ or $B = 0$.

If $ab = 0$, then $a = 0$ or $b = 0$. (Zero Product Property)

Consider more than one strategy. How can you determine whether a suspect claim is false? Sometimes you are lucky and you already have a counterexample that you discovered while doing something else. For instance, you discovered in Exercise 13 of Lesson 4.06 that the Zero Product Property is false for dot products, and dot products are a special sort of matrix product. If you are not lucky, you should probably not start by trying random examples. If the first example or two shows the claim to be false, you have your answer, but you do not know why. On the other hand, if the claim works for the first five examples, were you lucky, or was this because the claim is true? There is no way to be sure.

A better approach is to try to prove the claim from the basic rules and any other known truths. Either you will succeed, in which case no search for counterexamples is necessary, or else you will discover how the proof breaks down. That will probably suggest how to find a counterexample.

A good navigation system will help you find what you are looking for.

How do you prove the Zero Product Property for real numbers? One proof goes this way.

Assume $ab = 0$. Either $a = 0$ or not. If it does, you are done. If it does not, multiply $ab = 0$ by $\frac{1}{a}$, getting $b = 0$. So, $a = 0$ or $b = 0$.

Aha! The proof uses the existence of a^{-1}, which works for numbers so long as $a \neq 0$. But it does not work for most matrices, so you might suspect that the Zero Product Property for matrices will fail when A is not invertible.

For You to Do

2. According to Exercise 14 in Lesson 4.08, $A = \begin{pmatrix} 1 & 2 \\ 3 & 6 \end{pmatrix}$ is not invertible, because $1 \cdot 6 - 3 \cdot 2 = 0$. Find a nonzero 2×2 matrix B such that $AB = 0$.

> **Habits of Mind**
>
> **Make strategic choices.** The Zero Product Property will not necessarily fail for matrices. There might be a proof that does not use inverses and still works. But you should be very suspicious that the property will fail for matrices. It is now worth looking for a counterexample.

The Zero Product Property is a property that eliminates a product. You go from a statement about ab to a statement about a or b. All such properties involve inverses somewhere, and all are suspect (and usually false) in matrix algebra. The following problem gives one more property that would be useful if it were true for matrices, but it is not.

For You to Do

3. One of the cancellation laws of number algebra is

    If $ab = ac$, then $b = c$ (unless $a = 0$).

    Show that the corresponding matrix statement is false.

    If $AB = AC$, then $B = C$ (unless $A = 0$).

    (*Hint:* Subtract AC from both sides and set up a zero product.)

Exercises Practicing Habits of Mind

The exercises give some more examples of rules involving multiplication that break down. Be prepared for them to break down every time, except if special matrices like I are involved.

Check Your Understanding

1. Let $A = \begin{pmatrix} 1 & 2 & 3 \\ 4 & 5 & 6 \end{pmatrix}$.

   a. Find a matrix I such that $IA = A$.

   b. Find a matrix I such that $AI = A$.

This exercise confirms the fact that a matrix can have different identities on the left and the right.

2. Show that every square matrix A commutes under multiplication with itself. Does A also commute with A^2? Explain.

3. You usually state the Distributive Property for number algebra in just one equation.
$$a(b + c) = ab + ac$$
Explain why the Distributive Property for matrices was stated in two equations.
$$A(B + C) = AB + AC \text{ and } (B + C)A = BA + CA$$

4. Let $A = \begin{pmatrix} 1 & 2 \\ 3 & 6 \end{pmatrix}$.

   a. Find all 2×1 column matrices B such that $AB = 0$.

   b. Find all 2×2 matrices B such that $AB = 0$.

5. **What's Wrong Here?** In number algebra,
$$(x + y)^2 = x^2 + 2xy + y^2$$
Below is a proposed proof that the statement is also true for matrices. For each line that is correct, explain why. For each line that is wrong, explain why.
$$(X + Y)^2 = (X + Y)(X + Y)$$
$$= X(X + Y) + Y(X + Y)$$
$$= (XX + XY) + (YX + YY)$$
$$= X^2 + (XY + YX) + Y^2$$
$$= X^2 + 2XY + Y^2$$

6. Does the expansion principle hold for matrix algebra?

7. Show that the following revised cancellation law is valid for matrix algebra: If A is invertible and $AB = AC$, then $B = C$.

See the first Developing Habits of Mind section in this lesson for an explanation of the expansion principle.

8. Follow up on Tony's thought at the end of the dialog. Can you use Sasha's pictures to explain why AI is equal to IA? Explain.

As Sasha did, assume that A is a square matrix.

On Your Own

9. Is $A + A = 2A$ true for all matrices? You can use the definitions of *sum* and *scalar multiple* for matrices. However, if you note that $1A = A$, then you can also use one of the basic rules for matrices.

10. Consider the special binomial expansion $(X + I)^2 = X^2 + 2X + I$. This is the matrix version of $(x + 1)^2 = x^2 + 2x + 1$. Is this special matrix binomial expansion correct for all square matrices? Explain.

Habits of Mind

Detect the key characteristics. Here, the matrix X must be square. Explain.

11. Show that $(X + Y)^2 = X^2 + 2XY + Y^2$ if and only if X and Y commute.

12. Explain why $A(B + C) = AB + AC$. That is, justify the Distributive Property for matrix algebra.

13. **a.** Show that the all-0's matrix Z never has a multiplicative inverse, no matter what its size.

    b. Show that there exist infinitely many 2×2 matrices A that do not have an inverse. In fact, show that there are infinitely many 2×2 matrices in which all four entries are nonzero and yet A^{-1} does not exist.

14. Consider again one of the basic rules of matrix algebra.
$$a(BC) = (aB)C = B(aC)$$
This rule says that three different computations give the same result. You can describe the first computation as, "First you multiply the two matrices and then you scale." Describe in your own words the three different computations.

15. Show that the claim $(X + bI)^2 = X^2 + 2bX + b^2I$ is correct for any square matrix X and scalar b.

16. **Write About It** What have you learned in this lesson about rules for matrix algebra?

17. **Standardized Test Prep** Suppose X is a 2×2 matrix. Cynthia has a system for constructing a 2×2 matrix Y such that $XY = YX$. She says if
$X = \begin{pmatrix} a & b \\ c & d \end{pmatrix}$, then $Y = \begin{pmatrix} f & kb \\ kc & f - k(a - d) \end{pmatrix}$.
Suppose $X = \begin{pmatrix} 5 & 2 \\ 1 & 4 \end{pmatrix}$, $y_{11} = 4$, and $y_{12} = 6$. What is YX?

A. $\begin{pmatrix} 4 & 6 \\ 3 & 1 \end{pmatrix}$ **B.** $\begin{pmatrix} 20 & 12 \\ 3 & 4 \end{pmatrix}$ **C.** $\begin{pmatrix} 26 & 32 \\ 16 & 10 \end{pmatrix}$ **D.** $\begin{pmatrix} 26 & 54 \\ 16 & 54 \end{pmatrix}$

Go Online
Pearsonsuccessnet.com

Maintain Your Skills

18. The multiplication formula for 1×1 matrices is especially simple. What is it? Are there any pairs of 1×1 matrices that do not commute?

19. Use the matrices A and D below.

$$A = \begin{pmatrix} a & 0 & 0 \\ 0 & b & 0 \\ 0 & 0 & c \end{pmatrix} \qquad D = \begin{pmatrix} d & 0 & 0 \\ 0 & e & 0 \\ 0 & 0 & f \end{pmatrix}$$

Compute AD and DA. What do you notice?

> The nonzero entries in A and D are on the main diagonal. Matrices with nonzero entries only along the main diagonal are *diagonal matrices*. You can display them with spaces instead of 0's to avoid visual clutter.
>
> $$A = \begin{pmatrix} a & & \\ & b & \\ & & c \end{pmatrix}$$

20. **a.** Find all matrices that commute under multiplication with $\begin{pmatrix} 0 & \\ & 1 \end{pmatrix}$.

b. Find all matrices that commute under multiplication with $\begin{pmatrix} 0 & & \\ & 0 & \\ & & 1 \end{pmatrix}$.

c. Expand $(X + I)^3$.

d. Expand $(X + I)^4$.

e. Expand $(X + Y)^3$. Compare this expansion with the expansion of $(X + Y)^2$ in Exercise 5. See if you can find a pattern.

f. Expand $(X + Y + Z)^2$. Compare this expansion with the expansion of $(X + Y)^2$ in Exercise 5. See if you can find a pattern.

Mathematical 4B Reflections

In this investigation, you learned how to compute sums, differences, dot products, products, and inverses of matrices. You also explored the properties of matrix algebra. These questions will help you summarize what you have learned.

1. Use the following matrices.

$$A = \begin{pmatrix} 3 & 1 \\ -1 & 0 \end{pmatrix} \qquad B = (4 \quad 2) \qquad C = \begin{pmatrix} 0 \\ -2 \end{pmatrix} \qquad D = \begin{pmatrix} 5 & 0 \\ 1 & -2 \end{pmatrix}$$

For each part, either do the calculation or explain why it does not make sense.

   a. $3D$
   b. $A + B$
   c. $A - D$
   d. $B \cdot C$
   e. $A \cdot C$
   f. AB
   g. AC
   h. AD

2. Find a 3-tuple $E = (a \quad b \quad c)$ such that $E \cdot (-2 \quad 1 \quad 4) = 0$. Is the E you found the only possible answer? If so, explain why. If not, give another example.

3. For the following matrices, show that $F(G + H) = FG + FH$.

$$F = \begin{pmatrix} 1 & -1 \\ 2 & 0 \end{pmatrix} \qquad G = \begin{pmatrix} -3 & 1 \\ 0 & 4 \end{pmatrix} \qquad H = \begin{pmatrix} 0 & 1 \\ -2 & 0 \end{pmatrix}$$

4. Use the following matrices.

$$J = \begin{pmatrix} 1 & -1 \\ 0 & 2 \\ 3 & 1 \end{pmatrix} \qquad K = \begin{pmatrix} 2 & -1 & 0 \\ 0 & -2 & 1 \end{pmatrix}$$

   Is JK equal to KJ? Make a prediction and then find both products to check.

5. Give an example of a 2×2 matrix that does not have an inverse. Explain how you know.

6. What is a dot product? How can you represent matrix multiplication using dot products?

7. What are some special cases in which $AB = BA$ is true for matrices A and B?

8. How can you solve this system of equations using matrix inverses? What is the solution?

$$x + 4y - z = -3$$
$$2x - 2y + z = 0$$
$$3x + y - 3z = -9$$

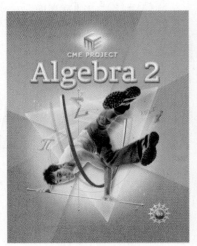

The final color at each point on the cover is the sum of the individual colors at that point.

Vocabulary and Notation

In this investigation, you learned these terms and symbols. Make sure you understand what each one means and how to use it.

- determinant
- dot product
- identity matrix, *I*
- inverse, A^{-1}
- linear combination
- matrix multiplication
- *n*-tuple
- scalar multiplication
- zero matrix, 0

Chapter 4 Mid-Chapter Test

Multiple Choice

1. What is the solution to the following system?

$$2x - 5y = 1$$
$$3x - 4y = 5$$

A. $(-7, 3)$ **B.** $(3, 1)$

C. $(1, 3)$ **D.** $(-2, -1)$

2. A local soccer team placed the following order at their favorite restaurant.

Item	Hot Dog	Hamburger	Drink
Cost ($)	3.00	4.00	1.50
Number Ordered	5	6	11

What is the cost of the entire order?

A. $8.50   **B.** $22.00

C. $50.55   **D.** $55.50

3. Find the dot product $(-1, 3, 5) \cdot (2, -4, 6)$.

A. 11   **B.** 16   **C.** 20   **D.** 240

4. After using Gaussian Elimination to solve a system of equations, you get this matrix.

$$\begin{pmatrix} 1 & 0 & 2 & | & 3 \\ 0 & 1 & 0 & | & 7 \\ 0 & 0 & 0 & | & 0 \end{pmatrix}$$

What can you conclude?

A. The only solution is $(2, 4, 0)$.

B. One possible solution is $(-1, 7, 2)$.

C. One possible solution is $(3, 0, 0)$.

D. There is no solution.

5. Suppose $A = (a_{ij})$, as shown below.

$$A = \begin{pmatrix} 4 & 3 & -1 & 2 \\ 1 & 5 & 0 & 8 \\ 7 & 11 & -3 & 10 \end{pmatrix}$$

Find a_{32}.

A. -3 **B.** 0   **C.** 8   **D.** 11

Open Response

6. The graph of a quadratic function $f(x) = ax^2 + bx + c$ passes through the points $(-2, 21)$, $(1, 6)$, and $(2, 9)$. Find a, b, and c.

7. Consider the augmented matrix below.

$$\begin{pmatrix} 1 & -2 & 1 & | & -9 \\ 2 & 1 & -3 & | & 7 \\ 1 & 2 & 4 & | & -3 \end{pmatrix}$$

 a. To what system of equations does this matrix correspond?

 b. Solve the system in matrix form.

8. Let $A = (a_{ij})$ be a 2×3 matrix where $a_{ij} = i + 2j$.

 a. Find A.

 b. Find $2A$.

 c. Find AB, where $B = \begin{pmatrix} 2 \\ -3 \\ 0 \end{pmatrix}$.

9. Use the following matrices.

$$A = \begin{pmatrix} 3 & -1 \\ 2 & 0 \\ -4 & 5 \end{pmatrix} \qquad B = \begin{pmatrix} 2 & -5 & 4 \\ 6 & -4 & -2 \\ 3 & 0 & 8 \\ 4 & 6 & -2 \end{pmatrix}$$

$$C = \begin{pmatrix} 3 & 1 \\ 6 & -2 \\ 0 & 4 \end{pmatrix}$$

 Find each matrix, if possible.

 a. $A + C$ **b.** $-B$

 c. AB **d.** BA

10. Let $D = \begin{pmatrix} 2 & 1 \\ 8 & 3 \end{pmatrix}$.

 a. Find D^{-1}.

 b. Suppose $\begin{pmatrix} 2 & 1 \\ 8 & 3 \end{pmatrix}\begin{pmatrix} x \\ y \end{pmatrix} = \begin{pmatrix} 2 \\ 4 \end{pmatrix}$. Find x and y.

 c. Write the system of equations that you just solved.

11. Why is it possible to solve systems of linear equations in matrix form?

Applications of Matrix Multiplication

In *Applications of Matrix Multiplication*, you will use matrices and matrix multiplication to model various situations, such as geometric transformations, transition problems, and probability problems.

By the end of this investigation, you will be able to answer questions like these.

1. Is it true that a matrix associated with a reflection must be its own inverse? If so, what are some relationships that must hold for the entries a, b, c, and d in a 2×2 reflection matrix $R = \begin{pmatrix} a & b \\ c & d \end{pmatrix}$?

2. What is an absorbing state, and what does such a state look like in a transition matrix?

3. A transition matrix for a fixed population of 150 is $\begin{pmatrix} 0.2 & 0.7 \\ 0.8 & 0.3 \end{pmatrix}$

   Does this matrix have a steady state? If so, what is it? If not, why not?

You will learn how to

- flexibly transition between systems of real-variable equations and matrices
- model the evolution of a system over time
- analyze sequences of repeated probabilities

You will develop these habits and skills:

- Reason about matrices as mathematical objects, like numbers, that you can compute with.
- Analyze a multistep process in several variables as a series of transition steps expressed as matrix multiplication.
- Visualize the result of matrix multiplication as a geometric transformation in the coordinate plane.

Look for patterns as you complete the following problems.

For You to Explore

1. Consider two sequences s and t, defined as follows.

$$s(0) = t(0) = 1$$
$$s(n) = s(n - 1) + t(n - 1) \quad \text{for } n \geq 1 \quad (15)$$
$$t(n) = s(n - 1) - t(n - 1) \quad \text{for } n \geq 1$$

> A *sequence* is a function with a domain that is the nonnegative integers.

   a. Compute several terms of each sequence until you see a pattern. You might want to line up the two sequences this way.

$$s(0) \quad s(1) \quad s(2) \quad s(3) \ldots$$
$$t(0) \quad t(1) \quad t(2) \quad t(3) \ldots$$

   b. Since the equations that define the sequences are all linear, you can replace them with a single matrix equation. Let $S(n) = \begin{pmatrix} s(n) \\ t(n) \end{pmatrix}$ and $M = \begin{pmatrix} 1 & 1 \\ 1 & -1 \end{pmatrix}$.

   Verify that you can rewrite (15) as

$$S(n) = \begin{cases} \begin{pmatrix} 1 \\ 1 \end{pmatrix} & \text{if } n = 0 \\ MS(n - 1) & \text{if } n > 0 \end{cases}$$

> Model the sequence S. See the TI-Nspire Handbook, p. 804.

   c. Note that $S(2) = MS(1) = M(MS(0)) = M^2 S(0)$, since matrix multiplication is associative. Explain why $S(n) = M^n S(0)$.

   d. Compute M, M^2, M^3, ... until you see a pattern. For as far as you computed powers of M, verify that $S(n) = M^n S(0)$.

2. Let $A = \begin{pmatrix} 1 & 1 \\ 0 & 1 \end{pmatrix}$. Compute powers of A until you can make a conjecture about a pattern.

3. Consider two sequences $u_0, u_1, \ldots$ and $v_0, v_1, \ldots$, defined as follows.

$$u(0) = v(0) = 1$$
$$u(n + 1) = u(n) + v(n) \quad \text{for } n \geq 0$$
$$v(n + 1) = v(n) \quad \text{for } n \geq 0$$

   a. Compute several terms of each sequence until you see a pattern.

   b. You can replace the system of equations that defines these sequences with a single matrix equation. Define $U(n) = \begin{pmatrix} u(n) \\ v(n) \end{pmatrix}$ and find the matrix M such that $U(n + 1) = MU(n)$.

   c. Compute M, M^2, M^3, ... until you see a pattern. For the powers n that you computed, verify that $U(n) = M^n U(0)$.

A geometric mapping is a function that maps points in the plane to other points in the plane in some organized way. One of the topics in this investigation is to understand what sorts of mappings of the plane you can describe with matrix multiplication.

For Exercises 4 and 5, let $M = \begin{pmatrix} -1 & 0 \\ 0 & 1 \end{pmatrix}$. If you think of $\begin{pmatrix} x \\ y \end{pmatrix}$ as a point in the plane, you can think of the following mapping as a geometric mapping.

$$X = \begin{pmatrix} x \\ y \end{pmatrix} \mapsto X' = M\begin{pmatrix} x \\ y \end{pmatrix} = \begin{pmatrix} -x \\ y \end{pmatrix}$$

4. One way to find out how a particular matrix M maps the plane is to choose several points X_1, X_2, ... that form a nice pattern and then see what patterns $X'_1 = MX_1$, $X'_2 = MX_2$, ... exhibit.

   Consider the following points. These are the integer points on the sides of a certain rectangle.

   $$\begin{pmatrix} 0 \\ 0 \end{pmatrix}, \begin{pmatrix} 1 \\ 0 \end{pmatrix}, \begin{pmatrix} 1 \\ 1 \end{pmatrix}, \begin{pmatrix} 1 \\ 2 \end{pmatrix}, \begin{pmatrix} 0 \\ 2 \end{pmatrix}, \begin{pmatrix} 0 \\ 1 \end{pmatrix}$$

   a. Plot each point.

   b. For each point X you plotted, compute and plot MX as well. Indicate which points pair up. You can draw an arrow from X to MX.

   c. What does the mapping seem to do to lines? To polygons?

   d. Describe what you think M does to the whole plane.

   e. Plot a few more points X that form a nice pattern. What do you think M will do to this pattern? Plot MX for your points and see if you are right.

5. If $X \mapsto MX$ maps the plane to itself, you can repeat the mapping.

   $$X \mapsto MX \mapsto M(MX) = M^2X \mapsto M(M^2X) = M^3X$$

   a. Consider M again. In Exercise 4, you probably decided that M reflects the plane over a certain line. If so, what should be the net effect if you repeat the mapping a second time?

   b. Compute M^2 and M^2X, where $X = \begin{pmatrix} x \\ y \end{pmatrix}$. Did you confirm your answer to part (a)?

6. Now consider the x-axis as a line and reflect points of the plane over that line.
   a. What are the images of the points $\begin{pmatrix} 2 \\ 1 \end{pmatrix}$, $\begin{pmatrix} -1 \\ -2 \end{pmatrix}$, and $\begin{pmatrix} 0 \\ 0 \end{pmatrix}$?

   What is the image of the generic point $\begin{pmatrix} x \\ y \end{pmatrix}$?

   b. Find a matrix M such that $X' = MX$ is the image of X after reflection over the x-axis for every point X.

   c. Determine, with and without matrices, the effect of doing this reflection twice.

You usually write points as horizontal ordered pairs (x, y). If you want to multiply them by a matrix on the left, then you must write them as columns. Doing so ensures that the matrix multiplication is defined.

Habits of Mind

Look for relationships. This repetition is the same function iteration that you have seen many times for numerical functions.

7. Now consider points in space and reflect them over the *xy*-plane.

   a. What are the images of the points $(1, 2, 3)$, $(1, 2, -3)$, $(2, -1, 4)$, $(0, 0, 0)$, and (x, y, z)?

   b. State how to express this reflection as a matrix multiplication. As usual, you will have to write points as columns. This time they are 3-tuple columns.

   c. Determine, with and without matrices, the effect of doing this reflection twice.

8. A certain car rental agency has two locations, one in Boston and one in Cambridge. All rentals are for one week, and the agency allows cars from both locations to be returned to either location. Experience shows that 80% of the cars rented in Boston return there, but only 50% of the cars rented in Cambridge return there. At the start of a certain month, the agency has 70 cars in each location. What will be the situation one week later? Two weeks later? Three weeks later? What happens many weeks into the future?

> Model the rental car inventories problem. See the TI-Nspire Handbook, p. 804.

Exercises *Practicing Habits of Mind*

On Your Own

9. Let $M = \begin{pmatrix} 3 & 0 \\ 0 & 3 \end{pmatrix}$. Consider the mapping $X = \begin{pmatrix} x \\ y \end{pmatrix} \mapsto X' = M\begin{pmatrix} x \\ y \end{pmatrix} = \begin{pmatrix} 3x \\ 3y \end{pmatrix}$.

Think of $\begin{pmatrix} x \\ y \end{pmatrix}$ as a point in the plane and $X \mapsto MX$ as a geometric mapping.

As in Problem 4, consider the points $\begin{pmatrix} 0 \\ 0 \end{pmatrix}$, $\begin{pmatrix} 1 \\ 0 \end{pmatrix}$, $\begin{pmatrix} 1 \\ 1 \end{pmatrix}$, $\begin{pmatrix} 1 \\ 2 \end{pmatrix}$, $\begin{pmatrix} 0 \\ 2 \end{pmatrix}$, and $\begin{pmatrix} 0 \\ 1 \end{pmatrix}$.

   a. Plot each point.

   b. For each point *X* you plotted, compute and plot *MX* as well. Indicate which points pair up. You can draw an arrow from *X* to *MX*.

   c. What does the mapping seem to do to lines? To polygons?

   d. Describe what you think *M* does to the whole plane.

   e. Plot a few more points *X* that form a nice pattern. What do you think *M* will do to this pattern? Plot *MX* for your points and see if you are right.

   f. Explain why you might call this mapping $X \mapsto MX$ a scaling mapping with scale factor 3.

10. **a.** Consider again M from Exercise 9. What do you expect the net effect to be if you repeat the mapping a second time?

   b. Compute M^2 and M^2X, where $X = \begin{pmatrix} x \\ y \end{pmatrix}$. Did you confirm your answer to part (a)?

   c. What do you expect the net effect to be if you repeat the mapping a third time? Compute M^3 and then M^3X to confirm your answer.

11. Consider rotation of the plane by $180°$ counterclockwise around the origin.

   a. What are the images of the points $\begin{pmatrix} 2 \\ 1 \end{pmatrix}$, $\begin{pmatrix} -1 \\ -2 \end{pmatrix}$, and $\begin{pmatrix} 0 \\ 0 \end{pmatrix}$?

   What is the image of the generic point $\begin{pmatrix} x \\ y \end{pmatrix}$?

   b. Find M such that this rotation is the mapping $X \mapsto MX$.

   c. Determine, with and without matrices, the effect of doing this rotation twice.

12. Suppose there is a matrix M such that the mapping of the plane $X \mapsto MX$ is a $30°$ counterclockwise rotation around the origin. What would the mapping $X \mapsto M^2X$ accomplish?

   There is such a matrix, but do not worry for now what it is. This exercise is meant to be a thought experiment.

13. Suppose that in a certain developing country, 35% of the people in the countryside move to the cities each year, and only 5% of the people in the cities move to the countryside. Assume there are no births and deaths, and nobody moves to or from other countries. If there were 8 million people in the countryside and 4 million in the cities at the beginning of 2007, what will be the situation at the start of 2008? At the start of 2009? At the start of 2010? What will happen many years into the future?

   These assumptions are unreasonable, but it is always a good idea to start with a simple model and, once you understand that model, later build in more complications.

14. Use matrix M from For You to Explore Problem 1. Let $X(0) = \begin{pmatrix} 1 + \sqrt{2} \\ 1 \end{pmatrix}$, $X(1) = MX(0)$, $X(2) = MX(1)$, and so on.

a. Compute $X(1)$, $X(2)$, $X(3)$, and $X(4)$.

b. Now define $Y(0) = X(0)$, $Y(1) = \sqrt{2}Y(0)$, $Y(2) = \sqrt{2}Y(1)$, and so on. Compute $Y(1)$, $Y(2)$, $Y(3)$, and $Y(4)$.

c. Now define $Z(0) = \begin{pmatrix} 1 - \sqrt{2} \\ 1 \end{pmatrix}$, $Z(1) = MZ(0)$, $Z(2) = MZ(1)$, and so on. Compute $Z(1)$, $Z(2)$, $Z(3)$, and $Z(4)$.

d. Now define $W(0) = Z(0)$, $W(1) = -\sqrt{2}W(0)$, $W(2) = -\sqrt{2}W(1)$, and so on. Compute $W(1)$, $W(2)$, $W(3)$, $W(4)$.

15. Use the following matrices.

$$D = \begin{pmatrix} \frac{\sqrt{2}}{2} & -\frac{\sqrt{2}}{2} \\ \frac{\sqrt{2}}{2} & \frac{\sqrt{2}}{2} \end{pmatrix} \qquad P = \begin{pmatrix} 1 \\ 0 \end{pmatrix} \qquad Q = \begin{pmatrix} 2 \\ 1 \end{pmatrix}$$

Compute and plot $DP, D^2P, D^3P, \ldots$ and $DQ, D^2Q, D^3Q, \ldots$ until you see from your plot what is happening. What is the pattern?

16. Let $B = \begin{pmatrix} 1 & 1 \\ 1 & 0 \end{pmatrix}$.

a. Compute B^2.

b. Compute B^3.

c. Compute several more powers. What patterns do you see?

d. Define a sequence of column vectors $S(n) = \begin{pmatrix} s(n) \\ t(n) \end{pmatrix}$ as

$$S(n) = \begin{cases} \begin{pmatrix} 2 \\ 1 \end{pmatrix} & \text{if } n = 0 \\ BS(n-1) & \text{if } n > 0 \end{cases}$$

Compute several terms of the sequence. What patterns do you see?

e. Find a system of nonmatrix equations for finding the next pair of values $s(n)$ and $t(n)$ from the previous values.

This is the reverse of For You to Explore Problem 1.

4.11 Geometric Transformations

In Lesson 4.10, you studied geometric transformations, where each point in the plane gets mapped to another. For instance, the mapping $(x, y) \mapsto (x + 1, y)$ translates points in the plane (shifts everything over) one unit in the positive x-direction.

You can express many geometric transformations (mappings) with matrix multiplication. A transformation is a **matrix transformation** if you can express it in the form $X \mapsto AX$, where A is a 2×2 matrix and a point X is represented as a column vector $\begin{pmatrix} x \\ y \end{pmatrix}$. You use column vectors so that you can multiply them by matrices on the left. You say this mapping is associated with the matrix A.

In this lesson, you will get a feel for what matrices can do geometrically. The work will be exploratory. You will do examples, often by plotting many points.

> There are also geometric transformations of three-dimensional space, or even higher dimensions, using bigger matrices. Indeed, with the right methods, every matrix of any size can be analyzed geometrically!

Example 1

Problem Let $A = \begin{pmatrix} 2 & 0 \\ 0 & 2 \end{pmatrix}$. What does the map $X \mapsto AX$ do?

Solution Let $X = \begin{pmatrix} x \\ y \end{pmatrix}$. Then

$$AX = \begin{pmatrix} 2 & 0 \\ 0 & 2 \end{pmatrix} \begin{pmatrix} x \\ y \end{pmatrix} = \begin{pmatrix} 2x \\ 2y \end{pmatrix} = 2X$$

This map scales everything by the factor 2 with the dilation centered at the origin. Every point moves twice as far from the origin. As a consequence, every length doubles in size as well, since every length is a distance between points. For instance, look at the graph below. When you dilate all the points in the small triangle by 2, the result is the large triangle. The lower left vertex (2, 1) of the smaller triangle maps to (4, 2), which is the lower left vertex of the larger triangle. The point (4, 2) is twice as far as (2, 1) from the origin. Similarly, the small quarter circle maps to the larger quarter circle.

> Experimenting with transformations can help you understand the effects of mappings. See the TI-Nspire Handbook, p. 804.

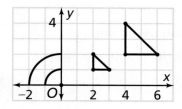

Experiment. Other matrix transformations in this lesson may be harder to interpret geometrically. How do you figure them out? Experiment! Start with several points in some sort of familiar shape. Plot them and plot all their images. You may need to use more than one figure and more than one shape.

For Discussion

1. Let $B = \begin{pmatrix} 1 & 0 \\ 0 & -1 \end{pmatrix}$. What does the map $X \mapsto BX$ do?

Example 2

Problem Let $R = \begin{pmatrix} 0 & -1 \\ 1 & 0 \end{pmatrix}$. What does the map $X \mapsto RX$ do?

Solution First, let $X = \begin{pmatrix} x \\ y \end{pmatrix}$. Then $RX = \begin{pmatrix} 0 & -1 \\ 1 & 0 \end{pmatrix} \begin{pmatrix} x \\ y \end{pmatrix} = \begin{pmatrix} -y \\ x \end{pmatrix}$.

You can rewrite the map $X \mapsto RX$ as $(x, y) \mapsto (-y, x)$. But it is still not so obvious what is going on. Plot some points and their images. Call the original points A, B, C, and D and their images A', B', C', and D'.

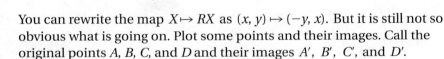

It seems the unit square has been rotated $90°$ counterclockwise around the origin $A = A'$. You could check this out with more points, for example, the points on the line with equation $x = 2$ or the points on the unit circle. Here is the result for the line with equation $x = 2$.

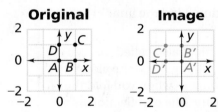

Indeed, the points on the line have been rotated, too.

However, you need a general argument to show that every point (x, y) is rotated 90° counterclockwise around the origin when it is mapped to $(-y, x)$. The next figure should help. What can you say about angles α, β, and γ?

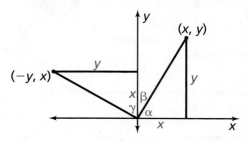

More on Reflections and Rotations

Any reflection over a line through the origin can be done by matrix multiplication. Any rotation around the origin can also be done by matrix multiplication. It is complicated to prove this with what you know, but the following examples illustrate it.

Example 3

Problem Use the matrix below.

$$M = \tfrac{1}{5}\begin{pmatrix} 3 & 4 \\ 4 & -3 \end{pmatrix} = \begin{pmatrix} \tfrac{3}{5} & \tfrac{4}{5} \\ \tfrac{4}{5} & -\tfrac{3}{5} \end{pmatrix}$$

It turns out that the mapping $X \mapsto MX$ is a reflection. Find the line of reflection.

Solution Any reflection in the plane has a line of reflection, also called the axis of reflection. You can visualize this by thinking of folding the plane along this line and mapping each point to the point it touches when you fold the plane. Another way to visualize it is by thinking of the line of reflection as a two-sided mirror. Then each point in the plane is mapped to its reflection in that mirror.

A reflection fixes a point if and only if the point is on the line of reflection. Assuming this mapping $X \mapsto MX$ is a reflection, a point $X = (x, y)$ is on the line of reflection if and only if $MX = X$. So write out this matrix equation as two real-number equations and solve them.

> If you fold a piece of paper, points on the fold do not touch other points. Only points not on the fold line will touch different points on the paper.

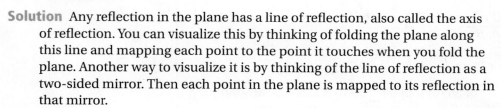

$$\tfrac{3}{5}x + \tfrac{4}{5}y = x \qquad 3x + 4y = 5x \qquad -2x + 4y = 0$$
$$\Rightarrow \qquad \qquad \Rightarrow$$
$$\tfrac{4}{5}x - \tfrac{3}{5}y = y \qquad 4x - 3y = 5y \qquad 4x - 8y = 0$$

The bottom equation on the right is a multiple of the top equation. They are equivalent equations, so you can write them both as $y = \tfrac{1}{2}x$. This is the equation of the line of slope $\tfrac{1}{2}$ through the origin.

For You to Do

2. Let $N = \frac{1}{2}\begin{pmatrix} 1 & \sqrt{3} \\ -\sqrt{3} & 1 \end{pmatrix}$.

It turns out (though it is not obvious) that N is the matrix of a rotation around the origin. Plot some points to convince yourself it is a rotation and to discover the angle of rotation.

(*Hint:* Every point X will be rotated by the same angle, so you do not need to solve for X as in the last example. Instead, just pick some points X, compute NX, and see how much the original points are rotated.)

Example 2 suggests some points to pick, but you can also choose other points. You also need to check that NX is the same distance from the origin as X. Otherwise, the mapping is doing more than just rotating.

In fact, you only need one point X, but just to confirm that this mapping really is a rotation, and to catch any arithmetic errors, use several points.

Other Matrix Transformations

Matrices can do much more than scaling, reflecting, and rotating. For example, they can do scaling by different factors in different directions.

For Discussion

3. Let $A = \begin{pmatrix} 3 & 0 \\ 0 & 2 \end{pmatrix}$. Predict what A does to the plane. Then show that you are right by computing what A does to the corners of the unit square. The unit square is the square with corners at $(0, 0)$, $(1, 0)$, $(1, 1)$ and $(0, 1)$.

Many matrices do this sort of multiple stretching, but not always in an obvious way.

Example 4

Problem Analyze the transformation $X \mapsto AX$, where

$$A = \begin{pmatrix} -2.7 & 1.4 \\ -2.1 & 2.2 \end{pmatrix}$$

Solution A few points may not make the pattern clear, but it gets clearer as you show more points. The graph on the left shows the original points and the graph on the right shows their images. Rather than label so many dots, a few of them are made different sizes. The biggest dot in the figure on the left maps to the biggest dot in the figure on the right.

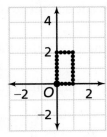
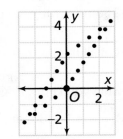

You can see that the segments of the rectangle get stretched, but the directions also get changed. For instance, in the left figure on the preceding page, take a sequence of points starting at the origin and moving along the positive *x*-axis. The images of these points in the right figure get flipped over and move down and left from the origin.

It turns out that the original shape does not clearly show what is happening. Look what happens to the parallelogram in the graph below. The parallelogram on the right is its image, using the same matrix *A*.

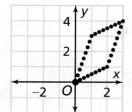 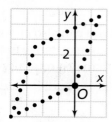

So the stretching is in a direction parallel to the sides of the parallelogram, with either a positive or negative scaling factor. For instance, the point (2, 1) on the left parallelogram gets mapped to $(-4, -2) = -2(2, 1)$ on the right. On the left side of the left parallelogram, the point (1, 3) gets mapped to $(1.5, 4.5) = \frac{3}{2}(1, 3)$ on the right.

How do you find these special directions, in which the map $X \mapsto AX$ just stretches? It turns out that most matrix transformations have them. You will be able to find them for many 2×2 matrices. See Exercises 10, 11, and 21.

When $AX = kX$, X is an *eigenvector* for *A* and *k* is its *eigenvalue*. This is an important concept in more advanced matrix algebra. It is the basis on which you can give every matrix a geometric interpretation.

Matrices can do all sorts of things geometrically. You will explore this more in the exercises. Perhaps the important thing to remember is that you can use matrices to describe several key geometric transformations: scaling, reflection, and rotation.

What is common to all these transformations?

It is impressive, if confusing, that matrices can do all these different transformations. Fortunately, there are some common aspects to all the transformations $X \mapsto AX$. Have you noticed that, in all the matrix transformations so far, lines get mapped to lines and parallel lines get mapped to parallel lines? Some of the exercises address the reasons for this fact.

Can matrices describe translations? Well, see below.

Another common aspect of all matrix transformations is that the origin gets mapped to the origin.

You can prove this with what you know. If $X \mapsto AX$, then substitute $\begin{pmatrix} 0 \\ 0 \end{pmatrix}$ for X and simply note that $A \begin{pmatrix} 0 \\ 0 \end{pmatrix} = \begin{pmatrix} 0 \\ 0 \end{pmatrix}$ for any 2×2 matrix *A*.

The fact that lines map to lines can save you time when you are plotting points to see what a matrix transformation does. Just find the image of two distinct points. The image is the line through the two image points.

The fact that (0, 0) always gets mapped to itself is an important restriction. The first geometric transformation mentioned in this lesson, $(x, y) \mapsto (x + 1, y)$, is a translation, and it maps (0, 0) to (1, 0). So translations are not matrix transformations. In fact, neither are rotations if they are not centered at the origin. Think about it—in such a rotation, the origin will be rotated to somewhere else. Reflections are not matrix transformations either, unless the line of reflection goes through the origin.

So, are matrix methods in geometry only of limited use? No! You can fix this problem. One way is to shift coordinates so that a rotation, for instance, is centered at the origin. Another way avoids shifting coordinates by using 3×3 matrices.

See Exercise 23.

Exercises *Practicing Habits of Mind*

Check Your Understanding

1. Determine what each matrix does. That is, describe the geometric transformation associated with it.

    a. $A = \begin{pmatrix} -1 & 0 \\ 0 & 1 \end{pmatrix}$ **b.** $B = \begin{pmatrix} 0 & 1 \\ 1 & 0 \end{pmatrix}$

2. Let $A = \begin{pmatrix} 2 & 0 \\ 0 & 2 \end{pmatrix}$. In Example 1, you showed that the mapping $X \mapsto AX$ scales every point by the factor 2. What do you think the mapping $X \mapsto A^{-1}X$ does? Confirm your conjecture by computing A^{-1} and then plotting a few pairs X and $A^{-1}X$.

3. Use matrix A from Exercise 2. What does the mapping $X \mapsto A^2X$ do? What does the mapping $X \mapsto A^{-2}X$ do? (As with numbers, A^{-2} means $(A^{-1})^2$.)

4. **Take It Further** Now think of each ordered pair $\begin{pmatrix} a \\ b \end{pmatrix}$ as representing a point $a + bi$ on the complex plane. Let $M = \begin{pmatrix} c & -d \\ d & c \end{pmatrix}$. Use your knowledge of complex plane geometry to describe geometrically what the mapping $X \mapsto MX$ does. Begin by computing $M\begin{pmatrix} a \\ b \end{pmatrix}$.

5. Example 3 claimed that $M = \frac{1}{5}\begin{pmatrix} 3 & 4 \\ 4 & -3 \end{pmatrix}$ is the matrix of a reflection over the line with equation $y = \frac{1}{2}x$. Plot this line and several points off the line. Pick points on either side of the line. For each of these points X, compute and plot MX. Are they reflections as claimed?

6. Continue with Example 3. If the mapping $X \mapsto MX$ reflects over the line with equation $y = \frac{1}{2}x$, what do you think the mapping $X \mapsto M^{-1}X$ does? How should M and M^{-1} be related? Confirm your conjectures by computing M^{-1}.

7. If $M = \frac{1}{5}\begin{pmatrix} 3 & 4 \\ 4 & -3 \end{pmatrix}$ is the matrix of a reflection, then it turns out there are points X such that $MX = -X$.

   a. Use the method of Example 3, where this matrix was introduced, to find all such points X. Plot several of them and their images MX.

   b. Let X be any one of the points you just plotted. Draw the vector to it from the origin.

   Let Y be any of the points on the line of reflection. Draw the vector to it from the origin. What is the angle between these two vectors? Why does this make sense?

   c. Take the dot product of your two points X and Y from part (b).

8. In light of Exercises 5 and 7, explain why reflections are examples of transformations that scale, but by different factors in different directions.

9. The text showed that you can represent a 90° rotation counterclockwise around the origin as

$$\begin{pmatrix} x' \\ y' \end{pmatrix} = \begin{pmatrix} 0 & -1 \\ 1 & 0 \end{pmatrix}\begin{pmatrix} x \\ y \end{pmatrix}$$

where (x, y) is the original point and (x', y') is the resulting point.

If you can rotate once, you can rotate twice. Call the original point X, the new point X', and the rotation matrix R. Then, to rotate twice, compute

$$X'' = RX' = R(RX) = (RR)X = R^2X$$

In this exercise, *rotate* always means counterclockwise around the origin.

   a. Without any use of matrices, determine the result if the point (x, y) is rotated by 90° twice.

   b. Confirm that you get the same answer as in part (a) using the matrix R^2.

   c. Without any use of matrices, determine the result if the point (x, y) is rotated by 90° three times.

   d. Determine how to do part (c) again with a power of R. Confirm that you get the same answer.

   e. Determine, with and without R, the result of rotating the point (x, y) by 90° four times.

10. This exercise shows, given a 2 × 2 matrix A, how to find scalars k and vectors X such that $AX = kX$. Use the matrix A below.

$$A = \begin{pmatrix} 1 & 1 \\ 2 & 0 \end{pmatrix}$$

a. Write out the equation $AX = kX$ as two real-number equations and rewrite them so that both equations equal 0. Your equations will involve three unknowns, the unknown coordinates x and y and the unknown scalar k.

b. In general, two linear equations in x and y equaling 0 will have only one solution $(x, y) = (0, 0)$. However, if the two equations turn out to be different equations for the same line, then there will be other solutions. When are two equations in the form below just different equations for the same line?

$$ax + by = 0$$
$$cx + dy = 0$$

The first equation describes the line with equation $y = (-\frac{a}{b})x$ and the second equation describes the line with equation $y = (-\frac{c}{d})x$, so set $\frac{a}{b} = \frac{c}{d}$. Plug in the values of a, b, c, and d you found in part (a). Then solve the equation for k. The equation is quadratic, so you will get two solutions.

> Assume $b \neq 0$ and $d \neq 0$.

c. Now, for each value of k, solve $AX = kX$ for x and y.

11. In Example 4, you were given the matrix below.

$$A = \begin{pmatrix} -2.7 & 1.4 \\ -2.1 & 2.2 \end{pmatrix}$$

The text made the claim that A stretches $(2, 1)$ by the factor -2 and stretches $(1, 3)$ by the factor 1.5 without any explanation. These claims were easy enough to check, but where did they come from? Using the method of Exercise 10, discover these facts for yourself.

12. Figure out the matrix that represents reflection over the line with equation $y = -x$.

(*Hint:* Figure out what the reflection does to a few points that are easy to compute with, such as $\begin{pmatrix} 1 \\ 0 \end{pmatrix}$ and $\begin{pmatrix} 0 \\ 1 \end{pmatrix}$. Then find a matrix that accomplishes the same thing by multiplication.)

13. **Take It Further** The design at the right was made using 45° counterclockwise rotations. Figure out the matrix for 45° rotation counterclockwise around the origin.

14. **Take It Further** If the 2×2 matrix M is invertible, then the geometric mapping $X \mapsto MX$ maps lines to lines and parallel lines to parallel lines. (Even if M is not invertible, M generally maps lines to lines, but it maps some lines to points and some parallel lines to the same line or to a point.) It is easy to prove these facts once you describe lines in matrix form, but you have not done that yet. So here is the outline of a proof using what you know.

You know that a set of points (x, y) form a line if they are the solutions to an equation $ax + by = c$, where a and b are not both 0.

Now, if $\begin{pmatrix} x' \\ y' \end{pmatrix} = M\begin{pmatrix} x \\ y \end{pmatrix}$ is the typical point in the image set of the line and M is invertible, then $\begin{pmatrix} x \\ y \end{pmatrix} = M^{-1}\begin{pmatrix} x' \\ y' \end{pmatrix}$.

Also, M^{-1} is some matrix $\begin{pmatrix} p & q \\ r & s \end{pmatrix}$ and $\begin{matrix} x = px' + qy' \\ y = rx' + sy' \end{matrix}$

Substitute these expressions into $ax + by = c$ and regroup until you have something of the form $a'x' + b'y' = c'$. At that point, you have shown that the points (x', y') also form a line. (You also have to argue that a' and b' are not both 0.)

> And you also need to show that any point satisfying
> $a'x' + b'y' = c'$ is in the image set.

On Your Own

15. Let $A = \begin{pmatrix} 3 & 0 \\ 0 & 2 \end{pmatrix}$. In Problem 3, you showed that the mapping $X \mapsto AX$ stretches the plane by the factor 3 in the x-direction and by the factor 2 in the y-direction. What do you think the mapping $X \mapsto A^{-1}X$ does? Confirm your conjecture by computing A^{-1} and then plotting a few pairs X and $A^{-1}X$.

16. Continue with Example 2. If this mapping is indeed associated with rotation by 90° counterclockwise around the origin, then, for every point X, its image ought to be the same distance from the origin. Pick some points and compare the distances of X and AX from the origin.

17. Determine what each matrix does.

   a. $B = \begin{pmatrix} 1 & 0 \\ 0 & 0 \end{pmatrix}$

   b. $C = \begin{pmatrix} \frac{1}{2} & \frac{1}{2} \\ \frac{1}{2} & \frac{1}{2} \end{pmatrix}$

> These transformations are different from all those discussed in the text, because they are not one-to-one. That is, $X \mapsto AX$ maps many points to the same point.

18. Continue with the transformations associated with matrices B and C from Exercise 17. Also consider the lines with the following equations.

$$L_1\colon x = 1 \qquad L_2\colon x = 2 \qquad L_3\colon y = 1$$
$$L_4\colon y = -1 \qquad L_5\colon y = x \qquad L_6\colon y = x + 2$$

a. Find the image of each line under multiplication by B.

b. Find the image of each line under multiplication by C.

19. Suppose all you know about the matrix transformation $X \mapsto AX$ is that $(2, 1) \mapsto (-4, -2)$ and $(1, 3) \mapsto (1.5, 4.5)$. That is, you know only that

$$A\begin{pmatrix} 2 \\ 1 \end{pmatrix} = \begin{pmatrix} -4 \\ -2 \end{pmatrix} \quad \text{and} \quad A\begin{pmatrix} 1 \\ 3 \end{pmatrix} = \begin{pmatrix} 1.5 \\ 4.5 \end{pmatrix}$$

a. What does $(6, 3)$ map to? (*Hint:* What properties do you know about the matrix product $A(kB)$?)

b. What does $(2, 1) + (1, 3) = (3, 4)$ map to?

c. What does $(-1, 2)$ map to?

d. Explain why you can figure out what any point (x, y) maps to.

e. In fact, you know all about this matrix transformation. It is the mapping from Example 4 and $A = \begin{pmatrix} -2.7 & 1.4 \\ -2.1 & 2.2 \end{pmatrix}$. Confirm your answers to parts (a)–(c) by direct multiplication.

20. **Take It Further** Consider A from Exercise 19 again. Suppose there is another matrix B such that $B\begin{pmatrix} 2 \\ 1 \end{pmatrix} = \begin{pmatrix} -4 \\ -2 \end{pmatrix}$ and $B\begin{pmatrix} 1 \\ 3 \end{pmatrix} = \begin{pmatrix} 1.5 \\ 4.5 \end{pmatrix}$. How are A and B related? Explain your reasoning.

21. **Take It Further** Let $R = \begin{pmatrix} 0 & -1 \\ 1 & 0 \end{pmatrix}$. This is the matrix from Example 2. Using the method of Exercise 10, find scalars k and points X such that $RX = kX$.

22. This lesson began with the mapping $(x, y) \mapsto (x + 1, y)$, which shifts everything over by one unit in the x-direction. It is not a matrix multiplication transformation because $(0, 0) \mapsto (1, 0)$. However, it is still a transformation that uses matrix algebra, because you can write it in the form $X \mapsto MX + B$, where $M = I$ and $B = \begin{pmatrix} 1 \\ 0 \end{pmatrix}$.

Show how to write the geometric transformation below in the form $X \mapsto MX + B$.

$$\begin{pmatrix} x \\ y \end{pmatrix} \mapsto \begin{pmatrix} x + 2y + 3 \\ 3x + 4 \end{pmatrix}$$

Go Online
Pearsonsuccessnet.com

You may think that because the transformation associated with this matrix is a 90° rotation, there is no point X that is scaled by any scalar k. Do the algebra and see what happens.

23. You can often handle transformations that do not fix the origin with matrix multiplication methods by using the following method of adding a dimension. It works this way:

$$\begin{pmatrix} x \\ y \end{pmatrix} \rightarrow \begin{pmatrix} x \\ y \\ 1 \end{pmatrix} \rightarrow A \begin{pmatrix} x \\ y \\ 1 \end{pmatrix} = \begin{pmatrix} x' \\ y' \\ 1 \end{pmatrix} \rightarrow \begin{pmatrix} x' \\ y' \end{pmatrix}$$

You insert a third component in your starting point. Typically you insert 1. Then, you act on your new point with a 3×3 matrix A. Finally, you strip off the third component to get the final transformation.

Show that if you use this method on (x, y) with the matrix A below, then (x, y) maps to $(x, y) + (a, b)$. That is, show that the matrix A represents the translation by (a, b).

$$A = \begin{pmatrix} 1 & 0 & a \\ 0 & 1 & b \\ 0 & 0 & 1 \end{pmatrix}$$

> The method of adding a dimension is used in computer graphics routines. Computer graphics routines need to handle motions like translations and rotations around arbitrary points in space. So you can start with 3×3 matrices and add a dimension to get 4×4 matrices.

24. Imagine rotating the xy-plane $90°$ counterclockwise through the origin and then reflecting over the x-axis.

    a. Without any use of matrices, determine where the following points end up.

    $$(1, 0), (0, 1), (1, 1), (-1, 1), (x, y)$$

    b. Find a matrix M such that the mapping $X \mapsto MX$ accomplishes what you did in part (a).

    c. Using your knowledge of matrices for rotations and reflections, find a matrix R for the rotation part of this exercise. Find another matrix R' for the reflection part.

    d. Verify that $M = R'R$. Explain why this makes sense.

    e. Express this transformation (the rotation followed by the reflection) as a single geometric action. It might be a rotation or a reflection.

25. Prove that if M is invertible (meaning the inverse M^{-1} exists), then the mapping of the plane $X \mapsto MX$ is one-to-one. That is, show that if $MX = MY$, then $X = Y$.

26. Prove the inverse of Exercise 25: If M is not invertible, then the mapping of the plane $X \mapsto MX$ is not one-to-one. (*Hint:* If $M = \begin{pmatrix} p & q \\ r & s \end{pmatrix}$ is not invertible, then you know that $ps - qr = 0$.)

> A mapping is not one-to-one if you can find two points X_1 and X_2 such that $X_1 \neq X_2$ but $MX_1 = MX_2$.

27. Prove that, if M is invertible, then the mapping of the plane $X \mapsto MX$ is *onto*. A mapping is onto if for every X', there exists some X such that $MX = X'$. In other words, some point X is mapped to X'.

28. Take It Further A set of points forms a line if and only if you can represent the points on the line in the form $X = P + tD$, with P any point on the line, D a nonzero ordered pair called the direction vector for the line, and t a parameter that can be any real number. Two lines are parallel (or the same line) if you can represent them in this form using the same D but different points P.

So if a set of points forms a line, then you can represent the set of images under M as the set with points that have the form $MX = M(P + tD)$.

But $P + tD$ is a matrix, so you can apply the Distributive Property, $MX = MP + t(MD)$. If M has an inverse, why does this identity prove that the set of image points MX forms a line?

> For each line, P and D are fixed. This way of thinking about lines is *vector representation*. This representation works just as well in three dimensions, or in any number of dimensions.

29. Standardized Test Prep Which of the following statements is NOT true?

A. The sum of the squares of the elements of each row of a 2×2 matrix is 1 for a rotation with no dilation.

B. The square of a reflection matrix is the identity matrix. $(AA = I)$

C. Divide $360°$ by the angle of rotation. If the remainder is 0, then you must raise the transformation matrix to that quotient to get an identity matrix.

D. For a rotation, the inverse of a matrix must equal itself. $(M^{-1} = M)$

Maintain Your Skills

30. Use the following matrix descriptions.

$$R = \text{the matrix for rotation } 90° \text{ counterclockwise around the origin}$$
$$F = \text{the matrix for reflection over the } x\text{-axis}$$
$$S_{-1} = \text{the matrix for dilating by } k = -1 \text{ around the origin}$$
$$S_2 = \text{the matrix for dilating by } k = 2 \text{ around the origin}$$

$(S_2R)X$ first rotates X by $90°$ and then scales by 2.

Describe a geometric transformation for each product matrix.

a. R^2 **b.** R^3 **c.** R^4 **d.** R^5 **e.** $(S_2)^2$

f. $S_{-1}S_2$ **g.** S_2S_{-1} **h.** $(S_{-1})^2$ **i.** F^2 **j.** S_2R

k. RS_2 **l.** FR **m.** RF

31. Many transformations of 3-dimensional space are matrix transformations. Points have the form $X = (x, y, z)$ and the matrices are 3×3. For each matrix M, figure out what the transformation $X \mapsto MX$ does.

a. $M = \begin{pmatrix} 2 & 0 & 0 \\ 0 & 2 & 0 \\ 0 & 0 & 2 \end{pmatrix}$ **b.** $M = \begin{pmatrix} 1 & 0 & 0 \\ 0 & 2 & 0 \\ 0 & 0 & 3 \end{pmatrix}$ **c.** $M = \begin{pmatrix} 1 & 0 & 0 \\ 0 & 1 & 0 \\ 0 & 0 & -1 \end{pmatrix}$

d. $M = \begin{pmatrix} 0 & -1 & 0 \\ 1 & 0 & 0 \\ 0 & 0 & 1 \end{pmatrix}$ **e.** $M = \begin{pmatrix} -1 & 0 & 0 \\ 0 & 1 & 0 \\ 0 & 0 & -1 \end{pmatrix}$ **f.** $M = \begin{pmatrix} 0 & 0 & 1 \\ 1 & 0 & 0 \\ 0 & 1 & 0 \end{pmatrix}$

Transition Matrices

There are many situations where you want to study what happens when something happens over and over again—an object rotates again and again, a rental car agency has its cars move between locations week after week, and so on. You would like to know what happens after any number of iterations into the future. And if there is a long-term pattern, you would like to know that, too.

In the past, you may have looked at an iteration when there was one variable.

For instance, if you iterate $x \rightarrow 1.01x + 50$, you learn what happens when you add \$50 to your bank account each month and the money already there grows by 1% monthly interest.

Now, with the help of matrices, you will analyze iteration with more variables.

Example 1

Return to Problem 8 from Lesson 4.10, about the car rental company with locations in Boston and Cambridge. They wanted to know where their cars would be at the end of each week. Solve their problem with matrices.

Solution Let $b(n)$ be the number of the company's cars in Boston at the end of week n. Similarly, let $c(n)$ be the number in Cambridge at the end of week n. Since each location has 70 cars to start, you have $b(0) = c(0) = 70$. In symbols, this is what the problem says about how cars move around each week:

$$b(n) = 0.8b(n - 1) + 0.5c(n - 1)$$

$$c(n) = 0.2b(n - 1) + 0.5c(n - 1)$$

The problem does not say 20% of cars in Boston at the start of one week are returned to Cambridge at the end of the week, but, since there are only two locations, that is where the rest of the cars have to go.

So what are the matrices? Well, the equations are linear. Define $A(n)$ (A for auto) by

$$A(n) = \begin{pmatrix} b(n) \\ c(n) \end{pmatrix}$$

The system above becomes

$$A(n) = \begin{pmatrix} 0.8 & 0.5 \\ 0.2 & 0.5 \end{pmatrix} A(n - 1)$$

You are assuming there are no new cars, no crashes, and no thefts. It is also unrealistic to assume that all rentals are for one week. However, more realistic models can be built using larger matrices.

So, if you let $M = \begin{pmatrix} 0.8 & 0.5 \\ 0.2 & 0.5 \end{pmatrix}$, then the information in the problem boils down to this:

$$A(n) = \begin{cases} \begin{pmatrix} 70 \\ 70 \end{pmatrix} & \text{if } n = 0 \\ MA(n-1) & \text{if } n > 0 \end{cases}$$

Therefore,

$A(1) = MA(0)$	(Substitute 0 for n.)
$A(2) = MA(1) = M(MA(0)) = M^2 A(0)$	(Substitute 1 for n.)
$A(3) = MA(2) = M(M^2 A(0)) = M^3 A(0)$	(Substitute 2 for n.)

In general, $A(n) = M^n A(0)$.

Because you use the same matrix M to transition from each time period to the next (you multiply by M one more time), M is a **transition matrix.**

> This is a simple equation for a complicated situation. Matrix notation is powerful because of its simplicity.

Using technology, you can compute the following values.

$$A(1) = \begin{pmatrix} 91 \\ 49 \end{pmatrix} \qquad A(2) = \begin{pmatrix} 97.3 \\ 42.7 \end{pmatrix} \qquad A(3) = \begin{pmatrix} 99.19 \\ 40.81 \end{pmatrix}$$

Do you have a conjecture about what is happening? Check out $A(10)$. To four decimal places, it is

$$\begin{pmatrix} 99.9998 \\ 40.0002 \end{pmatrix}$$

It seems that as the weeks go by, the distribution of cars is stabilizing, with 100 cars in Boston and 40 cars in Cambridge. When this happens, you call it a **steady state.**

For Discussion

Example 1 raises more questions than it answers. Here are a few. You may have more.

1. What do you make of these decimal values? You cannot have decimal numbers of cars!

2. What does it mean to say "stabilizing with 100 in Boston"? There cannot be 100 cars that always stay in Boston.

For You to Do

3. What happens if the company starts with 30 cars in Boston and 110 in Cambridge?

4. What happens if the company starts with 100 cars in Boston and 40 in Cambridge?

5. Consider the matrices M^2, M^3, and so on. Describe what happens to M^n for greater and greater values of n.

The rental example is about a fixed population of cars in which the total number does not change. Another use for repeated transition matrices is to model changes in living populations.

Example 2

Problem A certain beetle has three life stages: egg, larva, and adult. During each time period, each adult alive at the start of the period lays 15 eggs and then dies, 80% of the live eggs at the start of the period hatch into larvae, and 20% of the larvae alive at the start of the period survive and become adults. The remaining eggs never hatch and the rest of the larvae die.

Suppose a certain garden initially harbors 50 eggs, 20 larvae, and 10 adults. What will be the situation at the end of one time period? At the end of two time periods? At the end of three time periods?

Solution First define the functions.

$e(n)$ = number of eggs at the end of time period n

$l(n)$ = number of larvae at the end of time period n

$a(n)$ = number of adults at the end of time period n

The given information is

$$e(0) = 50 \qquad e(n) = 15a(n-1)$$
$$l(0) = 20 \quad \text{and} \quad l(n) = 0.8e(n-1)$$
$$a(0) = 10 \qquad a(n) = 0.2l(n-1)$$

You can turn this into a matrix equation.

$$P(n) = \begin{pmatrix} e(n) \\ l(n) \\ a(n) \end{pmatrix} \qquad M = \begin{pmatrix} 0 & 0 & 15 \\ 0.8 & 0 & 0 \\ 0 & 0.2 & 0 \end{pmatrix}$$

$$P(n) = \begin{cases} \begin{pmatrix} 50 \\ 20 \\ 10 \end{pmatrix} & \text{if } n = 0 \\ MP(n-1) & \text{if } n > 0 \end{cases}$$

Use the matrix M to calculate $P(n)$ for a few iterations.

$$P(1) = MP(0) = \begin{pmatrix} 150 \\ 40 \\ 4 \end{pmatrix}$$

$$P(2) = MP(1) = M(MP(0)) = M^2P(0) = \begin{pmatrix} 60 \\ 120 \\ 8 \end{pmatrix}$$

$$P(3) = M^3P(0) = \begin{pmatrix} 120 \\ 48 \\ 24 \end{pmatrix}$$

> Actually, each female adult lays 30 eggs and each male lays 0, but the average works fine in this model. Sometimes scientists just model the female population and use the fact that the male population is some constant multiple of the female population.

It is instructive to look at the powers of M.

$$M^2 = \begin{pmatrix} 0 & 3 & 0 \\ 0 & 0 & 12 \\ 0.16 & 0 & 0 \end{pmatrix} \quad M^3 = \begin{pmatrix} 2.4 & 0 & 0 \\ 0 & 2.4 & 0 \\ 0 & 0 & 2.4 \end{pmatrix}$$

What do these equations tell you?

M^3 tells us that every three periods, the beetle population grows by 2.4 times in every category. In other words, the population is cyclical. Every three periods it returns to the ratio of eggs to larvae to adults that it had three periods ago, but at 2.4 times the population. You call this a periodic growth cycle. You can check it out by actually computing $P(4)$, $P(5)$, ... and comparing. For instance, at the end of periods 1, 4, 7, ... the ratio of larvae to adults is always 10 to 1, whereas after periods 3, 6, 9, ... it is always just 2 to 1.

> Actually, some factor you have not been told about, such as crowding or insecticide, must take over. Otherwise, with its population more than doubling every three time periods, these beetles are going to take over the world, not just this garden. This raises an important point. Transition models rarely model the real world forever.

For You to Do

6. You do not really need matrices to solve the problem in the example. Show that the equations

$$e(n) = 15a(n - 1) \tag{16}$$

$$l(n) = 0.8e(n - 1) \tag{17}$$

$$a(n) = 0.2l(n - 1) \tag{18}$$

lead directly to

$$e(n + 3) = 2.4e(n)$$

$$l(n + 3) = 2.4l(n)$$

$$a(n + 3) = 2.4a(n)$$

For instance, here is most of the calculation for $e(n + 3)$.

$e(n + 3) = 15a(n + 2)$	from (16)
$= 15(0.2l(n + 1))$	from (17)
$= 15(0.2(0.8e(n)))$	from (18)

However, for populations where there is not such a rigid separation between life-cycle stages, the matrix approach is much easier.

You can use transition matrices to model the population cycles of sea turtles.

Exercises *Practicing Habits of Mind*

Check Your Understanding

1. In Example 1, suppose you assumed there was a steady state $A = (b, c)$, but you did not know what it was. That is, suppose you assumed there was a way to divide the 140 cars, b in Boston and c in Cambridge, so that $MA = A$. Use this matrix equation to solve for A.

2. Consider again Example 1. Given M and $A(0)$, one way to compute $A(1)$, $A(2)$, $A(3)$, . . . is to compute M, M^2, M^3, . . . and then multiply each of them by $A(0)$. But note that $M^2 A(0) = M(MA(0))$, $M^3 A(0) = M(M(MA(0)))$, and so on. Explain how this allows you to compute $A(1)$, $A(2)$, $A(3)$, . . . with fewer multiplications.

3. Another auto rental company has three locations A, B, and C. Let $a(n)$ be the number of cars at A at the end of week n, $b(n)$ be the number at B, and $c(n)$ be the number at C. Suppose the following equations describe the movement of cars.

$$a(n) = 0.7a(n - 1) + 0.2b(n - 1) + 0.3c(n - 1)$$

$$b(n) = 0.2a(n - 1) + 0.5b(n - 1) + 0.1c(n - 1)$$

$$c(n) = 0.1a(n - 1) + 0.3b(n - 1) + 0.6c(n - 1)$$

   a. Describe this situation in words. (*Hint:* It is similar to the situation in Example 1.)

   b. Find the transition matrix.

   c. Initially, the company has 100 cars in each location. How many cars are in each location two weeks later? Three weeks later? In the long run?

4. You can turn recurrences involving several terms into transition matrix problems with a nice method. Consider the Fibonacci sequence.

$$f(n) = \begin{cases} 1 & \text{if } n = 0 \text{ or } 1 \\ f(n - 1) + f(n - 2) & \text{if } n \geq 2 \end{cases}$$

   a. Let $X(n) = \begin{pmatrix} f(n) \\ f(n - 1) \end{pmatrix}$. Show that $X(n) = \begin{pmatrix} 1 & 1 \\ 1 & 0 \end{pmatrix} X(n - 1)$.

   b. Use your result from part (a) to compute $f(10)$.

5. Use the method in Exercise 4 to turn the second-order recurrence below into a matrix equation.

$$g(n) = 3g(n - 1) - 4g(n - 2)$$

> By using this method, you turn a second-order recurrence for a sequence of numbers (f_n) into a first-order recurrence for a sequence of ordered pairs (the X_n).

6. Now reverse the process of Exercises 4 and 5. Turn the following matrix equation into a third-order recurrence for the sequence h_n.

$$\begin{pmatrix} h(n) \\ h(n-1) \\ h(n-2) \end{pmatrix} = \begin{pmatrix} 2 & -3 & 4 \\ 1 & 0 & 0 \\ 0 & 1 & 0 \end{pmatrix} \begin{pmatrix} h(n-1) \\ h(n-2) \\ h(n-3) \end{pmatrix}$$

On Your Own

7. Suppose, each year, 3% of the people east of the Mississippi move west and 2% of the people west of the Mississippi move east. Assume initially there are 150 million people on each side. Find the transition matrix and figure out what happens in the long run.

> This is not a very realistic problem about American population because it is a closed system: There is no flow in or out of the whole country, and the total population of the country is fixed. But it is always a good idea to start with a simple model. You can set up more realistic models with bigger matrices.

8. Another species of beetle, related to the one in Example 2, also has three life stages: egg, larva, and adult. The reproduction and survival rates for each time period are also the same, with one exception. Instead of 80% of eggs surviving to larvae in one period, 70% of the eggs hatch out as larvae, 2% of the eggs mature so quickly that they emerge as adults at the end of the period, and the rest do not survive.

a. What is the transition matrix M for this beetle?

b. Compute M^2, M^3, and so on. Can you find any patterns or stability in long-term growth for this second kind of beetle? Explain. How does the pattern compare with the pattern for the first kind of beetle?

9. Let $M = \begin{pmatrix} 0.6 & 0.25 \\ 0.4 & 0.75 \end{pmatrix}$.

a. Come up with a scenario involving a fixed population that uses M as the transition matrix.

b. Suppose that the total population is 260. Assuming that your scenario has a steady state $X = (x, y)$, find it using the method from Exercise 1.

10. Take It Further Consider the translation on the line with equation $f(x) = x + 1$. You cannot represent this directly with a transition matrix because of the constant term. But note that

$$\begin{pmatrix} 1 & 1 \\ 0 & 1 \end{pmatrix} \begin{pmatrix} x \\ 1 \end{pmatrix} = \begin{pmatrix} x+1 \\ 1 \end{pmatrix}$$

Then $f(x)$ is the first coordinate of TX, where T is the 2×2 matrix above, and $X = \begin{pmatrix} x \\ 1 \end{pmatrix}$. Therefore $f(f(x))$ is the first coordinate of T^2X, and so on.

a. Without any use of matrices, determine what 10 iterations of $f(x)$ do to x.

b. Verify your result with the matrix method.

> **Habits of Mind**
>
> **Consider more than one strategy.**
> By going up one dimension, a problem with constant terms becomes a matrix problem. For more explanation of this method, see Exercise 23 in Lesson 4.11.

11. **Standardized Test Prep** A store has two hat displays: a bin and a table. Each day, customers move 15% of the hats from the bin to the table and 65% of the hats from the table to the bin. If each display starts with 200 hats, how many hats are in the bin after 10 days?

Go Online
Pearsonsuccessnet.com

   A. 76   **B.** 200   **C.** 300   **D.** 324

Maintain Your Skills

In Exercises 12–15, you will consider several bugs, each constrained to sit at one vertex of an equilateral triangle. Each minute, each bug either moves to another vertex or stays put, according to certain probabilities.

12. Bug 1 is antsy and does not like to stay put.

   No matter where she is now, in one minute she will move with equal probability to one of the other two vertices.

   Find the probability of each event.

   a. During the next two minutes, she moves clockwise both times.

   b. Two minutes from now, she will be one vertex counterclockwise from where she is now.

   c. Two minutes from now, she will be back to where she is now.

13. Bug 2 is also antsy, but favors the top vertex. When at vertices L or R, he will go to T $\frac{2}{3}$ of the time and to the other vertex $\frac{1}{3}$ of the time. From T, he will head to L or R with equal probability. The figure summarizes this information.

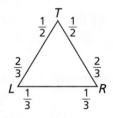

   Assume Bug 2 is currently at T. Find the probability of each event.

   a. In the next two minutes, Bug 2 moves clockwise both times.

   b. Two minutes from now, Bug 2 will be back to where he is now.

   c. Same as part (a), but assume Bug 2 starts at L.

   d. Same as part (b), but assume Bug 2 starts at L.

14. Bug 3 is lazy and prefers to stay put. No matter where he is now, at the next stage, he will stay put with probability $\frac{1}{2}$ and move to either of the other vertices with probability $\frac{1}{4}$. Find the probability of each event described in exercise 12, parts (a)–(c).

15. Bug 4 prefers to move clockwise. No matter where she is now, she will move one vertex clockwise with probability $\frac{3}{6}$, will stay put with probability $\frac{2}{6}$, and will move one vertex counterclockwise with probability $\frac{1}{6}$. Find the probability of each event described in Exercise 12, parts (a)–(c).

Why is it convenient to call this $\frac{3}{6}$ instead of $\frac{1}{2}$?

Probability Models

Consider all those bugs from the Lesson 4.12 Maintain Your Skills exercises. They all were moving around among the three corners of a triangle, named T, L, and R. The bugs had different probabilities for the direction of their moves in the next minute. For each bug, you used his or her transition probabilities to figure out the probabilities for his or her location after two minutes. There was nothing special about the number two. You could do it for 10 minutes or 100 minutes, although the calculations would get much longer.

The bug problems are multistep transition problems, just as the other problems in Lesson 4.12 are. Only now the questions are about probabilities instead of numbers of things. So matrix methods ought to work equally well to simplify the notation and the calculations, for any number of minutes.

To see this, here is notation that works for all the bugs at once. Let p_{AB} be the probability of moving to position A from position B in one minute. So, for each bug you have a **probability transition matrix.**

$$M = \begin{array}{c} \\ T \\ L \\ R \end{array} \begin{array}{c} T \quad\quad L \quad\quad R \\ \begin{pmatrix} p_{TT} & p_{TL} & p_{TR} \\ p_{LT} & p_{LL} & p_{LR} \\ p_{RT} & p_{RL} & p_{RR} \end{pmatrix} \end{array}$$

For instance, for Bug 1 the probability transition matrix is

$$M = \begin{array}{c} \\ T \\ L \\ R \end{array} \begin{array}{c} T \quad L \quad R \\ \begin{pmatrix} 0 & \frac{1}{2} & \frac{1}{2} \\ \frac{1}{2} & 0 & \frac{1}{2} \\ \frac{1}{2} & \frac{1}{2} & 0 \end{pmatrix} \end{array}$$

> The columns represent where the bug was and the rows represent where the bug goes.

For You to Do

1. Determine the transition matrix for Bug 2 from Exercise 12 of Lesson 4.12.

Now suppose at some time (not necessarily the start), a bug has probabilities p_T, p_L, and p_R of being at T, L, and R, respectively. Note that you are using just one subscript now. You want to figure out the probabilities of the bug being at T, L, and R one minute later. Call these probabilities p'_T, p'_L, and p'_R.

To see how these probabilities are related, ask, How can Bug 1 get to, say, vertex T one minute later? There are three ways: During that minute she could either stay put if she was at T already, she could move there from L, or she could move there from R. Therefore p'_T is the sum of three terms:

- the probability she stays put at T for the minute times the probability she was already at T

- the probability she moves to T from L times the probability she was already at L

- the probability she moves to T from R times the probability she was already at R

Therefore, $p'_T = p_{TT}p_T + p_{TL}p_L + p_{TR}p_R$.

Remember...

To find the probability of a compound event, where first one event happens and then another event happens, you multiply the probability of the first event by the probability of the second event.

For Discussion

2. Come up with similar formulas for p'_L and p'_R.

You can write the three equations for p'_T, p'_L, and p'_R as one matrix equation:

$$\begin{pmatrix} p'_T \\ p'_L \\ p'_R \end{pmatrix} = \begin{pmatrix} p_{TT} & p_{TL} & p_{TR} \\ p_{LT} & p_{LL} & p_{LR} \\ p_{RT} & p_{RL} & p_{RR} \end{pmatrix} \begin{pmatrix} p_T \\ p_L \\ p_R \end{pmatrix}$$

If you let P' stand for the column of probabilities on the left and P for the column of probabilities on the right, you get $P' = MP$.

By the same reasoning as in the previous lesson, $P(1) = MP(0)$ and $P(2) = MP(1) = M(MP(0)) = M^2P(0)$.

In general, $P(n) = M^nP(0)$. $P(n)$ is the column of probabilities that the bug is at T, L, or R after n minutes.

Example 1

Problem Exercise 13 from Lesson 4.12 was about Bug 2, who prefers vertex T of the triangle. Use matrix methods to solve parts (b) and (d) of this exercise again. Then take it further: What can you say about Bug 2's location 3 minutes from now? 4 minutes from now? In the long run?

Solution In part (b), Bug 2 starts at T, so

$$P(0) = \begin{pmatrix} 1 \\ 0 \\ 0 \end{pmatrix}$$

The probability transition matrix for Bug 2 is

$$M = \begin{pmatrix} 0 & \frac{2}{3} & \frac{2}{3} \\ \frac{1}{2} & 0 & \frac{1}{3} \\ \frac{1}{2} & \frac{1}{3} & 0 \end{pmatrix}$$

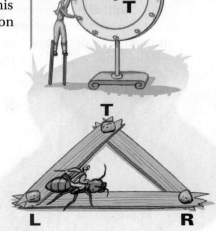

Therefore

$$P(2) = \begin{pmatrix} p_T(2) \\ p_L(2) \\ p_R(2) \end{pmatrix} = M^2 \begin{pmatrix} 1 \\ 0 \\ 0 \end{pmatrix} = \begin{pmatrix} \frac{2}{3} & \frac{2}{9} & \frac{2}{9} \\ \frac{1}{6} & \frac{4}{9} & \frac{1}{3} \\ \frac{1}{6} & \frac{1}{3} & \frac{4}{9} \end{pmatrix} \begin{pmatrix} 1 \\ 0 \\ 0 \end{pmatrix} = \begin{pmatrix} \frac{2}{3} \\ \frac{1}{6} \\ \frac{1}{6} \end{pmatrix}$$

So, the answer to part (b) is $\frac{2}{3}$.

To answer part (d), you compute $M^2 \begin{pmatrix} 0 \\ 1 \\ 0 \end{pmatrix}$. But note that this is just the second column of M^2, which you have already computed. You want the middle entry of that column. So the answer is $\frac{4}{9}$.

To take the problem further, you just need to compute M^3, M^4, and enough higher powers to look for a pattern.

$$M^3 = \begin{pmatrix} \frac{2}{9} & \frac{14}{27} & \frac{14}{27} \\ \frac{7}{18} & \frac{2}{9} & \frac{7}{27} \\ \frac{7}{18} & \frac{7}{27} & \frac{2}{9} \end{pmatrix} \qquad M^4 = \begin{pmatrix} \frac{14}{27} & \frac{26}{81} & \frac{26}{81} \\ \frac{13}{54} & \frac{28}{81} & \frac{1}{3} \\ \frac{13}{54} & \frac{1}{3} & \frac{28}{81} \end{pmatrix}$$

> This is about as far as you will want to take exact fractions. The denominators are getting too big. The next computation is approximated to three decimal places.

For instance, if Bug 2 starts at T, the probability of his being at T after 3 minutes is $\frac{2}{9}$, and his probability of being at R after 4 minutes is $\frac{13}{54}$. If he starts at L, his probability of being at R after 4 minutes is $\frac{1}{3}$.

For a long-term pattern, you can compute higher powers of M.

$$M^{10} = \begin{pmatrix} 0.410 & 0.393 & 0.393 \\ 0.295 & 0.303 & 0.303 \\ 0.295 & 0.303 & 0.303 \end{pmatrix} \qquad M^{100} = \begin{pmatrix} 0.400 & 0.400 & 0.400 \\ 0.300 & 0.300 & 0.300 \\ 0.300 & 0.300 & 0.300 \end{pmatrix}$$

It seems that in the long run, Bug 2 has probabilities of 0.4, 0.3, and 0.3 of being at T, L, and R, regardless of where he starts, because the columns of M^{100} are the same.

For Discussion

3. Does this matrix method also answer parts (a) and (c) of Exercise 12 from Lesson 4.12? Explain.

For You to Do

4. Figure out where Bug 1 will be after 3 minutes. That is, figure out the probabilities, depending on where she starts. Do the same thing for 10 minutes.

In the examples so far, the moves could go on forever, but many situations have rules that tell you when to stop. These are taken care of in matrix models by **absorbing states.**

Example 2

Problem Alice and Bob play the following game. They take turns tossing a number cube. The first person to toss a 6 loses. Alice goes first. Find the probability of each event.

   a. Alice loses right away.

   b. The game ends in 5 or fewer moves.

   c. Bob loses on the fourth toss.

Solution To model this problem with a probability transition matrix, you need to identify the states. What happens next depends on who is tossing, but to cover all possibilities, you also need an absorbing state. So, let the three states be

   A. Alice is about to toss.

   B. Bob is about to toss.

   E. The game has ended (just a moment ago or earlier).

Each toss marks a transition. The probability transition matrix is

$$G = \begin{matrix} & \begin{matrix} A & B & E \end{matrix} \\ \begin{matrix} A \\ B \\ E \end{matrix} & \begin{pmatrix} 0 & \frac{5}{6} & 0 \\ \frac{5}{6} & 0 & 0 \\ \frac{1}{6} & \frac{1}{6} & 1 \end{pmatrix} \end{matrix}$$

> Take time to make sense of this matrix before you move on.

Consider the first column (the A column), for instance. If Alice is about to toss, either she does toss a 6, with probability $\frac{1}{6}$, and the game passes to the end state, or she does not toss a 6. So with probability $\frac{5}{6}$, the game passes to the state where Bob is about to toss.

Notice that E is an absorbing state. Once the game has ended, it remains ended. It never gets out of state E. Mathematically, this is represented by the fact that the E column is all 0's except for a 1 on the main diagonal.

> Think of the game as having infinitely many rounds, but nothing happens in any round after someone tosses a 6.

Let $P(n)$ be the column of probabilities that states A, B, and E occur after n tosses. Then you have

$$P(n) = G^n P(0) \text{ with } P(0) = \begin{pmatrix} 1 \\ 0 \\ 0 \end{pmatrix}$$

The entries in $P(0)$ reflect the fact that Alice goes first. Therefore, $P(n)$ is given by the first column (the A column) of G^n.

a. You have already found the probability of the first event. The probability that Alice loses right away is the probability that the game passes in one step to the E state. This probability is $\frac{1}{6}$.

b. This probability is the entry in column A and row E of G^5.

$$G^5 = \begin{pmatrix} 0 & 0.402 & 0 \\ 0.402 & 0 & 0 \\ 0.598 & 0.598 & 1 \end{pmatrix}$$

You find that the game ends on or before the fifth toss with probability 0.598.

c. You cannot find this probability directly from any power of G because there is no state for "just lost" (but see Exercise 10). However, for Bob to lose on the fourth toss, he must get the fourth toss and then toss a 6. The probability that he is about to toss in round 4 is the entry in the A column and B row of G^3. Compute G^3, and you will find that this entry is 0.579. Multiply by $\frac{1}{6}$ and you get the probability 0.097.

> Column A says that there is a 0% chance it is Alice's turn, about a 40% chance it is Bob's turn, and about a 60% chance the game is over.

For You to Do

In the game above, what is the probability that Alice loses?

This is not a question that you can answer with the matrix you used above, because that matrix lumps all losses together into one state, E. So, separate the states. Turn the state E into two absorbing states, "Alice lost" (not necessarily on the most recent toss) and "Bob lost." Now the probability transition matrix is

$$M = \begin{matrix} & \begin{matrix} A & B & AL & BL \end{matrix} \\ \begin{matrix} A \\ B \\ AL \\ BL \end{matrix} & \begin{pmatrix} 0 & \frac{5}{6} & 0 & 0 \\ \frac{5}{6} & 0 & 0 & 0 \\ \frac{1}{6} & 0 & 1 & 0 \\ 0 & \frac{1}{6} & 0 & 1 \end{pmatrix} \end{matrix}$$

Explain the entries in this new matrix. Use it to determine the probability of each of the following events. Continue to assume that Alice goes first.

5. Alice loses on or before the fifth toss.

6. Bob loses on or before the tenth toss.

7. Bob loses on the tenth toss.

8. Alice loses.

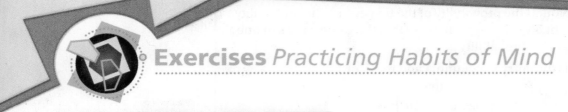

Exercises Practicing Habits of Mind

Check Your Understanding

Use probability transition matrices to solve the following exercises from Lesson 4.12 again. If you cannot answer some parts of each exercise using matrix methods, explain why.

1. Exercise 12   **2.** Exercise 14   **3.** Exercise 15

4. Write About It In every probability transition matrix in this lesson, each column had only nonnegative entries and they summed to 1. Explain why.

5. The weather tomorrow is influenced by the weather today. If it is sunny today, suppose the probability is 0.6 that it will be sunny tomorrow. If it is rainy today, suppose the probability is only 0.3 that it will be rainy tomorrow. Assume that the only choices are sunny or rainy.

Set up this situation as a matrix transition problem: Assume it is sunny today. Find the probabilities of sun and rain at each time.

a. 2 days from now   **b.** 5 days from now

c. 10 days from now   **d.** in the long run

e. If it is rainy today, find the probability of sunny weather 5 days from now.

> Any transition problem in which the matrix has nonnegative entries and each column sums to 1 is a *Markov chain*. Probability transition problems are automatically Markov chains.

6. Everyone has good moods and bad moods. Some people have a very hard time getting out of a bad mood.

Suppose Bob has thought a lot about his mental state and has made the following observations. If he is in a good mood now, the probability he will still be in a good mood in an hour is 0.8. But if he is in a bad mood now, the probability that he will still be in a bad mood in an hour is 0.9.

a. Describe Bob's moods with a probability transition matrix.

b. Suppose Bob wakes up in a good mood. What is the probability he will be in a good mood 12 hours later?

c. Suppose Bob wakes up in a bad mood. What is the probability he will be in a bad mood 12 hours later?

> Assume that Bob has only two moods, good or bad.

7. Suppose Alice and Bob take turns tossing a fair coin instead of a number cube. Again Alice goes first. The first player to toss heads loses the game. Set up a matrix. Find the probability of each event you found in Example 2.

8. Return to Bug 3 from Exercise 14 of Lesson 4.12. What are the probabilities of where he will be after three moves? After four? In the long run? Do the answers depend on the vertex at which he starts?

9. Return to Bug 4 from Exercise 15 of Lesson 4.12. What are the probabilities of where she will be after three moves? After four? In the long run? Do the answers depend on the vertex at which she starts?

10. Redo Example 2 with five states: Alice about to toss, Bob about to toss, Alice just lost, Bob just lost, and the game ended earlier. Use this matrix to determine the probability that Bob loses in the 4th round and the probability that he loses in the 8th round. Explain why you do not need the five-state matrix to find the probability that Bob loses in the 9th round.

11. **Take It Further** Alice and Bob slightly change the rules to their number-cube tossing game. If you toss a 6, you still lose. But if you toss a 1, you must toss again right away. In all other cases, the number cube passes to the other player, as before. Find the probability for each event in this variation. Before you compute, decide what matrix model will give you all the answers you want. (Recall that you have used three different models for the original game between Alice and Bob.)

    a. The game ends on or before the fifth toss.

    b. The game ends on or before the fifth toss, and Alice loses.

    c. Bob makes the fifth toss.

    d. Bob loses the game on the fifth toss.

    e. Alice loses the game.

12. **Take It Further** Change the rules for Alice and Bob again.

    • If you toss a 1, you get to toss again right away.

    • If you toss a 2 or a 3, you win.

    • If you toss a 4 or a 5, you pass the number cube to the other player.

    • If you toss a 6, you lose.

    Use these rules to find the probability of each event below. Before computing, decide what matrix model will give you all the answers you want.

    a. The game ends on or before the fifth toss.

    b. The game ends on or before the fifth toss, and Alice loses.

    c. There is a fifth toss, and Bob makes it.

    d. Bob loses the game on the fifth toss.

    e. Alice loses the game.

> So now you have modeled this same situation with a 3 × 3 matrix, a 4 × 4 matrix, and a 5 × 5 matrix. Depending on what you want to find, different models may work best, even for the same problem.

13. Alice gets tired of playing these games with Bob, so she decides to play alone. If she tosses a 2 or 3, she wins. If she tosses a 6, she loses. For any other toss, she tosses again.

Go Online
Pearsonsuccessnet.com

   a. What is the probability that Alice wins in four or fewer tosses?

   b. What is the probability that Alice loses in four or fewer tosses?

   c. What is the probability that the game never ends?

   d. What is the probability that Alice wins?

14. **Standardized Test Prep** Suppose A and B are both 2×2 invertible matrices, and I is the 2×2 identity matrix. Let det A represent the determinant of matrix A. Which of the following statements is NOT true?

   A. $\det A = \det A^{-1}$ for all A in which $\det A \neq 0$.

   B. $\det A \cdot \det A^{-1} = 1$ for all A in which $\det A \neq 0$.

   C. $\det B = -1$ if B is a transformation matrix for a reflection over a line that passes through the origin.

   D. $\det I = 1$

Maintain Your Skills

15. Recall that the determinant of a 2×2 matrix $A = \begin{pmatrix} a & b \\ c & d \end{pmatrix}$ is given by $\det(A) = ad - bc$.

   For each pair of matrices, compute

   $\det(A)$ $\det(B)$ $\det(AB)$

   a. $A = \begin{pmatrix} 1 & 2 \\ 3 & 4 \end{pmatrix}$, $B = \begin{pmatrix} 5 & 6 \\ 7 & 8 \end{pmatrix}$

   b. $A = \begin{pmatrix} -2 & 1 \\ 5 & -3 \end{pmatrix}$, $B = \begin{pmatrix} 7 & 1 \\ 4 & -2 \end{pmatrix}$

   c. $A = \begin{pmatrix} 6 & 2 \\ 3 & 1 \end{pmatrix}$, $B = \begin{pmatrix} 4 & 1 \\ 8 & 3 \end{pmatrix}$

   d. $A = \begin{pmatrix} 1 & 2 \\ 2 & 4 \end{pmatrix}$, $B = \begin{pmatrix} x & y \\ z & w \end{pmatrix}$

Go Online
Video Tutor
Pearsonsuccessnet.com

16. Recall that if $A = \begin{pmatrix} a & b \\ c & d \end{pmatrix}$ with $\det(A) \neq 0$, then its inverse is

   $A^{-1} = \dfrac{1}{\det(A)} \begin{pmatrix} d & -b \\ -c & a \end{pmatrix}$.

   For each matrix, compute $\det(A)$ and $\det(A^{-1})$.

   a. $A = \begin{pmatrix} 3 & 1 \\ 4 & 2 \end{pmatrix}$

   b. $A = \begin{pmatrix} 3 & 10 \\ 1 & 5 \end{pmatrix}$

   c. $A = \begin{pmatrix} 2 & 1 \\ 1 & 2 \end{pmatrix}$

   d. $A = \begin{pmatrix} x & 0 \\ 0 & 1 \end{pmatrix}$ with $x \neq 0$

Experiments and Simulations

Often mathematicians and scientists want to determine whether or not a particular item or treatment is really effective. Examples of products that may claim benefits include a new drug, a fuel additive, a new variety of corn, or a speed-reading. In any situation, some randomness occurs and is expected. Even when we see an impact from the item, how do we know that the item caused the effect and it wasn't random?

For Discussion

1. Suppose your friend flips a coin and it lands showing heads. Do you believe the coin is a fair coin?

2. Suppose your friend flips the coin twice in a row and it shows heads both times. Do you believe the coin is fair?

3. What if the coin is flipped 15 times in a row and it shows heads every time? Do you believe the coin is fair?

When the coin comes up heads enough times in a row, we start to suspect the coin is not fair. The field of statistics has grown up around questions like, "How many heads do I need to get in a row before I should think the coin is not fair?" In this lesson, we will explore this idea in the context of a scientific study.

> Statisticians do not answer questions like these as definitively as you might expect. Instead of saying "The coin is rigged!", they are more likely to say something like "The coin is probably not fair." or "The evidence suggests we reject the idea the coin is fair."

For Discussion

A TV commercial advertises the "amazing power of magnetic power bands." In this commercial, the advertiser claims that wearing magnetic power bands will improve athletes' balance. Is it possible to find scientific evidence to support this claim?

A university researcher in sports medicine decides to test this claim. Forty-eight college athletes volunteer and participate in the study. At the beginning of the study, each athlete's name is written on a slip of paper. The researcher mixes up all of the 48 names and randomly selects 24 of them. These 24 subjects are assigned to the Magnet Group. The remaining subjects are assigned to the Control Group. The name for this process is *randomization*. The athletes are not told whether they are in the Magnet Group or the Control Group.

> In a scientific study, the *control group* does not receive the treatment. This allows the researcher to compare subjects who received the treatment to those who did not.

4. Why might randomization of subjects be important for a study such as this one?

5. The researcher considered randomizing by having all 48 students line up, and then having the first athlete flip a coin. The athlete is placed in the Magnet Group if heads is flipped and in the Control Group if tails is flipped. The next athlete in line flips the coin, and this continues until there are 24 students in either the Magnet Group or the Control Group. Then the remaining students are placed in the group that has not yet been filled. Why might the researcher reject this plan for randomization?

6. Why would the researcher not tell the athletes which group they have been assigned to?

Once the students are randomly assigned to either the Magnet Group or the Control Group (without knowing which group they are in), each student is given a wristband. If the student was assigned to the Magnet Group, the wristband contains power magnets. If the student was assigned to the Control Group, the wristband has the same weight as the Magnet Group wristband but no power magnets.

Each student is given two hours for the body to "adjust" to the power magnets, and then takes a balance test designed by the researcher.

Here is a table with some of the information from the study filled in:

	Passed Balance Test	Failed Balance Test	Total
Magnet			24
Control			24
Total	36	12	48

For You to Do

7. Suppose that there is *little or no evidence* that the magnets are effective in improving balance. Complete the table with possible values under this assumption.

8. Are there other ways to complete the table such that there is little or no evidence that the magnets are effective in improving balance? Describe any changes that could be made while maintaining little or no evidence in the effectiveness of the magnets.

9. Suppose that there is *strong evidence* that the magnets are effective in improving balance. Complete the table with possible values under this assumption.

10. Are there other ways to complete the table such that there is strong evidence that the magnets are effective in improving balance? Describe any changes that could be made while maintaining strong evidence in the effectiveness of the magnets.

11. Suppose that there is *possible evidence* that the magnets are effective in improving balance. Complete the table with possible values. Could there be different answers to this question?

The idea that there could be a range of possible values for *strong evidence, possible evidence,* and *little or no evidence* is an important idea, but how can these ranges be mathematically justified? Given a set of initial conditions, any outcome is theoretically possible. A fair coin could flip heads 15 times in a row, or everyone in the Magnet Group could have passed the balance test without magnets. In order to more accurately interpret our results, we need to know how likely different outcomes are assuming randomness. To do this, we can use a *simulation*.

Tony, Sasha, and Derman are discussing their ranges of values for strong evidence, possible evidence, and little or no evidence of magnet effectiveness.

Derman So now that we have the different ranges, we just see which category the actual data fall in, right?

Sasha But how do we know our ranges are correct? Maybe they are really far off.

Tony Well, the *little or no evidence* category makes sense. If the magnets don't work, half of the athletes who passed the balance test should be from the Magnet Group and the other half should be from the Control Group.

Derman Yeah, 18 and 18!

Sasha But even if the magnets don't work, we won't necessarily get 18 and 18 each time. Maybe we get 19 and 17.

Derman Well, sure, but the magnets still won't work with 19 and 17.

Sasha But what about 20 and 16?

Derman Umm, they probably don't work . . . I think—

Sasha What about 21 and 15? Then do they work?

Derman Maybe, I don't know. If the number gets high enough, then we think they work, right?

Tony Right, but how high is high enough? And what about those middle numbers, like 20 and 21? Are those *no evidence* or *possible evidence*? How can we tell?

Sasha Let's run a simulation to replicate this experiment, assuming the power magnets don't work.

Derman Why would we do that?

Sasha We want to rule out luck as a cause for the data we got. But to do this, we need to get a plausible range of values for the number of people from the Magnet Group who passed the balance test if the magnets don't work, and everything is just random.

Tony Okay, I see. If the number of athletes in the Magnet Group who passed the balance test is too high to be caused by random chance, then we can probably rule out luck as a cause for the high value. Something else must have caused the high value . . .

Derman Well, maybe the Magnet Group had the better balancers in the first place.

Sasha Maybe, but we randomly assigned everybody into one of the two groups. For that reason, the balance levels of each group are probably the same entering the treatments.

Derman Oh, I see—the two groups in the experiment are as similar as possible before entering the treatments.

Sasha Right, so if the percent of passers in the Magnet Group is too high to be caused by chance, then we can probably conclude that the magnets work!

Tony Cool! So we need to know how likely it is to get 18, or 19, or 20, or 21, etc. . . . That seems hard to calculate directly. Let's create a simulation.

For Discussion

12. How should this simulation work? Describe a possible way to set up and carry out this simulation.

Tony, Sasha, and Derman are discussing their idea for this simulation.

Tony We have 48 people in our experiment altogether, so we need something with a lot of choices. How about a deck of cards?

Sasha Okay, suppose you let a red card be someone in the Magnet Group, and a black card is someone in the Control Group. How would we represent somebody who passed and somebody who failed?

Derman Wait, aren't there 52 cards in a deck?

Tony That's true. Well, let's leave out two red cards and two black cards—then we have 48.

Sasha So if I shuffle the cards, then deal out 36—those ones passed the test, and the rest failed.

Derman Then what?

Sasha Then I count out how many red cards I dealt to figure out how many people in the Magnet Group would have passed the test. That's replicating the situation where the power magnets don't work.

Tony Because the only thing making someone from each group pass or fail the balance test is random chance. Cool! Let's try it.

Derman This will be faster if we all do the simulation. Here are two more decks of cards.

Sasha Great! Let's each simulate this 30 times and keep track of the number of people from the Magnet Group who pass the balance test.

Tony, Sasha, and Derman each run the simulation 30 times. They graph their individual data in the dot plots shown below.

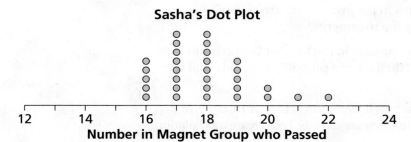

Sasha's Dot Plot

Number in Magnet Group who Passed

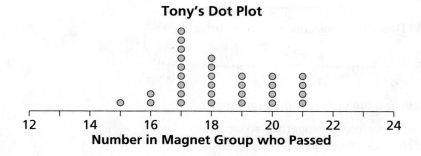

Tony's Dot Plot

Number in Magnet Group who Passed

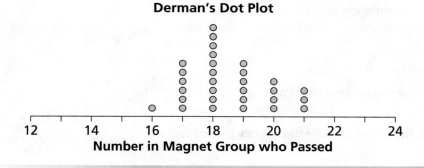

Derman's Dot Plot

Number in Magnet Group who Passed

For You to Do

13. How many times out of 30 did Sasha have 17 athletes in the Magnet Group pass the balance test?

14. How many times out of 30 did Tony have 17 athletes in the Magnet Group pass the balance test?

15. Neither Sasha, Tony, nor Derman had a simulation where 23 athletes in the Magnet Group passed the balance test. Does this mean it is impossible for 23 athletes in the Magnet Group to pass the balance test? Explain.

16. In the actual experiment, 21 of the 24 athletes in the Magnet Group passed the test. Based on these simulations of 30 trials, what would you conclude? Do you believe the power magnets assist balance?

17. What makes it difficult to make a definite conclusion?

Even though we might consider 90 trials a fairly large number of simulations, we usually will need more, depending on the frequency of particular outcomes and the number of possible outcomes. Using a computer, Sasha replicated the card simulation many more times. Here is a histogram of her results:

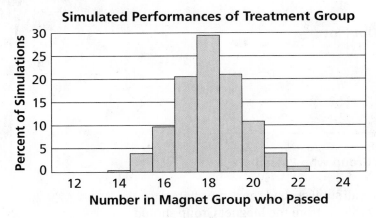

For You to Do

18. Do you believe having 21 of 24 athletes in the Magnet Group pass the balance test is sufficient evidence that power magnets improve balance? Explain.

Exercises *Practicing Habits of Mind*

Check Your Understanding

1. Using Sasha's histogram, create a range of values for the number of athletes in the Magnet Group who passed the balance test showing the following. Justify your answers with evidence from the histogram.

    a. *little or no evidence* that the magnets work

    b. *possible evidence* that the magnets work

    c. *strong evidence* that the magnets work

2. What number of athletes in the Magnet Group who passed the balance test would convince you that the magnets had a *detrimental* effect on balance? Justify your answer.

    > Some synonyms for *detrimental* are *adverse, harmful,* and *negative.*

3. The mode of Tony's dot plot data is 17 athletes in the Magnet Group who passed the balance test.

Tony's Dot Plot

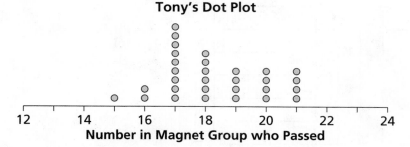

Number in Magnet Group who Passed

    a. Tony ran his simulations assuming all subjects had the same chance to pass the balance test. How many athletes from the Magnet Group should Tony expect to pass the balance test?

    b. Did Tony do something wrong with his simulations? Explain.

4. Can the university researcher know for sure whether or not power magnets improve balance as a result of an experiment like this one? Explain.

On Your Own

5. **What's Wrong Here?** Tony and Sasha have 15 playing cards: 10 black and 5 red. Two cards will be selected without replacement from this group. Tony and Sasha are interested in the number of red cards drawn. Sasha proposes the following simulation: use a calculator to randomly generate 0, 1, or 2, with this number representing the number of red cards drawn. Why is this not a good simulation for this scenario?

6. Heidi suspects a number cube with numbers 1 through 6 is weighted such that "1" occurs more often than it should. To test this, she rolls the number cube five times, and four of the five times the number "1" is rolled.

   a. Do you believe this number cube is fair? Explain.

   b. Design a simulation to replicate this situation.

   c. Carry out your simulation 100 times. Record your data as you go.

   d. Create a histogram of your results.

   e. Do you believe this number cube is fair? Explain.

7. A dropout prevention program is being pilot-tested at a high school. The guidance counselors have identified 20 seniors as being at risk for dropping out and have randomly divided them into two equal groups. One group will participate in the program and the other will not. At the end of the year, 15 of the 20 students graduate from high school.

   a. Explain why a valid simulation for this scenario is to generate a random list of 5 whole numbers and count the number of odd numbers that occur. This number represents the number of students in the prevention program who did not graduate from high school.

   b. Carry out this simulation 50 times. Create a histogram for these data.

8. **Take It Further** A fair coin is flipped eight times. Without running a simulation, determine the probability of getting each number of heads.

   a. 8

   b. 7

   c. 4

9. A new meditation exercise has been advertised to "significantly improve memory." Thirty-six volunteers agree to participate in a study to test this claim and are divided equally into two groups: the Treatment Group and the Control Group.

   a. Describe an effective and valid way to randomize the participants into the Treatment Group and Control Group.

   b. Describe what should occur if a participant is in the Treatment Group or Control Group.

c. Overall, 15 of the participants in the study improved their score on a memory test. Consider the partially completed table below. Complete the table under each of the following conditions.

- *little or no evidence* the meditation exercise improves memory
- *possible evidence* the meditation exercise improves memory
- *strong evidence* the meditation exercise improves memory

	Improved Memory	Did Not Improve Memory	Total
Treatment			18
Control			18
Total	15	21	36

d. Design a simulation for this scenario.

e. Carry out this simulation 100 times. Record your data and create a histogram of the results.

f. Revisit your answer to part (c) above, and create a range of values for the number of participants from the Treatment Group who improved their memory that demonstrates each of the following.

- *little or no evidence* the meditation exercise improves memory
- *possible evidence* the meditation exercise improves memory
- *strong evidence* the meditation exercise improves memory

g. In the experiment, 10 out of the 18 participants in the Treatment Group successfully improved their memory. Do you believe the claim in the advertisements to be valid? Explain.

Maintain Your Skills

10. Suppose you repeatedly flip a fair coin. Find the probability of getting each result.

   a. a head on your first flip

   b. 2 heads on your first 2 flips

   c. 3 heads on your first 3 flips

   d. n heads on your first n flips

11. For what values of n is the probability of getting n heads on your first n flips of a coin less than 1%?

In this investigation, you used matrix multiplication to describe geometric transformations. You used matrices and matrix multiplication to model situations that change over time. You also used experimental data to compare the effect of two treatments. These exercises will help you summarize what you have learned.

1. Use the matrix transformation $X \to AX$ with the matrix $A = \begin{pmatrix} 0 & 1 \\ 1 & 0 \end{pmatrix}$.

   a. Graph the triangle with vertices (2, 1), (4, 1), and (2, 0). Find the image of this triangle after the transformation.

   b. Describe what this transformation does to any point (x, y) in the plane, both algebraically and geometrically.

2. Find a matrix B such that the mapping $X \to BX$ is a 90° clockwise rotation around the origin. Graph the three points from Exercise 1 both before and after this mapping to show the effect of your matrix.

3. Tori sets up a mountain bike rental business with stations at the north and south ends of the town forest. She starts with 50 bikes at each location. She notices that 90% of the bikes that start at the south end and 60% of the bikes that start at the north end are returned to the north station.

   a. Set up a transition matrix for this situation.

   b. How many bikes would you predict to be at each station after 2 weeks?

   c. How many bikes would you predict to be at each station after 4 weeks?

   d. Will this situation settle down in the long term? If so, what number of bikes will be at each station in the steady state?

4. A researcher considered randomly assigning 58 participants to two equal groups by lining up the participants and choosing every other person for the treatment group. Explain why the researcher was right to reject this plan for randomization.

5. Wrongway Wainwright plays for the Hapless Losers baseball team. He stands still in the batter's box and earns a walk every time he is at bat. When this happens, the first base coach calls to him until he makes it to first base. From there, however, he is on his own.

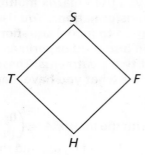

Wrongway prefers to run to the next base in a counterclockwise direction (which is also what his team prefers) and does so 80% of the time. However, the other 20% of the time, he runs clockwise. He will move to a new base each time one of his teammates gets a hit or a walk. Once he gets to home plate (from either direction), he will return to the dugout.

a. Set up a transition matrix for Wrongway that you can use to compute his probability of being at any of the four bases.

b. What are the probabilities for Wrongway being at each of the four bases after two of his teammates have gotten hits?

c. What is the probability that he has reached home plate (one way or another) after three of his teammates have gotten hits?

d. What is the probability that he still has not made it home after six of his teammates have gotten hits?

6. Is it true that a matrix associated with a reflection must be its own inverse? If so, what are some relationships that must hold for the entries a, b, c, and d in a

2 × 2 reflection matrix $R = \begin{pmatrix} a & b \\ c & d \end{pmatrix}$?

7. What is an absorbing state, and what does such a state look like in a transition matrix?

8. A transition matrix for a fixed population of 150 is $\begin{pmatrix} 0.2 & 0.7 \\ 0.8 & 0.3 \end{pmatrix}$.

Does this matrix have a steady state? If so, what is it? If not, why not?

Vocabulary

In this investigation, you learned these terms. Make sure you understand what each one means and how to use it.

- **absorbing state**
- **matrix transformation**
- **probability transition matrix**
- **steady state**
- **transition matrix**

Project: Using Mathematical Habits

More Matrix Operations

In this chapter, you looked at several applications of matrix algebra, including Gaussian Elimination, matrix addition, and matrix multiplication. There are several other operations on matrices that have proved very useful in mathematics and other disciplines. In this project, you will look at three of these operations: determinant, trace, and transpose. First, you will look at the definitions of these operations. In the problems, you will look at some of their properties.

You can carry out each of the three operations on a matrix of any size. They are functions that take a matrix as input and produce either a number or a matrix as output. In this project, you will only worry about 2×2 matrices. Here are the definitions.

Suppose $A = \begin{pmatrix} a & b \\ c & d \end{pmatrix}$.

- The determinant of A, written either as det A or $|A|$, is the number defined by

$$\det A = \begin{vmatrix} a & b \\ c & d \end{vmatrix} = ad - bc$$

- The trace of A, written as $\text{Tr}(A)$, is the number defined by

$$\text{Tr}(A) = \text{Tr}\begin{pmatrix} a & b \\ c & d \end{pmatrix} = a + d$$

$\text{Tr}(A)$ is the sum of the diagonal entries in A.

- The transpose of A, written as ^tA, is the matrix defined by

$$^tA = {}^t\begin{pmatrix} a & b \\ c & d \end{pmatrix} = \begin{pmatrix} a & c \\ b & d \end{pmatrix}$$

^tA is the matrix you get by "flipping" A over its main diagonal.

1. Consider the following system of linear equations.
$$x + 2y = 4$$
$$3x - y = -7$$

   Show that

$$x = \frac{\begin{vmatrix} 4 & 2 \\ -7 & -1 \end{vmatrix}}{\begin{vmatrix} 1 & 2 \\ 3 & -1 \end{vmatrix}} \text{ and } y = \frac{\begin{vmatrix} 1 & 4 \\ 3 & -7 \end{vmatrix}}{\begin{vmatrix} 1 & 2 \\ 3 & -1 \end{vmatrix}}$$

2. Consider the following system of linear equations.
$$ax + by = e$$
$$cx + dy = f$$

   If $\begin{vmatrix} a & b \\ c & d \end{vmatrix} \neq 0$, show that

$$x = \frac{\begin{vmatrix} e & b \\ f & d \end{vmatrix}}{\begin{vmatrix} a & b \\ c & d \end{vmatrix}} \text{ and } y = \frac{\begin{vmatrix} a & e \\ c & f \end{vmatrix}}{\begin{vmatrix} a & b \\ c & d \end{vmatrix}}$$

3. Consider the parallelogram below with vertices $(0, 0)$, (a, b), (c, d), and $(a + c, b + d)$.

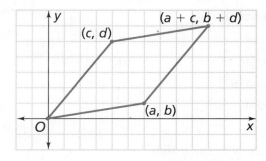

   Show that the area of the parallelogram is $\begin{vmatrix} a & b \\ c & d \end{vmatrix}$.

This square dance suggests how to find the transpose of a 2×2 matrix.

4. Suppose that A and B are 2×2 matrices. Show that

$$\det(AB) = \det(A)\det(B)$$

5. Suppose P is a matrix that has an inverse. By Exercise 14 from Lesson 4.08, $\det(P) \neq 0$. Show that

$$\det(P^{-1}) = \frac{1}{\det(P)}$$

6. Use the following matrices.

$$A = \begin{pmatrix} 3 & 4 \\ 3 & 8 \end{pmatrix} \quad B = \begin{pmatrix} 3 & 4 \\ 1 & 2 \end{pmatrix} \quad C = \begin{pmatrix} 3 & 4 \\ 6 & 8 \end{pmatrix}$$

Find each value.

a. $\det(AB)$ b. $\det(B^{-1})$

c. $\det(AB^{-1})$ d. $\det(BAB^{-1})$

e. $\det(B^5)$ f. $\det(C^5)$

g. $\det(A^2 B^3 C)$

7. Suppose A and B are 2×2 matrices and $\det(B) \neq 0$. Show that

$$\det(BAB^{-1}) = \det A$$

8. Suppose A is a 2×2 matrix. Show that

$$\det(A) = \det({}^t A)$$

9. **Write About It** Suppose that A and B are 2×2 matrices. Which of the following statements are true? For those that are true, state the result as a theorem and prove it. For those that are not true, explain why.

a. $\mathrm{Tr}(A + B) = \mathrm{Tr}(A) + \mathrm{Tr}(B)$

b. $\mathrm{Tr}(AB) = \mathrm{Tr}(A)\mathrm{Tr}(B)$

c. $\mathrm{Tr}(AB) = \mathrm{Tr}(BA)$

d. ${}^t(A^{-1}) = ({}^t A)^{-1}$

e. $\mathrm{Tr}(A^{-1}) = \frac{1}{\mathrm{Tr}(A)}$

10. Suppose A and B are 2×2 matrices and $\det(B) \neq 0$. Show that

$$\mathrm{Tr}(BAB^{-1}) = \mathrm{Tr}(A)$$

11. **Take It Further** Use the matrices below.

$$A = \begin{pmatrix} 19 & -12 \\ 20 & -12 \end{pmatrix} \text{ and } P = \begin{pmatrix} 4 & -3 \\ -5 & 4 \end{pmatrix}$$

Find $PA^6 P^{-1}$.

Review

Go Online
Pearsonsuccessnet.com

In **Investigation 4A,** you learned how to

- solve a system of three equations in three unknowns
- write a system of linear equations in matrix form or translate a matrix into a system of equations
- describe the process of Gaussian Elimination and apply it both by hand and with technology to solve a system

The following questions will help you check your understanding.

1. Solve the following system of equations.

$$x - y + 4z = 7$$
$$2x + 3y - 2z = 4$$
$$x + 2y + 8z = 6$$

2. a. Write the following system of equations as an augmented matrix.

$$2x + 3y + z = 5$$
$$x - y = 7$$
$$x + 2z = 16$$

   b. Solve the system using Gaussian Elimination.

3. Find the row-reduced echelon form of this matrix.

$$\begin{pmatrix} 2 & 5 & -3 & | & -8 \\ 1 & -4 & 0 & | & 9 \\ 3 & -2 & 1 & | & 7 \end{pmatrix}$$

In **Investigation 4B,** you learned how to

- communicate and prove results about matrices
- compute dot products, sums, differences, products, and inverses of matrices
- interpret and solve problems using matrix calculations

The following questions will help you check your understanding.

4. Various clubs at a high school are selling boxes of cookies for a fundraiser. They are reporting their weekly sales in tables.

Week 1

	Chocolate Chip	Sugar	Oatmeal
Art Club	10	12	5
Spanish Club	8	8	3
Math Club	15	12	10
Science Club	14	8	9

Week 2

	Chocolate Chip	Sugar	Oatmeal
Art Club	18	10	7
Spanish Club	12	9	5
Math Club	19	13	4
Science Club	15	8	11

a. Copy and complete the following table showing the total sales after two weeks. Use matrix algebra.

Total

	Chocolate Chip	Sugar	Oatmeal
Art Club	▦	▦	▦
Spanish Club	▦	▦	▦
Math Club	▦	▦	▦
Science Club	▦	▦	▦

b. Suppose chocolate chip cookies are $4 per box, sugar cookies are $3 per box, and oatmeal cookies are $3.50 per box. Copy and complete the following table. Use a matrix product to find the entries.

	Revenue ($)
Art Club	▦
Spanish Club	▦
Math Club	▦
Science Club	▦

5. Let A be a 2×2 matrix where $a_{ij} = i + j$, B be a 2×3 matrix where $b_{ij} = 2j$, and C be a 3×1 matrix where $c_{ij} = (2i - j)^2$. Find each matrix, if possible.

a. A, B, and C **b.** AB

c. BC **d.** $A + B$

e. $3B$ **f.** A^{-1}

6. Use the following matrix equation.

$$\begin{pmatrix} 3 & 2 \\ 5 & 6 \end{pmatrix}\begin{pmatrix} x \\ y \end{pmatrix} = \begin{pmatrix} 4 \\ 20 \end{pmatrix}$$

a. Find x and y.

b. Translate the matrix equation into a system of linear equations.

In **Investigation 4C,** you learned how to

- make transitions between systems of equations and matrices
- use matrices to model the evolution of a system over time
- analyze sequences of repeated probabilities
- used experimental data to compare the effect of two treatments

The following questions will help you check your understanding.

7. Let $A = \begin{pmatrix} -1 & 0 \\ 0 & 1 \end{pmatrix}$, $B = \begin{pmatrix} 0 & -2 \\ 2 & 0 \end{pmatrix}$, and $C = \begin{pmatrix} 0 & 1 \\ 1 & 0 \end{pmatrix}$.

a. Find $A \cdot \begin{pmatrix} 2 \\ -3 \end{pmatrix}$. What does matrix A do?

b. Find $B \cdot \begin{pmatrix} 2 \\ -3 \end{pmatrix}$. What does matrix B do?

c. Find $C \cdot \begin{pmatrix} 2 \\ -3 \end{pmatrix}$. What does matrix C do?

8. Suppose that the following matrix is a transition matrix for a fixed population.

$$M = \begin{pmatrix} 0.7 & 0.4 \\ 0.3 & 0.6 \end{pmatrix}$$

Assume that the total population is 700 and that there is a steady state $X = (x, y)$. Find X.

9. Marcie baby-sits for a very temperamental toddler named Joey. She has noticed that if Joey is happy when she arrives, the probability that he will still be happy in one hour is 0.6. If he is unhappy when she arrives, the probability that he will still be unhappy in one hour is 0.9.

a. Describe Joey's temperament with a probability transition matrix.

b. If Joey is happy when Marcie arrives, what is the probability that he will still be happy when his parents come home in 4 hours?

Multiple Choice

1. Which matrix is the row-reduced echelon form of the following matrix?

$$\begin{pmatrix} 1 & 2 & | & 4 \\ 2 & -1 & | & 3 \end{pmatrix}$$

A. $\begin{pmatrix} 1 & 0 & | & 1 \\ 0 & 1 & | & 1 \end{pmatrix}$
B. $\begin{pmatrix} 1 & 2 & | & 4 \\ 0 & -5 & | & -5 \end{pmatrix}$

C. $\begin{pmatrix} 1 & 0 & | & 2 \\ 0 & 1 & | & 1 \end{pmatrix}$
D. $\begin{pmatrix} 1 & 1 & | & 2 \\ 1 & 1 & | & 1 \end{pmatrix}$

2. Use the following matrix.

$$A = (a_{ij}) = \begin{pmatrix} 4 & -9 & 8 \\ -2 & 7 & 5 \\ 1 & -3 & 0 \end{pmatrix}$$

Find a_{12}.

A. 0
B. -9
C. -2
D. -36

3. Find the following dot product.

$$(2, 0, 0) \cdot (a, b, c)$$

A. $2a + b + c$
B. $2a$
C. 0
D. $2(a + b + c)$

4. Translate the following matrix equation into a linear system.

$$\begin{pmatrix} a \\ b \end{pmatrix} = \begin{pmatrix} 7 & 2 \\ -5 & 3 \end{pmatrix} \begin{pmatrix} x \\ y \end{pmatrix}$$

A. $7x - 5y = a$
   $2x + 3y = b$
B. $7a - 5b = x$
   $2a + 3b = y$
C. $7x + 2y = a$
   $-5x + 3y = b$
D. $7a + 2b = x$
   $-5a + 3b = y$

5. Which matrix results in a reflection across the y-axis?

A. $\begin{pmatrix} -1 & 0 \\ 0 & 1 \end{pmatrix}$
B. $\begin{pmatrix} 1 & 0 \\ 0 & -1 \end{pmatrix}$

C. $\begin{pmatrix} 0 & 1 \\ 1 & 0 \end{pmatrix}$
D. $\begin{pmatrix} 0 & 1 \\ -1 & 0 \end{pmatrix}$

Open Response

6. Solve the following system using Gaussian Elimination.

$$\begin{aligned} x - y + z &= 8 \\ 2y + z &= -12 \\ x + 4z &= 12 \end{aligned}$$

7. Use the matrices below.

$$A = \begin{pmatrix} 4 & -1 \\ 0 & 3 \\ 6 & 5 \end{pmatrix} \quad B = \begin{pmatrix} 10 & -4 \\ 3 & 2 \\ -5 & -20 \end{pmatrix} \quad C = \begin{pmatrix} 1 & 4 \\ -5 & 6 \end{pmatrix}$$

Find each value or matrix, if possible.

a. the size of A
b. $A + 2B$
c. BC
d. CB
e. C^2
f. C^{-1}

8. Solve the following matrix equation for x and y.

$$\begin{pmatrix} 3 & -2 \\ 6 & 5 \end{pmatrix} \begin{pmatrix} x \\ y \end{pmatrix} = \begin{pmatrix} 24 \\ 21 \end{pmatrix}$$

9. Let $X \mapsto AX = X'$ and $X = \begin{pmatrix} -2 \\ 5 \end{pmatrix}$. For each matrix A, describe the geometric transformation and find X'.

a. $A = \begin{pmatrix} 0 & 1 \\ 1 & 0 \end{pmatrix}$
b. $A = \begin{pmatrix} 1 & 0 \\ 0 & -1 \end{pmatrix}$

c. $A = \begin{pmatrix} 2 & 0 \\ 0 & 2 \end{pmatrix}$
d. $A = \begin{pmatrix} -\frac{1}{2} & 0 \\ 0 & \frac{1}{2} \end{pmatrix}$

10. There are two different routes from a certain town into the city. If Stella chooses the first route today, there is a 0.8 probability she will choose the first route tomorrow. If she chooses the second route today, there is a 0.4 probability that she will choose the first route tomorrow.

a. Express this situation as a transition matrix.

b. If Stella chooses the first route Monday, what is the probability that she will choose the second route Friday? Assume she goes to the city each weekday.

c. What can you say about Stella's choice of routes in the long run?

11. What is the process of Gaussian Elimination?

Multiple Choice

1. Simplify $\sqrt{3} \cdot \sqrt{-27}$.

    A. 9   **B.** -9 **C.** $9i$ **D.** $-9i$

2. Suppose $z = -3 + 2i$. Find $z - \bar{z}$.

    A. $-6 + 4i$ **B.** $4i$

    C. 0   **D.** $-12i$

3. If $z = a + bi$ is in Quadrant II, then $-z$ is in which quadrant?

    A. I   **B.** II   **C.** III   **D.** IV

4. Simplify $|-5 + 4i|$.

    A. 4   **B.** 5   **C.** $\sqrt{41}$ **D.** -1

5. If one solution of a quadratic equation with real coefficients is $3 - 4i$, which of the following numbers must be the other solution?

    A. $3 + 4i$ **B.** $-3 + 4i$

    C. $-3 - 4i$ **D.** 5

Open Response

6. a. Find the solutions of $x^4 - 81 = 0$ that are in $\mathbb{R}$.

    b. Find the solutions of $x^4 - 81 = 0$ that are in $\mathbb{C}$ but not in $\mathbb{R}$.

7. Solve each equation over $\mathbb{C}$. Express your answer in the form $a + bi$, where a and b are real numbers.

    a. $z + (3 - 5i) = -9 + 2i$

    b. $z \cdot (6 - 4i) = 1$

8. Let $z = \sqrt{3} + i$ and $w = 4i$.

    a. Find $z \cdot w$.

    b. On the complex plane, graph z, w, and $z \cdot w$.

    c. Find the magnitude and direction of z, w, and $z \cdot w$.

9. A complex number z has magnitude 3 and direction $120°$. Find the magnitude and direction of each number.

    a. z^2 **b.** z^3 **c.** z^4

10. Find the magnitude and direction of all the solutions to the equation $x^4 - 16 = 0$.

11. Rewrite the matrix $\begin{pmatrix} 2 & -1 & | & 5 \\ 1 & 3 & | & 8 \end{pmatrix}$ in row-reduced echelon form.

12. Let $A = (a_{ij}) = \begin{pmatrix} 3 & 2 & 0 \\ -4 & 6 & -1 \\ 1 & 5 & 2 \end{pmatrix}$. Find a_{13} and a_{21}.

13. Simplify $(5, 7, -1) \cdot (a, b, c)$.

14. Rewrite each matrix equation as a linear system of equations.

    a. $\begin{pmatrix} 3a \\ 7b \end{pmatrix} = \begin{pmatrix} 2 & 5 \\ -1 & 4 \end{pmatrix}\begin{pmatrix} x \\ y \end{pmatrix}$

    b. $\begin{pmatrix} -a \\ 2b \\ 5c \end{pmatrix} = \begin{pmatrix} 4 & 3 & -1 \\ 2 & 8 & 5 \\ 6 & -3 & 1 \end{pmatrix}\begin{pmatrix} x \\ y \\ z \end{pmatrix}$

15. What matrix results in a reflection across the y-axis?

16. What matrix results in a counterclockwise rotation of $90°$?

17. Solve the following system using Gaussian Elimination.

$$4x + 8z = 0$$
$$3x - 2y + z = 0$$
$$-2x + y - z = -1$$

18. Use the following matrices.

$$A = \begin{pmatrix} 3 & -2 & 1 \\ 5 & 0 & 4 \end{pmatrix} \quad B = \begin{pmatrix} -4 & 2 \\ 0 & 3 \end{pmatrix} \quad C = \begin{pmatrix} 5 & -6 \\ 9 & 2 \end{pmatrix}$$

Find each matrix, if possible.

    a. $B + C$ **b.** AC **c.** CB

    d. A^{-1} **e.** B^{-1}

19. Solve the following equation for x and y.

$$\begin{pmatrix} y \\ y - 3 \end{pmatrix} = \begin{pmatrix} 4x \\ 2x + 1 \end{pmatrix}$$

20. Let $X \mapsto AX = X'$ and $X = \begin{pmatrix} 5 \\ -2 \end{pmatrix}$. For each matrix A, describe the geometric transformation and find X'.

a. $A = \begin{pmatrix} 0 & -1 \\ -1 & 0 \end{pmatrix}$ **b.** $A = \begin{pmatrix} 1 & 0 \\ 0 & -1 \end{pmatrix}$

c. $A = \begin{pmatrix} -4 & 0 \\ 0 & 4 \end{pmatrix}$ **d.** $A = \begin{pmatrix} 3 & 0 \\ 0 & 5 \end{pmatrix}$

21. There are only two exits that buses can take to leave a college campus. Suppose each bus driver leaves the campus once per day. If a driver chooses the first exit today, there is a 0.3 probability she will choose the first exit tomorrow. If a driver chooses the second exit today, there is a 0.6 probability that she will choose the first exit tomorrow.

a. Express this situation as a probability transition matrix.

b. If a driver chooses the first exit Monday, what is the probability that she will choose the first exit again on Thursday?

c. What can you determine about a driver's choice of exits in the long run?

22. Copy and complete this difference table.

Input, n	Output, $a(n)$	Δ	Δ^2
0	■	4	1
1	9	■	1
2	■	■	1
3	■	■	
4	■		

23. Use the input-output table for the function $a(n)$. The function has a constant first difference. Find $a(50)$ and $a(100)$.

Input, n	Output, $a(n)$
0	83
1	■
2	■
3	■
4	■
5	−2

24. Find a recursive function that agrees with the following table of values.

Input, n	Output, $a(n)$
0	−1
1	4
2	9
3	14
4	19

25. Find the mean absolute error, mean squared error, and standard error for this data set, using the line with equation $y = 2x + 5$.

x	y
0	4
1	5
2	6
3	7
4	8

26. Use the following function definitions.

$$f(x) = 2x^2 - 3$$
$$g(x) = -5x + 1$$

Find each value.

a. $f(-2)$ **b.** $f \circ g(3)$

c. $g \circ f(x)$ **d.** $g^{-1}(x)$

27. Factor each polynomial.

a. $81x^2 - 49y^2$ **b.** $64x^3 + 27y^3$

28. Let $f(x) = 4x + 1$. Find the inverse of f and show that $f \circ f^{-1}(x) = x$.

29. Let $p(x) = 2x^3 - x^2 + 4x - 1$.

a. Find the quotient and remainder when you divide $p(x)$ by $x + 1$.

b. Use your answer from part (a) to find $p(-1)$.

30. Factor each polynomial over $\mathbb{Z}$.

a. $5x^2 - 16x + 12$

b. $6x^2 + 21x + 9$

c. $9x^4 - 35x^2 - 4$

Exponential and Logarithmic Functions

In the 1930s, Charles Richter developed the Richter scale at the California Institute of Technology. The Richter scale measures the magnitude of earthquakes. Earthquake magnitudes vary widely, from tiny microearthquakes that only sensitive seismographs can detect to catastrophic events that cause widespread destruction.

The wide variation of magnitude led Richter and his colleagues to use the base-10 logarithm in their formula. This limits the possible values of the magnitude to a more manageable and understandable range.

To calculate the magnitude M_L of an earthquake, you measure the maximum amplitude A of the wave pattern that your seismograph records. Richter used the formula $M_L = \log_{10} A - \log_{10} A_0$, where A_0 is a correction value based on the seismograph's distance from the earthquake and local conditions.

A small earthquake can have a negative magnitude. The largest magnitude ever recorded was 9.5, during the Great Chilean Earthquake on May 22, 1960. Instruments detect over a million earthquakes every year. Humans can only feel about one third of these.

Vocabulary and Notation

- base
- common logarithm, log x
- exponential decay
- exponential function
- exponential growth

- logarithm function, $x \mapsto \log_b x$
- logarithmic scale
- negative exponent, a^{-m}
- nth root, $\sqrt[n]{r}$
- zero exponent, a^0

5A

Working with Exponents

In *Working with Exponents*, you will use the basic rules of algebra to discover the laws of exponents. You will learn how to extend the rules to work with zero, negative, and rational exponents.

By the end of this investigation, you will be able to answer questions like these.

1. What is the Fundamental Law of Exponents? What are some of its corollaries?

2. How do you extend the laws of exponents to define zero, negative, and rational exponents?

3. What are the simplified forms of the expressions 4^0, 7^{-2} and $5^{\frac{27}{3}}$?

You will learn how to

- evaluate expressions involving exponents, including zero, negative, and rational exponents

- find missing terms in a geometric sequence and generate geometric sequences to interpret expressions involving rational exponents

- convert between exponential and radical forms for rational exponents

You will develop these habits and skills:

- Extend the laws of exponents to allow evaluation of zero, negative, and rational exponents.

- Reason logically to verify that a particular interpretation of an exponent follows the laws of exponents.

- Generalize from specific examples to develop and verify identities.

Radiographers use X-rays for medical imaging. X-rays have wavelengths between 10^{-7} and 10^{-10} cm.

Expressions or equations may contain variables as exponents.

For You to Explore

1. Copy and complete this table for the function $f(n) = 2^n$.

Input, n	Output, $f(n)$
6	64
5	32
4	16
3	8
2	▨
1	▨
0	▨
−1	▨
−2	▨
−3	▨

2. Solve each equation.

   a. $2^3 \cdot 2^5 = 2^a$ **b.** $2^b \cdot 2^8 = 2^{14}$

   c. $3^c \cdot 3^c = 3^{12}$ **d.** $(3^d)^2 = 3^8$

   e. $\dfrac{5^7}{5^f} = 5^6$ **f.** $3^g = 9^5$

   g. $5^{3h} = 5^7$ **h.** $(5^k)^3 = 5^4$

3. **Write About It** What are some rules of exponents? Give examples.

A *geometric sequence* is a list of numbers in which you get each term by multiplying the previous one by a constant. For example, the sequence below is a geometric sequence, since each term is three times as great as the previous term.

$$4, 12, 36, 108, 324, \ldots$$

For Problems 4 and 5, find the missing terms in each geometric sequence.

4. a. $4, 8, 16, \blacksquare, \blacksquare, \blacksquare, \ldots$ **b.** $4, -8, 16, \blacksquare, \blacksquare, \blacksquare, \ldots$

   c. $2, 2\sqrt{3}, \blacksquare, \blacksquare, \blacksquare, \blacksquare, \ldots$ **d.** $a, 2a, \blacksquare, \blacksquare, \blacksquare, \blacksquare, \ldots$

   e. $k, 3k, \blacksquare, \blacksquare, \blacksquare, \blacksquare, \ldots$

5. a. $1, \blacksquare, \blacksquare, 8, \blacksquare, \blacksquare, \ldots$ **b.** $\blacksquare, \blacksquare, 1, \frac{1}{2}, \blacksquare, \blacksquare, \ldots$

   c. $2, \blacksquare, 18, \blacksquare, \blacksquare, \blacksquare, \ldots$ **d.** $1, \blacksquare, \blacksquare, \blacksquare, 9, \blacksquare, \ldots$

Habits of Mind

Look for relationships. What is a closed form for the function g with this sequence of outputs?

Input	Output
0	4
1	12
2	36
3	108
4	324

Exercises Practicing Habits of Mind

6. Decide whether each equation is true for all positive integers a, b, and c.

a. $a^b \stackrel{?}{=} b^a$

b. $a^{b+c} \stackrel{?}{=} a^b + a^c$

c. $a^{b+c} \stackrel{?}{=} a^b \cdot a^c$

d. $a^b \cdot a^c \stackrel{?}{=} a^{bc}$

e. $(a^b)^c \stackrel{?}{=} a^{bc}$

f. $(a^b)^c \stackrel{?}{=} a^{(b^c)}$

g. $\dfrac{a^b}{a^c} \stackrel{?}{=} a^{b-c}$

h. $(ab)^c \stackrel{?}{=} a(b^c)$

Habits of Mind

Experiment.
If the equation is not true for all positive integers, is it true for some values of a, b, and c?

7. Determine whether each expression is equal to 2^{12}. Explain.

a. $2^{10} + 2^2$

b. $(2^4)(2^4)(2^4)$

c. $2^6 \cdot 2^6$

d. $2^9 + 2^3$

e. $(2^{10})(2^2)$

f. $2^{11} + 2^{11}$

g. $(2^4)(2^3)$

h. $4(2^{10})$

Try this without a calculator.

8. Copy and complete the table for the function $g(n) = 3^n$.

9. Problem 1 shows a table for $f(n) = 2^n$. Exercise 8 shows a table for $g(n) = 3^n$. Consider the function $h(n) = f(n) \cdot g(n)$.

a. Calculate $h(3)$.

b. Use the completed tables to calculate $h(0)$, $h(1)$, and $h(2)$.

c. Find a simple rule for $h(n)$.

10. **Take It Further**

a. Explain why there are no positive integers a and b such that $2^a = 5^b$.

b. Find the number x that makes $2^x = 5$. Round to four decimal places.

c. Find the number y that makes $2 = 5^y$. Round to four decimal places.

d. What is the relationship between x and y?

Input, n	Output, $g(n)$
5	243
4	81
3	27
2	▧
1	▧
0	▧
−1	▧
−2	▧
−3	▧

Maintain Your Skills

11. Solve each equation.

a. $3^x = 81$

b. $3^{x+1} = 81$

c. $3^{2x} = 81$

d. $3^{-x} = 81$

e. $3^{4x-1} = 81$

f. $3^{x^2} = 81$

Laws of Exponents

If n is a positive integer, then a^n (read as "a to the n") is the product of n factors of a.

$$a^n = \underbrace{a \cdot a \cdot a \cdots \cdot a}_{n \text{ factors of } a}$$

This lesson develops the rules for working with expressions in the form a^n. These rules are built on the basic rules for multiplication and division.

For You to Do

1. Use a product model like the one above to demonstrate that $a^3 \cdot a^5 = a^8$.

2. How can you use a product model to write out $(a^2)^5$? What is the result?

Multiplication has the any-order, any-grouping properties, but not all operations do. Division and subtraction do not have either property. Neither does exponentiation.

$$2^{20} \neq 20^2 \text{ and } (2^3)^4 \neq 2^{(3^4)}$$

You will review some of the rules for calculating with exponents and look at why they work.

Theorem 5.1 The Fundamental Law of Exponents

If b and c are positive integers, then
$$a^b \cdot a^c = a^{b+c}$$

Proof Use a product model to expand a^b and a^c.

$$(a^b)(a^c) = \underbrace{(a \cdot a \cdots \cdot a)}_{b \text{ factors}} \cdot \underbrace{(a \cdot a \cdots \cdot a)}_{c \text{ factors}} = \underbrace{(a \cdot a \cdots \cdot a)}_{(b+c) \text{ factors}} = a^{b+c}$$

It is important to notice that you can use Theorem 5.1 only if the base numbers are the same.
$$7^3 \cdot 7^8 = 7^{3+8} = 7^{11} \text{ but } 6^3 \cdot 7^8 \neq (6 \cdot 7)^{3+8}$$

For Discussion

3. Use Theorem 5.1 to prove that $a^b \cdot a^c \cdot a^d = a^{b+c+d}$.

A second law of exponents follows from Theorem 5.1.

Corollary 5.1.1

If b and c are positive integers such that $b > c$ and $a \neq 0$, then

$$\frac{a^b}{a^c} = a^{b-c}$$

Later in this investigation, you will find a way to remove the restriction $b > c$.

Proof By Theorem 5.1, you have

$$a^c \cdot a^{b-c} = a^{c+(b-c)} = a^b$$

Note that $b - c$ is positive, which allows you to use Theorem 5.1. Since $a^c \neq 0$, you can divide each side by a^c.

$$a^{b-c} = \frac{a^b}{a^c}$$

A third law of exponents applies when you raise an expression with an exponent to another power.

Corollary 5.1.2

For all numbers a and positive integers b and c,

$$\left(a^b\right)^c = a^{bc}$$

Proof Write c factors of a^b and then use Theorem 5.1.

$$\left(a^b\right)^c = \underbrace{\left(a^b\right)\left(a^b\right) \cdot \cdots \cdot \left(a^b\right)}_{c \text{ factors of } a^b}$$
$$= a^{(b+b+\cdots+b)}$$
$$= a^{bc}$$

In the expression $a^{(b+b+\cdots+b)}$, the exponent is the sum of c values of b.

Developing Habits of Mind

Use a different process to get the same result. These three laws come from the properties you learned for multiplication and division. So, if you are unsure about the rules of exponents while doing calculations, you can rewrite the expressions as products of factors. For example, you can rewrite

$$\frac{(b^4)^2}{b^7} \text{ as } \frac{(b \cdot b \cdot b \cdot b) \cdot (b \cdot b \cdot b \cdot b)}{b \cdot b \cdot b \cdot b \cdot b \cdot b \cdot b}$$

Then, you can cancel the factors of b to get the answer: b^1, or just b.

Remember...

The expression $(b^4)^2$ means b^4 times itself. So, $(b^4)^2 = (b^4)(b^4)$.

For now, these rules apply only to positive integer exponents. The rest of this investigation will focus on how to extend the definition of exponents to zero, negative integers, rational numbers, and real numbers. Some of the exercises in this lesson ask you to work with exponents that are not positive integers. Try them and see what happens.

Exercises *Practicing Habits of Mind*

Check Your Understanding

1. Explain why $(ab)^n = a^n b^n$. It may help to make models similar to the ones at the beginning of this lesson.

2. Use a product model to show that $\dfrac{3^{11}}{3^5} = 3^6$.

3. Use a product model to prove Corollaries 5.1.1 and 5.1.2.

4. Decide whether each expression equals 3^{15}. Explain.

   a. $3^{14} + 3^{14} + 3^{14}$ **b.** $(3^6)^9$

   c. $(3^{10})(3^5)$ **d.** $(3^3)(3^5)$

   e. $(3^{15})(3^1)$ **f.** $(3^5)(3^5)(3^5)$

   g. $3^9 + 3^6$ **h.** $(3^5)^3$

   i. $(3^3)^5$ **j.** $9(3^{13})$

   k. $(3^5)^{10}$ **l.** $(3^1)^{15}$

Habits of Mind

Look for a relationship. Your calculator will just slow you down in exercises like this one.

5. Suppose $M = c^4$ and $N = c^3$. Find at least two different ways to write c^{15} in terms of M and N.

6. **Write About It** Describe how you can use the Fundamental Law of Exponents (Theorem 5.1) to expand the product $(x^7 - 3x^2 + 6)(x^5 + 2x^3 + 3)$.

7. Write the following expression as a single power of 3.
$$3 \cdot 3^2 \cdot 3^4 \cdot 3^8 \cdot 3^{16}$$

8. Solve each equation.

   a. $2^x = 8$ **b.** $2^{y-1} = 16$

   c. $2^{5z} = 64$ **d.** $(2^w)(2^w) = 64$

9. Find a function that fits this table.

Input	Output
0	3
1	15
2	75
3	375
4	1875

10. Find the mean and the median of the following list of numbers.

$$5 \cdot 10^4 \qquad 5 \cdot 10^3 \qquad 5 \cdot 10^2 \qquad 5 \cdot 10^1 \qquad 5$$

11. Compute each quotient.

a. $\dfrac{10^9}{10^8}$

b. $\dfrac{3^2 y^8}{(2y)^3}$

c. $\dfrac{6^3 x^9}{3^3 2^2 x^5}$

d. $\dfrac{2^2}{2^5}$

12. Solve each equation for x.

a. $(x - 1)(x + 1) = 15$

b. $(2^x - 1)(2^x + 1) = 15$

On Your Own

13. Simplify each expression.

a. $5^3 \cdot 2^3$

b. $4^6 \cdot 25^6$

c. $9^{10} \cdot \left(\frac{1}{9}\right)^{10}$

d. $20^4 \cdot \left(\frac{1}{10}\right)^4$

e. $20^4 \cdot 5^4$

f. $\left(\frac{4}{3}\right)^4 \cdot \left(\frac{15}{2}\right)^4$

14. Use each method to prove the following statement.

If $n > 1$ is a positive integer and $a \neq 0$, then $\dfrac{a^n}{a} = a^{n-1}$.

a. The Fundamental Law of Exponents (Theorem 5.1)

b. a product model

15. Find a function that fits this table.

Input	Output
0	5
1	15
2	45
3	135
4	405

16. Suppose $A = c^3$ and $B = c^2$. Find two different ways to write c^8 in terms of A and B.

17. The number 2^{10} is close to 1000. Use this fact to estimate the value of 2^{21}.

18. Decide whether each expression equals 2^3. Explain.

a. $\dfrac{2^6}{2^2}$ **b.** $\dfrac{2^6}{2^3}$ **c.** $(2^2)^1$ **d.** $\dfrac{(2^2)^5}{2^7}$

e. $\dfrac{2^9}{2^6}$ **f.** $\dfrac{2^9}{2^3}$ **g.** $\dfrac{2^7 2^8}{2^5}$

19. Use the fact $2^8 = 256$ to find the units digit of each number.

a. 2^9 **b.** 2^{10} **c.** 2^{16} **d.** 2^7

20. Find the units digit of $(2^5)^2 + (5^2)^2$.

21. Decide whether each expression equals 5^6. Explain.

a. $5 \cdot 5 \cdot 5 \cdot 5 \cdot 5 \cdot 5$ **b.** $5^4 5^2$

c. $(5^3)(3^5)$ **d.** $\dfrac{5^{15}}{5^9}$

e. $\dfrac{(5^2)(5^2)(5^3)}{5}$ **f.** $5^5 + 5$

g. $\dfrac{5^{18}}{5^{12}}$ **h.** $(5^2)^3$

i. $(5^6)^1$ **j.** $(5^3)^3$

k. $\dfrac{(5^3)^3}{5^3}$ **l.** $5 + 5 + 5 + 5 + 5 + 5$

22. Write each expression as a single power of x.

a. $(x^2)^6$ **b.** $(x^2)^5$ **c.** $(x^3)^9$ **d.** $(x^{10})^{10}$

e. $\dfrac{x^8}{x^2}$ **f.** $\dfrac{x^9}{x^7}$ **g.** $\dfrac{1}{x^6}(x^{14})$

23. **Standardized Test Prep** Which value of x satisfies the equation $6^{x-1} = \frac{3}{2} \cdot 12^2$?

A. 2 **B.** 3 **C.** 4 **D.** 5

Maintain Your Skills

24. Determine whether each relationship is an identity.

a. $(-x)^1 \overset{?}{=} -x^1$ **b.** $(-x)^2 \overset{?}{=} -x^2$

c. $(-x)^3 \overset{?}{=} -x^3$ **d.** $(-x)^4 \overset{?}{=} -x^4$

e. $(-x)^5 \overset{?}{=} -x^5$ **f.** $(-x)^{13} \overset{?}{=} -x^{13}$

> **Remember...**
> The units digit is the rightmost digit of an integer. For example, the units digit of 256 is 6.

> **Habits of Mind**
> **Look for relationships.**
> Try it without a calculator.

> **Remember...**
> An identity must be true for every possible choice of variable: positive, negative, zero, rational, irrational, etc.

5.03 Zero and Negative Exponents

In the last lesson, you studied the three basic rules for working with exponents.

Laws of Exponents

Let $a \neq 0$ and let b and c be positive integers.

The Fundamental Law of Exponents

- $a^b \cdot a^c = a^{b+c}$

Corollaries

- $\dfrac{a^b}{a^c} = a^{b-c}$, provided $b > c$
- $(a^b)^c = a^{bc}$

These rules apply when b and c are positive integers. However, you can extend the definition to allow for other numbers as exponents. Each equation below uses a law of exponents in a way that was not defined in the last lesson.

$$2^5 \cdot 2^0 = 2^5 \qquad \frac{3^5}{3^7} = 3^{-2} \qquad \left(7^{\frac{1}{3}}\right)^3 = 7^1$$

You must define symbols, such as 2^0, 3^{-2}, and $7^{\frac{1}{3}}$, in a way that is consistent with the rules. In this lesson, you will find that there is only one way to define zero and negative integral exponents that is consistent with these rules.

> You will explore rational exponents, such as $7^{\frac{1}{3}}$, later in this investigation.

For Discussion

1. Tony thinks that he should define 2^0 to equal 0. Use the laws of exponents to explain why this cannot work.

2. Explain why the equation $2^5 \cdot 2^0 = 2^5$ suggests that you should define 2^0 to equal 1.

Minds in Action   episode 18

Tony wants to make up his own definition of negative exponents.

Tony   We're learning the definitions for zero and negative exponents, but why can't I make up my own definition?

Nina   Like what?

Tony   Well, the calculator says 10^{-2} is 0.01, which is $\frac{1}{100}$, but I think that's confusing. I think a negative exponent should give a negative answer, so 10^{-2} should be -100, the opposite of 10^2.

Nina	All right, but it better work.
Tony	What do you mean? I just defined it, so it must work.
Nina	I mean it has to be consistent with other exponents. All right, let's check it. What's 10^{-2} times 10^3?
Tony	I use the Fundamental Law of Exponents for that.

$$10^{-2} \cdot 10^3 = 10^{(-2+3)} = 10^1$$

The answer is 10.

Nina	Wait a second! What number did you define 10^{-2} to be?
Tony	-100.
Nina	I'm going to fill in your number for 10^{-2} and see what happens. If I use your number for 10^{-2}, I get $10^{-2} \cdot 10^3 = (-100) \cdot (1000) = -100{,}000$.

If I use your definition, the product is $-100{,}000$! You said it should be 10.

Tony	It should be 10. That's what the Fundamental Law of Exponents gives. Fine, I guess 10^{-2} can't be -100.

For You to Do

3. Use the example $10^{-2} \cdot 10^3 = 10^1$ to explain why 10^{-2} should equal $\frac{1}{100}$.

The following definitions allow the laws of exponents to work for any integer exponents, positive, negative, or zero.

Definitions

Zero exponent: If $a \neq 0$, then $a^0 = 1$.

Negative exponent: If $a \neq 0$ and m is a positive integer, then $a^{-m} = \frac{1}{a^m}$.

For Discussion

4. Here is a statement that uses both negative and zero exponents. Is it true? Explain.

$$a^b \cdot a^{-b} = a^0$$

With the proper definitions of zero and negative exponents, you can extend the laws of exponents to include all integer exponents.

Laws of Exponents

Let $a \neq 0$ and let b and c be integers.

The Fundamental Law of Exponents

- $a^b \cdot a^c = a^{b+c}$

Corollaries

- $\dfrac{a^b}{a^c} = a^{b-c}$ • $(a^b)^c = a^{bc}$

> Some of the exercises that follow ask you to justify extending the laws in this fashion.

There are still other exponents unaccounted for. Why is $9^{\frac{1}{2}}$ equal to 3, for example? The next two lessons look at how you can make the extension to include these exponents.

Exercises *Practicing Habits of Mind*

Check Your Understanding

1. Decide whether each expression equals 7^{-10}. Explain.

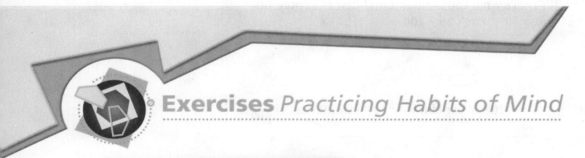

   a. $\left(\frac{1}{7}\right)^{10}$ **b.** $7^{-4} \cdot 7^{-3}$ **c.** $(7^{13})(7^{-6})$ **d.** $\frac{7^3}{7^{13}}$

   e. $\frac{7^2}{7^3 7^4 7^4}$ **f.** $\left(\frac{1}{7^{-10}}\right)$ **g.** $7^5 \cdot 7^{-2}$ **h.** $\left(\frac{1}{7^2}\right)^5$

   i. $(7^5)^{-15}$ **j.** $(7^5)^{-2}$ **k.** $(7^{-2})^5$ **l.** $\left(\frac{1}{7^{10}}\right)$

2. Use the definition of a negative exponent to show that $10^{-2} \cdot 10^3 = 10^1$.

3. **Write About It** Show that each of the three laws of exponents continues to work when one of the exponents is zero.

4. Suppose a is a number that satisfies the equation $3^a = 2$. Use the laws of exponents to simplify each expression.

   a. 3^{a+1} **b.** 3^{a-1} **c.** 3^{2a} **d.** 3^{3a} **e.** 3^{0a}

   f. **Take It Further** $3^{\frac{a}{2}}$

5. Find the units digit of $13^9 10^3 + (117 + 921)^0$.

6. The table below gives the minimum distance from the Earth to some astronomical objects.

Object	Distance From Earth (miles)
Moon	2.25×10^5
Mars	3.46×10^7
Pluto	2.66×10^9

A garden snail can move at the rate of 3×10^{-2} miles per hour. If a garden snail could fly through space at that rate, how many hours would it take to reach the Moon? To reach Mars? To reach Pluto?

7. Find the missing terms in each geometric sequence.

   a. 16, 8, 4, ■, ■, ■, . . .
           b. 2, ■, 18, ■, ■, ■, . . .

   c. 1, a, a^2, ■, ■, ■, . . .
           d. b^6, b^3, 1, ■, ■, ■, . . .

   e. c^{10}, ■, ■, c^4, ■, ■, . . .

8. Here is a table for a function $h(x)$.

   a. Find a rule $h(x)$ in the form $h(x) = c \cdot a^x$ that matches the table.

   b. Copy and complete the table using this rule.

x	$h(x)$
-3	■
-2	■
-1	■
0	2
1	10
2	50
3	250
4	1250

9. Explain why $(2^3)(2^{-3}) = 1$.

On Your Own

10. Find each variable.

   a. $2^5 \cdot 2^{-3} = 2^a$
     b. $2^5 \cdot 2^{-7} = 2^b$
     c. $\frac{2^5}{2^7} = 2^c$

   d. $\frac{2^5}{2^{-7}} = 2^d$
     e. $\frac{2^5}{2^f} = 2^8$

11. Decide whether each expression is equal to 5^3. Explain.

   a. $\left(\frac{1}{5}\right)^{-3}$
     b. $5^{-3} \cdot 5^3$
     c. $\left(5^8\right)\left(5^{-2}\right)$

   d. $\frac{5^6}{5^9}$
     e. $\frac{5^{10}}{5^2 5^3 5^2}$
     f. $\left(\frac{1}{5^3}\right)$

   g. $5^5 \cdot 5^{-2}$
     h. $\left(\frac{1}{5^3}\right)^{-1}$
     i. $\left(5^{15}\right)^{\frac{1}{5}}$

   j. $\left(5^2\right)^1$
     k. $\left(5^4\right)^{-1}$
     l. $\left(\frac{1}{5^{-3}}\right)$

Go Online
Pearsonsuccessnet.com

12. **Write About It** This lesson lists the laws of exponents twice, at the beginning and at the end of the lesson. Describe the differences between the first list and the second list.

13. Find the normal form of this polynomial.

$$(4x + 5y - 6z)^0 + (3xy^2 - 5z)^1$$

14. Expand each expression.

   a. $(3^x + 3^{-x})^2$ **b.** $(3^x - 3^{-x})^2$ **c.** $(3^x + 3^{-x})^2 - (3^x - 3^{-x})^2$

15. Write each expression as a single power of z.

   a. $(z^{-2})(z^4)$ **b.** $((z^3)^3)^{-3}$ **c.** $\dfrac{(z^2)(z^{-4})}{z^2}$

   d. $\dfrac{(z^0)^4}{z^{10}}$ **e.** $\dfrac{(z^7)^0}{(z^0)(z^{11})}$

16. Suppose $f(x) = 3^x$ and $g(x) = x^2$. Find each value.

   a. $(g \circ f)(1)$ **b.** $(g \circ f)(-1)$ **c.** $(g \circ f)(2)$

   d. $(g \circ f)(x)$ **e.** $(f \circ g)(1)$ **f.** $(f \circ g)(-1)$

   g. $(f \circ g)(2)$ **h.** $(f \circ g)(x)$

17. Copy and complete this table for $f(x) = 2^x$.

Input	Output
-3	▦
-2	▦
-1	▦
0	▦
1	▦
2	4
3	▦

18. Copy and complete this table for $g(x) = \left(\frac{1}{2}\right)^x$.

Input	Output
-3	▦
-2	4
-1	▦
0	▦
1	▦
2	▦
3	▦

19. Describe a relationship between the two tables in Exercises 17 and 18. Explain why the relationship holds.

20. Copy and complete this table for
$$w(x) = \left(\frac{-1 + i\sqrt{3}}{2}\right)^x.$$

Input	Output
−3	■
−2	■
−1	■
0	■
1	■
2	■
3	1
4	■
5	■

Knowing that $w(3) = 1$ will help.

21. Standardized Test Prep Simplify $\dfrac{5^2 \cdot (5^{-3})^0}{5^{-6}}$.

A. 5^{-4} **B.** 5^5 **C.** 5^6 **D.** 5^8

Maintain Your Skills

22. Find the missing values in each geometric sequence.

   a. 1, ■, ■, 125, . . .   **b.** 1, ■, ■, 27, ■, . . .

   c. 1, ■, 64, . . .   **d.** 1, ■, ■, 64, . . .

   e. 1, ■, ■, ■, ■, ■, 64, . . .

23. Solve each equation.

   a. $x^3 = 125$ **b.** $x^3 = 27$

   c. $x^2 = 64$ **d.** $x^3 = 64$

   e. $x^6 = 64$

24. Calculate each sum. Express each result as a mixed number, such as $1\frac{2}{3}$.

   a. 2^0

   b. $2^0 + 2^{-1}$

   c. $2^0 + 2^{-1} + 2^{-2}$

   d. $2^0 + 2^{-1} + 2^{-2} + 2^{-3}$

   e. $2^0 + 2^{-1} + 2^{-2} + 2^{-3} + 2^{-4}$

   f. What is the sum if this pattern continues forever? Explain.

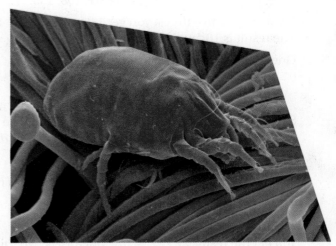

A dust mite is about 4.5×10^{-2} cm long.

Sequences and Operations

So far, the laws and definitions about exponents apply only to integer exponents—expressions like 5^{-2} or $(-3)^0$. An expression like $8^{\frac{2}{3}}$ is still undefined. This lesson seeks to build a conceptual understanding of how you can define expressions like $8^{\frac{2}{3}}$. One way to approach this is to look at the connections between repeated addition and repeated multiplication.

$$3 + 3 + 3 + 3 + 3 = 3 \cdot 5 \qquad 3 \cdot 3 \cdot 3 \cdot 3 \cdot 3 = 3^5$$

You can apply these types of calculations to fractions.

Repeated Addition

If you start with a number and keep adding the same quantity, you get a sequence with constant differences. Such a sequence is an arithmetic sequence.

Definition

A list of numbers is an **arithmetic sequence** if the difference d between any two consecutive terms is constant.

You can use an arithmetic sequence to list the integer multiples of any number by starting with 0 and repeatedly adding that number. Here are the multiples of 27.

$$0, 27, 54, 81, 108, 135, \ldots$$

If you add 27 five times, you get 135, so $27 \cdot 5 = 135$. But what is $27 \cdot \frac{2}{3}$? The result is 18, but how can you add something $\frac{2}{3}$ of one time?

One way is to insert extra terms in the arithmetic sequence between 0 and 27.

$$0, \blacksquare, \blacksquare, 27, \blacksquare, \blacksquare, 54, \blacksquare, \ldots$$

Since it remains an arithmetic sequence, you can replace the first blank with d. Then you can find the others in terms of d.

$$0, d, 2d, 3d, 4d, 5d, 6d, 7d, \ldots$$

Find d by setting up the equation $3d = 27$. So, d must be 9. Then you know that the sequence is

$$0, 9, 18, 27, 36, 45, 54, 63, \ldots$$

You get the result $27 \cdot \frac{2}{3} = 18$, since 18 is two thirds of the way from 0 to 27 in an arithmetic sequence.

The following lists are examples of arithmetic sequences.

$$1, 4, 7, 10, \ldots$$
$$5, 1, -3, -7, \ldots$$
$$3, 3 + 2i, 3 + 4i, \ldots$$
$$a, a + d, a + 2d, a + 3d, \ldots$$

Chapter 7 will deal with these sequences in depth.

Start with 0, the identity for addition.

For You to Do

1. Build an arithmetic sequence that shows that $16 \cdot \frac{3}{4} = 12$.

Repeated Multiplication

When you start with a number and keep multiplying by the same quantity, you get a sequence with constant ratios. This sequence is a *geometric sequence*.

Definition

A list of numbers is a **geometric sequence** if the ratio r between any two consecutive terms is constant.

> The following lists are examples of geometric sequences.
>
> 1, 4, 16, 64, . . .
>
> 2, 1, $\frac{1}{2}$, $\frac{1}{4}$, . . .
>
> -3, -6, -12, . . .
>
> a, ar, ar^2, ar^3, . . .

You can use a geometric sequence to list the integer powers of any number by starting with 1 and repeatedly multiplying by that number. Here are the powers of 27.

$$1;\ 27;\ 729;\ 19{,}683;\ 531{,}441;\ \ldots$$

If you multiply 1 by 27 four times, or multiply 4 factors of 27, you get 531,441. So, $27^4 = 531{,}441$. But what is $27^{\frac{2}{3}}$? How can you multiply 1 by something $\frac{2}{3}$ of one time?

One way is to insert extra terms in the geometric sequence between 1 and 27.

$$1,\ \blacksquare,\ \blacksquare,\ 27,\ \blacksquare,\ \blacksquare,\ 729,\ \blacksquare,\ \ldots$$

Assume it remains a geometric sequence. If you replace the first blank with r, you can find the other numbers in the sequence in terms of r.

$$1,\ r,\ r^2,\ r^3,\ r^4,\ r^5,\ r^6,\ r^7,\ \ldots$$

Find r by setting up the equation $r^3 = 27$. So, one possible value of r is 3. Then the sequence is

$$1,\ 3,\ 9,\ 27,\ 81,\ 243,\ 729,\ 2187,\ \ldots$$

Look at the sequence. The number 9 is two thirds of the way from 1 to 27. Then it makes sense to say that $27^{\frac{2}{3}} = 9$.

For You to Do

2. What is $27^{\frac{1}{3}}$? $27^{\frac{4}{3}}$? $27^{\frac{3}{3}}$?

3. Build a geometric sequence that shows that $16^{\frac{3}{4}} = 8$.

For Discussion

4. For $r^3 = 27$, the text says "one possible value of r is 3." Are there other possible values of r? Why does it make sense to pick $r = 3$ instead of the others?

The concept set forth here is an informal way of working with rational exponents. You will find a more formal definition in the next lesson. For the exercises that follow, use the laws of exponents or a geometric sequence model to work with expressions like $8^{\frac{2}{3}}$.

> **Habits of Mind**
>
> **Check your method.** You need to make sure that this way of thinking about fractional exponents is consistent with the laws of exponents.

Example 1

Problem Between what two integers is $17^{\frac{1}{3}}$?

Solution Build a geometric sequence starting with 1 and with the fourth term equal to 17.

$$1, \blacksquare, \blacksquare, 17, \blacksquare, \blacksquare, 289, \blacksquare, \ldots$$

The number for the first blank is $17^{\frac{1}{3}}$, the next is $17^{\frac{2}{3}}$, and so on.

If the ratio from one term to the next is r, the terms are

$$1, r, r^2, r^3, \ldots$$

If you match the two sequences, you can see that r equals $17^{\frac{1}{3}}$.

Since $2^3 = 8$ and $3^3 = 27$, the value of r is between 2 and 3. You can find a more accurate answer by solving $r^3 = 17$. Take the cube root:

$$r = \sqrt[3]{17} \approx 2.5713$$

For You to Do

5. Use the value of $17^{\frac{1}{3}}$ to find $17^{\frac{2}{3}}$ to three decimal places.

6. Between what two integers is $39^{\frac{1}{2}}$?

Example 2

Problem Solve $16^x = 32$ for x.

Solution Note that 16 and 32 are both powers of 2.

$$16^x = 32$$
$$(2^4)^x = 2^5$$
$$2^{4x} = 2^5$$
$$4x = 5$$
$$x = \frac{5}{4}$$

Another method is to write the geometric sequence of powers of 2, starting with $2^0 = 1$.

$$1, 2, 4, 8, 16, 32, 64, 128, \ldots$$

16 is 2^4. Counting by one-fourth powers, $16^{\frac{1}{4}} = 2$ and $16^{\frac{5}{4}} = 32$.

> **Habits of Mind**
>
> **Use a key characteristic.** To deduce $4x = 5$ from $2^{4x} = 2^5$, you can use the fact that the function $f(x) = 2^x$ is one-to-one. You will prove this later.

7. Solve $32^y = 16$ for y.

This lesson gives some ideas about the meaning of symbols like $27^{\frac{1}{3}}$. A big question remains: Does this method of extending the use of exponents still preserve the important laws of exponents? That question, along with the formal definition of rational exponents, is the subject of the next lesson.

Exercises *Practicing Habits of Mind*

Check Your Understanding

1. Find the missing terms in each arithmetic sequence.

a. 0, 3, 6, ▩, ▩, ▩, . . .

b. 0, ▩, ▩, ▩, ▩, 30, . . .

c. 1, ▩, ▩, ▩, 81, ▩, . . .

d. 5, ▩, ▩, −7, ▩, ▩, ▩, . . .

2. Write About It Describe how you can use the arithmetic sequence in Exercise 1b to show that $30 \cdot \frac{3}{5} = 18$.

3. Find the missing terms in each geometric sequence.

a. 2, −6, 18, ▩, ▩, ▩, . . .

b. 1, i, −1, ▩, ▩, ▩, . . .

c. 1, ▩, 5, ▩, ▩, ▩, . . .

d. 1, ▩, ▩, 125, ▩, . . .

e. 1, ▩, ▩, ▩, 9, ▩, ▩, . . .

4. Write About It Describe how you can use the geometric sequence in Exercise 3d to show that $125^{\frac{2}{3}} = 25$.

5. Let a, $b > 0$. For each type of sequence, find an expression in terms of a and b for the missing number in the sequence below.

$$a, \blacksquare, b$$

a. arithmetic sequence

b. geometric sequence

6. a. Copy and complete the following table.

(a, b)	$\frac{a+b}{2}$	$\sqrt{ab}$
(1, 2)	1.5	1.4142
(2, 5)	■	■
(4, 1)	■	■
(3, 3)	■	■
(6, 9)	■	■
(8, 10)	■	■
(7, 7)	■	■

> Approximate the square roots to 4 decimal places.

b. Take It Further Let $a > 0$ and $b > 0$. Which is greater, $\frac{a+b}{2}$ or $\sqrt{ab}$? Explain your reasoning.

7. Here is a geometric sequence with three missing terms.

$$1, \blacksquare, \blacksquare, \blacksquare, 16, \ldots$$

Alan says that there is more than one possible way to fill in the missing terms. Is he right? Find as many ways as you can to fill in the missing terms.

8. Suzanne has another method for calculating expressions like $81^{\frac{3}{4}}$. She says, "The Fundamental Law of Exponents says that I add exponents when I multiply, so I write down as many $81^{\frac{3}{4}}$ terms as I need to get rid of the denominator. The number of terms is always whatever the denominator is. So here it's 4 of them.

$$81^{\frac{3}{4}} \cdot 81^{\frac{3}{4}} \cdot 81^{\frac{3}{4}} \cdot 81^{\frac{3}{4}}$$

"The result is 81^3. So I have to multiply it four times. If we let x denote $81^{\frac{3}{4}}$, then $x^4 = 81^3$.

"Then I find the root on the calculator, if it's too big for me to figure out in my head: $x = \sqrt[4]{81^3} = 27$."

Use Suzanne's method to calculate $64^{\frac{2}{3}}$ and $625^{\frac{1}{4}}$.

9. Find each value to the nearest integer. Do not use a calculator.
   a. $17^{\frac{1}{2}}$ **b.** $25^{\frac{1}{3}}$ **c.** $84^{\frac{1}{4}}$ **d.** $32^{\frac{4}{5}}$

On Your Own

10. Simplify each expression.
   a. $81^{\frac{1}{2}} \cdot 81^{\frac{1}{2}}$ **b.** $\left(27^{\frac{1}{3}}\right)^3$ **c.** $16^{\frac{3}{4}} \cdot 16^{\frac{1}{4}}$ **d.** $\left(9^{\frac{1}{2}}\right)^3$

11. Find each value to the nearest integer. Do not use a calculator.
   a. $27^{\frac{1}{2}}$ **b.** $7^{\frac{1}{3}}$ **c.** $64^{\frac{5}{6}}$ **d.** $117^{\frac{1}{3}}$

12. Sarah invests \$500 in a savings account that grows by 3% per year.

   a. Copy and complete the table. Round to the nearest cent.

   b. Does the balance follow an arithmetic or a geometric sequence? Explain.

Years	Balance (dollars)
0	500.00
1	515.00
2	530.45
3	▩
4	▩
5	▩
6	▩

Go Online
Pearsonsuccessnet.com

13. Suppose $f(x) = x^{\frac{1}{2}}$. Calculate each value.

   a. $f(25)$ **b.** $f(100)$ **c.** $f(49)$ **d.** $f(1)$ **e.** $f(f(256))$

14. a. Based on your work in Exercise 13, write another function rule that could be equivalent to $f(x) = x^{\frac{1}{2}}$.

   b. Take It Further Write a function rule that could be equivalent to $f(f(x))$.

15. Standardized Test Prep What is the next term in the geometric sequence $4, 6, 9, \ldots$?

   A. $\frac{3}{2}$ **B.** 12   **C.** $\frac{27}{2}$ **D.** 15

16. Are there any sequences that are both arithmetic and geometric? Explain.

17. Solve each equation.

   a. $8^x = 4$ **b.** $5^x = 25^{x-3}$ **c.** $3^{2x-1} = 9^{x+1}$

   d. $8^{2x} = 4^{x-1}$ **e.** $8^x = 3^x$

18. Take It Further Find all solutions to each equation.

   a. $4^x + 2^x - 6 = 0$ **b.** $9^x - 12 \cdot 3^x + 27 = 0$

   c. $16^x - 6 \cdot 4^x + 8 = 0$

Maintain Your Skills

19. Simplify each expression.

   a. $\dfrac{8^{\frac{4}{3}}}{8^{\frac{1}{3}}}$ **b.** $\dfrac{27}{27^{\frac{2}{3}}}$ **c.** $\dfrac{125^{\frac{1}{3}}}{125^{\frac{2}{3}}}$ **d.** $\dfrac{49^{\frac{1}{2}}}{49^{\frac{3}{2}}}$ **e.** $\dfrac{17^{\frac{7}{5}}}{17^{\frac{2}{5}}}$

Go Online
Video Tutor
Pearsonsuccessnet.com

20. Find the number of real solutions to each equation.

   a. $x^3 = 8$ **b.** $x^4 = 16$ **c.** $x^3 = 7$

   d. $x^5 = -32$ **e.** $x^4 = -4$ **f.** $x^3 = -27$

21. Given a real number $a \neq 0$ and a positive integer n, how many real solutions does $x^n = a$ have? Explain.

Defining Rational Exponents

The previous lesson introduced a way of thinking about rational exponents. This lesson focuses on rational exponents from an algebraic perspective. It also covers how you should define rational exponents for the laws of exponents to apply. This idea of extension is extremely important in algebra. You will extend the set of possible exponents from integers to rational numbers in a way that ensures the laws of exponents and the related formulas still hold.

Consider the expression $8^{\frac{1}{3}}$. Corollary 5.1.2 says,

$$(a^b)^c = a^{bc}$$

Suppose you apply this rule to $8^{\frac{1}{3}}$. Try cubing it.

$$\left(8^{\frac{1}{3}}\right)^3 = 8^{\left(\frac{1}{3} \cdot 3\right)} = 8^1 = 8$$

So, if $8^{\frac{1}{3}}$ means anything at all, it has to be a number with a cube that is 8. There is only one real number with a cube that is 8. Therefore, it makes sense to define

$$8^{\frac{1}{3}} = 2$$

For You to Do

1. Use Corollary 5.1.2 to determine what $8^{\frac{2}{3}}$ should mean.
2. What should $8^{-\frac{2}{3}}$ mean? Explain.

What is $7^{\frac{1}{3}}$? The same reasoning tells you that it should mean a number with a cube that is 7. The only real number with a cube that is 7 is $\sqrt[3]{7}$, so it makes sense to define

$$7^{\frac{1}{3}} = \sqrt[3]{7}$$

In general, if a is any real number, then $a^{\frac{1}{3}}$ is equal to $\sqrt[3]{a}$.

Minds in Action   episode 19

Tony wonders what to do when there is more than one real-number choice for a root.

Tony   So I realize I should pick the real number when I can. What can I do about $16^{\frac{1}{4}}$? It's a number with fourth power 16. But there's more than one choice.

$$2^4 = 16 \quad (-2)^4 = 16 \quad (2i)^4 = 16 \quad (-2i)^4 = 16$$

There are four numbers with a fourth power of 16. So now I have to pick one. I know I should pick a real number, but then I still have to decide between 2 and −2. I'll just pick 2. It's the positive one. Besides, it's the one I get when I type $16^{\frac{1}{4}}$ into a calculator.

Establish a process. Consider the expression $a^{\frac{1}{n}}$. If $a^{\frac{1}{n}}$ equals a number x, then you can use Corollary 5.1.2 to remove the fraction.

$$x = a^{\frac{1}{n}}$$
$$x^n = \left(a^{\frac{1}{n}}\right)^n$$
$$x^n = a$$

The value of x comes from the equation $x^n = a$. This equation has n complex solutions, and either 0, 1, or 2 of these solutions are real numbers.

Tony had to make a choice when there were two real solutions. He picked the one that is commonly used. The choice is arbitrary. It makes just as much sense to let $16^{\frac{1}{4}}$ equal -2. In general, you use the positive solution.

Overall, to find the value of an expression like $a^{\frac{1}{n}}$, look at the real solutions to $x^n = a$.

- If there is one real solution to the equation $x^n = a$, use it. For example, $(-8)^{\frac{1}{3}} = -2$.

- If there are two real solutions to the equation $x^n = a$, use the positive solution. For example, $9^{\frac{1}{2}}$ is 3 and not -3.

- If there are no real solutions to the equation $x^n = a$, then $a^{\frac{1}{n}}$ is left undefined in this course. For example, $(-4)^{\frac{1}{4}}$ is undefined.

> There is more to the story. In later courses, you will learn that you can choose one of the n roots in the complex plane. For example, you can define $(-4)^{\frac{1}{4}}$ to be equal to $1 + i$.

Definitions

Unit fraction exponent: The expression $a^{\frac{1}{n}}$ is defined, when possible, as the real ***n*th root** of a.

$$a^{\frac{1}{n}} = \sqrt[n]{a}$$

If there is no real *n*th root of a, then $a^{\frac{1}{n}}$ is undefined in this course.

Most scientific calculators have a square root key. Some have a cube root key. A few have keys for fourth roots or larger roots. This definition of rational exponents explains why: you can always evaluate $\sqrt[6]{5}$ on a calculator as $5^{\frac{1}{6}}$.

What is $8^{\frac{2}{3}}$? Use the laws of exponents. The rule $a^b \cdot a^c = a^{b+c}$ gives
$$8^{\frac{2}{3}} = 8^{\frac{1}{3}} \cdot 8^{\frac{1}{3}} = \sqrt[3]{8} \cdot \sqrt[3]{8} = \left(\sqrt[3]{8}\right)^2$$

You can also use the rule $\left(a^b\right)^c = a^{bc}$.

$$8^{\frac{2}{3}} = \left(8^{\frac{1}{3}}\right)^2 = \left(\sqrt[3]{8}\right)^2$$

Applying this logic to the general case gives the following definition.

> Calculators may give different answers to some expressions with fractional exponents, depending on what mode they are in. For example, a calculator may say $(-4)^{\frac{1}{2}}$ is an error in normal mode, but is equal to $2i$ when the calculator is in complex mode.

Definition

Rational exponent: For integers p and q with $q > 0$, if $a^{\frac{1}{q}}$ is a real number, then

$$a^{\frac{p}{q}} = \left(a^{\frac{1}{q}}\right)^p = \left(\sqrt[q]{a}\right)^p$$

So, $a^{\frac{1}{2}} = \sqrt{a}$,

$a^{\frac{2}{3}} = \left(a^{\frac{1}{3}}\right)^2 = \left(\sqrt[3]{a}\right)^2$,

and $a^{\frac{3}{3}} = \sqrt[3]{a^3} = a$.

For You to Do

Simplify each expression in two different ways. Evaluate the rational exponents and use the laws of exponents.

3. $27^{\frac{2}{3}} \cdot 27^{\frac{1}{3}}$
4. $\dfrac{64^{\frac{1}{2}}}{64^{\frac{1}{3}}}$
5. $\left(16^{\frac{3}{4}}\right)^2$

The laws of exponents leave little choice for these definitions. If $9^{\frac{1}{2}}$ means anything at all, it must satisfy the equation

$$\left(9^{\frac{1}{2}}\right)^2 = 9$$

The only decision left is whether to let this expression equal 3 or -3. You learned to use the positive value when there is an option.

In the next investigation, you will see a few examples that the rules still do not cover. For example, how should you define $3^{\sqrt{2}}$?

Exercises Practicing Habits of Mind

Check Your Understanding

1. a. Give an approximation for $37^{\frac{1}{2}}$.

b. Give an approximation for $37^{\frac{3}{2}}$.

2. Simplify each expression.

a. $3^{\frac{1}{3}} \cdot 9^{\frac{1}{3}}$ **b.** $64^{\frac{5}{6}}$ **c.** $\left(7^{\frac{1}{3}}\right)^6$ **d.** $81^{\frac{1}{3}} \cdot 81^{\frac{1}{6}}$

3. Suppose two numbers a and b satisfy this relationship.

$$a^{\frac{2}{5}} = b$$

a. Find possible values for a and b, not including $a = b = 1$ or $a = b = 0$.

b. Is the equation $a^2 = b^5$ true for all numbers a and b that satisfy the equation $a^{\frac{2}{5}} = b$? Explain.

4. Use the definition of a rational exponent to prove that $1^{\frac{p}{q}} = 1$ for any integers p and q, with $q > 0$.

5. Take It Further The graph of $f(x) = 1^x$ is a horizontal line. Describe the graph of $g(x) = (-1)^x$.

6. Consider the functions $a(x) = x^2$ and $b(x) = x^{\frac{1}{2}}$.

   a. Calculate $a(b(9))$ and $b(a(7))$.

   b. Are $a(x)$ and $b(x)$ inverse functions? Explain.

7. Prove this statement.

   If $a, b, c, d, \ldots$ is an arithmetic sequence, then $10^a, 10^b, 10^c, 10^d, \ldots$ is a geometric sequence.

On Your Own

8. Write About It Explain why $(-25)^{\frac{1}{2}}$ is undefined in this course.

9. Simplify each expression.

   a. $7^{\frac{1}{3}} \cdot 7^{-\frac{1}{3}}$ **b.** $27^{-\frac{2}{3}}$

   c. $\left(9^{\frac{2}{3}}\right)^{\frac{3}{4}}$ **d.** $\left(62^{\frac{a}{3}}\right)^{\frac{3}{a}}$

10. Find all four solutions to the equation $x^4 = 81$.

11. a. What number is defined to be $81^{\frac{1}{4}}$?

   b. What is $81^{-\frac{1}{4}}$? Use a law of exponents.

12. Take It Further Suppose a function $E(x)$ is defined for all real numbers x. Let $E(1) = 3$. The function follows the rule below for any numbers a and b.

$$E(a + b) = E(a) \cdot E(b)$$

   a. Show that $E(0) = 1$.

   b. Find $E(4)$.

   c. Show that $E(n) = 3 \cdot E(n - 1)$ for any n.

   d. Write a function rule for $E(x)$.

13. Show that $8^{\frac{1}{6}} = \sqrt{2}$.

14. Here is a geometric sequence.

$$1, \blacksquare, \blacksquare, a^2, \blacksquare, \blacksquare, \blacksquare, \blacksquare, \ldots$$

Write the missing terms as expressions of a.

15. Consider the functions $f(x) = x^3$ and $g(x) = x^{\frac{1}{3}}$.

  a. Copy and complete this table. Round to three decimal places.

x	$f(x) = x^3$	$g(x) = x^{\frac{1}{3}}$
-8	▦	▦
-2	▦	▦
-1	▦	▦
$-\dfrac{1}{2}$	▦	▦
$-\dfrac{1}{8}$	▦	▦
0	▦	▦
$\dfrac{1}{8}$	▦	▦
$\dfrac{1}{2}$	▦	▦
1	▦	▦
2	▦	▦
8	▦	▦

  b. Using the table, sketch the graphs of $f(x) = x^3$ and $g(x) = x^{\frac{1}{3}}$ on the same axes.

> Use the same scale on both axes.

  c. How are the two graphs related to each other?

  d. How many solutions are there to the equation $f(x) = g(x)$?

16. Standardized Test Prep Which expression is equal to $x^{\frac{2}{3}}$?

  A. $\frac{2}{3}x^{-1}$ **B.** $\dfrac{1}{x^{\frac{1}{3}}}$ **C.** $\sqrt{x^3}$ **D.** $\sqrt[3]{x^2}$

Maintain Your Skills

For Exercises 17 and 18, use a calculator to find each solution. Round to three decimal places.

17. a. $10^a = 2$ **b.** $10^b = 4$ **c.** $10^c = 8$ **d.** $10^d = 16$

18. a. $10^a = 2$ **b.** $10^b = 3$ **c.** $10^c = 6$ **d.** $10^d = 12$ **e.** $10^f = 36$

In this investigation, you evaluated and simplified exponents. You developed the laws of exponents by extending exponents from positive integers to include zero, negative, and rational numbers. You also used sequences to explore exponents. These exercises will help you summarize what you have learned.

1. Use a product model to show why $\dfrac{b^6}{b^2} = b^{6-2}$.

2. Simplify each expression given $p, q, r, s, t, u \neq 0$.

   a. $p^6 \cdot p^{-6}$ b. $q^8 \cdot q^{\frac{1}{8}}$ c. $\left(r^2\right)^{-2}$

   d. $\left(s^4\right)^{\frac{1}{4}}$ e. $\dfrac{t^5}{t^{-2}}$ f. $\dfrac{u^6}{u^{\frac{1}{3}}}$

3. Suppose m is a number that satisfies the equation $2^m = 3$. Use the laws of exponents to find each value.

   a. 2^{m+1} b. 2^{3m}

   c. 2^{m-1} d. $\left(2^2\right)^m$

4. a. Build a geometric sequence that shows that $64^{\frac{2}{3}} = 16$. Show at least six terms of the sequence.

   b. What is the ratio between successive terms in your sequence? Why did you choose that ratio?

   c. Find $64^{\frac{4}{3}}$. Explain your method.

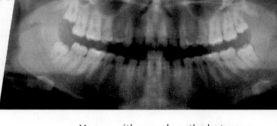

X-rays with wavelengths between 10^{-9} cm and 5×10^{-9} cm are used in dental radiography.

5. Simplify each expression.

   a. $81^{\frac{3}{4}}$ b. $32^{\frac{4}{5}}$

   c. $\left(11^4\right)^{\frac{1}{2}}$ d. $\left(\sqrt[3]{64}\right)^2$

6. What is the Fundamental Law of Exponents? What are some of its corollaries?

7. How do you extend the laws of exponents to define zero, negative, and rational exponents?

8. Simplify the expressions 4^0, 7^{-2}, and $5^{\frac{2}{3}}$.

Vocabulary and Notation

In this investigation, you learned these terms and symbols. Make sure you understand what each one means and how to use it.

- arithmetic sequence
- geometric sequence
- negative exponent, a^{-m}
- nth root, $\sqrt[n]{r}$

- rational exponent, $a^{\frac{p}{q}}$
- unit fraction exponent, $a^{\frac{1}{n}}$
- zero exponent, a^0

Exponential Functions

In *Exponential Functions*, you will use the laws of exponents to explore exponential functions. You will sketch the graphs of exponential functions and write exponential function rules from tables and points on graphs. You will also explore the properties of the inverse of the function $y = b^x$.

By the end of this investigation, you will be able to answer questions like these.

1. For $f(x) = b^x$, why is it true that $f(m) \cdot f(n) = f(m + n)$?

2. Why must an exponential function have an inverse function?

3. If you invest $1000 in an account at 6% interest, compounded annually, how much money will you have after 30 years?

You will learn how to

• graph an exponential function and determine the equation of an exponential function given two points on its graph

• identify an exponential function from the table it generates and use the table to create a closed-form or recursive definition of the function

• evaluate the inverse of the function $y = b^x$ either exactly or by approximation

You will develop these habits and skills:

• Reason by continuity to extend the definition of exponent to include all real numbers.

• Visualize exponential growth by examining graphs and tables of exponential functions.

• Draw logical conclusions from the laws of exponents and properties of exponential functions to solve problems and prove conjectures.

Archaeologists use exponential functions that model radioactive decay to determine the age of objects.

A difference table can help you find a function rule that fits a table. For some tables, a ratio table will help you find a rule that fits the table.

For You to Explore

For each function in Problems 1–5, make a difference table. Show the outputs for the inputs 0 through 5 and the differences between terms.

1. $a(x) = 3x + 1$

2. $b(x) = x^2 - x + 1$

3. $c(x) = 3^x$

4. $d(x) = 3 \cdot 5^x$

5. $f(x) = \left(\frac{1}{2}\right)^x$

6. Find a function $g(x)$ for which the difference column is equal to the output column.

Input	Output	Δ
0	▪	▪
1	▪	▪
2	▪	▪
3	▪	▪
4	▪	▪
5	▪	

Note that $d(x)$ is not equal to 15^x, since only the 5 is raised to the xth power.

Instead of calculating the difference between one term and the next, it sometimes makes sense to calculate the ratio of one term to the next.

7. **a.** Copy and complete this ratio table for $a(x) = 3x + 1$. Round to the nearest hundredth.

   b. What happens to the numbers in the ratio column if you continue the table for larger inputs? Explain.

Input	Output	÷
0	1	4
1	4	▪
2	7	▪
3	10	1.3
4	13	▪
5	16	

8. For each function from Problems 2–5, build a ratio table with the inputs from 0 to 5.

9. **Write About It** Suppose you have an input-output function table with integer inputs from 0 to 5.

   a. Describe how to find a rule that fits the table if the table has constant differences.

   b. Describe how to find a rule that fits the table if the table has constant ratios.

10. **Take It Further** Find a function $h(x)$ for which the ratio column is equal to the output column.

Exercises *Practicing Habits of Mind*

On Your Own

11. Solve each equation any way you choose. Then, decide which equation was the most difficult for you to solve. Explain.

   a. $5 = x^2$ **b.** $5 = 2^x$

   c. $x = 5^2$ **d.** $8 = 2^x$

12. Sketch the graph of $c(x) = 3^x$.

> You will need more input-output pairs than the ones you found in Problem 3.

The expression $3^{\sqrt{2}}$ is undefined so far, since you cannot write $\sqrt{2}$ as a rational number.

13. Use your graph of $c(x) = 3^x$ to explain why $3^{\sqrt{2}}$ should be between 3 and 9.

14. **Write About It** Describe how you can make a more accurate estimate of $3^{\sqrt{2}}$.

15. Copy and complete the table of values for each exponential function.

   a. $f(a) = 3 \cdot 2^a$

Input, a	Output, f(a)
−2	
−1	
0	
1	
2	

   b. $g(a) = 30 \cdot 2^a$

Input, a	Output, g(a)
−2	
−1	
0	
1	
2	

   c. $h(a) = \frac{1}{5} \cdot 5^a$

Input, a	Output, h(a)
0	
1	
2	
3	
4	

   d. $j(a) = 27 \cdot \left(\frac{1}{3}\right)^a$

Input, a	Output, j(a)
−1	
0	
1	
2	
3	

16. Find an exponential function that agrees with each table.

a.

Input, a	Output, $k(a)$
0	4
1	12
2	36
3	108
4	324

b.

Input, h	Output, $L(h)$
0	100
1	50
2	25
3	12.5
4	6.25

> An *exponential function* is a function that you can write in the form $f(x) = a \cdot b^x$.

c.

Input, x	Output, $p(x)$
0	2
1	$\frac{1}{2}$
2	$\frac{1}{8}$
3	$\frac{1}{32}$
4	$\frac{1}{128}$

d.

Input, n	Output, $Q(n)$
0	8
1	12
2	18
3	27
4	40.5

17. Copy and complete this input-output table for $f(x) = 2^x$. Round to three decimal places.

x	$f(x) = 2^x$
0	1
1	▣
1.4	▣
1.41	▣
1.414	▣
1.4142	▣
1.41421	▣
1.414213	▣

18. a. Explain why there are no integers a and b other than $a = b = 0$ that satisfy the equation $2^a = 5^b$.

b. Determine whether there are integers c and d other than $c = d = 0$ that satisfy the equation $4^c = 8^d$. If so, what are c and d?

Maintain Your Skills

19. Consider the function $f(x) = 2^x$. State whether you believe each value is a rational number. Find each rational value exactly, without using a calculator.

a. $f(0)$　　　　**b.** $f\left(\frac{1}{2}\right)$　　　　**c.** $f(\pi)$　　　　**d.** $f(f(2))$

e. all values of a such that $f(a) = \frac{1}{8}$

f. all values of a such that $f(a) = 7$

g. all values of a such that $f(a) = -1$

5.07 Graphs of Exponential Functions

Several of the functions in the Getting Started lesson of this investigation are *exponential functions*.

Definitions

An **exponential function** is a function *f* that you can write in the form $f(x) = a \cdot b^x$, where $a \neq 0$, $b > 0$, and $b \neq 1$. The number *b* is the **base**.

> The function $d(x) = 3 \cdot 5^x$ is exponential. What is its domain?

For Discussion

1. What happens if $a = 0$? What happens if $b = 1$?

Here are the graphs of $f(x) = 2^x$ and $g(x) = 5^x$.

Both graphs have their *y*-intercept at (0, 1). Both graphs pass through Quadrants I and II. Both functions are increasing. The greater *x* is, the greater the corresponding *y* is.

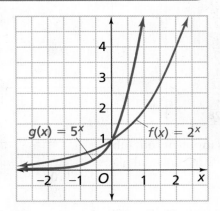

> **Habits of Mind**
>
> **Establish a process.**
> How can you decide whether the point $(-3.5, 0.1)$ is on the graph of $f(x)$?

For You to Do

2. According to the graphs, for what values of *x* is $2^x > 5^x$?

Here are the graphs of $h(x) = \left(\frac{1}{2}\right)^x$ and $j(x) = \left(\frac{1}{5}\right)^x$.

Both graphs have their *y*-intercept at (0, 1). Both graphs pass through Quadrants I and II. Both functions are decreasing. The greater *x* is, the less the corresponding *y* is.

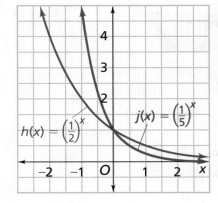

> **Habits of Mind**
>
> **Establish a process.**
> How can you decide whether the point (3.5, 0.1) is on the graph of $h(x)$?

3. Graph $f(x) = 2^x$ and $k(x) = 3 \cdot 2^x$. How are the graphs related?

4. Graph $k(x) = 3 \cdot 2^x$ and $m(x) = -3 \cdot 2^x$. How are the graphs related?

5. Graph $f(x) = 2^x$ and $h(x) = \left(\frac{1}{2}\right)^x$. How are the graphs related?

Monotonic Functions

As you have seen, the graph of $f(x) = 2^x$ seems to indicate that this function is **strictly increasing.** In other words, if $s > t$, then $f(s) > f(t)$. You will now verify this observation.

Lemma 5.1

Let $b > 1$ and let x be a positive rational number. Then $b^x > 1$.

Proof Since x is positive and rational, you can write $x = \frac{p}{q}$ for some positive integers p and q. First, use the following fact about power functions.

Let $g(x) = x^n$, where n is a positive integer. Then $g(x)$ is strictly increasing on nonnegative inputs. In other words, if s and t are nonnegative, then $s^n > t^n$ if and only if $s > t$.

Now, let $s = b^{\frac{1}{q}}$, $t = 1$, and $n = q$. By the above fact,

$$\left(b^{\frac{1}{q}}\right)^q > 1^q \iff b^{\frac{1}{q}} > 1$$

But $\left(b^{\frac{1}{q}}\right)^q = b$, so

$$b > 1 \iff b^{\frac{1}{q}} > 1$$

Since $b > 1$ is given, then $b^{\frac{1}{q}} > 1$.

Now use the above fact again, with $n = p$.

$$\left(b^{\frac{1}{q}}\right)^p > 1^p \iff (b)^{\frac{1}{q}} > 1$$

Therefore $b^{\frac{p}{q}} > 1$ for any positive integers p and q.

So $b^x > 1$, as desired.

> **Remember...**
>
> A function of the form $y = x^n$ is a polynomial function and not an exponential function.

Theorem 5.2

If $b > 1$, then the function $f(x) = b^x$ is strictly increasing on rational-number inputs. In other words, if s and t are rational numbers such that $s > t$, then $f(s) > f(t)$.

Proof Suppose s and t are rational numbers such that $s > t$. Then $s - t > 0$, so Lemma 5.4 gives

$$b^{s-t} > 1$$

You know b^t is positive. You can multiply each side of the inequality by b^t.

$$b^{s-t} \cdot b^t > 1 \cdot b^t$$

$$b^{s-t+t} > b^t \quad \text{using Theorem 5.1}$$

$$b^s > b^t$$

$$f(s) > f(t)$$

This is the desired result.

Similarly, you have observed from its graph that the function $h(x) = \left(\frac{1}{2}\right)^x$ is **strictly decreasing.** In general, if $0 < b < 1$, the function $g(x) = b^x$ is strictly decreasing on rational number inputs. See Exercise 4 for the proof.

Domain and Range

You can draw the graph of $f(x) = 2^x$ without any gaps. This suggests that its domain should be the set of all real numbers, $\mathbb{R}$, but the work in Investigation 5A only defines exponents for integers and rational numbers. The real numbers include irrational numbers such as $\sqrt{2}$ and π. How should you define $2^{\sqrt{2}}$?

You want to define $2^{\sqrt{2}}$ in such a way that the function $f(x) = 2^x$ is increasing on all real-number inputs. For example, since

$$1 < \sqrt{2} < 2$$

you must have

$$2^1 < 2^{\sqrt{2}} < 2^2$$

Thus, you must define $2^{\sqrt{2}}$ to be a number between 2 and 4. In fact, the graph suggests $2^{\sqrt{2}}$ should be between 2 and 3.

The key to defining irrational exponents is that, even though $\sqrt{2}$ is irrational, you can pick rational numbers that are as close to $\sqrt{2}$ as desired. As the rational numbers on either side get closer to $\sqrt{2}$, the outputs of $f(x) = 2^x$ get closer to a specific real number. You use this number for $2^{\sqrt{2}}$.

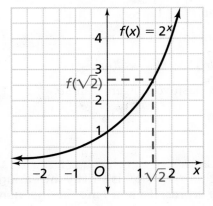

Habits of Mind

Extend what you know. This type of reasoning is *extension by continuity*. You can often use it to take things that work for integers or rational numbers and apply them to real numbers.

Establish a process. Evaluate $2^{\sqrt{2}}$ by approximating it with nearby rational exponents. Terminating decimals work well, since they are all rational numbers. Since $\sqrt{2} \approx 1.41421356$, you can get a good estimate for $2^{\sqrt{2}}$ by finding $2^{1.41}$ and $2^{1.42}$.

$$2^{1.41} < 2^{\sqrt{2}} < 2^{1.42}$$

You can do even better using better approximations.

$$2^{1.414} < 2^{\sqrt{2}} < 2^{2.415}$$

This table shows how you can approximate $2^{\sqrt{2}}$ by using decimals close to $\sqrt{2}$ as inputs to the function $f(x) = 2^x$, with outputs rounded to five decimal places.

Input, x	Output, $f(x) = 2^x$
1.41	2.65737
1.414	2.66475
1.4142	2.66512
1.41421	2.66514
1.414213	2.66514
1.4142135	2.66514

The value of $2^{\sqrt{2}}$ to five decimal places is 2.66514. As the inputs get closer to $\sqrt{2}$, the outputs get closer to a number, and you take that number as the value of $2^{\sqrt{2}}$. It is possible to approximate any irrational number with rational numbers. Therefore, it is possible to define $f(x) = 2^x$ for any real number x. So, the domain of f is the set of all real numbers.

This limiting process only works for positive bases. Therefore, you cannot define expressions like $(-2)^{\sqrt{2}}$ in a reasonable way.

Habits of Mind

Make strategic choices. In Chapter 7, you will explore further this concept of calculating a result as a limit of other results.

Based on this extension, the domain of an exponential function is the set of all real numbers. The range of $f(x) = b^x$ is restricted to positive numbers as long as $b > 0$ (see Exercise 20). Then the value of a determines whether the range of $f(x) = a \cdot b^x$ is all positive numbers or all negative numbers.

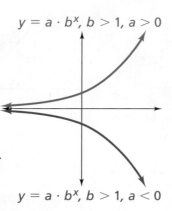

$y = a \cdot b^x, b > 1, a > 0$

$y = a \cdot b^x, b > 1, a < 0$

As the input x becomes more negative, the corresponding output y approaches but never reaches 0. This behavior—approaching but not reaching $f(x) = 0$—is very different from the behavior of any polynomial function.

Summary Properties of Exponential Functions

An exponential function $f : \mathbb{R} \mapsto \mathbb{R}$ is defined as $f(x) = a \cdot b^x$.

- The value of a cannot be zero, and b must be positive and not 1.

- The domain of f is $\mathbb{R}$.

- The range of f is all positive real numbers if $a > 0$, and all negative real numbers if $a < 0$.

- The graph of $y = f(x)$ has one y-intercept at $(0, a)$ and no x-intercepts.

- If $a > 0$, the graph of $y = f(x)$ is strictly increasing when $b > 1$ and strictly decreasing when $0 < b < 1$.

Exercises *Practicing Habits of Mind*

Check Your Understanding

1. Match each graph with its equation.

$$f(x) = 3 \cdot 2^x \qquad f(x) = 3 \cdot \left(\tfrac{1}{2}\right)^x \qquad f(x) = 3 \cdot 5^x \qquad f(x) = -3 \cdot 2^x$$

a.
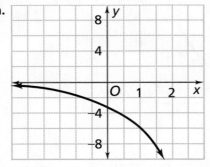

b.
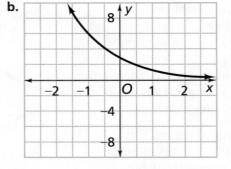

c.
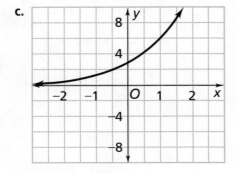

d.
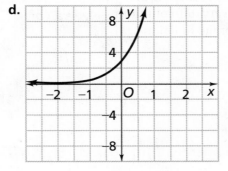

2. **a.** The graph of an exponential function contains the points $(0, 12)$ and $(2, 3)$. Find its equation.

   b. The graph of an exponential function contains the points $(2, 12)$ and $(4, 3)$. Find its equation.

3. **a.** Write the equations for at least two exponential functions with graphs that contain the point $(2, 72)$.

   b. Take It Further Write the general form for any exponential function with a graph that contains the point $(2, 72)$.

4. Prove the following lemma and theorem.

Lemma 5.2

Let $0 < b < 1$ and let x be a positive rational number. Then $b^x < 1$.

Theorem 5.3

Let $0 < b < 1$. Then the function $f(x) = b^x$ is strictly decreasing on rational-number inputs.

5. The graphs of $f(x) = 2^x$ and $g(x) = \left(\frac{1}{2}\right)^x$ are reflections of each other in the y-axis.

   Explain why this reflection property makes sense, using the definition of a negative exponent.

   $$b^{-x} = \frac{1}{b^x}$$

   If $f(x) = 2^x$ is increasing and $g(x) = \left(\frac{1}{2}\right)^x$ is its reflection over the y-axis, what can you say about $g(x)$?

   For Exercises 6 and 7, estimate the solution to each equation.

6. $2^x = 7$

7. $2^x = \frac{1}{7} \cdot 4^x$

8. **a.** Sketch the graph of each function for $-10 \le x \le 10$ and $-10 \le y \le 10$.

   $$f(x) = 5 \cdot (1.07)^x$$
   $$g(x) = (1.12)^x$$

   Do the graphs intersect in this window?

   b. Determine the total number of intersections of the two graphs.

   For advice on how to find an intersection point, see the TI-Nspire™ Handbook, p. 804.

9. In the lesson, you learned that $2^{\sqrt{2}}$ is a number $a \approx 2.66514$.

   a. Calculate $a^{\sqrt{2}}$.

   b. Is there a way to directly calculate $\left(2^{\sqrt{2}}\right)^{\sqrt{2}}$? Explain.

10. Try to use the method in the Developing Habits of Mind section to define $(-2)^{\sqrt{2}}$. What happens?

11. Explain why the y-intercept of the graph of $f(x) = a \cdot b^x$ is $(0, a)$.

12. **Standardized Test Prep** Which of these points is on the graph of $f(x) = -3 \cdot 2^x$?

 A. $(0, 1)$ **B.** $(-1, 6)$

 C. $(-2, -0.75)$ **D.** $(2, 36)$

13. Due to inflation, the cost of a Big Burger grows by 3% every year. This year a Big Burger costs $3.99.

 a. How much will a Big Burger cost next year and the year after that?

 b. How can you find the cost of a Big Burger ten years from now?

 c. Will a Big Burger ever cost more than $20? Explain.

 d. Find a rule for the function $C(n)$, with an output that is the cost of a Big Burger n years from now.

14. **What's Wrong Here?** Cody says, "The graph of $y = 2^x$ can't get to *every* positive number if it doesn't make it to zero. It has to stop somewhere. I'll bet it never gets below one millionth."

 Show that Cody is mistaken by finding a number x such that 2^x is positive but less than $\frac{1}{1,000,000}$.

15. Explain why $3^{\sqrt{6}}$ must be greater than 9 and less than 27.

16. Dorris claims the solution x in Exercise 6 must be an irrational number. She says, "If $2^x = 7$ is solved by a fraction, then it looks like $2^{\frac{p}{q}} = 7$. Then I raise both sides to a power of q.

$$2^{\frac{p}{q}} = 7$$
$$\left(2^{\frac{p}{q}}\right)^q = 7^q$$
$$2^p = 7^q$$

 "And p and q have to be integers. I'm pretty sure that can't happen unless p and q are both zero."

 Is it possible for $2^p = 7^q$ if p and q are nonzero integers? Explain.

17. Dorris's explanation above shows that the solution to $2^x = 7$ must be irrational. How does her argument break down if you try to apply it to the equation $2^x = 8$?

Go ◯**nline**
Pearsonsuccessnet.com

18. a. Copy and complete this table for $f(x) = (-2)^x$.

b. What happens if you try to make a smooth graph for $f(x) = (-2)^x$?

Input	Output
-2	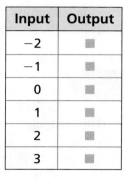
-1	
0	
1	
2	
3	

19. Take It Further The equation

$$a \cdot b^x = c \cdot d^x$$

may have a different number of solutions, depending on the values of a, b, c, and d. Describe the conditions on these parameters that make the equation have each number of solutions.

- exactly one

- none

- more than one

20. a. If $b > 0$ and x is an integer, explain why b^x must be positive.

b. If $b > 0$ and x is rational, use the definition of rational exponent to explain why b^x must be positive.

Maintain Your Skills

21. Simplify each expression.

a. $\left(3^{\sqrt{2}}\right)^{\sqrt{2}}$ **b.** $\left(3^{\sqrt{2}}\right)^2$ **c.** $\left(3^{-\sqrt{2}}\right)^{-1}$

d. $\left(3^{\sqrt{8}}\right)^{\sqrt{2}}$ **e.** $3^{\sqrt{2}} \cdot 3^{-\sqrt{2}}$ **f.** $\left(3^{-\sqrt{2}}\right)^{-\sqrt{2}}$

g. $3^{\sqrt{2}} \cdot 5^{\sqrt{2}}$ **h.** $\left(3^{\sqrt[3]{2}}\right)^{\sqrt[3]{2}}$ **i.** $\left(3^{\sqrt[3]{2}}\right)^{\sqrt[3]{4}}$

> Decide for yourself what *simplify* means, but your answer cannot be identical to the given expression.

22. Graph each function on the same set of axes. Let $-10 \leq x \leq 10$ and let $0 \leq y \leq 10$.

- $a(x) = 3^x$

- $b(x) = 3 \cdot 3^x$

- $c(x) = 9 \cdot 3^x$

- $d(x) = 27 \cdot 3^x$

- $f(x) = 81 \cdot 3^x$

How are these graphs related?

The logarithmic spiral is the graph of $r = ae^{b\theta}$ in polar coordinates. The arrangement of seeds in a sunflower approximates the logarithmic spiral.

5.08 Tables of Exponential Functions

This lesson focuses on exponential functions from a tabular perspective. It also focuses on how recursive rules can generate exponential functions.

In-Class Experiment

Consider this function defined on nonnegative integers.

$$B(n) = \begin{cases} 500 & \text{if } n = 0 \\ 1.06 \cdot B(n-1) & \text{if } n > 0 \end{cases}$$

1. Use the definition to calculate $B(10)$. Then figure out a more direct way to get $B(10)$.

2. Calculate $B(50)$.

3. Find the smallest integer n such that $B(n) > 4000$.

> This recursive function can be modeled. See the TI-Nspire Handbook, p. 804.

The exponential function $L(h) = 100 \cdot \left(\frac{1}{2}\right)^h$ is decreasing. If $h = 0$, $L = 100$.

> If the base b is between 0 and 1, it is an **exponential decay** function. If the base is greater than 1, it is an **exponential growth** function.

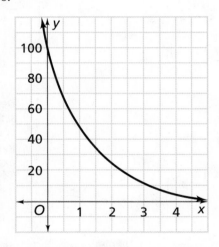

Here is a table for $L(h)$ for integer values of h from 0 to 4.

h	L(h)
0	100
1	50
2	25
3	12.5
4	6.25

Tony thinks he can start with the table and find an exponential function rule.

Tony If you just gave me that table, I could find an exponential function that matches it. There's an exponential that matches the table, since it has a constant ratio between any pair of successive terms. Here's a ratio table.

h	L(h)	÷
0	100	$\frac{1}{2}$
1	50	$\frac{1}{2}$
2	25	$\frac{1}{2}$
3	12.5	$\frac{1}{2}$
4	6.25	

> You calculate the ÷ column by computing ratios of successive terms.
> $$\frac{50}{100} = \frac{1}{2}$$

And I know $L(0) = 100$, so $L(h)$ is 100 times one half to the h. Now, that's not the only function that matches the table, but it's probably the simplest one. And I can describe $L(h)$ term by term. Start with 100 and divide by 2 each time the input increases by 1.

For You to Do

4. Find a rule that fits this table.

x	f(x)
0	12
1	18
2	27

Make strategic choices. Tony describes $L(h)$ using a recursive rule: Start with $L(0) = 100$ and divide by 2 each time. You can describe any exponential function $f(x) = a \cdot b^x$ in this way. In this case, the value of a is 100 and the base b is $\frac{1}{2}$, since dividing by 2 is the same as multiplying by one half.

Exponential functions arise naturally in situations like the following.

- the number of teams in an elimination tournament (Half of the teams move on to the next round.)

- the growth of money in a bank account (with 6% interest compounded annually)

- the growth of a population over time (The population doubles every 50 years.)

The function L is connected to the concept of a half-life in biology. Specifically, $L(h)$ outputs the percentage remaining of an element after h half-lives.

The recursive definition for $L(h)$ looks like this.

$$L(h) = \begin{cases} 100 & \text{if } h = 0 \\ 0.5 \cdot L(h-1) & \text{if } h > 0 \end{cases}$$

There is an important concern about domain here. The recursive rule for $L(h)$ limits its domain to nonnegative integers, since it fails to give a value for something like $L(1.5)$ or $L(-2)$. In some situations, it may make sense to use only nonnegative integers as inputs. However, remember that there is a difference between this version of $L(h)$ and the closed-form definition $L(h) = 100 \cdot \left(\frac{1}{2}\right)^h$, which has all real numbers as its domain.

> **Habits of Mind**
>
> **Experiment.** Build a model for *L* in your function-modeling language.

If you have a table for an exponential function, but the inputs do not start at 0 or they have gaps, you can still find the function using algebra if you know at least two input-output pairs.

Example

Problem An exponential function P defined as $P(x) = a \cdot b^x$ has this table of inputs and outputs. Find the values of a and b.

x	P(x)
−2	108
−1	36
2	$\frac{4}{3}$

> The outputs are positive and decreasing, so it must be exponential decay. The base b must be between 0 and 1.

Solution

Method 1 When two terms have inputs that differ by 1, you can calculate the base b directly as the ratio between these successive terms.

$$b = \frac{36}{108} = \frac{1}{3}$$

Then $P(x) = a \cdot \left(\frac{1}{3}\right)^x$. You can find a using any of the input-output pairs. Use $(-1, 36)$.

$$
\begin{aligned}
P(x) &= a \cdot \left(\tfrac{1}{3}\right)^x \\
36 &= a \cdot \left(\tfrac{1}{3}\right)^{-1} \\
36 &= a \cdot 3 \\
12 &= a
\end{aligned}
$$

The function is $P(x) = 12 \cdot \left(\frac{1}{3}\right)^x$.

Method 2 Pick any two points and set up the equation $P(x) = a \cdot b^x$ for each. For example, take $(-1, 36)$ and $\left(2, \frac{4}{3}\right)$.

$$
\begin{aligned}
36 &= a \cdot b^{-1} \\
\tfrac{4}{3} &= a \cdot b^2
\end{aligned}
$$

Then divide to build an equation for b.

$$
\begin{aligned}
\frac{36}{\frac{4}{3}} &= \frac{a \cdot b^{-1}}{a \cdot b^2} \\
27 &= b^{-3}
\end{aligned}
$$

Solve for b. If $b^{-3} = 27$, then $b^3 = \frac{1}{27}$ and $b = \frac{1}{3}$. Then find a.

For You to Do

5. Find the exponential function with a graph that contains the points $(1, 36)$ and $(2, 108)$.

Minds in Action   episode 21

Tony has another way to think about finding an exponential function from two points on its graph.

Tony   I guess the example does the same thing, but I like to think of it as how far apart the points are in a geometric sequence. Say the points are $(-3, 10)$ and $(2, 20)$. The x-values have a difference of 5, so it's a geometric sequences with five steps from 10 to 20.

$$10, \blacksquare, \blacksquare, \blacksquare, \blacksquare, 20$$

So whatever the base is, the output doubles from 10 to 20 in five terms. That means the base has to solve the equation $b^5 = 2$. And once you find b, you can use either point to find a.

Exercises Practicing Habits of Mind

1. For each table, find the exponential function that matches the table or explain how you know that an exponential function cannot fit the table.

a.

n	A(n)
0	18
1	6
2	2
3	$\frac{2}{3}$

b.

x	B(x)
0	−2
1	−8
2	−32
3	−128

c.

t	C(t)
0	4
1	6
2	9
3	12

d.

z	D(z)
1	2
2	12
3	72
4	432

2. For each exponential function in Exercise 1, build a recursive model in your function-modeling language.

3. Suppose q is an exponential function with $q(3) = 100$ and $q(5) = 4$. Find $q(x)$.

4. **What's Wrong Here?** George says there are two possible values of the base b for the exponential function in Exercise 3.

   George says, "The function goes from 100 to 4 in two steps, which means dividing by 25. So $b^2 = \frac{1}{25}$. But then there are two possible values of b. It could be either $\frac{1}{5}$ or $\frac{-1}{5}$. Either could be right."

   Do you agree or disagree with George's statement? Explain.

5. Find two functions for which $f(-3) = 10$ and $f(2) = 20$.

> The function $f(x)$ does not need to be an exponential function.

6. T is an exponential function with this table.

    a. If $T(x) = a \cdot b^x$, find a and b.

    b. Copy and complete the table.

x	T(x)	÷
0	100	▦
1	▦	▦
2	▦	▦
3	▦	▦
4	▦	▦
5	300	

7. Suppose a new car that costs $20,000 depreciates in value about 20% each year.

    a. How much will the car be worth after 1 year? After 2 years? After 3 years?

    b. Find a rule for $V(n)$, the value of the car after n years of driving.

    c. Will the car ever be worth less than $1000? Explain.

> Most cars actually depreciate more than 20% the first year.

8. **Take It Further** The graph of an exponential function passes through the points (x_1, y_1) and (x_2, y_2). Find the function in terms of these coordinates.

> **Habits of Mind**
>
> **Generalize.** Exercise 8 is a generalization of the type of problem found in Exercises 3 and 12.

On Your Own

9. **Standardized Test Prep** Suppose f is an exponential function $f(x) = a \cdot b^x$ with $f(0) = 4$ and $f(2) = 25$. What are the values of a and b?

    A. $a = 1, b = 5$ **B.** $a = 1, b = 10$

    C. $a = 4, b = 2.5$ **D.** $a = 4, b = 5$

10. The ratio column of this table is filled in.

n	M(n)	÷
0	16	1.5
1	▦	1.5
2	▦	1.5
3	▦	1.5
4	▦	

Copy and complete the table. Define $M(n)$ with both a closed-form rule and a recursive rule.

11. This table has the first output and the ratio column filled in.

n	F(n)	÷
0	1	1
1	▪	2
2	▪	3
3	▪	4
4	▪	5
5	▪	6
6	▪	

Go Online
Pearsonsuccessnet.com

a. Copy and complete the table.

b. Is F an exponential function? Explain.

c. Describe how to calculate $F(10)$ if the pattern in the ratio column continues.

12. Here are the graphs of three exponential functions. Find a closed-form rule that defines each function.

a.
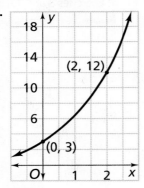

b.
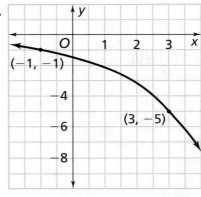

c.
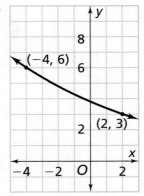

13. Money in a savings account typically grows by about 3% per year. Kara's savings account has $1000 in it.

   a. Find the amount of money in Kara's account after 1 year, 2 years, and 3 years.

   b. Find the amount of money in Kara's account after 20 years.

So, Kara will earn $30 (3% of $1000) interest during the first year. Why will she earn more than $30 interest during the second year?

14. Some credit cards offer 0% interest on their balance for 12 months, as long as you make a required monthly payment of at least 2% of the balance. Suppose you owe $2000 on one of these cards and make only the minimum payment each month.

   a. Find the balance after 1 month, 2 months, and 3 months.

   b. Find a rule for $B(n)$, the balance after n months.

   c. What is the domain of $B(n)$? Explain.

15. Suppose you have the credit card in Exercise 14, but want to be sure to pay off half the total balance by the end of the first year. If you plan to pay the same percentage of the remaining balance each month, about what percent of the balance do you need to pay?

16. **Write About It** Use the two function definitions below.

$$f(x) = 5 \cdot 2^x$$

$$g(x) = \begin{cases} 5 & \text{if } x = 0 \\ 2 \cdot g(x - 1) & \text{if } x > 0 \end{cases}$$

Explain why the graphs of these functions do not look the same.

Maintain Your Skills

17. Suppose $b(x) = 3^x$. Calculate each value.

   a. $b(5)$
   b. $b(3) \cdot b(2)$
   c. $b(1)$
   d. $\dfrac{b(3)}{b(2)}$
   e. $b(6)$
   f. $(b(2))^3$

18. Suppose $f(x) = b^x$ for $b > 0$ with $f(3) = p$ and $f(5) = q$. Find each value in terms of p and q.

   a. $f(0)$
   b. $f(-3)$
   c. $f(8)$
   d. $f(6)$
   e. $f(15)$

Habits of Mind

Look for relationships. How is $f(8)$ related to $f(3)$ and $f(5)$? Use the fact that $f(x) = b^x$.

Properties of Exponential Functions

This lesson explores several properties of exponential functions that are dictated by the laws of exponents.

In-Class Experiment

1. Sketch the graph of $f(x) = 2^x$. Then sketch the graphs of each pair of functions.

- $f(x + 1)$ and $2 \cdot f(x)$
- $f(x - 2)$ and $\dfrac{f(x)}{4}$

2. How are the graphs of each pair related?

You can now apply the laws of exponents to any real-number exponent.

Laws of Exponents

Let base $b > 0$ and let x and y be real numbers.

The Fundamental Law of Exponents

- $b^{x+y} = b^x \cdot b^y$

Corollaries

- $b^{x-y} = \dfrac{b^x}{b^y}$
- $b^{xy} = (b^x)^y$

> See the discussion on how you extend exponents from rational numbers to real numbers in the Developing Habits of Mind section in Lesson 5.07.

The graphs for each pair of functions in the In-Class Experiment were identical. A similar example is the graph of $f(x) = 3^x$. The graphs of $f(x + 1)$ and $3 \cdot f(x)$ are identical.

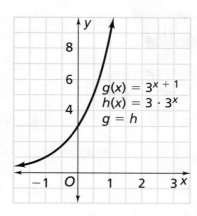

$g(x) = 3^{x+1}$
$h(x) = 3 \cdot 3^x$
$g = h$

This is not a coincidence. It is a consequence of the Fundamental Law of Exponents. If $f(x) = 3^x$, then

$$f(x + 1) = 3^{x+1} = 3^x \cdot 3^1 = 3 \cdot 3^x = 3f(x)$$

You can rewrite the laws of exponents using function notation. It is important to note that none of the results below is new. They are just written using the language of functions.

Laws of Exponents *Function Version*

Let $f(x) = b^x$ with $b > 0$ and domain $\mathbb{R}$.

The Fundamental Law of Exponents

- $f(x + y) = f(x) \cdot f(y)$

Corollaries

- $f(x - y) = \dfrac{f(x)}{f(y)}$
- $f(xy) = (f(x))^y$

The definitions for zero and negative exponents give these equations.

- $f(0) = 1$
- $f(-x) = \dfrac{1}{f(x)}$

> A **functional equation** is an equation that relates some values of a function to other values of the function. For example, $g(n) = g(n - 1) + 3$ is a functional equation for a linear function with a slope of 3. This list of functional equations relates values of the function $f(x) = b^x$.

For Discussion

3. Let $f(x) = b^x$ with $b > 0$. Prove that $f(x + y) = f(x) \cdot f(y)$.

The statement that $f(x + 1) = 3 \cdot f(x)$ for $f(x) = 3^x$ is the Fundamental Law of Exponents, with 1 replacing y.

Example

Problem Let $g(x) = 4^x$. Solve each equation exactly, if possible. Otherwise, round to four decimal places.

   a. $g(a) = 5$ **b.** $g(b) = 8$ **c.** $g(c) = 40$

Solution

a. You cannot find the solution $g(a) = 5$ exactly as an integer or as a fraction. The exact solution to $4^x = 5$ is irrational. Approximate the solution by successive guesses at a. Use the fact that $g(x) = 4^x$ is increasing.

> If the solution is rational, then $4^{\frac{p}{q}} = 5$, and $4^p = 5^q$. This is impossible if p and q are nonzero integers.

Guess, a	$g(a) = 4^a$	The next guess should be . . .
1	4	Higher
1.2	5.2780	Lower
1.15	4.9246	Higher
1.16	4.9933	Higher (close!)

Successive approximations give the value $a \approx 1.1610$ to four decimal places.

b. The solution to $g(b) = 8$ is exactly $\frac{3}{2}$. Both 8 and 4 are powers of 2, so you can solve $4^b = 8$ by rewriting each number as a power of 2.

$$(2^2)^b = 2^3$$

Then $2b = 3$ and $b = \frac{3}{2}$.

c. The solution to $g(c) = 40$ is irrational, since you cannot write 40 as a rational power of 2. Approximate the solution by successive guesses at c.

Guess, c	$g(c) = 4^c$	The next guess should be . . .
2	16	Higher
2.5	32	Higher
2.7	42.2243	Lower
2.65	39.3966	Higher
2.66	39.9466	Higher (close!)

Successive approximations give the value $c \approx 2.6610$ to four decimal places.

You can find the value of c more quickly by using the Fundamental Law of Exponents. It says that the following equation is true for any choices of a and b.

$$g(a + b) = g(a) \cdot g(b)$$

If $g(a) = 5$ and $g(b) = 8$, then $g(a + b) = 40$, which is exactly what you need for this problem. Then $c = a + b \approx 2.6610$ is the solution.

For You to Do

Use the information that $g(1.1610) \approx 5$ and $g(1.5) = 8$ to solve each equation.

4. $g(m) = 25$

5. $g(n) = 1.6$

6. $g(p) = 200$

7. $g(q) = 0.2$

8. $g(r) = 1$

In the next lesson, you will look at another important property of exponential functions: They are one-to-one, and therefore have inverse functions. An inverse function for something like $g(x) = 4^x$ is very useful, since it allows you to solve equations such as $g(x) = 5$ more quickly.

$$g(x) = 5$$
$$g^{-1}(g(x)) = g^{-1}(5)$$
$$x = g^{-1}(5)$$

Exponential functions are one-to-one because they are **monotonic**. This means these functions are either increasing for all inputs or decreasing for all inputs.

For now, that inverse function is unknown, but you will study its properties in the next investigation.

Exercises Practicing Habits of Mind

Check Your Understanding

For Exercises 1–4, use the equation $C = a \cdot b^x$. This equation has four variables. If you know three of them, you can find the fourth.

1. Describe how to find C if you know a, b, and x.
2. Describe how to find a if you know C, b, and x.
3. Describe how to find b if you know C, a, and x.
4. Describe how to find x if you know C, a, and b.
5. Let $f(x) = 2^x$. The solution of $f(a) = 3$ is approximately 1.5850. The solution to $f(b) = 5$ is approximately 2.3219.

   a. You can use the information above and the properties of exponents to find all but one of this table's missing entries. Copy and complete the table, except for that entry. Give all answers to four decimal places.

   b. Find the last missing entry by approximating it to four decimal places.

x	$f(x) = 2^x$
0	1
1	2
1.5850	3
▦	4
2.3219	5
▦	6
▦	7
▦	8
▦	9
▦	10

6. The function versions of the laws of exponents work only for functions in the form $f(x) = b^x$. Other exponential functions have the form $f(x) = a \cdot b^x$. How do the rules change if $f(x) = a \cdot b^x$ instead? For example, is it still true that $f(x + y) = f(x) \cdot f(y)$? If not, what adjustments can you make?

7. Binh tells you that by investing, he expects to have ten times as much money in 30 years as he has now. He expects his investment to grow by about the same percentage every year. He says he can break the 30 years into 15-year halves, where each half has the same proportional growth.

Earnings per Dollar Invested

Years Invested	Earnings	÷
0	$1	k
15	▨	k
30	$10	

a. Find k to three decimal places.

b. Find the exact value of k using a radical or rational exponent.

c. If Binh invests $1500, how much money does he expect to have after 15 years?

8. Binh goes on to explain that he can also break the 30 years of investing into three groups of 10 years each.

Earnings per Dollar Invested

Years Invested	Earnings	÷
0	$1	j
10	▨	j
20	▨	j
30	$10	

Financial analysts use exponential functions to model the growth of investments.

a. Find j to three decimal places.

b. Find the exact value of j using a radical or rational exponent.

c. If Binh invests $1500, how much money does he expect to have after 20 years?

9. **Take It Further** Find all real numbers x and y for which $x^y = 1$.

On Your Own

10. Using $g(x) = 5^x$, solve each equation for x.

   a. $g(x) = 25$ **b.** $g(x) = 5^{-11}$ **c.** $g(x) = 25^3$ **d.** $g(x) = 0$

11. Let $f(x) = 10^x$. Give examples to verify the function version of each law of exponents for this particular function.

Go Online
Pearsonsuccessnet.com

12. Sophie has made a deal with her father. She can deposit any amount of money with him, and he will guarantee her 6% interest per year. She deposits $100. The amount of money she can withdraw from the Bank of Dad after x years is given by the exponential function $f(x) = 100(1.06)^x$.

    a. How long will it take for Sophie's money to double in value?

    b. How long will it take for Sophie's money to triple in value?

    c. How long will it take for Sophie's money to sextuple in value, or in other words, for her original deposit to be worth $600?

13. Sketch the graph of each function.

    - $a(x) = 3^x$
    - $b(x) = 3 \cdot 3^x$
    - $c(x) = 9 \cdot 3^x$
    - $d(x) = 27 \cdot 3^x$
    - $f(x) = 81 \cdot 3^x$

    How are these graphs related? Explain.

See Exercise 22 in Lesson 5.07.

14. The table in Exercise 5 stops when the output is 10. Give three other examples of outputs N for which you can solve $f(x) = N$ by using the solutions to $f(a) = 3$ and $f(b) = 5$.

15. If x is an integer, $f(x) = i^x$ is a function that calculates the powers of the imaginary unit $i = \sqrt{-1}$.

    a. Calculate $f(2)$, $f(3)$, and $f(5)$. Is it true that $f(2) \cdot f(3) = f(5)$?

    b. Do all the laws of exponents work for this function f?

16. Alicia gets her first full-time job with a starting salary of $25,000. She is offered two compensation plans for the future.

    Plan 1: Alicia will earn a raise of $3000 every year.

    Plan 2: Alicia will earn an 8% raise every year.

    Determine how many years it will take for Alicia's salary to reach each amount under the two plans.

    a. at least $30,000

    b. at least $40,000

    c. at least $50,000

    d. at least $100,000

17. **What's Wrong Here?** Stacy says the function versions of the laws of exponents do not always work. "Here's one example. I take an exponential function $f(x) = x^3$. It says $f(x)$ times $f(y)$ equals $f(x + y)$, but that doesn't work. Take $x = 1$ and $y = 2$, for example: $f(x)$ times $f(y)$ is 8, but $f(x + y)$ is 27. I've got plenty of these."

What is wrong with Stacy's reasoning?

18. **Take It Further** Suppose a one-to-one function $L(x)$ has $L(2) = 1$ and follows the rule below for any positive numbers a and b.

$$L(a) + L(b) = L(ab)$$

a. Show that $L(4) = 2$ and $L(1) = 0$.

b. Find x if $L(x) = 6$.

c. Show that if n is an integer, then $L(a^n) = n \cdot L(a)$.

d. Find x if $L(x) = \frac{1}{2}$.

19. **Standardized Test Prep** Suppose a restaurant's sales increase 15% each year for 8 years. Use the approximations $(1.15)^3 \approx 1.521$ and $(1.15)^8 \approx 3.059$. What is the ratio of the restaurant's sales in the sixth year to the restaurant's sales in the first year?

A. 1.538   **B.** 2.011   **C.** 2.136   **D.** 4.580

Maintain Your Skills

20. Solve each equation. Round to three decimal places.

    a. $2^x = 7$ b. $4^x = 7$

    c. $8^x = 7$ d. $16^x = 7$

    e. $1024^x = 7$

Go Online
Video Tutor
Pearsonsuccessnet.com

21. Solve each equation. Round to three decimal places.

    a. $6^x = 35$ b. $35^x = 6$

    c. $3^x = 28$ d. $28^x = 3$

    e. $9^x = 28$ f. $28^x = 9$

Exponential Functions, One-to-One

Consider the equation $8^x = 32$. You can solve this equation by writing 8 and 32 as powers of 2.

$$8^x = 32$$
$$(2^3)^x = 2^5$$
$$2^{3x} = 2^5$$
$$3x = 5$$
$$x = \frac{5}{3}$$

The step that removes the exponent is an interesting one. If $2^x = 2^y$, is it always true that $x = y$? This has been an assumption throughout the chapter. This lesson provides a proof, as well as some initial exploration of the inverse functions of exponential functions.

Recall the definition of *one-to-one* from Chapter 2: A function is one-to-one if there is a unique input that produces a given output. Algebraically, a function f is one-to-one if $f(a) = f(b)$ only when $a = b$.

The graph of a function can suggest whether it is one-to-one. For example, $f(x) = x^3 - 4x$ is not one-to-one. You can see this from its graph.

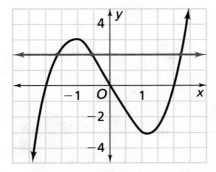

This function cannot be one-to-one since there is more than one input that gives the output $y = 2$. However, the graph of $f(x) = 2^x$ suggests that this function is one-to-one.

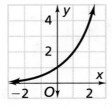

Remember...

Since you use a horizontal line to find such counterexamples, this is the horizontal-line test. A function is not one-to-one if a horizontal line intersects the graph more than once.

You can state the fact that all exponential functions are one-to-one as a theorem.

Theorem 5.4 One-to-One Property for Exponential Functions

If f is an exponential function, then f is one-to-one.

Proof Suppose that $f(a) = f(b)$, where a and b are real numbers. Recall from Lesson 5.07 that an exponential function is either strictly increasing or strictly decreasing. Assume that f is strictly increasing. If $a < b$, you have $f(a) < f(b)$, which contradicts the assumption that $f(a) = f(b)$. You get a similar contradiction if $a > b$. Thus, $a = b$. The proof is almost identical for the case in which f is strictly decreasing.

> You must show that $a = b$.

For Discussion

1. Complete the missing cases in the proof.

The fact that exponential functions are one-to-one provides an algebraic corollary. The algebraic step of "undoing the exponent" is valid as long as the base is positive and not equal to 1.

Corollary 5.4.1

If $b > 0$, $b \neq 1$, and $b^x = b^y$, then $x = y$.

Developing Habits of Mind

Detect the key characteristics. One other important property of a one-to-one function is that it has an inverse function. That means that any exponential function has an inverse function.

So, consider this table for the function $f(x) = 2^x$.

x	f(x)
−1	$\frac{1}{2}$
0	1
1	2
2	4
3	8
4	16

There is another function, which you can call $L_2(x)$, that is the inverse function. So its table would include these input-output pairs.

x	$L_2(x)$
$\frac{1}{2}$	-1
1	0
2	1
4	2
8	3
16	4

The use of the subscript 2 helps remind you that the original function had base 2. So, you could give the inverse function of $f(x) = 10^x$ the name $L_{10}(x)$. You will learn the more standard notation for this function in Investigation 5C.

Note that these are the same pairs listed for $f(x) = 2^x$ with the inputs and outputs switched.

But what can you do for other inputs to $L_2(x)$? For example, what is $L_2(3)$? The value of $L_2(3)$ is the number that solves $2^x = 3$, since 3 would appear as the output in the 2^x table. That value is an irrational number, about 1.5850 (see Exercise 5 in Lesson 5.09). So $L_2(3)$ is about 1.5850, which seems reasonable, given the table. You expect it to be somewhere between 1 and 2.

For You to Do

2. What two integers is $L_2(9)$ between? Find its value to three decimal places.

Any one-to-one function has an inverse function. If the point (x, y) is on the graph of the function f, then the point (y, x) is on the graph of the inverse f^{-1}. You can draw the graph of the inverse by reflecting the graph of the function across the line $y = x$.

As in Chapter 2, the -1 in the notation $f^{-1}(x)$ means "inverse with respect to function composition."

Here are the graphs of $f(x) = 2^x$ and its inverse function, which you will temporarily call $L_2(x)$.

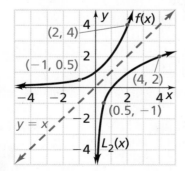

The next investigation focuses on functions such as $L_2(x)$, their properties, and how they are used to solve equations in algebra.

 **Exercises** *Practicing Habits of Mind*

Check Your Understanding

Throughout these exercises, $L_b(x)$ refers to the inverse of $f(x) = b^x$.

1. Based on what you know about $f(x) = 2^x$, find the domain and range of the inverse function $L_2(x)$.

2. Find each value. Each result is an integer.

   a. $L_5(25)$ **b.** $L_7(1)$ **c.** $L_{11}(11^6)$

   d. $L_{0.1}(0.001)$ **e.** $L_3\!\left(\frac{1}{9}\right)$

3. Find each value, either exactly or to four decimal places.

   a. $L_4(5)$ **b.** $L_4(8)$ **c.** $L_4(40)$ **d.** $L_4\!\left(\frac{8}{5}\right)$

4. Copy the graph below of $f(x) = (0.5)^x$. Sketch the graph of the inverse function.

   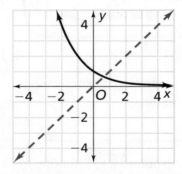

5. Let $f(x) = 2^x$. Determine which value in each pair is greater. (*Hint:* Use the graph of $f(x) = 2^x$.)

   a. the mean of $f(3)$ and $f(5)$ $f(4)$

   b. the mean of $f(5)$ and $f(7)$ $f(6)$

   c. the mean of $f(-4)$ and $f(-2)$ $f(-3)$

   d. the mean of $f(x)$ and $f(y)$ $f\!\left(\frac{x+y}{2}\right)$

6. **a.** Sketch the graphs of $y = 2^x$ and $y = x^2$.

   b. How many numbers x satisfy $2^x = x^2$?

7. As x increases, 2^x becomes greater than x^2. Consider the values of 1.06^x. Use the graphs of $y = x^2$ and $y = 1.06^x$.

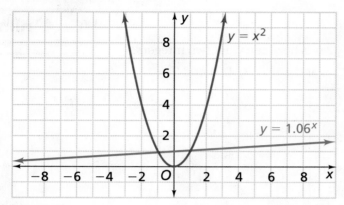

As x increases, will x^2 always be greater than 1.06^x?

8. As x increases, 2^x becomes greater than x^2. Consider the values of x^{10}. Use the graphs of $y = x^{10}$ and $y = 2^x$.

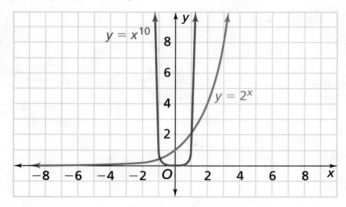

a. As x increases, will x^{10} always be greater than 2^x?

b. As x increases, will x^{10} always be greater than 1.06^x?

c. As x increases, will 2^x always be greater than 1.06^x?

9. Take It Further The graph of $y = 2^x$ does not intersect the graph of $y = x$. The graph of $y = 1.06^x$ intersects the graph of $y = x$ in two places. Approximate the greatest number b such that the graph of $y = b^x$ intersects the graph of $y = x$. Approximate the coordinates of the one point at which $y = b^x$ intersects $y = x$.

On Your Own

10. Is $L_2(x)$ a one-to-one function? Explain.

11. **Standardized Test Prep** The value of $L_3(28)$ is between what two integers?

    A. 1 and 2   **B.** 2 and 3   **C.** 3 and 4   **D.** 4 and 5

12. Copy and complete this table for $L_2(x)$. Give approximations to four decimal places.

x	$L_2(x)$
1	0
2	1
3	1.5850
4	■
5	■
6	■
7	■
8	■
9	■

13. **a.** Explain why $L_8(8) = 1$.

    b. Explain why $L_8(2) = \frac{1}{3}$.

    c. Copy and complete this table for $L_8(x)$. Give approximations to four decimal places.

x	$L_8(x)$
1	0
2	0.3333
3	0.5283
4	■
5	■
6	■
7	■
8	1
9	■

14. **Take It Further** Prove that $L_2(x) = 3 \cdot L_8(x)$ for any positive real number x.

15. Ariela puts $500 in an investment account. She earns 9% interest per year. After how many years will she be closest to doubling her starting investment?

16. Ariela wonders what will happen with higher or lower interest rates. Copy the table at the right. For each interest rate, find out after how many years Ariela will be closest to doubling her starting $500 investment.

Doubling Time

APR	Years to Double
3%	■
4%	■
5%	■
6%	12
7%	■
8%	■
9%	■
10%	■
11%	■
12%	■

Any APR will show exponential growth. See the TI-Nspire Handbook, p. 804.

Remember...
APR stands for "annual percentage rate."

17. Many financial advisors use the Rule of 72 when offering advice about long-term investments.

Rule of 72 To find the number of years it takes to double an investment's value, divide 72 by the annual percentage rate.

Go Online
Pearsonsuccessnet.com

a. Recopy the table from Exercise 16 and use the Rule of 72 to complete it. How do your results using the Rule of 72 compare to the results you found in Exercise 16?

b. According to the Rule of 72, how long will it take a credit card balance to double if the interest rate is 18% APR?

c. If Ariela invests $500 in an account at 9% APR for 40 years, how many times will her money double in value? How much money does the Rule of 72 suggest she will have after 40 years?

Maintain Your Skills

In Exercises 18 and 19, find each value to four decimal places.

18. a. $L_5(3)$ **b.** $L_5(9)$ **c.** $L_5(27)$ **d.** $L_5(81)$

19. a. $L_2(7)$ **b.** $L_4(7)$ **c.** $L_8(7)$ **d.** $L_{16}(7)$ **e.** $L_{1024}(7)$

Mathematical
5B
Reflections

In this investigation, you graphed exponential functions. You wrote rules for exponential functions, given a table of inputs and outputs or two points on the graph of the function. These exercises will help you summarize what you have learned.

1. Give the definition of *exponential function*. Pay special attention to any restrictions on the variables in your definition. Give an example of an exponential function and describe its domain and range. Describe where your function is increasing and where it is decreasing.

2. Use this table for the exponential function $g(x)$.

   a. Write a recursive definition for $g(x)$.

   b. Write a closed-form definition for $g(x)$.

   c. Do your answers for parts (a) and (b) define the same function? Explain.

x	g(x)
0	−5
1	−10
2	−20
3	−40
4	−80

3. a. Copy and complete this ratio table for $h(x)$.

   b. Find $h(23)$ to four decimal places.

   c. Could $h(x)$ be an exponential function? Explain.

x	h(x)	÷
0	▨	$\frac{2}{3}$
1	6	$\frac{2}{3}$
2	▨	$\frac{2}{3}$
3	▨	$\frac{2}{3}$
4	▨	

4. Find the exact values of x that solve each equation.

   a. $12 = 3x^2$

   b. $x = 5 \cdot 4^{-\frac{1}{2}}$

   c. $16 = 4 \cdot 32^x$

   d. $-5 = x \cdot 27^{\frac{2}{3}}$

5. $L_3(x)$ is the inverse of the function $f(x) = 3^x$.

   a. Find $L_3(1)$.

   b. Find $L_3(81)$.

   c. If $L_3(2) \approx 0.6309$, find $L_3(4)$ and $L_3(8)$.

   d. Approximate $L_3(5)$ to four decimal places.

6. For $f(x) = b^x$, why is it true that $f(m) \cdot f(n) = f(m + n)$?

7. Why must an exponential function have an inverse function?

8. If you invest $1000 in an account at 6% interest, compounded annually, how much money will you have in 30 years?

Vocabulary

In this investigation, you learned these terms. Make sure you understand what each one means and how to use it.

- base
- exponential decay
- exponential function
- exponential growth
- functional equation
- monotonic
- strictly decreasing
- strictly increasing

Multiple Choice

1. Which of the following expressions is NOT equal to 5^{12}?

   A. $(5^6)^2$ **B.** $(5^3)(5^4)$

   C. $\dfrac{5^{24}}{5^{12}}$ **D.** $(5^{10})(5^2)$

2. Simplify $((x^{-2})^2)^2$.

   A. x^{-8} **B.** x^{-6}

   C. x^2 **D.** x^{16}

3. Simplify $64^{\frac{3}{2}}$.

   A. 16   **B.** 96

   C. 512   **D.** 32,768

4. Which of these points is NOT on the graph of $f(x) = 4 \cdot \left(\frac{1}{2}\right)^x$?

   A. $(-2, 16)$ **B.** $(0, 4)$

   C. $\left(1, \frac{1}{2}\right)$ **D.** $(2, 1)$

5. Let $L_4(x)$ be the inverse of the function $f(x) = 4^x$. What is the value of $L_4(16)$?

   A. -4 **B.** -2

   C. 2   **D.** 4

Open Response

6. Use this table of the function $h(x)$.

x	h(x)	÷
0	3	▩
1	6	▩
2	12	▩
3	▩	▩
4	▩	▩
5	▩	

   a. Find a rule for $h(x)$ in the form $h(x) = c \cdot a^x$ that matches the table.

   b. Copy and complete the table.

   c. Find a recursive definition for $h(x)$.

7. Use the sequence below.

   $$3, 6, \blacksquare, \blacksquare, \blacksquare, \ldots$$

   a. Find the missing terms if the sequence is arithmetic.

   b. Find the missing terms if the sequence is geometric.

8. Simplify each expression. Assume $x, y, z \neq 0$.

   a. $x^{-4} \cdot x^6$ **b.** $\left(y^{\frac{1}{3}}\right)^3$

   c. $\dfrac{x^{-2}}{x^6}$ **d.** $z^{-7} \cdot z^7$

   e. $x^{\frac{1}{2}} \cdot x^2$ **f.** $(x^{-6})^{-5}$

9. **a.** Suppose q is an exponential function with $q(2) = 9$ and $q(3) = 27$. Find $q(x)$.

   b. Sketch the graph of $q(x)$.

   c. Let $t(x) = -2 \cdot q(x)$. Find a rule for $t(x)$. Find $t(2)$ and $t(3)$.

   d. Sketch the graph of $t(x)$.

10. Find the exact values of x that solve each equation.

    a. $16 = 4x^2$

    b. $16 = 4 \cdot 2^x$

    c. $x = 4 \cdot 16^{-\frac{1}{2}}$

11. Simplify the expressions $4^0, 7^{-2}$, and $5^{\frac{2}{3}}$.

Logarithmic Functions

In *Logarithmic Functions*, you will learn that logarithms are the inverses of exponential functions. You will use logarithms to solve exponential equations.

By the end of this investigation, you will be able to answer questions like these.

1. What are some reasons to use logarithms?

2. What is a logarithmic scale and when do you use it?

3. If you invest $1000 at 6% interest, compounded annually, how many years will it take until your money grows to $10,000?

You will learn how to

- evaluate logarithms of any base using a calculator

- use logarithms to solve exponential equations

- graph logarithmic functions

You will develop these habits and skills:

- Reason logically from the definition of a logarithmic function and the laws of exponents to develop the laws of logarithms.

- Visualize the graph of a logarithmic function from the graph of the corresponding exponential function.

- Convert flexibly and strategically between logarithmic form and exponential form, and choose the best form to solve problems.

The Krumbein scale is a logarithmic scale used to classify the size of particles. A boulder with diameter 256 mm or greater has a scale value of −8 or less.

Activating Prior Knowledge
Exploring New Ideas

In this lesson, you will investigate a function on your calculator called LOG. There may be a LOG key on your calculator. If there is not, look in your calculator's function library. You use the notation log x for this function.

> Although you use parentheses in $f(x)$ function notation, the parentheses are optional for the log function. You can write log (x) or log x. You still must use parentheses when needed to avoid confusion, for example in expressions such as log $(x + 1)$.

For You to Explore

1. Use your calculator to find the output when you use the LOG key for each integer input from 0 to 10. Copy and complete the table below. Record each output to four decimal places.

2. Find the value of log 2 + log 3 to four decimal places.

3. **a.** Calculate log 2 + log 6.

   b. Calculate log 3 + log 4.

   c. Calculate log 3 + log 2 + log 2.

   d. Find the number x such that log x = log 2 + log 6.

4. Estimate each result using the table from Problem 1 and any patterns you have seen so far. Then use a calculator to confirm the answer.

   a. log 15   **b.** log 24   **c.** log 36   **d.** log 63

5. Find a rule for calculating log MN in terms of log M and log N. (*Hint:* Refer to the results from Problem 4.)

x	log x
0	▦
1	▦
2	▦
3	▦
4	▦
5	▦
6	▦
7	▦
8	▦
9	▦
10	▦

6. Estimate each result using the table from Problem 1 and any patterns you have seen so far. Then use a calculator to confirm the answer.

   a. log 16   **b.** log 32   **c.** log 64   **d.** log 2^{10} **e.** log 3^5

7. Find a rule for calculating log M^p in terms of p and log M. (*Hint:* Refer to the results from Problem 6.)

8. **Write About It** Explain how you can use the result from Problem 7 and the table from Problem 1 to estimate log $\frac{1}{8}$.

9. Determine the domain and range of the function $x \mapsto \log x$.

10. **Take It Further** Use the rules that govern the function $x \mapsto \log x$ to find the solution to the following equation.

$$2^x = 5$$

Exercises *Practicing Habits of Mind*

On Your Own

11. You have seen that $\log 10 = 1$. Now calculate each of the following values.

Try evaluating these expressions without using a calculator.

a. $\log 10^2$ **b.** $\log 10^3$ **c.** $\log 10^6$

d. $\log 10^{10}$ **e.** $\log 10^{-3}$

12. Calculate each value.

a. $10^{\log 2}$ **b.** $10^{\log 3}$ **c.** $10^{\log 6}$

d. $10^{\log 10}$ **e.** $10^{\log -3}$

13. Describe the relationship between the functions $x \mapsto \log x$ and $x \mapsto 10^x$. Give examples.

14. Solve each equation for x.

a. $\log \frac{5}{4} + \log 4 = \log x$ **b.** $\log \frac{7}{3} + \log 3 = \log x$

c. $\log \frac{6}{17} + \log 17 = \log x$ **d.** $\log x + \log 2 = \log 5$

e. $\log x + \log 7 = \log 3$ **f.** $\log x = \log 11 - \log 4$

15. Find a rule for calculating $\log \frac{M}{N}$ in terms of $\log M$ and $\log N$.

Refer to the results from Exercise 14.

16. On the same axes, sketch the graphs of $f(x) = 3^x$ and its inverse function.

17. On the same axes, sketch the graphs of $f(x) = \log x$ and its inverse function.

18. Suppose $\log(A) = 1.6$ and $\log(B) = 2.7$. Find each value.

a. $\log AB$ **b.** $\log A^2$ **c.** $\log \frac{1}{A}$

d. $\log \frac{B}{A}$ **e.** $\log AB^2$ **f.** $\log \sqrt{A}$

Maintain Your Skills

19. Find a pair of consecutive integers j and k that satisfy each inequality.

- $j < \log 7 < k$
- $j < \log 70 < k$
- $j < \log 7000 < k$
- $j < \log 143{,}265 < k$

5.12 Defining Logarithms

Until now, you had to solve an equation such as $2^x = 5$ by trial and error. Knowledge that the graph of $y = 2^x$ is increasing can help, but you can only closely approximate the solution by making many guesses. This lesson introduces logarithms, including their definition. It gives an example of how you can use logarithms to solve equations, such as $2^x = 5$, where the variable is in the exponent.

In the last investigation, you learned that exponential functions such as $g(x) = 2^x$ are one-to-one, and therefore have inverse functions. The inverse function of an exponential function is a *logarithmic function*.

Definition

The **logarithmic function** $x \mapsto \log_b x$ is the inverse function of the exponential function $x \mapsto b^x$.

> In the last investigation, you used the notation $L_b(x)$ for logarithmic functions. So, you have actually already seen them. This is just a version of the standard notation.

The logarithmic function is often called the logarithm.

The output $\log_b M$ is the exponent k that solves $b^k = M$. In other words, $\log_b M$ is the power to which you have to raise b in order to get M. So these two statements are equivalent.

$$b^k = M \Leftrightarrow \log_b M = k$$

The base b must be positive and cannot equal 1 in order for $x \mapsto b^x$ to be an exponential function. Therefore, the same restriction applies to logarithmic functions. The base of a logarithm must be positive and cannot equal 1.

Exponential and logarithmic functions are closely related. You can see this by looking at tables and graphs. Consider the function $f(x) = \log_3 x$ and its inverse function $g(x) = 3^x$. The tables for the functions show reversed pairs of values. This is true for any function and its inverse.

x	$g(x) = 3^x$	x	$f(x) = \log_3 x$
-1	$\frac{1}{3}$	$\frac{1}{3}$	-1
0	1	1	0
1	3	3	1
2	9	9	2
3	27	27	3

The two graphs are reflections of each other over the line with equation $y = x$.

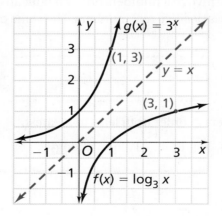

For You to Do

1. Explain why $\log_3 9 = 2$. Find $\log_3 \frac{1}{9}$ and $\log_3 81$.

Facts and Notation

The expression log x without a base generally refers to base 10. This is the **common logarithm**. In this course, if the base is not given for a logarithm, assume the base is 10.

Not all books or software use log x to mean base 10.

Example

Problem Find the exact value of each expression, if possible. Otherwise, give an approximation.

 a. $\log_5 26$ **b.** $\log \frac{1}{10}$ **c.** $\log_4 32$ **d.** $\log_3 -1$

Solution For each expression, write an equivalent expression involving an exponent.

a. If $\log_5 26 = x$, then $5^x = 26$. You cannot find the value of $\log_5 26$ exactly. It is a little greater than 2, since $5^2 = 25$.

b. If $\log \frac{1}{10} = x$, then $10^x = \frac{1}{10}$. You can solve the equation exactly, since $\frac{1}{10}$ is an exact power of 10. The value of $\log \frac{1}{10}$ is exactly -1.

Remember...

In this course, if no base is given for a logarithm, assume the base is 10.

c. If $\log_4 32 = x$, then $4^x = 32$. Both 4 and 32 are powers of 2, so you can find x exactly.

$$4^x = 32$$
$$(2^2)^x = 2^5$$
$$2^{2x} = 2^5$$
$$2x = 5$$
$$x = \frac{5}{2}$$

The value of $\log_4 32$ is exactly $\frac{5}{2}$.

d. If $\log_3 -1 = x$, then $3^x = -1$. This is impossible, since the range of the function $g(x) = 3^x$ is positive real numbers only. That means that the domain of $f(x) = \log_3 x$ is positive real numbers. The value of $\log_3 -1$ does not exist.

Look at the graphs of $f(x) = \log_3 x$ and $g(x) = 3^x$ on the previous page. You can use either graph to show that $\log_3 -1$ does not exist.

For You to Do

2. Put the following numbers in order from least to greatest.

$$\log_{11} 10, \ \log_7 8, \ \log_5 1, \ \log_3 10, \ \log_2 \tfrac{1}{4}$$

Establish a process. Now you can write the solution to $2^x = 5$ using logarithms.

$$\text{If } 2^x = 5, \text{ then } x = \log_2 5.$$

This is useful because it gives an expression for the exact value of x, just as $\sqrt{5}$ is one of the exact solutions of $x^2 = 5$. This process happens frequently in mathematics. You have a useful function, such as the inverse of $x \mapsto 2^x$, that you cannot express in terms of the standard functions at your disposal. So, you invent a new name for this function, in this case $\log_2$. You incorporate it into the toolkit of standard functions. You study its behavior, build it into calculators and computers, and use it until it becomes as familiar as $x \mapsto \sqrt{x}$.

You can find an approximate value for an expression such as $\log_2 5$ by finding other nearby logarithmic outputs with exact values you know. For example, $\log_2 4 = 2$, so $\log_2 5$ must be a bit more than 2.

But this does not help find the value of $\log_2 5$ accurately. Calculators can work with logarithms, but many can only use those with base 10. What can you do? You can argue as follows: Suppose $\log 2 = c$ and $\log 5 = d$. Then

$$10^c = 2 \text{ and } 10^d = 5$$

If $\log_2 5 = x$, then $2^x = 5$ and

$$(10^c)^x = 10^d$$

$$\text{or}$$

$$10^{cx} = 10^d$$

> Use the logarithm template to work in any positive base. See the TI-Nspire Handbook, p. 804.

But then, since exponential functions are one-to-one, you have

$$cx = d$$

$$x = \frac{d}{c} = \frac{\log 5}{\log 2}$$

This is another way to write $x = \log_2 5$. This is a way that calculators can calculate the value of x.

$$x = \log_2 5 = \frac{\log 5}{\log 2} \approx \frac{0.6990}{0.3010} \approx 2.322$$

By using logarithms, you can quickly solve equations that were once unsolvable to any degree of accuracy except by trial and error.

If you carry out the steps above in general for any base, you end up with a useful theorem.

Theorem 5.5 Change-of-Base Rule

If $b, x, y > 0$, and $b, x \neq 1$. then

$$\log_x y = \frac{\log_b y}{\log_b x}$$

You will prove this theorem in the next lesson. The Developing Habits of Mind section on the previous page gives the proof for a specific case.

When working with a calculator, the choice $b = 10$ is often the most practical. The change-of-base rule is the reason why every calculator does not need to have a way to work with logarithms of other bases.

Summary Properties of Logarithmic functions

A logarithmic function $f: \mathbb{R}^+ \to \mathbb{R}$ is defined as $f(x) = \log_b x$.

- The base b must be positive and not 1.
- The domain of f is $\mathbb{R}^+$, positive real numbers.
- The range of f is all real numbers.
- The graph of $y = f(x)$ has one x-intercept at $(1, 0)$ and no y-intercepts.
- The graph of $y = f(x)$ is increasing when $b > 1$ and decreasing when $0 < b < 1$.

Exercises Practicing Habits of Mind

Check Your Understanding

1. **a.** Sketch the graphs of $f(x) = \log_2 x$ and its inverse on the same axes.

    b. What is the inverse of $f(x) = \log_2 x$?

2. Which of these statements is true?

    A. $\log_2 9 = 3$

    B. $\log_{16} 4 = 2$

    C. $\log_5 10 > \log_5 9$

    D. $\log_4 0 = 1$

3. Find each value.

    a. $\log_4 2$

    b. $\log_4 2 + \log_4 32$

    c. $\log_4 64$

    d. $\log_9 27$

    e. $\log_9 27 + \log_9 3$

    f. $\log_9 81$

Go Online
Pearsonsuccessnet.com

4. **Write About It** Explain why $\log_b 0$ does not exist, no matter what the base is.

5. Put these expressions in order from least to greatest.

$$\log_4 18, \log 99, \log_2 0.1, \log_{100} 10, \log_{73} 1, \log_5 \frac{1}{5}, \log_2 18$$

6. Suppose $\log_b 9 = 4$ for some base b.

   a. Write an equation involving b that does not include a logarithm.

   b. Find the exact value of b.

7. Find the value of $3^{\log_3 75}$.

8. Suppose $\log_b 2 = 1.35$ and $\log_b 3 = 2.14$, to two decimal places. Evaluate each expression without finding the value of b.

   a. $b^{1.35}$ b. $b^{2.14}$ c. $b^{3.49}$

   d. $b^{6.42}$ e. $\log_b 6$ f. $\log_b 27$

9. Use the method from the Developing Habits of Mind section to find the solution to $4^x = 25$ to three decimal places.

10. **Take It Further** The value of $\log 20{,}000$ to four decimal places is 4.3010. Traditionally, the value 4.3010 is considered as two pieces—the characteristic 4, which is the greatest integer less than the number, and the mantissa .3010, which is the decimal part of the number. Experiment to figure out how to interpret these two pieces. For example, if a number M has $\log M = 3.6435$, what does the characteristic 3 tell you about M? What does the mantissa .6435 tell you about M?

Sometimes, people write the mantissa without the decimal point.

On Your Own

11. Explain why $\log_b b = 1$ for any base b.

12. Explain why $\log_b 1 = 0$ for any base b.

13. Suppose $b^x = M$.

   a. If $b^y = M^2$, what is the relationship between y and x?

   b. Find the missing exponent in the equation below.

$$b^{(\blacksquare)} = M^{10}$$

   c. Explain why this statement is true.

$$\log_b M^2 = 2 \log_b M$$

14. **Standardized Test Prep** Which of these points is on the graph of $f(x) = \log x$?

   A. $(0, 1)$ B. $(100, 2)$

   C. $(100, 10)$ D. $(2, 0.3)$

15. a. Sketch the graph of $f(x) = \log x$. Include the coordinates of three points on the graph.

 b. Sketch the graph of the inverse function f^{-1} on the same axes.

 c. Find the domain and range of f and the domain and range of f^{-1}.

 d. What is the inverse function of $f(x) = \log x$?

16. Use the change-of-base rule and the LOG key on your calculator to find each value to three decimal places.

 a. $\log_4 18$ **b.** $\log_2 0.1$ **c.** $\log_{73} 1$

 d. $\log_1 9$ **e.** $\log_3 7$ **f.** $\log_9 49$

17. Find each value.

 a. $\log_2 \frac{1}{8}$ **b.** $\log_2 8$ **c.** $\log_4 16$

 d. $\log_4 \frac{1}{16}$ **e.** $\log_{\frac{1}{2}} 8$ **f.** $\log_{\frac{1}{4}} \frac{1}{16}$

> Try to do this without using a calculator!

18. Prove each statement using the definition of logarithm.

 a. If $\log_b M = k$, then $\log_b \frac{1}{M} = -k$.

 b. $\log_b M = \log_{\frac{1}{b}} \frac{1}{M}$ for any valid base b and $M > 0$.

19. Take It Further Exercise 16 suggests that $\log_3 7 = \log_9 49$. Generalize this fact. Then prove it using the definition of logarithm.

20. What's Wrong Here? Sharon says there should be two solutions for b in Exercise 6. Sharon explains, "I rewrote the log equation as $b^4 = 9$. Since it's an even exponent, there are two real numbers b that make it true: b is close to plus or minus 1.73. Actually, now that I think about it, I don't need a decimal, it's $\sqrt{3}$ that works. So $b = \pm\sqrt{3}$."

There is only one correct value of b. Explain.

Maintain Your Skills

21. Find each value.

 a. $\log_4 2$ **b.** $\log_2 4$ **c.** $\log_9 27$

 d. $\log_{27} 9$ **e.** $\log_2 32$ **f.** $\log_{32} 2$

 g. A calculator gives the value of $\log_{10} 2$ as approximately 0.3010. Use this to approximate the value of $\log_2 10$.

22. Find each number to three decimal places.

 a. $\log 7.3$ **b.** $\log 73$

 c. $\log 730$ **d.** $\log\left(7.3 \times 10^6\right)$

 e. Find $\log 300{,}000$ to four decimal places using the table from Exercise 1 of Lesson 5.11.

Laws of Logarithms

Review the laws of exponents from earlier in this chapter.

Laws of Exponents

Let base $b > 0$, $b \neq 1$, and x and y be real numbers.

The Fundamental Law of Exponents

- $b^{x+y} = b^x \cdot b^y$

Corollaries

- $b^{x-y} = \dfrac{b^x}{b^y}$
- $b^{xy} = (b^x)^y$

In this lesson you will learn the laws of logarithms, which are restatements of the laws of exponents.

For You to Do

Let $b^x = M$ and $b^y = N$.

1. Find b^{x+y} in terms of M and N.

2. Find b^{x-y} in terms of M and N.

3. Find b^{px} in terms of M and p.

The results from Problems 1–3 follow from the laws of exponents.
For example,

$$\text{If } b^x = M \text{ and } b^y = N, \text{ then } b^{x+y} = MN.$$

You can rewrite each of the three equations in the above statement, using the definition of logarithm.

$$\text{If } \log_b M = x \text{ and } \log_b N = y, \text{ then } \log_b MN = x + y.$$

Add the first two statements.

$$\log_b M + \log_b N = x + y$$

Now you have two expressions for $x + y$, so they must be equal.

$$\log_b M + \log_b N = \log_b MN$$

You can restate each of the three laws of exponents in terms of logarithms. This gives you the laws of logarithms.

Laws of Logarithms

Let base $b > 0$, $b \neq 1$ and M and N be positive real numbers.

The Fundamental Law of Logarithms

- $\log_b MN = \log_b M + \log_b N$

Corollaries

- $\log_b \frac{M}{N} = \log_b M - \log_b N$
- $\log_b M^p = p \log_b M$

In other words, a logarithm $g(x) = \log_b x$ satisfies the functional equation $g(xy) = g(x) + g(y)$.

You can prove the laws of logarithms with arguments like the one above, or a set of statements like this proof of the third law.

Proof Let $\log_b M = x$. Then

$b^x = M$	Convert the form.
$(b^x)^p = M^p$	Build M^p.
$b^{px} = M^p$	Use a law of exponents.
$\log_b M^p = px$	Convert the form.
$\log_b M^p = p \log_b M$	Substitute for x.

Convert the form means to change from exponent notation to logarithm notation, or vice versa.

The three laws of logarithms provide the means to solve many equations that you previously had to solve by trial and error.

Example 1

Problem Ariela puts \$500 in an investment account. She earns 9% interest per year, compounded annually. How many years will it take to double her initial investment?

Solution The money Ariela invests grows by 9% per year, so after each year, the money invested is multiplied by 1.09. You need to find the number of years it takes for the investment to at least double, so you need to solve the equation below, where n is the number of years.

$$1000 = 500 \cdot 1.09^n$$

Apply the laws of logarithms to find n.

Method 1 Divide through by 500. Then find the base-10 logarithm of each side.

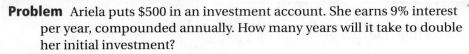
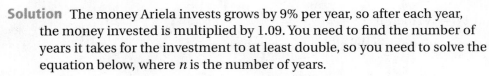

$$1000 = 500 \cdot 1.09^n$$
$$2 = 1.09^n$$
$$\log 2 = \log 1.09^n$$
$$\log 2 = n \log 1.09$$
$$\frac{\log 2}{\log 1.09} = n$$
$$8.043 \approx n$$

Why do you find the base-10 logarithm, and not some other base?

Method 2 Apply the base-10 logarithm first. Then apply the laws of logarithms.

$$1000 = 500 \cdot 1.09^n$$
$$\log 1000 = \log (500 \cdot 1.09^n)$$
$$\log 1000 = \log 500 + \log 1.09^n$$
$$\log 1000 = \log 500 + n \log 1.09$$
$$\log 1000 - \log 500 = n \log 1.09$$
$$\frac{\log 1000 - \log 500}{\log 1.09} = n$$
$$8.043 \approx n$$

Either equation produces the solution $n \approx 8.043$, but this is not the correct answer. Ariela's account compounds annually, so after the end of the eighth year, there is no further interest paid until the ninth year is complete. It will take 9 years to at least double her initial investment, even though the account is very close to $1000 after 8 years.

> The balance at the end of 8 years is $500 \cdot 1.09^8 \approx 996.28$. That is not quite enough.

For Discussion

4. The two methods generate two different expressions for n.

Method 1 $n = \dfrac{\log 2}{\log 1.09}$ **Method 2** $n = \dfrac{\log 1000 - \log 500}{\log 1.09}$

Is there a way to show these are equivalent using the laws of logarithms? Explain.

Developing Habits of Mind

Use a different process to get the same answer. Method 1 above solves the equation $2 = 1.09^n$ to get $n = \dfrac{\log 2}{\log 1.09}$. But the definition of logarithms gives another solution: $n = \log_{1.09} 2$. So, you can write the following equation.

$$\log_{1.09} 2 = \frac{\log 2}{\log 1.09}$$

This is an example of the change-of-base rule.

$$\log_x y = \frac{\log_b y}{\log_b x}$$

Here is a quick proof of the change-of-base rule. Let $\log_x y = k$. Then $x^k = y$. Find the base-b logarithm of each side.

$$x^k = y$$
$$\log_b x^k = \log_b y$$
$$k \log_b x = \log_b y$$
$$k = \frac{\log_b y}{\log_b x}$$

Then, since you also know $\log_x y = k$, the proof is complete.

> **Habits of Mind**
>
> **Look for relationships.** Note that these are the same steps you use to solve a problem involving actual numbers. So your work with numbers basically provides the proof.

Fractions such as $\dfrac{\log 2}{\log 1.09}$ lead to one of the most common mistakes made with logarithms. It is tempting to look at the corollary

$$\log_b \frac{M}{N} = \log_b M - \log_b N$$

and say that it applies to a fraction like $\dfrac{\log 2}{\log 1.09}$, so that

$$\frac{\log 2}{\log 1.09} = \log 2 - \log 1.09$$

This is incorrect reasoning. It is also incorrect to cancel the word *log* from the top and bottom of a fraction. It is generally not true that $\dfrac{\log M}{\log N}$ is equal to $\dfrac{M}{N}$.

When you solve equations that involve logarithms, it is important to check the solutions for validity. The logarithmic function is only defined for positive real numbers.

Example 2

Problem Find all values of x that solve the equation
$$\log (x + 7) + \log (x + 22) = 2$$

Solution First, rewrite 2 using a logarithm. The base is not given, so by convention it is 10. Since $10^2 = 100$, you have $\log 100 = 2$.

$$\log (x + 7) + \log (x + 22) = \log 100$$

Then use one of the laws of logarithms.

$$\log (x + 7) + \log (x + 22) = \log 100$$
$$\log ((x + 7)(x + 22)) = \log 100$$
$$(x + 7)(x + 22) = 100$$

Now solve by factoring or using the quadratic formula.

$$(x + 7)(x + 22) = 100$$
$$x^2 + 29x + 154 = 100$$
$$x^2 + 29x + 54 = 0$$
$$(x + 2)(x + 27) = 0$$

This equation has two solutions, $x = -2$ and $x = -27$. However, consider the domain of the logarithmic function. It can only accept positive inputs. Letting $x = -27$ in the original equation gives the result

$$\log -20 + \log -5 = 2$$

This makes no sense. Neither $\log -20$ nor $\log -5$ exists. So you reject the solution $x = -27$. The solution $x = -2$ is still valid. It gives the result

$$\log 5 + \log 20 = 2$$

All the inputs to the logarithmic function are positive.

Note that x may still be negative. It is the inputs to the logarithmic function that must be positive. Reject any solutions that result in negative inputs to a logarithm.

Laws and Properties of Logarithms

Let base $b > 0$, $b \neq 1$ and M and N be positive real numbers.

The Fundamental Law of Logarithms

- $\log_b MN = \log_b M + \log_b N$

Corollaries

- $\log_b \frac{M}{N} = \log_b M - \log_b N$
- $\log_b M^p = p \log_b M$

Other Properties

- change-of-base rule: $\log_M N = \dfrac{\log_b N}{\log_b M}$, if $M \neq 1$
- $\log_b 1 = 0$ and $\log_b b = 1$
- $\log_b \frac{1}{N} = -\log_b N$
- $\log_b M = \log_b N \Leftrightarrow M = N$, since the logarithm function is one-to-one.
- $\log_b(b^x) = x = b^{\log_b x}$, since the logarithm and the exponential are inverse functions.

Exercises *Practicing Habits of Mind*

Check Your Understanding

1. Let $\log_b M = 2$ and $\log_b N = 5$. Calculate each value.

   a. $\log_b M^2$ **b.** $\log_b MN$ **c.** $\log_b \frac{M^3}{N}$

   d. $\log_b (MN)^3$ **e.** $\log_b \sqrt{MN}$

2. Find the value of this product.

$$\log_2 3 \cdot \log_3 4 \cdot \log_5 6 \cdot \log_6 25$$

> See if you can do this one without a calculator.

3. **What's Wrong Here?** Explain what is wrong with the reasoning in the calculation below. Then determine the correct value.

$$\frac{\log_2 32}{\log_2 8} = \log_2 32 - \log_2 8 = 5 - 3 = 2$$

4. Prove the second law of logarithms in two ways.

$$\log_b \frac{M}{N} = \log_b M - \log_b N$$

a. Use the definition.

$$b^x = M \Leftrightarrow \log_b M = x$$

b. Use the Fundamental Law of Logarithms.

$$\log_b MN = \log_b M + \log_b N$$

5. Prove each statement.

a. $\log_b 1 = 0$ **b.** $\log_b b = 1$ **c.** $\log_b \frac{1}{N} = -\log_b N$

6. Due to inflation, the cost of a Big Burger grows by 3% every year. This year a Big Burger costs $3.99.

a. Write a rule for the function $C(n)$, where $C(n)$ is the cost of a Big Burger n years from now.

b. Using logarithms, find how long, to the nearest year, it will take for the cost of a Big Burger to reach $20.

7. Find the solution to this equation.

$$2 \cdot 5^x = 7$$

Give an exact answer. Then approximate the answer to three decimal places.

> The solutions to the next few exercises will include the logarithmic function in some way.

8. Find the solution to this equation in terms of the constants a, b, and c.

$$a \cdot b^x = c$$

9. Find the solution to this equation.

$$2 \cdot 5^x = 7 \cdot 3^x$$

Give an exact answer. Then approximate the answer to three decimal places.

10. In terms of the constants a, b, c, and d, find the solution to this equation.

$$a \cdot b^x = c \cdot d^x$$

11. In Exercise 21 in Lesson 5.09, you saw that the solution to the equation $6^x = 35$ is the reciprocal of the solution to $35^x = 6$. Use logarithms to explain why this makes sense.

> Can you explain it without using logarithms?

12. Find all solutions of each equation.

a. $\log x + \log (x + 1) = \log 6$

b. $\log (x^2 + x) = \log 6$

c. $\log 2x - \log x = \log 2$

d. $\log_2 (x - 3) + \log_2 (x + 3) = 4$

e. $\log_2 (x - 3) - \log_2 (x + 3) = 4$

13. Take It Further Suppose $\log 2 = 0.3$ exactly and $\log 3 = 0.5$ exactly. Assume both of these equations are true and prove that $0 = 1$.

14. Take It Further Recall the Rule of 72 from Lesson 5.10, Exercise 17.

Rule of 72 To find the number of years it takes to double an investment's value, divide 72 by the annual percentage interest rate.

Explain why the Rule of 72 gives fairly accurate results for relatively low interest rates (for example, from 6% to 12%).

On Your Own

15. Which is greater, $\log_5 135$ or $\log_7 300$? Explain completely without relying on a calculator answer.

16. Copy and complete this table for $f(x) = \log_3 x$. Use a calculator and the change-of-base rule. Give any approximate answers to four decimal places.

x	$\log_3 x$
1	0
2	0.6309
3	▨
4	▨
5	▨
6	▨
7	▨
8	▨
9	▨

> Even if your calculator can work with a base-3 logarithm, use the change-of-base rule here.

17. The value of $\log_3 7 + \log_9 81$ is between which two integers?

A. 0 and 1   **B.** 1 and 2
C. 2 and 3   **D.** 3 and 4

> Try this one without a calculator.

18. Suppose $\log_b 297{,}736 = 7$. Find the base b.

19. Let $a = \log 2$ and $b = \log 3$. Find each value in terms of a and b.

a. $\log 6$ **b.** $\log 1.5$
c. $\log 27$ **d.** $\log 200$
e. $\log \sqrt{3}$

Go Online
Pearsonsuccessnet.com

20. Each value below is between 1 and 2. Put them in order from least to greatest.

Be sure to do this exercise with a calculator.

$$\log_3 7, \log_9 50, \log 60, \log_8 40, \log_{12} 83, \log_2 3.44$$

21. What's Wrong Here? Explain what is wrong with the reasoning in the calculation below. Then determine the correct value.

$$\log 100 + \log_2 8 = \log 800 \approx 2.903$$

22. Use logarithms to find the solution to the equation $2^x = \frac{1}{1,000,000}$ to three decimal places.

23. Let $L(h) = 100 \cdot 0.5^h$.

a. If $L(h) = 50$, find h.

b. If $L(h) = 20$, find h.

c. If $L(h) = 10$, find h. How is the answer here related to your answers in parts (a) and (b)?

d. If $L(h) = c$, find h in terms of c.

e. If $L(h) = 1$, find h. How is the answer here related to your answer in part (d)?

24. Write About It Is $(\log x)^2$ the same as $\log x^2$? Explain.

25. Find all solutions to each equation.

a. $\log_2 x^2 - 5\log_2 x + 6 = 0$

b. $(\log_2 x)^2 - 5\log_2 x + 6 = 0$

c. **Take It Further** $\log x = 1 + \frac{6}{\log x}$

26. Show that the result $\log_b \frac{1}{N} = -\log_b N$ follows from the second law of logarithms.

27. Take It Further The Developing Habits of Mind section, earlier in this lesson, says that it is generally not true that $\frac{\log M}{\log N}$ equals $\frac{M}{N}$. When is it true? Explain.

Maintain Your Skills

28. Standardized Test Prep Which of the following expressions is equal to $\log \frac{xy^2}{z}$?

A. $\log x + 2\log y + \log z$

B. $\log x + 2\log y - \log z$

C. $\log z - \log x - 2\log y$

D. $2\log xy - \log z$

29. The government of Justinia reports that the current population is 10 million. The population is growing at 2.5% per year. Experts report the population will keep growing at this rate. Give the number of years it will take for the population to reach each milestone. Round to two decimal places.

a. 20 million   **b.** 30 million

c. 40 million   **d.** 60 million

e. 120 million   **f.** 240 million

> So, a sample answer is 16.43 years.

Historical Perspective

Logarithms used to play a much larger role in second-year algebra courses, because you can use them for arithmetic calculation. Consider the Fundamental Law of Logarithms.

$$\log_b MN = \log_b M + \log_b N$$

You can use it to transform a multiplication problem into an addition problem. To multiply two numbers M and N, you can use base-10 logarithms.

This may seem like a much more complicated way to multiply two numbers, but suppose M and N both have five digits. Adding five-digit numbers by hand is much faster than multiplying five-digit numbers by hand. The other laws of logarithms allow you to reduce division to subtraction and exponentiation to multiplication, which you can then reduce further to addition.

For example, here is how to calculate $\frac{6.453}{2.179}$ using logarithms.

- Call the numerator $M = 6.453$ and the denominator $N = 2.179$.
- Calculate $\log M \approx 0.8098$ and $\log N \approx 0.3383$.
- Subtract: $\log M - \log N \approx 0.4715$.
- This is $\log \frac{M}{N}$, so undo the logarithm: $10^{0.4715} \approx 2.961$.

The result at each step has four significant figures, so the answer is correct to four significant figures. Compare that to the task of dividing these decimals by hand. You reduce the division step to subtraction by using the laws of logarithms.

Go Online
Pearsonsuccessnet.com

5.14 Graphing Logarithmic Functions

This lesson focuses on some properties of the graphs of logarithmic functions. It includes a method for graphing a logarithm for any given base.

Minds in Action   episode 22

Tony wants to know how to graph a logarithmic function.

Tony   I've got a question. Exercise 16 in Lesson 5.13 asked us to make a table of values for $f(x) = \log_3 x$. And I can do that.

Sasha   So what's your question?

Tony   What I want to know is, how do I graph $y = \log_3 x$ on the graphing calculator? Do I have to just enter all these points as data and live with that?

Sasha   There has to be a way. How did you make the table?

Tony   Some of the numbers I can just fill in, like $\log_3 9 = 2$. For the others, I had to use the change-of-base rule.

Sasha   Give me an example.

Tony   Take 7. To calculate $\log_3 7$, I split it so it's $\log 7$ divided by $\log 3$. I type that on the calculator and I get 1.7712.

Sasha   Did you do it the same way each time?

Tony   Yes, except the ones that I did in my head. But I could even do those with the change-of-base rule.

Sasha   Then that's it. That's how you make the graph. Just take your number x and calculate $\log x$ divided by $\log 3$. That works for any number.

Tony   And I can type that in as a function on the calculator! The function is
$$f(x) = \frac{\log x}{\log 3}$$

Sasha types in the equation.

Sasha   Hey, that fraction worked! And the graph goes through the point (9, 2).

> Assume that Tony's calculator can work with base-10 logarithms only.

> You can program this version of Tony's $f(x)$ into your function-modeling language. Define $f(x) = \dfrac{\log x}{\log 3}$.

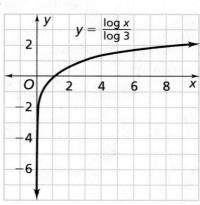

You can graph the logarithm for any base by using the relationship $\log_b x = \dfrac{\log x}{\log b}$. One interesting consequence of this fact is that the graphs of all logarithmic functions are related to each other by a vertical stretch.

Every one of these functions has the same domain and range. The domain is all positive reals. The range is all real numbers.

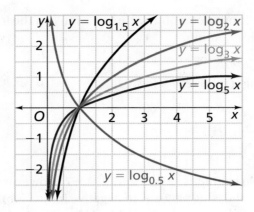

For You to Do

1. Find and graph a function $f(x) = \log_b x$ with a graph that contains the point (2, 5).

Hint: If $y = \log_b x$ contains the point (2, 5), what equation must b solve?

You can use graphs to find the number of solutions of some equations that involve logarithms.

Example

Problem

a. How many solutions are there to the equation
$\log_3 (x - 2) + \log_3 x = \log_3 63?$

b. Find all values of x that make $\log_3 (x - 2) + \log_3 x = \log_3 63$ true.

Solution

a. Graph each side of the equation. You can use the equation
$y_1 = \dfrac{\log (x - 2)}{\log 3} + \dfrac{\log x}{\log 3}$ to graph the left side.
The right side is the horizontal line $y_2 = \dfrac{\log 63}{\log 3}$.

Plot the two graphs on the same axes.

Each solution to the original equation corresponds to an intersection between the two graphs. The graphs intersect once, so there is one solution.

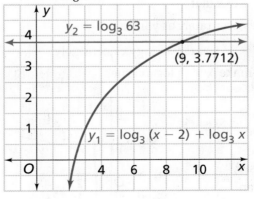

Why is the graph of $y_2 = \dfrac{\log 63}{\log 3}$ a horizontal line?

b. Use the laws of logarithms to combine the expressions on the left side. Then build a quadratic equation.

$$\log_3 (x - 2) + \log_3 x = \log_3 63$$

$$\log_3 (x(x - 2)) = \log_3 63$$

$$x(x - 2) = 63$$

$$x^2 - 2x - 63 = 0$$

$$(x - 9)(x + 7) = 0$$

The equation gives two solutions, $x = 9$ and $x = -7$. However, the solution $x = -7$ is invalid, since it leads to negative inputs for the logarithms in the original equation. The only solution is $x = 9$.

Exercises *Practicing Habits of Mind*

Check Your Understanding

1. Find all solutions to this equation.

$$\log_2 (3x + 1) - \log_2 (2x - 3) = 2$$

2. The **LN** key on a calculator also performs logarithms, but not to base 10. So, $\ln x = \log_b x$ for some unknown base b.

   a. Without using a calculator, determine what $\ln 1$ and $\ln 0$ should be. Then verify your results with a calculator.

   b. Determine the base b as accurately as you can.

3. **a.** Sketch the graphs of $y = \sqrt{x}$ and $y = \log_2 x$ accurately.

   b. How many numbers x make $\sqrt{x} = \log_2 x$ true?

4. As x increases, $\log_2 x$ becomes less than $\sqrt{x}$. Consider the values of $\log_{1.06} x$. Use the graphs of $y = \sqrt{x}$ and $y = \log_{1.06} x$. As x increases, will $\sqrt{x}$ always be less than $\log_{1.06} x$?

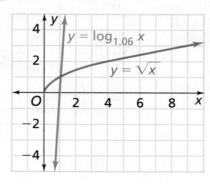

You can locate intersection points on a graph. See the TI-Nspire Handbook, p. 804.

5. As x increases, $\log_2 x$ becomes less than $\sqrt{x}$. Consider the values of $\sqrt[10]{x}$. Use the graphs of $y = \sqrt[10]{x}$ and $y = \log_2 x$.

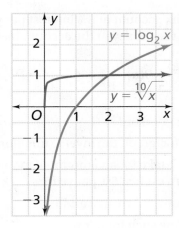

a. As x increases, will $\sqrt[10]{x}$ always be less than $\log_2 x$?

b. As x increases, will $\sqrt[10]{x}$ always be less than $\log_{1.06} x$?

c. As x increases, will $\log_2 x$ always be less than $\log_{1.06} x$?

6. Find the number of solutions to each equation.

a. $\log x^2 = 1$

b. $2 \log x = 1$

c. $\log_3 x = \sqrt{x} - 1$

d. $\log_2 x = 2^x$

e. $\log_{1.4} x = 1.4^x$

7. Take It Further The graphs of $y = \log_2 x$ and $y = 2^x$ do not intersect, but the graphs of $y = \log_{1.4} x$ and $y = 1.4^x$ do. For some base b such that $b > 1$, the graphs of $y = \log_b x$ and $y = b^x$ intersect exactly once. Find such a value of b and the intersection point of the two graphs as accurately as you can.

On Your Own

8. Use this detail of the graph of $x \mapsto \log_2 x$ with x between 1.3 and 1.4.

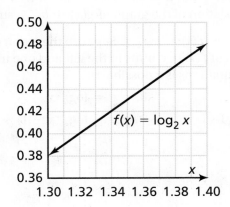

a. Approximate $\log_2 1.383$.

b. Approximate the solution to the equation $\log_2 x = 0.4$.

9. Asako says, "According to one of the laws of logarithms, $\log x^2 = 2 \log x$. So the graphs of $f(x) = \log x^2$ and $g(x) = 2 \log x$ should look exactly the same."

Do you agree or disagree with Asako's statement? Explain.

10. If you put money in a bank account at 6% interest per year, the function below outputs the factor the money in the account has grown by after n years.

Go Online
Pearsonsuccessnet.com

$$D(n) = 1.06^n$$

a. Sketch the graph of $D(n)$.

b. What is the inverse function of $D(n)$?

c. On a graphing calculator, graph the inverse function of $D(n)$.

d. How many years does it take for an amount of money to grow to 10 times its initial value if you invest it at 6% per year?

11. Let $f(x) = \log_b x$ with base b between 0 and 1.

a. Graph an example of one such function.

b. Explain why all such functions are decreasing.

12. Show that $f(x) = \log_2 x$ is exactly three times greater than $g(x) = \log_8 x$.

13. a. Sketch the graph of $y = \log 10^x$. Give another name for a function that is equivalent to $f(x) = \log 10^x$. Explain your reasoning.

b. Sketch the graph of $y = 10^{\log x}$. Explain why this graph is not the same as the graph of $y = \log 10^x$.

14. Take It Further

a. For $a > 0$, show that the graph of $f(x) = a \cdot 3^x$ is a translation of the graph of $g(x) = 3^x$.

b. For numbers a and b such that $a > 0$ and $b > 0$, show that the graph of $f(x) = a \cdot b^x$ is a translation of the graph of $g(x) = b^x$. Assume $b \neq 1$.

Compare with Exercise 22 from Lesson 5.07.

15. Standardized Test Prep Let $f(x) = \log_4 x$. Suppose the graph of $g(x)$ is a translation of the graph of $f(x)$ two units to the left and one unit down. Which of the following equations is a possible rule for $g(x)$?

A. $g(x) = \log_4 (x - 2) + 1$　　　**B.** $g(x) = \log_4 (x - 2) - 1$

C. $g(x) = \log_4 (x + 2) - 1$　　　**D.** $g(x) = \log_4 (x - 1) - 2$

16. Sketch each graph on the same axes.

   a. $y = \log_3 x$ **b.** $y = \log_3 (x - 3)$ **c.** $y = \log_3 (x + 4)$

   d. $y = \log_3 x - 3$ **e.** $y = \log_3 x + 4$

   f. Explain why the graph of $y = \log_3 (x - 3)$ is not the same as the graph of $y = \log_3 x - 3$.

Historical Perspective

In 1938, physicist Frank Benford published a paper describing something he had noticed in scientific data: Numbers started with the digit 1 much more frequently than 2 or 3, and far more frequently than 9. He compiled numeric information from many sources. He found that, on average, just over 30% of numbers started with the digit 1, while fewer than 5% started with the digit 9.

This numeric phenomenon is known as Benford's Law. It works for many sources of data, but not all. For example, it does not work for ZIP codes or telephone numbers, which are assigned to produce an even distribution of initial digits.

So, how do you find the expected frequencies? You use logarithms.

For example, take a number n with a first digit 4. The decimal part of $\log n$ must be between 0.6020 and 0.6990. If Benford's Law is true, then about 9.70% of the numbers observed should start with 4. And this is what actually happens with many sources of data. Numbers starting with 4 are less than one third as common as numbers starting with 1, which occur 30.1% of the time. The diagram at the right shows the relative frequency with which each digit occurs.

Accountants often use Benford's Law in investigating financial fraud. If the data in a financial report do not come close to the frequencies predicted by Benford's Law, they may be dishonest data.

5.15 The Logarithmic Scale

You can use different scales for the axes of a graph.

In-Class Experiment

1. Your teacher will give you four pieces of graph paper with the scales on the axes already marked. On the piece with the standard scales, plot the following graphs. On each other piece, plot only the graphs that are straight lines on that set of axes. (*Hint:* The graphs of nonlinear equations can be straight lines when you plot them on axes with different scales. Try to predict which graphs will be straight lines on each piece of graph paper.)

   a. $y = x$ **b.** $y = x^2$

   c. $y = x^3$ **d.** $y = 2^x$

   e. $y = 2 \cdot 3^x$ **f.** $y = 8 \cdot 0.5^x$

   g. $y = \log x$ **h.** $y = \log_2 x$

When you measure with a ruler, you use a **linear scale** to keep track of the number of inches, centimeters, yards, or other units you measure. You count by adding: 1 inch, 2 inches, 3 inches . . .

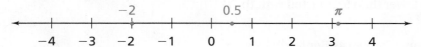

The linear scale is not the only choice. You can also use a **logarithmic scale.** You count by multiplying: 1 unit, 10 units, 100 units, 1000 units . . .

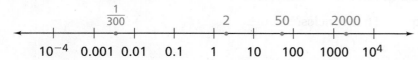

Note that zero and negative numbers do not appear on the logarithmic scale.

You can use a logarithmic scale when working with data that have widely varying values or when relative change is more important than absolute change. Well-known and frequently used logarithmic scales include the pH scale for acidity and the Richter scale for earthquakes.

So, you might consider using a logarithmic scale if a change from 1 to 2 is just as important as a change from 100 to 200. The scale for Benford's Law is logarithmic.

Logarithmic scales are so named because the logarithm outputs of the numbers on the axis increase linearly. For example, the numbers 1, 10, 100, and 1000 are equally spaced. The base-10 logarithms of these numbers are 0, 1, 2, and 3.

Example

Problem The U.S. Census has been taken every 10 years since 1790. It counts the number of people living in the United States. Here are two graphs of the data from the census. One uses a linear scale on both axes. The other uses a logarithmic scale on the *y*-axis.

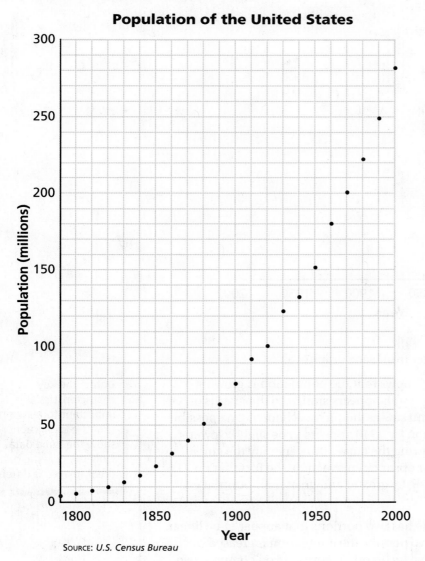

Population of the United States

SOURCE: *U.S. Census Bureau*

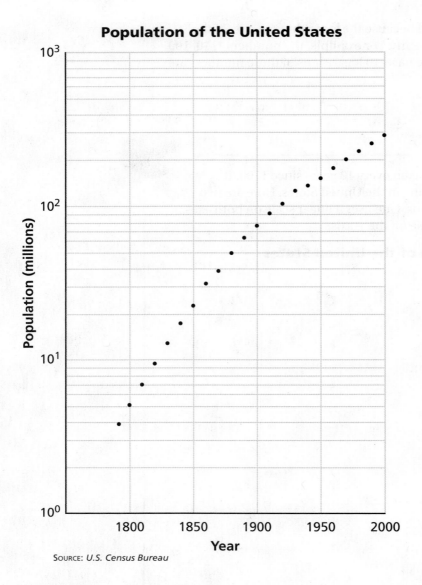

Population of the United States

SOURCE: *U.S. Census Bureau*

What information can you gather from each graph?

Solution The graph on a linear scale shows that the population is growing roughly exponentially, since the graph appears similar to the graphs of exponential growth functions you saw earlier in this chapter. One possible observation is that the population for 1940 appears to be slightly lower than might be expected by following the curve. But generally the curve seems to rise consistently. Other observations include the fact that the U.S. population appears to be growing by greater and greater amounts at each census, at least since 1950.

The graph on a logarithmic scale has two portions that appear to be linear. This means that during these two periods the population increased by the same growth factor every n years. In other words, if you compare two populations n years apart, they will have the same ratio as any other pair of populations n years apart.

Habits of Mind

Detect the key characteristics. It is important to remember that the two graphs show the same data. Only the way the data are displayed is different.

The noticeable change in the slope occurs at around 1900. The ratio appears to have changed. This suggests that the U.S. population has grown at a slower rate since 1900. Note that this observation is very difficult to make when viewing the data on a linear scale. This is the advantage of working with a logarithmic scale: ratios between successive outputs, whether equal or different, become immediately visible.

> You can also use a logarithmic scale on the x-axis to show the ratios between successive inputs more clearly.

For Discussion

2. The linear scale suggests the U.S. population grew by its greatest amount between 1990 and 2000, but the logarithmic scale suggests the population grew more slowly during that decade than in the past. Is this a contradiction? Explain.

You can use a logarithmic scale on the vertical or the horizontal axis, or on both. Some people prefer to say that you are actually graphing the logarithms of the values when you use this scale.

> Graph paper with one logarithmic axis is called *semilog* graph paper. Graph paper with two logarithmic axes is *log-log* graph paper.

Proving the Relationships

The In-Class Experiment and the U.S. Census example both show that when you plot an exponential function using a logarithmic y-axis, the function appears linear. For example, this graph is $y = 3 \cdot 2^x$ plotted with a logarithmic scale on the y-axis.

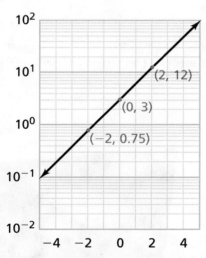

You can prove that the function $y = 3 \cdot 2^x$ should appear as a straight line on a logarithmic scale on the y-axis using the laws of logarithms.

Theorem 5.6

When you use a logarithmic *y*-axis and a linear *x*-axis, the graph of an exponential function $y = a \cdot b^x$ with $a > 0$ and $b > 0$ appears as a straight line.

Proof Consider any exponential function $y = a \cdot b^x$ with $a > 0$ and $b > 0$. When you use this scale, you display the logarithms of the *y*-values. So, calculate log *y* in terms of *b* and *x* using the laws of logarithms.

$$y = a \cdot b^x$$
$$\log y = \log (a \cdot b^x)$$
$$\log y = \log a + \log b^x$$
$$\log y = \log a + x \log b$$

This may not look like much, but remember that log *a* and log *b* are just numbers. If log $a = A$ and log $b = B$, then log $y = A + Bx$. This is an equation for a line in the plane. The graph of log *y* against *x* is linear.

There is an interesting corollary to this theorem. It has to do with two exponential functions graphed on the same set of axes. They appear as lines. Any two lines intersect unless they have the same slope. For example, there is exactly one solution to $2 \cdot 3^x = 8 \cdot 0.5^x$, since they are two lines with different slopes when graphed on this kind of scale. Here is the general statement.

Remember...

When making a graph, you choose to graph one thing against another. Here, choosing to graph log *y* against *x* gives a different picture than graphing *y* against *x*.

Corollary 5.6.1

The graphs of two exponential functions $f_1(x) = a_1 \cdot b_1{}^x$ and $f_2(x) = a_2 \cdot b_2{}^x$, with all a_i and b_i positive, must intersect exactly once unless $b_1 = b_2$.

This is true no matter what scale you use.

Overall, a logarithmic scale is another way of presenting data, one that stresses proportion instead of magnitude. You can use it to recognize graphically whether a function is exponential or logarithmic, or whether it makes sense to represent a set of data with an exponential or logarithmic function.

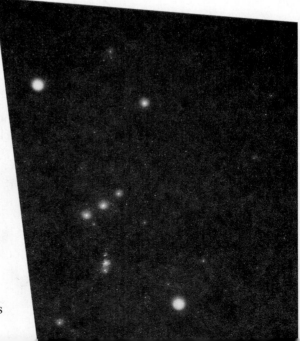

The stellar magnitude scale is a logarithmic scale. Brighter stars have lower values on the scale.

Check Your Understanding

The following table gives outputs for $\pi(x)$, the number of prime numbers less than or equal to x. The third column is a measure of the likelihood of choosing a prime among the integers from 1 to x. Out of all the integers from 1 to x, one in every $\frac{x}{\pi(x)}$ will be prime.

1. According to the table, do prime numbers become more or less frequent among larger integers? Explain.

2. Graph x against $\pi(x)$ using logarithmic x- and y-axes. Is there any observable pattern?

x	$\pi(x)$	$\frac{x}{\pi(x)}$
2	1	2
5	3	1.6667
10	4	2.5
50	15	3.3333
100	25	4
1000	168	5.9524
10,000	1229	8.1367
100,000	9592	10.4254
10^{10}	455,052,511	21.9755

For example, $\pi(6) = 3$ for the three primes 2, 3, and 5. This function's name is unrelated to the constant π that you know from studying circles. Amazingly, the primes from 1 to 100 million were calculated in the mid 1800s.

3. Graph x against $\frac{x}{\pi(x)}$ using a logarithmic x-axis and a linear y-axis. Is there any observable pattern?

4. The graph below shows the closing price of a stock from April 1, 2002, through April 1, 2004. Financial graphs use either linear or logarithmic scales on their vertical axis. Which scale does this graph use? Explain.

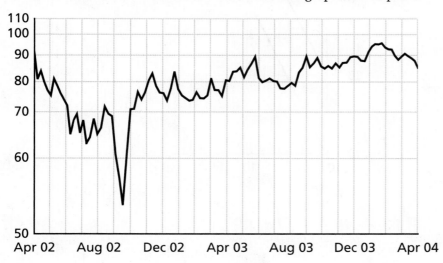

5. a. Use Theorem 5.6 as a model to prove the following result.

When you use a logarithmic x-axis and a linear y-axis, the logarithmic function $y = \log_b x$ appears as a straight line.

b. What is the slope of the line in part (a)? Assume that you use the base-10 logarithm for the x-axis.

6. a. Prove the following result.

When you use a logarithmic x-axis and a logarithmic y-axis, the power function $y = a \cdot x^b$ appears as a straight line.

b. What is the slope of the line in part (a)? Assume that you use the base-10 logarithm for both axes.

7. What's Wrong Here? Stephanie graphs $y = x^2$ and $y = 10x^2$ on the same piece of graph paper with both axes logarithmic.

Stephanie says, "Now wait a minute, these look parallel. Parallel lines don't intersect. But I know the graphs of $y = x^2$ and $y = 10x^2$ intersect at the point $(0, 0)$. Shouldn't these intersect too?"

What happened? Why do the graphs not appear to intersect?

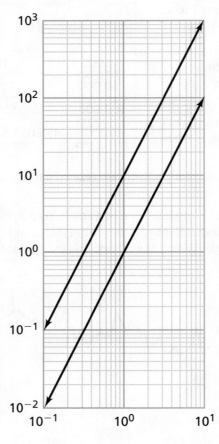

On Your Own

8. Is $f(x) = \log_2 x$ a one-to-one function? Explain.

9. a. Sketch the graph of $y = x$ on a logarithmic y-axis. Describe what the graph looks like.

    b. Sketch the graph of $y = \frac{1}{x}$ on the same axes.

    c. Take It Further Explain how the two graphs are related and why they are related in this way.

10. Find all solutions to each equation.

    a. $\log_3 x = \log_3 7$ **b.** $\log_3 x + \log_3 (x + 1) = \log_3 12$

    c. $\log x^2 = 4$ **d.** $\log_5 (x + 1) - \log_5 x = 1$

11. Standardized Test Prep Without a calculator, determine which of these four numbers is the greatest.

    A. $\log_4 17$ **B.** $\log_3 27$ **C.** $\log_5 117$ **D.** $\log_2 9$

12. This table includes the frequency for each of the eight A notes on a piano.

Note	Frequency (Hz)
A0	27.5
A1	55
A2	110
A3	220
A4	440
A5	880
A6	1760
A7	3520

Hz (or *hertz*) is a unit measuring cycles per second of a periodic event. In this case, it measures vibrations of a piano string.

Consider the function $F(n)$, where n is the note's octave (0 through 7), and $F(n)$ is the frequency of that note.

    a. Is $F(n)$ an exponential function, a logarithmic function, or neither? Explain.

    b. Graph $F(n)$. Choose the appropriate graph paper to make the graph of $F(n)$ appear as a straight line.

13. Take It Further Find or graph all the solutions to the equation $x^y = y^x$ with $x > 0$, $y > 0$, and $x \neq y$.

14. a. Copy and complete the following table.

x	$\log_2 x$	$\log_8 x$
0	■	■
1	■	■
2	■	■
3	■	■
4	■	■
5	■	■
6	■	■
7	■	■
8	■	■
9	■	■
10	■	■

    b. A calculator gives the value of $\log_8 23$ as approximately 1.5079. Approximate the value of $\log_2 23$.

15. Sketch each graph on a linear x-axis and logarithmic y-axis.

    a. $y = 2^x$ **b.** $y = 10 \cdot 2^x$

    c. $y = 1.5^x$ **d.** $y = 10 \cdot 1.5^x$

16. Sketch each graph on a logarithmic x-axis and logarithmic y-axis.

    a. $y = x^2$ **b.** $y = x^3$

    c. $y = 10x^2$ **d.** $y = 10x^3$

Mathematical 5C Reflections

In this investigation, you learned to evaluate logarithms of any base, to use logarithms in solving exponential equations, and to graph logarithmic functions. These questions will help you summarize what you have learned.

1. Solve each equation for x.

   a. $\log \frac{5}{6} + \log 6 = \log x$

   b. $\log_3 2 + \log_3 \frac{1}{2} = \log_3 x$

   c. $\log 10 \cdot \log x = \log 30$

   d. $\log_2 4 \cdot \log_2 \frac{1}{2} = \log_2 x$

2. Arrange the following numbers in order from least to greatest.
   $$\log_4 \frac{5}{2}, \ \log_2 \frac{1}{8}, \ \log 0.3, \ \log_7 1, \ \log_{\frac{1}{2}} 4$$

3. Let $N = \log_3 17$.

   a. Find two consecutive integers j and k such that $j < N < k$. Explain how you made your choice.

   b. Show how to use the change-of-base rule to evaluate N on a calculator that can only compute base-10 logarithms.

   c. Express $\log_3 (3 \cdot 17^2)$ in terms of N.

4. Find all values of x that are solutions of the equation $\log (x - 20) + \log (x - 50) = 3$.

5. Let $f(x) = \log_b x$, with $b > 0$ and $b \neq 1$.

   a. What do you know about b if the graph of $y = f(x)$ is increasing? If the graph is decreasing?

   b. For what values of x is $f(x) = 0$?

   c. Give the coordinates of one point on the graph of $f(x)$ without using any variables.

   d. How can you use the graph of $f(x)$ to determine the base b of the logarithm?

6. What are some reasons to use logarithms?

7. What is a logarithmic scale and when do you use it?

8. If you invest $1000 at 6% interest, compounded annually, how many years will it take until your money grows to $10,000?

Sand particles with diameters between $\frac{1}{4}$ mm and $\frac{1}{2}$ mm have values between 2 and 1 on the Krumbein scale.

Vocabulary and Notation

In this investigation, you learned these terms and symbols. Make sure you understand what each one means and how to use it.

- **common logarithm, log x**
- **linear scale**
- **logarithmic function, $x \mapsto \log_b x$**
- **logarithmic scale**

Project: Using Mathematical Habits

Functional Equations

Recall that a functional equation is an equation that relates some values of a function to other values of the function. In other words, the unknowns in a functional equation can be functions.

Suppose $f(x) = b^x$, with $b > 0$ and $b \neq 1$. Then you know that

- $f(1) = b$

- $f: \mathbb{R} \to \mathbb{R}$ is either strictly increasing (for $b > 1$) or strictly decreasing (for $0 < b < 1$)

- $f(x)$ satisfies the functional equation $f(x + y) = f(x) \cdot f(y)$

Conversely, suppose you are given an unknown function $g(x)$. All you know about $g(x)$ is that it satisfies the following three properties.

- $g(1) = b$, with $b > 0$

- $g : \mathbb{R} \to \mathbb{R}$ is strictly increasing

- $g(x)$ satisfies the functional equation $g(x + y) = g(x) \cdot g(y)$

Can you conclude that $g(x) = b^x$, with $b > 1$?

1. Show that $g(0) = 1$. (*Hint:* $0 + 1 = 1$)

2. Show that $b > 1$.

3. Show that each equation is true.

   a. $g(4) = b \cdot g(3)$

   b. $g(4) = b^2 \cdot g(2)$

   c. $g(4) = b^4$

   d. $g(n) = b^n$, for any nonnegative integer n

4. Show that for nonnegative integers m and n, $g(mn) = (g(m))^n$.

5. a. Show that $g(-1) = \frac{1}{b}$. (*Hint:* $1 + (-1) = 0$)

   b. Show that $g(n) = b^n$, for all integers n.

6. Let n be a positive integer. Show that
$$g\left(\left(\tfrac{1}{n} \right) \right)^n = b$$

7. Suppose $n = 4$ and $b = 81$. You know $g\left(\tfrac{1}{4}\right)$ must be a real number, because you assume that $\mathbb{R}$ is the target of g. From Exercise 6, you know $g\left(\tfrac{1}{4}\right)$ is a real number satisfying the equation below.
$$\left(g\left(\tfrac{1}{4}\right) \right)^4 = 81$$
So $g\left(\tfrac{1}{4}\right) = 3$ or -3.

   a. Use the fact that $g(x)$ is increasing to explain why $g\left(\tfrac{1}{4}\right)$ must equal 3 and not -3.

   b. Andy gives another reason why $g\left(\tfrac{1}{4}\right)$ must equal 3. He says, "Suppose we set $g\left(\tfrac{1}{4}\right) = -3$. Then $g\left(\tfrac{1}{8}\right)$ is not a real number, which doesn't work." Explain Andy's reasoning.

8. a. Show that $g(x) = b^x$ for all rational numbers x.

   b. Show that $g(x) = b^x$ for all real numbers x.

9. Suppose $h(x)$ has all the properties that $g(x)$ has, except that $h(x)$ is strictly decreasing. Show that $h(x) = b^x$ and $0 < b < 1$.

10. Suppose $k(x)$ has all the properties that $g(x)$ has, except that $k(x)$ does not have to be monotonic. Can you still conclude that $k(x) = b^x$?

11. Match each function in column A with a functional equation in column B.

A	B
$x \mapsto 2^x$	$f(a + b) = f(a) + f(b)$
$z \mapsto |z|$	$f(a + b) = f(a) \cdot f(b)$
$z \mapsto \arg z$	$f(ab) = f(a) \cdot f(b)$
$x \mapsto 2x$	$f(ab) = f(a) + f(b)$
$x \mapsto \log_3 x$	

Chapter 5 Review

Go Online
Pearsonsuccessnet.com

In **Investigation 5A,** you learned how to
- evaluate expressions involving exponents, including zero, negative, and rational exponents
- find the missing terms in a geometric sequence and make a geometric sequence to interpret expressions involving rational exponents
- convert between exponential and radical forms for rational exponents

The following questions will help you check your understanding.

1. Write each expression as a single power of x. Assume $x \neq 0$.

   a. $x^{-2} \cdot x^{-1}$ **b.** $\left(\frac{1}{x}\right)^{-2}$

   c. $\left((x^3)^{-2}\right)^{-5}$ **d.** $\frac{x^4}{x^{-4}}$

   e. $\left(x^6\right)^0 \cdot x^3$ **f.** $\frac{(x^5)(x^{-2})}{x^{10}}$

2. Find the missing terms in each geometric sequence.

   a. 5, 20, ■, ■, ■

   b. 6, ■, 24, ■, ■

   c. 1, ■, 6, ■

   d. 1, ■, ■, 125

   e. Use the sequence in part (d) to find $125^{\frac{2}{3}}$.

3. Simplify each expression.

   a. $49^{\frac{1}{2}}$ **b.** $81^{\frac{3}{4}}$

   c. $8^{-\frac{4}{3}}$ **d.** $\left(\sqrt[4]{16}\right)^5$

In **Investigation 5B,** you learned how to
- graph an exponential function and determine the equation of an exponential function given two points on its graph
- identify an exponential function from the table it generates and use the table to write a closed-form or recursive definition of the function
- evaluate the inverse of the function $y = b^x$, either exactly or by approximation

The following questions will help you check your understanding.

4. **a.** Suppose f is an exponential function with $f(2) = \frac{9}{2}$ and $f(3) = \frac{27}{2}$. Find $f(x)$.

   b. Sketch the graph of $y = f(x)$.

5. Copy this table for the exponential function $g(x)$.

x	$g(x)$	÷
0	-2	■
1	-20	■
2	-200	■
3	-2000	

   a. Complete the ratio column and write a recursive definition for $g(x)$.

   b. Write a closed-form definition for $g(x)$.

   c. Find $g(4)$ and $g(6)$.

6. Let $L_4(x)$ be the inverse of the function $h(x) = 4^x$.

   a. Find $L_4(1)$.

   b. Find $L_4(64)$.

   c. Find $L_4\left(\frac{1}{16}\right)$.

In **Investigation 5C,** you learned how to

- evaluate logarithms of any base using a calculator
- use logarithms to solve exponential equations
- graph logarithmic functions

The following questions will help you check your understanding.

7. Arrange the following numbers in order from least to greatest.

$\log_2 16$, $\log 5$, $\log_3 8$, $\log_4 \frac{1}{8}$, $\log_{\frac{1}{2}} 16$

8. Solve each equation. Give decimal answers to three places.

   a. $\log x - \log 5 = \log 15$

   b. $\log_2 (x - 1) + \log_2 (x + 1) = 3$

   c. $5^x = 7$

   d. $3 \cdot 2^x = 20$

9. Let $f(x) = \log_3 x$ and $g(x) = -2x + 3$.

   a. Graph $f(x)$ and $g(x)$ on the same set of axes.

   b. From the graph, determine the number of solutions to the equation $\log_3 x = -2x + 3$.

   c. Use the graph to estimate the solution(s) to $\log_3 x = -2x + 3$.

Go **Online**
Pearsonsuccessnet.com

Multiple Choice

1. Which of the following expressions is NOT equal to 1?

   A. $(2^3)^{\frac{1}{3}}$ **B.** $\dfrac{5^2 \cdot 5^4}{(5^2)^3}$

   C. $3^2 \cdot 3^{-2}$ **D.** $\left(\frac{1}{2}\right)^{-1} \cdot 2^{-1}$

2. Let $3^m = 2$. Find 3^{m+1}.

   A. 3   **B.** 4

   C. 5   **D.** 6

3. Which of the following expressions represents the smallest number?

   A. $25^{\frac{1}{2}}$ **B.** 4^{-2}

   C. $\log_2 8$ **D.** $\log_{\frac{1}{2}} 8$

4. Which of the following expressions is NOT equal to $\log_2(60)$?

   A. $\log_2 10 + \log_2 6$

   B. $\log_2 120 - \log_2 2$

   C. $\log_2 30 \cdot \log_2 2$

   D. $\log_2 12 + \log_2 5$

5. Which point is on the graph of $f(x) = \log_3 x$?

   A. $(0, 1)$ **B.** $(2, 9)$

   C. $(9, 2)$ **D.** $(60, 20)$

Open Response

6. Copy this table for the exponential function $h(x)$.

x	h(x)	÷
0	6	
1	3	
2	$\frac{3}{2}$	
3	$\frac{3}{4}$	
4	$\frac{3}{8}$	

   a. Complete the ratio column.

   b. Find a recursive definition for $h(x)$.

   c. Find a closed-form definition for $h(x)$.

   d. Find the exact value of $h(8)$.

7. Use the two function definitions below.

   $$f(x) = 4^x$$
   $$g(x) = \log_4 x$$

   a. Copy and complete each table.

x	f(x)
−1	▨
0	▨
$\frac{1}{2}$	▨
1	▨
2	▨

x	g(x)
$\frac{1}{4}$	▨
1	▨
2	▨
4	▨

   b. On a single set of axes, sketch the graphs of f and g.

   c. Is the graph of f increasing or decreasing?

   d. Is the graph of g increasing or decreasing?

8. Suppose $N = \log_2 28$.

   a. Find two consecutive integers j and k such that $j < N < k$.

   b. Express $\log_2 7$ in terms of N. (*Hint:* $7 = \frac{28}{4}$)

   c. Find the value of N to three decimal places.

9. Solve each equation. Give exact answers when possible, or round your answer to three decimal places.

   a. $x \cdot 16^{\frac{1}{2}} = 64^{\frac{4}{3}}$

   b. $45 = 5 \cdot 27^x$

   c. $2 \cdot 7^x = 24$

   d. $\log x + \log(x - 2) = \log 8$

10. If you invest $10,000 at 5.5% interest, compounded annually, how many years will it take until your money grows to $15,000?

11. Let $f(x) = b^x$. Explain why $f(m) \cdot f(n) = f(m + n)$.

Graphs and Transformations

The field of computer graphics depends heavily on mathematics, because mathematics is the language that computers speak. Computers store drawings as a series of coordinate pairs or triples, along with functions that define relationships and connections between them. In other words, every drawing is a graph.

You can animate a computer drawing using transformations of these graphs.

- Translations produce an identical copy of a drawing in a different location.

- Dilations produce a mathematically similar copy of a drawing that can be larger or smaller than the original.

- Reflections produce a mirror image of a drawing. A line acts as the mirror.

- Rotations produce an identical copy of a drawing that is turned relative to some center of rotation.

In this chapter, you will explore how changes in an equation result in transformations of its graph and how a transformation applied to a graph changes its equation. Computer animators use transformations to make objects appear to move and change shape. They do this either by manipulating the equations that define them or by using tools to change the object directly while the computer keeps track of the calculations. The work you will do in this chapter is at the foundation of computer graphics.

Vocabulary and Notation

- **affine recursive definition**
- **affine transformation, $\mathcal{A}_{(a, b)}$**
- **completing the square**
- **dilation, D_s**
- **even function**
- **fixed point**
- **identity transformation**
- **iteration**
- **odd function**
- **reflection transformation**
- **stabilizer, S_x**
- **translation, T_a**
- **unit circle**

Transforming Basic Graphs

In *Transforming Basic Graphs*, you will sketch basic graphs. You will explore the effects, on both the graphs and on their equations of translating, stretching, shrinking, and reflecting the basic graphs.

By the end of this investigation, you will be able to answer questions like these.

1. How are the graphs of $y = x^2$ and $y = (x - 3)^2$ related?

2. What does the graph of $(x + 1)^2 + (y - 4)^2 = 36$ look like?

3. What does the graph of $-2y = x^3 - x$ look like?

You will learn how to

- sketch basic graphs

- describe the effect of a translation of one of the basic graphs on both the graph and the equation of the graph

- describe the effect of scaling an axis or reflection on both the graph and the equation of the graph

- compose transformations and sketch the effect of such a composition

You will develop these habits and skills:

- Visualize variations of the basic graphs under translations, reflections, scaling, and compositions of those transformations.

- Match a transformation of a graph to a corresponding transformation of its equation.

- Analyze the operation of function compositions on transformations.

6.01 Getting Started

As you graph equations, you may notice that related equations have similar graphs.

For You to Explore

1. Sketch the graph of $y = x^2$.

2. Here are four equations related to $y = x^2$. Sketch the graph of each equation. Describe how the graph is related to the graph of $y = x^2$.

   a. $y + 5 = x^2$ **b.** $y = (x + 5)^2$

   c. $y = x^2 + 5$ **d.** $y - 3 = (x + 2)^2$

3. Sketch the graph of $y = x^3$.

4. Here are four equations related to $y = x^3$. Sketch the graph of each equation. Describe how the graph is related to the graph of $y = x^3$.

   a. $y + 5 = x^3$ **b.** $y = (x + 5)^3$

   c. $y = x^3 + 5$ **d.** $y - 3 = (x + 2)^3$

5. **Write About It** Compare the graphs of $y = x^2$ and $y = x^3$. In particular, address the following questions.

   • What type of symmetry does each graph have?

   • Through which quadrants does each graph pass?

   • How do the graphs compare near the origin? Away from the origin?

6. Sketch the graph of $y = \sqrt{x}$.

7. Here are four equations related to $y = \sqrt{x}$. Sketch the graph of each equation. Describe how the graph is related to the graph of $y = \sqrt{x}$.

   a. $y + 5 = \sqrt{x}$ **b.** $y = \sqrt{x + 5}$

   c. $y = \sqrt{x} + 5$ **d.** $y - 3 = \sqrt{x + 2}$

8. Sketch the graph of $y = |x|$, the absolute value function.

9. Here are four equations related to $y = |x|$. Sketch the graph of each equation. Describe how the graph is related to the graph of $y = |x|$.

   a. $y + 5 = |x|$ **b.** $y = |x + 5|$

   c. $y = |x| + 5$ **d.** $y - 3 = |x + 2|$

For help defining the absolute value function, see the TI-Nspire™ Handbook, p. 804.

10. **a.** Sketch the graph of $y = 3^x$ and $y = \log_3 x$ on the same axes.

    b. How are the two graphs related?

11. **Take It Further** Find three different equations with graphs that pass through the points $(6, 0)$ and $(-3, 0)$.

On Your Own

For Exercises 12–15, use this list of instructions.

- Connect endpoints (0, 0) and (3, 3).
- Connect endpoints (2, 2) and (3, 1).
- Connect endpoints (3, 3) and (5, 1).

12. a. Follow the instructions to plot figure *F*.

   b. Make a new list of instructions by replacing each point (x, y) in the list above with the point $(-x, -y)$.

   c. Follow your new instructions to plot figure *G* on the same set of axes.

   d. Describe how figures *F* and *G* are related to each other.

13. Think of figures *F* and *G* from Exercise 12 together as a single figure *O*. What kind of symmetry does figure *O* have?

14. a. Follow the instructions to plot figure *F* again on a new set of axes.

   b. Make a new list of instructions by replacing each point (x, y) in the list with the point $(-x, y)$.

   c. Follow your new instructions to plot figure *H* on the same set of axes.

   d. Describe how figures *F* and *H* are related to each other.

15. Think of figures *F* and *H* from Exercise 14 together as a single figure *E*. What kind of symmetry does figure *E* have?

16. Sketch each graph.

   a. $y = x^2$

   c. $y = x^2 - 3$

   b. $y = x^2 + 7$

   d. $y = x^2 - 10$

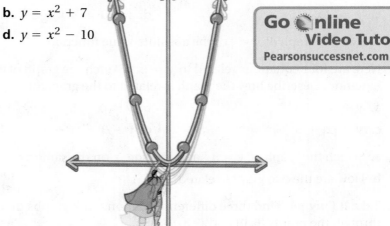

Go Online
Video Tutor
Pearsonsuccessnet.com

17. Write About It Describe the relationship between the graphs of $y = x^2$ and $y = x^2 + C$ for any number C.

18. Sketch each graph.

    a. $y = |x|$ **b.** $y = |x| + 7$

    c. $y = |x| - 3$ **d.** $y = |x| - 10$

19. Write About It Describe the relationship between the graphs of $y = |x|$ and $y = |x| + C$ for any number C.

20. Here are four equations related to $y = 3^x$. Sketch the graph of each equation. Describe how the graph is related to the graph of $y = 3^x$.

    a. $y + 5 = 3^x$ **b.** $y = 3^{x+5}$

    c. $y = 3^x + 5$ **d.** $y - 3 = 3^{x+2}$

21. a. Sketch the graph of $y = \frac{1}{x}$.

    b. Explain why the graph never intersects the x-axis or the y-axis.

22. Here are four equations related to $y = \frac{1}{x}$. Sketch the graph of each equation. Describe how the graph is related to the graph of $y = \frac{1}{x}$.

    a. $y + 5 = \frac{1}{x}$ **b.** $y = \frac{1}{x + 5}$

    c. $y = \frac{1}{x} + 5$ **d.** $y - 3 = \frac{1}{x + 2}$

23. Plot all the points on the xy-plane that are exactly 1 unit from the origin.

> You use the capital letter C here to show that C is a parameter rather than one of the variables you are graphing with. It is a value that you can change to produce different graphs. The idea is to see how different values of C change the graph.

Maintain Your Skills

24. Find the solutions to each equation.

    a. $5x - 7 = 2x + 5$ **b.** $5 \cdot \frac{x}{3} - 7 = 2 \cdot \frac{x}{3} + 5$

    c. $5 \cdot \frac{x}{10} - 7 = 2 \cdot \frac{x}{10} + 5$ **d.** $5 \cdot \frac{x}{100} - 7 = 2 \cdot \frac{x}{100} + 5$

25. Describe what happens to the solutions of an equation when you replace the variable x with $\frac{x}{C}$.

You have worked with the graphs of the following equations before, in this course or in your first-year algebra course.

- $y = x$

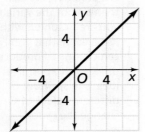

- $y = \frac{1}{x}$

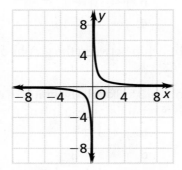

- $y = x^2$

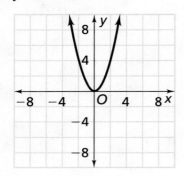

- $y = x^3$

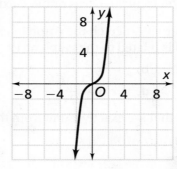

- $y = \sqrt{x}$

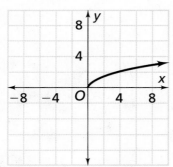

- $y = |x|$

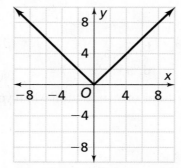

- $y = 3^x$

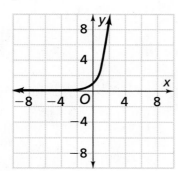

- $y = \log_3 x$

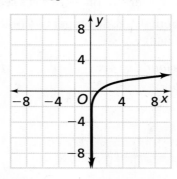

Any graph of $y = b^x$ with $b > 1$ looks similar to the graph of $y = 3^x$. Any graph of $y = \log_b x$ with $b > 1$ looks similar to the graph of $y = \log_3 x$.

You saw in the Getting Started lesson how, by changing these equations slightly, you can translate—move up, down, left, or right—the corresponding graphs without changing their shapes. In this lesson, you will learn three new basic graphs, namely the graphs of the equations $x^2 + y^2 = 1$ and $y = x^3 \pm x$.

The notation $y = x^3 \pm x$ really refers to two different equations: $y = x^3 + x$ and $y = x^3 - x$.

Graphing $x^2 + y^2 = 1$

The graph of the equation $x^2 + y^2 = 1$ is a shape you are familiar with.

Minds in Action   episode 23

Tony and Sasha are working on Exercise 23 from Lesson 6.01.

"Plot all points on the xy-plane that are exactly 1 unit from the origin."

Tony   Well, there are four obvious ones: $(1, 0)$, $(-1, 0)$, $(0, 1)$, and $(0, -1)$.

Sasha   Is there a point that has x-coordinate $\frac{1}{2}$?

Tony   Well, we would write it $\left(\frac{1}{2}, b\right)$. Then we need to find b. And we want its distance to $(0, 0)$ to be 1. What was the distance formula again?

Sasha   The distance between the points $\left(x_1, y_1\right)$ and $\left(x_2, y_2\right)$ is
$$d = \sqrt{(x_1 - x_2)^2 + (y_1 - y_2)^2}$$

Tony   Right. So we want
$$\sqrt{\left(\frac{1}{2} - 0\right)^2 + (b - 0)^2} = 1$$
We can get rid of the square root by squaring both sides. So we get
$$\frac{1}{4} + b^2 = 1$$
If we solve for b, we get
$$b^2 = \frac{3}{4}$$
$$b = \frac{\sqrt{3}}{2}$$

Sasha   Don't forget the negative root.

Tony   Oh, right. Thanks. So b is either $\dfrac{\sqrt{3}}{2}$ or $-\dfrac{\sqrt{3}}{2}$. Let's see, my calculator says $\dfrac{\sqrt{3}}{2}$ is about 0.866. So we get two points, $(0.5, 0.866)$ and $(0.5, -0.866)$.

Tony plots the six points they have found so far.

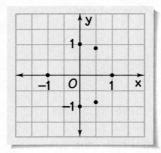

Sasha   Hey, shouldn't we also have $(-0.5, 0.866)$ and $(-0.5, -0.866)$ in there?

Tony   That makes sense. This picture should be symmetric. So we can also plot $(0.866, 0.5)$, $(0.866, -0.5)$, $(-0.866, 0.5)$, and $(-0.866, -0.5)$, right?

Sasha   Yeah, that sounds good.

Sasha plots the six new points.

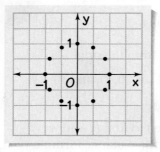

Sasha   Hey, it looks like a circle!

Suppose (a, b) is a point on the xy-plane that is exactly 1 unit from the origin. You can write this statement in symbols, using the distance formula.

$$\sqrt{(a - 0)^2 + (b - 0)^2} = 1$$

Square both sides and simplify.

$$a^2 + b^2 = 1$$

In other words, the point (a, b) satisfies the equation $x^2 + y^2 = 1$. Conversely, any point (a, b) that satisfies the equation $x^2 + y^2 = 1$ must be exactly 1 unit away from the origin. Therefore, you have just shown that the graph of the equation below is the unit circle.

$$x^2 + y^2 = 1$$

One such point is $\left(\dfrac{1}{2}, \dfrac{\sqrt{3}}{2}\right)$.

The **unit circle** is a circle of radius 1, centered at the origin.

For You to Do

1. Verify that $\left(\frac{3}{5}, \frac{4}{5}\right)$ is a point on the unit circle.

2. Using the point $\left(\frac{3}{5}, \frac{4}{5}\right)$, find as many other points on the unit circle as you can.

Using the distance formula, you can find an equation of a circle with any center and radius.

Example

Problem

a. Write an equation that describes the set of points that are exactly 1 unit away from $(3, -4)$, and sketch its graph.

b. Write an equation of the circle centered at the origin with radius r.

Solution

a. Using the distance formula as before, you know a point (a, b) is 1 unit away from $(3, -4)$ when

$$\sqrt{(a - 3)^2 + (b - (-4))^2} = 1$$

Square both sides and simplify.

$$(a - 3)^2 + (b + 4)^2 = 1$$

In other words, the desired equation is

$$(x - 3)^2 + (y + 4)^2 = 1$$

The graph is a circle of radius 1, centered at $(3, -4)$.

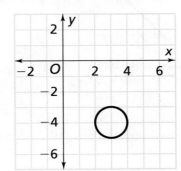

b. A point (a, b) is on a circle centered at the origin when it is r units away from the origin. In symbols,

$$\sqrt{(a - 0)^2 + (b - 0)^2} = r$$

Square both sides and simplify.

$$a^2 + b^2 = r^2$$

In other words, the desired equation is

$$x^2 + y^2 = r^2$$

For Discussion

3. If you square both sides of the equation $x = 3$, you introduce solutions that do not satisfy $x = 3$. So, $x^2 = 9$ and $x = 3$ are not equivalent equations.

Explain why the following two equations are equivalent.
$$\sqrt{(a - 3)^2 + (b + 4)^2} = 1 \text{ and } (a - 3)^2 + (b + 4)^2 = 1$$

The Equation $y = x^3 + x$

Here is the graph of the equation $y = x^3 + x$.

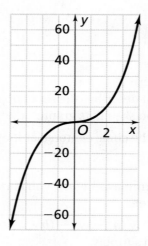

Zoom in on this graph near the origin.

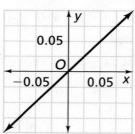

It looks like a straight line with slope 1. In other words, it looks like the graph of $y = x$. Why does it look that way? Well, when x is close to zero, say $x = 0.1$, you have

$$x^3 = (0.1)^3 = 0.001$$

This is very small. Most important, it is much smaller than x itself. Thus, you get

$$
\begin{aligned}
x^3 + x &= 0.001 + 0.1 \\
&= 0.101 \\
&\approx 0.1 \\
&\approx x
\end{aligned}
$$

In other words, when x is close to zero, you have

$$x^3 + x \approx x$$

And so the graph of $y = x^3 + x$ looks like the graph of $y = x$ near the origin.

> You could also say that when x is small, the term x^3 becomes *negligible* in the expression $x^3 + x$.

For Discussion

4. Explain why the graph of $y = x^3 + x$ starts to look like the graph of $y = x^3$ far away from the origin, as shown below.

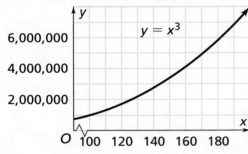

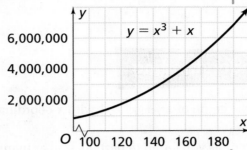

Here is a graph of $y = x^3 - x$.

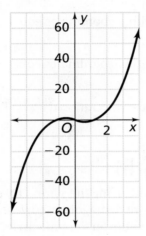

Again, zoom in near the origin.

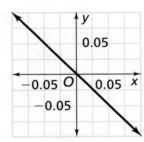

It looks like the graph of $y = -x$. And far away from the origin, the graph of $y = x^3 - x$ starts to resemble the graph of $y = x^3$, as shown below.

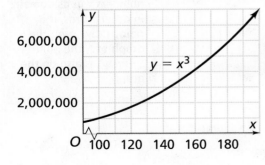

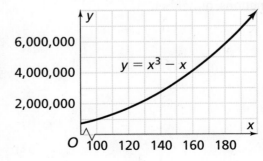

Exercises *Practicing Habits of Mind*

Check Your Understanding

1. a. Find all points on the graph of $x^2 + y^2 = 1$ with x-coordinates equal to $\frac{4}{5}$.

b. Using the point or points you found in part (a), find as many other points on the unit circle as you can.

2. a. Find all points on the graph of $x^2 + y^2 = 1$ with y-coordinates equal to $\frac{5}{13}$.

b. Find all points on the graph of $x^2 + y^2 = 1$ with x-coordinates equal to $\frac{8}{17}$.

3. Mariko writes down some points on the unit circle with rational coordinates.

Mariko says, "Let's see, so far I've found

$$\left(\tfrac{3}{5}, \tfrac{4}{5}\right), \left(\tfrac{12}{13}, \tfrac{5}{13}\right), \left(\tfrac{8}{17}, \tfrac{15}{17}\right)$$

I've also found all the points I could get from these using the symmetry of the circle. Wait, I recognize those numbers. They're Pythagorean triples! So we can use Pythagorean triples to find rational points on the unit circle."

What does Mariko mean? Explain.

Here are some other
Pythagorean triples.
• 7, 24, and 25
• 9, 40, and 41
• 20, 21, and 29

4. Let $f(x) = x^2$.

a. Show that f is an **even function** by showing that $f(-x) = f(x)$.

b. Show that f is an even function using the graph of $y = x^2$.

5. Let $f(x) = x^3 + x$.

a. Show that f is an odd function by showing that $f(-x) = -f(x)$.

b. Show that f is an odd function by using the graph of $y = x^3 + x$.

A function f is an **odd function** if it satisfies $f(-x) = -f(x)$ for all numbers x in its domain. In other words, if a point (x, y) is on the graph of f, the point $(-x, -y)$ is also on the graph.

6. Classify all of the basic graphs shown in this lesson as graphs of odd functions, even functions, or neither.

7. Explain why the graph of $y = x^3 + x$ has no x-intercept other than the origin.

8. a. Copy and complete the following table.

x	$x - 3$	$(x - 3)^2$
-1		
0		
1		
2		
3		
4		
5		
6		
7		

b. Using the table from part (a), sketch the graph of $y = (x - 3)^2$.

c. How are the graphs of $y = x^2$ and $y = (x - 3)^2$ related?

On Your Own

9. Let $g(x) = x^3 - x$.

a. Show that g is an odd function by showing that $g(-x) = -g(x)$.

b. Show that g is an odd function by using the graph of $y = x^3 - x$.

10. a. Explain why the graph of $y = x^3 - x$ resembles the graph of $y = -x$ near the origin.

b. Explain why the graph of $y = x^3 - x$ resembles the graph of $y = x^3$ far away from the origin.

11. Find the x-intercepts of the graph of $y = x^3 - x$.

12. a. Sketch the graph of $y = (x - 3)^3 - (x - 3)$.

b. Find the x-intercepts of the graph of $y = (x - 3)^3 - (x - 3)$.

c. How are the graphs of $y = x^3 - x$ and $y = (x - 3)^3 - (x - 3)$ related?

13. Write an equation for a circle with radius 5, centered at the origin.

14. Write an equation of a circle with radius 5, centered at the point $(3, 0)$.

Remember...

An intercept is a point where a graph intersects one of the axes.

Go Online
Pearsonsuccessnet.com

15. Serge takes the following approach to Exercise 14.

Serge says, "Let's see, in Exercise 13, I found an equation of a circle with radius 5, centered at the origin. It was $x^2 + y^2 = 25$.

"Now they're asking for the same circle translated three units to the right. Wait, this is just like the way the graphs of $y = x^2$ and $y = (x - 3)^2$ in Exercise 8 are related! So the equation of the new circle must be $(x - 3)^2 + y^2 = 25$."

Use Serge's method to find an equation of each circle.

a. radius 5, center at $(6, 0)$ **b.** radius 4, center at $(-3, 0)$

c. radius 1, center at $(0, -4)$ **d.** radius 1, center at $(3, -4)$

e. radius 3, center at $(-2, 3)$ **f.** radius r, center at (a, b)

16. Take It Further Sketch the graph of $(3x)^2 + y^2 = 1$. How is this graph related to the graph of $x^2 + y^2 = 1$?

17. Standardized Test Prep Which translation transforms the graph of $y = x^3 + x$ into the graph of $y = (x - 2)^3 + (x - 2)$?

A. 2 units up   **B.** 2 units down   **C.** 2 units left   **D.** 2 units right

Maintain Your Skills

18. Find the solutions to each equation.

a. $x^2 + 5x - 14 = 0$

b. $(x - 3)^2 + 5(x - 3) - 14 = 0$

c. $(x - 5)^2 + 5(x - 5) - 14 = 0$

d. $(x + 2)^2 + 5(x + 2) - 14 = 0$

19. Describe what happens to the solutions of an equation when the variable x is replaced by $x - C$.

6.03 Translating Graphs

Recall the lumping method of factoring from Chapter 2. You can also use the lumping technique to help you graph equations.

Minds in Action   episode 24

Sasha and Derman are trying to graph the equation $y = (x - 3)^2$.

Derman The equation $y = (x - 3)^2$ looks a lot like $y = x^2$. If I just cover the $x - 3$ part with my hand, it's easier, it is

$$y = M^2$$

Sasha That's pretty neat! And $y = M^2$ is one of the basic graphs we've already seen. Let me start with a table first.

M	y
−3	9
−2	4
−1	1
0	0
1	1
2	4
3	9

Derman Oh, I can graph that . . .

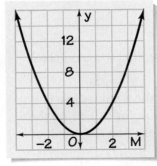

Are we done? I just graphed $y = M^2$, and since $M = x - 3$, is this the graph of $y = (x - 3)^2$?

Sasha Not quite. This is the graph of y against M. For example, the point $(2, 4)$ is on this graph, because when $M = 2$, we have $y = 4$. But what we need is a graph of y against x.

Derman Oh . . . When $x = 2$, we have $y = (2 - 3)^2 = 1$, but the point $(2, 1)$ is not on this graph. So what can we do?

Sasha Well, since $M = x - 3$, we can solve for x and get

$$x = M + 3$$

Let me write this in our table.

Sasha includes a new column of x-values in the table.

$x = M + 3$	M	y
0	−3	9
1	−2	4
2	−1	1
3	0	0
4	1	1
5	2	4
6	3	9

Derman The table has $(2, 1)$ in it! Cool.

Sasha Now we can just ignore the middle column and plot the points (x, y).

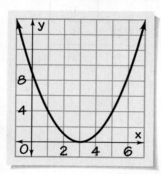

Derman It's the same graph as the graph of $y = M^2$, shifted three units to the right!

Sasha It makes sense, doesn't it? Since $x = M + 3$, the x-values just get shifted to the right by three. For example, the point $(-3, 9)$ on the graph of $y = M^2$ matches up with the point $(0, 9)$ on the graph of $y = (x - 3)^2$.

For Discussion

1. How are the graphs of $y = x^2$ and $y = (x + 5)^2$ related? Explain.

Developing Habits of Mind

Look for relationships In Exercise 18 of Lesson 6.02, you first solved the equation

$$x^2 + 5x - 14 = 0$$

The solutions are $x = -7$ and $x = 2$.

Next, you had to solve

$$(x - 3)^2 + 5(x - 3) - 14 = 0$$

An efficient way of solving this equation is to make the substitution $M = x - 3$. Then you get

$$M^2 + 5M - 14 = 0$$

Its solutions are $M = -7$ and $M = 2$. And since $x = M + 3$, you add three to each solution to get

$$x = -4 \text{ and } x = 5$$

Why does $x = M + 3$?

You can use the same idea to graph the equation $y = (x - 3)^2$. First make the substitution $M = x - 3$ so that $y = M^2$. Any point (M, y) that satisfies $y = M^2$ corresponds to a point (x, y) that satisfies $y = (x - 3)^2$. You can find the corresponding point by sending M to $x = M + 3$. For example, you translate the point $(-3, 9)$ on the graph of $y = M^2$ three units to the right to the point $(0, 9)$ on the graph of $y = (x - 3)^2$.

Similarly, you can translate graphs vertically (up or down) by making substitutions such as $N = y + 4$. Here are two examples.

Example

Problem Sketch the graph of each equation.

a. $x^2 + (y + 4)^2 = 1$

b. $y = (x - 3)^2 - 4$

Solution

a. With the substitution $N = y + 4$, this equation becomes

$$x^2 + N^2 = 1$$

The graph of this equation is the unit circle, which is a circle of radius 1 centered at the origin. The table at the right shows some points on the unit circle.

Since $N = y + 4$, solving for y gives

$$y = N - 4$$

x	N
1	0
−1	0
0	1
0	−1

Now, include a column of y-values in the table.

x	N	y = N − 4
1	0	−4
−1	0	−4
0	1	−3
0	−1	−5

Ignore the middle column and plot the points (x, y).

This is the unit circle, translated four units down. The key here is that since $y = N - 4$, you shift the y-values down by four.

> Use these points as the "corner points" of the new circle.

b. You can rewrite this equation as

$$(y + 4) = (x - 3)^2$$

With the substitution $N = y + 4$, the equation becomes

$$N = (x - 3)^2$$

The graph of this equation is the same as the graph of $N = x^2$, just translated three units to the right.

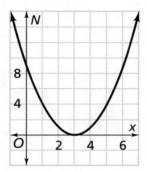

Since $N = y + 4$, solving for y gives $y = N - 4$. Therefore, the graph of $(y + 4) = (x - 3)^2$ is the same as the graph of $N = (x - 3)^2$, shifted down by four units.

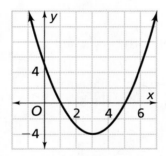

Or, you can compare these two expressions.

$$(x - 3)^2 \text{ and } (x - 3)^2 - 4$$

For each input x, the output $y = (x - 3)^2 - 4$ is four less than the output $y = (x - 3)^2$. So you can get the graph of the equation $y = (x - 3)^2 - 4$ by shifting the graph of $y = (x - 3)^2$ down by four units.

You can roll coins together in order to exchange them for bills.

Exercises Practicing Habits of Mind

Check Your Understanding

1. Consider the equation $y = \sqrt{x + 5}$. Let $M = x + 5$.

   a. Copy and complete the following table.

$x = M - 5$	M	$y = \sqrt{M}$
▪	0	▪
▪	1	▪
▪	4	▪
▪	9	▪
▪	16	▪
▪	25	▪

   > **Habits of Mind**
   >
   > **Look for relationships.**
   > Why are these good choices for values of M?

   b. Using the table from part (a), explain how the graphs of $y = \sqrt{x}$ and $y = \sqrt{x + 5}$ are related.

   c. Sketch the graph of $y = \sqrt{x + 5}$. According to the graph, what are the domain and the range of the function defined by $f(x) = \sqrt{x + 5}$?

2. Sketch the graph of each equation.

   a. $y = |x + 2|$

   b. $(x + 2)^2 + y^2 = 25$

   c. $(y - 3) = \log x$

   d. $y = \frac{1}{x} + 3$

3. Sketch the graph of each equation.

   a. $(y + 1) = |x + 2|$

   b. $(x + 2)^2 + (y - 4)^2 = 25$

   c. $y = \log(x - 5) + 3$

   d. $(x - 2)(y - 3) = 1$

4. **What's Wrong Here?** Walter is working on the following problem. The graph below is a graph of $y = x^3 - x$ translated two units to the right. Find its equation.

   Walter says, "Since it's two units to the right, I should replace x^3 with $(x - 2)^3$. So the equation I want is $y = (x - 2)^3 - x$."

   Do you agree or disagree with Walter? Explain.

   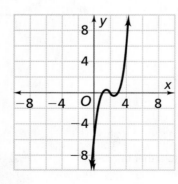

5. a. Explain how the graphs of the following equations are related.

- $y = x^3 + 6x^2 + 11x + 7$
- $y = (x - 2)^3 + 6(x - 2)^2 + 11(x - 2) + 7$

b. Expand $(x - 2)^3 + 6(x - 2)^2 + 11(x - 2) + 7$.

c. Using parts (a) and (b), sketch the graph of $y = x^3 + 6x^2 + 11x + 7$.

In Investigation 6B, you will see why you might want to replace x with $x - 2$.

6. a. Find the coordinates of the vertex of the parabola with equation $y = (x + 3)^2$.

b. Find the coordinates of the vertex of the parabola with equation $y - 2 = (x + 3)^2$.

c. In terms of h and k, find the coordinates of the vertex of the parabola with equation $y = (x + h)^2 + k$.

7. Sketch the graph of each equation.

a. $y = x^2 + 6x + 9$ **b.** $y = x^2 + 6x + 7$

On Your Own

8. Sketch the graph of each equation.

a. $y = (x - 2)^3 + (x - 2)$

b. $y + 1 = (x - 2)^3 + (x - 2)$

c. $y = (x - 2)^3 + x - 3$

d. Take It Further $y = x^3 - 6x^2 + 13x - 11$

9. Sketch the graph of each equation. Then find the slope of the graph.

a. $y = 3x$

b. $y = 3(x - 2)$

c. $y - 5 = 3(x - 2)$

d. How are the graphs in parts (a), (b), and (c) related? Explain.

10. a. Sketch the graph of $y = \frac{1}{2}x$.

b. Translate the graph of $y = \frac{1}{2}x$ three units to the right so that the origin $(0, 0)$ maps to the point $(3, 0)$ in the translated image. Find the equation of this new line.

c. Translate the graph of $y = \frac{1}{2}x$ three units to the right and one unit up so that the origin $(0, 0)$ maps to the point $(3, 1)$ in the translated image. Find the equation of this new line.

Go Online
Pearsonsuccessnet.com

11. **a.** Find an equation of the line with slope 4 that passes through the point $(3, 1)$.

b. Find an equation of the line with slope $\frac{2}{3}$ that passes through the point $(-2, -1)$.

c. Find an equation of the line with slope m that passes through the point (h, k).

12. The graph of the equation $y = x^2 + 6x + 7$ is a parabola with vertex at $(-3, -2)$.

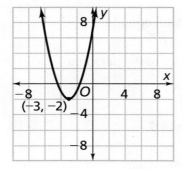

a. How are the graphs of $y = x^2 + 6x + 7$ and $y = (x - 3)^2 + 6(x - 3) + 7$ related? Explain.

b. How are the graphs of $y = (x - 3)^2 + 6(x - 3) + 7$ and $y - 2 = (x - 3)^2 + 6(x - 3) + 7$ related? Explain.

c. Simplify the expression below as much as possible.

$$y - 2 = (x - 3)^2 + 6(x - 3) + 7$$

13. **What's Wrong Here?** Susan is working on Exercise 11.

Susan says, "Let's see, I need a line with slope 4 that passes through the point $(3, 1)$. I can certainly start with $y = 4x$ and translate it to the right three and up one, so that the origin goes to $(3, 1)$. That gives me

$$y - 1 = 4(x - 3)$$

"But I can also take the point $(1, 4)$ on the graph of $y = 4x$ and move that to the point $(3, 1)$. That would mean translating the graph of $y = 4x$ to the right two and down 3, which gives me

$$y + 3 = 4(x - 2)$$

"I get two different answers. So this must mean there are at least two different lines with slope 4 that pass through the point $(3, 1)$."

Do you agree or disagree with Susan? Explain.

Go Online
Pearsonsuccessnet.com

14. Take It Further Derman is thinking about the graph of $y = (x - 3)^2$ again.

Derman thinks, "Instead of translating the graph of $y = x^2$ three units to the right, I can just keep it where it is and shift the coordinate axes three units to the left."

This figure shows the original axes in green and Derman's new axes in purple.

Use the substitution $M = x - 3$ to explain why Derman's method is valid.

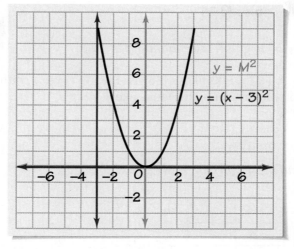

15. Standardized Test Prep Which equation has a graph that is a parabola with vertex at $(-1, -2)$?

A. $(y - 2) = (x - 1)^2$

B. $(y + 1) = (x - 2)^2$

C. $y = (x - 2)^2 + 1$

D. $y = (x + 1)^2 - 2$

Maintain Your Skills

16. a. Sketch the graphs of $y = 3^x$ and $y = \log_3 x$. How are the graphs related? Explain why they are related in this way.

Sketch the graphs of each equation. Explain how the graphs for each pair of equations are related to the graphs of $y = 3^x$ and $y = \log_3 x$, respectively. Then explain how the graphs of the two equations are related to each other.

b. $y = 3 \cdot 3^x$ and $y = \log_3 \frac{x}{3}$

c. $y = 9 \cdot 3^x$ and $y = \log_3 \frac{x}{9}$

d. $y = 27 \cdot 3^x$ and $y = \log_3 \frac{x}{27}$

e. $y = 3^n \cdot 3^x$ and $y = \log_3 \frac{x}{3^n}$, for a fixed positive integer n

Habits of Mind

Experiment. What do you find if n is negative?

6.04 Scaling and Reflecting Graphs

This lesson explores how to change an equation to resize its graph along either axis or reflect its graph over an axis.

Minds in Action   episode 25

Sasha and Derman are trying to graph the equation $y = \left(\frac{x}{3}\right)^2$.

Sasha   The equation $y = \left(\frac{x}{3}\right)^2$ looks like $y = x^2$ to me. If I cover $\frac{x}{3}$ with my hand like you did last time, this looks like $y = M^2 \ldots$

This time $M = \frac{x}{3}$.

Derman   We know this one pretty well.

Derman finds the table and the graph of $y = M^2$ in his notebook.

M	y
−3	9
−2	4
−1	1
0	0
1	1
2	4
3	9

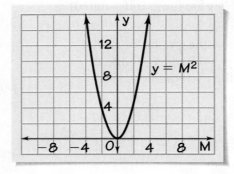

Sasha Great. Now, since $M = \frac{x}{3}$, solving for x gives us

$$x = 3M$$

Can you include this in your table?

Derman adds a column of x-values to his table.

$x = 3M$	M	y
-9	-3	9
-6	-2	4
-3	-1	1
0	0	0
3	1	1
6	2	4
9	3	9

Derman Oh, I can ignore the middle column and plot the points (x, y).

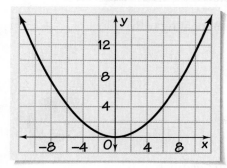

Sasha It looks just like the graph of $y = M^2$, stretched horizontally by a factor of 3.

Derman It makes sense to me. The x-values got tripled. $(2, 4)$ on the graph of $y = M^2$ became $(6, 4)$ on the new graph.

For You to Do

1. How are the graphs of $y = x^2$ and $y = \left(\frac{x}{5}\right)^2$ related?

2. How are the graphs of $y = x^2$ and $y = (5x)^2$ related?

Habits of Mind

Visualize. If $x = 3M$, each jump of one space in M corresponds to a jump of three spaces in x. If you look at a set of points on a graph that are all one unit apart in M, they are three units apart in x.

Developing Habits of Mind

Look for relationships. In Exercise 24 of Lesson 6.01, you solved the equation $5x - 7 = 2x + 5$. The solution is $x = 4$.

Next, you had to solve

$$5 \cdot \frac{x}{3} - 7 = 2 \cdot \frac{x}{3} + 5$$

You can solve this equation by making the substitution $M = \frac{x}{3}$.

$$5M - 7 = 2M + 5$$

The solution to this equation must be $M = 4$. But, since $x = 3M$,

$$x = 3(4) = 12$$

You can also use this idea to graph the equation $y = \left(\frac{x}{3}\right)^2$. Make the substitution $M = \frac{x}{3}$ to get the equation $y = M^2$. And by sending M to $x = 3M$, we find any point (M, y) on the graph of $y = M^2$ corresponds to a point (x, y) on the graph of $y = \left(\frac{x}{3}\right)^2$. For example, the point $(-1, 1)$ that is on the graph of $y = M^2$ gets scaled horizontally by the factor of 3 to the point $(-3, 1)$ on the graph of $y = \left(\frac{x}{3}\right)^2$.

You can use the same substitution technique when dealing with a reflection.

Example 1

Problem Sketch the graph of $y = 2^{-x}$.

Solution With the substitution $M = -x$, this equation becomes

$$y = 2^M$$

Here are the table and graph of this exponential function.

M	y
−3	$\frac{1}{8}$
−2	$\frac{1}{4}$
−1	$\frac{1}{2}$
0	1
1	2
2	4
3	8

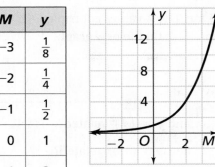

Since $M = -x$, solving for x gives

$$x = -M$$

Now, include a column of x-values in the table.

$x = -M$	M	y
3	−3	$\frac{1}{8}$
2	−2	$\frac{1}{4}$
1	−1	$\frac{1}{2}$
0	0	1
−1	1	2
−2	2	4
−3	3	8

Ignore the middle column and plot the points (x, y).

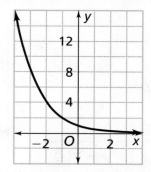

This graph is the same as the graph of $y = 2^M$ reflected over the y-axis. In other words, a point (M, y) on the graph of $y = 2^M$ corresponds to a point (x, y) on the graph of $y = 2^{-x}$, where $x = -M$.

You could also rewrite the equation.

$$y = 2^{-x} = \left(\frac{1}{2}\right)^x$$

Then you could use a relationship that you discovered in Chapter 5: the graph of $y = \left(\frac{1}{n}\right)^x$ is the reflection over the y-axis of the graph of $y = n^x$.

Similarly, you can scale graphs vertically, or reflect them over the *x*-axis, by making substitutions such as $N = -2y$.

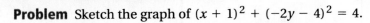

Example 2

Problem Sketch the graph of $(x + 1)^2 + (-2y - 4)^2 = 4$.

Solution With the substitution $N = -2y$, this equation becomes

$$(x + 1)^2 + (N - 4)^2 = 4$$

This is a circle of radius 2 with the center at the point $(-1, 4)$. Here is its graph and a table showing some of its points.

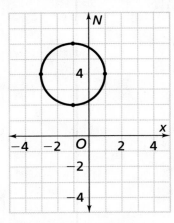

x	N
1	4
−3	4
−1	6
−1	2

Since $N = -2y$, solving for *y* gives

$$y = -\frac{N}{2}$$

Now, include a column of *y*-values in the table.

x	N	$y = -\frac{N}{2}$
1	4	−2
−3	4	−2
−1	6	−3
−1	2	−1

Ignore the middle column and plot the points (x, y).

To get this new graph, reflect the original circle over the *x*-axis and then scale it vertically by a factor of $\frac{1}{2}$. Algebraically, this corresponds to the fact that $y = -\frac{N}{2}$.

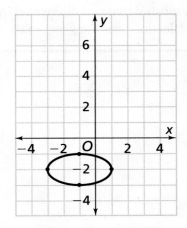

Check Your Understanding

1. Consider the equation $5y = x^2 + 1$.
   Let $N = 5y$.

   a. Copy and complete the following table.

   b. Using the table from part (a), explain how the graphs of $y = x^2 + 1$ and $5y = x^2 + 1$ are related.

   c. Sketch the graph of $5y = x^2 + 1$.

x	$N = x^2 + 1$	$y = \dfrac{N}{5}$
-2	▨	▨
-1	▨	▨
0	▨	▨
1	▨	▨
2	▨	▨
3	▨	▨

2. Sketch the graph of each equation.

   a. $x^2 + y^2 = 36$　　**b.** $(2x)^2 + y^2 = 36$　　**c.** $x^2 + (3y)^2 = 36$

   d. $(2x)^2 + (3y)^2 = 36$　　**e.** $\left(\dfrac{x}{2}\right)^2 + \left(\dfrac{y}{3}\right)^2 = 36$

   > For help graphing an equation in two variables, see the TI-Nspire Handbook, p. 804.

3. For each function f, sketch the graph of $y = f(x)$. Find the domain and range.

   a. $f(x) = -\sqrt{x}$　　　　　　**b.** $f(x) = -3\sqrt{x}$

   c. $f(x) = \sqrt{-3x}$　　　　　　**d.** $f(x) = \sqrt{1 - x}$

   > Hint:
   > $1 - x = -(x - 1)$.

4. This figure shows the basic graph of $y = x^2$ and the graph of another parabola.

   The second parabola is the image of the basic graph after a horizontal scaling by a factor of 2 and a translation of 3 units up and 4 units to the right. What is an equation for the second parabola?

   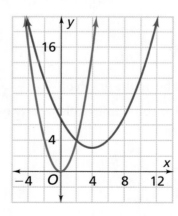

5. Sketch the graph of each equation.

    a. $y = (-x)^2$ **b.** $y = |-x|$ **c.** $(-x)^2 + y^2 = 1$

6. Tony and Sasha are arguing about the definition of an even function.

Tony says, "A function f is even if it has the property that $f(-x) = f(x)$ for all x in its domain."

Sasha says, "No, no. A function f is even if it looks the same when you reflect it over the y-axis."

Do you agree with Sasha or with Tony? Explain.

7. Explain how you can tell *without graphing* that the graph of $y = x^8 + 37x^6 - 71x^2 + 4$ looks the same when you reflect it over the y-axis.

8. **Take It Further** Given any function $f(x)$, explain why the function defined by $g(x) = f(x) + f(-x)$ looks the same when you reflect it over the y-axis.

9. Copy this graph of $x + y = 1$.

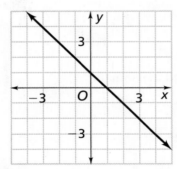

    a. Sketch the graph of $\frac{x}{5} + \frac{y}{3} = 1$.

    b. Sketch the graph of $\frac{x}{3} + \frac{y}{7} = 1$.

    c. Find two points that must be on the graph of $\frac{x}{-17} + \frac{y}{12} = 1$.

    d. The equation $\frac{x}{a} + \frac{y}{b} = 1$ is sometimes called the two-intercept form of a line. Explain.

Habits of Mind

Detect the key characteristics. Does every line have an equation of this form?

On Your Own

10. Sketch the graph of each equation.

    a. $y = (-x)^3 + (-x)$ **b.** $y = (-x)^3 - (-x)$ **c.** $y = -x^3 - x$

    d. $y = -x^3 + x$ **e.** $-y = (-x)^3 + (-x)$ **f.** $-y = (-x)^3 - (-x)$

11. Describe how the graph of each equation is related to the graph of $y = \frac{1}{x}$.

    a. $y = \frac{1}{-x}$ **b.** $y = \frac{1}{-4x}$ **c.** $y = \frac{4}{-x}$ **d.** $-y = \frac{1}{x}$

    e. $-4y = \frac{1}{x}$ **f.** $-\frac{y}{4} = \frac{1}{x}$ **g.** $-y = \frac{1}{-x}$ **h.** $-\frac{y}{4} = \frac{1}{-4x}$

12. This time, Tony, Sasha, and Derman are all arguing about odd functions.

    Tony says, "A function f is odd if it has the property that $f(-x) = -f(x)$ for all x in its domain."

    Sasha says, "No, no. A function f is odd if its reflection over the y-axis and its reflection over the x-axis look the same."

    Derman says, "I always thought that f was odd if rotating its graph $180°$ around the origin gave you a graph that looked the same as the original."

    Do you agree with Tony, Sasha, or Derman? Explain.

13. Explain how the graphs of the following equations are related.

    • $(x + 3)^2 + (y - 4)^2 = 1$

    • $(-x + 3)^2 + (-y - 4)^2 = 1$

14. Sketch the graph of each equation.

    a. $(3x)^2 + (2y)^2 = 36$

    b. $(3(x + 1))^2 + (2(y - 4))^2 = 36$

    c. $\dfrac{(x + 1)^2}{4} + \dfrac{(y - 4)^2}{9} = 1$

15. **Standardized Test Prep** Which equation can you use to graph the reflection of the graph of $y = \sqrt{x - 2} + 3$ over the y-axis?

    A. $y = \sqrt{x + 2} - 3$ **B.** $y = \sqrt{x - 2} - 3$

    C. $y = \sqrt{-x - 2} + 3$ **D.** $y = \sqrt{-x + 2} + 3$

16. **Write About It** Consider the equation $y = mx$. Its graph is a straight line through the origin. As the slope m increases, the line becomes more steep. On the other hand, you can rewrite the equation as

$$\frac{y}{m} = x$$

    Looking at it this way, you can say that as m increases, the line gets scaled vertically.

    Are these two ways of visualizing this situation geometrically consistent with each other? Explain.

Go Online
Pearsonsuccessnet.com

17. Take It Further

    a. Explain how the graphs of the following equations are related.

- $y = x^3 + 3x^2 + 7x + 13$
- $y = (x - 1)^3 + 3(x - 1)^2 + 7(x - 1) + 13$

    b. Expand $(x - 1)^3 + 3(x - 1)^2 + 7(x - 1) + 13$.

    c. If you divide the equation $y = x^3 + 4x + 8$ by 8, you get

$$\tfrac{1}{8} y = \left(\tfrac{1}{2} x \right)^3 + \left(\tfrac{1}{2} x \right) + 1$$

Use the second equation to explain how the graph of $y = x^3 + 4x + 8$ is related to the graph of $y = x^3 + x + 1$.

    d. Sketch the graph of $y = x^3 + x + 1$.

    e. Use parts (a)–(d) to sketch the graph of $y = x^3 + 3x^2 + 7x + 13$.

In Investigation 6B, you will see why you might want to replace x with $x - 1$.

18. Take It Further At home, Derman is thinking about the graph of $y = \left(\tfrac{x}{3} \right)^2$ again.

Derman thinks, "Instead of scaling the graph of $y = x^2$ horizontally by the factor of 3, I can just keep it where it is and scale the x-axis instead by the factor of $\tfrac{1}{3}$."

This figure shows the original axes in green and Derman's new axes in purple.

If the scale factor is greater than 1, the object stretches. If the scale factor is less than 1, the object shrinks.

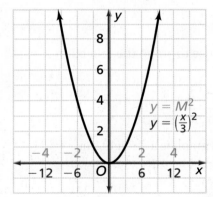

Use the substitution $M = \tfrac{x}{3}$ to explain why Derman's method is valid.

Maintain Your Skills

19. Determine whether each function is even, odd, or neither.

    a. $f(x) = x^2$ **b.** $f(x) = x^3$ **c.** $f(x) = x^4$ **d.** $f(x) = x^5$

    e. $f(x) = x^{10}$ **f.** $f(x) = x^{-1}$ **g.** $f(x) = x^n$, where n is an integer

In this investigation, you sketched basic graphs. You learned to relate the effects on a basic graph and on the equation of the graph of a translation, a scaling, or a reflection of the graph. These exercises will help you summarize what you have learned.

1. **a.** Explain what it means for a function to be even, both algebraically and graphically, and give an example of an even function.

   b. Explain what it means for a function to be odd, both algebraically and graphically, and give an example of an odd function.

2. Sketch the graph of $y = |x - 2| + 3$. How is your graph related to the graph of $y = |x|$?

3. Write an equation for a function with a graph that is the graph of $y = x^3$ after a translation 3 units to the left and 1 unit up.

4. Sketch the graph of $\left(\frac{x}{2}\right)^2 + (3y)^2 = 25$. How is your graph related to the graph of $x^2 + y^2 = 25$?

5. Write an equation for a function with a graph that is the graph of $y = \frac{1}{x}$ scaled horizontally by the factor 6.

6. How are the graphs of $y = x^2$ and $y = (x - 3)^2$ related?

7. What does the graph of $(x + 1)^2 + (y - 4)^2 = 36$ look like?

8. What does the graph of $-2y = x^3 - x$ look like?

Vocabulary

In this investigation, you learned these terms. Make sure you understand what each one means and how to use it.

- even function
- odd function
- unit circle

Affine Transformations

In *Affine Transformations*, you will continue to work with translations and dilations. You will learn to write the composition of a translation and a dilation as an affine transformation. You will use affine transformations to convert quadratic and cubic equations into the basic graph forms.

By the end of this investigation, you will be able to answer questions like these.

1. Why do dilations commute under function composition?

2. How do you compute the inverse of an affine transformation?

3. How do you transform an equation of the form $y = ax^3 + bx^2 + cx + d$ into one of the equations $y = x^3$, $y = x^3 + x$, or $y = x^3 - x$ by composing dilations and translations?

You will learn how to

- write any composition of translations and dilations as an affine transformation, and write any affine transformation as a composition of a dilation and a translation

- find the inverse of a dilation, a translation, or an affine transformation and use that inverse as a tool to solve equations

- find transformations for converting a general quadratic or cubic into one of the basic graph forms

You will develop these habits and skills:

- Generalize from a series of numerical calculations to produce a proof for a property of transformations.

- Extend the idea of finding an inverse of a function by undoing its steps in reverse order to find the inverse of an affine transformation.

- Find connections between algebraic calculations, such as using substitutions to make an equation monic or to complete the square and the affine transformations of translation and dilation.

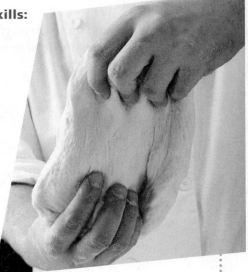

A vertical stretch is an affine transformation.

The compositions of some types of functions have special properties.

For You to Explore

Given a real number a, define a function T_a by the formula $T_a(x) = x + a$ for any real number x.

1. a. Compute each value.

$T_3(2)$ $T_3(5)$ $T_3(-1)$ $T_3(-7)$ $T_3(0)$

b. Why is T_a called a *translation by a*?

2. a. Compute each value.

$T_0(2)$ $T_0(5)$ $T_0(-1)$ $T_0(-7)$ $T_0(0)$

b. Why is T_0 called the **identity transformation**?

Suppose you have two functions, f and g where the target of g matches the domain of f.

As you saw in Chapter 2, you can build a new function $f \circ g$:

$$(f \circ g)(x) = f(g(x))$$

3. a. Compute each value.

$(T_3 \circ T_2)(4)$ $(T_3 \circ T_2)(-1)$ $(T_3 \circ T_2)(179)$

$(T_3 \circ T_2)(\pi)$ $(T_3 \circ T_2)(x)$, in terms of x

b. Find a such that $T_3 \circ T_2 = T_a$.

4. Two functions $f: \mathbb{R} \to \mathbb{R}$ and $g: \mathbb{R} \to \mathbb{R}$ are defined to be equal if $f(x) = g(x)$ for all real numbers x. Prove that $T_a \circ T_b = T_b \circ T_a$.

5. Compute each value.

a. $(T_{-4} \circ T_4)(3)$ **b.** $(T_{-4} \circ T_4)(-2)$

c. $(T_{-4} \circ T_4)(7)$ **d.** $(T_{-4} \circ T_4)(-1)$

e $(T_{-4} \circ T_4)(x)$, for any real number x

f. $(T_4 \circ T_{-4})(x)$, for any real number x

6. **Write About It** Explain how the functions T_a and T_{-a} are related to each other.

> **Remember...**
>
> You read $f \circ g$ as "f composed with g" or "f circle g." To find $f \circ g(a)$, you apply g to the input a and then apply f to the resulting output.

> In other words, prove that translations are commutative. In general, it is not always true that $f \circ g = g \circ f$.

On Your Own

For a nonzero real number s, a function D_s: $\mathbb{R} \to \mathbb{R}$ is defined by the formula $D_s(x) = sx$ for any real number x.

7. a. Compute each value.

$$D_3(2) \quad D_3(5) \quad D_3(-1) \quad D_3(-7) \quad D_3(0)$$

b. Explain why D_s is called a *dilation by s*.

8. a. Compute each value.

$$D_1(2) \quad D_1(5) \quad D_1(-1) \quad D_1(-7)$$

$D_1(x)$, in terms of x

b. Why is D_1 called the identity transformation?

9. a. Compute each value.

$$D_{-1}(2) \quad D_{-1}(5) \quad D_{-1}(-1) \quad D_{-1}(-7) \quad D_{-1}(0)$$

b. Why is D_{-1} called the **reflection transformation**?

The smooth surface of the water results in a reflection of the city.

10. a. Compute each value.

$$(D_3 \circ D_2)(4) \quad (D_3 \circ D_2)(-1) \quad (D_3 \circ D_2)(0) \quad (D_3 \circ D_2)(7) \quad (D_3 \circ D_2)(8)$$

b. Find k such that $D_3 \circ D_2 = D_k$.

11. Prove that $D_s \circ D_t = D_t \circ D_s$.

12. Compute each value.

a. $\left(D_{\frac{1}{4}} \circ D_4\right)(3)$ **b.** $\left(D_{\frac{1}{4}} \circ D_4\right)(-2)$

c. $\left(D_3 \circ D_{\frac{1}{3}}\right)(7)$ **d.** $\left(D_{\frac{1}{3}} \circ D_3\right)(-1)$

e. $\left(D_{\frac{1}{4}} \circ D_4\right)(x)$, for any real number x

f. $\left(D_4 \circ D_{\frac{1}{4}}\right)(x)$, for any real number x

13. Write About It Explain how the functions D_s and $D_{\frac{1}{s}}$ are related to each other.

14. Write each function in the form $x \mapsto ax + b$, where a and b are numbers.

a. $T_5 \circ D_2$ **b.** $D_2 \circ T_5$

> **Remember...**
>
> It is not usually the case that $f \circ g = g \circ f$. However, dilations commute under composition.

15. Take It Further Suppose r and s are numbers. Show that each function below can be defined by a linear polynomial with coefficients expressed in terms of r and s.

a. $T_r \circ D_s$

b. $D_s \circ T_r$

Remember...

A linear polynomial is a polynomial of the form $ax + b$, where the coefficients a and b are numbers.

Maintain Your Skills

16. Use the recursive definition below for a function f.

$$f(n) = \begin{cases} 2 & \text{if } n = 0 \\ T_3\left(f(n-1)\right) & \text{if } n > 0 \end{cases}$$

a. Copy and complete the following table.

n	f(n)
0	2
1	5
2	▦
3	▦
4	▦
5	▦
6	▦

b. Find a closed form for f.

17. Use the definition below for the linear function $f: \mathbb{R} \to \mathbb{R}$.

$$f(x) = 2x + 3$$

Find a closed form for each function.

a. $f \circ f$

b. $f \circ f \circ f$

c. $f \circ f \circ f \circ f$

d. $\underbrace{f \circ f \circ f \circ \cdots \circ f}_{7 \ f\text{'s}}$

6.06 Introducing Affine Transformations

Unlike the logarithmic functions in Chapter 5, you are probably familiar with the functions in Lesson 6.05. They are among the first functions you worked with in Algebra 1.

Developing Habits of Mind

Think about functions another way. The function D_5 is just $x \mapsto 5x$, and T_4 is just $x \mapsto x + 4$. These are examples of linear functions, which you have worked with before. However, in this investigation and the next, the perspective on these functions is a bit different.

You will study an algebraic structure, in which transformations of the form $x \mapsto ax + b$ are the objects, and the operation is function composition. Lesson 2.03 introduced you to the idea of algebra with functions. In this lesson, you will look much more closely at this idea.

Think of D_5 and T_4 as transformations of the number line. For example, T_4 translates numbers to the right by 4 units. The function D_5 dilates, or stretches, the number line by a factor of 5. Thinking about linear functions as transformations will help bring together many of the ideas about graph transformations from the previous investigation.

> A transformation on $\mathbb{R}$ is a function that maps $\mathbb{R}$ to itself.

Transformations of the form $x \mapsto ax + b$ are called *affine transformations*. An affine transformation can be built from two simpler types of transformation—translations and dilations.

> The word *affine* comes from the Latin *affinis*, which means "neighboring" or "related." It is related to the word *affinity*.

Facts and Notation

Let a be a real number. A **translation** by a is a transformation T_a of $\mathbb{R}$ given by the formula below, for any real number x.

$$T_a(x) = x + a$$

Let s be a nonzero real number. A **dilation** by s is a transformation D_s of $\mathbb{R}$ given by the formula below, for any real number x.

$$D_s(x) = sx$$

For Discussion

1. Why do you call T_a a translation? Why do you call D_s a dilation?

In Problem 3 from Lesson 6.05, you saw that $T_3 \circ T_2 = T_5$. This theorem is the generalization of that result.

Theorem 6.1

Let a and b be real numbers. Then $T_a \circ T_b = T_{a+b}$.

Developing Habits of Mind

Establish a process. Statements like Theorem 6.1 take some getting used to. Here is one way to think about building a proof. This is a series of questions you might ask yourself and steps you might take.

Step 1 What does the claim $T_a \circ T_b = T_{a+b}$ mean? It means that the two functions $T_a \circ T_b$ and T_{a+b} are the same. And what does that mean? It means that they have the same domain and that, given any input, they produce the same output.

Step 2 Try it with numbers. You did this in Exercise 3 of Lesson 6.05. There you showed that

- $(T_3 \circ T_2)(4) = 4 + 5 = T_5(4)$
- $(T_3 \circ T_2)(-1) = -1 + 5 = T_5(-1)$
- $(T_3 \circ T_2)(179) = 179 + 5 = T_5(179)$
- $(T_3 \circ T_2)(\pi) = \pi + 5 = T_5(\pi)$
- $(T_3 \circ T_2)(x) = x + 5 = T_5(x)$, for any number x

> You can check that the domains of $T_a \circ T_b$ and T_{a+b} are the same. Both domains are the real numbers.

This shows that $T_3 \circ T_2 = T_5$. Now generalize this result by replacing 3 and 2 with a and b. That is, show that

- $(T_a \circ T_b)(4) = 4 + a + b = T_{a+b}(4)$
- $(T_a \circ T_b)(-1) = -1 + a + b = T_{a+b}(-1)$
- $(T_a \circ T_b)(179) = 179 + a + b = T_{a+b}(179)$

Here is an example of the computation for $(T_a \circ T_b)(179)$.

$$
\begin{aligned}
(T_a \circ T_b)(179) &= T_a\big(T_b(179)\big) \\
&= T_a(179 + b) \\
&= (179 + b) + a \\
&= 179 + (a + b) \\
&= T_{a+b}(179)
\end{aligned}
$$

> ### Habits of Mind
>
> **Establish a process.** There is a rhythm to these calculations. Try to find it. The important thing is that there is nothing special about 179 or -1 or π. The same steps work for any input.

Similarly, you can show that

- $(T_a \circ T_b)(\pi) = \pi + a + b = T_{a+b}(\pi)$
- $(T_a \circ T_b)(x) = x + a + b = T_{a+b}(x)$ for any number x

The last equation does it. If the equation below is true for any number x, then the functions $T_a \circ T_b$ and T_{a+b} are the same.

$$(T_a \circ T_b)(x) = x + a + b = T_{a+b}(x)$$

From all your numerical work, you can easily put together the proof.

Proof Given any real number x,

$$(T_a \circ T_b)(x) = T_a\big(T_b(x)\big)$$
$$= T_a(x + b)$$
$$= (x + b) + a$$
$$= x + (a + b)$$
$$= T_{a+b}(x)$$

Therefore, $T_a \circ T_b = T_{a+b}$.

Habits of Mind

Check your assumptions. For a complete proof, you need to check that $T_a \circ T_b$ and T_{a+b} have the same domain. But they do, don't they?

For You to Do

2. Prove that, for any real numbers a and b, $T_a \circ T_b = T_b \circ T_a$.

Translations commute under composition.

In Exercise 10 from Lesson 6.05, you saw tha $D_3 \circ D_2 = D_6$. This theorem is the generalization of that result.

Theorem 6.2

Let s and t be nonzero real numbers. Then

$$D_s \circ D_t = D_{st}$$

The proof of this theorem is left as an exercise. (See Exercise 3.)

For You to Do

3. Prove that, if s and t are nonzero real numbers, $D_s \circ D_t = D_t \circ D_s$.

Dilations also commute under composition.

For Discussion

4. Do translations and dilations commute with each other? That is, is the equation below true for all real numbers a and $s \neq 0$? Explain.

$$T_a \circ D_s = D_s \circ T_a$$

In Lesson 6.05, you saw that the transformations T_0 and D_1 have the property below for all real numbers x.

$$T_0(x) = D_1(x) = x$$

First of all, this means that $T_0 = D_1$. Moreover, this transformation does not do anything to $\mathbb{R}$. It fixes every number. You met this identity function in Lesson 2.04 as "id."

$$T_0 = D_1 = \text{id}$$

In Problem 5 from Lesson 6.05, you saw that for all real numbers x,

$$(T_{-4} \circ T_4)(x) = (T_4 \circ T_{-4})(x) = x$$

So T_{-4} undoes the action of T_4, and vice versa. In other words, T_4 and T_{-4} are inverses of each other: $(T_4)^{-1} = T_{-4}$. This holds in general.

Example 1

Problem Show that $(T_a)^{-1} = T_{-a}$.

Solution In Lesson 2.04, you learned that the inverse of a function f is the function f^{-1} such that $f \circ f^{-1} = \mathrm{id}$.

By Theorem 6.1, you have

$$T_a \circ T_{-a} = T_{a+(-a)} = T_0 = \mathrm{id}$$

Thus, the inverse of T_a is T_{-a}. That is, $(T_a)^{-1} = T_{-a}$.

Habits of Mind

Consider more than one strategy. You can also show that $T_a \circ T_{-a} = \mathrm{id}$ by showing that $T_a \circ T_{-a}$ and id are equal as functions, as you did in the proof of Theorem 6.1. But the theorem allows you to generalize and work completely with function algebra.

For You to Do

5. Show that $(D_s)^{-1} = D_{\frac{1}{s}}$.

Minds in Action   episode 26

Tony and Sasha are talking during lunch about what they have learned so far.

Tony   So, for translations, we have some properties that seem very familiar.

- $T_a \circ T_b = T_b \circ T_a = T_{a+b}$
- $T_0 = \mathrm{id}$
- $(T_a)^{-1} = T_{-a}$

Sasha   These do seem familiar. They seem like the properties of addition with real numbers. And look at the properties of dilations.

- $D_s \circ D_t = D_t \circ D_s = D_{st}$
- $D_1 = \mathrm{id}$
- $(D_s)^{-1} = D_{\frac{1}{s}}$

They seem a lot like multiplication.

For Discussion

6. Compare the algebra of translations with the arithmetic of addition. Compare the algebra of dilations with the arithmetic of multiplication.

Go Online
Pearsonsuccessnet.com

The composition of two translations is another translation. The composition of two dilations is another dilation. But the composition of a translation and a dilation is an *affine transformation*.

$$(T_b \circ D_a)(x) = T_b(ax) = ax + b$$

You will use a special notation, $\mathcal{A}_{(a, b)}$, to stand for the function $x \mapsto ax + b$.

Definition

Let a and b be real numbers with $a \neq 0$. An **affine transformation** by (a, b) is a transformation $\mathcal{A}_{(a, b)}$ of $\mathbb{R}$ given by

$$\mathcal{A}_{(a, b)} = T_b \circ D_a$$

The following example illustrates what happens when you compose two affine transformations.

Example 2

Problem

a. Simplify $\mathcal{A}_{(2, 3)} \circ \mathcal{A}_{(-1, 4)}$.

b. Simplify $\mathcal{A}_{(-1, 4)} \circ \mathcal{A}_{(2, 3)}$.

Solution

a. For a real number x, you have

$$
\begin{aligned}
\left(\mathcal{A}_{(2, 3)} \circ \mathcal{A}_{(-1, 4)}\right)(x) &= \mathcal{A}_{(2, 3)}\left(\mathcal{A}_{(-1, 4)}(x)\right) \\
&= \mathcal{A}_{(2, 3)}(-x + 4) \\
&= 2(-x + 4) + 3 \\
&= -2x + 11 \\
&= \mathcal{A}_{(-2, 11)}(x)
\end{aligned}
$$

Therefore, $\mathcal{A}_{(2, 3)} \circ \mathcal{A}_{(-1, 4)} = \mathcal{A}_{(-2, 11)}$.

> For help modeling affine transformations, see the TI-Nspire Handbook, p. 804.

b. For a real number x, you have

$$
\begin{aligned}
\left(\mathcal{A}_{(-1, 4)} \circ \mathcal{A}_{(2, 3)}\right)(x) &= \mathcal{A}_{(-1, 4)}\left(\mathcal{A}_{(2, 3)}(x)\right) \\
&= \mathcal{A}_{(-1, 4)}(2x + 3) \\
&= -(2x + 3) + 4 \\
&= -2x + 1 \\
&= \mathcal{A}_{(-2, 1)}(x)
\end{aligned}
$$

Therefore, $\mathcal{A}_{(-1, 4)} \circ \mathcal{A}_{(2, 3)} = \mathcal{A}_{(-2, 1)}$.

From this example, you can conclude two things:

- This composition of two affine transformations produces another affine transformation.

- Affine transformations do not commute under composition.

You will explore these ideas further in the exercises.

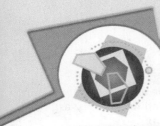 **Exercises** *Practicing Habits of Mind*

Check Your Understanding

1. Give another name for the transformation $\mathcal{A}_{(1,\,b)}$.

2. For which values of a and b is $\mathcal{A}_{(a,\,b)}$ a dilation only?

3. Prove Theorem 6.2.

4. Write each transformation in the form $x \mapsto ax + b$.

   a. $(T_3 \circ D_2)(x)$ **b.** $(D_2 \circ T_3)(x)$ **c.** $(T_{-5} \circ D_7)(x)$

   d. $(D_7 \circ T_{-5})(x)$ **e.** $(T_b \circ D_a)(x)$ **f.** $(D_a \circ T_b)(x)$

5. Find all values of a and b for which

$$T_b \circ D_a = D_a \circ T_b$$

6. Simplify each composition.

   a. $\mathcal{A}_{(2,\,-1)} \circ \mathcal{A}_{(3,\,5)}$ **b.** $\mathcal{A}_{(3,\,5)} \circ \mathcal{A}_{(2,\,-1)}$

   c. $\mathcal{A}_{(1,\,4)} \circ \mathcal{A}_{(-1,\,3)}$ **d.** $\mathcal{A}_{(-1,\,3)} \circ \mathcal{A}_{(1,\,4)}$

   e. $\mathcal{A}_{\left(\frac{1}{2},\,-3\right)} \circ \mathcal{A}_{(2,\,6)}$ **f.** $\mathcal{A}_{(2,\,6)} \circ \mathcal{A}_{\left(\frac{1}{2},\,-3\right)}$

7. Let $\mathcal{A}_{(a,\,b)} \circ \mathcal{A}_{(c,\,d)} = \mathcal{A}_{(e,\,f)}$. Express e and f in terms of a, b, c, and d.

8. Find numbers a and b that satisfy each equation.

   a. $\mathcal{A}_{(a,\,b)} \circ \mathcal{A}_{(4,\,1)} = \mathcal{A}_{(12,\,11)}$

   b. $\mathcal{A}_{(4,\,3)} \circ \mathcal{A}_{(a,\,b)} = \mathcal{A}_{(20,\,11)}$

   c. $\mathcal{A}_{(a,\,b)} \circ \mathcal{A}_{(2,\,3)} = \text{id}$

   d. $\mathcal{A}_{(2,\,3)} \circ \mathcal{A}_{(a,\,b)} = \text{id}$

Habits of Mind

Experiment. Try it with numbers! For example, give another name for $\mathcal{A}_{(1,\,3)}(x)$ and for $\mathcal{A}_{(1,\,-7)}(x)$.

Habits of Mind

Detect the key characteristics. Why does Exercise 7 show that a composition of two affine transformations is another affine transformation?

In Exercises 8c and 8d, you can write the identity transformation id as $\mathcal{A}_{(1,\,0)}$.

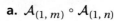

On Your Own

9. Simplify each composition.

   a. $\mathcal{A}_{(1,\,m)} \circ \mathcal{A}_{(1,\,n)}$

   b. $\mathcal{A}_{(s,\,0)} \circ \mathcal{A}_{(t,\,0)}$

   c. $\mathcal{A}_{(1,\,b)} \circ \mathcal{A}_{(a,\,0)}$

   d. $\mathcal{A}_{(a,\,0)} \circ \mathcal{A}_{(1,\,b)}$

10. **a.** Solve $4x + 8 = y$ for x in terms of y.

    b. Show that $\left(\mathcal{A}_{(4,\,8)}\right)^{-1} = \mathcal{A}_{\left(\frac{1}{4},\,-2\right)}$.

11. Find numbers c and d that satisfy each equation.

    a. $\left(\mathcal{A}_{(2,\,-1)}\right)^{-1} = \mathcal{A}_{(c,\,d)}$

    b. $\left(\mathcal{A}_{(3,\,5)}\right)^{-1} = \mathcal{A}_{(c,\,d)}$

    c. $\left(\mathcal{A}_{\left(\frac{1}{2},\,-3\right)}\right)^{-1} = \mathcal{A}_{(c,\,d)}$

    d. $\left(\mathcal{A}_{(2,\,6)}\right)^{-1} = \mathcal{A}_{(c,\,d)}$

    e. $\left(\mathcal{A}_{(a,\,b)}\right)^{-1} = \mathcal{A}_{(c,\,d)}$, for $a \neq 0$

12. Solve each equation for x in terms of y.

    a. $2x - 1 = y$

    b. $3x + 5 = y$

    c. $\frac{x}{2} - 3 = y$

    d. $2x + 6 = y$

    e. $ax + b = y$, where $a \neq 0$

13. Another way to find the inverse of an affine transformation is to think about it as a composition of a translation and a dilation.

    $$\mathcal{A}_{(a,\,b)} = T_b \circ D_a$$

    So an input is first dilated by a and then translated by b. The inverse undoes this process, working backward.

    $$\left(\mathcal{A}_{(a,\,b)}\right)^{-1} = \left(D_a\right)^{-1} \circ \left(T_b\right)^{-1}$$

    You know how to find the inverse of a dilation and a translation. Then you can write the resulting composition as an affine transformation. Use this method to find each inverse.

    a. $\left(\mathcal{A}_{(3,\,4)}\right)^{-1}$ **b.** $\left(\mathcal{A}_{(5,\,1)}\right)^{-1}$ **c.** $\left(\mathcal{A}_{(3,\,2)}\right)^{-1}$

You can also write the equation $4x + 8 = y$ as $\mathcal{A}_{(4,\,8)}(x) = y$.

When you put on your socks and shoes, which go on first? Which come off first when you take off your socks and shoes?

Now that you know how to find the inverse of an affine transformation, you can use these inverses to solve certain equations. But, affine transformations are not commutative under composition. So there is a difference between composing on the left and composing on the right. You need to make your choice strategically.

For example, suppose you want to solve this equation.

$$\mathcal{A}_{(a, b)} \circ \mathcal{A}_{(2, 8)} = \mathcal{A}_{(3, -4)}$$

Ideally, you want to isolate the $\mathcal{A}_{(a, b)}$ term, so it makes sense to compose each side with the inverse of $\mathcal{A}_{(2, 8)}$. If you do the composition on the left, this is what you get.

$$\left(\mathcal{A}_{(2, 8)}\right)^{-1} \circ \mathcal{A}_{(a, b)} \circ \mathcal{A}_{(2, 8)} = \left(\mathcal{A}_{(2, 8)}\right)^{-1} \circ \mathcal{A}_{(3, -4)}$$

You can simplify the right side of the equation, but the left side is more complicated than it was before. Because affine transformations are not commutative under composition, you cannot just rearrange the terms. This is what you get if you do the composition on the right.

$$\mathcal{A}_{(a, b)} \circ \mathcal{A}_{(2, 8)} \circ \left(\mathcal{A}_{(2, 8)}\right)^{-1} = \mathcal{A}_{(3, -4)} \circ \left(\mathcal{A}_{(2, 8)}\right)^{-1}$$

Now you can simplify the left side of the equation quite a bit, and the right side is still manageable.

> If you compose both sides of an equation with a function, you have to compose them on the same side to preserve equality.

> For this example, $\mathcal{A}_{(a, b)}$ turns out to be $\mathcal{A}\left(\frac{3}{2}, -16\right)$.

14. Find numbers a and b that satisfy each equation.

   a. $\mathcal{A}_{(a, b)} \circ \mathcal{A}_{(3, 4)} = \mathcal{A}_{(9, 6)}$

   b. $\mathcal{A}_{(3, 4)} \circ \mathcal{A}_{(a, b)} = \mathcal{A}_{(13, 6)}$

   c. $\mathcal{A}_{(a, b)} \circ \mathcal{A}_{(5, 1)} = \text{id}$

   d. $\mathcal{A}_{(3, 2)} \circ \mathcal{A}_{(a, b)} = \text{id}$

15. Simplify each composition.

   a. $\left(\mathcal{A}_{(2, -1)} \circ \mathcal{A}_{(3, 5)}\right)^{-1}$ b. $\left(\mathcal{A}_{(3, 5)}\right)^{-1} \circ \left(\mathcal{A}_{(2, -1)}\right)^{-1}$

   c. $\left(\mathcal{A}_{\left(\frac{1}{2}, -3\right)} \circ \mathcal{A}_{(2, 6)}\right)^{-1}$ d. $\left(\mathcal{A}_{(2, 6)}\right)^{-1} \circ \left(\mathcal{A}_{\left(\frac{1}{2}, -3\right)}\right)^{-1}$

16. a. Prove that $\left(\mathcal{A}_{(a, b)} \circ \mathcal{A}_{(c, d)}\right)^{-1} = \left(\mathcal{A}_{(c, d)}\right)^{-1} \circ \left(\mathcal{A}_{(a, b)}\right)^{-1}$.

   b. Make an analogy between the equation in part (a) and the act of putting on your socks and shoes and then taking them off.

17. Standardized Test Prep For which values of a and b does
$\mathcal{A}_{(a,\, b)} \circ \mathcal{A}_{(2,\, 4)} = \mathcal{A}_{(6,\, 6)}$?

A. $a = \frac{1}{2}, \; b = -2$ 　　　　　　**B.** $a = 3, \; b = \frac{3}{2}$

C. $a = 3, \; b = -6$ 　　　　　　**D.** $a = 4, \; b = 2$

18. Given a transformation F of $\mathbb{R}$ and a positive integer n, the *nth iterate* $F^{(n)}$ is defined as

$$F^{(n)} = \underbrace{F \circ F \circ \cdots \circ F}_{n \text{ copies of } F}$$

Simplify each transformation.

a. $\left(\mathcal{A}_{(a,\, b)}\right)^{(2)}(x)$

b. $\left(\mathcal{A}_{(a,\, b)}\right)^{(3)}(x)$

c. $\left(\mathcal{A}_{(a,\, b)}\right)^{(4)}(x)$

d. $\left(\mathcal{A}_{(a,\, b)}\right)^{(5)}(x)$

19. a. Use your work from Exercise 18 to find an expression for $\left(\mathcal{A}_{(a,\, b)}\right)^{(n)}$.

b. Suppose $a = 1$. What does your formula from part (a) look like? Why does it make sense?

c. Suppose $b = 0$. What does your formula from part (a) look like? Why does it make sense?

d. Suppose $a \neq 1$. Show that the formula from part (a) simplifies to

$$\left(\mathcal{A}_{(a,\, b)}\right)^{(n)} = \mathcal{A}_{\left(a^n,\; b \cdot \frac{a^n - 1}{a - 1}\right)}.$$

> Use this famous identity.
> $(a - 1)(a^{n-1} + a^{n-2} + \cdots + a + 1) = a^n - 1$

20. You showed in Exercise 19d that, for $a \neq 1$ and $n \geq 1$,

$$\left(\mathcal{A}_{(a,\, b)}\right)^{(n)}(x) = a^n x + b \cdot \frac{a^n - 1}{a - 1}.$$

a. Substitute $n = 0$ into this equation and simplify. Does your result make sense? Explain.

b. Substitute $n = -1$ into this equation and simplify. How does your result compare to that of Exercise 11e?

c. **Take It Further** Substitute $n = \frac{1}{2}$ into this equation and simplify. Use your result to compute

$$\left(\mathcal{A}_{(a,\, b)}\right)^{\left(\frac{1}{2}\right)} \circ \left(\mathcal{A}_{(a,\, b)}\right)^{\left(\frac{1}{2}\right)}.$$

21. Find numbers a and b that satisfy each equation.

a. $\mathcal{A}_{(3, 12)} = T_a \circ D_b$

b. $\mathcal{A}_{(3, 12)} = D_a \circ T_b$

22. If a and b are numbers and $a \neq 0$, show that each equation is true.

a. $T_b \circ D_a = D_a \circ T_{\frac{b}{a}}$

b. $T_b \circ D_a \circ T_{-\frac{b}{a}} = D_a$

Maintain Your Skills

23. Use the definition of function f below.
$$f(n) = \begin{cases} 2 & \text{if } n = 0 \\ D_3\left(f(n-1)\right) & \text{if } n > 0 \end{cases}$$

a. Copy and complete the following table.

n	f(n)
0	2
1	6
2	▨
3	▨
4	▨
5	▨
6	▨

b. Find a closed form for f.

Transforming Equations

In this lesson, you will transform equations into simpler forms through dilations and translations.

Transforming the Equation $y = ax^2 + bx + c$

You can transform any equation of the form $y = ax^2 + bx + c$ into an equation of the form $N = M^2$.

Minds in Action   episode 27

Tony and Sasha are working on the following problem.

Transform the equation $y = 8x^2 - 2x - 15$ into an equation of the form $N = M^2$ by first making it monic with a dilation and then **completing the square** with a translation.

Tony   I don't know about using dilations to make quadratics monic, but I do remember making monic quadratics in Chapter 2. You multiply through by a number that makes the x^2-term a perfect square. It's easiest just to use the coefficient. That gives us $8y = (8x)^2 - 2(8x) - 120$.

We can substitute $P = 8x$ and rewrite it as $8y = P^2 - 2P - 120$.

Sasha   But that's a dilation—in x and in y! Look, if $P = D_8(x) = 8x$ and $Q = D_8(y) = 8y$, we have $Q = P^2 - 2P - 120$.

Tony   Okay, but completing the square as a translation? I don't know about that one.

Sasha   So, let's just complete the square and see. We know how to do that. You look at the $P^2 - 2P$ part of the equation and figure out what constant to add to make it a perfect square. And that's 1, because $P^2 - 2P + 1 = (P - 1)^2$.

Tony   Then you go back to the equation and add and subtract that constant so you don't mess things up.

$$Q = P^2 - 2P + 1 - 1 - 120$$
$$Q = (P - 1)^2 - 121$$

Now, how is that a translation?

Sasha   Hmm. Oh, if I move the 121 . . .

$$Q + 121 = (P - 1)^2$$

So if $M = T_{-1}(P) = P - 1$ and $N = T_{121}(Q) = Q + 121$, then we have $N = M^2$.

Tony And you know what else? We used affine transformations on x and y as our substitutions!

- $M = (T_{-1} \circ D_8)(x) = \mathcal{A}_{(8, -1)}(x)$
- $N = (T_{121} \circ D_8)(y) = \mathcal{A}_{(8, 121)}(y)$

For You to Do

1. Consider the equation $y = 3x^2 + 4x - 2$. Find a, b, c, and d such that by making the substitutions below, you get the transformed equation $N = M^2$.

- $M = \mathcal{A}_{(a, b)}(x)$
- $N = \mathcal{A}_{(c, d)}(y)$

Now that you can transform an equation of the form $y = ax^2 + bx + c$ into a new equation of the form $y = x^2$, you can use the transformed equation to make other tasks easier. In the next investigation, you will see how this transformed form makes graphing easier. For now, you will learn how to use the transformed form to find the zeros of a quadratic polynomial.

Example 1

Problem Find the roots of the equation $8x^2 - 2x - 15 = 0$.

Solution Tony and Sasha transformed the equation $y = 8x^2 - 2x - 15$ into the form $N = M^2$ with these substitutions.

- $M = \mathcal{A}_{(8, -1)}(x)$
- $N = \mathcal{A}_{(8, 121)}(y)$

To find the zeros of the polynomial $8x^2 - 2x - 15$, you would normally just set $y = 0$ in the equation $y = 8x^2 - 2x - 15$. If you do that here, you get

$$N = \mathcal{A}_{(8, 121)}(0) = 121$$

And since $N = M^2$, you get

$$M = \pm 11$$

Now you have

$$M = (T_{-1} \circ D_8)(x)$$

Solve for x by taking the inverse.

$$x = \left(D_{\frac{1}{8}} \circ T_1\right)(M)$$

Since $M = \pm 11$,

$$x = \left(D_{\frac{1}{8}} \circ T_1\right)(\pm 11) = \frac{\pm 11 + 1}{8} = -\frac{5}{4} \text{ or } \frac{3}{2}.$$

The roots of the equation $8x^2 - 2x - 15 = 0$ are $-\frac{5}{4}$ and $\frac{3}{2}$.

Use the "socks-and-shoes" method of taking inverses.

For You to Do

2. Use the transformed equation you found in Problem 1 to find the roots of the equation $3x^2 + 4x - 2 = 0$.

Transforming the Equation $y = ax^3 + bx^2 + cx + d$

You can transform any equation of the form $y = ax^3 + bx^2 + cx + d$ into one of the equations $y = x^3$, $y = x^3 + x$, or $y = x^3 - x$.

Minds in Action   episode 28

Sasha and Tony are trying to transform the equation
$y = 10x^3 - 9x^2 - 13x + 6$ *into one of the basic forms, $S = R^3$, $S = R^3 + R$, or $S = R^3 - R$.*

Sasha   First, I want to make this equation monic. If I multiply through by 100, I'll make the x^3 term a perfect cube, and that should help.

$$100y = 1000x^3 - 900x^2 - 1300x + 600$$
$$100y = (10x)^3 - 9(10x)^2 - 130(10x) + 600$$

Tony   The substitutions we want to make are dilations again. Substituting $Q = D_{100}(y)$ and $P = D_{10}(x)$ makes it monic.

$$Q = P^3 - 9P^2 - 130P + 600$$

To make this into one of the basic other forms, we need to get rid of that quadratic term.

Sasha   With the other equation, we did a translation next, but I'm not sure which one will work here.

Tony   I know! We can just do a translation by some number k, and then we can pick the k that makes the quadratic term's coefficient 0.

Sasha   So if $M = T_k(P) = P + k$, we substitute $P = M - k$ into the equation.

$$Q = P^3 - 9P^2 - 130P + 600$$
$$= (M - k)^3 - 9(M - k)^2 - 130(M - k) + 600$$
$$= M^3 - 3M^2k + 3Mk^2 - k^3 - 9M^2 + 18Mk - \dots$$

Wait a minute. All I care about is the M^2 term, and I'm not going to get any more of those at this stage, so here's all I need.

$$-3M^2k - 9M^2 = (-3k - 9)M^2$$

Tony   We want that coefficient to be 0. If $-3k - 9 = 0$, then $k = -3$ and $M = T_{-3}(P) = P - 3$. So let's substitute $P = M + 3$ into $Q = P^3 - 9P^2 - 130P + 600$.

$$Q = (M + 3)^3 - 9(M + 3)^2 - 130(M + 3) + 600$$
$$= M^3 + 9M^2 + 27M + 27 - 9M^2 - 54M - 81 - 130M$$
$$\quad - 390 + 600$$
$$= M^3 - 157M + 156$$

Sasha   No quadratic term! Cool.

Tony   And $Q - 156 = M^3 - 157M$, so we can make $N = T_{-156}(Q)$ and have $N = M^3 - 157M$. Oh no, we're not done! How do we make the -157 into a -1 without messing all this up?

Sasha   It's got to be another dilation.

Tony and Sasha need a way to scale the equation to make the coefficient of the linear term of $N = M^3 - 157M$ equal to -1 while keeping it monic. This example shows how you can do it.

Example 2

Problem Use a dilation to transform $N = M^3 - 157M$ into an equation of the form $S = R^3 - R$.

Solution Multiply each side of the equation by a cube, say α^3.

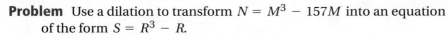

$$= (\alpha M)^3 - 157\alpha^2(\alpha M)$$

> You will figure out the value of α shortly.

Then, if $R = D_\alpha(M) = \alpha M$ and $S = D_{\alpha^3}(N) = \alpha^3 N$, the equation becomes

$$S = R^3 - 157\alpha^2 R$$

You want the coefficient of R to be -1.

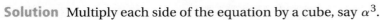

> You can also use $\alpha = -\dfrac{1}{\sqrt{157}}$, but choosing the positive root often makes the calculations a bit easier.

Tony and Sasha continue trying to transform the equation
$y = 10x^3 - 9x^2 - 13x + 6$ *into* $S = R^3 - R$.

Tony   Let's figure out where we are and see if we can answer the original question.

Sasha   So we started with $y = 10x^3 - 9x^2 - 13x + 6$.

To make that monic, we substituted $P = D_{10}(x)$ and $Q = D_{100}(y)$.

And we had

$$Q = P^3 - 9P^2 - 130P + 600$$

Tony   Then, to get rid of the quadratic term, we figured out what translation would work, and substituted $M = T_{-3}(P) = (T_{-3} \circ D_{10})(x)$ and $N = T_{-156}(Q) = (T_{-156} \circ D_{100})(y)$.

And we got

$$N = M^3 - 157M$$

Sasha   Then, to make the coefficient of M equal -1, we found $\alpha = \dfrac{1}{\sqrt{157}}$ and we substituted $R = D_\alpha(M) = (D_\alpha \circ T_{-3} \circ D_{10})(x)$ and $S = D_{\alpha^3}(N) = (D_{\alpha^3} \circ T_{-156} \circ D_{100})(y)$.

We ended up with $S = R^3 - R$.

Tony   Finally!

You should also note that, as with the quadratic equation, you can substitute your expressions for R and S in terms of x and y into the equation $S = R^3 - R$. By multiplying terms out and combining like terms, you can get back to your original cubic equation.

For You to Do

For Problems 3–5, give both the requested substitutions and the resulting equation.

3. Find substitutions that transform the equation $y = 4x^3 - 30x^2 + 59x + 15$ into a monic equation.

4. The equation $y = x^3 - 30x^2 + 236x + 240$ is already monic. Find substitutions that transform it into an equation without a quadratic term.

5. The equation $y = x^3 - 64x$ is already monic and has no quadratic term. Find substitutions that transform it into an equation of the form $S = R^3 - R$.

Extend the process. Can you find the zeros of the cubic polynomial below in the same way you found the zeros of the quadratic polynomial in Example 1?

$$10x^3 - 9x^2 - 13x + 6$$

Well, begin by setting $y = 0$. Then you have

$$S = \left(D_{\alpha^3} \circ T_{-156} \circ D_{100}\right)(0) = -156\alpha^3$$

And since $S = R^3 - R$, you get

$$R^3 - R + 156\alpha^3 = 0$$

Once you solve that equation for R, you can use the relationship below to find the values of x.

$$x = \left(D_\alpha \circ T_{-3} \circ D_{10}\right)^{-1}(R)$$

This gives you the zeros of the original polynomial $10x^3 - 9x^2 - 13x + 6$.

But solving an equation such as $R^3 - R + 156\alpha^3 = 0$ is no simple task. In later math courses, you may study how to solve equations of the form $R^3 \pm R + D = 0$, where D is a constant.

Exercises *Practicing Habits of Mind*

Check Your Understanding

1. Recall the work Tony and Sasha did in Minds in Action episode 27. By making the substitutions $M = \mathcal{A}_{(8,\,-1)}(x)$ and $N = \mathcal{A}_{(8,\,121)}(y)$, they transformed the equation $y = 8x^2 - 2x - 15$ into the equation $N = M^2$. Substitute $M = \mathcal{A}_{(8,\,-1)}(x)$ and $N = \mathcal{A}_{(8,\,121)}(y)$ into $N = M^2$. Then solve for y in terms of x.

> What should you get for y?

2. Consider the equation $y = 9x^2 + 12x - 5$.

   a. Find a, b, c, and d such that, by making the substitutions $M = \mathcal{A}_{(a,\,b)}(x)$ and $N = \mathcal{A}_{(c,\,d)}(y)$, you transform the equation to $N = M^2$.

   b. Let $y = 0$. Find, in order, the value or values of N, M, and x.

   c. Find the roots of $9x^2 + 12x - 5 = 0$.

3. Repeat Exercise 2 using the equation $y = 2x^2 + 4x + 5$.

4. For each equation, complete the square. That is, write it in the form below for some numbers k and D.

$$y = (x + k)^2 + D$$

a. $y = x^2 + 6x + 5$ **b.** $y = x^2 - 4x + 1$ **c.** $y = x^2 + 5x + 7$

5. **Take It Further** Consider the equation $y = x^2 + bx + c$.

a. If $M = T_k(x)$, then $x = T_{-k}(M) = M - k$.

Substitute $x = M - k$ into $y = x^2 + bx + c$. Find the value of k such that the coefficient of M is 0.

b. Use the value of k you found in part (a). Substitute $x = M - k$ into $y = x^2 + bx + c$. Simplify as much as possible.

c. Write the equation you found in part (b) in the form

$$y = (x + k)^2 + D$$

where D is some number. Find D in terms of b and c.

6. For each equation, find a, b, c, and d such that, by making the substitutions below, you get a transformed equation of the form $N = M^3$, $N = M^3 + M$, or $N = M^3 - M$.

- $M = A_{(a, b)}(x)$ • $N = A_{(c, d)}(y)$

a. $y = x^3 + 6x^2 + 11x + 7$ **b.** $y = x^3 + 3x^2 + 7x + 13$

On Your Own

7. Consider the equation $y = 5x^2 + 6x - 7$.

Go Online
Pearsonsuccessnet.com

a. Find a, b, c, and d such that, by making the substitutions below, you get the transformed equation $N = M^2$.

- $M = A_{(a, b)}(x)$ • $N = A_{(c, d)}(y)$

b. Let $y = 0$. Find, in order, the value or values of N, M, and x.

c. Find the roots of the equation $5x^2 + 6x - 7 = 0$.

8. Repeat Exercise 7 using the equation $y = 9x^2 - 12x + 4$.

9. Consider the equation $y = ax^2 + bx + c$, with $a \neq 0$.

a. Find e, f, g, and h such that, by making the substitutions below, you get the transformed equation $N = M^2$.

- $M = A_{(e, f)}(x)$ • $N = A_{(g, h)}(y)$

b. Let $y = 0$. Find, in order, the value or values of N, M, and x.

c. Find the roots of the equation $ax^2 + bx + c = 0$.

What should x be when $y = 0$?

10. Standardized Test Prep What are the roots of the equation
$2x^2 + 7x + 5 = 0$?

A. $x = -\frac{9}{2}$ and $x = 7$ 　　　　**B.** $x = -\frac{7}{2}$ and $x = -\frac{3}{2}$

C. $x = -\frac{5}{2}$ and $x = -1$ 　　　　**D.** $x = -\frac{3}{2}$ and $x = \frac{7}{2}$

11. Consider the equation $y = x^3 + bx^2 + cx + d$.

If $M = T_k(x)$, then $x = T_{-k}(M) = M - k$.

Substitute $x = M - k$ into $y = x^3 + bx^2 + cx + d$. Find the value of k such that the coefficient of M^2 is 0.

12. Consider this equation.

$$y = \left(M - \tfrac{b}{3}\right)^3 + b\left(M - \tfrac{b}{3}\right)^2 + c\left(M - \tfrac{b}{3}\right) + d$$

Expand the right side to get

$$y = M^3 + \left(-\tfrac{b^2}{3} + c\right)M + \text{(a number)}$$

a. Even before you expand the right side, why should you expect the quadratic term to vanish?

b. Given the equation $y = x^3 + bx^2 + cx + d$, you know that it transforms into one of the forms $N = M^3$, $N = M^3 + M$, or $N = M^3 - M$.

How can you tell which form from the coefficients b and c?

c. Given the equation $y = ax^3 + bx^2 + cx + d$, you know that it transforms into one of the forms $N = M^3$, $N = M^3 + M$, or $N = M^3 - M$.

How can you tell which form from the coefficients a, b, and c?

For Exercises 13 and 14, describe the substitutions required to transform each equation into one of the equations $N = M^3$, $N = M^3 + M$, or $N = M^3 - M$.

13. $y = 8x^3 - 6x^2 + 2x - 1$

14. Take It Further $y = ax^3 + bx^2 + cx + d$

Maintain Your Skills

15. Compute each composition.

a. $\mathcal{A}_{(2,\,3)} \circ T_4 \circ \left(\mathcal{A}_{(2,\,3)}\right)^{-1}$ 　　　　**b.** $\mathcal{A}_{(3,\,-7)} \circ T_{-3} \circ \left(\mathcal{A}_{(3,\,-7)}\right)^{-1}$

c. $\mathcal{A}_{(-1,\,8)} \circ T_5 \circ \left(\mathcal{A}_{(-1,\,8)}\right)^{-1}$ 　　　　**d.** $\mathcal{A}_{(-5,\,12)} \circ T_{-2} \circ \left(\mathcal{A}_{(-5,\,12)}\right)^{-1}$

16. Given an affine transformation $\mathcal{A}_{(a,\,b)}$ and a translation T_r, show that the composition below is a translation.

$$\mathcal{A}_{(a,\,b)} \circ T_r \circ \left(\mathcal{A}_{(a,\,b)}\right)^{-1}$$

In this investigation, you learned to write any composition of translations and dilations as an affine transformation and find the inverse of a dilation, a translation, or an affine transformation. These exercises will help you summarize what you have learned.

1. Write each composition as a single affine transformation, $\mathcal{A}_{(a,\, b)}$.

   a. $T_3 \circ T_{-1} \circ T_5$ **b.** $D_{-4} \circ D_2 \circ D_{-3}$ **c.** $D_{-4} \circ T_3$

   d. $T_3 \circ D_{-4}$ **e.** $T_3 \circ D_{-3} \circ (T_3)^{-1}$ **f.** $(D_{-4})^{-1} \circ T_5 \circ D_{-4}$

2. Write each expression as a single affine transformation, $\mathcal{A}_{(a,\, b)}$.

   a. $(\mathcal{A}_{(2,\, 5)})^{-1}$ **b.** $(\mathcal{A}_{(-3,\, 4)})^{-1}$ **c.** $\mathcal{A}_{(-3,\, 4)} \circ \mathcal{A}_{(2,\, 5)}$

   d. $\mathcal{A}_{(2,\, 5)} \circ \mathcal{A}_{(-3,\, 4)}$ **e.** $(\mathcal{A}_{(2,\, 5)} \circ \mathcal{A}_{(-3,\, 4)})^{-1}$

   f. Write an equation that relates $(\mathcal{A}_{(2,\, 5)})^{-1}$, $(\mathcal{A}_{(-3,\, 4)})^{-1}$, and $(\mathcal{A}_{(2,\, 5)} \circ \mathcal{A}_{(-3,\, 4)})^{-1}$.

3. Consider the equation $y = 3x^2 + 10x + 7$. Find a, b, c, and d such that, by making the substitutions $M = \mathcal{A}_{(a,\, b)}(x)$ and $N = \mathcal{A}_{(c,\, d)}(y)$, you get the transformed equation $N = M^2$.

4. The substitutions $M = \mathcal{A}_{(6,\, -5)}(x)$ and $N = \mathcal{A}_{(4,\, 1)}(y)$ transform a certain quadratic equation into the equation $N = M^2$.

   a. Substitute $M = \mathcal{A}_{(6,\, -5)}(x)$ and $N = \mathcal{A}_{(4,\, 1)}(y)$ into $N = M^2$. Solve for y in terms of x to find the original equation.

   b. Let $y = 0$ in the equation you found in part (a). Find, in order, the corresponding value or values of N, M, and x.

5. For $y = x^3 - 3x^2 + 12x + 17$, find a, b, c, and d such that, by making the substitutions $R = \mathcal{A}_{(a,\, b)}(x)$ and $S = \mathcal{A}_{(c,\, d)}(y)$, you get a transformed equation of the form $S = R^3$, $S = R^3 + R$, or $S = R^3 - R$.

6. Why do dilations commute under function composition?

7. How do you compute the inverse of an affine transformation?

8. How do you transform an equation of the form $y = ax^3 + bx^2 + cx + d$ into one of the equations $y = x^3$, $y = x^3 + x$, or $y = x^3 - x$ by composing dilations and translations?

Vocabulary and Notation

In this investigation, you learned these terms and symbols. Make sure you understand what each one means and how to use it.

- **affine transformation,** $\mathcal{A}_{(a,\, b)}$
- **completing the square**
- **dilation,** D_s
- **identity transformation**
- **reflection transformation**
- **translation,** T_a

Multiple Choice

1. Which translation transforms the graph of $y = x^2$ to the graph of $y = (x + 4)^2$?

   A. 4 units up   **B.** 4 units down

   C. 4 units left   **D.** 4 units right

2. What is the vertex of the parabola with equation $y - 4 = (x + 1)^2$?

   A. $(1, 4)$ **B.** $(-1, 4)$

   C. $(1, -4)$ **D.** $(-1, -4)$

3. Use the definitions of functions f and g below.

$$f(x) = x^2 + 4x$$
$$g(x) = x^3 + 4x$$

   Which of the following statements are true?

   I. f is an even function.

   II. f is an odd function.

   III. g is an even function.

   IV. g is an odd function.

   A. I and IV   **B.** II and III

   C. I only   **D.** IV only

4. For a nonzero real number s, the formula $D_s(x) = sx$ defines a function $D_s : \mathbb{R} \to \mathbb{R}$.

   What is $(D_2 \circ D_{-3})(5)$?

   A. -30 **B.** -5

   C. $-\dfrac{5}{6}$ **D.** 30

5. Which affine transformation is equal to $\mathcal{A}_{(2, 4)} \circ \mathcal{A}_{(-1, 3)}$?

   A. $\mathcal{A}_{(1, 12)}$ **B.** $\mathcal{A}_{(-2, 7)}$

   C. $\mathcal{A}_{(-2, 10)}$ **D.** $\mathcal{A}_{(-2, 12)}$

Open Response

6. a. Find all points on the unit circle $x^2 + y^2 = 1$ with x-coordinate $\dfrac{7}{25}$.

   b. Use your answer to find six more points on the unit circle.

7. a. Sketch a graph of $y = x^3 - x$.

   b. Write an equation for a function having a graph that is the graph of $y = x^3 - x$ after a translation 5 units to the right and 2 units down. Sketch the graph.

   c. Write an equation for a function having a graph that is the graph of $y = x^3 - x$ scaled horizontally by a factor of 3. Sketch the graph.

8. a. Sketch the graph of $y + 1 = 2|x - 4|$. How is your graph related to the graph of $y = |x|$?

   b. Sketch the graph of $\left(\dfrac{x}{2}\right)^2 + (y - 3)^2 = 25$. How is your graph related to the graph of $x^2 + y^2 = 25$?

9. Write each expression as a single affine transformation $\mathcal{A}_{(a, b)}$.

   a. $D_3 \circ T_1$ **b.** $T_1 \circ D_3$

   c. $D_2 \circ D_{-2} \circ T_6$ **d.** $T_4 \circ (D_2)^{-1}$

   e. $(\mathcal{A}_{(2, 6)})^{-1}$ **f.** $\mathcal{A}_{(2, -4)} \circ \mathcal{A}_{(-3, 5)}$

10. Consider the equation $y = 2x^2 + 6x - 3$. Find a, b, c, and d such that, by making the substitutions below, you get the transformed equation $N = M^2$.

   • $M = \mathcal{A}_{(a, b)}(x)$

   • $N = \mathcal{A}_{(c, d)}(y)$

11. What does the graph of $-2y = x^3 - x$ look like?

Investigation 6C

Graphing Using Affine Transformations

In *Graphing Using Affine Transformations*, you will use what you learned about affine transformations in the previous investigation to graph equations.

By the end of this investigation, you will be able to answer questions like these.

1. How do you use the replacing-the-axes method to sketch the graph of $y = x^3 + 3x^2 - x + 4$?

2. How do you use the replacing-the-axes method to explain the relationship between the graphs of $y = x^2$ and $y = (x - 3)^2$?

3. What is the fixed point for $\mathcal{A}_{(5, 3)}$?

You will learn how to

- use the techniques of Investigation 6B to transform an equation into one of the basic graph forms of Investigation 6A and use the information to graph the original equation

- describe the effect of an affine transformation on an axis and the effect of changes in axes on the graph of an equation

- identify the fixed points of an affine transformation and the set of affine transformations that fix a particular point

You will develop these habits and skills:

- Visualize transformations both as operations on graphs and as operations on coordinate axes.

- Make connections between transformations on graphs and on coordinate axes.

- Think algebraically to further examine the structure of the set of affine transformations.

You can use a dilation to relate the miles-per-hour scale and the kilometers-per-hour scale on the speedometer.

Getting Started

You can use number lines to show the result of an affine transformation.

For You to Explore

For each equation in Problems 1 and 2, find a, b, c, and d such that, by making the substitutions $M = \mathcal{A}_{(a, b)}(x)$ and $N = \mathcal{A}_{(c, d)}(y)$, you get the transformed equation $N = M^2$.

1. **a.** $y = 2x^2 - 12x + 17$ **b.** $y = -x^2 + 2x + 3$

2. **a.** $y = 3x^2 - 14x + 10$ **b.** $y = -\frac{1}{4}x^2 + 6x + 8$

3. Write each expression in the form $(x - h)^2 + k$.

     a. $x^2 + 4x$ **b.** $x^2 - 6x$ **c.** $x^2 + 5x$ **d.** $x^2 + 3x$

4. Write each equation in the form $(x - h)^2 + (y - k)^2 = r^2$.

     a. $x^2 + y^2 + 4x = 0$ **b.** $x^2 + y^2 - 6x + 4y - 12 = 0$

     c. $x^2 + y^2 + 5x = 0$ **d.** $x^2 + y^2 + 3x + 5y - \frac{1}{2} = 0$

5. Suppose $M = T_{-3}(x) = x - 3$. Then $x = T_3(M) = M + 3$.

Explain how the pair of number lines below shows the relationship between M and x.

6. For each expression, solve for x in terms of M. Then draw a pair of number lines like the one in Problem 5 showing the relationship between M and x.

     a. $M = T_4(x)$ **b.** $M = T_{-2}(x)$ **c.** $M = T_{\frac{3}{2}}(x)$ **d.** $M = T_0(x)$

     e. If $M = T_a(x)$, describe how the number lines for M and x are related.

On Your Own

7. Suppose $M = D_2(x) = 2x$. Then $x = D_{\frac{1}{2}}(M) = \frac{M}{2}$. Explain how the pair of number lines below shows the relationship between M and x.

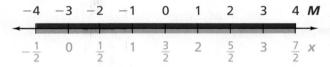

8. For each equation, solve for x in terms of M. Then draw a pair of number lines showing the relationship between M and x.

   a. $M = D_3(x)$ **b.** $M = D_{\frac{1}{2}}(x)$ **c.** $M = D_{-1}(x)$ **d.** $M = D_{-\frac{1}{2}}(x)$

   e. If $M = D_s(x)$, describe how the number lines for M and x are related.

9. Suppose $M = A_{(2, -3)}(x) = 2x - 3$. Then $x = A_{(\frac{1}{2}, \frac{3}{2})}(M) = \frac{1}{2}M + \frac{3}{2}$.

   Explain how the pair of number lines below shows the relationship between M and x.

   ```
   -4  -3  -2  -1   0   1   2   3   4  M
   ─────────────────────────────────────►

   -1/2  0  1/2  1  3/2  2  5/2  3  7/2  x
   ```

10. For each equation, solve for x in terms of M. Then draw a pair of number lines like the one in Exercise 9 showing the relationship between M and x.

    a. $M = A_{(3, -1)}(x)$ **b.** $M = A_{(\frac{1}{4}, 2)}(x)$

    c. $M = A_{(-1, -3)}(x)$ **d.** $M = A_{(-\frac{1}{2}, \frac{3}{2})}(x)$

11. For each equation, solve for x in terms of M. Then draw a pair of number lines like the one in Exercise 9 showing the relationship between M and x.

    a. $M = \left(A_{(3, -1)}\right)^{-1}(x)$ **b.** $M = \left(A_{(\frac{1}{4}, 2)}\right)^{-1}(x)$

    c. $M = \left(A_{(-1, -3)}\right)^{-1}(x)$ **d.** $M = \left(A_{(-\frac{1}{2}, \frac{3}{2})}\right)^{-1}(x)$

12. Simplify each expression using the socks-and-shoes method of taking inverses.

a. $(T_3 \circ D_2)^{-1}$ **b.** $(D_2 \circ T_3)^{-1}$ **c.** $(T_{-3} \circ D_{\frac{1}{2}})^{-1}$ **d.** $(D_{\frac{1}{2}} \circ T_{-3})^{-1}$

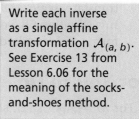

Write each inverse as a single affine transformation $\mathcal{A}_{(a,\, b)}$. See Exercise 13 from Lesson 6.06 for the meaning of the socks-and-shoes method.

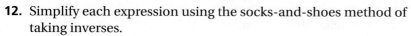
Maintain Your Skills

13. Expand the right side of each equation.

a. $y = (x-1)^3 + 3(x-1)^2 - (x-1) + 4$

b. $y = (x+2)^3 - 6(x+2)^2 - 4(x+2) + 1$

c. $y = (x-2)^3 + 6(x-2)^2 + 4(x-2) + 1$

d. $y = (x+1)^3 - 3(x+1)^2 + 2(x+1) + 4$

14. What is the coefficient of x^2 if you expand the following expression and write it as a polynomial in x?

$$\left(x - \frac{b}{3}\right)^3 + b\left(x - \frac{b}{3}\right)^2 + c\left(x - \frac{b}{3}\right) + d$$

Replacing the Axes

In this lesson, you will learn how you can use affine transformations to translate, scale, and reflect graphs with the "replacing-the-axes" method. In Investigation 6B, you found a way to transform equations into the basic forms. This resulted in a substitution such as $M = \mathcal{A}_{(2,\,-3)}(x)$.

For You to Do

For $M = \mathcal{A}_{(2,\,-3)}(x)$, show that each equation is true.

1. $x = (T_{\frac{3}{2}} \circ D_{\frac{1}{2}})(M)$

2. $x = (D_{\frac{1}{2}} \circ T_3)(M)$

You can use this affine transformation to create a pair of number lines that shows the relationship between the two variables.

$$
\begin{array}{ccccccccc}
-4 & -3 & -2 & -1 & 0 & 1 & 2 & 3 & 4 \ M \\
\end{array}
$$

$$
\begin{array}{ccccccccc}
-\frac{1}{2} & 0 & \frac{1}{2} & 1 & \frac{3}{2} & 2 & \frac{5}{2} & 3 & \frac{7}{2} \ x
\end{array}
$$

To describe this relationship in terms of translations and dilations, you might say that you dilated the M number line by the factor 2 and then translated it $\frac{3}{2}$ units left. This sequence of number lines shows that process.

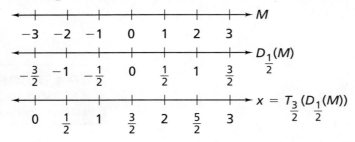

Each value on the $D_{\frac{1}{2}}(M)$ number line is half the corresponding value on the M number line. As a result, a unit on the $D_{\frac{1}{2}}(M)$ number line is twice as long as a unit on the M number line. You can think of the $D_{\frac{1}{2}}(M)$ number line as the image of the M number line after a dilation by the factor 2.

> **Habits of Mind**
>
> **Look for relationships.**
> Notice that $D_{\frac{1}{2}}$ multiplies numbers by $\frac{1}{2}$. From a geometric viewpoint, the result is a dilation of the number line by the factor 2.

Since $x = T_{\frac{3}{2}}(D_{\frac{1}{2}}(M)) = D_{\frac{1}{2}}(M) + \frac{3}{2}$, each value on the x number line is $\frac{3}{2}$ more than the corresponding value on the $D_{\frac{1}{2}}(M)$ number line. This means that the x number line is the image of the $D_{\frac{1}{2}}(M)$ number line after a translation of $\frac{3}{2}$ units to the left. You can check that corresponding values of M and x satisfy the equation $M = A_{(2, -3)}(x)$.

You can also think of the transformation from the M number line to the x number line as a translation followed by a dilation. This sequence of number lines shows that process.

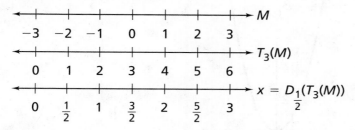

Notice that the number line for $T_3(M)$ is the image of the number line for M after a translation 3 units to the left. The number line for $x = D_{\frac{1}{2}}(T_3(M))$ is the image of the number line for $T_3(M)$ after a dilation by the factor 2.

Even though you follow a different process, the resulting pair of number lines for M and x is the same. You will use affine transformations on coordinate axes to graph some rather complicated equations.

Sasha and Derman are trying to graph the equation $y = (2x - 3)^2$.

Sasha   Okay, if we set $M = 2x - 3$, then this equation turns into $y = M^2$, which is a parabola. Here are its table and graph.

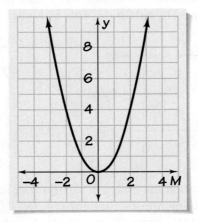

M	y
−3	9
−2	4
−1	1
0	0
1	1
2	4
3	9

Derman   We already have a pair of number lines showing the relationship $M = \mathcal{A}_{(2, -3)}(x)$.

We can use this relationship to show the labels for x that correspond to each value of M, right on the graph!

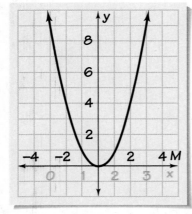

Sasha   With these new labels, we can figure out the (x, y) coordinates of lots of points on the graph of the parabola. For instance, we know its vertex is $\left(\frac{3}{2}, 0\right)$ and its line of symmetry has equation $x = \frac{3}{2}$.
We can label as many points as we want.

Derman   But wait. Doesn't the graph change at all?

Sasha Well, no, it is different. A graph is just a picture that lets us read off information about an equation. The picture itself tells us nothing about the equation unless we look at the axes. I can tell you anything you want to know about the pairs that satisfy the equation by looking at this picture. I can tell you if an (M, y) does or does not satisfy the equation, and I can do the same for an (x, y) pair. I just have to be careful that I read the information from the correct axes.

Derman But I can use this picture and all the points we found to make the usual kind of picture.

Derman makes a quick sketch.

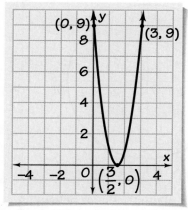

Sasha Sure, if that makes you feel better. But you can also learn to use the graph of y against M to get everything you can get from your graph. Try it. You'll get used to it.

For You to Do

Using the replacing-the-axes method, sketch the graph of each equation. You can stop at the replacing-the-axes graph if you want to, but be sure to label several points with their (x, y) coordinates. If you like, you can also make a sketch like Derman's, showing the graph in the xy-plane.

3. $y = |3x - 1|$

4. $y = \sqrt{\frac{1}{4}x + 2}$

As the following examples show, you can also transform a graph by replacing the vertical axis or by replacing both the horizontal and the vertical axes.

Example

Problems Sketch the graph of each equation.

    a. $x^2 + y^2 - 6x + 4y - 12 = 0$ **b.** $y = 2x^2 - 12x + 17$

Solutions

a. In Problem 4b of Lesson 6.08, you rewrote this equation as

$$(x - 3)^2 + (y + 2)^2 = 5^2$$

With the substitutions $M = x - 3$ and $N = y + 2$, the equation becomes

$$M^2 + N^2 = 5^2$$

The graph of this equation is a circle of radius 5 centered at the origin.

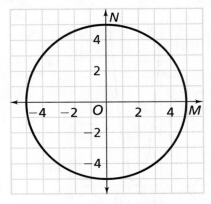

Since $M = x - 3$, you know $x = M + 3$. The pair of number lines below shows the relationship between M and x.

Likewise, $N = y + 2$ implies $y = N - 2$. The following pair of number lines relates N and y.

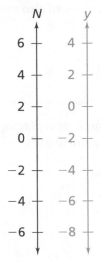

Using the graph of $M^2 + N^2 = 5^2$, replace the M-axis with the x-axis, and replace the N-axis with the y-axis.

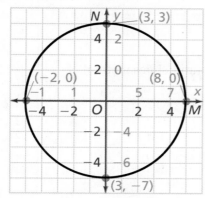

The resulting circle is centered at the point $(3, -2)$. Its radius is still 5. Note that the x-axis is the image of the M-axis translated to the left by three units. The y-axis is the image of the N-axis translated up by two units.

As a consequence, the graph of the circle $(x - 3)^2 + (y + 2)^2 = 5^2$ is the image of the basic circle of radius 5 translated three units to the right and two units down.

b. In Problem 1a from Lesson 6.08, you found that the following substitutions transform $y = 2x^2 - 12x + 17$ into $N = M^2$.

- $M = \mathcal{A}_{(2, -6)}(x)$
- $N = \mathcal{A}_{(2, 2)}(y)$

The graph of $N = M^2$ is just the basic parabola shown below.

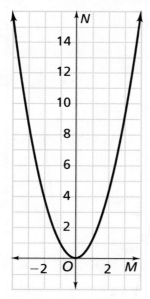

You have

$$x = \left(\mathcal{A}_{(2, -6)}\right)^{-1}(M)$$
$$= \mathcal{A}_{\left(\frac{1}{2}, 3\right)}(M)$$
$$= \tfrac{1}{2}M + 3$$

The pair of number lines shows the relationship between M and x.

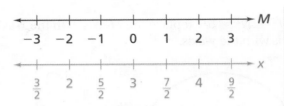

You also know that $N = (T_2 \circ D_2)(y)$, and the socks-and-shoes method of taking inverses gives

$$y = (D_{\frac{1}{2}} \circ T_{-2})(N) = \tfrac{1}{2}(N - 2)$$

So the following pair of number lines relates N and y.

Using the graph of $N = M^2$, replace the M-axis with the x-axis, and replace the N-axis with the y-axis.

The resulting parabola has its vertex at the point $(3, -1)$. The graph shows that the units on both the x- and y-axes are twice as big as those on the M- and N-axes.

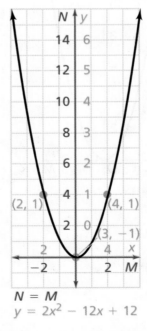

$N = M$
$y = 2x^2 - 12x + 12$

The usual graph of $y = 2x^2 - 12x + 17$ is the image of the basic parabola graph after horizontal and vertical scaling by a factor $\frac{1}{2}$ followed by a translation 3 units to the right and 1 unit down.

Exercises *Practicing Habits of Mind*

Check Your Understanding

For Exercises 1 and 2, suppose $M = -2x + 1$.

1. a. Show that $x = (T_{\frac{1}{2}} \circ D_{-\frac{1}{2}})(M)$.

   b. Copy and label the number lines for $D_{-\frac{1}{2}}(M)$ and x.

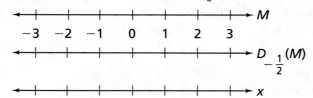

   c. Describe the relationship between the number lines in each pair.

     M and $D_{-\frac{1}{2}}(M)$ $D_{-\frac{1}{2}}(M)$ and x M and x

2. a. Show that $x = (D_{-\frac{1}{2}} \circ T_{-1})(M)$.

   b. Copy and label the number lines for $T_{-1}(M)$ and x.

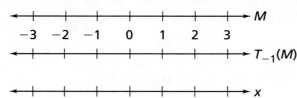

   c. Describe the relationship between the number lines in each pair.

     M and $T_{-1}(M)$ $T_{-1}(M)$ and x M and x

3. The figure shows the graph of $N = M^2$, but the corresponding x- and y-axes are not labeled.

The equation of this parabola in x and y is
$y = 3x^2 + 2x - 1$.

a. Find the substitutions that transform the equation $y = 3x^2 + 2x - 1$ into $N = M^2$.

b. Copy the figure to the right and label the x- and y-axes to show these substitutions. Show the (x, y) coordinates of several points on the graph.

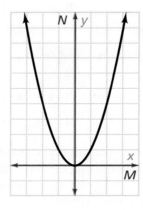

4. Write About It In Exercises 1 and 2, $x = \mathcal{A}_{(-\frac{1}{2}, \frac{1}{2})}(M)$.

You wrote $\mathcal{A}_{(-\frac{1}{2}, \frac{1}{2})}$ as a composition of translations and dilations in two different ways.

$$\mathcal{A}_{(-\frac{1}{2}, \frac{1}{2})} = T_{\frac{1}{2}} \circ D_{-\frac{1}{2}} = D_{-\frac{1}{2}} \circ T_{-1}$$

Are there other ways to decompose $\mathcal{A}_{(-\frac{1}{2}, \frac{1}{2})}$ into translations and dilations? Explain.

5. a. Confirm that the substitutions below transform the equation $y = 2x^2 + 6x + 5$ into the equation $N = M^2$. (To do this, write expressions for M and N in terms of x and y and plug them into the equation $N = M^2$. Multiply everything out and simplify your answer.)

$$M = \mathcal{A}_{(2, 3)}(x) \qquad N = \mathcal{A}_{(2, -1)}(y)$$

b. Sketch the graph of $y = 2x^2 + 6x + 5$ using the substitutions above and the replacing-the-axes method. Label several points on your graph with their (x, y) coordinates.

In Exercises 6–9, you will sketch some graphs. You can use any method, but try to use the replacing-the-axes method on at least two of the exercises, just to get used to it.

6. Sketch the graph of $y = 9x^2 + 12x - 5$. You may find your work from Exercise 2 in Lesson 6.07 helpful. Label several points on your graph with their (x, y) coordinates.

7. Sketch the graph of $y = -\frac{1}{4}x^2 + 6x + 8$. You may find your work from Problem 2b in Lesson 6.08 helpful. Label several points on your graph with their (x, y) coordinates.

8. Sketch the graph of each equation. Label several points on each graph with their (x, y) coordinates.

a. $(x + 5)^2 + y^2 = 9$ 　　　　　　**b.** $(-2x + 1)^2 + y^2 = 9$

c. $(x - 1)^2 + (-y + 4)^2 = 9$ 　　　**d.** $(x + 2)^2 + (4y - 16)^2 = 9$

9. Sketch the graph of each equation. Label several points on each graph with their (x, y) coordinates.

a. $y = \sqrt{x + 5}$ 　　　　　　　**b.** $y = \sqrt{-2x + 1}$

c. $y = -\sqrt{x - 1} + 4$ 　　　　　**d.** $y = \frac{1}{4}\sqrt{x + 2} + 4$

10. What's Wrong Here? Greg says that all of the graphs he drew in Exercise 8 are circles. Greg explains, "When using the replacing-the-axes method, I keep the original circle $M^2 + N^2 = 9$ where it is and just relabel the axes. The resulting graph has the same shape as the graph of $M^2 + N^2 = 9$, which is a circle of radius 3. So they must all be circles, too."

Do you agree with Greg? Explain.

In Exercises 11–16, you will sketch some graphs. You can use any method, but try to use the replacing-the-axes method on some of the exercises, just to get used to it.

Go Online
Pearsonsuccessnet.com

11. Sketch the graph of each equation. You may find your work from Exercise 6 in Lesson 6.07 helpful.

a. $y = x^3 + 6x^2 + 11x + 7$ **b.** $y = x^3 + 3x^2 + 7x + 13$

12. Sketch the graph of $y = 8x^3 - 6x^2 + 2x - 1$. You may find your work from Exercise 13 in Lesson 6.07 helpful.

13. Sketch the graph of each equation.

a. $y = 2x - 3$ **b.** $y - 1 = 2x - 3$

c. $-y + 1 = 2x - 3$ **d.** $2y - 3 = 2x - 3$

14. Sketch the graph of each equation.

a. $y = \dfrac{1}{2x - 3}$ **b.** $(2x - 3)(y - 1) = 1$

c. $(2x - 3)(-y + 1) = 1$ **d.** $(2x - 3)(2y - 3) = 1$

15. Sketch the graph of each equation.

a. $y = 10^{2x-3}$ **b.** $y - 1 = 10^{2x-3}$

c. $-y + 1 = 10^{2x-3}$ **d.** $2y - 3 = 10^{2x-3}$

16. Sketch the graph of each equation.

a. $2y - 3 = \log x$ **b.** $2y - 3 = \log(x - 1)$

c. $2y - 3 = \log(-x + 1)$ **d.** $2y - 3 = \log(2x - 3)$

17. Explain how the graphs in Exercises 15 and 16 are related to each other.

18. a. Sketch the graph of $y = (x - 3)^2$ using the replacing-the-axes method.

b. How are the number lines for $M = T_{-3}(x)$ and x related?

c. Using your answer from part (b), explain why you get the graph of $y = (x - 3)^2$ by translating the graph of $y = x^2$ three units to the right.

19. a. Sketch the graph of $y = \sqrt{2x}$ using the replacing-the-axes method.

b. How are the number lines for $M = D_2(x)$ and x related?

c. Using your answer from part (b), explain why you get the graph of $y = \sqrt{2x}$ by scaling the graph of $y = \sqrt{x}$ horizontally by the factor $\frac{1}{2}$.

20. a. Sketch the graph of $y = \left| \frac{1}{2} x \right|$.

   b. How are the number lines for $M = D_{\frac{1}{2}}(x)$ and x related?

   c. Using your answer from part (b), explain why you get the graph of $y = \left| \frac{1}{2} x \right|$ by scaling the graph of $y = |x|$ horizontally by the factor of 2.

21. a. Sketch the graph of $y = (-x)^3$ using the replacing-the-axes method.

   b. How are the number lines for $M = D_{-1}(x)$ and x related?

   c. Using your answer from part (b), explain why the graph of $y = (-x)^3$ is the image of the graph of $y = x^3$ after reflection over the y-axis.

22. Standardized Test Prep Which description best fits the graph of $(y - 7)^2 = -(x + 3)^2 + 25$?

   A. a parabola with vertex $(-3, 7)$

   B. a circle with center $(-3, 7)$

   C. a square with side length 5 units

   D. a circle with radius 25 units

Maintain Your Skills

23. For each affine transformation $\mathcal{A}_{(a, b)}$, find all x such that $\mathcal{A}_{(a, b)}(x) = 0$.

   a. $\mathcal{A}_{(2, -1)}$ **b.** $\mathcal{A}_{(4, -2)}$ **c.** $\mathcal{A}_{(6, -3)}$

   d. $\mathcal{A}_{\left(-1, \frac{1}{2}\right)}$ **e.** $\mathcal{A}_{\left(-3, \frac{3}{2}\right)}$

6.10 Advanced Affine Transformations

This lesson focuses on properties and applications of affine transformations.

In-Class Experiment

1. Find all x such that $\mathcal{A}_{(2, 3)}(x) = x$.

2. Find all x such that $\mathcal{A}_{(1, 3)}(x) = x$.

3. Find all x such that $\mathcal{A}_{(1, 0)}(x) = x$.

Fixed Points

Given an affine transformation $\mathcal{A}_{(a, b)}$, you are often interested in finding the values of x that are unchanged by $\mathcal{A}_{(a, b)}$. This gives rise to the following definition.

Definition

Let $\mathcal{A}_{(a, b)}$ be an affine transformation. A number x is a **fixed point** of $\mathcal{A}_{(a, b)}$ if $\mathcal{A}_{(a, b)}(x) = x$.

For Discussion

4. Which affine transformations have no fixed points?

The center of the potter's wheel is a fixed point.

Sasha and Tony are working on Exercise 19 from Lesson 6.06.

Tony We need to come up with a formula for $(\mathcal{A}_{(a,\, b)})^{(n)}$.

Sasha Let's try it for small values of n, like $n = 2$.

Tony Okay. The composition formula says $\mathcal{A}_{(a,\, b)} \circ \mathcal{A}_{(c,\, d)} = \mathcal{A}_{(ac,\, ad+b)}$. So we get

$$(\mathcal{A}_{(a,\, b)})^{(2)} = \mathcal{A}_{(a,\, b)} \circ \mathcal{A}_{(a,\, b)}$$
$$= \mathcal{A}_{(a^2,\, ab+b)}$$

Remember... This formula is from Exercise 7 of Lesson 6.06.

Sasha Great. Let's use this result to compute the next one.

$$\left(\mathcal{A}_{(a,\, b)}\right)^{(3)} = \mathcal{A}_{(a,\, b)} \circ \left(\mathcal{A}_{(a,\, b)}\right)^{(2)}$$
$$= \mathcal{A}_{(a,\, b)} \circ \mathcal{A}_{(a^2,\, ab+b)}$$
$$= \mathcal{A}_{(a^3,\, a(ab+b)+b)}$$
$$= \mathcal{A}_{(a^3,\, a^2b+ab+b)}$$

Tony Let me try one more.

$$\left(\mathcal{A}_{(a,\, b)}\right)^{(4)} = \mathcal{A}_{(a,\, b)} \circ \left(\mathcal{A}_{(a,\, b)}\right)^{(3)}$$
$$= \mathcal{A}_{(a,\, b)} \circ \mathcal{A}_{(a^3,\, a^2b+ab+b)}$$
$$= \mathcal{A}_{(a^4,\, a(a^2b+ab+b)+b)}$$
$$= \mathcal{A}_{(a^4,\, a^3b+a^2b+ab+b)}$$

Sasha I think I see a pattern. Let me double-check.

Sasha writes in her notebook.

Sasha Yup, I got $\left(\mathcal{A}_{(a,\, b)}\right)^{(5)} = \mathcal{A}_{(a^5,\, a^4b+a^3b+a^2b+ab+b)}$.

Tony And I bet we get $\left(\mathcal{A}_{(a,\, b)}\right)^{(6)} = \mathcal{A}_{(a^6,\, a^5b+a^4b+a^3b+a^2b+ab+b)}$.

Sasha That's right! And in general, we have

$$\left(\mathcal{A}_{(a,\, b)}\right)^{(n)} = \mathcal{A}_{(a^n,\, a^{n-1}b+a^{n-2}b+\cdots+ab+b)}$$
$$= \mathcal{A}_{(a^n,\, b(a^{n-1}+a^{n-2}+\cdots+a+1))}$$

Tony We can do even better. Remember? When $a \neq 1$, we know

$$a^{n-1} + a^{n-2} + \cdots + a + 1 = \frac{a^n - 1}{a - 1}$$

Sasha So when $a \neq 1$, we get $\left(\mathcal{A}_{(a,\, b)}\right)^{(n)}(x) = a^n x + b \cdot \dfrac{a^n - 1}{a - 1}$, just as the exercise says!

For You to Do

5. Using Tony's result for $(\mathcal{A}_{(a,\, b)})^{(4)}$, show that
$$\left(\mathcal{A}_{(a,\, b)}\right)^{(5)} = \mathcal{A}_{(a^5,\, a^4b+a^3b+a^2b+ab+b)}.$$

This is the calculation Sasha wrote in her notebook.

Here is a summary of the results from Lesson 6.06 and the dialog above.

- **Composition:**

  $\mathcal{A}_{(a,\ b)} \circ \mathcal{A}_{(c,\ d)} = \mathcal{A}_{(e,\ f)}$, **where** $e = ac$ **and** $f = ad + b$

- **Inverse:**

  $(\mathcal{A}_{(a,\ b)})^{-1} = \mathcal{A}_{\left(\frac{1}{a},\ -\frac{b}{a}\right)}$

- **Iteration:** For $a \neq 1$ **and positive integer** n,

  $(\mathcal{A}_{(a,\ b)})^{(n)} = \mathcal{A}_{\left(a^n,\ b \cdot \frac{a^n - 1}{a - 1}\right)}$

> This means that
> $(\mathcal{A}_{(a,\ b)})^{(n)}(x)$
> $= a^n(x) + b \cdot \dfrac{a^n - 1}{a - 1}.$

Stabilizers

In the In-Class Experiment, you had to find all numbers x that the affine transformation $\mathcal{A}_{(2,\ 3)}$ fixes. The only value that worked was $x = -3$. Now change the perspective a bit. Suppose you have a number, such as $x = -3$, and have to find all affine transformations $\mathcal{A}_{(a,\ b)}$ that fix x. Of course, $\mathcal{A}_{(2,\ 3)}$ is one such transformation. But there are many others—for example, the identity transformation $\mathcal{A}_{(1,\ 0)}$ fixes all points, so it certainly fixes $x = -3$. The following transformations all fix $x = -3$.

- $\mathcal{A}_{(3,\ 6)}(-3) = 3(-3) + 6 = -3$

- $\mathcal{A}_{(5,\ 12)}(-3) = 5(-3) + 12 = -3$

- $\mathcal{A}_{\left(\frac{1}{2},\ -\frac{3}{2}\right)}(-3) = \frac{1}{2}(-3) - \frac{3}{2} = -3$

For You to Do

6. Find at least three more affine transformations $\mathcal{A}_{(a,\ b)}$ that fix $x = -3$. Can you characterize all such transformations?

> To *characterize* something means to list its properties (or characteristics) so that another person could recognize it if he or she saw it.

Definition

Let x be a real number. Then the **stabilizer** of x, denoted S_x, is the set of all affine transformations that fix x.

$$S_x = \{\mathcal{A}_{(a,\ b)} \text{ such that } \mathcal{A}_{(a,\ b)}(x) = x\}$$

For example, the discussion above shows that S_{-3} contains the affine transformations $\mathcal{A}_{(2,\ 3)}$, $\mathcal{A}_{(1,\ 0)}$, $\mathcal{A}_{(3,\ 6)}$, $\mathcal{A}_{(5,\ 12)}$, $\mathcal{A}_{\left(\frac{1}{2},\ -\frac{3}{2}\right)}$, and perhaps many more.

For Discussion

7. Which affine transformation is in S_x for all values of x?

Affine Recursive Definition

Recall the following functions from Exercise 16 in Lesson 6.05 and Exercise 23 in Lesson 6.06.

- $f(n) = \begin{cases} 2 & \text{if } n = 0 \\ T_3\,(f(n-1)) & \text{if } n > 0 \end{cases}$

- $f(n) = \begin{cases} 2 & \text{if } n = 0 \\ D_3\,(f(n-1)) & \text{if } n > 0 \end{cases}$

Definition

Let $\mathcal{A}_{(a,\,b)}$ be an affine transformation of $\mathbb{R}$ and let p be a number. Then a recursive definition of the form below is an **affine recursive definition.**

$$f(n) = \begin{cases} p & \text{if } n = 0 \\ \mathcal{A}_{(a,\,b)}(f(n-1)) & \text{if } n > 0 \end{cases}$$

For Discussion

Find a closed form for each function in terms of a and b.

8. $f(n) = \begin{cases} 5 & \text{if } n = 0 \\ T_b\,(f(n-1)) & \text{if } n > 0 \end{cases}$

9. $f(n) = \begin{cases} 5 & \text{if } n = 0 \\ D_a\,(f(n-1)) & \text{if } n > 0 \end{cases}$

Example

Problem Consider the function below.

$$f(n) = \begin{cases} 1 & \text{if } n = 0 \\ \mathcal{A}_{(2,\,3)}\,(f(n-1)) & \text{if } n > 0 \end{cases}$$

Compute $f(5)$.

Solution Compute terms of the sequence in succession.

$$f(1) = \mathcal{A}_{(2,\,3)}(f(0)) = 2(1) + 3 = 5$$
$$f(2) = \mathcal{A}_{(2,\,3)}(f(1)) = 2(5) + 3 = 13$$
$$f(3) = \mathcal{A}_{(2,\,3)}(f(2)) = 2(13) + 3 = 29$$
$$f(4) = \mathcal{A}_{(2,\,3)}(f(3)) = 2(29) + 3 = 61$$
$$f(5) = \mathcal{A}_{(2,\,3)}(f(4)) = 2(61) + 3 = 125$$

Therefore, $f(5) = 125$.

Habits of Mind

Consider more than one strategy. Is there a more efficient approach?

Exercises Practicing Habits of Mind

Check Your Understanding

1. Find all the fixed points of each affine transformation.

   a. $\mathcal{A}_{(4, -2)}$ **b.** $\mathcal{A}_{(-2, 4)}$ **c.** $\mathcal{A}_{(-10, 22)}$

   d. $\mathcal{A}_{(a, 0)}$ **e.** $\mathcal{A}_{(1, -3)}$ **f.** $\mathcal{A}_{(a, b)}$

2. Determine which affine transformations $\mathcal{A}_{(a, b)}$ have the following number of fixed points: exactly one, more than one, or zero.

3. Find all affine transformations $\mathcal{A}_{(a, b)}$ such that $(\mathcal{A}_{(a, b)})^{-1} = \mathcal{A}_{(a, b)}$.

4. Find all affine transformations $\mathcal{A}_{(a, b)}$ such that $(\mathcal{A}_{(a, b)})^{(n)} = \mathcal{A}_{(a, b)}$ for all $n \geq 1$.

5. **What's Wrong Here?** Larry is solving the equation $3x + 7 = 3x - 2$ using affine transformations.

   Larry says, "Let's see, I first rewrite it as $\mathcal{A}_{(3, 7)}(x) = \mathcal{A}_{(3, -2)}(x)$.

   Then I apply $(\mathcal{A}_{(3, 7)})^{-1} = \mathcal{A}_{(\frac{1}{3}, -\frac{7}{3})}$ to each side. I get

   $$x = \left(\mathcal{A}_{(\frac{1}{3}, -\frac{7}{3})} \circ \mathcal{A}_{(3, -2)}\right)(x)$$

   $$= \mathcal{A}_{(1, -3)}(x)$$

   So x is a fixed point of $\mathcal{A}_{(1, -3)}$. But wait, I just did Exercise 1e, and I know that $\mathcal{A}_{(1, -3)}$ has no fixed point!"

   Where did Larry go wrong?

6. Find S_5. In other words, find all affine transformations $\mathcal{A}_{(a, b)}$ such that $\mathcal{A}_{(a, b)}(5) = 5$.

On Your Own

7. **Standardized Test Prep** Which point is a fixed point of $\mathcal{A}_{(3, 34)}$?

   A. -17 **B.** -3 **C.** 0 **D.** 34

8. **a.** Show that $\mathcal{A}_{(3, -4)}$ and $\mathcal{A}_{(-5, 12)}$ are in S_2.

   b. Without simplifying, show that $\mathcal{A}_{(3, -4)} \circ \mathcal{A}_{(-5, 12)}$ and $\mathcal{A}_{(-5, 12)} \circ \mathcal{A}_{(3, -4)}$ are both in S_2.

   c. Show that $(\mathcal{A}_{(3, -4)})^{-1}$ and $(\mathcal{A}_{(-5, 12)})^{-1}$ are both in S_2.

   d. Now simplify $\mathcal{A}_{(3, -4)} \circ \mathcal{A}_{(-5, 12)}$ and $\mathcal{A}_{(-5, 12)} \circ \mathcal{A}_{(3, -4)}$. What do you observe?

Go Online
Pearsonsuccessnet.com

You can do this without actually computing the inverses.

9. Suppose $A_{(a, b)}$ and $A_{(c, d)}$ are in S_x.

    a. Show that $A_{(a, b)} \circ A_{(c, d)}$ is in S_x.   **b.** Show that $(A_{(a, b)})^{-1}$ is in S_x.

    c. **Take It Further** Show that if $A_{(a, b)}$ and $A_{(c, d)}$ are in S_x, then

$$A_{(a, b)} \circ A_{(c, d)} = A_{(c, d)} \circ A_{(a, b)}$$

10. Find S_0. What special name do you use for this transformation?

11. Show that each transformation is in S_3.

    a. $T_3 \circ D_4 \circ (T_3)^{-1}$ **b.** $T_3 \circ D_{-1} \circ (T_3)^{-1}$ **c.** $T_3 \circ D_2 \circ (T_3)^{-1}$

    d. $T_3 \circ D_a \circ (T_3)^{-1}$ **e.** Explain why $T_x \circ D_a \circ (T_x)^{-1}$ is in S_x.

12. Use the affine recursive definition below.

$$f(n) = \begin{cases} 1 & \text{if } n = 0 \\ A_{(2, 3)}(f(n - 1)) & \text{if } n > 0 \end{cases}$$

    a. Compute $(A_{(2, 3)})^{(5)}(x)$.

    b. Explain why $f(5) = (A_{(2, 3)})^{(5)}(f(0))$.

    c. Use your answers from parts (a) and (b) to compute $f(5)$.

13. **Take It Further** Consider the function below.

$$g(n) = \begin{cases} 2 & \text{if } n = 0 \\ D_3(g(n - 1)) & \text{if } n > 0 \end{cases}$$

    Your goal is to find a closed form for the sum

$$\sigma(n) = g(0) + g(1) + g(2) + \cdots + g(n)$$

    a. Explain why $3\sigma(n - 1) = g(1) + g(2) + \cdots + g(n)$.

    b. Explain why the following equation is true.

$$\sigma(n) = g(0) + 3\sigma(n - 1)$$
$$= A_{(3, 2)}(\sigma(n - 1))$$

    c. Compute $\sigma(10)$. Verify your result by computing the sum below directly.

$$\sigma(10) = g(0) + g(1) + g(2) + \cdots + g(10)$$

    d. Find a closed form for $\sigma(n)$.

Maintain Your Skills

14. On the xy-plane, plot all points (a, b) such that $A_{(a, b)}$ is in S_{-4}.

In this investigation, you transformed an equation into one of the basic graph forms, described the effect of an affine transformation on an axis, and identified the fixed points of an affine transformation. These exercises will help you summarize what you have learned.

1. For each equation, copy and complete the pair of number lines showing the relationship between M and x.

   a. $M = T_4(x)$

   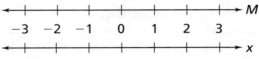

   b. $M = D_{\frac{1}{3}}(x)$

   c. $M = A_{(-1, 2)}(x)$

2. For each number-line pair you made in Exercise 1, describe the number line for x as a transformation of the number line for M.

3. Sketch the graph of $(2x - 1)^2 + (y + 3)^2 = 16$. Label several points on your sketch with their (x, y) coordinates. Then describe the graph as a transformation of the basic graph of $x^2 + y^2 = 16$.

4. The substitutions below transform the equation $y = -x^2 + 6x - 7$ into the equation $S = R^2$.

   $R = A_{(1, -3)}(x)$ $\qquad$ $S = A_{(-1, 2)}(y)$

   a. Confirm that the substitutions work by replacing R and S with expressions in x and y in the equation $S = R^2$ and simplifying.

   b. Sketch the graph of $y = -x^2 + 6x - 7$. Label several points on your graph with their (x, y) coordinates.

   c. Describe your graph from part (b) as a transformation of the basic graph of $y = x^2$.

5. Find at least four affine transformations that have 6 as a fixed point.

6. How do you use the replacing-the-axes method to sketch the graph of $y = x^3 + 3x^2 - x + 4$?

7. How do you use the replacing-the-axes method to explain the relationship between the graphs of $y = x^2$ and $y = (x - 3)^2$?

8. What is the fixed point for $A_{(5, 3)}$?

The transformation you use to convert from °C to °F has a fixed point at −40°.

Vocabulary and Notation

In this investigation, you learned these terms and this symbol. Make sure you understand what each one means and how to use it.

- affine recursive definition
- fixed point
- iteration
- stabilizer, S_x

Project Using Mathematical Habits

A Group of Functions

In Chapter 2, you learned that the function $f(x) = x$ is the identity function under the operation of composition. If $f(x) = x$ and g is any function, then $(f \circ g)(x) = g(x) = (g \circ f)(x)$.

Since $f(x) = x$ is the identity function, two functions g and h are inverse functions if $g \circ h = f = h \circ g$.

1. Give some examples of the use of *identity* and *inverse* in other mathematical contexts. Explain how the usage is similar to the usage with functions.

   Consider the following six functions.

   $$a(x) = \frac{1}{x}$$
   $$b(x) = \frac{1}{1 - x}$$
   $$c(x) = 1 - \frac{1}{x}$$
   $$d(x) = 1 - x$$
   $$e(x) = 1 + \frac{1}{x - 1}$$
   $$f(x) = x$$

2. Determine which of the six functions is equivalent to each composition.

   a. $e \circ f$

   b. $a \circ a$

   c. $b \circ e$

   d. $e \circ b$

   e. $b \circ a \circ a$

3. Copy and complete the following table with the results of composing the six functions. Some entries have been filled in to help you get started. For example, $a \circ b = d$ and $b \circ a = c$.

∘	a	b	c	d	e	f
a	▪	d	▪	▪	▪	▪
b	e	▪	▪	▪	▪	▪
c	▪	▪	▪	▪	a	▪
d	▪	▪	▪	▪	▪	▪
e	▪	▪	d	▪	▪	▪
f	▪	▪	▪	▪	▪	▪

4. Find the inverse function of each function a through f.

5. A set of elements under a binary operation ◇ has the associative property if, for any elements m, n, and p,

$$(m \diamond n) \diamond p = m \diamond (n \diamond p)$$

Pick three functions from Exercise 1, not including f, to test whether the associative property holds for those functions under composition. For example, you might check to see if $(a \circ b) \circ d = a \circ (b \circ d)$. Pay attention to the order of operations.

6. a. What four properties does a set need to have for it to be a group under a binary operation?

b. Do you think that the six functions in Exercise 1 form a group under composition? Explain.

c. A group is Abelian if it has the property of commutivity. Do you think that the six functions from Exercise 1 form an Abelian group under composition? Explain.

7. The order of an element in a group is the lowest number of copies of the element you need to operate together to get the identity element. For example, the order of *a* is 2, since $a \circ a = f$ and *f* is the identity element. Find the order of the functions *b* through *f* under the operation of composition.

8. Consider an equilateral triangle. There are six ways that you can map the triangle to itself.

- Reflect it around any of the three lines of symmetry (3 mappings).
- Rotate it 120° clockwise (1 mapping).
- Rotate it 120° counterclockwise (1 mapping).
- Leave the triangle the way it is (1 mapping).

Build a table for the operation "then," which means doing one of the mappings and then doing another of the mappings. For example, one output should be the result of doing a specific reflection and then doing a 120° rotation. (*Hint:* You can make a cutout of an equilateral triangle and label the three points.)

Is it possible to build this table to be the same as the table you completed in Exercise 3? If so, do it. If not, explain why not.

9. Consider a regular hexagon. There are six ways that you can map this hexagon onto itself while preserving its orientation. (*Hint:* In order to preserve orientation, you cannot reflect the hexagon.)

Build a table for the operation "then" as defined in Exercise 8. Is it possible to build this table to be the same as the one you completed in Exercise 3? If so, do it. If not, explain why not.

Go Online
Pearsonsuccessnet.com

In **Investigation 6A** you learned how to

- sketch the basic graphs
- relate the effect of a translation of a basic graph on both the graph and the equation of the graph
- relate the effect of a scale or reflection of a basic graph on both the graph and the equation of the graph
- compose transformations and sketch the effect of a composition on one of the basic graphs

The following questions will help you check your understanding.

1. **a.** Sketch the graph of $y - 2 = |x + 1|$. How is your graph related to the graph of $y = |x|$?
   b. Sketch the graph of $(x - 4)^2 + (y + 6)^2 = 4$. How is your graph related to the graph of $x^2 + y^2 = 4$?

2. **a.** Sketch the graph of $\frac{y}{2} = (x - 4)^2$. How is your graph related to the graph of $y = x^2$?
   b. Sketch the graph of $\left(\frac{x}{3}\right)^2 + (2y)^2 = 4$. How is your graph related to the graph of $x^2 + y^2 = 4$?
   c. Sketch the graph of $y = (-x)^3 - (-x)$. How is your graph related to the graph of $y = x^3 - x$?

3. Suppose you scale the graph of $y = |x|$ horizontally by the factor 2 and then translate the graph 3 units left and 7 units down. Write an equation to describe the resulting graph and sketch the graph of the equation.

In **Investigation 6B** you learned how to

- write any composition of translations and dilations as an affine transformation and write any affine transformation as a composition of a dilation and a translation
- find the inverse of a dilation, a translation, or an affine transformation and use inverses as a tool to solve equations
- find transformations to convert a general quadratic or cubic into one of the basic graph forms

The following questions will help you check your understanding.

4. Write each composition or inverse as a single affine transformation $\mathcal{A}_{(a, b)}$.
   a. $T_4 \circ D_3$
   b. $D_{-1} \circ T_6 \circ T_{-2}$
   c. $(T_7)^{-1}$
   d. $(D_7)^{-1}$
   e. $\mathcal{A}_{(2, -1)} \circ \mathcal{A}_{(-3, -5)}$
   f. $(\mathcal{A}_{(-2, 8)})^{-1}$

5. Find a and b that satisfy each equation.
   a. $\mathcal{A}_{(a, b)} \circ \mathcal{A}_{(3, 9)} = \mathcal{A}_{(15, 8)}$
   b. $\mathcal{A}_{(4, -1)} \circ \mathcal{A}_{(a, b)} = \mathcal{A}_{(16, 7)}$

6. Consider the equation $y = 5x^2 - 4x + 6$. Find a, b, c, and d such that, by making the substitutions below, you get the transformed equation $N = M^2$.
   - $M = \mathcal{A}_{(a, b)}(x)$
   - $N = \mathcal{A}_{(c, d)}(y)$

In **Investigation 6C** you learned how to

- use the techniques from Investigation 6B to transform an equation into one of the basic graph forms from Investigation 6A and use the information to graph the original equation

- describe the effect of an affine transformation on an axis and the effect of changes in axes on the graph of an equation

- identify the fixed points of an affine transformation and the set of affine transformations that fix a particular point.

The following questions will help you check your understanding.

7. For each equation, sketch a pair of number lines showing the relationship between M and x. Then describe the number line for x as a transformation of the number line for M.

    a. $M = T_2(x)$

    b. $M = D_4(x)$

    c. $M = A_{\left(\frac{1}{4},\, -2\right)}(x)$

8. Use the replacing-the-axes method to sketch the graph of $2y + 1 = \sqrt{3x - 4}$. Label the three points on your sketch that have (M, N) coordinates $(0, 0)$, $(1, 1)$, and $(4, 2)$ with their corresponding (x, y) coordinates. Then, describe the graph as a transformation of the basic graph of $y = \sqrt{x}$.

9. Find all the fixed points of each affine transformation.

    a. $A_{(2,\, -3)}$

    b. $A_{(-3,\, 2)}$

    c. $A_{\left(\frac{2}{3},\, 4\right)}$

    d. $A_{(1,\, 6)}$

Multiple Choice

1. Which equation describes the graph of $x^2 + y^2 = 4$ after a translation 2 units to the right and 7 units down?

   A. $(x - 2)^2 + (y - 7)^2 = 4$

   B. $(x + 2)^2 + (y - 7)^2 = 4$

   C. $(x - 2)^2 + (y + 7)^2 = 4$

   D. $(x + 7)^2 + (y - 2)^2 = 4$

2. Which equation describes the graph of $y = \frac{1}{x}$ after a horizontal scale by the factor 4?

   A. $y = \frac{4}{x}$

   B. $y = \frac{x}{4}$

   C. $y = 4x$

   D. $y = x + 4$

3. Find the value of $D_3 \circ T_{-2} \circ D_{\frac{1}{2}}(8)$.

   A. 5

   B. 6

   C. 12

   D. 13

4. Simplify $A_{(-4, 1)} \circ A_{(\frac{1}{4}, -1)}$.

   A. $A_{(-4, -\frac{1}{4})}$

   B. $A_{(-\frac{13}{4}, -1)}$

   C. $A_{(-1, 0)}$

   D. $A_{(-1, 5)}$

5. Which of the following affine transformations does NOT have a fixed point of 3?

   A. $A_{(-3, 12)}(x)$

   B. $A_{(-\frac{1}{2}, \frac{9}{2})}(x)$

   C. $A_{(2, 3)}(x)$

   D. $A_{(3, -6)}(x)$

Open Response

6. Sketch the graph of each equation. How is each graph related to the corresponding basic graph?

   a. $y - 1 = (2x)^2$

   b. $y = \left(\frac{x}{2}\right)^3 - \frac{x}{2}$

   c. $2y = |x - 5|$

   d. $y = 2^{x+1}$

7. Write each composition or inverse as a single affine transformation.

   a. $D_5 \circ (D_2)^{-1} \circ T_{-4}$

   b. $A_{(\frac{2}{3}, -8)} \circ A_{(6, -2)}$

   c. $(A_{(4, 8)})^{-1}$

8. Find a and b that satisfy each equation.

   a. $A_{(a, b)} \circ A_{(-1, 3)}(x) = A_{(-2, -4)}(x)$

   b. $A_{(4, -6)} \circ A_{(a, b)}(x) = A_{(12, 3)}(x)$

9. For each equation, find an equation for x in terms of M. Then sketch a pair of number lines showing the relationship between M and x.

   a. $M = T_{-5}(x)$

   b. $M = D_{10}(x)$

   c. $M = A_{(2, -6)}(x)$

10. Use the replacing-the-axes method to sketch the graph of $\frac{y}{2} = (3x + 2)^3 + (3x + 2)$. Label three points on your sketch with their (x, y) coordinates. Then describe the graph as a transformation of $y = x^3 + x$.

11. What does the graph of $(x + 1)^2 + (y - 4)^2 = 36$ look like?

Cumulative Review

Multiple Choice

1. Simplify the following expression.

$$\frac{x^{-5}y^{-9}}{x^{-11}y^{-7}}$$

   A. $\dfrac{x^{-16}}{y^{-16}}$ **B.** $\dfrac{y^2}{x^6}$

   C. $\dfrac{x^6}{y^2}$ **D.** x^6y^2

2. If $4^x = 32$, then which number is equal to 4^{4x}?

   A. 4^5 **B.** 4^{10}

   C. 2^5 **D.** 2^{10}

3. Place the following numbers in order from least to greatest.

   $$12^{-1} \qquad 9^{\frac{3}{2}} \qquad \left(\tfrac{2}{3}\right)^{-1} \qquad \log_2 8$$

   A. $12^{-1}, 9^{\frac{3}{2}}, \left(\tfrac{2}{3}\right)^{-1}, \log_2 8$

   B. $12^{-1}, \left(\tfrac{2}{3}\right)^{-1}, \log_2 8, 9^{\frac{2}{3}}$

   C. $9^{\frac{3}{2}}, \log_2 8, \left(\tfrac{2}{3}\right)^{-1}, 12^{-1}$

   D. $\left(\tfrac{2}{3}\right)^{-1}, 9^{\frac{3}{2}}, 12^{-1}, \log_2 8$

4. Which of the following expressions is equivalent to $\log 45$?

   A. $\log 9 + \log 5$ **B.** $\log 15 - \log 3$

   C. $\log 20 + \log 25$ **D.** $\log 100 - \log 55$

5. Which of the following points lies on the graph of $f(x) = \log_4 x$?

   A. $(4, 1)$ **B.** $(0, 1)$

   C. $(2, 16)$ **D.** $(8, 2)$

For Exercises 6 and 7, determine which equation describes the given transformation.

6. $y = x^3$ after a translation 4 units left and 5 units down

   A. $y = (x - 4)^3 + 5$

   B. $y = (x - 4)^3 - 5$

   C. $y = (x + 4)^3 + 5$

   D. $y = (x + 4)^3 - 5$

7. $y = |x|$ after a horizontal scaling by the factor $\frac{1}{3}$ and a reflection over the x-axis

   A. $y = 3|x|$ **B.** $y = -3|x|$

   C. $y = \frac{1}{3}|x|$ **D.** $y = -\frac{1}{3}|x|$

For Exercises 8 and 9, simplify each composition.

8. $(T_2 \circ D_4 \circ D_{\frac{1}{2}})(6)$

   A. 9   **B.** 11

   C. 13   **D.** 14

9. $\mathcal{A}_{(4, -6)} \circ \mathcal{A}_{(\frac{1}{2}, 3)}$

   A. $\mathcal{A}_{(8, 6)}$ **B.** $\mathcal{A}_{(2, 6)}$

   C. $\mathcal{A}_{(6, 2)}$ **D.** $\mathcal{A}_{(-2, -6)}$

10. Which affine transformation has a fixed point of 5?

   A. $\mathcal{A}_{(2, -5)}$ **B.** $\mathcal{A}_{(5, -1)}$

   C. $\mathcal{A}_{(-3, 5)}$ **D.** $\mathcal{A}_{(-1, 2)}$

Open Response

11. a. Copy and complete this ratio table for the exponential function $g(x)$.

x	g(x)	÷
0	−3	▪
1	6	▪
2	−12	▪
3	24	

   b. Find a recursive definition for the function.

   c. Find a closed-form definition for $g(x)$.

   d. Find the exact value of $g(5)$.

12. Let $f(x) = 6^x$ and $g(x) = \log_6 x$.

   a. Copy and complete each table.

x	f(x)
−2	▪
−1	▪
0	▪
1	▪
2	▪

x	g(x)
$\frac{1}{36}$	▪
$\frac{1}{6}$	▪
1	▪
6	▪
36	▪

   b. Sketch the graphs of f and g on the same axes.

   c. Is the graph of f increasing or decreasing? Explain.

   d. Is the graph of g increasing or decreasing? Explain.

13. Suppose $N = \log_3 15$.

   a. Find two consecutive integers j and k such that $j < N < k$.

   b. Express $\log_3 45$ in terms of N.

   c. Find the value of N to three decimal places.

14. Solve each equation. Give exact answers when possible, or round your answers to three decimal places.

   a. $3^x = 48$

   b. $x \cdot 8^3 = 16^2$

   c. $\log 2x + \log 8 = 3$

15. If you invest \$3000 at 6% interest compounded annually, how many years will it take until your money triples in value?

16. Sketch the graph of each equation. Then describe how each graph is related to its corresponding basic graph.

   a. $y = \dfrac{1}{x + 3} - 4$

   b. $y - 5 = -|x|$

   c. $2y = (x - 5)^2$

   d. $(x - 5)^2 + (y + 3)^2 = 16$

17. Write each expression as a single affine transformation $\mathcal{A}_{(a, b)}$.

   a. $(T_{-4})^{-1} \circ D_8 \circ D_7$

   b. $\mathcal{A}_{(-2, 3)} \circ \mathcal{A}_{(4, -7)}$

   c. $(\mathcal{A}_{(4, 5)})^{-1}$

18. Find numbers a and b such that the following equations are true.

   a. $\mathcal{A}_{(a, b)} \circ \mathcal{A}_{(2, 1)} = \mathcal{A}_{(-4, 9)}$

   b. $\mathcal{A}_{(2, -3)} \circ \mathcal{A}_{(a, b)} = \mathcal{A}_{(7, 1)}$

19. For each equation below, do the following.

   Solve for x in terms of M. Then draw a pair of number lines showing the relationship between M and x.

   a. $M = T_6(x)$

   b. $M = D_{\frac{1}{2}}(x)$

   c. $M = \mathcal{A}_{(-3, 5)}(x)$

20. a. Use the replacing-the-axes method to sketch the graph of $4y + 4 = (x + 2)^2$. Label three points with their (x, y) coordinates.

b. Describe the graph as a transformation of $y = x^2$.

21. Find all fixed points of the affine transformation $\mathcal{A}_{(4, 7)}$.

22. Multiply and simplify the following expression.

$$\sqrt{5} \cdot \sqrt{-20}$$

23. Let $z = 5 - 4i$. What is $-z + \bar{z}$?

24. Let $z = 3\sqrt{3} + 3i$ and $w = -2i$.

a. Find zw.

b. On the complex plane, graph z, w, and zw.

c. Find the magnitudes and directions of z, w, and zw.

25. Rewrite the following matrix in row-reduced echelon form.

$$\begin{pmatrix} 4 & -6 & | & -3 \\ 0 & -8 & | & 5 \end{pmatrix}$$

26. Let $A = \begin{pmatrix} 0 & -1 & -7 \\ 5 & 4 & 3 \end{pmatrix}$, $B = \begin{pmatrix} 4 & -2 \\ 2 & 0 \end{pmatrix}$, and $C = \begin{pmatrix} 3 & 6 \\ -9 & -2 \end{pmatrix}$.

If possible, find the following.

a. $B + C$ **b.** AC

c. CB **d.** A^{-1}

e. B^{-1}

27. Find a polynomial function in normal form for $f(x)$ that agrees with the following table.

Input, x	Output, $f(x)$
0	5
1	9
2	17

28. Let $p(x) = x^3 + 2x^2 - 5x + 10$.

a. Find the quotient and remainder when $p(x)$ is divided by $x + 4$.

b. Use your answer to part (a) to find $p(-4)$.

29. Use the table below to write a recursive definition for $a(n)$.

Input, n	Output, $a(n)$
0	-5
1	-2
2	1
3	4
4	7

Sequences and Series

If you win $1,000,000 in a state lottery, it is often buried in the contest rules that the prize is not really a check for $1,000,000. Instead, it is $50,000 a year for 20 years. Is your prize really worth $1,000,000?

No, it is not. If you got the $1,000,000 at the time you won the lottery, you might be able to invest it safely for at least a 6% return. That would give you not just $50,000 a year, but $60,000 a year, and not just for 20 years, but forever!

So your prize is not worth $1,000,000. How much is it worth? What is its present value? To find the present value of the lottery prize, assuming you invest it at an interest rate of 6%, you can compute this sum.

$$50{,}000 + 50{,}000\left(\tfrac{1}{1.06}\right) + 50{,}000\left(\tfrac{1}{1.06}\right)^2 + \cdots$$
$$+ 50{,}000\left(\tfrac{1}{1.06}\right)^{19}$$

That expression is an example of a geometric series. You can write it more compactly.

$$\sum_{k=0}^{19} 50{,}000\left(\tfrac{1}{1.06}\right)^k$$

And even though it is not really worth $1,000,000, you can see why the lottery does not advertise a big $\sum_{k=0}^{19} 50{,}000\left(\tfrac{1}{1.06}\right)^k$ prize. It is just not as impressive!

Vocabulary and Notation

- **arithmetic sequence**
- **arithmetic series**
- **definite sum**
- **geometric sequence**
- **geometric series**
- **identity**
- **Pascal's Triangle**
- **repeating decimal**
- **sequence**
- **series associated with** *f*
- **indefinite sum**
- **limit**
- $\sum_{k=0}^{n} f(k)$ **(summation)**

The Need to Sum

In *The Need to Sum,* you will explore sums. You will add a sum column to tables and find function rules to match the sum column. You will learn methods to calculate sums more easily.

By the end of this investigation, you will be able to answer questions like these.

1. Describe Gauss's method for summing all integers from 1 to n.

2. Find a formula for $\displaystyle\sum_{j=0}^{n} 2^j$ in terms of n.

3. Evaluate $\displaystyle\sum_{j=1}^{5} 4j$.

You will learn how to

- make a sum table for a function and write a closed-form rule for the sum column where appropriate

- use Gauss's method to find the sum of a sequence with a constant difference between successive terms

- use Euclid's method to find the sum of a sequence with a constant ratio between successive terms

- expand Σ notation or convert an expanded sum back to Σ notation

You will develop these habits and skills:

- Reason logically to understand how both Gauss's method and Euclid's method work, and choose which method to use for finding a particular sum.

- Visualize a sum geometrically to make sense of an algebraic pattern.

- Generalize a result from a series of numerical examples.

You can use Σ notation to describe sums with patterns, such as the total volume of successively smaller slices of watermelon.

For some problems, you need to look at the sums of all the outputs as well as the individual outputs.

For You to Explore

Emile got a letter in the mail saying that a wealthy relative had left him an inheritance. At a meeting the next week, a lawyer read the following statement.

To Emile, because he likes math problems, I leave a choice. He can have one of two inheritances. He must make his choice before leaving the office today.

Option 1 A starting amount of $10,000 and then, for the next 26 years, an annual payment at the end of each year that is $1000 more than the amount he received the previous year.

> For each option, there is a total of 27 payments.

Option 2 A starting amount of one cent and then, for the next 26 years, an annual payment at the end of each year that is twice the amount he received in the previous year.

Luckily, Emile brought his calculator to the meeting.

1. Suppose $f(n)$ is the amount of money Emile gets in Year n under Option 1 and $g(n)$ is the amount of money he gets in Year n under Option 2. Year 0 is the year in which Emile chooses one of the options and gets his first payment.

   a. Find closed-form rules for $f(n)$ and $g(n)$.

   b. For what values of n is $f(n) < g(n)$?

   c. For what values of n is $f(n) > g(n)$?

2. Suppose $F(n)$ is the total amount of money Emile has received after n years under Option 1, and $G(n)$ is the total amount of money he has received after n years under Option 2.

   a. Make a table of values for $F(n)$ with inputs 0 through 5.

   b. Make a table of values for $G(n)$ with inputs 0 through 5.

   c. For what values of n is $F(n) < G(n)$?

   d. For what values of n is $F(n) > G(n)$?

3. **a.** Write a closed-form rule for $F(n)$.

   b. Write a closed-form rule for $G(n)$.

4. If you were Emile, which option would you choose? Explain.

> **Habits of Mind**
>
> **Check your units.**
> When you compare the two functions, do not forget that you probably calculated f in dollars and g in cents.

Here is a table from Chapter 1, with a new column labeled Σ. The numbers in the Σ column are just the running totals of the outputs.

A closed-form rule for the Σ column in this case is $n \mapsto (n + 1)^2$.

n	f(n)	Σ
0	1	1
1	3	4
2	5	9
3	7	16
4	9	25
5	11	36

The symbol Σ is based on the capital Greek letter *sigma*. In mathematics, you often use Σ to stand for "sum."

5. a. Copy the table at the right. Add a Σ column to the table.

b. Find a closed-form rule for the Σ column.

n	h(n)
0	0
1	2
2	4
3	6
4	8
5	10

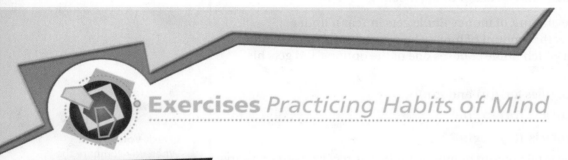

Exercises *Practicing Habits of Mind*

On Your Own

6. Ken and Maggie both start with 50 chips. One of them rolls a number cube. If the number is even, Maggie gives Ken that many chips. If the number is odd, Ken gives Maggie that many chips.

The table shows how many chips Maggie gains for each roll. If she loses chips, she records this as a negative gain.

a. Copy Maggie's table. Add a column that shows how many chips she has after each move.

b. Is this a fair game? Explain.

Maggie's Table

Roll	Gain
1	5
2	−2
3	−4
4	3
5	−6
6	1
7	−6

For Exercises 7–9, copy each table. Add a Σ column. Find a closed-form rule for the Σ column.

You can use a spreadsheet to make Σ columns. See the TI-Nspire™ Handbook, p. 804.

7.

n	t(n)
0	1
1	9
2	90
3	900
4	9000

8.

n	h(n)
0	5
1	5
2	5
3	5
4	5

9.

n	g(n)
0	−1
1	1
2	3
3	5
4	7
5	9

10. At the beginning of a bus route, 10 people get on the bus. At the first stop, 3 more people get on. At the second stop, 2 people get off and 5 others get on. At the third stop, 1 person gets off. At the next stop, 3 get off and 4 get on. At the next stop, 2 get on and 5 get off. At the next stop, 3 get on. How many passengers are on the bus?

11. A bakery manager asks employees to keep at least 6 dozen muffins in the display case at all times. The counter clerk has to keep track of the sales as well as how many muffins the baker brings out from the kitchen. Copy the table below. Add a Σ column to answer the questions.

Time	Baked or Bought	Amount
6:00 A.M.	Baked	144
6:10 A.M.	Bought	12
6:25 A.M.	Bought	2
6:45 A.M.	Bought	24
7:00 A.M.	Bought	5
7:15 A.M.	Baked	24
7:30 A.M.	Bought	36
8:15 A.M.	Baked	12
8:25 A.M.	Bought	6
8:30 A.M.	Bought	24

a. What was the total number of muffins in the case after the 8:30 A.M. count?

b. Did the clerk ever allow the total muffin count to go below the manager's requirement? If so, when?

Suppose that in Problem 1, the will gives Emile a third option.

Option 3 There is a starting amount of $0 and then, for the next 26 years, an annual payment at the end of each year that is the square of the year (1, 2, and so on) times $100.

12. Suppose $h(n)$ is the amount of money Emile gets in Year n under Option 3.

   a. What is a closed form for $h(n)$?

   b. Compare $h(n)$ to the functions $f(n)$ and $g(n)$ from Problem 1. For what values of n is each inequality true?

   $h(n) < f(n)$

   $h(n) > f(n)$

   $h(n) < g(n)$

   $h(n) > g(n)$

13. Suppose $H(n)$ is the total amount of money Emile gets after n years under Option 3. For what values of n is each inequality true?

   a. $H(n) < F(n)$

   b. $H(n) > F(n)$

   c. $H(n) < G(n)$

   d. $H(n) > G(n)$

Maintain Your Skills

14. Copy and complete the following difference tables. Write a closed-form rule for each function.

n	F(n)	Δ
0	1	▨
1	4	▨
2	9	▨
3	16	▨
4	25	▨
5	36	

n	T(n)	Δ
0	1	▨
1	10	▨
2	100	▨
3	1000	▨
4	10,000	▨
5	10,0000	

n	H(n)	Δ
0	5	▨
1	10	▨
2	15	▨
3	20	▨
4	25	▨
5	30	

Gauss's Method and Euclid's Method

Many stories are told about the mathematician Carl Friedrich Gauss. According to one story, one of his teachers gave Gauss and some classmates a problem to keep them busy for a while. The teacher asked the students to add all of the integers from 1 to 100. In just a few moments, Gauss wrote the number 5050 on his paper, and he was right!

Minds in Action   episode 32

For her history class, Sasha is doing a project about Gauss's life.

Sasha   So, Gauss had to solve the following problem.

Add up the integers from 1 to 100.

He probably did something like this.

You can write the sum two ways.

$$S = 1 + 2 + 3 + 4 + \cdots + 100$$

$$S = 100 + 99 + 98 + 97 + \cdots + 1$$

> Some people believe that he just added all the numbers up in his head.

Add the first numbers of each sum together, then the second numbers, then the third ones, and so on, and you'll get

$$
\begin{array}{ccccccccccccc}
S & = & 1 & + & 2 & + & 3 & + & 4 & + & \cdots & + & 100 \\
 & & \downarrow & & \downarrow & & \downarrow & & \downarrow & & & & \downarrow \\
+\ \ S & = & 100 & + & 99 & + & 98 & + & 97 & + & \cdots & + & 1 \\
\hline
2S & = & 101 & + & 101 & + & 101 & + & 101 & + & \cdots & + & 101
\end{array}
$$

There are one hundred 101's altogether, so

$$2S = 100 \cdot 101$$

$$S = 5050$$

For You to Do

Gauss found a way to add up the first 100 integers. Use his method to find the following sums.

1. Add up all integers from 1 to 371, inclusive.

2. Add up all integers from 0 to 789, inclusive.

Gauss's method allows you to add up certain kinds of lists of numbers. The method works when the numbers add up in the same way forward and backward. Not all sequences of numbers have this property.

For example, suppose $g(n) = 3^n$. A table for g looks fairly regular.

n	g(n)
0	$3^0 = 1$
1	$3^1 = 3$
2	$3^2 = 9$
3	$3^3 = 27$
4	$3^4 = 81$
5	$3^5 = 243$

How would you add up all the outputs of g between 1 and, say, 3^5? You might try Gauss's method.

$$S = 1 + 3 + 3^2 + 3^3 + 3^4 + 3^5$$

$$S = 3^5 + 3^4 + 3^3 + 3^2 + 3 + 1$$

$$
\begin{array}{ccccccccccccc}
S & = & 1 & + & 3 & + & 9 & + & 27 & + & 81 & + & 243 \\
& & \downarrow & & \downarrow & & \downarrow & & \downarrow & & \downarrow & & \downarrow \\
+ \quad S & = & 243 & + & 81 & + & 27 & + & 9 & + & 3 & + & 1 \\
\hline
2S & = & 244 & + & 84 & + & 36 & + & 36 & + & 84 & + & 244
\end{array}
$$

These sums are not all the same, so Gauss's trick does not work. What can you do?

Example

Problem Add up the numbers $3^0 + 3^1 + 3^2 + 3^3 + 3^4 + 3^5$.

Solution About B.C. 300, the Greek mathematician Euclid described a way of adding numbers like the outputs of g. Today's algebraic version of **Euclid's method** is to multiply the whole sum by 3. Since each output is 3 times the previous one, this shifts things over.

$$
\begin{array}{ccccccccccccc}
S & = & 3^0 & + & 3^1 & + & 3^2 & + & 3^3 & + & 3^4 & + & 3^5 \\
3S & = & & & 3^1 & + & 3^2 & + & 3^3 & + & 3^4 & + & 3^5 & + & 3^6
\end{array}
$$

Now subtract the top sum from the bottom one.

$$
\begin{array}{ccccccccccccc}
3S & = & & & 3^1 & + & 3^2 & + & 3^3 & + & 3^4 & + & 3^5 & + & 3^6 \\
- \quad S & = & - \, 3^0 & - & 3^1 & - & 3^2 & - & 3^3 & - & 3^4 & - & 3^5 & & \\
\hline
2S & = & - \, 3^0 & & & & & & & & & & & + & 3^6
\end{array}
$$

Almost everything cancels. You get the following result.

$$2S = -1 + 3^6$$

$$S = \frac{3^6 - 1}{2} = 364$$

Euclid described his method in Book IX, Proposition 35 of *Elements*. He based his demonstration on the theory of proportions.

For You to Do

Use Euclid's method to find each sum.

3. $1 + 2 + 2^2 + 2^3 + \cdots + 2^{12}$ **4.** $5^3 + 5^4 + 5^5 + 5^6 + 5^7 + 5^8$

Exercises *Practicing Habits of Mind*

Check Your Understanding

1. Use Gauss's method to find a formula for each sum.

  a. Add up all the integers from 0 to n.

  b. Add up all the integers from 1 to n.

  c. Add up all the integers from 0 to $n - 1$.

2. Add up the even integers in each range.

  a. 0 to 4, inclusive   **b.** 0 to 10, inclusive   **c.** 0 to 1000, inclusive

3. Add up the odd integers in each range.

  a. 1 to 7, inclusive   **b.** 1 to 13, inclusive   **c.** 1 to 999, inclusive

4. Find a formula for each sum.

  a. the even integers from 0 to $2n$ **b.** the odd integers from 1 to $2n + 1$

5. Use Euclid's method to find each sum.

  a. $2^5 + 2^6 + 2^7 + \cdots + 2^{15}$

  b. $3 \cdot 2^5 + 3 \cdot 2^6 + 3 \cdot 2^7 + \cdots + 3 \cdot 2^{15}$

  c. $\frac{9}{10} + \left(\frac{9}{10}\right)^2 + \left(\frac{9}{10}\right)^3 + \cdots + \left(\frac{9}{10}\right)^{10}$

  d. $\frac{9}{10} + \frac{9}{10^2} + \frac{9}{10^3} + \cdots + \frac{9}{10^{10}}$

  e. $1 - \frac{1}{2} + \left(\frac{1}{2}\right)^2 - \left(\frac{1}{2}\right)^3 + \cdots - \left(\frac{1}{2}\right)^7$

6. Write About It

  a. Give three sequences of numbers for which Gauss's method works. What do they have in common?

  b. Give three sequences of numbers for which Euclid's method works. What do they have in common?

7. Suppose r is some number. Find a formula for each sum.

  a. $1 + r + r^2 + \cdots + r^n$ **b.** $a + ar + ar^2 + \cdots + ar^n$

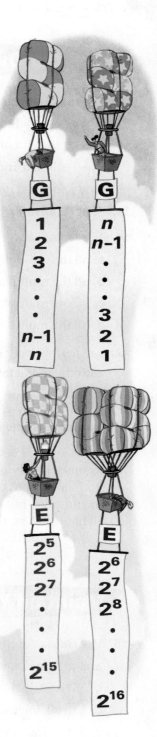

On Your Own

8. Add up all the integers in each range.

   a. −4 to 0, inclusive

   b. −10 to 0, inclusive

   c. −1000 to 0, inclusive

9. Find a formula for the sum of the integers from −n to 0.

10. Adapt a formula or formulas to find the sum of the integers from −10 to 8.

11. **Take It Further** Find a formula for each sum.

   a. all the multiples of 3 from 0 to $3n$

   b. all the multiples of 5 from 0 to $5n$

   c. all the multiples of 7 from 0 to $7n$

   d. all the multiples of k from 0 to kn

12. Let $f(n) = \left(\frac{1}{2}\right)^1 + \left(\frac{1}{2}\right)^2 + \left(\frac{1}{2}\right)^3 + \cdots + \left(\frac{1}{2}\right)^n$. Make a table for f starting with the initial term $f(1) = \frac{1}{2}$. Find a closed form for $f(n)$.

13. Let $g(n) = \left(\frac{1}{2}\right)^0 + \left(\frac{1}{2}\right)^1 + \left(\frac{1}{2}\right)^2 + \left(\frac{1}{2}\right)^3 + \cdots + \left(\frac{1}{2}\right)^n$. Make a table for g starting with the initial term $g(0) = \left(\frac{1}{2}\right)^0 = 1$. Find a closed form for $g(n)$.

14. **Standardized Test Prep** Rod went to a party. The host asked each guest to shake hands with every other guest exactly once. The next morning Rod's mother asked him how many guests attended the party. He forgot the number, but he remembered the host announced there had been 78 handshakes. How many guests attended the party?

   A. 10   **B.** 11   **C.** 12   **D.** 13

Maintain Your Skills

15. Use Gauss's method to add up the integers in each range.

   a. 3 to 5, inclusive

   b. 55 to 60, inclusive

   c. 5 to 80, inclusive

   d. −7 to 150, inclusive

   e. −31 to 131, inclusive

   f. n to m, inclusive

Many people like to think in images. Here are two In-Class Experiments that help you "see" what is going on with Gauss's and Euclid's methods.

In-Class Experiment

Suppose $f(n) = n$. The diagram at the right represents the first five outputs of f. The outputs are the number of squares in the towers.

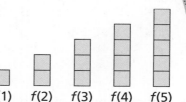

$f(1)$ $f(2)$ $f(3)$ $f(4)$ $f(5)$

Now you want to add these up, so you can think of pushing the towers together to form a staircase. Then you want to count the number of blocks that make up the staircase.

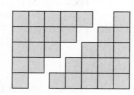

Step 1 Make two copies of the staircase above. Cut out the two copies of the staircase, made up of the blocks that you want to count. For now, just draw diagrams for the staircase that goes from $f(1)$ to $f(5)$.

Step 2 Flip one of the copies.

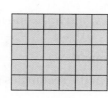

Step 3 Push them together to make a rectangle.

1. Find the height and length of the resulting rectangle. What is its area?
2. How many blocks are in the original staircase?
3. Use the staircase method to find $1 + 2 + 3 + 4 + 5 + 6$.

Euclid's method applies to functions in which each output is a multiple of the previous one, such as $f(n) = 3^n$. If that multiple is between 0 and 1, you can picture what is going on by ripping up a piece of paper.

In-Class Experiment

Get a piece of paper. Call the area of the paper 1.

Step 1 Take your piece of paper and fold it in half. Cut it into two pieces.

Step 2 Place one half on the desk in front of you. Keep the other half in your hand.

Step 3 Repeat Steps 1 and 2 using just the piece of paper that is in your hand now.

Repeat this process a few more times.

4. After doing Steps 1 and 2 three times, you have one rectangle in your hand and three on the desk.

   a. What is the area of each rectangle?

   b. What is the sum of the areas of the rectangles on the desk?

5. After doing Steps 1 and 2 eight times, you have one rectangle in your hand and eight on the desk.

   a. What is the area of each rectangle?

   b. What is the sum of the areas of the rectangles on the desk?

6. After doing Steps 1 and 2 n times, you have one rectangle in your hand and n rectangles on the desk.

   a. What is the area of each rectangle?

   b. What is the sum of the areas of the rectangles on the desk?

Consider more than one strategy. There are two useful ways to visualize the algebraic pattern that results when you find the product below.

$$P = (1 - x)(1 + x + x^2 + x^3 + x^4)$$

One is the telescoping sum model and the other is the shifting model.

The telescoping method works as follows.

$$
\begin{aligned}
P &= (1 - x)(1 + x + x^2 + x^3 + x^4) \\
&= (1 - x) + (x - x^2) + (x^2 - x^3) + (x^3 - x^4) + (x^4 - x^5) \\
&= 1 - x + x - x^2 + x^2 - x^3 + x^3 - x^4 + x^4 - x^5 \\
&= 1 + (-x + x) + (-x^2 + x^2) + (-x^3 + x^3) + (-x^4 + x^4) - x^5 \\
&= 1 - x^5
\end{aligned}
$$

The terms telescope as shown.

The shifting method works as follows.

$$
\begin{aligned}
P &= 1(1 + x + x^2 + x^3 + x^4) - x(1 + x + x^2 + x^3 + x^4) \\
&= 1 + x + x^2 + x^3 + x^4 - (x + x^2 + x^3 + x^4 + x^5) \\
&= 1 - x^5
\end{aligned}
$$

Shift and subtract.

Remember...

You saw and used the general identity in Chapter 2.

Habits of Mind

Detect the key characteristics. Each method corresponds to a different application of the Distributive Property.

Exercises *Practicing Habits of Mind*

Check Your Understanding

1. Referring to the second In-Class Experiment, Cori says, "If I add the areas of all these rectangles, I will never have a sum of more than the area of the piece of paper I started with."

   David replies, "That can't be right! If you repeat the process more times, you'll get more rectangles and the total area will grow."

   Who do you think is correct? Explain.

2. Take It Further When Emma does the second In-Class Experiment, she puts half of the paper (area $= 1$) on the table and keeps half for herself. She then cuts in half the piece that she kept, and again puts half on the table and keeps half for herself. Now, suppose that Emma repeats this process forever and ever. Explain why this suggests the following.

$$\frac{1}{2} + \frac{1}{4} + \frac{1}{8} + \frac{1}{16} + \frac{1}{32} + \frac{1}{64} + \cdots = 1$$

3. Use the staircase method to calculate each sum.

a. $1 + 2 + 3 + \cdots + 23 + 24$ **b.** $1 + 2 + 3 + \cdots + 55 + 56$

c. $1 + 2 + 3 + \cdots + 79 + 80$ **d.** $1 + 2 + 3 + \cdots + 122 + 123$

e. Use the staircase method to find a closed form for the following sum.

$$1 + 2 + 3 + \cdots + (n - 2) + (n - 1) + n$$

4. Expand each product.

a. $(1 - r)(1 + r)$ **b.** $(1 - r)(1 + r + r^2)$

c. $(1 - r)(1 + r + r^2 + r^3)$

d. $(1 - r)(1 + r + r^2 + r^3 + \cdots + r^n)$

Exercise 4 was more than just an exercise in algebraic calculation. The results give you the following identity.

$$(1 - r)(1 + r + r^2 + r^3 + \cdots + r^n) = 1 - r^{n+1}$$

You can divide both sides by $1 - r$.

$$1 + r + r^2 + r^3 + \cdots + r^n = \frac{1 - r^{n+1}}{1 - r}$$

This is an algebraic identity. It holds for any value of r that is allowed, which means all values of r such that $r \neq 1$. This formula allows you to add up certain sequences of numbers without working through the details of Euclid's method each time.

Remember...

You saw this identity in Chapter 2.

5. Use the formula above to find each sum.

a. $1 + \frac{2}{3} + \left(\frac{2}{3}\right)^2 + \left(\frac{2}{3}\right)^3 + \cdots + \left(\frac{2}{3}\right)^8$

b. $1 + \frac{1}{4} + \left(\frac{1}{4}\right)^2 + \left(\frac{1}{4}\right)^3 + \cdots + \left(\frac{1}{4}\right)^8$

c. $1 + 10 + 10^2 + 10^3 + \cdots + 10^{10}$

6. Show that $\frac{1 - r^{n+1}}{1 - r}$ is the same as $\frac{r^{n+1} - 1}{r - 1}$.

Habits of Mind

Make strategic choices. When would it be more convenient to use the $1 - r$ form? When would the $r - 1$ form be more convenient? Explain.

On Your Own

7. Standardized Test Prep What is the sum $1 + \frac{3}{4} + \left(\frac{3}{4}\right)^2 + \left(\frac{3}{4}\right)^3 + \left(\frac{3}{4}\right)^4$ rounded to two decimal places?

A. 2.15 **B.** 2.73 **C.** 3.05 **D.** 3.29

8. The diagram represents the first four outputs for a function *s*.

   a. Make a table for *s*, including a Σ column.

   b. Find a closed form for $s(n)$.

   c. Use a "cut and paste" argument to find a closed form for the Σ column.

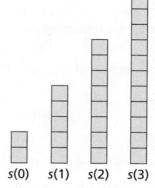

$s(0)$ $s(1)$ $s(2)$ $s(3)$

9. Use any piece of paper. Call its area 1. Follow these steps.

Step 1 Fold the paper in your hand into thirds. Cut it into 3 pieces.

Step 2 Put one piece in Pile 1, put one piece in Pile 2, and keep one piece in your hand.

Step 3 Repeat Steps 1 and 2 with just the piece of paper that is in your hand.

> This is similar to, but not exactly the same as, the last cutting activity you did.

   Repeat this process a few more times.

   a. After completing Steps 1 and 2 twice, you have two pieces of paper in each stack. What is the area of the paper in your hand? What is the sum of the areas of the rectangles in each pile?

   b. After completing Steps 1 and 2 three times, what is the area of the paper in your hand? What is the sum of the areas of the rectangles in each pile?

   c. After completing Steps 1 and 2 *n* times, what is the area of the paper in your hand? What is the sum of the areas of the rectangles in each pile?

   d. **Take It Further** Suppose you could do this process infinitely many times. Estimate the sum of the areas of the rectangles in each pile.

10. What is a closed form for $\frac{1}{3} + \frac{1}{9} + \frac{1}{27} + \cdots + \frac{1}{3^n}$?

Maintain Your Skills

11. Find each sum.

   a. $1 + 2 + 1$

   b. $1 + 2 + 3 + 2 + 1$

   c. $1 + 2 + 3 + 4 + 3 + 2 + 1$

   d. $1 + 2 + 3 + 4 + 5 + 4 + 3 + 2 + 1$

   e. $1 + 2 + \cdots + 23 + 24 + 25 + 24 + 23 + \cdots + 2 + 1$

   f. $1 + 2 + 3 + \cdots + (n - 1) + n + (n - 1) + 3 + 2 + 1$

7.04 The Σ Notation

You have been looking at ways to find sums—to add up sequences of numbers. You have already used the symbol Σ to describe sums in a table. You can also use this symbol as a shorthand notation to describe the sum of a sequence.

For now, think of a *sequence* as a list of numbers. The elements of this list are *terms*.

Example

Problem Find the sum of $2i$ as i goes from 1 to 4, that is, $\displaystyle\sum_{i=1}^{4} 2i$.

Solution
$$\sum_{i=1}^{4} 2i = 2 \cdot 1 + 2 \cdot 2 + 2 \cdot 3 + 2 \cdot 4$$
$$= 2 + 4 + 6 + 8$$
$$= 20$$

> You can model functions with Σ notation. See the TI-Nspire Handbook, p. 804.

Problem Find the sum of $2k + 3$ as k goes from 0 to 5, that is, $\displaystyle\sum_{k=0}^{5} (2k + 3)$.

Solution
$$\sum_{k=0}^{5} (2k + 3) = (2 \cdot 0 + 3) + (2 \cdot 1 + 3) + (2 \cdot 2 + 3)$$
$$+ (2 \cdot 3 + 3) + (2 \cdot 4 + 3) + (2 \cdot 5 + 3)$$
$$= 3 + 5 + 7 + 9 + 11 + 13$$
$$= 48$$

Problem Find the sum of 2^k as k goes from 0 to 5, that is, $\displaystyle\sum_{k=0}^{5} 2^k$.

Solution
$$\sum_{k=0}^{5} 2^k = 2^0 + 2^1 + 2^2 + 2^3 + 2^4 + 2^5$$
$$= 1 + 2 + 4 + 8 + 16 + 32 = 63$$

This is a general form of the notation.

final value $\longrightarrow \textcircled{n}$ ———— function to sum

$$\sum_{\textcircled{k}=\textcircled{0}} f(k) = f(0) + f(1) + \cdots + f(n)$$

index variable ——↗ ↖—— starting value

Go Online
Pearsonsuccessnet.com

For You to Do

Write each sum using Σ notation.

1. $2 + 4 + 6 + 8 + 10 + 12 + 14 + 16 + 18 + 20$

2. $1 + 4 + 9 + 16 + 25$

Exercises *Practicing Habits of Mind*

Check Your Understanding

1. Evaluate each sum.

   a. $\displaystyle\sum_{j=0}^{6} (3j + 4)$

   b. $\displaystyle\sum_{i=1}^{324} 1$

   c. $\displaystyle\sum_{i=0}^{4} i$

   d. $\displaystyle\sum_{i=12}^{45} i$

2. Ms. Take wrote Exercise 1 on the board. When Robin copied part (a), he accidentally changed all the *j*'s to *i*'s. Will Robin still get the correct answer? Explain.

3. Write each sum using $\sum$ notation.

   a. $1 + 4 + 9 + 16 + 25 + \ldots + n^2$

   b. $1 + 1 + 1 + 1 + 1 + 1$

   c. $1 + 2 + 3 + 4 + 5 + 6 + 7 + 8 + 9 + 10$

4. In Exercise 2 from Lesson 7.03, Emma cuts sheets of paper in half. Use $\sum$ notation to describe the sum of the areas of the pieces of paper on the table after Emma completes the steps the given number of times.

   a. 10 times

   b. *n* times

   c. **Take It Further** infinitely many times

5. Use your calculator to find the sum of the areas of the paper on the table after Emma completes the steps 10 times.

> **Habits of Mind**
>
> **Experiment.** In Exercises 4 and 5, you have to picture cutting the paper 10 times. Can you actually cut it 10 times?

6. For Exercise 9 in Lesson 7.03, you cut paper in thirds. Use Σ notation to describe the sum of the areas of the pieces of paper in each pile on the table after you complete the steps the given number of times.

Go Online
Pearsonsuccessnet.com

a. 10 times

b. n times

c. Take It Further infinitely many times

7. Use your calculator to find the sum of the areas of the pieces of paper on the table after you complete the steps 10 times.

8. Standardized Test Prep Which of the following sums is equivalent to
$3 + 5 + 7 + 9 + 11 + 13 + 15 + 17 + 19$?

A. $\displaystyle\sum_{i=1}^{9} (2i + 1)$

B. $\displaystyle\sum_{i=1}^{19} (2i - 1)$

C. $1 + \displaystyle\sum_{i=1}^{9} 2i$

D. $2 \cdot \displaystyle\sum_{i=0}^{8} (i + 3)$

Maintain Your Skills

9. Evaluate each sum. Look for patterns and general methods.

a. $\displaystyle\sum_{j=1}^{4} (5j - 1)$

b. $\displaystyle\sum_{j=4}^{10} (5j - 1)$

c. $\displaystyle\sum_{k=1}^{4} (5k - 1)$

d. $\displaystyle\sum_{i=0}^{6} 2i$

e. $\displaystyle\sum_{k=1}^{6} k(k + 1)$

f. $\displaystyle\sum_{i=0}^{15} 1$

g. $\displaystyle\sum_{i=0}^{16} 1$

h. $\displaystyle\sum_{i=1}^{15} 1$

Habits of Mind

Look for patterns. While evaluating a sum, see if you can use sums you have already evaluated. Which sums can you find using Gauss's method? Which can you find using Euclid's? Which can you find using arithmetic or other methods?

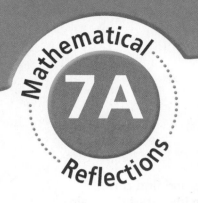

Mathematical 7A Reflections

In this investigation, you learned to make a sum table for a function, write closed-form rules for the sum column, and use $\sum$ notation. You used Gauss's method to find the sum of a sequence with constant differences and Euclid's method to find the sum of a sequence with constant ratios. These exercises will help you summarize what you have learned.

1. Copy and complete the following sum table. Find a closed-form rule for the $\sum$ column.

n	$g(n)$	$\sum$
0	-3	
1	1	
2	5	
3	9	
4	13	
5	17	

$$\sum_{i=1}^{4}\left(\frac{1}{2^i}\right) = \frac{15}{16}$$

2. Let $S = \frac{1}{3} + \frac{2}{3} + \frac{4}{3} + \cdots + \frac{256}{3}$.

   a. Explain why you can use Euclid's method to find the sum S.

   b. Find S using Euclid's method. Show your work.

3. Write an expression in $\sum$ notation for the sum in Exercise 2.

4. Find each sum.

   a. odd integers 3 to 33, inclusive

   b. powers of 4 from 4^0 to 4^{11}

5. Find each sum.

   a. $\sum_{i=1}^{8}\left(\frac{1}{2}\right)^i$ b. $\sum_{k=0}^{8}(9 - 3k)$

6. Describe Gauss's method for summing all integers from 1 to n.

7. Find a formula for $\sum_{j=0}^{n} 2^j$ in terms of n.

8. Evaluate $\sum_{j=1}^{5} 4j$.

Vocabulary and Notation

In this investigation, you learned these terms and symbols. Make sure you understand what each one means and how to use it.

- Euclid's method
- Gauss's method
- index

- $\sum_{k=0}^{n} f(k)$ (summation)

Investigation 7B

Sum Identities

In *Sum Identities*, you will evaluate definite sums and find closed-form formulas for indefinite su ms. You will learn identities that help you simplify sums. You will also use sums and these identities to find functions that agree with tables.

By the end of this investigation, you will be able to answer questions like these.

1. What is $\displaystyle\sum_{k=0}^{25} (k + 6^k)$?

2. What is a recursive rule for the series associated with $f(n) = 3n + 6$ having initial term $f(0)$?

3. What is a closed form for the following recursive rule?

$$f(n) = \begin{cases} 5 & \text{if } n = 0 \\ f(n-1) + 2n^2 + 3n + 2 & \text{if } n > 0 \end{cases}$$

You will learn how to

- find closed-form expressions for indefinite sums and use them to evaluate definite sums

- develop a list of Σ identities and recognize situations in which you can apply them

- find closed-form expressions for the series associated with a function

You will develop these habits and skills:

- Visualize a complicated sum as a combination of different simpler sums.

- Generalize the steps in calculating definite sums to find a closed form for an indefinite sum.

- Reason logically using a recursive definition of a function to develop a closed-form definition.

To complete the stack, she needs $(4 + 3 + 2 + 1)$ cups.

Getting Started

Look for patterns as you do the following problems.

For You to Explore

1. Copy and complete each table.

a.

n	f(n)	Σ
0	−2	▦
1	3	▦
2	8	▦
3	13	▦
4	18	▦
5	23	▦

b.

n	g(n)	Σ
0	0	▦
1	2	▦
2	4	▦
3	6	▦
4	8	▦
5	10	▦

c.

n	f(n) + g(n)	Σ
0	−2	▦
1	5	▦
2	▦	▦
3	▦	▦
4	▦	▦
5	▦	▦

d.

n	2f(n)	Σ
0	−4	▦
1	6	▦
2	▦	▦
3	▦	▦
4	▦	▦
5	▦	▦

e.

n	3g(n)	Σ
0	0	▦
1	6	▦
2	▦	▦
3	▦	▦
4	▦	▦
5	▦	▦

f.

n	f(n) · g(n)	Σ
0	0	▦
1	6	▦
2	▦	▦
3	▦	▦
4	▦	▦
5	▦	▦

2. Calculate each sum.

a. $\displaystyle\sum_{j=1}^{5} 1$

b. $\displaystyle\sum_{j=1}^{5} j$

c. $\displaystyle\sum_{j=1}^{5} 2j$

d. $\displaystyle\sum_{j=1}^{5} 3j$

e. $\displaystyle 2\sum_{j=1}^{5} j$

f. $\displaystyle 3\sum_{j=1}^{5} j$

g. $\displaystyle\sum_{j=1}^{5} (j+1)$

h. $\displaystyle\sum_{j=1}^{5} j^2$

i. $\displaystyle\left(\sum_{j=1}^{5} j\right)^2$

j. $\displaystyle\sum_{j=6}^{10} j$

k. $\displaystyle\sum_{j=1}^{10} j$

Exercises Practicing Habits of Mind

On Your Own

3. Tony is filling in a table like those in Problem 1.

n	q(n)	Σ
0	5	5
1	8	13
2	11	24
3	14	38
4	17	55
5	20	75

Tony says, "I can tell that $q(n)$ is linear. And I think Σ is a quadratic function of the inputs."

a. Show that $q(n)$ is a linear function.

b. Show that in this table, Σ is a quadratic function of the inputs.

c. Is it true that the Σ column in a table of any linear function is quadratic? Explain.

Maintain Your Skills

4. a. Copy and complete each table. The numbers in the Σ column are just the running totals of the outputs in the Δ column.

n	f(n)	Δ	Σ
0	0	1	1
1	1	3	4
2	4	■	■
3	9	■	■
4	16	■	■
5	25		

n	g(n)	Δ	Σ
0	1	■	■
1	2	■	■
2	5	■	■
3	10	■	■
4	17	■	■
5	26		

n	h(n)	Δ	Σ
0	5	■	■
1	6	■	■
2	9	■	■
3	14	■	■
4	21	■	■
5	30		

b. What is going on here?

Definite and Indefinite Sums

You have already learned at least two methods for finding certain kinds of sums. Using Gauss's method, Euclid's method, and a few new methods that you will learn in this investigation, you can solve very complicated sums.

Minds in Action   episode 33

Sasha and Derman are working on evaluating $\sum_{i=1}^{25} (3i + 2)$.

Derman I've got this one. $5 + 8 + 11 + 14 + \cdots$

Sasha Derman, we *could* figure out the 25 numbers and add them up. But let's try arranging the terms differently instead of writing out the whole list.

Sasha starts writing on the board.

$$\sum_{i=1}^{25} (3i + 2) = (3 \cdot 1 + 2) + (3 \cdot 2 + 2) + (3 \cdot 3 + 2)$$
$$+ (3 \cdot 4 + 2) + \cdots + (3 \cdot 25 + 2)$$

Sasha Now rearrange the numbers, grouping all the "3 ×" terms together and all the 2's together.

$$(3 \cdot 1 + 3 \cdot 2 + 3 \cdot 3 + 3 \cdot 4 + \cdots + 3 \cdot 25) + \underbrace{2 + 2 + \cdots + 2}_{\text{25 2's}}$$

Factor out a 3 from the first part of the sum.

$$3(1 + 2 + 3 + 4 + \cdots + 25) + \underbrace{2 + 2 + \cdots + 2}_{\text{25 2's}}$$

Derman I get it! You have three times the sum of the integers from 1 to 25, plus 25 two's.

- The sum of the integers from 1 to 25 is $\frac{25 \cdot 26}{2}$.

- 25 two's is $25 \cdot 2$ or 50.

So, the sum is $3 \cdot \frac{25 \cdot 26}{2} + 25 \cdot 2$, which simplifies to 1025.

You can summarize Sasha's method this way.

- Collect all the terms with a common factor of 3, factor out the 3, and use Gauss's method.

- Collect all the 2's, figure out how many there will be, and multiply.

For You to Do

Use Sasha's method to evaluate each sum.

1. $\displaystyle\sum_{k=1}^{30}(3k+2)$

2. $\displaystyle\sum_{k=1}^{13}3^k$

3. $\displaystyle\sum_{k=0}^{10}(f(k)+g(k))$, where $f(n)=5n-1$ and $g(n)=2n+3$

4. $\displaystyle\sum_{k=0}^{12}f(k)$, where $f(n)=5n-1$

> Write out each sum and rearrange it so that you can use the method of Gauss or the method of Euclid.

In all the problems so far, you knew where to start summing and where to stop. Sums like that are **definite sums.** Sometimes you have an **indefinite sum,** such as $\displaystyle\sum_{k=1}^{n}(3k+2)$, where n is a variable.

With an indefinite sum, you cannot find a number equal to the sum, but you can find a closed-form expression for it.

Example

Problem Find a closed form for $\displaystyle\sum_{k=1}^{n}(3k+2)$.

Solution
$$\sum_{k=1}^{n}(3k+2)=(3\cdot1+2)+(3\cdot2+2)+\ldots+(3\cdot n+2)$$
$$=(3\cdot1+3\cdot2+3\cdot3+3\cdot4+\cdots+3\cdot n)$$
$$+\underbrace{2+2+\cdots+2}_{n\,2\text{'s}}$$
$$=3(1+2+\ldots+n)+2n$$
$$=3\cdot\frac{n(n+1)}{2}+2n$$
$$=\frac{3n^2+7n}{2}$$

What good are indefinite sums? Well, if you can find a closed form for one, you can just plug numbers into that closed form to get values for many definite sums. For example, you know

$$\sum_{k=1}^{n}(3k+2)=\frac{3n^2+7n}{2}$$

So you can say with certainty that

$$\sum_{k=1}^{20}(3k+2)=\frac{3\cdot20^2+7\cdot20}{2}=670$$

You can also use indefinite sums to define new functions from old ones.

Definition

Given a function *f* having a domain that contains the nonnegative integers, the **series associated with *f*** is the function defined on nonnegative integers by

$$F(n) = \sum_{k=0}^{n} f(k) = f(0) + f(1) + f(2) + \cdots + f(n)$$

If you use a spreadsheet, you can make a summation column to tabulate the associated series. See the TI-Nspire Handbook, p. 804.

So, the series associated with *f* is a running total of the outputs of *f*. For example, in Exercise 3 from Lesson 7.05, the Σ column gives the outputs for the series associated with the function *q*.

Definition

An **identity** is a statement that two expressions that may seem different are actually equivalent under the basic rules of algebra.

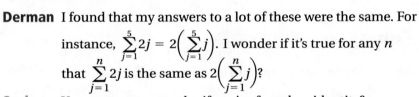

Minds in Action   episode 34

Derman is looking at his solutions to Problem 2 in Lesson 7.05.

Derman I found that my answers to a lot of these were the same. For instance, $\sum_{j=1}^{5} 2j = 2\left(\sum_{j=1}^{5} j\right)$. I wonder if it's true for any *n* that $\sum_{j=1}^{n} 2j$ is the same as $2\left(\sum_{j=1}^{n} j\right)$?

Sasha You mean, you wonder if you've found an identity?

In the Check Your Understanding exercises, you will get to investigate this very question, and others like it.

Exercises Practicing Habits of Mind

Check Your Understanding

1. Consider the statements below. Some of them are identities. Others are not, even though they may look as though they are true. Explore the statements and discover exactly which are identities and which are not.

   a. $\displaystyle\sum_{k=1}^{n} 2k \overset{?}{=} 2\sum_{k=1}^{n} k$

   b. $\displaystyle\sum_{k=0}^{n} 2f(k) \overset{?}{=} 2\sum_{k=0}^{n} f(k)$

In these exercises, n is some integer.

   c. $\displaystyle\sum_{k=1}^{n} k^2 \overset{?}{=} \left(\sum_{k=1}^{n} k\right)^2$

   d. $\displaystyle\sum_{k=0}^{n} k \overset{?}{=} \frac{n(n+1)}{2}$

   e. $\displaystyle\sum_{k=1}^{n} k \overset{?}{=} \frac{n(n+1)}{2}$

   f. $\displaystyle\sum_{k=0}^{n} 1 \overset{?}{=} n + 1$

   g. $\displaystyle\sum_{k=1}^{n} 1 \overset{?}{=} n$

   h. $\displaystyle\sum_{k=1}^{n} 1^2 \overset{?}{=} \left(\sum_{k=1}^{n} 1\right)^2$

   i. $\displaystyle\sum_{k=0}^{n} g(k)f(k) \overset{?}{=} \left(\sum_{k=0}^{n} g(k)\right) \times \left(\sum_{k=0}^{n} f(k)\right)$

   j. $\displaystyle\sum_{k=0}^{n} r^k \overset{?}{=} \frac{r^{n+1} - 1}{r - 1}$, where $r \neq 1$

   k. $\displaystyle\sum_{k=0}^{n} (f(k) + g(k)) \overset{?}{=} \sum_{k=0}^{n} f(k) + \sum_{k=0}^{n} g(k)$

2. Use Sasha's method from the dialog to evaluate the two sums in each part.

   a. $\displaystyle\sum_{k=1}^{16} (3k + 2), \ \sum_{k=0}^{16} (3k + 2)$

   b. $\displaystyle\sum_{k=1}^{13} 2 \cdot 3^k, \ \sum_{k=0}^{6} 2 \cdot 3^k$

   c. $\displaystyle\sum_{k=0}^{12} (f(k) - g(k)), \ \sum_{j=5}^{12} f(j)$, where $f(n) = 5n - 1$ and $g(n) = 2n + 3$

3. Find each sum.

   a. $\displaystyle\sum_{k=1}^{5} (2k - 1)$

   b. $\displaystyle\sum_{k=1}^{10} (2k - 1)$

   c. $\displaystyle\sum_{k=6}^{10} (2k - 1)$

   d. Find a closed form for $\displaystyle\sum_{k=1}^{n} (2k - 1)$.

   e. Use the closed form for $\displaystyle\sum_{k=1}^{n} (2k - 1)$ to calculate $\displaystyle\sum_{k=1}^{1000} (2k - 1)$.

Or find a closed form for the series associated with $x \mapsto 2x - 1$.

4. Find a closed form for the series associated with the function f, where $f(x) = 5x - 1$.

5. Use the closed form from Exercise 4 to find each sum.

   a. $\displaystyle\sum_{k=0}^{23}(5k - 1)$ **b.** $\displaystyle\sum_{k=0}^{7}(5k - 1)$

6. Find a closed form for $\left(\displaystyle\sum_{k=0}^{n}5k\right) - 1$.

7. Find each sum.

   a. $\displaystyle\sum_{k=0}^{5}7$ **b.** $\displaystyle\sum_{k=1}^{6}7$

   c. Find a closed form for $\displaystyle\sum_{k=1}^{n}7$.   **d.** Find a closed form for $\displaystyle\sum_{k=0}^{n-1}7$.

8. Suppose a and b are numbers. What is a closed form for $\displaystyle\sum_{k=1}^{n}(ak + b)$, in terms of a and b?

   > If you wanted to be fancy, you might restate the question as "Find a closed form for the series associated with the affine map $\mathcal{A}_{(a, b)}$."

9. Find each sum.

   a. $\displaystyle\sum_{k=0}^{4}9 \cdot 10^{k}$ **b.** $\displaystyle\sum_{k=0}^{12}9 \cdot 10^{k}$ **c.** $\displaystyle\sum_{k=5}^{12}9 \cdot 10^{k}$

   d. Find a closed form for $\displaystyle\sum_{k=0}^{n}9 \cdot 10^{k}$.

10. **Standardized Test Prep** Which expression is a closed form for $\displaystyle\sum_{k=0}^{n}\left(\frac{2}{3}\right)^{k}$?

   A. $\dfrac{1 - \left(\frac{2}{3}\right)^{n+1}}{3}$ **B.** $3\left(1 - \left(\frac{2}{3}\right)^{n+1}\right)$ **C.** $3 - \left(\frac{1}{3}\right)^{n+1}$ **D.** $\dfrac{\left(\frac{2}{3}\right)^{n+1} - 1}{\frac{1}{3}}$

Maintain Your Skills

11. Consider the statements below. Some of them are identities. Others are not, even though they may look as though they are true. Explore the statements and discover which are identities and which are not.

   > In these exercises, m and n are integers.

   a. $\displaystyle\sum_{k=1}^{m}f(k) + \sum_{k=m+1}^{n}f(k) \overset{?}{=} \sum_{k=1}^{n}f(k)$, where $m < n$

   b. $\displaystyle\sum_{k=1}^{n}ck^{2} \overset{?}{=} c\sum_{k=1}^{n}k^{2}$, where c is any real number

   c. $\displaystyle\sum_{k=1}^{n}k(k + 1) \overset{?}{=} \sum_{k=1}^{n}k^{2} + \sum_{k=1}^{n}k$

   d. $\displaystyle\sum_{k=1}^{n}k(k + 1) \overset{?}{=} \left(\sum_{k=1}^{n}k\right) \times \left(\sum_{k=1}^{n}(k + 1)\right)$

Σ Identities

Take stock of what you have done so far. There are several Σ identities that are so useful that you can list them in a theorem and refer to them by name. You have seen most of these in Exercise 1 of Lesson 7.06. And, as you go on, you will add to this list.

Theorem 7.1

The following are identities.

- **Factors come out.**

$$\sum_{k=0}^{n} cf(k) = c \times \sum_{k=0}^{n} f(k), \text{ where } c \text{ is any real number}$$

- **The sigma of a sum is the sum of the sigmas.**

$$\sum_{k=0}^{n} (f(k) + g(k)) = \sum_{k=0}^{n} f(k) + \sum_{k=0}^{n} g(k)$$

- **Splitting up a sum**

$$\sum_{k=0}^{n} f(k) = \sum_{k=0}^{m} f(k) + \sum_{k=m+1}^{n} f(k), \text{ where } 0 < m < n$$

- **Add a bunch of ones.**

$$\sum_{k=0}^{n} 1 = n + 1 \quad \text{or} \quad \sum_{k=1}^{n} 1 = n$$

- **Think Gauss.**

$$\sum_{k=0}^{n} k = \frac{n(n + 1)}{2}$$

- **Think Euclid.**

$$\sum_{k=0}^{n} r^k = \frac{r^{n+1} - 1}{r - 1}$$

> **Habits of Mind**
>
> **Detect the key characteristics.** You can use the first two identities together under the name *linearity*.

> It is a good idea to put these identities on a poster or in your notes.

For Discussion

1. Why are the "add a bunch of ones" identities different depending on whether the summation starts at $k = 0$ or $k = 1$?

2. How does a change of starting point from $k = 0$ to $k = 1$ affect the identities listed above as "Think Gauss" and "Think Euclid"?

Example

Problem Evaluate $\displaystyle\sum_{k=0}^{8} (3k + 2)$.

Solution You can calculate it this way.

$$\sum_{k=0}^{8} (3k + 2) = \sum_{k=0}^{8} 3k + \sum_{k=0}^{8} 2 \quad \text{(The sigma of a sum is the sum of the sigmas.)}$$

$$= 3\sum_{k=0}^{8} k + 2\sum_{k=0}^{8} 1 \quad \text{(Factors come out.)}$$

$$= 3 \cdot \frac{8 \cdot (8 + 1)}{2} + 2 \cdot (8 + 1) \quad \text{(Gauss and add a bunch of ones.)}$$

$$= 108 + 18 = 126$$

Problem Find a closed form for $\displaystyle\sum_{k=0}^{n} (3k + 2)$.

Solution

$$\sum_{k=0}^{n} (3k + 2) = \sum_{k=0}^{n} 3k + \sum_{k=0}^{n} 2 \quad \text{(The sigma of a sum is the sum of the sigmas.)}$$

$$= 3\sum_{k=0}^{n} k + 2\sum_{k=0}^{n} 1 \quad \text{(Factors come out.)}$$

$$= 3 \cdot \frac{n(n + 1)}{2} + 2(n + 1) \quad \text{(Gauss and add a bunch of ones.)}$$

> This is an example of an indefinite sum.

Habits of Mind

Use a different process to get the same answer. Your CAS can evaluate finite and indefinite sums. See the TI-Nspire Handbook on p. 804. But it is important to know how to use the sigma identities to break down complicated sums into simpler ones. Besides, why should the calculator have all the fun?

The last expression in the solution above is a fine way to represent the closed form for the sum. If you want, however, you can transform it even more.

$$\sum_{k=0}^{n} (3k + 2) = 3\frac{n(n + 1)}{2} + 2(n + 1)$$

$$= \frac{3n(n + 1) + 4(n + 1)}{2}$$

$$= \frac{(n + 1)(3n + 4)}{2}$$

Notice that if you substitute $n = 8$ in this formula, you get 126. This agrees with the earlier result. And, you can use this formula for the indefinite sum to do other definite sums, such as the following.

$$\sum_{k=0}^{205} (3k + 2) = \frac{(205 + 1)(3 \cdot 205 + 4)}{2} = 63{,}757$$

For You to Do

Evaluate each sum.

3. $\displaystyle\sum_{k=1}^{30} (3k - 2)$

4. $\displaystyle\sum_{k=1}^{n} (6k - 4)$, in terms of n

Jakob Bernoulli (1654–1705) was a member of a remarkable Swiss family that produced many mathematicians and scientists. Jakob studied the formulas for the sums of powers. These sums are the series associated with the functions $x \mapsto x^m$ for positive integers m. Johan Faulhaber published them in his 1631 work *Academia Algebrae*.

These sums are

$$\sum_{k=0}^{n} k = 0 + 1 + 2 + 3 + \cdots + n$$

$$\sum_{k=0}^{n} k^2 = 0^2 + 1^2 + 2^2 + 3^2 + \cdots + n^2$$

$$\sum_{k=0}^{n} k^3 = 0^3 + 1^3 + 2^3 + 3^3 + \cdots + n^3$$

$$\sum_{k=0}^{n} k^4 = 0^4 + 1^4 + 2^4 + 3^4 + \cdots + n^4$$

$$\vdots$$

$$\sum_{k=0}^{n} k^m = 0^m + 1^m + 2^m + 3^m + \cdots + n^m$$

You have seen a closed form for the first sum. Bernoulli studied all such sums. His definitive results were published in his book *Ars Conjectandi* in 1713, after his death. The coefficients in these formulas are related to an important sequence called the Bernoulli numbers. This book calls these formulas **Bernoulli's formulas** in his honor. Here are just the first few of the formulas Bernoulli gave.

$$\sum_{k=0}^{n} k = \frac{n(n+1)}{2}$$

$$\sum_{k=0}^{n} k^2 = \frac{n(n+1)(2n+1)}{6}$$

$$\sum_{k=0}^{n} k^3 = \frac{n^2(n+1)^2}{4}$$

$$\sum_{k=0}^{n} k^4 = \frac{n(n+1)(2n+1)(3n^2+3n-1)}{30}$$

$$\sum_{k=0}^{n} k^5 = \frac{n^2(n+1)^2(2n^2+2n-1)}{12}$$

It is useful to add these formulas to your list of Σ identities.

Bernoulli liked to brag that he could find the sum of the tenth powers of the first thousand numbers in less than 10 minutes. He would have been amazed at how his methods have continued to evolve over the last 300 years. A calculator uses Bernoulli's formulas and can find the sum of the first thousand tenth powers in seconds.

$$\sum_{k=0}^{1000} k^{10} = 91{,}409{,}924{,}241{,}424{,}243{,}424{,}241{,}924{,}242{,}500$$

None of this would have been possible without the work of mathematicians such as Bernoulli.

For You to Do

Use Bernoulli's formulas to evaluate each sum.

5. $\displaystyle\sum_{j=1}^{45} (4j + 3)$

6. $\displaystyle\sum_{k=0}^{100} (2k^2 + 1)$

Find a formula for each series.

7. $\displaystyle\sum_{j=1}^{n} (4j + 3)$

8. $\displaystyle\sum_{j=0}^{n} (4j + 3)$

Exercises *Practicing Habits of Mind*

Check Your Understanding

1. Evaluate $\displaystyle\sum_{k=1}^{50} 5(k + 1)$.

2. Evaluate each sum using the method in the example.

    a. $\displaystyle\sum_{k=0}^{16} (3k - 2)$ **b.** $\displaystyle\sum_{k=0}^{13} \left(\tfrac{1}{2}\right)^k$ **c.** $\displaystyle\sum_{k=1}^{13} \left(\tfrac{1}{2}\right)^k$

3. Suppose $f(n) = 5n - 1$ and $g(n) = 2n + 3$. Evaluate each sum.

    a. $\displaystyle\sum_{k=0}^{12} f(k)$ **b.** $\displaystyle\sum_{k=0}^{12} (f(k) + g(k))$

    c. $\displaystyle\sum_{k=0}^{12} (3f(k) + g(k))$ **d.** $\displaystyle\sum_{j=5}^{12} f(j)$

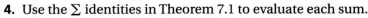

On Your Own

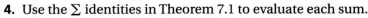

4. Use the Σ identities in Theorem 7.1 to evaluate each sum.

   a. $\displaystyle\sum_{j=1}^{12}(5j-1)$

   b. $\displaystyle\sum_{j=7}^{12}(5j-1)$

   c. $\displaystyle\sum_{j=1}^{n}(5j-1)$

   d. $\displaystyle\sum_{j=0}^{7}2^j$

   e. $\displaystyle\sum_{j=0}^{7}3\cdot2^j$

   f. $\displaystyle\sum_{j=0}^{n}3\cdot2^j$

Suppose you have a mystery function f, and all you know is a formula for its associated series.

$$\sum_{k=0}^{n}f(k)=n^2-3n$$

5. Find each sum.

   a. $\displaystyle\sum_{k=0}^{10}f(k)$

   b. $\displaystyle\sum_{k=5}^{10}f(k)$

   c. $\displaystyle\sum_{k=1}^{11}f(k-1)$

   d. $\displaystyle\sum_{k=0}^{10}(3f(k)+5^k)$

6. a. Find a polynomial g that agrees with f for all integers $n>0$.

   b. **Take It Further** Is there more than one polynomial g that works? Explain.

Suppose you have a mystery function g, and all you know is a formula for this indefinite sum.

$$\sum_{k=0}^{n}g(k)=2n^2-5n$$

7. Find each sum.

   a. $\displaystyle\sum_{k=0}^{10}g(k)$

   b. $\displaystyle\sum_{k=5}^{10}g(k)$

   c. $\displaystyle\sum_{k=1}^{11}g(k-1)$

   d. $\displaystyle\sum_{k=0}^{10}(3g(k)+7^k)$

8. a. Find a polynomial h that agrees with g for all integers $n>0$.

   b. **Take It Further** Is there more than one polynomial h that works? Explain.

9. What is the sum of all the multiples of 3 that are greater than 1 and less than 1000?

10. Use Bernoulli's formulas to evaluate each sum.

    a. $\displaystyle\sum_{k=1}^{30}k(k+1)(k+2)$

    b. $\displaystyle\sum_{k=1}^{100}(3k^2+5k-7)$

11. Find a formula for each indefinite sum.

a. $\displaystyle\sum_{k=0}^{n} k(k+1)$

b. $\displaystyle\sum_{k=0}^{n} k(k+1)(k+2)$

c. $\displaystyle\sum_{k=0}^{n} k(k+1)(k+2)(k+3)$

12. Evaluate each definite sum.

a. $\displaystyle\sum_{j=12}^{45} (4j+3)$

b. $5 + 9 + 13 + 17 + 21 + \cdots + 201$

c. $\displaystyle\sum_{k=1}^{36} k(k+1)$

d. $1 - 2 + 3 - 4 + 5 - \cdots - 1000$

e. $1 - 2 + 4 - 8 + 16 - \cdots + 1024$

13. Use Bernoulli's formulas to evaluate each sum.

a. $\displaystyle\sum_{k=1}^{5} 2k^3$

b. $\displaystyle\sum_{k=1}^{30} (k-1)^3$

c. $\displaystyle\sum_{k=1}^{30} (k+1)^3$

d. $\displaystyle\sum_{k=7}^{30} (k+2)^3$

14. **Standardized Test Prep** Which of the following closed-form formulas can you use to find the sum of all perfect squares less than or equal to 100?

A. $\dfrac{n(n-1)^2}{2}$

B. $\dfrac{10^3\left(1-\left(\frac{1}{10}\right)^{n+1}\right)}{3}$

C. $\dfrac{n(n+1)(2n+1)}{6}$

D. $\dfrac{n^2(n+1)^2}{4}$

Maintain Your Skills

15. a. Copy and complete each table. The numbers in the Σ column are just the running totals of the outputs in the Δ column.

n	f(n)	Δ	Σ
0	0	2	2
1	2	4	6
2	6	▨	▨
3	12	▨	▨
4	20	▨	▨
5	30		

n	g(n)	Δ	Σ
0	1	▨	▨
1	3	▨	▨
2	7	▨	▨
3	13	▨	▨
4	21	▨	▨
5	31		

n	h(n)	Δ	Σ
0	5	▨	▨
1	7	▨	▨
2	11	▨	▨
3	17	▨	▨
4	25	▨	▨
5	35		

b. What is going on here?

Tables and Figurate Numbers

In Chapter 1, you looked at tables like this one.

n	g(n)
0	7
1	8
2	10
3	13

Remember...

In Chapter 2, you studied Lagrange Interpolation, a method for fitting a function to any table. This lesson develops another method.

Your goal was to find a function that agreed with the table. Finding a closed-form function that agrees with a table is not always easy. But sometimes it is fairly easy to find a recursively defined function. For example, you can add a Δ column.

As you saw in Chapter 2, there are many functions (even polynomial functions) that agree with this table.

n	g(n)	Δ
0	7	1
1	8	2
2	10	3
3	13	

This leads to a function g, defined on positive integers, that agrees with the table above.

$$g(n) = \begin{cases} 7 & \text{if } n = 0 \\ g(n-1) + n & \text{if } n > 0 \end{cases}$$

You can sometimes use the ideas in this investigation to find a closed form for recursively defined functions. You can call this method *unstacking*.

Example

Problem Find a closed-form definition for a function G, defined on all of $\mathbb{R}$, that agrees with g.

Solution

Step 1 Calculate $g(5)$ the way a computer would.

$$g(5) = g(4) + 5 \qquad \text{but } g(4) = g(3) + 4 \qquad \text{so}$$

$$= g(3) + 4 + 5$$

$$= g(2) + 3 + 4 + 5$$

$$= g(1) + 2 + 3 + 4 + 5$$

$$= g(0) + 1 + 2 + 3 + 4 + 5$$

$$= 7 + 1 + 2 + 3 + 4 + 5$$

So $g(5) = 7 + 1 + 2 + 3 + 4 + 5$.

Step 2 Now, write $g(6)$ and $g(7)$ in the same form, just to get in the rhythm of the calculation.

Step 3 So, you can also write $g(n)$ using Σ notation.

$$g(n) = 7 + 1 + 2 + 3 + \cdots + n = 7 + \sum_{k=1}^{n} k$$

Step 4 Use Gauss's method to write $\displaystyle\sum_{k=1}^{n} k$ in a closed form.

Step 5 Now you can write a closed form for $G(n)$.

For You to Do

1. Complete the missing calculations in the Example above.

For Discussion

Tony is looking for a closed-form function $F(n)$ that agrees with the function $f(n)$ below.

$$f(n) = \begin{cases} 3 & \text{if } n = 0 \\ f(n-1) + 6n^2 + 2n + 5 & \text{if } n > 0 \end{cases}$$

Tony says, "After I unstacked $f(n)$, I ended up with

$$F(n) = 3 + 6\sum_{k=1}^{n} k^2 + 2\sum_{k=1}^{n} k + 5\sum_{k=1}^{n} 1."$$

Sasha circles the coefficients and draws some arrows.

$$f(n) = \begin{cases} \text{\textcircled{3}} & \text{if } n = 0 \\ f(n-1) + \text{\textcircled{6}}n^2 + \text{\textcircled{2}}n + \text{\textcircled{5}} & \text{if } n > 0 \end{cases}$$

$$F(n) = \text{\textcircled{3}} + \text{\textcircled{6}}\sum_{k=1}^{n} k^2 + \text{\textcircled{2}}\sum_{k=1}^{n} k + \text{\textcircled{5}}\sum_{k=1}^{n} 1$$

2. Does this happen for all functions like $f(n)$? Explain.

3. Find a closed form for f.

Figurate Numbers

Since the time of the Pythagoreans, around 500 B.C., people have classified numbers according to geometric shapes. The diagrams below show examples of **figurate numbers.** The triangular numbers are the numbers of dots needed to make up the equilateral triangles shown below.

The square numbers are the numbers of dots needed to make up the squares shown below.

And there are pentagonal numbers, hexagonal numbers, and so on.

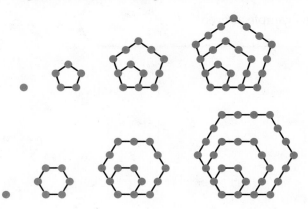

For You to Do

You can use the recursive definition below to find the nth triangular number.

$$t(n) = \begin{cases} 1 & \text{if } n = 1 \\ t(n-1) + n & \text{if } n > 1 \end{cases}$$

4. Verify that this recursive formula is correct for the diagrams above.

5. Find a closed form for the triangular numbers.

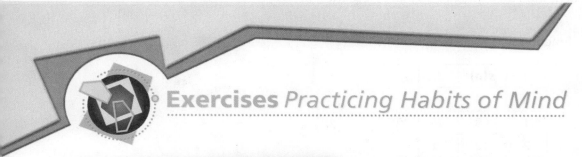

Exercises *Practicing Habits of Mind*

Check Your Understanding

In these exercises, *a closed-form definition for a function* means a closed-form definition for a function defined on all of $\mathbb{R}$. Also, *a closed-form definition for a function H that agrees with h* means a closed-form definition for a function H that agrees with h for all nonnegative integers.

1. Use the recursive definition for the function h below.

$$h(n) = \begin{cases} 3 & \text{if } n = 0 \\ h(n-1) + n & \text{if } n > 0 \end{cases}$$

Find a closed-form definition for a function H that agrees with h.

2. This table shows values of a function q.

n	$q(n)$	Δ
0	32	■
1	34	■
2	38	■
3	44	

a. Find a recursively defined formula for $q(n)$ that agrees with the table.

b. Find a closed-form definition for a function Q that agrees with your function from part (a).

3. Find a closed form for this recursive definition.

$$s(n) = \begin{cases} 1 & \text{if } n = 1 \\ s(n-1) + (2n-1) & \text{if } n > 1 \end{cases}$$

4. Use this recursive definition of the function m.

$$m(n) = \begin{cases} 28 & \text{if } n = 0 \\ m(n-1) + 2n - 1 & \text{if } n > 0 \end{cases}$$

Find a closed-form definition for a function M that agrees with the function m.

Go Online
Pearsonsuccessnet.com

5. Copy this table for a function s.

n	$s(n)$	Δ
0	7	■
1	8	■
2	12	■
3	21	

a. Complete the Δ column. Use it to find a recursive formula for $s(n)$.

b. Find a closed-form definition for a function S that agrees with your function s.

6. Use this recursive definition of a function t.

$$t(n) = \begin{cases} 1 & \text{if } n = 0 \\ t(n-1) + 2^n & \text{if } n > 0 \end{cases}$$

a. Express $t(n)$ as a sum of powers of 2.

b. Find a closed-form definition for a function T that agrees with t.

7. This table for some function g has a Δ column. Nina spilled ink over most of the $g(n)$ column.

n	$g(n)$	Δ
1	12	5
2		6
3		7
4		8
5		

a. What is $g(5)$?

b. How did you find it?

c. Find a recursive formula for $g(n)$.

d. Find a closed-form definition for a function G that agrees with g.

8. Standardized Test Prep Which of the following expressions is a closed-form rule for the recursively defined function below?

$$f(n) = \begin{cases} 5 & \text{if } n = 0 \\ f(n-1) + 8n^3 & \text{if } n > 0 \end{cases}$$

A. $8n^3(n+1)^2$ **B.** $5 + 4n(n+1)$

C. $8n^3 8n^3(n+1)^2$ **D.** $5 + 2n^2(n+1)^2$

9. a. Find two triangular numbers that are also square numbers.

   b. Take It Further Are there more than two such numbers?

10. a. Find a recursive formula $p(n)$ to describe the pentagonal numbers.

    b. Find a closed-form definition for a function P to describe the pentagonal numbers.

11. a. Find a recursive formula $h(n)$ to describe the hexagonal numbers.

    b. Find a closed-form formula $H(n)$ to describe the hexagonal numbers.

Maintain Your Skills

12. Let $T(n)$ be a formula for the nth triangular number. Show that $T(n-1) + T(n) = S(n)$. In other words, show that if you add two consecutive triangular numbers, you get a square number.

Here is a picture of the tetrahedral numbers. Notice that each level is made up of a triangular number of dots.

Let $T(n)$ be the nth triangular number. You can use the recursive formula below for the tetrahedral numbers.

$$a(n) = \begin{cases} 1 & \text{if } n = 1 \\ a(n-1) + T(n) & \text{if } n > 1 \end{cases}$$

13. a. Find a recursive definition for $a(n)$ that does not depend on $T(n)$.

    b. Find a closed-form function definition for a function A that agrees with the tetrahedral numbers at positive integers.

Go Online
Video Tutor
Pearsonsuccessnet.com

In this investigation, you learned to find closed-form definitions for indefinite sums and to use the definitions to evaluate definite sums, develop and use Σ identities, and find closed-form expressions for the series associated with a function. These questions will help you summarize what you have learned.

1. Evaluate each sum.

   a. $\displaystyle\sum_{k=2}^{21}(2k - 4)$

   b. $\displaystyle\sum_{k=3}^{10}(2 \cdot 5^k)$

2. Find a closed form for each indefinite sum.

   a. $\displaystyle\sum_{k=0}^{n}(2k - 4)$

   b. $\displaystyle\sum_{k=0}^{n}(2 \cdot 5^k)$

3. Suppose you know $\displaystyle\sum_{j=0}^{n} f(j) = 3n^2 + 4$ for a mystery function f.

   a. Copy and complete the table at the right for f.

   b. Find a polynomial g that agrees with f for all integers $n > 0$.

n	$f(n)$	Σ
0	4	4
1	3	■
2	■	16
3	■	■
4	■	■
5	■	■

4. Find a closed form for the series associated with $h(n) = 3 - 8n$, having initial term $h(0)$.

5. **a.** Explain why you can write the Σ identity "Think Euclid" as $\displaystyle\sum_{k=0}^{n} r^k = \frac{1 - r^{n+1}}{1 - r}$.

   b. Find a closed form for $\displaystyle\sum_{k=2}^{n} r^k$.

6. What is $\displaystyle\sum_{k=0}^{25}(k + 6^k)$?

7. What is a recursive rule for the series associated with $f(n) = 3n + 6$, having initial term $f(0)$?

8. What is a closed form for the following recursive rule?

$$f(n) = \begin{cases} 5 & \text{if } n = 0 \\ f(n - 1) + 2n^2 + 3n + 2 & \text{if } n > 0 \end{cases}$$

Vocabulary

In this investigation, you learned these terms. Make sure you understand what each one means and how to use it.

- **Bernoulli's formulas**
- **definite sum**
- **figurate number**
- **identity**
- **indefinite sum**
- **series associated with f**

Multiple Choice

1. What is the value of the following sum?

$$1 + \frac{1}{10} + \left(\frac{1}{10}\right)^2 + \left(\frac{1}{10}\right)^3 + \cdots + \left(\frac{1}{10}\right)^6$$

A. 1   **B.** 1.111111

C. 0.111111   **D.** 0.999999

2. Use Σ notation to write the sum
$1 + 2 + 4 + 8 + \cdots + 128$.

A. $\displaystyle\sum_{k=0}^{7} 2^k$

B. $\displaystyle\sum_{k=1}^{128} k$

C. $\displaystyle\sum_{k=1}^{64} 2k$

D. $\displaystyle\sum_{k=0}^{64} 2k$

3. What is the value of the sum $\displaystyle\sum_{j=3}^{5} (2j - 1)$?

A. 12   **B.** 14

C. 21   **D.** 25

4. What is the value of the sum $\displaystyle\sum_{k=1}^{n} 3$?

A. $3 + k$ **B.** $3k$

C. $3n$ **D.** $3n + 3$

5. Use the table below to find $h(2)$.

n	$h(n)$	Σ
0	5	5
1	8	▦
2	▦	30

A. 6   **B.** 8

C. 11   **D.** 17

Open Response

6. a. Find the sum of the integers from -5 to 75, inclusive.

   b. Find the sum: $5^0 + 5^1 + 5^2 + \cdots + 5^{12}$.

7. Copy and complete the following sum table. Find a closed-form rule for the Σ column.

n	$f(n)$	Σ
0	3	▦
1	5	▦
2	7	▦
3	9	▦
4	11	▦
5	13	▦

8. Evaluate each sum.

   a. $\displaystyle\sum_{k=6}^{8} (10k + 4)$ **b.** $\displaystyle\sum_{k=0}^{10} (3k - 1)$

   c. $\displaystyle\sum_{k=0}^{20} (k^2 + 2)$ **d.** $\displaystyle\sum_{k=5}^{18} (k^3)$

9. Find a closed-form rule for each indefinite sum.

   a. $\displaystyle\sum_{k=0}^{n} (5k + 3)$

   b. $\displaystyle\sum_{k=0}^{n} (3k^2 + k)$

10. What is a closed-form rule for the following recursive rule?

$$G(n) = \begin{cases} 3 & \text{if } n = 0 \\ G(n-1) + n^2 + 4 & \text{if } n > 0 \end{cases}$$

11. What is a recursive rule for the series associated with $f(n) = 3n + 6$, having initial term $f(0)$?

Arithmetic and Geometric Sequences and Series

In *Arithmetic and Geometric Sequences and Series,* you will explore the properties of arithmetic and geometric sequences. You will also investigate the series associated with arithmetic and geometric sequences.

By the end of this investigation, you will be able to answer questions like these.

1. What is an arithmetic sequence?

2. What is a geometric series?

3. How do you write the repeating decimal 0.121212121 . . . as a fraction?

You will learn how to

- find a closed-form representation for an arithmetic sequence and its associated series

- find a closed-form representation for a geometric sequence and its associated series

- determine whether a geometric sequence has a limit, and if it does, how to find the limit

- convert a repeating decimal into an exact fraction

You will develop these habits and skills:

- Visualize arithmetic and geometric series to better understand their behavior.

- Think about extreme cases as values of n become very large or as terms in a sequence become very small.

- Reason logically to understand, write, and analyze proofs.

You can use a geometric sequence with common ratio $\frac{1}{2}$ to model the number of teams in each round of a single-elimination tournament.

Recall the difference tables you made in Chapter 1.

For You to Explore

You have seen these two tables before.

1. **a.** Make a difference table for each function.

   b. Describe functions K and L as completely as you can.

Table K

n	K(n)
0	3
1	8
2	13
3	18
4	23

Table L

m	L(m)
0	3
1	9
2	15
3	21
4	27

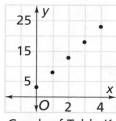

Graph of Table K   Graph of Table L

2. Thor and Pandora are bouncing a ball. Thor drops the ball from a height of 2 meters. Each time it bounces, Pandora measures the height of the bounce. The following table shows the results of this experiment.

Number of Bounces	Height (m)
0	2.00
1	1.68
2	1.41
3	1.19
4	1.00
5	0.84
6	0.71

> Does the ball ever stop bouncing?

a. Find a recursive rule for determining the height of a bounce based on the previous height.

b. How high would the ball bounce on its 100th bounce? Do you think Pandora would be able to measure this height?

3. Lisa is collecting soda cans to win a contest. She is storing her soda cans in her bedroom by making a stack like the one shown here. If she begins with a base of 75 soda cans (the number of cans that will fit across the length of her room), how many cans will she have in her finished stack?

4. Find the missing terms in each sequence. The ratio between each term and the previous one is constant. For each sequence, find this common ratio.

a. $1, 2, 4, \blacksquare, 16, \blacksquare, \blacksquare, \ldots$

b. $1, -2, 4, \blacksquare, 16, \blacksquare, \blacksquare, \ldots$

c. $1, -1, 1, \blacksquare, \blacksquare, \blacksquare, \ldots$

d. $2, 6, 18, \blacksquare, \blacksquare, \ldots$

e. $4, 1, \frac{1}{4}, \blacksquare, \blacksquare, \ldots$

f. $-1, \frac{2}{3}, -\frac{4}{9}, \blacksquare, \ldots$

Look back at Problem 4 from Lesson 5.01. How does this exercise compare to that one?

Exercises *Practicing Habits of Mind*

On Your Own

5. Suppose a snail moves 5 inches up a tree every day and 2 inches down the tree every night. In the morning of Day 0, the snail starts on the ground.

   a. Write a function for the snail's height in the morning and another function for the snail's height in the evening.

   b. Does either of these functions have a constant Δ column? Explain.

   c. If the tree is 40 feet tall, on what day does the snail reach the top?

6. The function $F(n)$ has a constant difference. Copy and complete the following table.

n	F(n)	Δ
0	8	▦
1	▦	▦
2	▦	▦
3	▦	▦
4	12	

7. A health club charges $70 for the first month's membership fee and reduces the monthly fee by $2 each month after that. What is the total membership fee for an entire year?

Maintain Your Skills

8. How many multiples of 9 are between each pair of numbers?

   a. 2 and 22   b. 2 and 62   c. 2 and 1000

   d. 2 and n, where n is some integer greater than 2

9. How many multiples of 3 are strictly between each pair of numbers?

   a. 2 and 22   b. 45 and 62   c. 45 and 1000

   d. integers m and n, where n is greater than m

7.10 Arithmetic Sequences and Series

Until now, a sequence has been a list of numbers. Another way to think about a **sequence** is as a function with a domain that is the set of nonnegative integers. So sequences are nothing new. If the domain of a function is $\{0, 1, 2, 3, 4, 5, \ldots\}$, then it is a sequence. For example, the function defined by $f(n) = 2n^2 + 3n + 5$ is a sequence, if you restrict its domain. You can then list the outputs of the function "in sequence."

$$\{f(0), f(1), f(2), f(3), f(4), \ldots\} = \{5, 10, 19, 32, 49, \ldots\}$$

The outputs of the function are the **terms** of the sequence. In this case, the initial term is 5, the next term is 10, and the fourth term is 32.

In this example, $f(0)$ is the initial term. Sometimes, you want the domain to be all integers n that are greater than 1, and then the initial term is $f(1)$.

Habits of Mind

Detect the key characteristics. In Chapter 2, you saw that to define a function, you must specify the domain. If the domain is the nonnegative integers, the function is a sequence.

Minds in Action   episode 35

Tony is working on Problem 1 from Lesson 7.09.

Tony $K(m)$ and $L(m)$ have a lot in common.

Table K

n	K(n)	Δ
0	3	5
1	8	5
2	13	5
3	18	5
4	23	

Table L

m	L(m)	Δ
0	3	6
1	9	6
2	15	6
3	21	6
4	27	

There's a constant difference of 5 in Table K.

There's a constant difference of 6 in Table L.

The two functions are defined on the set $\{0, 1, 2, 3, 4\}$.

Functions like $K(n)$ and $L(m)$ are special sequences called *arithmetic sequences*. They are defined by the property that their Δ columns are constant.

The constant value of an arithmetic sequence's Δ column is the *common difference d* for that sequence. The formal definition is on the following page.

When you use *arithmetic* as an adjective, the accent is on the third syllable: arithMETic.

Definitions

A sequence is an **arithmetic sequence** if

- its domain is the set of integers $n \geq 0$
- there is a number d, the **common difference** for the sequence, such that

$$f(n) = f(n-1) + d \text{ for all integers } n > 0$$

Habits of Mind

Detect the key characteristics. How does this definition compare to the definition in Lesson 5.04? You can also call arithmetic sequences *linear sequences*. Do their graphs suggest why? Is there an algebraic reason?

Examples of Arithmetic Sequences

Initial term	d	Sequence	Formula and Domain
$a(0) = 3$	3	3, 6, 9, 12, . . .	$a(n) = 3(n+1)$ for all $n \geq 0$
$b(1) = 10$	-1	10, 9, 8, 7, . . .	$b(n) = 11 - n$ for all $n \geq 1$
$w(3) = 180$	180	180, 360, 540, . . .	$w(n) = 180(n-2)$ for all $n \geq 3$

For You to Do

1. In an arithmetic sequence, $f(0) = 8$ and $f(1) = 12$. Write out the first several terms of such a sequence. Is there any other arithmetic sequence with first term 8 and second term 12?

2. Suppose r is an arithmetic sequence with $r(5) = 8$ and $r(12) = 29$.

   a. What is the common difference?

   b. Find $r(9)$.

   c. Find a closed form for r.

   d. Is 78,209,756 a term of r? If so, what term is it? If not, explain why you think it is not.

3. Give two different examples of an arithmetic sequence with common difference 0. How would you describe an arithmetic sequence with common difference 0?

You can denote the terms of a sequence by subscripts $t_0, t_1, t_2, \ldots$ Here, the ninth term is t_8. Explain.

For Discussion

4. Suppose f is an arithmetic sequence with initial term $f(0) = a$ and common difference d. Find a closed form for $f(n)$ in terms of a and d.

5. Suppose g is an arithmetic sequence with initial term $g(1) = b$ and common difference d. Find a closed form for $g(n)$ in terms of b and d.

Habits of Mind

Establish a process. It might help you to make a table for the sequence.

Arithmetic Series

Every arithmetic sequence has an associated arithmetic series.

Definition

If the sequence t is an arithmetic sequence with initial term $t(0)$, the associated series T defined on integers n, such that $n \geq 0$ by

$$T(n) = \sum_{k=0}^{n} t(k) \text{ is an } \textbf{arithmetic series.}$$

Example

Problem Consider the arithmetic sequence in Table K. The initial term is $f(0) = 3$. The common difference is 5. A closed form is $f(n) = 3 + 5n$.

Find a closed form for $F(n) = \sum_{k=0}^{n} f(k)$.

Solution

$$\sum_{k=0}^{n} (3 + 5k) = \sum_{k=0}^{n} 3 + \sum_{k=0}^{n} 5k$$

$$= 3(n + 1) + 5 \cdot \frac{n(n + 1)}{2}$$

$$= \frac{(5n + 6)(n + 1)}{2}$$

For You to Do

Here is Table L again.

m	L(m)	Σ
0	3	▦
1	9	▦
2	15	▦
3	21	▦
4	27	▦

6. Copy the table and complete the Σ column.

7. Find a closed form for the sequence.

8. Find a closed form for the series.

Exercises Practicing Habits of Mind

Check Your Understanding

1. In an arithmetic sequence, the first term is 8 and the nth term is 12. Find the common difference.

2. Can the numbers 1, $\frac{1}{2}$, and $\frac{1}{3}$ belong to the same arithmetic sequence? If so, give an example of such a sequence. If not, explain why not.

3. Can you find three numbers that cannot all belong to the same arithmetic sequence? If so, give an example. If not, explain why not.

4. For each table,
   - Copy the table and complete the Σ column.
   - Find a closed form for the sequence.
   - Find a closed form for the series.

   a.

n	$q(n)$	Σ
0	9	▩
1	15	▩
2	21	▩
3	27	▩
4	33	▩

   b.

n	$p(n)$	Σ
0	12	▩
1	7	▩
2	2	▩
3	-3	▩
4	-8	▩

5. In an arithmetic sequence, $f(0) = 8$ and $f(2) = 12$. Write the first several terms of such a sequence. Is there any other arithmetic sequence with first term 8 and third term 12?

6. Consider the arithmetic sequence g with $g(0) = 2$ and common difference 3.
   a. Write the first four terms of g.
   b. Write the first four terms of the series G associated with g.
   c. Find closed forms for $g(n)$ and for the associated series $G(n)$.

7. For each sequence with the given initial term and constant difference,
   - tabulate the sequence and the associated series
   - find closed forms for the sequence and the associated series
   a. $t(0) = 5, d = 9$ **b.** $h(0) = 7, d = -4$ **c.** $t(0) = 6, d = \frac{1}{2}$

8. Let $f(n) = a + dn$, where a is the initial term and d is the common difference.

   a. Copy and complete this table in terms of a and d.

n	$f(n)$	Σ
0	a	▦
1	$a + d$	▦
2	▦	$3a + 3d$
3	▦	▦
4	▦	▦
5	▦	▦

   b. Find a closed form for the series associated with f.

On Your Own

9. Suppose f is an arithmetic sequence with initial term $f(0) = 3$ and common difference 6.

   a. Find $f(8)$.

   b. Find a closed form for f.

   c. Is 78,209,756 a term of f? If so, what term is it? If not, explain why not.

Go Online
Pearsonsuccessnet.com

10. How would you describe the arithmetic sequence with initial term $f(0) = 1$ and common difference 1?

11. Show that the average of any three consecutive integers is equal to the middle number.

The diameters, in inches, of the cake's layers are part of an arithmetic sequence with initial term 6 and common difference 2.

12. Consider an arithmetic sequence t. Show that any term $t(n)$ is the average of the one before it, $t(n-1)$, and the one after it, $t(n+1)$.

In other words, in an arithmetic sequence, each term starting with the second one is the arithmetic mean of the preceding term and the following term. That is where the name "arithmetic sequence" comes from.

13. Below is an illustration of the first three pyramidal numbers. Each layer is a square.

a. Use this illustration to list the first five pyramidal numbers.

You count the dots here.

b. What series does the total number of dots in each figure represent? Is this series an arithmetic series? Explain.

c. Find the closed form for the number of dots n in a pyramid that is n rows high.

d. How many dots are in a pyramid ten levels high?

14. An arithmetic sequence with terms $a_1, a_2, \ldots, a_5$ satisfies both $a_1 + a_3 + a_5 = -12$ and $a_1 a_3 a_5 = 80$. Find the terms in this sequence.

Some of these exercises have more than one solution.

15. In an arithmetic sequence with a difference d, the product of the second term and d is 30. The sum of the third and fifth terms is 32. Find the first three terms in this sequence.

16. Give an example of a sequence with a Δ column that is an arithmetic sequence. Find a closed form for your sequence.

17. Give an example of a sequence with a Σ column that is an arithmetic sequence. Find a closed form for your sequence.

18. Can the Σ column of an arithmetic sequence ever be arithmetic? Explain.

19. The sum of the first and fifth terms of an arithmetic sequence is $\frac{5}{3}$. The product of the third and fourth terms of the same sequence is $\frac{65}{72}$. Find the sum of the first 17 terms of this sequence.

20. Standardized Test Prep Let $G(n) = \sum_{k=0}^{n} g(k)$, where $g(n) = 5 - 3n$. What is the value of $G(3)$?

A. -4 **B.** -3 **C.** -1 **D.** 2

Use this array for Exercises 21 and 22.

$$
\begin{array}{cccccccc}
1 & 2 & 3 & 4 & 5 & \cdots & k \\
2 & 2 & 3 & 4 & 5 & \cdots & k \\
3 & 3 & 3 & 4 & 5 & \cdots & k \\
4 & 4 & 4 & 4 & 5 & \cdots & k \\
5 & 5 & 5 & 5 & 5 & \cdots & k \\
\vdots & \vdots & \vdots & \vdots & \vdots & \ddots & \\
k & k & k & k & k & & k
\end{array}
$$

21. You can continue the pattern of numbers above indefinitely down and to the right. Let $S(n)$ be the number of entries that are less than or equal to n in this array.

   a. Find a sequence $s(n)$ such that $S(n) = \sum_{k=1}^{n} s(k)$. Is s an arithmetic sequence? Explain.

   b. Find a closed form for $S(n)$.

> So $S(2) = 4$ because there are one 1 and three 2's for a total of 4 entries.

22. **Take It Further** Let $G(n)$ be the sum of all of the entries in the array above that are less than or equal to n.

   a. Find a sequence $g(n)$ such that $G(n) = \sum_{k=1}^{n} g(k)$. Is g an arithmetic sequence? Explain.

   b. Find a closed form for $G(n)$.

> So $G(2) = 2 + 2 + 2 + 1 = 7$. It is the sum of the one 1 and the three 2's.

Maintain Your Skills

23. Suppose t is the sequence given by $t(n) = (n + 1)2^n$.

   a. Make a table for t for $n = 0$ through $n = 5$.

   b. Add a column to the table for the values of the ratio $\frac{t(n)}{t(n-1)}$.

   c. Is t an arithmetic sequence? Is the definition of each of its terms as $t(n) = (n + 1)2^n$ enough to decide? Explain.

   d. Find a closed form for $\sum_{k=0}^{n} t(k)$.

> To evaluate the indefinite sum, see the TI-Nspire Handbook, p. 804.

7.11 Geometric Sequences and Series

There are other types of sequences and series besides arithmetic sequences and series.

In-Class Experiment

Rolf was writing down the recursive formula for an arithmetic sequence *g* with initial term $g(0) = 1$ and common difference 2. As a result of a slip of a pen, he came up with the following definition.

$$g(n) = \begin{cases} 1 & \text{if } n = 0 \\ g(n-1) \cdot 2 & \text{if } n > 0 \end{cases}$$

1. a. Make a table and write down a few entries for *g*.

   b. Is *g* an arithmetic sequence? Explain.

   c. Write a closed form for $g(n)$.

2. a. Add a Δ column to the table for *g*. Describe a pattern in the Δ column.

   b. Add a Σ column to the table for *g*. Describe a pattern in the Σ column.

3. a. Add a ratio column to the table for *g*.

n	$g(n)$	$\dfrac{g(n+1)}{g(n)}$
0	1	$\frac{2}{1} = 2$
1	2	▪
2	4	▪
3	▪	▪
4	▪	▪

   b. Describe a pattern in the ratio column.

Remember...

Instead of what you must add to one output to get the next one, this column gives what you must multiply each output by to get the next one.

Functions like the ones that Rolf built and that Thor and Pandora recorded in Exercise 2 from Lesson 7.09 are *geometric sequences*. To be a geometric sequence, a function has to have two properties.

- It is a sequence, meaning a function defined on the nonnegative integers.
- The ratio column is constant.

Here is a formal definition.

Definitions

A sequence is a **geometric sequence** if

- its domain is the integers $n \geq 0$
- there is a number $r \neq 0$, called the **common ratio**, such that

$f(n) = r \cdot f(n - 1)$ for all integers $n > 0$

Compare this definition with the definition of arithmetic sequence in Lesson 7.10.

Examples of Geometric Sequences

Initial Term	r	Sequence	Formula and Domain
$a(0) = 3$	3	3, 9, 27, 81, . . .	$a(n) = 3^{n+1}$ for all $n \geq 0$
$b(1) = 1$	-1	1, -1, 1, -1, . . .	$b(n) = (-1)^{n-1}$ for all $n \geq 1$
$c(0) = 8$	$\frac{1}{2}$	8, 4, 2, 1, . . .	$c(n) = \frac{8}{(2^n)}$ for all $n \geq 0$

For You to Do

4. Suppose t is a geometric sequence.

   a. If $t(3) = 100$ and $t(5) = 10{,}000$, what is $t(4)$?

   b. If $t(3) = 100$ and $t(5) = 4$, what is $t(4)$?

   c. If $t(n - 1) = a$ and $t(n + 1) = b$, what is $t(n)$?

There could be more than one possibility for $t(4)$.

5. Write down the first four terms of a geometric sequence g with the given initial term and common ratio.

   a. $g(0) = 5$, $r = 2$ **b.** $g(0) = 5$, $r = -2$

   c. $g(0) = 5$, $r = 1$ **d.** $g(0) = 5$, $r = \frac{1}{2}$

Geometric Series

Just as an arithmetic sequence has an associated arithmetic series, a geometric sequence has an associated *geometric series*.

Definition

If the sequence g is a geometric sequence with initial term $g(0)$, the associated series $G(n) = \sum_{k=0}^{n} g(n)$ is a **geometric series.**

For You to Do

Suppose you have a table for a geometric sequence t. You can make a table for the series associated with t by adding a Σ column.

n	$t(n)$	Σ
0	3	3
1	6	9
2	12	21
3	24	45
4	48	93
5	96	189

6. Find both closed and recursive forms for t.

7. Find both closed and recursive forms for the associated series $T(n) = \sum\limits_{k=0}^{n} t(k)$.

8. Show that $T(n) = 2T(n-1) + 3 = \mathcal{A}_{(2,\,3)}(T(n-1))$.

9. What is $\sum\limits_{k=0}^{18} t(k)$?

Habits of Mind

Consider more than one strategy. Can you use Problem 8 to find a closed form for T?

Monthly Payments

In Lesson 1.11, you experimented with the monthly payment on a loan, modeled by a balance function like the one below.

$$b(n, m) = \begin{cases} 10{,}000 & \text{if } n = 0 \\ \left(1 + \frac{0.05}{12}\right)b(n-1, m) - m & \text{if } n > 0 \end{cases}$$

Suppose you have the following parameters.

- The amount borrowed is \$10,000.

- The interest rate is 5%.

- Payments are made at the end of each month.

Then $b(n, m)$ gives you the balance on the loan at the end of n months, with a monthly payment of m dollars.

For Discussion

10. Review the construction of this function and why it does what we say it does. Model it in your function-modeling language and experiment with it. You might want to introduce two more inputs for the initial amount of the loan and the interest rate so that you can control these things.

To model the monthly payment function b, see the TI-Nspire Handbook, p. 804.

For You to Do

Revisit Exercise 6 from Lesson 1.11.

Suppose you want to pay off a car loan in 36 months. Pick an interest rate and keep it constant. Investigate how the monthly payment changes with the cost of the car.

11. Make a table like the one below and complete it.

Cost of Car (thousands of dollars)	Monthly Payment
10	▨
11	▨
12	▨
13	▨
14	▨
15	▨
16	▨
17	▨
18	▨
⋮	⋮

12. Find either a closed-form or a recursive definition for a function that agrees with your table. Build a model of your function.

13. Use your model to find the monthly payment on a $26,000 car loan.

> If this function works for all inputs, you can use it to calculate the monthly payment in terms of the cost of the car in thousands of dollars.

It appears that the Δ column for this table is constant. That is, it seems that the monthly payment is a linear function of the cost of the car. You can use geometric series to see why.

Suppose you borrow C dollars at an interest rate of i, where i is a decimal so that you can calculate with it. Then the recursive definition below gives the more general function b.

$$b(n, m) = \begin{cases} C & \text{if } n = 0 \\ \left(1 + \frac{i}{12}\right)b(n - 1, m) - m & \text{if } n > 0 \end{cases}$$

Notice that $\left(1 + \frac{i}{12}\right)$ is a constant. You can cover it up with your hand and deal with it as if it is one piece q.

$$\text{Let } q = \left(1 + \frac{i}{12}\right).$$

So your function definition looks like this.

$$b(n, m) = \begin{cases} C & \text{if } n = 0 \\ q \cdot b(n - 1, m) - m & \text{if } n > 0 \end{cases}$$

> Notice that $b(n, m) = A_{(q, -m)}(b(n - 1, m))$.

Unstack this definition and look for some regularity in the calculation.

$$b(n, m) = q \cdot b(n - 1, m) - m$$

$$= q(q \cdot b(n - 2, m) - m) - m = q^2 \cdot b(n - 2, m) - qm - m$$

$$= q^2(q \cdot b(n - 3, m) - m) - qm - m$$

$$= q^3 \cdot b(n - 3, m) - q^2m - qm - m$$

$$\vdots$$

$$= q^n \cdot b(0, m) - q^{n-1}m - q^{n-2}m - \cdots - q^2m - qm - m$$

$$= C \cdot q^n - m(q^{n-1} + q^{n-2} + \cdots + q^2 + q + 1)$$

The last series is geometric. Summing it, you get

$$b(n, m) = Cq^n - m\frac{q^n - 1}{q - 1}$$

Setting $b(n, m)$ equal to 0 gives an explicit relationship between m and the cost of the car.

$$m = C\frac{(q - 1)q^n}{q^n - 1}$$

You can state the general result as a theorem.

Theorem 7.2

If you take out a loan for C dollars for n months at an interest rate of i, then the equation below gives the monthly payment.

$$m = C \cdot \frac{(q - 1)q^n}{q^n - 1}$$

where n is the term of the loan and

$$q = 1 + \frac{i}{12}$$

For Discussion

14. Why does this theorem say that the monthly payment is a linear function of the amount borrowed? If you write that linear function as $m = aC + b$, what is a? What is b?

Exercises Practicing Habits of Mind

Check Your Understanding

1. Find $g(7)$ for each geometric sequence.

   a. $g(1) = 5$, $r = 2$
   b. $g(1) = 5$, $r = -2$
   c. $g(1) = 5$, $r = 1$
   d. $g(1) = 5$, $r = \frac{1}{2}$
   e. $g(5) = 18$, $g(6) = 9$
   f. $g(3) = 12$, $g(5) = 30$
   g. $g(6) = 6$, $g(8) = 54$
   h. $g(5) = 6$, $g(9) = 54$

2. Can a sequence be geometric and arithmetic at the same time? Explain.

3. **Write About It** Write at least four pairs of sequences. A pair will consist of an arithmetic sequence a and a geometric sequence g with the same initial term and the common difference of a equal to the common ratio of g. For example,

   $$a_1 = 2, 5, 8, 11, 14, \ldots$$

   $$g_1 = 2, 6, 18, 54, 162, \ldots$$

   Both sequences have initial term 2. The common difference for the arithmetic series a is 3. The common ratio for geometric series g is 3.

   Compare the behavior of sequences in each pair. Do both sequences increase or decrease?

   > Make sure you have first terms, common differences, and common ratios with various signs and values.

4. Let $s(n) = 5 \cdot \left(\frac{1}{2}\right)^n$.

   a. Find a formula for $\displaystyle\sum_{i=0}^{n} s(i)$.
   b. Use the formula to find $\displaystyle\sum_{i=0}^{15} s(i)$.

5. Rosita took out a loan for a car that cost $11,000. She paid $1000 down and got a 4% interest rate.

   a. If the term of the loan is 36 months, what is the monthly payment?

   b. If Rosita pays $500 per month, which is more than the minimum monthly payment, how long will it take her to pay off the car?

On Your Own

6. Write a closed-form definition for a function that generates each sequence in Exercise 1.

   > That is, write a formula for $g(n)$.

7. **Standardized Test Prep** Suppose $a(n)$ is a geometric sequence with initial term $a(0) = 6$ and common ratio $\frac{3}{2}$. What is the value of $a(5)$?

   A. $\frac{15}{2}$
   B. $\frac{243}{32}$
   C. $\frac{27}{2}$
   D. $\frac{729}{16}$

8. Draw a square. Connect the midpoints of the sides of this square to form another square. Connect the midpoints of the sides of the second square to form the next one. You can continue to make more squares in this pattern.

   a. If the side length of the first square you draw is 1, what is the side length of the second square? Of the third square?

   b. Do these lengths form a geometric sequence? Explain. If they do, what are the first term and the common ratio of this geometric sequence?

   c. If the area of the first square you draw is 1, what is the area of the second square? Of third square?

   d. Do these areas form a geometric sequence? Explain. If they do, what are the first term and the common ratio of this geometric sequence? If they do not, what kind of a sequence do they form?

   e. **Take It Further** Prove that connecting the midpoints of the sides of a square really gives you another square.

9. a. Turn a blank piece of $8\frac{1}{2}$ in.-by-11 in. paper lengthwise and draw a 45° angle in the bottom left corner of the paper.

   b. Draw a small square, $\frac{1}{2}$ in. on each side, with one side on the horizontal side of the angle and a vertex on the other side of the angle.

   c. Extend the right side of this square vertically until it intersects the sloping side of the 45° angle. Draw a second square with this segment as its left side, as shown.

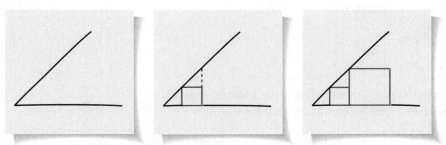

   d. Continue the process to draw two more squares.

   e. What are the lengths of the sides of the four squares?

   f. Find at least two geometric sequences in the diagram.

10. An old tale tells of a king who was tricked into paying an outrageous amount for a favor. The king was to pay by placing 1 grain of rice on the first square of a chessboard, 2 on the second square, 4 on the third square, 8 on the fourth square, and keep doubling the amount this way until all 64 squares had rice. The king thought this might take several pounds of rice.

   a. How many grains of rice would the king place on the last (64th) square?

   b. In all, how many grains of rice would the king place on the chessboard?

   c. If there are 8000 grains of rice in a pound, how many pounds of rice did the king have to pay for the favor?

11. Suppose you make up a joke. On Day 1, you tell your two best friends. They cannot stop laughing. The next day (Day 2), each of them tells two people, who also love the joke. On Day 3, the four people who heard the joke the day before all tell two new people. And so it continues. Each day, everyone who heard the joke yesterday tells two people who have never heard the joke. How quickly does the joke spread?

    a. How many people hear the joke for the first time on the 8th day?

    b. In all, how many people have heard the joke by the end of the 8th day?

    c. How long would it take all the students in your school to hear the joke?

    d. How long would it take all the students in your town or city to hear the joke?

    e. How long would it take everyone in the world to hear the joke?

> You can also model the spread of disease with geometric series, but the spread of jokes is more pleasant to think about.

> Assume there are about 6 billion people in the world.

12. Jaden wants to get a 3-year loan of $9000. He wants to know what monthly payment to expect for different interest rates.

    a. Copy and complete this table showing the monthly payments *m* for different interest rates *r*.

r	m
0%	▨
1%	▨
2%	▨
3%	▨
4%	▨
5%	▨

    b. If Jaden can afford to pay $300 per month, what is the greatest interest rate (to one tenth of a percent) that he can accept for his loan?

13. What price can Hector afford to pay for a car if he can put $1500 down and pay $500 per month on a 5-year, 4% loan?

14. To keep from getting in a rut, many athletes challenge themselves. Suppose Michelle runs 5 miles this week. She gives herself this challenge. In any week, she will never run a shorter distance than she did the week before, and she will try to increase her distance 10% each week.

    a. How far will Michelle run next week?

    b. How far will she run the week after next?

    c. Michelle plans to run in a marathon 32 weeks from now. How far will she run the week before the marathon?

    d. What total mileage will Michelle run between now and the week prior to the marathon, if she keeps her pact?

Do you remember this exercise from Lesson 7.01?

A wealthy relative left Emile an inheritance. The will read as follows.

To Emile, because he likes math problems, I leave a choice. He can have one of two inheritances.

Option 1 A starting amount of $10,000 with an annual payment at the end of each year that is $1000 more than the amount he received the previous year, for the next 26 years

Option 2 A starting amount of one cent with an annual payment at the end of each year that is twice the amount he received in the previous year, for the next 26 years

> Year 0 is the year in which Emile chooses an option and gets his first payment.

To find the total Emile gets under Option 1, you can sum an arithmetic series. After n years, he will get

$$10{,}000 + 11{,}000 + 12{,}000 + 13{,}000 + \cdots + (10{,}000 + 1{,}000n)$$

To find the total Emile gets under Option 2, you can sum a geometric series. After n years, he will get

$$0.01 + 0.02 + 0.04 + 0.08 + \cdots + (0.01) \cdot 2^n$$

15. **a.** What is n? That is, what is the last term you would add in each series?

b. Sum the arithmetic series to find the total Emile gets with Option 1.

c. Sum the geometric series to find the total Emile gets with Option 2.

Remember Thor and Pandora? They dropped a ball from a height of 2 meters and measured the height of each bounce. The following table shows the results of this experiment.

Number of Bounces	Height (m)
0	2.00
1	1.68
2	1.41
3	1.19
4	1.00
5	0.84
6	0.71

One question you might ask is what total distance the ball travels in, say, 100 bounces? The problem is more complicated than it might seem at first. Exercises 16–20 will help you answer this question.

16. First, just think about the distance the ball falls. Do not worry about the distance it travels bouncing up. When the ball first drops, it falls 2 meters. How far does it fall after the first bounce? After the second bounce? After the third bounce?

17. You saw that the bounce height was actually close to a geometric sequence. So you can rewrite your answers above as 2 meters, $2x$ meters, $2x^2$ meters, and $2x^3$ meters. What is the common ratio x?

18. To find the distance the ball falls in 100 bounces, you have to find this sum.

$$2 + 2x + 2x^2 + 2x^3 + \cdots + 2x^{100}$$

The value of x is whatever you found in Exercise 16. What is the sum?

19. What is the total distance the ball travels upward? Use any method you like to find out that total distance.

20. Find the total distance the ball travels upward and downward. Do you think your answer would be different if you calculated the distance for 1000 bounces instead? Explain.

Maintain Your Skills

21. Zeno starts 24 feet from a wall. He jumps half the distance to the wall. Then he jumps halfway across the remaining distance to the wall. Then he jumps half of that.

    This is a variation on a famous problem known as Zeno's paradox, named for a Greek mathematician who lived in the 400's B.C.

    a. How far does Zeno travel after 3 jumps? How far is he from the wall?

    b. How far does Zeno travel after 6 jumps? How far is he from the wall?

    c. How far does Zeno travel after n jumps? How far is he from the wall?

    d. Will Zeno ever get to the wall if he keeps up this "jumping halfway" scheme?

Limits

For some sequences and series, as the input values increase, the output values get closer and closer to a certain number.

In-Class Experiment

1. Suppose $f(n) = \frac{1}{2^n}$, and f is defined on the integers n such that $n \geq 1$.

n	$f(n)$
1	$\frac{1}{2^1} = \frac{1}{2}$
2	$\frac{1}{2^2} = \frac{1}{4}$
3	$\frac{1}{2^3} = \frac{1}{8}$
4	$\frac{1}{2^4} = \frac{1}{16}$
5	$\frac{1}{2^5} = \frac{1}{32}$

  a. How large do you have to make n to be sure that $f(n)$ is within 0.1 of 0?

  b. How large do you have to make n to ensure that $f(n)$ is within 0.01 of 0?

  c. How large do you have to make n to ensure that $f(n)$ is within 0.001 of 0?

2. Copy the table above and add a Σ column. Use it to answer these questions.

  a. Suppose $F(n)$ is the series associated with f.

  $$F(n) = \sum_{k=1}^{n} f(k) = \frac{1}{2} + \frac{1}{4} + \frac{1}{8} + \cdots + \frac{1}{2^n}$$

  Find a closed form for $F(n)$.

  b. How large do you have to make n to be sure that $F(n)$ is within 0.1 of 1?

  c. How large do you have to make n to ensure that $F(n)$ is within 0.01 of 1?

  d. How large do you have to make n to ensure that $F(n)$ is within 0.001 of 1?

You say that the sequence in Problem 1 of the In-Class Experiment has a **limit**, or ultimate value, of 0. This means that if you make n large enough, you can make $f(n)$ as close as you want to 0.

Similarly, the series in Problem 2 has a limit of 1. If you make n large enough, you can make $F(n)$ as close as you want to 1.

3. In Problem 1, is there any value of n for which $f(n) = 0$? In what sense is 0 a limit for the sequence?

4. In Problem 2, is there any value of n for which $F(n) = 1$? In what sense is 1 a limit for the series?

5. Can a sequence ever have more than one limit? Explain.

Minds in Action episode 36

Tony, Sasha, and Derman are working on the following questions.

Question 1 Suppose g is a geometric sequence with first term $g(0) = 1$ and common ratio $\frac{1}{5}$. Does g have a limit? If so, what is it?

Question 2 Using the same function g, does the associated series have a limit? If so, what is it?

n	$g(n)$
0	1
1	$\frac{1}{5}$
2	$\frac{1}{25}$
3	$\frac{1}{125}$

Sasha Let's try making a table for g, so we can see what's going on.

Tony I've already filled in values up to $n = 3$.

Derman Look—the outputs get smaller and smaller! They seem to approach 0, so I guess that's the limit.

Sasha It's not enough to say "they seem to approach 0." In order to say that the limit of the sequence is 0, we have to show that we can get as close as we want to 0. I mean, if we pick any number close to 0, we then have to find an n such that $g(n)$ is even closer to 0 than our number.

Tony Yes, look at this.

To get within 0.1 of 0, let $n = 2$.

$$g(2) = \left(\frac{1}{5}\right)^2 = \frac{1}{25} < 0.1$$

To get within 0.01 of 0, let $n = 3$.

$$g(3) = \left(\frac{1}{5}\right)^3 = \frac{1}{125} < 0.01$$

To get within 0.001 of 0, let $n = 5$.

$$g(5) = \left(\frac{1}{5}\right)^5 = \frac{1}{3125} < 0.001$$

Since you can get as close as you want to 0 by making n large enough, 0 is the limit of the sequence.

Derman Look—it seems that for every three steps in this process, we get another two places of accuracy. If that's true, I'm sure that the terms of the sequence converge to 0.

Sasha OK, so what's the answer to Question 2? I think we should find a formula for the associated series. We have $g(n) = \left(\frac{1}{5}\right)^n$, so we can write out $G(n)$ like this.

$$G(n) = \sum_{k=0}^{n} g(k)$$

$$= \sum_{k=0}^{n} \left(\frac{1}{5}\right)^k$$

$$= \frac{1 - \left(\frac{1}{5}\right)^{n+1}}{1 - \frac{1}{5}}$$

$$= \frac{1}{1 - \frac{1}{5}}\left(1 - \left(\frac{1}{5}\right)^{n+1}\right)$$

$$= \frac{1}{\frac{4}{5}}\left(1 - \left(\frac{1}{5}\right)^{n+1}\right)$$

$$= \frac{5}{4}\left(1 - \left(\frac{1}{5}\right)^{n+1}\right)$$

Habits of Mind

Look for relationships.
If g is a geometric sequence with first term $g(0) = a$ and common ratio r, then $g(n) = ar^n$, and

$$\sum_{k=0}^{n} g(k) = a \sum_{k=0}^{n} r^k$$

$$= a\left(\frac{1 - r^{n+1}}{1 - r}\right)$$

You can rewrite this as $\frac{a}{1 - r}(1 - r^{n+1})$.

This is equivalent to the "Think Euclid" identity multiplied by the constant a.

Derman Then I'll use the fact that $G(n) = \frac{5}{4}\left(1 - \left(\frac{1}{5}\right)^{n+1}\right)$ to fill in a Σ column.

n	$g(n)$	Σ
0	1	$\frac{5}{4}\left(1 - \frac{1}{5}\right)$
1	$\frac{1}{5}$	$\frac{5}{4}\left(1 - \frac{1}{25}\right)$
2	$\frac{1}{25}$	$\frac{5}{4}\left(1 - \frac{1}{125}\right)$
3	$\frac{1}{125}$	$\frac{5}{4}\left(1 - \frac{1}{625}\right)$
4	$\frac{1}{625}$	$\frac{5}{4}\left(1 - \frac{1}{3125}\right)$

Tony Well, $1 - \frac{1}{25}$ is within 0.1 of 1, $1 - \frac{1}{125}$ is within 0.01 of 1, and $1 - \frac{1}{3125}$ is within 0.001 of 1. Now it's clear that as n gets larger, the factor $\left(1 - \left(\frac{1}{5}\right)^{n+1}\right)$ gets closer and closer to 1. It's equal to 1 minus a tiny number.

Sasha Right, so you can get as close as anyone wants to $\frac{5}{4}$ by making n large enough. So the limit of the series is $\frac{5}{4}$.

For You to Do

Suppose $a = 12$. Pick three values for r from this list.

$$2, \frac{1}{2}, \frac{1}{3}, -1, -3, -\frac{1}{2}, -\frac{1}{3}, \frac{3}{8}, \frac{9}{8}, 10$$

6. For each r-value you select, decide whether the following series has a limit.

$$\sum_{k=0}^{n} g(k) = \frac{12}{1-r}\left(1 - r^{n+1}\right)$$

7. If it does, say what the limit is. If it does not, explain why not.

8. If $r = 1$, what happens with the formula? Does the series have a limit? Explain.

For Discussion

9. Explain how you can tell, just based on the value of r, if a geometric series has a limit.

10. Can an arithmetic series have a limit? Does the limit depend on the first term, the common difference, or both? Explain.

Exercises Practicing Habits of Mind

Check Your Understanding

1. For each geometric sequence described, do the following.
   - Write the first four terms of the sequence.
   - Write the first four terms of the series associated with the sequence.
   - Decide if the series has a limit.
   - If the series does have a limit, give that number.
   a. first term 7 and common ratio $\frac{2}{9}$
   b. first term 100 and common ratio $\frac{1}{2}$
   c. first term $\frac{3}{4}$ and common ratio 2
   d. first term 1 and common ratio 1

2. Pat and Sam are out for some exercise. They start off on a mile-long path. Sam starts walking at a steady rate. Pat starts running twice as fast as Sam walks. Pat runs to the end of the mile, runs back to Sam, turns around and runs to the end of the mile, turns around and runs to Sam, and so on. All the while Sam walks steadily along, laughing at Pat.

When Sam reaches the end of the mile-long path, how far has Pat run?

On Your Own

3. The diagrams below show the first three stages of the Koch curve. The segment of Stage 0 gets replaced by four segments, each $\frac{1}{3}$ the length of the original segment and arranged as shown in Stage 1. The same rule applies to each segment of Stage n as you pass to Stage $n + 1$.

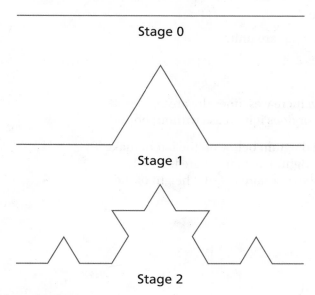

Stage 0

Stage 1

Stage 2

a. Draw the next stage.

b. Assume you start with length 1 at Stage 0. Find the length of the curve at Stages 1–3.

c. Find a closed form for the length of the curve at stage n.

d. Does the perimeter have a limit? That is, as n increases, does the perimeter of Stage n approach some fixed number, or does it increase without bound?

Go Online
Pearsonsuccessnet.com

4. You can close the shape at each stage by adding line segments. The diagram below shows closed shapes for Stage 1 and Stage 2. Then you can find the area within the curve.

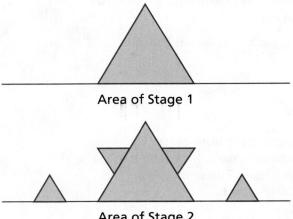

Area of Stage 1

Area of Stage 2

Assume that for Stage 1 above, the area is 1 square unit.

a. Find the area within the curve at Stages 2–4.

b. What is the area at Stage n?

c. Does the area have a limit? That is, as n increases, does the area of Stage n approach some fixed number, or does it increase without bound?

5. You can line up the squares shown in the diagram below on the left to make an infinite staircase, shown below on the right. The first square is 1 by 1. The second square is $\frac{2}{3}$ by $\frac{2}{3}$. Each successive square is $\frac{2}{3}$ the height of the previous square.

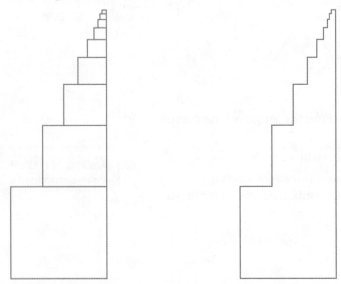

a. Find the area of the staircase.

b. Find the perimeter of the staircase.

6. To make the figure at the right, you connect the midpoints of the sides of a square of area 1 to form an inner square. You shade two opposite corners. You then repeat the process for the smaller square. Suppose you repeat this process an infinite number of times. Use a geometric series to find the total area of the shaded region. Does your answer make sense?

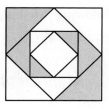

7. **Standardized Test Prep** What is the limit of the following geometric series?

$$1 + \frac{3}{5} + \frac{9}{25} + \frac{27}{125} + \frac{81}{625} + \cdots$$

A. $\frac{3}{2}$ **B.** 2   **C.** $\frac{5}{2}$ **D.** 3

Maintain Your Skills

8. Achilles and the tortoise run a race. Since Achilles is a faster runner (in fact, he can run 10 times faster than the tortoise), he gives the tortoise a 10-meter head start.

During the time it takes Achilles to run 10 meters, the tortoise covers 1 meter. Thus, the tortoise now has a 1-meter lead. During the time it takes Achilles to run another 1 meter, the tortoise runs 0.1 meter. Thus, the tortoise still has a 0.1-meter lead.

As Achilles runs the next 0.1 meter of the race, the tortoise goes 0.01 meter. Therefore, as small as the lead may be, the tortoise is still ahead in the race.

Does this mean Achilles never catches up to the tortoise? Explain.

9. **Take It Further** Suppose you divide a 3 inch-by-3 inch square into nine smaller squares and shade the center square. You then partition each unshaded square into nine squares and shade their centers. If you continue this process forever, how much area is shaded? (Note: The figures below are not full size.)

 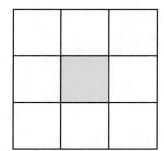 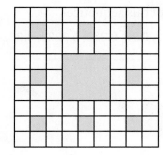

7.13 Repeating Decimals

You have learned the following two things in this investigation.

- If g is a geometric sequence $g(n) = a \cdot r^n$, then the formula for the associated series is

$$G(n) = \sum_{k=0}^{n} g(k) = \frac{a}{1-r}(1 - r^{n+1})$$

- If the common ratio of a geometric sequences is between -1 and 1—that is, $-1 < r < 1$—then the associated series has a limit. That limit is $\frac{a}{1-r}$.

Some decimals are geometric series. You can use the above facts to find fractions equivalent to them. For example, the decimal 0.2222 is

$$\frac{2}{10} + \frac{2}{100} + \frac{2}{1000} + \frac{2}{10{,}000} = \frac{2}{10} + \frac{2}{10^2} + \frac{2}{10^3} + \frac{2}{10^4}$$

$$= \frac{2}{10} + \frac{2}{10}\left(\frac{1}{10}\right) + \frac{2}{10}\left(\frac{1}{10}\right)^2 + \frac{2}{10}\left(\frac{1}{10}\right)^3$$

This is the sum of four terms of a geometric sequence with first term $\frac{2}{10}$ and common ratio $\frac{1}{10}$. You can use the formula below for the sum of $n + 1$ terms of a geometric series to get a fraction equivalent to 0.2222.

$$\left(\frac{a}{1-r}\right)(1 - r^{n+1})$$

Why are there $n + 1$ terms?

For You to Do

1. Think about the sequence that represents 0.2222.
   a. What is the initial term a?
   b. What is the common ratio r?
   c. What is n?
   d. Use the formula above to find a fraction equivalent to 0.2222.

2. Show that the following equations are true.

   $$0.22222 = \frac{2}{9}\left(1 - \left(\frac{1}{10}\right)^5\right)$$

   $$0.222222 = \frac{2}{9}\left(1 - \left(\frac{1}{10}\right)^6\right)$$

3. What is the limit of this sequence?

   $$\{0.2, 0.22, 0.222, 0.2222, 0.22222, 0.222222, \dots\}$$

Think about it another way. This is another way to think about **repeating decimals.** What you really want in Problem 3 above is the infinite decimal 0.222 . . . . Call this x. Then

$$10x = 2.22222 \ldots$$

$$x = 0.22222 \ldots$$

Subtract. You get $9x = 2$, so $x = \frac{2}{9}$.

What the argument really says is if 0.2222 . . . stands for anything, it has to stand for a number that when multiplied by 10, gives two more than itself. That is the 2.22222. . . . The only number with this property is $\frac{2}{9}$.

The important point is that the repeating decimal stands for something in the first place. Suppose you have an infinite string of 9's to the left of the decimal place.

$$\ldots 999999.00 \ldots$$

See where this leads you. In these calculations, make the decimal point large, as in **9.0**, so it is distinct from an ordinary decimal point.

Let $x = \ldots 9999.000 \ldots$

Then

$$x = \ldots 99999.000 \ldots$$

$$10x = \ldots 99990.000 \ldots$$

Subtract. You get $-9x = 9$, so $x = -1$.

That cannot be right. So a string of 9's to the left of the decimal point does not name a real number. You cannot call it x and do algebra with it.

> This trick does, in fact, work. You can use it to convert repeating decimals to fractions. But it rests on some properties of limits that you will not learn until you study calculus.

To be safe, use geometric series when dealing with repeating decimals. For example, think of the decimal 0.12121212 . . . as a series with first term $\frac{12}{100}$ and common ratio $\frac{1}{100}$.

Sometimes you can only successfully complete an action by going in a certain direction.

 **Exercises** *Practicing Habits of Mind*

Check Your Understanding

1. Consider the repeating decimal 0.123123123. . . .

    a. What is the initial term a?

    b. What is the common ratio r?

    c. Write this repeating decimal as a fraction.

2. Write each repeating decimal as a fraction.

    a. 0.121212 . . .

    b. 0.807807807 . . .

    c. 0.0123123123 . . .

    d. 0.075123123123 . . .

On Your Own

3. Write each repeating decimal as a fraction.

    a. 0.09090909 . . .

    b. 0.0370370370 . . .

    c. 0.0522222 . . .

4. Shannon says, "I know the series $1 + 2 + 4 + 8 + \cdots$ keeps increasing. But if I call it x, watch what happens.

$$2x = 2 + 4 + 8 + 16 + \cdots$$

$$x = 1 + 2 + 4 + 8 + \cdots$$

Subtract and I get $x = -1$."

Shannon is confused. What would you say to help?

5. **Standardized Test Prep** Which fraction is equivalent to the repeating decimal $0.25714\overline{714}$?

    A. $\dfrac{8563}{33,300}$

    B. $\dfrac{25,689}{99,000}$

    C. $\dfrac{25,714}{99,900}$

    D. $\dfrac{25,714}{99,999}$

Go Online
Pearsonsuccessnet.com

Maintain Your Skills

6. Write each repeating decimal as a fraction.

    a. 0.111 . . .

    b. 0.222 . . .

    c. 0.333 . . .

    d. 0.444 . . .

    e. 0.555 . . .

    f. 0.666 . . .

    g. 0.777 . . .

    h. 0.888 . . .

    i. 0.999 . . .

In this investigation, you learned to find closed forms for arithmetic and geometric sequences and their associated series. The following exercises will help you summarize what you have learned.

1. An arithmetic sequence s has second term 8 and fifth term 1.

   a. Explain why there is only one sequence that meets these requirements.

   For the sequence, find each of the following.

   b. the common difference **c.** the 28th term   **d.** a closed form

2. An arithmetic sequence g has $g(0) = -10$ and common difference 4.

   a. Make a Σ table for $g(n)$ for n-values 0 through 5.

   b. Find a closed form for the sequence.

   c. Find a closed form for the associated series.

3. Repeat Exercise 1 replacing *arithmetic sequence* with *geometric sequence*. In part (b), replace *common difference* with *common ratio*.

4. Repeat Exercise 2 replacing *arithmetic sequence* with *geometric sequence* and *common difference* with *common ratio*.

5. Derman wins a "million-dollar" prize, which he knows is not really worth $1,000,000. Instead of a check for $1,000,000, he is going to get $50,000 per year for 20 years. He wants to know what the present value of his prize is.

   a. Use $\sum\limits_{k=0}^{19} 50{,}000 \left(\dfrac{1}{1.06}\right)^k$ to find the present value. Assume a 6% interest rate.

   b. Suppose Derman is able to invest his money with an 8% rate of return. Would the present value of his prize be more or less than the amount you found for a 6% rate? Find the new present value to check your estimate. Explain why the interest rate affects the present value in the way it does.

6. What is an arithmetic sequence?

7. What is a geometric series?

8. How do you write the repeating decimal 0.121212121 . . . as a fraction?

Vocabulary

In this investigation, you learned these terms. Make sure you understand what each one means and how to use it.

- **arithmetic sequence**
- **arithmetic series**
- **common difference**
- **common ratio**
- **geometric sequence**

- **geometric series**
- **limit**
- **repeating decimal**
- **sequence**
- **term**

Pascal's Triangle and the Binomial Theorem

In *Pascal's Triangle and the Binomial Theorem*, you will explore the patterns in Pascal's Triangle. You will find patterns in the triangle and learn how the numbers in the triangle are related to powers of polynomials.

By the end of this investigation, you will be able to answer questions like these.

1. What is the sum of the entries in row 10 of Pascal's Triangle?

2. What is the expanded form of $(2d + 7)^8$?

3. What is the coefficient of x^7y^3 in the expansion of $(x + y)^{10}$?

You will learn how to

- generate Pascal's Triangle and evaluate the nth row, kth column entry as $\binom{n}{k}$

- notice and explain patterns in Pascal's Triangle

- use the Binomial Theorem for expanding expressions of the form $(a + b)^n$

You will develop these habits and skills:

- Seek invariants or regularity in calculation to develop a conjecture.

- Reason logically to prove conjectures.

- Apply previous results in new contexts.

There are $\binom{30}{2}$ ways to choose 2 socks from a pile of 30 socks.

7.14 Getting Started

Activating Prior Knowledge
Exploring New Ideas

You can find many patterns in the sums of sums and in the powers of polynomials.

For You to Explore

For Problems 1–5, use this big, but simple, table.

n	f(n)	Σ	ΣΣ	ΣΣΣ	ΣΣΣΣ
1	1				
2	2				
3	3				
4	4				
5	5				
6	6				
7	7				
8	8				
9	9				
10	10				

1. Copy and complete the table.

2. Find, describe, and explain several patterns in your table.

3. Find a closed form for f.

4. **a.** What is $\sum_{k=1}^{7} f(k)$?

   b. What is $\sum_{k=1}^{1000} f(k)$? Explain.

   c. Find a closed form for $\sum_{k=1}^{n} f(k)$.

5. **a.** Find a closed form for the $\Sigma\Sigma$ column.

   b. Find a closed form for the $\Sigma\Sigma\Sigma$ column.

   c. Where have you seen these closed forms before? What can you predict as a closed form for the $\Sigma\Sigma\Sigma\Sigma$ column?

Exercises Practicing Habits of Mind

On Your Own

6. Expand each expression.

   a. $(a + b)^2$

   b. $(a + b)^3$

   c. $(a + b)^4$

   d. $(a + b)^5$

   e. $(a + b)^6$

   f. What patterns do you observe?

Habits of Mind

Look for patterns. Use the answer to each part to help you with the next one.

7. Use your result from Exercise 6c to expand $(M + N)^4$, where $M = 2d$ and $N = 7$.

8. Expand each expression.

   a. $\left(\frac{1}{4}r + \frac{3}{4}s\right)^2$

   b. $\left(\frac{1}{4}r + \frac{3}{4}s\right)^3$

   c. $\left(\frac{1}{4}r + \frac{3}{4}s\right)^4$

   d. $\left(\frac{1}{4}r + \frac{3}{4}s\right)^5$

Maintain Your Skills

9. **a** Find the first five powers of 99.

   b. What patterns do you notice?

10. Tony is looking at differences of cubes. He says, "Let's see.

$$1^3 - 0^3 = 1 - 0 = 1$$

$$2^3 - 1^3 = 8 - 1 = 7$$

$$3^3 - 2^3 = 27 - 8 = 19$$

$$4^3 - 3^3 = 64 - 27 = 37$$

"I'm going to make a Σ table for these differences and see what happens."

n	$(n + 1)^3 - n^3$	Σ
0	1	1
1	7	8

Use Tony's idea to find the sum of the first 20 differences of cubes starting with $1^3 - 0^3$. The last one is $20^3 - 19^3$.

Pascal's Triangle

This triangular table below is **Pascal's Triangle.** It is a very famous triangle, named after mathematician Blaise Pascal, who is known for his studies of the relationships in the triangle.

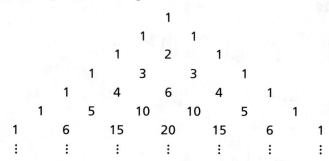

Pascal's Triangle shows up in many different areas of mathematics, including combinatorics. You will spend some time getting familiar with it and finding some of the many beautiful patterns it contains. You will also use it in other parts of this book, and in other mathematics courses throughout your life. An interesting thing to do with Pascal's Triangle is to see how many different patterns you can see in the rows and the columns of the triangle.

> Some people might even call it fun!

For Discussion

1. If you have seen Pascal's Triangle before, discuss anything you remember about it. What do the numbers represent?

2. What patterns can you find in the entries of Pascal's Triangle?

3. Describe in words how to find any entry in Pascal's Triangle.

4. Describe how Pascal's Triangle is related to the table in this investigation's Getting Started lesson.

You can label the entries of Pascal's Triangle with their row and column numbers, this way.

$$\binom{n}{k}$$

The top number n is the row number, starting with 0.

> The horizontal entries are the rows. The diagonals are the columns. Usually you number the first column and the first row 0.

The bottom number k is how far you go across in a row, starting with 0. So you label the entries in the sixth row this way.

row number (starting at 0)

$$\binom{n}{k}$$

column number (starting at 0)

1 ← row 0

1 1 ← row 1

1 2 1 ← row 2

1 3 3 1

1 4 6 4 1

1 5 10 10 5 1

1 6 15 20 15 6 1

↑ ↑ ↑ ↑ ↑ ↑ ↑

$\binom{6}{0}$ $\binom{6}{1}$ $\binom{6}{2}$ $\binom{6}{3}$ $\binom{6}{4}$ $\binom{6}{5}$ $\binom{6}{6}$

For You to Do

5. Find the value of each entry in the triangle.

a. $\binom{17}{1}$ **b.** $\binom{14}{14}$ **c.** $\binom{19}{0}$

6. Find all n and k such that $\binom{n}{k} = 15$.

Pascal's Triangle seems to have a kind of hockey stick property. If you draw a hockey stick on the triangle, the sum of the numbers on the handle is equal to the number on the tip.

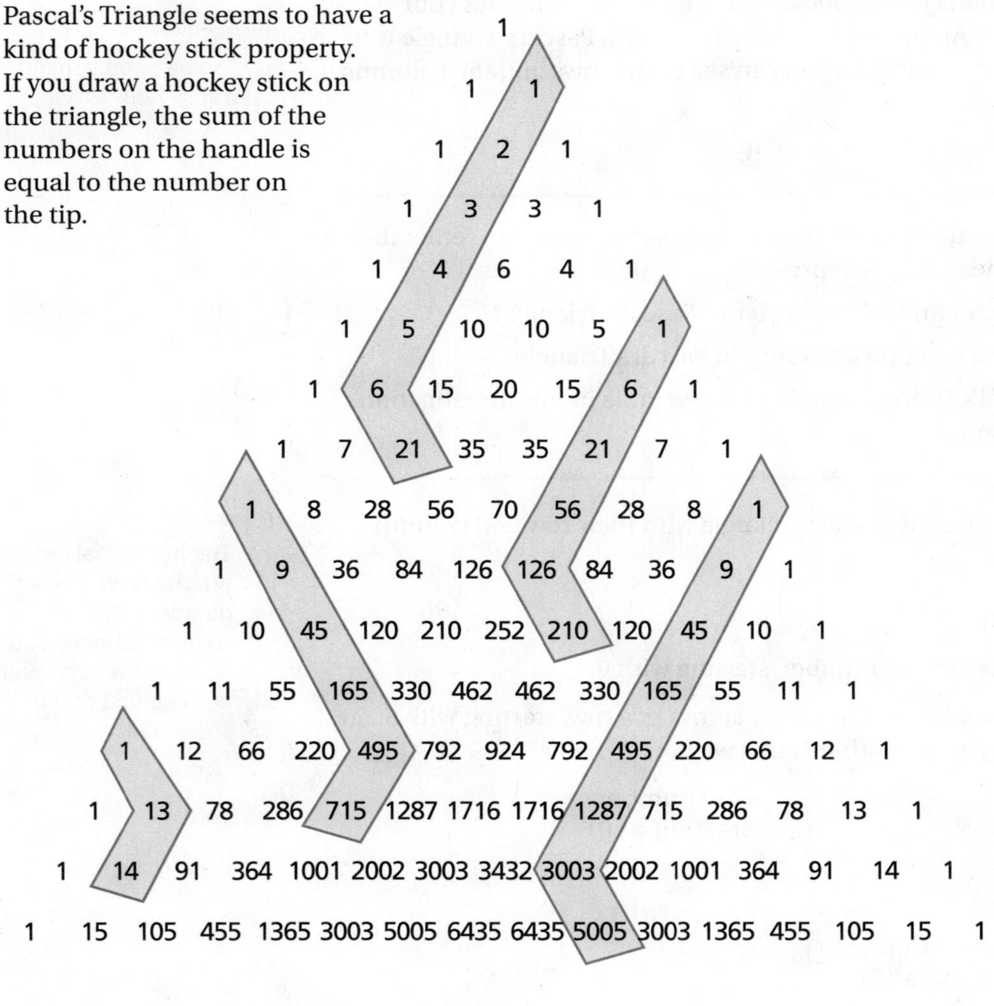

7. Does the hockey stick have to start on a one, or can it start anywhere in the triangle?

8. Does it matter if the hockey stick points left or right?

9. Does it matter if the hockey stick points up or down?

10. Explain the hockey stick property based on how you construct Pascal's Triangle.

For You to Do

11. Write the hockey stick property as an identity involving sums and the numbers $\binom{n}{k}$.

Exercises *Practicing Habits of Mind*

Check Your Understanding

1. Evaluate each sum.

   a. $\sum_{k=0}^{5} \binom{5}{k}$ b. $\sum_{k=0}^{6} \binom{6}{k}$ c. $\sum_{k=0}^{7} \binom{7}{k}$ d. $\sum_{k=0}^{n} \binom{n}{k}$

2. **Write About It** Explain why you get the sum you found in part (d) of Exercise 1. Think about how you get the numbers in Pascal's Triangle, or about what you know they represent.

On Your Own

3. Investigate the number of odd numbers in each row of Pascal's Triangle. If you continued the triangle out to row 64, how many odd numbers would you find in this row? In row 100? Explain.

Remember...
You start counting at row 0, so row 100 is really the 101st row you write down.

Go Online
Pearsonsuccessnet.com

4. Make three copies of the diagram below. Write in the values of Pascal's Triangle on your copies. You will use your copies to explore patterns in Pascal's Triangle.

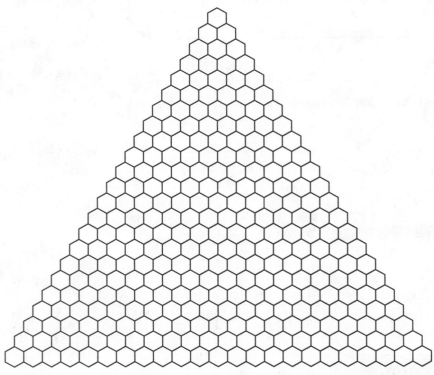

a. On one copy, color the odd numbers one color and the even numbers another color. Describe the patterns you find.

b. You can divide the integers up into three categories when you divide them by 3: those that leave a remainder of 1, those that leave a remainder of 2, and those that can be divided evenly by 3. On the second copy of the diagram, color each of these kinds of numbers a different color. Describe the patterns you find.

c. If you divide integers by 4, how many different kinds of numbers do you get? On the third copy of the diagram, color each of them a different color. Describe the patterns you find.

5. **Standardized Test Prep** The following list gives the first eight entries in the 15th row of Pascal's Triangle.

1   15   105   455   1365   3003   5005   6435

What is the value of $\binom{17}{6}$ in Pascal's Triangle?

A. 6188   **B.** 8008   **C.** 12,376   **D.** 19,448

6. **Take It Further** In Lesson 7.14, you found the closed forms for f, Σf, $\Sigma\Sigma f$, and $\Sigma\Sigma\Sigma f$, where $f(n) = n$. You can see these functions along diagonals in Pascal's Triangle.

Find a closed form for $\underbrace{\Sigma\Sigma\Sigma\Sigma \ldots \Sigma f(n)}_{k \text{ times}}$.

```
                1        ⟋ f
            1       1    ⟋ Σf
          1     2     1    ⟋ ΣΣf
        1     3     3     1   ⟋ ΣΣΣf
      1     4     6     4     1   ⟋ ΣΣΣΣf
    1     5    10    10     5     1
  1     6    15    20    15     6     1
1     7    21    35    35    21     7     1
 1     8    28    56    70    56    28     8     1
  1     9    36    84   126   126    84    36     9     1
   1    10    45   120   210   252   210   120    45    10     1
  1    11    55   165   330   462   462   330   165    55    11     1
 1    12    66   220   495   792   924   792   495   220    66    12     1
1    13    78   286   715  1287  1716  1716  1287   715   286    78    13     1
1   14    91   364  1001  2002  3003  3432  3003  2002  1001   364    91    14    1
1   15   105   455  1365  3003  5005  6435  6435  5005  3003  1365   455   105   15    1
```

Maintain Your Skills

7. Find the values of m and n that satisfy each equation.

a. $\binom{9}{4} = \binom{8}{4} + \binom{8}{m}$

b. $\binom{3}{2} = \binom{2}{2} + \binom{2}{m}$

c. $\binom{14}{8} = \binom{13}{8} + \binom{13}{m}$

d. $\binom{100}{15} = \binom{m}{15} + \binom{m}{n}$

Go Online
Video Tutor
Pearsonsuccessnet.com

7.16 The Binomial Theorem

In Exercise 6 of Lesson 7.14, you found some of these expansions.

$(a + b)^0 = 1$

$(a + b)^1 = a + b$

$(a + b)^2 = a^2 + 2ab + b^2$

$(a + b)^3 = a^3 + 3a^2b + 3ab^2 + b^3$

$(a + b)^4 = a^4 + 4a^3b + 6a^2b^2 + 4ab^3 + b^4$

$(a + b)^5 = a^5 + 5a^4b + 10a^3b^2 + 10a^2b^3 + 5ab^4 + b^5$

$(a + b)^6 = a^6 + 6a^5b + 15a^4b^2 + 20a^3b^3 + 15a^2b^4 + 6ab^5 + b^6$

Compare the coefficients of these polynomials to the entries of Pascal's Triangle.

```
                1
              1   1
            1   2   1
          1   3   3   1
        1   4   6   4   1
      1   5  10  10   5   1
    1   6  15  20  15   6   1
```

In fact, you find the coefficients for any binomial expansion $(a + b)^n$ in Pascal's triangle. The Binomial Theorem states this relationship.

Theorem 7.3 The Binomial Theorem

For $n \geq 0$,

$$(a + b)^n = \binom{n}{0}a^nb^0 + \binom{n}{1}a^{n-1}b^1 + \binom{n}{2}a^{n-2}b^2 + \cdots + \binom{n}{k}a^{n-k}b^k$$

$$+ \cdots + \binom{n}{n-1}a^1b^{n-1} + \binom{n}{n}a^0b^n$$

Go Online
Pearsonsuccessnet.com

You must admit, this connection is rather unexpected! But, as is usually the case in mathematics, it is no coincidence. The real question to ask is, "Why is there a connection?"

Establish a process. To see why this pattern holds, look closely at an example—multiplication by $(x + 1)$. Suppose you want to expand

$$(x + 1)(x^5 + 3x^4 + 7x^3 + 2x^2 + x + 1)$$

By the Distributive Property, this equals

$$x \cdot (x^5 + 3x^4 + 7x^3 + 2x^2 + x + 1) + 1 \cdot (x^5 + 3x^4 + 7x^3 + 2x^2 + x + 1)$$
$$= (x^6 + 3x^5 + 7x^4 + 2x^3 + x^2 + x) + (x^5 + 3x^4 + 7x^3 + 2x^2 + x + 1)$$
$$= x^6 + 4x^5 + 10x^4 + 9x^3 + 3x^2 + 2x + 1$$

Notice that the original polynomial has these coefficients.

$$1 \quad 3 \quad 7 \quad 2 \quad 1 \quad 1$$

To find the coefficients of the product, you can simply add Pascal-style, as follows.

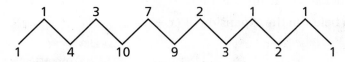

You should convince yourself why this method works. Look at another example. Suppose you want to expand

$$(x + 1)(7x^4 + 2x^3 + x^2 + 3x + 1)$$

You can obtain the coefficients of the product as follows.

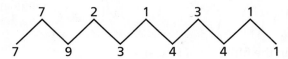

So the product is

$$7x^5 + 9x^4 + 3x^3 + 4x^2 + 4x + 1$$

For Discussion

1. Use the discussion above to explain why the fifth row of Pascal's Triangle gives the coefficients of $(x + 1)^5$, assuming that you know that the fourth row gives the coefficients of $(x + 1)^4$. (*Hint:* $(x + 1)^5 = (x + 1)(x + 1)^4$, and you already know what $(x + 1)^4$ looks like.)

Exercises *Practicing Habits of Mind*

Check Your Understanding

1. Use the Binomial Theorem to expand each binomial. Use your CAS to verify your answers.

   a. $(x + y)^7$ **b.** $(x + 2y)^5$

2. Consider the expansion of $(a + b)^8$.

   a. What is the coefficient of the term a^3b^5?

   b. What other term or terms share this coefficient?

   c. Which terms do not share their coefficients with any other terms?

3. Determine the coefficient of each term below in the expansion of $(x + y)^{10}$.

   a. x^3y^7 **b.** xy^9 **c.** x^5y^5

> You certainly should use your CAS to help evaluate these, but do not ask it to find all 11 terms! Use what you know, too, so the CAS does not have to do everything.

On Your Own

4. Compute the alternating sum below.

$$\binom{5}{0} - \binom{5}{1} + \binom{5}{2} - \binom{5}{3} + \binom{5}{4} - \binom{5}{5}$$

   This is the alternating sum of the numbers in the fifth row of Pascal's Triangle. What is the sum if the row number n is 6 instead of 5? If n is 11 instead of 5?

5. Write a polynomial that you can factor in the form $(a + b)^n$, satisfying the following criteria:

   • The constant term is not 1.

   • There is exactly one variable x.

   • There are at least five terms.

6. Simplify $(\sqrt{3} + \sqrt{2})^{100}(\sqrt{3} - \sqrt{2})^{100}$.

7. **Standardized Test Prep** What is the coefficient of the x^3 term in the expansion of $(a + b)^n$, where $a = 2x$, $b = -1$, and $n = 4$?

   A. −32   **B.** −4   **C.** 24   **D.** 21

> **Go Online**
> Pearsonsuccessnet.com

Maintain Your Skills

8. **Write About It** Look at the pattern in the powers of 11.

$$11^2 = 121$$

$$11^3 = 1331$$

$$11^4 = 14{,}641$$

Look at this more closely. You have $11^4 = 11^3 \times 11$, and since $11^3 = 1331$, you get

```
      1 3 3 1
    ×     1 1
    ─────────
      1 3 3 1
    1 3 3 1
    ─────────
    1 4 6 4 1
```

Or you can calculate Pascal-style.

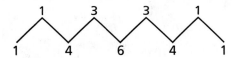

Now you may be tempted to conclude that $11^5 = 15{,}101{,}051$, but, in fact, $11^5 = 161{,}051$. What went wrong? Did anything really go wrong here?

9. **a.** Write out the first 7 powers of 101.

   b. Write out the first 7 powers of 1001.

Historical Perspective

Pascal's Triangle gets its name from Blaise Pascal, a famous French mathematician who wrote *Traité du triangle arithmétique* in 1654. Pascal showed many uses of the triangle and proved many things about its number patterns. He was not, however, the first person to discover or write about the triangle. The triangle was known in India as early as 1068—nearly 600 years before Pascal wrote his *Traité*. A mathematician named Bhattotpala used it to compute combinations of as many as sixteen things. The triangle was also known in China, probably as early as 1100, when Chia Hsien used something similar for finding binomial coefficients. It was certainly known there by 1303, when Chu Shih-Chieh used the triangle at the right.

Blaise Pascal

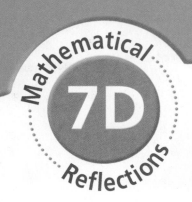

Mathematical 7D Reflections

In this investigation, you learned to generate Pascal's Triangle, to find and explain patterns in Pascal's Triangle, and to use the Binomial Theorem to expand expressions. These exercises will help you summarize what you have learned.

1. Give an example of the hockey stick property of Pascal's Triangle in which the sum on the tip is 20.

2. Find all values of m that satisfy each equation.

   a. $\dbinom{m}{1} = 27$

   b. $\dbinom{24}{m} = 1$

   c. $\dbinom{m}{31} = 32$

   d. $\dbinom{m}{4} + \dbinom{m}{5} = \dbinom{19}{5}$

3. Make an input-output table for the function $b(n) = \dbinom{n}{2}$ for $n = 2$ to $n = 6$. Find a polynomial function $p(n)$ that matches your table for $b(n)$, even if you continue the table.

4. Multiply $(x + 1)(5x^5 + 3x^4 - 2x^3 + 4x^2 + 6x - 7)$.

5. You can factor the polynomial below into the form $(a + b)^5$.

   $$32x^5 - 80x^4 + cx^3 - 40x^2 + 10x - 1$$

   Find a, b, and c.

6. What is the sum of the entries in row 10 of Pascal's Triangle?

7. What is the expanded form of $(2d + 7)^8$?

8. What is the coefficient of x^7y^3 in the expansion of $(x + y)^{10}$?

Vocabulary and Notation

In this investigation, you learned this term and this symbol. Make sure you understand what each one means and how to use it.

• **Pascal's Triangle**

• $\dbinom{n}{k}$ (the nth row, kth column entry of Pascal's triangle)

If you have 30 socks and 6 of them are striped, the probability of randomly choosing a matching pair of striped socks is $\dbinom{6}{2} \div \dbinom{30}{2}$.

Project: Using Mathematical Habits

The Line of Best Fit Contains the Centroid

The goal of this project is for you to prove Conjecture 1.1 from Lesson 1.09 of Investigation 1B.

For any set of data, the line of best fit contains the balance point.

As often happens in mathematics, it is easier to prove a related result. Exercises 3, 4, and 8 from Lesson 1.08 suggested a fascinating property:

Suppose you have a set of data points and you pick some number a. Then, the line with slope a that best fits the data is the one that contains the balance point $(\bar{x}, \bar{y})$ of the data.

You experimented with this idea in Investigation 1B, and you helped Tony verify it for a given data set and slopes 0, 1, 2, and 3. The first goal of this project is to prove that it is true in general.

Proofs of this kind often involve a careful analysis of an algebraic expression. In this case, the expression is for the calculation of the sum of the squares of the errors. A good algebraic habit is to carry out the calculations in numerical examples, keeping track of your steps. You did this in Lesson 1.08. A good next step is to make the slope a variable, keeping the same numerical data. After that, you can make the data itself variable. This kind of "ramping up" from numbers to variables is typical of how you develop many proofs in algebra.

For a numerical example to get started, go back to the data from Exercise 2 from Lesson 1.08. It has probably been quite a while since you first found a line of best fit for a data set, so take some time to go through the process.

Input	Output
1	3
2	4.5
3	8.1
4	8

1. Find the centroid of the data.

Next, you and Tony looked at all the lines of slope 3 and completed this table to find the one that minimized the error for this data set.

2. Copy and complete this table.

Data vs. Line Fit: $y = 3x + b$

Input	Output	Predicted	Error
1	3	$3 \cdot 1 + b$	$3 - (3 + b) = -b$
2	4.5	▩	▩
3	8.1	▩	▩
4	8	▩	▩

3. Write an expression for the sum of the squares of the errors. Simplify it to a quadratic expression in b.

4. A quadratic expression

$$px^2 + qx + r$$

takes on its minimum or maximum value at $x = -\dfrac{q}{2p}$.

a. Why does $x = -\dfrac{q}{2p}$ produce the minimum or maximum value?

b. How can you tell whether $x = -\dfrac{q}{2p}$ produces a minimum or maximum?

c. What value of b minimizes the sum of the squares of the errors you found in the previous exercise?

5. Find the equation for the line of slope 3 that is the best fit for the data. Does the centroid satisfy this equation? Explain.

You might try to carry out the same calculation with other slopes. You did this for slopes 0, 1, and 2 in Exercise 4 from Lesson 1.08.

To get more into the rhythm of the calculation, try it with some other slopes, say 4, 5, and 6. In each case, check that (2.5, 5.9) is on the best line with that slope.

Once you are comfortable with the calculations, you can carry out the process in general for any slope a.

6. Copy and complete this table.

Data vs. Line Fit: $y = ax + b$

Input	Output	Predicted	Error
1	3	$a \cdot 1 + b$	$3 - (a \cdot 1 + b) = 3 - a - b$
2	4.5	▨	▨
3	8.1	▨	▨
4	8	▨	▨

7. Show that the sum of squares of the errors is

$$(3 - a - b)^2 + (4.5 - 2a - b)^2$$
$$+ (8.1 - 3a - b)^2 + (8 - 4a - b)^2$$

Instead of squaring the four trinomials, look back at what happened with the numbers. The slope a is constant, so you can think of each term that you are squaring as a binomial.

$$((3 - a) - b)^2 + ((4.5 - 2a) - b)^2$$
$$+ ((8.1 - 3a) - b)^2 + ((8 - 4a) - b)^2$$

If you square each term, you get

$$(3 - a)^2 - 2(3 - a)b + b^2$$
$$+ (4.5 - 2a)^2 - 2(4.5 - 2a)b + b^2$$
$$+ (8.1 - 3a)^2 - 2(8.1 - 3a)b + b^2$$
$$+ (8 - 4a)^2 - 2(8 - 4a)b + b^2$$

Think about gathering up all the like terms, basically by "adding down."

An important habit in algebra is to predict the form of the result of a calculation without having to carry it out. The resulting expression will be a quadratic in b. The coefficient of b^2 will be 4 (look at the last column). The coefficient of b will be the sum of all the expressions in the middle column. And the constant term will be the sum of all the expressions in the left-most column.

But to find the value of b that minimizes the quadratic, you do not care what the constant term is. You just take the negative of the coefficient of b and divide it by twice the coefficient of b^2.

The coefficient of b is

$$-2(3 - a) - 2(4.5 - 2a)$$
$$- 2(8.1 - 3a) - 2(8 - 4a)$$
$$= -2((3 + 4.5 + 8.1 + 8)$$
$$- (1 + 2 + 3 + 4)a)$$

Notice how the sum of the x-values $(1 + 2 + 3 + 4)$ and the sum of the y-values $(3 + 4.5 + 8.1 + 8)$ show up in the calculation. Rather than simplifying this expression further, leave it like this—it will reveal more of what is going on behind the scenes.

The quadratic in b looks like this.

$$4b^2 - 2((3 + 4.5 + 8.1 + 8)$$
$$- (1 + 2 + 3 + 4)a)b + \text{something}$$

You know that the minimum value for this expression occurs when

$$b = -\frac{\text{the coefficient of } b}{2 \cdot \text{the coefficient of } b^2}$$

8. Find an expression in a for the value of b that minimizes the sum of the squares of the errors.

9. Find the equation of the line of best fit with slope a and show that the centroid is on this line, no matter what a is.

Everything so far has used the data in the table from Exercise 1. But the evidence suggests that the key to the proof is that the equation of the line with slope a that best fits any data set is

$$y = ax + (\bar{y} - \bar{x}a)$$

where $(\bar{x}, \bar{y})$ is the centroid for the data. If this were the case, you would be in business—you can show that $(\bar{x}, \bar{y})$ satisfies the equation

$$y = ax + (\bar{y} - \bar{x}a)$$

So the next step is to ramp up to any set of data, say

$$\{(x_1, y_1), (x_2, y_2), \ldots, (x_n, y_n)\}$$

Just follow what you did before.

10. Copy and complete this error table.

Data vs. Line Fit: $y = ax + b$

Input	Output	Predicted	Error
x_1	y_1	$ax_1 + b$	$y_1 - (ax_1 + b) = (y_1 - ax_1) - b$
x_2	y_2	■	■
x_3	y_3	■	■
$\vdots$	$\vdots$	$\vdots$	$\vdots$
x_n	y_n	■	■

Once you get the rhythm, the process becomes automatic.

11. Write an expression for the sum of the squares of the errors in Σ notation.

If you square each term in your sum, you get

$$(y_1 - ax_1)^2 - 2(y_1 - ax_1)b + b^2$$
$$+ (y_2 - ax_2)^2 - 2(y_2 - ax_2)b + b^2$$
$$\vdots \qquad \vdots \qquad \vdots$$
$$+ (y_n - ax_n)^2 - 2(y_n - ax_n)b + b^2$$

Or

$$\sum_{i=1}^{n} ((y_i - ax_i)^2 - 2(y_i - ax_i)b + b^2)$$

Again, think about gathering up all the like terms, basically by "adding down."

12. The sum of the squares of the errors will be a quadratic in b.

   a. What is the coefficient of b^2 in this quadratic?

   b. What is the coefficient of b in Σ notation?

13. To find the value of b that minimizes the quadratic, you do not care what the constant term is. Just take the negative of the coefficient of b and divide it by twice the coefficient of b^2.

   Show that the best value for b is when

$$b = -\frac{-2\left(\sum_{i=1}^{n} y_i - \left(\sum_{i=1}^{n} x_i\right)a\right)}{2 \cdot n}$$

$$= \bar{y} - \bar{x}a$$

   So, the equation of the best line with slope a is

$$y = ax + (\bar{y} - \bar{x}a)$$

14. Show that $(\bar{x}, \bar{y})$ satisfies $y = ax + (\bar{y} - \bar{x}a)$.

You are now in a position to prove Conjecture 1.1, by showing that the line of best fit for a set of data points contains the centroid of the data.

You can reason that, for reasonable data sets, there is one (and exactly one) line that best fits the data. You can prove this by generalizing the technique in Lesson 1.09. So you can argue that the line of best fit has some slope. For all lines of that slope, by the result you just proved, the best one contains the centroid.

15. In your own words, write out a proof of Conjecture 1.1.

16. **Take It Further** Now you know that the line of best fit has equation

$$y = ax + (\bar{y} - \bar{x}a)$$

for some slope a. You can go through the method of Lesson 1.09 with a generic slope and actually get a formula for the slope of the line of best fit—the one your calculator uses. Try it.

Review

Go Online
Pearsonsuccessnet.com

In **Investigation 7A,** you learned how to

- make a sum table for a function and write a closed-form rule for the sum column where appropriate
- use Gauss's method to find the sum of a sequence with a constant difference between successive terms
- use Euclid's method to find the sum of a sequence with a constant ratio between successive terms
- expand Σ notation or convert an expanded sum back to Σ notation

The following exercises will help you check your understanding.

1. Copy and complete the following sum table. Find a closed-form rule for the Σ column.

n	$g(n)$	Σ
0	1	▦
1	2	▦
2	6	▦
3	18	▦
4	54	▦
5	162	▦

2. Suppose $S = 3 + 6 + \cdots + 96$.

   a. If there is a constant difference between successive terms, what is the value of S? Use Gauss's method.

   b. If there is a constant ratio between successive terms, what is the value of S? Use Euclid's method.

3. a. Evaluate $\displaystyle\sum_{j=0}^{3} 3^j$.

   b. Evaluate $\displaystyle\sum_{k=1}^{5} (k + 2)$.

   c. Use Σ notation to write an expression for
   $S = \frac{1}{2} + 1 + \frac{3}{2} + 2 + \cdots + 6$.

In **Investigation 7B,** you learned how to

- find closed-form expressions for indefinite sums and use them to evaluate definite sums
- develop a list of Σ identities and recognize situations in which you can apply them
- find closed-form expressions for the series associated with a function

The following exercises will help you check your understanding.

4. Use the definitions below.
   $$S(n) = \sum_{k=0}^{n} (4 - 3k)$$
   $$T(n) = \sum_{k=0}^{n} \left(\frac{1}{2}\right)^k$$

   a. Find a closed form for $S(n)$.

   b. Find a closed form for $T(n)$.

   c. Use the closed form for $S(n)$ to find $\displaystyle\sum_{k=0}^{100} (4 - 3k)$.

   d. Use the closed form for $T(n)$ to find $\displaystyle\sum_{k=0}^{4} \left(\frac{1}{2}\right)^k$.

5. Find a closed form for the series associated with $g(n) = 4 - 5n$, with initial term $g(0)$.

In **Investigation 7C,** you learned how to

- find a closed-form representation for an arithmetic sequence and its associated series
- find a closed-form representation for a geometric sequence and its associated series
- determine whether a geometric sequence has a limit, and if it does, how to find it
- convert a repeating decimal into an exact fraction

The following exercises will help you check your understanding.

6. Suppose f is a sequence with initial term $f(0) = 5$.

n	$f(n)$	Σ
0	5	5
1	▦	▦
2	▦	▦
3	▦	▦
4	▦	▦
5	▦	▦

a. • Copy and complete the table if f is an arithmetic sequence with a constant difference of 2.
  - Find a closed form for the sequence.
  - Find a closed form for the series
    $$F(n) = \sum_{k=0}^{n} f(k).$$
  - Find $f(10)$ and $F(10)$.

b. • Copy and complete the table if f is a geometric sequence with a constant ratio of 2.
  - Find a closed form for the sequence.
  - Find a closed form for the series
    $$F(n) = \sum_{k=0}^{n} f(k).$$
  - Find $f(10)$ and $F(10)$.

7. For each geometric sequence t, do the following:

- Write the first four terms of the sequence.
- Find $T(0)$, $T(1)$, $T(2)$, and $T(3)$, where $T(n) = \sum_{k=0}^{n} t(k)$ is the series associated with the sequence.
- Decide if the series has a limit.
- If the series does have a limit, find it.

a. first term 10 and common ratio $\frac{1}{10}$

b. second term 3 and fifth term $\frac{81}{8}$

8. Write each repeating decimal as a fraction.

a. $0.151515\ldots$

b. $0.100100100\ldots$

In **Investigation 7D,** you learned how to

- generate Pascal's Triangle and write the nth row, kth column entry as $\binom{n}{k}$
- notice and explain patterns in Pascal's Triangle
- use the Binomial Theorem to expand expressions of the form $(a + b)^n$

The following exercises will help you check your understanding.

9. a. Make a copy of Pascal's Triangle through Row 5.

b. On your copy, show two examples of the hockey stick property in which the sum on the tip is 10.

c. Find the value of $\binom{4}{2} + \binom{5}{4}$.

10. a. What is the expanded form for $(3x + 2)^5$?

b. What is the coefficient of x^2y^4 in the expansion of $(x + 2y)^6$?

Multiple Choice

1. What is the sum of the odd integers from 7 to 55, inclusive?

   A. 62   **B.** 775

   C. 850   **D.** 1550

2. Suppose $\binom{j}{1} = 5$. What is j?

   A. 0   **B.** 4

   C. 5   **D.** 6

3. Which number is equivalent to $0.999\ldots$?

   A. 0   **B.** $\frac{1}{9}$

   C. $\frac{999}{1000}$ **D.** 1

4. In an arithmetic sequence, the second term is 9 and the eighth term is 33. What is the third term?

   A. 4   **B.** 12

   C. 13   **D.** 17

5. What is the coefficient of $x^4 y^5$ in the expansion of $(x + y)^9$?

   A. $\binom{5}{4}$

   B. $\binom{4}{5}$

   C. $\binom{9}{1}$

   D. $\binom{9}{5}$

Open Response

6. Find each sum.

   a. $\sum_{k=0}^{10} (7 - 4k)$

   b. $\sum_{j=0}^{8} \left(\frac{1}{3}\right)^j$

   c. $\sum_{k=3}^{12} 4k$

7. Find a closed form for each indefinite sum.

   a. $\sum_{k=0}^{n} (6k + 2)$ **b.** $\sum_{k=0}^{n} (k^2 + 1)$

8. Find a recursive rule and a closed-form rule for the series associated with $h(n) = 4 - 6n$, having initial term $h(0)$.

9. A geometric sequence h has $h(0) = 18$ and common ratio $\frac{1}{3}$.

   a. Make a $\sum$ table for $h(n)$ for $n = 0$ through $n = 4$.

   b. Find a closed form for the sequence.

   c. Find a closed form for the associated series.

10. You can factor the polynomial below into the form $(a + b)^7$.

    $$x^7 - 14x^6 + 84x^5 + cx^4 + 560x^3 - 672x^2 + 448x - 128$$

    Find a, b, and c.

11. What is a geometric series?

Introduction to Trigonometry

Trigonometry, at first glance, seems to be about triangles. With further study, you will see that it is also about waves and oscillations. When you graph $y = \sin x$ on your calculator and look at the function for $-720° \leq x \leq 720°$ and $-2 \leq y \leq 2$, you see a wave. This wave has properties in common with many natural systems such as a weight on a spring, a swinging pendulum, or a vibrating string on a musical instrument. You can use the sine function to describe movement in these systems.

In fact, Joseph Fourier, a French engineer, found a method for writing virtually any periodic function as a combination of sine and cosine functions. The entire graph of a periodic function consists of copies of one portion of the graph laid end to end. Light, sound, and even molecules in a solid move as waves. Trigonometry is at the heart of such diverse sciences as acoustics, optics, chemistry, seismology, meteorology, and electrical engineering.

Vocabulary and Notation

- cosine, $\cos \theta$
- discontinuity
- Heronian triangle
- Law of Cosines
- Law of Sines
- period

- periodic function
- sine, $\sin \theta$
- standard position
- tangent, $\tan \theta$
- trigonometric equation

In geometry, you learned about similarity and the AA Theorem: Two triangles are similar if two pairs of corresponding angles have the same measure.

If two right triangles have one pair of acute angles with the same measure, then they are similar. The ratio of any two side lengths in one of the triangles is the same as the ratio of the corresponding side lengths in the other triangle.

> If two triangles have two pairs of corresponding angles with the same measure, the third pair of angles also has the same measure, because the sum of the measures of the angles in a triangle is 180°.

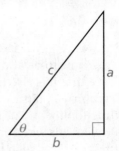

$$\frac{a}{c} = \frac{x}{z}$$

$$\frac{b}{c} = \frac{y}{z}$$

$$\frac{a}{b} = \frac{x}{y}$$

These ratios are determined by the marked angle in the triangle. In other words, each ratio is a function of the given angle. It helps to refer to the three sides of the triangle in terms of their position from the perspective of this angle. There are the leg opposite the angle, the leg adjacent to the angle, and the hypotenuse.

> Which side is which depends on which angle you are talking about. The side opposite one acute angle is adjacent to the other. The hypotenuse does not change.

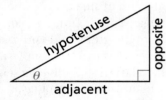

The three ratios are functions of the angle θ. Since they are helpful in many problems, they have standard names.

Definitions

The **sine** of an acute angle θ is the ratio of the opposite side to the hypotenuse in any right triangle that has θ as an acute angle. It is denoted by sin θ.

The **cosine** of an acute angle θ is the ratio of the adjacent side to the hypotenuse. It is denoted by cos θ.

The **tangent** of an acute angle θ is the ratio of the opposite side to the adjacent side. It is denoted by tan θ.

Here are those ratios again, written in the form of equations.

$$\sin \theta = \frac{\text{opposite}}{\text{hypotenuse}}$$

$$\cos \theta = \frac{\text{adjacent}}{\text{hypotenuse}}$$

$$\tan \theta = \frac{\text{opposite}}{\text{adjacent}}$$

Calculators have keys for all three of these functions. They also have keys for their inverse functions, which allow you to calculate an angle if you know its sine, cosine, or tangent.

Example 1

Problem A wheelchair ramp should not incline at an angle steeper than 5°. You are building a ramp next to a staircase that rises a total of 2 feet. How long will the ramp be if the angle is 5°?

Solution The picture below shows what the ramp would look like.

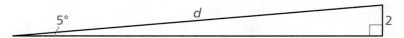

The hypotenuse and the side opposite the 5° angle are involved, so it is simplest to use the sine function. You know the angle measure, and that the length of the opposite side is 2. The hypotenuse is the unknown d.

$$\sin 5° = \frac{2}{d}$$

Solve for d: $d = \frac{2}{\sin 5°}$. You can use a calculator to find that $d \approx 23$ feet.

A 5° angle is quite small. How does the length of the ramp compare with the horizontal distance from the end of the ramp to the building?

For You to Do

1. For safety, a ladder manufacturer recommends that you should place a ladder's base a minimum distance from the wall. This distance is at least one foot for every 6 feet of ladder length. How high on the wall can a 20-foot ladder reach if the base is at the minimum distance from the wall?

Example 2

Problem For some angle θ, $\cos \theta = \frac{3}{5}$. Find $\sin \theta$ and $\tan \theta$.

Solution

Method 1 You can use any right triangle with this angle θ, so pick one that has convenient side lengths. Since the ratio given is $\frac{3}{5}$, set up a right triangle with a side of length 3 adjacent to angle θ and a hypotenuse of length 5.

> Method 1 gives exact answers.

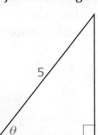

You can find the length of the remaining side with the Pythagorean Theorem or by recognizing the famous 3-4-5 right triangle. Since the third side's length is 4, you know the other ratios.

$$\sin \theta = \frac{\text{opposite}}{\text{hypotenuse}} = \frac{4}{5}$$

$$\tan \theta = \frac{\text{opposite}}{\text{adjacent}} = \frac{4}{3}$$

Method 2 Use the inverse function to find the angle θ.

$$\cos \theta = \frac{3}{5} \Rightarrow \theta = \cos^{-1}\left(\frac{3}{5}\right)$$

> Method 2 gives approximate answers.

The angle θ is approximately 53.130°. Once you know θ, you can find the other ratios with your calculator.

$$\sin 53.130° \approx 0.8000$$

$$\tan 53.130° \approx 1.3333$$

These values are very close to the exact fractions $\frac{4}{5}$ and $\frac{4}{3}$ you found using Method 1.

For Discussion

2. For this example, it seems that Method 1 gives more accurate answers, more quickly. Can you think of a situation in which Method 2 might be necessary?

Developing Habits of Mind

Look for relationships. You can express the Pythagorean Theorem using sine and cosine. Consider the triangle drawn at the right. The Pythagorean Theorem tells you that for this triangle,

$$a^2 + b^2 = c^2$$

Divide each side by c^2.

$$\frac{a^2}{c^2} + \frac{b^2}{c^2} = 1$$

The trigonometric functions define $\cos\theta$ as $\frac{a}{c}$ and $\sin\theta$ as $\frac{b}{c}$. So,

$$(\cos\theta)^2 + (\sin\theta)^2 = 1$$

The parentheses can get in the way. The exponent is frequently moved to appear next to the function name.

$$\cos^2\theta + \sin^2\theta = 1$$

You read this equation as "cosine squared theta plus sine squared theta equals 1." It is one of the most fundamental relationships in trigonometry.

How far is the point $(\cos\theta, \sin\theta)$ from the origin?

Exercises *Practicing Habits of Mind*

Check Your Understanding

1. A right triangle has a 40° angle and hypotenuse of length 10. Find the triangle's perimeter to two decimal places.

2. A right triangle has legs of lengths 20 and 21.

  a. What is the area of this triangle?

  b. How long is the hypotenuse?

  c. Draw an accurate picture of this triangle. Estimate the acute angle measures.

  d. Using a calculator, find the measure of each acute angle to the nearest degree.

3. In a right triangle, the value of $\cos\theta$ is $\frac{8}{17}$. Find the values of $\sin\theta$ and $\tan\theta$ exactly (without decimal approximations).

4. Show that for any angle measure θ such that $0° < \theta < 90°$,
$$\tan \theta = \frac{\sin \theta}{\cos \theta}$$

5. For some angle θ, $\sin \theta$ is exactly $\frac{1}{4}$. Find the exact value of $\cos \theta$ for this angle by drawing a right triangle.

6. **Take It Further** A right triangle has a 30° angle and one side length that is 12. Find all possible values for the area of the triangle.

On Your Own

7. A right triangle has an angle θ and a hypotenuse of length 1. Find the lengths of the other two sides in terms of θ.

8. Explain why it is true that for any angle θ, $0° < \theta < 90°$,
$$\sin \theta = \cos (90° - \theta)$$

Remember...

Angles with measure θ and $90° - \theta$ are complementary. Hence the name cosine.

9. Use this triangle to find the exact values of sine, cosine, and tangent for 30° and 60°.

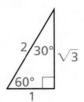

θ	$\sin \theta$	$\cos \theta$	$\tan \theta$
30°	■	■	■
60°	■	■	■

10. Use this triangle to find the exact values of sine, cosine, and tangent for 45°.

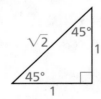

θ	$\sin \theta$	$\cos \theta$	$\tan \theta$
45°	■	■	■

11. Derman wants to extend the domain of sine and cosine so that he can give a value for sin 90° and cos 90°. What are good values for Derman to pick? Explain.

12. **a.** What are the largest and smallest possible values for $\sin \theta$? Explain.

b. What are the largest and smallest possible values for $\cos \theta$? Explain.

c. What are the largest and smallest possible values for $\tan \theta$? Explain.

For Exercise 12, assume $0° < \theta < 90°$.

13. For each triangle, find sin θ, cos θ, and tan θ.

a.

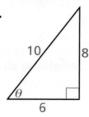

b.

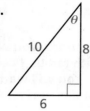

c.

d.

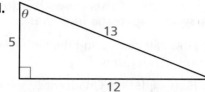

14. What's Wrong Here? Trent sees $\triangle TRI$.

Trent says, "So side *TI* is 10 and angle *T* is 70°, that means I can find side *RI* by using sine of 70°. So I know $\sin 70° = \frac{RI}{10}$."

What is wrong with Trent's reasoning?

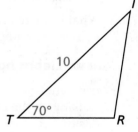

15. Take It Further Prove that for any angle θ such that $0° < \theta < 90°$, $\tan(90° - \theta) = \frac{1}{\tan \theta}$.

Maintain Your Skills

16. Copy the following table. Use a calculator to complete it for the sine, cosine, and tangent of angles in increments of 10°. Find each value to three decimal places.

θ	sin θ	cos θ	tan θ
10°	■	■	■
20°	■	■	■
30°	■	■	■
40°	■	■	■
50°	■	■	■
60°	■	■	■
70°	■	■	■
80°	■	■	■

Habits of Mind

Look for relationships.
Review Exercise 8.

17. Explain why sin 10° and cos 80° are equal.

Trigonometric Functions

In *Trigonometric Functions*, you will explore the relationships between points on a circle with radius 1 centered at the origin and angles with vertex at the origin. You will learn how to find the sine, cosine, and tangent of angles of any measure.

By the end of this investigation, you will be able to answer questions like these.

1. How can you extend the definitions of sine, cosine, and tangent to any angle, not just acute angles?

2. If an angle is in Quadrant IV, what can you say about the sign of its sine, cosine, and tangent?

3. What is the relationship between the equation of the unit circle and the Pythagorean Identity?

You will learn how to

- use right triangle trigonometry to find the coordinates of a person walking on the unit circle, given an angle through which an observer has turned

- evaluate the sine, cosine, and tangent functions for any angle

- solve equations involving trigonometric functions

You will develop these habits and skills:

- Visualize relationships between coordinates of a point on the unit circle and the angle that an observer at the origin must turn through to look at that point.

- Extend the sine, cosine, and tangent functions carefully, in order to preserve key properties.

- Use logical reasoning to find all possible solutions of a trigonometric equation.

As this drawbridge rises, the angle it forms with the river increases. The right end traces part of a circle.

The values of trigonometric functions are related to the coordinates of points on a circle with radius 1 centered at the origin.

For You to Explore

Olivia watches Paul walk around a circle. The circle's radius is 1 meter. Olivia stands at the center, and Paul begins walking counterclockwise. Consider a coordinate grid, with Olivia standing at the origin and Paul starting at the point $(1, 0)$.

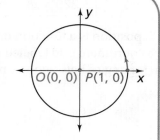

> **Remember...**
>
> This circle, with center $(0, 0)$ and radius 1, is the unit circle.

As Paul walks, Olivia watches Paul and keeps track of the angle she has turned. For example, when Olivia has turned 70°, the situation looks like this.

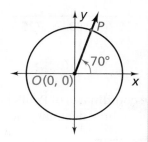

1. a. Explain why the distance between Olivia and Paul is always 1.

 b. Suppose Paul is at a point with coordinates (x, y). Write an equation in x and y to express the fact that Paul is 1 unit away from $(0, 0)$.

2. Find the coordinates of Paul's location when Olivia has turned 70°. Round to three decimal places.

3. Find the lengths of the other two sides of this triangle.

4. Find the coordinates of Paul's location when Olivia has turned 45°.

 (*Hint:* Your work in Problem 3 should be helpful here.)

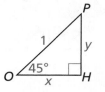

5. Find the coordinates of Paul's location when Olivia has turned 90°.

> Draw a diagram. You do not need to use triangles this time.

6. a. Explain why Paul will pass through the point $\left(\frac{3}{5}, \frac{4}{5}\right)$.

 b. When Paul is at $\left(\frac{3}{5}, \frac{4}{5}\right)$, find the angle Olivia has turned to the nearest degree.

7. Write About It Describe how the y-coordinate of Paul's location changes as Olivia's angle increases.

8. Copy and complete this table, giving the coordinates of Paul's location when Olivia has turned each angle.

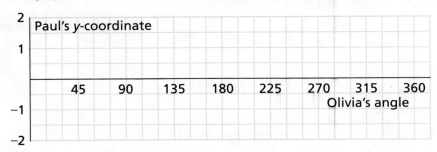

Angle	Coordinates	Angle	Coordinates
0°	(1, 0)	270°	▨
45°	▨	315°	▨
90°	▨	360°	▨
135°	▨	405°	▨
180°	(−1, 0)	450°	▨
225°	▨		

9. The *y*-coordinate of Paul's position is a function of the angle through which Olivia has turned. Make a coordinate grid labeled like the one below. Draw the graph of the function for angles between 0° and 360°.

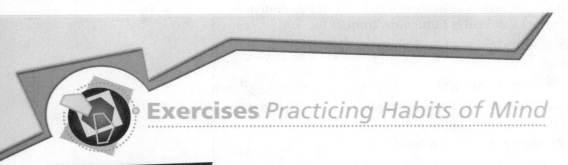

10. **Take It Further** Find the coordinates of Paul's location when Olivia has turned 10,000°. Calculate to three decimal places.

Exercises *Practicing Habits of Mind*

On Your Own

11. Copy and complete this table, giving the coordinates of Paul's location when Olivia has turned through each angle. Find each answer to three decimal places.

Angle	Coordinates	Angle	Coordinates
0°	(1, 0)	50°	▨
10°	▨	60°	▨
20°	▨	70°	▨
30°	▨	80°	▨
40°	▨	90°	(0, 1)

12. Find the magnitude and argument of each complex number.

    a. $3 + 4i$ **b.** $\frac{3}{5} + \frac{4}{5}i$

    c. $-5 + 12i$ **d.** $-\frac{5}{13} + \frac{12}{13}i$

Approximate the arguments to the nearest degree.

13. Which of these points is on the unit circle $x^2 + y^2 = 1$?

    A. $\left(\frac{1}{2}, -\frac{1}{2}\right)$ **B.** $(1, -1)$

    C. $\left(-\frac{5}{13}, \frac{12}{13}\right)$ **D.** $\left(\frac{2}{3}, -\frac{4}{5}\right)$

14. a. Find the coordinates of Paul's location to three decimal places when Olivia has turned $130°$.

    b. Find the coordinates of Paul's location to three decimal places when Olivia has turned $230°$.

15. Describe how the x-coordinate of Paul's location varies as Olivia's angle increases.

16. In Problem 9, you graphed Paul's y-coordinate as a function of the angle Olivia had turned. Now graph Paul's x-coordinate as a function of the angle Olivia has turned.

Include the points $(0, 1)$ and $(180, -1)$.

17. Find the coordinates of Paul's location to three decimal places when Olivia has turned $430°$.

18. Suppose a and b are real numbers and $z = a + bi$, a complex number. If $|z| = 2$ and $\arg z = 120°$, find a and b.

Maintain Your Skills

19. Draw the graphs of each pair of equations on the same axes. Find the number of intersections of the two graphs.

    a. $x^2 + y^2 = 1$ **b.** $x^2 + y^2 = 1$

           $x = 0.5$ $x = 0.9$

    c. $x^2 + y^2 = 1$ **d.** $x^2 + y^2 = 1$

           $x = 1$ $x = 1.3$

20. Draw the graphs of each pair of equations on the same axes. Find the number of intersections of the two graphs.

    a. $x^2 + y^2 = 1$ **b.** $x^2 + y^2 = 1$

           $y = 0.5$ $y = -0.5$

    c. $x^2 + y^2 = 1$ **d.** $x^2 + y^2 = 1$

          $y = -0.9$ $y = -1$

Go Online
Video Tutor
Pearsonsuccessnet.com

Right now, you can only find the sine, cosine, or tangent of an angle if the angle has measure between 0° and 90°, since these functions have been defined as ratios of sides in a right triangle. By following Olivia and Paul around their circle, you can extend the domain of these trigonometric functions to include all angles from 0° to 360°. Here is how.

Consider the situation in Lesson 8.01. Suppose Paul has moved along the circle, and Olivia has turned through an angle of 70°.

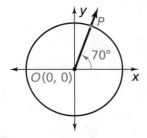

The 70° angle Olivia has turned is part of a right triangle with vertices at O and P. You complete the triangle by dropping an altitude from point P to the x-axis.

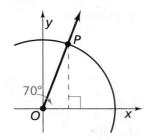

The hypotenuse of this right triangle has length 1, so the horizontal leg has length cos 70° and the vertical leg has length sin 70°. The coordinates of point P are (cos 70°, sin 70°).

In fact, this works for any angle in Quadrant I. Angles with measures between 0° and 90° are in Quadrant I. If the angle at the origin is θ, the coordinates of point P are (cos θ, sin θ).

In the other quadrants, you can draw right triangles to find Paul's coordinates, but one or both of the coordinates will be negative.

The position of the hammer at the moment of release is related to the angle the athlete has rotated.

You can find the approximate values of cos 70° and sin 70° on a calculator. Note that calculators typically have more than one way to measure angles. Refer to the TI-Nspire™ Handbook on p. 804 to see how to check that your calculator is in degree mode.

Example

Problem Find Paul's coordinates when Olivia has turned 210°.

Solution First, draw a diagram for the situation. The angle is in Quadrant III, so both coordinates will be negative. To find the exact coordinates, draw an altitude from P to the x-axis.

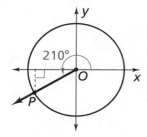

You can use sine and cosine to find the side lengths in this triangle. The triangle has a 30° angle at the origin, so it is a 30-60-90 triangle with hypotenuse length 1. Because this is a special right triangle, you can write exact expressions for its side lengths without using a calculator.

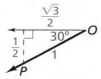

The side opposite the 30° angle has length $\frac{1}{2}$, and the side opposite the 60° angle has length $\frac{\sqrt{3}}{2}$.

To determine the coordinates of point P, use the side lengths of the triangle. Note that both coordinates are negative, since P is in Quadrant III. The coordinates of point P are $\left(-\frac{\sqrt{3}}{2}, -\frac{1}{2}\right)$.

Remember...

The values $\frac{1}{2}$ and $\frac{\sqrt{3}}{2}$ come up often in trigonometry.

For Discussion

1. Why does the hypotenuse of the triangle in the Example have length 1?

2. Find another angle in Quadrant III where you can find the coordinates of point P exactly without including a trigonometric function or using a calculator.

The unit circle gives you a way to extend the domain of sine and cosine.

Habits of Mind

Give an exact answer. Finding coordinates exactly means to use a rational number written as a fraction or an expression involving rational numbers and square roots. For example, $\cos 45° = \frac{\sqrt{2}}{2}$ is exact. But 0.707107 is an approximation of $\frac{\sqrt{2}}{2}$.

Definitions

Let θ be an angle centered at the origin and measured counter-clockwise from the positive *x*-axis. The left side of θ intersects the graph of $x^2 + y^2 = 1$ (the unit circle) in exactly one point.

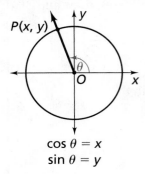

$$\cos \theta = x$$
$$\sin \theta = y$$

The **cosine** of angle θ is the *x*-coordinate of this intersection.

The **sine** of angle θ is the *y*-coordinate of this intersection.

This is the same as the situation with Olivia and Paul. You measure angles in the same way you measured the direction (or argument) of complex numbers in Chapter 3.

Remember...

The coordinates of a point P on the unit circle are $(\cos \theta, \sin \theta)$.

This definition is the one calculators use. For example, a calculator gives $\cos 180° = -1$.

For You to Do

3. Is $\sin 280°$ positive or negative? Answer without using a calculator.

4. In which quadrants is cosine negative?

For acute angles θ, one of the properties of the tangent function is that

$$\tan \theta = \frac{\sin \theta}{\cos \theta}$$

Since you now have a definition for the sine and cosine of any angle, you can use the above formula to extend the domain of the tangent function to any angle, as well. For example, you can say that

$$\tan 120° = \frac{\sin 120°}{\cos 120°} = \frac{\frac{\sqrt{3}}{2}}{-\frac{1}{2}} = -\sqrt{3}$$

Now you have a tentative definition. If θ is any angle, define $\tan \theta$ by the rule

$$\tan \theta = \frac{\sin \theta}{\cos \theta}$$

Check your definition. Why is this definition only tentative? The formula $\tan \theta = \frac{\sin \theta}{\cos \theta}$ is valid only for $0 \leq \theta < 90$, but is often used to define $\tan \theta$ for any angle.

In mathematics, it often happens that you can have a functional equation (in this case, $\tan \theta = \frac{\sin \theta}{\cos \theta}$) that is valid for certain values (in this case, for $0 \leq \theta < 90$). Sometimes the right side of the equation makes sense for many more values, so you define the left side for those additional values.

When you do this, you have to be careful. In the case of $\tan \theta = \frac{\sin \theta}{\cos \theta}$, you have to check two things:

- Does the right side make sense for all angles θ? Clearly, the numerator and denominator do, but does the fraction?

- You originally defined the left side of the equation to be "opposite over adjacent" for acute angles θ. Does this still make sense for angles with measure greater than $90°$?

For Discussion

5. As a class, discuss the two bullet points above and make a more precise definition of the tangent function.

Habits of Mind

Represent a function. To define a function, you have to give its domain.

Exercises *Practicing Habits of Mind*

Check Your Understanding

1. **What's Wrong Here?** Jo says that $\sin 45°$ should be $\frac{1}{2}$. Jo explains, "Well, $\sin 0° = 0$ and $\sin 90° = 1$. The same is true for cosine, except reversed. Halfway between, they should both be $\frac{1}{2}$." Use the unit circle to explain what is wrong with Jo's reasoning.

2. A complex number $w = a + bi$ has $|w| = 1$ and $\arg w = 70°$. Find a and b to three decimal places.

3. What complex number has magnitude 1 and direction 210°?

4. **Write About It** Write an identity that gives the relationship between the two expressions.

   a. $\cos \theta$ and $\cos (\theta + 180°)$

   b. $\sin \theta$ and $\sin (\theta + 180°)$

   c. $\tan \theta$ and $\tan (\theta + 180°)$

5. Find each value.

   a. $(\cos 150°)^2 + (\sin 150°)^2$

   b. $(\cos 52.696°)^2 + (\sin 52.696°)^2$

6. **Write About It** Suppose you know a complex number has magnitude 1, but you do not know its direction. Describe, with some examples, where that complex number can be located.

7. **a.** Find a formula for all values of θ such that $\sin \theta = 0$.

   b. Find a formula for all values of θ such that $\cos \theta = 0$.

   c. Find a formula for all values of θ such that $\tan \theta = 0$.

On Your Own

8. For each angle, draw the angle in standard position. Find the sine, cosine, and tangent of the angle.

   a. 210°

   b. 330°

   c. 40°

   d. 320°

   e. 360°

9. **Standardized Test Prep** If $\sin \theta = 0.57358$ and $\tan \theta = 0.70021$, what is $\cos \theta$?

   A. 0.40163   **B.** 0.81915   **C.** 1.22077   **D.** 1.27379

Remember...

An angle is in **standard position** when its vertex is at the origin and one of its sides lies along the positive *x*-axis. The angle opens counterclockwise from this fixed side.

10. For each angle in the table, find the cosine, sine, cosine squared, and sine squared. Look for rules and relationships that allow you to find the results more quickly.

11. Explain why $\sin 310° = -\sin 50°$.

12. Let $\theta = 150°$. Find each value.

   a. $\sin 2\theta$

   b. $2 \cdot \sin\theta \cdot \cos\theta$

13. Find a formula for all values of θ such that the given equation is true.

   a. $\sin\theta = 1$

   b. $\cos\theta = 1$

   c. $\tan\theta = 1$

θ	$\cos\theta$	$\sin\theta$	$\cos^2\theta$	$\sin^2\theta$
0°	▦	0	▦	0
30°	$\dfrac{\sqrt{3}}{2}$	▦	$\dfrac{3}{4}$	▦
45°	▦	$\dfrac{\sqrt{2}}{2}$	▦	$\dfrac{1}{2}$
60°	▦	▦	▦	▦
90°	0	1	0	1
120°	▦	▦	▦	▦
135°	▦	▦	▦	▦
150°	▦	$\dfrac{1}{2}$	▦	$\dfrac{1}{4}$
180°	▦	▦	▦	▦
210°	▦	▦	▦	▦
225°	$-\dfrac{\sqrt{2}}{2}$	▦	▦	$\dfrac{1}{2}$
240°	▦	▦	▦	▦
270°	0	▦	▦	▦
300°	▦	▦	▦	▦
315°	▦	▦	▦	▦
330°	▦	▦	▦	▦
360°	1	▦	▦	▦

Remember...

The notation $\cos^2 x$ means $(\cos x)^2$. You use this notation primarily for ease of reading. You read $\cos^2 x$ as "cosine squared of x."

Go Online
Pearsonsuccessnet.com

14. a. Find the magnitude and direction of $-6\sqrt{3} + 6i$.

   b. What complex number has magnitude 10 and direction 30°?

   c. What complex number has magnitude 1 and direction 60°?

Maintain Your Skills

15. Take It Further Find the value of θ in each equation.

   a. $\cos\theta + i\sin\theta = (\cos 40° + i\sin 40°)(\cos 50° + i\sin 50°)$

   b. $\cos\theta + i\sin\theta = (\cos 40° + i\sin 40°)(\cos 20° + i\sin 20°)$

   c. $\cos\theta + i\sin\theta = (\cos 40° + i\sin 40°)(\cos 80° + i\sin 80°)$

   d. $\cos\theta + i\sin\theta = (\cos 45° + i\sin 45°)^2$

8.03 Extending the Domain, Part 2

In the last lesson, you learned the meaning of cosine, sine, and tangent for values from 0° to 360°. This lesson extends the definitions to all real numbers.

For You to Do

1. Using a calculator, find cos 20°, cos 380°, and cos 1100°. Find another angle that produces the same value for the cosine.

The table in Exercise 10 from Lesson 8.02 only goes from 0° to 360°. The reason is that turning through any angle larger than 360° returns you to an angle between 0° and 360°. The coordinates after turning through a 20° angle are the same as the coordinates after turning 360° + 20° = 380° or 720° + 20° = 740°. It makes sense, then, to define the cosine of 740° to be the same as the cosine of 20°.

> Two numbers that differ by a multiple of 360 are *congruent modulo 360*. *Modulo* means "except for." The numbers 20 and 380 are the same, except for 360.

The same goes for negative angle measures: An angle of −35° puts you at the same place on the unit circle as an angle of 325°. So it makes sense to say that sin (−35°) = sin 325°.

With this extension, you can find the sine or cosine for any angle measure from the set of real numbers. For an angle θ with measure outside of 0° < θ < 360°, simply find another angle that is between 0° and 360° but has the same coordinates on the unit circle. You can use almost exactly the same definition as the one in Lesson 8.02 to extend the definition to any angle measure.

> **Habits of Mind**
>
> **Experiment.** Will the tangent of any angle be the same as the tangent of an angle between 0° and 360°?

Definitions

Let θ be an angle centered at the origin and measured from the positive *x*-axis. The terminal side of θ intersects the graph of $x^2 + y^2 = 1$ (the unit circle) in exactly one point.

The **cosine** of angle θ is the *x*-coordinate of this intersection.

The **sine** of angle θ is the *y*-coordinate of this intersection.

The **tangent** of angle θ is $\frac{\sin\theta}{\cos\theta}$, whenever cos $\theta \neq 0$.

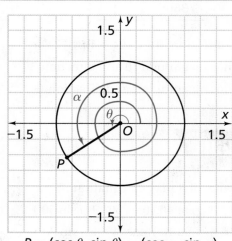

$P = (\cos\theta, \sin\theta) = (\cos\alpha, \sin\alpha)$

> One side of θ passes through (1, 0). This is its initial side. The other side is the terminal side. When are these two sides the same ray?

For You to Do

2. Using a calculator, find cos 20°, cos 160°, cos 200°, and cos 340°.

Theorem 8.1

If n is an integer and x is an angle in degrees,
- $\cos(x + 360n) = \cos x$
- $\sin(x + 360n) = \sin x$

For Discussion

3. The functions sine and cosine are periodic with period 360°. What does this mean? Is the tangent function a **periodic function**?

Developing Habits of Mind

Visualize. In Chapter 3, you learned how to calculate the direction of complex numbers. You noticed that the direction of $4 + 3i$ is related to the direction of $-4 + 3i$, $-4 - 3i$, and $4 - 3i$.

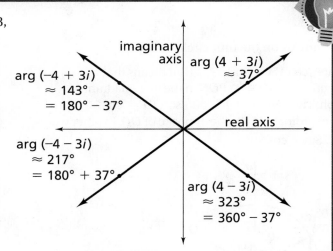

arg $(-4 + 3i)$
$\approx 143°$
$= 180° - 37°$

arg $(4 + 3i)$
$\approx 37°$

arg $(-4 - 3i)$
$\approx 217°$
$= 180° + 37°$

arg $(4 - 3i)$
$\approx 323°$
$= 360° - 37°$

This is the same picture you see now in the unit circle. Each quadrant has a related angle with coordinates that are the same, except for a sign.

For example, if you know the cosine and sine of a 20° angle, you automatically know the cosine and sine of a 160° angle, as well as a 200° angle and a 340° angle, and many other angles.

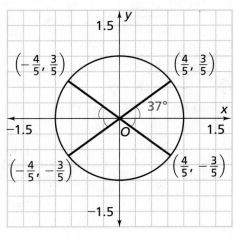

Habits of Mind

Look for relationships. Equations like $\cos x = -\cos(180° - x)$ express a symmetry of the cosine function.

Knowing about the signs of the coordinates in each quadrant will help you decide quickly about whether the cosine, sine, or tangent of an angle is positive or negative. For example, in Quadrant I, cosine is positive and sine is positive. Therefore, tangent is positive.

Habits of Mind

Look for relationships. If you are familiar with angles in Quadrant I, then you can handle any other angle using these relationships.

For You to Do

Find the sign of the sine, cosine, and tangent for angles in each quadrant.

4. Quadrant II

5. Quadrant III

6. Quadrant IV

Example

Problem Express each value as the value of the sine or cosine of an acute angle.

    a. $\cos 150°$

    b. $\sin 460°$

    c. $\sin 290°$

Solution It helps to draw the angles on the unit circle:

    a. The coordinates of P are $(\cos 150°, \sin 150°)$. That means that $m\angle POC = 30°$. Imagine $\triangle QOD \cong \triangle POC$ in the first quadrant, oriented as in the graph. Then $m\angle DOQ = 30°$, so $OD = \cos 30°$. But $OC = OD$, and the x-coordinate of P is the opposite of OD. In other words, $\cos 150° = -\cos 30°$. Since $\cos 30° = \frac{\sqrt{3}}{2}$, $\cos 150° = -\frac{\sqrt{3}}{2}$.

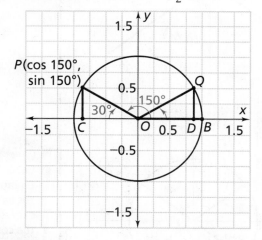

    b. Note that $\sin 460°$ is the same as $\sin 100°$, since traveling around the circle $460°$ is the same as making one complete revolution ($360°$) with an additional $100°$. Now draw a graph like the one above and convince yourself that $\sin 100° = \sin 80°$.

c. The graph shows that $\sin 290° = -\sin 70°$.

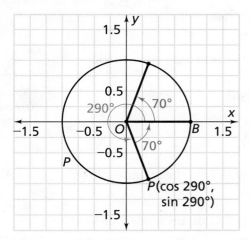

Habits of Mind

Generalize. Convince yourself that $\sin (-x) = -\sin x$ for any angle measure x.

Exercises *Practicing Habits of Mind*

Check Your Understanding

1. **Write About It** Explain why $\sin 160° = \sin 20°$ but $\cos 160° = -\cos 20°$.

2. Suppose $\sin \theta = \frac{20}{29}$ for some angle θ.
   a. In what quadrants can θ be located?
   b. Find both possible values for $\cos \theta$.
   c. Find both possible values for $\tan \theta$.

3. Find an angle θ for which $\tan \theta > 100$, or explain why no such angle exists.

4. **What's Wrong Here?** Herb wants to calculate $\cos (-60°)$. He says, "I know that $\cos 60°$ is $\frac{1}{2}$. So $\cos (-60°)$ should just be the negative. The answer is $-\frac{1}{2}$."
   What is wrong with Herb's reasoning? What is the correct value of $\cos (-60°)$?

5. List the following values in order from least to greatest.
   $$\tan 70° \quad \sin 120° \quad \cos 120° \quad \cos 720° \quad \tan 110° \quad \sin 210°$$

6. Find the two angles between $0°$ and $360°$ for which $\sin \theta + \sin (180° - \theta) = 1$.

7. Given that $\sin 50° \approx 0.7660$ and $\cos 50° \approx 0.6428$, find each value to four decimal places.

a. $\sin 130°$

b. $\cos 130°$

c. $\cos 230°$

d. $\sin 310°$

e. $\cos^2 230° + \sin^2 230°$

f. $\sin 40°$

You do not need a calculator for any of the parts of this exercise.

8. a. There is a relationship between $\tan^2 \theta$ and $\frac{1}{\cos^2 \theta}$. Find the relationship by calculating each expression for several angles.

b. Take It Further Prove that this relationship holds for any angle θ, as long as $\tan \theta$ is defined.

On Your Own

9. Find the values of $\cos(-30°)$, $\sin(-30°)$, and $\tan(-30°)$.

10. Express each value as a sine or cosine of an acute angle.

a. $\sin 400°$

b. $\cos 400°$

c. $\cos 300°$

d. $\sin 315°$

e. $\sin(-100°)$

11. Express each value as a sine or cosine of θ.

a. $\sin(180° - \theta)$

b. $\cos(180° - \theta)$

c. $\sin(180° + \theta)$

d. $\cos(180° + \theta)$

e. $\sin(270° - \theta)$

f. $\cos(270° - \theta)$

g. $\sin(270° + \theta)$

h. $\cos(270° + \theta)$

Habits of Mind

Use what you know. There is no need to memorize these identities. You can reconstruct them by looking at the unit circle.

12. Is this statement true or false? Explain.

For any two angles a and b, $\sin(a + b) = \sin a + \sin b$ and $\cos(a + b) = \cos a + \cos b$.

This statement says that addition is distributive over the sine and cosine functions. But maybe it is not!

13. Suppose an angle θ is unknown, but it is between $300°$ and $350°$. Determine whether each expression is positive or negative.

a. $\cos \theta$

b. $\sin \theta$

c. $\tan \theta$

d. $\cos^2 \theta + \sin^2 \theta$

e. $\tan^3 \theta$

14. What is the value of $\cos 120° + \sin 120°$?

A. 0

B. $\frac{\sqrt{3} - 1}{2}$

C. 1

D. $\frac{\sqrt{3} + 1}{2}$

15. Find this sum: $\sin 60° + \sin 120° + \sin 180° + \cdots + \sin 360°$.

16. For which angles between $0°$ and $360°$ can you find the sine and cosine exactly without using a calculator or an approximation?

17. Suppose θ is an angle in Quadrant II with $\sin \theta = \frac{35}{37}$.

   a. Find the value of $\cos \theta$.

   b. Find the value of $\tan \theta$.

   c. Suppose θ is between $0°$ and $360°$. Find θ to the nearest degree.

18. a. There is a relationship between $\frac{1}{\tan^2 \theta}$ and $\frac{1}{\sin^2 \theta}$. Find the relationship by calculating each expression for several angles.

   b. **Take It Further** Prove that this relationship holds for any angle θ, as long as $\tan \theta$ is defined and $\tan \theta$ and $\sin \theta$ are not equal to 0.

19. **Standardized Test Prep** Lindsay has a four-function calculator $(+, -, \times, \div)$. She also has a printed table showing values of $\sin \theta$ for values of θ from $0°$ to $90°$ in increments of $1°$. Which formula will allow her to use this table and her calculator to compute the values of $\cos \theta$ for several different angles between $0°$ and $90°$?

   A. $\cos \theta = 1 - \sin \theta$ **B.** $\cos \theta = \sin (90 - \theta)$ **C.** $\cos \theta = -\sin \theta$

   D. No relation exists between $\cos \theta$ and $\sin \theta$ for values of θ between $0°$ and $90°$.

The missing terms all follow the arithmetic sequence set up by 60, 120, and 180.

Go Online
Pearsonsuccessnet.com

Maintain Your Skills

20. Find an angle θ, not equal to $30°$, that satisfies each equation.

   a. $\cos \theta = \cos 30°$ **b.** $\sin \theta = \sin 30°$ **c.** $\tan \theta = \tan 30°$

   d. Describe how you can find ten other angles θ such that $\cos \theta = \cos 30°$.

The Pythagorean Identity

While solving Exercise 10 in Lesson 8.02, you may have noticed the following equation is true for all angles between 0° and 360°.

$$\cos^2 \theta + \sin^2 \theta = 1$$

Since then, you have extended the domain for sine and cosine to include all angles. Does the identity still hold? Happily, it does.

Theorem 8.2 *The Pythagorean Identity*

If α is any angle, then

$$\cos^2 \alpha + \sin^2 \alpha = 1$$

The symbol α is the Greek letter alpha. You pronounce it AL fuh.

Proof For any angle α, $\cos \alpha$ and $\sin \alpha$ are the coordinates of the point P on the unit circle, where the left side of α intersects the unit circle.

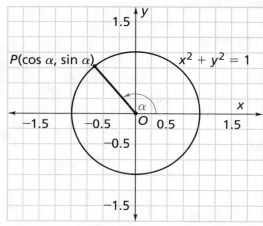

There are several ways to see that the sum of the squares of the coordinates of P is 1.

Method 1 The equation of the unit circle is $x^2 + y^2 = 1$, and the coordinates of P satisfy this equation.

Method 2 The distance from P to the origin is 1.

Method 3 Drop a perpendicular from P to the x-axis and use the Pythagorean Theorem.

For You to Do

1. Pick one of the methods above (or one of your own) and finish the proof of Theorem 8.2.

Problem If $\sin \gamma = \frac{1}{2}$, find $\cos \gamma$.

Solution Think of $(\cos \gamma, \sin \gamma)$ as a point P on the unit circle. Then $\sin \gamma$ is the y-coordinate of P. How many points have a y-coordinate of $\frac{1}{2}$ on the unit circle?

In Exercise 20a from Lesson 8.01, you saw that there are two points on the unit circle with y-coordinate $\frac{1}{2}$. The x-coordinates of these two points are precisely the values of $\cos \gamma$ for which $\sin \gamma = \frac{1}{2}$.

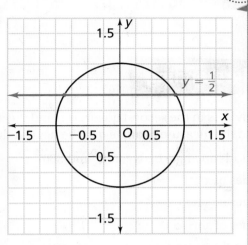

> The symbol γ is the Greek letter gamma. You pronounce it GAM uh.

To find the two intersection points, you can do one of two equivalent things.

Method 1 In the equation $x^2 + y^2 = 1$, substitute $y = \frac{1}{2}$ and solve for x.

$$x^2 + \left(\tfrac{1}{2}\right)^2 = 1$$
$$x^2 + \tfrac{1}{4} = 1$$
$$x^2 = \tfrac{3}{4}$$
$$x = \pm\sqrt{\tfrac{3}{4}} = \pm\tfrac{\sqrt{3}}{2}$$

Method 2 Use the Pythagorean Identity.

$$\cos^2 \gamma + \sin^2 \gamma = 1$$

Substitute $\sin \gamma = \frac{1}{2}$.

$$\cos^2 \gamma + \left(\tfrac{1}{2}\right)^2 = 1$$
$$\cos^2 \gamma + \tfrac{1}{4} = 1$$
$$\cos^2 \gamma = \tfrac{3}{4}$$
$$\cos \gamma = \pm\sqrt{\tfrac{3}{4}} = \pm\tfrac{\sqrt{3}}{2}$$

> Methods 1 and 2 really are the same. On the unit circle, if (x, y) is the point where a radius that forms an angle γ with the x-axis intersects the circle, then $\cos \gamma = x$ and $\sin \gamma = y$.

For You to Do

2. Solve $\sin \gamma = \frac{1}{2}$ for γ.

Habits of Mind

Consider more than one solution. If you ask your calculator for $\sin^{-1}(0.5)$, it will probably return $30°$. It is true that $\sin 30° = 0.5$, but is that the only solution for γ? The calculator picks its values for $\sin^{-1}$ from a restricted sine domain.

Exercises *Practicing Habits of Mind*

Check Your Understanding

1. Suppose $\sin q = 0.72$ and q is in the second quadrant. Find the approximate value of $\cos q$. Then find the measure of angle q to the nearest degree.

2. Suppose $\cos x = \frac{1}{2}$ and x is an angle between $0°$ and $360°$.

   a. Find all possible values of x.

   b. Find all possible values of $\sin x$.

   c. Find all possible values of $\sin^2 x$.

3. Graph both equations on the same axes.

   $$x^2 + y^2 = 1$$
   $$y = 0.6$$

4. Find all solutions to the system of equations in Exercise 3.

5. Suppose $\cos x = 0.6$ and x is an angle between $0°$ and $360°$.

   a. Find all possible values of x.

   b. Find all possible values of $\sin x$.

   c. Find all possible values of $\sin^2 x$.

6. Suppose that $z = \cos 30° + i \sin 30°$. Show that $\frac{1}{z} = \bar{z}$.

> Approximate to one decimal place if necessary.

> **Remember...**
>
> The notation $\bar{z}$ means the complex conjugate of z.

On Your Own

7. Suppose that $z = \cos \theta + i \sin \theta$. Show that $\frac{1}{z} = \bar{z}$.

8. Solve each equation or system for $0 \le x \le 360°$.

   a. $\sin x = \frac{\sqrt{2}}{2}$

   b. $\begin{cases} \sin x = \frac{\sqrt{2}}{2} \\ \cos x > 0 \end{cases}$

   c. $\begin{cases} \sin x = \frac{\sqrt{2}}{2} \\ \cos x < 0 \end{cases}$

   d. $\begin{cases} \sin x = -\frac{\sqrt{2}}{2} \\ \cos x < 0 \end{cases}$

9. Find ten pairs of rational numbers (a, b) such that $a^2 + b^2 = 1$.

10. **Write About It** The Pythagorean Identity says that, if θ is any angle, $\cos^2 \theta + \sin^2 \theta = 1$.

Suppose you have numbers a and b such that $a^2 + b^2 = 1$. Is there an angle θ such that $\sin \theta = a$ and $\cos \theta = b$? Explain.

11. a. Show that
$$\tan^2 30° = \frac{1}{\cos^2 30°} - 1.$$

b. If α is any angle, is the equation below true? Explain.

$$\tan^2 \alpha = \frac{1}{\cos^2 \alpha} - 1$$

12. a. Calculate $\cos^2 30° - \sin^2 30°$.

b. Calculate $\cos^4 30° - \sin^4 30°$.

c. Verify that $\cos^2 \theta - \sin^2 \theta = \cos^4 \theta - \sin^4 \theta$ for a new choice of θ.

d. Prove that for any angle θ, it must be true that
$$\cos^2 \theta - \sin^2 \theta = \cos^4 \theta - \sin^4 \theta.$$

13. **Standardized Test Prep** If $\cos \theta = \frac{1}{3}$ and $0° < \theta < 90°$, what is the value of $\sin \theta$?

A. $\frac{2}{3}$

B. $\frac{4}{9}$

C. $\frac{2\sqrt{2}}{3}$

D. $\frac{8}{9}$

Alpha is the first letter of the Greek alphabet. The alpha wolf is the leader of the pack.

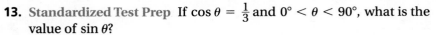

Pick a θ, any θ.

Go Online
Pearsonsuccessnet.com

14. Copy and complete the table without using a calculator.

θ	$\cos \theta$	$\sin \theta$	$\tan \theta$
0°	■	0	■
30°	$\frac{\sqrt{3}}{2}$	■	$\frac{1}{\sqrt{3}}$
45°	■	$\frac{\sqrt{2}}{2}$	1
60°	■	■	■
90°	0	1	■
120°	■	■	■
135°	■	■	■
150°	■	$-\frac{1}{2}$	■
180°	■	■	■
210°	■	■	■
225°	$-\frac{\sqrt{2}}{2}$	■	■
240°	■	■	■
270°	0	■	■
300°	■	■	■
315°	■	■	■
330°	■	■	■
360°	1	■	■

You have done much of the work for this table before.

Solving Trigonometric Equations

You solve equations with trigonometric functions in much the same way you solve other equations.

Minds in Action   episode 37

Tony and Sasha are trying to solve the equation 5 cos x + 6 = 9 for x between 0° and 360°.

Tony   I'm not sure what to do with the cos x.

Sasha   It's like in Chapter 2, when we lumped things.

Sasha goes to the board and covers up the cos x with her hand.

$$5 \text{ co} \quad x + 6 = 9$$

Sasha   See? Now it looks like it's saying "5 times something plus 6 is 9."

So, let z stand for cos x, for the time being, and solve

$$5z + 6 = 9$$

Tony   I know how to do that. You get $z = \frac{3}{5} = 0.6$.

Sasha   But z is just an alias for cos x, so our equation is cos x = 0.6.

Tony   And I know how to do that, too. In fact, we have already done it in Exercise 5 in the last lesson. You just use the inverse cosine button and get 53.13°. That's an approximation, I know.

Sasha   Yes, but that's not the only answer. Look:

Sasha draws on the board.

Sasha   See? Cosine is the x-coordinate, and there are two points on the unit circle with x-coordinate 0.6. One has a central angle of about 53.13°.

Tony   And the other is −53.13°.

Sasha   Or, if you want your angles to measure between 0° and 360°, the second angle is about 306.87°.

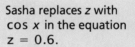

Sasha replaces z with cos x in the equation z = 0.6.

Habits of Mind

Make strategic choices. What happens when you allow angles with measure greater than 360°?

For You to Do

1. Solve $5 \sin x + 3 = 7$ for x between $0°$ and $360°$.

Developing Habits of Mind

Look for patterns. The lumping idea is often used to solve trigonometric equations that look like ordinary algebraic equations.

For example, the trigonometric equation below is a quadratic equation in $\sin x$.

$$10 \sin^2 x - 3 \sin x = 4$$

That is, if you let $z = \sin x$, the equation becomes

$$10z^2 - 3z = 4$$

You can solve this with the methods of Chapter 2. When you find two values for z, replace z with $\sin x$. Then solve for x.

A **trigonometric equation** is an equation that involves trigonometric functions.

For You to Do

2. Solve the equation $10 \sin^2 x - 3 \sin x = 4$ for x, where $0° \le x \le 360°$.

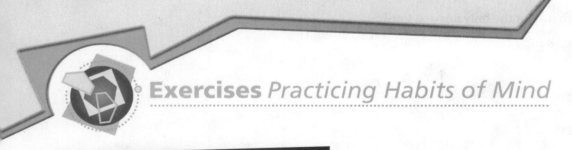

Exercises *Practicing Habits of Mind*

Check Your Understanding

1. Suppose $\sin x = \sin 50°$. Find all possible values of x.

2. **a.** Find, to the nearest degree, the two angles between $0°$ and $360°$ that make $\sin x = 0.6$.

   b. Find, to the nearest degree, the two angles between $0°$ and $360°$ that make $\sin x = -0.6$.

3. a. Find, to the nearest degree, all angles between 0° and 360° that make cos x = 0.8.

b. Find, to the nearest degree, all angles between 0° and 360° that make cos x = −1.2.

4. Find all solutions to each equation for 0° ≤ x ≤ 360°.

a. 3 cos x + 4 = 0

b. 6 sin x − 1 = 3

c. 4 sin$^2 x$ = 1

d. 4 sin$^2 x$ = 4 sin x + 3

5. a. Find, to the nearest degree, all angles between 0° and 360° that make sin x = cos x.

b. Find, to the nearest degree, all angles between 0° and 360° that make sin x = −cos x.

c. *Take It Further* Find, to the nearest degree, all angles between 0° and 360° that make sin x = tan x.

6. Solve the equation 6 cos$^2 x$ + sin x − 5 = 0 for x, where 0° ≤ x ≤ 360°. (*Hint:* cos$^2 x$ + sin$^2 x$ = 1)

7. Suppose z is a complex number and arg z = θ. Use geometry to show that $z + \bar{z} = 2|z| \cos \theta$.

8. In the isosceles triangle below, $OA = OB = 1$ and $m\angle O = 36°$.

Show that $z = 2 \cos 72°$.

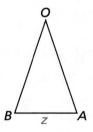

Habits of Mind

Detect the key characteristics. What is special about the parallelogram that has vertices 0, z, $z + \bar{z}$, and $\bar{z}$?

On Your Own

9. Find all solutions to each equation for 0° ≤ x ≤ 360°.

a. 5 cos x + 4 = 0

b. $\sqrt{2}$ sin x − 1 = 3

c. 4 cos$^2 x$ = 1

d. 4 cos$^2 x$ = 4 cos x + 3

10. Find all solutions to each equation for 0° ≤ x ≤ 360°.

a. 2 cos x + 1 = 0

b. tan x − 1 = 0

c. 1 − 3 sin x + 2 sin$^2 x$ = 0

d. 2 cos$^2 x$ − 5 cos x = 2

11. For what values of α between 0° and 360° is the following equation true?

$$2 \sin^2 \alpha + 5 \cos \alpha = 2$$

12. Find or approximate the complex number on the unit circle that has each argument. Write your answers in $a + bi$ form.

   a. 20°   **b.** 330°   **c.** −30°   **d.** 100°   **e.** 227°   **f.** 75°

13. For each complex number z, find arg z.

   a. $z = \frac{4}{5} + \frac{3}{5}i$ **b.** $z = \frac{3}{5} + \frac{4}{5}i$ **c.** $z = -\frac{3}{5} - \frac{4}{5}i$ **d.** $z = -\frac{4}{5} + \frac{3}{5}i$

14. Solve the equation $2 \sin^3 x - \sin^2 x - 2 \sin x + 1 = 0$ for x, where $0° \le x \le 360°$.

15. In the isosceles triangle below, $OA = OB = 1$ and $m\angle O = 36°$. $\overline{BC}$ bisects $\angle OBA$.

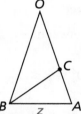

See Exercise 8.

Habits of Mind

Look for relationships. There are similar triangles in the figure.

   a. Show that $1 - z^2 = z$.

   b. Use the result of part (a) to find an exact value for z.

   c. Use parts (a) and (b) and the result of Exercise 8 to find an exact value for $\cos 72°$.

   d. **Take It Further** Find an exact value for $\sin 72°$.

16. **Take It Further** Solve the equation $5 \cos 2x + 6 = 9$, where $0° \le x \le 360°$.

17. **Standardized Test Prep** Solve, to the nearest hundredth of a degree, $\tan x - 10 = -\tan x$ for $-90° < x < 90°$.

   A. −80°   **B.** 1.37°   **C.** 78.69°   **D.** 84.29°

Maintain Your Skills

18. Here is a graph of the unit circle with a line ℓ that intersects the circle at the points $A(0, -1)$ and $P(a, b)$.

Find the coordinates of P for each slope of ℓ.

   a. 1   **b.** 2   **c.** $\frac{3}{2}$

   d. 4   **e.** $\frac{6}{5}$

   f. **Take It Further** $\frac{r}{s}$

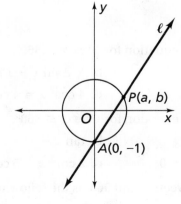

Mathematical 8A Reflections

In this investigation, you learned how to evaluate the sine, cosine, and tangent functions for any angle and to solve equations involving trigonometric equations. These questions will help you summarize what you have learned.

1. A line through the origin forms a 30° angle with the x-axis. What are the coordinates of the points where this line intersects the graph of the unit circle?

2. Sketch each angle in standard position. Find its sine, cosine, and tangent.

   a. 150°   **b.** 315°   **c.** 240°

3. Find five solutions to the equation $\sin x = -1$.

4. For some angle θ, $\sin \theta = \frac{12}{13}$.

   a. Find all possible values for $\cos \theta$.

   b. Find all possible values for $\tan \theta$.

   c. Find a possible θ between 0° and 360° to the nearest tenth of a degree.

5. Solve the following equation for α between 0° and 360°.

$$10 \cos^2 \alpha + \cos \alpha - 3 = 0$$

6. How can you extend the definitions of sine, cosine, and tangent to any angle, not just acute angles?

7. If an angle is in Quadrant IV, what can you say about the sign of its sine, cosine, and tangent?

8. What is the relationship between the equation of the unit circle and the Pythagorean Identity?

Vocabulary and Notation

In this investigation, you learned these terms and symbols. Make sure you understand what each one means and how to use it.

- cosine, $\cos \theta$
- periodic function
- sine, $\sin \theta$
- standard position
- tangent, $\tan \theta$
- trigonometric equation

Graphs of Trigonometric Functions

In *Graphs of Trigonometric Functions*, you will sketch the graphs of the sine, cosine, and tangent functions. You can use these graphs to explore trigonometric identities.

By the end of this investigation, you will be able to answer questions like these.

1. What do the graphs of the sine and cosine functions look like?

2. Why does the tangent function have a period of 180°?

3. What is a simple rule for finding the value of cos (90° + θ)?

You will learn how to

- sketch graphs of the sine, cosine, and tangent

- use the graphs of trigonometric functions to solve problems

- prove and use trigonometric identities

You will develop these habits and skills:

- Visualize relationships between graphs of trigonometric functions.

- Choose the appropriate representation—graph or unit circle— to understand and develop trigonometric identities.

- Reason logically to prove trigonometric identities.

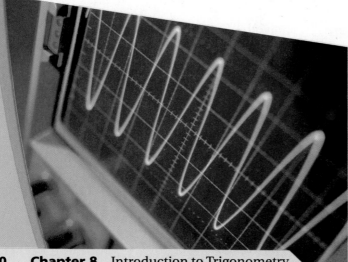

An oscilloscope displays voltage as a function of time. The graph is a sine wave.

8.06 **Getting Started**

The graphs of the sine, cosine, and tangent functions show the periodic nature of these functions.

For You to Explore

An exact value for a trigonometric function is an expression that may include square roots. If you use your calculator, it may return a decimal approximation and not an exact value.

1. Find the exact values of cos 30° and sin 30°.

2. Find the exact values of cos 45° and sin 45°.

3. Calculate each value.

   a. $\cos^2 30°$ **b.** $\sin^2 30°$

   c. $\cos^2 45°$ **d.** $\sin^2 45°$

   e. $\cos^2 30° + \sin^2 30°$ **f.** $\cos^2 45° + \sin^2 45°$

4. Describe how the cosine and sine of 60° are related to the cosine and sine of 30°.

5. Describe how the cosine and sine of 150° are related to the cosine and sine of 30°.

Exercises *Practicing Habits of Mind*

On Your Own

6. Use the information from Exercise 14 in Lesson 8.04 to draw a graph of $y = \cos x$ for $0° \leq x \leq 360°$.

7. Use the graph of $y = \cos x$ to answer this question: Is cos 230° greater or less than cos 190°?

8. Use the information from Exercise 14 in Lesson 8.04 to draw a graph of the function $y = \sin x$ for $0° \leq x \leq 360°$.

9. Use the graph of $y = \sin x$ to answer this question: Is $\sin 230°$ greater or less than $\sin 190°$?

10. Find and describe a relationship between $\sin \theta$ and $\sin (180° + \theta)$.

11. **Take It Further** Which is greater, $\tan 190°$ or $\tan 230°$? Determine the answer without a calculator. Justify your answer.

Maintain Your Skills

12. For each complex number, calculate the magnitude and direction.

   a. $3 + 2i$ **b.** $(3 + 2i)^2$ **c.** $1 + 2i$

   d. $(1 + 2i)^2$ **e.** $-\frac{8}{17} + \frac{15}{17}i$ **f.** $\left(-\frac{8}{17} + \frac{15}{17}i\right)^2$

   g. z^2, where z has magnitude 5 and direction 100°

Calculate the direction to the nearest tenth of a degree.

13. Here is the table you completed in Lesson 8.04, Exercise 14. What patterns can you find in each column?

θ	$\cos \theta$	$\sin \theta$	$\tan \theta$
0°	1	0	0
30°	$\frac{\sqrt{3}}{2}$	$\frac{1}{2}$	$\frac{1}{\sqrt{3}}$
45°	$\frac{\sqrt{2}}{2}$	$\frac{\sqrt{2}}{2}$	1
60°	$\frac{1}{2}$	$\frac{\sqrt{3}}{2}$	$\sqrt{3}$
90°	0	1	undefined
120°	$-\frac{1}{2}$	$\frac{\sqrt{3}}{2}$	$-\sqrt{3}$
135°	$-\frac{\sqrt{2}}{2}$	$\frac{\sqrt{2}}{2}$	-1
150°	$-\frac{\sqrt{3}}{2}$	$\frac{1}{2}$	$-\frac{1}{\sqrt{3}}$
180°	-1	0	0
210°	$-\frac{\sqrt{3}}{2}$	$-\frac{1}{2}$	$\frac{1}{\sqrt{3}}$
225°	$-\frac{\sqrt{2}}{2}$	$-\frac{\sqrt{2}}{2}$	1
240°	$-\frac{1}{2}$	$-\frac{\sqrt{3}}{2}$	$\sqrt{3}$
270°	0	-1	undefined
300°	$\frac{1}{2}$	$-\frac{\sqrt{3}}{2}$	$-\sqrt{3}$
315°	$\frac{\sqrt{2}}{2}$	$-\frac{\sqrt{2}}{2}$	-1
330°	$\frac{\sqrt{3}}{2}$	$-\frac{1}{2}$	$-\frac{1}{\sqrt{3}}$
360°	1	0	0

8.07 Graphing Cosine and Sine

In Lesson 8.03, you extended the domain of sine and cosine to all of ℝ. This means that you can graph sin x or cos x against x on a Cartesian graph. One way to do this is to use the completed table on the facing page.

Consider the sine function first. Notice that the second column in the table starts at 0, climbs to 1, then retreats backs to 0, plunges to −1, and then climbs back up to 0.

For You to Do

1. To get a feeling for the relative sizes, rewrite the sine values as decimal approximations.

Once you get the decimal approximations, you can plot points. If you use your calculator to get decimal approximations for even more sines, you will end up with a graph that looks like this.

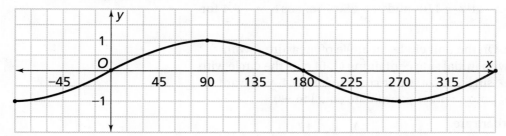

For Discussion

2. Use the fact that sine is periodic to extend the graph to $-360° \leq x \leq 720°$.

For You to Do

3. Sketch the graph of $y = \cos x$ for $-360° \leq x \leq 720°$. Describe how the graph of $y = \cos x$ is related to the graph of $y = \sin x$.

Along with the unit circle, the graphs of sine and cosine give you a toolkit that will help you think about the properties of the trigonometric functions.

Example

Problem For how many values of α between $0°$ and $360°$ is $\cos \alpha = -0.4$? What are they, approximately?

Solution There are two ways to think about this.

Method 1 Use the graph of the function $\cos x = y$. Just as on the graph of any function, the output at x is the y-height above or below x on the graph. So, to find α such that $\cos \alpha = -0.4$, find the intersections of the graphs of $y = -0.4$ and $y = \cos x$.

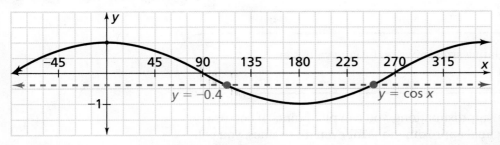

There are two such intersections in the interval $0° \leq x \leq 360°$. And it looks as if the intersections occur at $x \approx 110°$ and $x \approx 250°$. So, $\cos \alpha = -0.4$ for $\alpha \approx 110°$ and $\alpha \approx 250°$.

Method 2 Use the unit circle. On the unit circle, an angle of measure α with vertex at the origin and with initial side containing $(1, 0)$ cuts the circle with its terminal side at $(\cos \alpha, \sin \alpha)$. If you want $\cos \alpha$ to be -0.4, you want to look on the unit circle for points with x-coordinate equal to -0.4.

Once again, we see that there are two such angles between $0°$ and $360°$. They are approximately $110°$ and $250°$.

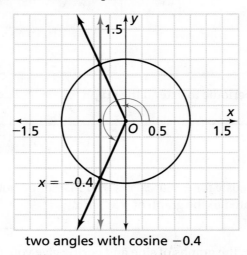

two angles with cosine -0.4

Go Online
Pearsonsuccessnet.com

For You to Do

4. Use your calculator's $\cos^{-1}$ key to get better approximations of the angles with cosine -0.4. Round to three decimal places.

Developing Habits of Mind

Consider more than one strategy. These two ways of thinking—using the graphs and using the unit circle—complement each other in many ways. The graph, because of its symmetry, is useful for discovering interesting things like the fact that $\cos 20° = \cos(-20°)$. But the proof of such a fact usually relies on the geometry of the unit circle.

The unit circle is ideal for figuring out exact values for things like $\sin 240°$, because you can use what you know from geometry. The graph is ideal for finding qualitative facts, such as the number of solutions to $\sin x = 0.7$.

For You to Do

5. Explain why $\cos 20° = \cos(-20°)$. Is it always true that $\cos x = \cos(-x)$?

For Discussion

For each question, decide whether it is a good idea to use the unit circle, the graph, or both. Then answer each question.

6. How many solutions are there to $|\sin x| = 1$ for $-360° \le x \le 360°$?

7. Find the solutions to $|\sin x| = 1$ for $-360° \le x \le 360°$.

8. Find a formula for all solutions of $|\sin x| = 1$.

Exercises *Practicing Habits of Mind*

Check Your Understanding

1. The values of $\sin 50°$ and $\sin(-50°)$ are related.

   a. Use the unit circle to describe and illustrate this relationship.

   b. Use the graph of $y = \sin x$ to describe and illustrate this relationship.

2. **What's Wrong Here?** Derman uses his graphing calculator to sketch the graph of $y = \sin x$. As is his custom, he sets the window so that x and y go from -10 to 10. He is surprised by what he sees. Describe what Derman sees. How can he fix the problem?

> To help Derman, see the TI-Nspire Handbook, p. 804.

3. Sketch the graph of $f(x) = \cos(x + 360°)$. Describe why the graph looks the way it does.

4. **a.** How many x-intercepts does the graph of $y = \cos x$ have?

   b. Explain why the cosine function cannot be a polynomial function.

   c. Where is the tangent function undefined? Explain.

5. Sketch the graph of $f(x) = \sin(30° + x) + \sin(30° - x)$.

6. Sketch the graph of $g(x) = \cos(x - 90°)$.

7. Here are the graphs of $y = \sin x$ and $y = 0.6$ on the same axes.

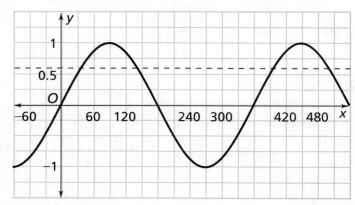

The least positive value of x that solves $\sin x = 0.6$ is about $37°$. Find the next two values of x, to the nearest degree, that solve the equation.

8. **Take It Further** Sketch the graph of $k(x) = \cos 2x$ without the aid of a graphing calculator. Then use a calculator to check your work.

9. **a.** Sketch the graphs of $f(x) = \cos x$ and $g(x) = \sin x$ on the same axes.

   b. Use the graphs to find two angles θ for which $\sin \theta = \cos \theta$.

10. **a.** For each angle θ you found in Exercise 9, find $\tan \theta$.

    b. If $\sin \theta = \cos \theta$, prove that $\tan \theta = 1$.

> Consider the entire graph, not just a small section.

On Your Own

11. Draw a picture to explain why $\cos(-\theta) = \cos \theta$.

12. Draw a picture to explain why $\sin(-\theta) = -\sin \theta$.

13. Sketch the graph of $s(x) = \cos^2 x + \sin^2 x$.

14. **Standardized Test Prep** Which function has the same graph as $y = \sin x$?

    A. $y = 180° + \cos x$ **B.** $y = -\sin x$

    C. $y = \sin(x + 360°)$ **D.** $y = 2\sin x$

> **Habits of Mind**
>
> **Make strategic choices.**
> For Exercises 11 and 12, should you draw a unit circle or a graph? You decide.

15. Below are the graphs of $y = \cos x$ and $y = 0.8$ on the same axes. The least positive value of x that solves $\cos x = 0.8$ is about $37°$. Find the next two values of x that solve the equation, to the nearest degree.

Go Online
Pearsonsuccessnet.com

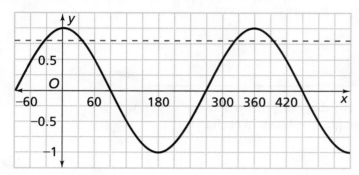

16. Use the unit circle or graphs to illustrate that each identity is true for all θ.

   a. $\sin(180° - \theta) = \sin\theta$ **b.** $\cos(180° - \theta) = -\cos\theta$

   c. $\sin(180° + \theta) = -\sin\theta$ **d.** $\cos(360° - \theta) = \cos\theta$

   e. $\sin\theta = \cos(\theta - 90°)$ **f.** $\cos\theta = -\sin(\theta - 90°)$

17. Sketch the graph of $h(x) = -\sin x$ for at least two periods.

18. Describe the graph of $h(x) = -\sin x$ as a translation of the graph of $g(x) = \sin x$.

19. Sketch an accurate graph of each function.

   a. $j(x) = \cos^2 x - \sin^2 x$ **b.** $r(x) = \cos 2x$

   c. $k(x) = \cos^4 x - \sin^4 x$

> A **period** is a full cycle of the wave: up, down, and back again. It is the smallest piece that you can repeat over and over to produce the entire graph.

Maintain Your Skills

20. The graph below in black shows a portion of the graph of $y = \cos x$. Find the coordinates of each marked point.

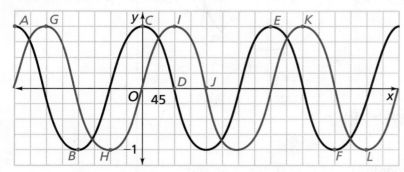

21. The graph above in red shows a portion of the graph of $y = \sin x$. Find the coordinates of each marked point.

Graphing the Tangent Function

You have extended the definition of tangent to $\tan x = \frac{\sin x}{\cos x}$, whenever $\cos x \neq 0$. In other words, tangent is defined for all real numbers except odd multiples of 90°. In this lesson, you will build the graph of $y = \tan x$. First, however, note this interesting way to picture the tangent.

Developing Habits of Mind

Visualize. Why do you call it *tangent?* The diagrams below show a tangent to the unit circle at (1, 0). The angle x is shown in each of the four quadrants.

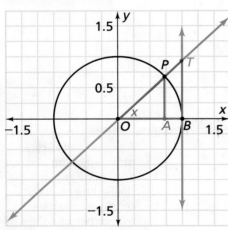
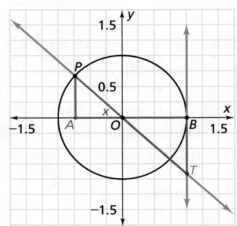

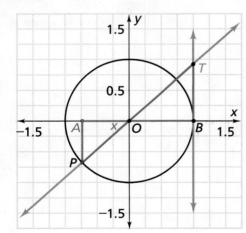
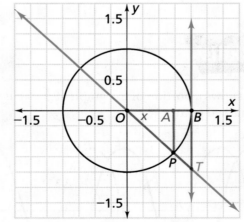

In each case, $\triangle POA \sim \triangle TOB$, so $\frac{TB}{OB} = \frac{PA}{OA}$.

But $OB = 1$, so $TB =$ the length of the tangent $= \frac{PA}{OA}$.

You can use this to show that the coordinates of T are $(1, \tan x)$. So you measure $\tan x$ along the tangent.

For Discussion

1. Finish the argument above by showing that the coordinates of T are $(1, \tan x)$.

2. What happens when the angle is 90° or 270°?

Check the signs.

For You to Do

3. What happens to $\tan x$ for values of x close to, but slightly less than, 90°?

4. What happens to $\tan x$ for values of x close to, but slightly greater than, 90°?

Along with the definition of the tangent function, some other information may help you think about the shape of the graph of $y = \tan x$.

The familiar completed table below shows some values of $\tan \theta$.

θ	$\cos \theta$	$\sin \theta$	$\tan \theta$
0°	1	0	0
30°	$\frac{\sqrt{3}}{2}$	$\frac{1}{2}$	$\frac{1}{\sqrt{3}}$
45°	$\frac{\sqrt{2}}{2}$	$\frac{\sqrt{2}}{2}$	1
60°	$\frac{1}{2}$	$\frac{\sqrt{3}}{2}$	$\sqrt{3}$
90°	0	1	undefined
120°	$-\frac{1}{2}$	$\frac{\sqrt{3}}{2}$	$-\sqrt{3}$
135°	$-\frac{\sqrt{2}}{2}$	$\frac{\sqrt{2}}{2}$	-1
150°	$-\frac{\sqrt{3}}{2}$	$\frac{1}{2}$	$-\frac{1}{\sqrt{3}}$
180°	-1	0	0
210°	$-\frac{\sqrt{3}}{2}$	$-\frac{1}{2}$	$\frac{1}{\sqrt{3}}$
225°	$-\frac{\sqrt{2}}{2}$	$-\frac{\sqrt{2}}{2}$	1
240°	$-\frac{1}{2}$	$-\frac{\sqrt{3}}{2}$	$\sqrt{3}$
270°	0	-1	undefined
300°	$\frac{1}{2}$	$-\frac{\sqrt{3}}{2}$	$-\sqrt{3}$
315°	$\frac{\sqrt{2}}{2}$	$-\frac{\sqrt{2}}{2}$	-1
330°	$\frac{\sqrt{3}}{2}$	$-\frac{1}{2}$	$-\frac{1}{\sqrt{3}}$
360°	1	0	0

Habits of Mind

Detect the key characterisitics. Notice that the tangent function is undefined for some angles. This happens when you try to divide by 0. Look at what happens close to these points of **discontinuity**.

The discussion and graphs in Developing Habits of Mind show that $\tan x$ is the coordinate of a point related to x.

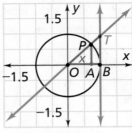
$T(1, \tan x)$

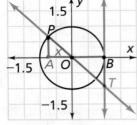
$T(1, \tan x)$

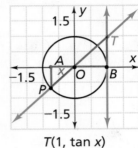
$T(1, \tan x)$

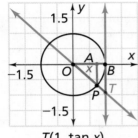
$T(1, \tan x)$

In-Class Experiment

5. Use these ideas or any other information you have to carefully draw the graph of $y = \tan x$. Label the coordinates of all points you plot.

For Discussion

6. Explain why the tangent function is periodic. What is its period?

The periods of the traffic lights are set to manage the flow of traffic.

Exercises *Practicing Habits of Mind*

Check Your Understanding

1. a. Explain why $\cos(180° + \theta) = -\cos\theta$.

    b. Explain why $\sin(180° + \theta) = -\sin\theta$.

2. Use the results from Exercise 1 to explain why $\tan(180° + \theta) = \tan\theta$.

3. Suppose θ is in Quadrant I and $\tan\theta = \frac{2}{3}$.

    a. Draw a right triangle in the unit circle to indicate the location of θ.

    b. Find the exact values of $\sin\theta$ and $\cos\theta$.

4. Suppose θ is in Quadrant I and $\tan\theta = \frac{2}{3}$.

    a. Find the value of $\tan(90° + \theta)$ in terms of $\tan\theta$.

    b. Suppose that ℓ is a line. Show that the slope of ℓ is the tangent of the angle ℓ makes with the positive x-axis.

    c. Show that two lines are perpendicular if and only if their slopes are negative reciprocals.

5. As stated at the beginning of this lesson, cosine is equal to 0 for odd multiples of 90°. Explain why this is true.

6. Find the argument of each complex number to the nearest degree.

    a. $4 + i$ **b.** $(4 + i)^2$

    c. $-1 + 4i$ **d.** $(-1 + 4i)^2$

7. Find each angle to the nearest degree.

    a. θ is in Quadrant I, and $\tan\theta = \frac{1}{4}$.

    b. θ is in Quadrant I, and $\tan\theta = \frac{8}{15}$.

    c. θ is in Quadrant II, and $\tan\theta = -4$.

    d. θ is in Quadrant III, and $\tan\theta = \frac{8}{15}$.

8. a. Calculate $(x + yi)^2$ and write the results in the form $\blacksquare + \blacksquare i$.

    b. Suppose $\tan\theta = \frac{y}{x}$. Find an expression for $\tan 2\theta$, the tangent of twice the given angle.

9. **Write About It** Give two different explanations for why $\tan \theta$ is positive when θ is in Quadrant III but negative when θ is in Quadrant II.

10. **a.** What is the domain of the tangent function? Give a complete answer, not just one for angles from 0° to 360°.

   b. What is the range of the tangent function?

This graph of $y = \tan x$ may be helpful for Exercises 11–13.

11. **a.** Approximate the solutions to the equation $\tan x = 2$.

   b. Approximate the solutions to the equation $\tan x = -2$.

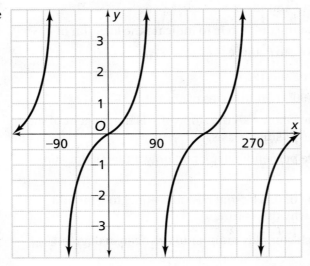

12. Explain how the graph of the tangent function suggests that $\tan (180° + x) = \tan x$.

13. **Take It Further** Use the graph of $y = \tan x$ to sketch an accurate graph of the function $y = \frac{1}{\tan x}$.

Habits of Mind

Experiment. Where is tangent undefined?

14. **Standardized Test Prep** Use the equation $\tan (A + B) = \frac{\tan A + \tan B}{1 - (\tan A)(\tan B)}$. What is the value of $\tan 2\theta$ if $\tan \theta = \frac{1}{2}$?

   A. $\frac{3}{4}$ **B.** 1   **C.** $\frac{4}{3}$ **D.** 2

Maintain Your Skills

15. For each angle θ, calculate $\sin (120° + \theta)$.

   a. $\theta = 0°$ **b.** $\theta = 30°$ **c.** $\theta = 60°$ **d.** $\theta = 90°$

   e. Suppose $\sin (120° + \theta) = A \cos \theta + B \sin \theta$. Find the values of A and B.

The Angle-Sum Identities

If you look back at the results of some of the problems you have solved in this chapter, you can see a thread that has woven its way through many of them. For example, Exercise 16 from Lesson 8.07 and Exercises 1 and 2 from Lesson 8.08 give some interesting identities.

For all x:

- $\sin(180° - x) = \sin x$
- $\cos(180° - x) = -\cos x$
- $\cos(360° - x) = \cos x$
- $\sin x = \cos(x - 90°)$
- $\cos x = -\sin(x - 90°)$
- $\cos(180° + x) = -\cos x$
- $\sin(180° + x) = -\sin x$
- $\tan(180° + x) = \tan x$

All of these identities have the same form. They give an alternate expression for $f(a + b)$, where f is a trigonometric function and a and b are numbers. Usually when you see a collection of identities with the same form, there are a few general identities lurking in the background that tie all the special identities together.

For You to Do

Derman says, "I bet $\sin(\alpha + \beta) = \sin \alpha + \sin \beta$ for all numbers α and β."

1. Help Derman see that this is not an identity.

2. Do any values of α and β make Derman's equation work? If so, find them.

3. Is $\cos(\alpha + \beta) = \cos \alpha + \cos \beta$ an identity for all α and β? Explain.

Can you find a function f such that $f(a + b) = f(a) + f(b)$ for all numbers a and b?

So, Derman's try at a formula for $\sin(\alpha + \beta)$, while simple, is not correct. The purpose of this lesson is to come up with formulas for $\sin(\alpha + \beta)$ and $\cos(\alpha + \beta)$ that are true for all values of α and β. The main result is the following theorem.

Theorem 8.3 Angle-Sum Identities

For all α and β,

- $\cos(\alpha + \beta) = \cos\alpha\cos\beta - \sin\alpha\sin\beta$
- $\sin(\alpha + \beta) = \sin\alpha\cos\beta + \cos\alpha\sin\beta$

Identities that involve functions, such as
$\cos(\alpha + \beta) = \cos\alpha\cos\beta - \sin\alpha\sin\beta$ or
$\log_2 ab = \log_2 a + \log_2 b$,
are functional equations.

Pick a Proof

This time, you will find the formula and build the proof. In this section, there are three sketches of a derivation for the formulas you want. Your job is to pick a method, study it, and write it up in your own words. You will fill in all the missing steps and explain all the statements.

Proof 1 (Rotated Triangles) This derivation uses the unit circle definitions of sine and cosine. Here you will look at sine. (You can look at cosine on your own.) In the graph below, $AD = \sin\alpha$ and $BK = \sin\beta$.

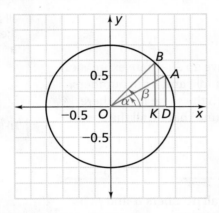

Habits of Mind

Work like a mathematician.
An important part of learning mathematics is learning to read mathematics and to fill in the gaps for yourself.

You want a picture of $\sin(\alpha + \beta)$. To get an $\alpha + \beta$ in the picture, rotate $\triangle OBK$ upward through an angle of α.

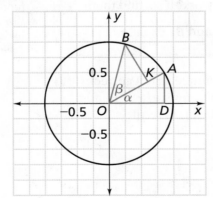

The sine of $\alpha + \beta$ is the y-height of B—the length of the perpendicular from B to the x-axis. Copy the diagram below. Make sure the segments are parallel and perpendicular to the appropriate axes.

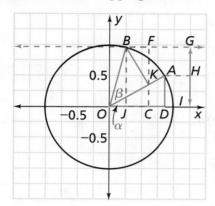

Here is where the work really starts. You need to justify these basic steps.

Step 1 $BJ = \sin(\alpha + \beta)$, $BK = \sin\beta$, and $AD = \sin\alpha$.

Step 2 Also, $KO = \cos\beta$ and $DO = \cos\alpha$.

Step 3 $\sin(\alpha + \beta) = IH + HG$

Step 4 $IH = KC$

Step 5 Now, to get KC, prove that $\triangle KCO \sim \triangle ADO$, so

$$\frac{KC}{KO} = \frac{AD}{AO}$$

Step 6 Use Steps 1 and 2 to conclude that

$$\frac{KC}{\cos\beta} = \frac{\sin\alpha}{1}$$

So, $KC = \sin\alpha\cos\beta$.

Step 7 Next, show $GH = FK$.

Step 8 To get FK, prove that $\triangle FKB \sim \triangle DOA$, so

$$\frac{FK}{BK} = \frac{DO}{AO}$$

Step 9 Use Steps 1 and 2 to conclude that

$$\frac{FK}{\sin\beta} = \frac{\cos\alpha}{1}$$

So $FK = \sin\beta\cos\alpha$.

Step 10 Now comes the grand finale. Combine Steps 3, 6, and 9 to conclude that

$$\sin(\alpha + \beta) = \sin\alpha\cos\beta + \cos\alpha\sin\beta$$

Step 11 To complete your proof, use the same diagram to prove that

$$\cos(\alpha + \beta) = \cos\alpha\cos\beta - \sin\alpha\sin\beta$$

In your description, you might want to explain why the same formulas work if α and β are in other quadrants. You can also show how some of the facts from the beginning of the lesson follow from your formulas.

Proof 2 (Coordinate Geometry) This derivation uses ideas from basic algebra (slope), geometry (coordinates and vectors), and Chapter 4 of this book.

The setup is in the graph below. In this picture of the unit circle, $(r, s) = (\cos \alpha, \sin \alpha)$, and $(a, b) = (\cos \beta, \sin \beta)$.

The segment $\overline{HO}$ is perpendicular to $\overline{AO}$. The coordinates of H are $(-s, r)$.

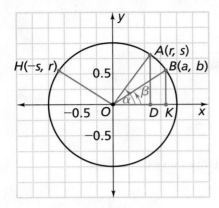

Step 1 Explain why the coordinates of H are $(-s, r)$.

Copy the graph. Now draw in some lines. Pick Q along $\overline{HO}$ such that $QO = BK$. Pick R along $\overline{AO}$ such that $RO = KO$. Then draw a line through Q parallel to $\overline{OA}$ and a line through R parallel to $\overline{OH}$. These segments intersect at S.

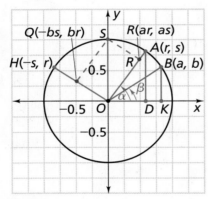

Step 2 Show that $Q = (-bs, br)$ and $R = (ar, as)$.

Step 3 Show that $S = (ar - bs, as + br)$.

Step 4 Show that S is on the circle by showing that it is 1 unit from O.

Step 5 Show that $\triangle OSR \cong \triangle OBK$. Then $m\angle SOR = \beta$ and $m\angle SOK = \alpha + \beta$.

Step 6 So, the coordinates of S are $(\cos (\alpha + b), \sin (\alpha + b))$.

Step 7 Combine steps 3 and 6 to get your formulas.

In your description, you might want to explain why the same formulas work if α and β are in other quadrants. You can also show how some of the facts from the beginning of the lesson follow from your formulas.

> **Remember...**
> You can use the distance formula.

Proof 3 (Complex Numbers) In Chapter 3, you saw a derivation of the fact that when you multiply two complex numbers, the length of the product is the product of the lengths of the factors. The argument (direction) of the product is the sum of the arguments of both factors.

Fact 1 $|zw| = |z| \cdot |w|$ **Fact 2** $\arg zw = \arg z + \arg w$

Step 1 Look back at this derivation in Chapter 3 and summarize it as part of your description.

The basic idea of this proof is to think of points on the unit circle in the complex plane. So, instead of $(\cos \alpha, \sin \alpha)$ and $(\cos \beta, \sin \beta)$, think of $z = \cos \alpha + i \sin \alpha$ and $w = \cos \beta + i \sin \beta$.

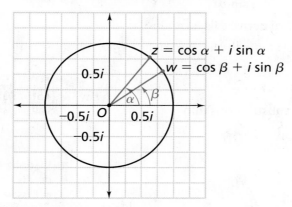

The idea is to write zw in two ways.

Step 2 Show that $|zw| = 1$. Then zw is on the unit circle.

If zw is on the unit circle, it is of the form $\cos x + i \sin x$ for some angle x. But what is the angle? By Fact 2 above, it is the sum of the angles of z and w.

$$zw = \cos(\alpha + \beta) + i \sin(\alpha + \beta)$$

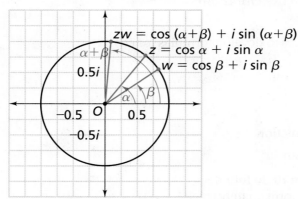

Step 3 Multiply $z = \cos \alpha + i \sin \alpha$ by $w = \cos \beta + i \sin \beta$, using the usual rules for multiplying complex numbers, to show that

$$zw = (\cos \alpha \cos \beta - \sin \alpha \sin \beta) + i(\sin \alpha \cos \beta + \cos \alpha \sin \beta)$$

Step 4 Combine the results from Steps 2 and 3 to get your formulas.

In your description, you might want to explain why the same formulas work if α and β are in other quadrants. You can also show how some of the facts from the beginning of the lesson follow from your formulas.

Exercises *Practicing Habits of Mind*

Check Your Understanding

1. One identity for cosine is
$$\cos(a - b) = \cos a \cos b + \sin a \sin b$$
   a. Use Exercises 11 and 12 from Lesson 8.07 to derive this formula.
   b. What happens in this identity if $a = b$? Evaluate the left and right sides separately.
   c. Use this identity to find an exact value for $\cos 15°$.

2. Prove each identity by making appropriate substitutions into the angle-sum identities.
   a. $\cos 2x = \cos^2 x - \sin^2 x$
   b. $\sin 2x = 2 \sin x \cos x$
   c. $\cos 2x = 2 \cos^2 x - 1$

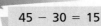

3. From the identity in Exercise 2c, you know $\cos 30° = 2 \cos^2 15° - 1$. Also, $\cos 30° = \frac{\sqrt{3}}{2}$. So if you let $z = \cos 15°$, this equation becomes
$$\frac{\sqrt{3}}{2} = 2z^2 - 1$$
   a. Use this equation to find an exact value for $\cos 15°$.
   b. Compare your answer with the answer to Exercise 1c. Are they equal? Explain.

4. **Take It Further** Use the angle-sum identities to develop formulas for $\cos 3x$ and $\sin 3x$ in terms of $\cos x$ and $\sin x$.

5. Find a complex number z such that
$$z^2 = \frac{1}{2} + i\frac{\sqrt{3}}{2}$$

6. Here is an interesting fact about the sine function.
$$\sin 10° + \sin 50° = \sin 70°$$
   a. Find the values of $\sin 10°$, $\sin 50°$, and $\sin 70°$ to four decimal places. Then verify that the above equation is approximately true.
   b. For some acute angle x, $\sin 20° + \sin 40° = \sin x$. Find x.
   c. For some acute angle x, $\sin 5° + \sin 55° = \sin x$. Find x.

7. **Take It Further** Find a general result from the examples in Exercise 6. Prove it using angle-sum identities.

Habits of Mind

Visualize. Check your results from Exercise 18 in Lesson 8.07.

$45 - 30 = 15$

8. Which expression is equal to $\cos(90° - \theta)$?

    A. $\cos\theta$ **B.** $-\cos\theta$ **C.** $\sin\theta$ **D.** $-\sin\theta$

Go Online
Pearsonsuccessnet.com

9. Derive a formula for $\sin(\alpha - \beta)$ in terms of sine and cosine of α and β.

10. Use the angle-sum identities to prove the following identities.

$$\cos(180° + \theta) = -\cos\theta$$
$$\sin(180° + \theta) = -\sin\theta$$

11. Simplify each expression.

    a. $\sin(360° + x)$ **b.** $\sin(90° + x)$ **c.** $\cos(90° + x)$

    d. $\sin(90° - x)$ **e.** $\sin(180° - x)$

12. Match each function in List A with its functional equation in List B.

    A   B

$$x \mapsto 2^x \qquad\qquad f(a + b) = f(a) + f(b)$$
$$z \mapsto |z| \qquad\qquad f(a + b) = f(a)f(b)$$
$$z \mapsto \arg z \qquad\qquad f(ab) = f(a)f(b)$$
$$x \mapsto 2x \qquad\qquad f(ab) = f(a) + f(b)$$
$$x \mapsto \log_3 x$$

> The matching is not one-to-one.

13. Use the angle-sum identities to find another expression for $\tan(45° + x)$.

14. Use the angle-sum identities to find a rule for $\tan(x + y)$ in terms of $\tan x$ and $\tan y$.

15. **Take It Further** Use your derivation of the formulas in Theorem 8.3, adjusting the diagrams if necessary, to justify the formulas for $\cos(a - b)$ and $\sin(a - b)$.

16. **Standardized Test Prep** If $\cos 2A = \frac{5}{8}$, what is the value of $\dfrac{1}{(\cos^2 A) - (\sin^2 A)}$?

    A. -4.57 **B.** 0.31 **C.** 1.6 **D.** 4

Maintain Your Skills

Go Online
Video Tutor
Pearsonsuccessnet.com

17. Rewrite each expression in the form $A\cos\theta + B\sin\theta$.

    a. $\sin(30° + \theta)$ **b.** $\sin(45° + \theta)$ **c.** $\sin(60° + \theta)$

    d. $\sin(120° + \theta)$ **e.** $\sin(150° + \theta)$

In this investigation, you learned how to use the graphs of trigonometric functions to solve problems and to prove and use trigonometric identities. These questions will help you summarize what you have learned.

1. Sketch a graph of $y = \cos x$ for $90° \leq x \leq 180°$. Label five points on your graph with exact coordinates.

2. For each interval below, state whether $\sin x$ is *positive* or *negative* in the interval and whether its value is increasing or decreasing as x increases through the interval.

   a. $0° < x < 90°$

   b. $90° < x < 180°$

   c. $180° < x < 270°$

   d. $270° < x < 360°$

3. Sketch a picture of the unit circle. Use it to locate and label points with coordinates $(\cos 210°, \sin 210°)$ and $(1, \tan 210°)$.

4. Sketch a graph of $y = \tan x$ that shows two periods of the function.

5. Simplify each expression.

   a. $\sin(270° - x)$

   b. $\cos(180° - x)$

6. What do the graphs of the sine and cosine functions look like?

7. Why does the tangent function have a period of 180°?

8. What is a simple rule for finding the value of $\cos(90° + \theta)$?

Vocabulary

In this investigation, you learned these terms. Make sure you understand what each one means and how to use it.

• discontinuity
• period

These two sine waves have the same period.

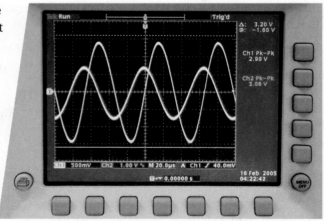

Multiple Choice

1. Which point is on the unit circle $x^2 + y^2 = 1$?

   A. $(-1, 1)$

   B. $\left(\frac{1}{4}, \frac{3}{4}\right)$

   C. $\left(\frac{3}{5}, -\frac{4}{5}\right)$

   D. $\left(\frac{2}{3}, \frac{2}{5}\right)$

2. If $\cos \theta = 0$, then which could NOT be the value of θ?

   A. $90°$

   B. $180°$

   C. $270°$

   D. $450°$

3. Suppose $\sin 80° = a$ and $\cos 80° = b$. Which expression is equal to $\sin 260°$?

   A. $-a$

   B. a

   C. b

   D. $a^2 + b^2$

4. Simplify $\cos^2 60° + \sin^2 60°$.

   A. $\cos^2 120°$

   B. $\sin^2 120°$

   C. 0

   D. 1

5. How many solutions does the equation $\cos x = -0.4$ have for $-90° \leq x \leq 180°$?

   A. 0

   B. 1

   C. 2

   D. 3

Open Response

6. Write each expression as the sine or cosine of an acute angle.

   a. $\sin 145°$

   b. $\cos 260°$

   c. $\cos 740°$

   d. $\sin(-78°)$

7. Write each expression as some multiple factor of the sine or cosine of α.

   a. $\sin(180° + \alpha)$

   b. $\cos(360° - \alpha)$

8. Suppose $\cos \theta = \frac{3}{5}$ and θ is an angle between $0°$ and $360°$.

   a. Find all possible values of $\sin \theta$.

   b. Find all possible values of $\tan \theta$.

   c. Find all possible values of θ to the nearest tenth.

9. Find all solutions of each equation for $0° \leq x \leq 360°$.

   a. $2 \cos x - 1 = 0$

   b. $2 \cos^2 x - 1 = 0$

   c. $2 \sin^2 x - 3 \sin x = 5$

10. Graph $y = \sin x$ for $-90° \leq x \leq 270°$. Label five points on your graph with exact coordinates.

11. If an angle is in Quadrant IV, what do you know about the sign of its sine, cosine, and tangent?

Applications to Triangles

In *Applications to Triangles*, you will use what you know about trigonometric functions to find the side lengths, angle measures, and areas of triangles.

By the end of this investigation, you will be able to answer questions like these.

1. What information do you need to find all of a triangle's side lengths and angle measures?

2. What information do you need to find the area of a triangle?

3. A triangle has sides of length 5, 8, and 10. What is the measure of its largest angle?

You will learn how to

- solve a triangle—find all of its side lengths and angle measures—given enough information

- state and use the Law of Sines

- state and use the Law of Cosines

- state and use Heron's Formula

You will develop these habits and skills:

- Analyze given information to choose a solution strategy.

- Reason logically to understand and produce a mathematical proof.

- Reason by continuity to examine extreme cases.

You can use triangle relationships to measure the width of the glacier.

8.10 Getting Started

You can use trigonometry to get the information you need to find the area of a triangle.

For You to Explore

1. **Write About It** Here is a triangle.

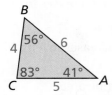

Describe some measurements you could use to find the area of the triangle.

2. In △*ABC*, *AC* = 10, *BC* = 12, and ∠*C* measures 50°.

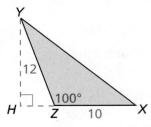

   a. Find the length of the altitude $\overline{BH}$.

   b. Find the area of △*ABC*.

   c. Find the length of side $\overline{AB}$.

3. In △*XYZ*, *XZ* = 10, *YZ* = 12, and ∠*Z* measures 100°.

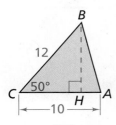

   a. Find the length of the altitude $\overline{YH}$.

   b. Find the area of △*XYZ*.

   c. Find the length of side $\overline{XY}$.

4. In △*PQR*, *PR* = 10, *QR* = 12, and ∠*R* measures 130°.

   a. Draw an accurate diagram of △*PQR*. Use your diagram to answer the next two questions.

   b. Which triangle has a greater perimeter, △*PQR* or △*XYZ* from Exercise 3?

   c. Which triangle has a larger area, △*PQR* or △*XYZ* from Exercise 3?

5. Determine whether each statement is true or false. Justify your answers with a diagram.

   a. The longest side in a triangle is opposite its largest angle.

   b. In △*ABC*, if $\overline{AC}$ and $\overline{BC}$ stay the same length but angle *C* increases in size, side $\overline{AB}$ increases in length.

   c. In △*ABC*, if $\overline{AC}$ and $\overline{BC}$ stay the same length but $\overline{AB}$ increases in length, the area of △*ABC* increases.

   d. Two triangles with the same perimeter must have the same area.

6. **Take It Further** Suppose two triangles have the same perimeter and the same area. Must the triangles be congruent? Justify your answer.

> **Remember...**
>
> The perimeter of a polygon is the sum of its side lengths.

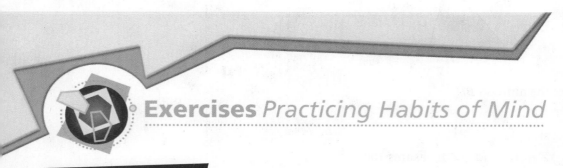

Exercises Practicing Habits of Mind

On Your Own

7. Suppose sin *θ* = sin 50° and *θ* is between 0° and 360°. What are the possible values of *θ*?

8. Suppose cos *θ* = cos 50° and *θ* is between 0° and 360°. What are the possible values of *θ*?

9. Which statement is true?

   A. cos 70° = cos 110°   **B.** sin 70° = sin 110°

   C. tan 70° = tan 110°   **D.** sin 70° = −sin 110°

10. Jan lives 5 miles away from Paul. Paul lives 8 miles away from Dwayne.

    a. What is the shortest possible distance between Jan's and Dwayne's houses? Draw a diagram to represent this situation.

    b. What is the longest possible distance between Jan's and Dwayne's houses? Draw a diagram to represent this situation.

    c. Is it possible for the distance between Jan's and Dwayne's houses to be 10 miles? If so, draw a diagram to represent the situation.

11. Consider the labeled diagram below.

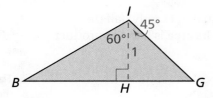

    a. Find all missing lengths.

    b. Use any method to find the area of $\triangle BIG$.

12. The diagram below gives variables for the side lengths of $\triangle ABC$.

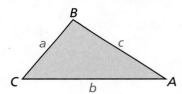

Find at least two different expressions for the area of $\triangle ABC$ in terms of its side lengths and angle measures.

Maintain Your Skills

13. For each set of three lengths, determine whether or not they can be the side lengths of a triangle.

    a. 8, 6, 10   **b.** 8, 6, 12   **c.** 8, 6, 14

    d. 8, 6, 16   **e.** 8, 6, 9   **f.** 8, 6, 5

    g. 8, 6, 3   **h.** 8, 6, 2   **i.** 8, 6, 1

8.11 The Area of a Triangle

In geometry, you learned the area formulas for many shapes, including triangles. For example, a right triangle is half of a rectangle.

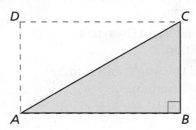

The area of this triangle is $A = \frac{1}{2}bh$, since it is equal to exactly half the rectangle's area. The same applies to any triangle. Its area is half the product of its base and height.

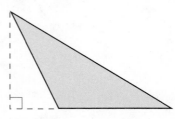

Remember...

The height is always measured perpendicular to the base. You can use any side of the triangle as the base.

You can often use trigonometry to find the height of a triangle when it is unknown.

Example

Problem In $\triangle BCU$, $BC = 10$, $UC = 12$, and $\angle C$ measures 50°. Find an expression for the exact area of this triangle. Then approximate the area to two decimal places.

Solution First, sketch the triangle. Here is an accurate sketch of $\triangle BCU$, including the altitude drawn to side $\overline{UC}$.

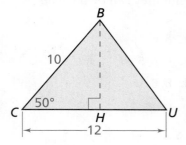

The area is $A = \frac{1}{2}bh$, and the base is 12. So $A = \frac{1}{2} \cdot 12 \cdot h$.

Find h by recognizing the right triangle BCH. The missing side h is opposite the 50° angle. You know the length of the hypotenuse. Use the sine ratio.

$$\sin 50° = \frac{h}{10}$$

The exact value of h is $10 \sin 50°$. The area is $\frac{1}{2} \cdot 12 \cdot 10 \sin 50°$. This simplifies to $A = 60 \sin 50°$, which is approximately 45.96.

For You to Do

1. Follow the same process as in the Example, but drop the altitude to the side of length 10. What happens?

You can generalize the process in the Example. Consider $\triangle ABC$ with no numbered sides.

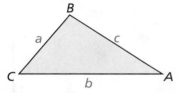

Drop the altitude to the side of length b. One expression for the altitude's length is $a \sin C$. Then the area of the triangle is $\frac{1}{2} ab \sin C$. Since a triangle has three altitudes, there are three possible area formulas.

Theorem 8.4 Area of a Triangle

For $\triangle ABC$ with $AB = c$, $AC = b$, and $BC = a$, the area of the triangle is equal to the expressions below.

$$\frac{1}{2} ab \sin C = \frac{1}{2} bc \sin A = \frac{1}{2} ac \sin B$$

What measurements can you use to calculate the area of this triangular lot?

Visualize. Angle *C* is acute in all the diagrams used to show that the area is $\frac{1}{2}ab \sin C$. But $\angle C$ might not be acute. It could be right or obtuse. What is the area formula then?

If $\angle C$ is a right angle, the triangle looks like this.

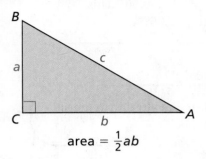

area $= \frac{1}{2}ab$

Since this is a right triangle, the area is $\frac{1}{2}ab$. But $\sin 90° = 1$, so this is also equal to $\frac{1}{2}ab \sin C$. The formula covers the case when $\angle C$ is a right angle.

If $\angle C$ is obtuse, the triangle looks like this.

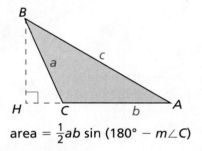

area $= \frac{1}{2}ab \sin (180° - m\angle C)$

To find the altitude, you use the sine of $\angle BCH$. This angle is the supplement of $\angle ACB$. If $\angle ACB$ measures θ, $\angle BCH$ measures $(180° - \theta)$. Then the altitude is $a \sin (180° - \theta)$.

Earlier, however, you learned that $\sin (180° - \theta) = \sin \theta$. So, the sine of $\angle ACB$ is the same as the sine of $\angle BCH$. The area is $\frac{1}{2}ab \sin C$, even for obtuse triangles.

Remember...

See, for example, Exercise 11 from Lesson 8.09.

The formula for the area of the triangle leads to an elegant proof of the formula for $\sin (a + b)$. Consider this diagram.

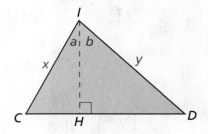

Now, what is the area of $\triangle CID$? There are two ways to find it.

- First, look at $\triangle CID$ as a whole. The area is $\frac{1}{2} xy \sin(a + b)$.
- Second, consider $\triangle CIH$ and $\triangle DIH$ separately. Within $\triangle CIH$, $CH = x \sin a$ and $IH = y \cos b$. The area of $\triangle CIH$ is $\frac{1}{2}(x \sin a)(y \cos b) = \frac{1}{2} xy \sin a \cos b$. Similarly, the area of $\triangle DIH$ is $\frac{1}{2} xy \cos a \sin b$.

The sum of the areas of the two smaller triangles is equal to the area of the larger triangle.

$$\frac{1}{2} xy \sin(a + b) = \frac{1}{2} xy \sin a \cos b + \frac{1}{2} xy \cos a \sin b$$

$$\frac{1}{2} xy \sin(a + b) = \frac{1}{2} xy (\sin a \cos b + xy \cos a \sin b)$$

$$\sin(a + b) = \sin a \cos b + \cos a \sin b$$

This expression for $\sin(a + b)$ is the one you found in Investigation 8B. All the proof uses is the rule for the area of a triangle and the definitions of sine and cosine for right triangles.

For Discussion

2. When finding the area of $\triangle CIH$, why did you write it as $y \cos b$ and not $x \cos a$? Both are equal, so what purpose is there in using one instead of the other?

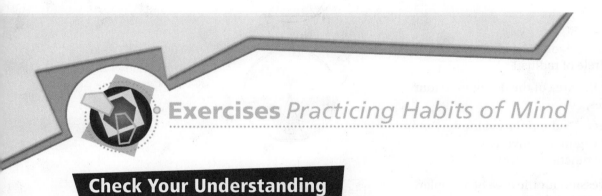

Exercises *Practicing Habits of Mind*

Check Your Understanding

1. Use the diagram of $\triangle EFG$ below.

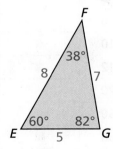

Find at least two different ways to calculate the area of $\triangle EFG$.

2. Use the diagram from Exercise 11 in Lesson 8.10.

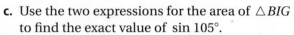

   a. Use the formula $A = \frac{1}{2}bh$ to find the exact area of $\triangle BIG$.

   b. Use the formula $A = \frac{1}{2}ab \sin C$ along with the measure of angle I to write another expression for the area of $\triangle BIG$.

   c. Use the two expressions for the area of $\triangle BIG$ to find the exact value of $\sin 105°$.

3. Find the area of a regular pentagon inscribed in a circle of radius 1.

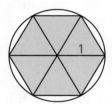

4. Find the exact area and perimeter of a regular hexagon inscribed in a circle of radius 1.

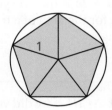

5. Here is a regular decagon (10-sided figure) inscribed in a circle of radius 1.

   a. Approximate the area of the decagon to four decimal places.

   b. Take It Further Find an exact value for the area of the decagon that involves no trigonometric functions.

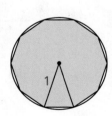

6. a. Write an expression for the area of a regular n-gon (n-sided figure) inscribed in a circle of radius 1.

   b. Copy and complete this table for the function $A(n)$, the area of the n-gon. Find all values to four decimal places.

Sides, n	Area, $A(n)$
4	2
5	▦
6	▦
10	▦
12	▦
20	▦
30	▦
50	▦
100	▦
360	▦

7. Write About It Use your completed table from Exercise 6. Describe what happens to the area of the *n*-gons as the number of sides increases. Explain why this happens.

On Your Own

8. In $\triangle MIB$, $MI = 12$ and $IB = 10$. Find the maximum possible area for this triangle.

9. Which statement is true?

   A. $\cos 20° = \cos 70°$ **B.** $\cos 20° = \cos^2 70°$

   C. $\cos 20° = \sin^2 70°$ **D.** $\cos 20° = \sin 70°$

10. Use this diagram of an isosceles triangle with legs of length 1.

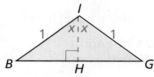

   a. Find the area of $\triangle BIG$ using the rule $A = \frac{1}{2}bh$.

   b. Find the area of $\triangle BIG$ using $\angle I$.

   c. Write a formula for $\sin 2x$ by using the two expressions for the area of $\triangle BIG$.

> You will have to find the base and height in terms of *x* first.

11. a. Can one side of a triangle be ten times as long as each of the other sides? Explain.

   b. Can one angle in a triangle be ten times as large as each of the other angles?

12. Use this diagram of $\triangle ONE$.

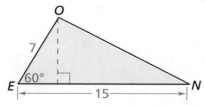

   a. Explain why there can be only one such $\triangle ONE$.

   b. Find the length of side $\overline{ON}$.

> **Habits of Mind**
>
> **Establish a process.** Keep track of your steps!

13. Use what you have learned in this lesson to find area formulas for each figure.

   a. a parallelogram   **b.** a rhombus

> **Remember...**
>
> A rhombus is a parallelogram with all four sides equal in length.

14. What's Wrong Here? Derman thinks he has found two different formulas for the area of a parallelogram.

Go Online
Pearsonsuccessnet.com

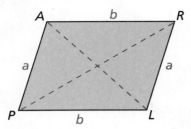

Derman says, "If I cut along one diagonal, I get that the area is $ab \sin P$, but if I cut along the other diagonal, I get that the area is $ab \sin L$. That doesn't seem possible—the areas should be the same. Angle L looks larger than angle P, so isn't $\sin L$ greater than $\sin P$?"

What is wrong with Derman's reasoning? Are both area formulas correct?

15. A rhombus has perimeter 36. What is the largest possible area it could have?

16. Standardized Test Prep A triangle has a side that is 8 cm long and a side that is 12 cm long. The included angle measures 65°. To the nearest hundredth, what is the area of the triangle?

A. 24 cm²   **B.** 40.57 cm²   **C.** 43.50 cm²   **D.** 81.14 cm²

Maintain Your Skills

17. Each set of three lengths forms a triangle. Determine whether the triangle is acute, right, or obtuse.

    a. 8, 6, 10   **b.** 8, 6, 12   **c.** 8, 6, 13   **d.** 8, 6, 9

    e. 8, 6, 8   **f.** 8, 6, 7   **g.** 8, 6, 6   **h.** 8, 6, 5

8.12 The Law of Sines

In the last lesson, you learned to find the area of a triangle using the rule $A = \frac{1}{2}ab \sin C$, where a and b are two side lengths and C is the angle between those sides. This lesson introduces the Law of Sines, which you can prove using that formula. The Law of Sines relates the side lengths in a triangle to their corresponding angle measures.

Remember...

You call the angle between two given sides the included angle. Similarly, you call the side between two given angles the included side.

For Discussion

1. If one angle in a triangle is twice as large as another, is the corresponding side twice as long? Give an example to justify your answer.

2. Can one side of a triangle be ten times as long as each of the other sides? Can one angle in a triangle be ten times as large as each of the other angles? Explain.

There is a correspondence between sides and angles in a triangle, but not a direct one. For example, it is possible for one angle in a triangle to be many times larger than both of the other angles (say, a triangle with angles 10°, 15°, and 165°). But it is not possible for one side of a triangle to be many times larger than both other sides. Still, the longest side in a triangle is opposite the largest angle, so there is a relationship.

That relationship is the **Law of Sines.**

Theorem 8.5 Law of Sines

Given $\triangle ABC$ with corresponding side lengths a, b, and c,

$$\frac{a}{\sin A} = \frac{b}{\sin B} = \frac{c}{\sin C}$$

Proof Consider $\triangle ABC$.

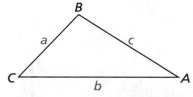

You can write the area of this triangle in three different ways. Choose two.

$$\text{area} = \frac{1}{2}ac \sin B \quad \text{and} \quad \text{area} = \frac{1}{2}bc \sin A$$

You can write the Law of Sines with the numerators and denominators switched. $\frac{\sin A}{a} = \frac{\sin B}{b} = \frac{\sin C}{c}$ It is true in either form. Work through Exercise 6 to see why you might want to use the form with $\frac{c}{\sin C}$.

A triangle cannot have two different areas, so these expressions must be equal.

$$\tfrac{1}{2}\,ac \sin B = \tfrac{1}{2}\,bc \sin A$$

You can cancel the factors of $\tfrac{1}{2}$ and c from each side. You know $c \neq 0$ since it is a side length.

$$a \sin B = b \sin A$$

$$\frac{a}{\sin A} = \frac{b}{\sin B}$$

Use the starting point $\tfrac{1}{2}\,ac \sin B = \tfrac{1}{2}\,ab \sin C$ to obtain the relationship $\frac{b}{\sin B} = \frac{c}{\sin C}$. This completes the proof.

Developing Habits of Mind

Look for relationships. The Law of Sines is useful whenever you know a side and its opposite angle measure. For one thing, it puts a limit on how long the other sides in the triangle can be. Suppose you know $a = 10$ and $\angle A$ measures $50°$. Then

$$\frac{a}{\sin A} \approx 13.05$$

The Law of Sines says that this also equals $\frac{b}{\sin B}$. Since $\sin B$ cannot be greater than 1, b cannot be greater than 13.05.

You can rewrite the proportions in the Law of Sines to discover more facts. Here is one way.

$$\frac{a}{b} = \frac{\sin A}{\sin B}$$

This proportion answers the For Discussion problem. If one side of a triangle is twice as long as another side, the sine of the angle opposite the longer side is twice as great.

You can see this in a 30-60-90 right triangle.

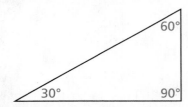

> Note that this does not say that the angle itself is twice as large.

The side opposite the right angle is twice as long as the side opposite the $30°$ angle. The Law of Sines confirms this: $\sin 90° = 1$ and $\sin 30° = \tfrac{1}{2}$.

Example

Problem Find all remaining side lengths and angle measures in this triangle.

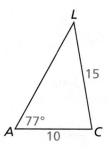

△*LAC* is not to scale. It could be acute, right, or obtuse.

Solution You know the measure of ∠*A* and the length of its opposite side. Use the Law of Sines.

$$\frac{a}{\sin A} = \frac{\ell}{\sin L} = \frac{c}{\sin C}$$

The variables *a*, *ℓ*, and *c* are the side lengths opposite angles *A*, *L*, and *C*. Fill in the known information.

$$\frac{15}{\sin 77°} = \frac{10}{\sin L} = \frac{c}{\sin C}$$

Use the first two equal expressions and solve for sin *L*.

$$\sin L = \frac{10 \sin 77°}{15} \approx 0.6496$$

A calculator gives $\sin^{-1}(0.6496)$ as approximately 40.5°. Note, though, that this is not the only angle with sine about 0.6496. The other angle is 180° − 40.5° = 139.5°.

So, are there two possible measures of ∠*L*? No, the 139.5° angle is impossible, since there is a 77° angle in the triangle. The measure of ∠*L* must be less than 103°.

That means ∠*L* measures 40.5°, and ∠*C* measures 62.5°.

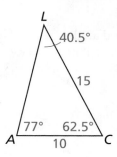

Then use the Law of Sines again to find *c*.

$$\frac{15}{\sin 77°} = \frac{c}{\sin 62.5°}$$

This gives *c* ≈ 13.66. Now you know all the side lengths and angle measures.

Habits of Mind

Check your work. This is an important check. Note that there is no other reason to reject the second angle. If both angles are possible, so be it. There would then be two cases to look at for the rest of the solution.

Note that you need at least three pieces of information about a triangle before you can use the Law of Sines to solve for the rest. And not all groups of three pieces will do. For example, if you only know the three side lengths, you have all the numerators and none of the denominators. So, the Law of Sines helps in solving triangles, but sometimes you need a different method. You will learn another method in the next lesson.

For You to Do

3. Use the Law of Sines to prove the Hinge Theorem: In a triangle, the longest side is opposite the largest angle and the shortest side is opposite the smallest angle.

> To *solve a triangle* just means to find its side lengths and angle measures. The example's direction line could have been "Solve $\triangle ALC$."

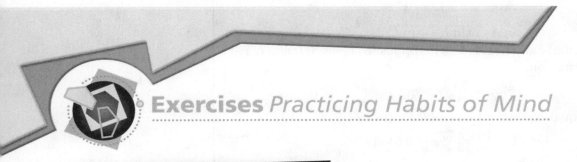

Exercises *Practicing Habits of Mind*

Check Your Understanding

Figures of triangles in this lesson are not to scale. Do not assume anything about the size of angles or the relative lengths of the sides of a triangle.

1. In $\triangle MIB$, $MI = 12$. This side is opposite a 30° angle. Find the maximum possible side length that this triangle can have.

For Exercises 2 and 3, find all the remaining side lengths and angle measures of the triangle. Round answers to one decimal place if necessary.

2.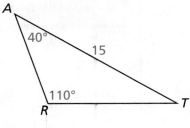

3.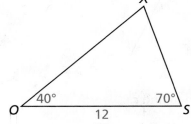

> How can you apply the Law of Sines in Exercise 3? You need a side and an opposite angle.

4. Use the triangle below. Find the two possible measures of $\angle K$. Explain why there are two possible answers.

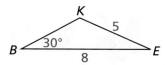

5. Write About It What do Exercises 2, 3, and 4 suggest about triangle congruence?

6. You can draw a circle through any three noncollinear points. Draw a circle through the vertices of a triangle such as $\triangle ABC$ below. Draw diameter $\overline{AD}$. Connect points B and D.

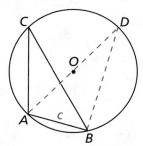

> You can state the result of Exercise 6 as part of the Law of Sines: In a triangle, the ratio of any side to the sine of its opposite angle is the diameter of a circle circumscribing the triangle.

  a. Why is $\angle ABD$ a right angle?

  b. Explain why $\angle C$ and $\angle D$ are congruent.

  c. Explain why $\sin C = \sin D$.

  d. Show that the diameter $\overline{AD}$ has length $\dfrac{c}{\sin C}$.

7. Copy the diagram below. Drop an altitude from any vertex of the triangle. Find two expressions for the length of the altitude. Use these expressions to prove the Law of Sines.

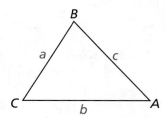

8. Use the diagram of $\triangle TWO$ below. Find the length of $\overline{TW}$. Keep track of your steps!

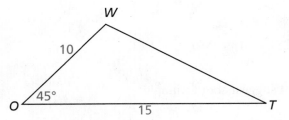

9. **Take It Further** Use the diagram of $\triangle ABC$ below. Find the length of side $\overline{AB}$ in terms of a, b, and $\angle C$.

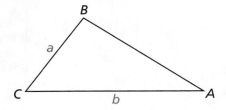

On Your Own

10. Verify that the Law of Sines is valid for a 30-60-90 right triangle.

11. Verify that the Law of Sines is valid for a 45-45-90 right triangle.

Go Online
Pearsonsuccessnet.com

12. In $\triangle ABC$, $AB = 7$, $AC = 15$, and $\angle A$ measures 60°. What happens if you try to use the Law of Sines to find the other sides and angles in this triangle?

13. **Standardized Test Prep** You are given $\triangle ABC$ with $AB = 14$ cm, $AC = 10$ cm, and $m\angle C = 110°$. What is the length of $\overline{BC}$?

A. 4.82 cm

B. 5.10 cm

C. 6.96 cm

D. 7.38 cm

The case in which you know two side lengths and a nonincluded angle measure of a triangle is the "ambiguous case." Exercises 14–18 explore this situation.

14. In △ABC, AB = 12, AC = 10, and ∠B measures 40°.

    a. According to the Law of Sines, what is the value of sin C to three decimal places?

    b. Find all possible measures of ∠C to the nearest degree.

    c. Find all possible measures of ∠A and all possible lengths of side $\overline{BC}$.

15. In △ABC, AB = 12, AC = 10, and ∠C measures 40°.

    a. According to the Law of Sines, what is the value of sin B to three decimal places?

    b. Find all possible measures of ∠B to the nearest degree.

    c. Find all possible measures of ∠A and all possible lengths of side $\overline{BC}$.

16. In △ABC, AB = 12, AC = 10, and ∠B measures 70°.

    a. According to the Law of Sines, what is the value of sin C to three decimal places?

    b. Find all possible measures of ∠C to the nearest degree.

    c. Find all possible measures of ∠A and all possible lengths of side $\overline{BC}$.

17. Write About It Tyler says that if the given angle in an ambiguous-case problem is obtuse, then there is exactly one solution. Do you agree? Explain.

18. Take It Further For the information given in an ambiguous-case problem, there can be 0, 1, or 2 possible triangles. Determine the conditions on the sides and angle that produce these possible outcomes.

Maintain Your Skills

19. For each set of measurements for △ABC, find the remaining side lengths and angle measures.

    a. BC = 10, ∠A measures 30°, and ∠B measures 45°.

    b. BC = 20, ∠A measures 30°, and ∠B measures 45°.

    c. AC = 10, ∠A measures 30°, and ∠B measures 45°.

    d. AC = 10, ∠A measures 30°, and ∠B measures 60°.

    e. AC = 10, ∠A measures 30°, and ∠B measures 120°.

Go Online
Video Tutor
Pearsonsuccessnet.com

In the last lesson, you learned the Law of Sines. It relates the side lengths of a triangle to their corresponding angle measures. In this lesson, you will learn the **Law of Cosines.** If you know two side lengths of a triangle and the measure of their included angle, the Law of Cosines can help you find the length of the third side. Alternatively, if you know three side lengths of a triangle, you can use the Law of Cosines to figure out the measure of any angle in the triangle.

Minds in Action   episode 38

Derman and Sasha are looking at △ONE.

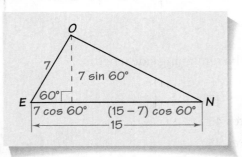

Sasha   We need to find the length of side $\overline{ON}$.

Derman Can't we just use that $a^2 + b^2 = c^2$ theorem? We know the two sides, so let's just find the length of the third. $(ON)^2 = 7^2 + 15^2$. So ON is about 16.55.

Sasha   The Pythagorean Theorem only works for right triangles!

Derman Oh, right. Well, there are two right triangles in our drawing. Too bad we don't know the height of the dotted line.

Sasha   We can figure that out. We can at least figure out the length of the legs of each triangle, using sine and cosine.

> What right triangles is Derman talking about?

Derman Now we can use the Pythagorean Theorem to find ON. It looks messy, though.

They write down their steps.

$$(ON)^2 = (7 \sin 60°)^2 + (15 - 7 \cos 60°)^2$$
$$= 49 \sin^2 60° + 225 - 2 \cdot 15 \cdot 7 \cos 60° + 49 \cos^2 60°$$

Sasha   I wonder if we can simplify this a bit.

Derman   Hey. There's 49 times sine squared, and 49 times cosine squared, and they're even the same angle. I'm going to combine those and see what happens.

$$(ON)^2 = 49\ (\sin^2 60° + \cos^2 60°) + 225 - 210 \cos 60°$$

$$= 49 + 225 - 210 \cos 60°$$

$$= 274 - 210\left(\frac{1}{2}\right)$$

$$= 169$$

Derman   Wow! $ON = 13$.

Sasha   Very smooth.

For You to Do

1. Find the length of side $\overline{TW}$ in the triangle below.

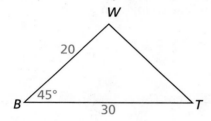

Sasha and Derman found the following equation.

$$c^2 = 49 + 225 - 210 \cos 60°$$

They can rewrite the equation this way.

$$(ON)^2 = 7^2 + 15^2 - 2 \times 7 \times 15 \cos 60°$$

In fact, a similar relationship holds for any triangle with sides of length *a*, *b*, and *c*.

Theorem 8.6 *The Law of Cosines*

Given △*ABC* with corresponding side lengths *a*, *b*, and *c*,

$$c^2 = a^2 + b^2 - 2\,ab \cos C$$

The following proof of the Law of Cosines closely follows what Derman and Sasha did in the dialog. There are three possible situations, depending on whether ∠*C* is acute, right, or obtuse.

Proof Case 1: Suppose $\angle C$ is an acute angle. Let $\triangle ABC$ be the triangle below.

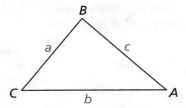

As Sasha did for her triangle, you can write down much more information about this triangle.

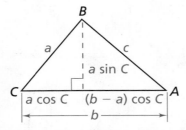

Now find c^2 by using the Pythagorean Theorem and the triangle on the right.

$$
\begin{aligned}
c^2 &= (a \sin C)^2 + (b - a \cos C)^2 \\
&= a^2 \sin^2 C + b^2 - 2\,ab \cos C + a^2 \cos^2 C \\
&= a^2 (\sin^2 C + \cos^2 C) + b^2 - 2\,ab \cos C \\
&= a^2 + b^2 - 2\,ab \cos C
\end{aligned}
$$

Case 2: Suppose $\angle C$ is a right angle. Let $\triangle ABC$ be the triangle below.

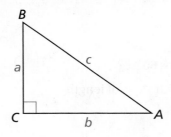

Since C is a right angle, by the Pythagorean Theorem $c^2 = a^2 + b^2$. Also, $\cos C = 0$. So, $c^2 = a^2 + b^2 + (\text{anything}) \cos C$.

In particular, $c^2 = a^2 + b^2 - 2\,ab \cos C$ is true.

Case 3: Suppose $\angle C$ is an obtuse angle. Let $\triangle ABC$ be the triangle below.

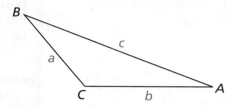

You can extend side $\overline{AC}$ to meet the altitude.

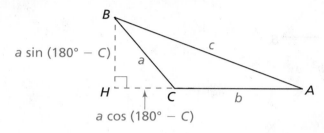

You know that $\sin(180° - C) = \sin C$ and $\cos(180° - C) = -\cos C$. So, you can relabel the diagram to use $\angle C$.

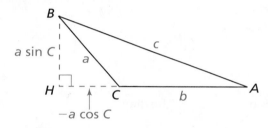

Why is the length of the altitude $a \sin(180° - C)$? Why does $CH = a \cos(180° - C)$?

Note that the length $-a \cos C$ is positive, since $\cos C$ is negative. Use the Pythagorean Theorem again. The length along the base is the sum of the two lengths b and $-a \cos C$.

$$c^2 = (a \sin C)^2 + (b + (-a \cos C))^2$$
$$= a^2 \sin^2 C + b^2 - 2ab \cos C + a^2 \cos^2 C$$
$$= a^2 (\sin^2 C + \cos^2 C) + b^2 - 2ab \cos C$$
$$= a^2 + b^2 - 2ab \cos C$$

Separating a proof into cases is similar to sorting your laundry into whites and colors.

The Law of Cosines looks very much like the Pythagorean Theorem. The only difference is the little correction of $-2ab \cos C$. This suggests that you can find a different proof using only ideas from geometry.

Proof Suppose you have $\triangle ABC$.

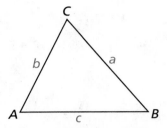

You can draw in squares with areas a^2, b^2, and c^2.

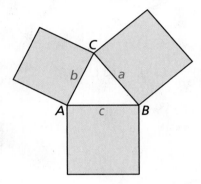

You want to find a way to describe c^2 in terms of a^2 and b^2. The diagram below shows the three altitudes of the triangle.

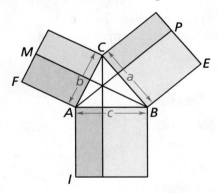

The area of each green rectangle is $ab \cos C$.

If you can show the purple rectangles have the same area and the yellow rectangles have the same area, then

$$c^2 = \text{purple} + \text{yellow} = b^2 - \text{green} + a^2 - \text{green}$$

In other words,

$$c^2 = a^2 + b^2 - 2ab \cos C$$

To show that the purple rectangles have the same area, you have to be a little tricky. Consider the diagram below.

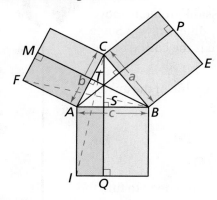

Triangles *CAI* and *FAB* are congruent.

The area of rectangle *AIQS* is twice the area of △*CAI*. The area of rectangle *FAMT* is twice the area of △*FAB*.

So rectangles *AIQS* and *FAMT* have the same area.

You can use a similar argument to show that the yellow rectangles have the same area. This proves the result.

Figure out why △*CAI* ≅ △*FAB*.

For Discussion

2. Use the Law of Cosines to find all the angle measures of this triangle.

Developing Habits of Mind

Consider more than one strategy. The For Discussion problem above required you to use the Law of Cosines in a slightly different way. Since you know the three side lengths, the only unknown is the cosine of the given angle.

You can rewrite the Law of Cosines to solve for the cosine of the angle.

$$c^2 = a^2 + b^2 - 2ab\cos C$$

$$2ab\cos C = a^2 + b^2 - c^2$$

$$\cos C = \frac{a^2 + b^2 - c^2}{2ab}$$

Use this form when you know the three side lengths and need to find the angle measure. You get the cosine of the angle. The $\cos^{-1}$ function on a calculator can give you the angle's approximate measure.

You may recall that the Law of Sines produces two possible angle measures when you know the sine. If $\sin\theta = 0.8$, the angle may be $53°$ or $127°$. This does not happen with the Law of Cosines. If $\cos\theta = 0.8$, the angle is either $37°$ or $323°$. An angle of $323°$ is impossible in a triangle!

This means that if you are faced with the option of using either the Law of Sines or the Law of Cosines, you might consider using the Law of Cosines. Its answers are always unique.

For You to Do

3. Find the missing side length and angle measures in the triangle below.

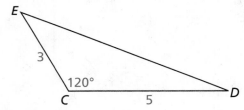

4. Find the measures of all three angles in the triangle below.

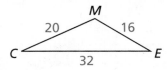

For Discussion

5. You have learned that if you know all three side lengths of a triangle, you can figure out the angle measures. If you have all three angle measures, can you figure out the side lengths? Explain.

Check Your Understanding

1. In $\triangle ABC$, $BC = a$ and $AC = b$. Write an expression for the length of side $\overline{AB}$ in terms of a, b, and the cosine of $\angle C$.

2. For $\triangle ABC$ from Exercise 1, use the properties of the cosine function to find upper and lower bounds on the length of side $\overline{AB}$. Your answers should be expressed in terms of a and b.

> It is possible to find expressions here that do not involve a square root. Try to figure it out!

3. In $\triangle OBT$, $OB = 3$, $BT = 4$, and $\angle B$ is obtuse. What can you say about the length of side $\overline{OT}$?

4. In $\triangle ACU$, $AC = 3$, $CU = 4$, and $\angle C$ is acute. What can you say about the length of side $\overline{AU}$?

5. **Take It Further** $\triangle FMB$ is acute, with $FM = 12$ and $MB = 5$. Find the range of possible lengths for side $\overline{FB}$.

6. **Write About It** There are six possible combinations of three pieces of information about a triangle. For each combination below, explain how you can find the remaining side lengths and angle measures, or explain why you cannot find them.

   a. SSS (three side lengths)

   b. SAS (two side lengths and the measure of the included angle)

   c. SSA (two side lengths and the measure of a nonincluded angle)

   d. AAS (two angle measures and the length of a nonincluded side)

   e. ASA (two angle measures and the length of the included side)

   f. AAA (three angle measures)

7. A triangle has side lengths 13, 14, and 15.

   a. Find the cosine of each angle in this triangle.

   b. Which is the largest angle, the one with the greatest cosine or the one with the least cosine?

   c. Suppose you draw an altitude to the side of length 14. Find the length of the altitude.

   d. What is the area of this triangle?

8. Suppose all the side lengths of $\triangle ABC$ are integers.

   a. Explain why $\cos C$ must be rational.

   b. **Take It Further** Show that you can write an expression for the area of $\triangle ABC$ in the form $x\sqrt{y}$, where x is rational and y is an integer.

Go ⊙nline
Pearsonsuccessnet.com

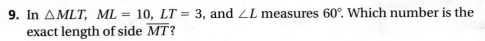

9. In $\triangle MLT$, $ML = 10$, $LT = 3$, and $\angle L$ measures 60°. Which number is the exact length of side $\overline{MT}$?

 A. 7 **B.** $\sqrt{79}$ **C.** $\sqrt{139}$ **D.** 13

10. In $\triangle ABC$, $BC = 10$ and $AC = 3$. Write an expression for the length of side $\overline{AB}$ in terms of the cosine of $\angle C$.

11. For $\triangle ABC$ from Exercise 10, use the properties of the cosine function. Find the upper and lower bounds of the length of side $\overline{AB}$.

12. A triangle has sides of length 12, 15, and 10. Find the measure of the smallest angle in the triangle to the nearest degree.

13. In $\triangle FOM$, $FO = 12$, $OM = 20$, and $\angle O$ measures 60°.

 a. Explain why $\angle O$ cannot be the smallest angle in the triangle.

 b. Use the Law of Cosines and the Law of Sines to find the measure of the smallest angle in the triangle to the nearest degree.

14. Let θ be an angle between 0° and 180°. Determine whether each statement is true or false.

 a. $\cos \theta > 0$ **b.** $\sin \theta > 0$

 c. $\sin^2 \theta = 1 + \cos^2 \theta$ **d.** $\sin \theta = \sqrt{1 - \cos^2 \theta}$

15. A triangle has side lengths 7, 10, and 12.

 a. Find the angles in the triangle to the nearest degree.

 b. Use the diagram at the right. Find x and h.

 c. Find the area of the triangle.

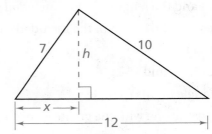

16. **Take It Further** The cosines of two angles of a triangle are $\frac{4}{5}$ and $\frac{5}{13}$. Find the exact cosine of the third angle.

17. **Standardized Test Prep** What is the measure of the smallest angle in a triangle with side lengths 5, 7, and 8 inches?

 A. 17.19° **B.** 34.38° **C.** 38.21° **D.** 60.00°

18. The diagram below shows $\triangle ABC$ with altitude $\overline{CD}$.

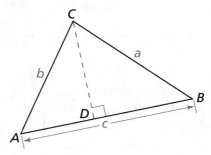

a. Show that $b \cos A + a \cos B = c$.

b. Use a similar diagram to show that $c \cos A + a \cos C = b$.

c. Show that $c \cos B + b \cos C = a$.

19. Take It Further Solve the system of equations below for $\begin{pmatrix} \cos A \\ \cos B \\ \cos C \end{pmatrix}$.

$$\begin{pmatrix} b & a & 0 \\ c & 0 & a \\ 0 & c & b \end{pmatrix} \begin{pmatrix} \cos A \\ \cos B \\ \cos C \end{pmatrix} = \begin{pmatrix} c \\ b \\ a \end{pmatrix}$$

This gives you another proof of the Law of Cosines.

This system comes from Exercise 18. For help in finding the inverse of a matrix, see the TI-Nspire Handbook, p. 804.

Maintain Your Skills

20. For each set of measurements for $\triangle ABC$, calculate the length of side $\overline{AB}$ to two decimal places.

a. $AC = 13$, $BC = 8$, and $\angle C$ measures $1°$.

b. $AC = 13$, $BC = 8$, and $\angle C$ measures $10°$.

c. $AC = 13$, $BC = 8$, and $\angle C$ measures $50°$.

d. $AC = 13$, $BC = 8$, and $\angle C$ measures $90°$.

e. $AC = 13$, $BC = 8$, and $\angle C$ measures $130°$.

f. $AC = 13$, $BC = 8$, and $\angle C$ measures $170°$.

g. $AC = 13$, $BC = 8$, and $\angle C$ measures $179°$.

h. Describe what happens to the length of side $\overline{AB}$ as $\angle C$ increases from $1°$ to $179°$.

8.14 Heron's Formula

For any three given side lengths, there is at most one triangle. That means that given the three side lengths, you should be able to find all the angle measures in the triangle, and its area.

The side lengths 10, 50, and 100 cannot form a triangle.

For You to Do

1. A triangle has side lengths 16, 25, and 31. Use the Law of Cosines to find the angles in this triangle to the nearest degree. Then use any of the angles and the two sides next to the angle to find the area of the triangle.

The Greek mathematician Heron developed a formula for the area of a triangle based only on its side lengths. In this lesson, you will see two proofs of Heron's Formula. The first proof uses algebra. You may have worked through this proof in the Chapter 2 project. The second proof uses trigonometry. Look for similarities between the proofs.

Theorem 8.7 Heron's Formula

Given a triangle with side lengths a, b, and c, the area of the triangle is

$$A = \sqrt{s(s - a)(s - b)(s - c)}$$

where s is the semiperimeter $\dfrac{a + b + c}{2}$.

For You to Do

2. Use Heron's Formula to find the area of a triangle with side lengths 16, 25, and 31. Find s first. Does the value for the area you get using the formula agree with the answer you got in Problem 1 above?

The two proofs of Heron's Formula rely on the known area formulas for triangles. The diagram for the first proof looks remarkably like the one you used to prove the Law of Cosines.

Proof 1 Draw a $\triangle ABC$. Label the side lengths. Drop an altitude to side $\overline{AB}$.

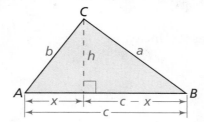

The area of the triangle is $A = \frac{1}{2}ch$. So, the task is to find h in terms of a, b, and c. Apply the Pythagorean Theorem to the right triangles formed by the altitude.

$$h^2 + x^2 = b^2$$
$$h^2 + (c - x)^2 = a^2$$

You can rewrite the second equation as $h^2 + c^2 - 2cx + x^2 = a^2$. Then subtract the first equation from the second to find an expression for x.

$$\left(h^2 + c^2 - 2cx + x^2\right) - \left(h^2 + x^2\right) = a^2 - b^2$$
$$c^2 - 2cx = a^2 - b^2$$
$$c^2 + b^2 - a^2 = 2cx$$
$$\frac{c^2 + b^2 - a^2}{2c} = x$$

Now that you have a formula for x, you can use the first equation to find h.

$$h^2 = b^2 - x^2$$
$$h^2 = b^2 - \left(\frac{c^2 + b^2 - a^2}{2c}\right)^2$$
$$h^2 = \frac{(4b^2c^2 - (c^2 + b^2 - a^2)^2)}{4c^2}$$

This looks unmanageable, but the key to success is recognizing that the numerator of the right side is a difference of squares.

$$h^2 = \frac{(2bc)^2 - (c^2 + b^2 - a^2)^2}{4c^2}$$
$$h^2 = \frac{(2bc + c^2 + b^2 - a^2)(2bc - c^2 - b^2 + a^2)}{4c^2}$$
$$h^2 = \frac{((b + c)^2 - a^2)(a^2 - (b - c)^2)}{4c^2}$$

And there are even *more* differences of squares. You can factor again to find a final formula for h^2 and then find h.

$$h^2 = \frac{(b + c + a)(b + c - a)(a + b - c)(a - b + c)}{4c^2}$$
$$h = \frac{\sqrt{(b + c + a)(b + c - a)(a - b + c)(a + b - c)}}{2c}$$

The area of the triangle is $A = \frac{1}{2}ch$. Substitute for h. You can cancel c in the numerator and denominator.

$$A = \frac{\sqrt{(b + c + a)(b + c - a)(a - b + c)(a + b - c)}}{4}$$

Pushing the 4 inside the square root as a 16 gives Heron's Formula.

$$A = \sqrt{s(s - a)(s - b)(s - c)}$$

The first proof relies primarily on algebra, but some of the work involved closely resembles the Law of Cosines. You can also use the Law of Cosines in a second proof.

You will explain this last step further in the exercises.

Proof 2 The formula $A = \frac{1}{2}ab\sin C$ gives the area of $\triangle ABC$. A handy formula already exists for the cosine of C in terms of side lengths. Use the Law of Cosines and solve for $\cos C$.

$$\cos C = \frac{a^2 + b^2 - c^2}{2ab}$$

You can use the relationship $\cos^2\theta + \sin^2\theta = 1$ here. Exercise 14 in Lesson 8.13 gives the following identity for angles between $0°$ and $180°$.

$$\sin\theta = \sqrt{1 - \cos^2\theta}$$

Use this identity to rewrite the formula for the area of the triangle.

$$A = \tfrac{1}{2}ab\sin C = \tfrac{1}{2}ab\sqrt{1 - \cos^2 C}$$

Now swap in the formula for cosine and work inside the square root.

$$A = \tfrac{1}{2}ab\sqrt{1 - \cos^2 C}$$

$$= \tfrac{1}{2}ab\sqrt{1 - \left(\frac{a^2 + b^2 - c^2}{2ab}\right)^2}$$

$$= \tfrac{1}{2}ab\sqrt{\frac{(2ab)^2 - (a^2 + b^2 - c^2)^2}{(2ab)^2}}$$

$$= \tfrac{1}{4}\sqrt{(2ab)^2 - (a^2 + b^2 - c^2)^2}$$

The remainder of the work under the square root is the same as the work in Proof 1, with a different ordering of the variables. You factor in two steps. Both times you find differences of squares.

$$A = \tfrac{1}{4}\sqrt{(2ab + a^2 + b^2 - c^2)(2ab - a^2 - b^2 + c^2)}$$

$$= \tfrac{1}{4}\sqrt{((a + b)^2 - c^2)(c^2 - (a - b)^2)}$$

$$= \tfrac{1}{4}\sqrt{(a + b + c)(a + b - c)(c + a - b)(c - a + b)}$$

If you start with the area as $\frac{1}{2}bc\sin A$, you actually end up with the same ordering of the variables as in Proof 1.

The algebra of the two proofs is quite similar, although the means to get there differs. Since you derived the Law of Cosines using a diagram similar to the one in the first proof, it is not surprising to find similar steps in the two proofs.

You can use Heron's Formula to find the area of the triangular sails. How can you find the area of the quadrilateral sails?

Exercises *Practicing Habits of Mind*

Check Your Understanding

1. In $\triangle QED$, $QE = 6$ and $ED = 8$.

   a. Suppose the remaining side length is x. Write a formula for the semiperimeter s in terms of x.

   b. Write a formula for $A(x)$, the area of $\triangle QED$ in terms of x.

   c. Find the zeros of $A(x)$.

   d. Find the maximum value of $A(x)$ and the value of x that produces it.

2. In $\triangle QEU$, $QE = 6$. The triangle's perimeter is 18.

   a. Suppose $QU = x$. Find the length of $\overline{EU}$ in terms of x.

   b. Write a formula for $A(x)$, the area of $\triangle QEU$ in terms of x.

   c. Find the zeros of $A(x)$.

   d. Find the maximum value of $A(x)$ and the value of x that produces it.

3. Find the area of this quadrilateral.

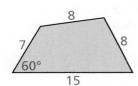

4. Peter thinks there is another way to draw the quadrilateral in Exercise 3 given only its marked side lengths and angle measure. He says the quadrilateral might be concave instead.

   a. What does *concave* mean? Draw an example of a concave quadrilateral.

   b. Could this quadrilateral be concave? If so, find its area. If not, explain why not.

5. Proof 1 in the lesson gives the formula below.

$$A = \frac{\sqrt{(b + c + a)(b + c - a)(a - b + c)(a + b - c)}}{4}$$

You can rewrite this formula as

$$A = \sqrt{s(s - a)(s - b)(s - c)}$$

where $s = \dfrac{a + b + c}{2}$.

a. Show that the two expressions below are equal.

$$\frac{\sqrt{(b + c + a)(b + c - a)(a - b + c)(a + b - c)}}{4}$$

$$\sqrt{\frac{b + c + a}{2} \cdot \frac{b + c - a}{2} \cdot \frac{a - b + c}{2} \cdot \frac{a + b - c}{2}}$$

b. Show the remaining steps you need to write the formula in the following form.

$$A = \sqrt{s(s - a)(s - b)(s - c)}$$

On Your Own

6. **Write About It** What happens when you try to use Heron's Formula to find the area of a triangle with sides of length 12, 25, and 11? Explain.

7. Suppose $\triangle ABT$ is equilateral with $AT = 10$.

a. Find the area of $\triangle ABT$. Use any method.

b. Find the area of $\triangle ABT$ using Heron's Formula.

c. **Take It Further** Use Heron's Formula to show that the formula below gives the area of an equilateral triangle with sides of length x.

$$Area = \frac{x^2 \sqrt{3}}{4}$$

A **Heronian triangle** is a triangle with integer side lengths and integer area.

8. Which sets of three lengths form a Heronian triangle?

a. 7, 10, 12

b. 6, 8, 9

c. 10, 15, 20

d. 10, 17, 21

9. **Standardized Test Prep** Which set of three lengths does NOT form a Heronian triangle?

A. 10, 13, 13 **B.** 9, 12, 16 **C.** 15, 37, 44 **D.** 5, 29, 30

10. Prove that an equilateral triangle cannot be Heronian.

11. Use the two right triangles below to form a Heronian triangle.

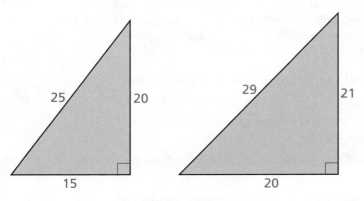

12. Take It Further The triangle with side lengths 13, 14, and 15 is Heronian. Its area is 84. Find some more Heronian triangles with side lengths that are consecutive integers.

Maintain Your Skills

13. In a triangle with side lengths 5 and 12, the third side can be any real number between 7 and 17.

a. Copy and complete this table for $A(c)$, the area of the triangle with sides 5, 12, and c. Find each answer to two decimal places.

Habits of Mind

Look for relationships. How do you know that the length of the third side must be between 7 and 17?

c	A(c)
7	■
8	■
9	■
10	■
11	■
12	■
13	■
14	■
15	■
16	■
17	■

b. What value of c appears to give the maximum area $A(c)$? Explain.

In this investigation, you learned to solve a triangle. You also proved and used the Law of Sines, the Law of Cosines, and Heron's Formula. These questions will help you summarize what you have learned.

1. In $\triangle DOG$, $DG = 10$, $GO = 8$, and $\angle G$ measures $20°$. Find the area of $\triangle DOG$.

2. Find the missing angle measures and side lengths for $\triangle DOG$ from Exercise 1. Give all possible solutions.

3. In $\triangle PIG$, $PI = 7$, $GI = 8$, and $\angle G$ measures $40°$. Solve the triangle. Give all possible solutions.

4. In $\triangle CAT$, $CA = 6$, $AT = 4$, and $CT = 8$. Find the angle measures of the triangle.

5. Find the area of $\triangle CAT$ from Exercise 4.

6. What information do you need to find all of a triangle's side lengths and angle measures?

7. What information do you need to find the area of a triangle?

8. A triangle has sides of length 5, 8, and 10. What is the measure of its largest angle?

Vocabulary

In this investigation, you learned these terms. Make sure you understand what each one means and how to use it.

- **Heronian triangle**
- **Law of Cosines**
- **Law of Sines**

You can use triangle relationships to measure how a glacier changes over time.

Project: Using Mathematical Habits

Brahmagupta's Formula

In the 600s, the Indian mathematician Brahmagupta found a generalization of Heron's Formula. It applies to cyclic quadrilaterals. A cyclic quadrilateral is a quadrilateral with four vertices that are all on the same circle. This is not true for most quadrilaterals.

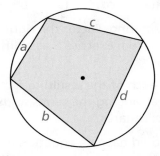

His formula relates the area of the quadrilateral to the lengths of its sides.

Theorem 8.8 Brahmagupta's Formula

Given a cyclic quadrilateral with side lengths a, b, c, and d the area of the quadrilateral is

$$A = \sqrt{(s-a)(s-b)(s-c)(s-d)}$$

where s is the semiperimeter $s = \dfrac{a+b+c+d}{2}$.

The goal of this project is for you to work through a proof of the theorem. You will write up the proof in your own words and supply reasons for the major steps.

1. Show that the opposite angles of a cyclic quadrilateral are supplementary. Two angles are supplementary if their measures sum to 180°.

2. Call one of the angles in the cyclic quadrilateral α. Let e be the length of the diagonal in the diagram.

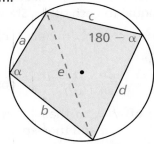

Let A be the area of the quadrilateral. Find expressions for the areas of the two triangles and add them to get a formula for A.

$$A = \tfrac{1}{2}(ab + cd)\sin\alpha$$

You can solve the equation for $\sin\alpha$.

$$\frac{2A}{ab + cd} = \sin\alpha$$

3. Now apply the Law of Cosines to each triangle to find expressions for e^2, where e is the length of the diagonal in the diagram. Set these expressions equal to each other. Show that

$$a^2 + b^2 - c^2 - d^2 = 2(ab + cd) \cos \alpha$$

Conclude that

$$\frac{a^2 + b^2 - c^2 - d^2}{2(ab + cd)} = \cos \alpha$$

There is a factor of $ab + cd$ that shows up in both the expression for $\cos \alpha$ and the expression for $\sin \alpha$. This is a good place to use the Pythagorean Identity or at least some form of it. Because the expressions for sine and cosine have so much in common, maybe you can cancel or combine some of the terms in their squares.

4. Use the fact that $\cos^2 \alpha = 1 - \sin^2 \alpha$ to write the following equation.

$$\left(\frac{a^2 + b^2 - c^2 - d^2}{2(ab + cd)}\right)^2 = 1 - \left(\frac{2A}{ab + cd}\right)^2$$

5. Rearrange the result of Exercise 4 to get the equation below.

$$\frac{4(ab + cd)^2 - (a^2 + b^2 - c^2 - d^2)^2}{4(ab + cd)^2} = \frac{16A^2}{4(ab + cd)^2}$$

So

$$16A^2 = 4(ab + cd)^2 - (a^2 + b^2 - c^2 - d^2)^2$$

6. The rest is factoring. Factor the right side of the equation from Exercise 5 as a difference of two squares.

Then factor each of the resulting factors some more. Try rearranging the terms so that you see some perfect squares.

7. Now you should have an equation like this.

$$16A^2 = (-a + b + c + d)(a - b + c + d) \cdot$$

$$(a + b - c + d)(a + b + c - d)$$

Put it all together to get Brahmagupta's Formula.

8. **Write About It** Explain how you can use Brahmagupta's Formula to prove Heron's Formula.

In **Investigation 8A,** you learned how to

- use right triangle trigonometry to find the coordinates of a person walking on the unit circle, given an angle through which an observer has turned
- evaluate the sine, cosine, and tangent functions for any angle
- solve equations involving trigonometric equations

The following questions will help you check your understanding.

1. Paul walks on the unit circle starting at the point (1, 0), in a counterclockwise direction. Olivia is the observer standing at the origin.

   a. Find the coordinates of Paul's location when Olivia has turned 240°.

   b. When Paul is at the point $\left(\frac{5}{13}, -\frac{12}{13}\right)$ for the first time, find the angle Olivia has turned to the nearest degree.

2. Sketch each angle in standard position. Find its sine, cosine, and tangent.

   a. 45°

   b. 90°

   c. 120°

   d. 180°

   e. 210°

   f. 330°

3. Solve each equation for α between 0° and 360°.

   a. $\sin \alpha - 1 = 0$

   b. $2 \sin \alpha = \sqrt{2}$

   c. $4 \cos^2 \alpha - 1 = 0$

   d. $3 \cos^2 \alpha + 2 \cos \alpha = 1$

In **Investigation 8B,** you learned how to

- sketch the graphs of sine, cosine, and tangent
- use the graphs of trigonometric functions to solve problems
- prove and use trigonometric identities

The following questions will help you check your understanding.

4. a. Copy and complete the table.

x	sin x
0°	▦
30°	▦
45°	▦
90°	▦
120°	▦
180°	▦
210°	▦
240°	▦
270°	▦
315°	▦

   b. Sketch a graph of $y = \sin x$ for $0° \le x \le 360°$. On your graph, label the points that you found for $x = 30°$, $x = 90°$, $x = 120°$, $x = 270°$, and $x = 315°$.

5. a. Sketch a graph of $y = \tan x$ for $0° \le x \le 360°$.

   b. Use the graph of $y = \tan x$ to determine the number of solutions to the equation below for $0° \le x \le 360°$.

   $$\tan x = \frac{1}{2}$$

   c. Use $x = \tan^{-1} \frac{1}{2}$ to find all values of x for $0° \le x \le 360°$ to the nearest degree.

6. Use the angle-sum identities to prove each identity.

   a. $\cos(180° + x) = -\cos x$

   b. $\sin(180° + x) = -\sin x$

   c. $\tan(180° + x) = \tan x$

In **Investigation 8C** you learned how to
   • solve a triangle
   • state and use the Law of Sines
   • state and use the Law of Cosines
   • state and use Heron's Formula

The following questions will help you check your understanding.

7. In $\triangle ABC$, $AB = 6$, $\angle A = 50°$, and $\angle B = 60°$.

   a. Find all remaining side lengths and angle measures in this triangle to the nearest tenth.

   b. Find the area of $\triangle ABC$ to the nearest tenth by drawing the altitude $\overline{CH}$ from $\angle C$ to side $\overline{AB}$.

8. In $\triangle DEF$, $DE = 12$, $EF = 10$, and $DF = 9$.

   a. Find the angle measure of the largest angle of this triangle to the nearest degree.

   b. Find the area of this triangle using Heron's Formula.

9. For each set of equations about $\triangle GHI$, find all possible values for the measure of $\angle G$.

   a. $GH = 3$, $GI = 8$, and $HI = 7$

   b. $GI = 8$, $HI = 7$, and $m\angle H = 50°$

   c. $GI = 18$, $HI = 21$, $m\angle H = 52°$

   d. $GI = 6$, $HI = 7$, and $m\angle H = 75°$

Test

Multiple Choice

1. If $\cos \theta > 0$ and $\sin \theta < 0$, then θ is in which quadrant?

    A. I **B.** II

    C. III **D.** IV

2. For some angle α in Quadrant II, $\sin \alpha = \frac{15}{17}$. What is $\cos \alpha$?

    A. $-\frac{15}{17}$ **B.** $-\frac{8}{17}$

    C. $\frac{8}{17}$ **D.** 1

3. For the interval $90° < x < 180°$, is $\sin x$ positive or negative? Is the value of $\sin x$ increasing or decreasing as x increases through the interval?

    A. positive, increasing

    B. positive, decreasing

    C. negative, increasing

    D. negative, decreasing

4. Which is equal to $\cos 200°$?

    A. $\cos 20°$ **B.** $-\cos 20°$

    C. $\sin 20°$ **D.** $-\sin 20°$

5. In $\triangle ABC$, $AB = 5$, $BC = 9$, and $AC = 8$. What is the area of $\triangle ABC$?

    A. $\sqrt{22}$ **B.** 11

    C. $11\sqrt{6}$ **D.** $6\sqrt{11}$

Open Response

6. Sketch each angle in standard position. Find its sine, cosine, and tangent. Give exact values, if possible. Otherwise, round to the nearest hundredth.

    a. $60°$ **b.** $90°$

    c. $150°$ **d.** $289°$

7. Solve each equation for $0° \leq \theta < 360°$.

    a. $2 \sin \theta + 1 = 0$

    b. $2 \cos^2 \theta - 1 = 0$

    c. $3 \cos^2 \theta - 5 \cos \theta + 2 = 0$

8. Simplify each expression.

    a. $\sin (180° - x)$

    b. $\cos (180° + x)$

    c. $\sin (270° + x)$

9. **a.** Sketch a graph of $y = \cos x$ for $0° \leq x \leq 450°$.

    b. Use your graph to determine the number of solutions to the equation $\cos x = \frac{1}{2}$.

    c. Find all solutions to $\cos x = \frac{1}{2}$ for $0° \leq x \leq 450°$.

10. For each set of information about $\triangle ABC$, find all the missing side lengths to the nearest tenth and angle measures to the nearest degree.

    a. $AB = 16$, $BC = 12$, and $AC = 8$

    b. $m\angle A = 34°$, $BC = 5$, and $AC = 7$

11. What information do you need about a triangle to find its area?

Multiple Choice

1. What is the sum of the odd integers from 9 to 101, inclusive?

A. 1242 **B.** 2484

C. 2585 **D.** 5076

2. If $\binom{20}{k} = 1$, what could k be?

A. 0 **B.** 1

C. 19 **D.** 20!

3. What is a rational expression for $0.131313\ldots$?

A. $\frac{1}{13}$ **B.** $\frac{13}{87}$

C. $\frac{13}{99}$ **D.** $\frac{13}{100}$

4. In an arithmetic sequence, the third term is 19 and the eighth term is 574. What is the sixth term?

A. 112 **B.** 352

C. 464 **D.** 688

5. What is the coefficient of x^4y^8 in the expansion of $(x + y)^{12}$?

A. $\binom{8}{4}$ **B.** $\binom{12}{6}$

C. $\binom{12}{8}$ **D.** $\binom{16}{12}$

6. If $\cos\theta > 0$ and $\sin\theta < 0$, which quadrant is θ in?

A. I **B.** II

C. III **D.** IV

7. For some angle α in Quadrant IV, $\cos\alpha = \frac{5}{13}$. What is $\sin\alpha$?

A. $\frac{5}{12}$ **B.** $-\frac{5}{12}$

C. $\frac{12}{13}$ **D.** $-\frac{12}{13}$

8. As x increases through the interval $-90° < x < 90°$, is $\cos\alpha$ positive or negative? Is the value of $\sin\alpha$ increasing or decreasing?

A. positive, increasing

B. positive, decreasing

C. negative, increasing

D. negative, decreasing

9. What is the value of $\cos 42°$?

A. $\cos 48°$ **B.** $-(\cos 48°)$

C. $\sin 48°$ **D.** $-\sin 48°$

10. In $\triangle ABC$, $AB = 16$, $BC = 23$, and $AC = 21$. What is the approximate area of $\triangle ABC$?

A. 41 **B.** 81

C. 163 **D.** 1654

Open Response

11. Find each sum.

a. $\displaystyle\sum_{k=1}^{10} (3k - 1)$

b. $\displaystyle\sum_{k=0}^{4} 6(-2)^k$

12. Find a closed-form rule for the following indefinite sum.

$$\sum_{k=0}^{n} (6k + 4)$$

13. Find a recursive rule and a closed-form rule for the series defined by $h(n) = 6n + 2$, with initial term $h(0)$.

14. A geometric sequence g has $g(0) = 8$ and common ratio $\frac{3}{2}$.

a. Make an output table for $g(n)$ for $n = 0$ through $n = 4$.

b. Find a closed-form rule for the sequence.

15. Use Pascal's Triangle to expand $(3x - 2y)^5$.

16. Sketch each angle in standard position and find its sine, cosine, and tangent. Give exact values if possible.

   a. 135°   **b.** 300°

17. Solve each equation over $0° \leq \theta \leq 360°$.

   a. $\cos \theta + 1 = 0$ **b.** $\sqrt{2} \sin \theta + 1 = 0$

   c. $\sin^2 \theta - 3 \sin \theta + 2 = 0$

18. Simplify each expression

   a. $\cos (360° - x)$ **b.** $\sin (90° - x)$

   c. $\sin (180° - x)$

19. Write each expression as the sine or cosine of an acute angle.

   a. $\sin 135°$ **b.** $\cos 330°$

   c. $\tan 240°$

20. Suppose $\sin \theta = -\frac{12}{13}$ and θ is an angle in the interval $0° \leq \theta \leq 360°$.

   a. Find all possible values of $\cos \theta$.

   b. Find all possible values of $\tan \theta$.

   c. Find all possible values of θ to the nearest tenth of a degree.

21. Find the center and radius of the circle with equation $(x - 3)^2 + (y + 4)^2 = 36$.

22. Determine whether the function $g(x) = 2x^3 - x$ is even, odd, or neither.

23. Describe the translation of $y = x^3$ to $y + 2 = (x + 1)^3$.

24. a. Write an equation for a function with a graph that is the graph of $y = x^2$ stretched vertically by a factor of $\frac{1}{2}$ and translated up 3 units.

   b. Sketch the graph.

25. Write each expression as a single affine transformation.

   a. $D_5 \circ T_{-3}$ **b.** $D_2 \circ D_6 \circ T_3$

   c. $\mathcal{A}_{(3, -2)} \circ \mathcal{A}_{(6, 3)}$

26. Simplify each expression.

   a. $8^{-\frac{5}{3}}$ **b.** $\dfrac{x^{-3}y^{-7}}{x^{-5}y^{-1}}$

27. You are given the sequence 15, ■, ■, 120.

   a. Find the missing terms if the sequence is arithmetic.

   b. Find the missing terms if the sequence is geometric.

28. Find the inverse of each function.

   a. $f(x) = 5^x$ **b.** $g(x) = \log_3 x$

29. Find the solution to the following system.

$$2x + 3y = 12$$
$$-3x - y = 3$$

30. Find the dot product.

   $(2, -1, 5) \cdot (6, -2, 0)$

31. Simplify each expression.

   a. $\sqrt{40} \cdot \sqrt{-5}$ **b.** $(3 - 2i)^2$

32. Find the magnitude of $6 + 2i$.

33. Suppose $f(x) = -2x + 4$. If possible, find a function $g(x)$ such that $f \circ g(x) = x$.

34. Find the line of best fit for the data set.

x	y
−1	4
2	7
4	10
7	14

.... TI-Nspire™ Technology Handbook ....

Recognizing how to use technology to support your mathematics is an important habit of mind. Although the use of technology in this course is independent of any particular hardware or software, this handbook gives examples of how you can apply the TI-Nspire™ handheld technology.

Handbook Contents

Setting the Handheld to Degree Mode, Lesson 8.02

1. Press **ctrl** **⌂**. Choose **File** and then **Document Settings**. Press **enter**.

2. Tab down to the **Angle** menu. Press **▽** until **Degree** is highlighted. Press **enter** **enter**.

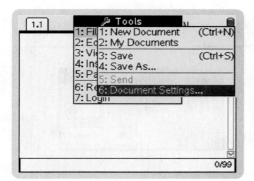

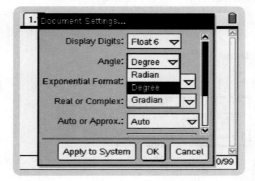

Modeling a Function, Lessons 1.02, 2.02

1. Choose **Define** from the **Actions** menu (or type **D** **E** **F** **I** **N** **E**).

2. Type the function. Press **enter**.

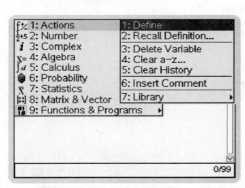

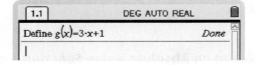

Modeling a Recursive Function I, Lessons 1.02, 5.08

1. Choose **Define** from the **Actions** menu. Name the function by typing **B** **(** **N** **)** **=**. Press **ctrl** **✕** to open the Templates palette. Select **▦**. Press **enter**.

2. Enter the function. Press **tab** to move from box to box. Press **enter** when done.

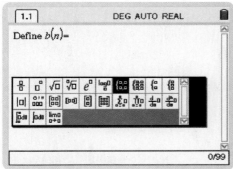

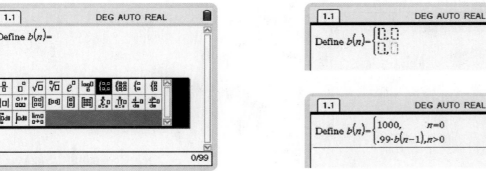

Modeling a Recursive Function II, Lesson 1.10

1. Choose **Define** from the **Actions** menu. Name the function by typing **G** **(** **N** **)** **=**. Press **ctrl** **X** to open the Templates palette. Select ▦. Press **enter**.

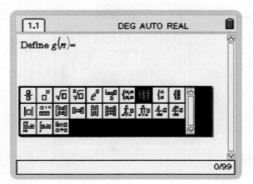

2. Select the number of pieces in the definition. Press **enter**.

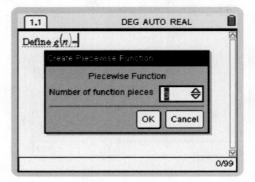

3. Enter the function. Press **tab** to move from box to box. Press **enter** when done.

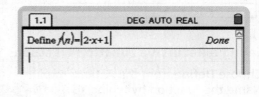

Modeling an Absolute Value Function, Lesson 6.01

1. Choose **Define** from the **Actions** menu. Name the function by typing **F** **(** **N** **)** **=**. Press **ctrl** **X** to open the Templates palette. Select |□|. Press **enter**.

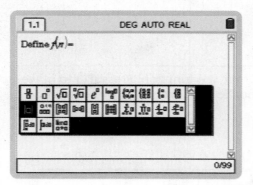

2. Enter the function. Press **enter** when done.

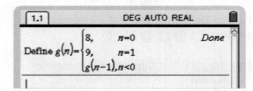

Modeling a Monthly Payment Function, Lessons 1.11, 7.11

1. Choose **Define** from the **Tools** menu. Name the function by typing Ⓑ Ⓒ Ⓝ , Ⓒ , Ⓘ , Ⓜ Ⓓ ⊜.Press **ctrl** **X** to open the Templates palette. Select ⌷. Press **enter**.

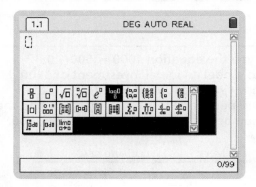

2. Enter the function. Press **tab** to move from box to box. Press **enter** when done.

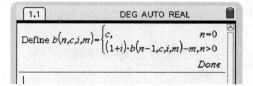

3. Enter values for the number of months, the initial principal, the interest rate, and the monthly payment. Press **enter** to calculate the current balance.

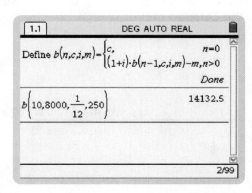

Using the Logarithm Template, Lesson 5.12

1. Press **ctrl** **X** to open the Templates palette. Select ⌷. Press **enter**.

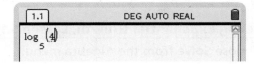

2. Press **tab** to move from box to box. Press **enter** when done.

Using Sigma Notation, Lessons 7.04, 7.07, 7.10

1. Choose **Sum** in the **Calculus** menu.

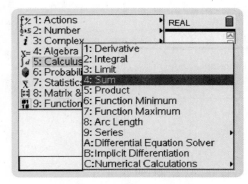

2. Press **tab** to move from box to box. Type the upper limit, the lower limit, and the expression for the sequence. Press **enter**.

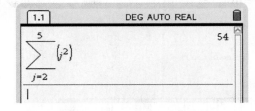

3. To evaluate an indefinite sum, Choose **Sum** in the **Calculus** menu.

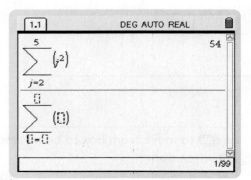

4. Press **tab** to move from box to box. Use a variable for the upper limit, and an integer for the lower limit. Type an expression for the sequence using the upper limit variable. Press **enter** to evaluate the sum.

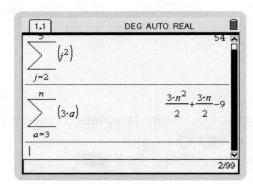

Modeling Exponential Growth, Lesson 5.10

1. Choose **Solve** from the **Algebra** menu.

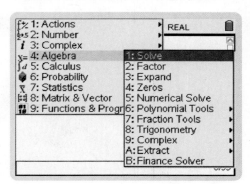

2. Type the equation $1000 = 500(1.03)^n$ to model an initial investment of \$500 growing to \$1000 at an interest rate of 3% per year. Press **,** **N**, **enter** to find the number of years needed to reach \$1000.

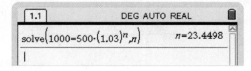

Modeling an Affine Transformation, Lesson 6.06

1. Choose **Delete Variable** from the **Actions** menu. Type 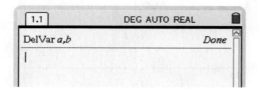 to delete two variables to use in the affine transformation.

2. Define the function $m(x,a,b) = ax + b$.

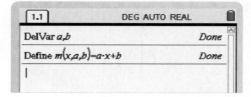

3. To define the affine transformation $x \mapsto A_{(3,4)}(x)$, define $f(x)$ as $m(x,3,4)$.

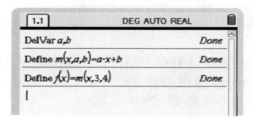

Graphing an Equation, Lesson 2.02

1. Use the **Text** tool in the **Actions** menu. Type the equation on the screen. Press **enter**.

2. Place the cursor on the equation. Press **ctrl** **✦** to grab the equation. Drag it to an axis. Press **enter**.

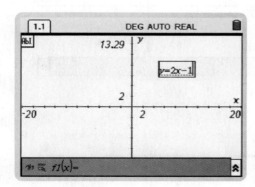

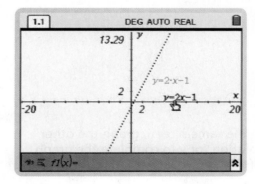

Graphing a Function, Lesson 2.02

1. Tab down to the entry line at the bottom of the screen. Type an expression in *x*.

2. Press `enter`.

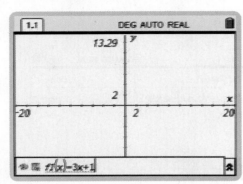

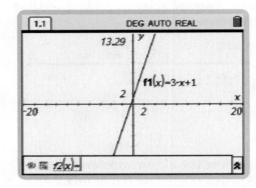

Graphing an Equation in Two Variables, Lesson 6.04

1. Type Ⓢ Ⓞ Ⓛ Ⓥ Ⓔ Ⓒ. Type the equation and then Ⓒ Ⓨ. Press `enter`.

2. In a graphing screen, graph one of the solutions for *y*.

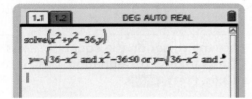

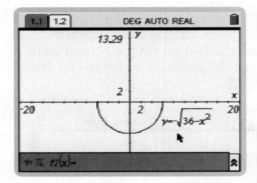

3. In the same screen, graph the other solution for *y* to complete the graph of $x^2 + y^2 = 36$.

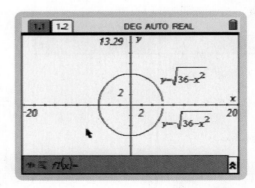

Finding the Intersection of Two Graphs, Lessons 5.07, 5.14

1. Choose **Intersection Point(s)** from the **Points & Lines** menu.

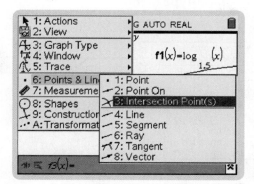

2. Place the cursor on one graph. Press **enter**.

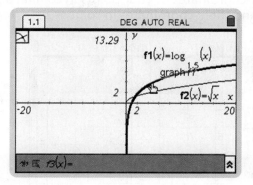

3. Place the cursor on the other graph. Press **enter**.

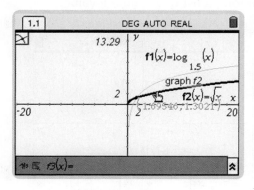

4. Move the cursor to drag the coordinates of the point of intersection. Press **enter** to anchor the coordinates.

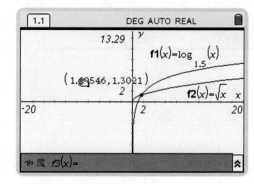

Using Zoom—Trig to View the Graph of a Trigonometric Function, Lesson 8.07

1. Choose **Zoom–Trig** from the **Window** menu.

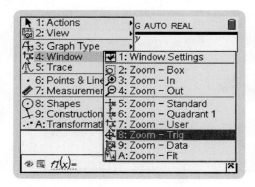

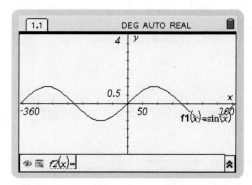

1. Name the first two columns of a spreadsheet *a* and *b*. Enter the *x*-coordinates of your points in column *a* and the *y*-coordinates in column *b*.

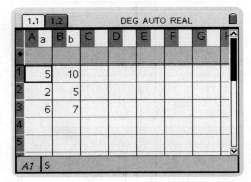

2. Navigate to the Graphs & Geometry application. Choose **Scatter Plot** from the **Graph Type** menu.

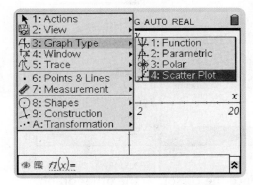

3. Press **enter** to select from among a list of possible *x*-values. Select *a*. Press **enter**.

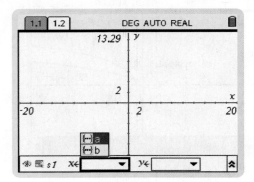

4. Press **tab** and then **enter** to select from among a list of possible *y*-values.

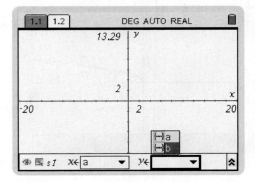

5. Select *b*. Press **enter** to view a scatter plot of the selected data.

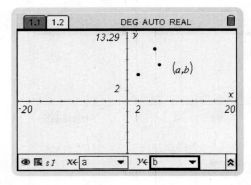

6. Choose **Function** from the **Graph Type** menu.

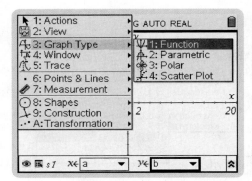

Finding the Line of Best Fit I, (continued)

7. Graph any linear function. Here the function is $f(x) = 2$.

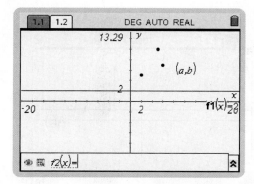

8. Choose **Parallel** from the **Constructions** menu.

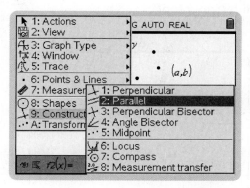

9. Select a scatter-plot point with the cursor. Press **enter**. Select the *y*-axis. Press **enter** to construct a vertical line that passes through the point.

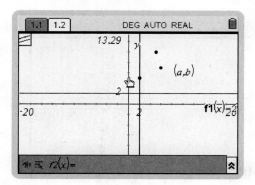

10. Choose **Segment** from the **Points & Lines** menu.

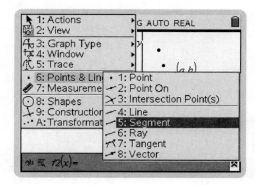

11. Select the point (Step 9) again. Press **enter**. Select the intersection point of its vertical line and the graph of the linear function. Press **enter** to construct a segment between the two points.

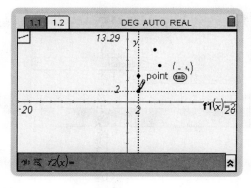

12. Choose **Hide/Show** from the **Actions** menu.

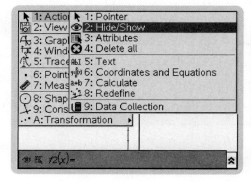

13. Select the vertical line (not the segment). Press **enter** to hide it. Press **esc** to exit the Hide/Show tool.

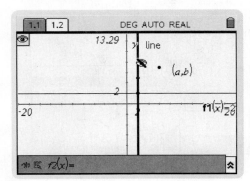

14. Repeat Steps 8–13 for the other points.

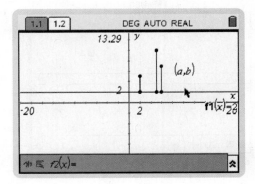

15. Choose **Length** from the **Measurement** menu.

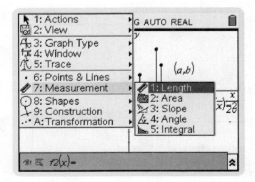

16. Select a segment. Press **enter**. Drag the measurement to the desired location on the screen. Press **enter** to anchor it.

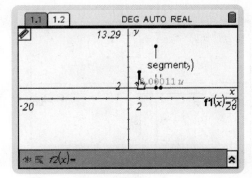

17. Repeat Step 16 for the other segments.

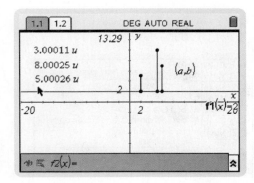

18. Choose **Text** from the **Actions** menu. Write $i^2 + k^2 + l^2$ on the screen.

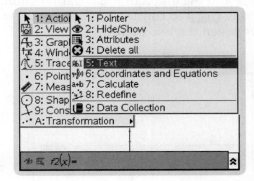

19. Choose **Calculate** from the **Actions** menu.

20. Position the cursor on $i^2 + k^2 + l^2$. Press **enter**.

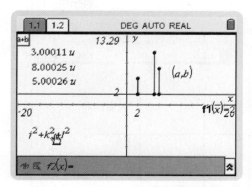

21. Select a value for each variable. Position the cursor over the respective length measurements and press **enter**.

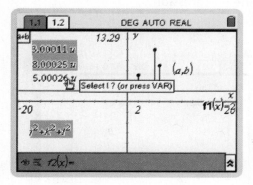

22. Drag the result of the calculation to the desired location. Press **enter** to anchor it. Press **esc** to exit the Text tool.

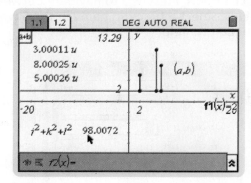

23. Use arrow keys to navigate to the horizontal line. Press **ctrl** **✷** to grab it. Drag the line to rotate and translate the line.

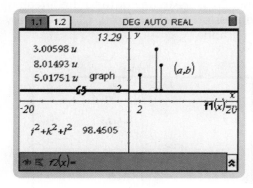

24. Move the line to make the sum of the squares of the segment lengths as small as possible. The line with the least value of $i^2 + k^2 + l^2$ is the line of best fit.

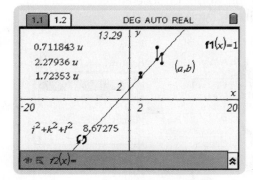

1. Make a scatter plot of the data you wish to use.

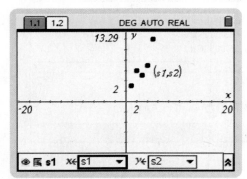

2. Navigate to the calculator application. Choose **Stat Calculations** from the **Statistics** menu. Choose **Linear Regression (mx + b)**. Press **enter**.

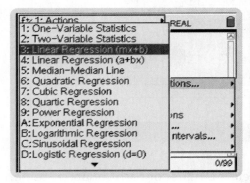

3. Select the data to use in the **X List** and **Y List** fields. Press **tab** to navigate between fields. Select a function name in the **Save RegEqn to** field.

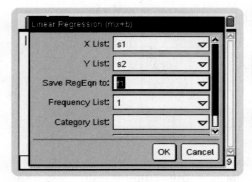

4. Press **enter** to show a summary of the linear regression.

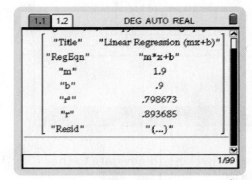

5. Navigate to the Graphs & Geometry application. Choose **Function** from the **Graph Type** menu.

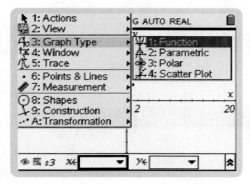

6. Press **tab** to navigate to the function entry line. Press △ to navigate to the linear regression function. Press **enter** to draw its graph.

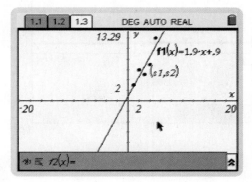

Finding the Quadratic Curve of Best Fit, Lesson 1.08

1. Navigate to the Calculator application. Choose **Stat Calculations** from the **Statistics** menu. Choose **Quadratic Regression**. Press **enter**.

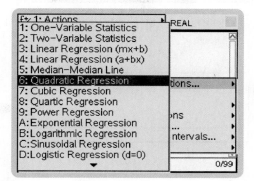

2. Select the data to use in the **X List** and **Y List** fields. Press **tab** to navigate between fields. Select a function name in the **Save RegEqn to** field.

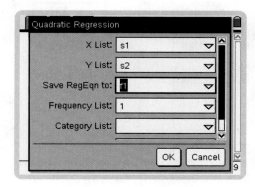

3. Press **enter** to show a summary of the quadratic regression. Navigate to the Graphs & Geometry application. Choose **Function** from the **Graph Type** menu.

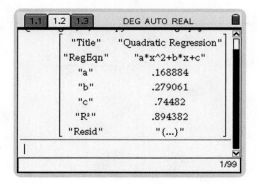

4. Press **tab** to navigate to the function entry line. Press **△** to navigate to the quadratic regression function. Press **enter** to draw its graph.

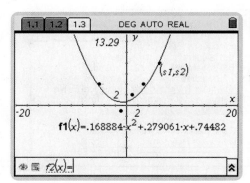

Making a Function Table, Lesson 2.02

1. Choose **Add Function Table** from the **View** menu . . .

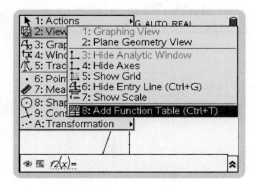

2. . . . to show a function table on the right side of the screen.

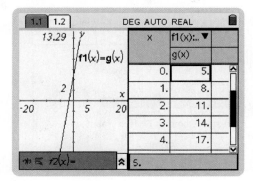

Expanding a Product of Polynomials, Lesson 3.10

1. Choose **Expand** from the **Algebra** menu.

2. Type a product of polynomials. Press **enter**.

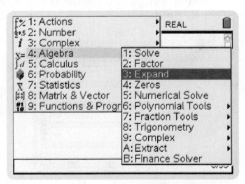

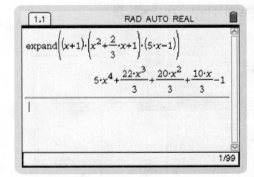

Dividing Polynomials, Lesson 2.10

1. Choose **Polynomial Tools** from the **Algebra** menu. Choose **Quotient of Polynomial**.

2. Type the polynomial to divide and then ●. Type the polynomial you are dividing by. Press **enter** to show the quotient without remainder.

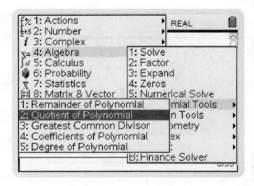

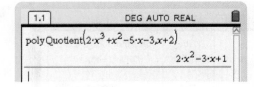

3. Choose **Polynomial Tools** from the **Algebra** menu. Choose **Remainder of Polynomial**.

4. Type the polynomial to divide and then ●. Type the polynomial you are dividing by. Press **enter** to find the remainder after dividing the polynomials.

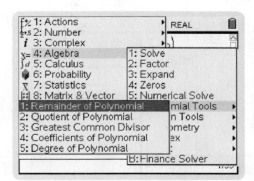

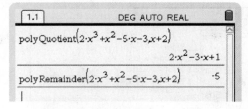

TI-Nspire™ Technology Handbook

Factoring a Polynomial, Lesson 2.12

1. Choose **Factor** from the **Algebra** menu.

2. Type the polynomial to be factored. Press **enter**.

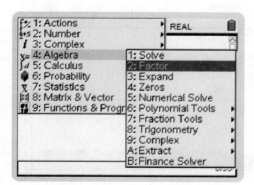

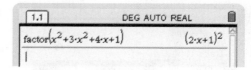

Calculating the Argument of a Complex Number, Lesson 3.09

1. Choose **Polar Angle** from the **Complex** menu.

2. Type the complex number. Press **enter**.

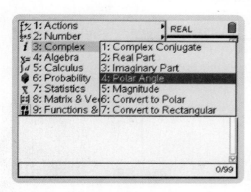

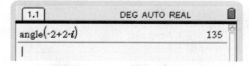

Calculating the Magnitude of a Complex Number, Lesson 3.09

1. Choose **Magnitude** from the **Complex** menu.

2. Type the complex number. Press **enter**.

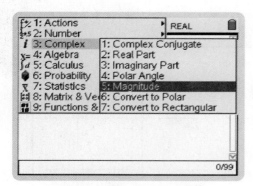

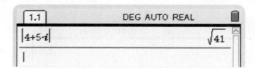

1. Choose **Point** from the **Points & Lines** menu.

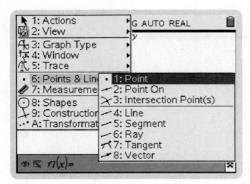

2. Press **enter** to place a point on the graphing screen.

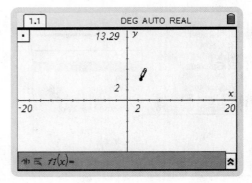

3. Choose **Coordinates and Equations** from the **Actions** menu.

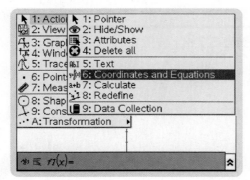

4. Select the point. Press **enter**. Drag the coordinates to the desired location. Press **enter**. Press **esc** to exit the Coordinates and Equations tool.

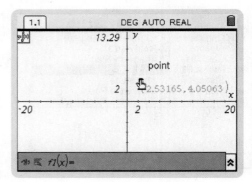

5. Double click on the first coordinate. Replace the existing number with the real part of the complex number. The point moves to reflect the new coordinates.

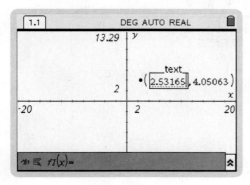

6. Replace the second coordinate with the imaginary part.

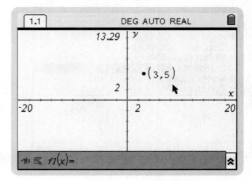

Calculating the Magnitude of a Complex Number Graphically (continued)

7. Choose **Vector** from the **Points & Lines** menu.

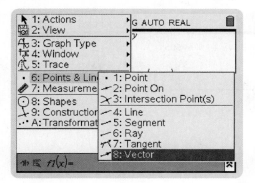

8. Select the origin. Press **enter** to set the tail of the vector.

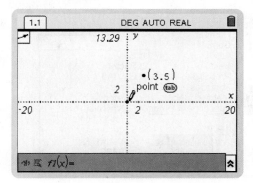

9. Select the point. Press **enter** to set the head of the vector.

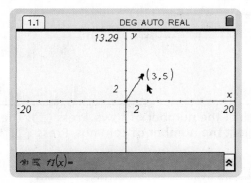

10. Choose **Length** from the **Measurement** menu.

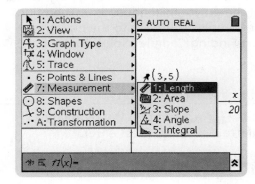

11. Select the vector. Press **enter**.

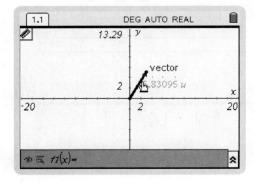

12. Drag the length measurement to the desired location. Press **enter** to anchor it. This is the magnitude of the complex number.

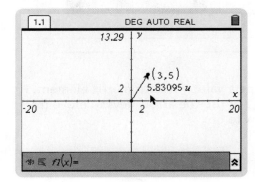

Finding Complex Solutions, Lesson 3.08

1. Choose **Complex** from the **Algebra** menu. Choose **Solve**.

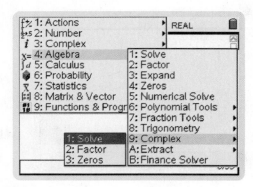

2. Type the equation and then ⊙. Type the variable to solve for. Press **enter**.

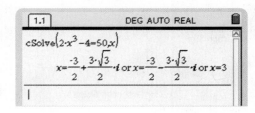

Finding Complex Zeros, Lesson 3.12

1. To find the complex roots of a polynomial, set the polynomial equal to 0. Then find the complex solutions to the equation. (See Finding Complex Solutions, above.)

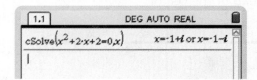

Entering a Matrix, Lesson 4.07

1. Press **ctrl** **x** to open the template palette. Select ⊞. Press enter.

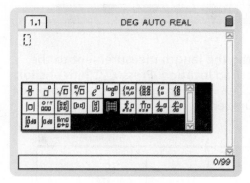

2. Select the number of rows. Press **tab**. Then select the number of columns. Press **enter**.

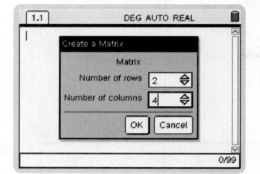

3. Type a value for each matrix element. Press **tab** or use the arrow keys to move from box to box.

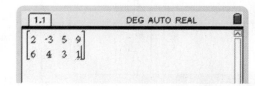

Adding or Subtracting Matrices, Lesson 4.07

1. Enter a matrix. Press ➕ or ➖. Enter a second matrix. Press **enter**.

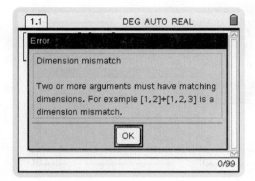

2. If the matrices do not have the same dimensions, you see this image.

Multiplying Matrices, Lesson 4.07

1. Enter a matrix. Press ❌. Enter a second matrix. Press **enter**.

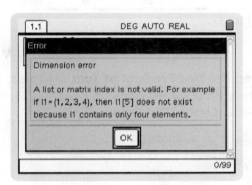

2. If the number of columns of the first matrix does not equal the number of rows of the second matrix, you see this image.

Finding the Inverse of a Matrix, Lesson 4.08

1. Enter a square matrix. Press ⌃ ➖ ❶ **enter**.

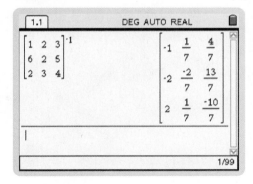

2. If the matrix has no inverse, you see this image.

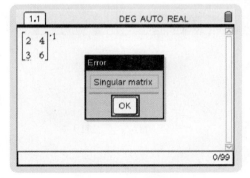

Using the rref Command, Lesson 4.03

1. Choose **Reduced Row-Echelon** Form from the **Matrix & Vector** menu.

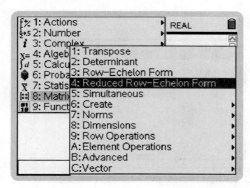

2. Enter a matrix. Press **enter**.

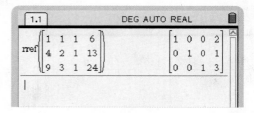

Adding or Subtracting *n*-tuples, Lesson 4.07

1. Press **ctrl** **( )**. Enter *n*-tuple elements separated by commas.

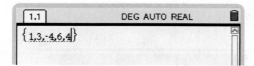

2. Press **+** or **−**. Then enter a second *n*-tuple (same *n* value as the first). Press **enter**.

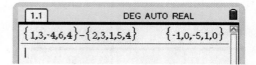

Finding the Dot Product of Two *n*-tuples, Lesson 4.07

1. Choose **Vector** from the **Matrix & Vector** menu. Choose **Dot Product**.

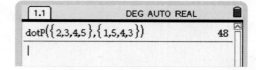

2. Enter two *n*-tuples (same value of *n*) separated by a comma. Press **enter**.

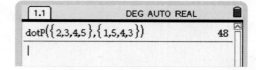

TI-Nspire™ Technology Handbook

Using a Spreadsheet to Make a Summation Column, Lesson 7.01, 7.06

1. In column A, make an index column with 1 in the first row, 2 in the second row, and so on. In column B, enter the data to be summed. In cell C1, type ⊜ Ⓢ Ⓤ Ⓜ ⦅ Ⓑ ⟨ctrl⟩ ⦅ 𝗿 ⟨ctrl⟩ ⟨"⟩ Ⓐ ⟨ctrl⟩ ⟨"⟩ ❶ , Ⓐ ❶. Press ⟨enter⟩.

2. Move the cursor back to cell C1. Choose **Fill Down** from the **Data** menu.

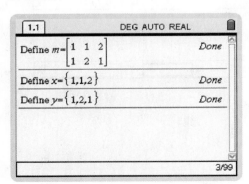

3. Press ▽ to extend highlighted cells to match the last data cell in column B. Press ⟨enter⟩.

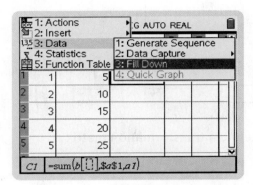

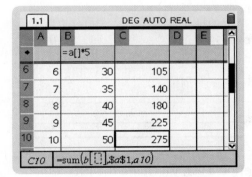

Using a Matrix to Transform Points, Lesson 4.11

1. Define a 2-by-*n* matrix to model a set of *n* points. The first row consists of the *x*-coordinates, and the second row consists of the corresponding *y*-coordinates. Define lists of the *x*-coordinates and *y*-coordinates, in order.

2. Navigate to the Graphs & Geometry application. Choose **Scatter Plot** from the **Graph Type** menu.

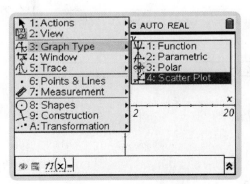

Using a Matrix to Transform Points (continued)

3. Select the data lists from Step 1 as the *x*- and *y*-values.

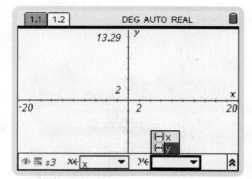

4. Press **enter** to see the points you will transform using a 2-by-2 matrix.

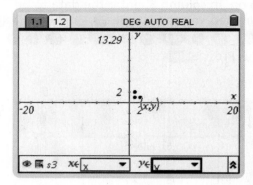

5. Define a transformation matrix *s*.

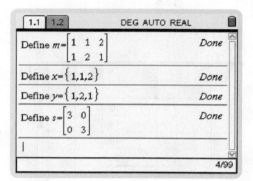

6. Define a list, *x*1. Name the list elements $(s \cdot m)[1,1]$, $(s \cdot m)[1,2]$, and so on.

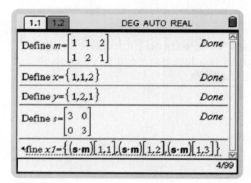

7. Define a list, *y*1. Name the list elements $(s \cdot m)[2,1]$, $(s \cdot m)[2,2]$, and so on.

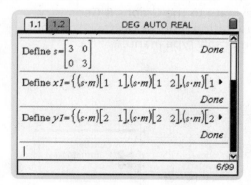

8. Make a scatter plot using *x*1 for the *x*-values and *y*1 for the *y*-values. The result is the original points transformed by the matrix *s*.

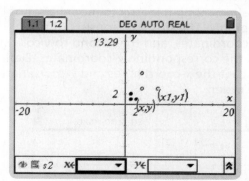

9. For a second transformation, press ▲ in the calculator screen until you highlight the definition of *s*. Press **enter** to copy it to the entry line.

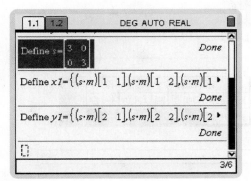

10. Use the arrow keys to change the values in *s*. Press **enter**.

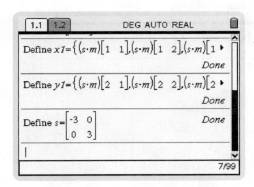

11. Press ▲ in the calculator screen until you highlight the definition of *x*1. Press **enter** to copy it to the entry line. Press **enter**.

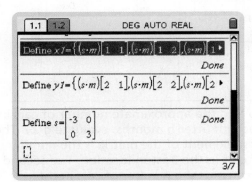

12. Repeat Step 11 with the definition of *y*1.

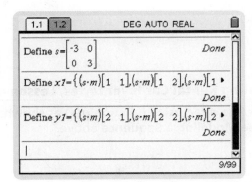

13. Navigate to the scatter plot from Step 8 to view the new transformation.

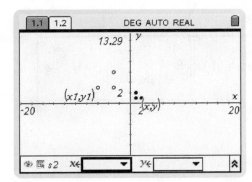

Modeling a Sequence, Lesson 4.10

1. Choose **Define** from the **Actions** menu. Press ⓜ ⊜. Enter the matrix shown. Press **enter**.

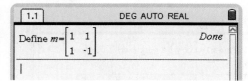

3. Enter the 2-by-1 matrix in the first box as shown. Complete the rest of the function. Press **enter**.

2. Choose **Define** from the **Actions** menu. Press ⓢ ⊜. Press **ctrl** **✕** to open the template palette. Select ▦. Press **enter**.

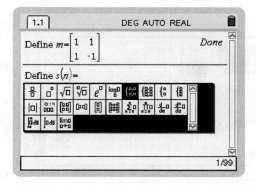

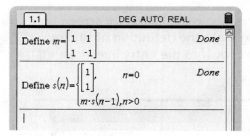

Modeling Rental Car Inventories, Lesson 4.10

1. Define a recursive function $g(x)$ as shown. See **Modeling a Sequence** above.

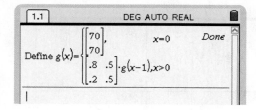

3. To find the approximate number of cars in each lot after n months, evaluate $g(n)$. The first element of the matrix is the number of cars in the Boston location. The second element is the number of cars in the Cambridge location.

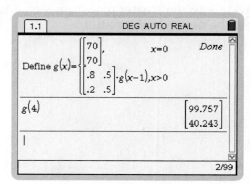

Tables

Table 1 Math Symbols

$\ldots$	and so on	$a : b, \frac{a}{b}$	ratio of a to b
$=$	is equal to	$\sin \theta$	sine of θ
$\approx$	is approximately equal to	$\cos \theta$	cosine of θ
$\neq$	is not equal to	$\tan \theta$	tangent of θ
$>$	is greater than	$\sin^{-1} x$	inverse sine of x
$\geq$	is greater than or equal to	$\cos^{-1} x$	inverse cosine of x
$<$	is less than	$\tan^{-1} x$	inverse tangent of x
$\leq$	is less than or equal to	$n!$	n factorial
$\pm$	plus or minus	$\binom{n}{k}$	the nth row, kth column entry of Pascal's triangle
$\mapsto$	which gives, leads to, maps to		
n^2	n squared	$\sum\limits_{n=1}^{5}$	summation notation
a^{-m}	$\frac{1}{a^m}, a \neq 0$		
a^0	1	$f^{-1}(x)$	inverse of function f
$a^{\frac{1}{n}}$	$\sqrt[n]{a}$	$g \circ f(x)$	$g(f(x))$
$a^{\frac{p}{q}}$	$(\sqrt[q]{a})^p$	$x \mapsto y$	x maps to y
$\sqrt{x}$	nonnegative square root of x	$\mathbb{N}$	set of natural numbers
$\sqrt[n]{r}$	nth root of r	$\mathbb{Z}$	set of integers
Δ	difference (delta)	$\mathbb{Q}$	set of rational numbers
$\Leftrightarrow$	if and only if	$\mathbb{R}$	set of real numbers
A	point A	i	$\sqrt{-1}$
A'	image of A, A prime	$a + bi$	complex number
$\overleftrightarrow{AB}$	line through A and B	$\bar{z}$	conjugate
$\overline{AB}$	segment from A to B	$|z|$	magnitude of a complex number
AB	length of $\overline{AB}$	I	identity matrix
$\angle A$	angle A	A^{-1}	inverse of matrix A
$\angle ABC$	angle with sides $\overrightarrow{BA}$ and $\overrightarrow{BC}$	0	zero matrix
$m\angle A$	measure of angle A	$\mathcal{A}_{(a,b)}$	affine transformation
$^\circ$	degree(s)	S_x	stabilizer
$\log_b x$	logarithm of x, base b	T_a	translation
$\arg z$	argument	D_s	dilation
$\triangle ABC$	triangle with vertices A, B, and C		
π	pi, the ratio of the circumference of a circle to its diameter		

Table 2 Measures

United States Customary	Metric

Length

12 inches (in.) = 1 foot (ft)	10 millimeters (mm) = 1 centimeter (cm)
36 in. = 1 yard (yd)	100 cm = 1 meter (m)
3 ft = 1 yard	1000 mm = 1 meter
5280 ft = 1 mile (mi)	1000 m = 1 kilometer (km)
1760 yd = 1 mile	

Area

144 square inches (in.^{2}) = 1 square foot (ft^2)	100 square millimeters (mm^2) = 1 square centimeter (cm^2)
9 ft^2 = 1 square yard (yd^2)	10,000 cm^2 = 1 square meter (m^2)
43,560 ft^2 = 1 acre (a)	10,000 m^2 = 1 hectare (ha)
4840 yd^2 = 1 acre	

Volume

1728 cubic inches (in.^{3}) = 1 cubic foot (ft^3)	1000 cubic millimeters (mm^3) = 1 cubic centimeter (cm^3)
27 ft^3 = 1 cubic yard (yd^3)	1,000,000 cm^3 = 1 cubic meter (m^3)

Liquid Capacity

8 fluid ounces (fl oz) = 1 cup (c)	1000 milliliters (mL) = 1 liter (L)
2 c = 1 pint (pt)	1000 L = 1 kiloliter (kL)
2 pt = 1 quart (qt)	
4 qt = 1 gallon (gal)	

Weight and Mass

16 ounces (oz) = 1 pound (lb)	1000 milligrams (mg) = 1 gram (g)
2000 pounds = 1 ton (t)	1000 g = 1 kilogram (kg)
	1000 kg = 1 metric ton

Temperature

32°F = freezing point of water	0°C = freezing point of water
98.6°F = normal body temperature	37°C = normal body temperature
212°F = boiling point of water	100°C = boiling point of water

Time

60 seconds (s) = 1 minute (min)	365 days = 1 year (yr)
60 minutes = 1 hour (h)	52 weeks (approx.) = 1 year
24 hours = 1 day (d)	12 months = 1 year
7 days = 1 week (wk)	10 years = 1 decade
4 weeks (approx.) = 1 month (mo)	100 years = 1 century

Tables

Table 3 Formulas From Geometry

You may need geometric formulas as you work through your algebra book. Here are some perimeter, area, and volume formulas.

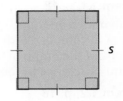

$$P = 2\ell + 2w$$
$$A = \ell w$$

Rectangle

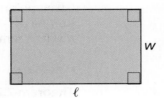

$$P = 4s$$
$$A = s^2$$

Square

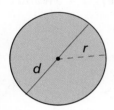

$$C = 2\pi r \ \text{ or } \ C = \pi d$$
$$A = \pi r^2$$

Circle

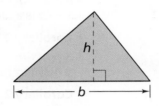

$$A = \tfrac{1}{2}bh$$

Triangle

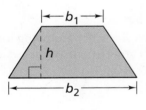

$$A = bh$$

Parallelogram

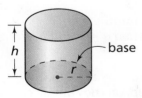

$$A = \tfrac{1}{2}(b_1 + b_2)h$$

Trapezoid

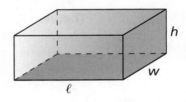

$$V = Bh$$
$$V = \ell wh$$

Rectangular Prism

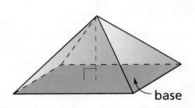

$$V = \tfrac{1}{3}Bh$$

Pyramid

$$V = Bh$$
$$V = \pi r^2 h$$

Cylinder

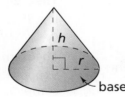

$$V = \tfrac{1}{3}Bh$$
$$V = \tfrac{1}{3}\pi r^2 h$$

Cone

$$V = \tfrac{4}{3}\pi r^3$$

Sphere

.... Properties and Theorems ....

Chapter 1

Theorem 1.1, p. 18

You can match an input-output table having constant differences with a linear function. The slope of the graph of the function is the constant difference in the table.

Theorem 1.2, p. 18

If $f(x) = ax + b$ is a linear function, its differences are constant.

Theorem 1.3, p. 32

For any quadratic function $p(x) = ax^2 + bx + c$, the second differences are constant. The constant second difference is $2a$, twice the coefficient of the squared term.

Theorem 1.4, p. 34

If a table has constant second differences, there is some quadratic function that agrees with the table.

Theorem 1.5 *Invariance Under Translation*, p. 56

Suppose a and b are fixed numbers and you have a set of data labeled (x, y). If you perform the transformation $(x, y) \mapsto (x + a, y + b)$ on the data set, the lines of best fit for the two data sets will have the same slope.

Conjecture 1.1, p. 62

For any set of data, the line of best fit contains the balance point.

Chapter 2

Theorem 2.0 *The Zero Product Property*, p. 92

If a and b are real numbers with a product of 0, then either a or b (or both) must be 0.

Theorem 2.1, p. 121

Suppose $f: A \rightarrow B$ is one-to-one. Then
- $f^{-1}: B \rightarrow A$ is one-to-one
- $(f^{-1})^{-1} = f$

Euclidean Property, p. 162

Given positive integers a and b, there are unique nonnegative integers q (the quotient) and r (the remainder) such that
- $b = a \cdot q + r$
- $0 \leq r < a$

Euclidean Property for Polynomials, p. 162

Given polynomials $f(x)$ and $g(x)$, there are unique polynomials $q(x)$ (the quotient) and $r(x)$ (the remainder) such that
- $f(x) = g(x) \cdot q(x) + r(x)$
- $\deg(r(x)) < \deg(g(x))$

Theorem 2.2 *The Remainder Theorem*, p. 163

If you divide a polynomial $f(x)$ by $x - a$, where a is a number, the remainder is the number $f(a)$.

Theorem 2.3 *The Factor Theorem*, p. 167

Suppose $f(x)$ is a polynomial. Then the number a is a root of the equation $f(x) = 0$ if and only if $x - a$ is a factor of $f(x)$.

Corollary 2.3.1, p. 168

A polynomial of degree n can have at most n distinct real-number zeros.

Corollary 2.3.2, p. 168

If two polynomials of degree n agree at $n + 1$ inputs, they are identical.

Corollary 2.3.3, p. 169

A polynomial of degree n is completely determined by its output values for $n + 1$ inputs.

Theorem 2.4, p. 181

The following identities show the factoring for the difference of cubes and the sum of cubes.
- $x^3 - y^3 = (x - y)(x^2 + xy + y^2)$
- $x^3 + y^3 = (x + y)(x^2 - xy + y^2)$

Theorem 2.5, p. 186

The following are identities.
- $(x + y)^3 = x^3 + 3x^2y + 3xy^2 + y^3$
- $(x - y)^3 = x^3 - 3x^2y + 3xy^2 - y^3$

Chapter 3

Theorem 3.1, p. 225

If a, b, c, and d are real numbers, then $a + bi = c + di$ only when $a = c$ and $b = d$.

Theorem 3.2, p. 247

Suppose $z = a + bi$ and $w = c + di$ are complex numbers. Then, on the complex plane, the numbers 0, z, w, and $z + w$ form the vertices of a parallelogram.

Theorem 3.3 *Multiplication by i*, p. 249

If z is a complex number, iz is obtained from z by rotating it 90° counterclockwise about the origin.

Theorem 3.4 *Magnitude and Conjugates,* **p. 254**

The magnitude $|z|$ of a complex number is given by $|z| = \sqrt{z\bar{z}}$.

Theorem 3.5, p. 272

Given complex numbers z and w, the following statements are true.
- $|zw| = |z| \cdot |w|$
- $\arg zw = \arg z + \arg w$

Theorem 3.6, p. 279

Suppose that z and w are complex numbers. Then the following statements are true.
$$\bar{z} + \bar{w} = \overline{z + w}$$
When you add conjugates, the result is the conjugate of the sum of the original numbers.
$$\bar{z} \cdot \bar{w} = \overline{zw}$$
When you multiply conjugates, the result is the conjugate of the product of the original numbers.
$$(\bar{z})^2 = \overline{z^2}$$
When you square a conjugate, the result is the conjugate of the square of the original number. If z is a real number, then $\bar{z} = z$.

Theorem 3.7 *Polynomials and Conjugates,* **p. 280**

For any polynomial f with real coefficients and any complex number z, $\overline{f(z)} = f(\bar{z})$.

Corollary 3.7.1 *Conjugate Pairs,* **p. 280**

If f is a polynomial with real coefficients, and $f(z) = 0$, then $f(\bar{z}) = 0$.

Chapter 4

Theorem 4.1, p. 341

Suppose matrix A represents a system where the z's are linear combinations of y's. Suppose B represents a system where these y's are linear combinations of x's. Then, by substitution, the z's are linear combinations of the x's, and the matrix that represents this system is the product AB.

Chapter 5

Theorem 5.1 *The Fundamental Law of Exponents,* **p. 427**

If b and c are positive integers, then
$$a^b \cdot a^c = a^{b+c}$$

Corollary 5.1.1, p. 428

If b and c are positive integers with $b > c$ and $a \neq 0$, then
$$\frac{a^b}{a^c} = a^{b-c}$$

Corollary 5.1.2, p. 428

For all numbers a and positive integers b and c,
$$(a^b)^c = a^{bc}$$

Lemma 5.1, p. 455

Let $b > 1$ and let x be a positive rational number. Then $b^x > 1$.

Theorem 5.2, p. 455

If $b > 1$, then the function $f(x) = b^x$ is strictly increasing on rational-number inputs. In other words, if s and t are rational numbers such that $s > t$, then $f(s) > f(t)$.

Lemma 5.2, p. 459

Let $0 < b < 1$ and let x be a positive number. Then $b^x < 1$.

Theorem 5.3, p. 459

Let $0 < b < 1$. Then the function $f(x) = b^x$ is strictly decreasing on rational-number inputs.

Theorem 5.4 *One-to-One Property for Exponential Functions,* **p. 478**

If f is an exponential function, then f is one-to-one.

Corollary 5.4.1, p. 478

If $b > 0$, $b \neq 1$, and $b^x = b^y$, then $x = y$.

Theorem 5.5 *Change-of-Base Rule,* **p. 492**

If $b, x, y > 0$, and $b, x, y \neq 1$, then
$$\log_x y = \frac{\log_b y}{\log_b x}$$

Theorem 5.6, p. 514

When you use a logarithmic y-axis and a linear x-axis, the graph of an exponential function $y = a \cdot b^x$ with $a > 0$ and $b > 0$ appears as a straight line.

Corollary 5.6.1, p. 514

The graphs of two exponential functions $f_1(x) = a \cdot b_1{}^x$ and $f_2(x) = a_2 \cdot b_2{}^x$, with all a_i and b_i positive, must intersect exactly once, unless $b_1 = b_2$.

Chapter 6

Theorem 6.1, p. 563

Let a and b be real numbers. Then
$$T_a \circ T_b = T_{a+b}$$

Theorem 6.2, p. 564

Let s and t be nonzero real numbers. Then
$$D_s \circ D_t = D_{st}$$

Chapter 7

Theorem 7.1, p. 640

The following are identities.
- Factors come out.
$$\sum_{k=0}^{n} cf(k) = c \times \sum_{k=0}^{n} f(k)$$
where c is any number
- The sigma of a sum is the sum of the sigmas.
$$\sum_{k=0}^{n} (f(k) + g(k)) = \sum_{k=0}^{n} f(k) + \sum_{k=0}^{n} g(k)$$
- Splitting up a sum
$$\sum_{k=0}^{n} f(k) = \sum_{k=0}^{m} f(k) + \sum_{k=m+1}^{n} f(k)$$
where $0 < m < n$
- Add a bunch of ones.
$$\sum_{k=0}^{n} 1 = n + 1 \text{ or } \sum_{k=1}^{n} 1 = n$$
- Think Gauss.
$$\sum_{k=0}^{n} k = \frac{n(n + 1)}{2}$$
- Think Euclid.
$$\sum_{k=0}^{n} r^k = \frac{r^{n+1} - 1}{r - 1}$$

Theorem 7.2, p. 669

If you take a loan for C dollars for n months at an interest rate of i, then the equation below gives the monthly payment.
$$m = C \cdot \frac{(q - 1)q^1}{q^n - 1}$$
where n is the term of the loan and $q = 1 + \frac{i}{12}$.

Theorem 7.3 *The Binomial Theorem*, p. 694

For $n \geq 0$,
$$(a + b)^n = \binom{n}{0}a^n b^0 + \binom{n}{1}a^{n-1}b^1 +$$
$$\binom{n}{2}a^{n-2}b^2 + \cdots + \binom{n}{k}a^{n-k}b^k + \cdots$$
$$+ \binom{n}{n-1}a^1 b^{n-1} + \binom{n}{n}a^0 b^n$$

Chapter 8

Theorem 8.1, p. 725

If n is an integer and x is an angle in degrees,
- $\cos(x + 360n) = \cos x$
- $\sin(x + 360n) = \sin x$

Theorem 8.2 *The Pythagorean Identity*, p. 730

If α is any angle, then $\cos^2 \alpha + \sin^2 \alpha = 1$.

Theorem 8.3 *Angle-Sum Identities*, p. 754

For all α and β,
- $\cos(\alpha + \beta) = \cos \alpha \cos \beta - \sin \alpha \sin \beta$
- $\sin(\alpha + \beta) = \sin \alpha \cos \beta + \cos \alpha \sin \beta$

Theorem 8.4 *Area of a Triangle*, p. 767

For $\triangle ABC$ with $AB = c$, $AC = b$, and $BC = a$, the area of the triangle is equal to the expressions below.
$$\frac{1}{2}ab \sin C = \frac{1}{2}bc \sin A = \frac{1}{2}ac \sin B$$

Theorem 8.5 *Law of Sines*, p. 773

Given $\triangle ABC$ with corresponding side lengths a, b, and c,
$$\frac{a}{\sin A} = \frac{b}{\sin B} = \frac{c}{\sin C}$$

Theorem 8.6 *The Law of Cosines*, p. 781

Given $\triangle ABC$ with corresponding side lengths a, b, and c,
$$c^2 = a^2 + b^2 - 2ab \cos C$$

Theorem 8.7 *Heron's Formula*, p. 790

Given a triangle with side lengths a, b, and c, the area of the triangle is
$$A = \sqrt{s(s - a)(s - b)(s - c)}$$
where s is the semiperimeter $\frac{a + b + c}{2}$.

Theorem 8.8 *Brahmagupta's Formula*, p. 797

Given a cyclic quadrilateral with side lengths a, b, c, and d, the area of the quadrilateral is
$$A = \sqrt{(s - a)(s - b)(s - c)(s - d)}$$
where s is the semiperimeter $s = \frac{a + b + c + d}{2}$.

Properties and Theorems

Glossary

A

absorbing state (p. 397) An absorbing state in a probability transition matrix brings an end to an infinite situation.

absolute value of a real number (p. 52) The absolute value of a real number is its distance from the origin on the number line.

additive inverse (p. 120) The additive inverse, or opposite, of any number a is $-a$.

affine recursive definition (p. 600) Let $\mathcal{A}_{(a,\,b)}$ be an affine transformation of $\mathbb{R}$ and let p be a number. Then a recursive definition of the form below is an affine recursive definition.

$$f(n) = \begin{cases} p & \text{if } n = 0 \\ \mathcal{A}_{(a,\,b)}(f(n-1)) & \text{if } n > 0 \end{cases}$$

affine transformation (p. 566) Let a and b be real numbers with $a \neq 0$. An affine transformation by (a, b) is a transformation $\mathcal{A}_{(a,\,b)}$ of $\mathbb{R}$ given by $\mathcal{A}_{(a,\,b)} = T_b \circ D_a$.

arithmetic mean (p. 662) The arithmetic mean of any two numbers is their sum divided by two.

arithmetic sequence (pp. 438, 659) A sequence is an arithmetic sequence if its domain is the set of integers $n \geq 0$, and there is a number d, the common difference, for the sequence such that $f(n) = f(n-1) + d$ for all integers $n > 0$.

arithmetic series (p. 660) If the sequence t is an arithmetic sequence with initial term $t(0)$, the associated series T defined on integers n, such that $n \geq 0$ by $T(n) = \sum_{k=0}^{n} t(k)$ is an arithmetic series.

augmentation line (p. 308) An augmentation line is the vertical bar in an augmented matrix that separates the coefficients from the constants.

augmented matrix (p. 308) An augmented matrix contains the coefficients and constants from a system of equations.

B

balance point (p. 44) The balance point $(\bar{x}, \bar{y})$ is the point with x-coordinate that is the average of the x-coordinates in a table and with y-coordinate that is the average of the y-coordinates in the table.

base (p. 454) In the exponential function $f(x) = a \cdot b^x$, b is the base.

Bernoulli's formulas (p. 642) Bernoulli's formulas give closed-form sums for series associated with the functions $x \mapsto x^m$ for positive integers m. For example, $\sum_{k=0}^{n} k = \dfrac{n(n+1)}{2}$, and $\sum_{k=0}^{n} k^2 = \dfrac{n(n+1)(2n=1)}{6}$.

binary operation (p. 110) A binary operation takes two inputs and produces one output.

C

centroid (p. 43) Centroid is another term for balance point. It is most commonly used in geometry.

circle (p. 306) A circle is a set of all points in a plane at a distance r from a given point. The standard form of the equation of a circle with center (h, k) and radius r is $(x - h)^2 + (y - k)^2 = r^2$.

circumcenter (p. 238) The circumcenter of a polygon is the center of the circle that contains the vertices of the polygon.

closed-form definition (p. 9) A closed-form definition of a function uses direct calculation to find an output for any input.

coefficient (p. 90) The coefficient is the numerical factor in a monomial.

coefficient matrix (p. 308) When representing a system of equations with a matrix equation, the matrix containing the coefficients of the system is the coefficient matrix.

collinear (p. 44) Points are collinear if they lie on the same line.

combination (p. 697) Any unordered selection of r objects from a set of n objects is a combination. The number of combinations of n objects taken r at a time is $_nC_r = \dfrac{n!}{r!(n-r)!}$ for $0 \leq r \leq n$.

common difference (p. 659) The common difference for a sequence is a number d such that $f(n) = f(n - 1) + d$ for all $n > 0$.

common logarithm (p. 490) A common logarithm is a logarithm that uses base 10. You can write the common logarithm $\log_{10} y$ as $\log y$.

common ratio (p. 666) The common ratio for a sequence is a number $r \neq 0$ such that $f(n) = r \cdot f(n - 1)$ for all integers $n > 0$.

completing the square (p. 572) Completing the square is a process for converting a quadratic equation into a perfect square trinomial.

complex conjugate (p. 285) The complex numbers $a + bi$ and $a - bi$ are complex conjugates.

complex numbers (p. 224) The system of complex numbers $\mathbb{C}$ consists of all expressions in the form $a + bi$ with the following properties.

- a and b are real numbers.
- $i^2 = -1$
- You can use addition and multiplication as if $a + bi$ were a polynomial.

complex plane (p. 241) The complex plane is used to represent a complex number geometrically. The real-number part of the number is located on the horizontal axis and the imaginary part on the vertical axis.

composite function (p. 110) For two functions $f : A \rightarrow B$ and $g : B \rightarrow C$, the composite function meets the following conditions.

- $g \circ f : A \rightarrow C$
- $g \circ f(x) = g(f(x))$

concurrent lines (p. 58) Concurrent lines all intersect at the same point.

conjugate (p. 230) Number pairs of the form $a + bi$ and $a - bi$ are conjugates. The symbol $\bar{z}$ represents the conjugate of z.

converge (p. 677) When the outputs of an iteration get closer and closer to a number, the iteration converges to that number.

cosine (pp. 720, 724) The cosine function, $y = \cos \theta$, matches the measure θ of an angle in standard position with the x-coordinate of a point on the unit circle. This point is where the terminal side of the angle intersects the unit circle.

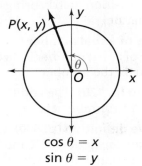

$$\cos \theta = x$$
$$\sin \theta = y$$

cubic function (p. 35) A cubic function is a polynomial in which the highest-degree term is cubed.

D

definite sum (p. 636) A definite sum is a summation with numbers for starting and ending values.

degree of a monomial (p. 90) The degree of a monomial is the sum of the exponents of each variable in the monomial.

degree of a polynomial (p. 90) The degree of a polynomial is the largest degree of any of its terms.

determinant (p. 356) The determinant of a 2×2 matrix $\begin{pmatrix} a & b \\ c & d \end{pmatrix}$ is the real number $ad - bc$.

difference of cubes (p. 181) A difference of cubes is an expression of the form $x^3 - y^3$. It can be factored as $(x - y)(x^2 + xy + y^2)$.

difference table (p. 10) A difference table shows the difference between consecutive outputs. It can help show patterns that lead to recursive definitions.

dilation (p. 562) A dilation is a transformation that changes the size of a figure. A dilation by s is a transformation D_s of $\mathbb{R}$ given by the formula $D_s(x) = sx$ for any real number x.

dimension (p. 308) The dimensions of a matrix tell the number of rows and columns. A matrix with m rows and n columns has dimensions $m \times n$.

discontinuity (p. 749) A point of discontinuity in a graph occurs whenever the function is undefined at that point.

domain (p. 104) The domain of a function is the set of all inputs. *See* **function**.

dot product (p. 331) The dot product is an operation over two n-tuples that returns a real number. If $A = (a_1, a_2, \ldots, a_n)$ and $B = (b_1, b_2, \ldots, b_n)$ then the dot product $A \cdot B$ is the real number $a_1 b_1 + a_2 b_2 + \ldots + a_n b_n$.

E

elimination (p. 302) Elimination is a method for solving a system of equations by using addition, subtraction, and multiplication to find an equation in one variable that can be solved.

equal functions (p. 105) Two functions f and g are equal functions if both of these conditions are satisfied.

- f and g have the same domain.

- $f(a) = g(a)$ for every a in the common domain.

error (p. 48) Error is the difference between the actual value and the predicted value.

Euclid's method (p. 620) Euclid's method tells how to find the sum of a sequence with a constant ratio.

evaluate (p. 9) To evaluate an expression, substitute numbers for the variables in the expression and follow the order of operations.

even function (p. 536) A function f is an even function if it satisfies $f(x) = f(-x)$ for all numbers x in its domain. If point (x, y) is on the graph of f, the point $(-x, y)$ is also on the graph.

exponential decay (p. 462) Given $f(x) = a \cdot b^x$, if $0 < b < 1$, the function shows exponential decay.

exponential equations (p. 486) An equation of the form $b^{cx} = a$, where the exponent includes a variable, is an exponential equation. You can solve an exponential equation by taking the logarithm of each side of the equation.

exponential function (p. 454) An exponential function is a function f that you can write in the form $f(x) = a \cdot b^x$, where $a \neq 0$, $b > 0$, and $b \neq 1$.

exponential growth (p. 462) Given $f(x) = a \cdot b^x$, if $b > 1$, the function $f(x)$ shows exponential growth.

F

factorial function (p. 78) The factorial function is defined by the recursive function
$$f(n) = \begin{cases} 1 & \text{if } n = 0 \\ n \cdot f(n - 1) & \text{if } n > 0 \end{cases}$$

factoring (p. 167) Factoring is rewriting an expression as the product of its factors.

figurate numbers (p. 648) Figurate numbers tell the number of dots needed to make a series of regular geometric shapes of increasing size. Examples of figurate numbers include the triangular, square, and pentagonal numbers.

fixed point (p. 597) Let $\mathcal{A}_{(a, b)}$ be an affine transformation. A number x is a fixed point of $\mathcal{A}_{(a, b)}$ if $\mathcal{A}_{(a, b)}(x) = x$.

function (p. 104) A function from set A to set B is a pairing between A and B such that each element in A pairs with exactly one element of B. A is the *domain* of f. B is the *target* of f. The set of objects in B that are paired with objects in A is the *range* of f.

function notation (p. 96) You read the function notation $f(x)$ as "f of x" or "a function of x." Note that $f(x)$ does *not* mean "f times x."

functional equation (p. 471) A functional equation is an equation with unknowns that are functions.

Fundamental Theorem of Algebra (p. 227) If $P(x)$ is a polynomial of degree $n \geq 1$ with complex coefficients, then $P(x) = 0$ has at least one complex root.

G

Gaussian Elimination (p. 310) Gaussian elimination is an algorithm that transforms the matrix of any given system of linear equations through a sequence of other matrices, ending in a final matrix form from which the solution to the corresponding system is obvious.

Gauss's method (p. 620) Gauss's method tells how to find the sum of a sequence with a constant difference.

geometric sequence (pp. 439, 666) A sequence is a geometric sequence if its domain is the integers $n \geq 0$, and there is a number $r \neq 0$, called the common ratio, such that $f(n) = r \cdot f(n - 1)$ for all integers $n > 0$.

geometric series (p. 666) If a sequence g is a geometric sequence with initial term $g(0)$, the associated series $G(n) = \sum_{k=0}^{n} g(n)$ is a geometric series.

H

Heronian triangle (p. 794) A Heronian triangle is a triangle with integer side lengths and integer area.

hockey stick property (p. 17) The hockey stick property states that, in a difference table, an output is the sum of all of the differences above it to the right and the single output at the top of the table.

hypotenuse (p. 237) The hypotenuse of a right triangle is the side opposite the right angle. It is always the longest side in a right triangle.

I

i (p. 220) The imaginary number i is defined as the number with square -1. So $i^2 = -1$ and $i = \sqrt{-1}$.

identity (p. 637) An identity is a statement that two expressions that may seem different are actually equivalent under the basic rules of algebra.

identity function (p. 119) The identity function on a set is the function id that simply returns its input.

identity matrix (pp. 312, 354) An identity matrix is a square matrix with all entries 0 except for 1's along the main diagonal from the top left to the bottom right. Multiplying a matrix by an identity matrix will result in the original matrix.

identity transformation (p. 559) An identity transformation leaves all inputs unchanged.

image (p. 372) An image is a figure obtained by a transformation of a preimage.

imaginary number (p. 241) An imaginary number is any number of the form $a + bi$, where $b \neq 0$.

indefinite sum (p. 636) An indefinite sum is a summation with a variable for the ending value of the index.

index (p. 628) The index of a summation indicates the range of the variable.

intercept (p. 215) An intercept is a point where a graph crosses either the x- or y-axis.

interest (p. 72) Interest is the amount of money paid regularly at a particular rate for the use of money lent.

initial side (of an angle) (p. 724) When an angle is in standard position, the side along the x-axis is the initial side of the angle, and the side not along the x-axis is the terminal side of the angle.

inverse function (f^{-1}) (p. 119) Suppose f is a one-to-one function with domain A and range B. The inverse function f^{-1} is a function with these properties:

- f^{-1} has domain B and range A.
- For all x in B, $f(f^{-1}(x)) = x$, or alternatively, $f \circ f^{-1} = $ id.

inverse matrix (A^{-1}) (p. 355) The inverse of matrix A is a matrix M such that $AM = I$. You write it as A^{-1}.

irrational numbers (p. 213) Irrational numbers cannot by expressed as the quotient of integers.

iteration (p. 599) An iteration is a repeated calculation that uses the previous result in the next calculation.

L

Lagrange interpolation (p. 147) Lagrange interpolation is a method of finding a polynomial to fit a data set.

Law of Cosines (p. 781) Given $\triangle ABC$ with corresponding side lengths a, b, and c, $c^2 = a^2 + b^2 - 2ab \cos C$.

Law of Sines (p. 773) Given $\triangle ABC$ with corresponding side lengths a, b, and c, $\frac{a}{\sin A} = \frac{b}{\sin B} = \frac{c}{\sin C}$.

leg (p. 240) The legs in a right triangle are the sides adjacent to the right angle.

limit (p. 675) A limit is a value a series or summation converges to as the input values increase.

line of best fit (p. 62) Given a set of data, the line of best fit is the line that minimizes the sum of the squares of the errors. It minimizes the mean squared error.

linear combination (p. 339) A linear combination of variables is a sum of multiples of the variables.

linear function (p. 18) A linear function is a function of the form $x \mapsto ax + b$ for some numbers a and b.

linear scale (p. 510) A linear scale increases by a constant amount.

logarithm (p. 489) A logarithm of a positive number y to the base b is defined as follows: If $y = b^x$, then $\log_b y = x$. If a base is not given, it is assumed to be 10. The logarithmic function is often called the logarithm.

logarithmic function (p. 489) The logarithmic function $x \mapsto \log_b x$ is the inverse function of the exponential function $x \mapsto b^x$.

logarithmic scale (p. 510) A logarithmic scale increases by a common multiple.

M

matrix (p. 308) A matrix is a rectangular array of numbers written within brackets. A matrix with m horizontal rows and n vertical columns is an $m \times n$ matrix.

matrix equation (p. 344) A matrix equation is an equation in which the variable is a matrix.

matrix multiplication (p. 340) Let A have as many columns as B has rows. Say, A is $m \times n$ and B is $n \times p$. Let the rows of A be called $R_1, R_2, \ldots, R_m$. Let the columns of B be called $C_1, C_2, \ldots, C_p$. The product AB is defined to be the $m \times p$ matrix for which the entry ij is the dot product $R_i \cdot C_j$.

$$AB = \begin{pmatrix} R_1 \cdot C_1 & R_1 \cdot C_2 & \cdots & R_1 \cdot C_p \\ R_2 \cdot C_1 & R_2 \cdot C_2 & \cdots & R_2 \cdot C_p \\ \vdots & \vdots & \ddots & \vdots \\ R_m \cdot C_1 & R_m \cdot C_2 & \cdots & R_m \cdot C_p \end{pmatrix}$$

matrix transformation (p. 376) A transformation is called a matrix transformation if it can be expressed in the form $X \mapsto AX$, where A is a 2×2 matrix and points X are represented as column vectors $\begin{pmatrix} x \\ y \end{pmatrix}$ so that they can be multiplied by matrices on the left.

mean (p. 43) The sum of the data values divided by the number of data values.

mean absolute error (p. 55) The mean absolute error is the average of the absolute values of the differences between the line of best fit and the actual data points.

mean squared error (p. 55) The mean squared error is the average of the squares of the differences between the line of best fit and the actual data points.

median (p. 59) The median is the middle value in a data set. If the data set contains an even number of values, the median is the mean of the two middle values.

mode (p. 59) The mode is the most frequently occurring value (or values) in a set of data.

monic (p. 124) A monic polynomial is a polynomial with a leading coefficient of one.

monomial (p. 90) A monomial is an expression that you can write as a product of a nonzero number and one or more variables, each raised to a nonnegative integer exponent.

monotonic (p. 472) A function is monotonic if it either increases or decreases over its domain.

multiplicative inverse (p. 120) The multiplicative inverse, or reciprocal, of any nonzero number a is $\frac{1}{a}$.

N

n factorial ($n!$) (p. 79) For any positive integer n, $n!$ is the product of all of the integers between n and 1. $0! = 1$.

n-tuple (p. 331) An n-tuple is a string of n numbers.

nth root (p. 445) For any real numbers a and b, and any positive integer n, if $a^n = b$, then a is the nth root of b.

natural domain (p. 97) The natural domain of a function is the largest set of inputs for which a function produces an output.

natural numbers (p. 213) The natural numbers, or counting numbers, are $1, 2, 3, \ldots$ and are represented by the symbol $\mathbb{N}$.

negative exponent (a^{-m}) (p. 433) If $a \neq 0$ and m is a positive integer, then $a^{-m} = \frac{1}{a^m}$.

normal form (p. 91) A polynomial is in normal form if it contains no parenthesis, like terms have been combined, and the degrees of the terms go from highest to lowest.

O

odd function (p. 536) A function f is an odd function if it satisfies $f(-x) = -f(x)$ for all numbers x in its domain. If the point (x, y) is on the graph of f, the point $(-x, -y)$ is also on the graph.

one-to-one (p. 117) A function is one-to-one if its outputs are unique. That is, a function f is one-to-one if $f(r) = f(s)$ only when $r = s$.

opposite (p. 120) The opposite, or additive inverse, of any number a is $-a$.

outlier (p. 46) An outlier is an item of data with a substantially different value from the rest of the items in the data set.

P

parabola (p. 545) A parabola is the graph of a quadratic function.

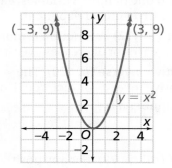

Pascal's Triangle (p. 689) Pascal's triangle is a pattern that can be used to find combinations of n things taken k at a time. Each entry can be labeled $\binom{n}{k}$, where n is the row number and k is the column number.

```
                1
              1   1
            1   2   1
          1   3   3   1
        1   4   6   4   1
      1   5   10  10   5   1
    1   6   15  20  15   6   1
```

period (p. 747) A period of a periodic function is one complete pattern of y-values.

periodic function (p. 725) A periodic function repeats a pattern of y-values at regular intervals.

piecewise-defined function (p. 128) A piecewise-defined function is a function in which the domain is split into at least two non-overlapping subsets, each with its own distinct function definition.

polynomial (p. 90) A polynomial is a sum of monomials.

polynomial function (p. 38) A polynomial function is a function defined on $\mathbb{R}$ by a polynomial.

probability transition matrix (p. 395) A probability transition matrix is a matrix that shows the probabilities of moving from one state or position to another.

Q

$\mathbb{Q}$ (p. 193) $\mathbb{Q}$ is the set of all rational numbers.

quadratic formula (p. 181) A quadratic equation written in standard form $ax^2 + bx + c = 0$, can be solved using the quadratic formula.

$$x = \frac{-b \pm \sqrt{b^2 - 4ac}}{2a}$$

quadratic function (p. 31) A quadratic function is a function defined by a polynomial of degree 2.

quartic (p. 188) A quartic polynomial is a fourth-degree polynomial.

quotient (p. 162) Given positive integers a and b, there are nonnegative integers q (the quotient) and r (the remainder) such that $b = a \cdot q + r$ and $0 \le r < a$. Given polynomials $f(x)$ and $g(x)$, there are unique polynomials $q(x)$ (the quotient) and $r(x)$ (the remainder) such that $f(x) = g(x) \cdot q(x) + r(x)$ and $\deg(r(x)) < \deg(g(x))$.

R

$\mathbb{R}$ (p. 102) $\mathbb{R}$ is the set of all real numbers.

radius (p. 97) The radius r of a circle is the distance between the center of the circle and any point on the circumference.

range (p. 104) The range of a function is the set of objects that are paired with objects from the domain. *See* **function**.

rational exponent $\left(a^{\frac{p}{q}}\right)$ (p. 446) For integers p and q with $q > 0$, if $a^{\frac{1}{q}}$ is a real number, then $a^{\frac{p}{q}} = \left(a^{\frac{1}{q}}\right)^p = \left(\sqrt[q]{a}\right)^p$.

rational expression (p. 196) A rational expression is a ratio of two expressions.

reciprocal (p. 120) The reciprocal, or multiplicative inverse, of any nonzero number a is $\frac{1}{a}$.

recursive definition (p. 9) A recursive definition of a function gives an output in terms of previous outputs.

reflection (p. 372) A reflection, or flip, is a transformation that maps a point in the plane to its mirror image, using a specific line as a mirror.

reflection transformation (p. 560) A reflection transformation on a function returns the opposite of the input.

relation (p. 104) A relation is any pairing between two sets A and B.

remainder (p. 162) Given positive integers a and b, there are nonnegative integers q (the quotient) and r (the remainder) such that $b = a \cdot q + r$ and $0 \le r < a$. Given polynomials $f(x)$ and $g(x)$, there are unique polynomials $q(x)$ (the quotient) and $r(x)$ (the remainder) such that $f(x) = g(x) \cdot q(x) + r(x)$ and $\deg(r(x)) < \deg(g(x))$.

repeating decimal (p. 683) A repeating decimal is a decimal that has a set of digits that repeat infinitely many times.

roots of unity (p. 287) The solutions to $x^n = 1$ are roots of unity. They will all have magnitude 1 and a direction n times the direction of x.

rotation (p. 249) A rotation is a transformation that turns a figure about a fixed point called the center of rotation.

row-reduced echelon form (rref) (p. 311) A matrix in row-reduced echelon form is the final matrix in an Gaussian elimination. There will be an identity matrix to the left of the augmentation line.

S

scalar multiplication (p. 325) Multiplying a matrix by a number (called a scalar) is scalar multiplication.

sequence (p. 658) A sequence is a function with a domain that is the set of nonnegative integers.

series associated with f (p. 637) Given a function having a domain that contains the nonnegative integers, the series associated with f is the function defined on nonnegative integers by

$$F(n) = \sum_{k=0}^{n} f(k) = f(0) + f(1) + f(2) + \cdots + f(n)$$

sine (pp. 720, 724) The sine function, $y = \sin\theta$, matches the measure θ of an angle in standard position with the y-coordinate of a point on the unit circle. This point is where the terminal side of the angle intersects the unit circle.

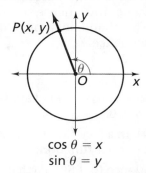

$$\cos\theta = x$$
$$\sin\theta = y$$

slope (p. 15) Slope is the ratio of the change in the y-coordinates to the change in the x-coordinates.

square matrix (p. 362) A square matrix is a matrix with equal numbers of columns and rows.

stabilizer (p. 599) Let x be a real number. Then the stabilizer of x, denoted S_x, is the set of all affine transformations that fix x.

standard error (p. 55) The standard error is a measure of error involving the square root of the mean squared error.

standard position (of an angle) (p. 722) An angle is in standard position when its vertex is at the origin and one of its sides lies along the positive x-axis. The angle opens counterclockwise from this fixed side.

steady state (p. 389) A steady state occurs when a variable in a system settles to a constant value.

strictly decreasing (p. 456) A function f is strictly decreasing if for any s and t such that $s > t$, then $f(s) < f(t)$.

strictly increasing (p. 455) A function f is strictly increasing if for any s and t such that $s > t$, then $f(s) > f(t)$.

substitution (p. 302) Substitution is a method for solving a system of equations by replacing one variable with an equivalent expression containing the other variable(s).

sum of cubes (p. 181) A sum of cubes is an expression of the form $x^3 + y^3$. It factors as $(x + y)(x^2 - xy + y^2)$.

summation notation (p. 628) The general form of summation notation is
$$\sum_{k=0}^{n} f(k) = f(0) + f(1) + \cdots f(n),$$ where k is the index variable, 0 is the starting value, and n is the final value. You can use summation notation as a shorthand notation to describe the sum of a sequence.

T

tangent (p. 724) The tangent of angle θ is $\frac{\sin \theta}{\cos \theta}$, whenever $\cos \theta \neq 0$.

target (p. 104) In a function f from A to B, B is the target of f. *See* **function**.

term of a sequence (p. 658) Each number in a sequence is a term.

terminal side (of an angle) (p. 724) When an angle is in standard position, the side along the x-axis is the initial side of the angle, and the side not along the x-axis is the terminal side of the angle.

terms of a polynomial (p. 90) Each monomial in a polynomial is a term.

transition matrix (p. 389) A transition matrix is used to model changes from one time period, or state, to another.

transformation (p. 562) A transformation is a change made to a figure. Four types of transformations are translations, rotations, reflections, and dilations.

translation (p. 562) A translation is a transformation that slides a graph or figure horizontally, vertically, or both without changing the size or shape of the graph. A translation by a is a transformation T_a of $\mathbb{R}$ given by the formula $T_a(x) = x + a$ for any real number x.

triangular numbers (p. 14) The triangular numbers are numbers determined by how many dots are needed to form a triangle with n dots on a side. The number of dots in a triangular pattern with n dots on a side is the nth triangular number.

trigonometric equation (p. 736) A trigonometric equation is an equation that involves trigonometric functions.

trigonometric identities (p. 740) A trigonometric identity is a trigonometric equation that is true for all values except those for which an expression on either side of the equal sign is undefined.

U

unit circle (p. 532) The unit circle has a radius of 1 unit and its center at the origin of the coordinate plane.

unit fraction exponent (p. 445) The expression $a^{\frac{1}{n}}$ is defined, when possible, as the real nth root of a.
$$a^{\frac{1}{n}} = \sqrt[n]{a}$$

up-and-over property (p. 17) The up-and-over property states that, in a difference table, an output is the sum of the two numbers above it: the output directly above and the difference above and to the right.

V

variable (p. 53) A variable is a symbol, usually a letter, that represents one or more variables.

vector (p. 246) A vector is any quantity that has magnitude and direction. It is represented as an arrow from the origin to a point.

vertex of a parabola (p. 545) The vertex of a parabola is the point at which the parabola intersects the line of symmetry. The y-value of the vertex is the maximum or minimum value of the function.

X

$x \mapsto y$ (p. 100) $x \mapsto y$ is read as "x maps to y." This uses arrow notation to represent a function.

x-intercept (p. 300) The point at which a line crosses the x-axis (or the x-coordinate of that point) is an x-intercept.

Y

y-intercept (p. 454) The point at which a line crosses the *y*-axis (or the *y*-coordinate of that point) is a *y*-intercept.

Z

ℤ (p. 175) ℤ is the set of all integers.

zero exponent (a^0) (p. 433) If $a \neq 0$, then $a^0 = 1$.

zero matrix (p. 345) The zero matrix 0, or $0_{m \times n}$, is the $m \times n$ matrix with elements that are all zeros. It is the additive identity matrix for the set of all $m \times n$ matrices.

zeros of a function (p. 123) The zeros of a function j are the numbers a that make $j(a) = 0$.

Selected Answers

Chapter 1
Lesson 1.01
On Your Own
3–18. Answers may vary. Samples are given.
3. $E(n) = 2n + 3$ **8.** $J(n) = 2n^2$
12. $N(n) = (n + 3)^2$ **16.** $R(n) = n^3$
18. $T(n) = 3^n$

Lesson 1.02
Check Your Understanding
1.

Input, n	Output, $B(n)$	Δ
0	0	2
1	2	4
2	6	6
3	12	8
4	20	

2a. no **b.** no **c.** yes **d.** no **3a.** no **b.** yes **c.** yes
d. no
4.

Input	Output	Δ
0	5	6
1	11	8
2	19	10
3	29	15
4	44	

5.

Input	Output	Δ
0	6	3
1	9	3
2	12	3
3	15	3
4	18	

6.

Input	Output	Δ
0	5	−3
1	2	15
2	17	−13
3	4	−5
4	−1	

7a. $f(1) = 1 \cdot f(0) = 1 \cdot 1 = 1$
$f(2) = 2 \cdot f(1) = 2 \cdot 1 = 2$
$f(3) = 3 \cdot f(2) = 3 \cdot 2 = 6$
$f(4) = 4 \cdot f(3) = 4 \cdot 6 = 24$
$f(5) = 5 \cdot f(4) = 5 \cdot 24 = 120$
$f(6) = 6 \cdot f(5) = 6 \cdot 120 = 720$
b. $f(n) = n!$
8a.

Input	Output
0	2
1	6
2	**10**
3	**14**
4	**18**

b–c.

Input	Output
0	2
1	6
2	**18**
3	**54**
4	**162**

d. see part (a) **9.** Answers may vary. Sample: Tables E, F, and G have a constant difference in the difference table; Tables I, J, and K include an x^2 term in the rule.

On Your Own
10.

Side Length	Number of Dots	Δ
0	0	**1**
1	1	**2**
2	3	**3**
3	6	**4**
4	10	**5**
5	15	

11a. $T(n) = T(n - 1) + n$
12a. The differences are all a.

Lesson 1.03
Check Your Understanding

1.

Input	Output	Δ
0	−7	3
1	−4	3
2	−1	3
3	2	3
4	5	3
5	8	

2. $f(n) = \begin{cases} -7 & \text{if } n = 0 \\ f(n-1) + 3 & \text{if } n > 0 \end{cases}$

3. $g(n) = 3n - 7$ **4a.** 23 **b.** 23.3 for closed form rule; the recursive rule cannot be applied if n is not a nonnegative integer. **5.** The differences are −6, 6, −6, and 6, which are not constant.

6.

n	p(n)	Δ
0	3	$-\frac{7}{4}$
1	$\frac{5}{4}$	$-\frac{7}{4}$
2	$-\frac{1}{2}$	$-\frac{7}{4}$
3	$-\frac{9}{4}$	$-\frac{7}{4}$
4	−4	

7. $p(10) = -\frac{29}{2}$; $p(100) = -172$;

$p(263) = -\frac{1829}{4}$ **8.** D

9a.

n	F(n)	Δ
0	1	0
1	1	1
2	2	1
3	3	2
4	5	3
5	8	5
6	13	

b. The differences are the same as the outputs except that $\Delta_1 = 0$ and $\Delta_n = F(n-1)$ for $n > 0$. **c.** $F(10) = 89$

14a.

n	D(n)	Δ
0	1	1
1	2	2
2	4	4
3	8	8
4	16	16
5	32	32
6	64	

b. The differences are directly related to the output. They are the same. $D(n + 1) - D(n) = D(n)$. They will never get to constant differences **17.** −1.5

Lesson 1.04
Check Your Understanding

1a. $\frac{7}{2}$ **b.** $-\frac{1}{2}$ **c.** $f(n) = \frac{7}{2}n - \frac{1}{2}$ **2a.** $\frac{7}{2}$

b. $y = \frac{7}{2}x - \frac{1}{2}$ or $2y = 7x - 1$ **3.** The slope for $(0, -12)$ and $(3, 5)$ is $\frac{17}{3}$, and the slope for $(3, 5)$ and $(4, 10)$ is 5, so one line cannot contain all three points. **4.** No; the difference for the last two outputs is 5, but using that as the constant difference, you would expect the point $(0, -10)$, so the table does not have a constant difference. **5.** $a = -1, b = -26$ **6.** $f(n) = \frac{n}{2} - 2$ **7a.** 2 **b.** −18 **7c.** $f(n) = 5n - 33$

8. The differences are 1, 3, 5, and 7. Since those differences are not constant, the table cannot match a linear function.

9.

x	K(x)	Δ	Δ²
0	1	1	2
1	2	3	2
2	5	5	2
3	10	7	
4	17		

10a. −5 **b.** $a = -1$

12a.

b. 0

17.

w	R(w)	Δ	Δ²	Δ³
0	0	1	6	6
1	1	7	12	6
2	8	19	18	6
3	27	37	24	6
4	64	61	30	6
5	125	91	36	
6	216	127		
7	343			

Lesson 1.05

Check Your Understanding

1. $y(n) = 5n^2 + 3n - 2$

2. $y(n) = -3n^2 + 15n + 10$

3.

w	R(w)	Δ	Δ²	Δ³
0	0	1	6	6
1	1	7	12	6
2	8	19	18	6
3	27	37	24	6
4	64	61	30	6
5	125	91	36	
6	216	127		
7	343			

4.

x	m(x)	Δ	Δ²	Δ³
0	4	−3	34	30
1	1	31	64	30
2	32	95	94	30
3	127	189	124	30
4	316	313	154	30
5	629	467	184	
6	1096	651		
7	1747			

5a. The column for Δ^3 should be constant. **b.** The constant third difference is 6 times the leading coefficient. **6.** Yes; for any table with constant third differences, calculate $f(x + 1) - f(x)$ and show that the result can be put into Sasha's form. **7.** The Δ column begins $a + b + c$, $7a + 3b + c$, $19a + 5b + c$; the Δ^2 column begins $6a + 2b$, $12a + 2b$, $18a + 2b$; the Δ^3 column begins $6a$, $6a$, $6a$. **8a.** $x = 3, x = 5, x = 6$ **b.** $x^3 - 14x^2 + 63x - 90$

9.

x	v(x)	Δ	Δ²	Δ³
0	−90	50	−22	6
1	−40	28	−16	6
2	−12	12	−10	6
3	0	2	−4	6
4	2	−2	2	6
5	0	0	8	
6	0	8		
7	8			

10. $y = 10x^2 - 23x + 7$ **11a.** No, the third differences are not constant. **b.** Except for the left column, each cell is equal to the cell that is one to the right and one down.

12. $f(n) = 2n^3 - 5n^2 + n - 3$

On Your Own

17. None of the first, second, or third differences are constant, so the table is not a linear, quadratic, or cubic function. **18.** The values of Rule 4 match the five input-output pairs in the table.

Lesson 1.06
On Your Own
8a. 86 **9a.** Answers will vary. Sample: More

people are living in the western regions of the country. **10a.** For each pair of points the slope is 3, so the points lie on a line. **b.** $y = 3x + 4$ **12a.** 5.9

Lesson 1.07
Check Your Understanding
1a. Answers may vary. Samples: $y = 2x$, $y = x + 3$, $y = 6$ **b.** $7x + 5y = 51$
2a–b.

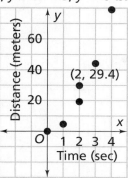

b. (2, 29.4) **c.** No; the points seem to lie on a curve, not a line.
3a-b.

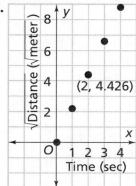

b. (2, 4.426) **c.** Yes, the points seem to lie on a line.

4.

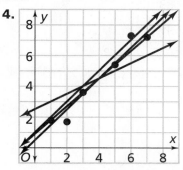

Lines (c) and (d) seem to fit the data.
5a. (667, −93) **b.** (629, 6) **6.** For 1900–1960: (1929, 233.2); a linear function is $f(x) = -0.5(x - 1929) + 233.3$. For 1960–2000: (1980, 216); a linear function is $f(x) = 216$. The two functions fit the data better than the single function $f(x) = -0.34x + 892.1$.

a. Using $f(x) = -0.5(x - 1929) + 233.3$ for the dates prior to 1960, $f(1916) \approx 240$, $f(1940) \approx 228$, $f(1944) \approx 226$.
b. Using $f(x) = 216$ for dates after 1960, $f(2623) = 216$.

On Your Own
7a. no **b.** below **9a.** The balance point is (4, 4.5); an equation is $y = x + 0.5$ or $y = 0.9x + 0.9$. **b.** For line (c), the sum of the errors is 0 and for line (d) the sum of the errors is 0. **11a.** 14 sixes **b.** mean: 3.5; median: 3; mode: 3 **13a.** Data vs. Line Fit: $y = 333.4476x - 26.2917$

Hours x	Actual Yeast Density, y	Predicted Yeast Density, y	Error
0	9.6	−26.3	35.9
1	18.3	7.2	11.1
2	29.0	40.6	−11.6
3	47.2	74.1	−26.9
4	71.1	107.5	−36.4
5	119.1	141.0	−21.9
6	174.6	174.4	−0.2
7	257.3	207.8	49.5

Lesson 1.08
Check Your Understanding
1. A **2a.** A **b.** For $y = 3x - 1$: sum of errors is −2.4; mean absolute error is 1.15; mean squared error is 2.565. For $y = -x + 8.4$: sum of errors is 1; mean absolute error is 2.9; mean squared error is 8.855.
3a.

Input	Output	Predicted	Error
1	3	$3 \cdot 1 + b = 3 + b$	$3 - (3 + b) = -b$
2	4.5	$3 \cdot 2 + b = 6 + b$	$4.5 - (6 + b) = -1.5 - b$
3	8.1	$3 \cdot 3 + b = 9 + b$	$8.1 - (9 + b) = -0.9 - b$
4	8	$3 \cdot 4 + b = 12 + b$	$-4 - b$

b. $4b^2 + 12.8b + 19.06$ **c.** −1.6
d. $y = 3x - 1.6$ **4a.** $y = x + 3.4$
b. $y = 2x + 0.9$ **c.** $y = 5.9$
5.

Slope	Equation of Best Line
0	$y = 5.9$
1	$y = x + 3.4$
2	$y = 2x + 0.9$
3	$y = 3x - 1.6$

As the slope increases by 1, the constant term decreases by 2.5.

On Your Own

6. Table 1.

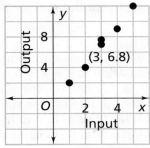

Table 2.

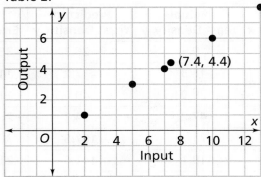

Table 3.

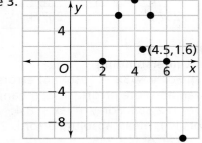

Table 4.

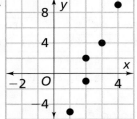

Tables 1, 2, and 4 show a linear trend.

7a. (3, 6.8) **9a.** 1.25 **10a.** 1.32

Lesson 1.09

Check Your Understanding

1. Table 1: $y = 4x - 7$; Table 2: $y = 4x - 19$; Table 3: $y = 12x - 5$; Table 4: $y = 12x - 29$

2. $y = 1.86x + 1.25$ **3a.** $y = 53.69x - 85.36$

b. quadratic: $y = 7.56x^2 - 14.35x + 28.04$; exponential: $y = 13.9 \cdot 1.55^x$; the quadratic has the smaller mean squared error.

On Your Own

5. Table 1

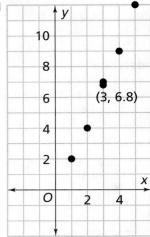

6. Table 1: (3, 6.8) **7.** Table 1: $y = 2.5x - 0.7$

Lesson 1.10

On Your Own

10.

n	$t(n)$
0	1
1	3
2	9
3	27
4	81
5	243
6	729
7	2187
8	6561
9	19,683
10	54,049

$t(n) = 3^n$; $t(103) \approx 1.39 \times 10^{49}$, $t(104) \approx 4.17 \times 10^{49}$, $t(245) \approx 7.8 \times 10^{116}$.

11.

n	j(n)
0	1
1	4
2	9
3	16
4	25
5	36
6	49
7	64
8	81
9	100
10	121

$j(n) = (n + 1)^2$; $j(103) = 10,816$, $j(104) = 11,025$, $j(245) = 60,516$.

13.

n	d(n)
0	1
1	1
2	2
3	6
4	24
5	120
6	720
7	5040
8	40,320
9	362,880
10	3,628,800

$$d(n) = \begin{cases} 1 & \text{if } n = 0 \\ n \cdot d(n - 1) & \text{if } n > 0 \end{cases}$$

Lesson 1.11
Check Your Understanding
1. $6390.74 **2.** no **3a.** $269.74 **b.** $250.51
c. $207.26 **4.** $8341.43 **5.** about 0.9%

On Your Own
7. Answers may vary. Sample: For cars that cost less than $33,200, you would pay less over the life of the loan if you chose the rebate deal. For cars that cost more than $33,200, you would pay less if you chose the low interest rate deal. The deals are the same if the car costs $33,200.

Lesson 1.12
Check Your Understanding
1.

n	g(n)
2	2
3	3
4	4
5	5
6	6
7	7
8	8
9	9
10	10

$g(n) = n$

2.

n	h(n)
3	6
4	12
5	20
6	30
7	42
8	56
9	72
10	90

$h(n) = n(n - 1)$ **3.** $k(n) = \dfrac{n!}{(n - 4)!}$
4. $q(n) = (n!)^2$ **5a.** 1 **b.** 2 **c.** 4

On Your Own

6a. 8 **7.** $f(n) = \begin{cases} 2 & \text{if } n = 1 \\ n \cdot f(n - 1) & \text{if } n > 1 \end{cases}$

10a.

n	r(n)
1	1
2	3
3	6
4	10
5	15

b. $r(n) = \begin{cases} 1 & \text{if } n = 1 \\ r(n - 1) + n & \text{if } n > 1 \end{cases}$

c. $r(n) = \dfrac{n(n + 1)}{2}$

12a.

n	$t(n)$
1	3
2	15
3	105
4	945
5	10,395

b. $t(n) = \begin{cases} 2 & \text{if } n = 1 \\ t(n-1) \cdot (2n+1) & \text{if } n > 1 \end{cases}$

Chapter 2

Lesson 2.0

Check Your Understanding

1a. no **b.** no **c.** yes **d.** yes **e.** no **2a.** 2 **b.** 27
3. $g(n) = n^3$ **4a.** $x^3 + x^2 + x + 1$
b. $x^7 + x^6 + x^5 + x^4 + x^3 + x^2 + x + 1$
c. $x^{15} + x^{14} + \ldots + x^2 + x + 1$
d. $x^{31} + x^{30} + \ldots + x^2 + x + 1$ **5a.** 3, 4
b. -20, 4 **c.** 4, 6

On Your Own

6a. 0 **b.** $f(1) = 0$, so $(x - 1)$ is a factor of $f(x)$.
8a. $f(3) = 16$ **b.** $x^2 + 4x - 21$
11a. deg $(fg) = $ deg $(f) + $ deg (g)

Lesson 2.01

On Your Own

6a. no **7a.** Answers may vary. Sample: -3
and 3 **8b.** 5 **9b.** 10

Lesson 2.02

Check Your Understanding

1a. all real numbers ≤ 1296
b.

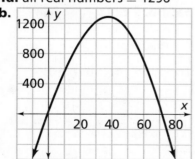

2a. $A(x) = x(72 - x)$ **b.** positive numbers less
than 72 **c.** positive numbers less than or
equal to 1296

d.

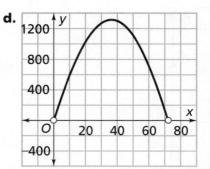

3. No; they have different domains and ranges.

4a.

Input	Output
0	3
1	8
2	13
3	18
4	23
5	28

b. H: all real numbers; K: all nonnegative
integers **c.** No; they have different domains
and ranges. **5a.** all nonnegative real numbers
b. all nonnegative real numbers **6a.** domain is
$\mathbb{R}^2$ and the target is $\mathbb{R}$ **b.** Answers may vary.
Sample: (0, 4), (6, 0), (3, 2), or any solution of
$b = \dfrac{12 - 2a}{3}$

c.

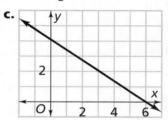

7a. $f(3) = 27$, $f(-3) = 27$ **b.** 2, -2 **c.** 63
d. $f(x + 1) = 3(x + 1)^2 = 3(x^2 + 2x + 1) =$
$3x^2 + 6x + 3$ **e.** $6x + 3$ **f.** 63 **8a.** 5 **b.** 5
c. 10 **d.** A **e.** $2x + 1$ **f.** $6x + 3$ **g.** $20x + 10$
h. $2x + 11$ **i.** $6x + 13$ **9a.** all real numbers ≤ 6
b.

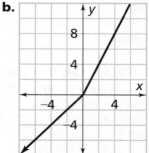

On Your Own

14a. domain: all real numbers; target: all real numbers; range: $f(x) \geq \frac{-49}{24}$ **b.** domain: $x \geq 3$; target: all real numbers; range: all nonnegative real numbers **15a.** 12

d. $z^2 - 4z - 6$ **16a.** $-\frac{1}{3}$ **17a.** 4096 **18b.** false

Lesson 2.03

Check Your Understanding

1a. 9 **b.** 16 **c.** 35 **d.** 35 **e.** 46 **f.** 144

2a. $g \circ f(x) = 10x + 16$ **b.** $f \circ g(x) = 10x + 5$

3a. $A = \pi r^2$ **b.** $A = 16\pi t^2$ **4a.** $f \circ g(x) =$ $f \circ g(x) = x^2 + 3$; $g \circ f(x) = x^2 + 3$

b. $f \circ g(x) = 2x - 7$; $g \circ f(x) = 2x - 7$

c. $f \circ g(x) = (x - 4)^3$; $g \circ f(x) = (x - 4)^3$

d. Sample: The function takes any input and produces that same value as the output.

5. $g(x) = \frac{x + 1}{3}$ **6.** $g(x) = \frac{x - 3}{2}$

7a. $g(x) = 2x^2 - 2$ **b.** $g(x) = \frac{4x^2 + 1}{2x + 5}$

8a. $f \circ g(x) = acx + ad + b$, $g \circ f(x) =$ $acx + bc + d$ **b.** $ad + b = bc + d$ or $\frac{a}{c} = \frac{b - 1}{d - 1}$ **9.** $a = 2$, $b = 3$ or $a = -2$, $b = -9$

On Your Own

12c. $a^2 - 9a + 20$ **g.** 4 or 5 **13a.** x^2

Lesson 2.04

Check Your Understanding

1a. Yes; $f^{-1}(x) = x$ **b.** Yes; $g^{-1}(x) = \frac{1}{x}$ **c.** No; $h(x) = x^2$ is not one-to-one. **d.** Yes; $k^{-1}(x) = x$ **e.** No; $l(x) = x^3 - x$ is not one-to-one. **f.** Yes; $m^{-1}(x) = x^2$ with $x \geq 0$. **g.** No; $n(x) = |x|$ is not one-to-one. **2a.** (5, 1) **b.** Answers may vary. Sample: Reflect the graph over the line $y = x$. **c.** Answers may vary. Sample: Each graph represents a one-to-one function, and if you reflect either graph over the line $y = x$, you get the other graph. **3a.** $x \leq 6$

b.

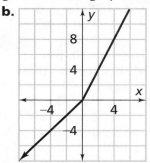

c. Answers may vary. Sample:
$f(x) = \begin{cases} x & \text{if } x < 0 \\ 2x & \text{if } x \geq 0 \end{cases}$ **d.** Answers may vary.

Sample: $f(x) = \begin{cases} x & \text{if } x < 0 \\ 2x & \text{if } 0 \leq x \leq 6 \\ -x & \text{if } x > 6 \end{cases}$

4a. Answers may vary. Sample: $x > 0$
b. $f^{-1}(x) = \sqrt{x}$ **5a.** the numbers 1, 5, 9, 13
b.

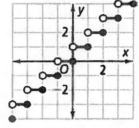

c. Each input is matched to a unique output.
d. $t(x)$ does not have an inverse because it contains (9, 11) and (13, 11). To make it a function, change one of the output 11's to a number other than 3, 7, or 11. **6.** $f^{-1}(x) = \frac{x}{x - 1}$ **7.** Yes, $h = j^{-1}$. **8a.** $g \circ f(x) =$ $25x^2 - 85x + 30$ **b.** $x^2 - 17x + 30$

c. f: parabola opening up with vertex $\left(\frac{17}{10}, -\frac{169}{20}\right)$ and x-intercepts $\left(\frac{2}{5}, 0\right)$ and (3, 0) h: parabola opening up with vertex $\left(\frac{17}{2}, -\frac{169}{4}\right)$ and x-intercepts (2, 0) and (15, 0)

d. f: $\frac{2}{5}$ and 3; h: 2 and 15. **9.** False; Answers may vary. Sample: See Exercise 6, in which $f(x) = f^{-1}(x) = \frac{x}{x - 1}$.

On Your Own

10. a and d **14a.** $m^{-1}(x) = \frac{x - 3}{5}$

16a. $g \circ f(x) = 125x^3 - 300x^2 - 275x + 150$

Lesson 2.05

Check Your Understanding

1. Answers may vary. Samples are given.

a. $f(x) = \left[x + \frac{1}{2}\right]$

b. $f(x) = \frac{\left[100x + \frac{1}{2}\right]}{100}$

c. $f(x) = 5 \cdot \left[\frac{x}{5} + \frac{1}{2}\right]$

2. The domain is all real numbers, and the range is all integers. The inverse of the floor function is not a function; infinitely many numbers map to the same integer, so you cannot uniquely determine what input corresponds to a particular output.

On Your Own

9. a.

b. Answers may vary. Sample:
$[x] = -[-x]$

10. a. $f(x) = \begin{cases} \frac{x}{2} + 1, & \text{if } -6 \le x \le -2 \\ x + 2, & \text{if } -2 < x \le 0 \\ \frac{x}{8} + 2, & \text{if } 0 < x \le 8 \end{cases}$

b. $f_1(x) = \begin{cases} \frac{x-3}{2}, & \text{if } -1 \le x \le 3 \\ x - 3, & \text{if } 3 < x \le 5 \\ \frac{x+11}{8}, & \text{if } 5 < x \le 13 \end{cases}$

c. $f_2(x) = \begin{cases} \frac{x}{2} + 4, & \text{if } -6 \le x \le -2 \\ x + 5, & \text{if } -2 < x \le 0 \\ \frac{x}{8} + 5, & \text{if } 0 < x \le 8 \end{cases}$

Lesson 2.06
On Your Own
10a. $A = 6$, $B = -2$, $C = 3$ **12a.** The $f(x)$ values are -5, -2, 1, 4, 7, 10, 13, and 16; the $g(x)$ values are 499, -2, -55, 4.7, -46, 13, 520. **13a.** Answers may vary. Sample: $g(x) = 5$ (or any polynomial function for which $g(2) = 5$).

Lesson 2.07
Check Your Understanding
1. $f(x) = 6x^2 - 22x + 28$
2. $f(x) = 9x - 7$ **3.** $f(x) = 4x^2 - 3x + 1$
4. $f(x) = x^3 + 3x^2 + 5x - 8$ **5a.** $A = 1$, $B = 21$, $C = 9$, $D = 1$ **b.** yes **6.** Answers may vary. Sample: As in Exercise 18 in Lesson 2.05, when $A = -3$, $B = 1$, and $C = 2$, the final coefficient of x^2 was 0 so the equation was linear. Whenever the coefficient of the leading term is 0, the degree will be smaller than expected.

On Your Own
10. greatest degree: 4; least degree: 0
11. Answers may vary. Sample:
$h(x) = (x - 1)(x - 2)(x - 3)(x - 4)$
$= x^4 - 10x^3 + 35x^2 - 50x + 24$

Lesson 2.08
Check Your Understanding
1. The graphs intersect at $(1, 4)$, $(2, 6)$, and $(3, 8)$.
2. $j(x) = 2x + 2 + T(x - 1)(x - 2)(x - 3)$ where T is a polynomial or a constant.
3a. $f(x) = 2x - 1$; the next term is 7.
b. Answers may vary. Sample: For the rule $g(x) = 2x - 1 + (x - 1)(x - 2)(x - 3)$, the next term $g(4)$ is 13. **c.** $g(x) = 2x - 1 + 2(x - 1)(x - 2)(x - 3)$ or $g(x) = 2x^3 - 12x^2 + 24x - 13$ **d.** $g(x) = 2x - 1 - (x - 1)(x - 2)(x - 3)$ or $g(x) = -x^3 + 6x^2 - 9x + 5$

4a. $f(4) = 8$ if $f(x) = 2x$ **b.** $f(4) = 10$ if $f(x) = 2x + \frac{1}{3}(x - 1)(x - 2)(x - 3)$ or $f(x) = \frac{x^3}{3} - 2x^2 + \frac{17}{3}x - 2$ **c.** $f(4) = 80$ if $f(x) = 2x + 12(x - 1)(x - 2)(x - 3)$ or $f(x) = 12x^3 - 72x^2 + 134x - 72$ **d.** $f(4) = 0$ if $f(x) = 2x + \frac{4}{3}(x - 1)(x - 2)(x - 3)$ or $f(x) = -\frac{4}{3}(x^3 + 8x^2 - \frac{38}{3}x + 8)$ **5a.** 3 points
b. 6 points **c.** $(n + 1)$ points

On Your Own
8. Answers may vary. Sample:
$p(x) = 4 - x^2 - 3x(x - 1)(x - 2)(x - 3)$ The graphs intersect at $(0, 4)$, $(1, 3)$, $(2, 0)$, and $(3, -5)$. **11a.** Yes; a sample is $f(x) = 3(x - 2)^2$.

Lesson 2.09
On Your Own
8a. 1 and -3 **9.** $x^3 - a^3$

Lesson 2.10
Check Your Understanding
1a. quotient: $x^2 - 3$; remainder: 0 **b.** 0 **2.** 3
3. -1 **4.** 0 **5a.** Answers may vary. Sample: 8
b. Answers may vary. Samples: 113 and 218, or any number of the form $8 + 105n$, where n is a nonnegative integer. **6a.** Answers may vary. Sample: $f(x) = 2x^2 - 3x + 7$ **b.** Answers may vary. Sample: any polynomial of the form $g(x) = 2x^2 - 3x + 7 + p(x)(x - 3)(x - 5)(x - 7)$, where $p(x)$ is a polynomial

On Your Own
8a. 26 **9a.** 11 **10a.** 8

Lesson 2.11
Check Your Understanding
1. By Corollary 2.4, a polynomial of degree 2 can have at most 2 real roots. **2a.** Checking 5 values, $P(0) = R(0) = -2$, $P(1) = R(1) = -2$, $P(-1) = R(-1) = -2$, $P(\sqrt{2}) = R(\sqrt{2}) = 0$, and $P(-\sqrt{2}) = R(-\sqrt{2}) = 0$. So $P(x) = R(x)$.
b. Checking 3 values, $P(1) = R(1) = 0$, $P(0) = R(0) = 0$, $P(-1) = R(-1) = 0$, but $P(2) \ne R(2)$. So $P(x) \ne R(x)$. **c.** Checking three values, $P(-3) = R(-3) = -7$, $P(0) = R(0) = 2$, $P(-2) = R(-2) = -6$. So $P(x) = R(x)$. **3.** -5
4. $a = 7$, $b = 1$ **5.** -3, -1, 1, 2 **6.** Answers may vary. Sample: Checking 3 values, for $x = 1$ both sides are 2; for $x = 3$ both sides are 2, and for $x = 2$ both sides are -1. So the expressions are equivalent. **7.** Answers may vary. Sample: Checking 3 values, for $x = 1$ both sides are 20; for $x = 3$ both sides are 12; and for $x = 6$ both sides are 60. So the two expressions are equivalent. **8.** $P(x) = 1$

On Your Own

12a. $f(2) = 0$, so $(x - 2)$ is a factor of $f(x)$.
b. $g(x) = \frac{f(x)}{x-2} = 3x^3 - 6x^2 + x - 2$ and $g(2) = 0$, so $x - 2$ is a factor of $g(x)$.

Lesson 2.12
On Your Own

5a. $(x + 1)(x + 5)$ **d.** It doesn't factor; there are no rational numbers with sum 10 and product -20. **6a.** $x^3 - 1$ **7c.** $(x - 2)$ $(x^2 + 2x + 4)$ **f.** $(2x + 1)(4x^2 - 2x + 1)$
i. $x(x^2 + 3x + 3)$

Lesson 2.13
Check Your Understanding

1a. $(3x + 7)(3x - 1)$ **b.** $(2x - 7)(3x - 5)$
c. $(3x - 1)(5x + 7)$ **d.** $(9x - 1)(x + 7)$
e. $-(9x + 1)(2x + 7)$ **f.** $-(9x + 1)(2x - 7)$
g. $(3x + 1)(3x - 1)(x^2 + 7)$ **h.** $(5 - 2x)(5 + 2x)$
i. $x(9x + 1)(2x - 7)$ **2a.** $(3x + 7y)(3x - y)$
b. $(2x - 7y)(3x - 5y)$ **c.** $(3x - a)(5x + 7a)$
d. $(9x - b)(x + 7b)$ **e.** $-(9x + a)(2x + 7a)$
f. $-(9x + y)(2x - 7y)$ **g.** $(5y + 2x)(5y - 2x)$
h. $x(9x + y)(2x - 7y)$

On Your Own

3d. $(2x + 5)(2x + 1)$
e. $(2x + 1)(2x - 1)(x^2 - 3)$ **5a.** $z^2 = 2$

Lesson 2.14
Check Your Understanding

1. Expand the left sides: $(x + y)^3 =$
$(x + y)(x^2 + 2xy + y^2) = x^3 + 3x^2y + 3xy^2 + y^3$, and $(x - y)^3 = (x - y)(x^2 - 2xy + y^2) = x^3 - 3x^2y + 3xy^2 - y^3$
2a. $(x - 4)(x^2 + 4x + 16)$
b. $(x + 4)(x^2 - 4x + 16)$
c. $(3x - 4)(9x^2 + 12x + 16)$
d. $(3x - 4)(9x^2 - 12x + 16)$
e. $(x - 3)(x^2 - 2x + 21)$
f. $(2x + 1)(4x^2 - 20x + 37)$
g. $(x + 3)(x - 3)(x + 3)$
h. $(x + a)(x - a)(x + a)$ **i.** $(-2x - 1)(4x + 1)$
j. $(x - y + z)(x + y - z)$
k. $(x - 2)(x - 7)(x + 5)$
l. $(x - 2y)(x - 7y)(x + 5y)$
m. $(x + 1)(x^2 - x + 1)$ **3.** Multiply each term by 25 to get $125x^3 + 75x^2 + 75x - 50$; that can be rewritten as $(5x)^3 + 3(5x)^2 + 15(5x) - 50$, which can be factored as $25(5x - 2)(x^2 + x + 1)$. Divide by 25 to get $(5x - 2)(x^2 + x + 1)$.

On Your Own

4l. $(x - 2)(x^2 - x + 1)$ **5.** $(x - 4)(x^2 + 4x + 1)$

Lesson 2.15
Check Your Understanding

1a. $(x^2 + 2)(x^2 - 3)$
b. $(x - 1)(x^2 + x + 1)(x - 2)(x^2 + 2x + 4)$
c. $(x^2 + 4)(x + 2)(x - 2)$
d. $(x^2 - 2)(x^4 + 2x^2 + 4)$
e. $(x^2 + 4y^2)(x + 2y)(x - 2y)$
f. $(x^2 + 2)(x^4 - 2x^2 + 4)$
g. $(x^2 + x - 4)(x^2 - x - 4)$
h. $(x^2 + x + 1)(x^2 - x + 1)$
2a. $(x - 1 - \sqrt{5})(x - 1 + \sqrt{5})$
b. $\left(x - 0.5 - \frac{\sqrt{5}}{2}\right)\left(x - 0.5 + \frac{\sqrt{5}}{2}\right)$
3a. Answers may vary. Sample: $x^2 - 4x + 1$
b. Answers may vary. Sample: $x^2 - 4x + 1$
c. $x^4 - 10x^2 + 1 = 0$ **4.** yes; Sample:
$x^2 - \frac{1}{4} = (x - \frac{1}{2})(x + \frac{1}{2})$

On Your Own

5e. $(x^2 - x + 5)(x^2 + x + 5)$ **6a.** 49 **c.** 81

Lesson 2.16
Check Your Understanding

1a. $\frac{3}{x}$ **b.** $x - y$ **c.** $\frac{x - y}{x + y}$ **d.** $\frac{1}{x^2 + 1}$ **e.** $\frac{2x - 3}{3x - 2}$
f. $\frac{(x + 1)(x^2 + 1)}{x^2 + x + 1}$ **2.** $f(x) = \frac{(2x - 3)(x + 2)}{(3x - 2)(x + 2)}$ and
$g(x) = \frac{2x - 3}{3x - 2}$. The graph of $f(x)$ will have a "hole" at $f(-2)$, or $(-2, 0.875)$, since $f(-2)$ is undefined. The graph of $g(x)$ will not have a hole, since $g(-2)$ is defined. **3a.** 1
b. $\frac{1}{(x - a)(x - b)}$ **4a.** $\frac{2x^2 - 10x + 1}{3(x - 1)(x - 4)}$ **b.** $\frac{-x^2 + 12x + 9}{x(x - 3)(x + 3)}$
c. 0 **5.** $A = -\frac{1}{2}$, $B = \frac{1}{2}$

On Your Own

6c. $x^3 + 1$ **7a.** $\frac{x^2 + 1}{x^2 - 1}$

Chapter 3
Lesson 3.01
On Your Own

9a. 102 **14c.** $\frac{3}{2}$ and $\frac{1}{2}$

Lesson 3.02
Check Your Understanding

1a. 4, 6 **b.** 10 **c–g.** no solution **h.** 1 **2a.** no additional solutions **b.** 0 **c.** $-6, -4$
d–h. no additional solutions **3a–c.** no additional solutions **d.** $\frac{1}{4}, \frac{1}{6}$ **e–h.** no additional solutions **4a–d.** no additional solutions
e. $\sqrt{10}, -\sqrt{10}$ **f–h.** no additional solutions
5a–e. no additional solutions
f. $\sqrt{-10}, -\sqrt{-10}$ **g.** $\frac{-1 \pm \sqrt{-3}}{2}$ **h.** $\frac{-1 \pm \sqrt{-3}}{2}$
6a. 2 **b.** 1 **c.** 0 **d.** 2

7a.

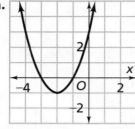

x-intercepts $(-3, 0)$, $(-1, 0)$, y-intercept $(0, 3)$

b.

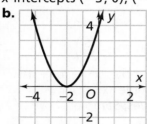

x-intercept $(-2, 0)$, y-intercept $(0, 4)$

c.

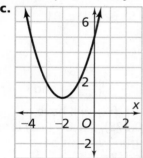

no x-intercept, y-intercept $(0, 5)$

d.

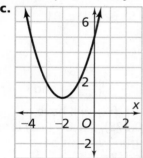

x-intercepts $(\frac{4}{3}, 0)$, $(2, 0)$, y-intercept $(0, 8)$

8a. 0 **b.** If $f(x) = x^2 - 2x + 2$, then $f(1 + i) = 0$ (by Exercise 8a). **9a.** $a(0) = 2$, $a(1) = 0$, $a(2) = 6$, $a(3) = 0$, $a(4) = 18$, $a(5) = 0$, $a(6) = 54$ **b.** $a(10) = 486$, $a(101) = 0$ **c.** No; Answers may vary. Sample: $a(n) = 0$ for all odd values of n, and since there are an infinite number of odd positive integers, $a(n)$ cannot be a polynomial. **10a.** rational **b.** irrational **c.** irrational

d. $f(0) = 2$, $f(1) = 2$, $f(2) = 6$, $f(3) = 14$, $f(4) = 34$, $f(5) = 82$, $f(6) = 198$ **e.** Answers may vary. Sample: $x^2 - 2x - 1 = 0$ **f.** Answers may vary. Sample: $2 \cdot f(n - 1) + f(n - 2)$

$$= 2[(1 + \sqrt{2})^{n-1} + (1 - \sqrt{2})^{n-1}]$$
$$+ (1 + \sqrt{2})^{n-2} + (1 - \sqrt{2})^{n-2}$$
$$= 2(1 + \sqrt{2})^{n-1} + (1 + \sqrt{2})^{n-2}$$
$$+ 2(1 - \sqrt{2})^{n-1} + (1 - \sqrt{2})^{n-2}$$
$$= (1 + \sqrt{2})^{n-2}[2(1 + \sqrt{2}) + 1]$$
$$+ (1 + \sqrt{2})^{n-2}[2(1 - \sqrt{2}) + 1]$$
$$= (1 + \sqrt{2})^{n-2}[(3 + 2\sqrt{2})] +$$
$$(1 - \sqrt{2})^{n-2}[(3 - 2\sqrt{2})]$$
$$= (1 + \sqrt{2})^{n-2}(1 + \sqrt{2})^2$$
$$+ (1 - \sqrt{2})^{n-2}(1 - \sqrt{2})^2$$
$$= (1 + \sqrt{2})^n + (1 - \sqrt{2})^n$$
$$= f(n)$$

11a. $g(0) = 2$, $g(1) = 4$, $g(2) = 6$, $g(3) = 4$, $g(4) = -14$, $g(5) = -76$, $g(6) = -234$
b. $(2 + \sqrt{-1})^2 = 4 + (-1) + 4\sqrt{-1} = 3 + 4\sqrt{-1}$ **c.** Answers may vary. Sample: $x^2 - 4x + 5 = 0$ **d.** $4g(n - 1) - 5g(n - 2)$

$$= 4(2 + \sqrt{-1})^{n-1} + 4(2 - \sqrt{-1})^{n-1}$$
$$- 5(2 + \sqrt{-1})^{n-2} - 5(2 - \sqrt{-1})^{n-2}$$
$$= (2 + \sqrt{-1})^{n-2}[4(2 + \sqrt{-1}) - 5]$$
$$+ (2 - \sqrt{-1})^{n-2}[4(2 - \sqrt{-1}) - 5]$$
$$= (2 + \sqrt{-1})^{n-2}(8 + 4\sqrt{-1} - 5)$$
$$+ (2 - \sqrt{-1})^{n-2}(8 - 4\sqrt{-1} - 5)$$
$$= (2 + \sqrt{-1})^{n-2}(3 + 4\sqrt{-1})$$
$$+ (2 - \sqrt{-1})^{n-2}(3 - 4\sqrt{-1})$$
$$= (2 + \sqrt{-1})^{n-2}(2 + \sqrt{-1})^2$$
$$+ (2 - \sqrt{-1})^{n-2}(2 - \sqrt{-1})^2$$
$$= (2 + \sqrt{-1})^n + (2 - \sqrt{-1})^n$$
$$= g(n)$$

On Your Own
12. Answers may vary. Samples are given.
a. $(-10) - (-20) = 10$, $(-10)(-20) = 200$
b. $\frac{5}{4} \cdot \frac{4}{5} = 1$, $\frac{5}{4} + \frac{3}{4} = 2$
d. $(1 + \sqrt{-2}) + (1 - \sqrt{-2}) = 2$, $\sqrt{-1} \cdot \sqrt{-1} = -1$
15c. The sum is 2, and the product is -2.

Lesson 3.03
Check Your Understanding
1a. $a^2 - b^2$ **b.** $a^2 - 2b^2$ **c.** $a^2 - 3b^2$

d. $a^2 - cb^2$ **e.** $a^2 + b^2$

2.

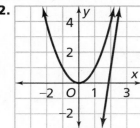

The graphs do not intersect. **3a.** $3 \pm \sqrt{-2}$
b. The sum is 6, and the product is 11. **4.** Yes;
Answers may vary. Sample: The Quadratic
Formula gives the solutions to any quadratic
equation. **5.** $\sqrt{34} = 5.83$ and $-\sqrt{34} = -5.83$
6. No; 0 is nonnegative and has only one
number whose square is 0. **7.** Answers may
vary. Sample: $x^3 - 5x^2 + 8x - 6 =$
$(x - 3)(x^2 - 2x + 2) = 0$, and the solutions to
$x^2 - 2x + 2 = 0$ are $1 + \sqrt{-1}$ and $1 - \sqrt{-1}$.
8a. 5 **b.** 8 **c.** 6

On Your Own
9a. -6 **e.** $-3 + 2\sqrt{-3}$
11b. $7 + 9\sqrt{-1}$ **c.** $23 + 15\sqrt{-1}$
13a. $x^3 - 8 = (x - 2)(x^2 + 2x + 4)$

Lesson 3.04
Check Your Understanding
1a. $12 + i$ **b.** $25 + 21i$ **c.** $10 + 0i$
d. $29 + 0i$ **e.** $6 + 6i$ **f.** $0 + 20i$ **2a.** 6 **b.** 34
c. -14 **d.** 53 **e.** 24 **f.** 169 **3a.** $(a - bi)$
b. $(a + bi) + (a - bi) = a + a + (b - b)i$
$= 2a$, and if a is real, $2a$ is also real.
c. $(a + bi)(a - bi) = a^2 - b^2i^2 + abi - abi =$
$a^2 + b^2$, and if a and b are real, $a^2 + b^2$ is
also real. **d.** when $a = 0$ in $a + bi$ and $a - bi$
e. when $a = 0$ and $b = 0$ **4.** No; Derman is
wrong because a and b must be real numbers
in $a + bi$. **5.** $4 - 7i$ **6a.** Yes; the opposite of
$2 + 3i$ is $-2 - 3i$. **b.** All complex numbers
have opposites. **7.** If $z = a + bi$,
then $z^2 + \bar{z}^2 = (a + bi)^2 + (a - bi)^2$
$= (a^2 + 2abi - b^2) + (a^2 - 2abi - b^2)$
$= 2a^2 - 2b^2$, which is a real number.
8a. $x^2 - 6x + 13 = 0$ **b.** $x^2 - 6x + 13 = 0$
c. $(x^2 - 6x + 13)(x^2 - 2x + 26) = 0$
d. $(x^2 - 2x + 26)(x^2 + 2x + 26) = 0$
e. $x^2 - 2x + 4 = 0$ **f.** $x - (\sqrt{2} + \sqrt{3}) = 0$, or
$x^4 - 10x^2 + 1 = 0$ **g.** $x^2 - (2\sqrt{2})x + 5 = 0$

On Your Own
10a. $-i$ **b.** 1 **11a.** $3 + 3i$ **d.** $3 \pm 5i$
13. Answers may vary. Samples are given.
a. $1 + i$ **14a.** $(x + i)(x - i) = x^2 - i^2 + xi -$
$xi = x^2 - (-1) = x^2 + 1$

Lesson 3.05
Check Your Understanding
1. $z + \bar{z}$ is a real number. **2a.** $-2i$
b. 7 **c.** $\overline{z + w} = \overline{7 + 2i} = 7 - 2i$, and
$\bar{z} + \bar{w} = -2i + 7 = 7 - 2i$, so they are equal.
3a. $\bar{z} = a - bi$, and $\bar{w} = c - di$
b. $\overline{z + w} = \overline{(a + c) + (b + d)i} =$
$(a + c) - (b + d)i$; $\bar{z} + \bar{w} =$
$(a - bi) + (c - di) = (a + c) - (b + d)i$
4a. $3 - 2i$ **b.** $3 + 2i$ **c.** $7 + 3i$ **d.** $7 + 3i$
e. $22 + 7i$ **f.** $22 + 7i$ **g.** 6 **h.** 41 **5a.** $4 - 7i$
b. $\frac{7}{5} + \frac{6}{5}i$ **c.** $4 + 0i$ **d.** $\frac{4}{5} + \frac{3}{5}i$ **e.** $\frac{4}{5} - \frac{3}{5}i$
f. $\frac{ac + bd}{a^2 + b^2} + \frac{ad - bc}{a^2 + b^2}i$ **6a.** $-9 + 38i$
b. $-9 - 38i$ **c.** $37 + 50i$ **d.** $37 - 50i$ **e.** $1 + 76i$
f. $1 - 76i$ **7.** If $z = a + bi$ and $w = c + di$,
then $\overline{zw} = \overline{(ac - bd) + (ad + bc)i} =$
$(ac - bd) - (ad + bc)i$, and $(\bar{z})(\bar{w}) =$
$(a - bi)(c - di) = (ac - bd) + (-ad - bc)i$
$= (ac - bd) - (ad + bc)i$.
8a. $z + \bar{z} = (a + bi) + (a - bi) = 2a$
b. $z\bar{z} = (a + bi)(a - bi) = a^2 - b^2i^2 +$
$(ab - ab)i = a^2 + b^2$ **9a.** $a = 7, b = 5$ or
$a = 7, b = -5$ **b.** $7 + 5i, 7 - 5i$

On Your Own
10a. $\frac{1}{2} - \frac{1}{2}i$ **12a.** -1 **g.** $9 - 40i$
16a. $(a + bi)^2 = a^2 + abi + abi + b^2i^2 =$
$(a^2 - b^2) + (2ab)i$

Lesson 3.06
On Your Own
7a. $\sqrt{17}$ **8a.** 17 **d.** 85 **9a.** $14.04°$ **10a.** $4\sqrt{2}$
d. $2\sqrt{2}$ **11a.** $A(8, 0)$, $B(8, 8)$

Lesson 3.07
Check Your Understanding
1a–d.

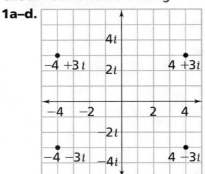

2a. $a > 0, b > 0$ **b.** $a < 0, b > 0$
c. $a < 0, b < 0$ **d.** $a > 0, b < 0$

3a.

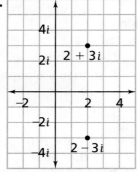

b. The sum is 4, and the product is 13.

4a.

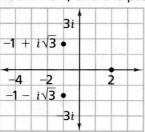

b. Equilateral; the length of each side of the triangle is 2. **c.** The sum is 0, and the product is 8. **5.** Answers may vary. Sample: $1 + i, 1 - i, -1 - i, -1 + i$

6a–f.

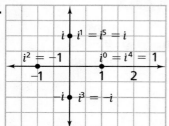

On Your Own
8a–d.

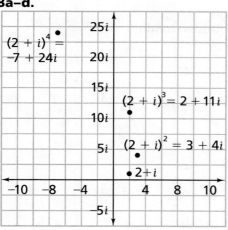

9a.

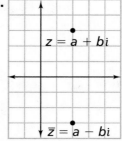

b.

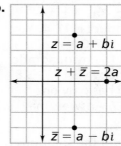

10c. $-3 + i, -3 - i$

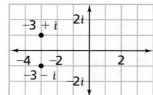

11a. $\pm i, \pm 1$

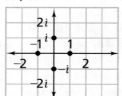

13a. $w = 2 - i,\ 2w = 4 - 2i,\ 3w = 6 - 3i$

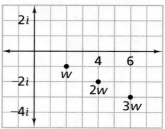

Lesson 3.08
Check Your Understanding
1a.

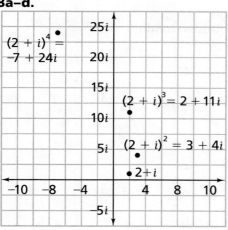

b.

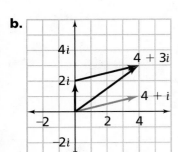

c.

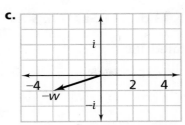

c.

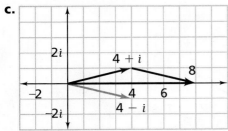

d.

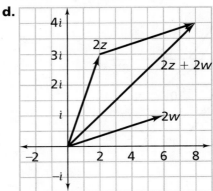

d.

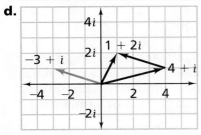

e.

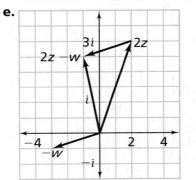

e.

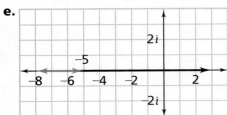

f.

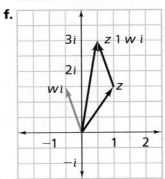

2a.

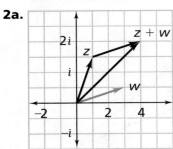

3. $z = a + bi$ is $\sqrt{a^2 + b^2}$ units from the origin, and $iz = -b + ai$ is $\sqrt{b^2 + a^2}$ units from the origin. The distances are equal.

b.

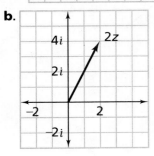

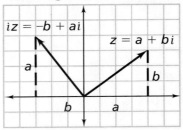

4a. $\sqrt{17}$ **b.** $\sqrt{5}$ **c.** $\sqrt{13}$ **d.** $\sqrt{61}$ **5a.** 17 **b.** 5
c. 13 **d.** 61
6a. 65, 17, 80 **b.** rotated 180°

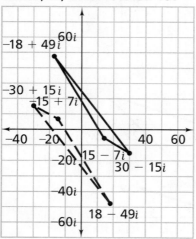

c. rotated 90°

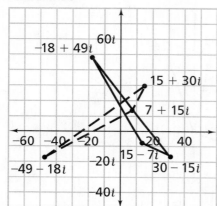

7a.

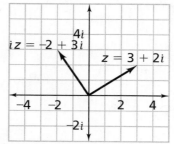

b.

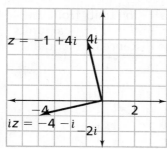

c.

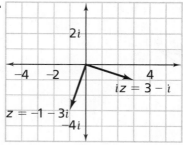

d.

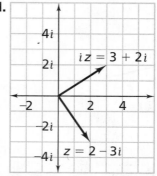

8a. a rotation of 180° about the origin
b. a rotation of 270° counterclockwise about
the origin **9.** Answers may vary. Samples are
given. **a.** Points; the vertices of a square are
points.

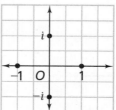

b. Vectors; you use vectors to illustrate the
parallelogram law.

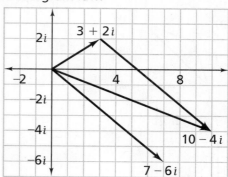

c. Points; the vertices of each triangle are points.

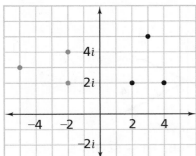

d. Vectors; distances can be represented by vectors.

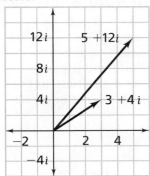

On Your Own

10.

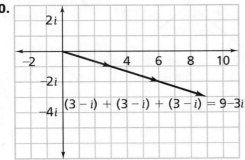

13. $5 + 3i$, $-6 - 4i$, $2 - 7i$, 8

15a. $(1 + i)z = \sqrt{2}i$

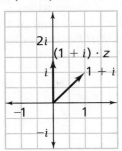

Lesson 3.09

Check Your Understanding

1a. 5, 37° **b.** 5, 323° **c.** 5, 143° **d.** 5, 217°

2a. $|w| = 2\sqrt{2}$, arg $w = 45°$ **b.** $|w| = 2\sqrt{2}$, arg $w = 315°$ **c.** $|w| = 2\sqrt{2}$, arg $w = 135°$ **d.** $|w| = 2\sqrt{2}$, arg $w = 225°$ **3.** Answers may vary. Samples are given. **a.** 40° **b.** 140° **c.** 320° **d.** 220° **4.** The magnitude is doubled, and the direction stays the same. **5.** The property holds for complex numbers. **6a.** $|z| = 2$; arg $z = 90°$ $|z^2| = 4$; arg $z^2 = 180°$ **b.** $|z| = \sqrt{2}$; arg $z = 135°$ $|z^2| = 2$; arg $z^2 = 270°$ **c.** $|z| = \sqrt{17}$; arg $z \approx 14°$ $|z^2| = 17$; arg $z^2 \approx 28°$ **d.** $|z| = \sqrt{17}$; arg $z \approx 166°$ $|z^2| = 17$; arg $z^2 \approx 332°$

7a. $\frac{1}{z} = \frac{1}{2} - \frac{1}{2}i$

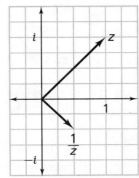

b. $\frac{1}{z} = \frac{2}{5} - \frac{1}{5}i$

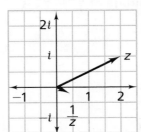

c. $\frac{1}{z} = \frac{1}{4} - \frac{\sqrt{3}}{4}i$

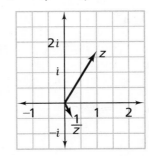

d. $\frac{1}{z} = -\frac{1}{2} + \frac{1}{2}i$

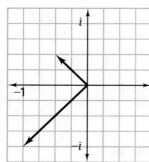

8a. $|z| = \sqrt{2}$, arg $z = 45°$; $\left|\frac{1}{z}\right| = \frac{\sqrt{2}}{2}$, arg $\frac{1}{z}$ $= 315°$ **b.** $|z| = \sqrt{5}$, arg $z = 27°$; $\left|\frac{1}{z}\right| = \frac{\sqrt{5}}{5}$, arg $\frac{1}{z} = 333°$ **c.** $|z| = 2$, arg $z = 60°$; $\left|\frac{1}{z}\right| = \frac{1}{2}$, arg $\frac{1}{z} = 300°$ **d.** $|z| = \sqrt{2}$, arg $z = 225°$; $\left|\frac{1}{z}\right| = \frac{\sqrt{2}}{2}$, arg $\frac{1}{z} = 135°$

9a. $5\left(\frac{4}{5} + \frac{3}{5}i\right)$ **b.** $13\left(\frac{5}{13} + \frac{12}{13}i\right)$ **c.** $\sqrt{2}\left(\frac{\sqrt{2}}{2}\right.$ $+ \left.\frac{\sqrt{2}}{2}i\right)$ **d.** $\sqrt{2}\left(\frac{\sqrt{2}}{2} - \frac{\sqrt{2}}{2}i\right)$ **e.** $\sqrt{13}\left(\frac{2\sqrt{13}}{13}\right.$ $+ \left.\frac{3\sqrt{13}}{13}i\right)$ **f.** $2\left(-\frac{1}{2} + \frac{\sqrt{3}}{2}i\right)$

10. For $z = a + bi$ with $|z| = k$, rewrite z as $z = k\left(\frac{a}{k} + \frac{b}{k}i\right)$. Then k is a positive real number and the magnitude of $\frac{a}{k} + \frac{b}{k}i$ is $\sqrt{\frac{a^2}{k^2} + \frac{b^2}{k^2}} = \sqrt{\frac{a^2 + b^2}{k^2}} = \sqrt{\frac{k^2}{k^2}} = 1$.

On Your Own
12c. 2, 240°
14a–b.

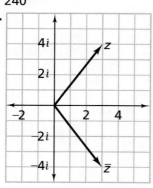

16a. 0° **b.** 26.565° **17a.** $|z| = \sqrt{5}$, $|w| = \sqrt{10}$, $|zw| = 5\sqrt{2}$

Lesson 3.10
On Your Own
8.

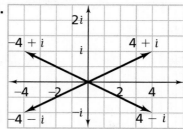

a. 14° **9a.** 30° **10b.** $-1 - 5i$ **d.** $-5 + 12i$

Lesson 3.11
Check Your Understanding
1a. magnitude 9, direction 240° **b.** magnitude 27, direction 0° **c.** $x^2 + 3x + 9 = 0$
2. Answers may vary. Sample: For z^2, square the magnitude and double the direction. For z^3, cube the magnitude and triple the direction. For z^n raise the magnitude to the nth power and multiply the direction by n.
3. options b, c, or d
4.

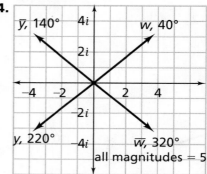

5a. magnitude $5\sqrt{2}$, direction 355°
b. magnitude $5\sqrt{2}$, direction 355°
c. $yz = (-w)(-x) = wx$ **6.** Answers may vary. Sample: The magnitude is about $(3.5)(4.5) = 16$, and the direction is about $50° + 110° = 160°$ **7.** The magnitude of the product is the product of the magnitudes. The direction of the product is the sum of the directions, but subtract 360° if necessary to express the angle between 0° and 360°.
8a.

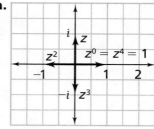

Consecutive powers of i rotate 90° counterclockwise; if you raise $z = i$ to the nth power, you multiply the direction, 90°, by n, and there is no change to the magnitude. So consecutive powers of i rotate 90° counterclockwise.

b.

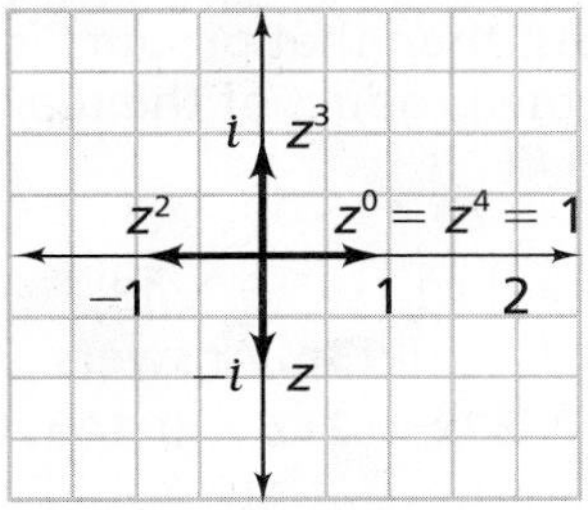

Consecutive powers of $-i$ rotate 90° clockwise; if you raise $z = -i$ to the nth power, you multiply the direction, 270°, by n, and there is no change to the magnitude. So consecutive powers of $-i$ rotate 270° counterclockwise, which is equivalent to rotating by 90° clockwise.

c.

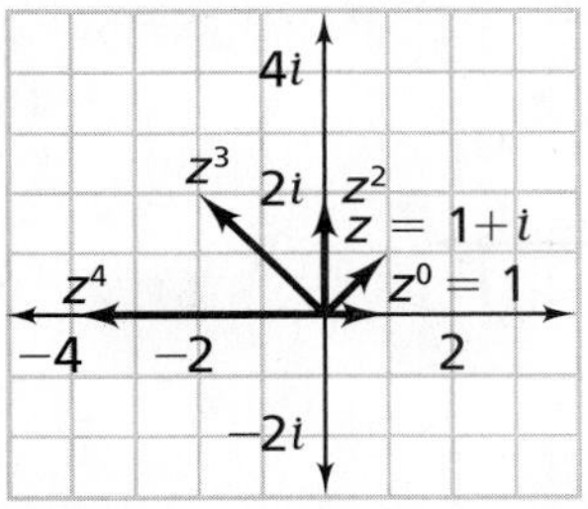

Consecutive powers of $1 + i$ rotate 45° counterclockwise, with the magnitudes increasing by a factor of $\sqrt{2}$; if you raise $z = 1 + i$ to the nth power, you multiply the direction, 45°, by n, and you raise the magnitude, $\sqrt{2}$, to the nth power. So consecutive powers of $1 + i$ rotate 45° counterclockwise, and increase the magnitude by a factor of $\sqrt{2}$.

d.

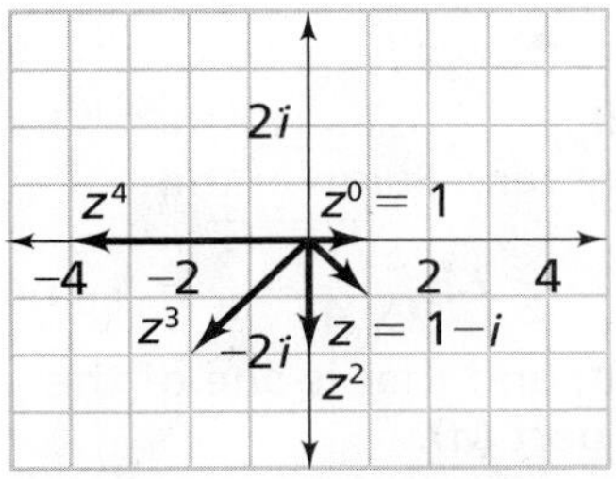

The powers of $1 - i$ rotate 45° clockwise, with the magnitudes increasing by a factor of $\sqrt{2}$; if you raise $z = 1 - i$ to the nth power, you multiply the direction, 315°, by n, and you raise the magnitude, $\sqrt{2}$, to the nth power. So consecutive powers of $1 - i$ rotate 315° counterclockwise (which is equivalent to rotating by 45° clockwise), and increase the magnitude by a factor of $\sqrt{2}$.

e.

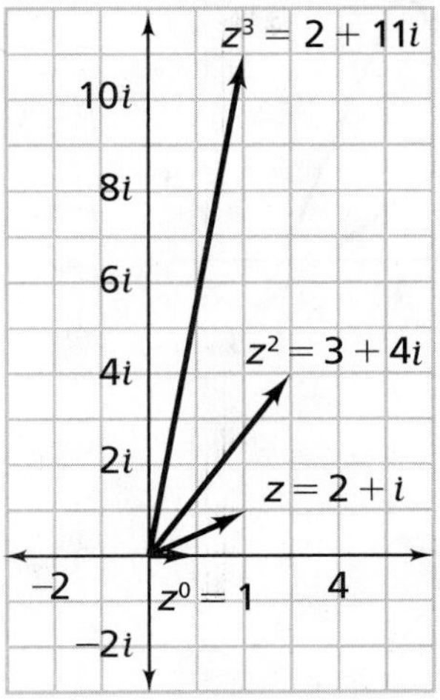

The powers of $2 + i$ rotate about 26.6° counterclockwise, with the magnitudes increasing by a factor of $\sqrt{5}$; if you raise $z = 2 + i$ to the nth power, you multiply the direction, 26.6°, by n, and you raise the magnitude, $\sqrt{5}$, to the nth power. So consecutive powers of $2 + i$ rotate 26.6° counterclockwise, and increase the magnitude by a factor of $\sqrt{5}$.

f.

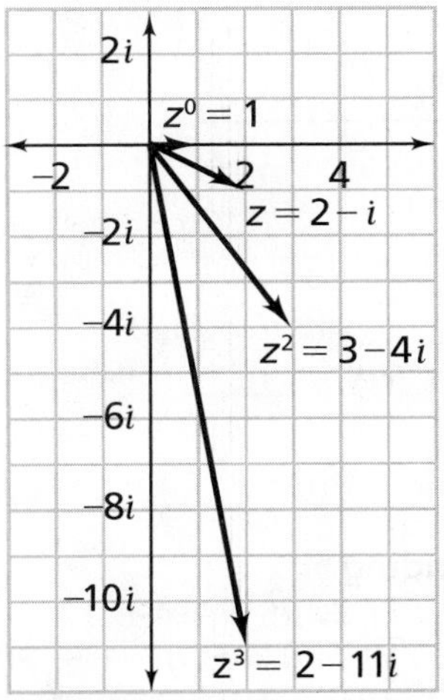

The powers of $2 - i$ rotate about 26.6° clockwise, with the magnitudes increasing by a factor of $\sqrt{5}$; if you raise $z = 2 - i$ to the nth power, you multiply the direction, 333.4°, by n and you raise the magnitude, $\sqrt{5}$, to the nth power. So consecutive powers of $2 - i$ rotate 333.4° counterclockwise (which is equivalent to rotating by 26.6° clockwise), and increase the magnitude by a factor of $\sqrt{5}$.

On Your Own

9. a, c, d, and e must have magnitude 1.

10a.

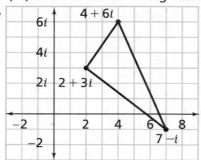

b.

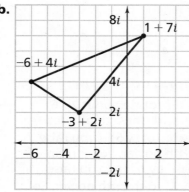

11a. Answers may vary. Sample: $1 + i$, $5 + 5i$

13a. Answers may vary. Sample:

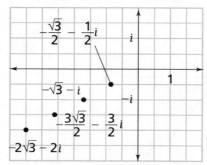

16a. $\frac{7}{5} + \frac{1}{5}i$

Lesson 3.12
Check Your Understanding

1a. $x = -2$ **b.** $x = 1 \pm 3i$ **2.** $x^2 - 8x + 17 = 0$
3. $x^3 - 15x^2 + 73x - 119 = 0$ **4a.** $g(-1 + 2i)$
$= (-1 + 2i)^3 - 4(-1 + 2i)^2 - 7(-1 + 2i) - 30$
$= (11 - 2i) - (-12 - 16i) - (-7 + 14i) - 30$
$= 0$ So $(-1 + 2i)$ is a root of $g(x)$. **b.** $-1 - 2i$, 6

5a. $f(3 + i) = (3 + i)^2 - (8 + 6i) = (8 + 6i) - (8 + 6i) = 0$, so $3 + i$ is a solution. **b.** No;
The equation does not have real coefficients, which is a requirement for the conjugate to be

a root. When you test $x = 3 - i$, it does not make the equation true. **6.** All the complex roots come in pairs, $a + bi$ and $a - bi$, and the product of each pair of complex roots is $a^2 + b^2$, which is positive. Since the product of all the roots is the product of the complex roots and the real roots, then that product is positive if and only if the product of the real roots is positive.

On Your Own

7a. $|z| = \sqrt{26}$, arg $z \approx 11°$; $|w| = \sqrt{13}$, arg $w \approx 56°$ **10a.** 0 **c.** $1 - 3i$ **13a.** Answers may vary. Sample: $x^3 + 37x + 212 = 0$ **14a.** 0 **b.** 0

Lesson 3.13
Check Your Understanding

1a. $(w^2)^n = w^{2n} = (w^n)^2 = 1^2 = 1$
b. $(w^k)^n = w^{nk} = (w^n)^k = 1^k = 1$

2.

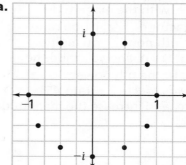

3a.

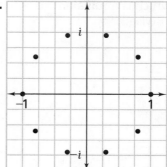

b. Yes; Answers may vary. Sample: the magnitude of $-\frac{1}{2} - \frac{\sqrt{3}}{2}i$ is $\sqrt{\frac{1}{4} + \frac{3}{4}} = 1$ and the direction is 240°, and that is one of the solutions shown in part (a).

4a.

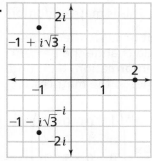

b. Each solution to $x^3 = 8$ is doubled in magnitude. **5.** $\frac{\sqrt{2}}{2} + \frac{\sqrt{2}}{2}i$, $-\frac{\sqrt{2}}{2} - \frac{\sqrt{2}}{2}i$

6a. Answers may vary. Sample: $\frac{\sqrt{3}}{2} + \frac{1}{2}i$

b. $-i$, $\frac{\sqrt{3}}{2} + \frac{1}{2}i$, $\frac{\sqrt{3}}{2} - \frac{1}{2}i$

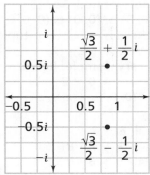

c. Rotate the solutions to $x^3 = 1$ $30°$ counterclockwise to get the solutions to $x^3 = i$. **7.** 0 **8.** Yes; complex roots of polynomials come in conjugate pairs.

9a.

Equation	Number of New Roots
$x = 1$	1
$x^2 = 1$	1
$x^3 = 1$	2
$x^4 = 1$	2
$x^5 = 1$	4
$x^6 = 1$	2
$x^7 = 1$	6
$x^8 = 1$	4
$x^9 = 1$	6
$x^{10} = 1$	4

b. Answers may vary. Sample: Beginning with $x^3 = 1$, the number of new roots is even.

11. 18 sides **12a.** $|z| = 1$, arg $z = 60°$ **13a.** The magnitudes are 1, and the directions are 0°, 45°, 90°, 135°, 180°, 225°, 270°, and 315°.

Chapter 4
Lesson 4.01
On Your Own

7. $x = \frac{16}{5}$, $y = -\frac{9}{5}$ **9.** $p(1) = 4$ so $a + b = 4$; $p(3) = 2$ so $3a + b = 2$; $a = -1$ and $b = 5$ so $p(x) = -x + 5$. **12a.** The two equations represent the same line, so any point on $x + 2y = 3$ is a solution to the system. **b.** The two equations represent parallel lines, so the system has no solution.

Lesson 4.02
Check Your Understanding

1. $(2, 1, -1)$ **2.** $(2, 1, -1)$ **3.** $(2, 1, -1)$

4. $(2, 1, -1)$ **5.** $a = \frac{1}{2}$, $b = \frac{1}{2}$, $c = 0$.

On Your Own

8. $(-4, 1, -1, 2)$ **9.** The system has no solution.

Lesson 4.03
Check Your Understanding

1a. $x - y + 2z = 5$, $2x - 3y + z = 3$, $x + 7z = 16$

b. $\begin{pmatrix} 1 & 0 & 0 & | & 2 \\ 0 & 1 & 0 & | & 1 \\ 0 & 0 & 1 & | & 2 \end{pmatrix}$ or $(x, y, z) = (2, 1, 2)$

2. $\begin{pmatrix} 1 & 0 & 0 & | & -\frac{1}{2} \\ 0 & 1 & 0 & | & \frac{1}{2} \\ 0 & 0 & 1 & | & 1 \end{pmatrix}$

3. Yes, $\begin{pmatrix} 1 & 0 & 0 & | & 1 \\ 0 & 1 & 0 & | & -1 \\ 0 & 0 & 1 & | & 2 \end{pmatrix}$ represents the same solution.

4. $\begin{pmatrix} 1 & 0 & 0 & | & 1 \\ 0 & 1 & 0 & | & -1 \\ 0 & 0 & 1 & | & 2 \end{pmatrix} \xrightarrow[(1)+(3)]{(1)+(2)} \begin{pmatrix} 1 & 1 & 1 & | & 2 \\ 0 & 1 & 0 & | & -1 \\ 0 & 0 & 1 & | & 2 \end{pmatrix}$

$\xrightarrow{(2)+2(3)} \begin{pmatrix} 1 & 1 & 1 & | & 2 \\ 0 & 1 & 2 & | & 3 \\ 0 & 0 & 1 & | & 2 \end{pmatrix}$; then reverse the steps shown in the middle of page 517 to get $A = \begin{pmatrix} 1 & 1 & 1 & | & 2 \\ 2 & -1 & 1 & | & 5 \\ 1 & 2 & 3 & | & 5 \end{pmatrix}$.

5. Answers may vary. Sample: Adding a positive multiple is the same as subtracting the same multiple with the opposite sign(s).

6. $\begin{pmatrix} 1 & 0 & | & 1 \\ 0 & 1 & | & -2 \end{pmatrix}$

7. $a = -\frac{7}{2}$, $b = \frac{8}{3}$ **8a.** Each equation in the system is a line in the xy-plane, and the intersection of the lines is the solution to the system. **b.** The solution represents m lines in the xy-plane; if the lines have point(s) in common, that point or points is the solution to the system. **c.** Each equation represents a plane in 3-space; the common intersection of the m planes (if it exists) is the solution to the system.

On Your Own

12. $f(x) = 2x - 2$ **13.** $(2, 0, 4)$

15. $x + 2y + 2z = 3$, $x - \frac{1}{2}y - \frac{1}{2}z = 1$, $x + \frac{1}{3}y + \frac{1}{6}z = 1$ **19.** 4 in. by 6 in. by 8 in.

Lesson 4.04
On Your Own

7.

	A	B	C	D	E
EUR	0.6	0.25	0.3	0.3	1.3
US	4.6	3.3	1.4	2.2	0.4
ASIA	0.3	0.15	1.3	4.5	0.1

8a.

	A	B	C	D	E
EUR	1	0.5	0	1	6
US	2	-0.5	2	3	0
ASIA	-1	-0.5	8	11	-1

b.

A	B	C	D	E
2	-0.5	10	15	5

c.

EUR	8.5
US	6.5
ASIA	16.5

10. 1239 mi

Lesson 4.05
Check Your Understanding

1a. 2×3 **b.** 2 **c.** 4 **d.** 6 **e.** There is no 3rd row.

2a. $\begin{pmatrix} 3 \\ 6 \\ 11 \\ 18 \end{pmatrix}$ **b.** $(3 \quad 5 \quad 9 \quad 17)$ **3a.** $a_{ij} = i + j$

b. $b_{ij} = 2(i - 1) + j$ **c.** $c_{ij} = (i + j - 1)^i$

4a. $A + B = (c_{ij})$, where $c_{ij} = a_{ij} + b_{ij}$.

b. $A - B = (c_{ij})$, where $c_{ij} = a_{ij} - b_{ij}$.

c. $k \cdot A = (c_{ij})$, where $c_{ij} = k \cdot a_{ij}$.

5. $3 \cdot \begin{pmatrix} 6 \\ 8 \\ 10 \end{pmatrix} = \begin{pmatrix} 18 \\ 24 \\ 30 \end{pmatrix}$ or

$3 \cdot (6 \quad 8 \quad 10) = (18 \quad 24 \quad 30)$

6. $\begin{pmatrix} 271 & 282 & 233 \\ 365 & 362 & 340 \end{pmatrix}$ This is matrix addition.

7. The matrices cannot be added term-by-term; the teacher could change the percent information to point information, then find the means of the entries in the matrices.

On Your Own

9. $\begin{pmatrix} 1 & 2 & 3 & 4 \\ 1 & 4 & 9 & 16 \end{pmatrix}$ **10a.** $\begin{pmatrix} 1 & 0 & 0 & 0 \\ 0 & 1 & 0 & 0 \\ 0 & 0 & 1 & 0 \\ 0 & 0 & 0 & 1 \end{pmatrix}$

12. matrix addition

Lesson 4.06
Check Your Understanding

1. In Lesson 4.04, Exercises 5, 6, 10, and 11 were dot products. **2a.** 32 **b.** 32 **c.** 32 **d.** 32 **e.** 32 **f.** The dot product is not defined. **3a.** 25 **b.** $a^2 + b^2$ **c.** 29 **4a.** $(0, 0)$ **b.** $(0, 0)$ **c.** $(0, 0, 0, 0)$ **5.** For any n-tuple X, there is a unique n-tuple $Z = (0, 0, \dots, 0)$ such that $X + Z = X$.

6a. 0 **b.** Answers may vary. Sample: Rewrite the expression as $(1 + 0 - 1, 0 + 2 - 2, 1 + 1 - 2) \cdot (x, y, z) = (0, 0, 0) \cdot (x, y, z) = 0$.

7. $(A + B) \cdot (A + B)$
$= (A + B) \cdot A + (A + B) \cdot B$
$= A \cdot A + B \cdot A + A \cdot B + B \cdot B$
$= A \cdot A + A \cdot B + A \cdot B + B \cdot B$
$= A \cdot A + 2A \cdot B + B \cdot B$

8. $(A + B) \cdot (A - B)$
$= A \cdot (A - B) + B \cdot (A - B)$
$= A \cdot A - A \cdot B + B \cdot A - B \cdot B$
$= A \cdot A - A \cdot B + A \cdot B - B \cdot B$
$= A \cdot A - B \cdot B$

9. If X is the n-tuple $(x_1, x_2, \dots, x_n)$, then $(-1)X = (-1)(x_1, x_2, \dots, x_n) = (-x_1, -x_2, \dots, -x_n)$. Then $X + (-1)X = (0, 0, \dots, 0)$ so $-1(X) = -X$.

10. We know that $A \cdot (kB) = k(A \cdot B) = (kA) \cdot B$, so $A \cdot ((-1)B) = A \cdot (-B)$ by Exercise 9, and $A \cdot (-B) = -(A \cdot B) = (-A) \cdot B$.

On Your Own

13. No **14a.** 0 **b.** 0 **c.** 0 **d.** 0 The Zero Product Property, that if a product is zero then at least one of the factors is zero, does not hold for dot products. **18a.** $(-1, -2)$ **b.** $(-x, -y)$ **c.** $(-1, -2, 3, -\pi)$

Lesson 4.07
Check Your Understanding

1a. $\begin{pmatrix} a & b \\ c & d \end{pmatrix}$ **b.** $\begin{pmatrix} a & b \\ c & d \end{pmatrix}$ **c.** $\begin{pmatrix} 2a & -3b \\ 2c & -3d \end{pmatrix}$

d. $\begin{pmatrix} 2a & 2b \\ -3b & -3d \end{pmatrix}$

2a.

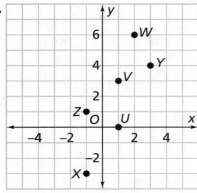

b. $AU = \begin{pmatrix} 1 \\ 0 \end{pmatrix}$, $AV = \begin{pmatrix} 1 \\ -3 \end{pmatrix}$, $AW = \begin{pmatrix} 2 \\ -6 \end{pmatrix}$,

$AX = \begin{pmatrix} -1 \\ 3 \end{pmatrix}$, $AY = \begin{pmatrix} 3 \\ -4 \end{pmatrix}$, $AZ = \begin{pmatrix} -1 \\ -1 \end{pmatrix}$

c.

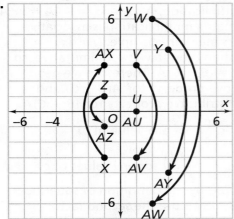

Corresponding points are reflections of each other over the x-axis.

d. $BU = \begin{pmatrix} 0 \\ 1 \end{pmatrix}$, $BV = \begin{pmatrix} -3 \\ 1 \end{pmatrix}$, $BW = \begin{pmatrix} -6 \\ 2 \end{pmatrix}$,

$BX = \begin{pmatrix} 3 \\ -1 \end{pmatrix}$, $BY = \begin{pmatrix} -4 \\ 3 \end{pmatrix}$, $BZ = \begin{pmatrix} -1 \\ -1 \end{pmatrix}$

Each point in part (d) is a rotation of the original point by 90° counterclockwise.

3a. $\begin{pmatrix} 2 \\ 5 \\ 3 \end{pmatrix}$ **b.** $\begin{pmatrix} 6 \\ 15 \\ 9 \end{pmatrix}$ **c.** $(5 \quad 3 \quad 1)$ **d.** $(-4 \quad -1 \quad 2)$

e. $\begin{pmatrix} 0 & 0 \\ 0 & 0 \\ 0 & 0 \end{pmatrix}$ **f.** $\begin{pmatrix} 0 & 0 \\ 0 & 0 \\ 0 & 0 \end{pmatrix}$ **4a.** $p = x - y$,

$q = 3x - 2y$ **b.** $2a + b = 3$, $4a + 3b = 5$, $6b = 7$

5a. $\begin{pmatrix} x \\ y \\ z \end{pmatrix} = \begin{pmatrix} 2 & -3 & 4 \\ -1 & 2 & \pi \\ 7 & -4 & -2 \end{pmatrix}\begin{pmatrix} u \\ v \\ w \end{pmatrix}$

b. $\begin{pmatrix} p \\ q \end{pmatrix} = \begin{pmatrix} 2 & 3 & -4 \\ 1 & -3 & 0 \end{pmatrix}\begin{pmatrix} x \\ y \\ z \end{pmatrix}$ **c.** $\begin{pmatrix} y_1 \\ y_2 \\ y_3 \end{pmatrix} = x\begin{pmatrix} 3 \\ -1 \\ 4 \end{pmatrix}$

6a. possible **b.** not possible **c.** possible **d.** not possible **e.** possible **f.** not possible **g.** possible **h.** not possible **7.** Answers may vary.

8a. Matrix B must have 3 rows. **b.** Matrix B must have 2 columns. **c.** Matrix B must have 3 rows and 2 columns. **9.** any square matrix **10.** any square matrix

11. $z_1 = 8x_1 + x_2$, $z_2 = -6x_1 - 7x_2$

12. To add down the columns, you can multiply on the left by a 1×3 matrix of 1's. To add across columns, you can multiply on the right by a 5×1 matrix of 1's.

13a. $\begin{pmatrix} 5 & 10 \\ 1 & 1 \end{pmatrix}\begin{pmatrix} 200 & 150 & 50 \\ 100 & 100 & 85 \end{pmatrix} = \begin{pmatrix} 2000 & 1750 & 1100 \\ 300 & 250 & 135 \end{pmatrix}$

b. $\begin{pmatrix} 2000 & 1750 & 1100 \\ 300 & 250 & 135 \end{pmatrix}\begin{pmatrix} 1 \\ 1 \\ 1 \end{pmatrix} = \begin{pmatrix} 3850 \\ 685 \end{pmatrix}$

14. $BA = \begin{pmatrix} 2 & 1 & 3 \\ 3 & 4 & 2 \\ 2 & 2 & 1 \end{pmatrix}\begin{pmatrix} 0.3 & 0.5 \\ 0.3 & 0.2 \\ 0.3 & 0.3 \end{pmatrix} = \begin{pmatrix} 1.8 & 2.1 \\ 2.7 & 2.9 \\ 1.5 & 1.7 \end{pmatrix}$

On Your Own

15. $\begin{pmatrix} a & b & c \\ d & e & f \\ g & h & i \end{pmatrix}$, $\begin{pmatrix} a & b & c \\ d & e & f \\ g & h & i \end{pmatrix}$

19a. $AB + AC = \begin{pmatrix} 0 \\ 2 \end{pmatrix} + \begin{pmatrix} 11 \\ 25 \end{pmatrix} = \begin{pmatrix} 11 \\ 27 \end{pmatrix}$

b. $A(B + C) = \begin{pmatrix} 1 & 2 \\ 3 & 4 \end{pmatrix}\begin{pmatrix} 5 \\ 3 \end{pmatrix} = \begin{pmatrix} 11 \\ 27 \end{pmatrix}$

21a. $\begin{pmatrix} -3 & -26 \\ -7 & -58 \end{pmatrix}$ **b.** $\begin{pmatrix} -3 & -26 \\ -7 & -58 \end{pmatrix}$

25a. 74.5 g protein, 50.2 g fat, 128.4 g carbohydrates **b.** The problem (and solution) can be written as

$\begin{pmatrix} 5.5 & 0.5 & 3 \\ 5.5 & 0.03 & 0.02 \\ 0.1 & 6 & 1.5 \end{pmatrix}\begin{pmatrix} 9 \\ 20 \\ 5 \end{pmatrix} = \begin{pmatrix} 74.5 \\ 50.2 \\ 128.4 \end{pmatrix}$.

Lesson 4.08
Check Your Understanding

1. $\begin{pmatrix} x \\ y \\ z \end{pmatrix} = \begin{pmatrix} 1 \\ -1 \\ 2 \end{pmatrix}$

2. $\begin{pmatrix} a \\ b \\ c \\ d \end{pmatrix} = \begin{pmatrix} 0 \\ \frac{1}{2} \\ \frac{1}{2} \\ 0 \end{pmatrix}$

3a. The two lines $x + 2y = 1$ and $2x + 4y = 1$ are parallel, so the system has no solution.

b. Gaussian Elimination results in $\left(\begin{array}{cc|c} 1 & 2 & 1 \\ 0 & 0 & -1 \end{array}\right)$, and the second row indicates that the system has no solution. **c.** The inverse does not exist $(ad - bc = 0)$. **4.** Answers may vary. Sample: To solve $AX = B$, find A^{-1} and write $A^{-1}AX = A^{-1}B$ or $X = A^{-1}B$.

5. $MA = \begin{pmatrix} 1 & 0 & 0 \\ 0 & 0 & 1 \end{pmatrix}\begin{pmatrix} 1 & 0 \\ 3 & 4 \\ 0 & 1 \end{pmatrix} = \begin{pmatrix} 1 & 0 \\ 0 & 1 \end{pmatrix}$ and

$AM = \begin{pmatrix} 1 & 0 \\ 3 & 4 \\ 0 & 1 \end{pmatrix}\begin{pmatrix} 1 & 0 & 0 \\ 0 & 0 & 1 \end{pmatrix} = \begin{pmatrix} 1 & 0 \\ 3 & 4 \\ 0 & 1 \end{pmatrix}$, so

$MA \neq AM$.

6. $AM = \begin{pmatrix} 1 & 2 \\ 3 & 4 \end{pmatrix}\begin{pmatrix} -2 & 1 \\ \frac{3}{2} & -\frac{1}{2} \end{pmatrix} =$

$\begin{pmatrix} -2 + 3 & 1 - 1 \\ -6 + 6 & 3 - 2 \end{pmatrix} = \begin{pmatrix} 1 & 0 \\ 0 & 1 \end{pmatrix} = I$

7. No, zero is a real number but it does not have an inverse.

8. No; for example, $\begin{pmatrix} 3 & -1 \\ -2 & 2 \end{pmatrix}\begin{pmatrix} 1 \\ 1 \end{pmatrix} = \begin{pmatrix} 2 \\ 0 \end{pmatrix}$ and $\begin{pmatrix} 1 \\ 1 \end{pmatrix} \neq \begin{pmatrix} 2 \\ 0 \end{pmatrix}$.

On Your Own

10. Using $M = \begin{pmatrix} 5.5 & 0.5 & 3 \\ 5.5 & 0.03 & 0.02 \\ 0.1 & 6 & 1.5 \end{pmatrix}$, the system is

$M\begin{pmatrix} m \\ p \\ c \end{pmatrix} = \begin{pmatrix} 45 \\ 35 \\ 120 \end{pmatrix}$. Then $\begin{pmatrix} m \\ p \\ c \end{pmatrix} = M^{-1}\begin{pmatrix} 45 \\ 35 \\ 120 \end{pmatrix}$

$\approx \begin{pmatrix} 6.3 \\ 19.8 \\ 0.2 \end{pmatrix}$. 6.3 oz meat, 19.8 oz potatoes, 0.2 oz cabbage

11. If $\begin{pmatrix} a & b \\ c & d \end{pmatrix}\begin{pmatrix} x \\ y \end{pmatrix} = \begin{pmatrix} x \\ y \end{pmatrix}$, then $ax + by = x$ and $cx + dy = y$. The only values of a, b, c, and d that satisfy both equations simultaneously are $a = 1$, $b = 0$, $c = 0$, and $d = 1$ or $\begin{pmatrix} 1 & 0 \\ 0 & 1 \end{pmatrix}$.

12. $\begin{pmatrix} x & y \\ z & w \end{pmatrix} = \begin{pmatrix} -2 & 1 \\ \frac{3}{2} & -\frac{1}{2} \end{pmatrix}$

Lesson 4.09
Check Your Understanding

1a. $I = \begin{pmatrix} 1 & 0 \\ 0 & 1 \end{pmatrix}$ **b.** $I = \begin{pmatrix} 1 & 0 & 0 \\ 0 & 1 & 0 \\ 0 & 0 & 1 \end{pmatrix}$

2. If $A = B$, then by substitution $AB = AA = BA$, so square matrices commute with themselves under multiplication. Also, $AA^2 = AAA = A^2A$ because matrix multiplication is associative.
3. Answers may vary. Sample: Matrix multiplication is not always commutative, so $A(B + C) \neq (B + C)A$. Therefore we need a distributive property for $A(B + C)$ and another distributive property for $(B + C)A$.

4a. $B = \begin{pmatrix} -2c \\ c \end{pmatrix}$ for any value of c.

b. $B = \begin{pmatrix} -2c & -2d \\ c & d \end{pmatrix}$ for any values of c and d.

5. Line 1: OK, by the definition of squaring; Line 2: OK; distribute the second factor $(X + Y)$ over the two terms of the first factor; Line 3: OK; distributive property; Line 4: OK, by the definition of squaring; Line 5: wrong because $XY \neq YX$. The last line should be $X^2 + XY + YX + Y^2$. **6.** yes **7.** Since A^{-1} exists and $AB = AC$, $A^{-1}(AB) = A^{-1}(AC)$. Then $(A^{-1}A)B = (A^{-1}A)C$ or $B = C$. **8.** Answers may vary. Sample: When you multiply a square matrix M by its appropriate identity matrix, there is only one element in each row of M that results in a nonzero term, and that is the same whether the identity is to the left or to the right of M.

On Your Own
9. Answers may vary. Sample: $A + A = 1A + 1A = (1 + 1)A = 2A$ **10.** Answers may vary. Sample: From Exercise 5, $(X + Y)^2 = X^2 + XY + YX + Y^2$. Substituting I for Y gives us $(X + I)^2 = X^2 + XI + IX + I^2 = X^2 + 2X + I$. **13a.** For a zero matrix Z and another matrix B, $ZB = Z$. Since $ZB \neq I$ for any B, matrix Z cannot have an inverse.

Lesson 4.10
On Your Own
9b.

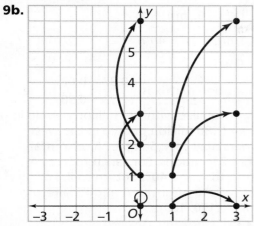

c. The mapping dilates line and polygons by a factor of 3, with the origin as the centre of the dilation.

11a. The images are $\begin{pmatrix} -2 \\ -1 \end{pmatrix}$, $\begin{pmatrix} 1 \\ 2 \end{pmatrix}$, $\begin{pmatrix} 0 \\ 0 \end{pmatrix}$, and $\begin{pmatrix} -x \\ -y \end{pmatrix}$, respectively. **b.** $M = \begin{pmatrix} -1 & 0 \\ 0 & -1 \end{pmatrix}$

Lesson 4.11
Check Your Understanding
1a. $(x, y) \mapsto (-x, y)$, which is a reflection over the y-axis. **b.** $(x, y) \mapsto (y, x)$, which is a reflection over the line $y = x$.

2. $A^{-1} = \begin{pmatrix} \frac{1}{2} & 0 \\ 0 & \frac{1}{2} \end{pmatrix}$; $A^{-1}\begin{pmatrix} x \\ y \end{pmatrix} = \begin{pmatrix} \frac{1}{2} & 0 \\ 0 & \frac{1}{2} \end{pmatrix}$

$\begin{pmatrix} x \\ y \end{pmatrix} = \begin{pmatrix} \frac{1}{2}x \\ \frac{1}{2}y \end{pmatrix}$

3. $A^2 = \begin{pmatrix} 4 & 0 \\ 0 & 4 \end{pmatrix}$, so $A^2\begin{pmatrix} x \\ y \end{pmatrix} = \begin{pmatrix} 4x \\ 4y \end{pmatrix}$;

$A^{-2} = \begin{pmatrix} \frac{1}{4} & 0 \\ 0 & \frac{1}{4} \end{pmatrix}$, so $A^{-2}\begin{pmatrix} x \\ y \end{pmatrix} = \begin{pmatrix} \frac{1}{4}x \\ \frac{1}{4}y \end{pmatrix}$.

4. $M\begin{pmatrix} a \\ b \end{pmatrix} = \begin{pmatrix} c & -d \\ d & c \end{pmatrix}\begin{pmatrix} a \\ b \end{pmatrix} = \begin{pmatrix} ac - bd \\ ad + bc \end{pmatrix}$, or M maps the point $a + bi$ to $ac - bd + (ad + bc)i = (a + bi)(c + di)$. **5.** The result of the matrix is to reflect each point over the line $y = \frac{1}{2}x$.

6. The mapping $X \mapsto M^{-1}X$ reflects a preimage

over the line $y = \frac{1}{2}x$; $M^{-1} = \begin{pmatrix} \frac{3}{5} & \frac{4}{5} \\ \frac{4}{5} & -\frac{3}{5} \end{pmatrix}$ so

$M^{-1} = M$. **7a.** If a point is on the line $y = -2x$, then its image is also on that line. **b.** 90°
c. $(2t)s + t(-2s) = 0$ **8.** A reflection scales by 1 in the direction of the line of reflection (points on this line are not moved) and scales by -1 in the perpendicular direction identified in exercise 7. **9a.** 180° (counterclockwise) rotation

b. $R^2 = \begin{pmatrix} -1 & 0 \\ 0 & -1 \end{pmatrix}$, so $R^2\begin{pmatrix} x \\ y \end{pmatrix} = \begin{pmatrix} -x \\ -y \end{pmatrix}$.

c. 270° counterclockwise rotation

d. $R^3 = \begin{pmatrix} 0 & 1 \\ -1 & 0 \end{pmatrix}$, so $R^3\begin{pmatrix} x \\ y \end{pmatrix} = \begin{pmatrix} y \\ -x \end{pmatrix}$.

e. $R^4 = \begin{pmatrix} 1 & 0 \\ 0 & 1 \end{pmatrix}$, which is the same as a (clockwise) rotation of 360° **10a.** $x + y = kx$, $2x = ky$; $(1 - k)x + y = 0$, $2x - ky = 0$
b. $k = 2$, $k = -1$ **c.** If $k = 2$, the equations are $-x + y = 0$ and $2x - 2y = 0$; the solution to that system is any point on the line $y = x$. If $k = -1$, the equations are $2x + y = 0$ and $2x + y = 0$; the solution to that system is any point on the line $y = -2x$. **11.** Answers may vary. Sample: Using the technique from Exercise 10 results in the proportion $\frac{-2.7 - k}{-1.4} = \frac{2.1}{2.2 - k}$; solving that proportion gives $k = -2$ or $k = \frac{3}{2}$. The value $k = -2$ results in a system of equations with a solution of all points on the line $y = \frac{1}{2}x$. The value $k = \frac{3}{2}$ results in a system of equations with a solution of all points on the line $y = 3x$.

12. $M = \begin{pmatrix} 0 & -1 \\ -1 & 0 \end{pmatrix}$ **13.** $M = \begin{pmatrix} \frac{\sqrt{2}}{2} & -\frac{\sqrt{2}}{2} \\ \frac{\sqrt{2}}{2} & \frac{\sqrt{2}}{2} \end{pmatrix}$

14. Answers may vary.
On Your Own
15. $X \mapsto A^{-1}X$ dilates the plane by a factor of $\frac{1}{3}$ horizontally and by a factor of $\frac{1}{2}$ vertically;

$A^{-1} = \begin{pmatrix} \frac{1}{3} & 0 \\ 0 & \frac{1}{2} \end{pmatrix}$. **16.** Answers may vary.

Sample: Using the general point $\begin{pmatrix} x \\ y \end{pmatrix}$,

$\begin{pmatrix} 0 & -1 \\ 1 & 0 \end{pmatrix}\begin{pmatrix} x \\ y \end{pmatrix} = \begin{pmatrix} -y \\ x \end{pmatrix}$, and the distance from the origin to $\begin{pmatrix} x \\ y \end{pmatrix}$ or to $\begin{pmatrix} -y \\ x \end{pmatrix}$ is $\sqrt{x^2 + y^2}$.

19a. $(-12, -6)$ **b.** $(-2.5, 2.5)$

24a. The images are $(0, -1)$, $(-1, 0)$,

$(-1, -1)$, $(-1, 1)$, $(-y, -x)$. **b.** $\begin{pmatrix} 0 & -1 \\ -1 & 0 \end{pmatrix}$

Lesson 4.12
Check Your Understanding

1. Rewriting $MA = A$ as $\begin{pmatrix} 0.8 & 0.5 \\ 0.2 & 0.5 \end{pmatrix} \begin{pmatrix} b \\ c \end{pmatrix} = \begin{pmatrix} b \\ c \end{pmatrix}$, then $A = \begin{pmatrix} 100 \\ 40 \end{pmatrix}$.

2. Answers may vary. Sample: Refer to the TI-Nspire™ Handbook, p. 778 to see how to calculate each expression. **3a.** For the cars that start at location A, 70% of them are returned to A, 20% are returned to B, and 10% are returned to C. For the cars that start at location B, 20% of them are returned to A, 50% are returned to B, and 30% are returned to C. For the cars that start at location C, 30% of them are returned to A, 10% are returned to B, and 60% are returned to C. **b.**

$$M = \begin{pmatrix} 0.7 & 0.2 & 0.3 \\ 0.2 & 0.5 & 0.1 \\ 0.1 & 0.3 & 0.6 \end{pmatrix}$$

c. $P(2) = \begin{pmatrix} 130 \\ 74 \\ 96 \end{pmatrix}$, $P(3) = \begin{pmatrix} 134.6 \\ 72.6 \\ 92.8 \end{pmatrix}$; the distribution seems to settle at about $\begin{pmatrix} 138 \\ 73 \\ 89 \end{pmatrix}$.

4a. Answers may vary. Sample: We know that

$X(n) = \begin{pmatrix} f(n) \\ f(n - 1) \end{pmatrix}$. Also, $\begin{pmatrix} 1 & 1 \\ 1 & 0 \end{pmatrix} \begin{pmatrix} f(n - 1) \\ f(n - 2) \end{pmatrix} = \begin{pmatrix} f(n - 1) + f(n - 2) \\ f(n - 1) \end{pmatrix}$. But $f(n - 1) + f(n - 2) = f(n)$ by definition, so

$\begin{pmatrix} f(n - 1) + f(n - 2) \\ f(n - 1) \end{pmatrix} = \begin{pmatrix} f(n) \\ f(n - 1) \end{pmatrix}$. So the transitive property of equality lets us conclude that $X(n) = \begin{pmatrix} 1 & 1 \\ 1 & 0 \end{pmatrix} \begin{pmatrix} f(n - 1) \\ f(n - 2) \end{pmatrix}$ or

$X(n) = \begin{pmatrix} 1 & 1 \\ 1 & 0 \end{pmatrix} X(n - 1)$. **b.** Let $M = \begin{pmatrix} 1 & 1 \\ 1 & 0 \end{pmatrix}$.

Then $X(9) = \begin{pmatrix} f(10) \\ f(9) \end{pmatrix} = M^9 X(0) =$

$\begin{pmatrix} 55 & 34 \\ 34 & 31 \end{pmatrix} \begin{pmatrix} 1 \\ 1 \end{pmatrix} = \begin{pmatrix} 89 \\ 55 \end{pmatrix}$, or $f(10) = 89$. **5.** For

$n > 1$, $Y(n) = \begin{pmatrix} g(n) \\ g(n - 1) \end{pmatrix}$; $Y(n + 1) = \begin{pmatrix} 3 & -4 \\ 1 & 0 \end{pmatrix} Y(n)$. **6.** $h(n + 1) = 2h(n) - 3h(n - 1) + 4h(n - 2)$

On Your Own

7. The transition matrix is $\begin{pmatrix} 0.97 & 0.02 \\ 0.03 & 0.98 \end{pmatrix}$; the migrations stabilize with 120 million people in the east and 180 million people in the west. **9a.** Answers may vary. Sample: A car rental agency has 2 locations. For cars rented at A, 60% return to A and 40% return to B. For cars rented at B, 25% return to A and 75% return to B. **b.** $X = (100, 160)$

Lesson 4.13
Check Your Understanding

1a. $\frac{1}{4}$ **b.** $\frac{1}{4}$ **c.** $\frac{1}{2}$ **2a.** This cannot be answered using a matrix because the matrix does not describe how to move one vertex counterclockwise in 2 steps. **b.** $\frac{5}{16}$ **c.** $\frac{3}{8}$ **3a.** This cannot be answered using a matrix because the matrix does not describe how to move one vertex counterclockwise in 2 steps. **b.** $\frac{13}{36}$ **c.** $\frac{5}{18}$ **4.** Answers may vary. Sample: Probabilities cannot be negative; each column represents *all* the possibilities for a particular situation, so the sum of the entries in a column must be 1.

5. The weather transition matrix is $\begin{pmatrix} 0.6 & 0.7 \\ 0.4 & 0.3 \end{pmatrix}$.

a. 0.64 **b.** 0.636 **c.** 0.636 **d.** 0.636 **e.** 0.636

6a. $\begin{pmatrix} 0.8 & 0.1 \\ 0.2 & 0.9 \end{pmatrix}$ **b.** 0.343 **c.** 0.671

7. The matrix is $\begin{pmatrix} 0 & \frac{1}{2} & 0 \\ \frac{1}{2} & 0 & 0 \\ \frac{1}{2} & \frac{1}{2} & 0 \end{pmatrix}$.

(1) $\frac{1}{2}$ (2) 0.696 (3) $\frac{1}{16}$

On Your Own

8. $M^3 = \begin{pmatrix} 0.344 & 0.328 & 0.328 \\ 0.328 & 0.344 & 0.328 \\ 0.328 & 0.328 & 0.344 \end{pmatrix}$,

$M^4 = \begin{pmatrix} 0.366 & 0.332 & 0.332 \\ 0.332 & 0.336 & 0.332 \\ 0.332 & 0.332 & 0.336 \end{pmatrix}$;

in the long run, all the entries will be 0.333, regardless of the starting vertex. **13a.** 0.625 **b.** 0.312

Lesson 4.14

Check Your Understanding

1. a. 17–19; about half of the simulations had fewer than 17–19 athletes in the Magnet Group who passed, and about half had more. **b.** 20; a majority of the simulations had fewer than 20 athletes in the Magnet Group pass the test, so 20 is a less likely result than 17–19. But it is not so far from the most likely results that you can confidently rule out it happening by chance along. **c.** 21–24; a great majority of simulations had fewer than 21–24 athletes pass the test. These results are very unlikely to happen due to chance alone.

2. Answers may vary. Sample: If only 15 athletes from the Magnet Group passed the balance test, this could be evidence that the magnets have a detrimental effect on balance. It is unlikely that only 15 athletes would pass the balance test if the results were impacted by chance alone.

3. a. Tony would expect 18 athletes in the Magnet Group to pass the balance test. **b.** No; Tony did not do anything wrong in his simulation. There is always randomness in a simulation, so you can expect Tony's results to vary slightly from the expectation.

On Your Own

5. Sasha's simulation assumes the outcomes of drawing 0, 1, or 2 red cards are all equally likely. This is not the case, since drawing 0 red cards is more likely than drawing exactly 1 red card, which in turn is more likely than drawing 2 red cards.

8. a. $\frac{1}{256}$ **b.** $\frac{1}{32}$ **c.** $\frac{35}{128}$

Chapter 5

Lesson 5.01

On Your Own

6a. no **c.** yes **f.** no **7a.** No; $2^{10} + 2^2 \neq 2^{10+2}$. This sum cannot be written as a single power of 2. **c.** Yes; $2^{10} \cdot 2^2 = 2^{10+2} = 2^{12}$ **h.** Yes; $4 \cdot 2^{10} = 2^2 \cdot 2^{10} = 2^{2+10} = 2^{12}$

Lesson 5.02

Check Your Understanding

1. $(ab)^n = \underbrace{(ab) \cdot (ab) \cdot \cdots \cdot (ab)}_{n \text{ copies of } ab}$

$= \underbrace{(a \cdot a \cdot \cdots \cdot a)}_{n \text{ copies of } a} \underbrace{(b \cdot b \cdot \cdots \cdot b)}_{n \text{ copies of } b}$

$= a^n \cdot b^n$

2. $\frac{3^{11}}{3^5} = \frac{3 \cdot 3 \cdot 3 \cdot 3 \cdot 3 \cdot 3 \cdot 3 \cdot 3 \cdot 3 \cdot 3 \cdot 3}{3 \cdot 3 \cdot 3 \cdot 3 \cdot 3}$

$= \frac{3 \cdot 3 \cdot 3 \cdot 3 \cdot 3}{3 \cdot 3 \cdot 3 \cdot 3 \cdot 3} \cdot \frac{3 \cdot 3 \cdot 3 \cdot 3 \cdot 3 \cdot 3}{1}$

$= 1 \cdot 3^6 = 3^6$

3. Corollary 5.1.1:

$$\frac{a^b}{a^c} = \frac{\overbrace{(a \cdot a \cdot \cdots \cdot a)}^{b \text{ copies of } a}}{\underbrace{(a \cdot a \cdot \cdots \cdot a)}_{c \text{ copies of } a}}$$

$$= \frac{\overbrace{(a \cdot a \cdot \cdots \cdot a)}^{c \text{ copies of } a}}{\underbrace{(a \cdot a \cdot \cdots \cdot a)}_{c \text{ copies of } a}} \cdot \frac{\overbrace{(a \cdot a \cdot \cdots \cdot a)}^{b-c \text{ copies of } a}}{1}$$

$$= 1 \cdot a^{b-c} = a^{b-c}$$

Corollary 5.1.2: $(a^b)^c =$

$$\overbrace{(a \cdot a \cdot \cdots \cdot a)}^{b \text{ copies of } a} \cdot \overbrace{(a \cdot a \cdot \cdots \cdot a)}^{b \text{ copies of } a} \cdot \cdots \cdot \overbrace{(a \cdot a \cdot \cdots \cdot a)}^{b \text{ copies of } a}$$

$$\underbrace{}_{c \text{ copies of } a^b}$$

$$= \underbrace{\frac{a \cdot a \cdot \cdots \cdot a}{}}_{bc \text{ copies of } a} = a^{bc}$$

4a. Yes; $3^{14} + 3^{14} + 3^{14} = 3 \cdot 3^{14} = 3^1 + 3^{14} = 3^{1+14} = 3^{15}$ **b.** No; $(3^6)^9 = 3^{6 \cdot 9} = 3^{54} \neq 3^{15}$
c. Yes; $(3^{10})(3^5) = 3^{10+5} = 3^{15}$
d. No; $(3^3)(3^5) = 3^{3+5} = 3^8 \neq 3^{15}$
e. No; $(3^{15})(3^1) = 3^{15+1} = 3^{16} \neq 3^{15}$
f. Yes; $(3^5)(3^5)(3^5) = 3^{5+5+5} = 3^{15}$
g. No; $3^9 + 3^6 \neq 3^{9+6}$. This sum cannot be written as a single power of 3. **h.** Yes; $(3^5)^3 = 3^{5 \cdot 3} = 3^{15}$ **i.** Yes; $(3^3)^5 = 3^{3 \cdot 5} = 3^{15}$
j. Yes; $9(3^{13}) = (3^2)(3^{13}) = 3^{2+13} = 3^{15}$
k. No; $(3^5)^{10} = 3^{5 \cdot 10} = 3^{50} \neq 3^{15}$ **l.** Yes; $(3^1)^{15} = 3^{1 \cdot 15} = 3^{15}$ **5.** Answers may vary.

Sample: M^3N, $\frac{M^6}{N^3}$ **6.** Each time you multiply a power of x from the first factor by a power of x from the second factor, you can use the Fundamental Law of Exponents to find the exponent to place on x in the resulting term of the product. **7.** 3^{31} **8a.** 3 **b.** 5 **c.** $\frac{6}{5}$ **d.** 3
9. $f(n) = 3 \cdot 5^n$ **10.** mean: 11,111; median: $5 \cdot 10^2$ or 500 **11a.** 10 **b.** $\frac{9y^5}{8}$ **c.** $2x^4$ **d.** $\frac{1}{8}$

12a. ± 4 **b.** 2

On Your Own

13a. 1000 **b.** 1,000,000,000,000 **d.** 16

f. 10,000 **17.** about 2,000,000 **18a.** No; $\frac{2^6}{2^2} = 2^{6-2} = 2^4 \neq 2^3$ **d.** Yes; $\frac{(2^2)^5}{2^7} = \frac{2^{2 \cdot 5}}{2^7} = \frac{2^{10}}{2^7} = 2^{10-7} = 2^3$ **22a.** x^{12} **g.** x^8

Lesson 5.03
Check Your Understanding

1a. Yes; $\left(\frac{1}{7}\right)^{10} = (7^{-1})^{10} = 7^{-1 \cdot 10} = 7^{-10}$

b. No; $7^{-4} \cdot 7^{-3} = 7^{-4 + (-3)} = 7^{-7} \neq 7^{-10}$

c. No; $(7^{13})(7^{-6}) = 7^{13 + (-6)} = 7^7 \neq 7^{-10}$

d. Yes; $\frac{7^3}{7^{13}} = 7^{3-13} = 7^{-10}$ **e.** No; $\frac{7^2}{7^3 \cdot 7^4 \cdot 7^4}$
$= \frac{7^2}{7^{3+4+4}} = \frac{7^2}{7^{11}} = 7^{2-11} = 7^{-9} \neq 7^{-10}$

f. No; $\frac{1}{7^{-10}} = 7^{-(-10)} = 7^{10} \neq 7^{-10}$

g. No; $7^5 \cdot 7^{-2} = 7^{5 + (-2)} = 7^3 \neq 7^{-10}$

h. Yes; $\left(\frac{1}{7^2}\right)^5 = (7^{-2})^5 = 7^{(-2) \cdot 5} = 7^{-10}$

i. No; $(7^5)^{-15} = 7^{5 \cdot (-15)} = 7^{-75} \neq 7^{-10}$

j. Yes; $(7^5)^{-2} = 7^{5 \cdot (-2)} = 7^{-10}$

k. Yes; $(7^{-2})^5 = 7^{-2 \cdot 5} = 7^{-10}$ **l.** Yes; $\frac{1}{7^{10}}$
$= 7^{-10}$ **2.** $10^{-2} \cdot 10^3 = \frac{1}{10^2} \cdot \frac{10^3}{1} = \frac{10^3}{10^2}$
$= 10^{3-2} = 10^1$ **3.** $a^b \cdot a^c = a^{b+c}$:
If $b = 0$, then $a^b \cdot a^c = a^0 \cdot a^c = a^c$
and $a^{b+c} = a^{0+c} = a^c$. $\frac{a^b}{a^c} = a^{b-c}$ $(b > c)$:
If $c = 0$, then $\frac{a^b}{a^c} = \frac{a^b}{a^0} = \frac{a^b}{1} = a^b$ and
$a^{b-c} = a^{b-0} = a^b$. $(a^b)^c = a^{bc}$: If $b = 0$, then
$(a^b)^c = (a^0)^c = 1^c = 1$ and $a^{bc} = a^{0 \cdot c} = a^0 = 1$.

4a. 6 **b.** $\frac{2}{3}$ **c.** 4 **d.** 8 **e.** 1 **f.** $2^{\frac{1}{2}}$ or $\sqrt{2}$ **5.** 1

6. 0.75×10^7h; 1.53×10^9h; 0.89×10^{11}h

7a. 16, 8, 4, **2, 1,** $\frac{1}{2}, \ldots$ **b.** 2, **6**, 18, **54, 162,**
486, ... **c.** 1, a, a^2, a^3, a^4, a^5, ...

d. b^6, b^3, 1, b^{-3}, b^{-6}, b^{-9}, ...

e. c^{10}, c^8, c^6, c^4, c^2, 1, ...
8a. $h(x) = 2 \cdot 5^x$ **b.** $h(x) = \frac{2}{125}, \frac{2}{25}, \frac{2}{5}$

9. $(2^3)(2^{-3}) = 2^{3 + (-3)} = 2^0 = 1$

On Your Own
10a. 2 **e.** -3 **14a.** $3^{2x} + 2 + 3^{-2x}$ **15b.** z^{-27}
16b. $\frac{1}{9}$ **f.** 3

Lesson 5.04
Check Your Understanding
1a. 0, 3, 6, 9, **12, 15,** ... **b.** 0, **6, 12, 18, 24,**
30, ... **c.** 1, **21, 41, 61,** 81, **101,** ... **d.** 5, **1, −3,**
−7, −11, −15, −19 ... **2.** There are five
"steps" from 0 to 30, so the third step, 18, is
three fifths of the way from 0 to 30. **3a.** 2, −6,
18, **−54, 162,** −486, ... **b.** 1, i, −1, −i, **1**, i, ...
c. 1, $\pm\sqrt{5}$, 5, $\pm5\sqrt{5}$, 25, $\pm25\sqrt{5}$, ... **d.** 1, **5,**
25, 125, **625,** ... **e.** 1, $\pm\sqrt{3}$, 3, $\pm3\sqrt{3}$, 9, ±9
$\sqrt{3}$, 27, ... **4.** There are three "steps" from 1

to 125, so the second step, 25, is two thirds of
the way from 1 to 125. **5a.** $\frac{a+b}{2}$ **b.** $\pm\sqrt{ab}$

6a.

(a, b)	$\dfrac{a+b}{2}$	$\sqrt{ab}$
$(1, 2)$	1.5	1.4142
$(2, 5)$	3.5	3.1623
$(4, 1)$	2.5	2
$(3, 3)$	3	3
$(6, 9)$	7.5	7.3485
$(8, 10)$	9	8.9443
$(7, 7)$	7	7

b. $\frac{a+b}{2}$; Answers may vary. Sample: The
square of any real number is positive, so
$(a - b)^2 \geq 0$. Then, $a^2 - 2ab + b^2 \geq 0$,
$a^2 + 2ab + b^2 \geq 4ab$, $\frac{a^2 + 2ab + b^2}{4} \geq ab$, and
$\frac{(a+b)^2}{4} \geq ab$. Taking the square root of each
side (since a, $b > 0$) gives $\frac{a+b}{2} \geq \sqrt{ab}$. **7.** Yes;
the missing terms could be 2, 4, 8, or −2, 4, −8.

8. $64^{\frac{2}{3}} = 16$, $625^{\frac{1}{4}} = 5$ **9a.** 4 **b.** 3 **c.** 3 **d.** 16

On Your Own
10a. 81 **b.** 27 **12a.** Balance: 546.36, 562.75,
579.64, 597.03 **13a.** 5 **17a.** $\frac{2}{3}$ **b.** 6

Lesson 5.05
Check Your Understanding
1a. a little more than 6 **b.** Answers may vary.
Sample: a little more than 222 **2a.** 3 **b.** 32 **c.** 49
d. 9 **3a.** Answers may vary. Sample: $a = 32$,
$b = 4$ **b.** Yes; if $a^{\frac{2}{5}} = b$, then $\left(a^{\frac{2}{5}}\right)^5 = b^5$,
which simplifies to $a^2 = b^5$.

4. $1^{\frac{p}{q}} = (1^p)^{\frac{1}{q}} = 1^{\frac{1}{q}} = \sqrt[q]{1} = 1$

5. The graph is made up of points from the
horizontal lines $y = 1$ and $y = -1$. It consists
of the points $(x, 1)$ when x is an even integer
and $(x, -1)$ when x is an odd integer. If x is not
an integer, the output is sometimes
defined (for example, $(-1)^{\frac{1}{3}} = -1$) and
sometimes not defined (for example, $(-1)^{\frac{1}{2}}$
is not a real number). **6a.** $a(b(9)) = 9$,
$b(a(7)) = 7$ **b.** No; Answers may vary. Sample:
It is not always true that $b(a(x)) = x$. For
example, $b(a(-7)) = b(49) = 7$. **7.** If $a, b, c, d,$
... is an arithmetic sequence, then $b = a + k$,
$c = a + 2k$, $d = a + 3k, \ldots$, for some
number k. Then $10^b = 10^{a+k} = 10^a \cdot 10^k$,

$10^c = 10^{a+2k} = 10^a \cdot 10^{2k}$, and
$10^d = 10^{a+3k} = 10^a \cdot 10^{3k}$. Thus
10^a, 10^b, 10^c, 10^d, ... is a geometric sequence with the common ratio 10^k.

On Your Own

10. ± 3, $\pm 3i$ **11a.** 3

15a.

x	$f(x) = x^3$	$g(x) = x^{\frac{1}{3}}$
-8	-512	-2
-2	-8	-1.26
-1	-1	-1
$-\frac{1}{2}$	-0.125	-0.794
$-\frac{1}{8}$	-0.002	-0.5
0	0	0
$\frac{1}{8}$	0.002	0.5
$\frac{1}{2}$	0.125	0.794
1	1	1
2	8	1.26
8	512	2

Lesson 5.06
On Your Own

11a. $\pm\sqrt{5}$ **b.** 2.32

12.

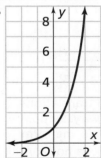

15a. outputs: $\frac{3}{4}$, $\frac{3}{2}$, 3, 6, 12

16b. $L(h) = 100 \cdot \left(\frac{1}{2}\right)^h$

Lesson 5.07
Check Your Understanding

1a. $f(x) = -3 \cdot 2^x$ **b.** $f(x) = 3 \cdot \left(\frac{1}{2}\right)^x$
c. $f(x) = 3 \cdot 2^x$ **d.** $f(x) = 3 \cdot 5^x$

2a. $f(x) = 12 \cdot \left(\frac{1}{2}\right)^x$ **b.** $f(x) = 48 \cdot \left(\frac{1}{2}\right)^x$

3a. Answers may vary. Sample: $f(x) = 2 \cdot 6^x$,
$g(x) = 8 \cdot 3^x$ **b.** $f(x) = a \cdot \left(\sqrt{\frac{72}{a}}\right)^x$

4. Lemma: The proof uses the fact that b^x is strictly decreasing for nonnegative integer inputs. Let $x = \frac{p}{q}$ for some positive integers p and q, and then suppose that $b^{\frac{1}{q}} \geq 1$.
Then $b = (b^{\frac{1}{q}})^q \geq 1^q = 1$, which implies $b \geq 1$.
But this contradicts the hypothesis of the lemma that $b < 1$. Thus $b^{\frac{1}{q}} < 1$, and therefore $b^x = (b^{\frac{p}{q}}) = (b^{\frac{1}{q}})^p < 1^p = 1$. So, $b^x < 1$.

Theorem: Let s and t be rational numbers such that $s > t$. Then $s - t > 0$, so (using the Lemma) $b^{s-t} < 1$. Since $b^t > 0$, multiplying both sides of the inequality by b^t does not reverse the inequality symbol. So,
$b^{s-t} \cdot b^t < 1 \cdot b^t$
$b^{s-t+t} < b^t$
$b^s < b^t$
Thus, if $s > t$, then $f(s) < f(t)$, which means that f is strictly decreasing on rational number inputs.

5. Answers may vary. Sample: If $f(x) = 2^x$,
then $f(-x) = 2^{-x} = \frac{1}{2^x} = \left(\frac{1}{2}\right)^x = g(x)$.

6. 2.807 **7.** 2.807

8a.

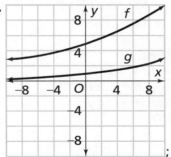

; no

b. one **9a.** 4 **b.** Yes; $\left(2^{\sqrt{2}}\right)^{\sqrt{2}} = 2^{\sqrt{2} \cdot \sqrt{2}} = 2^2 = 4$ **10.** Answers may vary. Sample: A calculator gives error messages because b^a is not defined for $b < 0$.

On Your Own

11. $f(0) = a \cdot b^0 = a \cdot 1 = a$, so the graph contains $(0, a)$. **13a.** \$4.11, \$4.23
15. $2 < \sqrt{6} < 3$, so $3^2 < 3^{\sqrt{6}} < 3^3$ or
$9 < 3^{\sqrt{6}} < 27$. **18a.** outputs: $\frac{1}{4}$, $-\frac{1}{2}$, 1, -2, 4, -8

Lesson 5.08
Check Your Understanding

1a. $A(n) = 18 \cdot \left(\frac{1}{3}\right)^n$ **b.** $B(x) = -2 \cdot (4)^n$

c. No exponential function fits the table because the ratio between consecutive outputs is not constant. **d.** $D(z) = \frac{1}{3} \cdot 6^z$

2a. $A(n) = \begin{cases} 18 & \text{if } n = 0 \\ \frac{1}{3} \cdot A(n-1) & \text{if } n > 0 \end{cases}$

b. $B(x) = \begin{cases} -2 & \text{if } x = 0 \\ 4 \cdot B(x-1) & \text{if } x > 0 \end{cases}$

c. not an exponential function

d. $D(z) = \begin{cases} \frac{1}{3} & \text{if } z = 0 \\ 6 \cdot D(z-1) & \text{if } z > 0 \end{cases}$

3. $q(x) = 12{,}500 \cdot \left(\frac{1}{5}\right)^x$ **4.** Disagree; a value of $-\frac{1}{5}$ for b is not possible because the base of an exponential function must be positive.
5. Answers may vary. Sample: $f(x) = 2x + 16$; $f(x) = (10 \cdot 2^{\frac{3}{5}})(2^{\frac{1}{5}})^x$ **6a.** $a = 100$, $b = 3^{\frac{1}{5}}$

b.

x	$T(x)$	$\div$
0	100	$\approx$**1.246**
1	$\approx$**124.57**	$\approx$**1.246**
2	$\approx$**155.18**	$\approx$**1.246**
3	$\approx$**193.32**	$\approx$**1.246**
4	$\approx$**240.82**	$\approx$**1.246**
5	300	

7a. $16,000; $12,800; $10,240
b. $V(n) = 20{,}000 \cdot (0.8)^n$ **c.** Yes; $V(14) = \$879.61$, so after 14 yr the car will be worth less than $1000.

8. $y = y_1^{\frac{-x_2}{x_1 - x_2}} \cdot y_2^{\frac{x_1}{x_1 - x_2}} \cdot \left(\left(\frac{y_1}{y_2}\right)^{\frac{1}{x_1 - x_2}}\right)^x$

On Your Own
10. $M(n) = 24, 36, 54, 81$; $M(n) = 16 \cdot \left(\frac{3}{2}\right)^n$,
$M(n) = \begin{cases} 16 & \text{if } n = 0 \\ \frac{3}{2} \cdot M(n-1) & \text{if } n > 0 \end{cases}$

12b. $y = -5^{\frac{1}{4}} \cdot \left(5^{\frac{1}{4}}\right)^x$ or $y = -5^{\frac{x+1}{4}}$

Lesson 5.09
Check Your Understanding
1. Multiply a by the power b^x. **2.** Divide C by the power b^x. **3.** Find the $\frac{1}{x}$ power of the quotient $C \div a$. **4.** Find $C \div a$, and then find the power of b that results in the value $C \div a$.

5a.

x	$f(x) = 2^x$
0	1
1	2
1.5850	3
2	4
2.3219	5
2.5850	6
■	7
3	8
3.1700	9
3.3219	10

b. 2.8074
6a. $f(x + y) = \frac{f(x) \cdot f(y)}{a}$ **b.** $f(x - y) = a \cdot \frac{f(x)}{f(y)}$
c. $f(xy) = a^{1-y} \cdot (f(x))^y$ **7a.** 3.162 **b.** $\sqrt{10}$
c. $4743.42 **8a.** 2.154 **b.** $\sqrt[3]{10}$ **c.** $6962.38
9. If $x = 1$, then $x^y = 1$ for all real number values of y; if $x = -1$, then $x^y = 1$ for all even values of y, or for all fractions $\frac{p}{q}$ where p and q are relatively prime and p is even; if $y = 0$, then $x^y = 1$ for all values of x except $x = 0$.
On Your Own
10a. 2 **d.** no solution **12a.** 11.9 yr
13.

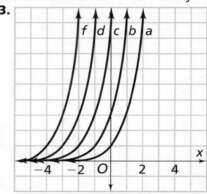

The graphs are all horizontal translations of each other. Answers may vary. Sample: Each function can be written in the form $F(x) = 3^{x+n}$, which represents a horizontal translation of $a(x) = 3^x$. For example, $c(x) = 9 \cdot 3^x = 3^2 + 3^x = 3^{2+x}$, so the graph of $c(x) = 3^{x+2}$ is a horizontal translation of two units to left of the graph of $a(x) = 3^x$.
16a. Plan 1: 2 yr, Plan 2: 3 yr

Lesson 5.10
Check Your Understanding
1. domain: positive real numbers, range: all real numbers **2a.** 2 **b.** 0 **c.** 6 **d.** 3 **e.** -2
3a. 1.1610 **b.** 1.5 **c.** 2.6610 **d.** 0.3390
4.

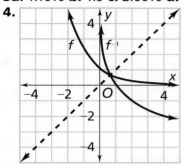

5a. the mean of $f(3)$ and $f(5)$ **b.** the mean of $f(5)$ and $f(7)$ **c.** the mean of $f(-4)$ and $f(-2)$ **d.** the mean of $f(x)$ and $f(y)$

6a.

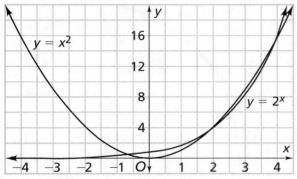

b. 3 solutions **7.** no **8a.** no **b.** no **c.** yes
9. $b \approx 1.4$; about (2.7, 2.7)

On Your Own
10. Yes; $L_2(x)$ is the inverse of $f(x) = 2^x$. Since $f(x)$ is one-to-one, its inverse is one-to-one.

12.

x	$L_2(x)$
1	0
2	1
3	1.5850
4	2
5	2.3219
6	2.5850
7	2.8074
8	3
9	3.1699

13b. $8^{\frac{1}{3}} = 2$, so $L_8(2) = \frac{1}{3}$. **15.** 8 yr

Lesson 5.11
On Your Own
11a. 2 **12a.** 2 **14a.** 5 **d.** $\frac{5}{2}$

16.

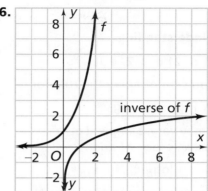

18a. 4.3 **b.** 3.2

Lesson 5.12
Check Your Understanding
1a.

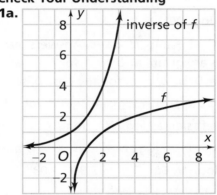

b. $f^{-1}(x) = 2^x$ **2.** C **3a.** $\frac{1}{2}$ **b.** 3 **c.** 3 **d.** $\frac{3}{2}$ **e.** 2 **f.** 2
4. If $\log_b 0 = x$, then $b^x = 0$. But $b^x = 0$ only when $b = 0$. Since $b = 0$ is not a valid base for logarithms, $\log_b 0$ does not exist. **5.** $\log_2 0.1$, $\log_5 \frac{1}{5}$, $\log_{73} 1$, $\log_{100} 10$, $\log 99$, $\log_4 18$, $\log_2 18$ **6a.** $b^4 = 9$ **b.** $\sqrt{3}$ **7.** 75 **8a.** 2 **b.** 3 **c.** 6 **d.** 27 **e.** 3.49 **f.** 6.42 **9.** 2.322 **10.** Answers may vary. Sample: The characteristic of $\log M$ is a good indicator of the size of the number M. For example, if $\log M = 3.6435$, then the characteristic 3 means M is between $10^3 = 1000$ and $10^4 = 10,000$. The mantissa of $\log M$ is always the logarithm of the number between 1 and 10 that $10^{\text{characteristic}}$ is multiplied by to get M. For example, the number 0.6465 in $\log M = 3.6435$ tells us that $10^{0.6435}$ is the number that must be multiplied by 10^3 to get M. The mantissa in combination with the characteristic provides a way to find M from a logarithm table that gives logarithms of numbers between 1 and 10.

On Your Own

12. $b^0 = 1$ for any nonzero value of b, so $\log_b 1 = 0$ for any base b. **13a.** $y = 2x$
16a. 2.085

Lesson 5.13
Check Your Understanding

1a. 4 **b.** 7 **c.** 1 **d.** 21 **e.** $\frac{7}{2}$ **2.** 4 **3.** $\frac{\log_2 32}{\log_2 8} \neq$

$\log_2 \frac{32}{8}$, so you cannot apply the rule for

$\log_b \frac{M}{N}$ to get $\log_2 32 - \log_2 8$; $\frac{5}{3}$.

4a. Answers may vary. Sample: Let $b^x = M$
and $b^y = N$ so $x = \log_b M$ and

$y = \log_b N$. Then $\log_b \frac{M}{N} = \log_b \frac{b^x}{b^y}$

$= \log_b b^{x-y} = x - y = \log_b M - \log_b N$.

b. Answers may vary. Sample: $\log_b \frac{M}{N}$

$= \log_b \left(M \cdot \frac{1}{N} \right) = \log_b M + \log_b \frac{1}{N}$

$= \log_b M + \log_b N^{-1} = \log_b M + (-1) \cdot$

$\log_b N = \log_b M - \log_b N$. **5a–c.** Answers may
vary. Samples are given. **a.** $b^0 = 1$ for any base
b, so $\log_b 1 = 0$. **b.** $b^1 = b$ for any base b, so

$\log_b b = 1$. **c.** Start with $\log_b (N \cdot \frac{1}{N}) = \log_b 1$.

Rewrite the left side as $\log_b N + \log_b \frac{1}{N}$.

The right side is 0, so $\log_b N + \log_b \frac{1}{N} = 0$ and

$\log_b \frac{1}{N} = -\log_b N$. **6a.** $C(n) = 3.99 \cdot 1.03^n$

b. 55 yr **7.** $\frac{\log 3.5}{\log 5}$; 0.778 **8.** $\frac{\log \frac{c}{a}}{\log b}$ or $\frac{\log c - \log a}{\log b}$

9. $\frac{\log \frac{7}{2}}{\log \frac{5}{3}}$; 2.452 **10.** $\frac{\log \frac{c}{a}}{\log \frac{b}{d}}$ or $\frac{\log c - \log a}{\log b - \log d}$

11. Answers may vary. Sample: If $6^x = 35$, then

$x = \frac{\log 35}{\log 6}$, while if $35^x = 6$ then $x = \frac{\log 6}{\log 35}$;

the fractions are reciprocals. **12a.** 2 **b.** -3, 2
c. all real numbers greater than 0 **d.** 5 **e.** no
solution **13.** If $\log 2 = 0.3$ then $5 \cdot \log 2 = 1.5$,
and if $\log 3 = 0.5$ then $3 \cdot \log 3 = 1.5$. Then
$5 \cdot \log 2 = 3 \cdot \log 3$, so $\log 2^5 = \log 3^3$, which
implies that $32 = 27$. Subtracting 27 from each
side gives $5 = 0$. Dividing each side by 5 gives
$1 = 0$. **14.** If r is the annual interest rate, then
the situation of doubling an amount

A can be written as $2A = A \left(1 + \frac{r}{100} \right)^y$

or $2 = \left(1 + \frac{r}{100} \right)^y$. Then $\log 2 = y \cdot$

$\log \left(1 + \frac{r}{100} \right)$ and $y = \frac{\log 2}{\log \left(1 + \frac{r}{100} \right)}$. By letting

r take the values 6, 7, 8, 9, 10, 11, and 12,
you can calculate the corresponding
y-values 11.8957, 10.2448, 9.0065, 8.0432,
7.2725, 6.6419, and 6.1163. These values are
very close to the results given by the Rule of 72
(listed in Exercise 17, Lesson 5.10).

On Your Own

15. $\log_5 135$; $5^3 = 125$,
so $\log_5 135 > 3$. $7^3 = 343$, and $\log_7 300 < 3$.
Thus, $\log_5 135 > \log_7 300$. **16.** $\log_3 x = 1$,
1.2619, 1.4650, 1.6309, 1.7712, 1.8928, 2 **17.** D
19a. $a + b$ **23a.** 1

Lesson 5.14
Check Your Understanding

1. 2.6 **2a.** $\ln 1 = 0$; $\ln 0$ is undefined.
b. about 2.71728.

3a.

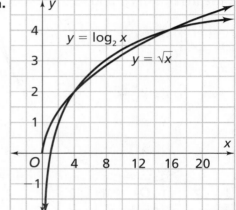

b. 2 **4.** no **5a.** no **b.** no **c.** yes **6a.** 1 **b.** 1 **c.** 2
d. 0 **e.** 2 **7.** $b \approx 1.4447$, intersect at about
(2.7183, 2.7183)

On Your Own

8a. 0.468 **9.** Disagree; the graphs are not the
same because the domain of $f(x) = \log x^2$
is all real numbers except 0, while the domain
of $g(x) = 2 \log x$ is only the positive real
numbers.

10a.

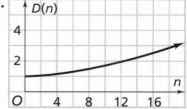

13a.

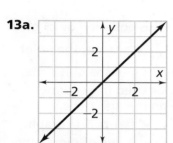

$y = x$; since $\log 10^x = x$ for all real numbers x, the graph of $y = \log 10^x$ is the same as the graph of $y = x$.

Lesson 5.15
Check Your Understanding
1. Less frequent; about 1 out of 10 integers are prime up to 10^5, but only 1 out of 22 are prime up to 10^{10}.

2.

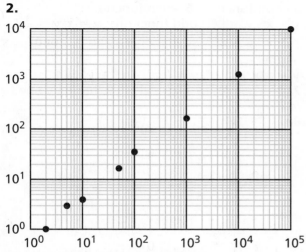

The points appear to lie on a line.

3.

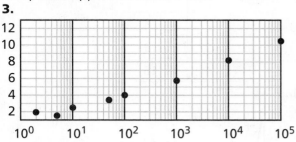

The points appear to lie on a line, especially as the values of x get larger. **4.** Logarithmic; on the vertical axis, equal differences are not represented by equal distances.

5a. Suppose $y = \log_b x$ with $b > 0$, $b \neq 1$. Rewrite the equation as $b^y = x$, and take the logarithm of each side: $\log b^y = \log x$.

Then $y \cdot \log b = \log x$, so $y = \dfrac{1}{\log b} \cdot \log x$. Since $\dfrac{1}{\log b}$ is a constant, say B, the equation becomes $y = B \cdot \log x$, which is in linear form. **b.** $\dfrac{1}{\log b}$

6a. If $y = a \cdot x^b$, then $\log y = \log (a \cdot x^b)$. So, $\log y = \log a + b \cdot \log x$. But $\log a$ is a constant, say A, so the equation becomes $\log y = A + b \cdot \log x$, which is in linear form. **b.** b **7.** The intersection of $y = x^2$ and $y = 10x^2$ is (0, 0). Because there is no value of 0 on the logarithmic axes, the intersection is not shown.

On Your Own
9a–b.

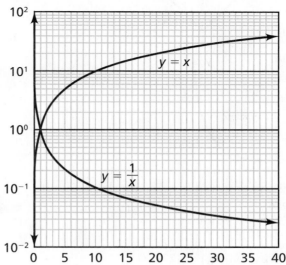

The graph of $y = x$, when shown using a logarithmic y-axis, looks like the graph of a logarithmic function when that function is shown on a standard coordinate plane.
10b. 3 **c.** ± 100 **12a.** Exponential; the ratio of successive outputs is constant.

Chapter 6
Lesson 6.01
On Your Own
12a, c.

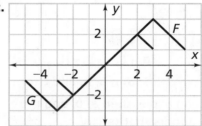

b. Connect (0, 0) and (−3, −3). Connect (−2, −2) and (−3, −1). Connect (−3, −3) and (−5, −1). **d.** Figure G is figure F rotated 180° about the origin. **13.** 180° rotational symmetry

16b.

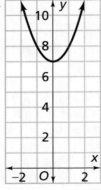

18c.

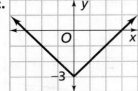

20a.

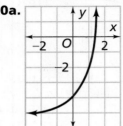

It is the graph of $y = 3^x$ translated 5 units down.

22c.

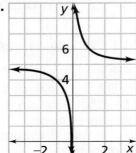

It is the graph of $y = \frac{1}{x}$ translated 5 units up.

Lesson 6.02
Check Your Understanding

1a. $\left(\frac{4}{5}, \frac{3}{5}\right)$, $\left(\frac{4}{5}, -\frac{3}{5}\right)$

b. $\left(-\frac{4}{5}, \frac{3}{5}\right)$, $\left(-\frac{4}{5}, -\frac{3}{5}\right)$, $\left(\frac{3}{5}, \frac{4}{5}\right)$, $\left(\frac{3}{5}, -\frac{4}{5}\right)$, $\left(-\frac{3}{5}, \frac{4}{5}\right)$, $\left(-\frac{3}{5}, -\frac{4}{5}\right)$ **2a.** $\left(\frac{12}{13}, \frac{5}{13}\right)$, $\left(-\frac{12}{13}, \frac{5}{13}\right)$

b. $\left(\frac{8}{17}, \frac{15}{17}\right)$, $\left(\frac{8}{17}, -\frac{15}{17}\right)$ **3.** If a, b, and c form a Pythagorean triple, then a, b, and c are positive integers that satisfy $a^2 + b^2 = c^2$.

Dividing both sides of this equation by c^2 gives $\frac{a^2}{c^2} + \frac{b^2}{c^2} = \frac{c^2}{c^2}$, or $\left(\frac{a}{c}\right)^2 + \left(\frac{b}{c}\right)^2 = 1$. Thus, the point $\left(\frac{a}{c}, \frac{b}{c}\right)$ satisfies the equation of the unit circle, $x^2 + y^2 = 1$, and can be used to generate other points that are on the unit circle.
4a. $f(-x) = (-x)^2 = x^2 = f(x)$ **b.** The graph of $y = x^2$ has the y-axis as a line of symmetry, so if (x, y) is on the graph, then $(-x, y)$ is also on the graph. Since opposite inputs have the same output, $f(x) = x^2$ is an even function.
5a. $f(-x) = (-x)^3 + (-x) = -x^3 - x = -(x^3 + x) = -f(x)$ **b.** The graph of $y = x^3 + x$ has $180°$ rotational symmetry about the origin, so if (x, y) is on the graph, then $(-x, -y)$ is also on the graph. Since opposite inputs have opposite outputs, $f(x) = x^3 + x$ is an odd function. **6.** even functions: $y = x^2$, $y = |x|$; odd functions: $y = x$, $y = \frac{1}{x}$, $y = x^3$, $y = x^3 - x$, $y = x^3 + x$; both: none; neither: $y = \sqrt{x}$, $y = b^x$, $y = \log_b x$, $x^2 + y^2 = 1$
7. $x^3 + x = 0$, or $x(x^2 + 1) = 0$, has only one real root, 0.

8a.

x	$x-3$	$(x-3)^2$
-1	-4	16
0	-3	9
1	-2	4
2	-1	1
3	0	0
4	1	1
5	2	4
6	3	9
7	4	16

b.

c. The graph of $y = (x - 3)^2$ is the graph of $y = x^2$ translated 3 units to the right.

On Your Own

10a. Near the origin $|x| < 1$, so $|x^3|$ is much less than $|x|$. Thus the x^3-term has very little effect on the value of $x^3 - x$. **11.** $(-1, 0)$, $(0, 0)$, $(1, 0)$

12a.

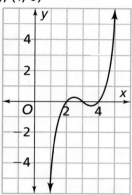

15a. $(x - 6)^2 + y^2 = 25$ **b.** $(x + 3)^2 + y^2 = 16$

Lesson 6.03
Check Your Understanding

1a.

$x = M - 5$	M	$y = \sqrt{M}$
-5	0	0
-4	1	1
-1	4	2
4	9	3
11	16	4
20	25	5

b. The graph of $y = \sqrt{x + 5}$ is the graph of $y = \sqrt{x}$ translated 5 units to the left.

c.

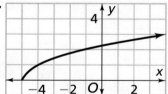

domain: $x \geq -5$, range: $y \geq 0$

2a.

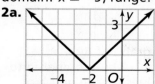

b.

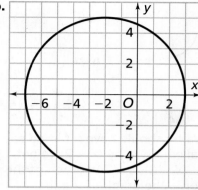

c.

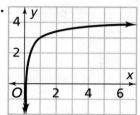

d.

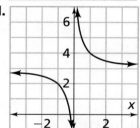

3a.

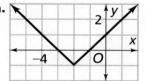

b.

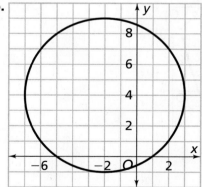

c.

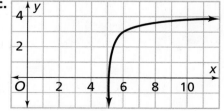

d.

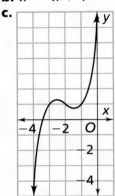

4. Disagree; Walter should have replaced each x in the original equation by $(x - 2)$ to get $y = (x - 2)^3 - (x - 2)$. **5a.** The graph of the second equation is the graph of the first equation translated 2 units to the right.

b. $x^3 - x + 1$

c.

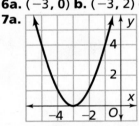

6a. $(-3, 0)$ **b.** $(-3, 2)$ **c.** $(-h, k)$

7a.

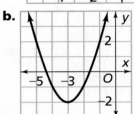

b.

On Your Own

8a.

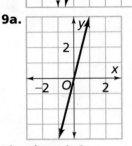

9a.

The slope is 3.

11a. $y = 4(x - 3) + 1$ or $y = 4x - 11$

12a. The graph of $y = (x - 3)^2 + 6(x - 3) + 7$ is the graph of $y = x^2 + 6x + 7$ translated 3 units to the right; Answers may vary. Sample: In the equation $y = (x - 3)^2 + 6(x - 3) + 7$, each x in the equation $y = x^2 + 6x + 7$ is replaced by $M = x - 3$, so each point on the graph of $y = M^2 + 6M + 7$ corresponds to the point on the graph of $y = x^2 + 6x + 7$ with x-coordinate 3 units less.

Lesson 6.04
Check Your Understanding

1a.

x	$N = x^2 + 1$	$y = \frac{N}{5}$
-2	5	1
-1	2	$\frac{2}{5}$
0	1	$\frac{1}{5}$
1	2	$\frac{2}{5}$
2	5	1
3	10	2

b. The y-values for the graph of $5y = x^2 + 1$ are smaller by the factor 5 when compared to the corresponding y-values for the graph of $y = x^2 + 1$, so the graph of $5y = x^2 + 1$ is the graph of $y = x^2 + 1$ scaled vertically by the factor $\frac{1}{5}$.

c.

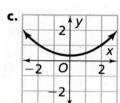

2a.

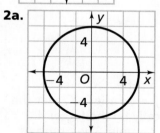

b.

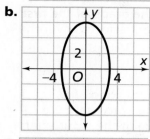

c.

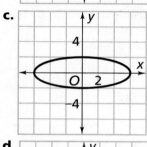

d.

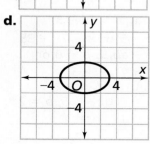

e.

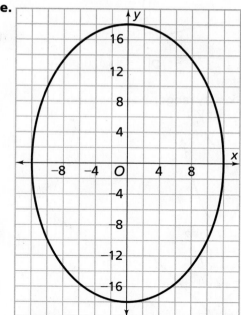

3a.

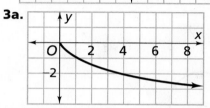

domain: $x \geq 0$, range: $y \leq 0$

b.

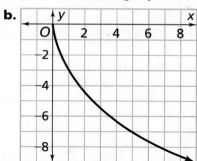

domain: $x \geq 0$, range: $y \leq 0$

c.

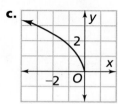

domain: $x \leq 0$, range: $y \geq 0$

d.

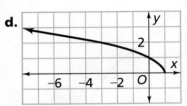

domain: $x \leq 1$, range: $y \geq 0$

4. $y = \left(\frac{1}{2}x - 2\right)^2 + 3$

5a.

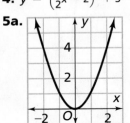

b.

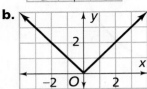

c.

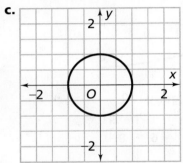

6. Agree with both; the statement $f(-x) = f(x)$ is equivalent to saying the graph of f has the y-axis as a line of symmetry.

7. Because all the exponents are even the y-values for x and $-x$ are the same, so the function is even. **8.** $g(-x) = f(-x) + f(-(-x)) = f(-x) + f(x) = g(x)$, so g is an even function.

9a–b.

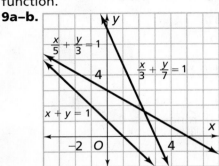

c. Answers may vary. Sample: $(0, 12)$, $(-17, 0)$

d. The intercepts of $\frac{x}{a} + \frac{y}{b} = 1$ are $(0, b)$ and $(a, 0)$.

10a.

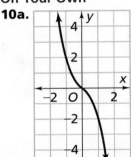

11a. the graph of $y = \frac{1}{x}$ reflected over the y-axis **c.** the graph of $y = \frac{1}{x}$ reflected over the y-axis and scaled vertically by the factor 4
13. Answers may vary. Sample: The graph of the second equation is the graph of the first equation after it has been reflected over the y-axis and then over the x-axis.

Lesson 6.05
On Your Own
7a. 6; 15; -3; -21; 0 **b.** Thinking of D_s as mapping the number line onto itself, the output of D_s is the image of the input after a dilation by the factor s (using the origin of the number line as the center of dilation).
10a. 24; -6; 0; 42; 48 **12a.** 3 **14a.** $x \mapsto 2x + 5$
17a. $(f \circ f)(x) = 4x + 9$

Lesson 6.06
Check Your Understanding
1. T_b **2.** $a \neq 0$, $b = 0$
3. $(D_s \circ D_t)(x) = D_s(D_t(x)) = D_s(tx)$ $= s(tx) = (st)x = D_{st}(x)$ **4a.** $x \mapsto 2x + 3$
b. $x \mapsto 2x + 6$ **c.** $x \mapsto 7x - 5$ **d.** $x \mapsto 7x - 35$
e. $x \mapsto ax + b$ **f.** $x \mapsto ax + ab$ **5.** $b = 0$ or $a = 1$ **6a.** $\mathcal{A}_{(6, 9)}$ **b.** $\mathcal{A}_{(6, 2)}$ **c.** $\mathcal{A}_{(-1, 7)}$
d. $\mathcal{A}_{(-1, -1)}$ **e.** $\mathcal{A}_{(1, 0)}$ **f.** $\mathcal{A}_{(1, 0)}$ **7.** $e = ac$, $f = ad + b$ **8a.** $a = 3$, $b = 8$ **b.** $a = 5$, $b = 2$
c. $a = \frac{1}{2}$, $b = -\frac{3}{2}$ **d.** $a = \frac{1}{2}$, $b = -\frac{3}{2}$

On Your Own
10a. $x = \frac{1}{4}y - 2$ **b.** $\left(\mathcal{A}_{(4, 8)} \circ \mathcal{A}_{\left(\frac{1}{4}, -2\right)}\right)(x) =$

$\mathcal{A}_{(4, 8)}\left(\mathcal{A}_{\left(\frac{1}{4}, -2\right)}(x)\right) = \mathcal{A}_{(4, 8)}\left(\frac{1}{4}x - 2\right) =$

$4\left(\frac{1}{4}x - 2\right) + 8 = x - 8 + 8 = x$, and

$\left(\mathcal{A}_{\left(\frac{1}{4}, -2\right)} \circ \mathcal{A}_{(4, 8)}\right)(x) = \mathcal{A}_{\left(\frac{1}{4}, -2\right)}\left(\mathcal{A}_{(4, 8)}(x)\right) =$

$\mathcal{A}_{\left(\frac{1}{4}, -2\right)}(4x + 8) = \frac{1}{4}(4x + 8) - 2 = x + 2 -$

$2 = x$. Thus, $\mathcal{A}_{(4, 8)}$ and $\mathcal{A}_{\left(\frac{1}{4}, -2\right)}$ are inverses,

so $\left(A_{(4, 8)}\right)^{-1} = \mathcal{A}_{\left(\frac{1}{4}, -2\right)}$. **11a.** $c = \frac{1}{2}$, $d = \frac{1}{2}$

13a. $\mathcal{A}_{\left(\frac{1}{3}, -\frac{4}{3}\right)}$ **14a.** $a = 3$, $b = -6$

15a. $A_{\left(\frac{1}{6},\,-\frac{3}{2}\right)}$ **18a.** $A_{\left(a^2,\,ab+b\right)}(x)$

Lesson 6.07

Check Your Understanding

1. $y = 8x^2 - 2x - 15$ **2a.** $a = 9$, $b = 6$,
$c = 9$, $d = 81$ **b.** $N = 81$, $M = \pm 9$, $x = \frac{1}{3}$
or $-\frac{5}{3}$ **c.** $\frac{1}{3}, -\frac{5}{3}$ **3a.** $a = 2$, $b = 2$, $c = 2$,
$d = -6$ **b.** $N = -6$, no real values for M or x
c. no real roots **4a.** $y = (x + 3)^2 + (-4)$

b. $y = (x + (-2))^2 + (-3)$ **c.** $y = \left(x + \frac{5}{2}\right)^2 + \frac{3}{4}$
5a. $\frac{b}{2}$ **b.** $y = M^2 - \frac{b^2}{4} + c$
c. $y = \left(x + \frac{b}{2}\right)^2 + \left(-\frac{b^2}{4} + c\right);$ $D = -\frac{b^2}{4} + c$
6a. $a = 1$, $b = 2$, $c = 1$, $d = -1$ **b.** $a = \frac{1}{2}$,
$b = \frac{1}{2}$, $c = \frac{1}{8}$, $d = -1$

On Your Own

9a. $e = a$, $f = \frac{b}{2}$, $g = a$, $h = \frac{b^2 - 4ac}{4}$
11. $\frac{b}{3}$ **12a.** The equation shown is the result
of substituting $\left(M - \frac{b}{3}\right)$ into the equation
$y = x^3 + bx^2 + cx + d$. In Exercise 11, we
found that $\frac{b}{3}$ is the value of k for which the
substitution of $(M - k)$ into the equation
$y = x^3 + bx^2 + cx + d$ makes the coefficient
of M^2 0.

Lesson 6.08

Exercises

On Your Own

7. Answers may vary. Sample: Each value
on the x number line is one-half the
corresponding value on the M number line.
8c. $x = -M$

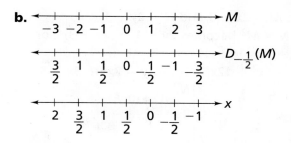

9. Answers may vary. Sample: For each value
on the M number line, the corresponding value
on the x number line is $\frac{1}{2}M + \frac{3}{2}$.
11a. $x = 3M - 1$

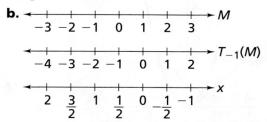

12a. $A_{\left(\frac{1}{2},\,\frac{-3}{2}\right)}$

Lesson 6.09

Check Your Understanding

1a. If $M = -2x + 1$, then $x = -\frac{1}{2}M + \frac{1}{2} =$
$T_{\frac{1}{2}}\left(-\frac{1}{2}M\right) = \left(T_{\frac{1}{2}} \circ D_{-\frac{1}{2}}\right)(M)$.

b.

-3	-2	-1	0	1	2	3	M

$D_{-\frac{1}{2}}(M)$

| $\frac{3}{2}$ | 1 | $\frac{1}{2}$ | 0 | $-\frac{1}{2}$ | -1 | $-\frac{3}{2}$ | |

| 2 | $\frac{3}{2}$ | 1 | $\frac{1}{2}$ | 0 | $-\frac{1}{2}$ | -1 | x |

c. The $D_{-\frac{1}{2}}(M)$ number line is the image of the
M number line reflected over 0 and dilated by
the factor 2; the x number line is the image of
the $D_{-\frac{1}{2}}(M)$ number line translated $\frac{1}{2}$ unit to
the right; the x number line is the image of the
M number line reflected over 0, dilated by the
factor 2, and translated $\frac{1}{2}$ unit to the right.
2a. If $M = -2x + 1$, then $x = -\frac{1}{2}M + \frac{1}{2} =$
$-\frac{1}{2}(M - 1) = D_{-\frac{1}{2}}(M - 1) =$
$\left(D_{-\frac{1}{2}} \circ T_{-1}\right)(M)$.

b.

-3	-2	-1	0	1	2	3	M

$T_{-1}(M)$

| -4 | -3 | -2 | -1 | 0 | 1 | 2 | |

| 2 | $\frac{3}{2}$ | 1 | $\frac{1}{2}$ | 0 | $-\frac{1}{2}$ | -1 | x |

c. The $T_{-1}(M)$ number line is the image of the
M number line translated 1 unit to the right;
the x number line is the image of the $T_{-1}(M)$
number line reflected over 0 and dilated by
the factor 2; the x number line is the image of
the M number line translated 1 unit right,
reflected over 0, and dilated by the factor 2.
3a. $M = A_{(3,\,1)}(x)$, $N = A_{(3,\,4)}(y)$

b.

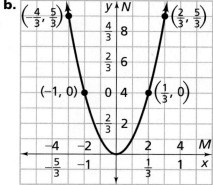

4. Yes; Answers may vary. Sample: You can use
more than two transformations. For example,

$A_{\left(-\frac{1}{2},\,\frac{1}{2}\right)} = D_{\frac{1}{2}} \circ T_1 \circ D_{-1}$.

5a. $M = 2x + 3$ and $N = 2y - 1$,
so $N = M^2$ becomes $2y - 1 = (2x + 3)^2$, or
$2y + 1 = 14x^2 + 12x + 9$. Then
$2y = 4x^2 + 12x + 10$, so $y = 2x^2 + 6x + 5$.

b.

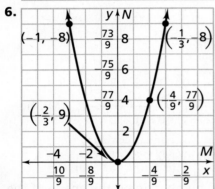

6.

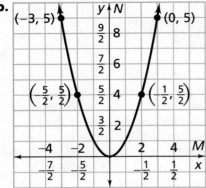

7.

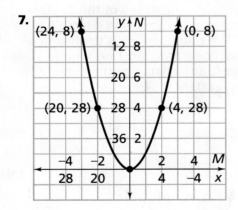

8a.

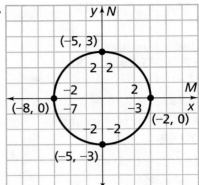

b.

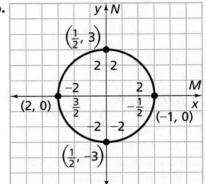

c.

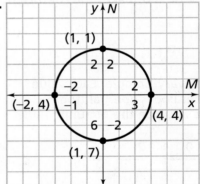

d.

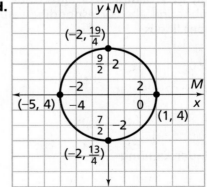

9a.

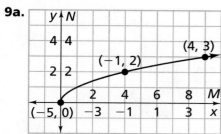

b.

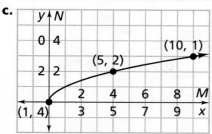

c.

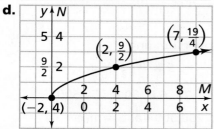

d.

10. Disagree; Answers may vary. Sample: If you dilate the graph of a circle horizontally and vertically by factors with different absolute values, the distances between the transformed intercepts are no longer equal and the transformed graph is no longer a circle. So, the graphs for Exercises 8b and 8d are not circles.

On Your Own

11a.

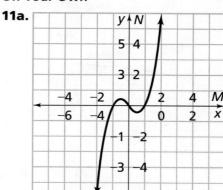

13b.

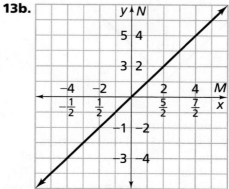

14a.

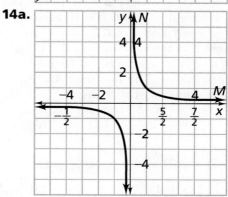

15a.

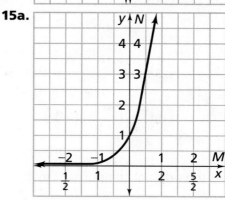

16a.

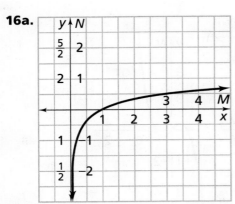

20a.

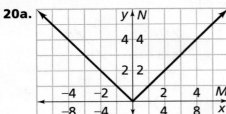

Lesson 6.10
Check Your Understanding
1a. $\frac{2}{3}$ **b.** $\frac{4}{3}$ **c.** 2 **d.** $a = 1$: all real numbers, $a \neq 1$: 0 **e.** none **f.** $a = 1$ and $b = 0$: all real numbers, $a = 1$ and $b \neq 0$: none, $a \neq 1$: $\frac{-b}{a-1}$
2. exactly one: $\mathcal{A}_{(a, b)}$ where $a \neq 1$; more than one: $\mathcal{A}_{(a, b)}$ where $a = 1$ and $b = 0$; zero: $\mathcal{A}_{(a, b)}$ where $a = 1$ and $b \neq 0$ **3.** $\mathcal{A}_{(1, 0)}$ and $\mathcal{A}_{(-1, b)}$ where b is any real number **4.** $\mathcal{A}_{(1, 0)}$
5. Larry just needs to use his result to draw the correct conclusion. The fact that $\mathcal{A}_{(1, -3)}$ has no fixed point implies that the original equation, $3x + 7 = 3x - 2$, has no solution.
6. $\mathcal{A}_{(a, 5-5a)}$

On Your Own
8a. $\mathcal{A}_{(3, -4)}(2) = 3(2) - 4 = 2$, $\mathcal{A}_{(-5, 12)}(2) = -5(2) + 12 = 2$ **b.** $\left(\mathcal{A}_{(3, -4)} \circ \mathcal{A}_{(-5, 12)}\right)(2) = \mathcal{A}_{(3, -4)}(\mathcal{A}_{(-5, 12)}(2)) = \mathcal{A}_{(3, -4)}(2) = 2$, $(\mathcal{A}_{(-5, 12)} \circ \mathcal{A}_{(3, -4)})(2) = \mathcal{A}_{(-5, 12)}(\mathcal{A}_{(3, -4)}(2)) = \mathcal{A}_{(-5, 12)}(2) = 2$
c. Answers may vary. Sample: $(\mathcal{A}_{(3, -4)})^{-1}(2) = \mathcal{A}_{\left(\frac{1}{3}, \frac{4}{3}\right)}(2) = 2\left(\frac{2}{3}\right) + \frac{4}{3} = \frac{2}{3} + \frac{4}{3} = \frac{6}{3} = 2$, $(\mathcal{A}_{(-5, 12)})^{-1}(2) = \mathcal{A}_{\left(-\frac{1}{5}, \frac{12}{5}\right)}(2) = 2\left(-\frac{1}{5}\right) + \frac{12}{5} = -\frac{2}{5} + \frac{12}{5} = \frac{10}{5} = 2$
11a. $T_3 \circ D_4 \circ \left(T_3\right)^{-1}(3) = T_3 \circ D_4(0) = T_3(0) = 3$, so the original composite is in S_3.
12a. $\left(\mathcal{A}_{(2,3)}\right)^{(5)} = \mathcal{A}_{\left(2^5, 3 \cdot \frac{2^5-1}{2-1}\right)} = \mathcal{A}_{(32, 93)}$

6a.

Roll	Gain	Total
1	5	55
2	−2	53
3	−4	49
4	3	52
5	−6	46
6	1	47
7	−6	41

7.

n	$t(n)$	Σ
0	1	1
1	9	10
2	90	100
3	900	1000
4	9,000	10,000

$\sum = 10^n$ **12a.** $h(n) = 100n^2$

Lesson 7.02
Check Your Understanding

1a. $S = \frac{n(n+1)}{2}$ **b.** $S = \frac{n(n+1)}{2}$

c. $S = \frac{(n-1) \cdot n}{2}$ **2a.** 6 **b.** 30 **c.** 250,500

3a. 16 **b.** 49 **c.** 250,000 **4a.** $S = n(n+1)$

b. $S = (n+1)^2$ **5a.** 65,504 **b.** 196,512

c. ≈ 5.862 **d.** $1 - \frac{1}{10^{10}} \approx 1$ **e.** ≈ 0.664

6a. Answers may vary. Sample:
$1 + 2 + 3 + \cdots + 10 = 55$;
$2 + 4 + 6 + \cdots + 22 = 132$;
$4 + 7 + 10 + \cdots + 31 = 175$; Gauss's method works when there is a constant difference between successive terms. **b.** Answers may vary. Sample: $2 + 4 + 8 + \cdots + 64 = 126$;
$5 + 10 + 20 + 40 + \cdots + 640 = 1275$;
$4 + 12 + 36 + \cdots + 4 \cdot 3^{100} = 2 \cdot 3^{101} - 2 \approx 3.09 \cdot 10^{48}$; Euclid's method works when there is a constant ratio between successive terms. **7a.** $S = \frac{r^{n+1} - 1}{r - 1}$

b. $S = a \cdot \frac{r^{n+1} - 1}{r - 1}$

On Your Own

8a. −10 **10.** −19

12.

n	$f(n)$
1	$\frac{1}{2}$
2	$\frac{3}{4}$
3	$\frac{7}{8}$
4	$\frac{15}{16}$
5	$\frac{31}{32}$
n	$\frac{2^n-1}{2^n}$

$f(n) = \dfrac{2^n - 1}{2^n}$

Lesson 7.03
Check Your Understanding

1. Answers may vary. Sample: Cori is correct that the sum is never more than the whole sheet. David is correct that the total area of the rectangles on the desk increases, although by smaller and smaller amounts. **2.** Answers may vary. Sample: The area of the piece of paper in her hand keeps getting smaller and smaller, so the area of the "rest" of the paper gets closer to the starting area of 1. **3a.** 300

b. 1596 **c.** 3240 **d.** 7626 **e.** $\frac{n(n+1)}{2}$ **4a.** $1 - r^2$

b. $1 - r^3$ **c.** $1 - r^4$ **d.** $1 - r^{n+1}$ **5a.** ≈ 2.92

b. ≈ 1.33 **c.** 11,111,111,111 **6.** $\dfrac{1 - r^{n+1}}{1 - r} =$

$\dfrac{-1}{-1} \cdot \dfrac{1 - r^{n+1}}{1 - r} = \dfrac{-1 + r^{n+1}}{-1 + r} = \dfrac{r^{n+1} - 1}{r - 1}$

On Your Own
8a.

n	$s(n)$	Σ
0	2	2
1	5	7
2	8	15
3	11	26

b. $s(n) = 3n + 2$ **9a.** $\frac{1}{9}$ in hand, $\frac{4}{9}$ in pile 1,

$\frac{4}{9}$ in pile 2

Lesson 7.04
Check Your Understanding
1a. 91 **b.** 324 **c.** 10 **d.** 969 **2.** Yes; Answers may vary. Sample: After you substitute values for the placeholder, the placeholder does not appear in the sequence.

3a. $\displaystyle\sum_{i=1}^{n} n^2$ **b.** $\displaystyle\sum_{i=1}^{6} 1$ **c.** $\displaystyle\sum_{i=1}^{10} i$ **4a.** $\displaystyle\sum_{i=1}^{10} \frac{1}{2^i}$ **b.** $\displaystyle\sum_{i=1}^{n} \frac{1}{2^i}$

c. $\displaystyle\sum_{i=1}^{\infty} \frac{1}{2^i}$ **5.** $\frac{1023}{1024} \approx 0.999023438$

On Your Own

6a. $\displaystyle\sum_{i=1}^{10} \frac{1}{3^i}$ **7.** $\frac{29,524}{59,049} \approx 0.499991532$

Lesson 7.05
On Your Own
3a. $q(n) = 3n + 5$, which is linear.

Lesson 7.06
Check Your Understanding
1a. yes **b.** yes **c.** no **d.** yes **e.** yes **f.** yes
g. yes **h.** no **i.** no **j.** yes **k.** yes **2a.** 440; 442
b. 4,782,966; 2186 **c.** 182; 332 **3a.** 25 **b.** 100

c. 75 **d.** $\displaystyle\sum_{k=1}^{n} (2k - 1) = n^2$ **e.** 1,000,000

On Your Own

4. $\displaystyle\sum_{k=0}^{n} (5k - 1) = \dfrac{(n+1)(5n-2)}{2}$ **7a.** 42

9a. 99,999

Lesson 7.07
Check Your Understanding
1. 6625 **2a.** 374 **b.** 1.99988 **c.** 0.99988 **3a.** 377
b. 572 **c.** 1326 **d.** 332

On Your Own
4e. 765 **5a.** 70 **b.** 66 **c.** 70 **d.** 12,207,241

10b. 1,039,600 **11a.** $\dfrac{n(n+1)(n+2)}{3}$ **13a.** 450

Lesson 7.08
Check Your Understanding

1. $H(n) = \dfrac{n^2 + n + 6}{2}$

2a. $q(n) = \begin{cases} 32 & \text{if } n = 0 \\ q(n-1) + 2n & \text{if } n > 0 \end{cases}$

b. $Q(n) = n(n+1) + 32$ **3.** $S(n) = n^2$

On Your Own
5a.

n	$s(n)$	Δ
0	7	1
1	8	4
2	12	9
3	21	

$s(n) = \begin{cases} 7 & \text{if } n = 0 \\ s(n-1) + n^2 & \text{if } n > 0 \end{cases}$

6a. $t(n) = \displaystyle\sum_{k=0}^{n} 2^k$

10a. $p(n) = \begin{cases} 1 & \text{if } n = 1 \\ p(n - 1) + (3n - 2) & \text{if } n > 1 \end{cases}$

b. $P(n) = \frac{3n^2 - n}{2}$

Lesson 7.09
On Your Own
5a. A.M.: $h(n) = 3n$; P.M.: $g(n) = 3n + 5$
7. $708

Lesson 7.10
Check Your Understanding

1. $\frac{4}{n - 1}$ **2.** Yes; $\frac{1}{6}, \frac{1}{3}, \frac{1}{2}, \frac{2}{3}, \frac{5}{6}, 1, \ldots$ **3.** Yes;
1, 3, π; Any multiple of the difference between 3 and π cannot equal a multiple of the difference between 1 and 3.

4a.

n	q(n)	Σ
0	9	9
1	15	24
2	21	45
3	27	72
4	33	105

$q(n) = 6n + 9$;
$Q(n) = 3n^2 + 2n + 9$

b.

n	p(n)	Σ
0	12	12
1	7	19
2	2	21
3	−3	18
4	−8	10

$p(n) = 12 - 5n$; $P(n) = -\frac{5}{2}n^2 + \frac{19}{2}n + 12$

5. 8, 10, 12, 14, 16, . . . ; there is no other arithmetic sequence with the same 0th and 2nd terms. **6a.** 2, 5, 8, 11, 14, . . . **b.** 2, 7, 15, 26, 40, . . . **c.** $g(n) = 2 + 3n$; $G(n) = \frac{3}{2}n^2 + \frac{7}{2}n + 2$

7a.

n	t(n)	Σ
0	5	5
1	14	19
2	23	42
3	32	74
4	41	115

$t(n) = 5 + 9n$; $T(n) = \frac{9}{2}n^2 + \frac{19}{2}n + 5$

b.

n	h(n)	Σ
0	7	7
1	3	10
2	−1	9
3	−5	4
4	−9	−5

$h(n) = 7 - 4n$; $H(n) = -2n^2 + 5n + 7$

c.

n	t(n)	Σ
0	6	6
1	6.5	12.5
2	7	19.5
3	7.5	27
4	8	35

$t(n) = 6 + \frac{1}{2}n$; $T(n) = \frac{1}{4}n^2 + \frac{25}{4}n + 6$

8a.

n	f(n)	Σ
0	a	a
1	a + d	2a + d
2	a + 2d	3a + 3d
3	a + 3d	4a + 6d
4	a + 4d	5a + 10d
5	a + 5d	6a + 15d

b. $F(n) = \frac{1}{2}(n + 1)(2a + nd)$

On Your Own
11. If the integers are n, $n + 1$, and $n + 2$, then the average is $\frac{n + (n + 1) + (n + 2)}{3} = \frac{3n + 3}{3}$ $= n + 1$, which is the middle number.
13a. 1, 5, 14, 30, 55 **15.** 1, 6, 11, 21, . . . or 7, 10, 13, 16, 19, . . . **16.** Answers may vary. Sample: for the sequence 1, 4, 9, 16, 25, 36, . . . , the Δ values are 3, 5, 7, 9, 11, . . . , which is an arithmetic sequence. A closed form is $f(n) = n^2$.

Lesson 7.11
Check Your Understanding

1a. 320 **b.** 320 **c.** 5 **d.** $\frac{5}{64}$ **e.** 4.5 **f.** 75 **g.** ± 18 **h.** 18 **2.** Yes; Any constant sequence such as 3, 3, 3, 3, . . . has a constant difference (0) and a constant ratio (1), so it is both arithmetic and geometric. **3.** Answers may vary. Sample:

$a_1 = 2, 4, 6, 8, \ldots$ and $g_1 = 2, 4, 8, 16, 32, \ldots$, the common difference is greater than 1 and the terms of the sequence increase, the common ratio is greater than 1, if the first term is positive the terms will increase, if the first term is negative the terms will decrease; $a_2 = 1, 2, 3, 4, 5, \ldots$ and $g_2 = 1, 1, 1, 1, 1, \ldots$, the common difference is 1 and the terms of the sequence increase, the common ratio is 1 and the terms of the sequence remain constant; $a_3 = 6, 5, 4, 3, 2, \ldots$ and $g_3 = 6, -6, 6, -6, 6, \ldots$ the common difference is negative 1 and the terms of the sequence decrease, the common ratio is -1, the terms will alternate between positive and negative values with the same absolute value; $a_4 = 5, 2, -1, -4, -7, \ldots$ and $g_4 = 5, -15, 45, -135, 405, \ldots$ the common difference is less than -1 and the terms of the sequence decrease, the common ratio is less than -1, the terms will alternate between positive and negative values; $a_5 = 10, 9.5, 9, 8.5, 8, 7.5, \ldots$ and $g_5 = 10, 5, \frac{5}{2}, \frac{5}{4}, \frac{5}{8}, \ldots$, the common difference is between 0 and 1, and the terms of the sequence decrease, the common ratio is between 0 and 1, if the first term is positive the terms will decrease towards zero, if the first term is negative the terms will increase towards zero

4a. $\displaystyle\sum_{i=0}^{n} 5 \cdot \left(\frac{1}{2}\right)^n = -10\left[\left(\frac{1}{2}\right)^{n+1} - 1\right]$ or $\displaystyle\sum_{i=0}^{n} 5 \cdot \left(\frac{1}{2}\right)^n = 10\left[1 - \left(\frac{1}{2}\right)^{n+1}\right]$ **b.** ≈ 9.999847

5a. \$295.24 **b.** 21 months

On Your Own

6a. $g(n) = 5 \cdot 2^{n-1}$ **e.** $g(n) = 576 \cdot \left(\frac{1}{2}\right)^n$

8.

a. $\frac{\sqrt{2}}{2}; \frac{1}{2}$ **b.** Yes, the first term is 1 and the common ratio is $\frac{\sqrt{2}}{2}$. **10a.** $2^{63} \approx 9.22 \cdot 10^{18}$ **13.** about \$28,650 **14a.** at least 5.5 mi

Lesson 7.12
Check Your Understanding

1a.

n	$t(n)$	$T(n)$
1	7	7
2	$7 \cdot \left(\frac{2}{9}\right) = \frac{14}{9}$	$8\frac{5}{9}$
3	$7 \cdot \left(\frac{2}{9}\right)^2 = \frac{28}{81}$	$8\frac{73}{81}$
4	$7 \cdot \left(\frac{2}{9}\right)^3 = \frac{56}{729}$	$8\frac{713}{729}$

$T(n)$ has a limit, which is 9.

b.

n	$t(n)$	$T(n)$
1	100	100
2	$100 \cdot \frac{1}{2} = 50$	150
3	$100 \cdot \left(\frac{1}{2}\right)^2 = 25$	175
4	$100 \cdot \left(\frac{1}{2}\right)^3 = 12.5$	187.5

$T(n)$ has a limit, which is 200.

c.

n	$t(n)$	$T(n)$
1	$\frac{3}{4}$	$\frac{3}{4}$
2	$\frac{3}{4} \cdot 2 = \frac{3}{2}$	$2\frac{1}{4}$
3	$\frac{3}{4} \cdot 2^2 = 3$	$5\frac{1}{4}$
4	$\frac{3}{4} \cdot 2^3 = 6$	$11\frac{1}{4}$

$T(n)$ does not have a limit.

d.

n	$t(n)$	$T(n)$
1	1	1
2	1	2
3	1	3
4	1	4

$T(n)$ does not have a limit.
2. 2 miles (she is traveling twice as fast, so in the same time period she will travel twice as far).

On Your Own
3a.

b. The lengths of the ends of Stages 0, 1, 2, and 3 are 1, $\frac{4}{3}$, $\frac{16}{9}$, and $\frac{64}{27}$, respectively.

5a. $\frac{9}{5}$ square units

Lesson 7.13
Check Your Understanding

1a. $a = 0.123$ **b.** $r = 0.001$ **c.** $\frac{123}{999}$ (or $\frac{41}{333}$)

2a. $\frac{12}{99}$ (or $\frac{4}{33}$) **b.** $\frac{807}{999}$ (or $\frac{269}{333}$) **c.** $\frac{123}{9990}$ (or $\frac{41}{3330}$)

d. $\frac{75,048}{999,000}$ (or $\frac{3127}{41,625}$)

On Your Own

4. The series $1 + 2 + 3 + 4 + \ldots$ does not have a finite value, so it was not possible to "call it x."

Lesson 7.14
On Your Own

6a. $(a + b)^2 = a^2 + 2ab + b^2$

b. $(a + b)^3 = a^3 + 3a^2b + 3ab^2 + b^3$

8a. $\frac{1}{16}r^2 + \frac{3}{8}rs + \frac{9}{16}s^2$ **b.** $\frac{1}{64}r^3 + \frac{9}{64}r^2s + \frac{27}{64}rs^2 + \frac{27}{64}s^3$

Lesson 7.15
Check Your Understanding

1a. 32 or 2^5 **b.** 64 or 2^6 **c.** 128 or 2^7 **d.** 2^n

2. Answers may vary. Sample: Each element in row $(n - 1)$ contributes twice to row n, so the sum of entries in row n is twice the sum of entries in row $(n - 1)$.

Lesson 7.16
Check Your Understanding

1a. $(x + y)^7 = x^7 + 7x^6y + 21x^5y^2 + 35x^4y^3 + 35x^3y^4 + 21x^2y^5 + 7xy^6 + y^7$

b. $(x + 2y)^5 = x^5 + 10x^4y + 40x^3y^2 + 80x^2y^3 + 80xy^4 + 32y^5$ **2a.** 56 **b.** a^5b^3

c. entry $\begin{pmatrix} 8 \\ 4 \end{pmatrix}$ **3a.** 120 **b.** 10 **c.** 252

On Your Own

4. 0; 0; 0

Chapter 8
Lesson 8.0
Check Your Understanding

1. 24.09 **2a.** 210 **b.** 29

c.

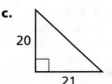

20

21

Each angle measures about 45°. **d.** 46°, 44°

3. $\sin \theta = \frac{15}{17}$, $\tan \theta = \frac{15}{8}$ **4.** $\sin \theta = \frac{\text{opp}}{\text{hyp}}$

and $\cos \theta = \frac{\text{adj}}{\text{hyp}}$, so $\frac{\sin \theta}{\cos \theta} = \frac{\frac{\text{opp}}{\text{hyp}}}{\frac{\text{adj}}{\text{hyp}}} = \frac{\text{opp}}{\text{adj}} = \tan \theta$.

5. $\frac{\sqrt{15}}{4}$ **6.** $72\sqrt{3} \approx 124.71$, $24\sqrt{3} \approx 41.57$, or $18\sqrt{3} \approx 31.2$

On Your Own

9.

θ	$\sin \theta$	$\cos \theta$	$\tan \theta$
30°	$\frac{1}{2}$	$\frac{\sqrt{3}}{2}$	$\frac{\sqrt{3}}{3}$
60°	$\frac{\sqrt{3}}{2}$	$\frac{1}{2}$	$\sqrt{3}$

12a. The largest value is 1 and the smallest is 0. As θ gets close to 90°, $\sin \theta$ gets close to 1, and as θ gets close to 0, $\sin \theta$ gets close to 0.

13a. $\sin \theta = \frac{4}{5}$, $\cos \theta = \frac{3}{5}$, $\tan \theta = \frac{4}{3}$ **14.** You do not know that $\triangle TRI$ is a right triangle.

Lesson 8.01
On Your Own

11.

Angle	Coordinates
0°	(1, 0)
10°	(0.985, 0.174)
20°	(0.940, 0.342)
30°	(0.866, 0.5)
40°	(0.766, 0.643)
50°	(0.643, 0.766)
60°	(0.5, 0.866)
70°	(0.342, 0.940)
80°	(0.174, 0.985)
90°	(0, 1)

12a. magnitude 5, argument $\approx 53°$

15. Answers may vary. Sample: The x-coordinate starts at 1 when Olivia's angle is 0°, decreases to 0 as her angle increases to 90°, decreases to -1 as her angle increases to 180°, increases to 0 as her angle increases to 270°, and increases to 1 as her angle increases to 360°. This pattern will repeat from 360° to 720°, from 720° to 1080°, and so on.

18. $a = -1$, $b = \sqrt{3}$

Lesson 8.02

Check Your Understanding

1. Answers may vary. Sample: If Jo's reasoning were correct, then the point $\left(\frac{1}{2}, \frac{1}{2}\right)$ should be on the unit circle and satisfy the equation $x^2 + y^2 = 1$. However, $\left(\frac{1}{2}\right)^2 + \left(\frac{1}{2}\right)^2 \neq 1$, so the point $\left(\frac{1}{2}, \frac{1}{2}\right)$ is not on the circle. **2.** $a = 0.342$, $b = 0.940$ **3.** $-\frac{\sqrt{3}}{2} - \frac{1}{2}i \approx -0.866 - 0.5i$ **4a.** $\cos \theta = -\cos(\theta + 180°)$
b. $\sin \theta = -\sin(\theta + 180°)$
c. $\tan \theta = \tan(\theta + 180°)$ **5a.** 1 **b.** 1 **6.** If the magnitude of a complex number is 1, such as i or $-i$, then it must lie on the unit circle.
7a. $\theta = 0°$ or $180°$, or $\theta = 180° \cdot k$, where k is an integer. **b.** $\theta = 90°$ or $270°$, or $\theta = 90° + 180° \cdot k$, where k is an integer.
c. $\theta = 0°$ or $180°$, or $\theta = 180° \cdot k$, where k is an integer.

On Your Own
8a.

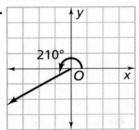

$\sin 210° = -\frac{\sqrt{3}}{2}$, $\cos 210° = -\frac{1}{2}$, $\tan 210° = \frac{\sqrt{3}}{3}$ **11.** Answers may vary. Sample: Since $310°$ is the same as $-50°$ on the unit circle, we know that $\sin 310° = \sin(-50°)$. And because $-50°$ is in Quadrant IV, where sine is negative, $\sin(-50°) = -\sin 50°$. So, $\sin 310° = -\sin 50°$.
12a. $-\frac{\sqrt{3}}{2}$

Lesson 8.03

Check Your Understanding
1. Answers may vary. Sample: $160°$ is in Quadrant II and $20°$ is in Quadrant I. Since $\sin \theta$ is positive in both quadrants, $\sin 160° = \sin 20°$. Since $\cos \theta$ is positive in Quadrant I and negative in Quadrant II, then $\cos 160° = -\cos 20°$. **2a.** I or II **b.** $\cos \theta = \pm\frac{21}{29}$
c. $\tan \theta = \pm\frac{20}{21}$ **3.** Answers may vary. Sample: $\theta \approx 89.5°$ **4.** Answers may vary. Sample: Since $-60°$ intersects the unit circle in Quadrant IV, the cosine will be positive. In general, $\cos(-\theta) = \cos \theta$. So $\cos(-60°) = \cos 60° = \frac{1}{2}$.
5. $\tan 110°$; $\cos 120° = \sin 210°$; $\sin 120°$; $\cos 720°$; $\tan 70°$ **6.** $30°$, $150°$ **7a.** 0.7660

b. -0.6428 **c.** -0.6428 **d.** -0.7660 **e.** 1
f. 0.6428 **8a.** $\tan^2 \theta = \frac{1}{\cos^2 \theta} - 1$ or
$\tan^2 \theta + 1 = \frac{1}{\cos^2 \theta}$ **b.** $\tan^2 \theta + 1 = \frac{\sin^2 \theta}{\cos^2 \theta} + 1 = \frac{\sin^2 \theta}{\cos^2 \theta} + \frac{\cos^2 \theta}{\cos^2 \theta} = \frac{\sin^2 \theta + \cos^2 \theta}{\cos^2 \theta} = \frac{1}{\cos^2 \theta}$.
So, $\tan^2 \theta = \frac{1}{\cos^2 \theta} - 1$ or $\tan^2 \theta + 1 = \frac{1}{\cos^2 \theta}$.

On Your Own
9. $\cos(-30°) = \frac{\sqrt{3}}{2}$, $\sin(-30°) = -\frac{1}{2}$, $\tan(-30°) = -\frac{\sqrt{3}}{3}$ **10a.** $\sin 40°$ **d.** $-\sin 45°$
11a. $\sin \theta$ **f.** $-\sin \theta$ **13a.** positive **c.** negative
17a. $-\frac{12}{37}$

Lesson 8.04

Check Your Understanding
1. $\cos q \approx -0.69$; $m \angle q \approx 134°$

2a. $60°$, $300°$ **b.** $\pm\frac{\sqrt{3}}{2}$ **c.** $\frac{3}{4}$

3.

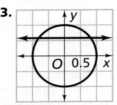

4. $(0.8, 0.6)$, $(-0.8, 0.6)$ **5a.** $53.1°$, $306.9°$
b. ± 0.8 **c.** 0.64 **6.** Answers may vary. Sample:
$\frac{1}{z} = \frac{1}{\cos 30° + i \sin 30°} = \frac{1}{\frac{\sqrt{3}}{2} + \frac{1}{2}i} = \frac{1}{\frac{\sqrt{3}}{2} + \frac{1}{2}i} \cdot$
$\frac{\frac{\sqrt{3}}{2} - \frac{1}{2}i}{\frac{\sqrt{3}}{2} - \frac{1}{2}i} = \frac{\frac{\sqrt{3}}{2} - \frac{1}{2}i}{\frac{3}{4} + \frac{1}{4}} = \frac{\sqrt{3}}{2} - \frac{1}{2}i = \bar{z}$

On Your Own
8a. $45°$, $135°$ **11a.** Answers may vary. Sample:
$\tan 30° = \frac{\sqrt{3}}{3}$ and $\cos 30° = \frac{\sqrt{3}}{2}$, so $\frac{1}{\cos^2 30°} - 1 = \frac{1}{\left(\frac{\sqrt{3}}{2}\right)^2} - 1 = \frac{1}{\frac{3}{4}} - 1 = \frac{4}{3} - \frac{3}{3} = \frac{1}{3} = \frac{3}{9} = \left(\frac{\sqrt{3}}{3}\right)^2 = \tan^2 30°$. **12a.** $\frac{1}{2}$

Lesson 8.05

Check Your Understanding
1. $x = 50° + 360° \cdot k$, where k is an integer.
2a. $37°$, $143°$ **b.** $217°$, $323°$ **3a.** $37°$, $323°$
b. no solution **4a.** no solution **b.** $41.8°$, $138.2°$
c. $30°$, $150°$, $210°$, $330°$ **d.** $210°$, $330°$ **5a.** $45°$, $225°$ **b.** $135°$, $315°$ **c.** $0°$, $180°$, $360°$ **6.** $30°$, $150°$, $199.47°$, $340.53°$ **7.** Using the Parallelogram Law from Chapter 3, you find the vertices of the parallelogram formed by z and $\bar{z}$ are $(0, 0)$, (a, b), $(a, -b)$, and $(2a, 0)$. So $z + \bar{z} = 2a$. Also, if $\arg z = \theta$, then $\cos \theta = \frac{a}{|z|}$ (because a is the value of the x-coordinate and

$|z|$ is the distance from the origin to z). So $a = |z| \cos \theta$ and $2a = 2|z| \cos \theta$. **8.** Drop a perpendicular from O to $\overline{AB}$ to form two congruent right triangles with acute angles $18°$ and $72°$, legs $\frac{z}{2}$ and $\frac{z\sqrt{3}}{2}$, and hypotenuse 1.

Then $\cos 72° = \frac{\text{adjacent}}{\text{hypotenuse}} = \frac{z}{2}$, so $z = 2 \cdot \cos 72°$.

On Your Own
10b. $45°$, $225°$ **12a.** $0.940 + 0.342i$
e. $-0.682 - 0.731i$ **13a.** $36.87°$

Lesson 8.06
On Your Own
6.

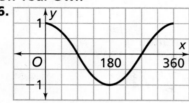

7. $\cos 230° > \cos 190°$

Lesson 8.07
Check Your Understanding
1a. The points on the unit circle that represent $\sin 50°$ and $\sin (-50°)$ have opposite y-values. So, $\sin 50° = -\sin (-50°)$. **b.** The y-values for $x = 50°$ and $x = -50°$ on the graph of $y = \sin x$ are opposites. So, $\sin 50° = -\sin (-50°)$.
2. Answers may vary. Sample: Derman sees only a portion of $y = \sin x$, and all the y-values are close to the x-axis. He should reset his window so that $-360 \leq x \leq 360$ and $-2 \leq y \leq 2$.
3.

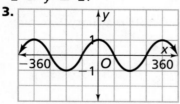

The graph looks like $y = \cos x$ because $\cos (x + 360°) = \cos x$. **4a.** There are infinitely many x-intercepts of $y = \cos x$.
b. A polynomial function must have a finite degree and a finite number of x-intercepts, so the cosine function cannot be written as a polynomial function. **c.** The tangent function, $\frac{\sin \theta}{\cos \theta}$, is undefined when $\cos \theta = 0$, that is when $\theta = 90° + k \cdot 180°$, where k is an integer.

5.

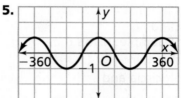

6.

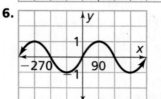

7. $143°$, $397°$

8.

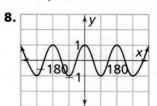

9a.

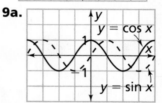

b. Answers may vary. Sample: $45°$, $225°$. Any angle of the form $45° + k \cdot 180°$, where k is an integer. **10a.** 1 **b.** $\tan \theta = \frac{\sin \theta}{\cos \theta}$ and if $\sin \theta = \cos \theta$, then the tangent must be 1.

On Your Own
11. Answers may vary. Sample:

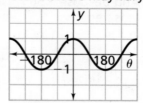

The graph of $y = \cos \theta$ is symmetric about the y-axis, so $\cos (-\theta) = \cos \theta$. **16.** Answers may vary. Samples:
a.

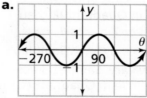

From the graph, $\sin x$ and $\sin (180° - x)$ are equal for any given x, so $\sin (180° - x) = \sin x$.

17. Answers may vary. Sample:

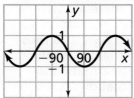

Lesson 8.08
Check Your Understanding
1a.

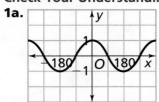

From the graph, $\cos(180° + x)$ and $-\cos x$ are equal for any given x, so $\cos(180° + x) = -\cos x$.

b.

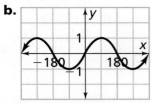

From the graph, $\sin(180° + x)$ and $-\sin x$ are equal for any given x, so $\sin(180° + x) = -\sin x$.

2. $\tan(180° + x) = \dfrac{\sin(180° + x)}{\cos(180° + x)} = \dfrac{-\sin x}{-\cos x} = \tan x$

3a.

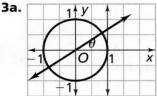

b. $\sin \theta = \dfrac{2\sqrt{13}}{13}$, $\cos \theta = \dfrac{3\sqrt{13}}{13}$

4a. $\tan(90° + \theta) = -\dfrac{3}{2} = -\dfrac{1}{\tan \theta}$ **b.** Answers may vary. Sample: The slope of the line is $\frac{y}{x}$, which is the same as the tangent of the angle formed by the line and the positive x-axis. **c.** Answers may vary. Sample: If two perpendicular lines intersect at the origin and are not the x- and y-axes, and if (a, b) is a point on one line, then $(-b, a)$ is a point on the other line. So the slopes are $\frac{b}{a}$ and $-\frac{a}{b}$, which are negative reciprocals. Now suppose two lines have slopes that are negative reciprocals $\frac{b}{a}$ and $-\frac{a}{b}$. Using the results of Exercise 4a, $\tan(90° + \theta) = -\dfrac{1}{\tan \theta}$. If the line through $(a,$

$b)$ forms an angle of θ with the positive x-axis, then the line through $(-b, a)$ forms an angle of $(\theta + 90°)$, so the two lines are perpendicular. **5.** Answers may vary. Sample: $\cos \theta$ is 0 for $\theta = 90° + k \cdot 180°$, where k is an integer. We can rewrite $90 + 180k$ as $90(1 + 2k)$. The values $2k + 1$ are the odd integers, so the values $90°(1 + 2k)$ are the odd multiples of 90°. **6a.** 14° **b.** 28° **c.** 104° **d.** 208° **7a.** 14° **b.** 28° **c.** 104° **d.** 208°

8a. $(x^2 - y^2) + (2xy)i$ **b.** $\dfrac{2xy}{x^2 - y^2}$

On Your Own
10a. All real numbers except $90° + k \cdot 180°$, where k is an integer **11a.** $x \approx 65° + k \cdot 180°$, where k is an integer.

Lesson 8.09
Check Your Understanding
1a. $\cos(-x) = \cos x$ and $\sin(-x) = -\sin x$. So, $\cos(a - b) = \cos(a + (-b)) = \cos a \cos(-b) - \sin a \sin(-b) = \cos a \cos b - (\sin a)(-\sin b) = \cos a \cos b + \sin a \sin b$. **b.** If $a = b$, then $\cos(a - b) = \cos 0° = 1$ and $\cos a \cos b + \sin a \sin b = \cos^2 a + \sin^2 a = 1$.

c. $\dfrac{\sqrt{2} + \sqrt{6}}{4}$ **2a.** $\cos(2x) = \cos(x + x) = \cos x \cos x - \sin x \sin x = \cos^2 x - \sin^2 x$ **b.** $\sin(2x) = \sin(x + x) = \sin x \cos x + \cos x \sin x = 2\sin x \cos x$ **c.** $\cos 2x = \cos^2 x - \sin^2 x = \cos^2 x - (1 - \cos^2 x) = \cos^2 x - 1 + \cos^2 x = 2\cos^2 x - 1$ **3a.** $\dfrac{\sqrt{2 + \sqrt{3}}}{2}$

b. Yes; if $A = \dfrac{\sqrt{2 + \sqrt{3}}}{2}$, then $4A = 2\sqrt{2 + \sqrt{3}}$ and $(4A)^2 = (4)(2 + \sqrt{3}) = 8 + 4\sqrt{3}$. If $B = \dfrac{\sqrt{2} + \sqrt{6}}{4}$, then $4B = \sqrt{6} + \sqrt{2}$ and $(4B)^2 = 6 + 2\sqrt{12} + 2 = 8 + 2\sqrt{4} \cdot \sqrt{3}$ $= 8 + 4\sqrt{3}$. So, $\dfrac{\sqrt{2 + \sqrt{3}}}{2} = \dfrac{\sqrt{2} + \sqrt{6}}{4}$.

4. $\cos 3x = \cos^3 x - 3\sin^2 x \cos x$, $\sin 3x = 3\sin x \cos^2 x - \sin^3 x$ **5.** $\dfrac{\sqrt{3}}{2} + \dfrac{1}{2}i$

6a. $\sin 10° = 0.1736$, $\sin 50° = 0.7660$, and $\sin 70° = 0.9397$; $\sin 10° + \sin 50° = 0.1736 + 0.7660 = 0.9396$, which is about 0.9397. **b.** 80° **c.** 65°

7. $\sin x + \sin(60° - x) = \sin(60° + x)$; to prove that result, the left side is $\sin x + \sin(60° - x) = \sin x + (\sin 60°)(\cos x) - (\cos 60°)(\sin x) = \sin x + \left(\dfrac{\sqrt{3}}{2}\right)(\cos x) - \left(\dfrac{1}{2}\right)(\sin x) = \left(\dfrac{1}{2}\right)(\sin x) + \left(\dfrac{\sqrt{3}}{2}\right)(\cos x)$. The right side is $(\sin 60°)(\cos x) + (\cos 60°)(\sin x) =$ $\left(\frac{\sqrt{3}}{2}\right)(\cos x) + \left(\frac{1}{2}\right)(\sin x)$. The two sides are equal, so $\sin x + \sin(60° - x) = \sin(60° + x)$.

On Your Own
8. C **11a.** $\sin x$ **d.** $\cos x$ **12.** $x \mapsto 2^x$ matches $f(a + b) = f(a) \cdot f(b)$.

Lesson 8.10
On Your Own
7. 50°, 130° **9.** B

10a. 3 miles;
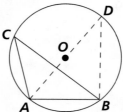

11a. $BH = \sqrt{3}$, $BI = 2$, $HG = 1$, $IG = \sqrt{2}$, $BG = 1 + \sqrt{3}$

Lesson 8.11
Check Your Understanding
1. Answers may vary. Sample: You can use $\frac{1}{2}(8)(5 \sin 60°)$ or $\frac{1}{2}(5)(7 \sin 82°)$ to find the area. **2a.** $\frac{\sqrt{3} + 1}{2}$ **b.** $\sqrt{2} \sin 105°$ **c.** $\frac{\sqrt{6} + \sqrt{2}}{4}$
3. $\frac{5}{2} \sin 72° \approx 2.38$ **4.** $A = \frac{3\sqrt{3}}{2}$, $P = 6$
5a. 2.9389 **b.** $\frac{5\sqrt{10 - 2\sqrt{5}}}{4}$ **6a.** $\frac{n}{2} \cdot \sin\left(\frac{360°}{n}\right)$

b.

Sides n	Area A(n)
4	2
5	2.3776
6	2.5981
10	2.9389
12	3
20	3.0902
30	3.1187
50	3.1333
100	3.1395
360	3.1414

7. As n increases, the polygon approaches a circle with radius 1, so the area approaches π.

On Your Own
8. 60 **10a.** $\sin x \cos x$ **11a.** No; the sides cannot have lengths x, x, and 10x because $x + x < 10x$, and the sum of any two sides of a triangle must be greater than the third side.
12a. Any other triangle with the same SAS would be congruent by SAS.

Lesson 8.12
Check Your Understanding
1. 24 **2.** $m \angle S = 30°$, $RS = 10.3$, $AR = 8.0$

3. $m \angle W = 70°$, $WS = 8.2$, $WO = 12$
4. $m \angle K = 53.1°$ or 126.9°; there are two solutions for $\sin K = 0.8$. **5.** The situations in Exercises 2 and 3 are AAS and ASA, and those situations result in a unique triangle, so they are congruence theorems. The situation in Exercise 4 is SSA, and that situation results in two triangles, so it is not a congruence theorem.

6.
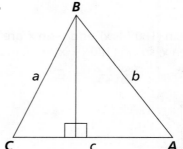

a. $\angle ABD$ is inscribed in a semicircle, so it is a right angle. **b.** $\angle C$ and $\angle D$ intercept the same arc, $\overset{\frown}{AB}$, so they are congruent.
c. $m \angle C = m \angle D$, so $\sin C = \sin D$ **d.** We know $\frac{c}{\sin C} = \frac{AD}{\sin \angle ABD}$. $\angle ABD$ is a right angle, so $\sin \angle ABD = 1$. Thus $AD = \frac{c}{\sin C}$.

7.

The length of the altitude from vertex B is $a \sin C$ or $c \sin A$. Therefore the area of the triangle is $\frac{1}{2} a \sin C \cdot c$ or $\frac{1}{2} c \sin A \cdot c$. The expressions are equal, so $\frac{1}{2} a \sin C \cdot c = \frac{1}{2} c \sin A \cdot c$, and $a \sin C = c \sin A$. Then $\frac{a}{\sin A} = \frac{c}{\sin C}$. By using a different altitude you can make a similar argument to prove $\frac{a}{\sin A} = \frac{b}{\sin B}$. Therefore $\frac{a}{\sin A} = \frac{b}{\sin B} = \frac{c}{\sin C}$.
8. $TW = \sqrt{325 - 150\sqrt{2}}$
9. $AB = \sqrt{a^2 + b^2 - 2ab \cos C}$

On Your Own
10. Answers may vary. Sample: The sides 1, $\sqrt{3}$, and 2 are opposite the angles with measures 30°, 60°, and 90°, so $\frac{1}{\sin 30°} = 2$, $\frac{\sqrt{3}}{\sin 60°} = 2$, $\frac{2}{\sin 90°} = 2$. **12.** To use the Law of Sines, you need to know a side and the

angle opposite that side. There is not enough information for this exercise, so you cannot use the Law of Sines. **14a.** $\sin C = 0.771$ **b.** $50°$, $130°$ **c.** $m \angle A = 90°$ or $10°$; $BC = 15.6$ or 2.7

Lesson 8.13
Check Your Understanding
1. $\sqrt{a^2 + b^2 - 2ab \cos C}$
2. $|a - b| < AB < a + b$ **3.** $5 < OT < 7$
4. $1 < AU < 5$ **5.** $\sqrt{119} < FB < 13$
6a. Use the Law of Cosines to find one angle. Then use the Law of Cosines or the Law of Sines to find a second angle. Subtract the sum of the angles from $180°$ to find the third angle. **b.** Use the Law of Cosines to find the third side. Then use the Law of Cosines or the Law of Sines to find a second angle. Subtract the sum of the angles from $180°$ to find the third angle. **c.** Use the Law of Sines to find the angle opposite the other given side (there may be 0, 1, or 2 values). Subtract the sum of the angles from $180°$ to find the third angle. Use the Law of Sines or the Law of Cosines to find the third side length. **d.** Subtract the sum of the angles from $180°$ to find the third angle. Use the Law of Sines to find a second side. Use the Law of Sines or the Law of Cosines to find the length of the third side. **e.** Subtract the sum of the angles from $180°$ to find the third angle. Use the Law of Sines to find a second side. Use the Law of Sines or the Law of Cosines to find the length of the third side. **f.** This cannot be solved. The triangle will not be unique because you are not given the length of a side. **7a.** The cosines opposite the sides of length 13, 14, and 15 are 0.6, 0.5077, and 0.3846, respectively. **b.** The largest angle has the smallest cosine. **c.** 12 **d.** 84 **8a.** $\cos C = \dfrac{a^2 + b^2 - c^2}{2ab}$, and the numerator and denominator must be integers, so $\cos C$ must be rational. **b.** The area of a triangle can be written as $\frac{1}{2}ab \sin C$. We know that ab is an integer, and part a showed that $\cos C$ is rational. So $\dfrac{1 - \cos^2 C}{4} = \dfrac{\sin^2 C}{4}$ is rational. Therefore $\sqrt{\dfrac{\sin^2 C}{4}} = \frac{1}{2} \sin C$ is the square root of a rational number. So the area of a triangle, $\frac{1}{2}ab \sin C$ or $ab \cdot \frac{1}{2} \sin C$, is the product of an integer times the square root of a rational number.

On Your Own
12. $42°$ **13a.** If $\angle O$ is the smallest angle, the measures of angles F and M would be greater

than $60°$. But the sum of the angles in a triangle cannot be greater than $180°$. So $\angle O$ cannot be the smallest angle. **14a.** false **15a.** The angles opposite the sides of length 7, 10, and 12 are $36°$, $56°$, and $88°$, respectively.

Lesson 8.14
Check Your Understanding
1a. $s = \dfrac{x + 14}{2}$ **b.** $A(x) = \frac{1}{4}\sqrt{(x + 14)(-x + 14)(x - 2)(x + 2)}$ **c.** 2, 14
d. The maximum of $A(x)$ is 24 when $x = 10$.
2a. $12 - x$ **b.** $A(x) = \sqrt{27(9 - x)(-3 + x)}$
c. 3, 9 **d.** The maximum of $A(x) \approx 15.6$ when $x = 6$. **3.** 75.8
4a.

b. No; if you fold the figure on its diagonal, you do not get a concave quadrilateral.
5a. The denominator 4 is outside the radical. You can move the denominator into the radical and change it to 16, which can be expressed as a denominator 2 for each of the four factors. **b.** If $a + b + c = 2s$, then $b + c - a = 2s - 2a$; $a - b + c = 2s - 2b$; $a + b - c = 2s - 2c$. Therefore $\dfrac{a + b + c}{2} = s$, $\dfrac{b + c - a}{2} = s - a$, $\dfrac{a + c - b}{2} = s - b$, and $\dfrac{a + b - c}{2} = s - c$. Then substitute each expression above into the second expression in part (a) to get the expression $\sqrt{s(s - a)(s - b)(s - c)}$.

On Your Own
7a. $25\sqrt{3}$ **8.** D

Index

454, 463, 465, 472, 479,
490, 491, 495, 505, 533,
549, 564 (2), 565, 573, 574,
576, 586, 589, 598, 599,
619, 621, 628, 636, 641,
643, 647, 649, 659, 660,
666, 667, 668, 678, 682,
690, 691, 709, 720, 724,
725, 726, 730, 731, 736 (2),
743 (2) 744, 745, 749, 753,
767, 776, 781, 786, 790 (2)

For You to Explore 5, 41, 69,
97, 139, 159, 175, 211, 237,
269, 299, 319, 371, 425,
451, 487, 527, 559, 583,
615, 633, 655, 687, 715,
741, 763

Fourier, Joseph 707
fractal 209
frequency(ies)
  piano A-notes 515, 518
  prime numbers 515
function(s) 100, 104
  absolute value 101
  to agree with table 5, 6–7, 8
  arrow notation, $x \mapsto y$ 100
  associated series 637, 660
  calculator, computer model
    for 9, 10
  closed-form definition 9, 10,
    79, 649
  composite 110
  composition of 109, 559
  composition of, with
    inverse 119, 121
  cosine 720, 724
  cubic 35
  decreasing 454
  different 103
  domain 8, 102, 104, 105
  equal (same) 103, 105, 559
  even 536, 746
  extension of 103
  factorial 78, 79
  group of 604
  identity 112, 119
  increasing 42, 124
  input 5, 100
  inverse 118, 119, 479
  linear 5, 18, 113
  loan-balance 667, 668
  monotonic 472
  naming 101
  natural domain 97, 102,
    104
  notation 104
  odd 536, 746
  one-to-one 117, 477
  output 5, 100

periodic 725
period of 725
polynomial 455
potato-and-arrow diagram
  104, 118
product of two numbers 97
quadratic 31, 32
quotient of two numbers 97
range 98, 104
rational 195
reciprocal 5, 97
recursive definition 9, 10
restricted domain 97
restriction of 103
rule for 5
square 97
square root 5, 97, 101
strictly decreasing 456, 460
strictly increasing 455, 456
sum 97
table for 5, 6–7, 8
table form 122
tangent 720, 724
target of 104, 105
trigonometric 715
unequal 105
zero of 123, 168
functional equation 471, 520,
  754
function-modeling language
  9, 78, 101
  using, for recursive
    definition 10
Fundamental
  Law of Exponents 427, 432,
    434, 470, 495
  Law of Logarithms 496, 499
  Theorem of Algebra 227,
    283

G

Gauss, Carl Friedrich 227, 241,
  283, 619
Gaussian elimination 310, 355
Gauss's method 620
geometric mapping 372
  onto 386
  See also geometric
    transformations.
geometric sequence 425, 439,
  442, 665, 666
  associated series 666
  common ratio of 439
  sum of 677
geometric series 666
  associated sequence 666
  formula for 682
geometric transformations
  376–381

See also geometric
  mapping.
graph(s)
  basic 530–531
  of cosine function 741, 743
  of exponential function
    454–458
  intersection of 514
  of logarithmic functions
    504–506
  using logarithmic scale 513
  reflecting 550–552
  scaling 548–552
  of sine function 741, 743
  of tangent function 741,
    748–750
  transforming 586–592
  translating 539–543
graphing
  complex number 242
  of inverse and piecewise
    functions, 125–131
  lumping method 539
graph paper
  loglog 513
  semilog 513
greatest integer function, 130
Greek letters
  delta (Δ) 11
  sigma (Σ) 616
grouping, to factor 101
group of functions 604

H

Habits of Mind, 259, 260
height of triangle 766
Heronian triangle 794
Heron of Alexandria 200
Heron's Formula 200, 790
hertz (cycles per seconds) 518
hexagonal numbers 648
Hinge Theorem 776
Historical Perspective 111, 147,
  217, 283, 357, 503, 697
hockey-stick property 17, 18,
  647, 690
horizontal line test 117, 477
hypotenuse of right triangle
  237, 708

I

i $(\sqrt{-1})$ 216, 220, 224
identity(ies) (equations) 7,
  431, 637
  difference-of-squares 181
  equation 91
  perfect-square 181
  sigma (Σ) 640
  sum-and-product 181

Index

W

U

V

X

Y

Z

Index

Staff Credits

The Pearson people on the CME Project team—representing design, editorial, editorial services, digital product development, publishing services, and technical operations—are listed below. Bold type denotes the core team members.

Ernest Albanese, Scott Andrews, Carolyn Artin, Michael Avidon, Margaret Banker, Suzanne Biron, Beth Blumberg, Stacie Cartwright, Carolyn Chappo, Casey Clark, Bob Craton, Sheila DeFazio, Patty Fagan, **Frederick Fellows**, **Patti Fromkin**, Paul J. Gagnon, Cynthia Harvey, Gillian Kahn, Jonathan Kier, Jennifer King, Elizabeth Krieble, Sara Levendusky, Lisa Lin, Clay Martin, **Carolyn McGuire**, Rich McMahon, Eve Melnechuk, **Hope Morley**, Jen Paley, Mairead Reddin, Marcy Rose, Rashid Ross, Carol Roy, Jewel Simmons, Ted Smykal, Kara Stokes, Richard Sullivan, Tiffany Taylor-Sullivan, Catherine Terwilliger, Mark Tricca, Lauren Van Wart, Paula Vergith, **Joe Will**, **Kristin Winters**, Allison Wyss

Additional Credits

Gina Choe, Cynthia Metallides, Christine Nevola, Lillian Pelaggi, Deborah Savona

Cover Design and Illustration
9 Surf Studios

Cover Photography
Alamy/RubberBall

Illustration
Kerry Cashman, Rich McMahon, Deborah Savona, Ted Smykal

Photography
Photo locators denoted as follows: Top (T), Center (C), Bottom (B), Left (L), Right (R), Background (Bkgd)

Front Matter: i: RubberBall/Alamy; **vi**: Oxford Scientific/Getty Images; **ix**: MedioImages/Corbis; **x**: Kevin Schafer/Alamy; **xi**: Allan Baxter/Digital Vision/Getty Images; **xvii**: William Sallaz/Corbis.

2–3: Don Mason/Corbis; **4**: Oxford Scientific/Getty Images; **27**: Science Source; **39**: A. & J. Visage/Getty Images; **45**: Ryan McVay/Exactostock1598/SuperStock; **59**: Steve Gschmeissner/Science Photo Library/Getty Images; **64**: Felix Lipov/Shutterstock; **68**: Lili K./Corbis; **71**: Richard Megna/Fundamental Photographs; **81**: Lili K./Corbis; **82**: Steven May/Alamy; **88–89**: William Sallaz/Corbis; **96**: James Baigrie/Photolibrary/Getty Images; **111**: Olympia/SIPA/Newscom; **138**: Leroy Francis/hemis.fr/Getty Images; **142**: ML Harris/The Image Bank/Getty Images; **147**: The Granger Collection, New York; **148**: Charles Krupa/AP Images; **173**: Ellen McKnight/Alamy; **174**: Bo Rader/KRT/Newscom; **177T**: Dirk Anschütz/Corbis; **177B**: C Squared Studios/Exactostock1598/SuperStock; **190**: Chuck Eckert/Alamy; **201**: Arcaid/Corbis; **208–209**: ©Kris Northern/Phidelity; **210**: Stefano Bianchetti/Corbis; **217L**: North Wind Picture Archive; **217R**: The Granger Collection, New York; **236**: Mehau Kulyk/Science Source; **250**: Eric Feferberg/AFP/Getty Images; **266**: Gregory Sams/Science Source;

276T: Gusto/Science Source; **276B**: Alexei Sysoev/Fotolia; **296–297**: Derek Henthorn/AGE Fotostock; **298**: Al Bello/Getty Images Sport/Getty Images; **307**: MedioImages/Corbis; **317**: Anthony John West/Corbis; **318**: RubberBall/Alamy; **346**: Valueline/Getty Images; **364**: Christian Lagereek/The Image Bank/Getty Images; **368**: RubberBall/Alamy; **391**: Foryouinf/Shutterstock; **416**: Stacey Wescott/MCT/Newscom; **422–423**: Daren Fentiman/ZUMA Press/Newscom; **423**: Craig Mitchelldyer/ Stringer/Getty Images News/Getty Images; **424**: A. Inden/Corbis; **437**: Andrew Syred/Science Source; **449**: ArcticImages/Corbis; **450**: David Lyons/Alamy; **461**: Artifacts Images/Ocean/Corbis; **474**: Gerald Holubowicz/Alamy; **486**: Kevin Schafer/Alamy; **514**: Eckhard Slawik/Science Source; **519**: John Lund/Sam Diephuis/Blend Images/Corbis; **524–525**: Small_frog/E+/Getty Images; **558**: Oodcollection/Alamy; **560**: Allan Baxter/Digital Vision/Getty Images; **582**: William Whitehurst/Corbis; **597**: Magdalena Rehova/Alamy; **603**: StockImages/Alamy; **612–613**: Ian McKinnell/Photographer's Choice/Getty Images; **614**: Tobbe/Corbis; **632**: Walter Michot/KRT/Newscom; **654**: Ann Heisenfelt/AP Images; **662**: VStock/Alamy; **683**: SheldonCreative/Alamy; **697**: Georgios Kollidas/Fotolia; **700–701**: Allen Eyestone/ZUMA Press/Newscom; **706–707**: Michael Jenner/Alamy; **714**: VisionsofAmerica/Joe Sohm/Photodisc/Getty Images; **718**: Sue Ogrocki/AP Images; **733**: Design Pics/Alamy; **740**: Tek Image/Science Source; **750**: Grant V. Faint/Photodisc/Getty Images; **760**: Enremimages/Alamy; **762**: Jay Boucher/Shutterstock; **767**: Bruce Dale/National Geographic/Getty Images; **783**: Howard Shooter/Getty Images; **792**: Navy Pier, Matt Ferguson, ho/AP Images; **796**: Andrew Haliburton/Alamy.

Text Acknowledgments
Grateful acknowledgment is made to the following for copyrighted material: **40, 46, 66**, "Gold Medal Times (in seconds) from the Men's 1500-Meter Run" from *Sports Illustrated 2007 Almanac*. Copyright © 2006 Time Inc. Home Entertainment.

Note: Every effort has been made to locate the copyright owner of material reprinted in this component. Omissions brought to our attention will be corrected in subsequent editions.

Additional Credits:
Chapter 1: Whole chapter taken from Chapter 1 of CME Project: Algebra 2.

Chapter 2: Lessons 2.0 through 2.04 and 2.06 through 2.16 taken from Chapter 2 of CME Project: Algebra 2. Lesson 2.05 taken from CME Project: Algebra 2 Common Core Additional Lessons.

Chapter 3: Lessons 3.01 through 3.08 and 3.10 through 3.13 taken from Chapter 3 of CME Project: Algebra 2. Lesson 3.09 taken from CME Project: Algebra 2 Common Core Additional Lessons.

Chapter 4: Lessons 4.01 through 4.13 taken from Chapter 4 of CME Project: Algebra 2. Lesson 4.14 taken from CME Project: Algebra 2 Common Core Additional Lessons.

Chapter 5: Whole chapter taken from Chapter 5 of CME Project: Algebra 2.

Chapter 6: Whole chapter taken from Chapter 6 of CME Project: Algebra 2.

Chapter 7: Whole chapter taken from Chapter 7 of CME Project: Algebra 2.

Chapter 8: Whole chapter taken from Chapter 8 of CME Project: Algebra 2.